Microsoft® OFFICE 2011 FOR MAC

INTRODUCTORY

Gary B. Shelly

Mali B. Jones

COURSE TECHNOLOGY
CENGAGE Learning™

SHELLY
CASHMAN
SERIES®

Australia • Brazil • Japan • Korea • Mexico • Singapore • Spain • United Kingdom • United States

COURSE TECHNOLOGY
CENGAGE Learning™

Microsoft Office 2011 for Mac: Introductory
Gary B. Shelly, Mali B. Jones

Vice President, Publisher: Nicole Pinard

Executive Editor: Kathleen McMahon

Product Manager: Jon Farnham

Associate Product Manager: Caitlin Womersley

Editorial Assistant: Angela Giannopoulos

Director of Marketing: Cheryl Costantini

Marketing Manager: Tristen Kendall

Marketing Coordinator: Adrienne Fung

Print Buyer: Julio Esperas

Director of Production: Patty Stephan

Content Project Manager: Matthew Hutchinson

Development Editor: Deb Kaufmann

Proofreader: Kim Kosmatka

Indexer: Rich Carlson

QA Manuscript Reviewers: Jeff Schwartz, Ashlee Welz Smith, Susan Whalen

Art Director: Marissa Falco

Cover Designer: Lisa Kuhn, Curio Press, LLC

Cover Photo: Tom Kates Photography

Text Design: Joel Sadagursky

Compositor: PreMediaGlobal

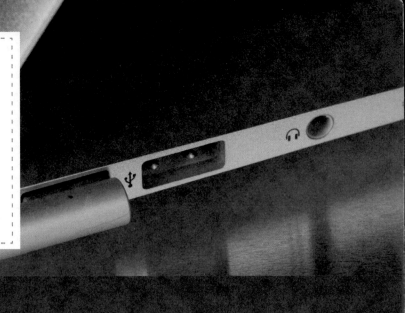

Microsoft® OFFICE 2011 FOR MAC
INTRODUCTORY

Contents

Microsoft **Office for Mac 2011**

Office for Mac 2011 and Mac OS X: Essential Concepts and Skills

Microsoft **Word for Mac 2011**

CHAPTER ONE
Creating, Formatting, and Editing a
Word Document with Pictures

Microsoft **PowerPoint for Mac 2011**

CHAPTER ONE
Creating and Editing a Presentation with Clip Art

CHAPTER TWO
Enhancing a Presentation with Pictures, Shapes, and WordArt

Microsoft **Excel for Mac 2011**

CHAPTER ONE
Creating a Worksheet and an Embedded Chart

Microsoft **Outlook for Mac 2011**

CHAPTER ONE
Managing E-Mail Messages with Outlook

CHAPTER TWO
Managing Calendars

Appendices

Capstone Projects

Preface

The Shelly Cashman Series® offers the finest textbooks in computer education. We are proud that since Mircosoft Office 4.3, our series of Microsoft Office textbooks have been the most widely used books in education. With each new edition of our Office books, we make significant improvements based on the software and comments made by instructors and students. For this Microsoft Office 2011 for Mac text, the Shelly Cashman Series development team carefully reviewed our pedagogy and analyzed its effectiveness in teaching today's Office student. Students today read less, but need to retain more. They need not only to be able to perform skills, but to retain those skills and know how to apply them to different settings. Today's students need to be continually engaged and challenged to retain what they're learning.

With this Microsoft Office 2011 for Mac text, we continue our commitment to focusing on the user and how they learn best.

Objectives of This Textbook

Microsoft Office 2011 for Mac: Introductory is intended for a first course on Office 2011 applications. No experience with a computer is assumed, and no mathematics beyond the high school freshman level is required. The objectives of this book are:

- To offer an introduction to Mac OS X Lion and Microsoft Office 2011 for Mac

- To expose students to practical examples of the computer as a useful tool

- To acquaint students with the proper procedures to create documents, worksheets, and presentations suitable for coursework, professional purposes, and personal use

- To help students discover the underlying functionality of Office 2011 so they can become more productive

- To develop an exercise-oriented approach that allows learning by doing

New to This Edition

Microsoft Office 2011 for Mac: Introductory offers a number of new features and approaches, which improve student understanding, retention, transference, and skill in using Office 2011 programs. The following enhancements will enrich the learning experience:

- Office for Mac 2011 and Mac OS X: Essential Concepts and Skills chapter prevents repetitive coverage of basic skills in the application chapters.

- Streamlined first chapters for each application allow the ability to cover more advanced skills earlier.

- Chapter topic redistribution offers concise chapters that ensure complete skill coverage.

- Expanded coverage of PowerPoint and Outlook gives exposure to the numerous enhancements made to these applications.

- New pedagogical elements enrich material creating an accessible and user-friendly approach.

  - Break Points, a new boxed element, identify logical stopping points and give students instructions regarding what they should do before taking a break.

  - Within step instructions, Tab | Group Identifiers, such as (Home tab | Bold button), help students more easily locate elements in the groups and on the tabs on the Ribbon.

  - Modified step-by-step instructions tell the student what to do and provide the generic reason why they are completing a specific task, which helps students easily transfer given skills to different settings.

The Shelly Cashman Approach

A Proven Pedagogy with an Emphasis on Project Planning

Each chapter presents a practical problem to be solved, within a project planning framework. The project orientation is strengthened by the use of Plan Ahead boxes, which encourage critical thinking about how to proceed at various points in the project. Step-by-step instructions with supporting screens guide students through the steps. Instructional steps are supported by the Q&A and BTW features.

A Visually Engaging Book that Maintains Student Interest

The step-by-step tasks, with supporting figures, provide a rich visual experience for the student. Call-outs on the screens that present both explanatory and navigational information provide students with information they need when they need to know it.

Supporting Reference Materials (Appendices, Capstones, Quick Reference)

The appendices provide additional information about the Application at hand and include such topics as project planning guidelines and publishing Web pages. With the Quick Reference, students can quickly look up information about a single task, such as keyboard shortcuts, and find page references of where in the book the task is illustrated. The Capstone Projects allow students to demonstrate mastery of skills across the Introductory content for Word, PowerPoint, and Excel.

Integration of the World Wide Web

The World Wide Web is integrated into the Office 2011 learning experience by (1) BTW annotations; (2) BTW, Q&A, and Quick Reference Summary Web pages; and (3) the Learn It Online section for each chapter.

End-of-Chapter Student Activities

Extensive end-of-chapter activities provide a variety of reinforcement opportunities for students where they can apply and expand their skills.

Instructor Resources

The Instructor Resources include both teaching and testing aids and can be accessed via CD-ROM or at www.cengage.com/login.

Instructor's Manual Includes lecture notes summarizing the chapter sections, figures and boxed elements found in every chapter, teacher tips, classroom activities, lab activities, and quick quizzes in Microsoft Word files.

Syllabus Easily customizable sample syllabi that cover policies, assignments, exams, and other course information.

Figure Files Illustrations for every figure in the textbook in electronic form.

PowerPoint Presentations A multimedia lecture presentation system that provides slides for each chapter. Presentations are based on chapter objectives.

Solutions to Exercises Includes solutions for all end-of-chapter and chapter reinforcement exercises.

Test Bank & Test Engine Test Banks include 112 questions for every chapter, featuring objective-based and critical thinking question types, and including page number references and figure references, when appropriate. Also included is the test engine, ExamView, the ultimate tool for your objective-based testing needs.

Data Files for Students Includes all the files that are required by students to complete the exercises.

Additional Activities for Students Consists of Chapter Reinforcement Exercises, which are true/false, multiple-choice, and short answer questions that help students gain confidence in the material learned.

SAM: Skills Assessment Manager

SAM 2010 is designed to help bring students from the classroom to the real world. It allows students to train on and test important computer skills in an active, hands-on environment.

SAM's easy-to-use system includes powerful interactive exams, training, and projects on the most commonly used Microsoft Office applications. SAM simulates the Microsoft Office 2010 application environment, allowing students to demonstrate their knowledge and think through the skills by performing real-world tasks such as bolding word text or setting up slide transitions. Add in live-in-the-application projects, and students are on their way to truly learning and applying skills to business-centric documents.

Designed to be used with the Shelly Cashman Series, SAM includes handy page references so that students can print helpful study guides that match the Shelly Cashman textbooks used in class. For instructors, SAM also includes robust scheduling and reporting features.

Content for Online Learning

Course Technology has partnered with the leading distance learning solution providers and class-management platforms today. To access this material, instructors will visit our password-protected instructor resources available at www.cengage.com/coursetechnology. Instructor resources include the following: additional case projects, sample syllabi, PowerPoint presentations per chapter, and more. For additional information or for an instructor user name and password, please contact your sales representative. For students to access this material, they must have purchased a WebTutor PIN-code specific to this title and your campus platform. The resources for students may include (based on instructor preferences), but are not limited to: topic review, review questions, and practice tests.

CourseNotes

Course Technology's CourseNotes are six-panel quick reference cards that reinforce the most important and widely used features of a software application in a visual and user-friendly format. CourseNotes serve as a great reference tool during and after the student completes the

course. CourseNotes are available for software applications such as Microsoft Office for Mac 2011, Microsoft Office 2010, and Windows 7. Topic-based CourseNotes are available for Best Practices in Social Networking, Hot Topics in Technology, and Web 2.0. Visit www.cengage.com/ct/coursenotes to learn more!

A Guided Tour

Add excitement and interactivity to your classroom with "*A Guided Tour*" product line. Play one of the brief mini-movies to spice up your lecture and spark classroom discussion. Or, assign a movie for homework and ask students to complete the correlated assignment that accompanies each topic. "*A Guided Tour*" product line takes the prep work out of providing your students with information about new technologies and applications and helps keep students engaged with content relevant to their lives; all in under an hour!

About Our Covers

The Shelly Cashman Series is continually updating our approach and content to reflect the way today's students learn and experience new technology. This focus on student success is reflected on our covers, which feature real students from the University of Rhode Island using the Shelly Cashman Series in their courses, and reflect the varied ages and backgrounds of the students learning with our books. When you use the Shelly Cashman Series, you can be assured that you are learning computer skills using the most effective courseware available.

Textbook Walk-Through

The Shelly Cashman Series Pedagogy: Project-Based — Step-by-Step — Variety of Assessments

Plan Ahead boxes prepare students to create successful projects by encouraging them to think strategically about what they are trying to accomplish before they begin working.

Step-by-step instructions now provide a context beyond the point-and-click. Each step provides information on why students are performing each task, or what will occur as a result.

Overview

As you read this chapter, you will learn how to create the flyer shown in Figure 1–1 on the previous page by performing these general tasks:

- Enter text in the document.
- Format the text in the document.
- Insert the pictures in the document.
- Format the pictures in the document.
- Enhance the page with a border and additional spacing.
- Correct errors and revise the document.
- Print the document.

Plan Ahead

General Project Guidelines

When creating a Word document, the actions you perform and decisions you make will affect the appearance and characteristics of the finished document. As you create a flyer, such as the project shown in Figure 1–1, you should follow these general guidelines:

1. **Choose the words for the text.** Follow the *less is more* principle. The less text, the more likely people will read the flyer. Use as few words as possible to make a point.

2. **Identify how to format various elements of the text.** The overall appearance of a document significantly affects its ability to communicate clearly. Examples of how you can modify the appearance, or **format**, of text include changing its shape, size, color, and position on the page.

3. **Find the appropriate graphical image(s).** An eye-catching graphical image should convey the flyer's overall message. It could show a product, service, result, or benefit, or visually convey a message that is not expressed easily with words.

4. **Establish where to position and how to format the graphical image(s).** The position and format of the graphical image(s) should grab the attention of passersby and draw them into reading the flyer.

5. **Determine whether the page needs enhancements such as a border or spacing adjustments.** A graphical, color-coordinated page border can further draw attention to a flyer and nicely frame its contents. Increasing or decreasing spacing between elements on a flyer can improve its readability and overall appearance.

6. **Correct errors and revise the document as necessary.** Post the flyer on a wall and make sure all text and images are legible from a distance. Ask someone else to read the flyer and give you suggestions for improvements.

7. **Determine the best method for distributing the document.** You can distribute documents on paper or electronically. A flyer should be printed on paper so it can be posted. When necessary, more specific details concerning the above guidelines are presented at appropriate points in the chapter. The chapter also will identify the actions performed and decisions made regarding these guidelines during the creation of the flyer shown in Figure 1–1.

For an introduction to Mac OS X and instruction about how to perform basic Mac OS X tasks, read the Office 2011 and Mac OS X chapter at the beginning of this book, where you can learn how to resize windows, change screen resolution, create folders, move and rename files, use Mac OS X Help, and much more.

To Start Word

If you are using a computer to step through the project in this chapter and you want your screens to match the figures in this book, you should change your screen's resolution to 1280 × 800. For information about how to change a computer's resolution, refer to the Office 2011 and Mac OS X chapter at the beginning of this book.

To Center a Paragraph

The headline in the flyer currently is left-aligned (Figure 1–17). You wa
is, positioned horizontally between the left and right margins on the page. Re
line of text, such as the two-word headline, a paragraph. Thus, you will center
The following steps center a paragraph.

 1

- Click somewhere in the paragraph to be centered (in this case, the headline) to position the insertion point in the paragraph to be formatted (Figure 1–17).

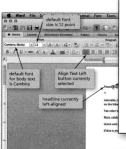

Figure 1–17

2

- On the Home tab, under Paragraph, click the Center Text button to center the paragraph containing the insertion point (Figure 1–18).

Q&A What if I want to return the paragraph to flush left-aligned? You would click the Center Text button again; or on the Home tab, under Paragraph, click the Align Text Left button.

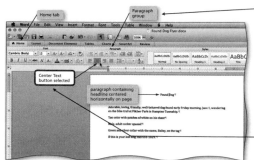

Figure 1–18

Other Ways

1. CONTROL-click paragraph, choose Paragraph in shortcut menu, click Indents and Spacing tab (Paragraph dialog), click Alignment box, click Centered, click OK button

2. Choose Format > Paragraph in menu bar, click Indents and Spacing tab (Paragraph dialog), click Alignment box, click Centered, click OK button

3. Press COMMAND-E

Explanatory callouts summarize what is happening on screen.

Navigational callouts in red show students where to click.

Q&A boxes offer questions students may have when working through the steps and provide additional information about what they are doing right where they need it.

To Bold Text

Bold characters appear somewhat thicker and darker than those that are not bold. To further emphasize the signature line, it is bold in the flyer. To format the line, as you have learned previously, you select the line first. The following steps format the signature line bold.

1

• Move the mouse pointer to the left of the line to be selected (in this case, the signature line) until the mouse pointer changes to a right-pointing black arrow and then click the mouse to select the text to be formatted.

• With the text selected, on the Home tab, under Font, click the Bold button to bold the selected text (Figure 1–45).

Q&A How would I remove a bold format? You would click the Bold button a second time, or you immediately could click the Undo button on the Standard toolbar.

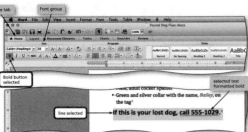

Figure 1–45

2

• Click anywhere in the document window to remove the selection from the screen.

Other Ways

1. CONTROL-click selected text, choose Font in shortcut menu, click Font tab (Font dialog), select Bold in Font style list, click OK button

2. Choose Format > Font in menu bar, click Font tab, under Font style select Bold, click OK button

3. Press COMMAND-B

To Change Theme Colors

text, background, simple way to select

ades of browns scheme from the

Table 1–3 Techniques for Selecting Text

Item to Select	Mouse	Keyboard (where applicable)
Block of text	Click at beginning of selection, scroll to end of selection, position mouse pointer at end of selection; hold down SHIFT key and then click; or drag through the text.	
Character(s)	Drag through character(s).	SHIFT-RIGHT ARROW or SHIFT-LEFT ARROW
Document	Move mouse to left of text until mouse pointer changes to a right-pointing black arrow and then triple-click.	COMMAND-A
Graphic	Click the graphic.	
Line	Move mouse to left of line until mouse pointer changes to a right-pointing black arrow and then click.	FN-LEFT ARROW, then SHIFT-COMMAND-RIGHT ARROW or FN-RIGHT ARROW, then SHIFT-COMMAND-LEFT ARROW
Lines	Move mouse to left of first line until mouse pointer changes to a right-pointing black arrow and then drag up or down.	FN-LEFT ARROW, then SHIFT-DOWN ARROW or FN-RIGHT ARROW, then SHIFT-UP ARROW
Paragraph	Triple-click paragraph; or move mouse to left of paragraph until mouse pointer changes to a right-pointing black arrow and then double-click.	COMMAND-SHIFT-DOWN ARROW
Paragraphs	Move mouse to left of paragraph until mouse pointer changes to a right-pointing black arrow, double-click, and then drag up or down.	COMMAND-SHIFT-DOWN ARROW (repeatedly)
Sentence	Press and hold down COMMAND key and then click sentence.	
Word	Double-click the word.	OPTION-SHIFT-RIGHT ARROW
Words	Drag through words.	OPTION-SHIFT-RIGHT ARROW (repeatedly)

To Save an Existing Document with the Same File Name

You have made several modifications to the document since you last saved it. Thus, you should save it again. The following step saves the document again. For an example of the step listed below, refer to the Office 2011 and Mac OS X chapter at the beginning of this book.

1 Click the Save button on the Standard toolbar to overwrite the previously saved file.

Break Point: If you wish to take a break, this is a good place to do so. You can quit Word now (refer to page WD 48 for instructions). To resume at a later time, start Word (refer to pages WD 4 and WD 49 for instructions), open the file called Found Dog Flyer (refer to page WD 49 for instructions), and continue following the steps from this location forward.

Inserting and Formatting Pictures in a Word Document

With the text formatted in the flyer, the next step is to insert digital pictures in the flyer and format the pictures. Flyers usually contain graphical images, such as a picture, to attract the attention of passersby. In the following pages, you will perform these tasks:

1. Insert the first digital picture into the flyer and then reduce its size.
2. Insert the second digital picture into the flyer and then reduce its size.
3. Change the look of the first picture and then the second picture.

Break Points identify logical breaks in the chapter if students need to stop before completing the project.

Textbook Walk-Through

To Quit Word

The project now is complete. Thus, the following steps quit Word. For an example of the step listed below, refer to the Office 2011and Mac OS X chapter at the beginning of this book.

1 Click Word in the menu bar and then choose Quit Word to close all open documents and quit Word.

2 If a Word dialog appears, click the Save button to save any changes made to the document since the last save.

Chapter Summary

In this chapter, you have learned how to enter text in a document, format text, insert a picture, format a picture, add a page border, and print a document. The items listed below include all the new Word skills you have learned in this chapter.

1. Start Word (WD 4)
2. Change Line and Paragraph Spacing (WD 6)
3. Adjust the Margins (WD 7)
4. Type Text (WD 9)
5. Display Formatting Marks (WD 10)
6. Insert a Blank Line (WD 10)
7. Wordwrap Text as You Type (WD 11)
8. Check Spelling and Grammar as You Type (WD 12)
9. Save a Document (WD 15)
10. Center a Paragraph (WD 18)
11. Select a Line (WD 20)
12. Change the Font Size of Selected Text (WD 20)
13. Change the Font of Selected Text (WD 21)

23. Underline Text (WD 32)
24. Bold Text (WD 33)
25. Change Theme Colors (WD 33)
26. Save an Existing Document with the Same File Name (WD 35)
27. Insert a Picture (WD 36)
28. Zoom the Document (WD 37)
29. Resize a Graphic (WD 38)
30. Resize a Graphic by Entering Exact Measurements (WD 40)
31. Apply a Picture Style (WD 41)
32. Apply Picture Effects (WD 42)
33. View One Page (WD 44)
34. Add a Page Border (WD 45)
35. Change Spacing before and after a Paragraph (WD 46)
36. Quit Word (WD 48)
37. Open a Document from Word (WD 49)
38. Insert Text in an Existing Document (WD 50)
39. Delete Text (WD 50)
40. Move Text (WD 51)
41. Change Document Properties (WD 52)
42. Print a Document (WD 55)

profile, your instructor may have assigned an autogradable
, log into the SAM 2010 Web site at www.cengage.com/sam2010
d start files.

Learn It Online

Test your knowledge of chapter content and key terms.

Instructions: To complete the Learn It Online exercises, please visit **www.cengagebrain.com**. At the CengageBrain.com home page, search for *Office 2011 for Mac* using the search box at the top of the page. This will take you to the product page for this book. On the product page, click the Access Now button below the Study Tools heading. On the Book Companion Site Web page, select Word Chapter 1, and then click the link for the desired exercise.

Chapter Reinforcement TF, MC, and SA
A series of true/false, multiple choice, and short answer questions that test your knowledge of the chapter content.

Flash Cards
An interactive learning environment where you identify chapter key terms associated with displayed definitions.

Practice Test
A series of multiple choice questions that test your knowledge of chapter content and key terms.

Who Wants To Be a Computer Genius?
An interactive game that challenges your knowledge of chapter content in the style of a television quiz show.

Wheel of Terms
An interactive game that challenges your knowledge of chapter key terms in the style of the television show *Wheel of Fortune*.

Crossword Puzzle Challenge
A crossword puzzle that challenges your knowledge of key terms presented in the chapter.

Apply Your Knowledge

Reinforce the skills and apply the concepts you learned in this chapter.

Modifying Text and Formatting a Document
Note: To complete this assignment, you will be required to use the Data Files for Students. See the inside back cover of this book for instructions on downloading the Data Files for Students, or contact your instructor for information about accessing the required files.

Instructions: Start Word. Open the document, Apply 1–1 Buffalo Photo Shoot Flyer Unformatted, from the Data Files for Students. The document you open is an unformatted flyer. You are to modify text, format paragraphs and characters, and insert a picture in the flyer.

Perform the following tasks:

1. Delete the word, single, in the sentence of body copy below the headline.
2. Insert the word, Creeks, between the words, Twin Buffalo, in the sentence of body copy below the headline.
3. At the end of the signature line, change the period to an exclamation point.
4. Center the headline and the signature line.
5. Change the theme colors to the Pushpin color scheme.
6. Change the font size of the headline to 48-point. Change the case of the headline text to all capital letters. Apply the text effect located at row 4, column 4 of the Text Effects pop-up menu to the headline. Change the font of the headline to Market Felt Thin, or a similar font.
7. Change the font size of body copy between the headline and the signature line to 20 point.
8. Change the font size of the signature line to 26 point.

Continued >

Extend Your Knowledge

Extend the skills you learned in this chapter and experiment with new skills. You may need to use Help to complete the assignment.

Modifying Text and Picture Formats and Adding Page Borders

Note: To complete this assignment, you will be required to use the Data Files for Students. See the inside back cover of this book for instructions on downloading the Data Files for Students, or contact your instructor for information about accessing the required files.

Instructions: Start Word. Open the document, Extend 1–1 TVC Cruises Flyer, from the Data Files for Students. You will enhance the look of the flyer shown in Figure 1–80. *Hint:* Remember, if you make a mistake while formatting the picture, you can reset it by clicking the Reset button on the Format Picture tab, under Adjust.

Perform the following tasks:

1. Use Help to learn about the following formats: remove bullets, increase font size, decrease font size, art page borders, decorative underline(s), picture bullets, picture border shading, shadow picture effects, and color saturation and tone.

2. Remove the bullet from the paragraph below the picture.

3. Select the text, 10 percent, and use the Increase Font size button to increase its font size.

4. Add an art page border to the flyer. If the border is not in color, add color to it.

5. Change the solid underline below the word, cruises, to a decorative underline. Change the color of the underline.

6. Change the style of the bullets to picture bullet(s).

7. Change the color of the picture border. Add a shadow picture effect to the picture.

8. Change the color saturation and color tone of the picture.

9. Change the document properties, including keywords, as specified by your instructor. Save the revised document with a new file name and then submit it in the format specified by your instructor.

add art page border

NEED AN ESCAPE?

change border color and add shadow effect; change color saturation and color tone

use Grow Font button to increase font size

Tango Vacatio...
→**10 percent disc...**
during May. Se...
destinations.

An experience...

change to picture bullets

• **Ultimate rel...**
• **Endless fun...**
• **Breathtakin...**
• **Friendly, at...**
• **Clean facili...**

Interested?...

STUDENT ASSIGNMENTS

Make It Right

Analyze a document and correct all errors and/or improve the design.

Correcting Spelling and Grammar Errors

Note: To complete this assignment, you will be required to use the Data Files for Students. See the inside back cover of this book for instructions on downloading the Data Files for Students, or contact your instructor for information about accessing the required files.

Instructions: Start Word. Open the document, Make It Right 1–1 Karate Academy Flyer Unchecked, from the Data Files for Students. The document is a flyer that contains spelling and grammar errors, as shown in Figure 1–81. You are to correct each spelling (red wavy underline) and grammar error (green and blue wavy underlines) by right-clicking the flagged text and then clicking the appropriate correction in the shortcut menu.

If your screen does not display the wavy underlines, click Word in the menu bar and then select Preferences. When the Word Preferences dialog is displayed, click Spelling and Grammar in the Author and Proofing tools pane to display the Spelling and Grammar dialog, be sure the 'Hide spelling errors in this document' and 'Hide grammatical errors in this document' check boxes do not contain checkmarks, click the back arrow to go back to the main Word Preferences dialog and then click the OK button. If your screen still does not display the wavy underlines, redisplay the Spelling and Grammar dialog, and then click the Recheck Document button.

Change the document properties, including keywords, as specified by your instructor. Save the revised document with the name, Make It Right 1–1 Karate Academy Flyer, and then submit it in the format specified by your instructor.

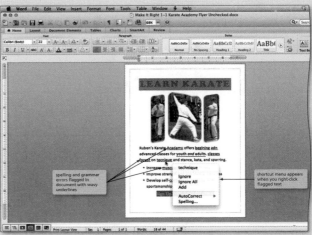

spelling and grammar errors flagged in document with wavy underlines

shortcut menu appears when you right-click flagged text

Figure 1–81

Textbook Walk-Through

In the Lab

Design and/or create a document using the guidelines, concepts, and skills presented in this chapter. Labs are listed in order of increasing difficulty.

Lab 1: Creating a Flyer with a Picture

Problem: As a part-time employee in the Student Services Center at school, you have been asked to prepare a flyer that advertises study habits classes. First, you prepare the unformatted flyer shown in Figure 1–82a, and then you format it so that it looks like Figure 1–82b. *Hint:* Remember, if you make a mistake while formatting the flyer, you can click the Undo button on the Standard toolbar to undo your last action.

Note: To complete this assignment, you will be required to use the Data Files for Students. See the inside back cover of this book for instructions on downloading the Data Files for Students, or contact your instructor for information about accessing the required files.

Instructions: Perform the following tasks:
1. Start Word and open a new, blank document. Display formatting marks on the screen.
2. Set line spacing to 1.15, and space after to 10 pt. Set margins to Normal.
3. Type the flyer text, unformatted, as shown in Figure 1–82a, inserting a blank line between the headline and the body copy. If Word flags any misspelled words as you type, check their spelling and correct them.
4. Save the document using the file name, Lab 1–1 Study Habits Flyer.
5. Center the headline and the signature line.
6. Change the theme colors to Sketchbook.
7. Change the font size of the headline to 48 point and the font to Mistral, or a similar font. Apply the text effect found in row 4, column 2 of the Text Effects pop-up menu.
8. Change the font size of body copy between the headline and the signature line to 20 point.
9. Change the font size of the signature line to 22 point. Bold the text in the signature line.

In the Lab Three all new in-depth assignments per chapter require students to utilize the chapter concepts and techniques to solve problems on a computer.

Studying All Night?

Let us help you! Our expert instructors teach effective [...]
management skills, and energy-building techniques.

Classes are $15.00 per session

Sessions last four weeks

Classes meet in the Student Services Center twice a w[...]

Call 555-2838 or stop by to sign up today!

Figure 1–82 (a) Unformatted Text

Cases & Places exercises call on students to create open-ended projects that reflect academic, personal, and business settings.

In the Lab *continued*

Instructions: Start Word and open a new, blank document. Set line spacing to 1.15, and space after to 10 pt. Set margins to Normal. Enter the text in the flyer, checking spelling as you type, and then format it as shown in Figure 1–84 on the previous page. The pictures to be inserted are called Train and Scenery and are available on the Data Files for Students. Adjust spacing before and after paragraphs and resize pictures as necessary so that the flyer fits on a single page.

Change the document properties, including keywords, as specified by your instructor. Save the document using the file name, Lab 1–3 Train Ride Flyer. Submit the document, shown in Figure 1–84, in the format specified by your instructor.

Cases and Places

Apply your creative thinking and problem solving skills to design and implement a solution.

Note: To complete these assignments, you may be required to use the Data Files for Students. See the inside back cover of this book for instructions on downloading the Data Files for Students, or contact your instructor for information about accessing the required files.

1: Design and Create a Spring Break Flyer

Academic

As secretary of your school's Student Government Association, you are responsible for creating and distributing flyers for spring break group outings. This year, you have planned a trip to Settlers Resort. The flyer should contain two digital pictures appropriately resized; the Data Files for Students contains two pictures called Cabin 1 and Cabin 2, or you can use your own digital pictures if they are appropriate for the topic of the flyer. The flyer should contain the headline, Feeling Adventurous?, and this signature line: Call Lyn at 555–9901 to sign up. The body copy consists of the following, in any order: Spring Break – Blast to the Past. Settlers Resort is like a page right out of a history textbook! Spend five days living in the 1800s. The bulleted list in the body copy is as follows: One-room cabins with potbelly stoves, Campfire dining with authentic meals, and Horseback riding and much more.

Use the concepts and techniques presented in this chapter to create and format this flyer. Be sure to check spelling and grammar. Submit your assignment in the format specified by your instructor.

2: Design and Create a Yard Sale Flyer

Personal

You are planning a yard sale and would like to create and post flyers around town advertising the upcoming sale. The flyer should contain two digital pictures appropriately resized; the Data Files for Students contains two pictures called Yard Sale 1 and Yard Sale 2, or you can use your own digital pictures if they are appropriate for the topic of the flyer. The flyer should contain the headline, Yard Sale!, and this signature line: Questions? Call 555–9820. The body copy consists of the following, in any order: Hundreds of items for sale. After 20 years, we are moving to a smaller house and are selling anything that won't fit. Everything for sale must go! The bulleted list in the body copy is as follows: When: August 7, 8, 9 from 9:00 a.m. to 7:00 p.m.; Where: 139 Ravel Boulevard; and What: something for everyone – from clothing to collectibles.

Use the concepts and techniques presented in this chapter to create and format this flyer. Be sure to check spelling and grammar. Submit your assignment in the format specified by your instructor.

Introduction to Computers

and How to Purchase Computers and Mobile Devices

Introduction to Computers

What Is a Computer?

Computers are everywhere: at work, at school, and at home. In the workplace, employees use computers to create correspondence such as e-mail messages, memos, and letters; manage calendars; calculate payroll; track inventory; and generate invoices. At school, teachers use computers to assist with classroom instruction. Students use computers to complete assignments and research. People also spend hours of leisure time using a computer. They play games, communicate with friends and relatives online and using e-mail, purchase goods online, converse in chat rooms, listen to music or radio broadcasts, watch or create videos and movies, read books and magazines, share stories, research genealogy, retouch photos, and plan vacations. At work, at school, and at home, computers are helping people do their work faster, more accurately, and in some cases, in ways that previously would not have been possible.

A **computer** is an electronic device, operating under the control of instructions stored in its own memory, that can accept data (input), process the data according to specified rules (process), produce results (output), and store the results (storage) for future use. Generally, the term is used to describe a collection of electric, electronic, and mechanical components known as hardware. Figure 1 shows some common hardware components that are used on different types of computers, such as notebook computers (Figure 1a), all-in-one desktop computers (Figure 1b), and traditional desktop computers (Figure 1c). These components are discussed in more depth later in this chapter.

Computers perform four basic operations — input, process, output, and storage. These operations comprise the **information processing cycle**. Collectively, these operations process data into information and store it for future use.

A computer derives its power from its capability to perform the information processing cycle with amazing speed, reliability (low failure rate), and accuracy; its capacity to store huge amounts of data and information; and its capability to communicate with other computers.

For a computer to perform operations, it must be given a detailed set of instructions that tells it exactly what to do. These instructions are called a program, or software. Before processing for a specific activity begins, the program corresponding to that activity is stored in the computer. Once the program is stored, the computer can begin to execute the program's first instruction. The computer executes one program instruction after another until the activity is complete.

All computer processing requires data. **Data** is a collection of unprocessed items, which can include text, numbers, images, audio, and video. Computers manipulate data to create information. **Information** conveys meaning and is useful to people. During the output operation, the information that has been created is put into some form, such as a printed report, or it can be stored on the

🖑 Computers

For more information, visit the Office 2011 for Mac Online Companion Web page at www.cengagebrain.com, click Web Links, and then click Computers.

🖑 Programs

For more information, visit the Office 2011 for Mac Online Companion Web page at www.cengagebrain.com, click Web Links, and then click Computer Programs.

🖑 Information

For more information, visit the Office 2011 for Mac Online Companion Web page at www.cengagebrain.com, click Web Links, and then click Information.

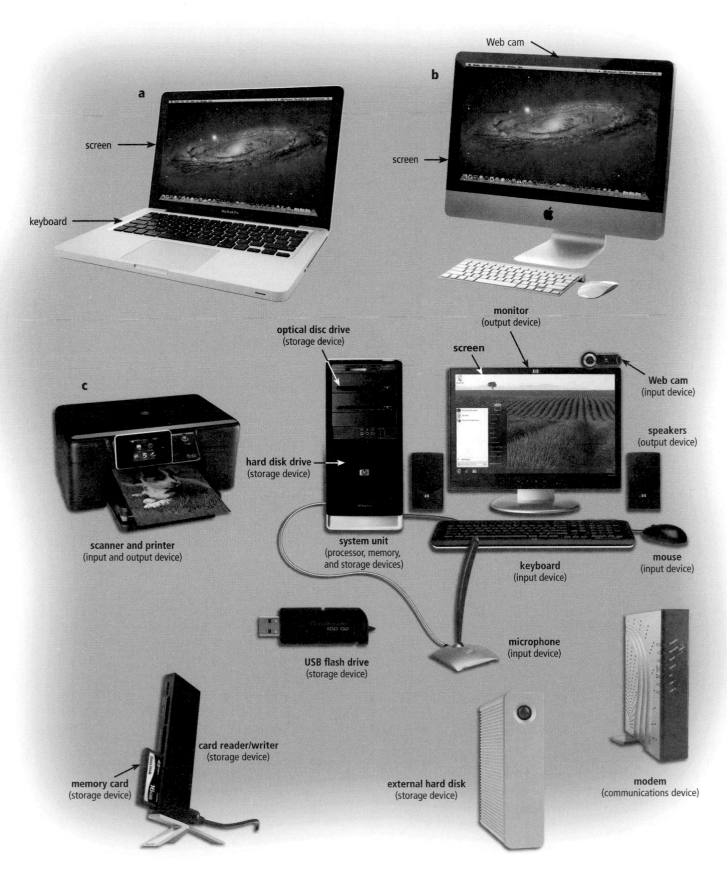

Figure 1 Common computer hardware components include the keyboard, mouse, microphone, all-in-one device, Web cam, monitor, speakers, system unit, hard disk drive, external hard disk, optical disc drive(s), USB flash drive, card reader/writer, memory cards, and modem.

computer for future use. As shown in Figure 2, a computer processes several data items to produce a cash register receipt.

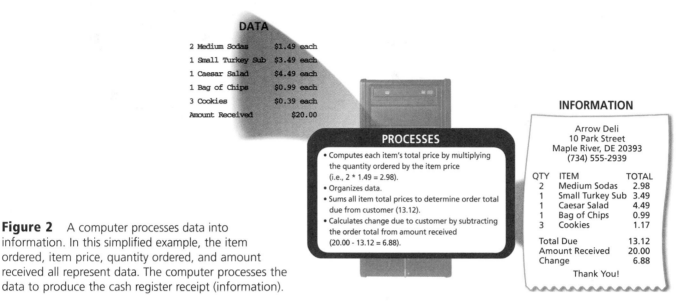

DATA

2 Medium Sodas	$1.49	each
1 Small Turkey Sub	$3.49	each
1 Caesar Salad	$4.49	each
1 Bag of Chips	$0.99	each
3 Cookies	$0.39	each
Amount Received		$20.00

PROCESSES

- Computes each item's total price by multiplying the quantity ordered by the item price (i.e., 2 * 1.49 = 2.98).
- Organizes data.
- Sums all item total prices to determine order total due from customer (13.12).
- Calculates change due to customer by subtracting the order total from amount received (20.00 - 13.12 = 6.88).

INFORMATION

Arrow Deli
10 Park Street
Maple River, DE 20393
(734) 555-2939

QTY	ITEM	TOTAL
2	Medium Sodas	2.98
1	Small Turkey Sub	3.49
1	Caesar Salad	4.49
1	Bag of Chips	0.99
3	Cookies	1.17
	Total Due	13.12
	Amount Received	20.00
	Change	6.88

Thank You!

Figure 2   A computer processes data into information. In this simplified example, the item ordered, item price, quantity ordered, and amount received all represent data. The computer processes the data to produce the cash register receipt (information).

People who use the computer directly or use the information it provides are called **computer users**, **end users**, or sometimes, just **users**. Users and computer manufacturers can reduce the environmental impact of computers through green computing. **Green computing** involves reducing the electricity consumed and environmental waste generated when using a computer.

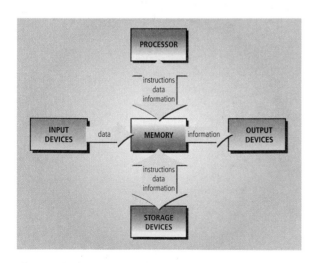

Figure 3   Most devices connected to the computer communicate with the processor to carry out a task. When a user starts a program, for example, its instructions transfer from a storage device to memory. Data needed by the program enters memory either from an input device or a storage device. The processor interprets and executes instructions in memory and also performs calculations on the data in memory. Resulting information is stored in memory, from which it can be sent to an output device or a storage device for future access, as needed.

The Components of a Computer

The six primary components of a computer are input devices, the processor (control unit and arithmetic/logic unit), memory, output devices, storage devices, and communications devices. The processor, memory, and storage devices are housed in the system unit (shown in Figure 1c). A **peripheral** is a device that connects to the system unit and is controlled by the processor in the computer. Peripherals can include input devices and output devices, as well as some storage devices and communications devices.

Figure 3 shows how the components of a computer interact to carry out a task. The following sections describe the types of personal computers and mobile devices, as well as their primary components (input devices, processor, memory, output devices, and communications devices).

Personal Computers and Mobile Devices

A **personal computer** is a computer that can perform all of its input, processing, output, and storage activities by itself. A personal computer contains a processor, memory, and one or more input, output, and storage devices. Personal computers also often contain a communications device. A **mobile computer** is a personal computer you can carry from place to place. Similarly, a **mobile device** is a computing device small enough to hold in your hand. The most popular type of mobile computer is the notebook computer.

Notebook Computers

A **notebook computer**, also called a **laptop computer**, is a portable, personal computer often designed to fit on your lap. These computers are thin and lightweight, yet can be as powerful as the average desktop computer. A **netbook**, which is a type of notebook computer, is smaller, lighter, and often not as powerful as a traditional notebook computer. Resembling a letter-sized slate, the **tablet PC** is a special type of notebook computer that allows you to write or draw on the screen using a digital pen or stylus. A **stylus** is a small metal or plastic device that looks like a tiny ink pen but uses pressure instead of ink.

Desktop Computers

A **desktop computer** is designed so that the system unit, input devices, output devices, and any other devices fit entirely on or under a desk or table. An **all-in-one computer** is a type of desktop computer that houses the monitor and system unit in the same case. The Apple iMac is an example of an all-in-one computer, and is the most common desktop computer among Mac users.

Tablet Slate Computers

A **tablet slate computer** is similar to a notebook computer, but often has less functionality. Tablet slate computers typically have touch-sensitive screens between seven and ten inches, and are extremely lightweight (Figure 4). Unlike tablet PCs, tablet slate computers do not have a separate keyboard. Most tablet slate computers also have an integrated Web cam and microphone to facilitate taking pictures and videos, and participating in video chat sessions. The Apple iPad and Samsung Galaxy Tab are examples of tablet slate computers. In addition, some eReaders, such as the Kindle Fire and Nook Tablet, also can be classified as tablet slate computers.

Mobile Devices

Mobile devices, which are small enough to carry in a pocket, usually store programs and data permanently on memory inside the system unit or on small storage media such as memory cards. You often can connect a mobile device to a personal computer to exchange information. Three popular types of mobile devices are smart phones, portable media players, and digital cameras.

Figure 4　A tablet slate computer.

A **smart phone** is a phone that can connect to the Internet and usually also provides personal information management functions such as a calendar, an appointment book, an address book, a calculator, and a notepad (Figure 5). A **portable media player** is a mobile device on which you can store, organize, and play digital media. For example, you can listen to music; watch videos, movies, and television shows; and view photos on the device's screen. A **digital camera** is a device that allows users to take pictures and store the photographed images digitally, instead of on traditional film. Digital cameras typically allow users to review, and sometimes modify, images while they are in the camera. Many of today's smart phones, such as the iPhone, have a built-in portable media player and digital camera.

Figure 5　A smart phone is a popular mobile device.

Input Devices

An **input device** is any hardware component that allows you to enter data and instructions into a computer. Depending on your particular program and requirements, the input device you use may vary. Five widely used input devices are the keyboard, mouse, microphone, scanner, and Web cam (shown in Figure 1c on page COM 3). The two primary input devices used are the keyboard and the mouse.

Keyboard

A **keyboard** is an input device that contains keys users press to enter data and instructions into the computer. All desktop computer keyboards have a typing area that includes the letters of the alphabet, numbers, punctuation marks, and other basic keys. Many desktop computer keyboards also have a numeric keypad on the right side of the keyboard. Most of today's desktop computer

Input Devices

For more information, visit the Office 2011 for Mac Online Companion Web page at www.cengagebrain.com, click Web Links, and then click Input Devices.

keyboards are enhanced keyboards. An enhanced keyboard has 12 or more function keys along the top and a set of arrow and additional keys between the typing area and the numeric keypad (Figure 6). Function keys are special keys programmed to issue instructions to a computer. On some keyboards, such as the one shown in Figure 6, function keys also can serve an alternate purpose, such as adjusting the volume or screen brightness.

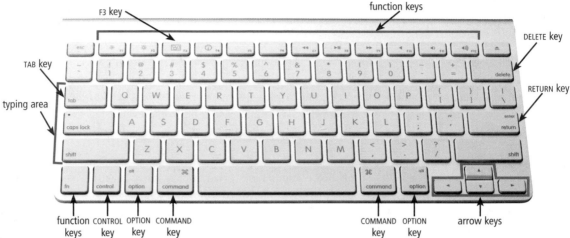

Figure 6 On a desktop computer keyboard, you type using keys in the typing area and on the numeric keypad.

A variety of options are available for typing on a smart phone (Figure 7). Many can display an on-screen keyboard, where you press the on-screen keys using your finger. Some smart phones have one key for each letter of the alphabet, often called a mini-keyboard. Other phones have keypads that contain fewer keys than there are letters in the alphabet. For these phones, each key on the keypad represents multiple characters, which are identified on the key.

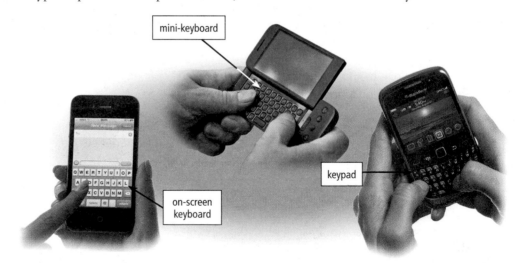

Figure 7 Users have a variety of options for typing on a phone.

Mouse and Other Pointing Devices

A **mouse** is a pointing device that fits comfortably under the palm of your hand (Figure 8). With a mouse, users control the movement of the **pointer**, which is a small symbol on the screen whose location and shape change as a user moves a pointing device. As you move a mouse, for example, the pointer on the screen also moves. Generally, you use the mouse to move the pointer on the screen to an object such as a button, a menu, an icon, a link, or text. Then, you press a mouse button to perform a certain action

Figure 8 The touchpad and Magic Mouse are common pointing devices used on most Apple notebook computers.

associated with that object. The bottom of a mouse is flat and contains a mechanism (ball, optical sensor, or laser sensor) that detects movement of the mouse. Most notebook computers have a **touchpad**, also shown in Figure 8, which is a small, flat, rectangular pointing device near the keyboard that allows you to move the pointer by sliding a fingertip on the surface of the pad.

If you own a desktop computer and want the same functionality of a touchpad, Apple's Magic Trackpad allows you to perform the same gestures that you would on a notebook computer's touchpad (Figure 9).

Magic Trackpad

Figure 9   The Magic Trackpad is a pointing device that is similar to a touchpad, and typically is used on Apple desktop computers.

Other Input for Mobile Devices   Most mobile devices, such as smart phones, and some notebook computers, such as tablet PCs, use a variety of alternatives for entering data and instructions (Figure 10). Some have touch screens, enabling you to touch the screen to perform tasks.

speak into the microphone that wirelessly communicates with the phone

take a picture using the digital camera built into the back of the phone

enter text messages via a wireless keyboard

transfer data and instructions to and from the computer and phone by connecting it to the computer with a cable

Figure 10   Besides a touch screen, users have a variety of other options for entering data and instructions into a smart phone.

System Unit

The **system unit** is a case that contains electronic components of the computer used to process data (Figure 11). System units are available in a variety of shapes and sizes. The case of the system unit, also called the chassis, is made of metal or plastic and protects the internal components from damage. The **motherboard**, sometimes called a system board, is the main circuit board of the system unit. Many electronic components attach to the motherboard; others are built into it. The sound card and video card shown in Figure 11 are examples of adapter cards, which are circuit boards that provide connections and functions not built into the motherboard or expand on the capability of features integrated into the motherboard.

Processor

Processor

For more information, visit the Office 2011 for Mac Online Companion Web page at www.cengagebrain.com, click Web Links, and then click Processor.

The **processor** (bottom of Figure 11), also called the **central processing unit** (**CPU**), interprets and carries out the basic instructions that operate a computer. Processors contain a control unit and an arithmetic/logic unit. The **control unit** directs and coordinates most of the operations in the computer. The **arithmetic/logic unit** (**ALU**) performs arithmetic, comparison, and other operations.

On a personal computer, all functions of the processor usually are on a single chip. A computer chip is a small piece of semiconducting material that contains many microscopic pathways capable of carrying electrical current. Today's processors can perform some operations in less than the time it takes to blink your eye.

Memory

Memory

For more information, visit the Office 2011 for Mac Online Companion Web page at www.cengagebrain.com, click Web Links, and then click Memory.

Memory consists of electronic components that store instructions waiting to be executed and data needed by those instructions. Most memory keeps data and instructions temporarily, which means its contents are erased when the computer is shut off. When discussing computer memory, users typically are referring to RAM. Also called main memory, **RAM** (random access memory) consists of memory chips that can be read from and written to by the processor and other devices. These chips are placed on a memory module (lower left of Figure 11) that fits in a slot on the motherboard in the system unit.

The amount of memory in computers is measured in kilobytes, megabytes, gigabytes, or terabytes. A **byte** usually stores one character, such as the letter A. One **kilobyte** (**KB or K**) equals exactly 1,024 bytes, and one **megabyte** (**MB**) equals approximately one million bytes. One **gigabyte** (**GB**) equals approximately one billion bytes, and one **terabyte** (**TB**) equals approximately

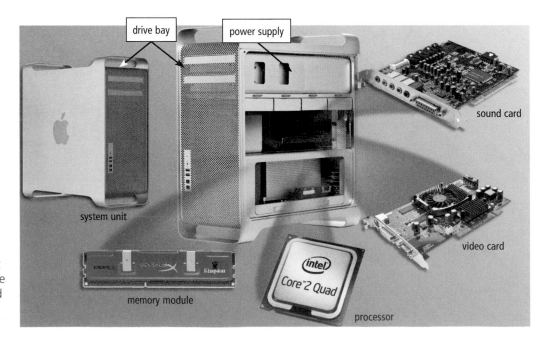

Figure 11 The system unit on a typical personal computer consists of numerous electronic components, some of which are shown in this figure. The sound card and video card are two types of adapter cards.

one trillion bytes. A computer with 4 GB of RAM, therefore, can store approximately four billion characters. For reference, one megabyte can hold approximately 500 letter-size pages of text information, and one gigabyte can hold approximately 500,000 letter-size pages of text information.

Output Devices

Output devices are hardware components that convey information to one or more people. Commonly used output devices include display devices; printers; speakers, headphones, and earbuds; data projectors; and interactive whiteboards. When a computer is used for processing tasks such as creating documents, the two output devices widely used are the printer and a display device.

Output Devices

For more information, visit the Office 2011 for Mac Online Companion Web page at www.cengagebrain.com, click Web Links, and then click Output Devices.

Printers

A **printer** is an output device that produces text and graphics on a physical medium such as paper. Ink-jet printers and laser printers often are used with personal computers.

Ink-jet printers produce text and graphics in both black and white and color on a variety of paper types and sizes (Figure 12). Some ink-jet printers, called **photo printers**, produce photo-lab-quality pictures and are ideal for home or small-business use. The speed of an ink-jet printer is measured by the number of pages per minute (ppm) it can print. Most ink-jet printers print from 12 to 36 pages per minute. Graphics and colors print at the slower rate.

A laser printer is a high-speed, high-quality printer that operates in a manner similar to a copy machine. Laser printers typically use individual sheets of paper stored in one or more removable trays that slide in the printer case. It creates images using a laser beam and powdered ink, called toner, on a special drum inside the printer, forming the images to be printed. Laser printers can cost from a couple hundred dollars to a few thousand dollars for the home and small office user, to several hundred thousand dollars for large business users. Generally, the more expensive the laser printer, the more pages it can print per minute.

A **multifunction peripheral**, also called an **all-in-one device**, is a single device that looks like a printer or copy machine but provides the functionality of a printer, scanner, copy machine, and perhaps a fax machine (Figure 13). Some use color ink-jet printer technology, while others include a black-and-white or color laser printer.

Figure 12　Ink-jet printers are a popular type of color printer used in the home.

Figure 13　A multifunction peripheral.

Display Devices

A **display device** is an output device that visually conveys text, graphics, and video information. A **monitor** is a display device that is packaged as a separate peripheral. A widely used monitor is an LCD monitor. The **LCD monitor** shown in Figure 14 uses a liquid crystal display to produce images on the screen. The surface of the screen of an LCD monitor is composed of individual picture elements called **pixels**. **Resolution** is the number of horizontal and vertical pixels in a display device. For example, a screen set to a resolution of 2560 × 1440 pixels displays up to 2560 pixels per horizontal row and 1440 pixels per vertical row, for a total of 3,686,400 pixels to create a screen image. A higher resolution provides a smoother, sharper, clearer image.

Mobile computers such as notebook computers, including netbooks and tablet PCs, and mobile devices such as smart phones, portable media players, handheld game consoles, and digital cameras, have built-in LCD screens (Figure 15).

Figure 14   The LCD monitor is widely used with desktop computers.

notebook computer

smart phone

portable media player

handheld game console

digital camera

Figure 15   Notebook computers, smart phones, handheld game consoles, portable media players, and digital cameras have color LCD screens.

Storage Devices

A **storage device** is the computer hardware that records and/or retrieves items to and from storage media. A **storage medium** (media is the plural) is the physical material on which a computer keeps data, instructions, and information. Three common types of storage media are hard disks, flash memory, and optical discs.

Hard Disks

A **hard disk** is a storage device that contains one or more inflexible, circular platters that use magnetic particles to store data, instructions, and information. The system unit on most personal computers contains at least one hard disk, sometimes called an internal hard disk because it is not portable. Users store documents, spreadsheets, presentations, databases, e-mail messages, Web pages, digital photos, music, videos, and software on hard disks.

Hard disks store data and instructions in tracks and sectors on a platter (Figure 16). A **track** is a narrow recording band that forms a full circle on the surface of the disk. The disk's storage locations consist of pie-shaped sections, which break the tracks into small arcs called **sectors**. On a hard disk, a sector typically stores up to 512 bytes of data. Storage capacities of internal hard disks for personal computers range from 160 GB to more than 2 TB.

On desktop computers, platters most often have a size of approximately 3.5 inches in diameter. On notebook computers and mobile devices, the diameter is 2.5 inches or less. A typical hard disk has multiple platters stacked on top of one another. Each platter has two read/write heads, one for each side. The hard disk has arms that move the read/write heads to the proper location on the platter (Figure 17). The hard disk platters spin at a high rate of speed, typically 5,400 to 15,000 revolutions per minute. On today's computers, the platters typically stop spinning or slow down after a specified time to save power.

When reading or writing, the read/write heads on a hard disk do not actually touch the surface of the disk. The distance between the read/write heads and the platters is about two millionths of one inch. This close clearance means that dirt, hair, dust, smoke, or other particles could cause the hard disk to have a **head crash**, when a read/write head touches a platter, usually resulting in loss of data or sometimes the entire disk. Although current hard disks are sealed tightly to keep out contaminants, head crashes do occur occasionally. Thus, it is crucial that you back up your hard disk regularly. A **backup** is a duplicate of a file, program, or disk placed on a separate storage medium that you can use in case the original is lost, damaged, or destroyed.

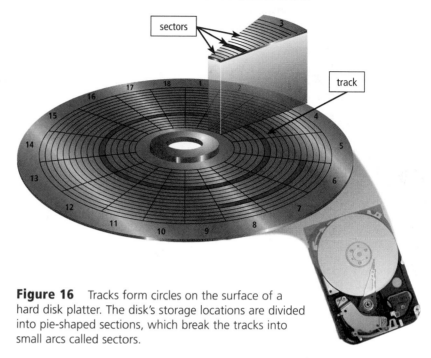

Figure 16 Tracks form circles on the surface of a hard disk platter. The disk's storage locations are divided into pie-shaped sections, which break the tracks into small arcs called sectors.

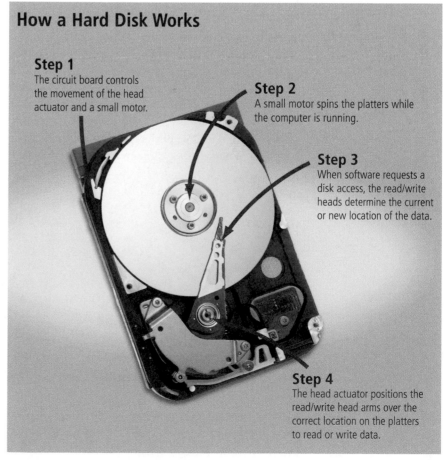

How a Hard Disk Works

Step 1
The circuit board controls the movement of the head actuator and a small motor.

Step 2
A small motor spins the platters while the computer is running.

Step 3
When software requests a disk access, the read/write heads determine the current or new location of the data.

Step 4
The head actuator positions the read/write head arms over the correct location on the platters to read or write data.

Figure 17 How a hard disk works.

Portable Hard Disks   Some hard disks are portable. An **external hard disk** (Figure 18) is a separate freestanding hard disk that connects with a cable to a port on the system unit or communicates wirelessly. A **removable hard disk** (Figure 19) is a hard disk that you insert and remove from a drive. Both internal and external hard disks are available in compact sizes to allow users to transport their data easily.

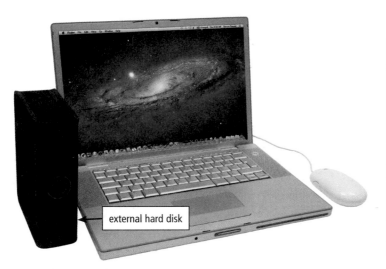

Figure 18   An external hard disk.

Figure 19   A removable hard disk.

Flash Memory Storage

🖑 **Flash Memory Storage**

For more information, visit the Office 2011 for Mac Online Companion Web page at www.cengagebrain.com, click Web Links, and then click Flash Memory Storage.

Flash memory is a type of memory that can be erased electronically and rewritten. Flash memory chips are a type of **solid state media**, which means they consist entirely of electronic components and contain no moving parts. Types of flash memory storage include solid state drives, memory cards, USB flash drives, and ExpressCard modules.

A **solid state drive** (**SSD**) is a storage device that typically uses flash memory to store data, instructions, and information (Figure 20). With available sizes of 3.5 inches, 2.5 inches, and 1.8 inches, SSDs are used in all types of computers, including desktop computers, mobile computers, and mobile devices such as portable media players and digital video cameras. Storage capacities of current SSDs range from 16 GB to 512 GB and more.

Figure 20   As the price of SSDs drops, experts estimate that increasingly more users will purchase computers and devices that use this media.

A **memory card** is a removable flash memory device, usually no bigger than 1.5 inches in height or width, that you insert and remove from a slot in a computer, mobile device, or card reader/writer (Figure 21). Memory cards enable mobile users easily to transport digital photos, music, or files to and from mobile devices and computers or other devices.

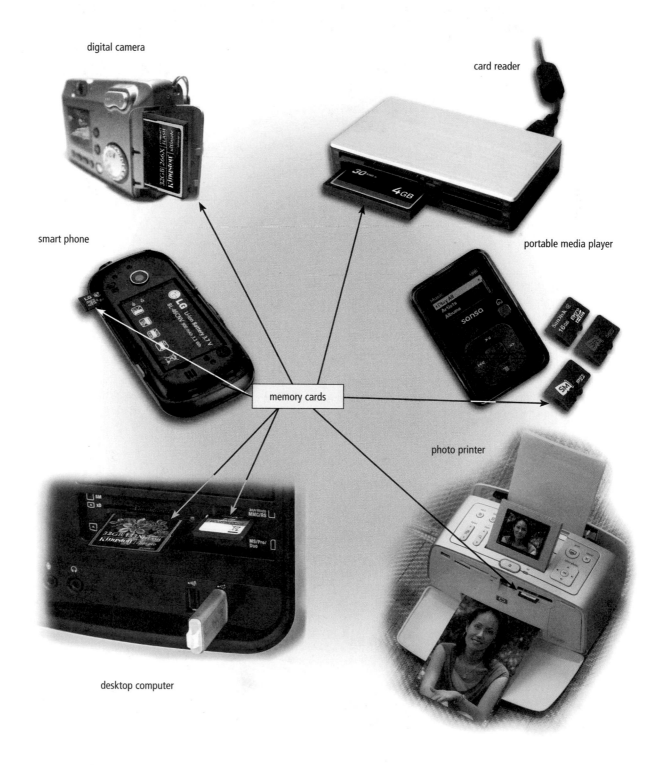

digital camera

card reader

smart phone

portable media player

memory cards

photo printer

desktop computer

Figure 21   Many types of computers and devices have slots for memory cards.

Common types of memory cards include CompactFlash (CF), Secure Digital High Capacity (SDHC), Secure Digital Extended Capacity (SDXC), microSD, microSDHC, xD Picture Card, and microSDXC (Figure 22).

Various Memory Cards

Media Type		Storage Capacity	Use
CompactFlash (CF)		512 MB to 100 GB	Digital cameras, smart phones, photo printers, portable media players, notebook computers, desktop computers
SDHC		4 to 32 GB	Digital cameras
SDXC		64 GB to 2 TB	Digital cameras, digital video cameras, photo printers, portable media players
microSD		1 to 2 GB	Smart phones, portable media players, handheld game consoles, eReaders, handheld navigation devices
microSDHC		4 to 16 GB	Smart phones, portable media players, handheld game consoles, eReaders, handheld navigation devices
xD Picture Card		256 MB to 2 GB	Digital cameras, photo printers
microSDXC		64 GB to 2 TB	Digital cameras, smart phones, notebook computers, desktop computers

Figure 22 A variety of memory cards.

A **USB flash drive**, sometimes called a thumb drive, is a flash memory storage device that plugs into a USB port on a computer or mobile device (Figure 23). USB flash drives are convenient for mobile users because they are small and lightweight enough to be transported on a keychain or in a pocket. Current USB flash drives have storage capacities ranging from 512 MB to 64 GB.

An **ExpressCard module** is a removable device, about 75 mm long and 34 mm wide or L-shaped with a width of 54 mm, that fits in an ExpressCard slot (Figure 24). ExpressCard modules can be used to add memory, storage, communications, multimedia, and security capabilities to a computer. ExpressCard modules commonly are used in notebook computers.

Figure 23 A close-up of the flash memory and circuitry inside a USB flash drive.

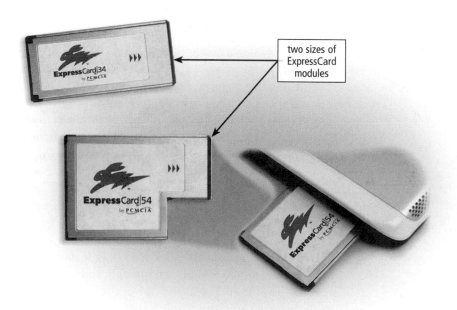

two sizes of ExpressCard modules

Figure 24 ExpressCard modules are available in two sizes.

Optical Discs

An **optical disc** is a flat, round, portable metal disc with a plastic coating. CDs, DVDs, and Blu-ray Discs are three types of optical discs. A CD can hold from 650 million to 1 billion characters. Some DVDs can store two full-length movies or 17 billion characters. Blu-ray Discs can store about 46 hours of standard video, or 100 billion characters. Optical discs used in personal computers are 4.75 inches in diameter and less than one-twentieth of an inch thick. Nearly every personal computer today has some type of optical disc drive installed in a drive bay. On some, you push a button to slide out a tray, insert the disc, and then push the same button to close the tray; others are slot loaded, which means you insert the disc in a narrow opening on the drive (Figure 25).

Figure 25 A slot-loaded optical disc drive.

Optical Disc Formats

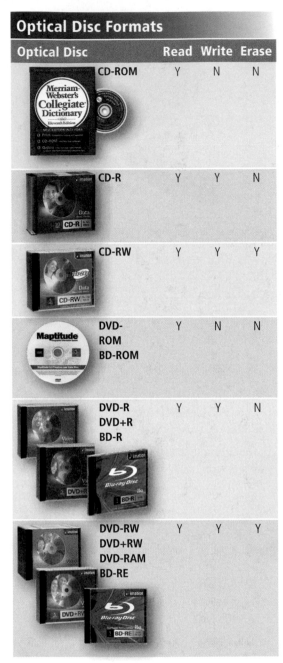

Optical Disc	Read	Write	Erase
CD-ROM	Y	N	N
CD-R	Y	Y	N
CD-RW	Y	Y	Y
DVD-ROM BD-ROM	Y	N	N
DVD-R DVD+R BD-R	Y	Y	N
DVD-RW DVD+RW DVD-RAM BD-RE	Y	Y	Y

Figure 26 Manufacturers sell CD-ROM, DVD-ROM, and BD-ROM media prerecorded (written) with audio, video, and software. Users cannot change the contents of these discs. Users, however, can purchase the other formats of optical discs as blank media and record (write) their own data, instructions, and information on these discs.

👆 **CDs**

For more information, visit the Office 2011 for Mac Online Companion Web page at www.cengagebrain.com, click Web Links, and then click CDs.

Many different formats of optical discs exist today. Figure 26 identifies a variety of optical disc formats and specifies whether a user can read from the disc, write on the disc, and/or erase the disc.

A **CD-ROM,** or compact disc read-only memory, is a type of optical disc that users can read but not write (record) or erase — hence, the name read-only. Manufacturers write the contents of standard CD-ROMs. A standard CD-ROM is called a single-session disc because manufacturers write all items on the disc at one time. Software manufacturers often distribute programs using CD-ROMs.

A typical CD-ROM holds from 650 MB to 1 GB of data, instructions, and information. To read a CD-ROM, insert the disc in a CD-ROM drive or a CD-ROM player. Because audio CDs and CD-ROMs use the same laser technology, you may be able to use a CD-ROM drive to listen to an audio CD while using the computer.

A **CD-R** (compact disc-recordable) is a multisession optical disc on which users can write, but not erase, their own items such as text, graphics, and audio. Multisession means you can write on part of the disc at one time and another part at a later time. Each part of a CD-R can be written on only one time, and the disc's contents cannot be erased.

A **CD-RW** (compact disc-rewritable) is an erasable multisession disc you can write on multiple times. To write on a CD-RW disc, you must have optical disc burning software and a CD-RW drive. Burning is the process of writing on an optical disc. A popular use of CD-RW and CD-R discs is to create audio CDs. For example, users can record their own music and save it on a CD, purchase and download songs from the Web to their computer and then burn the songs on a CD, or rearrange tracks on a purchased music CD. The process of copying audio and/or video data from a purchased disc and saving it on a storage medium is called ripping.

Although CDs have large storage capacities, even a CD cannot hold many of today's complex programs. Thus, some software companies have moved from CDs to the larger DVDs — a technology that can be used to store large amounts of text and even videos (Figure 27).

A **DVD-ROM** (digital versatile disk-read-only memory or digital video disc-read-only memory) is a high-capacity optical disc on which users can read but not write or erase. Manufacturers write the contents of DVD-ROMs and distribute them to consumers. DVD-ROMs store movies, music, huge databases, and complex software. To read a DVD-ROM, you need a **DVD-ROM drive** or DVD player. Most DVD-ROM drives also can read audio CDs, CD-ROMs, CD-Rs, and CD-RWs.

Figure 27 A DVD-ROM is a high-capacity optical disc.

A newer, more expensive DVD format is Blu-ray, which is a higher capacity and better quality than standard DVDs, especially for high-definition audio and video. A **Blu-ray Disc** (BD) has storage capacities of 100 GB, with expectations of exceeding 200 GB in the future.

Many types of recordable and rewritable DVD formats are available. DVD-R, DVD+R, and BD-R allow users to write on the disc once and read (play) it many times. **DVD-RW, DVD+RW, and DVD+RAM** are three competing rewritable DVD formats. Similarly, **BD-RE** is a high-capacity rewritable Blu-ray format. To write on these discs, you must have a compatible drive or recorder.

DVDs

For more information, visit the Office 2011 for Mac Online Companion Web page at www.cengagebrain.com, click Web Links, and then click DVDs.

Cloud Storage

Cloud storage is an Internet service that provides hard disk storage to computer users (Figure 28). Fee arrangements vary. For example, one cloud storage service provides 25 GB of storage free to registered users; another charges $5 per month for 150 GB of storage. For organizations, cloud storage services typically charge for storage on a per gigabyte basis, such as 15 cents per gigabyte.

Types of services offered by cloud storage providers vary. Figure 29 identifies a variety of cloud storage providers.

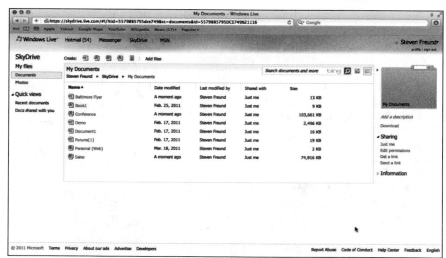

Figure 28 An example of one Web site advertising its storage service.

Cloud Storage Providers	
Web Site Names	**Type of Storage Provided**
Box.net, IDrive, Windows Live SkyDrive	Backup or additional storage for any type of file
iCloud	Backup of most files generated or purchased on Apple products such as MacBook Pro, iPhone, iPod Touch, or iPad.
Flickr, Picasa	Digital photos
YouTube	Digital videos
Facebook, MySpace	Digital photos, digital videos, messages, and personal information
Google Docs	Documents, spreadsheets, presentations
Gmail, Windows Live Hotmail, Yahoo! Mail	E-mail messages
Amazon EC2, Amazon S3, Nirvanix	Enterprise-level storage

Figure 29 Some of the more widely used cloud storage providers.

Communications Devices

A **communications device** is a hardware component that enables a computer to send (transmit) and receive data, instructions, and information to and from one or more computers or mobile devices. A widely used communications device is a modem (Figure 1c on page COM 3).

Communications occur over **transmission media** such as cables, telephone lines, cellular radio networks, and satellites. Some transmission media, such as satellites and cellular radio networks, are **wireless**, which means they have no physical lines or wires. People around the world use computers and communications devices to communicate with each other using one or more transmission media.

Computer Software

Software, also called a **program,** consists of a series of related instructions, organized for a common purpose, that tells the computer what tasks to perform and how to perform them. You interact with a program through its user interface. The user interface controls how you enter data and instructions and how information is displayed on the screen. Software today often has a graphical user interface. With a **graphical user interface** (**GUI,** pronounced gooey), you interact with the software using text, graphics, and visual images such as icons.

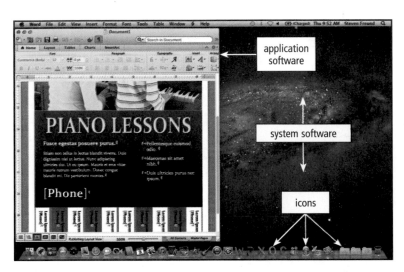

When you buy a computer, it usually has some software on its hard disk. This enables you to use the computer the first time you turn it on. Programs also can be installed after you purchase the computer. **Installing** is the process of adding software to a computer, and **uninstalling** is the process of removing programs and all associated files from the hard disk.

Much software is available at retail stores and on the Web for purchase and/or download. As an alternative, some people use a **Web application,** which is a Web site that allows users to access and interact with software from any computer or device that is connected to the Internet. Software can be divided into two categories: system software and application software (Figure 30).

Figure 30   Today's system software and application software usually have a graphical user interface.

System Software

System software consists of programs that control the operations of the computer and its devices. Two types of system software are operating systems and utility programs.

An **operating system** is a set of programs that coordinates all the activities among computer hardware devices. It provides a means for users to communicate with the computer and other software. Many of today's computers use Mac OS, the latest version of which is shown in Figure 30, or Microsoft Windows, Microsoft's operating system. When a user starts a computer, portions of the operating system are copied into memory from the computer's hard disk. These parts of the operating system remain in memory while the computer is on.

A **utility program** allows a user to perform maintenance-type tasks usually related to managing a computer, its devices, or its programs. For example, you can use a utility program to burn digital photos on an optical disc. Most operating systems include several utility programs for managing disk drives, printers, and other devices and media. You also can buy utility programs that allow you to perform additional computer management functions.

 **Operating Systems**

For more information, visit the Office 2011 for Mac Online Companion Web page at www.cengagebrain.com, click Web Links, and then click Operating Systems.

Application Software

Application software consists of programs designed to make users more productive and/or assist them with personal tasks. These include personal information management, note taking, project management, accounting, document management, computer-aided design, desktop publishing, paint/image editing, audio and video editing, multimedia authoring, Web page authoring, personal finance, legal, tax preparation, home design/landscaping, travel and mapping, education, reference, and entertainment (e.g., games or simulations). Software is available at stores that sell computer products and at many Web sites.

Computer users regularly use application software. Some of the more commonly used programs are word processing, presentation, spreadsheet, and e-mail. These programs often are sold together as a unit, called a business suite. When you purchase a collection of programs as a suite, the suite usually costs significantly less than purchasing them individually. Suites also provide ease of use because the programs in the suite normally use a similar interface and share features.

Word Processing   **Word processing software** is used to create, edit, format, and print documents (Figure 31). A key advantage of word processing software is that users easily can make changes in documents, such as correcting spelling; changing margins; and adding, deleting, or relocating words, sentences, or entire paragraphs.

🖑 **Word Processing Software**

For more information, visit the Office 2011 for Mac Online Companion Web page at www.cengagebrain.com, click Web Links, and then click Word Processing Software.

Figure 31   Word processing software is used to create letters, memos, newsletters, and other documents.

Presentation   **Presentation software** is application software that allows users to create visual aids for presentations to communicate ideas, messages, and other information to a group (Figure 32). The presentations can be viewed as slides, sometimes called a slide show, that are displayed on a large monitor or on a projection screen.

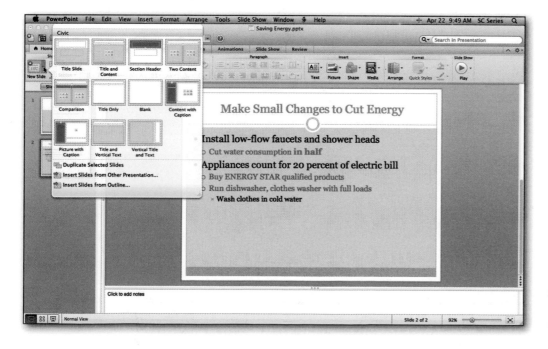

🖑 **Presentation Software**

For more information, visit the Office 2011 for Mac Online Companion Web page at www.cengagebrain.com, click Web Links, and then click Presentation Software.

Figure 32   Presentation software allows the user to produce professional-looking presentations.

Spreadsheet   **Spreadsheet software** allows users to organize data in rows and columns and perform calculations on the data (Figure 33). These rows and columns collectively are called a **worksheet**. Most spreadsheet software has basic features to help users create, edit, and format worksheets.

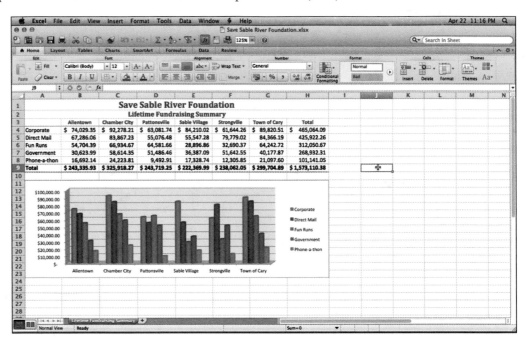

Figure 33   With spreadsheet software, you create worksheets that contain data arranged in rows and columns, and you can perform calculations on the data in the worksheets.

E-Mail   E-mail (short for electronic mail) is the transmission of messages and files via a computer network. Today, e-mail is a primary communications method for both personal and business use. You use an **e-mail program** to create, send, receive, forward, store, print, and delete e-mail messages (Figure 34). Mac OS X Mail and Outlook are two popular desktop e-mail programs. Just as you address a letter when using the postal system, you address an e-mail message with the e-mail address of your intended recipient. Likewise, when someone sends you a message, he or she must have your e-mail address.

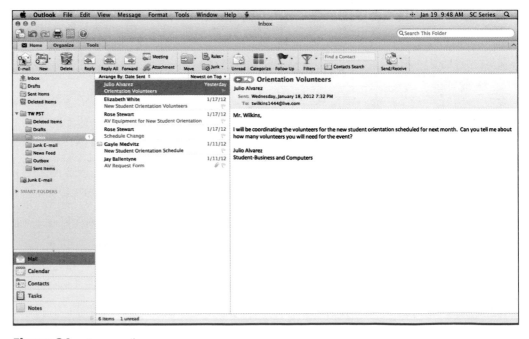

Figure 34   An e-mail program.

Networks and the Internet

A **network** is a collection of computers and devices connected together, often wirelessly, via communications devices and transmission media. When a computer connects to a network, it is **online**. Networks allow users to share resources, such as hardware, software, data, and information. Sharing resources saves time and money. For example, instead of purchasing one printer for every computer in a company, the firm can connect a single printer and all computers via a network; the network enables all of the computers to access the same printer.

Most business computers are networked. These networks can be relatively small or quite extensive. A **local area network** (**LAN**) is a network that connects computers and devices in a limited geographical area such as a home, school computer laboratory, office building, or closely positioned group of buildings. A **wireless LAN** (**WLAN**) is a LAN that uses no physical wires. Often, a WLAN communicates with a wired LAN (Figure 35).

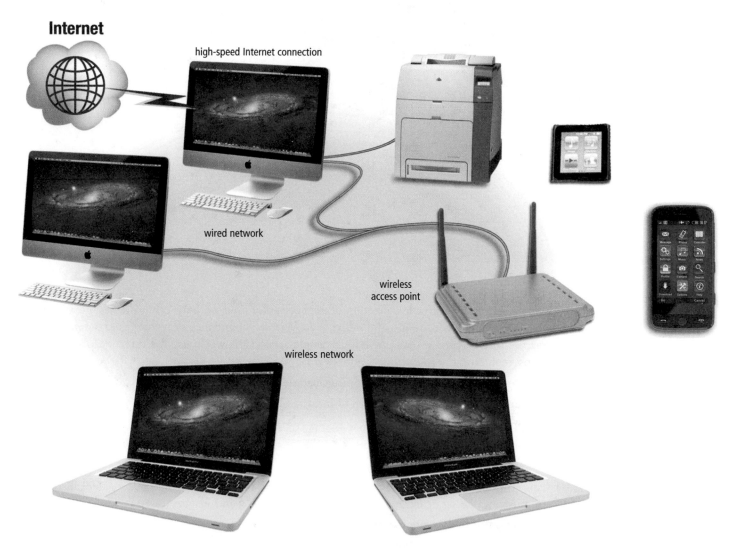

Internet

high-speed Internet connection

wired network

wireless access point

wireless network

Figure 35   Computers and mobile devices on a wireless LAN often communicate via an access point with a wired LAN to access its software, printer, the Internet, and other resources.

A **wide area network (WAN)** is a network that covers a large geographic area (such as a city, country, or the world) using a communications channel that combines many types of media such as telephone lines, cables, and radio waves (Figure 36). The Internet is the world's largest WAN.

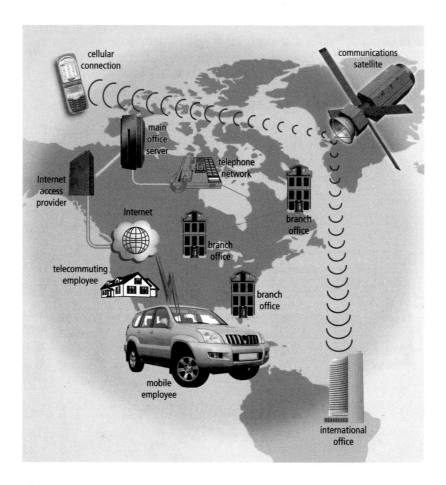

Figure 36 An example of a WAN.

The Internet

The **Internet** is a worldwide collection of networks that links millions of businesses, government agencies, educational institutions, and individuals. With an abundance of resources and data accessible via the Internet, more than one billion people around the world use the Internet for a variety of reasons, including the following (Figure 37):

- Communicating with and meeting other people
- Researching and accessing a wealth of information and news
- Shopping for goods and services
- Banking and investing
- Participating in online training
- Engaging in entertaining activities, such as planning vacations, playing online games, listening to music, watching or editing videos, and reading books and magazines
- Sharing information, photos, and videos
- Downloading music and videos
- Accessing and interacting with Web applications

An **access provider** is a business that provides individuals and organizations access to the Internet free or for a fee. Access providers are categorized as ISPs, online service providers, and wireless Internet service providers. An **ISP (Internet service provider)** is a regional or national access provider. A regional ISP usually provides Internet access to a specific geographic area.

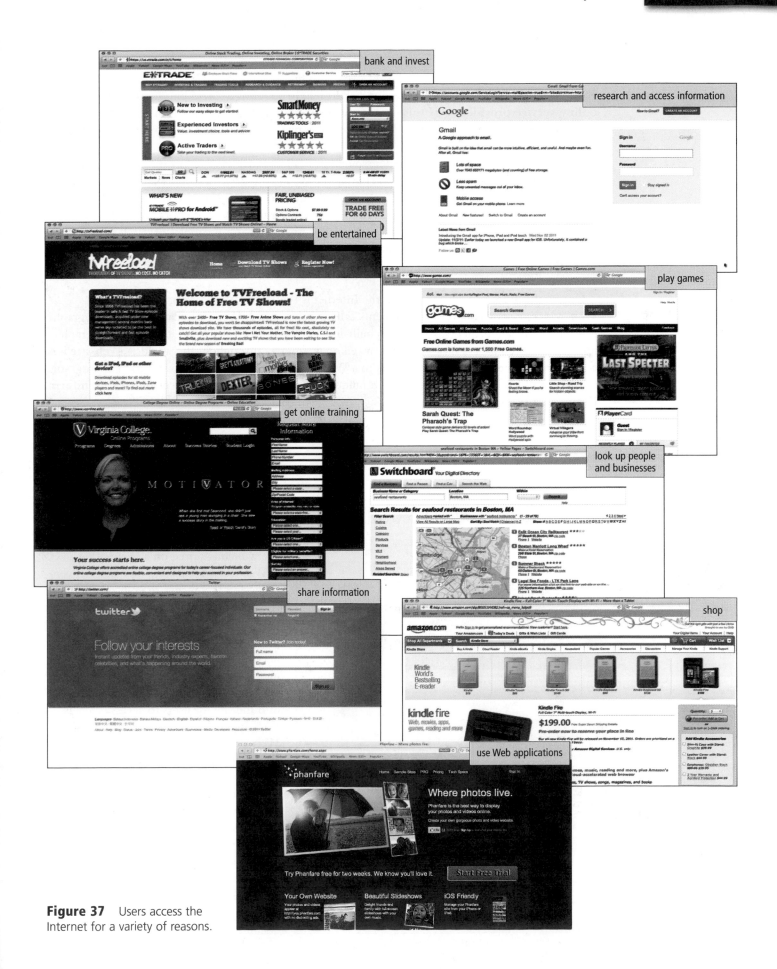

Figure 37   Users access the Internet for a variety of reasons.

A national ISP is a business that provides Internet access in cities and towns nationwide. National ISPs usually offer more services and have a larger technical support staff than regional ISPs. Examples of national ISPs are AT&T and EarthLink. In addition to providing Internet access, an **online service provider** (**OSP**) also has many members-only features such as instant messaging or their own customized version of a Web browser. The two more popular OSPs are AOL (America Online) and MSN (Microsoft Network).

A **wireless Internet service provider**, sometimes called a wireless data provider, is a company that provides wireless Internet access to computers and mobile devices, such as smart phones and portable media players, with built-in wireless capability (such as Wi-Fi) or to computers using wireless modems or wireless access devices. Wireless modems usually are in the form of a USB flash drive or a card that inserts in a slot in a computer or mobile device. Examples of wireless Internet service providers include AT&T, Sprint, and Verizon Wireless.

The World Wide Web

👆 **World Wide Web**

For more information, visit the Office 2011 for Mac Online Companion Web page at www.cengagebrain.com, click Web Links, and then click World Wide Web.

One of the more popular services on the Internet is the **World Wide Web**, also called the **Web**, which contains billions of documents called Web pages. A **Web page** can contain text, graphics, animation, audio, and video, and has built-in connections, or links, to other documents, graphics, or other Web pages. Web pages are stored on computers throughout the world. A **Web site** is a collection of related Web pages. Visitors to a Web site access and view Web pages using a program called a **Web browser**. A Web page has a unique address, called a **Web address** or **URL** (**Uniform Resource Locator**).

As shown in Figure 38, a Web address consists of a protocol, a domain name, sometimes the path to a specific Web page or location in a Web page, and the Web page name. Many Web page addresses begin with **http://**, which stands for **Hypertext Transfer Protocol**, the set of rules that defines how pages transfer on the Internet. The domain name identifies the Web site, which is stored on a Web server. A **Web server** is a computer that delivers requested Web pages to your computer.

The term **Web 2.0** refers to Web sites that provide a means for users to share personal information (such as social networking Web sites), allow users to modify the Web site contents (such as some blogs), and/or have software built into the site for users to access (such as Web applications). A **social networking Web site** or **online social network** is an online community that encourages members to share their interests, ideas, stories, photos, music, and videos with other registered users. A **blog** is an informal Web site consisting of time-stamped articles in a diary or journal format. Examples of software available as Web applications include those that allow you to send and receive e-mail messages, prepare your taxes, organize digital photos, create documents, and play games.

Figure 38   After entering http://www.nps.gov/grsm/planyourvisit/wildlifeviewing.htm as the Web address in the Address bar, this Web page at the United States National Park Service Web site is displayed.

E-commerce, short for electronic commerce, is a business transaction that occurs over an electronic network such as the Internet. Anyone with access to a computer or mobile device, an Internet connection, and a means to pay for purchased goods or services can participate in e-commerce.

Searching the Web

The Web is a worldwide resource of information. A primary reason that people use the Web is to search for specific information, including text, pictures, music, and video. The first step in successful searching is to identify the main idea or concept in the topic about which you are seeking information. Determine any synonyms, alternate spellings, or variant word forms for the topic. Then, use a search tool to locate the information.

Two types of search tools are search engines and subject directories. A **search engine** is a program that finds Web sites, Web pages, images, videos, news, maps, and other information related to a specific topic. A search engine is helpful in locating information for which you do not know an exact Web address or are not seeking a particular Web site. Search engines require that you enter a word or phrase, called **search text**, that describes the item you want to find. Figure 39 shows one way to use the Google search engine to search for the phrase, Aspen Colorado ski resorts. A **subject directory** classifies Web pages in an organized set of categories or groups, such as sports or

E-Commerce
For more information, visit the Office 2011 for Mac Online Companion Web page at www.cengagebrain.com, click Web Links, and then click E-Commerce.

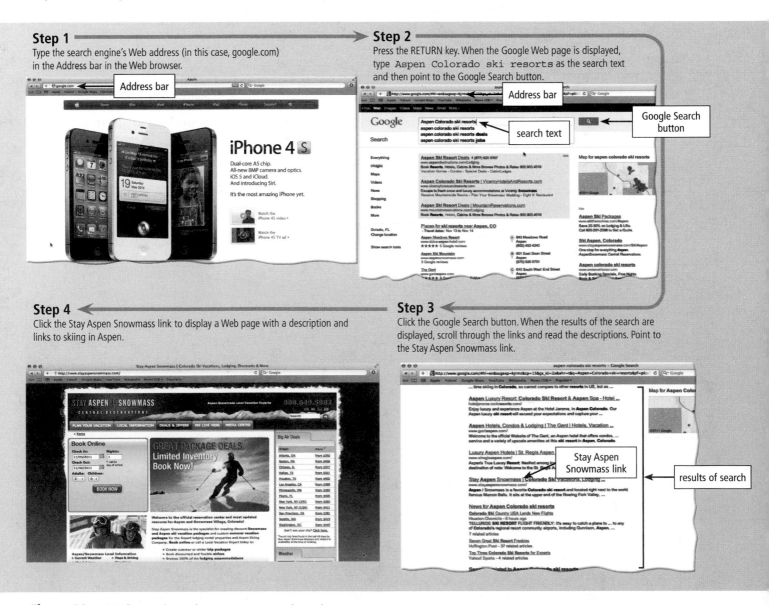

Step 1
Type the search engine's Web address (in this case, google.com) in the Address bar in the Web browser.

Step 2
Press the RETURN key. When the Google Web page is displayed, type Aspen Colorado ski resorts as the search text and then point to the Google Search button.

Step 4
Click the Stay Aspen Snowmass link to display a Web page with a description and links to skiing in Aspen.

Step 3
Click the Google Search button. When the results of the search are displayed, scroll through the links and read the descriptions. Point to the Stay Aspen Snowmass link.

Figure 39   This figure shows how to use a search engine.

shopping, and related subcategories. A subject directory provides categorized lists of links arranged by subject. Using this search tool, you locate a particular topic by clicking links through different levels, moving from the general to the specific.

Computer Viruses and Other Malware

Today, people rely on computers to create, store, and manage critical information. Thus, it is crucial users take measures to protect their computers and data from loss or damage, especially for information that is transmitted over networks. Every unprotected computer is susceptible to a computer virus, worm, Trojan horse, and/or rootkit.

- A computer **virus** is a potentially damaging computer program that affects, or infects, a computer negatively by altering the way the computer works without the user's knowledge or permission. Once the virus infects the computer, it can spread throughout and may damage files and system software, including the operating system.

- A **worm** is a program that copies itself repeatedly, for example in memory or on a network, using up resources and possibly shutting down the computer or network.

- A **Trojan horse** (named after the Greek myth) is a program that hides within or looks like a legitimate program. A certain condition or action usually triggers the Trojan horse. Unlike a virus or worm, a Trojan horse does not replicate itself to other computers.

- A **rootkit** is a program that hides in a computer and allows someone from a remote location to take full control of the computer. Once the rootkit is installed, the rootkit author can execute programs, change settings, monitor activity, and access files on the remote computer.

Computer viruses, worms, Trojan horses, and rootkits are classified as **malware** (short for malicious software), which are programs that act without a user's knowledge and deliberately alter the computer's operations. Users can take several precautions to protect their home and work computers and mobile devices from these malicious infections. For example, users should install an antivirus program and update it frequently. An **antivirus program** protects a computer against viruses by identifying and removing any computer viruses found in memory, on storage media, or on incoming files. Most antivirus programs also protect against other malware. When you purchase a new computer, it often includes antivirus software. The list in Figure 40 summarizes important tips for protecting your computer from viruses and other malware.

Tips for Preventing Viruses and Other Malware

1. Never start a computer with removable media inserted in the drives or plugged in the ports, unless the media are uninfected.

2. Never open an e-mail attachment unless you are expecting it *and* it is from a trusted source.

3. Set the macro security in programs so that you can enable or disable macros. Enable macros only if the document is from a trusted source and you are expecting it.

4. Install an antivirus program on all of your computers. Update the software and the virus signature files regularly.

5. Scan all downloaded programs for viruses and other malware.

6. If the antivirus program flags an e-mail attachment as infected, delete or quarantine the attachment immediately.

7. Before using any removable media, scan the media for malware. Follow this procedure even for shrink-wrapped software from major developers. Some commercial software has been infected and distributed to unsuspecting users.

8. Install a personal firewall program.

9. Stay informed about new virus alerts and virus hoaxes.

10. Do not click links in e-mail messages.

11. Avoid navigating to unknown Web sites.

Figure 40   With the growing number of new viruses and other malware, it is crucial that users take steps to protect their computers.

Buyer's Guide: How to Purchase Computers and Mobile Devices

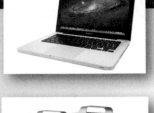

AT SOME POINT, perhaps while you are taking this course, you may decide to buy a computer or mobile device (Figure 41). The decision is an important one and will require an investment of both time and money. Like many buyers, you may have little experience with technology and find yourself unsure of how to proceed. You can start by talking to your friends, coworkers, and instructors about their computers and mobile devices. What type of computers and mobile devices did they buy? Why? For what purposes do they use their computers and mobile devices?

notebook computer

desktop computer

tablet slate computer

smart phone

portable media player

digital camera

Figure 41 Computers and mobile devices.

How to Purchase a Notebook Computer

If you need computing capability when you travel or to use in lectures or meetings, you may find a notebook computer to be an appropriate choice. The guidelines mentioned in the previous section also apply to the purchase of a notebook computer. The following are additional considerations unique to notebook computers, including netbooks and tablet PCs.

❶ Determine which computer fits your mobile computing needs.

Before purchasing a notebook computer, you need to determine whether a traditional notebook computer, netbook, or tablet PC will meet your needs. If you spend most of your time working on spreadsheets, writing and/ or editing documents, sending and responding to e-mail messages, or using the Internet, then a traditional notebook computer will suffice. If your primary use will be to access the Internet while traveling and you are not concerned as much with processing power or hard disk capacity, you might consider a netbook or tablet slate computer (tablet slate computers are covered in the next section). If you need a computer in class or you spend more time in meetings than in your office, then the tablet PC may be the answer. Before you invest money in a tablet PC, however, determine which programs you plan to use on it. You should not buy a tablet PC simply because it is an interesting type of computer.

❷ Purchase a notebook computer with a sufficiently large screen.

Notebook computers typically include an 11.6-inch, 13.3-inch, 15.4-inch, or 17-inch display. Netbooks have screens as small as 7 inches. For most users, a 13.3-inch display is satisfactory. If you intend to use the notebook computer as a desktop computer replacement, however,

you may opt for a 15.4-inch or 17-inch display. Some notebook computers with larger displays weigh more, however, so if you travel a lot and portability is essential, you might want a lighter computer with a smaller display. The lightest notebook computers, which weigh less than 3 pounds, are equipped with an 11.6-inch display.

❸ Experiment with different keyboards, pointing devices, and digital pens.

Notebook computer keyboards, especially netbook keyboards, are far less standardized than those for desktop computers. Some notebook computers, for example, have wide wrist rests, while others have none, and keyboard layouts on notebook computers often vary. Notebook computers also use a range of pointing devices, including touchpads, pointing sticks, trackballs, and, in the case of tablet PCs, digital pens.

Before purchasing a notebook computer, try various types of keyboards and pointing devices to determine which is easiest for you to use. Regardless of the device you select, you also may want to purchase a standard mouse to use when you are working at a desk or other large surface.

❹ Make sure the notebook computer you purchase has an optical disc drive.

Most mobile computers include an optical disc drive. Although DVD/Blu-ray Disc drives are slightly more expensive, they allow you to play CDs, DVDs, and Blu-ray Discs using your notebook computer and hear the sound through earbuds. If you decide to purchase a netbook or MacBook Air, it might not include an optical disc drive. Instead, you might need to purchase an external optical disc drive.

❺ If necessary, upgrade the processor, memory, and disk storage at the time of purchase.

As with a desktop computer, upgrading a notebook computer's memory and disk storage usually is less expensive at the time of initial purchase. Some disk storage is custom designed for notebook computer manufacturers, meaning an upgrade might not be available in the future. If you are purchasing a lightweight notebook computer or tablet PC, then it should include at least an Intel Core i3, 2 GB RAM, and 250 GB of storage. If you are purchasing a netbook, it should have an Intel Atom processor, at least 1 GB RAM, and 120 GB of storage.

❻ The availability of built-in ports and slots and a USB hub on a notebook computer is important.

A notebook computer does not have much room, if any, to add adapter cards. If you know the purpose for which you plan to use the notebook computer, then you can determine the ports you will need. Netbooks typically have fewer ports than traditional notebook computers and tablet PCs. Most notebook computers include common ports, such as a video port, audio port, network port, FireWire port, and multiple USB ports. If you plan to connect the notebook computer to a television, however, then you will need a PC to TV port. To optimize television viewing, you may want to consider DisplayPort, DVI, or HDMI ports. If you want to connect to wired networks at school or in various offices via a network cable, make sure the notebook computer you purchase has a network port.

❼ If you plan to use your notebook computer for note-taking at school or in meetings, consider a convertible tablet PC.

Some computer manufacturers have developed convertible tablet PCs that allow the screen to rotate 180 degrees on a central hinge and then fold down to cover the keyboard (Figure 42). You then can use a digital pen to enter text or drawings into the computer by writing on the screen. Some notebook computers have wide screens for better viewing and editing, and some even have a screen on top of the unit in addition to the regular screen.

Figure 42 A convertible tablet PC.

❽ If you purchase a tablet PC, determine whether you require multi-touch technology.

Newer operating systems now support hardware with multi-touch technology. If you choose an operating system that supports this technology, the tablet PC also must support this technology.

❾ Purchase a notebook computer with an integrated Web cam.

If you will be using a notebook computer to connect to the Internet and chat with friends online, consider purchasing one with an integrated Web cam.

❿ Check with your wireless carrier to see if it offers netbooks for sale.

Most wireless carriers now offer wireless data plans allowing you to connect to the Internet from almost anywhere with a cell phone signal. Some wireless carriers now

are selling netbooks with built-in capability to connect wirelessly to the Internet using a wireless data plan.

⓫ Purchase a notebook computer with a built-in wireless network connection.

A wireless network connection (Bluetooth, Wi-Fi a/b/g/n, WiMAX, etc.) can be useful when you travel or as part of a home network. Increasingly more airports, hotels, schools, and cafés have wireless networks that allow you to connect to the Internet. Many users today are setting up wireless home networks. With a wireless home network, your notebook computer can access the Internet, as well as other computers in the house, from any location to share files and hardware, such as a printer, and browse the Web. Most home wireless networks allow connections from distances of 150 to 800 feet.

⓬ Purchase a well-padded and well-designed carrying case.

An amply padded carrying case will protect your notebook computer from the bumps it will receive while traveling. A well-designed carrying case will have room for accessories such as spare optical discs, pens, and paperwork (Figure 43). Although a netbook may be small enough to fit in a handbag, make sure that the bag has sufficient padding to protect the computer.

Figure 43 A well-designed notebook computer carrying case.

⓭ If you plan to connect your notebook computer to a video projector, make sure the notebook computer is compatible with the video projector.

You should check, for example, to be sure that your notebook computer will allow you to display an image on the computer screen and projection device at the same time. Also, ensure that the notebook computer has the ports required to connect to the video projector. You may need to purchase a special adapter to connect your notebook computer to a video projector.

How to Purchase a Desktop Computer

A desktop computer sits on or below a desk or table in a stationary location such as a home, office, or dormitory room. Desktop computers are a good option if you work mostly in one place and have plenty of space in a work area. Desktop computers generally provide more performance for your money. Today, manufacturers are placing more emphasis on style by offering bright colors, stylish displays, and theme-based displays so that the computer looks attractive if it is in an area of high visibility. Once you have decided that a desktop computer is most suited to your computing needs, the next step is to determine specific software, hardware, peripheral devices, and services to purchase, as well as where to buy the computer.

❶ Determine the specific software to use on your computer.

Before deciding to purchase software, be sure it contains the features necessary for the tasks you want to perform. Rely on the computer users in whom you have confidence to help you decide on the software to use. In addition, consider purchasing software that might help you perform tasks at home that you otherwise would perform at another location, such as at school or at work. The minimum requirements of the software you select may determine the operating system (Mac OS, Microsoft Windows, etc.) you need. If you decide to use a particular operating system that does not support software you want to use, you may be able to purchase similar software from other manufacturers.

Many Web sites and trade magazines provide reviews of software products. These Web sites frequently have articles that rate computers and software on cost, performance, and support.

Your hardware requirements depend on the minimum requirements of the software you will run on your computer. Some software requires more memory and disk space than others, as well as additional input, output, and storage devices. For example, if you want to store all your digital photos and videos on your computer and edit them using photo and video editing software, the computer will need a large hard disk and an upgraded video card. If you plan to run software that allows your computer to function as an entertainment system, then you will need an optical disc drive, quality speakers, and an upgraded sound card.

❷ Know the system requirements of the operating system.

After determining the software you want to run on your new computer, the next step is to determine the operating system to use. If, however, you purchase a new computer, chances are it will have the latest version of your preferred operating system (Mac OS, Windows, etc.).

❸ Look for bundled software.

When you purchase a computer, it may include bundled software. Some sellers even let you choose which software you want. Remember, however, that bundled software has value only if you would have purchased the software even if it had not been included with the computer. At the very least, you probably will want word processing software. If you need additional programs, such as a spreadsheet, presentation software, or an e-mail program, consider purchasing the latest version of Microsoft Office 2011, which includes several programs at a reduced price.

❹ Avoid buying the least powerful computer available.

Once you know the application software you want to use, then consider the following important criteria about the computer's components: (1) processor speed, (2) size and types of memory (RAM) and storage, (3) types of input/output devices, (4) types of ports and adapter cards, and (5) types of communications devices. You also should consider if the computer is upgradeable and to what extent you are able to upgrade. For example, all manufacturers limit the amount of memory you can add. The information in Figure 44 on page COM 31 and Figure 45 on page COM 32 can help you determine which computer components are best for you and outlines considerations for specific hardware components. It is important to consider the base components listed in Figure 44 when you are making your initial computer purchase. If, at a later time you wish to increase the functionality and performance of your computer, you can consider the optional components (Figure 45).

Considerations for Core Hardware Components

Hard Disk: It is recommended that you buy a computer with at least a 320 GB hard disk if your primary interests are browsing the Web and using e-mail and Microsoft Office suite-type programs; 1 TB if you also want to edit digital photos or if you plan to edit digital video or manipulate large audio files even occasionally; and 2 TB if you will edit digital video, movies, or photos often; store audio files and music; or consider yourself to be a power user.

Keyboard: The keyboard is one of the more important devices used to communicate with the computer. For this reason, make sure the keyboard you purchase is comfortable and easy to use, and has a USB connection. A wireless keyboard should be considered, especially if you have a small desk area.

Monitor: The monitor is where you will view documents, read e-mail messages, and view pictures. A minimum of a 19" LCD flat-panel monitor is recommended, but if you plan to use the computer for graphic design or game playing, then you may want to purchase something larger, such as a 27" monitor.

Mouse: While working with a desktop computer, you use the mouse constantly. Make sure the mouse has an ergonomic design, which is important because your hand is on the mouse most of the time when you are using the computer. A wireless mouse should be considered to eliminate the cord and allow you to work at short distances from the computer.

Optical Disc Drives: Most computers include a DVD±RW combination drive. A DVD±RW drive allows you to read optical discs and to write data on (burn) an optical disc. It also will allow you to store and share video files, digital photos, and other large files with other people who have access to a DVD drive. A DVD has a capacity of at least 4.7 GB, versus the 650 MB capacity of a CD.

Ports: Depending on how you use the computer, you may need multiple USB ports. USB ports have become the connection of choice in the computer industry. They offer an easy way to connect peripheral devices such as printers, digital cameras, and portable media players.

Processor: For a personal computer, an Intel Core i7 processor at 2.4 GHz is more than enough processor power for most home and small office/home office users. Higher-end users, such as large businesses or people who use the computer to play games, should upgrade to faster, more powerful processors.

RAM: RAM plays a vital role in the speed of a computer. Make sure the computer you purchase has at least 4 GB of RAM. If you have extra money to invest in a computer, consider increasing the RAM. The extra money for RAM will be well spent because more RAM typically translates into more speed.

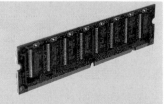

Video Card: Most standard video cards satisfy the monitor display needs of most home and small office users. If you use your home computer to play games or if you are a graphic designer, you will want to upgrade to a higher quality video card. The higher refresh rates will further enhance the display of games, graphics, and movies.

Figure 44 Core hardware components.

Considerations for Optional Hardware Components

Card Reader/Writer: A card reader/writer is useful for transferring data directly to and from a memory card, such as the type used in a digital camera, smart phone, or portable media player. Make sure the card reader/writer can read from and write on the memory cards that you use. Before purchasing a card reader/writer, make sure the computer you are purchasing does not already support the type of memory card you plan to use.

Digital Video Capture Device: A digital video (DV) capture device allows you to connect a computer to a video camera or VCR and record, edit, manage, and then write video back on an optical disc or VCR tape. To create quality video (true 30 frames per second, full-sized TV), the digital video capture device should have a USB or FireWire port.

External Hard Disk: An external hard disk can serve many purposes: it can serve as extra storage for your computer, provide a way to store and transport large files or large quantities of files, and provide a convenient way to back up data on other internal and external hard disks. External hard disks can be purchased with the same capacity as any internal disk.

Fingerprint Reader: For added security, you may want to consider purchasing a fingerprint reader. It helps prevent unauthorized access to your computer and also allows you to log onto Web sites quickly via your fingerprint, rather than entering a user name and password each time you access the site. Most use a USB connection and require software installation.

Joystick/Wheel: If you use the computer to play games, then you will want to purchase a joystick or a wheel. These devices, especially the more expensive ones, provide for realistic game play with force feedback, programmable buttons, and specialized levers and wheels.

Microphone: If you plan to record audio or use speech recognition to enter text and commands, then purchase a close-talk headset with gain adjustment support.

Multifunction Peripheral: Your two basic choices for printing are ink-jet and laser. Multifunction peripherals with laser printers typically print faster, but are more expensive. Multifunction peripherals that print with ink-jet technology typically are slower, but also cost less.

Speakers: Once you have a good sound card, quality speakers and a separate subwoofer that amplifies the bass frequencies of the speakers can turn the computer into a premium stereo system.

USB Flash Drive: If you work on different computers and need access to the same data and information, then this portable flash memory device is ideal. USB flash drive capacity typically varies from 2 GB to 32 GB.

USB Hub: If you plan to connect several peripheral devices to the computer at the same time, then you need to be concerned with the number of ports available on the computer. If the computer does not have enough ports, then you should purchase a USB hub. A USB hub plugs into a single USB port and provides several additional ports.

Web Cam: A Web cam is a small digital video camera that can capture and display live video on a Web page. You also can capture, edit, and share video and still photos. Recommended minimum specifications include 640 × 480 resolution, a video with a rate of 30 frames per second, and a USB or FireWire port. Some Web cams are built into computer monitors.

Wireless LAN Access Point: A wireless LAN access point allows you to network several computers, so that multiple users can share files and access the Internet through a single Internet connection. Each device that you connect requires a wireless card or wireless capability. A wireless LAN access point can offer a range of operations up to several hundred feet, so be sure the device has a high-powered antenna.

Figure 45　Optional hardware components.

Computer technology changes rapidly, meaning a computer that seems powerful enough today may not serve your computing needs in several years. In fact, studies show that many users regret not buying a more powerful computer. To avoid this, plan to buy a computer that will last for at least two to three years. You can help delay obsolescence by purchasing the fastest processor, the most memory, and the largest hard disk you can afford. If you must buy a less powerful computer, be sure you can upgrade it with additional memory, components, and peripheral devices as your computer requirements grow.

⑤ Consider upgrades to the mouse, keyboard, monitor, printer, microphone, and speakers.

You use these peripheral devices to interact with the computer, so make sure they are up to your standards. Review the peripheral devices listed in Figure 44 on page COM 31 and Figure 45, and then visit both local computer dealers and large retail stores to test the computers and devices on display. Ask the salesperson which input and output devices would be best for you and whether you should upgrade beyond the standard product. Consider purchasing a wireless keyboard and wireless mouse to eliminate wires on your desktop. A few extra dollars spent on these components when you initially purchase a computer can extend its usefulness by years.

⑥ Determine what kind of desktop computer you prefer.

Desktop computers include those with both large and small system units, as well as all-in-one computers (Figure 46). Traditional desktop computers with a separate system unit often are more powerful and easier to upgrade. However, all-in-one computers, which are becoming more popular than traditional desktop computers, are sufficient for most everyday computer use, take up less desk space, and are very attractive. All-in-one computers sometimes cost more than traditional desktop computers, and often are more difficult to upgrade.

⑦ If you are buying a new computer, you have several purchasing options: buying from a school bookstore, a local computer dealer, a local large retail store, or ordering by mail via telephone or the Web.

Each purchasing option has certain advantages. Many college bookstores, for example, sign exclusive pricing agreements with computer manufacturers and, thus, can offer student discounts. Local dealers and local large retail stores, however, more easily can provide hands-on support. Mail-order companies that sell computers by telephone or online via the Web (Figure 47) often provide the lowest prices, but extend less personal service. Some major mail-order companies, however, have started to provide next-business-day, on-site services. A credit card usually is required to buy from a mail-order company.

⑧ If you are buying a used computer, stay with name brands such as Apple, Dell, and HP.

Although brand-name equipment can cost more, most brand-name computers have longer, more comprehensive warranties, are better supported, and have more authorized centers for repair services. As with new computers, you can purchase a used computer from local computer dealers, local large retail stores, or mail order via the telephone or the Web. Classified ads and used computer sellers offer additional outlets for purchasing used computers.

Figure 46   Different types of desktop computers.

Figure 47   Mail-order companies, such as Apple, sell computers online.

9 If you have a computer and are upgrading to a new one, then consider selling or trading in the old one.

If you are a replacement buyer, your older computer still may have value. If you cannot sell the computer through the classified ads, via a Web site, or to a friend, then ask if the computer dealer will buy your old computer.

An increasing number of companies are taking trade-ins, but do not expect too much money for your old computer. Other companies offer to recycle your old computer free or for a fee.

10 Be aware of hidden costs.

Before purchasing, be sure to consider any additional costs associated with buying a computer, such as an additional telephone line, a broadband modem, an uninterruptible power supply (UPS), computer furniture, a USB flash drive, paper, and computer training classes you may want to take. Depending on where you buy the computer, the seller may be willing to include some or all of these in the computer purchase price.

11 Consider more than just price.

The lowest-cost computer may not be the best long-term buy. Consider such intangibles as the vendor's time in business, regard for quality, and reputation for support. If you need to upgrade a computer often, you may want to consider a leasing arrangement, in which you pay monthly lease fees, but can upgrade or add on to your computer as your equipment needs change. No matter what type of buyer you are, insist on a 30-day, no-questions-asked return policy on the computer.

12 Avoid restocking fees.

Some companies charge a restocking fee of 10 to 20 percent as part of their money-back return policy. In some cases, no restocking fee for hardware is applied, but it is applied for software. Ask about the existence and terms of any restocking policies before you buy.

13 Use a credit card to purchase a new computer.

Many credit cards offer purchase protection and extended warranty benefits that cover you in case of loss of or damage to purchased goods. Paying by credit card also gives you time to install and use the computer before you have to pay for it. Finally, if you are dissatisfied with the computer and are unable to reach an agreement with the seller, paying by credit card gives you certain rights regarding withholding payment until the dispute is resolved. Check your credit card terms for specific details.

14 Consider purchasing an extended warranty or service plan.

If you use your computer for business or require fast resolution to major computer problems, consider purchasing an extended warranty or a service plan through a local dealer or third-party company. Most extended warranties cover the repair and replacement of computer components beyond the standard warranty. Most service plans ensure that your technical support calls receive priority response from technicians. You also can purchase an on-site service plan that states that a technician will arrive at your home, work, or school within 24 hours. If your computer includes a warranty and service agreement for a year or less, consider extending the service for two or three years when you buy the computer.

How to Purchase a Tablet Slate Computer

If you are always out and about and do not have a need for a full-featured notebook computer, consider a tablet slate computer. Tablet slate computers, such as the Apple iPad, do not offer the same functionality as a notebook computer, but are suitable for everyday tasks such as browsing the Web, checking e-mail messages, and playing media files. The following section lists guidelines to consider when purchasing a tablet slate computer.

❶ Determine the operating system you prefer.

Tablet slate computers come with various operating systems. For example, the iPad uses the iOS operating system, and the Samsung Galaxy Tab has the Android operating system installed. Research the advantages and disadvantages of operating systems on tablet slate computers, and choose the one that works best for you. You might consider features such as the Web browser and its capabilities, the e-mail program, and the number of apps available for installation.

❷ Pick a screen size.

Once you choose your preferred operating system, decide the screen size that will meet your needs. Tablet slate computers with larger screen sizes can display more content, but also may be heavier and more difficult to hold in one hand. Devices with smaller screens may be easier to transport, but display less content at one time without scrolling.

❸ Choose a device with adequate storage space.

As with smart phones and portable media players, tablet slate computers come with varying amounts of internal storage. Some tablet slate computers also allow you to expand the storage capacity by inserting a memory card. When choosing a tablet slate computer, select one with adequate storage for your needs. Because many tablet slate computers also can function as portable media players, consider the amount of space you might require to store audio and video files.

❹ Think about how you plan to connect to the Internet.

Tablet slate computers such as the iPad offer different options for connecting to the Internet. Some models only allow you to connect using Wi-Fi, but others also contain hardware that allows you to connect to the Internet through a cell phone company's data network. Although connecting to the Internet using a cell phone data network allows you access to the Internet from almost anywhere, it also carries a monthly fee. In addition, devices with this capability often are more expensive. Consider a tablet slate computer with data network access if you think you will require Internet access where Wi-Fi is not be available. Otherwise, choose one that connects using only Wi-Fi.

❺ Protect your investment.

Because you most likely will be carrying your tablet slate computer from place to place, you might consider purchasing a case to protect it. Some cases also function as a stand, so that you can set your device on a flat surface and view it at an angle. Figure 48 shows various cases that can protect your tablet slate computer.

Figure 48   One type of case for a tablet slate computer.

How to Purchase a Smart Phone

You probably will use a smart phone more often than other mobile devices. For this reason, it is important to choose a phone that is available through your preferred wireless carrier, available in your price range, and offers access to the features you will use most frequently. This section lists guidelines you should consider when purchasing a smart phone.

❶ Choose a wireless carrier and plan that satisfies your needs and budget.

Multiple wireless carriers exist today, and each one offers a different line of smart phones. For example, the HTC Evo 3D is available only through Sprint. Alternatively, some smart phones, such as the iPhone line of smart phones, are available from multiple wireless carriers. Before deciding on a smart phone, you first should research the wireless carriers in your area, and be sure to ascertain whether the coverage is acceptable. Additionally, compare the calling plans for the various carriers and determine which one best meets your needs. Once you have determined the wireless carrier to use, you then can choose from one of their available smart phones. Once you purchase a smart phone, most carriers allow you to perform a risk-free evaluation for 30 days. If you are not satisfied with the phone or its performance, you can return the phone and pay only for the service you have used.

2 Decide on the size, style, and weight of the smart phone that will work best for you.

Smart phones are available in various sizes, weights, shapes, and colors. Some people prefer larger, heavier phones because they feel that they are more durable, while others prefer smaller, lightweight phones for easy portability. Some smart phones are flip phones, meaning that you have to open the phone (like a clamshell) to display the screen and keypad, some open by sliding the phone, and others do not need to be opened to use them. Figure 49 shows various smart phone styles.

Figure 49   Various smart phone styles.

3 Determine whether you prefer a touch screen, keypad, or mini-keyboard.

Modern smart phones provide various ways to enter text. A touch screen is the primary input device on most of today's smart phones. Some smart phone users prefer touch screens because the phone does not require additional space for a keypad or mini-keyboard, but others find it more difficult to type on a touch screen. Most newer smart phones with touch screens also include handwriting and/or voice recognition. Smart phones with keypads might make it easier to type for some users, but others do not like the unfamiliar feeling of keys arranged in alphabetical order. In addition, you often have to press the keys multiple times before reaching the letter you want to type. Mini-keyboards are available on some smart phones, such as the BlackBerry. Mini-keyboards provide a key for each letter, but the keys are significantly smaller than those on a standard keyboard. Most smart phone users type on mini-keyboards using their thumbs.

4 If you will be synchronizing your smart phone with a program on your computer, select a smart phone that is compatible with the program you wish to use.

Programs such as Microsoft Outlook allow you to synchronize your e-mail messages, contacts, and calendar with your smart phone. If you would like this functionality, purchase a smart phone that can synchronize with Microsoft Outlook. Similarly, if your company uses a BlackBerry Enterprise server or Microsoft Exchange server, you should consider purchasing a smart phone that can synchronize, either using wires or wirelessly, with those servers.

5 Compare battery life.

Any smart phone is useful only if it has the power required to run. Talking and using the Internet on your smart phone will shorten battery life more quickly than when the phone is powered on but not in use. If you have a choice, be sure to purchase a battery that will allow the phone to function all day. Pay particular attention to the talk time and standby time. If you plan to talk on the phone more than the advertised talk time, you might consider purchasing a second battery or an extended battery if your phone supports it.

6 Consider whether you also want your smart phone to function as your primary portable media player or digital camera.

Many newer smart phones contain portable media player and digital camera capabilities, thus reducing the number of mobile devices you might have to carry. If it is important for you to have one device that functions as multiple devices, consider a smart phone that also works as a portable media player and/or digital camera.

7 Make sure your smart phone has enough memory and storage.

If you are using the smart phone to send and receive pictures, video, and e-mail messages, and to store music, purchase a memory card that not only is compatible with your computer and smart phone, but also has adequate storage space for your messages and files. Some smart phones allow you to insert memory cards to expand the storage capacity, but others do not. If you are purchasing a smart phone that does not allow added storage, such as the iPhone, be sure it has enough built-in storage.

8 Check out the accessories.

Determine which accessories you want for the smart phone. Accessories include carrying cases, screen protectors, synchronization cradles and cables, and car chargers.

How to Purchase a Portable Media Player

Portable media players are the preferred devices for listening to music and watching videos on the go. This section lists guidelines you should consider when purchasing a portable media player.

❶ Choose a device with sufficient storage capacity.

Audio and video files can consume a great deal of storage space, so be sure to purchase a portable media player that has enough capacity to store your audio and video files. You also should consider approximately how many media files you acquire each year, and make sure that your device has enough storage space to accommodate these files for years to come.

❷ Determine which file formats your new portable media player should support and how you will add files to your library.

Some portable media players are designed to accept new audio and video files only through a program installed on a computer. For example, it is easiest to add media files to an iPod using the iTunes program. Other portable media players connect to a computer using a cable and are displayed in Windows as a removable disk. You then can add files to the media player by dragging the files to the removable disk icon in Windows. The portable media player must support the file formats you are using. You can determine the file format by looking at the file extension on the media files you wish to transfer to your portable media player. Before purchasing a portable media player, make sure that it can support the file formats you are using.

❸ Consider a portable media player that can play video.

Some users prefer to watch videos on their portable media player in addition to playing music. You typically can download videos for portable media players less expensively than purchasing the movie on a DVD/Blu-ray Disc. Although the display on a portable media player is small, many still find entertainment value because they are able to watch videos while waiting for a bus, on an airplane, or at other locations where they otherwise might not have anything to occupy them.

❹ Read reviews about the sound quality on the portable media players you are considering.

Sound quality may vary greatly among portable media players. If you are unable to try the portable media player before buying it, read reviews and make sure that those reviewing the devices find the sound quality to be acceptable. You also may consider purchasing higher-quality earbuds or headphones to enhance the sound quality.

❺ Select a size and style that works best for you.

Portable media players are available in various shapes and styles. For example, Apple offers the iPod shuffle, iPod nano, iPod classic, and iPod touch (Figure 50). Each type of iPod varies in size and style, and some have capabilities (such as video) that others do not. Choose a size and style that meets your needs and fits your personality.

Figure 50 Portable media players are available in different shapes, styles, and colors.

❻ Check out additional memory cards.

Most portable media players have internal storage for your media files. If you wish to increase the available storage, consider purchasing a portable media player that allows you to increase storage capacity by inserting memory cards. Similar to most computers, it is less expensive initially to purchase the largest amount of storage that you can afford, but it is helpful to be able to increase your storage at a later date.

❼ Consider rechargeable batteries.

Although most portable media players include rechargeable batteries, some still use traditional alkaline batteries. Portable media players sometimes can last for only a few hours on alkaline batteries, and battery replacement can be costly. Rechargeable batteries often last longer and create less waste. If you are not near a power source, you are unable to recharge the batteries when they die. With alkaline batteries, you simply can insert new ones and continue enjoying your player.

❽ Stay within your budget.

As previously mentioned, portable media players are available in a variety of shapes and sizes, and they also are available with various storage capacities. When shopping for a portable media player, be realistic when you consider how you will use the device, as well as how much storage you require. Purchasing the latest and greatest device is not always the best option, and the cost can exceed what you care to spend.

How to Purchase a Digital Camera

Both amateur and professional photographers now are mostly purchasing digital cameras to meet their photography needs. Because digital cameras with new and improved features regularly are introduced to the marketplace, consumers should know how to compare the differences among the multiple cameras that are available. This section lists guidelines you should consider when purchasing a digital camera.

❶ Determine the type of digital camera that meets your needs.

Various types of digital cameras exist, including point-and-shoot cameras, field cameras, and studio cameras. Point-and-shoot cameras typically fit in your pocket and meet the needs of most general consumers. Field cameras, which often are used by photojournalists, are portable but flexible. Field cameras allow photographers to change lenses and use other attachments, and also are more customizable than point-and-shoot cameras. Studio cameras are used in photo studios and are stationary. These cameras give you the widest range of lenses and settings.

❷ The digital camera with the highest resolution is not always the best.

Many consumers mistakenly believe that the digital camera with the highest resolution is the best camera for their needs. A higher resolution increases quality and clarity of your photos, as well as the size at which you can print the photos before noticing degradation in quality. If you never plan to print photos larger than 8" × 10", for example, you do not need a camera with a resolution greater than 5 megapixels. Many cameras available today advertise higher resolutions, but taking pictures at these high resolutions can use valuable storage space. Just because your camera can take a 10-megapixel photo does not mean that you always should set the resolution to 10 megapixels.

❸ Consider size and weight.

Digital cameras are available in various sizes and weights. Some people prefer smaller, lighter cameras because they are easier to transport and take up less space. Others prefer bulkier, heavier cameras because the weight helps steady them to take a clearer picture. Many digital cameras also include an image stabilization feature that reduces the possibility of a blurry picture if you move your hands slightly while taking the picture. Some also believe that heavier cameras are of better quality, although that seldom is true. When choosing a digital camera, practice taking pictures with it and select one that feels comfortable and natural.

❹ Different cameras require different memory cards.

When purchasing a digital camera, pay careful attention to the type of memory card the camera uses. Many use SD cards, some use xD Picture cards, and some use CompactFlash memory cards. Some memory cards are more expensive to replace than others, and some have a higher capacity than other cards. If you take a lot of pictures, purchase a camera that supports a memory card with a higher storage capacity so that you can avoid carrying multiple memory cards. You also might consider purchasing a camera that uses a memory card that is compatible with your other mobile devices.

❺ Photo editing features can save you time.

Some digital cameras have integrated tools that allow you to edit photos directly from the camera. For instance, you may be able to crop photos, change the brightness, or remove red-eye effects. Editing photos directly on the camera after taking them can save you from editing multiple photos at once when you transfer them to a computer. The photo editing capabilities available on digital cameras are limited when compared to photo editing programs, but in many cases they can edit a photo to your satisfaction.

❻ Make sure that you can see the LCD screen easily.

LCD screens on digital cameras allow you to configure the settings, frame a shot before taking it, and preview photos after taking them. LCD screens vary by inches, so select a camera with a screen that does not require you to strain your eyes to view. This is especially important if the camera you are considering does not have a viewfinder, because you then will be required to use the display to frame your shots.

❼ Determine whether your pictures will require you to zoom.

If you plan to take pictures of people or objects that require you to zoom in, select a digital camera that has a high optical zoom. An optical zoom enlarges the subject by adjusting the camera lens, whereas a digital zoom uses formulas built into the camera to magnify images. Optical zooms, as opposed to digital zooms, often result in a higher quality photo. While a digital zoom might be capable of magnifying objects that are 100 feet away, the photo will suffer a loss of quality.

8 Price is important.

As with all other devices, purchase a digital camera that does not exceed your budget. If you find a great camera that is available for more than you are willing to spend, consider locating a camera with a slightly lower resolution, an alternate brand, or a smaller screen. Digital cameras can last well beyond five years if properly maintained, so consider this a longer-term investment that will create memories lasting you a lifetime.

9 Know your batteries.

Some digital cameras require replaceable alkaline or rechargeable batteries (often AA or AAA), and others have a rechargeable battery. Similar to batteries in portable media players, using disposable batteries in digital cameras can get expensive, and they may not last as long as rechargeable battery packs. Digital camera battery life is not measured in hours (as is the case with smart phones and portable media players); instead, it is measured in how many pictures can be taken on a single charge or set of batteries. Turning off the LCD screen and flash when you take pictures can help to extend battery life.

10 Purchase accessories.

Accessories that are available for digital cameras include carrying cases, extra batteries and battery chargers, and extra memory cards (Figure 51). Carrying cases can help protect your digital camera, especially while traveling, and the extra batteries and chargers can stay inside your carrying case so that they are readily available should you need them. Screen protectors can help protect the LCD screen on your digital camera.

Figure 51   Digital camera accessories include memory cards, cases, batteries, and battery chargers.

Learn It Online

Instructions

To complete the Learn It Online exercises, please visit www.cengagebrain.com. At the CengageBrain home page, search for *Office 2011 for Mac* using the search box at the top of the page. This will take you to the product page for this book. On the product page, click the Access Now button below the Study Tools heading. On the Book Companion Site Web page, select Introduction to Computers, and then click the link for the desired exercise.

1 Chapter Reinforcement TF, MC, and SA

A series of true/false, multiple choice, and short answer questions that test your knowledge of the chapter content.

2 Flash Cards

An interactive learning environment where you identify key terms associated with displayed definitions.

3 Practice Test

A series of multiple choice questions that test your knowledge of chapter content and key terms.

4 Who Wants To Be a Computer Genius?

An interactive game that challenges your knowledge of chapter content in the style of a television quiz show.

5 Wheel of Terms

An interactive game that challenges your knowledge of chapter key terms in the style of the television show *Wheel of Fortune*.

6 Crossword Puzzle Challenge

A crossword puzzle that challenges your knowledge of key terms presented in the chapter.

Case Studies

1. Computers are ubiquitous. Watching television, driving a car, using a credit card, ordering fast food, and the more obvious activity of typing a research paper all involve interaction with computers. Make a list of every computer you can recall that you encountered over the past week (be careful not to limit yourself just to the computers you see). Consider how each computer is used. How were the tasks the computers performed done before computers existed? Do you feel computers have a positive impact on people and organizations? Write a brief report and submit it to your instructor.

2. The Internet has had a tremendous impact on organizations. For some organizations, that influence has not been positive. For example, surveys suggest that as a growing number of people make their own travel plans online, travel agents are seeing fewer customers. Use the Web to research organizations that have been affected negatively by the Internet. What effect has the Internet had? How can the organization compete with the Internet? Do you feel that computers might replace humans entirely in the workforce? Why or why not? Write a brief report and submit it to your instructor.

3. As tablet slate computers become more affordable, an increasing number of college students are purchasing them to use instead of using notebook computers. As a new college student, you also would like to purchase a tablet slate computer for your coursework. Shop online for a tablet slate computer that you believe will be sufficient for your major. Once you find a tablet slate computer, write a brief report describing the computer (include the brand, model, configuration information, and price), and submit it to your instructor.

4. Today, the functional lines among mobile devices seem blurred. Your cell phone has a digital camera; your portable media player has wireless Internet access; and your game console plays videos and connects to the Internet. These are examples of technological convergence, a process in which separate technologies merge in single products. Write a brief report on how your favorite mobile device is an example of convergence, listing the various technologies that it uses.

Photo Credits

Office for Mac 2011 and Mac OS X: Essential Concepts and Skills

Objectives

You will have mastered the material in this chapter when you can:

Perform basic mouse operations

Start Mac OS X and log in to the computer

Identify the objects on the Mac OS X desktop

Identify the programs in and versions of Microsoft Office for Mac

Start a program

Identify the components of the Microsoft Office for Mac ribbon

Create folders

Save files

Change screen resolution

Perform basic tasks in Microsoft Office for Mac programs

Manage files

Use Microsoft Office for Mac Help and Mac OS X Help

Office for Mac 2011 and Mac OS X: Essential Concepts and Skills

This introductory chapter covers features and functions common to Office for Mac 2011 programs, as well as the basics of Mac OS X Lion.

Overview

As you read this chapter, you will learn how to perform basic tasks in Mac OS X and Office for Mac programs by performing these general activities:

- Start programs using Mac OS X.
- Use features common across Office for Mac programs.
- Organize files and folders.
- Change screen resolution.
- Quit Office programs.

Introduction to the Mac OS X Lion Operating System

Mac OS X v 10.7 Lion, referred to as **Lion,** is the newest version of the Mac OS X operating system. An **operating system** is a computer program (set of computer instructions) that coordinates all the activities of computer hardware such as memory, storage devices, and printers, and provides the capability for you to communicate with the computer.

The Mac OS X Lion operating system simplifies the process of working with documents and programs by organizing the manner in which you interact with the computer. Lion is used to run **application software,** which consists of programs designed to make users more productive and/or assist them with personal tasks, such as word processing. Figure 1 shows the Mac OS X Lion desktop.

Using a Mouse or Trackpad

Current Mac models come with either a single-button mouse (iMac models) or with a Multi-Touch trackpad (MacBook models). Mouse operations can be accomplished using the mouse or trackpad in its default state, or by customizing the mouse or trackpad configuration. Table 1 explains how to perform a variety of operations using both the single-button mouse and the trackpad. Table 2 lists additional operations specific to the trackpad.

Figure 1

Table 1 Mouse and Trackpad Operations			
Operation	**Mouse Action**	**Trackpad Action**	**Example**
Point	Move the mouse until the pointer on the desktop is positioned on the item of choice	Move one finger on the trackpad until the pointer on the desktop is positioned on the item of choice	Position the pointer on the screen
Click	Press and release the mouse button	Press and release on the trackpad with one finger	Select or deselect items on the screen or start a program or program feature
Secondary click	Hold the CONTROL key on the keyboard and click the mouse	Press and release on the trackpad with two fingers	Display a shortcut menu
Double-click	Press and release the mouse twice in rapid succession without moving the mouse	Press and release on the trackpad twice in rapid succession	Start a program or program feature
Triple-click	Press and release the mouse three times in rapid succession without moving the mouse	Press and release on the trackpad three times in rapid succession	Select a paragraph
Drag	Point to an item, hold down the mouse button, move the item to the desired location on the screen, and then release the mouse button	Point to an item, press down and hold on the trackpad, move the item to the desired location on the screen, and then release the trackpad	Move an object from one location to another

Table 2 Additional Trackpad Operations	
Operation	**Trackpad Gesture**
Scroll up or down	Drag with two fingers up or down on the trackpad
Zoom in	Pinch with thumb and finger
Zoom out	Spread with thumb and finger
Rotate	Rotate with thumb and finger
Swipe between pages	Scroll left or right with two fingers
Swipe between full-screen applications	Swipe left or right with three fingers
Launchpad	Pinch with thumb and three fingers
Show desktop	Spread with thumb and three fingers

Scrolling

Minimize Wrist Injury

BTW Computer users frequently switch between the keyboard and the mouse during a word processing session; such switching strains the wrist. To help prevent wrist injury, minimize switching. For instance, if your fingers already are on the keyboard, use keyboard keys to scroll. If your hand already is on the mouse, use the mouse to scroll.

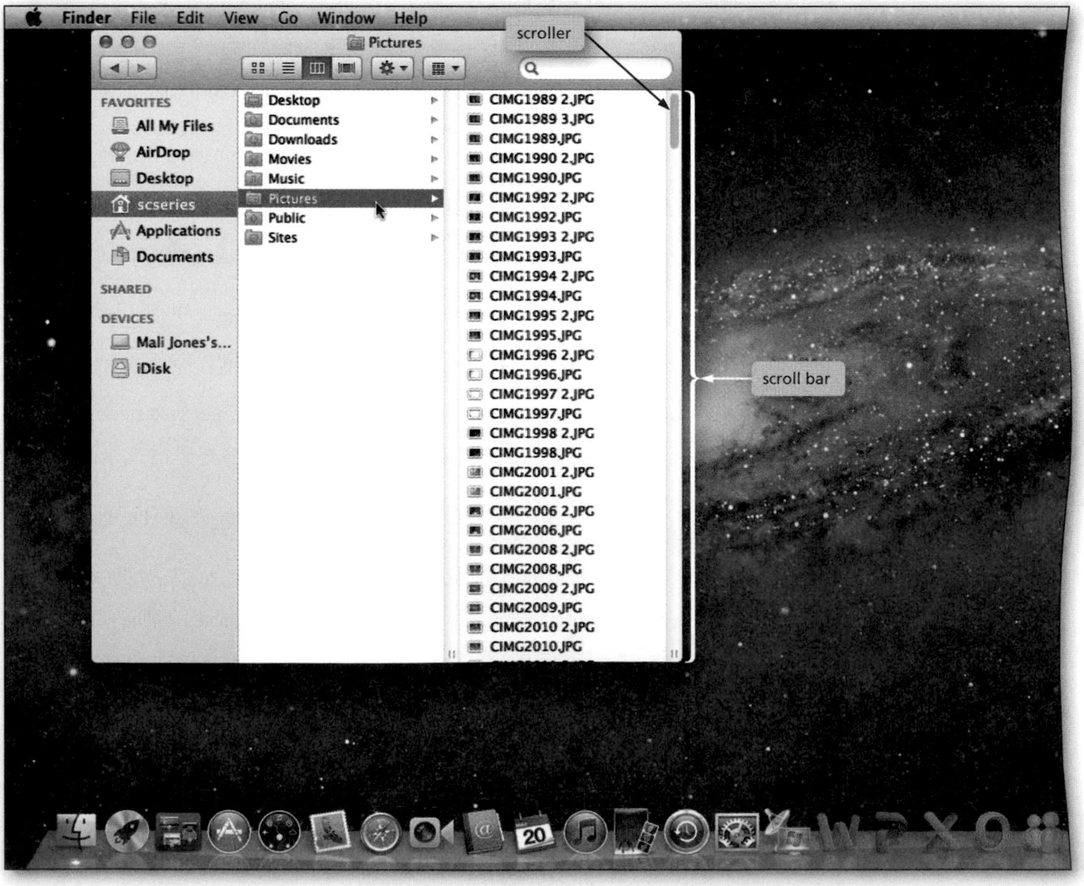

A **scroll bar** is a horizontal or vertical bar that appears when the contents of an area may not be visible completely on the screen (Figure 2). A scroll bar contains a **scroller** that enables you to view areas that currently cannot be seen. You can click above or below the scroller to move up or down a section, or drag the scroller up or down to move to a specific location. You also can use two fingers on the trackpad to scroll up or down. In addition, you can use other **gestures** with two or three fingers to perform additional Multi-Touch operations with the trackpad (Table 2).

Figure 2

Shortcut Keys

In many cases, you can use the keyboard instead of the mouse to accomplish a task. To perform tasks using the keyboard, you press one or more keyboard keys, sometimes identified as a **shortcut key** or **keyboard shortcut**. Some shortcut keys consist of a single key, such as the F1 key. For example, to dim the screen on a MacBook Pro, you can press the F1 key. Other shortcut keys consist of multiple keys, in which case a hyphen separates the key names, such as CONTROL-V. This notation means to press and hold down the first key listed, press one or more additional keys, and then release all keys. For example, to open a new window or document, press COMMAND-N, that is, hold down the COMMAND key, press the N key, and then release both keys.

Starting Mac OS X Lion

It is not unusual for multiple people to use the same computer in a work, educational, recreational, or home setting. Lion enables each user to establish a **user account**, which identifies to Lion the resources, such as programs and storage locations, a user can access when working with a computer.

Each user account has a user name and may have a password and an icon, as well. A **user name** is a unique combination of letters or numbers that identifies a specific user to Lion. A **password** is a private combination of letters, numbers, and special characters associated with the user name that allows access to a user's account resources. A **user icon** is a picture associated with a user name.

When you turn on a Mac, an introductory screen consisting of the Apple logo is displayed. An animated, rotating cursor appears below the Apple logo as the operating system is loaded. Once loaded, a login screen may appear, depending on your computer's settings. **Logging in** to a computer opens your user account and makes the computer available for use. If you are required to log in to the computer, the display shows the user names of users on the computer (Figure 3). Clicking the user name or picture begins the process of logging in to the computer.

Figure 3

At the bottom of the screen are the Sleep, Restart, and Shut Down buttons. The following list identifies the functions of the buttons and commands that typically appear on the initial startup screen:

- The **Sleep command** waits for Lion to save your work and then turns off the computer fans and hard disk. To wake the computer from the Sleep state, press the power button or lift a notebook computer's cover, and log in to the computer.
- The **Restart command** closes open programs, shuts down Lion, and then restarts Lion and displays the Welcome screen.
- The **Shut Down command** shuts down and turns off the computer.

To Log In to the Computer

After starting Lion, you might need to log in to the computer. The following steps log in to the computer based on a typical installation. You may need to ask your instructor how to log in to your computer. This set of steps uses SC Series as the user name. The list of user names on your computer will be different.

- Click the user icon (SC Series, in this case) on the Welcome screen (shown in Figure 3 on the previous page); depending on settings, this either will display a password text box (Figure 4) or will log in to the computer and display the Lion desktop.

Q&A   Why do I not see a user icon?
Your computer may require you to type a user name instead of clicking an icon, or your system may be set to automatically log you in.

Q&A   What is a text box?
A text box is a rectangular box in which you type text.

Q&A   Why does my screen not show a password text box?
Your account does not require a password.

Figure 4

2

- If Lion displays a password text box, type your password in the text box and then click the arrow button to log in to the computer and display the Lion desktop (Figure 5).

Q&A   Why does my desktop look different from the one in Figure 5?
The Lion desktop is customizable, and your school or employer may have modified the desktop to meet its needs. Also, your screen resolution, which affects the size of the elements on the screen, may differ from the screen resolution used in this book. Later in this chapter, you learn how to change screen resolution.

Figure 5

The Mac OS X Lion Desktop

The Lion desktop (Figure 5) and the objects on the desktop emulate a work area in an office. Think of the desktop as an electronic version of the top of your desk. You can perform tasks such as placing objects on the desktop, moving the objects around the desktop, and removing items from the desktop.

When you start a program in Lion, it appears on the desktop. The **Dock**, a row of icons, appears at the bottom of the desktop. Icons that appear in the Dock include all open programs and windows, certain Apple programs and utilities that come with Lion, and the **Trash**, where files that have been deleted are located. A **file** is a named unit of storage. Files can contain text, images, audio, and video. You can customize your desktop so that icons representing programs and files you use often appear on your desktop.

Introduction to Microsoft Office for Mac 2011

Microsoft Office for Mac 2011 is the newest version of Microsoft Office for Mac, offering features that provide users with better functionality and easier ways to work with the various files they create. These features include enhanced design tools, such as improved picture formatting tools and new themes, coauthoring and collaboration tools for working in groups, mobile versions of Office programs, broadcast presentation for the Web, and improved photo and media editing options.

Microsoft Office for Mac 2011 Programs

Microsoft Office for Mac 2011 includes four programs:

- **Microsoft Word for Mac 2011**, or Word, is a full-featured word processing program that allows you to create professional-looking documents and revise them easily.
- **Microsoft PowerPoint for Mac 2011**, or PowerPoint, is a complete presentation program that allows you to produce professional-looking presentations.
- **Microsoft Excel for Mac 2011**, or Excel, is a powerful spreadsheet program that allows you to organize data, complete calculations, make decisions, graph data, develop professional-looking reports, publish organized data to the Web, and access real-time data from Web sites.
- **Microsoft Outlook for Mac 2011**, or Outlook, is a communications and scheduling program that allows you to manage e-mail accounts, calendars, contacts, and access to other Internet content.

In addition, Microsoft Office Web App support, Messenger for Mac 8, and Remote Desktop for Mac 2 are bundled with Microsoft Office for Mac 2011.

Microsoft Office for Mac 2011 Suites

A **suite** is a collection of individual programs available together as a unit. Microsoft offers two Office for Mac 2011 suites. Table 3 lists the Office 2011 suites and their components.

Programs in a suite, such as Microsoft Office, typically use a similar interface and share features. In addition, Microsoft Office programs use **common dialogs** for performing actions such as opening and saving files. Once you are comfortable working with these elements and this interface and performing tasks in one program, the similarity can help you apply the knowledge and skills you have learned to another Office program(s). For example, the process for saving a file in Word is the same in PowerPoint, Excel, and the other Office programs. While briefly showing how to use several Office programs, this chapter illustrates some of the common functions across the programs and also identifies the characteristics unique to these programs.

Table 3 Microsoft Office for Mac 2011 Suites		
	Microsoft Office for Mac Home and Business 2011	**Microsoft Office for Mac Home and Student 2011**
Microsoft Word 2011	✓	✓
Microsoft PowerPoint 2011	✓	✓
Microsoft Excel 2011	✓	✓
Microsoft Outlook 2011	✓	✗
Microsoft Messenger for Mac 8	✗	✗
Microsoft Remote Desktop for Mac 2	✗	✗

Starting and Using a Program

To use a program, you must instruct the operating system to start the program. Lion provides many different ways to start a program, one of which is presented in this section (other ways to start a program are presented throughout this chapter). After starting a program, you can use it to perform a variety of tasks. The following pages use Word to discuss some elements of the Office 2011 interface and to perform tasks that are common to other Office programs.

Word

Word is a full-featured word processing program that allows you to create many types of personal and business documents, including flyers, letters, memos, resumes, reports, fax cover sheets, mailing labels, and newsletters. Word also provides tools that enable you to create Web pages and save these Web pages directly on a Web server. Word has many features designed to simplify the production of documents and add visual appeal. Using Word, you easily can change the shape, size, and color of text. You also can include borders, shading, tables, images, pictures, charts, and Web addresses in documents.

To Start a Program Using the Dock

Across the bottom of the Lion desktop is the Dock. The Dock is divided into two sections by a dashed divider line. On the left are icons for applications and utilities installed on the Mac. On the right are two folders containing icons for Applications and Documents respectively, an icon for accessing the Downloads folder, and the Trash. A **folder** is a named location on a storage medium that usually contains related documents.

On the far left side of the dock is the **Finder icon**, which you use to access applications, files, folders, and settings on a computer. The Dock also displays an icon for each program currently running on a computer.

The following steps, which assume Lion is running, use the Applications folder to start an Office program based on a typical installation. You may need to ask your instructor how to start Office programs for your computer. Although the steps illustrate starting the Word program, the steps to start any Office program are similar.

1

- Click the Applications folder in the Dock to display the contents of the Applications folder in a window on the desktop.

- If necessary, use the scroller to scroll down in the window until the Microsoft Office 2011 folder icon is visible (Figure 6).

Q&A Why does my Applications folder look different?
It may look different depending on the applications you have installed on your computer.

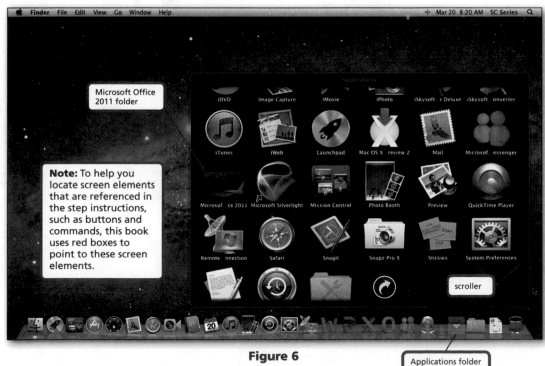

Figure 6

● Click the Microsoft
Office 2011 folder to
open the folder in a
new window (Figure 7).

Q&A Why is the Microsoft
Office 2011 folder on
my computer?
During installation of
Microsoft Office 2011,
the Microsoft Office
2011 folder was added
to the Applications
folder.

Figure 7

● Click the Microsoft
Word icon to start
the Word application
and open the Word
Document Gallery
(Figure 8).

Figure 8

4

- Double-click Word
  Document in the Word
  Document Gallery to
  open a blank Word
  document (Figure 9).

Figure 9

Q&A   What happens when
you start a program?
Many programs
initially display
a blank document
in a program window;
others provide
a means for you
to create a blank
document, as shown
in the Word window
in Figure 8. A **window**
is a rectangular area
that displays data
and information. The
top of a window has
a **title bar**, which is a
horizontal space that contains the window's name.

Q&A   Why is my program window a different size?
The Word window shown in Figure 9 is not maximized. Your Word
window already may be maximized. The next steps maximize a window.

Other Ways

1. Click program icon in Dock,
   if one is present

2. Choose Finder > Go in menu
   bar, choose Applications,
   double-click Microsoft

3. Double-click file created
   using program you want to
   start

Office 2011 folder, double-
click program icon

4. Press SHIFT-COMMAND-A to
   open Applications folder,
   double-click Microsoft
   Office 2011 folder, double-
   click program icon

To Maximize a Window

Sometimes content is not visible completely in a window. One method of displaying the entire contents of
a window is to **maximize** it, or enlarge the window so that it fills the entire screen. The steps on the next page
maximize the Word document window; however, any Office program's window can be maximized using a subset of
these steps.

1

- If the document window is not maximized already, click the green Zoom button (+) on the window's title bar (the Word window title bar, in this case) to move the window so that the top and left edges of the window are in the leftmost and uppermost positions possible.

- Move the mouse pointer to the right border of the window. The pointer will change to a double-headed horizontal arrow (Figure 10).

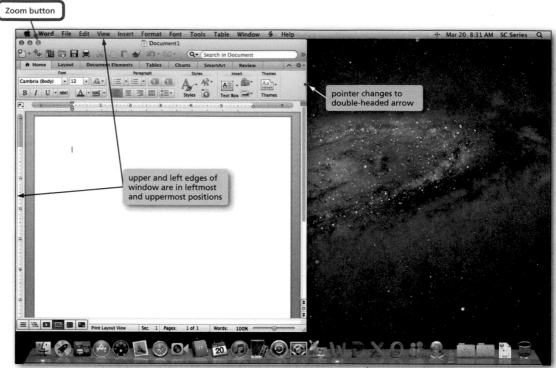

Figure 10

Q&A My pointer won't change to a double-headed arrow. It is a single-headed horizontal arrow pointing to the center of the document. Why?

A single-headed arrow here indicates that the window is already at its maximum width. A single-headed arrow when pointing to the bottom border would indicate that the window is at its maximum height.

2

- Drag the right border of the window to its rightmost position. The arrow will change to a single-headed arrow pointing left.

- Position the mouse pointer over the bottom border of the window. The pointer will change to a double-headed vertical arrow (Figure 11).

3

- Drag the bottom border of the window to its bottommost position. The arrow will change to a single-headed arrow pointing up, and the window will be maximized.

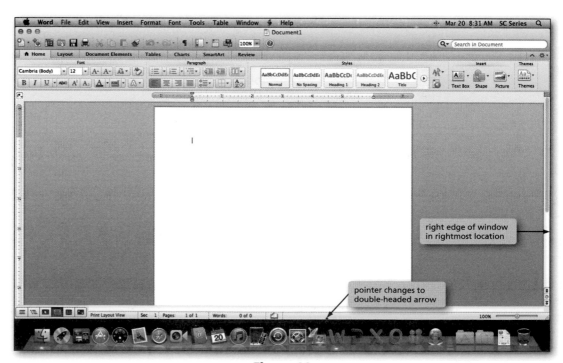

Figure 11

To Hide the Dock

For some documents, you may want to have more space for the Word window than is currently available. The following steps hide the Dock, making it visible only when needed. To make the Dock visible, hover the mouse pointer over the bottom of the screen when it is hidden.

- Click the System Preferences icon in the Dock to open the System Preferences window (Figure 12).

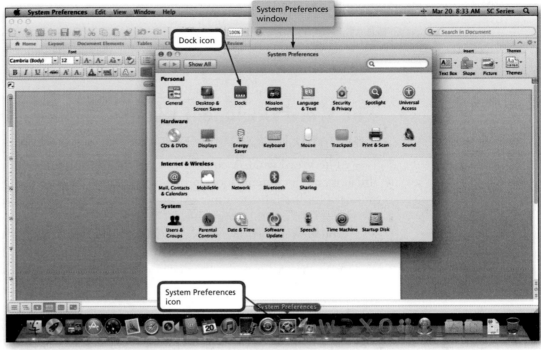

Figure 12

- In the System Preferences dialog, under Personal, click the Dock icon to open the Dock window. Click to check Automatically hide and show the Dock (Figure 13).

- Click the Close button to close the Dock window.

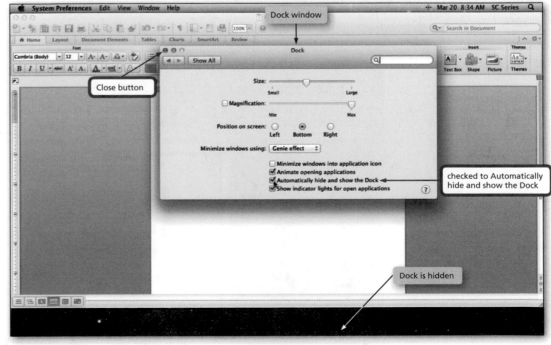

Figure 13

To Maximize a Window

After hiding the Dock, the Word window no longer is maximized. The following steps maximize the Word document window to take up the space freed up by hiding the Dock.

1 Position the mouse pointer over the bottom border of the Word window. The pointer will change to a double-headed vertical arrow.

2 Drag the bottom border of the Word window to its bottommost position. The arrow will change to a single-headed arrow pointing up, and the window will be maximized.

The Word Document Window, Ribbon, and Elements Common to Office Programs

The Word window consists of a variety of components to make your work more efficient and documents more professional. These include the document window, ribbon, Standard toolbar, shortcut menus, and menu bar. These components are common to other Microsoft Office 2011 programs.

You view a portion of a document on the screen through a **document window** (Figure 14a). The default (preset) view is **Print Layout view**, which shows the document on a mock sheet of paper in the document window. Figure 14b shows how the document would appear when printed.

Scroll Bars You use a scroll bar to display different portions of a document in the document window. At the right edge of the document window is a vertical scroll bar. If a document is too wide to fit in the document window, a horizontal scroll bar also appears at the bottom of the document window. On a scroll bar, the position of the scroller reflects the location of the portion of the document that is displayed in the document window.

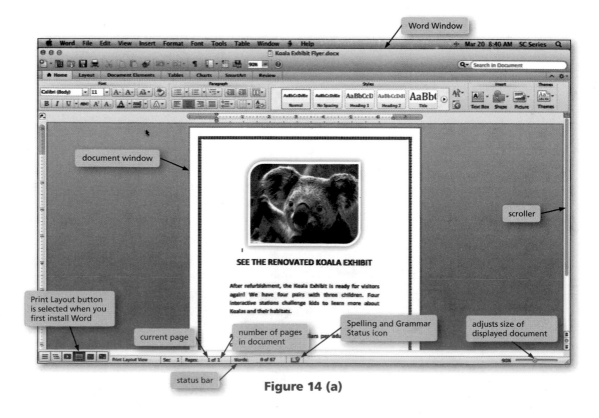

Figure 14 (a)

stored document

SEE THE RENOVATED KOALA EXHIBIT

After refurbishment, the Koala Exhibit is ready for visitors again! We have four pairs with three children. Four interactive stations challenge kids to learn more about Koalas and their habitats.

Admission is now just $30 dollars per adult and $20 for children under 12.

Join us for an exciting adventure at the Parkville Zoo!

1892 Parkville Town Center Blvd, Parkville, USA 55789

Figure 14 (b)

Status Bar The **status bar**, located at the bottom of the document window, presents information about the document, the progress of current tasks, and the status of certain commands and keys; it also provides controls for viewing the document. As you type text or perform certain tasks, various indicators and buttons may appear on the status bar.

The left side of the status bar in Figure 14 contains buttons to change the view of a document. The center left of the status bar shows the current page followed by the total number of pages in the document, the number of words in the document, and an icon to check spelling and grammar. The right side of the status bar shows a Zoom slider to adjust the size of the displayed document.

Ribbon   The **ribbon**, located near the top of the window below the title bar, in conjunction with the Standard toolbar and menu bar, is the control center in Word and other Office programs (Figure 15). The ribbon provides easy, central access to many of the tasks you perform while creating a document. The ribbon consists of tabs, groups, and commands. Each **tab** contains a collection of groups, and each **group** contains related functions. When you start an Office program, such as Word, it initially displays several main tabs, also called default tabs. All Office programs have a **Home tab**, which contains the more frequently used commands.

In addition to the main tabs, Office programs display **contextual tabs**, also called tool tabs (Figure 16), when you perform certain tasks or work with objects such as pictures or tables. If you insert a picture in a Word document, for example, the Format Picture tab appears. When you are finished working with the picture, the Format Picture tab disappears from the ribbon. Word and other Office programs determine when contextual tabs should appear and disappear based on tasks you perform.

Items on the ribbon include buttons, boxes (text boxes, check boxes, etc.), and galleries (Figure 16). A **gallery** is a set of choices, usually graphical, arranged in a grid or in a list. You can scroll through choices in an in-ribbon gallery by clicking the gallery's scroll arrows. Or, you can click a gallery's More button to view more gallery options on the screen at a time.

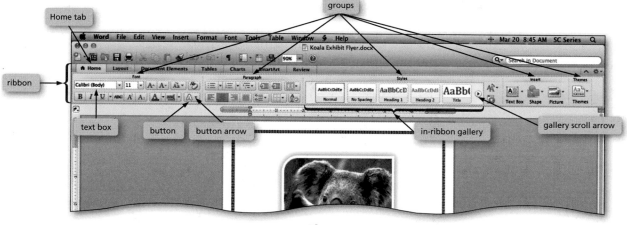

Figure 15

Some buttons and boxes have arrows that, when clicked, also display a gallery; others always cause a gallery to be displayed when clicked (Figure 16).

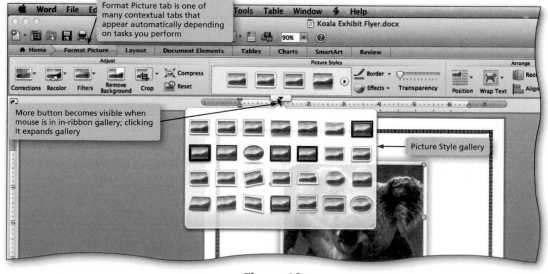

Figure 16

Some commands on the ribbon display an image to help you remember their function. When you point to a command on the ribbon, the command becomes outlined or shaded, and a ScreenTip appears on the screen (Figure 17). A typical ScreenTip displays the name or a description of the command.

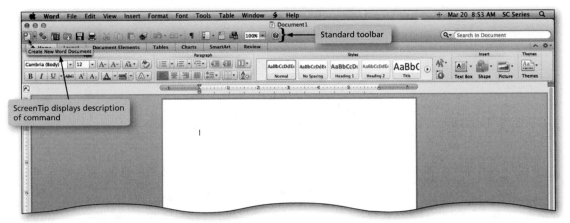

Figure 17

Standard Toolbar The **Standard toolbar**, located above the ribbon, provides convenient, one-click access to frequently used commands (Figure 17). The commands in the Standard toolbar always are available, regardless of the task you are performing.

Menu Bar The **menu bar**, located at the top of the Word window, provides menu access to all the Word commands. The commands in the Standard toolbar and the ribbon usually are also available via the menus in the menu bar. Click a menu name once to display the pull-down menu (Figure 18).

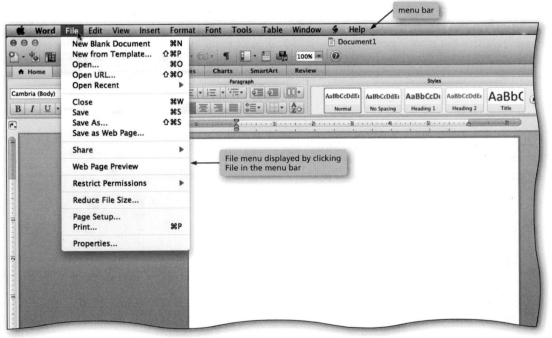

Figure 18

To Display a Different Tab on the Ribbon

When you start Word, the ribbon displays seven main tabs: Home, Layout, Document Elements, Tables, Charts, SmartArt, and Review. The tab currently displayed is called the **active tab**.

The following step displays the Layout tab, that is, makes it the active tab.

1

- Click Layout on the ribbon to display the Layout tab (Figure 19).

 Experiment

- Click the other tabs on the ribbon to view their contents. When you are finished, click the Layout tab to redisplay the Layout tab.

Q&A   If I am working in a different Office program, such as PowerPoint or Access, how do I display a different tab on the ribbon?
Follow this same procedure; that is, click the desired tab on the ribbon.

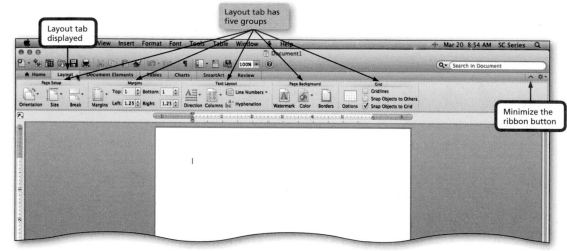

Figure 19

To Minimize, Display, and Restore the Ribbon

To display more of a document or other item in the window of an Office program, some users prefer to minimize the ribbon, which hides the groups on the ribbon and displays only the main tabs. Each time you start an Office program, the ribbon appears the same way it did the last time you used that Office program. The chapters in this book, however, begin with the ribbon appearing as it did at the initial installation of the software.

The following steps minimize, display, and restore the ribbon in an Office program.

1

- Click the Minimize the ribbon button on the ribbon (shown in Figure 19) to minimize the ribbon (Figure 20).

Q&A   What happened to the groups on the ribbon?
When you minimize the ribbon, the groups disappear so that the ribbon does not take up as much space on the screen.

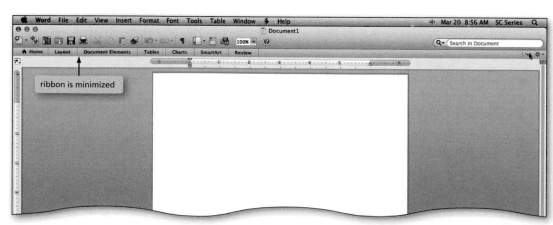

Figure 20

Q&A   What happened to the Minimize the ribbon button?
The Expand the ribbon button replaces the Minimize the ribbon button when the ribbon is minimized.

2

- Click Home on the ribbon to display the Home tab (Figure 21).

Q&A   Why would I click the Home tab?
If you want to use a command on a minimized ribbon, click any tab to display the groups for that tab. After you select a command on the ribbon, the groups will be hidden once again. If you decide not to use a command on the ribbon, you can hide the groups by clicking the same tab or clicking in the program window.

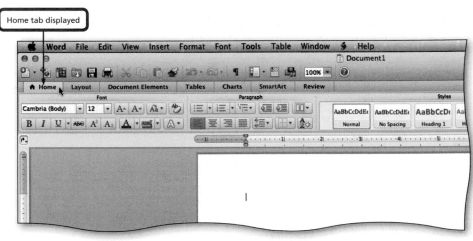

Home tab displayed

Figure 21

> **Other Ways**
> 1. Double-click Home on ribbon
> 2. Press OPTION-COMMAND-R

To Display a Menu in the Menu Bar

When you start Word, the menu bar displays 12 menus. The contents of any menu are accessible using the same process.

The following steps display the contents of the Format menu.

1

- Click Format in the menu bar to display the Format menu (Figure 22).

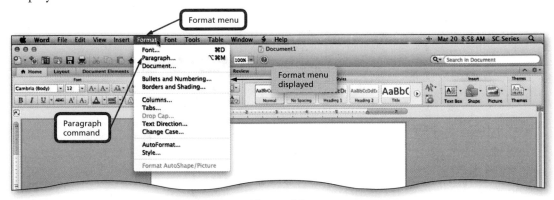

Format menu

Format menu displayed

Paragraph command

Figure 22

2

- Choose Paragraph in the Format menu to display the Paragraph dialog (Figure 23).

3

- Click the Cancel button (Paragraph dialog) to close the dialog.

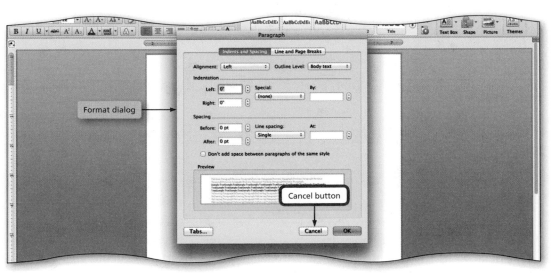

Format dialog

Cancel button

Figure 23

To Display and Use a Shortcut Menu

When you CONTROL-click certain areas of the Word and other program windows, a shortcut menu will appear. A **shortcut menu** is a list of frequently used commands that relate to the CONTROL-clicked object. When you CONTROL-click the Standard toolbar, for example, a shortcut menu appears with commands related to the Standard toolbar. You can use shortcut menus to access common commands quickly. The following steps use a shortcut menu to add descriptive text to the Standard toolbar, which by default has icons only.

- CONTROL-click the Standard toolbar to display a shortcut menu that presents a list of commands related to the Standard toolbar (Figure 24).

Figure 24

- Choose Icon and Text in the shortcut menu to display both icons and text on the Standard toolbar (Figure 25).

- CONTROL-click the Standard toolbar to display a shortcut menu.

- Choose Icon Only in the shortcut menu to return the Standard toolbar to display only icons.

Other Ways

1. With insertion point in Standard toolbar, press with two fingers on the Multi-Touch trackpad to display shortcut menu

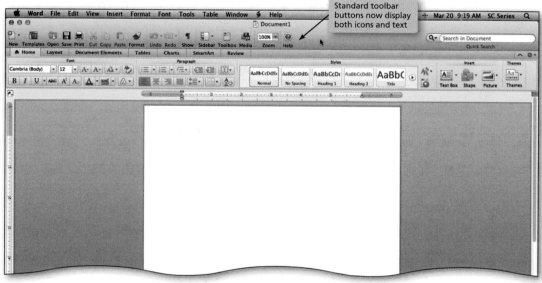

Figure 25

To Customize the Standard Toolbar

The Standard toolbar provides easy access to some of the more frequently used commands in Office programs. You can customize the Standard toolbar by changing it to display both icons and text, or by adding more buttons to reflect commands you would like to access easily. The following steps add the New Web page button to the Standard toolbar and then reset the toolbar.

1

- CONTROL-click the Standard toolbar to display a shortcut menu.

- Choose Customize Toolbars and Menus from the shortcut menu.

- Click the Commands tab to display the Commands pane (Customize Toolbars and Menus dialog).

- Click File under Categories.

- Drag New Web Page under Commands to the right of the New icon the Standard toolbar, but do not release the mouse button (Figure 26).

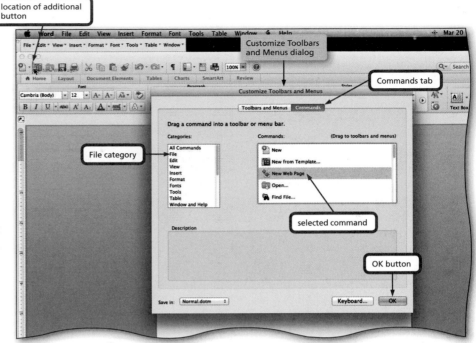

Figure 26

2

- Release the mouse button to place the New Web Page icon in the Standard toolbar.

- Click the OK button to close the Customize Toolbars and Menus dialog (Figure 27).

3

- CONTROL-click the Standard toolbar to display a shortcut menu.

- Choose Reset Toolbar in the shortcut menu to reset the Standard toolbar to the default settings.

- Click the OK button to reset the changes made to the Standard toolbar.

4

- Drag the bottom border of the Word window to its bottommost position to maximize the Word window.

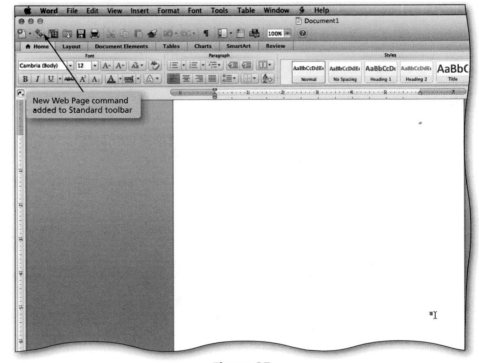

Figure 27

To Enter Text in a Document

The first step in creating a document is to enter its text by typing on the keyboard. By default, Word positions text at the left margin as you type. To begin creating a flyer, for example, you type the headline in the document window. The steps on the next page type this first line of text, a headline, in a document.

- Type **SEE THE RENOVATED KOALA EXHIBIT** as the text (Figure 28).

Q&A What is the blinking vertical bar to the right of the text?
The insertion point. It indicates where text, graphics, and other items will be inserted in the document. As you type, the insertion point moves to the right, and when you reach the end of a line, it moves downward to the beginning of the next line.

Q&A What if I make an error while typing?
You can press the DELETE key until you have deleted the text in error and then retype the text correctly.

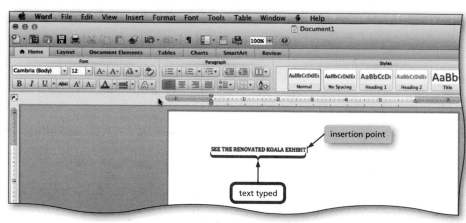

Figure 28

- Press the RETURN key to move the insertion point to the beginning of the next line (Figure 29).

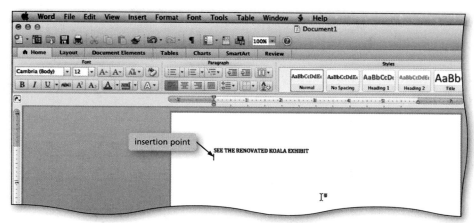

Figure 29

Saving and Organizing Files

While you are creating a document, the computer stores it in memory. When you save a document, the computer places it on a storage medium such as a hard disk, USB flash drive, or optical disc. A saved document is referred to as a file. A **file name** is the name assigned to a file when it is saved. It is important to save a document frequently for the following reasons:

- The document in memory might be lost if the computer is turned off or you lose electrical power while a program is running.
- If you run out of time before completing a project, you may finish it at a future time without starting over.

When saving files, you should organize them so that you easily can find them later. Mac OS X Lion provides tools to help you organize files.

File Type

BTW Depending on your Mac OS settings, the file type .docx may be displayed immediately to the right of the file name after you save the file. The file type .docx is a Word 2011 document.

Organizing Files and Folders

A file contains data. This data can range from a research paper to an accounting spreadsheet to an electronic math quiz. You should organize and store these files in folders to avoid misplacing a file and to help you find a file quickly.

If you are a freshman taking an introductory computer class (CIS 101, for example), you may want to design a series of folders for the different subjects covered in the class. To accomplish this, you can arrange the folders in a hierarchy for the class, as shown in Figure 30.

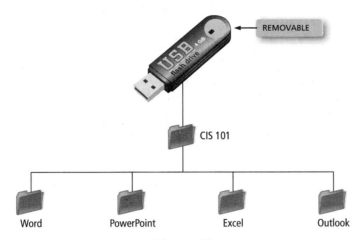

Figure 30

The hierarchy contains three levels. The first level contains the storage device, in this case a USB flash drive. Lion identifies the storage device with a name. In Figure 30, the USB flash drive is identified as REMOVABLE.

The second level contains the class folder (CIS 101, in this case), and the third level contains four folders, one each for a different Office program that will be covered in the class (Word, PowerPoint, Excel, and Outlook).

When the hierarchy in Figure 30 is created, the USB flash drive is said to contain the CIS 101 folder, and the CIS 101 folder is said to contain the separate Office folders (i.e., Word, PowerPoint, Excel, and Outlook). In addition, this hierarchy easily can be expanded to include folders from other classes taken during additional semesters.

The vertical and horizontal lines in Figure 30 form a pathway that allows you to navigate to a drive or folder on a computer or network. A **path** consists of the name of the device you are interested in, in this case the USB flash drive, followed by the folders from top to bottom, each item separated by a slash. Each drive or folder in the hierarchy has a corresponding path.

Table 3 shows examples of paths and their corresponding drives and folders.

Saving Online

Instead of saving files on [BTW] a USB flash drive, some people prefer to save them online so that they can access the files from any computer with an Internet connection. For more information, read Appendix C.

Table 3 Paths and Corresponding Drives and Folders	
Path	**Drive and Folder**
/REMOVABLE/	REMOVABLE drive
REMOVABLE/CIS101	CIS 101 folder on REMOVABLE drive
REMOVABLE/CIS 101/Word	The Word folder in the CIS 101 folder on the REMOVABLE drive

The following pages illustrate the steps to organize the folders for this class and save a file in one of those folders:

1. Create the folder identifying your class.
2. Create the Word folder in the folder identifying your class.
3. Create the remaining folders in the folder identifying your class (one each for PowerPoint, Excel, Access, and Outlook).
4. Save a file in the Word folder.
5. Verify the location of the saved file.

To Create a Folder

When you create a folder, such as the CIS 101 folder shown in Figure 30 on the previous page, you must name the folder. A folder name should describe the folder and its contents. A folder name can contain spaces and any uppercase or lowercase characters, except a backslash (\), slash (/), colon (:), asterisk (*), question mark (?), quotation marks ("), less than symbol (<), greater than symbol (>), or vertical bar (|). The same rules for naming folders also apply to naming files.

To store files and folders on a USB flash drive, you must connect the USB flash drive to an available USB port on a computer. The following steps create your class folder (CIS 101, in this case) on a USB flash drive called REMOVABLE. If the name of your flash drive is different, substitute it for REMOVABLE in these steps.

1

- Connect the USB flash drive to an available USB port on the computer.

- Click the Finder icon in the Dock to open a Finder window (Figure 31).

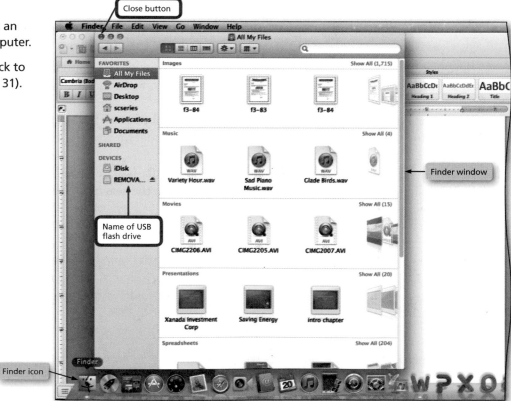

Figure 31

2

- Click REMOVABLE under DEVICES to make the flash drive the active device.

- Click the Action button (gear icon) to display the Action pop-up menu (Figure 32).

Figure 32

3

- Choose New Folder in the menu to create a new folder on the USB drive (Figure 33).

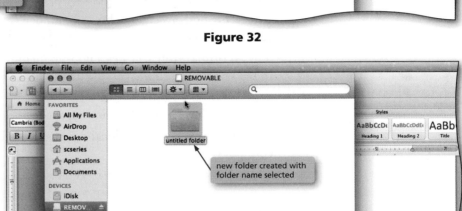

Figure 33

4

- Type **CIS 101** (or your class code) in the text box to name the folder.

- Press the RETURN key to create a folder identifying your class on the selected drive (Figure 34).

Q&A   What happens when I press the RETURN key?

The class folder (CIS 101, in this case) is displayed as a folder on the REMOVABLE drive.

Figure 34

The Finder

The window shown in Figure 34 on the previous page is called a Finder window. Recall that a folder is a specific named location on a storage medium that contains related files. Most users rely on the **Finder** for finding, viewing, and managing information on their computer. Finder windows have common design elements, including the following:

- The **title bar** contains the name of the folder whose contents are shown in the window. In addition, it contains three window controls: the Close button, which closes the window, the Minimize button, which minimizes the Finder window to an icon in the Dock, and the Zoom button, which, in the Finder, toggles between the current window size and the size at which the window had previously been set.

- The **toolbar** contains buttons used to accomplish tasks in the Finder window.

- The **View** buttons change how the Finder window presents the items of the selected device.

- The **Action** button accesses a pop-up menu with commands for actions meaningful in the current location.

- The **Arrange** button accesses a pop-up menu with options for how to arrange content within the Finder window, such as sorting by name, size, or Date Created.

- The **Sidebar** displays the local devices, shared devices, and favorite locations on your computer.

- The **navigation buttons** allow you to navigate back and forward through the previous screens in the Finder window you visited.

- The **Path bar** shows the path, or location, of the current folder. If the Path bar is not visible, click View in the menu bar and choose Show Path bar in the menu.

- The **Spotlight search box** provides a search utility for locating files by file name or content.

To Create a Folder within a Folder

With the class folder created, you can create folders that will store the files you create using each Office program. The following steps create a Word folder in the CIS 101 folder (or the folder identifying your class).

- If necessary, click the icon or folder name for the CIS 101 folder (or the folder identifying your class) in the File list to make it active.

- Click the Column view button to display the contents of the CIS 101 folder in column view.

- Click the Action button to display the Action pop-up menu (Figure 35).

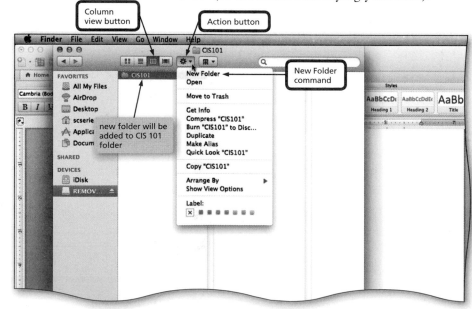

Figure 35

2

- Choose New Folder in the menu to display a new folder icon and text box for the folder.

- Type `Word` in the text box to name the folder.

- Press the RETURN key to create the folder (Figure 36).

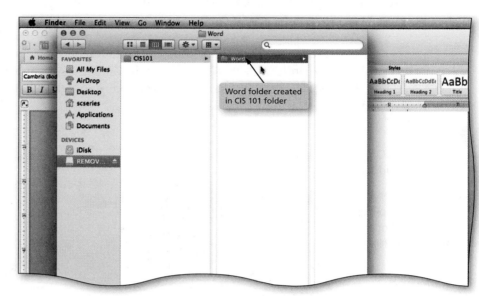

Figure 36

To Create the Remaining Folders

The following steps create the remaining folders in the folder identifying your class (in this case, CIS 101).

1 Click the CIS 101 folder in the Finder window to make it the active folder, and then choose New Folder from the Action menu to display a new folder icon and text box.

2 Type `PowerPoint` in the text box to name the folder.

3 Repeat Steps 1 and 2 to create each of the remaining folders, using the names Excel and Outlook as the folder names (Figure 37).

Q&A Why doesn't the Finder show the folders in the order in which I created them?
By default, folder names are shown in alphabetical order.

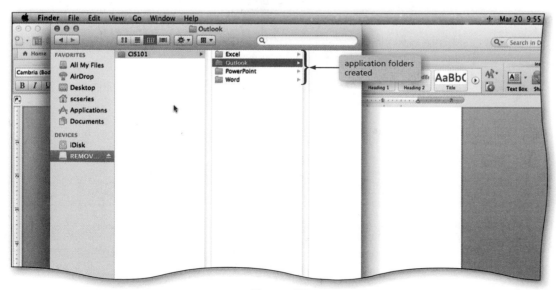

Figure 37

To Use Cover Flow View to Expand a Folder, Scroll through Folder Contents, and Collapse a Folder

Different views in the Finder window provide you with different ways to navigate the contents of drives and folders. When a folder is expanded, it lists all the folders it contains. By contrast, a collapsed folder does not list the folders it contains. The following steps expand, scroll through, and then collapse the folder identifying your class (CIS 101, in this case) in Cover Flow and List views.

- Click the REMOVABLE drive in the Sidebar.

- Click the Cover Flow view button to switch the view to Cover Flow view (Figure 38).

Figure 38

- Click the disclosure triangle beside the CIS101 folder to display the subfolders contained in the CIS 101 folder (Figure 39).

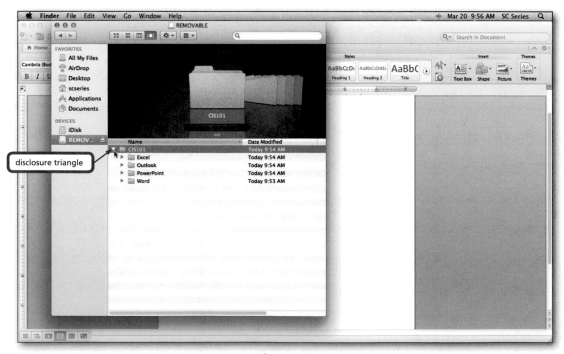

Figure 39

● Click the List view
button to display the
flash drive contents in
List view (Figure 40).

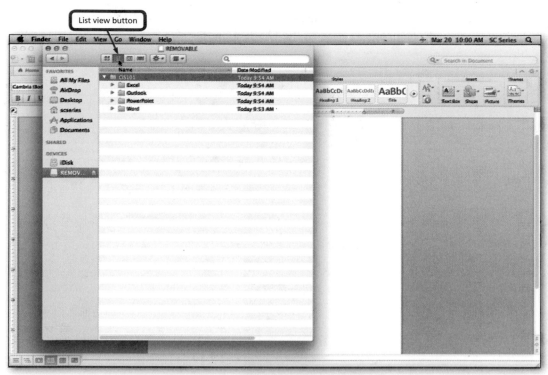

Figure 40

④

● Click the disclosure
triangle beside the
folder identifying your
class (CIS 101, in this
case) to collapse the
folder (Figure 41).

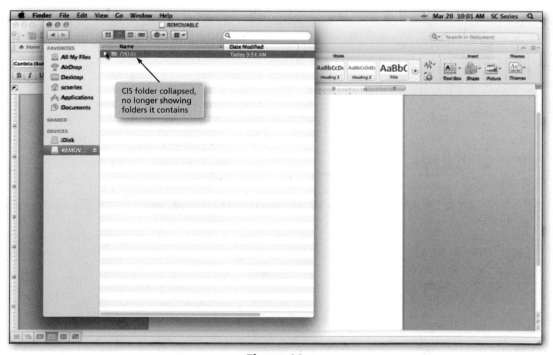

Figure 41

To Switch from One Program to Another

The next step is to save the Word file containing the headline you typed earlier. Word, however, currently is
not the active window. You can use the program icon in the Dock to switch to Word and then save the document in
the Word document window.

The step below uses the Word program; however, the steps are the same for any active Office program currently displayed as a program icon in the Dock. The following step switches to the Word window.

1
- Click the program icon (in this case, the Word icon) in the Dock to make the program associated with the program icon the active window (Figure 42).

Q&A What if multiple documents are open in a program?
If multiple documents are open in a program, Lion will show the most recently accessed document in the active window.

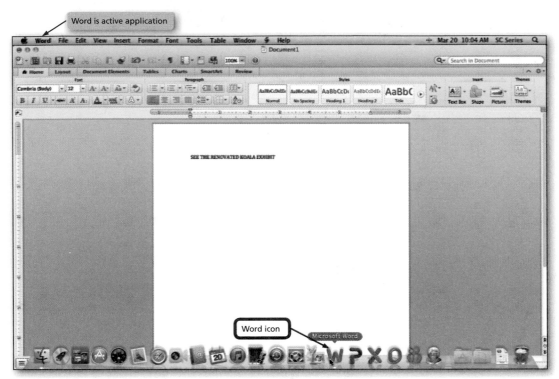

Figure 42

To Save a File in a Folder

Now that you have created the folders for storing files, you can save the Word document. The following steps save a file on a USB flash drive in the Word folder contained in your class folder (CIS 101, in this case) using the file name, Koala Exhibit.

1
- With a USB flash drive connected to one of the computer's USB ports, click the Save button in the Standard toolbar to display the Save dialog (Figure 43).

Q&A Why does a file name already appear in the Save As text box?
Word automatically suggests a file name the first time you save a document. The file name normally consists of the first few words contained in the document. Because the suggested file name is selected, you do not need to delete it; as soon as you begin typing, the new file name replaces the selected text.

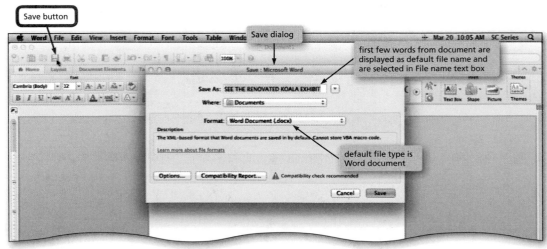

Figure 43

• Type **Koala Exhibit** in the Save As text box (Save dialog) to change the file name. Do not press the RETURN key after typing the file name because you do not want to close the dialog at this time (Figure 44).

Q&A What characters can I use in a file name?

The only invalid characters are the backslash (\), slash (/), colon (:), asterisk (*), question mark (?), quotation mark ("), less than symbol (<), greater than symbol (>), and vertical bar (|).

Figure 44

• Navigate to the desired save location (in this case, the Word folder in the CIS 101 folder [or your class folder] on the USB flash drive) by performing the tasks in Steps 3a, 3b, and 3c.

3a

• If necessary, click the Save As disclosure button to expand the dialog.

• If necessary, click the Column view button to show items in Column view.

• If necessary, scroll through the Sidebar until your USB flash drive appears in the list of available devices (Figure 45).

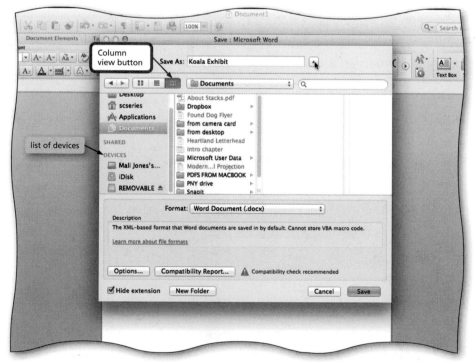

Figure 45

• Click the USB flash drive in the list of available devices to select that drive as the new save location and display its contents in the right pane.

• If your class folder (CIS 101, in this case) is not expanded, click the CIS 101 folder to select the folder and display its contents in the right pane.

Q&A What if I do not want to save in a folder?

Although storing files in folders is an effective technique for organizing files, some users prefer not to store files in folders. If you prefer not to save this file in a folder, skip all instructions in Step 3c and proceed to Step 4.

• Click the Word folder to select the folder and display its contents in the next pane to the right (Figure 46).

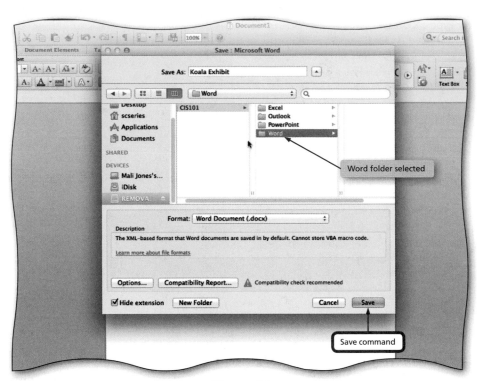

Figure 46

• Click the Save button (Save dialog) to save the document in the selected folder on the selected drive with the entered file name (Figure 47).

Q&A How do I know that the file is saved?

While an Office program is saving a file, it briefly displays a message on the status bar indicating the amount of the file saved. In addition, the USB flash drive may have a light that flashes during the save process.

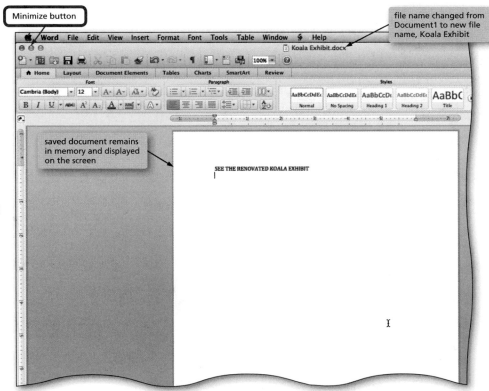

Figure 47

Other Ways

1. Choose File > Save, type file name, navigate to desired save location, click Save button

2. Press COMMAND-S, type file name, navigate to desired save location, click Save button

Navigating in Dialogs

Navigating is the process of finding a location on a storage device. While saving the Koala Exhibit file, for example, Steps 3a–3c in the previous set of steps navigated to the Word folder located in the CIS 101 folder. When performing certain functions, such as saving a file, opening a file, or inserting a picture in an existing document, you most likely will have to navigate to the location where you want to save the file or to the folder containing the file you want to open or insert. Most dialogs requiring navigation follow a similar procedure; that is, the way you navigate to a folder in one dialog such as the Save As dialog, is similar to how you might navigate in another dialog, such as the Open dialog. If you chose to navigate to a specific location in a dialog, you would follow the instructions in Steps 3a–3c on pages OFF 31 and OFF 32.

To Minimize and Restore a Window

Before continuing, you can verify that the Word file was saved properly. To do this, you will minimize the Word window and then open the USB flash drive window so that you can verify the file is stored on the USB flash drive. A **minimized window** is an open window hidden from view but that can be displayed quickly by clicking the window's program icon in the Dock.

In the following example, Word is used to illustrate minimizing and restoring windows; however, you would follow the same steps regardless of the Office program you are using.

The following steps minimize the Word window, verify that the file is saved, and then restore the minimized window.

- Click the Minimize button on the document's title bar (shown in Figure 47 on the previous page) to minimize the document window to the Dock (Figure 48).

Q&A   Is the minimized window still available? The minimized window, Word in this case, remains available but no longer is the active window. It is minimized as a document in the Dock.

- If necessary, double-click the REMOVABLE flash drive icon on the desktop to open the USB flash drive window.

Figure 48

2

- If necessary, click the disclosure arrow beside the CIS 101 folder to expand it.

- Click the disclosure arrow beside the Word folder to display its contents (Figure 49).

3

- After viewing the contents of the Word folder, click the Close button to close the Finder window.

- Click the Word icon in the Dock to restore the minimized window (as shown in Figure 47 on page OFF 32).

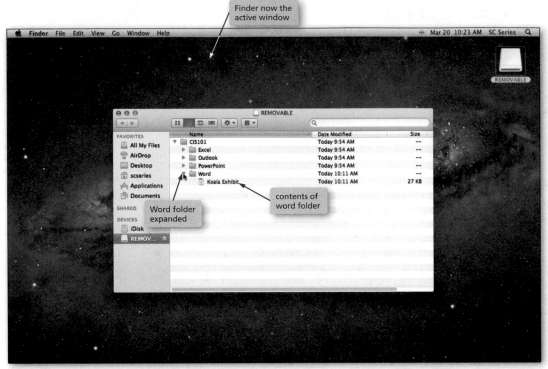

Figure 49

Screen Resolution

Screen resolution indicates the number of pixels (dots) that the computer uses to display the letters, numbers, graphics, and background you see on the screen. When you increase the screen resolution, Lion displays more information on the screen, but the information decreases in size. The reverse also is true: as you decrease the screen resolution, Lion displays less information on the screen, but the information increases in size.

Screen resolution usually is stated as the product of two numbers, such as 1280×800 (pronounced "twelve eighty by eight hundred"). A 1280×800 screen resolution results in a display of 1,200 distinct pixels on each of 800 lines, or about 1,024,000 pixels. Changing the screen resolution affects how the ribbon appears in Office programs. Figure 50 shows the Word ribbon at screen resolutions of 800×600 and 1280×800. All of the same commands are available regardless of screen resolution. Word, however, makes changes to the groups and the buttons within the groups to accommodate the various screen resolutions. The result is that certain commands may need to be accessed differently depending on the resolution chosen.

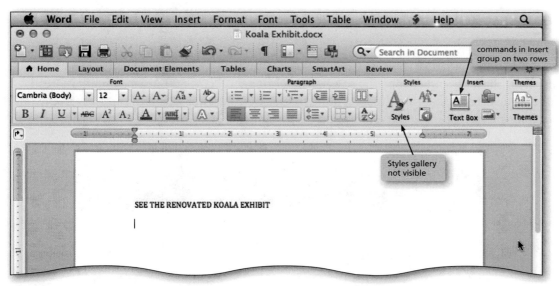

Figure 50 (a) Ribbon at Resolution of 800 × 600

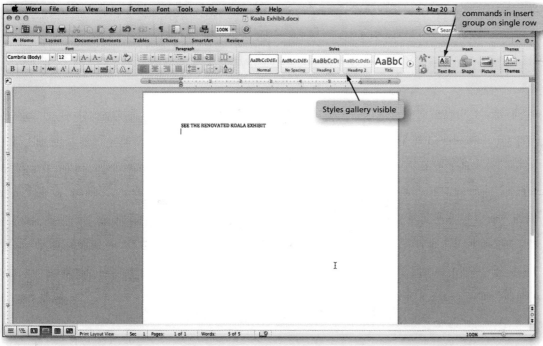

Figure 50 (b) Ribbon at Resolution of 1280 × 800

Comparing the two ribbons in Figure 50, notice the changes in content and layout of the groups and galleries. In some cases, the content of a group is the same in each resolution, but the layout of the group differs. For example, the same buttons appear in the Styles groups in the two resolutions, but the layouts differ. In other cases, the content and layout are the same across the resolution, but the level of detail differs with the resolution. In the Insert group, when the resolution increases to 1280 × 800, the names of all the buttons in the group appear in addition to the buttons themselves. At the lower resolution, only some names appear.

To Change the Screen Resolution

If you are using a computer to step through the chapters in this book and you want your screen to match the figures, you may need to change your screen's resolution. The figures in this book use a screen resolution of 1280×800. The following steps show how to change the screen resolution to 1280×800. Your computer already may be set to 1280×800 or some other resolution. Keep in mind that many computer labs prevent users from changing the screen resolution; in that case, read the following steps for illustration purposes.

- Minimize the Koala Exhibit Word document to the Dock to display the Lion desktop.

- Click the System Preferences icon in the Dock to open the System Preferences window (Figure 51).

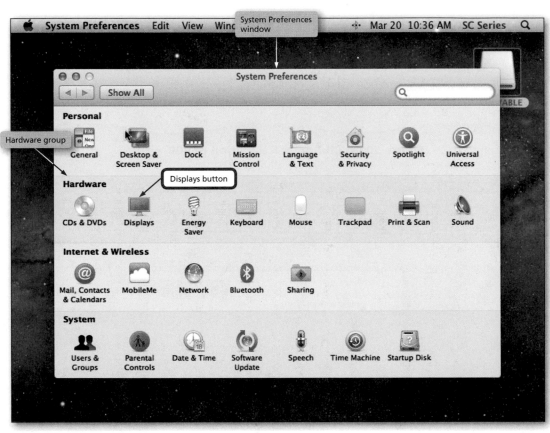

Figure 51

- Under Hardware, click Displays to open the Color LCD dialog.

- If necessary, choose the desired resolution (1280×800 in this case) from the Resolutions list (Figure 52).

Q&A What if my computer does not support the 1280×800 resolution?
Some computers do not support the 1280×800 resolution. In this case, select a resolution that is close to the 1280×800 resolution.

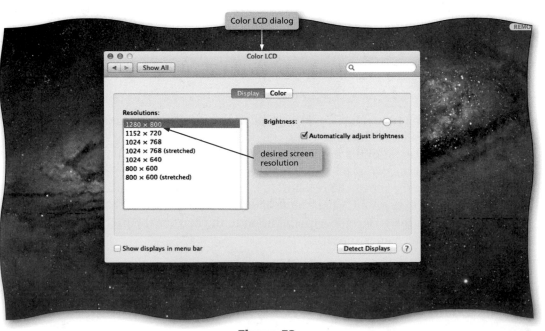

Figure 52

- If the 'About to change the display mode' dialog displays, click the OK button, and then click the Close button to close the Color LCD dialog and change the screen resolution (Figure 53).

- If necessary, repeat steps 1–3 to reset the screen resolution to the original screen setting.

Figure 53

To Quit an Office Program with One Document Open

When you quit an Office program, such as Word, if you have made changes to a file since the last time the file was saved, the Office program displays a dialog asking if you want to save the changes you made to the file before it closes the program window. The dialog contains three buttons with these resulting actions: the Save button saves the changes and then quits the Office program, the Don't Save button quits the Office program without saving changes, and the Cancel button closes the dialog and redisplays the file without saving the changes.

If no changes have been made to an open document since the last time the file was saved, the Office program will close the window without displaying a dialog.

The following steps quit an Office program. In the following example, Word is used to illustrate quitting an Office program; however, you would follow the same steps regardless of the Office program you were using.

- If necessary, click the Word program icon in the Dock to display the Word window on the desktop.

- Click Word in the menu bar to display the Word menu (Figure 54).

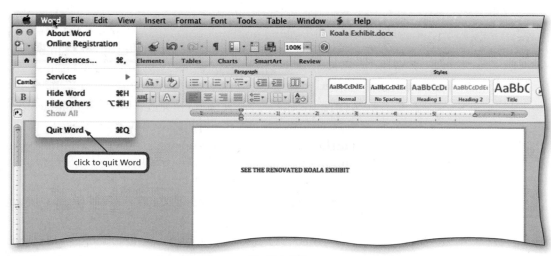

Figure 54

• Choose Quit Word from the Word menu to close the document and quit Word.

Q&A What if I have more than one document open in an Office program?

You will see a dialog prompting you to save changes for each open Word document with unsaved changes. After choosing to save or not save any unsaved changes for each document, the application will be closed. If there are no unsaved changes in any of the documents, all documents and the Word application will be closed with the Quit Word command.

• If a Microsoft Word dialog appears, click the Save button to save any changes made to the document since the last save.

Other Ways

1. CONTROL-click the Office program button in Dock, click Quit in shortcut menu

2. On trackpad, two-finger press the Office icon in Dock, click Quit in shortcut menu

3. Press COMMAND-Q

Break Point: If you wish to take a break, this is a good place to do so. To resume at a later time, continue to follow the steps from this location forward.

Additional Microsoft Office Programs

The previous section used Word to illustrate common features of Office and some basic elements unique to Word. The following sections present elements unique to PowerPoint and Excel, as well as illustrate additional common features of Office.

In the following pages, you will learn how to do the following:

1. Start an Office program (PowerPoint) using the search box.
2. Create two small documents in the same Office program (PowerPoint).
3. Close one of the documents.
4. Reopen the document just closed.
5. Create a document in a different Office program (Excel).
6. Save the document with a new file name.

PowerPoint

PowerPoint is a complete presentation program that allows you to produce professional-looking presentations (Figure 55). A PowerPoint **presentation** also is called a **slide show**. PowerPoint contains several features to simplify creating a slide show. To make presentations more impressive, you can add diagrams, tables, pictures, video, sound, and animation effects. Additional PowerPoint features include the following:

• **Word processing** — Create bulleted lists, combine words and images, find and replace text, and use multiple fonts and font sizes.

• **Outlining** — Develop a presentation using an outline format. You also can import outlines from Microsoft Word or other word processing programs, including single-level and multilevel lists.

• **Charting** — Create and insert charts into presentations and then add effects and chart elements.

• **Drawing** — Create and modify diagrams using shapes such as arcs, arrows, cubes, rectangles, stars, and triangles. Then, customize and add effects to the diagrams, and arrange these objects by sizing, scaling, and rotating them.

- **Inserting multimedia** — Insert artwork and multimedia effects into a slide show. The Microsoft Clip Organizer, included with Office programs, contains hundreds of media files, including pictures, sounds, and movies.
- **Saving to the Web** — Save presentations or parts of a presentation so that they can be viewed in a Web browser. You can publish your slide show to the Internet or to an intranet.
- **E-mailing** — Send an entire slide show as an attachment to an e-mail message.
- **Collaborating** — Share a presentation with friends and coworkers. Ask them to review the slides and then insert comments that offer suggestions to enhance the presentation.
- **Preparing delivery** — Rehearse integrating PowerPoint slides into your speech by setting timings, using presentation tools, showing only selected slides in a presentation, and packaging the presentation for an optical disc.

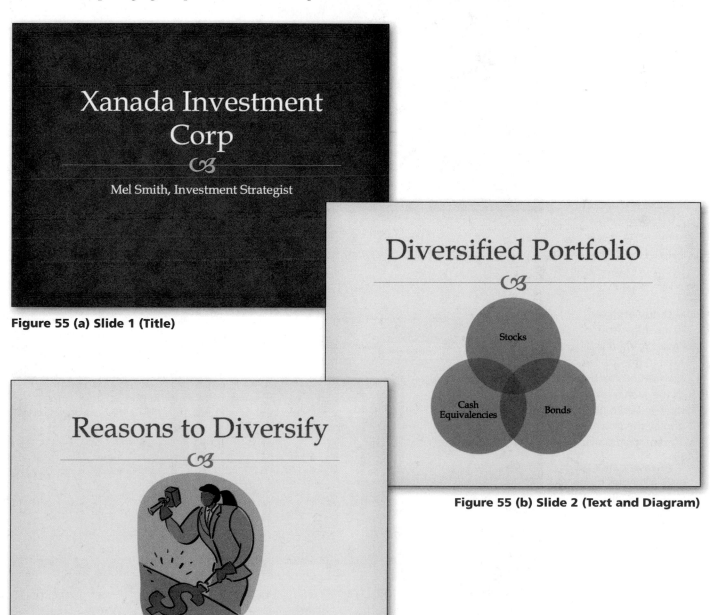

Figure 55 (a) Slide 1 (Title)

Figure 55 (b) Slide 2 (Text and Diagram)

Figure 55 (c) Slide 3 (Text and Picture)

To Start a Program Using the Spotlight Search Box

The following steps, which assume Mac OS X Lion is running, use the Spotlight search box to start the PowerPoint Office program based on a typical installation; however, you would follow similar steps to start any Office program. You may need to ask your instructor how to start programs for your computer.

1

- Click the Search (magnifying glass) icon in the upper-right corner of the Finder window to open the Spotlight text box.

- In the Spotlight text box, type **Microsoft PowerPoint** as the search text and watch the search results appear below the text box (Figure 56).

Q&A Do I need to type the complete program name or correct capitalization?
No, just enough of it for the program name to appear in the search results. For example, you may be able to type PowerPoint or powerpoint, instead of Microsoft PowerPoint.

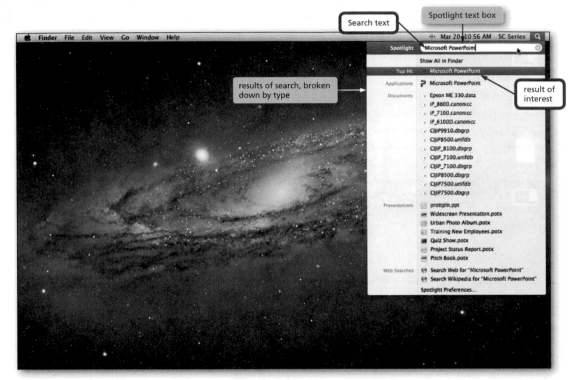

Figure 56

2

- Click the program name, Microsoft PowerPoint in this case, in the Top Hit or Applications section of the search results to start PowerPoint and display the PowerPoint Presentation Gallery.

- If necessary, click All under Themes in the Sidebar to select all PowerPoint themes (Figure 57).

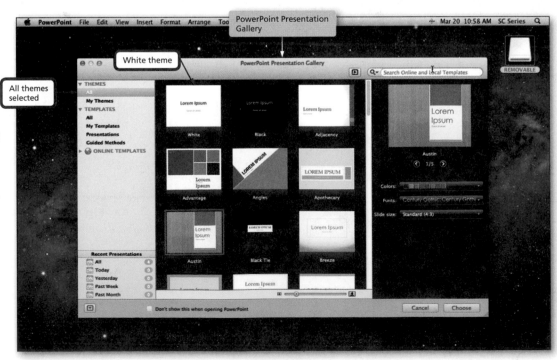

Figure 57

3

- Double-click the White theme to close the gallery and display a blank presentation in the PowerPoint window.

- If the presentation window is not maximized, click the Zoom button on its title bar to maximize the window (Figure 58).

Q&A Does Zoom work differently in PowerPoint than in Word?
Yes. Clicking the Zoom button in PowerPoint zooms the window to fill the screen.

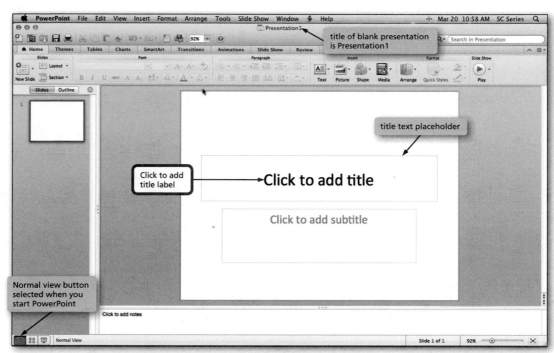

Figure 58

The PowerPoint Window and Ribbon

The PowerPoint window consists of a variety of components to make your work more efficient and documents more professional: the window, ribbon, Standard toolbar, shortcut menus, and menu bar. Many of these components are common to other Office programs and have been discussed earlier in this chapter. Other components, discussed in the following paragraphs and later in subsequent chapters, are unique to PowerPoint.

The basic unit of a PowerPoint presentation is a **slide**. A slide may contain text and objects, such as graphics, tables, charts, and drawings. **Layouts** are used to position this content on the slide. When you create a new presentation, the default **Title Slide** layout appears (Figure 58). The purpose of this layout is to introduce the presentation to the audience. PowerPoint includes 10 other built-in standard layouts.

The default slide layouts are set up in **landscape orientation**, where the slide width is greater than its height. In landscape orientation, the slide size is preset to 10 inches wide and 7.5 inches high when printed on a standard sheet of paper measuring 11 inches wide and 8.5 inches high.

Portrait Orientation | BTW

If your slide content is dominantly vertical, such as a skyscraper or a person, consider changing the slide layout to a portrait orientation. To change the orientation to portrait, choose Page Setup in the file menu and then click the Portrait icon for slides.

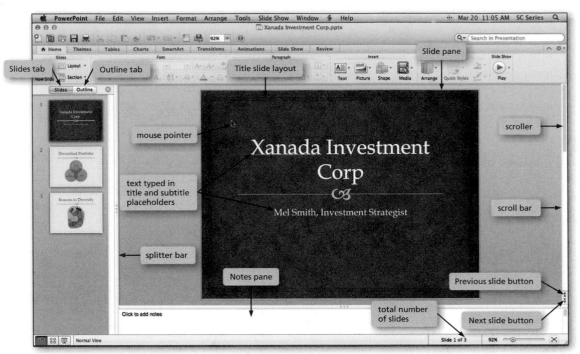

Figure 59

Placeholders **Placeholders** are boxes with dotted or hatch-marked borders that are displayed when you create a new slide. All layouts except the Blank slide layout contain placeholders. Depending on the particular slide layout selected, title and subtitle placeholders are displayed for the slide title and subtitle; a content text placeholder is displayed for text, art, or a table, chart, picture, graphic, or movie. The title slide in Figure 59 has two text placeholders for the main heading, or title, of a new slide and the subtitle.

Ribbon The ribbon in PowerPoint is similar to the one in Word and the other Microsoft Office programs. When you start PowerPoint, the ribbon displays nine main tabs: Home, Themes, Tables, Charts, SmartArt, Transitions, Animations, Slide Show, and Review.

To Enter Content in a Title Slide

With the exception of a blank slide and a slide with a picture and caption, PowerPoint assumes every new slide has a title. Many of PowerPoint's layouts have both a title text placeholder and at least one content placeholder. To make creating a presentation easier, any text you type after a new slide appears becomes title text in the title text placeholder. As you begin typing text in the title text placeholder, the title text also is displayed in the Slide 1 thumbnail in the Slides pane. The presentation title for this presentation is Xanada Investments. The following steps enter a presentation title on the title slide.

- Click the label 'Click to add title' located inside the title text placeholder (shown in Figure 58 on the previous page) to select the placeholder (Figure 60).

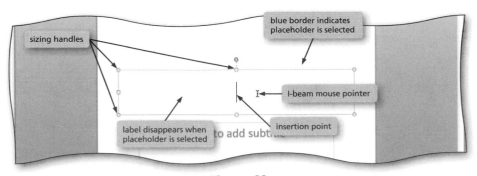

Figure 60

2

- Type **Xanada Investments** in the title text placeholder. Do not press the RETURN key because you do not want to create a new line of text (Figure 61).

Q&A What are the white squares and circles that appear around the title text placeholder as I type the presentation title?

The white squares and circles are sizing handles, which you can drag to change the size of the title text placeholder. Sizing handles also can be found around other placeholders and objects within a presentation.

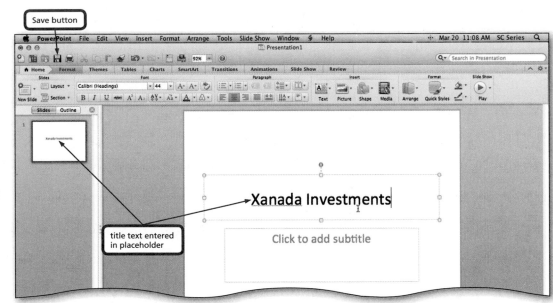

Figure 61

To Save a File in a Folder

The following steps save the presentation in the PowerPoint folder in the class folder (CIS 101, in this case) on a USB flash drive using the file name, Xanada Investments.

1 With a USB flash drive connected to one of the computer's USB ports, click the Save button on the Standard toolbar to display the Save As dialog.

2 If necessary, type **Xanada Investments** in the File name text box to change the file name. Do not press the RETURN key after typing the file name because you do not want to close the dialog at this time.

3 Navigate to the desired save location (in this case, the PowerPoint folder in the CIS 101 folder [or your class folder] on the USB flash drive). For specific instructions, perform the tasks in Steps 3a through 3d.

3a If necessary, click the disclosure button to expand the dialog. If necessary, scroll through the Sidebar until your USB flash drive appears in the list of available devices.

3b Click the USB flash drive in the list of available devices to select that drive as the new save location and display its contents in the right pane.

3c If your class folder (CIS 101, in this case) is not expanded, double-click the CIS 101 folder to select the folder and display its contents in the right pane.

3d Click the PowerPoint folder to select the folder and display its contents in the next pane to the right.

4 Click the Save button (Save As dialog) to save the document in the selected folder on the selected drive with the entered file name.

To Create a New Office Document from the File Menu

As discussed earlier, the File menu contains a set of commands that enable you to manage documents and data about the documents. From the File menu in PowerPoint, for example, you can create, open, print, and save presentations. You also can share documents, manage versions, set permissions, and modify document properties. In other Office 2011 programs, the File menu may contain features specific to those programs. The steps on the following pages create a file, a blank presentation in this case, from the File menu.

- Click File in the menu bar to open the File menu (Figure 62).

Q&A What is the purpose of the File menu? The **File** menu is used to display file management commands for each Office program.

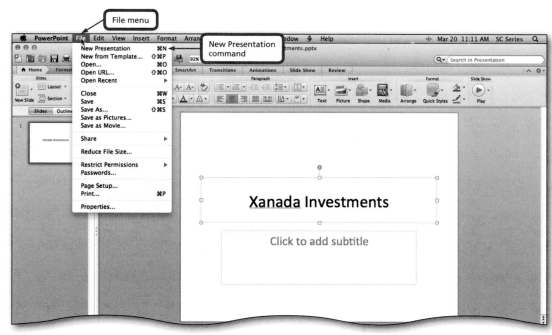

Figure 62

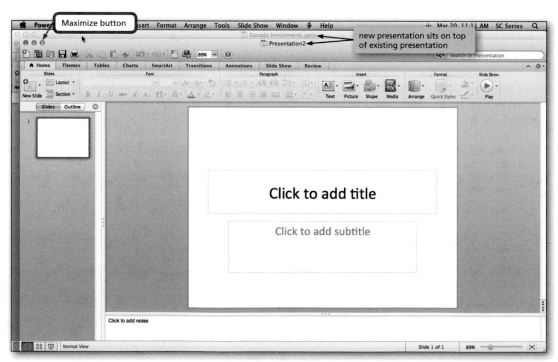

- Choose New Presentation in the File menu to display a new presentation (Figure 63).

Figure 63

3

• Click the Maximize button to maximize the window (Figure 64).

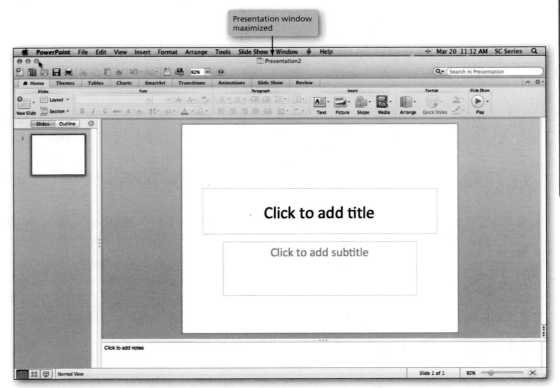

Figure 64

To Enter Content in a Title Slide of a Second PowerPoint Presentation

The presentation title for this presentation is Koala Exhibit Gala. The following steps enter a presentation title on the title slide.

1 Click the title text placeholder (shown in Figure 64) to select it.

2 Type **Koala Exhibit Gala** in the title text placeholder. Do not press the RETURN key (Figure 65).

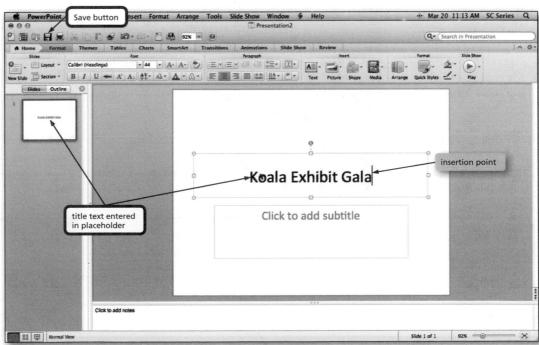

Figure 65

To Save a File in a Folder

The following steps save the second presentation in the PowerPoint folder in the class folder (CIS 101, in this case) on a USB flash drive using the file name, Koala Exhibit Gala.

1 With a USB flash drive connected to one of the computer's USB ports, click the Save button in the Standard toolbar to display the Save As dialog.

2 If necessary, type `Koala Exhibit Gala` in the Save As text box to change the file name. Do not press the RETURN key after typing the file name because you do not want to close the dialog at this time.

3 If necessary, navigate to the desired save location (in this case, the PowerPoint folder in the CIS 101 folder [or your class folder] on the USB flash drive).

4 Click the Save button (Save As dialog) to save the presentation in the selected folder on the selected drive with the entered file name.

To Close an Office File and Leave the Application Open

Sometimes, you may want to close an Office file, such as a PowerPoint presentation, entirely and start over with a new file. You also may want to close a file when you are finished working with it so that you can begin a new file. The following steps close the current active Office file, that is, the Koala Exhibit Gala presentation, without quitting the active program (PowerPoint in this case).

1

- Click the Close button (see Figure 65) to close the Koala Exhibit Gala file without quitting the active program (Figure 66).

Q&A What if the Office program displays a dialog about saving? Click the Save button if you want to save the changes, click the Don't Save button if you want to ignore the changes since the last time you saved, and click the Cancel button if you do not want to close the document.

Q&A Can I use the File menu to close an open file in other Office programs, such as Word and Excel? Yes.

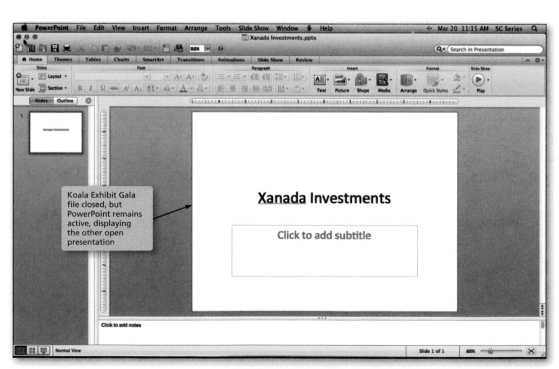

Figure 66

To Open a Recent Office File Using the File Menu

You sometimes need to open a file that you recently modified. You may have more changes to make such as adding more content or correcting errors. The File menu allows you to access recent files easily. The following steps reopen the Koala Exhibit Gala file just closed.

1

- Click File in the menu bar to display the File menu.

- Point to Open Recent in the File menu to display the submenu containing a list of recently opened files (Figure 67).

2

- Click the desired file name in the submenu, Koala Exhibit Gala in this case, to open the file (shown in Figure 65 on page OFF 45).

Q&A   Can I use the File menu to open a recent file in other Office programs, such as Word and Excel?
Yes, as long as the file name appears in the list of recent files in the submenu.

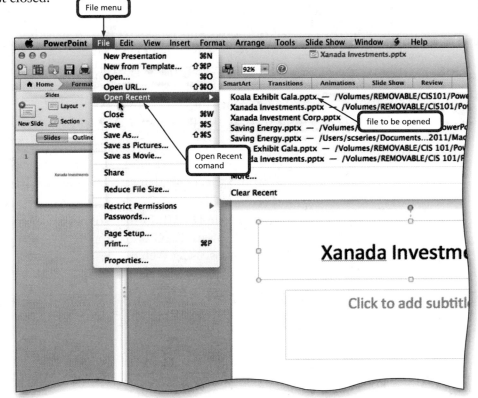

Figure 67

Other Ways

1. Click Open button in Standard toolbar, navigate to file (Open dialog), click Open button

2. Click Documents folder in Dock, choose file to open

3. Choose File > Open in menu bar, navigate to file (Open dialog), click Open button

---

To Quit an Office Program

You are finished using PowerPoint. Thus, you should quit this Office program. The following steps quit PowerPoint.

1 Click PowerPoint in the menu bar to display the PowerPoint menu.

2 Choose Quit PowerPoint from the PowerPoint menu to close the document and quit PowerPoint.

3 If a dialog appears, click the Save button to save any changes made to the document since the last save.

Excel

Excel is a powerful spreadsheet program that allows users to organize data, complete calculations, make decisions, graph data, develop professional-looking reports (Figure 68), publish organized data to the Web, and access real-time data from Web sites. The four major parts of Excel are:

- **Workbooks and Worksheets** — A **workbook** is like a notebook. Inside the workbook are sheets, each of which is called a **worksheet**. In other words, a workbook is a collection of worksheets. Worksheets allow users to enter, calculate, manipulate, and analyze data such as numbers and text. The terms worksheet and spreadsheet are interchangeable.

- **Charts** — Excel can draw a variety of charts.

- **Tables** — Tables organize and store data within worksheets. For example, once a user enters data into a worksheet, an Excel table can sort the data, search for specific data, and select data that satisfies defined criteria.

- **Web Support** — Web support allows users to save Excel worksheets or parts of a worksheet in HTML format, so that a user can view and manipulate the worksheet using a browser. Excel Web support also provides access to real-time data, such as stock quotes, using Web queries.

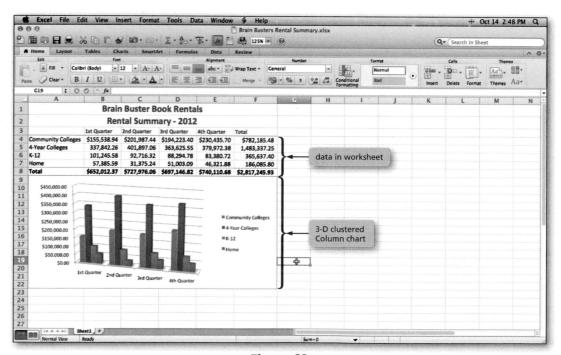

Figure 68

To Start a Program from a Finder Window and Open an Existing File

Previously, you learned how to start an Office program using the Dock and the Spotlight search box. Another way to start an Office program is to open an existing file from a Finder window, which causes the program in which the file was created to start and then open the selected file. The following steps, which assume Mac OS X Lion is running, use the Finder to start the Excel Office program based on a typical installation. You may need to ask your instructor how to start Office programs for your computer. You will need to use the Data Files for Students to complete this set of steps. See the inside back cover of this book for instructions on downloading the Data Files for Students, or contact your instructor for information about accessing the required files.

1

- Click the Finder icon in the Dock to open a Finder window.

- Navigate to the location where you have saved the Data Files for Students, the Excel folder on the USB flash drive REMOVABLE in this example, and select the file you want to open, Brain Busters in this case.

- Click the Action button in the Finder toolbar to display a menu (Figure 69).

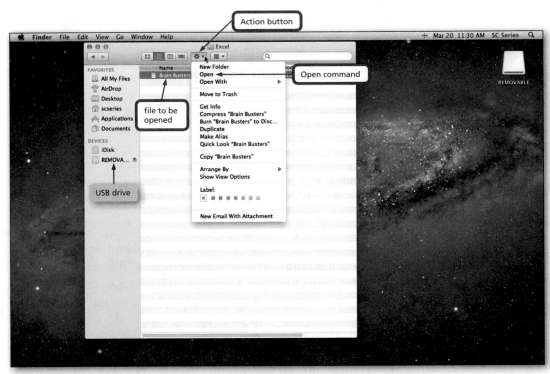

Figure 69

2

- Choose Open in the Action menu to open the selected file in the program used to create the file, Microsoft Excel in this case (Figure 70).

- If the worksheet window in Excel is not maximized, click the worksheet window Zoom button to maximize the worksheet window within Excel.

Q&A   Instead of using a Finder window, can I start Excel using the same method shown previously for Word and PowerPoint?
Yes, you can use any method of starting an Office program to start Excel.

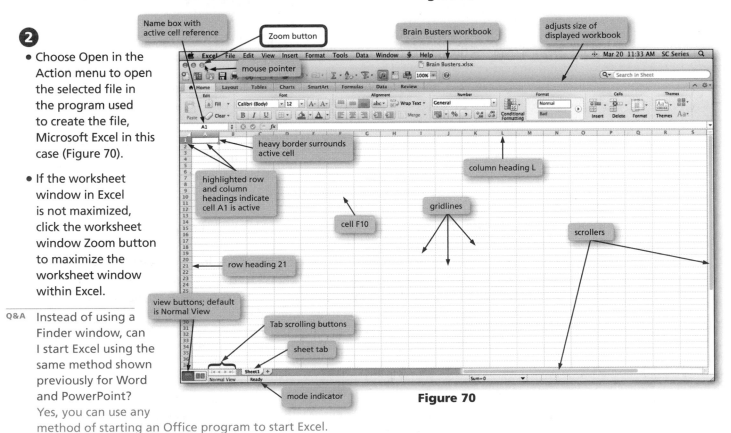

Figure 70

Unique Features of Excel

The Excel window consists of a variety of components to make your work more efficient and worksheets more professional. These include the document window, ribbon, Standard toolbar, shortcut menus, and menu bar. Some of these components are common to other Microsoft Office 2011 programs; others are unique to Excel.

Excel opens a new workbook with one worksheet. If necessary, you can add additional worksheets as long as your computer has enough memory to accommodate them.

Each worksheet has a sheet name that appears on a **sheet tab** at the bottom of the workbook. For example, Sheet1 is the name of the active worksheet displayed in the Brain Busters workbook. Additional worksheets are named Sheet2, Sheet3, and so on.

The Worksheet   The worksheet is organized into a rectangular grid containing vertical columns and horizontal rows. A column letter above the grid, also called the **column heading**, identifies each column. A row number on the left side of the grid, also called the **row heading**, identifies each row. With the screen resolution set to 1280 × 800, the Excel window maximized, and a zoom set at 100%, Excel displays 19 columns (A through S) and 37 rows (1 through 37) of the worksheet on the screen, as shown in Figure 70 on the previous page.

The intersection of each column and row is a cell. A **cell** is the basic unit of a worksheet into which you enter data. Each worksheet in a workbook has 16,384 columns and 1,048,576 rows for a total of 17,179,869,180 cells. Only a small fraction of the active worksheet appears on the screen at one time.

A cell is referred to by its unique address, or **cell reference**, which is the coordinates of the intersection of a column and a row. To identify a cell, specify the column letter first, followed by the row number. For example, cell reference F10 refers to the cell located at the intersection of column F and row 10 (Figure 70).

One cell on the worksheet, designated the **active cell**, is the one into which you can enter data. The active cell in Figure 70 is A1. The active cell is identified in three ways. First, a heavy border surrounds the cell; second, the active cell reference shows immediately above column A in the Name box; and third, the column heading A and row heading 1 are highlighted so it is easy to see which cell is active (Figure 70).

The horizontal and vertical lines on the worksheet itself are called **gridlines**. Gridlines make it easier to see and identify each cell in the worksheet. If desired, you can turn the gridlines off so that they do not show on the worksheet, but it is recommended that you leave them on for now.

The mouse pointer in Figure 70 has the shape of a block plus sign. The mouse pointer appears as a block plus sign whenever it is located in a cell on the worksheet. Another common shape of the mouse pointer is the black arrow. The mouse pointer turns into the black arrow when you move it outside the worksheet or when you drag cell contents between rows or columns. The other mouse pointer shapes are described when they appear on the screen.

Ribbon   When you start Excel, the ribbon displays eight main tabs: Home, Layout, Tables, Charts, SmartArt, Formulas, Data, and Review. The Formulas and Data tabs are specific to Excel. The Formulas tab allows you to work with Excel formulas, and the Data tab allows you to work with data processing features such as importing and sorting data.

Standard Toolbar   The **Standard toolbar**, located above the ribbon, provides convenient, one-click access to frequently used commands (Figure 71). The commands on the Standard toolbar always are available, regardless of the task you are performing.

The Worksheet Size and Window

BTW The 16,384 columns and 1,048,576 rows in Excel make for a huge worksheet that – if you could imagine – takes up the entire side of a building to display in its entirety. Your computer screen, by comparison, is a small window that allows you to view only a minute area of the worksheet at one time. While you cannot see the entire worksheet, you can move the window over the worksheet to view any part of it.

Customizing the Ribbon

BTW In addition to customizing the Standard toolbar, you can add items to and remove items from the ribbon. To customize the ribbon, choose Preferences from the Excel (or other Office application) menu, and then click the Ribbon icon in the Preferences dialog. More information about customizing the ribbon is presented in a later chapter.

Menu Bar   The **menu bar**, located at the top of the Excel window, provides menu access to Excel commands (Figure 71). The commands on the Standard toolbar and the ribbon always are available via the menus in the menu bar. Click a menu name once to display the pull-down menu.

Formula Bar   The formula bar appears below the ribbon (Figure 71). As you type, Excel displays the entry in the **formula bar**. You can make the formula bar larger by dragging the sizing handle at the bottom of the formula bar or clicking the expand button to the right of the formula bar. Excel also displays the active cell reference in the **Name box** on the left side of the formula bar.

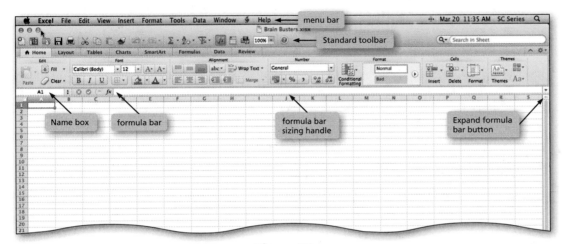

Figure 71

To Enter a Worksheet Title

To enter data into a cell, you first must select it. The easiest way to select a cell (make it active) is to use the mouse to move the block plus sign mouse pointer to the cell and then click. An alternative method is to use the keyboard arrow keys. An arrow key selects the cell adjacent to the active cell in the direction of the arrow on the key.

In Excel, any set of characters containing a letter, hyphen (as in a telephone number), or space is considered text. **Text** is used to place titles, such as worksheet titles, column titles, and row titles, on the worksheet. The following steps enter the worksheet title in cell A1.

1
• If it is not already the active cell, click cell A1 to make it the active cell.

2
• Type **Brain Buster Book Rentals** in cell A1 (Figure 72).

Q&A   Why did the appearance of the formula bar change?
Excel displays the title in the formula bar and in cell A1. When you begin typing a cell entry, Excel displays two additional buttons in the formula bar: the Cancel button and the Enter button. Clicking the Enter button completes an entry. Clicking the Cancel button cancels an entry.

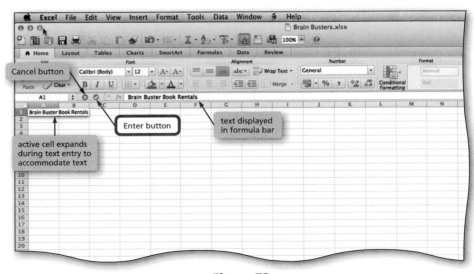

Figure 72

• Click the Enter button to complete the entry and enter the worksheet title in cell A1 (Figure 73).

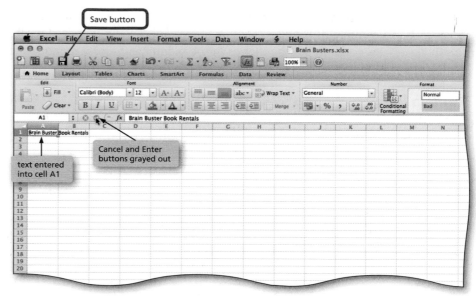

Figure 73

Other Ways

1. To complete entry, click any cell other than active cell

2. To complete entry, press RETURN, HOME, PAGE UP,

PAGE DOWN, END, UP, DOWN, LEFT ARROW, or RIGHT ARROW

To Save an Existing Office Document with the Same File Name

Saving frequently cannot be overemphasized. You have made modifications to the file (spreadsheet) since you created it. Thus, you should save again. Similarly, you should continue saving files frequently so that you do not lose your changes since the time you last saved the file. You can use the same file name, such as Brain Busters, to save the changes made to the document. The following step saves a file again.

• Click the Save button in the Standard toolbar to overwrite the previously saved file (Brain Busters, in this case) on the USB flash drive.

Q&A Why did the Save dialog not appear?

Office programs, including Excel, overwrite the document using the setting specified the first time you saved the document.

Other Ways

1. Press COMMAND-S

To Use Save As to Change the Name of a File

You might want to save a file with a different name and even to a different location. For example, you might start a homework assignment with a data file and then save it with a final file name for submitting to your instructor, saving it to a location designated by your instructor. The following steps save a file with a different file name.

1 With your USB flash drive connected to one of the computer's USB ports, click File in the menu bar to display the File menu.

2 Choose Save As in the menu to display the Save As dialog.

3 Type **Brain Busters Rental Summary** in the Save As text box to change the file name. Do not press the RETURN key after typing the file name because you do not want to close the dialog at this time (Figure 74).

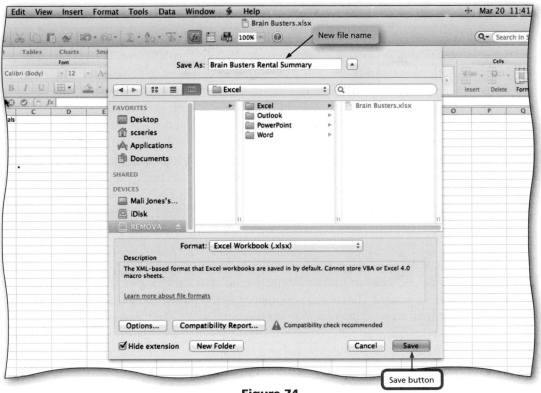

Figure 74

4 Navigate to the desired save location (the Excel folder in the CIS 101 folder [or your class folder] on the USB flash drive, in this case). For specific instructions, perform the tasks in steps 4a through 4d.

4a If necessary, click the disclosure button to expand the dialog. If necessary, scroll through the Sidebar until your USB flash drive appears in the list of available devices.

4b Click the USB flash drive in the list of available devices to select that drive as the new save location and display its contents in the right pane.

4c If your class folder (CIS 101, in this case) is not expanded, double-click the CIS 101 folder to select the folder and display its contents in the right pane.

4d Click the Excel folder to select the folder and display its contents in the next pane to the right.

5 Click the Save button (Save As dialog) to save the file in the selected folder on the selected drive with the new file name.

To Quit an Office Program

You are finished using Excel. The following steps quit Excel.

1 Click Excel in the menu bar to display the Excel menu.

2 Choose Quit Excel from the Excel menu to close the document and quit Excel.

3 If a dialog appears, click the Save button to save any changes made to the document since the last save.

Outlook

In addition to the Office programs discussed thus far, Office 2011 for Mac includes one other program that is useful for managing personal information and communicating with others: Outlook. **Outlook** is a powerful communications and scheduling program that helps you communicate with others, keep track of contacts, and organize your calendar. Personal information manager (PIM) programs such as Outlook provide a way for individuals and workgroups to organize, find, view, and share information easily. Outlook allows you to send and receive electronic mail (e-mail) and permits you to engage in real-time messaging with family, friends, or coworkers using instant messaging. Outlook also provides a means to organize contacts. Users can track e-mail messages, meetings, and notes related to a particular contact. Outlook's Calendar, Contacts, Tasks, and Notes components aid in this organization. Contact information readily is available from the Outlook Calendar, Mail, Contacts, and Task components by accessing the Find a Contact feature.

Electronic mail (e-mail) is the transmission of messages and files over a computer network. E-mail has become an important means of exchanging information and files between business associates, classmates and instructors, friends, and family. Businesses find that using e-mail to send documents electronically saves both time and money. Parents with students away at college or relatives who live across the country find that communicating by e-mail is an inexpensive and easy way to stay in touch with their family members. Exchanging e-mail messages is one of the more widely used features of the Internet.

The Outlook Window   Figure 75 shows an Outlook window, which is divided into three panes: the Navigation pane on the left side of the window, the Message list to the left of center, and the Reading pane to the right of center.

When an e-mail message is open in Outlook, it is displayed in a Message window (Figure 76). When you open a message, the Message window ribbon displays the Message tab, menu bar, and the toolbar, which contain the more frequently used commands. All commands are accessible in the menus found in the menu bar.

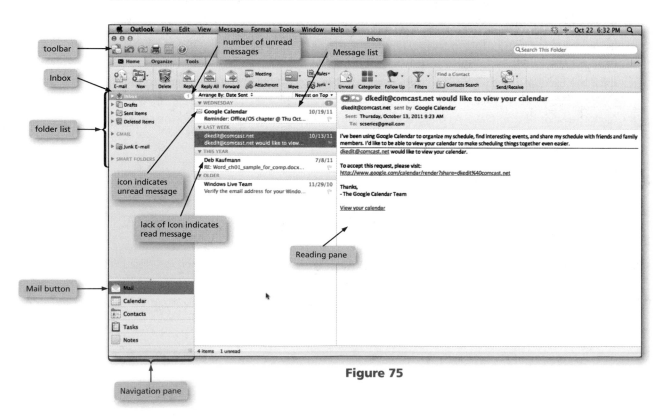

Figure 75

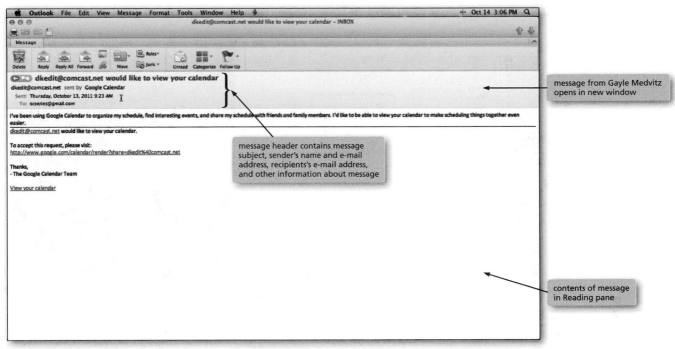

Figure 76

Break Point: If you wish to take a break, this is a good place to do so. To resume at a later time, continue to follow the steps from this location forward.

Moving, Renaming, and Deleting Files

Earlier in this chapter, you learned how to organize files in folders, which is part of a process known as **file management**. The following sections cover additional file management topics including renaming, moving, and deleting files.

To Rename a File

In some circumstances, you may want to change the name of, or rename, a file or a folder. For example, you may want to distinguish a file in one folder or drive from a copy of a similar file, or you may decide to rename a file to better identify its contents. The Word folder shown in Figure 77 contains the Word document, Koala Exhibit. The following steps change the name of the Koala Exhibit file in the Word folder to Koala Exhibit Flyer.

- If necessary, open a Finder window by clicking the Finder icon in the Dock.

- If necessary, switch to Column view. Navigate to the location of the file to be renamed (in this case, the Word folder in the CIS 101 [or your class folder] folder on the USB flash drive) to display the file(s) it contains.

- Click to select the file (Figure 77).

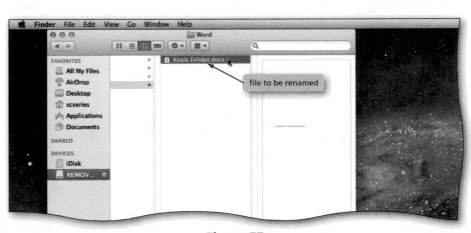

Figure 77

- Click the Koala Exhibit file name to select the file name (Figure 78).

Figure 78

- Type **Koala Exhibit Flyer** in the text box and then press the RETURN key (Figure 79).

Q&A Are any risks involved in renaming files that are located on a hard disk?

Yes. If you inadvertently rename a file that is associated with certain programs, the programs may not be able to find the file and, therefore, may not execute properly. Always use caution when renaming files.

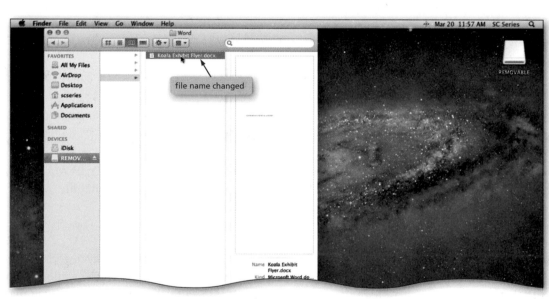

Figure 79

Q&A Can I rename a file when it is open?

No, a file must be closed to change the file name.

To Move a File

At some time, you may want to move a file from one folder, called the source folder, to another, called the destination. When you move a file, it no longer appears in the original folder. If the destination and the source folders are on the same disk drive, you can move a file by dragging it. If the folders are on different disk drives, then you will need to COMMAND-drag the file. The following step moves the Koala Exhibit Flyer file from the Word folder to the Excel folder.

- In a Finder window, navigate to the location of the file to be moved (in this case, the Word folder in the CIS 101 folder [or your class folder] on the USB flash drive).

- Click the Word folder in the Column view to display the files it contains in the right pane (Figure 80).

- Drag the Koala Exhibit Flyer file in the right pane to the Excel folder in the middle pane.

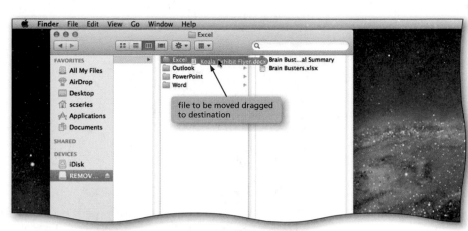

Figure 80

To Delete a File

A final task you may want to perform is to delete a file. Exercise extreme caution when deleting a file or files. When you delete a file from a hard disk, the deleted file is stored in the Trash where you can recover it until you empty the Trash. If you delete a file from removable media, such as a USB flash drive, the file is deleted permanently. The next steps delete the Koala Exhibit Gala file from the PowerPoint folder.

- Use Finder to navigate to the location of the file to be deleted (in this case, the PowerPoint folder in the CIS 101 folder [or your class folder] on the USB flash drive).

- Click the PowerPoint folder to display the files it contains.

- CONTROL-click the Koala Exhibit Gala icon or file name in the right pane to select the file and display a shortcut menu (Figure 81).

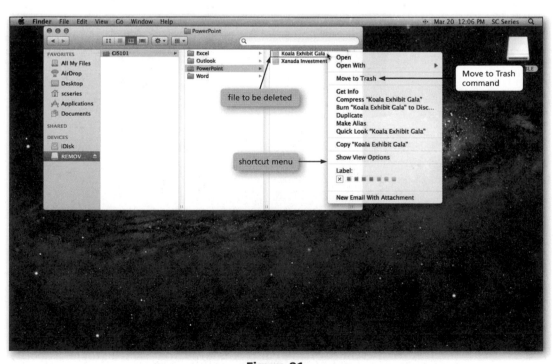

Figure 81

- Choose Move to Trash in the shortcut menu to delete the selected file.

- Click Finder in the menu bar to display the Finder menu (Figure 82).

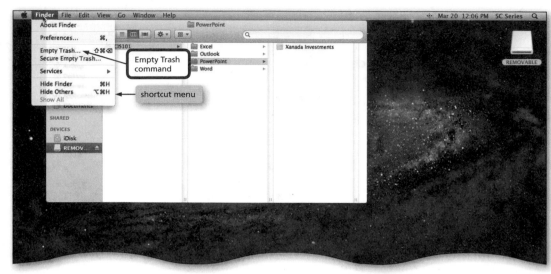

Figure 82

- Choose Empty Trash to permanently delete the file (Figure 83).

- Click the Empty Trash button in the dialog to permanently delete the file.

- Click the Close button to close the Finder window.

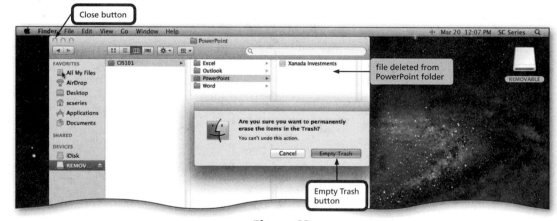

Figure 83

Q&A Can I use this same technique to delete a folder?

Yes. CONTROL-click the folder and then click Move to Trash in the shortcut menu. When you delete a folder, all of the files and folders contained in the folder you are deleting, together with any files and folders on lower hierarchical levels, are deleted as well.

Q&A What if I delete a file in error?

Files will remain in the Trash until you empty it. You can open the Trash and drag any files from it to other locations.

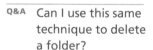

Other Ways

1. Select file in Finder, press SHIFT-COMMAND-DELETE

Microsoft Office and Windows Help

At any time while you are using one of the Microsoft Office 2011 programs, you can use Office Help to display information about all topics associated with the program. To illustrate the use of Office Help, this section uses Word. Help in other Office 2011 programs operates in a similar fashion.

In Office 2011, Help is presented in a window that has Web-browser-style navigation buttons. Each Office 2011 program has its own Help home page, which is the starting Help page that is displayed in the Help window. If your computer is connected to the Internet, you can click the Go Online button to see a more complete set of Help, tutorials, and videos from Microsoft's Web site.

To Open the Help Center in an Office Program

The following step opens the Word Help Center window.

1

- Start an Office program, in this case Word.

- Click the Office program's Help button in the Standard toolbar (the Microsoft Word Help button, in this case) to open the program's Help Center window (Figure 84).

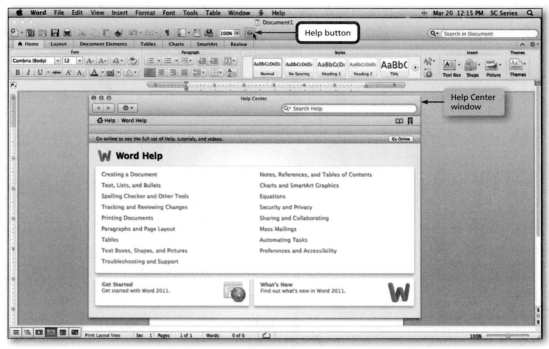

Figure 84

Other Ways

1. Choose Help > Word Help in menu bar
2. Press COMMAND-?

Moving and Resizing Windows

Up to this point, this chapter has used minimized and maximized windows. At times, however, it is useful, or even necessary, to have more than one window open and visible on the screen at the same time. You can resize and move these open windows so that you can view different areas of and elements in the window. In the case of the Help window, for example, it could be covering document text in the Word window that you need to see.

To Move a Window by Dragging

You can move any open window that is not maximized to another location on the desktop by dragging the title bar of the window. The following step drags the Word Help Center window to the top left of the desktop.

1

- Drag the window title bar (the Help Center window title bar, in this case) so that the window moves to the top right of the desktop, as shown in Figure 85.

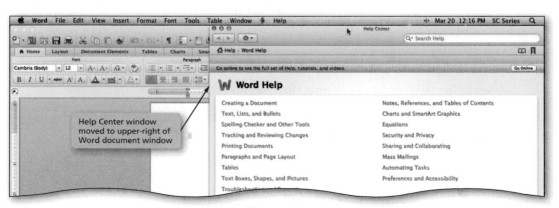

Figure 85

To Resize a Window by Dragging

Sometimes, information is not visible completely in a window. A method used to change the size of the window is to drag the window borders. The following step changes the size of the Word Help window by dragging its borders.

- Point to the lower-left corner of the window (the Word Help window, in this case) until the mouse pointer changes to a two-headed diagonal arrow.

- Drag the bottom border downward to display more of the active window (Figure 86).

Q&A Can I drag other borders on the window to enlarge or shrink the window?
Yes, you can drag the left, right, and top borders and any window corner to resize a window.

Q&A Will Lion remember the new size of the window after I close it?
Yes. When you reopen the window, Lion will display it at the same size it was when you closed it.

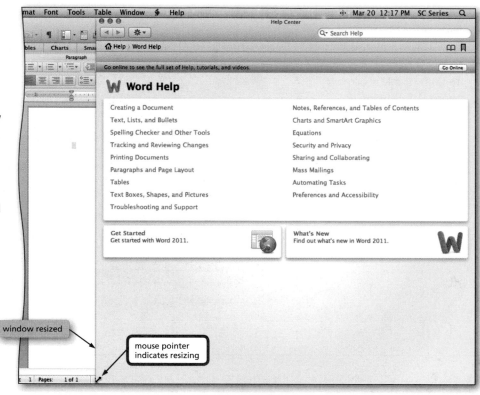

Figure 86

Using Office Help

Once an Office program's Help window is open, several methods exist for navigating Help. You can search for help by using either of the following methods from the Help window:

1. Enter search text in the 'Search Help' text box
2. Click the links in the Help window

To Obtain Help Using the 'Search Help' Text Box

Assume for the following example that you want to know more about the ribbon. The following steps use the 'Search Help' text box to obtain useful information about the ribbon by entering the word, ribbon, as search text.

- Type **ribbon** in the text box at the top of the Word Help window to enter the search text (Figure 87).

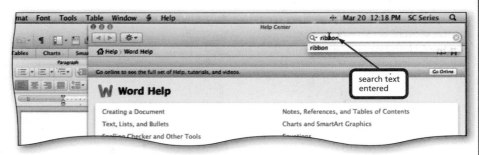

Figure 87

- Press the RETURN key to display the search results (Figure 88).

Q&A Why do my search results differ?
If you do not have an Internet connection, your results will reflect only the content of the Help files on your computer. When searching for help online, results also can change as material is added, deleted, and updated on the online Help Web pages maintained by Microsoft.

Q&A Why were my search results not very helpful?
When initiating a search, be sure to check the spelling of the search text; also, keep your search specific, with fewer than seven words, to return the most accurate results.

Figure 88

- Click the Familiarize yourself with the ribbon link to open the Help document associated with the selected topic (Figure 89).

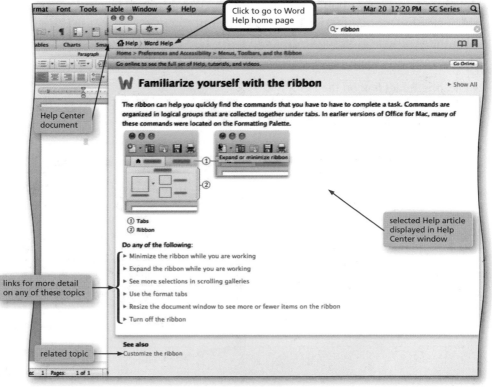

Figure 89

- Click Word Help in the path to clear the search results and redisplay the Word Help home page (Figure 90).

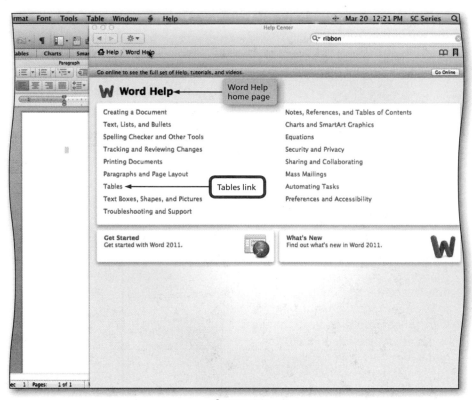

Figure 90

To Obtain Help Using the Help Links

If your topic of interest is listed on the Word Help home page, you can click the link to begin browsing the Help categories instead of entering search text. You browse Help just as you would browse a Web site. If you know which category contains your Help information, you may wish to use these links. The following step finds the Tables Help information using the category link from the Word Help home page.

- Click the Tables link on the Help home page (shown in Figure 90) to display the Tables page (Figure 91).

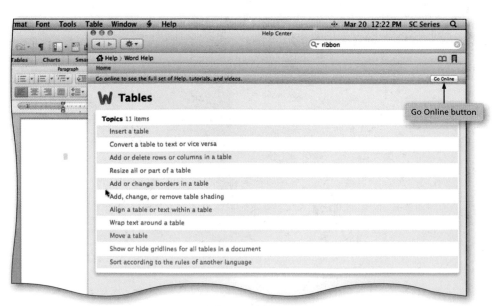

Figure 91

Accessing Online Help

Microsoft Office has a strong online Help feature. To access the online Help feature, click the Go Online button (see Figure 91) from any of the Help Center windows. The online help center will open in your default browser. Figure 92 shows the introductory screen to the Office for Mac Online Help feature.

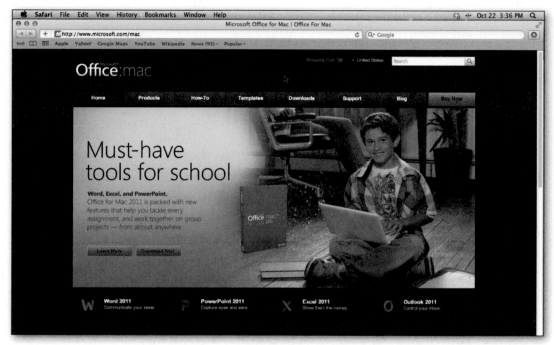

Figure 92

Using Mac OS X Lion Help and Support

One of the more powerful Lion features is Help. **OS X Lion Help** is available when using Lion or any program running under Lion. This feature is designed to assist you in using Lion or the various programs.

To Access Mac OS X Lion Help

The following steps start OS X Lion Help and display the OS X Lion Help window containing links to more information about Lion, and to all installed applications with a Help feature.

1

- If necessary, click the Help button in the Standard toolbar in an open application to display the Help Center window.

- Click the Home button on the path to open the OS X Lion Help Center (Figure 93).

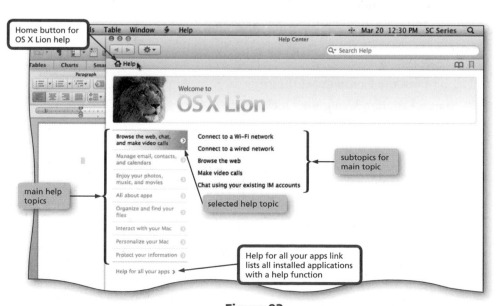

Figure 93

- Click the 'Help for all your apps' link to display the list of all applications installed on your Mac that have a Help function (Figure 94).

- After reviewing the Help Center window, click the Close button to quit the Help Center.

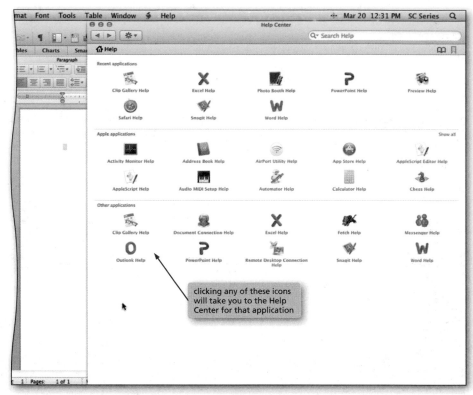

Figure 94

Chapter Summary

In this chapter, you learned about the Mac OS X Lion interface. You started Lion, were introduced to the components of the desktop, and learned several mouse and trackpad operations. You opened, closed, moved, resized, minimized, maximized, and scrolled a window. You used Finder windows to expand and collapse drives and folders, display drive and folder contents, create folders, and rename and then delete a file.

You also learned some basic features of some Microsoft Office 2011 programs, including Word, PowerPoint, and Excel. As part of this learning process, you discovered the common elements that exist among these different Office programs. You now can save basic document, presentation, and spreadsheet files. The additional Office program, Outlook, was discussed.

Microsoft Office for Mac Help was demonstrated, and you learned how to use the Office for Mac Help Center window. You were introduced to the Mac OS X Lion Help Center and learned how to use it to obtain more information about Lion and installed applications on your Mac.

The items listed below include all of the new Lion and Office 2011 skills you have learned in this chapter.

1. Log In to the Computer (OFF 6)
2. Start a Program Using the Dock (OFF 9)
3. Maximize a Window (OFF 11)
4. Hide the Dock (OFF 13)
5. Display a Different Tab on the Ribbon (OFF 18)
6. Minimize, Display, and Restore the Ribbon (OFF 18)
7. Display a Menu in the Menu Bar (OFF 19)
8. Display and Use a Shortcut Menu (OFF 20)
9. Customize the Standard Toolbar (OFF 20)
10. Enter Text in a Document (OFF 21)
11. Create a Folder (OFF 24)
12. Create a Folder within a Folder (OFF 26)
13. Use Cover Flow View to Expand a Folder, Scroll through Folder Contents, and Collapse a Folder (OFF 28)
14. Switch from One Program to Another (OFF 29)
15. Save a File in a Folder (OFF 30)
16. Minimize and Restore a Window (OFF 33)
17. Change the Screen Resolution (OFF 36)

18. Quit an Office Program with One Document Open (OFF 37)

19. Start a Program Using the Spotlight Search Box (OFF 40)

20. Enter Content in a Title Slide (OFF 42)

21. Create a New Office Document from the File Menu (OFF 44)

22. Close an Office File and Leave the Application Open (OFF 46)

23. Open a Recent Office File Using the File Menu (OFF 47)

24. Start a Program from a Finder Window and Open an Existing File (OFF 48)

25. Enter a Worksheet Title (OFF 51)

26. Save an Existing Office Document with the Same File Name (OFF 52)

27. Rename a File (OFF 55)

28. Move a File (OFF 56)

29. Delete a File (OFF 57)

30. Open the Help Center in an Office Program (OFF 58)

31. Move a Window by Dragging (OFF 59)

32. Resize a Window by Dragging (OFF 60)

33. Obtain Help Using the 'Search Help' Text Box (OFF 60)

34. Obtain Help Using the Help Links (OFF 62)

35. Access Mac OS X Lion Help (OFF 63)

 If you have a SAM 2010 user profile, your instructor may have assigned an autogradable version of this assignment. If so, log into the SAM 2010 Web site at www.cengage.com/sam2010 to download the instruction and start files.

Learn It Online

Test your knowledge of chapter content and key terms.

Instructions: To complete the Learn It Online exercises, please visit **www.cengagebrain.com.** At the CengageBrain.com home page, search for *Office 2011 for Mac* using the search box at the top of the page. This will take you to the product page for this book. On the product page, click the Access Now button below the Study Tools heading. On the Book Companion Site Web page, select Office and Mac OS, and then click the link for the desired exercise.

Chapter Reinforcement TF, MC, and SA
A series of true/false, multiple choice, and short answer questions that test your knowledge of the chapter content.

Flash Cards
An interactive learning environment where you identify chapter key terms associated with displayed definitions.

Practice Test
A series of multiple choice questions that test your knowledge of chapter content and key terms.

Who Wants To Be a Computer Genius?
An interactive game that challenges your knowledge of chapter content in the style of a television quiz show.

Wheel of Terms
An interactive game that challenges your knowledge of chapter key terms in the style of the television show *Wheel of Fortune*.

Crossword Puzzle Challenge
A crossword puzzle that challenges your knowledge of key terms presented in the chapter.

Apply Your Knowledge

Reinforce the skills and apply the concepts you learned in this chapter.

Creating a Folder and a Document

Instructions: You will create a Word folder and then create a Word document and save it in the folder.

Perform the following tasks:

1. Connect a USB flash drive to an available USB port and then open the USB flash drive window.
2. Choose the New Folder command in the Action pop-up menu to display a new folder icon and text box for the folder name.
3. Type **Word** in the text box to name the folder. Press the RETURN key to create the folder on the USB flash drive.
4. Start Word.
5. Enter the text shown in Figure 95.
6. Click the Save button on the Standard toolbar. Navigate to the Word folder on the USB flash drive and then save the document using the file name, Apply 1 Class List.
7. Print the document using the Quick Print button on the Standard toolbar.
8. Submit the printout to your instructor.
9. Quit Word.

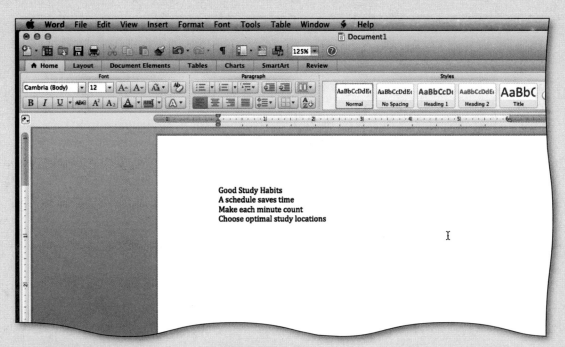

Figure 95

Extend Your Knowledge

Extend the skills you learned in this chapter and experiment with new skills. You will use Help to complete the assignment.

Using Help

Instructions: Use Office Help to perform the following tasks.

Perform the following tasks:
1. Start Word.
2. Click the Microsoft Word Help button to open the Word Help window (Figure 96).

Figure 96

3. Search Word Help to answer the following questions.
   a. What are the steps to rearrange tabs on the ribbon?
   b. What is AutoText?
4. Close the Help windows, and then, with the Word program still running, start PowerPoint.
5. Click the Microsoft PowerPoint Help button on the title bar to open the PowerPoint Help window.
6. Search PowerPoint Help to answer the following questions.
   a. What is a slide master?
   b. How do you insert slides from another presentation into the existing presentation?
7. Quit PowerPoint.
8. Start Excel.
9. Click the Microsoft Excel Help button to open the Excel Help window.
10. Search Excel Help to answer the following questions.
    a. What are three different functions available in Excel?
    b. What are sparklines?

Continued >

Extend Your Knowledge *continued*

11. Quit Excel.

12. Type the answers from your searches in the Word document. Save the document with a new file name and then submit it in the format specified by your instructor.

13. Quit Word.

Make It Right

Analyze a file structure and correct all errors and/or improve the design.

Organizing Vacation Photos

Note: To complete this assignment you will be required to use the Data Files for Students. See the inside back cover of this book for instructions on downloading the Data Files for Students, or contact your instructor for information on accessing the required files.

Instructions: Traditionally, you have stored photos from past vacations together in one folder. The photos are becoming difficult to manage, and you now want to store them in appropriate folders. You will create the folder structure shown in Figure 97. You then will move the photos to the folders so that they will be organized properly.

1. Connect a USB flash drive to an available USB port to open the USB flash drive window and locate the folder Vacation Photos from the Data Files for Students.

2. Using the techniques presented in the chapter, create the hierarchical folder structure shown in Figure 97.

3. Using the techniques presented in the chapter, move the vacation photos to their appropriate folders.

4. Submit your work in the format specified by your instructor.

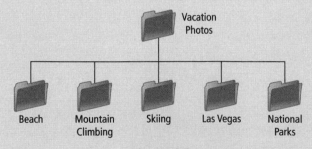

Figure 97

In the Lab

Use the guidelines, concepts, and skills presented in this chapter to increase your knowledge of Mac OS X Lion and Office 2011. Labs are listed in order of increasing difficulty.

Lab 1: Using Windows Help and Support

Problem: You have a few questions about using Mac OS X Lion and would like to answer these questions using the Help Center.

Instructions: Use the OS X Lion Help Center to perform the following tasks:

1. Open the OS X Lion Help Center from the Help menu in the Finder.

2. Use the Help Center page to answer the following questions.

   a. How do you change your desktop picture?

   b. What is the launchpad?

   c. What are the steps to create an alias?

   d. What are some tips for creating secure passwords?

3. Use the Search Help text box in the OS X Lion Help Center to answer the following questions.

   a. How do you reduce computer screen flicker?

   b. How do you change the appearance of the mouse pointer?

   c. How do you hide all windows?

   d. What is a VPN?

4. Mac OS X Lion has a group of small apps called **widgets** that can be used for a variety of tasks. They are found within an app called **Dashboard.** Use the Help Center to find a list of widgets that are preinstalled (Figure 98), and answer the following questions.

   a. How do you use Dashboard widgets?

   b. How do you install more Dashboard widgets?

   c. List five Lion Dashboard widgets that are not listed in Figure 98.

6. Close the Help Center.

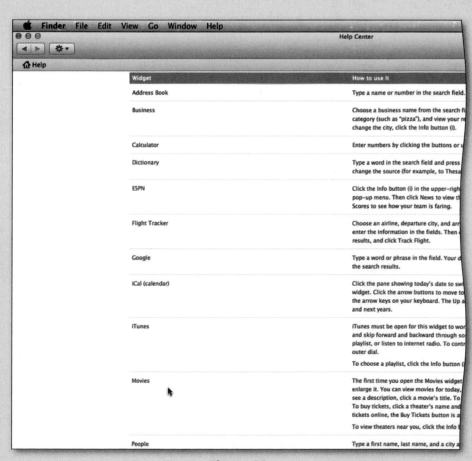

Figure 98

In the Lab

Lab 2: Creating Folders for a Pet Supply Store

Problem: Your friend works for Pete's Pet Supplies. He would like to organize his files in relation to the types of pets available in the store. He has five main categories: dogs, cats, fish, birds, and exotic. You are to create a folder structure similar to Figure 99.

Instructions: Perform the following tasks:
1. Connect a USB flash drive to an available USB port and then open the USB flash drive window.
2. Create the main folder for Pete's Pet Supplies.
3. Navigate to the Pete's Pet Supplies folder.
4. Within the Pete's Pet Supplies folder, create a folder for each of the following: Dogs, Cats, Fish, Birds, and Exotic.
5. Within the Exotic folder, create two additional folders, one for Primates and the second for Reptiles.
6. Submit the assignment in the format specified by your instructor.

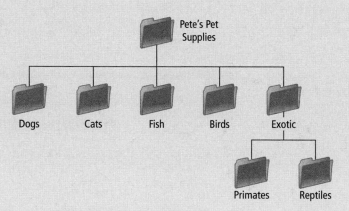

Figure 99

In the Lab

Lab 3: Creating Office Documents

Problem: You are taking a class that requires you to create a Word, PowerPoint, and Excel file. You will save these files to folders named for three different Office programs (Figure 100).

Instructions: Create the folders shown in Figure 100. Then, using the respective Office program, create a small file to save in each folder (i.e., create a Word document to save in the Word folder, a PowerPoint presentation to save in the PowerPoint folder, and so on).
1. Connect a USB flash drive to an available USB port and then open the USB flash drive window.
2. Create the folder structure shown in Figure 100.

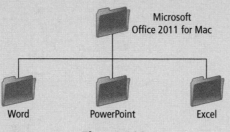

Microsoft
Office 2011 for Mac

Word   PowerPoint   Excel

Figure 100

3. Navigate to the Word folder.

4. Create a Word document containing the text, My First Word Document, and then save it in the Word folder.

5. Navigate to the PowerPoint folder.

6. Create a PowerPoint presentation containing the title text, My First PowerPoint Presentation, and then save it in the PowerPoint folder.

7. Navigate to the Excel folder.

8. Create an Excel spreadsheet containing the text, My First Excel Spreadsheet, in cell A1 and then save it in the Excel folder.

9. Close all open Office programs.

10. Submit the assignment in the format specified by your instructor.

Cases and Places

Apply your creative thinking and problem solving skills to design and implement a solution.

Note: To complete these assignments, you may be required to use the Data Files for Students. See the inside back cover of this book for instructions on downloading the Data Files for Students, or contact your instructor for information about accessing the required files.

1: Creating Beginning Files for Classes

Academic

You are taking the following classes: Introduction to Engineering, Beginning Psychology, Introduction to Biology, and Accounting. Create folders for each of the classes. Use the following folder names: Engineering, Psychology, Biology, and Accounting, when creating the folder structure. In the Engineering folder, use Word to create a Word document with the name of the class and the class meeting location and time (MW 10:30 – 11:45, Room 317). In the Psychology folder, use PowerPoint to create your first lab presentation. It should begin with a title slide containing the text, Behavioral Observations. In the Biology folder, save a database named Research in the Biology folder. In the Accounting folder, create an Excel spreadsheet with the text, Tax Information, in cell A1. Use the concepts and techniques presented in this chapter to create the folders and files.

Continued >

Cases and Places *continued*

2: Using Help

Personal

Your parents enjoy working and playing games on their home computers. Your mother uses a note-book computer downstairs, and your father uses a desktop computer upstairs. They expressed interest in sharing files between their computers and sharing a single printer, so you offered to research various home networking options. Start Mac OS X Help and search Help using the keywords, sharing files with others on your network. Read the Help information on File Sharing, and open the suggested menus to find the file sharing options. Start Word and then type the main steps for sharing files. Use the concepts and techniques presented in this chapter to use Help and create the Word document.

3: Creating Folders

Professional

Your boss at the bookstore where you work part-time has asked for help with organizing her files. After looking through the files, you decided upon a file structure for her to use, including the follow-ing folders: books, magazines, tapes, DVDs, and general merchandise. Within the books folder, create folders for hardback and paperback books. Within magazines, create folders for special issues and periodicals. In the tapes folder, create folders for celebrity and major release. In the DVDs folder, cre-ate a folder for book to DVD. In the general merchandise folder, create folders for novelties, posters, and games. Use the concepts and techniques presented in this chapter to create the folders.

1 Creating, Formatting, and Editing a Word Document with Pictures

Objectives

You will have mastered the material in this chapter when you can:

- Enter text in a Word document
- Check spelling as you type
- Format paragraphs
- Format text
- Undo and redo commands or actions
- Change the color scheme
- Insert digital pictures in a Word document
- Format pictures
- Add a page border
- Correct errors and revise a document
- Change document properties
- Print a document

1 Creating, Formatting, and Editing a Word Document with Pictures

Introduction

To advertise a sale, promote a business, publicize an event, or convey a message to the community, you may want to create a flyer and hand it out in person or post it in a public location. Libraries, schools, religious organizations, grocery stores, coffee shops, and other places often provide bulletin boards or windows for flyers. These flyers announce personal items for sale or rent (car, boat, apartment); garage or block sales; services being offered (animal care, housecleaning, lessons); membership, sponsorship, or donation requests (club, religious organization, charity); and other messages such as a lost or found pet.

Project Planning Guidelines

The process of developing a document that communicates specific information requires careful analysis and planning. As a starting point, establish why the document is needed. Once the purpose is determined, analyze the intended readers of the document and their unique needs. Then, gather information about the topic and decide what to include in the document. Finally, determine the document design and style that will be most successful at delivering the message. Details of these guidelines are provided in Appendix A. In addition, each project in this book provides practical applications of these planning considerations.

Project — Flyer with Pictures

Individuals and businesses create flyers to gain public attention. Flyers, which usually are a single page in length, are an inexpensive means of reaching the community. Many flyers, however, go unnoticed because they are designed poorly.

The project in this chapter follows general guidelines and uses Word to create the flyer shown in Figure 1–1. This colorful, eye-catching flyer announces that a dog has been found. The pictures of the dog, taken with a camera phone, entice passersby to stop and look at the flyer. The headline on the flyer is large and colorful to draw attention into the text. The body copy below the pictures briefly describes where and when the dog was found, along with a bulleted list that concisely highlights important identifying information. The signature line of the flyer calls attention to the contact phone number. The dog's name, Bailey, and signature line are in a different color so that they stand apart from the rest of the text on the flyer. Finally, the graphical page border nicely frames and complements the contents of the flyer.

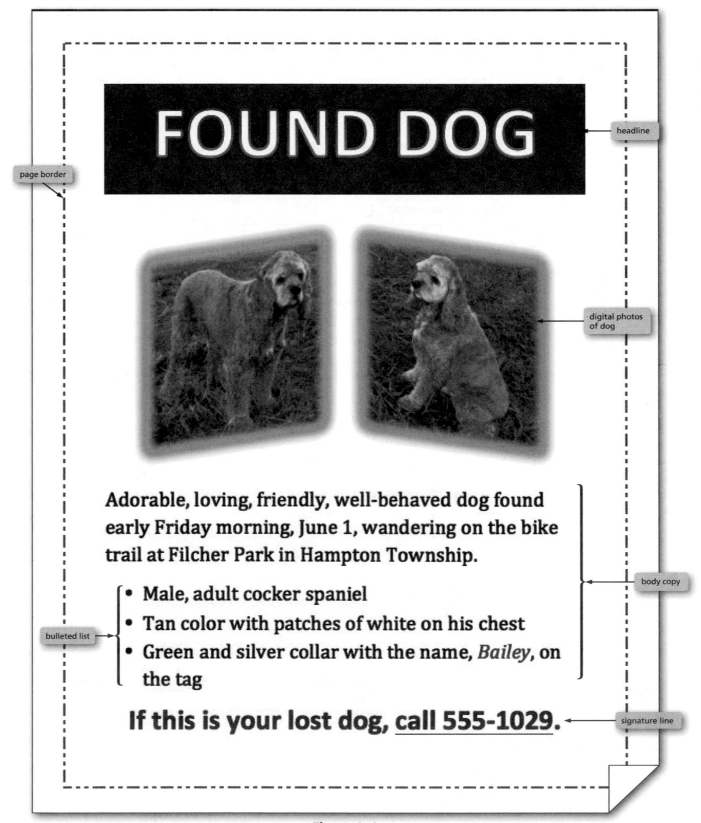

page border

headline

digital photos of dog

body copy

bulleted list

signature line

Figure 1–1

Overview

As you read this chapter, you will learn how to create the flyer shown in Figure 1–1 on the previous page by performing these general tasks:

- Enter text in the document.
- Format the text in the document.
- Insert the pictures in the document.
- Format the pictures in the document.
- Enhance the page with a border and additional spacing.
- Correct errors and revise the document.
- Print the document.

Plan Ahead

General Project Guidelines

When creating a Word document, the actions you perform and decisions you make will affect the appearance and characteristics of the finished document. As you create a flyer, such as the project shown in Figure 1–1, you should follow these general guidelines:

1. **Choose the words for the text.** Follow the *less is more* principle. The less text, the more likely people will read the flyer. Use as few words as possible to make a point.

2. **Identify how to format various elements of the text.** The overall appearance of a document significantly affects its ability to communicate clearly. Examples of how you can modify the appearance, or **format**, of text include changing its shape, size, color, and position on the page.

3. **Find the appropriate graphical image(s).** An eye-catching graphical image should convey the flyer's overall message. It could show a product, service, result, or benefit, or visually convey a message that is not expressed easily with words.

4. **Establish where to position and how to format the graphical image(s).** The position and format of the graphical image(s) should grab the attention of passersby and draw them into reading the flyer.

5. **Determine whether the page needs enhancements such as a border or spacing adjustments.** A graphical, color-coordinated page border can further draw attention to a flyer and nicely frame its contents. Increasing or decreasing spacing between elements on a flyer can improve its readability and overall appearance.

6. **Correct errors and revise the document as necessary.** Post the flyer on a wall and make sure all text and images are legible from a distance. Ask someone else to read the flyer and give you suggestions for improvements.

7. **Determine the best method for distributing the document.** You can distribute documents on paper or electronically. A flyer should be printed on paper so it can be posted. When necessary, more specific details concerning the above guidelines are presented at appropriate points in the chapter. The chapter also will identify the actions performed and decisions made regarding these guidelines during the creation of the flyer shown in Figure 1–1.

For an introduction to Mac OS X and instruction about how to perform basic Mac OS X tasks, read the Office 2011 and Mac OS X chapter at the beginning of this book, where you can learn how to resize windows, change screen resolution, create folders, move and rename files, use Mac OS X Help, and much more.

To Start Word

If you are using a computer to step through the project in this chapter and you want your screens to match the figures in this book, you should change your screen's resolution to 1280 × 800. For information about how to change a computer's resolution, refer to the Office 2011 and Mac OS X chapter at the beginning of this book.

The following steps, which assume Mac OS X is running, start Word based on a typical installation. You may need to ask your instructor how to start Word for your computer. For a detailed example of the procedure summarized below, refer to the Office 2011 and Mac OS X chapter.

1 Click the Word icon on the Dock to display the Word Document Gallery.

Q&A What is the Welcome to Word screen I see?
The first time you start Word, you may see the Welcome to Word screen. Click Continue to move to the Word Document Gallery.

Q&A Why do I see a blank Word document rather than the Word Document Gallery?
The default setting is to show the Word Document Gallery. If you do not see it, your Word application has a setting other than the default. You can skip to step 4.

2 If All is not selected in the Templates pane on the left, click to select it.

3 Double-click the Word Document icon in the Word Document Gallery to display a new blank document in the Word window.

4 If the Word window is not sized properly, as described in the Office and Mac OS X chapter, size the window properly.

5 If the Print Layout View button in the lower left of the document window is not selected (shown in Figure 1–2 on the next page), click it so that your screen is in Print Layout View.

Q&A What is Print Layout View?
The default (preset) view in Word is **Print Layout View**, which shows the document on a mock sheet of paper in the document window.

6 On the Home tab, under Styles, if Normal is not selected in the Quick Style gallery (shown in Figure 1–2), click it so that your document uses the Normal style.

Q&A What is the Normal style?
When you create a document, Word formats the text using a particular style. The default style in Word is called the **Normal style**, which is discussed later in this book.

For an introduction to Office 2011 and instruction about how to perform basic tasks in Office 2011 programs, read the Office 2011 and Mac OS X chapter at the beginning of this book, where you can learn how to start a program, use the ribbon, save a file, open a file, quit a program, use Help, and much more.

The Word Window

The chapters in this **BTW** book begin with the Word window appearing as it did at the initial installation of the software. Your Word window may look different depending on your screen resolution and other Word settings.

Adjusting Line and Paragraph Spacing

Line spacing is the amount of vertical space between lines of text in a paragraph. **Paragraph spacing** is the amount of space above and below a paragraph. By default, the Normal style places 0 pts (points) of blank space after each paragraph and inserts a vertical space equal to 1.0 lines between each line of text. It also automatically adjusts line height to accommodate various font sizes and graphics.

You can adjust line and paragraph spacing at any point during document creation. If the default line and paragraph spacing are not suitable for the document you are creating, you can adjust spacing before you create your document, and make adjustments as necessary. The steps on the next page adjust line spacing and paragraph spacing to provide additional spacing between lines and paragraphs, to make the flyer more readable.

Zooming

If text is too small for you **BTW** to read on the screen, you can zoom the document by dragging the Zoom slider in the lower right of the document window. Changing the zoom has no effect on the printed document.

To Change Line and Paragraph Spacing

The lines of the flyer should have enough space between them to allow the casual viewer to determine easily what the flyer is about. The following steps change the line spacing to 1.15.

- On the Home tab, under Paragraph, click the Line Spacing button to display the Line Spacing pop-up menu (Figure 1–2).

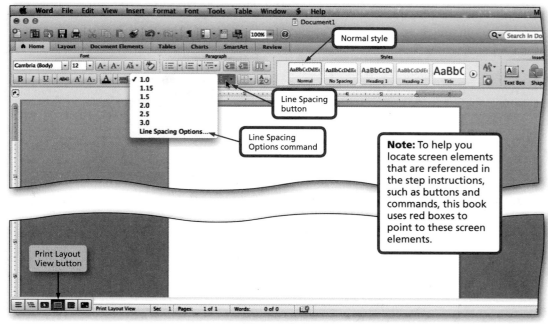

Figure 1–2

- Choose Line Spacing Options to display the Paragraph dialog.

- In the After text box, press DELETE as needed to delete the current entry, then type **10 pt** to add 10 points of space following each paragraph.

- In the At text box, type **1.15** to set line spacing to 1.15 lines (Figure 1–3).

- Click the OK button to apply the Line and Paragraph spacing to the document.

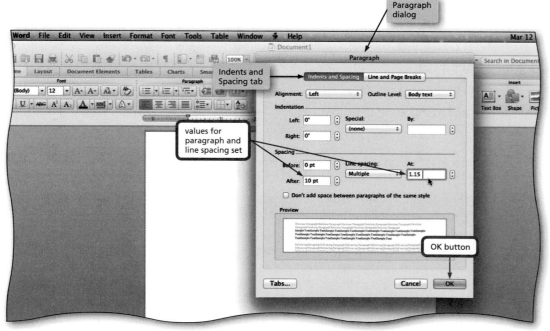

Figure 1–3

Other Ways

1. CONTROL-click paragraph, choose Paragraph in shortcut menu, click Indents and Spacing tab (Paragraph dialog), set desired spacing, click OK button

2. Choose Format > Paragraph in menu bar, click Indents and Spacing tab (Paragraph dialog), set desired spacing, click OK button

3. Press OPTION-COMMAND-M, set desired spacing, click OK button

To Adjust the Margins

The flyer should not have large amounts of white space around the edges. The following steps reduce the size of the margins.

1

• Click the Layout tab on the ribbon (Figure 1–4).

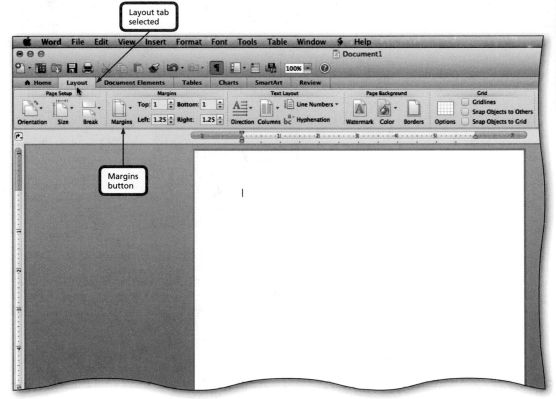

Figure 1–4

2

• On the Layout tab, click the Margins button to display the Margins pop-up menu (Figure 1–5).

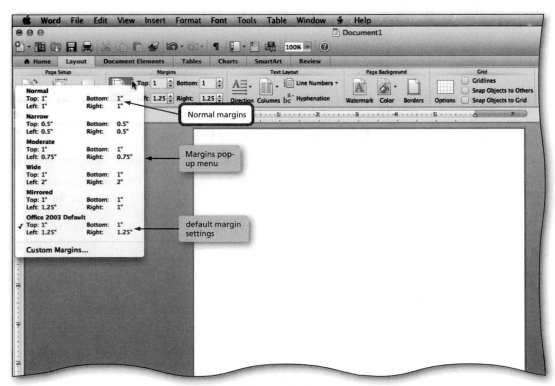

Figure 1–5

3

- Click Normal to apply the Normal margin settings to the document (Figure 1–6).

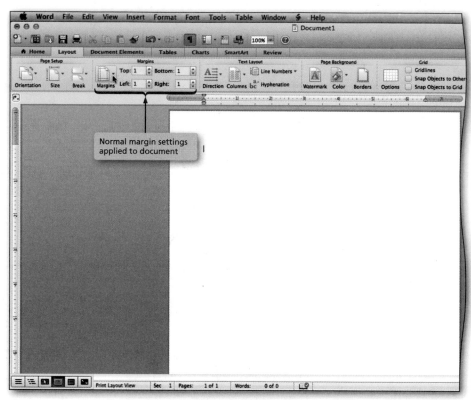

Figure 1–6

Entering Text

After preparing the initial settings, the next step in creating a document is to enter its text. With the projects in this book, you enter text by typing on the keyboard. By default, Word positions text you type at the left margin. In a later section of this chapter, you will learn how to format, or change the appearance of, the entered text.

Plan Ahead

Choose the words for the text.

The text in a flyer is organized into three areas: headline, body copy, and signature line.

- The **headline** is the first line of text on the flyer. It conveys the product or service being offered, such as a car for sale or personal lessons, or the benefit that will be gained, such as a convenience, better performance, greater security, higher earnings, or more comfort; or it can contain a message such as a lost or found pet.

- The **body copy** consists of all text between the headline and the signature line. This text highlights the key points of the message in as few words as possible. It should be easy to read and follow. While emphasizing the positive, the body copy must be realistic, truthful, and believable.

- The **signature line**, which is the last line of text on the flyer, contains contact information or identifies a call to action.

To Type Text

To begin creating the flyer in this chapter, type the headline in the document window. The following steps type this first line of text in the document.

1

- Click the Home tab to make it the active tab.

- Type **Found Dog** as the headline (Figure 1–7).

Q&A What if I make an error while typing?
You can press the DELETE key until you have deleted the text in error and then retype the text correctly.

Q&A Why does the Spelling and Grammar Status icon appear in the status bar?
The **Spelling and Grammar Status icon** appears in the status bar with an animated pencil writing on paper to indicate that Word is checking for spelling and grammar errors. When you stop typing, the pencil changes to a green check mark (no errors) or a red X (potential errors found). Word flags potential errors in the document with a red or green wavy underline. Later in this chapter, you will learn how to fix flagged errors.

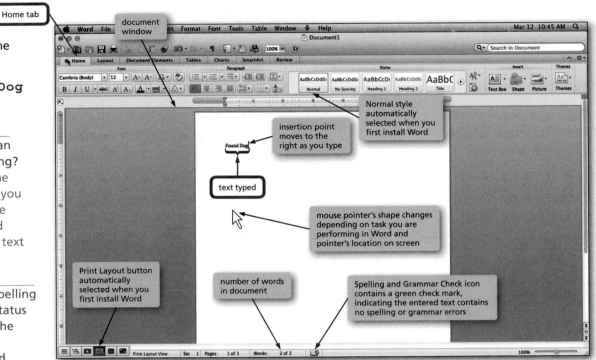

Figure 1–7

2

- Press the RETURN key to move the insertion point to the beginning of the next line (Figure 1–8).

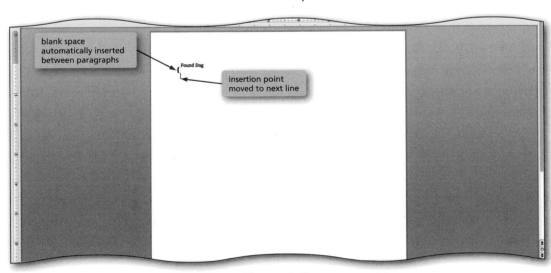

Figure 1–8

To Display Formatting Marks

To indicate where in a document you pressed RETURN or SPACE BAR, you may find it helpful to display formatting marks. A **formatting mark**, sometimes called a **nonprinting character**, is a character that Word displays on the screen but is not visible on a printed document. For example, the paragraph mark (¶) is a formatting mark that indicates where you pressed RETURN. A raised dot (·) shows where you pressed SPACE BAR. Other formatting marks are discussed as they appear on the screen.

Depending on settings made during previous Word sessions, your Word screen already may display formatting marks (Figure 1–9). The following step displays formatting marks, if they do not show already on the screen.

1

- If it is not selected already, click the Show (¶) button on the Standard toolbar to display formatting marks on the screen (Figure 1–9).

Q&A What if I do not want formatting marks to show on the screen?
You can hide them by clicking the Show button on the Standard toolbar so the button is not selected. It is recommended that you display formatting marks so that you visually can identify when you press RETURN, SPACE BAR, and other keys associated with nonprinting characters; therefore, most of the document windows presented in this book show formatting marks.

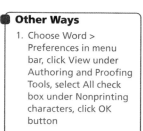

Other Ways

1. Choose Word > Preferences in menu bar, click View under Authoring and Proofing Tools, select All check box under Nonprinting characters, click OK button

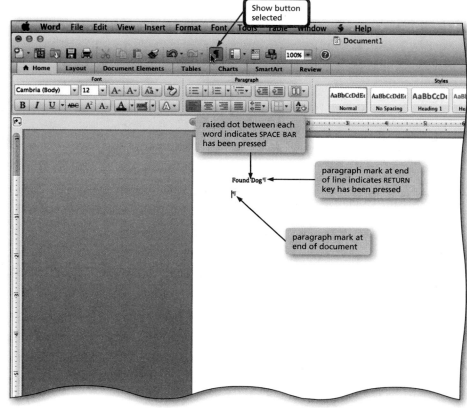

Figure 1–9

To Insert a Blank Line

In the flyer, the digital pictures of the dog appear between the headline and body copy. You will not insert these pictures, however, until after you enter and format all text. Thus, you must leave a blank line in the document as a placeholder for the pictures. To enter a blank line in a document, press RETURN without typing any text on the line. The following step inserts one blank line below the headline.

- Press RETURN to insert a blank line in the document (Figure 1–10).

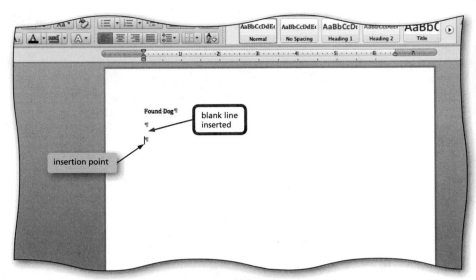

Figure 1–10

Wordwrap

Wordwrap allows you to type words in a paragraph continually without pressing RETURN at the end of each line. As you type, if a word extends beyond the right margin, Word also automatically positions that word on the next line along with the insertion point.

Word creates a new paragraph each time you press RETURN. Thus, as you type text in the document window, do not press RETURN when the insertion point reaches the right margin. Instead, press RETURN only in these circumstances:

1. To insert a blank line(s) in a document (as shown in the step on the previous page)

2. To begin a new paragraph

3. To terminate a short line of text and advance to the next line

4. To respond to questions or prompts in Word dialogs and other on-screen objects

The Ribbon and Screen Resolution

Word may change how the groups and buttons under the groups appear on the ribbon, depending on the computer's screen resolution. Thus, your ribbon may look different from the ones in this book if you are using a screen resolution other than 1280 × 800. | BTW

To Wordwrap Text as You Type

The next step in creating the flyer is to type the body copy. The following step illustrates how the body copy text wordwraps as you enter it in the document.

- Type the first sentence of the body copy: `Adorable, loving, friendly, well-behaved dog found early Friday morning, June 1, wandering on the bike trail at Filcher Park in Hampton Township.`

Q&A   Why does my document wrap on different words?

The printer connected to a computer is one factor that can control where wordwrap occurs for each line in a document. Thus, it is possible that the same document could wordwrap differently if printed on different printers.

• Press RETURN to position the insertion point on the next line in the document (Figure 1–11).

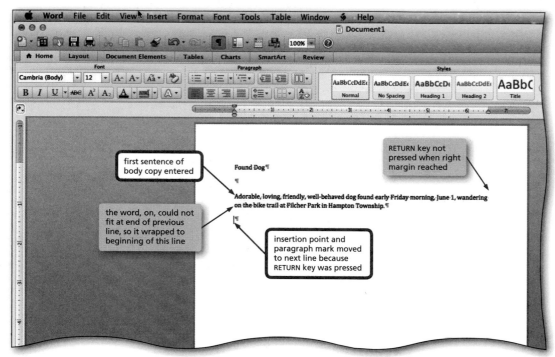

Figure 1–11

Spelling and Grammar Check

As you type text in a document, Word checks your typing for possible spelling and grammar errors. If all of the words you have typed are in Word's dictionary and your grammar is correct, as mentioned earlier the Spelling and Grammar Status icon in the status bar displays a green check mark. Otherwise, the icon shows a red X. In this case, Word flags the potential error in the document window with a red or green wavy underline. A red wavy underline means the flagged text is not in Word's dictionary (because it is a proper name or is misspelled). A green wavy underline indicates the text may be incorrect grammatically. Although you can check the entire document for spelling and grammar errors at once, you also can check flagged errors as they appear on the screen.

A flagged word is not necessarily misspelled. For example, many names, abbreviations, and specialized terms are not in Word's main dictionary. In these cases, you can instruct Word to ignore the flagged word. As you type, Word also detects duplicate words while checking for spelling errors. For example, if your document contains the phrase, to the the store, Word places a red wavy underline below the second occurrence of the word, the.

To Check Spelling and Grammar as You Type

In the following steps, the word, patches, has been misspelled intentionally as paches to illustrate Word's 'check spelling as you type' feature. If you are doing this project on a computer, your flyer may contain different misspelled words, depending on the accuracy of your typing.

- Type **Tan color with paches** and then press SPACE BAR so that a red wavy line appears below the misspelled word (Figure 1–12).

Q&A What if Word does not flag my spelling and grammar errors with wavy underlines?
To verify that the 'check spelling and grammar as you type' features are enabled, click Tools in the menu bar to open the Tools menu and then choose AutoCorrect to open the AutoCorrect dialog. When the AutoCorrect dialog appears, ensure the 'Automatically correct spelling and formatting as you type' check box contains a check mark. Close the AutoCorrect dialog.

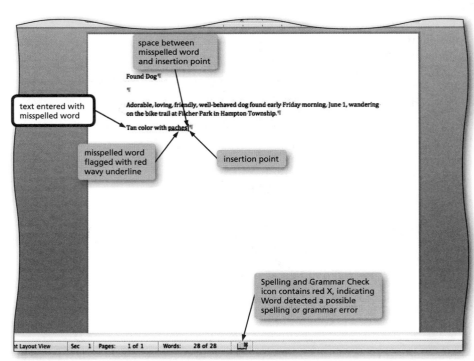

Figure 1–12

2

- CONTROL-click the flagged word (paches, in this case) to display a shortcut menu that presents a list of suggested spelling corrections for the flagged word (Figure 1–13).

Q&A What if, when I CONTROL-click the misspelled word, my desired correction is not in the list in the shortcut menu?
You can click outside the shortcut menu to close the shortcut menu and then retype the correct word, or you can choose Spelling in the shortcut menu to display the Spelling dialog. Chapter 2 discusses the Spelling dialog.

Q&A What if a flagged word actually is, for example, a proper name and spelled correctly?
CONTROL-click it and then choose Ignore All in the shortcut menu to instruct Word not to flag future occurrences of the same word in this document.

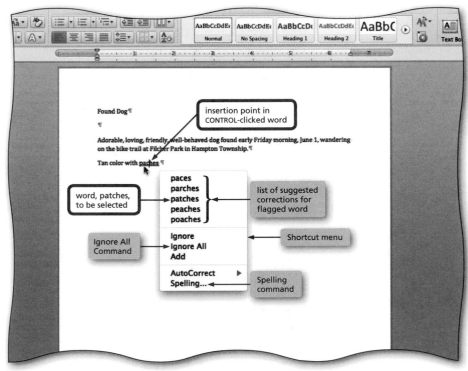

Figure 1–13

③

- Choose patches in the shortcut menu to replace the misspelled word in the document with a correctly spelled word (Figure 1–14).

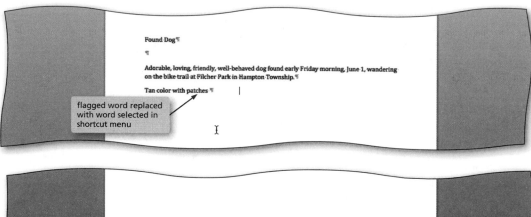

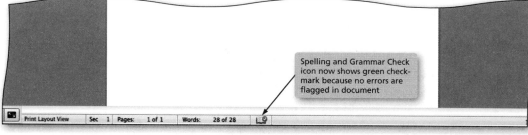

Figure 1–14

Other Ways

1. Click Spelling and Grammar Status icon in status bar, choose desired word in shortcut menu
2. Choose Tools > Spelling and Grammar in menu bar
3. Press OPTION-COMMAND-L

Character Widths

BTW Many word processing documents use variable character fonts, where some characters are wider than others; for example, the letter w is wider than the letter i.

To Enter More Text

In the flyer, the text yet to be entered includes the remainder of the body copy, which will be formatted as a bulleted list, and the signature line. The next steps enter the remainder of text in the flyer.

① Press COMMAND-RIGHT ARROW key (or the END key) to move the insertion point to the end of the current line.

② Type `of white on his chest` and then press RETURN.

③ Type `Male, adult cocker spaniel` and then press RETURN.

④ Type `Green and silver collar with the name, Bailey, on the tag` and then press RETURN.

⑤ Type the signature line in the flyer (Figure 1–15): `If this is your lost dog, call 555-1029.`

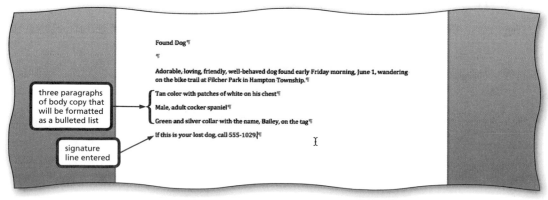

Figure 1–15

Navigating a Document

You view only a portion of a document on the screen through the document window. At some point when you type text or insert graphics, Word probably will **scroll** the top or bottom portion of the document off the screen. Although you cannot see the text and graphics once they scroll off the screen, they remain in the document.

You can use either the keyboard or the mouse to scroll to a different location in a document and/or move the insertion point around a document. When you use the keyboard, the insertion point automatically moves when you press the desired keys. For example, the previous steps used the END key (or the COMMAND-RIGHT ARROW keys) to move the insertion point to the end of the current line. Table 1–1 outlines various techniques to navigate a document using the keyboard.

With the mouse, you can use the scroll arrows or the scroller on the scroll bar to display a different portion of the document in the document window and then click in the document to move the insertion point to that location. Table 1–2 explains various techniques for using the scroll bar to scroll vertically with the mouse. If you click the Select Browse Object button (circle between the up and down scroll arrows at the bottom of the scroll bar), you can use the scroll arrows to browse by page, heading, graphic, or other object.

Keyboard Keys | BTW

Depending on the type of keyboard you have, you may or may not have the HOME, END, PAGE UP, PAGE DOWN, and DELETE FORWARD keys. Extended keyboards (keyboards that include numeric keypads) include these keys, but other keyboards, such as some MacBook Pro laptop keyboards, do not.

Table 1–1 Moving the Insertion Point with the Keyboard

Insertion Point Direction	Key(s) to Press	Insertion Point Direction	Key(s) to Press
Left one character	LEFT ARROW	Up one paragraph	COMMAND-UP ARROW
Right one character	RIGHT ARROW	Down one paragraph	COMMAND-DOWN ARROW
Left one word	OPTION-LEFT ARROW	Up one screen	FN-UP ARROW (or PAGE UP)
Right one word	OPTION-RIGHT ARROW	Down one screen	FN-DOWN ARROW (or PAGE DOWN)
Up one line	UP ARROW	To top of document window	COMMAND-FN-UP ARROW
Down one line	DOWN ARROW	To bottom of document window	COMMAND-FN-DOWN ARROW
To end of line	COMMAND-RIGHT ARROW (or END)	To beginning of document	COMMAND-FN-LEFT ARROW
To beginning of line	COMMAND-LEFT ARROW (or HOME)	To end of document	COMMAND-FN-RIGHT ARROW

Table 1–2 Using the Scroll Bar to Scroll Vertically with the Mouse

Scroll Direction	Mouse Action	Scroll Direction	Mouse Action
Up	Drag the scroller upward.	Down one screen	Click anywhere below the scroller on the vertical scroll bar.
Down	Drag the scroller downward.	Up one object	Click the Browse By Object button, select object, click up scroll arrow.
Up one screen	Click anywhere above the scroller on the vertical scroll bar.	Down one object	Click the Browse by Object button, click the down scroll arrow.

To Save a Document

You have performed many tasks while creating this flyer and do not want to risk losing work completed thus far. Accordingly, you should save the document.

The steps on the next page assume you already have created folders for storing your files, for example, a CIS 101 folder (for your class) that contains a Word folder (for your assignments). Thus, these steps save the document in the Word folder in the CIS 101

Organizing Files and Folders

BTW You should organize and store files in folders so that you easily can find the files later. For example, if you are taking an introductory computer class called CIS 101, a good practice would be to save all Word files in a Word folder in a CIS 101 folder. For a discussion of folders and detailed examples of creating folders, refer to the Office 2011 and Mac OS X chapter at the beginning of this book.

folder on a USB flash drive using the file name, Found Dog Flyer. For a detailed example of the procedure summarized below, refer to the Office 2011 and Mac OS X chapter at the beginning of this book.

1 With a USB flash drive connected to one of the computer's USB ports, click the Save button on the Standard toolbar to display the Save dialog.

2 Type **Found Dog Flyer** in the Save As text box to change the file name. Do not press RETURN after typing the file name because you do not want to close the dialog at this time.

3 Navigate to the desired save location (in this case, the Word folder in the CIS 101 folder [or your class folder] on the USB flash drive).

4 Click the Save button (Save: Microsoft Word dialog) to save the document in the selected folder on the selected drive with the entered file name.

Formatting Paragraphs and Characters

With the text for the flyer entered, the next step is to **format**, or change the appearance of, its text. A paragraph encompasses the text from the first character in the paragraph up to and including its paragraph mark (¶). **Paragraph formatting** is the process of changing the appearance of a paragraph. For example, you can center or add bullets to a paragraph. Characters include letters, numbers, punctuation marks, and symbols. **Character formatting** is the process of changing the way characters appear on the screen and in print. You use character formatting to emphasize certain words and improve readability of a document. For example, you can color or underline characters. Often, you apply both paragraph and character formatting to the same text. For example, you may center a paragraph (paragraph formatting) and underline some of the characters in the same paragraph (character formatting).

Although you can format paragraphs and characters before you type, many Word users enter text first and then format the existing text. Figure 1–16a shows the flyer in this chapter before formatting its paragraphs and characters. Figure 1–16b shows the flyer after formatting. As you can see from the two figures, a document that is formatted is easier to read and looks more professional. The following pages discuss how to format the flyer so that it looks like Figure 1–16b.

Characters that appear on the screen are a specific shape and size. The **font**, or typeface, defines the appearance and shape of the letters, numbers, and special characters. In Word 2011 for Mac, the default font usually is Cambria (shown in Figure 1–17 on page WD 18). You can leave characters in the default font or change them to a different font. **Font size** specifies the size of the characters and is determined by a measurement system called points. A single **point** is about 1/72 of one inch in height. The default font size in Word typically is 12 (Figure 1–17). Thus, a character with a font size of 12 is about 12/72 or 1/6 of one inch in height. You can increase or decrease the font size of characters in a document.

A document **theme** is a set of unified formats for fonts, colors, and graphics. Word includes a variety of document themes to assist you with coordinating these visual elements in a document. The default theme fonts are Calibri for headings and Cambria for body text. By changing the document theme, you quickly can give your document a new look. You also can define your own document themes.

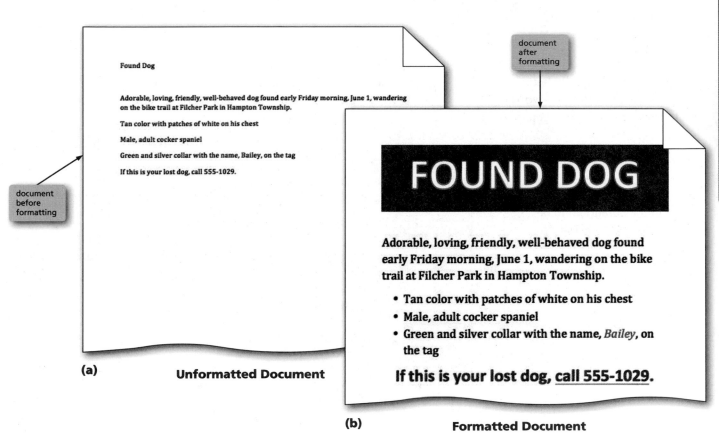

(a)   **Unformatted Document**

(b)   **Formatted Document**

Figure 1–16

Identify how to format various elements of the text.   ☐ **Plan Ahead**

By formatting the characters and paragraphs in a document, you can improve its overall appearance. In a flyer, consider the following formatting suggestions.

- **Increase the font size of characters.** Flyers usually are posted on a bulletin board or in a window. Thus, the font size should be as large as possible so that passersby easily can read the flyer. To give the headline more impact, its font size should be larger than the font size of the text in the body copy. If possible, make the font size of the signature line larger than the body copy but smaller than the headline.

- **Change the font of characters.** Use fonts that are easy to read. Try to use only two different fonts in a flyer, for example, one for the headline and the other for all other text. Too many fonts can make the flyer visually confusing.

- **Change paragraph alignment.** The default alignment for paragraphs in a document is left-aligned, that is, flush at the left margin of the document with uneven right edges. Consider changing the alignment of some of the paragraphs to add interest and variety to the flyer.

- **Highlight key paragraphs with bullets.** A bulleted paragraph is a paragraph that begins with a dot or other symbol. Use bulleted paragraphs to highlight important points in a flyer.

- **Emphasize important words.** To call attention to certain words or lines, you can underline them, italicize them, or bold them. Use these formats sparingly, however, because overuse will minimize their effect and make the flyer look too busy.

- **Use color.** Use colors that complement each other and convey the meaning of the flyer. Vary colors in terms of hue and brightness. Headline colors, for example, can be bold and bright. Signature lines should stand out more than body copy but less than headlines. Keep in mind that too many colors can detract from the flyer and make it difficult to read.

To Center a Paragraph

The headline in the flyer currently is left-aligned (Figure 1–17). You want the headline to be **centered**, that is, positioned horizontally between the left and right margins on the page. Recall that Word considers a single short line of text, such as the two-word headline, a paragraph. Thus, you will center the paragraph containing the headline. The following steps center a paragraph.

- Click somewhere in the paragraph to be centered (in this case, the headline) to position the insertion point in the paragraph to be formatted (Figure 1–17).

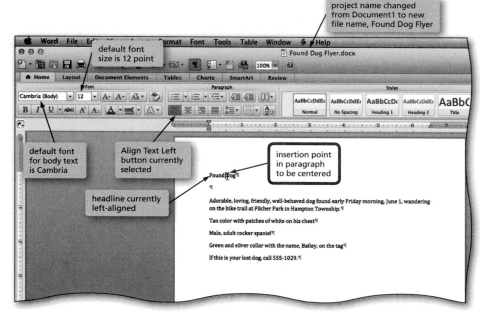

Figure 1–17

- On the Home tab, under Paragraph, click the Center Text button to center the paragraph containing the insertion point (Figure 1–18).

Q&A What if I want to return the paragraph to flush left-aligned? You would click the Center Text button again; or on the Home tab, under Paragraph, click the Align Text Left button.

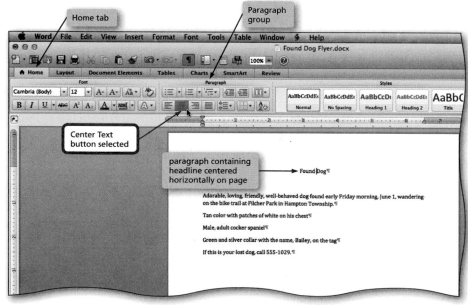

Figure 1–18

Other Ways

1. CONTROL-click paragraph, choose Paragraph in shortcut menu, click Indents and Spacing tab (Paragraph dialog), click Alignment box, click Centered, click OK button

2. Choose Format > Paragraph in menu bar, click Indents and Spacing tab (Paragraph dialog), click Alignment box, click Centered, click OK button

3. Press COMMAND-E

To Center Another Paragraph

In the flyer, the signature line is to be centered to match the paragraph alignment of the headline. The following steps center the signature line.

1 Click somewhere in the paragraph to be centered (in this case, the signature line) to position the insertion point in the paragraph to be formatted.

2 On the Home tab, under Paragraph, click the Center Text button to center the paragraph containing the insertion point (Figure 1–19).

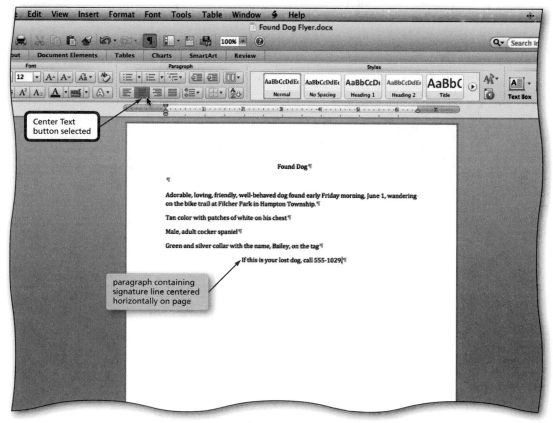

Figure 1–19

File Type

BTW

Depending on your computer settings, the file type .docx may appear on the title bar immediately to the right of the file name after you save the file. The file type .docx is a Word 2011 document.

Formatting Single versus Multiple Paragraphs and Characters

As shown on the previous pages, to format a single paragraph, simply move the insertion point in the paragraph to make it the current paragraph, and then format the paragraph. Similarly, to format a single word, position the insertion point in the word to make it the current word, and then format the word.

To format multiple paragraphs or words, however, you first must select the paragraphs or words you want to format and then format the selection. If your screen normally displays dark letters on a light background, which is the default setting in Word, then selected text displays dark letters on a color background.

Selecting Nonadjacent Items

BTW

In Word, you can select nonadjacent items, that is, items not next to each other. This is helpful when you are applying the same formatting to multiple items. To select nonadjacent items (text or graphics), select the first item, such as a word or paragraph, as usual; then, press and hold down the COMMAND key. While holding down the COMMAND key, select additional items.

To Select a Line

The default font size of 12 point is too small for a headline in a flyer. To increase the font size of the characters in the headline, you first must select the line of text containing the headline. The following step selects a line.

- Move the pointer to the left of the line to be selected (in this case, the headline) until the pointer changes to a right-pointing black arrow.

- While the pointer is a right-pointing black arrow, click to select the entire line to the right of the pointer (Figure 1–20).

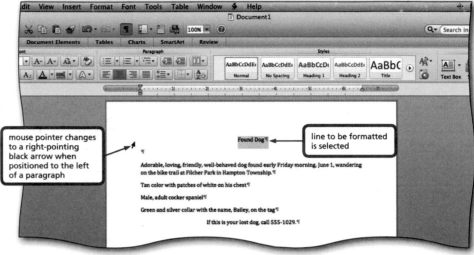

Figure 1–20

Other Ways

1. Drag pointer through line

2. With insertion point at beginning of line, triple-click

To Change the Font Size of Selected Text

The next step is to increase the font size of the characters in the selected headline. You would like the headline to be as large as possible and still fit on a single line, which in this case is 72 point. The following steps increase the font size of the headline from 12 to 72 point.

- With the text selected, on the Home tab, under Font, click the Font Size box arrow to display the Font Size pop-up menu (Figure 1–21).

Q&A Why are the font sizes in my Font Size list different from those in Figure 1–16?

Font sizes may vary depending on the current font and printer.

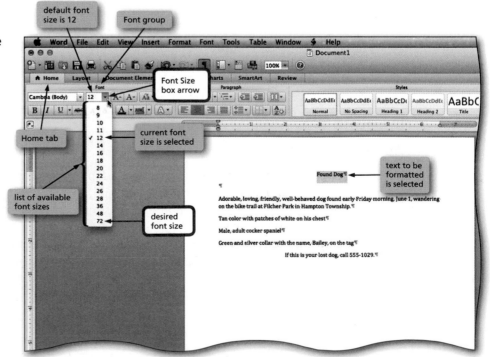

Figure 1–21

2

- Choose 72 in the Font Size pop-up menu to increase the font size of the selected text to 72 point (Figure 1–22).

Figure 1–22

Other Ways

1. CONTROL-click selected text, click Font in shortcut menu, click Font tab (Font dialog), select desired font size in Size list, click OK button

2. Choose Format > Font in menu bar, click Font tab (Font dialog), select desired font size in Size list, click OK button

3. Press COMMAND-D, click Font tab (Font dialog), select desired font size in Size list, click OK button

To Change the Font of Selected Text

The default theme font for headings is Calibri and for all other text, called body text in Word, is Cambria. Many other fonts are available, however, so that you can add variety to documents.

To draw more attention to the headline, you change its font so that it differs from the font of other text in the flyer. The following steps change the font of the headline from Cambria to Calibri.

1

- With the text selected, on the Home tab, under Font, click the Font box arrow to display the Font pop-up menu (Figure 1–23).

Q&A Will the fonts in my Font pop-up menu be the same as those in Figure 1–23?
Your list of available fonts may differ, depending on the type of printer you are using and other settings.

Q&A What if the text is no longer selected?
Follow the steps on the previous page to select a line.

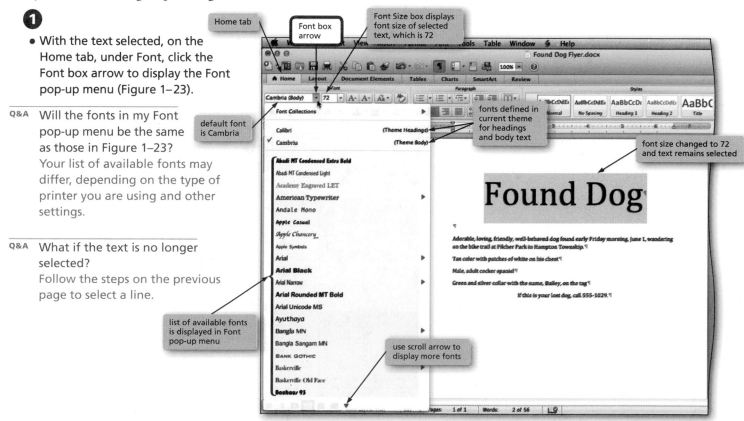

Figure 1–23

2

- Scroll through the Font pop-up menu, if necessary, and then choose Calibri to change the font of the selected text to Calibri (Figure 1–24).

Figure 1–24

Other Ways

1. CONTROL-click selected text, choose Font in shortcut menu, click Font tab (Font dialog), select desired font in Font list, click OK button

2. Choose Format > Font in menu bar, click Font tab (Font dialog), select desired font in Font list, click OK button

3. Click Font in menu bar, select desired font

4. Press COMMAND-D, click Font tab (Font dialog), select desired font in the Font list, click OK button

To Change the Case of Selected Text

The headline currently shows the first letter in each word capitalized, which sometimes is referred to as initial cap. To draw more attention to the headline, you would like the entire line of text to be capitalized, or in uppercase letters. The following steps change the headline to uppercase.

1

- With the text selected, on the Home tab, under Font, click the Change Case button to display the Change Case pop-up menu (Figure 1–25).

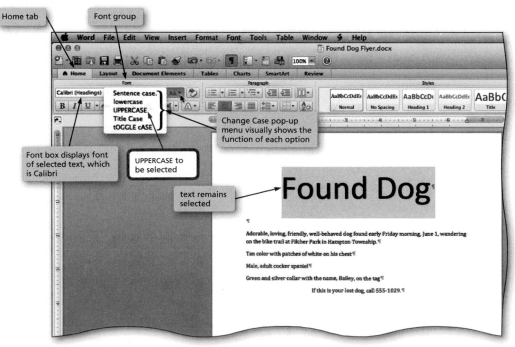

Figure 1–25

2

- Choose UPPERCASE in the Change Case pop-up menu to change the case of the selected text to uppercase (Figure 1–26).

Q&A What if the pointer shape changes? Depending on the position of your pointer and locations you click on the screen, the pointer shape may change. Simply move the pointer and the pointer shape will change.

Figure 1–26

Other Ways

1. CONTROL-click selected text, click Font in shortcut menu, click Font tab (Font dialog), under Effects select All caps, click OK button

2. Choose Format > Font in menu bar, click Font tab (Font dialog), under Effects select All caps, click OK button

To Apply a Text Effect to Selected Text

You would like the text in the headline to be even more noticeable. Word provides many text effects to add interest and variety to text. The following steps apply a text effect to the headline.

1

- With the text selected, on the Home tab, under Font, click the Text Effects button to display the Text Effects gallery (Figure 1–27).

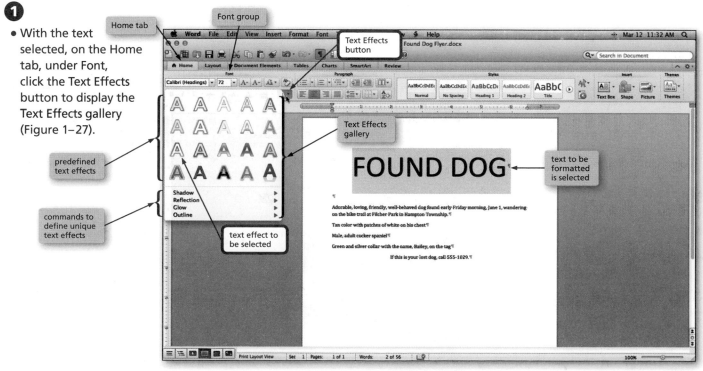

Figure 1–27

- Click the first text effect in the third row to change the text effect of the selected text.

- Click anywhere in the document window to remove the selection from the selected text (Figure 1–28).

Figure 1–28

Other Ways

1. CONTROL-click selected text, click Font in shortcut menu, click Font tab (Font dialog), click Text Effects button, select desired text effects (Format Text Effects dialog), click OK button (Format Text Effects dialog), click OK button (Font dialog)

2. Choose Format > Font in menu bar, click Font tab (Font dialog), click Text Effects button, select desired text effects (Format Text Effects dialog), click OK button (Format Text Effects dialog), click OK button (Font dialog)

To Shade a Paragraph

To make the headline of the flyer more eye-catching, you would like to shade it. When you **shade** text, Word colors the rectangular area behind any text or graphics. If the text to shade is a paragraph, Word shades the area from the left margin to the right margin of the current paragraph. To shade a paragraph, place the insertion point in the paragraph. To shade any other text, you must first select the text to be shaded. This flyer uses brown as the shading color for the headline. The following steps shade a paragraph.

- Click somewhere in the paragraph to be shaded (in this case, the headline) to position the insertion point in the paragraph to be formatted.

- Click Format in the menu bar to display the Format menu (Figure 1–29).

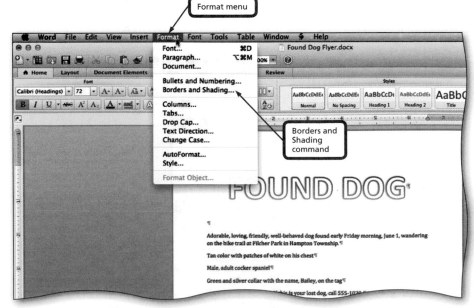

Figure 1–29

2

- Choose Borders and Shading to display the Borders and Shading dialog. If necessary, click the Shading tab to display the Shading pane.

- Click Brown (fourth row, second column) to select the shading color (Figure 1–30).

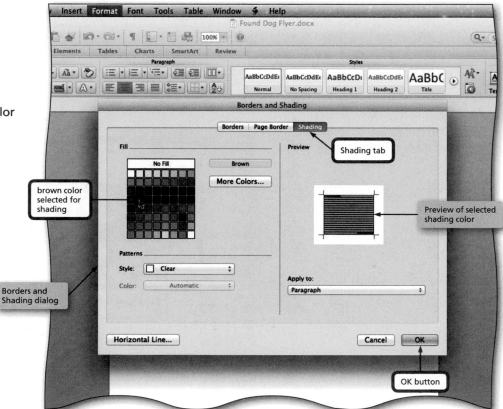

Figure 1–30

3

- Click the OK button (Borders and Shading dialog) to shade the current paragraph (Figure 1–31).

 Q&A What if I apply a dark shading color to dark text?

When the font color of text is Automatic, it usually is black. If you select a dark shading color, Word automatically may change the text color to white so that the shaded text is easier to read.

Other Ways

1. CONTROL-click selected text, choose Borders and Shading, Shading tab, select desired shading (Borders and Shading dialog), click OK button

Figure 1–31

To Select Multiple Lines

The next formatting step for the flyer is to increase the font size of the characters between the headline and the signature line so that they are easier to read from a distance. To change the font size of the characters in multiple lines, you first must select all the lines to be formatted. The following steps select multiple lines.

- Move the pointer to the left of the first paragraph to be selected until the pointer changes to a right-pointing black arrow (Figure 1–32).

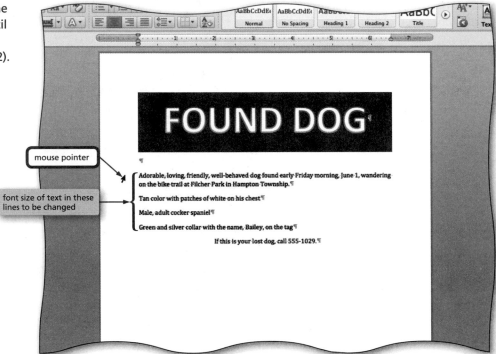

Figure 1–32

- Drag downward to select all lines that will be formatted (Figure 1–33).

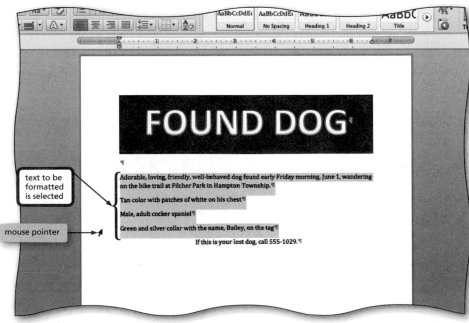

Figure 1–33

Other Ways

1. With insertion point at beginning of desired line, press SHIFT-DOWN ARROW repeatedly until all lines are selected

To Change the Font Size of Selected Text

The characters between the headline and the signature line in the flyer currently are 12 point. To make them easier to read from a distance, this flyer uses 20 point for these characters. The following steps change the font size of the selected text.

1 With the text selected, on the Home tab, under Font, click the Font Size box arrow to display the Font Size pop-up menu.

2 Choose 20 in the Font Size pop-up menu to increase the font size of the selected text.

3 Click anywhere in the document window to remove the selection from the text.

4 If necessary, scroll so that you can see all the text on the screen (Figure 1–34).

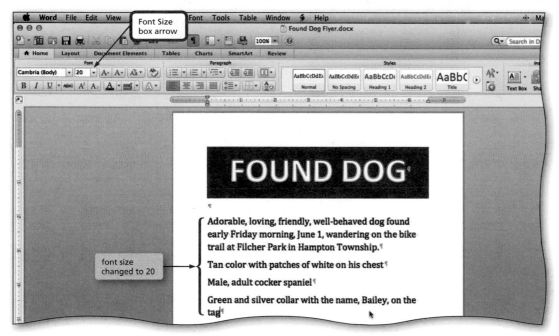

Formatting Marks

BTW

With some fonts, formatting marks may not appear properly on the screen. For example, the raised dot that signifies a blank space between words may appear behind a character instead of in the blank space, causing the characters to look incorrect.

Figure 1–34

To Bullet a List of Paragraphs

The next step is to format as a bulleted list the three paragraphs of identifying information that are above the signature line in the flyer. A **bulleted list** is a series of paragraphs, each beginning with a bullet character.

To format a list of paragraphs with bullets, you first must select all the lines in the paragraphs. The following steps bullet a list of paragraphs.

1

- Move the pointer to the left of the first paragraph to be selected until the mouse pointer changes to a right-pointing black arrow.

- Drag downward until all paragraphs that will be formatted with a bullet character are selected (Figure 1–35).

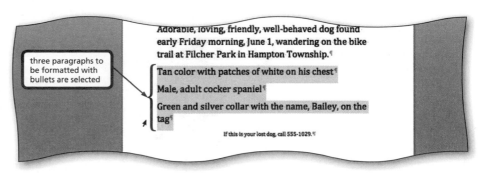

Figure 1–35

- On the Home tab, under Paragraph, click the Bulleted List button to place a bullet character at the beginning of each selected paragraph (Figure 1–36).

Q&A How do I remove bullets from a list or paragraph?
Select the list or paragraph and then click the Bulleted List button again.

Q&A What if I accidentally click the arrow next to the Bulleted List button?
Press the ESC key to remove the Bullet Library from the screen and then repeat Step 2.

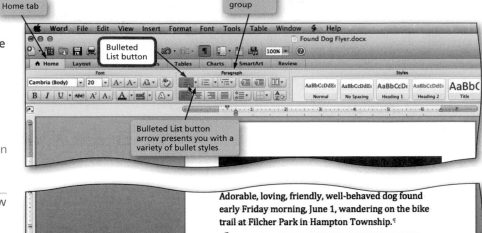

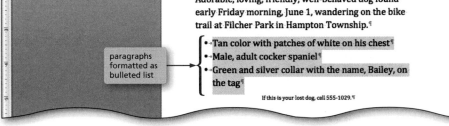

Figure 1–36

Other Ways

1. CONTROL-click paragraphs, choose Bullets and Numbering in shortcut menu, click Bulleted tab (Bullets and Numbering dialog), select desired bullet style, click OK button

2. Choose Format > Bullets and Numbering in menu bar, click Bulleted tab (Bullets and Numbering dialog), select desired bullet style, click OK button

To Undo and Redo an Action

Word provides a means of canceling your recent command(s) or action(s). For example, if you format text incorrectly, you can undo the format and try it again. When you point to the Undo button, Word displays the action you can undo as part of a ScreenTip.

If, after you undo an action, you decide you did not want to perform the undo, you can redo the undone action. Word does not allow you to undo or redo some actions, such as saving or printing a document. The next steps undo the bullet format just applied and then redo the bullet format.

- Click the Undo button on the Standard toolbar to reverse your most recent action (in this case, remove the bullets from the paragraphs) (Figure 1–37).

- Click the Redo button on the Standard toolbar to reverse your most recent undo (in this case, place a bullet character on the paragraphs again) (shown in Figure 1–36).

Other Ways

1. Press COMMAND-Z to undo; press COMMAND-Y to redo

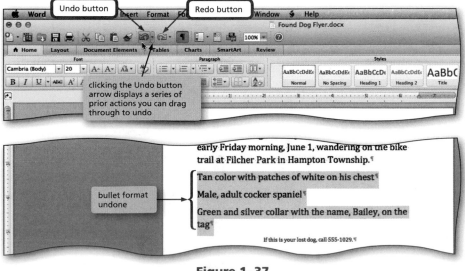

Figure 1–37

To Italicize Text

The next step is to italicize the dog's name, Bailey, in the flyer to further emphasize it. **Italicized** text has a slanted appearance. As with a single paragraph, if you want to format a single word, you do not need to select it. Simply position the insertion point somewhere in the word and apply the desired format. The following step formats a word in italics.

1

- Click somewhere in the word to be italicized (Bailey, in this case) to position the insertion point in the word to be formatted.

- On the Home tab, under Font, click the Italic button to italicize the word containing the insertion point (Figure 1–38).

Q&A   How would I remove an italic format?
You would click the Italic button a second time, or you immediately could click the Undo button on the Standard toolbar or press COMMAND-Z.

Q&A   How can I tell what formatting has been applied to text?
The selected buttons and boxes on the Home tab show formatting characteristics of the location of the insertion point. With the insertion point in the word, Bailey, the Home tab shows these formats: 20-point Cambria italic font, bulleted paragraph.

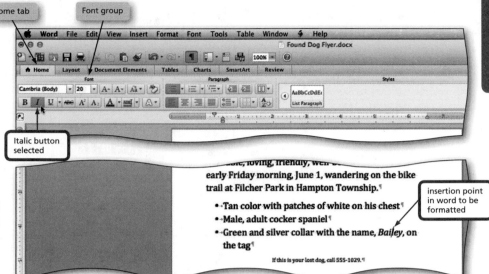

Figure 1–38

Other Ways

1. CONTROL-click selected text, choose Font in shortcut menu, click Font tab (Font dialog), select Italic in Font style list, click OK button

2. Choose Format > Font in menu bar, click Font tab (Font dialog), under Font style select Italic, click OK button

3. Press COMMAND-I

Use color.

When choosing color, associate the meaning of color to your message:

- Red expresses danger, power, or energy, and often is associated with sports or physical exertion.

- Brown represents simplicity, honesty, and dependability.

- Orange denotes success, victory, creativity, and enthusiasm.

- Yellow suggests sunshine, happiness, hope, liveliness, and intelligence.

- Green symbolizes growth, healthiness, harmony, blooming, and healing, and often is associated with safety or money.

- Blue indicates integrity, trust, importance, confidence, and stability.

- Purple represents wealth, power, comfort, extravagance, magic, mystery, and spirituality.

- White stands for purity, goodness, cleanliness, precision, and perfection.

- Black suggests authority, strength, elegance, power, and prestige.

- Gray conveys neutrality and thus often is found in backgrounds and other effects.

Plan Ahead

Q&As

For a complete list of the **BTW** Q&As found in many of the step-by-step sequences in this book, visit the Office 2011 for Mac Online Companion Web page at www.cengagebrain.com, navigate to the desired chapter, and click Q&As.

To Color Text

To emphasize the dog's name even more, its color is changed to a shade of blue. The following steps change the color of the word, Bailey.

- With the insertion point in the word to format, on the Home tab, under Font, click the Font Color button arrow to display the Font Color pop-up menu (Figure 1–39).

Q&A What if I click the Font Color button by mistake?
Click the Font Color button arrow and then proceed with Step 2.

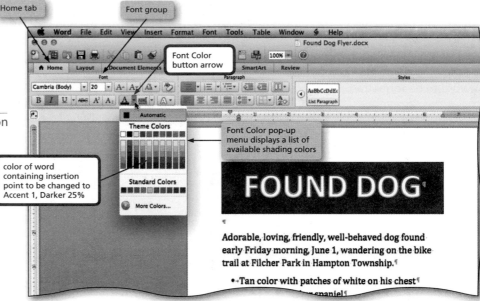

Figure 1–39

- Choose Accent 1, Darker 25% (fifth color in the fifth row) to change the font color of the selected text (Figure 1–40).

Q&A How would I change the text color back to black?
You would position the insertion point in the word or select the text, click the arrow next to the Font Color box again, and then click Automatic in the Font Color pop-up menu.

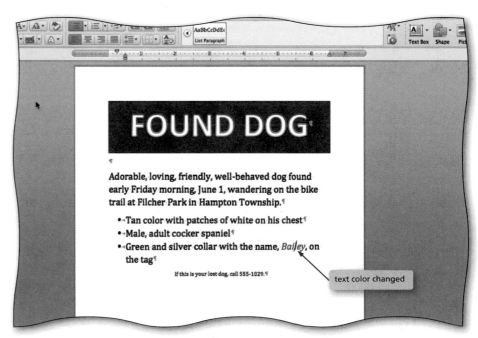

Figure 1–40

Other Ways

1. CONTROL-click selected text, choose Font in shortcut menu, click Font tab (Font dialog), click Font color disclosure button, select desired color, click OK button

2. Choose Format > Font in menu bar, click Font tab (Font dialog), click Font Color button, select desired color, click OK button

To Change the Font, Font Color, and Font Size of Additional Text

The following steps change the font, font color, and font size of text in the signature line of the flyer.

1 Move the mouse pointer to the left of the line to be selected (in this case, the signature line) until the mouse pointer changes to a right-pointing black arrow and then click to select the line.

2 On the Home tab, under Font, click the Font box arrow to display the Font pop-up menu. Choose Calibri to change the font of the selected text.

3 Under Font, click the Font Size box arrow to display the Font Size pop-up menu. Choose 28 in the Font Size pop-up menu to increase the font size of the selected text to 28 point.

4 With the text still selected, click the Font Color button arrow to display the Font Color pop-up menu. Choose Accent 4, Darker 50% (eighth color in the sixth row) to change the color of the selected text. Click anywhere in the document window to remove the selection from the text. (Figure 1–41).

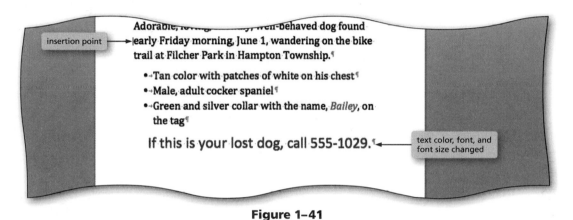

Figure 1–41

To Select a Group of Words

To emphasize the contact information (call 555-1029), these words are underlined in the flyer. To format a group of words, you first must select them. The following steps select a group of words.

1

- Position the mouse pointer immediately to the left of the first character of the text to be selected, in this case, the c in call (Figure 1–42).

Q&A Why did the shape of the mouse pointer change?
The mouse pointer's shape is an I-beam when positioned in unselected text in the document window.

Figure 1–42

- Drag the mouse pointer through the last character of the text to be selected, in this case, the 9 in the phone number (Figure 1–43).

Q&A Why did the mouse pointer shape change again?
When the mouse pointer is positioned in selected text, its shape is a left-pointing black arrow.

Other Ways
1. With insertion point at beginning of first word in group, press OPTION-SHIFT-RIGHT ARROW repeatedly until all words are selected

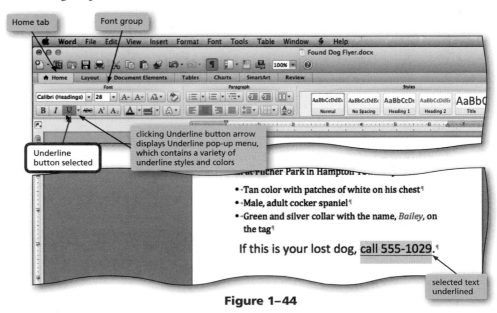

Figure 1–43

To Underline Text

Underlines are used to emphasize or draw attention to specific text. **Underlined** text prints with an underscore (_) below each character. In the flyer, the contact information, call 555-1029, in the signature line is emphasized with an underline. The following step formats selected text with an underline.

- With the text selected, on the Home tab, under Font, click the Underline button to underline the selected text (Figure 1–44).

Q&A How would I remove an underline?
You would click the Underline button a second time, or you immediately could click the Undo button on the Standard toolbar.

Figure 1–44

Other Ways
1. CONTROL-click selected text, choose Font in shortcut menu, click Font tab (Font dialog), select desired underline in Underline style list, click OK button
2. Choose Format > Font in menu bar, click Font tab, under Underline style select desired style, click OK button
3. Press COMMAND-U

To Bold Text

Bold characters appear somewhat thicker and darker than those that are not bold. To further emphasize the signature line, it is bold in the flyer. To format the line, as you have learned previously, you select the line first. The following steps format the signature line bold.

- Move the mouse pointer to the left of the line to be selected (in this case, the signature line) until the mouse pointer changes to a right-pointing black arrow and then click the mouse to select the text to be formatted.

- With the text selected, on the Home tab, under Font, click the Bold button to bold the selected text (Figure 1–45).

Q&A How would I remove a bold format?
You would click the Bold button a second time, or you immediately could click the Undo button on the Standard toolbar.

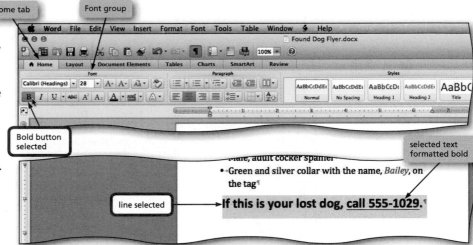

Figure 1–45

- Click anywhere in the document window to remove the selection from the screen.

Other Ways

1. CONTROL-click selected text, choose Font in shortcut menu, click Font tab (Font dialog), select Bold in Font style list, click OK button

2. Choose Format > Font in menu bar, click Font tab, under Font style select Bold, click OK button

3. Press COMMAND-B

To Change Theme Colors

A **color scheme** in Word is a document theme that identifies 12 complementary colors for text, background, accents, and links in a document. With more than 20 predefined color schemes, Word provides a simple way to select colors that work well together.

In the flyer, you want all the colors to convey honesty, dependability, and healing, that is, shades of browns and greens. In Word, the Pushpin color scheme uses these colors. Thus, you will change the color scheme from the default, Office, to Pushpin. The next steps change theme colors.

1

- Click the Publishing Layout View button at the bottom left of the document window (Figure 1–46).

Figure 1–46

2

- Click the Continue button (shown in Figure 1–46 on the previous page) to display the document in Publishing Layout view.

- On the Home tab, under Themes, click the Colors button to display the Colors gallery (Figure 1–47).

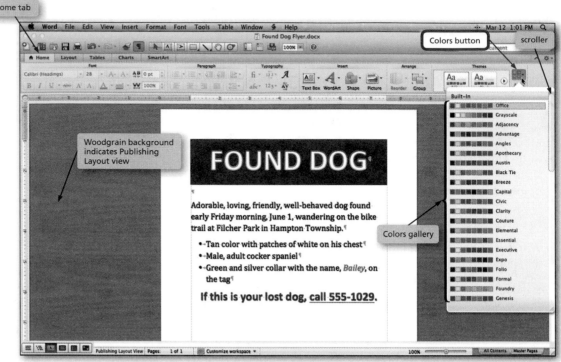

Figure 1–47

3

- Scroll to display the Pushpin color scheme.

- Click Pushpin in the Colors gallery to change the document theme colors.

- Click the Print Layout View button at the bottom left of the document window to return to Print Layout view (Figure 1–48).

Q&A What if I want to return to the original color scheme?
You would return to the Colors gallery in Publishing Layout view, and then click Office in the Colors gallery.

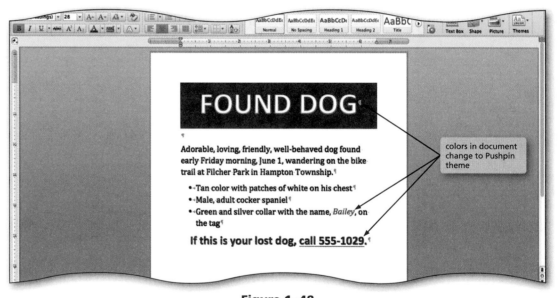

Figure 1–48

Other Ways
1. Choose View > Publishing Layout in menu bar, click Continue, click Colors button on Home tab under Themes, select Pushpin

Selecting Text

In many of the previous steps, you have selected text. Table 1–3 summarizes the techniques used to select various items.

Table 1–3 Techniques for Selecting Text

Item to Select	Mouse	Keyboard (where applicable)
Block of text	Click at beginning of selection, scroll to end of selection, position mouse pointer at end of selection; hold down SHIFT key and then click; or drag through the text.	
Character(s)	Drag through character(s).	SHIFT-RIGHT ARROW or SHIFT-LEFT ARROW
Document	Move mouse to left of text until mouse pointer changes to a right-pointing black arrow and then triple-click.	COMMAND-A
Graphic	Click the graphic.	
Line	Move mouse to left of line until mouse pointer changes to a right-pointing black arrow and then click.	FN-LEFT ARROW, then SHIFT-COMMAND-RIGHT ARROW or FN-RIGHT ARROW, then SHIFT-COMMAND-LEFT ARROW
Lines	Move mouse to left of first line until mouse pointer changes to a right-pointing black arrow and then drag up or down.	FN-LEFT ARROW, then SHIFT-DOWN ARROW or FN-RIGHT ARROW, then SHIFT-UP ARROW
Paragraph	Triple-click paragraph; or move mouse to left of paragraph until mouse pointer changes to a right-pointing black arrow and then double-click.	COMMAND-SHIFT-DOWN ARROW
Paragraphs	Move mouse to left of paragraph until mouse pointer changes to a right-pointing black arrow, double-click, and then drag up or down.	COMMAND-SHIFT-DOWN ARROW (repeatedly)
Sentence	Press and hold down COMMAND key and then click sentence.	
Word	Double-click the word.	OPTION-SHIFT-RIGHT ARROW
Words	Drag through words.	OPTION-SHIFT-RIGHT ARROW (repeatedly)

To Save an Existing Document with the Same File Name

You have made several modifications to the document since you last saved it. Thus, you should save it again. The following step saves the document again. For an example of the step listed below, refer to the Office 2011 and Mac OS X chapter at the beginning of this book.

1 Click the Save button on the Standard toolbar to overwrite the previously saved file.

Break Point: If you wish to take a break, this is a good place to do so. You can quit Word now (refer to page WD 48 for instructions). To resume at a later time, start Word (refer to pages WD 4 and WD 49 for instructions), open the file called Found Dog Flyer (refer to page WD 49 for instructions), and continue following the steps from this location forward.

Inserting and Formatting Pictures in a Word Document

With the text formatted in the flyer, the next step is to insert digital pictures in the flyer and format the pictures. Flyers usually contain graphical images, such as a picture, to attract the attention of passersby. In the following pages, you will perform these tasks:

1. Insert the first digital picture into the flyer and then reduce its size.

2. Insert the second digital picture into the flyer and then reduce its size.

3. Change the look of the first picture and then the second picture.

Plan Ahead	**Find the appropriate graphical image.**

To use a graphical image, also called a graphic, in a Word document, the image must be stored digitally in a file. Files containing graphical images are available from a variety of sources:

- Word includes a collection of predefined graphical images that you can insert in a document.
- Microsoft has free digital images on the Web for use in a document. Other Web sites also have images available, some of which are free, while others require a fee.
- You can take a picture with a digital camera or camera phone and download it, which is the process of copying the digital picture from the camera or phone to your computer.
- With a scanner, you can convert a printed picture, drawing, or diagram to a digital file. If you receive a picture from a source other than yourself, do not use the file until you are certain it does not contain a virus. A virus is a computer program that can damage files and programs on your computer. Use an antivirus program to verify that any files you use are virus free.

Plan Ahead	**Establish where to position and how to format the graphical image.**

The content, size, shape, position, and format of a graphic should capture the interest of passersby, enticing them to stop and read the flyer. Often, the graphic is the center of attraction and visually the largest element on a flyer. If you use colors in the graphical image, be sure they are part of the document's color scheme.

To Insert a Picture

The next step in creating the flyer is to insert one of the digital pictures of the dog so that it is centered on the blank line below the headline. The picture, which was taken with a camera phone, is available on the Data Files for Students. See the inside back cover of this book for instructions on downloading the Data Files for Students, or contact your instructor for information about accessing the required files.

The following steps insert a centered picture, which, in this example, is located in the Chapter 01 folder in the Word folder in the Data Files for Students folder on a USB flash drive.

- Position the insertion point on the blank line below the headline, which is the location where you want to insert the picture.

- On the Home tab, under Paragraph, click the Center Text button to center the paragraph that will contain the picture.

- Under Insert, click the Picture button to display the pop-up menu (Figure 1–49).

Figure 1–49

2

- With your USB flash drive connected to one of the computer's USB ports, click the Picture from File command in the pop-up menu (shown in Figure 1–49) to display the Choose a Picture dialog (shown in Figure 1–50).

3

- Navigate to the picture location (in this case, the Chapter 01 folder in the Word folder in the Data Files for Students folder on a USB flash drive). For a detailed example of this procedure, refer to Steps 1–4 in the To Save a File in a Folder section in the Office 2011 and Mac OS X chapter at the beginning of this book.

- Click Dog Picture 1 to select the Figure 1–50 file.

Q&A What if the picture is not on a USB flash drive?
Use the same process, but select the storage location containing the picture.

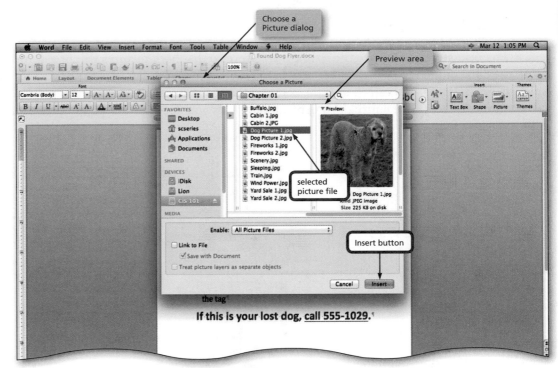

Figure 1–50

4

- Click the Insert button (Choose a Picture dialog) to insert the picture at the location of the insertion point in the document (Figure 1–51).

Q&A What are the symbols around the picture? A selected graphic appears surrounded by a **selection rectangle**, which has small squares and circles, called **sizing handles**, at each corner and middle location.

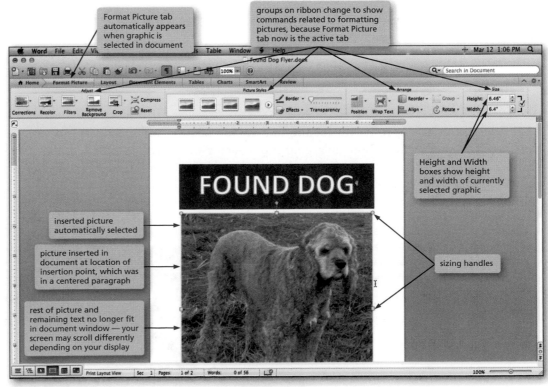

Figure 1–51

To Zoom the Document

The next step is to reduce the size of the picture so that both pictures will fit side-by-side on the same line. With the current picture size, the flyer now has expanded to two pages. The final flyer, however, should fit on a single page. In Word, you can change the zoom so that you can see the entire document (that is, both pages) on the screen at once. Seeing the entire document at once helps you determine the appropriate size for the picture. The following step zooms the document.

① Experiment

• Drag the zoom slider in the lower-right corner of the document window and watch the size of the document change in the document window.

• Drag the slider until the Zoom percentage displays 50% (Figure 1–52).

Q&A If I change the zoom percentage, will the document print differently? Changing the zoom has no effect on the printed document.

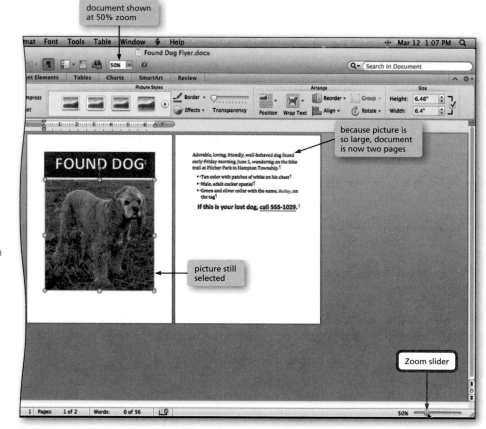

Figure 1–52

● Other Ways

1. Click Zoom box arrow in Standard toolbar, select desired Zoom option

2. Choose View > Zoom in menu bar, select desired Zoom option, click OK button

To Resize a Graphic

The next step is to resize the picture so that both pictures will fit side-by-side on the same line below the headline. **Resizing** includes both enlarging and reducing the size of a graphic. In this flyer, you will reduce the size of the picture. With the entire document displayed in the document window, you will be able to see how the resized graphic will look on the entire page. The following steps resize a selected graphic.

• With the graphic still selected, point to the upper-right corner sizing handle on the picture so that the mouse pointer shape changes to a two-headed arrow (Figure 1–53).

Q&A What if my graphic (picture) is not selected?
To select a graphic, click it.

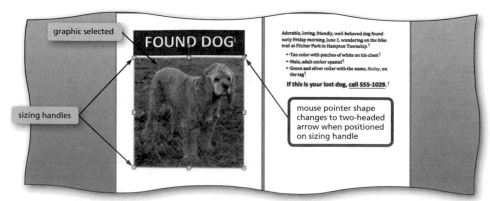

Figure 1–53

2

- Drag the sizing handle diagonally inward until the crosshair mouse pointer is positioned approximately as shown in Figure 1–54.

3

- Release the mouse button to resize the graphic, which in this case should have a height of about 2.72" and a width of about 2.7".

Q&A   How can I see the height and width measurements?

As you drag the sizing handle, a yellow box will appear beside the resized figure. This box will show you the changing height and width.

Q&A   What if the graphic is the wrong size?

Repeat Steps 1, 2, and 3; or until the desired height and width are reached.

Figure 1–54

4

- Click to the right of the graphic to deselect it (Figure 1–55).

Q&A   What happened to the Format Picture tab?

When you click outside of a graphic or press a key to scroll through a document, Word deselects the graphic and removes the Format Picture tab from the screen.

Q&A   What if I want to return a graphic to its original size and start again?

With the graphic selected, on the Format Picture tab, under Adjust, click the Reset button to undo all formatting changes made to the picture.

Figure 1–55

Other Ways

1. Enter height and width of graphic in Height and Width boxes on Format Picture tab under Size

To Insert Another Picture

The next step is to insert the other digital picture of the dog immediately to the right of the current picture. This second picture also is available on the Data Files for Students. See the inside back cover of this book for instructions on downloading the Data Files for Students, or contact your instructor for information about accessing the required files.

The following steps insert another picture immediately to the right of the current picture.

1 Position the insertion point as shown in Figure 1–55.

2 Under Insert, click the Insert a picture button to display the pop-up menu (Figure 1–49).

3 With your USB flash drive connected to one of the computer's USB ports, click the Picture from File command in the pop-up menu to display the Choose a Picture dialog.

4 Click Picture from File, and then navigate to the picture location in the Choose a Picture dialog.

5 Click Dog Picture 2 to select the file.

6 Click the Insert button (Choose a Picture dialog) to insert the picture at the location of the insertion point in the document.

To Resize a Graphic by Entering Exact Measurements

The next step is to resize the second picture so that it is the exact same size as the first picture. The height and width measurements of the first graphic are approximately 2.72" and 2.7", respectively. When a graphic is selected, its height and width measurements show in the Size group of the Picture Tools Format tab. The following steps resize a selected graphic by entering its desired exact measurements.

- With the second graphic still selected, on the Format Picture tab, under Size, click the Height box, select the contents in the box, and then type **2.72** as the height.

Q&A What if the Picture Tools Format tab no longer is displayed on my ribbon?
Click to select the picture and display the Picture Tools Format tab.

Q&A What if the contents of the Height box are not selected?
Triple-click the Height box.

2

- Click the picture to apply the settings (Figure 1–56).

Q&A Why did the contents of the Width box change when I clicked the picture?
The Lock Aspect Ratio check box is checked, which means that the relationship between height and width of the picture is kept intact. When you change one measurement, the other automatically changes to keep the ratio between height and width constant. This prevents you from distorting the image.

- If necessary, scroll up to display the entire document in the window.

Q&A Why did my measurements change slightly?
Depending on relative measurements, the height and width values entered may change slightly.

Figure 1–56

Other Ways

1. CONTROL-click picture, click Format Picture, click Size, enter height and width values in boxes, click OK button

2. Choose Format > Picture in menu bar, click Size, enter height and width values in boxes, click OK button

To Zoom the Document

You are finished resizing the graphics and no longer need to view the entire page in the document window. Thus, the following step changes the zoom back to 100 percent.

 Drag the zoom slider until the Zoom displays as 100% (shown in Figure 1–57).

To Apply a Picture Style

A **style** is a named group of formatting characteristics. Word provides more than 25 picture styles that enable you easily to change a picture's look to a more visually appealing style, including a variety of shapes, angles, borders, and reflections. The flyer in this chapter uses a style that applies soft edges to the picture. The following steps apply a picture style to a picture.

- Click the leftmost dog picture to select it.

- If necessary, click the Format Picture tab.

- On the Format Picture tab, under Picture Styles, click the downward-facing More button to display the Picture Styles gallery (Figure 1–57).

Q&A Why can't I see the More button on my ribbon?
The More button is only visible when you point to the Picture Styles scrolling gallery.

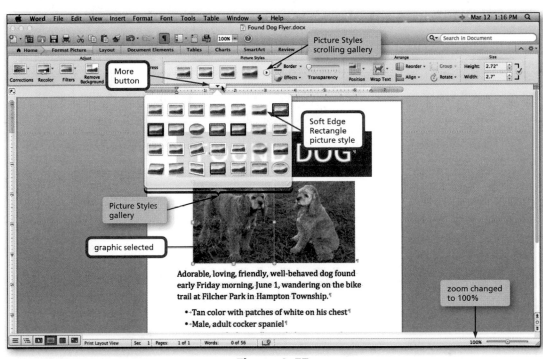

Figure 1–57

- Click Soft Edge Rectangle in the Picture Styles gallery to apply the style to the selected picture (Figure 1–58).

Q&A What is the green circle attached to the selected graphic?
It is called a rotate handle. When you drag a graphic's rotate handle, the graphic moves in either a clockwise or counterclockwise direction.

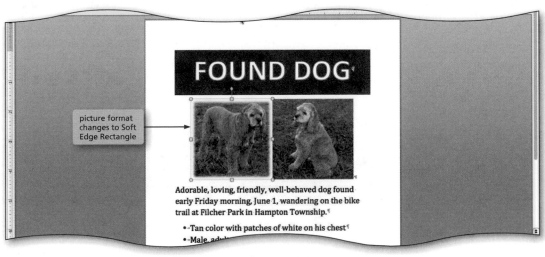

Figure 1–58

To Apply Picture Effects

Word provides a variety of picture effects so that you can further customize a picture. Effects include shadows, reflections, glow, soft edges, bevel, and 3-D rotation. The difference between the effects and the styles is that each effect has several options, providing you with more control over the exact look of the image.

In this flyer, the leftmost dog picture has a slight tan glow effect and is turned inward toward the center of the page. The following steps apply picture effects to the selected picture.

- On the Format Picture tab, under Picture Styles, click the Effects button to display the Effects menu.

- Point to Glow on the Effects menu to display the Glow gallery (Figure 1–59).

- Click Accent 6, 5 pt glow (fourth row, third column) to apply the selected picture effect.

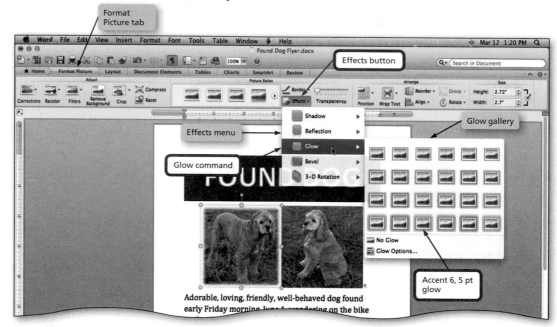

Figure 1–59

Q&A What if I wanted to discard formatting applied to a picture?
You would click the Reset Picture button on the Picture Tools Format tab, under the Adjust group. To reset formatting and size, you would click the Reset button on the Picture Tools Format tab, under Adjust.

- Click the Effects button to display the Effects menu again.

- Point to 3-D Rotation on the Effects menu to display the 3-D Rotation gallery (Figure 1–60).

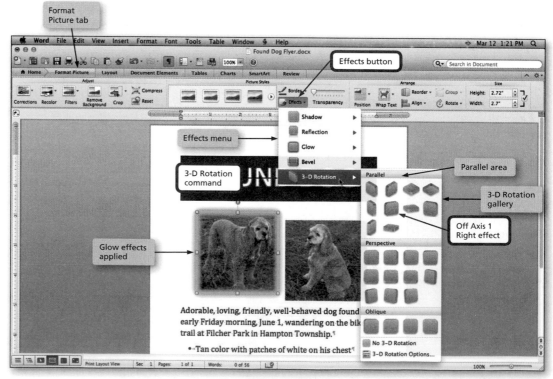

Figure 1–60

- Click Off Axis 1 Right (see Figure 1–60) in the 3-D Rotation gallery to apply the selected picture effect (Figure 1–61).

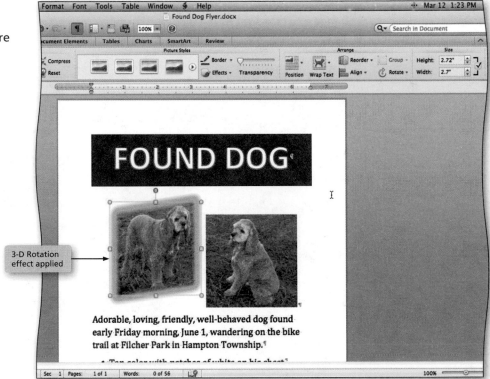

Figure 1–61

To Apply a Picture Style and Effects to Another Picture

In this flyer, the rightmost dog picture also uses the Soft Edge picture style, has a slight tan glow effect, and is turned inward toward the center of the page. The following steps apply the picture style and picture effects to the picture.

1. Click the rightmost dog picture to select it.

2. On the Picture Tools Format tab, under Picture Styles, click the downward-facing More button to display the gallery then click Soft Edge Rectangle to apply the selected style to the picture.

3. Click the Effects button to display the Effects menu and then point to Glow on the Effects menu to display the Glow pop-up menu.

4. Click Accent 6, 5 pt glow in the Glow pop-up menu to apply the picture effect to the picture.

5. Click the Effects button to display the Effects menu again and then point to 3-D Rotation on the Effects menu to display the 3-D Rotation pop-up menu.

6 Click Off Axis 2 Left (rightmost rotation in second row) in the Parallel area in the 3-D Rotation pop-up menu to apply the effect to the selected picture.

7 Click to the right of the picture to deselect it (Figure 1–62).

Figure 1–62

BTWs

BTW For a complete list of the BTWs found in the margins of this book, visit the Office 2011 for Mac Online Companion Web page at www.cengagebrain.com, navigate to the desired chapter, and click BTWs.

Enhancing the Page

With the text and graphics entered and formatted, the next step is to look at the page as a whole and determine if it looks finished in its current state. As you review the page, answer these questions:

- Does it need a page border to frame its contents, or would a page border make it look too busy?
- Is the spacing between paragraphs and graphics on the page adequate? Do any sections of text or graphics look as if they are positioned too closely to the items above or below them?

You determine that a graphical, color-coordinated border would enhance the flyer. You also notice that the flyer would look more proportionate if it had a little more space above and below the pictures. The following pages make these enhancements to the flyer.

To View One Page

Earlier in this chapter, you changed the zoom using the Zoom slider in the lower-right corner of the document window. If you want to display an entire page as large as possible in the document window, Word can compute the correct zoom percentage for you. The next steps display a single page in its entirety in the document window as large as possible.

1

- Click the Zoom box arrow in the Standard toolbar to display the menu.

2

- Click the Whole Page command to display the entire page in the document window as large as possible (Figure 1–63).

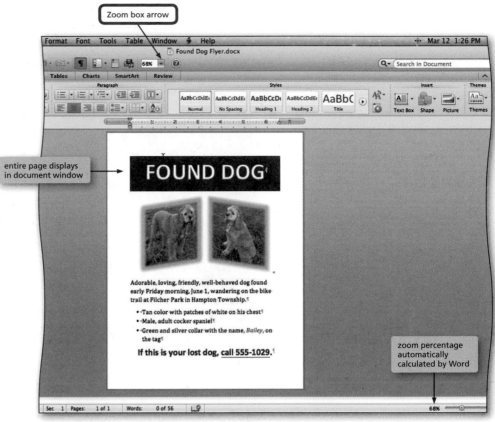

Figure 1–63

To Add a Page Border

In Word, you can add a border around the perimeter of an entire page. The flyer in this chapter has a light green dashed border. The following steps add a page border.

1

- On the Layout tab, under Page Background, click the Borders button to display the Borders and Shading dialog.

- If necessary, click the Page Border tab.

- Scroll through the Style list (Borders and Shading dialog) and select the style shown in Figure 1–64.

- Click the Color box to display a Color pop-up menu.

- Select Accent 6, Darker 25% (fifth row, tenth column).

- Click the Width box and then click 3 pt to select the thickness of the page border (Figure 1–64).

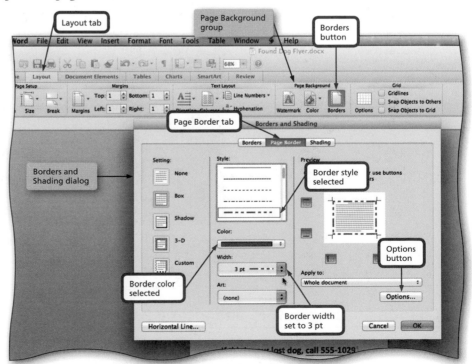

Figure 1–64

2

- Click the Options button to display the Border and Shading Options dialog.

- Click the Measure from box and select Edge of page to determine the placement of the border (Figure 1–65).

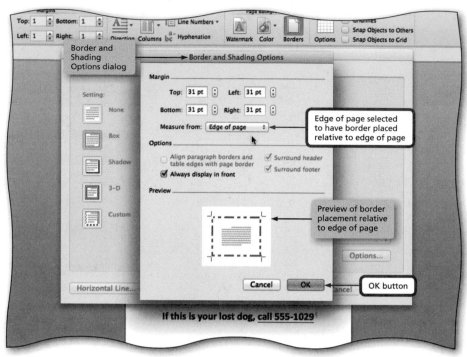

Figure 1–65

3

- Click the OK button to close the Border and Shading Options dialog, then click OK (Borders and Shading dialog) to add the border to the page (Figure 1–66).

Q&A What if I wanted to remove the border?
You would click None in the Setting list in the Borders and Shading dialog.

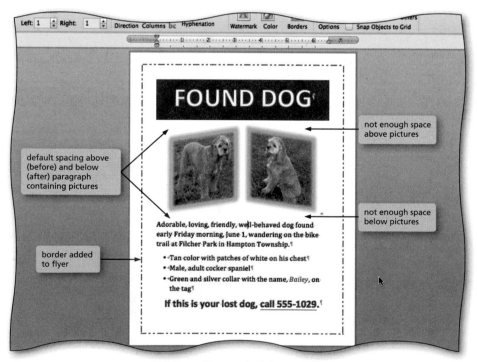

Figure 1–66

To Change Spacing before and after a Paragraph

In the flyer, you want to increase the spacing above and below the paragraph containing the pictures. The following steps change the spacing above and below a paragraph.

1

- Position the insertion point in the paragraph to be adjusted, in this case, the paragraph containing the pictures.

- Click Format in the menu bar, then choose Paragraph to open the Paragraph dialog. If necessary, click the Indents and Spacing tab.

- Enter `24 pt` in the Before text box, and `12 pt` in the After text box (Figure 1–67).

Q&A Do I have to type in the values in the text boxes?
You can also use the box arrow keys to increment or decrement the measurements in units of 6 points.

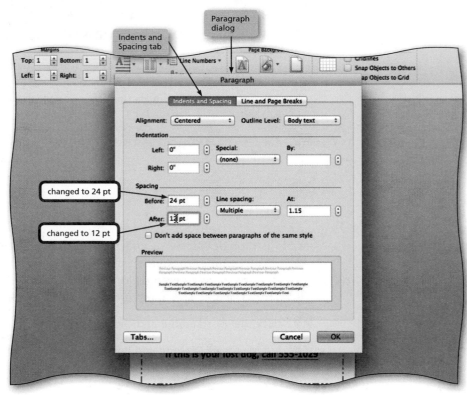

Figure 1–67

- Click OK to increase the spacing before and after the pictures. If the text flows to two pages, reduce the spacing above and below paragraphs as necessary (Figure 1–68).

Figure 1–68

Other Ways

1. CONTROL-click paragraph, choose Paragraph in shortcut menu, click Indents and Spacing tab (Paragraph dialog), enter spacing before and after values, click OK button

2. Choose Format > Paragraph in menu bar, click Indents and Spacing tab (Paragraph dialog), set desired spacing values, click OK button

3. Press OPTION-COMMAND-M, set desired spacing values, click OK button

To Save an Existing Document with the Same File Name

You have made several modifications to the document since you last saved it. Thus, you should save it again. The following step saves the document again. For an example of the step listed below, refer to the Office 2011 and Mac OS X chapter at the beginning of this book.

1   Click the Save button on the Standard toolbar to overwrite the previously saved file.

To Quit Word

Although you still need to make some edits to this document, you want to quit Word and resume working on the project at a later time. Thus, the following steps quit Word. For a detailed example of the procedure summarized below, refer to the Office 2011 and Mac OS X chapter at the beginning of this book.

1   Click the Word menu, and choose Quit Word.

2   If a Microsoft Word dialog appears, click the Save button to save any changes made to the document since the last save.

Quick Reference

 For a table that lists how to complete the tasks covered in this book using the mouse, ribbon, menus, toolbar, and keyboard, see the Quick Reference Summary at the back of this book, or visit the Office 2011 for Mac Online Companion Web page at www.cengagebrain.com, and click Quick Reference.

Other Ways

1. Press COMMAND-Q

Break Point: If you wish to take a break, this is a good place to do so. To resume at a later time, continue following the steps from this location forward.

Correcting Errors and Revising a Document

After creating a document, you may need to change it. For example, the document may contain an error, or new circumstances may require you to add text to the document.

Types of Changes Made to Documents

The types of changes made to documents normally fall into one of the three following categories: additions, deletions, or modifications.

Additions   Additional words, sentences, or paragraphs may be required in a document. Additions occur when you omit text from a document and want to insert it later. For example, you may want to add your e-mail address to the flyer.

Deletions   Sometimes, text in a document is incorrect or is no longer needed. For example, you may discover the dog's collar is just green. In this case, you would delete the words, and silver, from the flyer.

Modifications   If an error is made in a document or changes take place that affect the document, you might have to revise a word(s) in the text. For example, the dog may have been found in Hampton Village instead of Hampton Township.

To Start Word

Once you have created and saved a document, you may need to retrieve it from your storage medium. For example, you might want to revise the document or print it. The following steps, which assume Mac OS X is running, start Word so that you can open and modify the flyer. You may need to ask your instructor how to start Word for your computer. For a detailed example of the procedure summarized below, refer to the Office 2011 and Mac OS X chapter at the beginning of this book.

1 Click the Word icon on the Dock.

2 Double-click the Word Document icon in the Word Document Gallery to display a new blank document in the Word window.

3 If the Word window is not sized properly, as described in the Office 2011 and Mac OS X chapter, size the window properly.

4 If the Print Layout View button in the lower left of the document window is not selected, click it so that your screen is in Print Layout View.

To Open a Document from Word

Earlier in this chapter, you saved your project on a USB flash drive using the file name, Found Dog Flyer. The following steps open the Found Dog Flyer file from the Word folder in the CIS 101 folder on the USB flash drive. For a detailed example of the procedure summarized below, refer to the Office 2011 and Mac OS X chapter at the beginning of this book.

1 With your USB flash drive connected to one of the computer's USB ports, click File in the menu bar to display the File menu.

2 Choose Open to display the Open dialog.

3 Navigate to the location of the file to be opened (in this case, the Word folder in the CIS 101 folder [or your class folder] on the USB flash drive). For a detailed example of this procedure, refer to Steps 1–4 in the To Save a File in a Folder section in the Office 2011 and Mac OS X chapter at the beginning of this book.

4 Click Found Dog Flyer to select the file to be opened.

5 Click the Open button (Open dialog) to open the selected file and display the opened document in the Word window

Q&A Could I have clicked the Open Recent command to open the file?
Yes. Because the file was recently closed, it should appear in the Recent Documents list.

To Zoom the Document

While modifying the document, you prefer the document at 100 percent so that it is easier to read. Thus, the following step changes the zoom back to 100 percent.

1 Click the Zoom box arrow on the Standard toolbar and choose 100% from the pop-up menu. The Zoom slider shows 100% (as seen in Figure 1–69 on the next page).

To Insert Text in an Existing Document

Word inserts text to the left of the insertion point. The text to the right of the insertion point moves to the right and downward to fit the new text. The following steps insert the word, very, to the left of the word, early, in the flyer.

- Scroll through the document and then click to the left of the location of text to be inserted (in this case, the e in early) to position the insertion point where text should be inserted (Figure 1–69).

Figure 1–69

- Type **very** and then press the SPACE BAR to insert the word to the left of the insertion point (Figure 1–70).

Q&A Why did the text move to the right as I typed?

In Word, the default typing mode is **insert mode**, which means as you type a character, Word moves all the characters to the right of the typed character one position to the right.

Figure 1–70

Deleting Text from a Document

It is not unusual to type incorrect characters or words in a document. As discussed earlier in this chapter, you can click the Undo button on the Standard toolbar to undo a command or action immediately — this includes typing. Word also provides other methods of correcting typing errors.

To delete an incorrect character in a document, simply click next to the incorrect character and then press the DELETE key to erase to the left of the insertion point, or press FN-DELETE to erase to the right of the insertion point.

To Delete Text

To delete a word or phrase, you first must select the word or phrase. The following steps select the word, very, that was just added in the previous steps and then delete the selection.

- Position the mouse pointer somewhere in the word to be selected (in this case, very) and then double-click to select the word (Figure 1–71).

- With the text selected, press the DELETE key to delete the selected text (shown in Figure 1–69).

Figure 1–71

To Move Text

While proofreading the flyer, you realize that the body copy would read better if the first two bulleted paragraphs were reversed. An efficient way to move text a short distance, such as reversing two paragraphs, is drag-and-drop editing. With **drag-and-drop editing**, you select the text to be moved and then drag the selected item to the new location and then *drop*, or insert, it there. Another technique for moving text is the cut-and-paste technique, which is discussed in the next chapter. The following steps use drag-and-drop editing to move text.

- Position the mouse pointer in the paragraph to be moved (in this case, the second bulleted item) and then triple-click to select the paragraph.

- With the left-pointing black mouse pointer in the selected text, press and hold down the mouse button, which displays a solid insertion point with the mouse pointer (Figure 1–72).

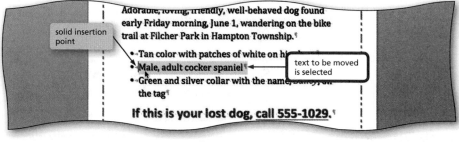

Figure 1–72

- Drag the insertion point to the location where the selected text is to be moved, as shown in Figure 1–73.

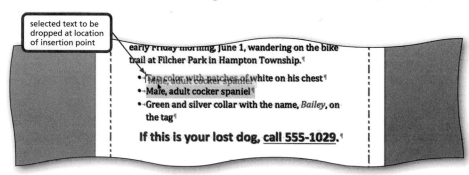

Figure 1–73

❸

- Release the mouse button to move the selected text to the location of the insertion point (Figure 1–74).

Q&A What if I accidentally drag text to the wrong location?
Click the Undo button on the Standard toolbar and try again.

Q&A Can I use drag-and-drop editing to move any selected item?
Yes, you can select words, sentences, phrases, and graphics and then use drag-and-drop editing to move them.

Q&A What is the purpose of the Paste Options button?
If you click the Paste Options button, a menu appears that allows you to change the format of the item that was moved. The next chapter discusses the Paste Options menu.

- Click anywhere in the document window to remove the selection from the bulleted item.

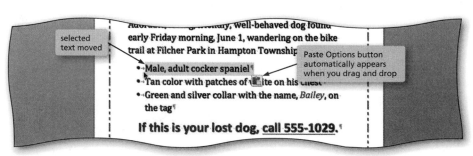

Figure 1–74

Other Ways

1. CONTROL-click selected text, click Cut in shortcut menu, CONTROL-click where text or object is to be pasted, click Keep Source Formatting in shortcut menu

2. Click Cut button in Standard toolbar, click where text or object is to be pasted, click Paste button in Standard toolbar

3. Press COMMAND-X, position insertion point where text or object is to be pasted, press COMMAND-V

Changing Document Properties

Word helps you organize and identify your files by using **document properties**, which are the details about a file. Document properties, also known as **metadata**, can include information such as the project author, title, subject, and keywords. A **keyword** is a word or phrase that further describes the document. For example, a class name or document topic can describe the file's purpose or content.

Document properties are valuable for a variety of reasons:

- Users can save time locating a particular file because they can view a document's properties without opening the document.

- By creating consistent properties for files having similar content, users can better organize their documents.

- Some organizations require Word users to add document properties so that other employees can view details about these files.

Five different types of document properties exist, but the more common ones used in this book are standard and automatically updated properties. **Standard properties** are associated with all Microsoft Office documents and include author, title, and subject. **Automatically updated properties** include file system properties, such as the date you create or change a file, and statistics, such as the file size.

To Change Document Properties

The **Properties dialog** contains areas where you can view and enter document properties. You can view and change information in this panel at any time while you are creating a document. Before saving the flyer again, you want to add your name and course information as document properties. The following steps use the Properties dialog to change document properties.

- Click File in the menu bar to display the File menu.

- Choose Properties to open the Properties dialog (Figure 1–75).

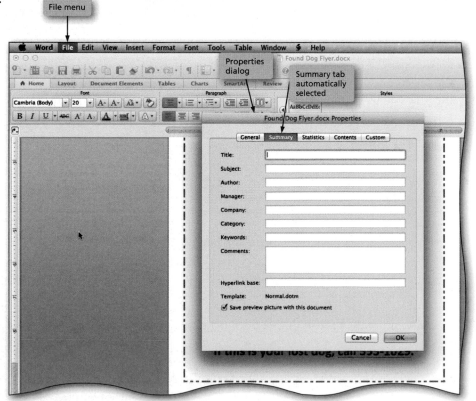

Figure 1–75

- Click the Author text box, if necessary, and then type your name as the Author property. If a name already is displayed in the Author text box, delete it before typing your name.

- Click the Subject text box, if necessary delete any existing text, and then type your course and section as the Subject property.

- If an AutoComplete dialog appears, click its Yes button. Click the Keywords text box, if necessary delete any existing text, and then type **cocker spaniel** as the Keywords property (Figure 1–76).

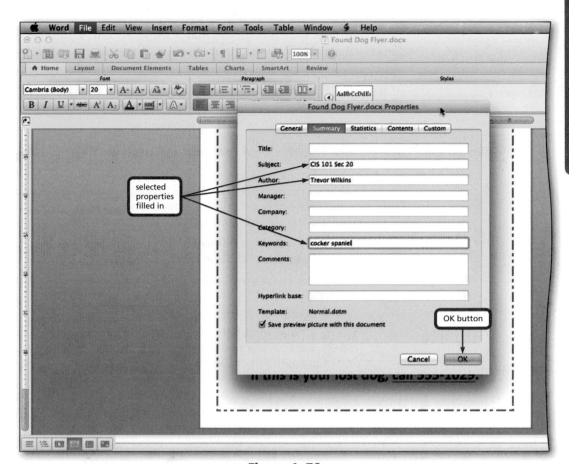

Figure 1–76

Q&A   What types of document properties does Word collect automatically?
Word records details such as time spent editing a document, the number of times a document has been revised, and the fonts and themes used in a document.

- Click the OK button to close the Properties dialog.

To Save an Existing Document with the Same File Name

You are finished editing the flyer. Thus, you should save it again. The following step saves the document again. For an example of the step listed below, refer to the Office 2011 and Mac OS X chapter at the beginning of this book.

1   Click the Save button on the Standard toolbar to overwrite the previously saved file.

Printing a Document

After creating a document, you may want to print it. Printing a document enables you to distribute the document to others in a form that can be read or viewed but typically not edited. It is a good practice to save a document before printing it, in the event you experience difficulties printing.

Plan Ahead

Determine the best method for distributing the document.

The traditional method of distributing a document uses a printer to produce a hard copy. A **hardcopy** or **printout** is information that exists on a physical medium such as paper. For users that can receive fax documents, you can elect to print a hard copy on a remote fax machine. Hard copies can be useful for the following reasons:

- Many people prefer proofreading a hard copy of a document rather than viewing it on the screen to check for errors and readability.

- Hard copies can serve as reference material if your storage medium is lost or becomes corrupted and you need to recreate the document.

- Instead of distributing a hard copy of a document, users can choose to distribute the document as an electronic image that mirrors the original document's appearance. The electronic image of the document can be e-mailed, posted on a Web site, or copied to a portable storage medium such as a USB flash drive. Two popular electronic image formats, sometimes called fixed formats, are PDF by Adobe Systems and XPS by Microsoft. In Word, you can create electronic image files through the Save as dialog. Electronic images of documents, such as PDF and XPS, can be useful for the following reasons:

  - Users can view electronic images of documents without the software that created the original document (e.g., Word). Specifically, to view a PDF file, you use a program called Acrobat Reader, which can be downloaded free from Adobe's Web site. Similarly, to view an XPS file, you use a program called an XPS Viewer, which is included in the latest versions of some browsers.

  - Sending electronic documents saves paper and printer supplies. Society encourages users to contribute to **green computing**, which involves reducing the environmental waste generated when using a computer.

Word Help

BTW At any time while using Word, you can find answers to questions and display information about various topics through Word Help. Used properly, this form of assistance can increase your productivity and reduce your frustrations by minimizing the time you spend learning how to use Word. For instruction about Word Help and exercises that will help you gain confidence in using it, read the Office 2011 and Mac OS X chapter at the beginning of this book.

To Print a Document

With the completed document saved, you may want to print it. Because this flyer is being posted, you will print a hard copy on a printer. The steps on the next page print a hard copy of the contents of the saved Found Dog Flyer document.

1

- Click File in the menu bar to display the File menu.

- Choose Print to display the Print dialog (Figure 1–77).

Q&A How can I print multiple copies of my document?
Increase the number in the Copies box.

Q&A What if I decide not to print the document at this time?
Click the Cancel button.

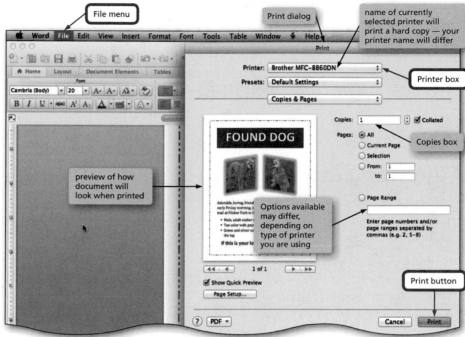

Figure 1–77

2

- Verify the printer name that appears in the Printer box will print a hard copy of the document. If necessary, click the Printer box to display a list of available printer options and then click the desired printer to change the currently selected printer.

3

- Click the Print button in the Print dialog to print the document on the currently selected printer.

- When the printer stops, retrieve the hard copy (Figure 1–78).

Q&A Do I have to wait until my document is complete to print it?
No, you can follow these steps to print a document at any time while you are creating it.

Figure 1–78

Other Ways

1. Click the Print icon on Standard toolbar

2. Choose File > Print on menu bar, click Print button (Print dialog)

3. Press COMMAND-P, click Print button (Print dialog)

To Quit Word

The project now is complete. Thus, the following steps quit Word. For an example of the step listed below, refer to the Office 2011and Mac OS X chapter at the beginning of this book.

1 Click Word in the menu bar and then choose Quit Word to close all open documents and quit Word.

2 If a Word dialog appears, click the Save button to save any changes made to the document since the last save.

Chapter Summary

In this chapter, you have learned how to enter text in a document, format text, insert a picture, format a picture, add a page border, and print a document. The items listed below include all the new Word skills you have learned in this chapter.

1. Start Word (WD 4)
2. Change Line and Paragraph Spacing (WD 6)
3. Adjust the Margins (WD 7)
4. Type Text (WD 9)
5. Display Formatting Marks (WD 10)
6. Insert a Blank Line (WD 10)
7. Wordwrap Text as You Type (WD 11)
8. Check Spelling and Grammar as You Type (WD 12)
9. Save a Document (WD 15)
10. Center a Paragraph (WD 18)
11. Select a Line (WD 20)
12. Change the Font Size of Selected Text (WD 20)
13. Change the Font of Selected Text (WD 21)
14. Change the Case of Selected Text (WD 22)
15. Apply a Text Effect to Selected Text (WD 23)
16. Shade a Paragraph (WD 24)
17. Select Multiple Lines (WD 26)
18. Bullet a List of Paragraphs (WD 27)
19. Undo and Redo an Action (WD 28)
20. Italicize Text (WD 29)
21. Color Text (WD 30)
22. Select a Group of Words (WD 31)
23. Underline Text (WD 32)
24. Bold Text (WD 33)
25. Change Theme Colors (WD 33)
26. Save an Existing Document with the Same File Name (WD 35)
27. Insert a Picture (WD 36)
28. Zoom the Document (WD 37)
29. Resize a Graphic (WD 38)
30. Resize a Graphic by Entering Exact Measurements (WD 40)
31. Apply a Picture Style (WD 41)
32. Apply Picture Effects (WD 42)
33. View One Page (WD 44)
34. Add a Page Border (WD 45)
35. Change Spacing before and after a Paragraph (WD 46)
36. Quit Word (WD 48)
37. Open a Document from Word (WD 49)
38. Insert Text in an Existing Document (WD 50)
39. Delete Text (WD 50)
40. Move Text (WD 51)
41. Change Document Properties (WD 52)
42. Print a Document (WD 55)

 If you have a SAM 2010 user profile, your instructor may have assigned an autogradable version of this assignment. If so, log into the SAM 2010 Web site at www.cengage.com/sam2010 to download the instruction and start files.

Learn It Online

Test your knowledge of chapter content and key terms.

Instructions: To complete the Learn It Online exercises, please visit   **www.cengagebrain.com**. At the CengageBrain.com home page, search for *Office 2011 for Mac* using the search box at the top of the page. This will take you to the product page for this book. On the product page, click the Access Now button below the Study Tools heading. On the Book Companion Site Web page, select Word Chapter 1, and then click the link for the desired exercise.

Chapter Reinforcement TF, MC, and SA
A series of true/false, multiple choice, and short answer questions that test your knowledge of the chapter content.

Flash Cards
An interactive learning environment where you identify chapter key terms associated with displayed definitions.

Practice Test
A series of multiple choice questions that test your knowledge of chapter content and key terms.

Who Wants To Be a Computer Genius?
An interactive game that challenges your knowledge of chapter content in the style of a television quiz show.

Wheel of Terms
An interactive game that challenges your knowledge of chapter key terms in the style of the television show *Wheel of Fortune*.

Crossword Puzzle Challenge
A crossword puzzle that challenges your knowledge of key terms presented in the chapter.

Apply Your Knowledge

Reinforce the skills and apply the concepts you learned in this chapter.

Modifying Text and Formatting a Document
Note: To complete this assignment, you will be required to use the Data Files for Students. See the inside back cover of this book for instructions on downloading the Data Files for Students, or contact your instructor for information about accessing the required files.

Instructions: Start Word. Open the document, Apply 1–1 Buffalo Photo Shoot Flyer Unformatted, from the Data Files for Students. The document you open is an unformatted flyer. You are to modify text, format paragraphs and characters, and insert a picture in the flyer.

Perform the following tasks:

1. Delete the word, single, in the sentence of body copy below the headline.
2. Insert the word, Creeks, between the words, Twin Buffalo, in the sentence of body copy below the headline.
3. At the end of the signature line, change the period to an exclamation point.
4. Center the headline and the signature line.
5. Change the theme colors to the Pushpin color scheme.
6. Change the font size of the headline to 48-point. Change the case of the headline text to all capital letters. Apply the text effect located at row 4, column 4 of the Text Effects pop-up menu to the headline. Change the font of the headline to Market Felt Thin, or a similar font.
7. Change the font size of body copy between the headline and the signature line to 20 point.
8. Change the font size of the signature line to 26 point.

Continued >

Apply Your Knowledge *continued*

9. Select the words, hundreds of buffalo, in the paragraph below the headline and underline them.

10. Italicize the word, every, in the paragraph below the headline. Undo this change and then redo the change.

11. Select the three lines (paragraphs) of text above the signature line and add bullets to the selected paragraphs.

12. Switch the last two bulleted paragraphs. That is, select the Questions bullet and move it so that it is the last bulleted paragraph.

13. Bold the first word of each bulleted paragraph. Change the font color of these same three words to Accent 4, Darker 50%.

14. Bold the text in the signature line. Shade the signature line Dark Green. If the font color does not automatically change to a lighter color, change it to a shade of white.

15. Change the zoom so that the entire page is visible in the document window.

16. Insert the picture of the buffalo centered on the blank line below the headline. The picture is called Buffalo and is available on the Data Files for Students. Apply the Snip Diagonal Corner, White picture style (row 3, column 1) to the inserted picture. Apply the glow called Accent 1, 18 pt glow (row 1, column 4) to the picture.

17. Change the spacing after the headline paragraph to 6 point.

18. The entire flyer now should fit on a single page. If it flows to two pages, resize the picture or decrease spacing before and after paragraphs until the entire flyer text fits on a single page.

19. Change the zoom to Page Width, then 100% and notice the differences.

20. Enter the text, Twin Creeks, as the keywords in the document properties. Change the other document properties, as specified by your instructor.

21. Click File in the menu bar and then click Save As. Save the document on your USB drive in the appropriate folder using the file name, Apply 1–1 Buffalo Photo Shoot Flyer Formatted.

22. Print the document. Submit the revised document, shown in Figure 1–79, in the format specified by your instructor.

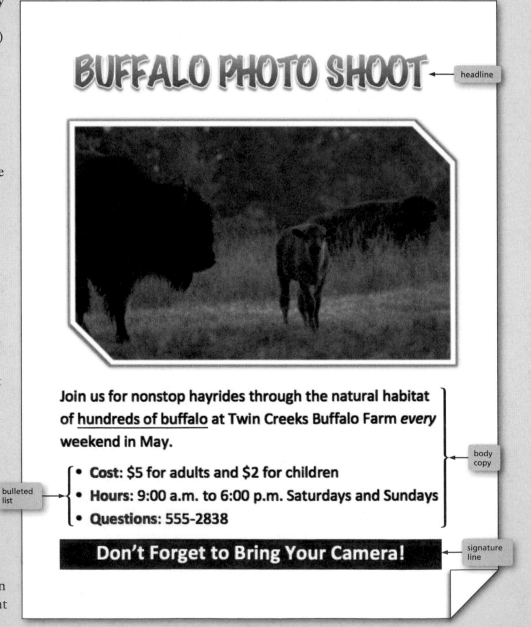

Figure 1–79

Extend Your Knowledge

Extend the skills you learned in this chapter and experiment with new skills. You may need to use Help to complete the assignment.

Modifying Text and Picture Formats and Adding Page Borders

Note: To complete this assignment, you will be required to use the Data Files for Students. See the inside back cover of this book for instructions on downloading the Data Files for Students, or contact your instructor for information about accessing the required files.

Instructions: Start Word. Open the document, Extend 1–1 TVC Cruises Flyer, from the Data Files for Students. You will enhance the look of the flyer shown in Figure 1–80. *Hint:* Remember, if you make a mistake while formatting the picture, you can reset it by clicking the Reset button on the Format Picture tab, under Adjust.

Perform the following tasks:

1. Use Help to learn about the following formats: remove bullets, increase font size, decrease font size, art page borders, decorative underline(s), picture bullets, picture border shading, shadow picture effects, and color saturation and tone.

2. Remove the bullet from the paragraph below the picture.

3. Select the text, 10 percent, and use the Increase Font size button to increase its font size.

4. Add an art page border to the flyer. If the border is not in color, add color to it.

5. Change the solid underline below the word, cruises, to a decorative underline. Change the color of the underline.

6. Change the style of the bullets to picture bullet(s).

7. Change the color of the picture border. Add a shadow picture effect to the picture.

8. Change the color saturation and color tone of the picture.

9. Change the document properties, including keywords, as specified by your instructor. Save the revised document with a new file name and then submit it in the format specified by your instructor.

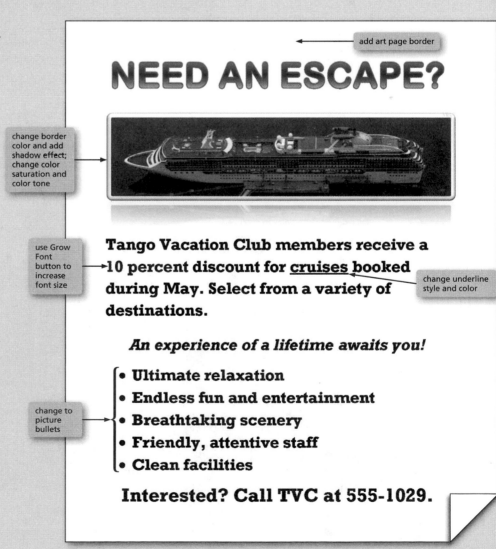

Figure 1–80

Make It Right

Analyze a document and correct all errors and/or improve the design.

Correcting Spelling and Grammar Errors

Note: To complete this assignment, you will be required to use the Data Files for Students. See the inside back cover of this book for instructions on downloading the Data Files for Students, or contact your instructor for information about accessing the required files.

Instructions: Start Word. Open the document, Make It Right 1–1 Karate Academy Flyer Unchecked, from the Data Files for Students. The document is a flyer that contains spelling and grammar errors, as shown in Figure 1–81. You are to correct each spelling (red wavy underline) and grammar error (green and blue wavy underlines) by right-clicking the flagged text and then clicking the appropriate correction in the shortcut menu.

If your screen does not display the wavy underlines, click Word in the menu bar and then select Preferences. When the Word Preferences dialog is displayed, click Spelling and Grammar in the Author and Proofing tools pane to display the Spelling and Grammar dialog, be sure the 'Hide spelling errors in this document' and 'Hide grammatical errors in this document' check boxes do not contain checkmarks, click the back arrow to go back to the main Word Preferences dialog and then click the OK button. If your screen still does not display the wavy underlines, redisplay the Spelling and Grammar dialog, and then click the Recheck Document button.

Change the document properties, including keywords, as specified by your instructor. Save the revised document with the name, Make It Right 1–1 Karate Academy Flyer, and then submit it in the format specified by your instructor.

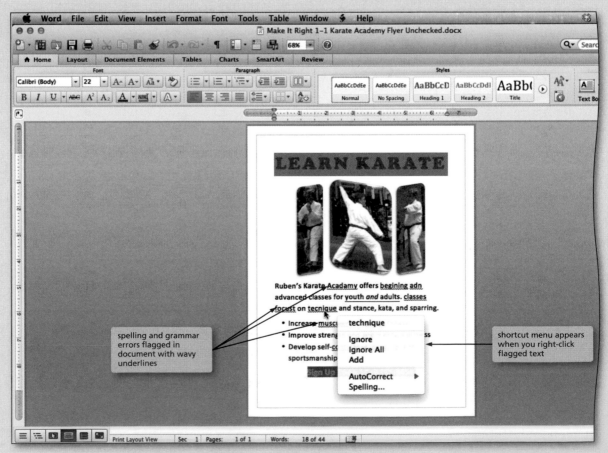

Figure 1–81

In the Lab

Design and/or create a document using the guidelines, concepts, and skills presented in this chapter. Labs are listed in order of increasing difficulty.

Lab 1: Creating a Flyer with a Picture

Problem: As a part-time employee in the Student Services Center at school, you have been asked to prepare a flyer that advertises study habits classes. First, you prepare the unformatted flyer shown in Figure 1–82a, and then you format it so that it looks like Figure 1–82b. *Hint:* Remember, if you make a mistake while formatting the flyer, you can click the Undo button on the Standard toolbar to undo your last action.

Note: To complete this assignment, you will be required to use the Data Files for Students. See the inside back cover of this book for instructions on downloading the Data Files for Students, or contact your instructor for information about accessing the required files.

Instructions: Perform the following tasks:

1. Start Word and open a new, blank document. Display formatting marks on the screen.

2. Set line spacing to 1.15, and space after to 10 pt. Set margins to Normal.

3. Type the flyer text, unformatted, as shown in Figure 1–82a, inserting a blank line between the headline and the body copy. If Word flags any misspelled words as you type, check their spelling and correct them.

4. Save the document using the file name, Lab 1–1 Study Habits Flyer.

5. Center the headline and the signature line.

6. Change the theme colors to Sketchbook.

7. Change the font size of the headline to 48 point and the font to Mistral, or a similar font. Apply the text effect found in row 4, column 2 of the Text Effects pop-up menu.

8. Change the font size of body copy between the headline and the signature line to 20 point.

9. Change the font size of the signature line to 22 point. Bold the text in the signature line.

> Studying All Night?
>
>
> Let us help you! Our expert instructors teach effective study habits, time management skills, and energy-building techniques.
>
> Classes are $15.00 per session
>
> Sessions last four weeks
>
> Classes meet in the Student Services Center twice a week|
>
> Call 555-2838 or stop by to sign up today!

Figure 1–82 (a) Unformatted Text

Continued >

In the Lab *continued*

10. Change the font of the body copy and signature line to Rockwell, and change the color of the signature line to Dark Purple.

11. Bullet the three lines (paragraphs) of text above the signature line.

12. Bold and capitalize the text, Let us help you!, and change its color to Dark Purple.

13. Italicize the word, or, in the signature line.

14. Underline the text, Student Services Center, in the third bulleted paragraph.

15. Change the zoom so that the entire page is visible in the document window.

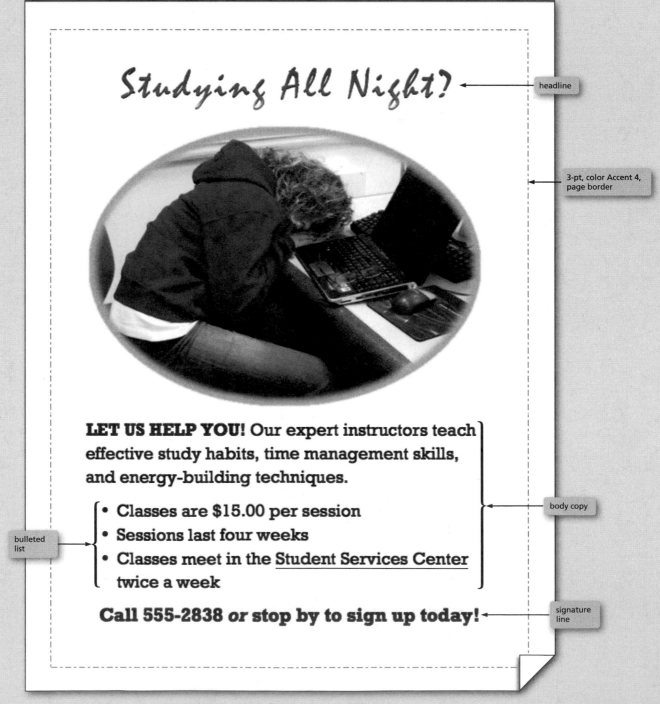

Figure 1–82 (b) Formatted Flyer

16. Insert the picture centered on a blank line below the headline. The picture is called Sleeping and is available on the Data Files for Students.

17. Apply the Soft Edge Oval picture style to the inserted picture. Apply the glow effect called Accent 1, 18 pt glow (row 1, column 4), to the picture.

18. The entire flyer should fit on a single page. If it flows to two pages, resize the picture or decrease spacing before and after paragraphs until the entire flyer text fits on a single page.

19. Add the page border shown in Figure 1–82b.

20. Change the document properties, including keywords, as specified by your instructor. Save the flyer again with the same file name. Submit the document, shown in Figure 1–82b, in the format specified by your instructor.

In the Lab

Lab 2: Creating a Flyer with a Resized Picture

Problem: Your boss at Granger Camera House has asked you to prepare a flyer that announces the upcoming photography contest. You prepare the flyer shown in Figure 1–83 on the next page. *Hint:* Remember, if you make a mistake while formatting the flyer, you can click the Undo button on the Standard toolbar to undo your last action.

Note: To complete this assignment, you will be required to use the Data Files for Students. See the inside back cover of this book for instructions on downloading the Data Files for Students, or contact your instructor for information about accessing the required files.

Instructions: Perform the following tasks:

1. Start Word and open a new, blank document. Set line spacing to 1.15, and space after to 10 pt. Set margins to Normal. Type the flyer text, unformatted. If Word flags any misspelled words as you type, check their spelling and correct them.

2. Save the document using the file name, Lab 1–2 Photography Contest Flyer.

3. Change the theme colors to the Inspiration color scheme.

4. Center the headline, the line that says RULES, and the signature line.

5. Change the font size of the headline to 36 point and the font to Stencil, or a similar font. Shade the headline paragraph Dark Blue. Change the headline text color to Background 1. Apply the text effect found in row 2, column 2 of the Text Effects pop-up menu.

6. Change the font and font size of body copy between the headline and the signature line to 18 point Calibri.

7. Change the font size of the signature line to 24 point and the font to Stencil. Bold the text in the signature line. Change the font color of the text in the signature line to Accent 4, Darker 50%.

8. Bullet the three paragraphs of text above the signature line.

9. Italicize the word, not.

10. Bold the word, landscape.

11. Underline the text, August 31.

12. Shade the line that says RULES to the Blue-Gray color. If the font color does not automatically change to a lighter color, change it to Background 1.

13. Change the zoom so that the entire page is visible in the document window.

14. Insert the picture on a blank line below the headline. The picture is called Wind Power and is available on the Data Files for Students. If necessary, center the picture.

Continued >

In the Lab *continued*

15. Resize the picture so that it is approximately 3.04" × 4.56". Apply the Rotated, White picture style to the inserted picture. Apply the glow effect called Accent 1, 18 pt. glow to the picture.

16. The entire flyer should fit on a single page. If it flows to two pages, resize the picture or decrease spacing before and after paragraphs until the entire flyer text fits on a single page.

17. Add the page border shown in Figure 1–83.

18. Change the document properties, including keywords, as specified by your instructor. Save the flyer again with the same file name. Submit the document, shown in Figure 1–83, in the format specified by your instructor.

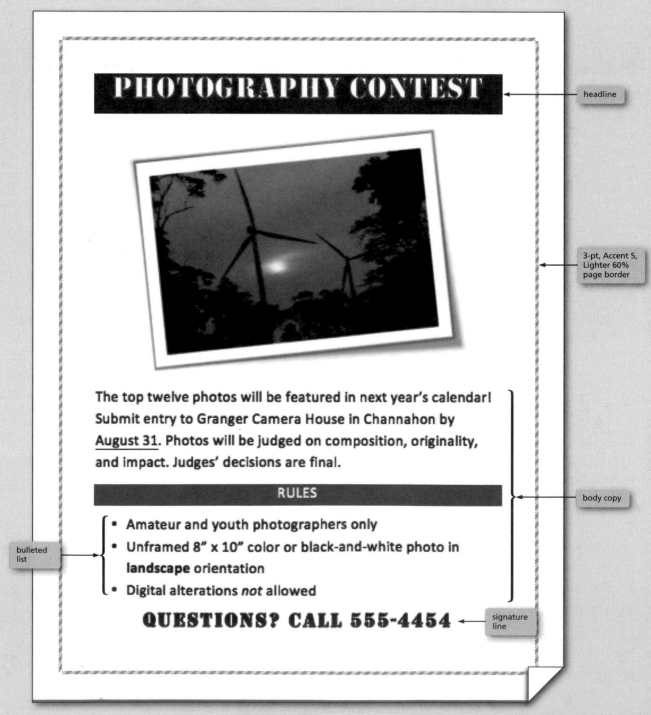

Figure 1–83

In the Lab

Lab 3: Creating a Flyer with Pictures

Problem: Your boss at Warner Depot has asked you to prepare a flyer that advertises its scenic train ride. You prepare the flyer shown in Figure 1–84.

Note: To complete this assignment, you will be required to use the Data Files for Students. See the inside back cover of this book for instructions on downloading the Data Files for Students, or contact your instructor for information about accessing the required files.

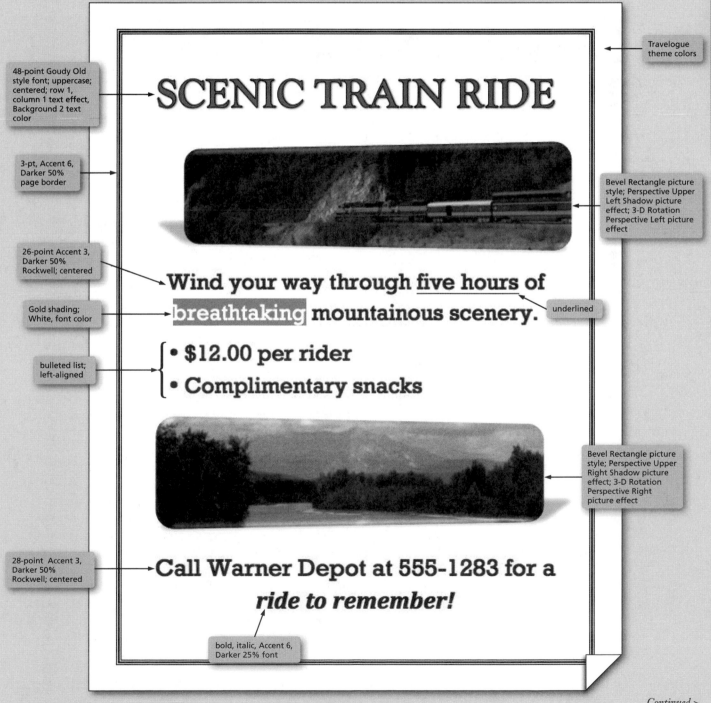

Figure 1–84

Continued >

In the Lab *continued*

Instructions: Start Word and open a new, blank document. Set line spacing to 1.15, and space after to 10 pt. Set margins to Normal. Enter the text in the flyer, checking spelling as you type, and then format it as shown in Figure 1–84 on the previous page. The pictures to be inserted are called Train and Scenery and are available on the Data Files for Students. Adjust spacing before and after paragraphs and resize pictures as necessary so that the flyer fits on a single page.

Change the document properties, including keywords, as specified by your instructor. Save the document using the file name, Lab 1–3 Train Ride Flyer. Submit the document, shown in Figure 1–84, in the format specified by your instructor.

Cases and Places

Apply your creative thinking and problem solving skills to design and implement a solution.

Note: To complete these assignments, you may be required to use the Data Files for Students. See the inside back cover of this book for instructions on downloading the Data Files for Students, or contact your instructor for information about accessing the required files.

1: Design and Create a Spring Break Flyer

Academic

As secretary of your school's Student Government Association, you are responsible for creating and distributing flyers for spring break group outings. This year, you have planned a trip to Settlers Resort. The flyer should contain two digital pictures appropriately resized; the Data Files for Students contains two pictures called Cabin 1 and Cabin 2, or you can use your own digital pictures if they are appropriate for the topic of the flyer. The flyer should contain the headline, Feeling Adventurous?, and this signature line: Call Lyn at 555–9901 to sign up. The body copy consists of the following, in any order: Spring Break – Blast to the Past. Settlers Resort is like a page right out of a history textbook! Spend five days living in the 1800s. The bulleted list in the body copy is as follows: One-room cabins with potbelly stoves, Campfire dining with authentic meals, and Horseback riding and much more.

Use the concepts and techniques presented in this chapter to create and format this flyer. Be sure to check spelling and grammar. Submit your assignment in the format specified by your instructor.

2: Design and Create a Yard Sale Flyer

Personal

You are planning a yard sale and would like to create and post flyers around town advertising the upcoming sale. The flyer should contain two digital pictures appropriately resized; the Data Files for Students contains two pictures called Yard Sale 1 and Yard Sale 2, or you can use your own digital pictures if they are appropriate for the topic of the flyer. The flyer should contain the headline, Yard Sale!, and this signature line: Questions? Call 555–9820. The body copy consists of the following, in any order: Hundreds of items for sale. After 20 years, we are moving to a smaller house and are selling anything that won't fit. Everything for sale must go! The bulleted list in the body copy is as follows: When: August 7, 8, 9 from 9:00 a.m. to 7:00 p.m.; Where: 139 Ravel Boulevard; and What: something for everyone – from clothing to collectibles.

Use the concepts and techniques presented in this chapter to create and format this flyer. Be sure to check spelling and grammar. Submit your assignment in the format specified by your instructor.

3: Design and Create a Village Fireworks Flyer

Professional

As a part-time employee at the Village of Crestwood, your boss has asked you to create and distribute flyers for the upcoming fireworks extravaganza. The flyer should contain two digital pictures appropriately resized; the Data Files for Students contains two pictures called Fireworks 1 and Fireworks 2, or you can use your own digital pictures if they are appropriate for the topic of the flyer. The flyer should contain the headline, Light Up The Sky, and this signature line: Call 555–2983 with questions. The body copy consists of the following, in any order: Join Us! The Village of Crestwood will present its tenth annual Light Up The Sky fireworks extravaganza on August 8 at 9:00 p.m. during the end of summer celebration in Douglas Park. The bulleted list in the body copy is as follows: Pork chop dinners will be sold for $3.00 beginning at 6:00 p.m., Bring chairs and blankets, and Admission is free.

Use the concepts and techniques presented in this chapter to create and format this flyer. Be sure to check spelling and grammar. Submit your assignment in the format specified by your instructor.

2 Creating a Research Paper with Citations and References

Objectives

You will have mastered the material in this chapter when you can:

- Describe the MLA documentation style for research papers
- Modify a style
- Use a header to number pages of a document
- Apply formatting using shortcut keys
- Modify paragraph indentation
- Insert and edit citations and their sources
- Add a footnote to a document
- Insert a manual page break
- Create a bibliographical list of sources
- Cut, copy, and paste text
- Find text and replace text
- Find a synonym
- Use the Reference Tools toolbox to look up information

2 Creating a Research Paper with Citations and References

Introduction

In both academic and business environments, you will be asked to write reports. Business reports range from proposals to cost justifications to five-year plans to research findings. Academic reports focus mostly on research findings.

A **research paper** is a document you can use to communicate the results of research findings. To write a research paper, you learn about a particular topic from a variety of sources (research), organize your ideas from the research results, and then present relevant facts and/or opinions that support the topic. Your final research paper combines properly credited outside information along with personal insights. Thus, no two research papers — even if about the same topic — will or should be the same.

Project — Research Paper

When preparing a research paper, you should follow a standard documentation style that defines the rules for creating the paper and crediting sources. A variety of documentation styles exists, depending on the nature of the research paper. Each style requires the same basic information; the differences in styles relate to requirements for presenting the information. For example, one documentation style uses the term bibliography for the list of sources, whereas another uses references, and yet a third prefers the title works cited. Two popular documentation styles for research papers are the **Modern Language Association of America** (**MLA**) and **American Psychological Association** (**APA**) styles. This chapter uses the MLA documentation style because it is used in a wide range of disciplines.

The project in this chapter follows research paper guidelines and uses Word to create the short research paper shown in Figure 2–1. This paper, which discusses triangulation, follows the MLA documentation style. Each page contains a page number. The first two pages present the name and course information (student name, instructor name, course name, and paper due date), paper title, an introduction with a thesis statement, details that support the thesis, and a conclusion. This section of the paper also includes references to research sources and a footnote. The third page contains a detailed, alphabetical list of the sources referenced in the research paper. All pages include a header at the upper-right edge of the page.

APA Appendix

BTW If your version of this book includes the Word APA Appendix and you are required to create a research paper using the APA documentation style instead of the MLA documentation style, the appendix shows the steps required to create the research paper in this chapter using the APA guidelines. If your version of this book does not include the Word APA Appendix, see print publications or search the Web for the APA guidelines.

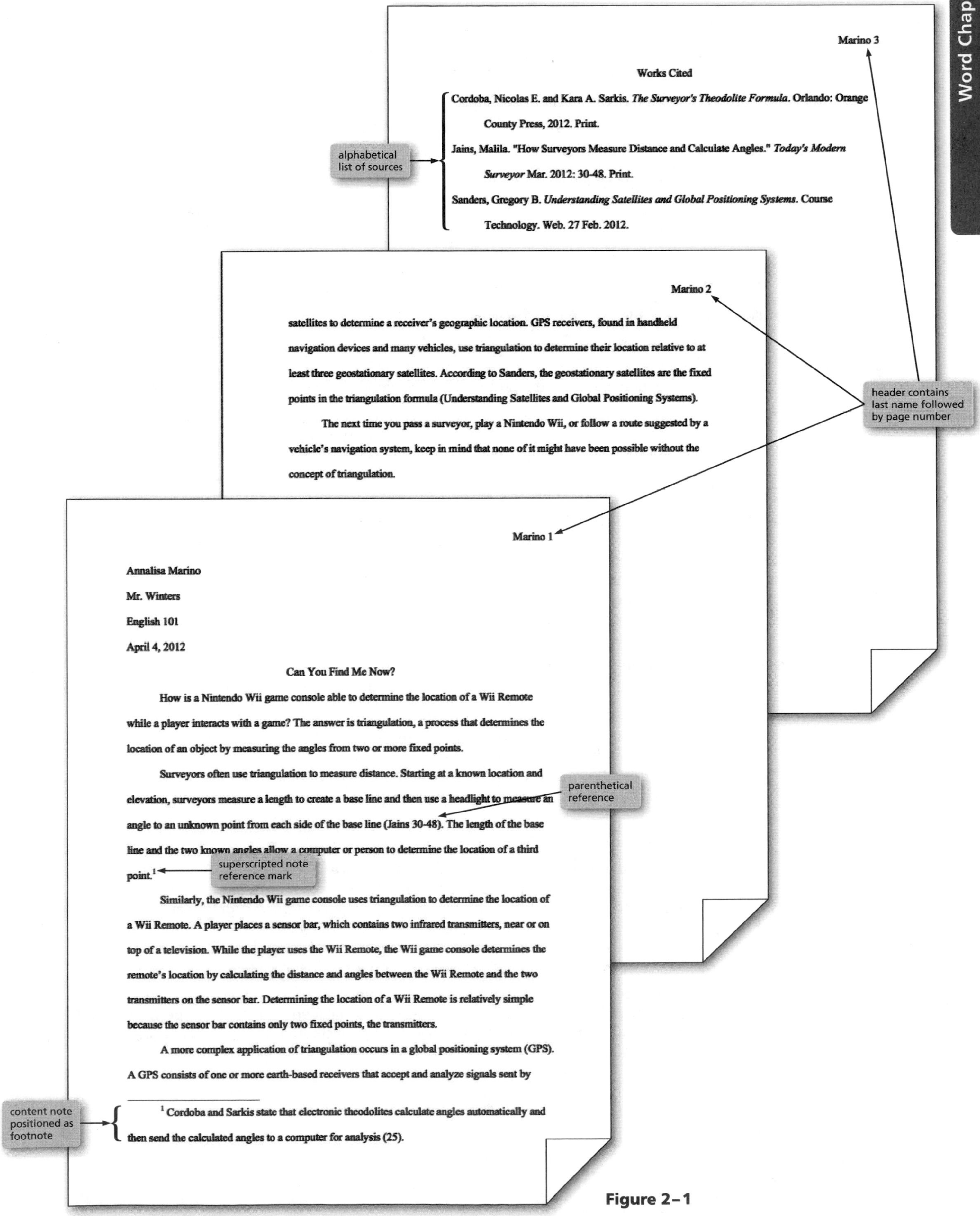

Marino 3

Works Cited

Cordoba, Nicolas E. and Kara A. Sarkis. *The Surveyor's Theodolite Formula*. Orlando: Orange

County Press, 2012. Print.

Jains, Malila. "How Surveyors Measure Distance and Calculate Angles." *Today's Modern*

Surveyor Mar. 2012: 30-48. Print.

Sanders, Gregory B. *Understanding Satellites and Global Positioning Systems*. Course

Technology. Web. 27 Feb. 2012.

alphabetical
list of sources

header contains
last name followed
by page number

Marino 2

satellites to determine a receiver's geographic location. GPS receivers, found in handheld

navigation devices and many vehicles, use triangulation to determine their location relative to at

least three geostationary satellites. According to Sanders, the geostationary satellites are the fixed

points in the triangulation formula (Understanding Satellites and Global Positioning Systems).

The next time you pass a surveyor, play a Nintendo Wii, or follow a route suggested by a

vehicle's navigation system, keep in mind that none of it might have been possible without the

concept of triangulation.

Marino 1

Annalisa Marino

Mr. Winters

English 101

April 4, 2012

Can You Find Me Now?

How is a Nintendo Wii game console able to determine the location of a Wii Remote

while a player interacts with a game? The answer is triangulation, a process that determines the

location of an object by measuring the angles from two or more fixed points.

Surveyors often use triangulation to measure distance. Starting at a known location and

elevation, surveyors measure a length to create a base line and then use a headlight to measure an

angle to an unknown point from each side of the base line (Jains 30-48). The length of the base

line and the two known angles allow a computer or person to determine the location of a third

point.[1]

parenthetical
reference

superscripted note
reference mark

Similarly, the Nintendo Wii game console uses triangulation to determine the location of

a Wii Remote. A player places a sensor bar, which contains two infrared transmitters, near or on

top of a television. While the player uses the Wii Remote, the Wii game console determines the

remote's location by calculating the distance and angles between the Wii Remote and the two

transmitters on the sensor bar. Determining the location of a Wii Remote is relatively simple

because the sensor bar contains only two fixed points, the transmitters.

A more complex application of triangulation occurs in a global positioning system (GPS).

A GPS consists of one or more earth-based receivers that accept and analyze signals sent by

content note
positioned as
footnote

[1] Cordoba and Sarkis state that electronic theodolites calculate angles automatically and

then send the calculated angles to a computer for analysis (25).

Figure 2–1

Overview

As you read through this chapter, you will learn how to create the research paper shown in Figure 2–1 on the previous page by performing these general tasks:

- Change the document settings.
- Type the research paper.
- Save the research paper.
- Create an alphabetical list of sources.
- Proof and revise the research paper.
- Print the research paper.

Plan Ahead

General Project Guidelines

When creating a Word document, the actions you perform and decisions you make will affect the appearance and characteristics of the finished document. As you create a research paper, such as the project shown in Figure 2–1, you should follow these general guidelines:

1. **Select a topic.** Spend time brainstorming ideas for a topic. Choose one you find interesting. For shorter papers, narrow the scope of the topic; for longer papers, broaden the scope. Identify a tentative thesis statement, which is a sentence describing the paper's subject matter.

2. **Research the topic and take notes.** Gather credible, relevant information about the topic that supports the thesis statement. Sources of research include books, magazines, newspapers, and the Internet. As you record facts and ideas, list details about the source: title, author, place of publication, publisher, date of publication, etc. When taking notes, be careful not to **plagiarize**. That is, do not use someone else's work and claim it to be your own. If you copy information directly, place it in quotation marks and identify its source.

3. **Organize your ideas.** Classify your notes into related concepts. Make an outline from the categories of notes. In the outline, identify all main ideas and supporting details.

4. **Write the first draft, referencing sources.** From the outline, compose the paper. Every research paper should include an introduction containing the thesis statement, supporting details, and a conclusion. Follow the guidelines identified in the required documentation style. Reference all sources of information.

5. **Create the list of sources.** Using the formats specified in the required documentation style, completely list all sources referenced in the body of the research paper in alphabetical order.

6. **Proofread and revise the paper.** If possible, proofread the paper with a fresh set of eyes, that is, at least one to two days after completing the first draft. Proofreading involves reading the paper with the intent of identifying errors (spelling, grammar, etc.) and looking for ways to improve the paper (wording, transitions, flow, etc.). Try reading the paper out loud, which helps to identify unclear or awkward wording. Ask someone else to proofread the paper and give you suggestions for improvements.

When necessary, more specific details concerning the above guidelines are presented at appropriate points in the chapter. The chapter also will identify the actions performed and decisions made regarding these guidelines during the creation of the research paper shown in Figure 2–1.

MLA Documentation Style

APA Documentation Style

In the APA documenta- **BTW** tion style, a separate title page is required instead of placing name and course information on the paper's first page. Double-space all pages of the paper with one-inch top, bottom, left, and right margins. Indent the first word of each paragraph one-half inch from the left margin. In the upper-right margin of each page, including the title page, place a running head that consists of the page number preceded by a brief summary of the paper title.

The research paper in this project follows the guidelines presented by the MLA. To follow the MLA documentation style, use 12-point Times New Roman, or a similar, font. Double-space text on all pages of the paper using one-inch top, bottom, left, and right margins. Indent the first word of each paragraph one-half inch from the left margin. At the right margin of each page, place a page number one-half inch from the top margin. On each page, precede the page number by your last name.

The MLA documentation style does not require a title page. Instead, place your name and course information in a block at the left margin beginning one inch from the top of the page. Center the title one double-spaced line below your name and course information.

In the text of the paper, place author references in parentheses with the page number(s) of the referenced information. The MLA documentation style uses in-text **parenthetical references** instead of noting each source at the bottom of the page or at the end of the paper. In the MLA documentation style, notes are used only for optional content or bibliographic notes.

If used, content notes elaborate on points discussed in the paper, and bibliographic notes direct the reader to evaluations of statements in a source or provide a means for identifying multiple sources. Use a superscript (raised number) both to signal that a note exists and to sequence the notes (shown in Figure 2–1 on page WD 71). Position notes at the bottom of the page as footnotes or at the end of the paper as endnotes. Indent the first line of each note one-half inch from the left margin. Place one space following the superscripted number before beginning the note text. Double-space the note text (shown in Figure 2–1).

The MLA documentation style uses the term **works cited** to refer to the bibliographic list of sources at the end of the paper. The works cited page alphabetically lists sources that are referenced directly in the paper. Place the list of sources on a separate numbered page. Center the title, Works Cited, one inch from the top margin. Double-space all lines. Begin the first line of each source at the left margin, indenting subsequent lines of the same source one-half inch from the left margin. List each source by the author's last name, or, if the author's name is not available, by the title of the source.

For an introduction to Mac OS X and instruction about how to perform basic Mac OS X tasks, read the Office 2011 and Mac OS X chapter at the beginning of this book, where you can learn how to resize windows, change screen resolution, create folders, move and rename files, use Mac OS X Help, and much more.

Changing Document Settings

The MLA documentation style defines some global formats that apply to the entire research paper. For example, MLA documentation style requires one inch margins for left, right, top, and bottom margins. You will modify, the margin, font, font size, line and paragraph spacing, and header formats as required by the MLA documentation style.

For an introduction to Office 2011 and instruction about how to perform basic tasks in Office 2011 programs, read the Office 2011 and Mac OS X chapter at the beginning of this book, where you can learn how to start a program, use the ribbon, save a file, open a file, quit a program, use Office 2011 Help, and much more.

To Start Word

If you are using a computer to step through the project in this chapter and you want your screens to match the figures in this book, you should change your screen's resolution to 1280 × 800. For information about how to change a computer's resolution, refer to the Office 2011 and Mac OS X chapter at the beginning of this book.

New Document Window

BTW If you wanted to open a new blank document window, you could press COMMAND-N or choose New Blank Document from the File menu.

The following steps, which assume Mac OS X is running, start Word based on a typical installation. You may need to ask your instructor how to start Word for your computer. For a detailed example of the procedure summarized below, refer to the Office 2011 and Mac OS X chapter.

1 Click the Word icon in the Dock to display the Word Document Gallery.

2 If All is not selected in the Templates pane on the left, click to select it.

3 Double-click the Word Document icon in the Word Document Gallery to display a new blank document in the Word window.

4 If the Word window is not sized properly, as described in the Office and Mac OS X chapter, size the window properly.

5 If the Print Layout View button in the lower left of the document window is not selected (shown in Figure 2–2), click it so that your screen is in Print Layout View.

6 On the Layout tab, under Margins, click the Margins button to display the Margins pop-up menu, and choose Normal to apply the Normal margin settings to the document.

7 On the Home tab, under Styles, if Normal is not selected in the Quick Style gallery (shown in Figure 2–2), click it so that your document uses the Normal style.

8 If your zoom percent is not 125, click the Zoom button arrow on the Standard toolbar and choose 125%.

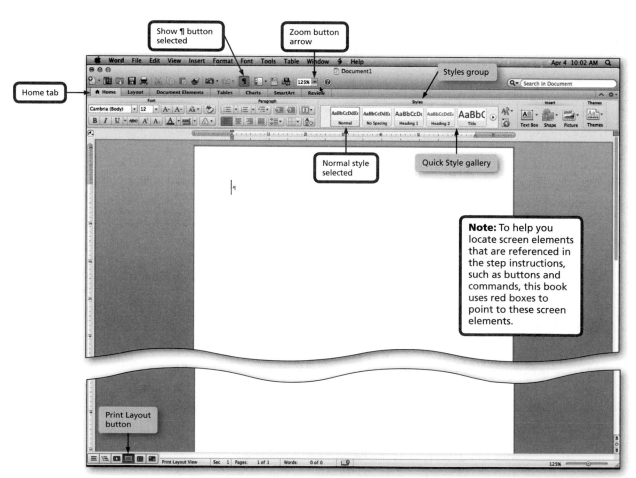

Figure 2–2

To Display Formatting Marks

As discussed in Chapter 1, it is helpful to display formatting marks that indicate where in the document you press the RETURN key, SPACE BAR, and other keys. The following step displays formatting marks.

1 If it is not selected already, click the Show (¶) button on the Standard toolbar to display formatting marks on the screen.

Styles

When you create a document, Word formats the text using a particular style. A **style** is a named group of formatting characteristics, including font and font size. The default style in Word is called the **Normal style**, which in Word 2011 uses 12-point Cambria font. If you do not specify a style for text you type, Word applies the Normal style to the text. In addition to the Normal style, Word has many other built-in, or predefined styles that you can use to format text. Styles make it easy to apply many formats at once to text. You can modify existing styles and create your own styles. Styles are discussed as they are used in this book.

Style Formats

BTW

To see the formats assigned to a particular style in a document, on the Home tab, under Styles, click the "Manage the styles that are used in this document" button to open the Toolbox with the Styles tab selected. Position the insertion point in the style in the document and then point to the outlined style in the 'Pick a style to apply' area in the Toolbox to display an Enhanced ScreenTip describing formats assigned to the location of the insertion point.

To Show the Toolbox

The Toolbox provides quick access to five different types of tools, each type presented on its own pane. The Styles pane on the Toolbox provides easy access to the styles available for a document, as well as easy access to the commands used to manage styles. The following step displays the Toolbox with the Style pane active.

1

- On the Home tab, under Styles, click the 'Manage the styles that are used in the document' button to open the Toolbox with the Styles pane selected. If necessary, using the Toolbox header, drag the toolbox to the right side of the document window (Figure 2–3).

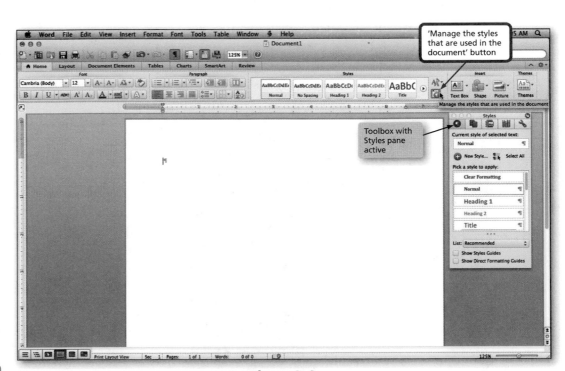

Figure 2–3

Other Ways
1. Click Toolbox button on Standard toolbar

To Modify a Style

The MLA documentation style requires that all text in the research paper use 12-point Times New Roman, or a similar, font. If you change the font and font size using buttons on the ribbon, you will need to make the change many times during the course of creating the paper because Word formats different areas of a document using the Normal style, which uses 12-point Cambria font. For example, body text, headers, and bibliographies all display text based on the Normal style. Thus, instead of changing the font and font size for each of these document elements, a more efficient technique would be to change the Normal style for this document to 12-point Times New Roman. By changing the Normal style, you ensure that all text in the document will use the format required by the MLA. The next steps change the Normal style.

- On the Home tab, under Styles, CONTROL-click Normal in the Quick Style gallery to display a shortcut menu related to styles (Figure 2–4).

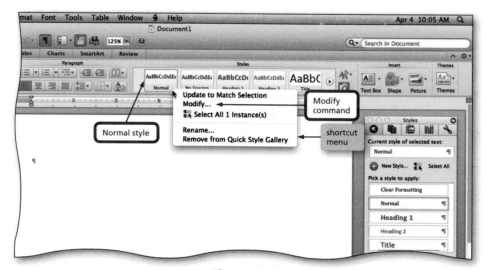

Figure 2–4

- Choose Modify in the shortcut menu to display the Modify Style dialog (Figure 2–5).

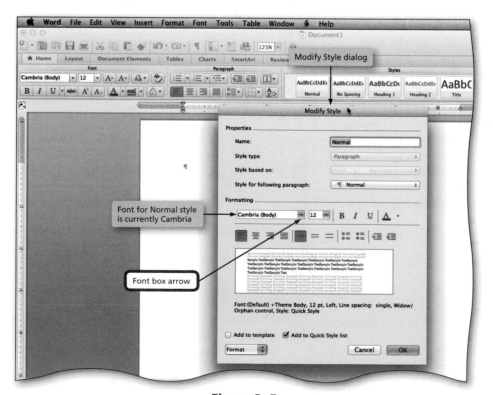

Figure 2–5

- Click the Font box arrow (Modify Style dialog) to display the Font list. Scroll to and then click Times New Roman in the list to change the font for the style being modified.

- If necessary, click the Font Size box arrow (Modify Style dialog) and then click 12 in the Font Size list to change the font size for the style being modified.

- Ensure that the 'Add to template' check box is not selected (Figure 2–6).

Q&A Will all future documents use the new font and font size?
No, because the 'Add to template' check box is not selected. If you want all future documents created using this template to use a new setting, you would select the 'Add to template' check box.

- Click the OK button (Modify Style dialog) to update the Normal style to the specified settings.

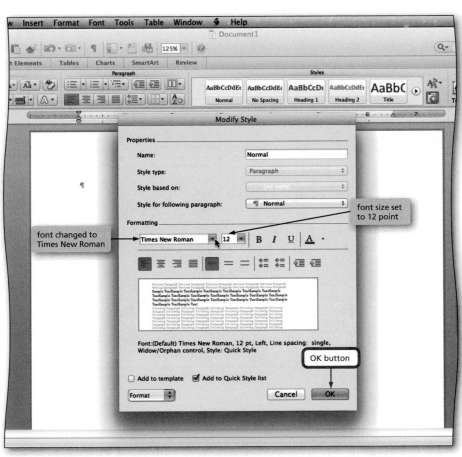

Figure 2–6

Other Ways

1. Choose Format > Style > Modify, change settings (Modify Style dialog), click OK button

Adjusting Line and Paragraph Spacing

Line spacing is the amount of vertical space between lines of text in a paragraph. **Paragraph spacing** is the amount of space above and below a paragraph. By default, the Normal style places 10 points of blank space after each paragraph and inserts a vertical space equal to 1.0 lines between each line of text. It also automatically adjusts line height to accommodate various font sizes and graphics.

The MLA documentation style requires that you **double-space** the entire research paper. That is, the amount of vertical space between each line of text and above and below paragraphs should be equal to one blank line. The sets of steps on the next page adjust line spacing and paragraph spacing according to the MLA documentation style.

Line Spacing

BTW

If the top of a set of characters or a graphical image is chopped off, then line spacing may be set to Exactly. To remedy the problem, change line spacing to 1.0, 1.15, 1.5, 2.0, 2.5, 3.0, or At least (in the Paragraph dialog), all of which accommodate the largest font or image.

To Change Line Spacing

The lines of the research paper should be double-spaced, according to the MLA documentation style. In Word, you change the line spacing to 2.0 to double-space lines in a paragraph. The following steps change the line spacing to double.

- On the Home tab, under Paragraph, click the Line Spacing button to display the pop-up menu (Figure 2–7).

Q&A What do the numbers in the Line Spacing pop-up menu represent?
The default line spacing is 1.0 lines. The options 1.0, 2.0, and 3.0 set line spacing to single, double, and triple, respectively. Similarly, the 1.15, 1.5, and 2.5 options set line spacing to 1.15, 1.5, and 2.5 lines. All these options adjust line spacing automatically to accommodate the largest font or graphic on a line.

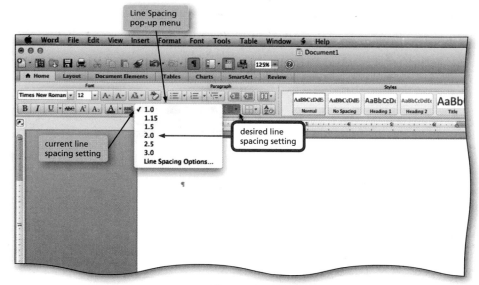

Figure 2–7

- Choose 2.0 in the pop-up menu to change the line spacing at the location of the insertion point.

Q&A Can I change the line spacing of existing text?
Yes. Select the text first and then change the line spacing as described in these steps.

Other Ways

1. CONTROL-click paragraph, choose Paragraph from shortcut menu, click Indents and Spacing tab (Paragraph dialog), click Line spacing box arrow, click desired spacing, click OK button

2. Choose Format > Paragraph, click Indents and Spacing tab (Paragraph dialog), click Line spacing box arrow, click desired spacing, click OK button

3. Press COMMAND-2 for double-spacing

TO REMOVE SPACE AFTER A PARAGRAPH

The research paper should not have additional blank space after each paragraph. In situations where the paragraph formatting is already set up for space to be added after each paragraph, use the following steps to remove space after a paragraph.

- On the Home tab, under Paragraph, click the Line Spacing button to display the Line Spacing pop-up menu.
- Choose Line Spacing Options from the pop-up menu to display the Paragraph dialog.
- In the Spacing section, in the After text box, enter 0 pt.
- Click the OK button.

Q&A Can I remove space after existing paragraphs?
Yes. Select the paragraphs first and then remove the space as described in these steps.

To Update a Style to Match a Selection

To ensure that all paragraphs in the paper will be double-spaced and do not have space after the paragraphs, you want the Normal style to include the line and paragraph spacing changes made in the previous two sets of steps. You can update a style to reflect the settings of the location of the insertion point or selected text. Because no text has yet been typed in the research paper, you do not need to select text prior to updating the Normal style. The following steps update the Normal style.

- CONTROL-click Normal in the Quick Style gallery to display a shortcut menu (Figure 2–8).

- Choose Update to Match Selection in the shortcut menu to update the selected (or current) style to reflect the settings at the location of the insertion point.

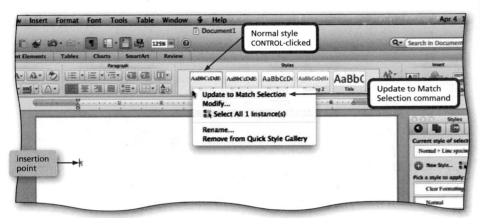

Figure 2–8

Headers and Footers

A **header** is text and graphics that print at the top of each page in a document. Similarly, a **footer** is text and graphics that print at the bottom of every page. In Word, headers print in the top margin one-half inch from the top of every page, and footers print in the bottom margin one-half inch from the bottom of each page, which meets the MLA documentation style. In addition to text and graphics, headers and footers can include document information such as the page number, current date, current time, and author's name. Word provides a selection of built-in headers from which you can choose. Figure 2–9 shows the Header gallery, with the header selection. If none of these headers suits your needs, you can create your own custom header in Word.

The Ribbon and Screen Resolution

Word may change how the groups and buttons within the groups appear on the ribbon, depending on the computer's screen resolution. Thus, your ribbon may look different from the ones in this book if you are using a screen resolution other than 1280 × 800. **BTW**

BTWs

For a complete list of the BTWs found in the margins of this book, visit the Office 2011 for Mac Online Companion Web page at www.cengagebrain.com, navigate to the desired chapter, and click BTWs. **BTW**

Q&As

For a complete list of the Q&As found in many of the step-by-step sequences in this book, visit the Office 2011 for Mac Online Companion Web page at www.cengagebrain.com, navigate to the desired chapter, and click Q&As. **BTW**

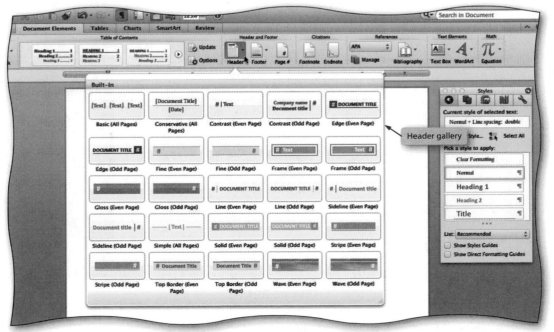

Figure 2–9

In this research paper, you are to precede the page number with your last name placed one-half inch from the upper-right edge of each page. The procedures on the following pages enter your name and the page number in the header, as specified by the MLA documentation style. There is not a built-in header for this particular setup, and so you will create a custom header for this paper.

To Switch to the Header

To enter text in the header, you instruct Word to edit the header. The following steps switch from editing the document text to editing the header.

- Move the mouse pointer above the paragraph marker, until the mouse pointer changes to a header icon (Figure 2–10).

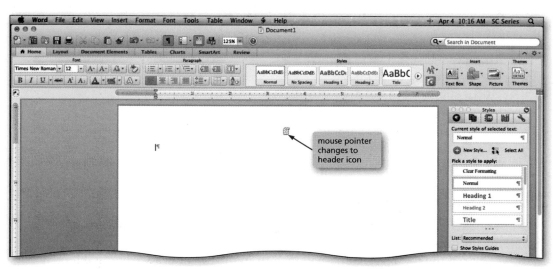

Figure 2–10

- Double-click to switch from the document text to the header, and to show the Header and Footer tab on the ribbon (Figure 2–11).

Q&A How do I remove the Header and Footer tab from the ribbon? When you are finished editing the header, you will close it, which removes the Header and Footer tab.

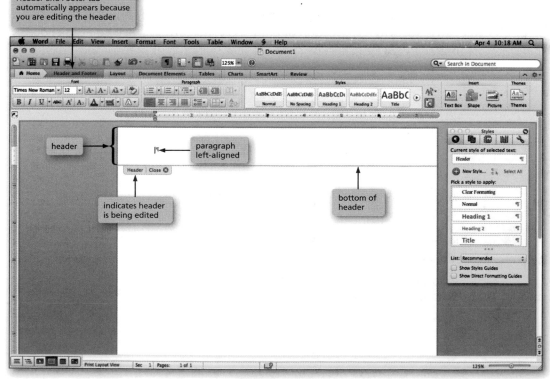

Figure 2–11

Other Ways
1. Choose View > Header and Footer in menu bar

To Right-Align a Paragraph

The paragraph in the header currently is left-aligned (Figure 2–11). Your last name and the page number should print **right-aligned**, that is, at the right margin. The following step right-aligns a paragraph.

- If necessary, click Home on the ribbon to display the Home tab.

- Under Paragraph, click the Align Text Right button to right-align the current paragraph (Figure 2–12).

Q&A What if I wanted to return the paragraph to left-aligned?
Click the Align Text Right button again, or click the Align Text Left button.

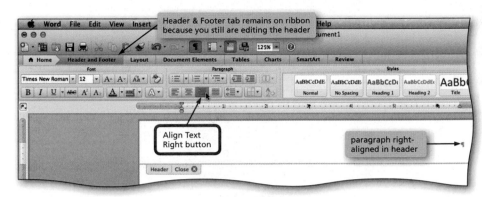

Figure 2–12

Other Ways

1. CONTROL-click paragraph, choose Paragraph in shortcut menu, click Indents and Spacing tab (Paragraph dialog), click Alignment box arrow, choose Right, click OK button

2. Choose Format > Paragraph in menu bar, click Indents and Spacing tab, click Alignment box arrow, choose Right, click OK button

3. Press COMMAND-R

To Enter Text

The following step enters your last name right-aligned in the header area.

 Type **Marino** and then press the SPACE BAR to enter the last name in the header.

To Insert a Page Number

The next task is to insert the current page number in the header. The following steps insert a page number at the location of the insertion point.

- Click Header and Footer on the ribbon to display the Header and Footer tab.

2

- Under Insert, click the Page # button to insert the page number at the insertion point in the header (Figure 2–13).

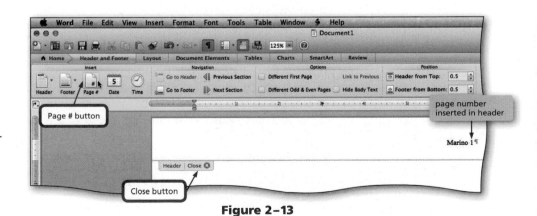

Figure 2–13

Other Ways

1. Click Document Elements on ribbon, click Page # button

2. Choose Insert > Page Numbers, under Position click Top of page (header), click OK button

To Close the Header

You are finished entering text in the header. Thus, the next task is to switch back to the document text. The following step closes the header.

- In the header, click the Close button (shown in Figure 2–13 on the previous page) to close the header and switch back to the document text (Figure 2–14).

Q&A How do I make changes to existing header text?

Switch to the header using the steps described on page WD 80, edit the header as you would edit text in the document window, and then switch back to the document text.

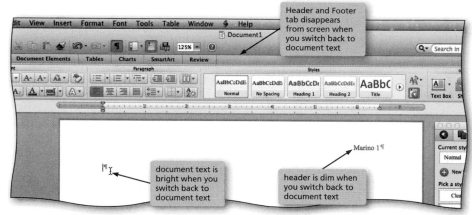

Figure 2–14

Typing the Research Paper Text

The text of the research paper in this chapter encompasses the first two pages of the paper. You will type the text of the research paper and then modify it later in the chapter, so that it matches Figure 2–1 on page WD 71.

Plan Ahead

Write the first draft, referencing sources.

As you write the first draft of a research paper, be sure it includes the proper components, uses credible sources, and does not contain any plagiarized material.

- **Include an introduction, body, and conclusion.** The first paragraph of the paper introduces the topic and captures the reader's attention. The body, which follows the introduction, consists of several paragraphs that support the topic. The conclusion summarizes the main points in the body and restates the topic.

- **Evaluate sources for authority, currency, and accuracy.** Be especially wary of information obtained from the Web. Any person, company, or organization can publish a Web page on the Internet. Ask yourself these questions about the source:

  - Authority: Does a reputable institution or group support the source? Is the information presented without bias? Are the author's credentials listed and verifiable?

  - Currency: Is the information up to date? Are dates of sources listed? What is the last date revised or updated?

  - Accuracy: Is the information free of errors? Is it verifiable? Are the sources clearly identified?

- **Acknowledge all sources of information; do not plagiarize.** Not only is plagiarism unethical, but it is considered an academic crime that can have severe punishments such as failing a course or being expelled from school.

  When you summarize, paraphrase (rewrite information in your own words), present facts, give statistics, quote exact words, or show a map, chart, or other graphical image, you must acknowledge the source. Information that commonly is known or accessible to the audience constitutes common knowledge and does not need to be acknowledged. If, however, you question whether certain information is common knowledge, you should document it — just to be safe.

To Enter Name and Course Information

As discussed earlier in this chapter, the MLA documentation style does not require a separate title page for research papers. Instead, place your name and course information in a block at the top of the page, below the header, at the left margin. The following steps enter the name and course information in the research paper.

1 Type **Annalisa Marino** as the student name and then press the RETURN key.

2 Type **Mr. Winters** as the instructor name and then press the RETURN key.

3 Type **English 101** as the course name and then press the RETURN key.

4 Type **April 4, 2012** as the paper due date and then press the RETURN key (Figure 2–15).

Date Formats

The MLA documenta- **BTW** tion style prefers the day-month-year (4 April 2012) or month-day-year (April 4, 2012) format.

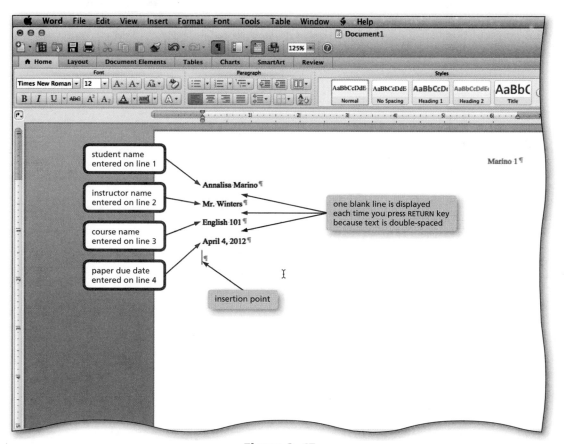

Figure 2–15

To Click and Type

The next step is to enter the title of the research paper centered between the page margins. In Chapter 1, you used the Center button to center text and graphics. As an alternative, you can use Word's **Click and Type** feature to format and enter text, graphics, and other items. To use Click and Type, you double-click a blank area of the document window. Word automatically formats the item you type or insert according to the location where you double-clicked. The steps on the next page use Click and Type to center and then type the title of the research paper.

1

 Experiment

- Move the mouse pointer around the document below the entered name and course information and observe the various icons that appear with the I-beam.

- Position the mouse pointer in the center of the document at the approximate location for the research paper title until a center icon appears to the right of the I-beam (Figure 2–16).

Q&A What are the other icons that appear in the Click and Type pointer?

A left-align icon appears to the right of the I-beam when the Click and Type pointer is in certain locations on the left side of the document window. A right-align icon appears to the left of the I-beam when the Click and Type pointer is in certain locations on the right side of the document window.

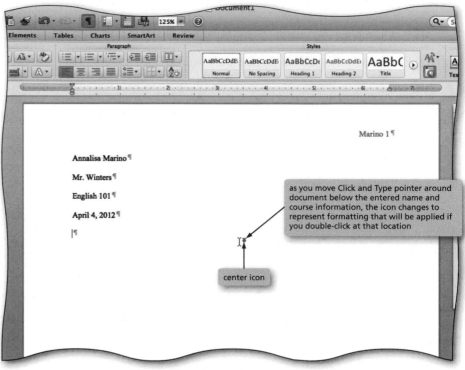

Figure 2–16

2

- Double-click to center the paragraph mark and insertion point between the left and right margins.

- Type **Can You Find Me Now?** as the paper title and then press RETURN to position the insertion point on the next line (Figure 2–17).

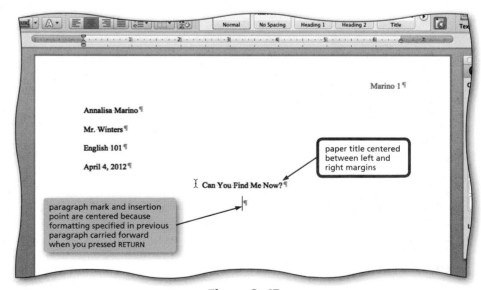

Figure 2–17

Shortcut Keys

Word has many **shortcut keys**, or keyboard key combinations, for your convenience while typing. Table 2–1 lists the common shortcut keys for formatting characters. Table 2–2 lists common shortcut keys for formatting paragraphs.

Table 2–1 Shortcut Keys for Formatting Characters

Character Formatting Task	Shortcut Keys	Character Formatting Task	Shortcut Keys
All capital letters	COMMAND-SHIFT-A	Italic	COMMAND-I
Bold	COMMAND-B	Remove character formatting (plain text)	CONTROL-SPACE BAR
Decrease font size	COMMAND-SHIFT-<	Small uppercase letters	COMMAND-SHIFT-K
Decrease font size 1 point	COMMAND-[	Subscript	COMMAND-EQUAL SIGN
Double-underline	COMMAND-SHIFT-D	Superscript	COMMAND-SHIFT-PLUS SIGN
Increase font size	COMMAND-SHIFT->	Underline	COMMAND-U
Increase font size 1 point	COMMAND-]	Underline words, not spaces	COMMAND-SHIFT-W

Table 2–2 Shortcut Keys for Formatting Paragraphs

Paragraph Formatting	Shortcut Keys	Paragraph Formatting	Shortcut Keys
1.5 line spacing	COMMAND-5	Increase paragraph indent	CONTROL-SHIFT-M
Add/remove one line above paragraph	COMMAND-0 (Zero)	Justify paragraph	COMMAND-J
Center paragraph	COMMAND-E	Left-align paragraph	COMMAND-L
Decrease paragraph indent	COMMAND-SHIFT-M	Remove hanging indent	COMMAND-SHIFT-T
Double-space lines	COMMAND-2	Right-align paragraph	COMMAND-R
Hanging indent	COMMAND-T	Single-space lines	COMMAND-1

To Format Text Using Shortcut Keys

The paragraphs below the paper title should be left-aligned, instead of centered. Thus, the next step is to left-align the paragraph below the paper title. When your fingers are already on the keyboard, you may prefer using shortcut keys to format text as you type it. The following step left-aligns a paragraph using the shortcut keys COMMAND-L. (Recall from Chapter 1 that a notation such as COMMAND-L means to press the letter L on the keyboard while holding down the COMMAND key.)

1 Press COMMAND-L to left-align the current paragraph, that is, the paragraph containing the insertion point (shown in Figure 2–18 on the next page).

Q&A   Why would I use a keyboard shortcut instead of the ribbon to format text?
Switching between the mouse and the keyboard takes time. If your hands are already on the keyboard, use a shortcut key. If your hand is on the mouse, use the ribbon.

Shortcut Keys

To see a more complete list of shortcut keys in Word, click Help in the Word menu bar, type shortcut keys in the Search text box at the top of the Word Help window, press RETURN, choose Word keyboard shortcuts, and choose from the list of types of keyboard shortcuts in the Help Center dialog. **BTW**

To Save a Document

You have performed many tasks while creating this research paper and do not want to risk losing work completed thus far. Accordingly, you should save the document. The steps on the next page assume you already have created folders for storing your files, for example, a CIS 101 folder (for your class) that contains a Word folder (for your assignments). Thus, these steps save the document in the Word folder in the CIS 101 folder on a USB flash drive using the file name, Triangulation Paper.

For an introduction to Office 2011 and instruction about how to perform basic tasks in Office 2011 programs, read the Office 2011 and Mac OS X chapter at the beginning of this book, where you can learn how to start a program, use the ribbon, save a file, open a file, quit a program, use Help, and much more.

1 With a USB flash drive connected to one of the computer's USB ports, click the Save button on the Standard toolbar to display the Save dialog.

2 Type **Triangulation Paper** in the Save As text box to change the file name. Do not press the RETURN key after typing the file name because you do not want to close the dialog at this time.

3 Navigate to the desired save location (in this case, the Word folder in the CIS 101 folder [or your class folder] on the USB flash drive).

4 Click the Save button (Save: Microsoft Word dialog) to save the document in the selected folder on the selected drive with the entered file name.

To Hide or Display the Rulers

According to the MLA documentation style, the first line of each paragraph in the research paper is to be indented one-half inch from the left margin. Although you can use a dialog to indent paragraphs, Word provides a quicker way through the **horizontal ruler**. This ruler is displayed at the top edge of the document window just below the ribbon. Word also provides a **vertical ruler** that is displayed along the left edge of the Word window. You can control the display of rulers from the View menu. When the ruler command in the View menu has a check mark next to it, the rulers are visible. The following step hides and then displays the rulers.

- Click the View menu (Figure 2–18).

- Choose Ruler to remove the check mark and hide the rulers.

- Click View again and choose Ruler to add the check mark and display the rulers.

Q&A For what tasks would I use the rulers?
You can use the rulers to indent paragraphs, set tab stops, change page margins, and adjust column widths.

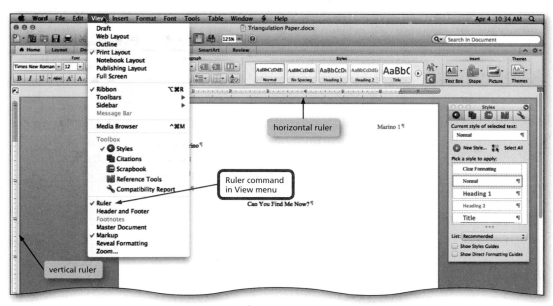

Figure 2–18

To First-Line Indent Paragraphs

The first line of each paragraph in the research paper is to be indented one-half inch from the left margin. You can use the horizontal ruler, usually simply called the **ruler**, to indent just the first line of a paragraph, which is called a **first-line indent**.

The left margin on the ruler contains two triangles above a rectangle. The **First Line Indent marker** is the top triangle at the 0" mark on the ruler (Figure 2–19). The bottom triangle is discussed later in this chapter. The small rectangle at the 0" mark is the Left Indent marker. The **Left Indent marker** allows you to change the entire left margin, whereas the First Line Indent marker indents only the first line of the paragraph. The following steps first-line indent paragraphs in the research paper.

1

- With the insertion point on the paragraph mark below the research paper title, point to the First Line Indent marker on the ruler (Figure 2–19).

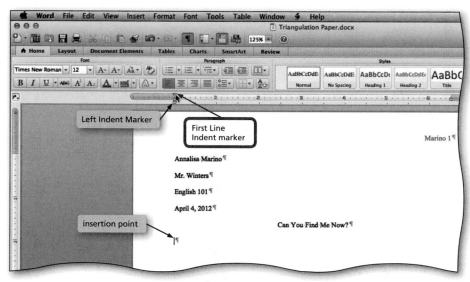

Figure 2–19

2

- Drag the First Line Indent marker to the .5" mark on the ruler to display a vertical line in the document window, which indicates the proposed location of the first line of the paragraph (Figure 2–20).

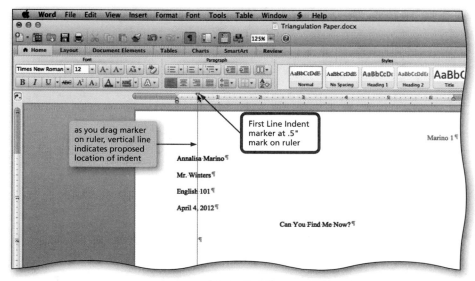

Figure 2–20

3

- Release the mouse button to place the First Line Indent marker at the .5" mark on the ruler, or one-half inch from the left margin (Figure 2–21).

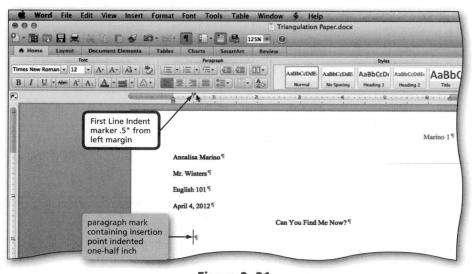

Figure 2–21

4

- Type `How is a Nintendo Wii console able to determine the location of a Wii Remote while a player interacts with a game?` and notice that Word automatically indented the first line of the paragraph by one-half inch (Figure 2–22).

Q&A   Will I have to set a first-line indent for each paragraph in the paper? No. Each time you press the RETURN key, paragraph formatting in the previous paragraph carries forward to the next paragraph. Thus, once you set the first-line indent, its format carries forward automatically to each subsequent paragraph you type.

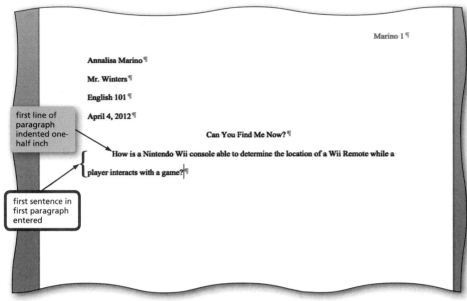

Figure 2–22

Other Ways

1. CONTROL-click paragraph, choose Paragraph in shortcut menu, click Indents and Spacing tab (Paragraph dialog), click Special box arrow, choose First line, click OK button

2. Choose Format > Paragraph, choose Indents and Spacing (Paragraph dialog), click Special box arrow, choose First line, click OK button

3. Press **TAB** key at beginning of paragraph

To AutoCorrect as You Type

As you type, you may make typing, spelling, capitalization, or grammar errors. For this reason, Word provides an **AutoCorrect** feature that automatically corrects these kinds of errors as you type them in the document. For example, if you type ahve, Word automatically changes it to the correct spelling, have, when you press the SPACE BAR or a punctuation mark key such as a period or comma.

Word has predefined many commonly misspelled words, which it automatically corrects for you. The following steps intentionally misspell the word, the, as teh to illustrate the AutoCorrect feature.

1

- Press the SPACE BAR.

- Type the beginning of the next sentence, misspelling the word, the, as follows: `The answer is triangulation, a process that determines teh` (Figure 2–23).

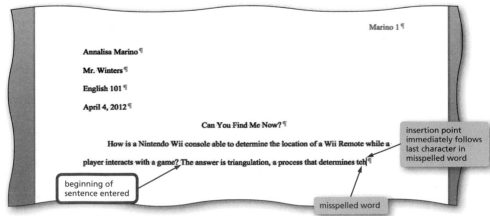

Figure 2–23

- Press the SPACE BAR and watch Word automatically correct the misspelled word.

- Type the rest of the sentence (Figure 2–24): `location of an object by measuring the angles from two or more fixed points.`

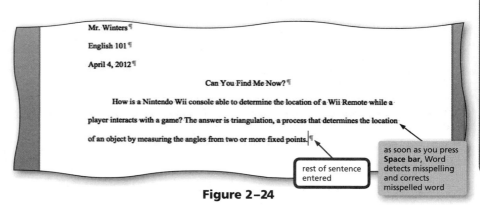

Figure 2–24

To Use the AutoCorrect Options Button

When you position the mouse pointer on text that Word automatically corrected, a small blue box appears below the text. If you point to the small blue box, Word displays the AutoCorrect Options button. When you click the **AutoCorrect Options button**, Word displays a menu that allows you to undo a correction or change how Word handles future automatic corrections of this type. The following steps illustrate the AutoCorrect Options button and menu.

- Position the mouse pointer in the text automatically corrected by Word (the word, the, in this case) to display a small blue box below the automatically corrected word (Figure 2–25).

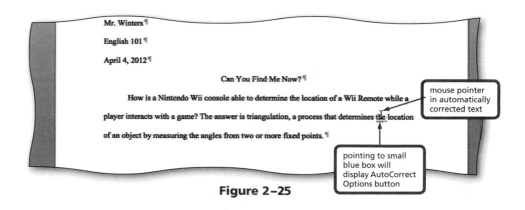

Figure 2–25

- Point to the small blue box to display the AutoCorrect Options button.

- Click the AutoCorrect Options button to display the AutoCorrect Options menu (Figure 2–26).

- Press the ESCAPE key to remove the AutoCorrect Options menu from the screen.

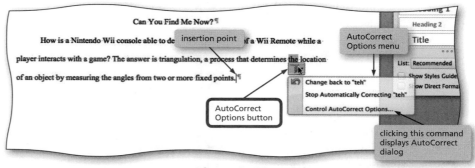

Figure 2–26

Q&A   Do I need to remove the AutoCorrect Options button from the screen?

No. When you move the mouse pointer, the AutoCorrect Options button will disappear from the screen. If, for some reason, you wanted to remove the AutoCorrect Options button from the screen, you could press the ESCAPE key a second time.

To Create an AutoCorrect Entry

In addition to the predefined list of AutoCorrect spelling, capitalization, and grammar errors, you can create your own AutoCorrect entries to add to the list. For example, if you tend to mistype the word sensor as senser, you should create an AutoCorrect entry for it. The following steps create an AutoCorrect entry.

- Click Tools in the menu bar to display the Tools menu (Figure 2–27).

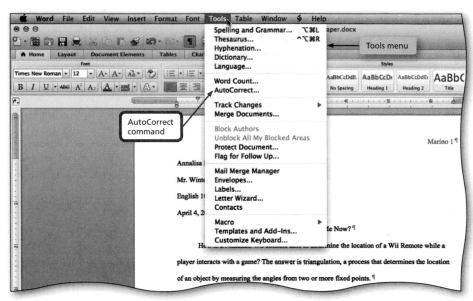

Figure 2–27

- Choose AutoCorrect to display the AutoCorrect dialog. If necessary, choose the AutoCorrect tab.

- Type **senser** in the Replace text box.

- Press the TAB key and then type **sensor** in the With text box (Figure 2–28).

Q&A How would I delete an existing AutoCorrect entry?

You would select the entry to be deleted in the list of defined entries in the AutoCorrect dialog and then click the Delete button.

- Click the Add button (AutoCorrect dialog) to add the entry alphabetically to the list of words to correct automatically as you type. (If your dialog displays a Replace button instead, click it and then click the Yes button in the Microsoft Word dialog to replace the previously defined entry.)

- Click the OK button to close the AutoCorrect dialog.

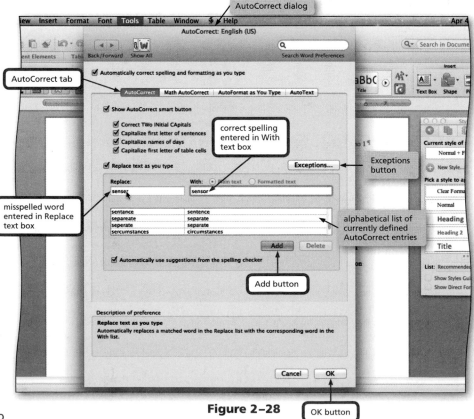

Figure 2–28

The AutoCorrect Dialog

In addition to creating AutoCorrect entries for words you commonly misspell or mistype, you can create entries for abbreviations, codes, and so on. For example, you could create an AutoCorrect entry for asap, indicating that Word should replace this text with the phrase, as soon as possible.

If, for some reason, you do not want Word to correct automatically as you type, you can turn off the 'Replace text as you type' feature by clicking Tools in the menu bar, choosing AutoCorrect to show the AutoCorrect dialog (Figure 2–28), removing the check mark from the 'Replace text as you type' check box, and then clicking the OK button.

The AutoCorrect tab in the AutoCorrect dialog (Figure 2–28) contains other check boxes that correct capitalization errors if the check boxes are selected. If you type two capital letters in a row, such as TH, Word makes the second letter lowercase, Th. If you begin a sentence with a lowercase letter, Word capitalizes the first letter of the sentence. If you type the name of a day in lowercase letters, such as tuesday, Word capitalizes the first letter in the name of the day, Tuesday. If you do not want Word to automatically perform any of these corrections, simply remove the check mark from the appropriate check box in the AutoCorrect dialog.

Sometimes you do not want Word to AutoCorrect a particular word or phrase. For example, you may use the code WD. in your documents. Because Word automatically capitalizes the first letter of a sentence, the character you enter following the period will be capitalized (in the previous sentence, it would capitalize the letter i in the word, in). To allow the code WD. to be entered into a document and still leave the AutoCorrect feature turned on, you would set an exception. To set an exception to an AutoCorrect rule, click Tools in the menu bar, choose AutoCorrect, click the Exceptions button in the AutoCorrect dialog (Figure 2–28), click the appropriate tab in the AutoCorrect Exceptions dialog, type the exception entry in the text box, click the Add button, click the Close button (AutoCorrect Exceptions dialog), and then click the OK button in each of the remaining dialogs.

To Enter More Text

The next step is to continue typing text in the research paper up to the location of the in-text parenthetical reference. The following steps enter this text.

1 With the insertion point positioned at the end of the first paragraph in the paper, as shown in Figure 2–26 on page WD 89, press the RETURN key, so that you can begin typing the text in the second paragraph.

2 Type `Surveyors often use triangulation to measure distance. Starting at a known location and elevation, surveyors measure a length to create a base line and then use a theodolite to measure an angle to an unknown point from each side of the base line` and then press the SPACE BAR.

Citations

Both the MLA and APA guidelines suggest the use of in-text parenthetical references (placed at the end of a sentence), instead of footnoting each source of material in a paper. These parenthetical references, called citations in Word, guide the reader to the end of the paper for complete information about the source.

Automatic Corrections BTW

If you do not want to keep a change automatically made by Word and you immediately notice the automatic correction, you can undo the change by clicking the Undo button on the Standard toolbar or pressing COMMAND-Z. You also can undo a correction through the AutoCorrect Options button, which was shown in the previous steps.

Character Widths BTW

Many word processing documents use variable character fonts, where some characters are wider than others; for example, the letter w is wider than the letter i.

Spacing after Punctuation BTW

Because word processing documents use variable character fonts, it often is difficult to determine in a printed document how many times someone has pressed the spacebar between sentences. Thus, the rule is to press the Space bar only once after periods, colons, and other punctuation marks.

Plan Ahead

Reference all sources.

During your research, be sure to record essential publication information about each of your sources. Following is a sample list of types of required information for the MLA documentation style.

- Book: full name of author(s), complete title of book, edition (if available), volume (if available), publication city, publisher name, publication year, publication medium

- Magazine: full name of author(s), complete title of article, magazine title, issue number (if available), date of magazine, page numbers of article, publication medium

- Web site: full name of author(s), title of Web site, Web site publisher or sponsor (if none, write N.p.), publication date (if none, write n.d.), publication medium, date viewed

Word provides tools to assist you with inserting citations in a paper and later generating a list of sources from the citations. With a documentation style selected, Word automatically formats the citations and list of sources according to that style. The process for adding citations in Word is as follows:

1. Modify the documentation style, if necessary.
2. Insert a citation placeholder.
3. Enter the source information for the citation.

You can combine Steps 2 and 3, where you insert the citation placeholder and enter the source information at once. Or, you can insert the citation placeholder as you write and then enter the source information for the citation at a later time. While creating the research paper in this chapter, you will use both methods.

To Change the Bibliography Style

The first step in inserting a citation is to be sure the citations and sources will be formatted using the correct documentation style, called the bibliography style in Word. The following steps change the specified documentation style.

- Click Document Elements on the ribbon to display the Document Elements tab (Figure 2–29).

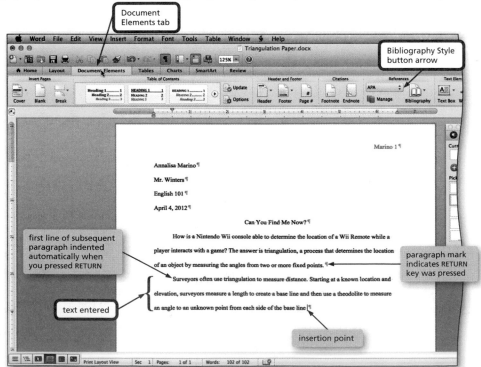

Figure 2–29

- On the Document Elements tab, under References, click the Bibliography Style button arrow to display a pop-up menu of predefined documentation styles (Figure 2–30).

- Click MLA in the Bibliography Style pop-up menu to change the documentation style to MLA.

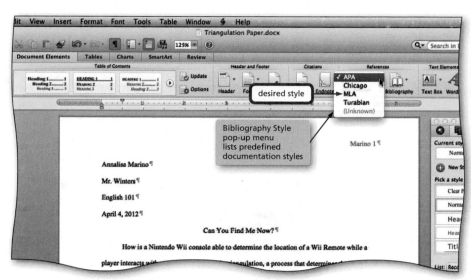

Figure 2–30

To Insert a Citation and Create Its Source

With the documentation style selected, the next task is to insert a citation placeholder and enter the source information for the citation. You can accomplish both of these steps at once by instructing Word to add a new source. The following steps add a new source for a magazine (periodical) article.

1

- On the Document Elements tab, under References, click the Manage button to display the Citations pane of the Toolbox (Figure 2–31).

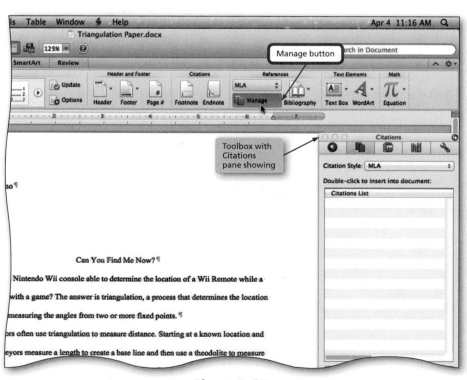

Figure 2–31

2

• Click the + button in the Citations Toolbox to display the Create New Source dialog (Figure 2–32).

Q&A What are the Bibliography Fields in the Create New Source dialog?
A **field** is a placeholder for data whose contents can change. You enter data in some fields; Word supplies data for others. In this case, you enter the contents of the fields for a particular source, for example, the author name in the Author field.

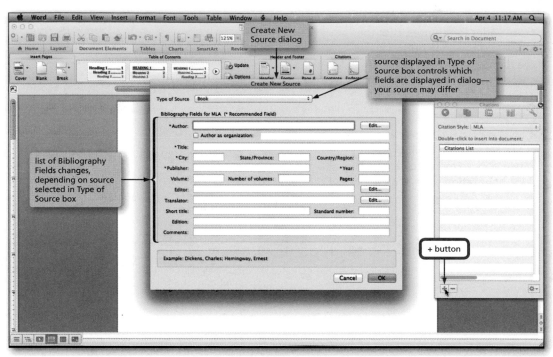

Figure 2–32

 Experiment

• Click the Type of Source box arrow and then click one of the source types in the list, so that you can see how the list of fields changes to reflect the type of source you selected.

3

• If necessary, click the Type of Source box arrow (Create New Source dialog) and then click Article in periodical, so that the list shows fields required for a magazine (periodical).

• If necessary, click the Author text box. Type **Jains, Malila** as the author.

• Click the Title text box. Type **How Surveyors Measure and Calculate Angles** as the article title.

• Press the TAB key and then type **Today's Modern Surveyor** as the periodical title.

• Press the TAB key three times and then type **2012** as the year.

• Press the TAB key and then type **Mar.** as the month.

• Press the TAB key four times and then type **30–48** as the pages (Figure 2–33).

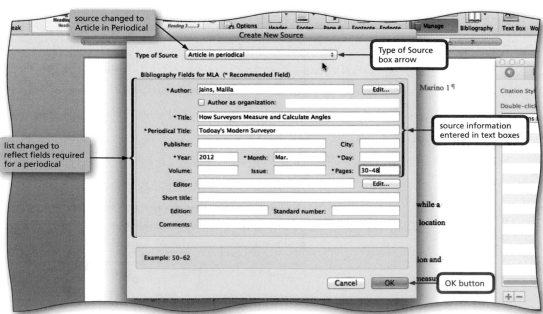

Figure 2–33

- Click the OK button to close the dialog, create the source, and insert the citation in the document at the location of the insertion point (Figure 2–34).

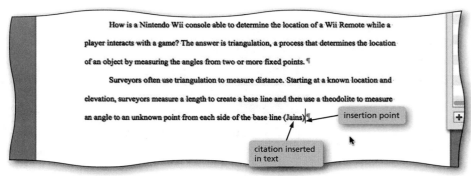

Figure 2–34

To Edit a Citation

In the MLA documentation style, if a source has page numbers, you should include them in the citation. Thus, Word provides a means to enter the page numbers to be displayed in the citation. The following steps edit a citation, so that the page numbers appear in it.

- Click somewhere in the citation to be edited, in this case somewhere in (Jains), which selects the citation and displays the Citation Options box arrow.

- Click the Citation Options box arrow to display the Citation Options menu (Figure 2–35).

Q&A What is the purpose of the tab to the left of the selected citation? If, for some reason, you wanted to move a citation to a different location in the document, you would select the citation and then drag the citation tab to the desired location.

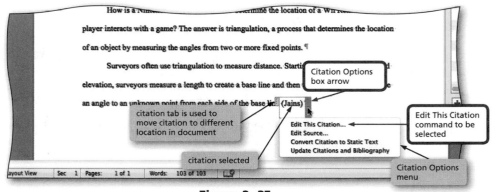

Figure 2–35

- Choose Edit this Citation in the Citation Options menu to display the Edit Citation dialog.

- Type 30–48 in the Pages text box (Edit Citation dialog) (Figure 2–36).

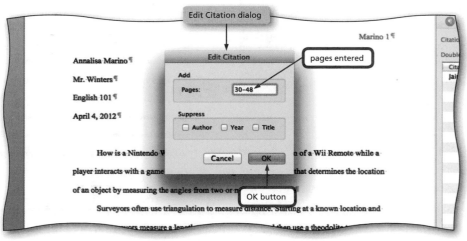

Figure 2–36

- Click the OK button to close the dialog and add the page numbers to the citation in the document (Figure 2–37).

- Press the COMMAND-RIGHT ARROW keys to move the insertion point to the end of the line, which also deselects the citation.

- Press . (period) key to end the sentence.

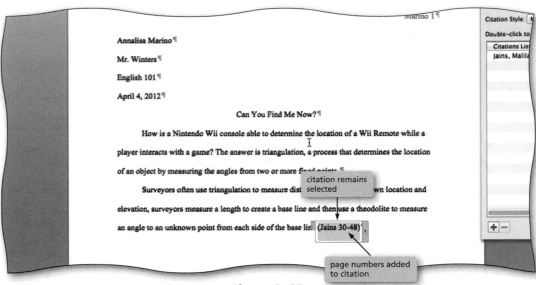

Figure 2–37

To Enter More Text

The next step is to continue typing text in the research paper up to the location of the footnote. The following steps enter this text.

1 Press the SPACE BAR.

2 Type the next sentence (Figure 2–38): `The length of the base line and the two known angles allow a computer or person to determine the location of a third point.`

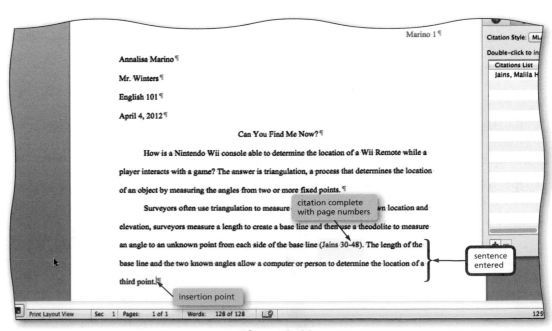

Figure 2–38

To Save an Existing Document with the Same File Name

You have made several modifications to the document since you last saved it. Thus, you should save it again. The following step saves the document again.

 Click the Save button on the Standard toolbar to overwrite the previously saved file.

Footnotes

As discussed earlier in this chapter, notes are optional in the MLA documentation style. If used, content notes elaborate on points discussed in the paper, and bibliographic notes direct the reader to evaluations of statements in a source or provide a means for identifying multiple sources. The MLA documentation style specifies that a superscript (raised number) be used for a **note reference mark** to signal that a note exists either at the bottom of the page as a **footnote** or at the end of the document as an **endnote**.

In Word, **note text** can be any length and format. Word automatically numbers notes sequentially by placing a note reference mark both in the body of the document and to the left of the note text. If you insert, rearrange, or remove notes, Word renumbers any subsequent note reference marks according to their new sequence in the document.

To Insert a Footnote Reference Mark

The following step inserts a footnote reference mark in the document at the location of the insertion point and at the location where the footnote text will be typed.

- With the insertion point positioned as shown in Figure 2–38, click Insert in the menu bar, then choose Footnote to display the Footnote and Endnote dialog.

- Under Location, if necessary, choose Bottom of page for the Footnotes location.

- Under Format, if necessary, choose 1,2,3, … as the number format (Figure 2–39).

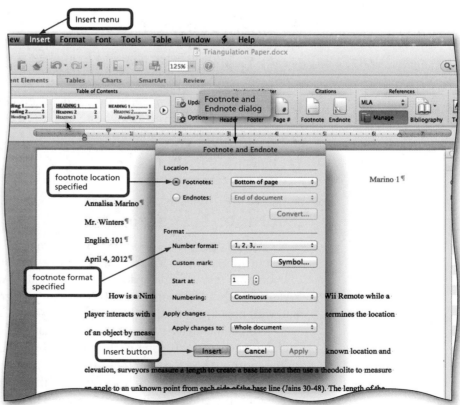

Figure 2–39

- Click the Insert button (Footnote and Endnote dialog) to display a note reference mark (a superscripted 1) in two places: (1) in the document window at the location of the insertion point and (2) at the bottom of the page where the footnote will be positioned, just below a separator line (Figure 2–40).

Q&A What if I wanted notes to be positioned as endnotes instead of as footnotes?
In the Footnotes and Endnotes dialog, you would choose Endnotes rather than Footnotes under Location, which places the separator line and the endnote text at the end of the document, instead of the bottom of the page containing the reference.

Other Ways
1. Press COMMAND-OPTION-F

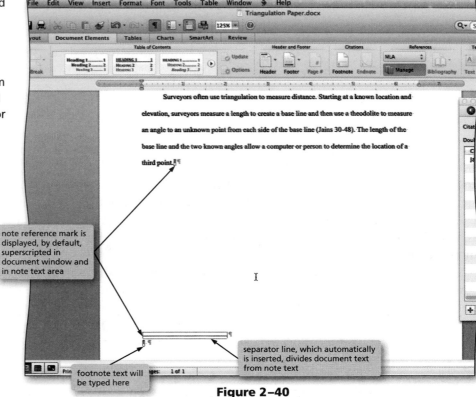

Figure 2–40

To Enter Footnote Text

The following step types the footnote text to the right of the note reference mark below the separator line.

1 Type the footnote text up to the citation: `Cordoba and Sarkis state that electronic theodolites calculate angles automatically and then send the calculated angles to a computer for analysis (25).` and then press the SPACE BAR.

Footnote Text Style

When you insert a footnote, Word formats it using the Footnote Text style, which does not adhere to the MLA documentation style. For example, notice in Figure 2–38 that the footnote text is single-spaced and left-aligned. According to the MLA documentation style, notes should be formatted like all other paragraphs in the paper; that is, double-spaced and with first-line indent.

You could change the paragraph formatting of the footnote text to first-line indent and double-spacing. If you use this technique, however, you will need to change the format of the footnote text for each footnote you enter into the document.

A more efficient technique is to modify the format of the Footnote Text style so that every footnote you enter in the document will use the formats defined in this style.

To Modify a Style Using a Shortcut Menu

The Footnote Text style specifies left-aligned single-spaced paragraphs with a 12-point font size for text. To meet MLA documentation style, the footnotes should be double-spaced with a first line indent and a 12-point font size for text. The following steps modify the Footnote Text style.

- CONTROL-click the note text in the footnote to display a shortcut menu related to footnotes (Figure 2–41).

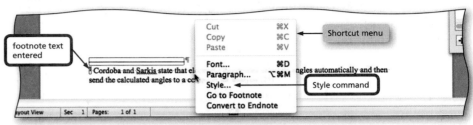

Figure 2–41

- Choose Style in the shortcut menu to display the Style dialog. If necessary, click the List arrow, click All styles in the Category list, and then click Footnote Text in the Styles list.

- Click the Modify button (Style dialog) to display the Modify Style dialog.

- Click the Double Space button (Modify Style dialog) to change the line spacing (Figure 2–42).

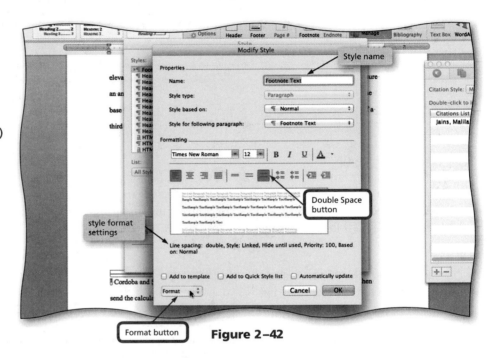

Figure 2–42

- Click the Format button to display the Format menu.

- Click Paragraph in the Format menu (Modify Style dialog) to display the Paragraph dialog.

- If necessary, click the Indents and Spacing tab (Paragraph dialog).

- Click the Special box arrow (Paragraph dialog) and then click First line (Figure 2–43).

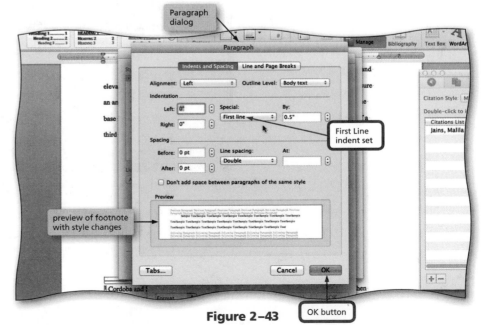

Figure 2–43

- Click the OK button (Paragraph dialog) to close the dialog.

- Click OK (Modify Style dialog) to close the dialog.

- Click the Apply button (Style dialog) to apply the style changes to the footnote text (Figure 2–44).

Q&A Will all footnotes use this modified style?
Yes. Any future footnotes entered in the document will use a 12-point font with the paragraphs first-line indented and double-spaced.

Other Ways
1. Choose Format > Style, select desired style, click Modify button (Style dialog)

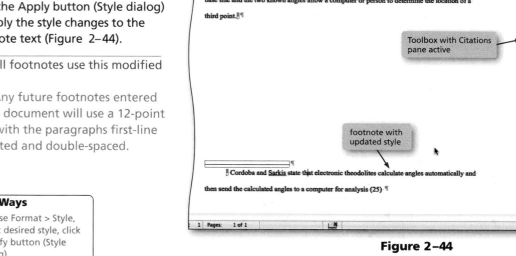

Figure 2–44

To Enter a Source

When you typed the footnote text for this research paper, you a cited a source that has not yet been added to the master source list. You need to enter the source information in order for it to be included in a bibliography or works cited list. The following steps add a source.

- On the Citations pane of the Toolbox, click the Action button to display the Citations menu.

- Choose Citation Source Manager to open the Source Manager dialog (Figure 2–45).

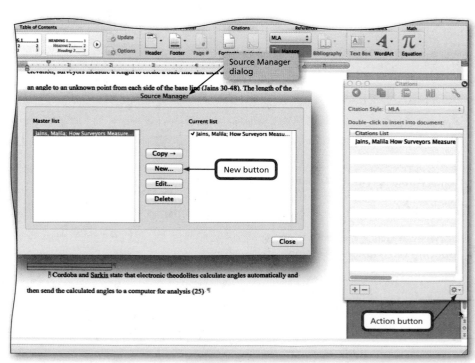

Figure 2–45

2

- Click the New button to open the Create New Source dialog.

- Click the Type of Source box arrow (Create New Source dialog) and then click Book, so that the list shows fields required for a book.

- If necessary, click the Author text box. Type `Cordoba, Nicolas E.; Sarkis, Kara A.` as the author.

 Q&A What if I do not know how to punctuate the author entry so that Word formats it properly? Click the Edit button (Create New Source dialog) to the right of the Author entry for assistance. For example, you should separate multiple author names with a semicolon as shown in Figure 2–46.

- Click the Title text box. Type `The Surveyor's Theodolite Formula` as the book title.

- Press the TAB key and then type `Orlando` as the city.

- Press the TAB key three times and then type `Orange County Press` as the publisher.

- Press the TAB key and then type `2012` as the year (Figure 2–46).

3

- Click the OK button to close the Create New Source dialog.

- Click the Close button to close the Source Manager dialog and create the source.

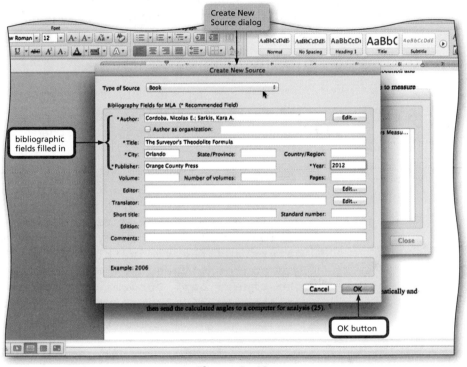

Figure 2–46

Working with Footnotes and Endnotes

You edit footnote text just as you edit any other text in the document. To delete or move a note reference mark, however, the insertion point must be in the document text (not in the footnote text).

To delete a note, select the note reference mark in the document text (not in the footnote text) by dragging through the note reference mark and then click the Cut button on the Standard toolbar. Or, click to place the insertion point immediately to the right of the note reference mark in the document text and then press the DELETE key twice, or click immediately to the left of the note reference mark in the document text and then press the FN-DELETE keys twice.

To move a note to a different location in a document, select the note reference mark in the document text (not in the footnote text), click the Cut button on the Standard toolbar, click the location where you want to move the note, and then click the Paste button on the Standard toolbar. You also can select the note reference mark and drag it to the desired location in the document. When you move or delete notes, Word automatically renumbers any remaining notes in the correct sequence.

Footnote and Endnote Location

BTW

You can change the location of footnotes from the bottom of the page to beneath the text by clicking Insert in the menu bar, choosing Footnotes to display the Footnote and Endnote dialog, clicking the Footnotes option button (Footnote and Endnote dialog), and then clicking Beneath text. Similarly, clicking the Endnotes option button (Footnote and Endnote dialog) enables you to change the location of endnotes from the end of the document to the end of a section.

If you position the mouse pointer on the note reference mark in the document text, the note text is displayed above the note reference mark as a ScreenTip. To remove the ScreenTip, move the mouse pointer.

If, for some reason, you wanted to change the format of note reference marks in footnotes or endnotes (i.e., from 1, 2, 3, to A, B, C), you would click Insert in the menu bar, and choose Footnote from the Insert menu to display the Footnote and Endnote dialog. In the Footnote and Endnote dialog, click the Number format box arrow, click the desired number format in the list, and then click the Apply button.

If, for some reason, you wanted to convert footnotes to endnotes, you would click Insert in the menu bar, and choose Footnote from the Insert menu to display the Footnote and Endnote dialog. In the Footnote and Endnote dialog, click the Convert button, select the 'Convert all footnotes to endnotes' option button, click the OK button, and then click the Insert button (Footnote and Endnote dialog).

To Enter More Text

The next step is to continue typing text in the body of the research paper. The following steps enter this text.

1 Position the insertion point after the note reference mark in the document and then press the RETURN key.

2 Type the third paragraph of the research paper (Figure 2–47): `Similarly, the Nintendo Wii console uses triangulation to determine the location of a Wii Remote. A player places a sensor bar, which contains two infrared transmitters, near or on top of a television. While the player uses the Wii Remote, the Wii console determines the remote's location by calculating the distance and angles between the Wii Remote and the two transmitters on the sensor bar. Determining the location of a Wii Remote is relatively simple because the sensor bar contains only two fixed points: the transmitters.`

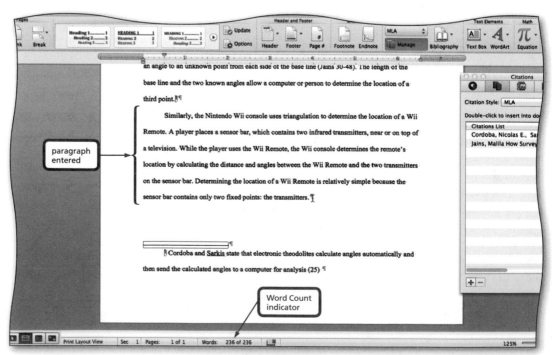

Figure 2–47

To Count Words

Often when you write papers, you are required to compose the papers with a minimum number of words. The minimum requirement for the research paper in this chapter is 325 words. You can look at the status bar at the bottom of the document window and see the total number of words thus far in a document. For example, Figure 2–47 shows the research paper has 236 words, but you are not sure if that count includes the words in your footnote. The following steps display the Word Count dialog, so that you can verify the footnote text is included in the count.

- Click the Word Count indicator in the status bar to display the Word Count dialog.

- If necessary, place a check mark in the 'Include footnotes and endnotes' check box (Word Count dialog) (Figure 2–48).

Q&A Why do the statistics in my Word Count dialog differ from Figure 2–48?
Depending on the accuracy of your typing, your statistics may differ.

- Click the OK button to close the dialog.

Q&A Can I display statistics for just a section of the document?
Yes. Select the section and then click the Word Count indicator in the status bar to display statistics about the selected text.

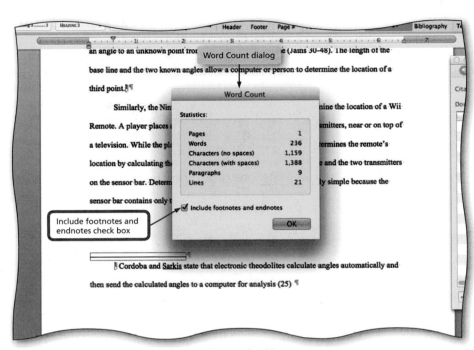

Figure 2–48

Other Ways
1. Choose Tools > Word Count in menu bar

Automatic Page Breaks

As you type documents that exceed one page, Word automatically inserts page breaks, called **automatic page breaks** or **soft page breaks**, when it determines the text has filled one page according to paper size, margin settings, line spacing, and other settings. If you add text, delete text, or modify text on a page, Word recomputes the location of automatic page breaks and adjusts them accordingly.

Word performs page recomputation between the keystrokes, that is, in between the pauses in your typing. Thus, Word refers to the automatic page break task as **background repagination**. The steps on the next page illustrate Word's automatic page break feature.

Page Break Locations

BTW As you type, your page break may occur at different locations depending on Word settings and the type of printer connected to the computer.

To Enter More Text and Insert a Citation Placeholder

The next task is to type the fourth paragraph in the body of the research paper. The following steps enter this text and a placeholder.

1 With the insertion point positioned at the end of the third paragraph as shown in Figure 2–47 on page WD 102, press the RETURN key.

2 Type the fourth paragraph of the research paper: **A more complex application of triangulation occurs in a global positioning system (GPS). A GPS consists of one or more earth-based receivers that accept and analyze signals sent by satellites to determine a receiver's geographic location. GPS receivers, found in handheld navigation devices and many vehicles, use triangulation to determine their location relative to at least three geostationary satellites. According to Sanders, the satellites are the fixed points in the triangulation formula** and then press the SPACE BAR.

Q&A Why does the text move from the second page to the first page as I am typing?
Word, by default, will not allow the first line of a paragraph to be by itself at the bottom of a page (an orphan) or the last line of a paragraph to be by itself at the top of a page (a widow). As you type, Word adjusts the placement of the paragraph to avoid orphans and widows.

3 Click the + button in the Citations pane of the Toolbox to display the Create new Source dialog. Type **Sanders** as the Author name for the source. You will add the rest of the source later.

4 Click the OK button to close the dialog and insert the Author name as a citation placeholder.

5 Press the **.** (period) key to end the sentence.

To Edit a Source

When you typed the fourth paragraph of the research paper, you inserted a citation placeholder, Sanders, for the source. You now have the source information, which is for a Web site, and are ready to enter it. The following steps edit the source for the Sanders citation placeholder.

1 Click somewhere in the citation placeholder to be edited, in this case (Sanders), to select the citation placeholder.

2 Click the Citation Options box arrow to display the Citation Options menu.

3 Choose Edit Source in the Citation Options menu to display the Edit Source dialog.

4 If necessary, click the Type of Source box arrow (Edit Source dialog); scroll to and then click Web site, so that the list shows fields required for a Web site.

5 Click the Author text box. Type **Sanders, Gregory B.** as the author.

6 Click the Name of Web Page text box. Type **Understanding Satellites and Global Positioning Systems** as the Web page name.

7 Click the Production Company text box. Type `Course Technology` as the production company.

8 Click the Year Accessed text box. Type `2012` as the year accessed.

9 Press the TAB key and then type `Feb.` as the month accessed.

10 Press the TAB key and then type `27` as the day accessed (Figure 2–49).

Q&A   Do I need to enter a Web address (URL)?
The latest MLA documentation style update does not require the Web address in the source.

11 Click the OK button to close the dialog. Click Yes to save changes to both master and current lists and complete the edits to the source.

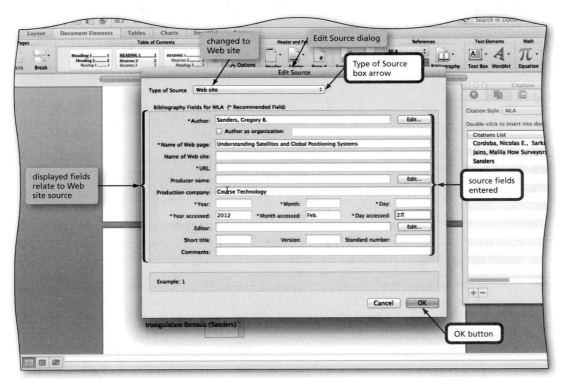

Figure 2–49

To Edit a Citation

In MLA documentation style, if you reference the author's name in the text, you should not list it again in the parenthetical citation. For Web site citations, when you suppress the author's name, the citation shows the Web site name. The following steps edit the citation, suppressing the author and displaying the name of the Web site instead.

1 If necessary, click somewhere in the citation to be edited, in this case (Sanders), to select the citation and display the Citation Options box arrow.

2 Click the Citation Options box arrow and then click Edit This Citation in the Citation Options menu to display the Edit Citation dialog.

3 Click the Author check box (Edit Citation dialog) to place a check mark in it (Figure 2–50).

4 Click the OK button to close the dialog, remove the author name from the citation, and show the name of the Web site in the citation (shown in Figure 2–51).

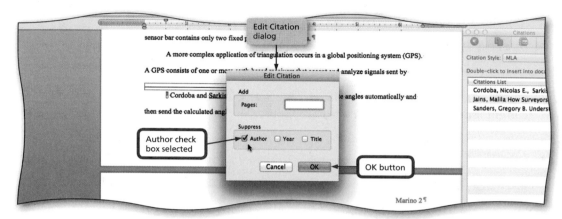

Figure 2–50

To Enter More Text

The next step is to type the last paragraph of text in the research paper. The following steps enter this text.

1 Press the COMMAND-RIGHT ARROW keys to position the insertion point at the end of the fourth paragraph and then press the RETURN key.

2 Type the last paragraph of the research paper (Figure 2–51): `The next time you pass a surveyor, play a Nintendo Wii, or follow a route prescribed by a vehicle's navigation system, keep in mind that none of it might have been possible without the con-cept of triangulation.`

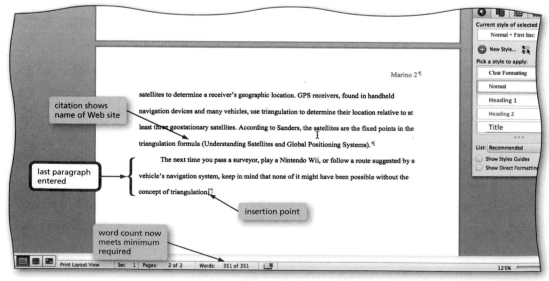

Figure 2–51

To Save an Existing Document with the Same File Name

You have made several modifications to the document since you last saved it. Thus, you should save it again. The following step saves the document again.

1 Click the Save button in the Standard toolbar to overwrite the previously saved file.

Break Point: If you wish to take a break, this is a good place to do so. You can quit Word now (refer to page WD 126 for instructions). To resume at a later time, start Word (refer to page WD 73 for instructions), open the file called Triangulation Paper (refer to page WD 49 for instructions), and continue following the steps from this location forward.

Creating an Alphabetical Works Cited Page

According to the MLA documentation style, the **works cited page** is a list of sources that are referenced directly in a research paper. You place the list on a separate numbered page with the title, Works Cited, centered one inch from the top margin. The works are to be alphabetized by the author's last name or, if the work has no author, by the work's title. The first line of each entry begins at the left margin. Indent subsequent lines of the same entry one-half inch from the left margin.

Plan Ahead

Create the list of sources.

A **bibliography** is an alphabetical list of sources referenced in a paper. Whereas the text of the research paper contains brief references to the source (the citations), the bibliography lists all publication information about the source. Documentation styles differ significantly in their guidelines for preparing a bibliography. Each style identifies formats for various sources, including books, magazines, pamphlets, newspapers, Web sites, television programs, paintings, maps, advertisements, letters, memos, and much more. You can find information about various styles and their guidelines in printed style guides and on the Web.

To Page Break Manually

The works cited are to be displayed on a separate numbered page. Thus, you must insert a manual page break following the body of the research paper so that the list of sources is displayed on a separate page. A **manual page break**, or **hard page break**, is one that you force into the document at a specific location.

Word never moves or adjusts manual page breaks. Word, however, does adjust any automatic page breaks that follow a manual page break. Word inserts manual page breaks immediately above or to the left of the location of the insertion point. The step on the next page inserts a manual page break after the text of the research paper.

1

• Verify that the insertion point is positioned at the end of the text of the research paper, as shown in Figure 2–51 on page WD 106.

• Click Layout on the ribbon to display the Layout tab.

• On the Layout tab, under Page Setup, click the Break button and then choose Page to insert a manual page break immediately to the left of the insertion point and position the insertion point immediately below the manual page break (Figure 2–52).

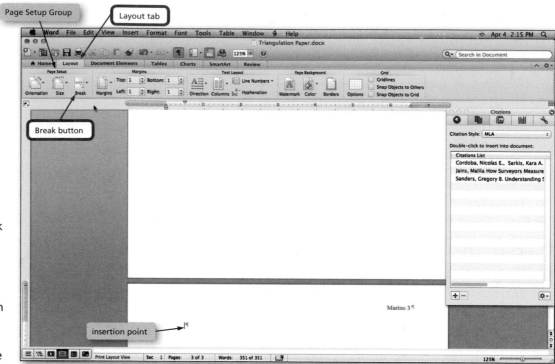

Figure 2–52

Other Ways

1. Choose Insert > Break > Page in menu bar
2. Press COMMAND-SHIFT-RETURN

To Create the Bibliographical List

While typing the research paper, you created several citations and their sources. Word can format the list of sources and alphabetize them in a **bibliographical list**, saving you time looking up style guidelines. That is, Word will create a bibliographical list with each element of the source placed in its correct position with proper punctuation, according to the specified style. For example, in this research paper, the book source will list, in this order, the author name(s), book title, publisher city, publishing company name, and publication year with the correct punctuation between each element according to the MLA documentation style. The following steps create an MLA-styled bibliographical list from the sources previously entered.

1

• Click Document Elements on the ribbon to display the Document Elements tab.

• With the insertion point positioned as shown in Figure 2–52, under References, click the Bibliography button to display the Bibliography pop-up menu (Figure 2–53).

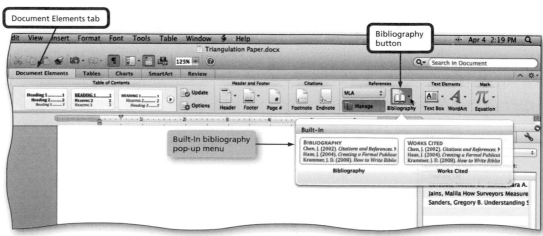

Figure 2–53

- Click Works Cited in the Bibliography pop-up menu to insert a list of sources at the location of the insertion point.

- If necessary, scroll to display the entire list of sources in the document window (Figure 2–54).

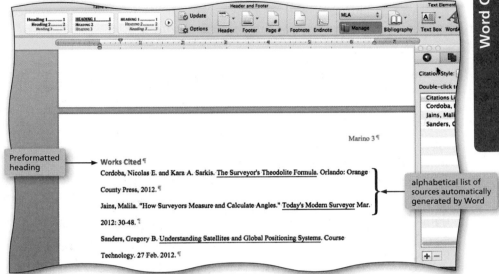

Figure 2–54

To Format Paragraphs with a Hanging Indent

MLA styled bibliographies require use of a hanging indent for each entry. With a hanging indent, the first line of each source entry begins at the left margin, and subsequent lines in the same paragraph are indented one-half inch from the left margin. In essence, the first line hangs to the left of the rest of the paragraph; thus, this type of paragraph formatting is called a **hanging indent**. The following step formats the entries in the bibliographical list with a hanging indent.

- Select the three source entries.

- Drag the Hanging Indent marker (the bottom triangle) on the ruler to the .5" mark on the ruler to set the hanging indent at that location from the left margin.

- Click outside of the works cited to deselect the source entries (Figure 2–55).

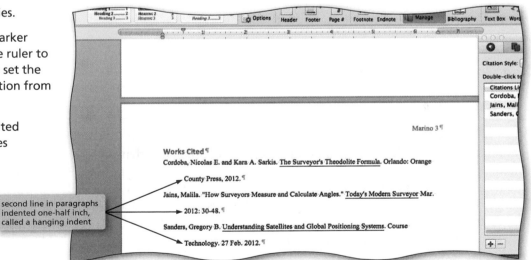

Figure 2–55

Other Ways

1. COMMAND-click paragraph to format, click Paragraph in shortcut menu, click Indents and Spacing tab (Paragraph dialog), click Special box arrow, click Hanging, click OK button

2. Choose Format > Paragraph in menu bar, click Indents and Spacing tab (Paragraph dialog), click Special box arrow, click Hanging, click OK button

To Modify a Source and Update the Bibliographical List

If you modify the contents of any source, the list of sources automatically updates because the list is a field. The following steps modify the title of the magazine article.

- If necessary, on the Document Elements tab, under References, click the Manage button to display the Citations toolbox.

- Click the source you wish to edit in the Citations List, in this case the article by Jains, to select the source.

- Click the Action button in the lower-right corner of the Citations toolbox and choose Edit Source from the menu to display the Edit Source dialog.

- In the Title text box, insert the word, Distance, between the words, Measure and, in the title (Figure 2–56).

- Click the OK button (Edit Source dialog) to close the dialog.

- If a Microsoft Word dialog appears, click its Yes button to update all occurrences of the source.

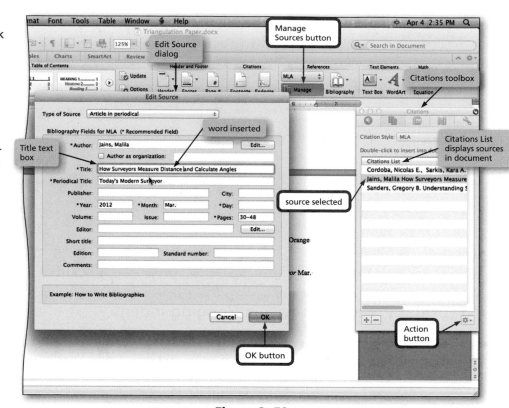

Figure 2–56

Q&A What if the list of sources in the document is not updated automatically?
Click in the list of sources and then click the Bibliography box arrow that appears in the upper left of the frame. Select Update Citations and Bibliography from the list.

To Convert a Field to Regular Text

Word may use an earlier version of the MLA documentation style to format the bibliography. The latest guidelines for the MLA documentation style, for example, state that titles should be italicized instead of under-lined, and each work should identify the source's publication medium (e.g., Print for printed media, Web for online media, etc.). If you format or add text to the bibliography, Word automatically will change it back to the Bibliography style's predetermined formats when the bibliography field is updated. To preserve modifications you make to the format of the bibliography, you can convert the bibliography field to regular text. Keep in mind, though, once you convert the field to regular text, it no longer is a field that can be updated. The following steps convert a field to regular text.

● Click somewhere in the field to select it, in this case, somewhere in the bibliography. Click the box arrow that appears in the upper left of the frame to display the Bibliography options menu (Figure 2–57).

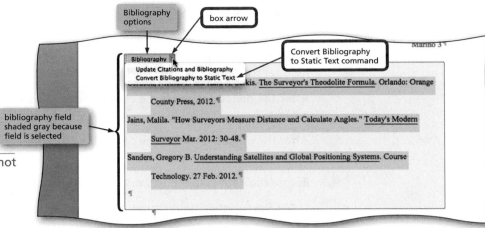

Figure 2–57

 Q&A What if the bibliography field is not shaded?
Click Word in the menu bar to display the Word menu. Choose Preferences to display the Word Preferences dialog. Under Authoring and Proofing Tools, choose View, and make sure that under Show, the Field Shading is set to When selected, and then click the OK button.

Q&A Why are all the words in the bibliography shaded?
The bibliography field consists of all text in the bibliography.

2

● Select Convert Bibliography to Static Text from the list.

Q&A Why did the shading disappear?
The bibliography no longer is a field, so it is not shaded.

● Click anywhere outside the Works Cited to remove the selection from the text (Figure 2–58).

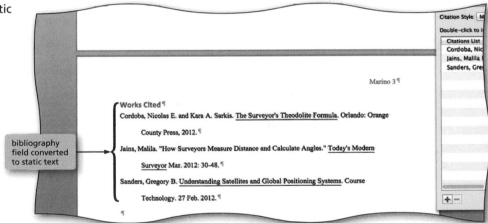

Figure 2–58

To Format the Works Cited to the Latest MLA Documentation Style

As mentioned earlier, the latest MLA documentation style guidelines state that titles should be italicized instead of underlined, and each work should identify the source's publication medium (e.g., Print, Web, Radio, Television, CD, DVD, Film, etc.). The following steps format and modify the Works Cited as specified by the latest MLA guidelines, if yours are not already formatted this way.

1 Drag through the book title, The Surveyor's Theodolite Formula, to select it.

2 On the Home tab, under Font, click the Underline button to remove the underline from the selected text and then click the Italic button to italicize the selected text.

3 Select the magazine title, Today's Modern Surveyor. Remove the underline from the selected title and then italicize the selected title.

4 Select the Web page title, Understanding Satellites and Global Positioning Systems. Remove the underline from the selected title and then italicize the selected title.

5 After the period following the year in the first work, press the SPACE BAR and then type `Print.`

6 After the period following the page range in the second work, press the SPACE BAR and then type `Print.`

7 Before the date in the third work, type `Web.` and then press the SPACE BAR.

8 Select the heading, Works Cited. Format the text to 12 point Times New Roman, automatic font color. Remove the bold formatting and center the heading (Figure 2–59).

9 Select the heading and set line spacing to 2.

10 Click the close button to close the toolbox. Click outside the Works Cited to deselect the text.

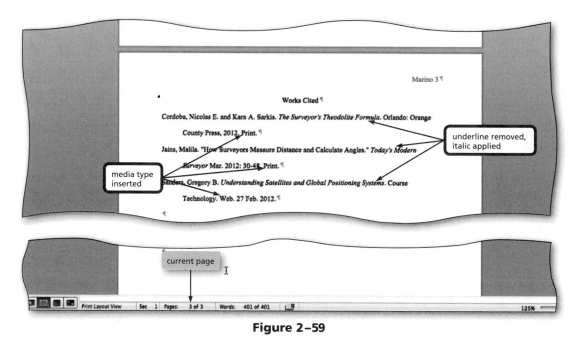

Figure 2–59

To Save an Existing Document with the Same File Name

You have made several modifications to the document since you last saved it. Thus, you should save it again. The following step saves the document again.

1 Click the Save button on the Standard toolbar to overwrite the previously saved file.

Proofing and Revising the Research Paper

As discussed in Chapter 1, once you complete a document, you might find it necessary to make changes to it. Before submitting a paper to be graded, you should proofread it. While **proofreading**, look for grammatical errors and spelling errors. You also should ensure the transitions between sentences flow smoothly and the sentences themselves make sense.

Proofread and revise the paper. **Plan Ahead**

As you proofread the paper, look for ways to improve it. Check all grammar, spelling, and punctuation. Be sure the text is logical and transitions are smooth. Where necessary, add text, delete text, reword text, and move text to different locations. Ask yourself these questions:

- Does the title suggest the topic?
- Is the thesis clear?
- Is the purpose of the paper clear?
- Does the paper have an introduction, body, and conclusion?
- Does each paragraph in the body relate to the thesis?
- Is the conclusion effective?
- Are all sources acknowledged?

To assist you with the proofreading effort, Word provides several tools. You can browse through pages, copy text, find text, replace text, insert a synonym, check spelling and grammar, and look up information. The following pages discuss these tools.

To Scroll Page by Page through a Document

The next step is to modify text on the second page of the paper. Currently, the third page is the active page (Figure 2–59). The following step scrolls up one page in the document.

- With the insertion point on the third page of the paper, click the Previous Page button on the vertical scroll bar to position the insertion point at the top of the previous page (Figure 2–60).

Q&A The button on my screen shows a ScreenTip different from Previous Page. Why?
By default, the functions of the buttons above and below the Select Browse Object button are Previous Page and Next Page, respectively. You can change the commands associated with these buttons by clicking the Select Browse Object button and then clicking the desired browse object. The Browse by Page command in the Select Browse Object menu, for example, changes the buttons back to Previous Page and Next Page.

Q&A How do I display the next page?
Click the Next Page button on the vertical scroll bar.

Figure 2–60

Other Ways

1. Click Page Number indicator on status bar, click Page in 'Go to what' list (Find and Replace dialog), type desired page number in 'Enter page number' text box, click Go To button

2. Press COMMAND-PAGE UP or COMMAND-PAGE DOWN (extended keyboards only)

Copying, Cutting, and Pasting

While proofreading the research paper, you decide it would read better if the word, geostationary, appeared in front of the word, satellites, in the last sentence of the fourth paragraph. You could type the word at the desired location, but because this is a difficult word to spell, you decide to use the Clipboard. The **Clipboard** is a temporary storage area that holds any single item copied or cut until such time as you copy or cut another item.

Copying is the process of placing items on the Clipboard, leaving the item in the document. **Cutting**, by contrast, removes the item from the document before placing it on the Clipboard. **Pasting** is the process of copying an item from the Clipboard into the document at the location of the insertion point.

To Copy and Paste

In the research paper, you copy a word from one sentence to another. The following steps copy and paste a word.

- Select the item to be copied (the word, geostationary, in this case).

- Click the Copy button in the Standard toolbar to copy the selected item in the document to the Clipboard (Figure 2–61).

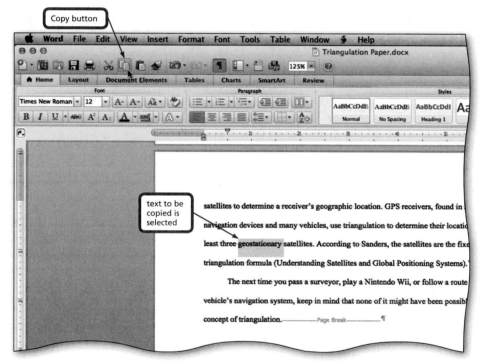

Figure 2–61

- Position the insertion point at the location where the item should be pasted (immediately to the left of the word, satellites, in this case) (Figure 2–62).

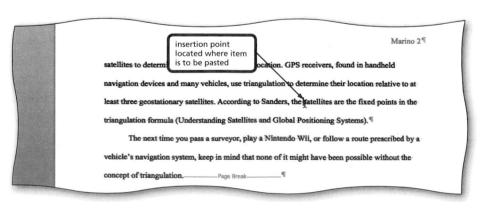

Figure 2–62

3

- In the Standard toolbar, click the Paste button to paste the copied item in the document at the location of the insertion point (Figure 2–63).

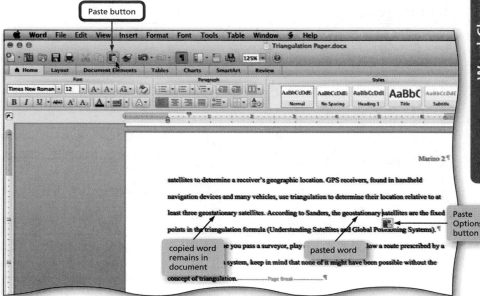

Figure 2–63

● **Other Ways**

1. CONTROL-click selected item, choose Copy in shortcut menu, CONTROL-click where item is to be pasted, choose Paste

2. Select item, choose Edit > Copy in menu bar, position insertion point at paste location, choose Edit > Paste

3. Select item, press COMMAND-C, position insertion point at paste location, press COMMAND-V

To Display the Paste Options Menu

When you paste an item or move an item using drag-and-drop editing, which was discussed in the previous chapter, Word automatically displays a Paste Options button near the pasted or moved text (Figure 2–63). The Paste Options button allows you to change the format of a pasted item. For example, you can instruct Word to format the pasted item the same way as where it was copied, or format it the same way as where it is being pasted. The following steps display the Paste Options menu.

1

- Click the Paste Options button to display the Paste Options menu (Figure 2–64).

Q&A   What are the functions of the options in the Paste Options menu? In general, the Keep Source Formatting option indicates the pasted item should look the same as it did in its original location. The Match Destination Formatting option formats the pasted text to match the rest of the item where it was pasted. The Keep Text Only option removes all formatting from the pasted item. Keep in mind that the options shown in a Paste Options menu will vary, depending on the item being pasted.

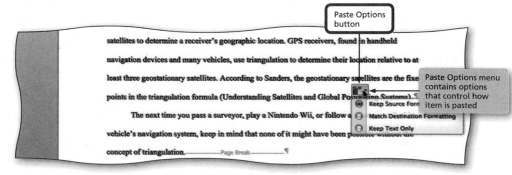

Figure 2–64

2

- Press the ESCAPE key to remove the Paste Options menu from the window.

To Find Text

While proofreading the paper, you would like to locate all occurrences of Wii console because you are contemplating changing this text to Wii game console. The following steps find all occurrences of specific text in a document.

- Press FUNCTION-COMMAND-LEFT ARROW to place the insertion point at the top of the document.

- Click in the Search in Document text box, and type Wii console to highlight all occurrences of the typed text, called the search text, in the document window (Figure 2–65).

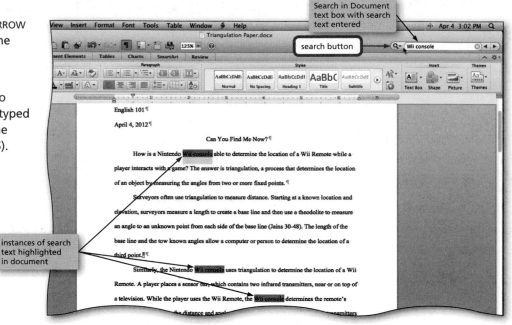

Figure 2–65

- Click the search button and choose List Matches in Sidebar to highlight all occurrences of the search text in the Sidebar Search pane and in the document (Figure 2–66).

Q&A What is the Sidebar?
The Sidebar is a window that provides you with four different panes within which to accomplish tasks. The Search pane allows you to search for and replace text in a document.

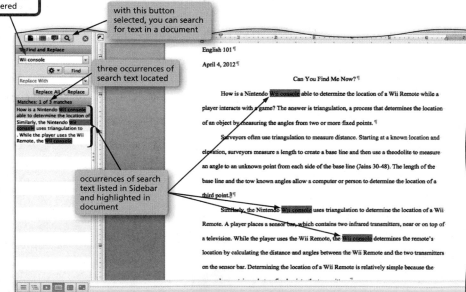

Figure 2–66

 Experiment

- Type various search text in the Search Document text box, and watch Word list matches in the Sidebar and highlight matches in the document window. When you are finished experimenting, search again for Wii console.

Other Ways

1. Choose View > Sidebar > Search Pane, enter search text in Search Pane

2. Choose Edit > Find > Find, enter search text in Search in Document text box, click the search button and choose List Matches in Sidebar

3. Click Page Number indicator in status bar, click Find tab (Find and Replace dialog), enter search text, click Find All button

4. Press COMMAND-F

To Replace Text

You decide to change all occurrences of Wii console to Wii game console. To do this, you can use Word's find and replace feature, which automatically locates each occurrence of a word or phrase and then replaces it with specified text. The following steps replace all occurrences of Wii console with Wii game console.

- If necessary, type `Wii console` in the Search Document text box in the Sidebar.
- Type `Wii game console` in the Replace With text box (Figure 2–67).

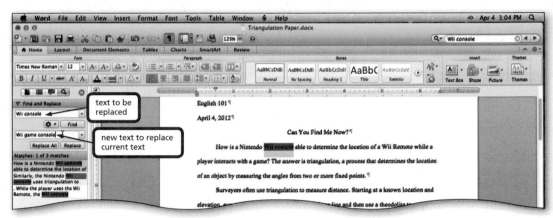

Figure 2–67

- Click the Replace All button to instruct Word to replace all occurrences of the Search document text with the Replace With text (Figure 2–68). If Word displays a dialog asking if you want to continue searching from the beginning of the document, click the Yes button.

Q&A Does Word search the entire document?
If the insertion point is at the beginning of the document, Word searches the entire document; otherwise, Word searches from the location of the insertion point to the end of the document and then displays a dialog asking if you want to continue searching from the beginning. You also can search a section of text by selecting the text before clicking the Replace button.

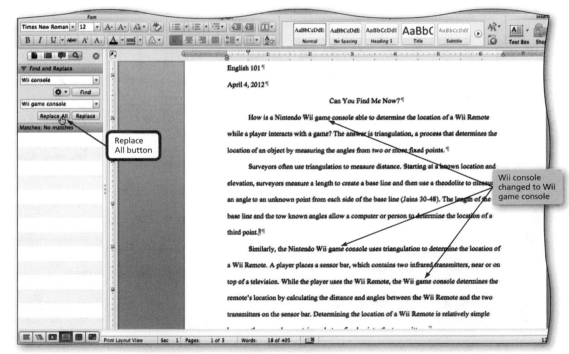

Figure 2–68

Other Ways

1. Choose View > Sidebar > Search Pane
2. Choose Edit > Find > Replace
3. Click Page Number indicator in status bar, click Replace tab (Find and Replace dialog), enter search text, click Replace All button
4. Press COMMAND-SHIFT-H

Finding Formatting

BTW To search for formatting or a special character, click Edit in the menu bar, choose Find > Advanced Find and Replace to expand the Find dialog. To find formatting, use the Format button in the expanded Find dialog. To find a special character, use the Special button.

Find and Replace Sidebar and Search Pane

The Replace All button (Find and Replace sidebar) replaces all occurrences of the Search Document text with the Replace With text. In some cases, you may want to replace only certain occurrences of a word or phrase, not all of them. To instruct Word to confirm each change, click the Find button (Find and Replace sidebar) (Figure 2–68 on the previous page), instead of the Replace All button. When Word locates an occurrence of the text, it pauses and waits for you to click either the Replace button or the Find button. Clicking the Replace button changes the text; clicking the Find Next button instructs Word to disregard the replacement and look for the next occurrence of the Find what text.

If you accidentally replace the wrong text, you can undo a replacement by clicking the Undo button on the Standard toolbar. If you used the Replace All button, Word undoes all replacements. If you used the Replace button, Word undoes only the most recent replacement.

To Go to a Page

The next step in revising the paper is to change a word on the second page of the document. You could scroll to the location in the document, or as mentioned earlier, you can use the Sidebar to browse through pages in a document. The following steps display the top of the second page in the document window and position the insertion point at the beginning of that page.

- In the Search pane, delete the search text from the text box. Click the Thumbnails Pane button to display thumbnail images of the document pages in the Sidebar (Figure 2–69).

Q&A Why did I have to delete the search text?
If there is search text specified, only the thumbnails for the pages containing the search text will display. Deleting the search text results in thumbnails of all pages in the document being displayed.

- Click the thumbnail of the second page, even if the second page already is selected, to display the top of the selected page in the top of the document window (shown in Figure 2–70).

- Click the Close button in the Sidebar to close the Thumbnails pane.

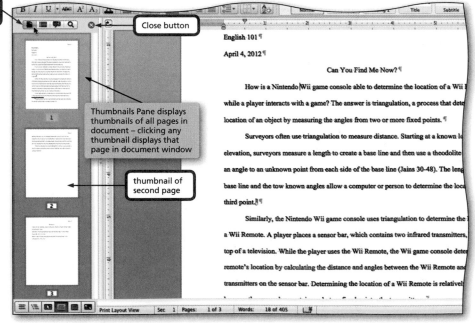

Figure 2–69

Other Ways

1. Choose Edit > Find > Go To to display Find and Replace dialog, enter page number, click Go To button
2. Click Select Browse Object button in vertical scroll bar, click Go To icon on

Select Browse Object menu, enter page number (Find and Replace dialog), click Go To button
3. Click Page Number indicator on status bar, click Go To tab (Find and

Replace dialog), enter page number, click Go To button
4. Press COMMAND-OPTION-G, enter page number, click Go To button

To Find and Insert a Synonym

When writing, you may discover that you used the same word in multiple locations or that a word you used was not quite appropriate. In these instances, you will want to look up a **synonym**, or a word similar in meaning, to the duplicate or inappropriate word. A **thesaurus** is a book of synonyms. Word provides synonyms and a thesaurus for your convenience.

In this project, you would like a synonym for the word, prescribed, in the fourth paragraph of the research paper. The following steps find a suitable synonym.

- Locate and then CONTROL-click the word for which you want to find a synonym (in this case, prescribed) to display a shortcut menu related to the word you CONTROL-clicked.

- Point to Synonyms in the shortcut menu to display a list of synonyms for the word you CONTROL-clicked (Figure 2–70).

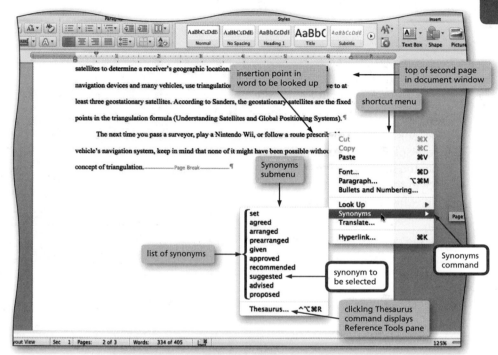

Figure 2–70

- Click the synonym you want (in this case, suggested) in the Synonyms submenu to replace the selected word in the document with the selected synonym (Figure 2–71).

Q&A — What if the synonyms list in the shortcut menu does not display a suitable word?
You can display the thesaurus in the Reference Tools toolbox by clicking Thesaurus in the Synonyms submenu. The Reference Tools toolbox displays a thesaurus, in which you can look up synonyms for various meanings of a word. The Reference Tools toolbox is discussed later in this chapter.

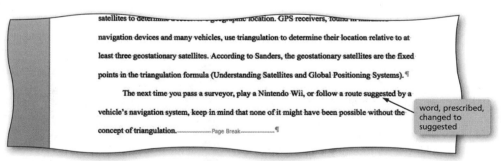

Figure 2–71

Other Ways

1. Click Toolbox button in Standard toolbar, click Reference Tools icon, enter word in Word or Phrase text box, click Thesaurus

2. Choose Tools > Thesaurus

3. Press CONTROL-OPTION-COMMAND-R

To Check Spelling and Grammar at Once

As discussed in Chapter 1, Word checks spelling and grammar as you type and places a wavy underline below possible spelling or grammar errors. Chapter 1 illustrated how to check these flagged words immediately. As an alternative, you can wait and check the entire document for spelling and grammar errors at once. The next steps check spelling and grammar at once.

Note: In the following steps, the word, theodolite, has been misspelled intentionally as theadalight to illustrate the use of Word's check spelling and grammar at once feature. If you are completing this project on a personal computer, your research paper may contain different misspelled words, depending on the accuracy of your typing.

- Press FUNCTION-COMMAND-LEFT ARROW because you want the spelling and grammar check to begin from the top of the document.

- Click Tools in the menu bar, then choose Spelling and Grammar to begin the spelling and grammar check at the location of the insertion point, which in this case, is at the beginning of the document.

- Click the desired spelling in the Suggestions list (theodolite, in this case) (Figure 2–72).

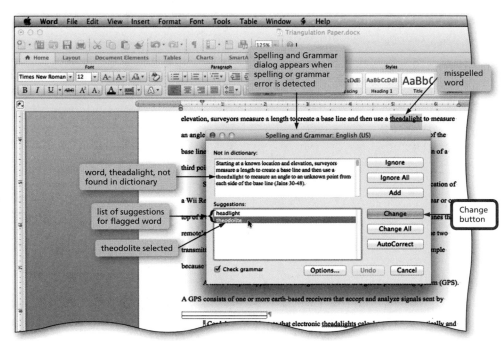

Figure 2–72

- With the word, theodolite, selected in the Suggestions list, click the Change button (Spelling and Grammar dialog) to change the flagged word to the selected suggestion and then continue the spelling and grammar check until the next error is identified or the end of the document is reached (Figure 2–73).

- Click the Ignore All button (Spelling and Grammar dialog) to ignore this and future occurrences of the flagged proper noun and then continue the spelling and grammar check until the next error is identified or the end of the document is reached.

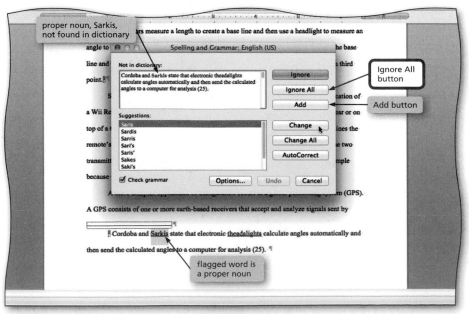

Figure 2–73

4

- When the spelling and grammar check is finished and Word displays a dialog, click its OK button.

Q&A Can I check spelling of just a section of a document?
Yes, select the text before starting the spelling and grammar check.

● Other Ways

1. CONTROL-click flagged word, click Spelling in shortcut menu

2. Choose Tools > Spelling and Grammar in menu bar

3. Click Spelling and Grammar Status icon in status bar

4. Press OPTION-COMMAND-L

The Main and Custom Dictionaries

As shown in the steps on the previous page, Word may flag a proper noun as an error because the proper noun is not in its main dictionary. To prevent Word from flagging proper nouns as errors, you can add the proper nouns to the custom dictionary. To add a correctly spelled word to the custom dictionary, click the Add button (Spelling and Grammar dialog) or CONTROL-click the flagged word and then click Add in the shortcut menu. Once you have added a word to the custom dictionary, Word no longer will flag it as an error.

TO VIEW OR MODIFY ENTRIES IN A CUSTOM DICTIONARY

To view or modify the list of words in a custom dictionary, you would follow these steps.

1. Click Word in the menu bar, and then click Preferences to display the Preferences dialog.

2. Choose Spelling and Grammar to display the Spelling and Grammar dialog.

3. Click the Dictionaries button.

4. When Word displays the Custom Dictionaries dialog, place a check mark next to the dictionary name to view or modify. Click the Edit button (Custom Dictionaries dialog) and then click OK in the dialog to display the Custom dictionary as a document. (In this dialog, you can add or delete entries to and from the selected custom dictionary.)

5. When finished viewing and/or modifying the list, click the Save button in the dialog.

6. Click the OK button (Custom Dictionaries dialog).

7. If the 'Suggest from main dictionary only' check box is selected in the Word Options dialog, remove the check mark. Click the OK button (Word Options dialog).

TO SET THE DEFAULT CUSTOM DICTIONARY

If you have multiple custom dictionaries, you can specify which one Word should use when checking spelling. To set the default custom dictionary, you would follow these steps.

1. Click Word in the menu bar, and then click Preferences to display the Preferences dialog.

2. Choose Spelling and Grammar to display the Spelling and Grammar dialog.

3. Click the Dictionaries button.

4. When the Custom Dictionaries dialog is displayed, place a check mark next to the desired dictionary name. Click the Change Default button (Custom Dictionaries dialog).

Readability Statistics

You can instruct Word to display readability statistics when it has finished a spelling and grammar check on a document. Three readability statistics presented are the percent of passive sentences, the Flesch Reading Ease score, and the Flesch-Kincaid Grade Level score. The Flesch Reading Ease score uses a 100-point scale to rate the ease with which a reader can understand the text in a document. A higher score means the document is easier to understand. The Flesch-Kincaid Grade Level score rates the text in a document on a U.S. school grade level. For example, a score of 10.0 indicates a student in the tenth grade can understand the material. To show readability statistics when the spelling and grammar check is complete, choose Preferences from the Word menu, and then click Spelling and Grammar under Authoring and Proofing Tools. In the Spelling and Grammar dialog, under Grammar, place a check mark in the 'Show readability statistics' check box, and then click the OK button. Readability statistics will be displayed the next time you check spelling and grammar at once in the document.

5. Click the OK button (Custom Dictionaries dialog).

6. If the 'Suggest from main dictionary only' check box is selected in the Word Options dialog, remove the check mark. Click the OK button (Word Options dialog).

To Use the Reference Tools Toolbox to Look Up Information

From within Word, you can search through various forms of reference information. Earlier, this chapter discussed the Reference Tools toolbox with respect to looking up a synonym in a thesaurus. Other services available in the Reference Tools toolbox include a dictionary, bilingual dictionary, translation, and, if you are connected to the Web, a Web Search tool.

Assume you want to know more about the word, geostationary. The following steps use the Reference Tools toolbox to look up a definition of a word.

- Locate the word you want to look up.

- While holding down the CONTROL key, click the word you want to look up (in this case, geostationary) and choose Look Up and then choose Definition from the shortcut menu to open the toolbox and display a dictionary entry for the CONTROL-clicked word. Release the CONTROL key.

- If necessary, in the toolbox, click Web Search to display the results of a search on your search term from a list of search locations (Figure 2–74).

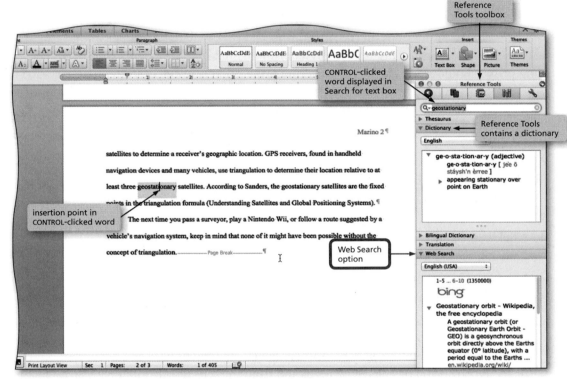

Figure 2–74

Q&A   Why does my Reference Tools toolbox look different?
Depending on your settings and Microsoft's Web site search settings, your Reference Tools pane may appear different from the figure shown here. For example, you may need to click to allow access to online Reference tools.

Q&A   Can I copy information from the Reference Tools pane into my document?
Yes, you can use the Copy and Paste commands. When using Word to insert material from the Reference Tools pane or any other online reference, however, be careful not to plagiarize. You can also double-click an online reference to open it in your Web browser.

- Click the Close button in the toolbox.

To Change Document Properties

Before saving the research paper again, you want to add your name, course information, and some keywords as document properties. The following steps use the Properties dialog to change document properties.

1 Click File in the menu bar to display the File menu.

2 Choose Properties to open the Properties dialog.

3 On the Summary tab, click the Author text box, if necessary, and then type your name as the Author property. If a name already is displayed in the Author text box, delete it before typing your name.

4 Click the Subject text box, if necessary delete any existing text, and then type your course and section as the Subject property.

5 If an AutoComplete dialog appears, click its Yes button.

6 Click the Keywords text box, if necessary delete any existing text, and then type `surveyor, Wii, GPS` as the Keywords property.

7 Click the OK button to close the Properties dialog.

Conserving Ink and Toner

If you want to conserve ink or toner, you can instruct Word to print draft quality documents by choosing File > Print in the menu bar, clicking the Presets box arrow (Print dialog), and selecting Plain paper, Fast draft, or Plain paper, Fast draft, black and white, and then clicking the Print button to print the document. **BTW**

To Save an Existing Document with the Same File Name

You have made several modifications to the document since you last saved it. Thus, you should save it again. The following step saves the document again.

1 Click the Save button on the Standard toolbar to overwrite the previously saved file.

To Print Document Properties

With the document properties entered and the completed document saved, you may want to print the document properties along with the document. The following steps print the document properties for the Triangulation Paper.

1

- Click File in the menu bar to display the File menu.

- Choose Print to open the Print dialog.

- Verify the printer name that appears in the Printer text box will print a hard copy of the document. If necessary, click the Printer box arrow to display a list of available printer options and then click the desired printer to change the currently selected printer (Figure 2–75).

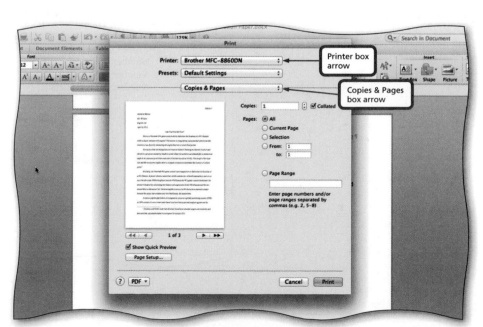

Figure 2–75

2

- Click the Copies & Pages box arrow and select Microsoft Word from the list.

- Click the Print What box arrow to display a list of options specifying what you can print (Figure 2–76).

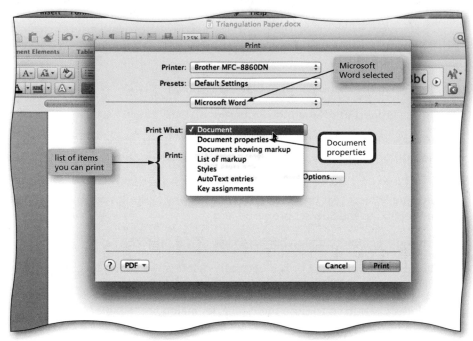

Figure 2–76

3

- Click Document properties in the list to specify you want to print the document properties instead of the actual document.

- Click the Print button in the dialog to print the document properties on the selected printer (Figure 2–77).

Q&A What if the currently updated document properties do not print on the hard copy?
Try closing the document, reopening the document, and then repeating these steps.

Filename:	Triangulation Paper.docx
Folder:	CIS 101:Word
Template:	Macintosh HD:Users:scseries:Library:Application Support:Microsoft:Office:User Templates:Normal.dotm
Title:	Triangulation Paper
Subject:	English 101
Author:	Annalisa Marino
Keywords:	surveyor, Wii, GPS
Comments:	
Creation Date:	4/4/13 9:54 AM
Change Number:	2
Last Saved On:	4/4/13 5:02 PM
Last Saved By:	Mac User
Total Editing Time:	105 Minutes
Last Printed On:	4/4/13 6:45 PM

As of Last Complete Printing
- Number of Pages: 3
- Number of Words: 420 (approx.)
- Number of Characters: 2,210 (approx.)

Figure 2–77

 Other Ways

1. Press COMMAND-P, click Copies & Pages (Print dialog), choose Microsoft Word, click Print What, choose Document properties, click Print button

To Preview a Document and Then Print It

Before printing the research paper, you want to verify the page layouts. The following steps change the print option to print the document (instead of the document properties), preview the printed pages in the research paper, and then print the document.

1

- With the insertion point at the top of the document, click File in the menu bar to display the File menu.

- Select Print to open the Print dialog that includes a Quick Preview of the printed document.

- Verify the printer name that appears on the Printer text box will print a hard copy of the document. If necessary, select a different printer.

- Ensure that the All option is selected for Pages to specify you want to print all pages in the actual document.

- Click the Next Page button under the Quick Preview to preview the second page of the research paper in the Print dialog.

- Click the Next Page button again to preview the third page of the research paper (Figure 2–78).

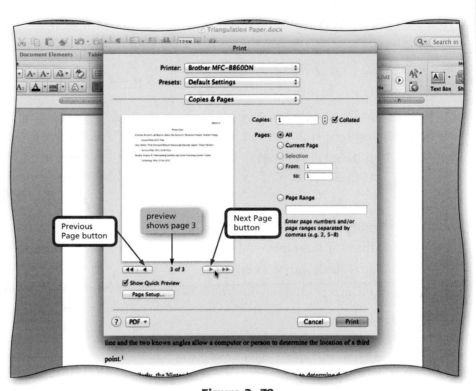

Figure 2–78

2

- Click the Print button in the Print dialog to print the research paper on the currently selected printer (shown in Figure 2–1 on page WD 71).

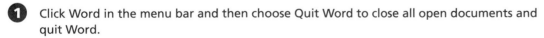

Other Ways

1. Press COMMAND-P, press RETURN

To Quit Word

This project now is complete. The following steps quit Word. For a detailed example of the procedure summarized below, refer to the Office 2011 and Mac OS X chapter at the beginning of this book.

1 Click Word in the menu bar and then choose Quit Word to close all open documents and quit Word.

2 If a Word dialog appears, click the Save button to save any changes made to the document since the last save.

Quick Reference

For a table that lists how **BTW** to complete the tasks covered in this book using the mouse, ribbon, shortcut menu, and keyboard, see the Quick Reference Summary at the back of this book, or visit the Office 2011 for Mac Online Companion Web page at www.cengagebrain.com, navigate to the desired application, and click Quick Reference.

Chapter Summary

In this chapter, you have learned how to change document settings, use headers to number pages, modify a style, insert and edit citations and their sources, add footnotes, create a bibliographical list of sources, and use the Reference Tools toolbox. The items listed below include all the new Word skills you have learned in this chapter.

1. Show the Toolbox (WD 75)
2. Modify a Style (WD 76)
3. Change Line Spacing (WD 78)
4. Remove Space after a Paragraph (WD 78)
5. Update a Style to Match a Selection (WD 79)
6. Switch to the Header (WD 80)
7. Right-Align a Paragraph (WD 81)
8. Insert a Page Number (WD 81)
9. Close the Header (WD 82)
10. Click and Type (WD 83)
11. Hide or Display the Rulers (WD 86)
12. First-Line Indent Paragraphs (WD 86)
13. AutoCorrect as You Type (WD 88)
14. Use the AutoCorrect Options Button (WD 89)
15. Create an AutoCorrect Entry (WD 90)
16. Change the Bibliography Style (WD 92)
17. Insert a Citation and Create Its Source (WD 93)
18. Edit a Citation (WD 95)
19. Insert a Footnote Reference Mark (WD 97)
20. Modify a Style Using a Shortcut Menu (WD 99)
21. Enter a Source (WD 100)
22. Count Words (WD 103)
23. Page Break Manually (WD 107)
24. Create the Bibliographical List (WD 108)
25. Format Paragraphs with a Hanging Indent (WD 109)
26. Modify a Source and Update the Bibliographical List (WD 110)
27. Convert a Field to Regular Text (WD 110)
28. Scroll Page by Page through a Document (WD 113)
29. Copy and Paste (WD 114)
30. Display the Paste Options Menu (WD 115)
31. Find Text (WD 116)
32. Replace Text (WD 117)
33. Go to a Page (WD 118)
34. Find and Insert a Synonym (WD 119)
35. Check Spelling and Grammar at Once (WD 120)
36. View or Modify Entries in a Custom Dictionary (WD 121)
37. Set the Default Custom Dictionary (WD 121)
38. Use the Reference Tools Toolbox to Look Up Information (WD 122)
39. Print Document Properties (WD 123)
40. Preview a Document and Then Print It (WD 125)

If you have a SAM 2010 user profile, your instructor may have assigned an autogradable version of this assignment. If so, log into the SAM 2010 Web site at www.cengage.com/sam2010 to download the instruction and start files.

Learn It Online

Test your knowledge of chapter content and key terms.

Instructions: To complete the Learn It Online exercises, please visit **www.cengagebrain.com.** At the CengageBrain.com home page, search for *Office 2011 for Mac* using the search box at the top of the page. This will take you to the product page for this book. On the product page, click the Access Now button below the Study Tools heading. On the Book Companion Site Web page, select Word Chapter 2, and then click the link for the desired exercise.

Chapter Reinforcement TF, MC, and SA
A series of true/false, multiple choice, and short answer questions that test your knowledge of the chapter content.

Flash Cards
An interactive learning environment where you identify chapter key terms associated with displayed definitions.

Practice Test
A series of multiple choice questions that test your knowledge of chapter content and key terms.

Who Wants To Be a Computer Genius?
An interactive game that challenges your knowledge of chapter content in the style of a television quiz show.

Wheel of Terms
An interactive game that challenges your knowledge of chapter key terms in the style of the television show *Wheel of Fortune*.

Crossword Puzzle Challenge
A crossword puzzle that challenges your knowledge of key terms presented in the chapter.

Apply Your Knowledge

Reinforce the skills and apply the concepts you learned in this chapter.

Revising Text and Paragraphs in a Document
Note: To complete this assignment, you will be required to use the Data Files for Students. See the inside back cover of this book for instructions on downloading the Data Files for Students, or contact your instructor for information about accessing the required files.

Instructions: Start Word. Open the document, Apply 2–1 Space Paragraph Draft, from the Data Files for Students. The document you open contains a paragraph of text. You are to revise the document as follows: move a word, move another word and change the format of the moved word, change paragraph indentation, change line spacing, find all occurrences of a word, replace all occurrences of a word with another word, locate a synonym, and edit the header.

Perform the following tasks:
1. Copy the word, exploration, from the first sentence and paste it in the last sentence after the word, space, so that it is the eighth word in the sentence.
2. Select the underlined word, safe, in the paragraph. Use drag-and-drop editing to move the selected word, safe, so that it is before the word, mission, in the same sentence. Click the Paste Options button that displays to the right of the moved word, safe. Remove the underline format from the moved sentence by clicking Keep Text Only in the Paste Options menu.
3. Display the ruler, if necessary. Use the ruler to indent the first line of the paragraph one-half inch.
4. Change the line spacing of the paragraph to double.

Continued >

Apply Your Knowledge *continued*

5. Use the Sidebar to find all occurrences of the word, sensors. How many are there?

6. Use the Find and Replace dialog to replace all occurrences of the word, issues, with the word, problems. How many replacements were made?

7. Use Word to find the word, height. Use Word's thesaurus to change the word, height, to the word, altitude.

8. Switch to the header so that you can edit it. In the first line of the header, change the word, Draft, to the word, Modified, so that it reads: Space Paragraph Modified.

9. In the second line of the header, insert the page number (with no formatting) one space after the word, Page.

10. Change the alignment of both lines of text in the header from left-aligned to right-aligned. Switch back to the document text.

11. Change the document properties, as specified by your instructor.

12. Click File in the menu bar and then choose Save As. Save the document using the file name, Apply 2–1 Space Paragraph Modified.

13. Print the document properties and then print the revised document, shown in Figure 2–79.

14. Use the Reference Tools in the toolbox to look up the definition of the word, NASA, in the paragraph. Handwrite the definition of the word on your printout, as well as your responses to the questions in #5 and #6.

15. Print an article from one of the sites listed in the Web Search section of the Reference Tools.

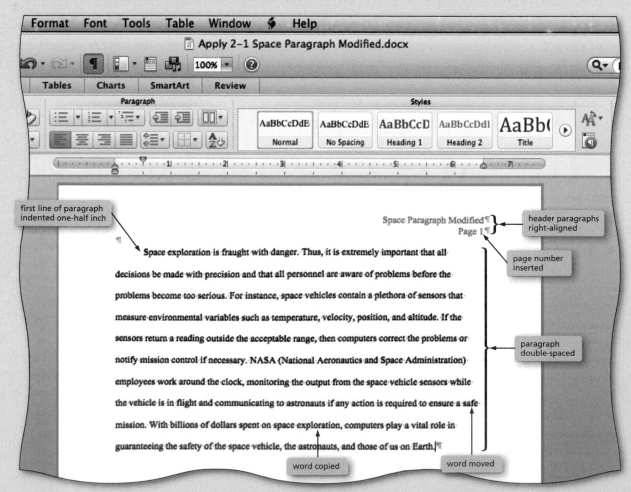

Figure 2–79

Extend Your Knowledge

Extend the skills you learned in this chapter and experiment with new skills. You may need to use Help to complete the assignment.

Working with References and Proofing Tools

Note: To complete this assignment, you will be required to use the Data Files for Students. See the inside back cover of this book for instructions on downloading the Data Files for Students, or contact your instructor for information about accessing the required files.

Instructions: Start Word. Open the document, Extend 2–1 Digital Camera Paper Draft, from the Data Files for Students. You will add another footnote to the paper, use the thesaurus, convert the document from MLA to APA documentation style, convert the footnotes to endnotes, modify the Endnote Text style, change the format of the note reference marks, and translate the document to another language (Figure 2–80).

research paper translated from English to German

Figure 2–80

Perform the following tasks:

1. Use Help to learn more about footers, footnotes and endnotes, bibliography styles, AutoCorrect, and the Translation feature.

2. Delete the footer from the document.

3. Insert a second footnote at an appropriate place in the research paper. Use the following footnote text: For instance, Adams states that you may be able to crop photos, change the brightness, or remove red eye effects.

4. Change the location of the footnotes from the bottom of the page to beneath text.

5. Use the Find and Replace Sidebar to find the word, small, in the document and then replace it with a word of your choice.

6. Save the document with a new file name and then print it. On the printout, write the number of words, characters without spaces, characters with spaces, paragraphs, and lines in the document. Be sure to include footnote text in the statistics.

7. Select the entire document and then change the documentation style of the citations and bibliography to APA. Save the APA version of the document with a new file name and then print it. Compare the two versions. Circle the differences between the two documents.

8. Convert the footnotes to endnotes.

Continued >

Extend Your Knowledge *continued*

9. Modify the Endnote Text style to 12-point Times New Roman font, double-spaced text with a hanging-line indent.

10. Change the format of the note reference marks to capital letters (A, B, etc.).

11. Add an AutoCorrect entry that replaces the word, camora, with the word, camera. Add this sentence, A field camora usually is more than sufficient for most users., to the end of the second paragraph, misspelling the word camera to test the AutoCorrect entry. Delete the AutoCorrect entry that replaces camora with the word, camera.

12. Display readability statistics. What are the Flesch-Kincaid Grade Level, the Flesch Reading Ease score, and the percent of passive sentences?

13. Save the revised document with endnotes with a new file name and then print it. On the printout, write your response to the question in #12.

14. If you have an Internet connection, translate the research paper into a language of your choice using the Translate feature on the Reference Tools pane of the Toolbox. Submit the translated document in the format specified by your instructor.

Make It Right

Analyze a document and correct all errors and/or improve the design.

Inserting Missing Elements in an MLA-Styled Research Paper

Note: To complete this assignment, you will be required to use the Data Files for Students. See the inside back cover of this book for instructions on downloading the Data Files for Students, or contact your instructor for information about accessing the required files.

Instructions: Start Word. Open the document, Make It Right 2–1 Biometrics Paper Draft, from the Data Files for Students. The document is a research paper that is missing several elements. You are to insert these missing elements, all formatted according to the MLA documentation style: header with a page number, name and course information, paper title, footnote, and source information for a citation.

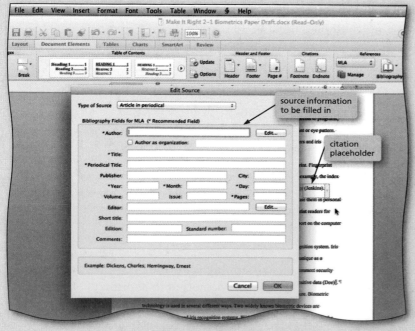

Figure 2–81

Perform the following tasks:

1. Insert a header with a page number (use your own last name), name and course information (your name, your instructor name, your course name, and today's date), and an appropriate paper title, all formatted according to the MLA documentation style.

2. The Jenkins citation placeholder is missing its source information (Figure 2–81). Use the following source information to edit the source: magazine article titled "Fingerprint Readers" written by Arthur D. Jenkins and Marissa K. Weavers, magazine name is *Security Today*, publication date is February 20, 2013, article is on pages 55–60. Edit the citation so that it displays the author name and the page numbers of 55–56 for this reference.

3. Modify the source of the book authored by Carolina Doe, so that the publisher city is Chicago instead of Dallas.

4. Change the Footnote Text style to 12-point Times New Roman, double-spaced paragraphs with a first-line indent.

5. Insert the following footnote with the note reference at an appropriate place in the paper, formatted according to the MLA documentation style: Parlor states that one use of fingerprint readers is for users to log on to programs and Web sites via their fingerprint instead of entering a user name and password.

6. Use the Thumbnails pane on the Sidebar to display page 3. Use Word to insert the bibliographical list (bibliography). Convert the works cited to regular text. Change the underline format on the titles of the works to the italic format, and insert the correct publication medium for each work. Change the Works Cited title format to match the formatting of the references, and center it.

7. Change the document properties, as specified by your instructor. Save the revised document with the file name, Make It Right 2–1 Biometrics Paper Modified, and then submit it in the format specified by your instructor.

In the Lab

Design and/or create a document using the guidelines, concepts, and skills presented in this chapter. Labs are listed in order of increasing difficulty.

Lab 1: Preparing a Short Research Paper

Problem: You are a college student currently enrolled in an introductory business class. Your assignment is to prepare a short research paper (275–300 words) about video or computer games. The requirements are that the paper be presented according to the MLA documentation style and have three references. One of the three references must be from the Web. You prepare the paper shown in Figure 2–82 on pages WD 132 and WD 133, which discusses game controllers.

Instructions: Perform the following tasks:

1. Start Word. If necessary, display formatting marks on the screen.

2. Modify the Normal style to 12-point Times New Roman font.

3. Adjust line spacing to double. If necessary, remove space below (after) paragraphs.

4. Set margins to Normal.

5. Update the Normal style to reflect the adjusted line and paragraph spacing.

6. Create a header to number pages.

7. Type the name and course information at the left margin. Center and type the title.

8. Set a first-line indent to one-half inch for paragraphs in the body of the research paper.

9. Type the research paper as shown in Figures 2–82a and 2–82b. Set the bibliography style to MLA. As you insert citations, enter their source information (shown in Figure 2–82c). Edit the citations so that they are displayed according to Figures 2–82a and 2–82b.

10. At the end of the research paper text, press the RETURN key and then insert a manual page break so that the Works Cited page begins on a new page. Use Word to insert the Works Cited list (bibliography). Convert the bibliography field to text. Format the Works Cited heading to match Figure 2–82c. Change the underline format on the titles of the works to the italic format and insert the correct publication medium for each work (shown in Figure 2–82c).

11. Check the spelling and grammar of the paper at once.

Continued >

In the Lab *continued*

(a) Page 1

Kimble 1

Harley Kimble

Ms. Longherst

English 101

April 30, 2012

From One Controller to Another

Video games and computer games use a game controller as the input device that directs

movements and actions of on-screen objects. Two commonly used game controllers are

gamepads and motion-sensing game controllers (Joyce). Game controllers not only enrich the

gaming experience but also aid in the movements and actions of players.

A gamepad is held by the player with both hands, allowing the player to control the

movement or actions of the objects in the video or computer games. Players press buttons on the

gamepad, often with their thumbs, to carry out actions. Some gamepads have swiveling sticks

that also can trigger events during game play (Cortez 20-24). Some gamepads include wireless

capabilities; others connect via a cable directly to the game console or a personal computer.

Motion-sensing game controllers allow the user to guide on-screen elements or trigger

events by moving a handheld input device in predetermined directions through the air. These

controllers communicate with a game console or personal computer via wired or wireless

technology. A variety of games, from sports to simulations, use motion-sensing game controllers.

Some of these controllers, such as baseball bats and golf clubs, are designed for only one specific

kind of game; others are general purpose. A popular general-purpose, motion-sensing game

controller is Nintendo's Wii Remote. Shaped like a television remote control and operated with

one hand, the Wii Remote uses Bluetooth wireless technology to communicate with the Wii

game console (Bloom 56-59).

(b) Page 2

Kimble 2

Game controllers are used primarily to direct movement and actions of on-screen objects.

Two popular types are gamepads and motion-sensing game controllers. Games become more

enjoyable everyday with the use of new and exciting game controllers. What will be next?

Figure 2–82

(c) Page 3

Kimble 3

Works Cited

Bloom, June. *The Gaming Experience*. New York: Buffalo Works Press, 2012. Print.

Cortez, Dom I., and Mark W. Mathews. "Today's Game Controllers." *Gaming, Gaming, Gaming*
Jan. 2012: 12-34. Print.

Joyce, Andrea D. *What Gamers Want*. 15 Feb. 2012. Web. 28 Mar. 2012.

Figure 2–82 *(continued)*

12. Change the document properties, as specified by your instructor. Save the document using Lab 2–1 Game Controllers Paper as the file name.

13. Print the research paper. Handwrite the number of words, paragraphs, and characters in the research paper above the title of your printed research paper.

In the Lab

Lab 2: Preparing a Research Report with a Footnote

Problem: You are a college student enrolled in an introductory English class. Your assignment is to prepare a short research paper in any area of interest to you. The requirements are that the paper be presented according to the MLA documentation style, contain at least one note positioned as a footnote, and have three references. One of the three references must be from the Internet. You prepare a paper about trends in agriculture (Figure 2–83 on the next page).

Instructions: Perform the following tasks:

1. Start Word. Modify the Normal style to 12-point Times New Roman font. Adjust line spacing to double and remove space below (after) paragraphs. Update the Normal style to include the adjusted line and paragraph spacing. Create a header to number pages. Type the name and course information at the left margin. Center and type the title. Set a first-line indent for paragraphs in the body of the research paper.

2. Type the research paper as shown in Figures 2–83a and 2–83b. Insert the footnote as shown in Figure 2–83a. Change the Footnote Text style to the format specified in the MLA documentation style. Change the bibliography style to MLA. As you insert citations, use the source information listed below and on page WD 135:

   a. Type of Source: Article in a Periodical
      Author: Barton, Blake
      Title: Computers in Agriculture
      Periodical Title: Agriculture Today and Tomorrow
      Year: 2012
      Month: Feb.
      Pages 53–86
      Publication Medium: Print

Continued >

(a) Page 1

Gander 1

Samuel Gander

Mr. Dunham

English 102

April 25, 2012

Farming on a Whole New Level

Although people have worked in agriculture for more than 10,000 years, advances in

technology assist with maintaining and protecting land, crops, and animals. The demand to keep

food prices affordable encourages those working in the agriculture industry to operate as

efficiently as possible (Newman 33-47).

Almost all people and companies in this industry have many acres of land they must

maintain, and it is not always feasible for farmers to take frequent trips around the property to

perform basic tasks such as watering soil in the absence of rain. The number of people-hours

required to water soil manually on several thousand acres of land might result in businesses

spending thousands of dollars in labor and utility costs. If the irrigation process is automated,

sensors detect how much rain has fallen recently, as well as whether the soil is in need of

watering. The sensors then send this data to a computer that processes it and decides when and

how much to water.[1]

In addition to keeping the soil moist and reducing maintenance costs, computers also can

utilize sensors to analyze the condition of crops in the field and determine whether pests or

diseases are affecting the crops. If sensors detect pest and/or diseases, computers send a

———————————

[1] Barton states that many automated home irrigation systems also are programmable and

use rain sensors (67-73).

(b) Page 2

Gander 2

notification to the appropriate individual to take corrective action. In some cases, according to

Brewster, the discovery of pests might trigger a pesticide to discharge in the affected area

automatically (Agriculture: Expanding and Growing).

Many farmers use technology on a daily basis to regulate soil moisture and to keep their

crops pest free. With technology, farming can be much more convenient and efficient.

Figure 2–83

    b. Type of Source: Book
       Author: Newman, Albert D., and Carmen W. Ruiz
       Title: The Agricultural Industry Today
       Year: 2012
       City: New York
       Publisher: Alabama Press
       Publication Medium: Print

    c. Type of Source: Web site
       Author: Brewster, Letty
       Name of Web page: Agriculture: Expanding and Growing
       Year: 2012
       Month: Jan.
       Day: 3
       Publication Medium: Web
       Year Accessed: 2013
       Month Accessed: Feb.
       Day Accessed: 9

3. At the end of the research paper text, press the RETURN key once and insert a manual page break so that the Works Cited page begins on a new page. Use Word to insert the Works Cited list. Convert the bibliography field to text. Format the works cited title. Change the underline format on the titles of the works to the italic format, and insert the correct publication medium for each work.

4. Check the spelling and grammar of the paper.

5. Save the document using Lab 2–2 Agriculture Paper as the file name.

6. Print the research paper. Handwrite the number of words, including the footnotes, in the research paper above the title of your printed research paper.

In the Lab

Lab 3: Composing a Research Paper from Notes

Problem: You have drafted the notes shown in Figure 2–84 on the next page. Your assignment is to prepare a short research paper from these notes.

Instructions: Perform the following tasks:

1. Start Word. Review the notes in Figure 2–84 and then rearrange and reword them. Embellish the paper as you deem necessary. Present the paper according to the MLA documentation style.

    Create an AutoCorrect entry that automatically corrects the spelling of the misspelled word, digtal, to the correct spelling, digital. Set an AutoCorrect exception for CD, so that Word does not lowercase the next typed letter.

    Insert a footnote that refers the reader to the Web for more information. Enter citations and their sources as shown.

    Create the Works Cited page (bibliography) from the listed sources. Convert the bibliography field to text. Format the Works Cited heading. Change the underline format on the titles of the works to the italic format, and insert the correct publication medium for each work.

2. If necessary, set the default dictionary. Add the word, Flickr, to the dictionary. Check the spelling and grammar of the paper.

Continued >

3. Use the Reference Tools toolbox to look up a definition of a word in the paper. Copy and insert the definition into the document as a footnote. Be sure to quote the definition and cite the source. *Hint:* Use a Web site as the type of source.

4. Save the document using Lab 2–3 Cloud Storage Paper as the file name. Print the research paper. Handwrite the number of words, including the footnotes, in the research paper above the title of the printed research paper.

Cloud Storage:

- When storing data using cloud storage, the user must locate the appropriate Web site. Some sites only support certain file types. Other sites provide more than just storage.
- Cloud storage is one of the many different features available on the Internet.
- Cloud storage allows users to store files on Web sites.
- Computer users may use this type of storage if they do not want to store their data locally on a hard disk or other type of media.

Different Web sites provide different types of cloud storage. Three are Google's Gmail, YouTube, and Windows Live SkyDrive (source: "Cloud Storage and the Internet," an article on pages 23-37 in March 2012 issue of *Internet Usage and Trends* by Leona Carter.)

- Google's e-mail program, Gmail, is cloud storage that stores e-mail messages.
- YouTube is different from Gmail, however, because it stores only digital videos (source: a book called *Working with the Internet: Cloud Storage* by Robert M Gaff, published at Jane Lewis Press in New York in 2012)
- Windows Live SkyDrive is a cloud storage provider that accepts any type of file. This type of Web site is used mainly for backup or additional storage space.

Some cloud storage Web sites also provide other services (source: a Web site titled *The Internet: Cloud Storage* by Rebecca A. Ford and Harry I. Garland of Course Technology dated January 2, 2012, viewed on March 7, 2012.)

- Flickr provides cloud storage for digital photos and also enables users to manage their photos and share them with others.
- Facebook provides cloud storage for a number of different file types including digital photos, digital videos, messages, and personal information. Facebook also provides a means of social networking.
- Google Docs not only stores documents, spreadsheets, and presentations in its cloud, it also enables its users to create these documents (Ford).

Figure 2–84

Cases and Places

Apply your creative thinking and problem solving skills to design and implement a solution.

Note: To complete these assignments, you may be required to use the Data Files for Students. See the inside back cover of this book for instructions on downloading the Data Files for Students, or contact your instructor for information about accessing the required files.

1: Create a Research Paper about Preparing for a Career in the Computer Industry

Academic

As a student in an introductory computer class, your instructor has assigned a research paper that discusses educational options available for students pursuing a career in the computer industry. The source for the text in your research paper is in a file called Preparing for a Career in the Computer Industry, which is located on the Data Files for Students. In addition to this source, if your instructor requests, use the Reference Tools toolbox to obtain information from another source. Include a note positioned as a footnote. Add an AutoCorrect entry to correct a word you commonly mistype.

Using the concepts and techniques presented in this chapter, along with the text in the file on the Data Files for Students, create and format this research paper according to the MLA documentation style. Be sure to check spelling and grammar of the finished paper. Submit your assignment in the format specified by your instructor.

2: Create a Research Paper about Computer Viruses

Personal

The computer you recently purchased included an antivirus program. Because you need practice writing research papers and you want to learn more about computer viruses, you decide to write a paper about computer viruses. The source for the text in your research paper is in a file called Computer Viruses, which is located on the Data Files for Students. In addition to this source, if your instructor requests, use the Reference Tools toolbox to obtain information from another source. Include a note positioned as a footnote. Add an AutoCorrect entry to correct a word you commonly mistype.

Using the concepts and techniques presented in this chapter, along with the text in the file on the Data Files for Students, create and format this research paper according to the MLA documentation style. Be sure to check spelling and grammar of the finished paper. Submit your assignment in the format specified by your instructor.

3: Create a Research Paper about a Disaster Recovery Plan

Professional

Your boss has asked you to research the components of a disaster recovery plan. Because you learned in college how to write research papers, you decide to present your findings in a research paper. The source for the text in your research paper is in a file called Disaster Recovery Plan, which is located on the Data Files for Students. In addition to this source, if your instructor requests, use the Reference Tools toolbox to obtain information from another source. Include a note positioned as a footnote. Add an AutoCorrect entry to correct a word you commonly mistype.

Using the concepts and techniques presented in this chapter, along with the text in the file on the Data Files for Students, create and format this research paper according to the MLA documentation style. Be sure to check spelling and grammar of the finished paper. Submit your assignment in the format specified by your instructor.

3 Creating a Business Letter with a Letterhead and Table

Objectives

You will have mastered the material in this chapter when you can:

- Change margins
- Insert and format a shape
- Change text wrapping
- Find and download clip art
- Insert and format a clip art image
- Insert a symbol
- Add a border to a paragraph
- Clear formatting
- Convert a hyperlink to regular text

- Create a file from an existing file
- Apply a Quick Style
- Set and use tab stops
- Insert the current date
- Create and insert an AutoText entry
- Insert a Word table, enter data in the table, and format the table
- Address and print an envelope

3 Creating a Business Letter with a Letterhead and Table

Introduction

In a business environment, people use documents to communicate with others. Business documents can include letters, memos, newsletters, proposals, and resumes. An effective business document clearly and concisely conveys its message and has a professional, organized appearance. You can use your own creative skills to design and compose business documents. Using Word, for example, you can develop the content and decide on the location of each item in a business document.

Project — Business Letter with a Letterhead and Table

At some time, you will prepare some type of business letter. Contents of business letters include requests, inquiries, confirmations, acknowledgements, recommendations, notifications, responses, invitations, offers, referrals, complaints, and more.

The project in this chapter follows generally accepted guidelines for writing letters and uses Word to create the business letter shown in Figure 3–1. This business letter to a potential advertiser (Wilcox Tractor Restorations) includes a custom letterhead, as well as all essential business letter components: date line, inside address, salutation, body, complimentary close, and signature block. To easily present the advertisement rates, this information appears in a table, and the discounts are in a bulleted list.

Overview

As you read through this chapter, you will learn how to create the business letter in Figure 3–1 by performing these general tasks:

- Design and create a letterhead.
- Compose a business letter.
- Print the business letter.
- Address and print an envelope.

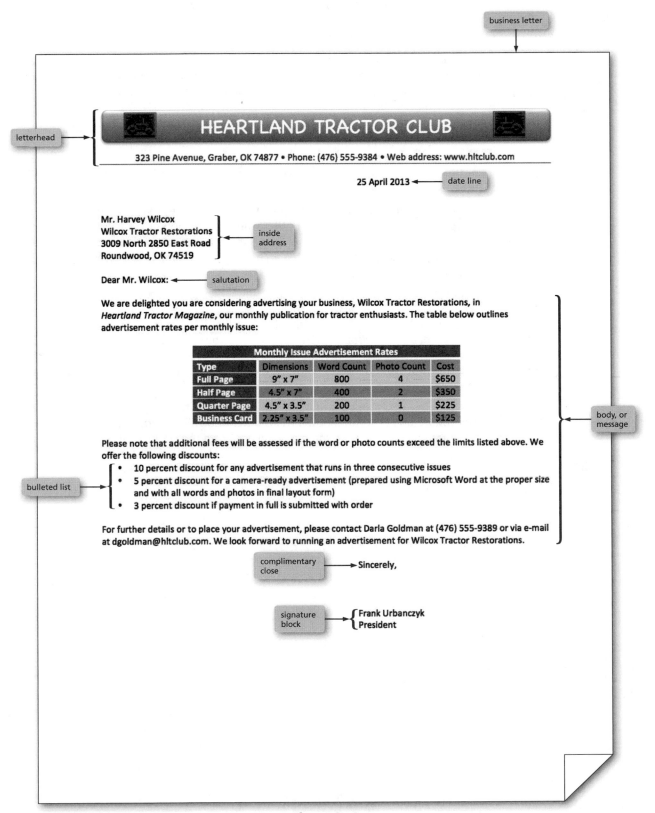

Figure 3–1

Plan Ahead

General Project Guidelines

When creating a Word document, the actions you perform and decisions you make will affect the appearance and characteristics of the finished document. As you create a business letter, such as the project shown in Figure 3–1 on the previous page, you should follow these general guidelines:

1. **Determine how to create a letterhead.** A **letterhead** is the section of a letter that identifies an organization or individual. Often, the letterhead appears at the top of a letter. Although you can design and print a letterhead yourself, many businesses pay an outside firm to design and print their letterhead, usually on higher-quality paper. They then use the professionally preprinted paper for external business communications.

2. **If you do not have preprinted letterhead paper, design a creative letterhead.** Use text, graphics, formats, and colors that reflect the organization or individual. Include the organization's or individual's name, postal mailing address, and telephone number. If the organization or individual has an e-mail address and Web address, you may include those as well.

3. **Compose an effective business letter.** A finished business letter should look like a symmetrically framed picture with evenly spaced margins, all balanced below an attractive letterhead. The letter should be well-written, properly formatted, logically organized, and use visuals where appropriate. The content of a letter should contain proper grammar, correct spelling, logically constructed sentences, flowing paragraphs, and sound ideas. If possible, keep the length of a business letter to one page. Be sure to proofread the finished letter carefully.

When necessary, more specific details concerning the above guidelines are presented at appropriate points in the chapter. The chapter also will identify the actions performed and decisions made regarding these guidelines during the creation of the business letter shown in Figure 3–1.

For an introduction to Mac OS X and instruction about how to perform basic Mac OS X tasks, read the Office 2011 and Mac OS X chapter at the beginning of this book, where you can learn how to resize windows, change screen resolution, create folders, move and rename files, use Mac OS X Help, and much more.

For an introduction to Office 2011 and instruction about how to perform basic tasks in Office 2011 programs, read the Office 2011 and Mac OS X chapter at the beginning of this book, where you can learn how to start a program, use the ribbon, save a file, open a file, quit a program, use Help, and much more.

To Start Word and Display Formatting Marks

If you are using a computer to step through the project in this chapter and you want your screens to match the figures in this book, you should change your screen's resolution to 1280 × 800. For information about how to change a computer's resolution, refer to the Office 2011 and Mac OS X chapter at the beginning of this book.

The following steps start Word and display formatting marks.

1 Start Word and open a blank Word document if necessary. If necessary, size the Word window as described in the Office 2011 and Mac OS X chapter.

2 If the Print Layout View button in the bottom left of the document window is not selected (shown in Figure 3–2), click it so that your screen is in Print Layout view.

3 Change your zoom to 125% (or a percent where the document is large enough for you easily to see its contents).

4 If the Show (¶) button on the Standard toolbar is not selected already, click it to display formatting marks on the screen.

To Change Margin Settings

Word is preset to use standard 8.5-by-11-inch paper, with 1-inch top and bottom, and 1.25-inch left and right margins. Changing the document theme can alter the margins. If you change the default (preset) margin settings, the new margin settings affect every page in the document.

The business letter in this chapter uses .75-inch left and right margins and 1-inch top and bottom margins, so that more text can fit from left to right on the page. The following steps change margin settings.

1 On the Layout tab, under Page Setup, click the Margins button to display the Margins pop-up menu (Figure 3–2).

2 Click Moderate in the Margins pop-up menu to change the margins to the specified settings.

Q&A What if the margin settings I want are not in the Margins pop-up menu?
You can click Custom Margins in the Margins pop-up menu and then enter your desired margin values in the top, bottom, left, and right text boxes in the dialog.

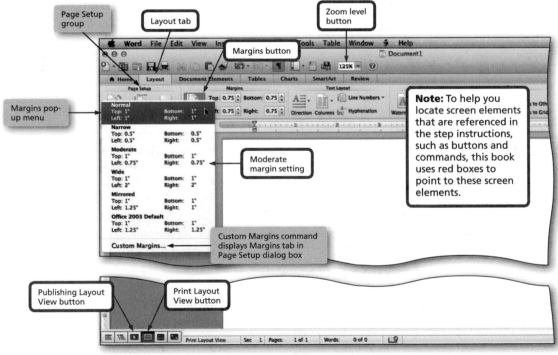

Figure 3–2

Other Ways
1. Position mouse pointer on margin boundary on ruler; when mouse pointer changes to two-headed arrow, drag margin boundary on ruler

To Change the Color Scheme

The next steps change the color scheme for the letterhead.

1 Click the Publishing Layout View button, and click the Continue button in the dialog that displays to open the existing document in Publishing Layout View.

2 On the Home tab, under Themes, click the Colors button and select the Executive color scheme from the Colors gallery.

3 Click the Print Layout View button at the bottom left of the document window to return to Print Layout view.

Creating a Letterhead

The cost of preprinted letterhead can be high. Thus, an alternative is to create your own letterhead and save it in a file. When you want to create a letter at a later time using the letterhead, simply create a new document from the letterhead file. In this chapter, you create a letterhead and then save it in a file for future use.

Plan Ahead

The Ribbon and Screen Resolution

BTW Word may change how the groups and buttons within the groups appear on the ribbon, depending on the computer's screen resolution. Thus, your ribbon may look different from the ones in this book if you are using a screen resolution other than 1280 × 800.

Design a creative letterhead.

A letterhead often is the first section a reader notices on a letter. Thus, it is important the letterhead appropriately reflect the essence of the business or individual (i.e., formal, technical, creative, etc.). The letterhead should leave ample room for the contents of the letter. When designing a letterhead, consider its contents, placement, and appearance.

- **Contents of letterhead.** A letterhead should contain these elements:
  - Complete legal name of the individual, group, or company
  - Complete mailing address: street address including building, room, suite number, or post office box, along with city, state, and postal code
  - Telephone number(s) and fax number, if one exists

  Many letterheads also include a Web address, an e-mail address, and a logo or other image. If you use an image, select one that expresses your personality or goals.

- **Placement of elements in the letterhead.** Many letterheads center their elements across the top of the page. Others align some or all of the elements with the left or right margins. Sometimes, the elements are split between the top and bottom of the page. For example, a name and logo may be at the top of the page with the address at the bottom of the page.

- **Appearance of letterhead elements.** Use fonts that are easy to read. Give the organization or individual name impact by making its font size larger than the rest of the text in the letterhead. For additional emphasis, consider formatting the name in bold, italic, or a different color. Choose colors that complement each other and convey the goals of the organization or individual.

  When finished designing the letterhead, determine if a divider line would help to visually separate the letterhead from the remainder of the letter.

The letterhead for the business letter in this chapter consists of the organization name, appropriate graphics, postal address, telephone number, and Web address. The name and graphics are enclosed in a rectangular shape (Figure 3–1 on page WD 141), and the contact information is below the shape. You will follow these general steps to create the letterhead for the business letter:

1. Insert and format a shape.
2. Enter and format the organization name in the shape.
3. Insert, format, and position the images in the shape.
4. Enter the contact information below the shape.
5. Add a border below the contact information.

To Insert a Shape

The first step in creating the letterhead in this chapter is to draw a rectangular shape. Word has a variety of predefined shapes, which are a type of drawing object, that you can insert in documents. A **drawing object** is a graphic that you create using Word. Examples of shape drawing objects include rectangles, circles, triangles, arrows, flowcharting symbols, stars, banners, and callouts. The next steps insert a rounded rectangle shape.

1

- On the Home tab, under Insert, click the Shape button and then point to Rectangles to display the Rectangles gallery (Figure 3–3).

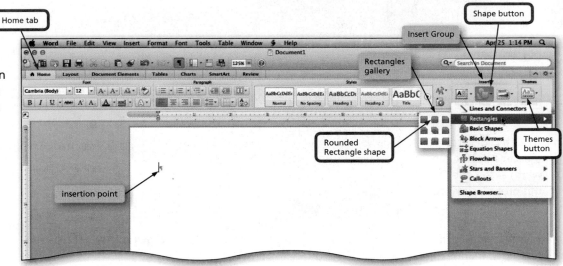

Figure 3–3

2

- Click the Rounded Rectangle shape in the Rectangles gallery (first row, second column), which removes the gallery and changes the mouse pointer to the shape of a crosshair.

- Position the mouse pointer (a crosshair) by the insertion point in the document window, as shown in Figure 3–4, which is the location for the upper-left corner of the desired shape.

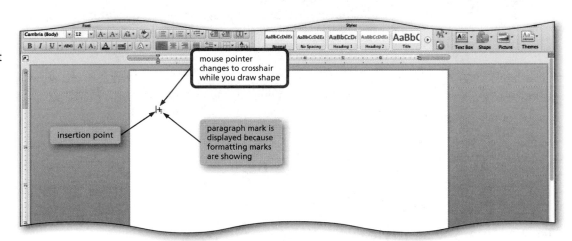

Figure 3–4

Q&A What is the purpose of the crosshair mouse pointer?
In the document window, you will drag the crosshair mouse pointer from the upper-left corner to the lower-right corner to form the desired location and size of the shape.

- Drag the mouse to the right and downward to form the boundaries of the shape, as shown in Figure 3–5, until the measurements match those in the figure. Do not release the mouse button.

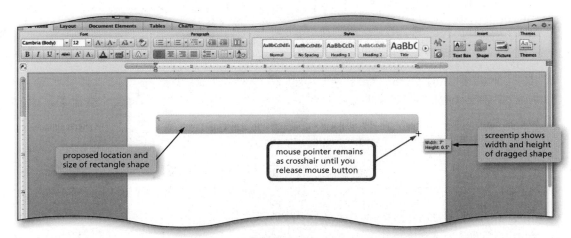

Figure 3–5

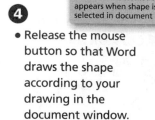

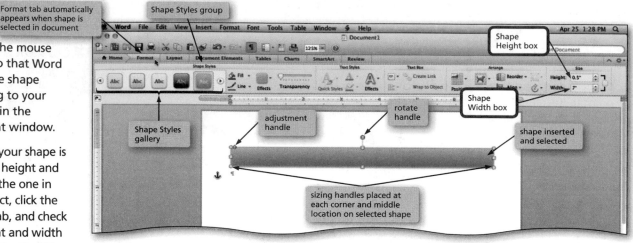

4

- Release the mouse button so that Word draws the shape according to your drawing in the document window.

- To verify your shape is the same height and width as the one in this project, click the Format tab, and check the height and width boxes under Size. If necessary, change the values in the Height and Width boxes to 0.5"and 7", respectively (Figure 3–6).

Figure 3–6

Q&A What is the purpose of the rotate and adjustment handles?
When you drag an object's **rotate handle**, which is the green circle, Word rotates the object in the direction you drag the mouse. When you drag an object's **adjustment handle**, which is the yellow diamond, Word changes the object's shape.

Q&A What is the anchor on the screen?
The anchor indicates that the object you just drew is anchored to a paragraph marker. Edits affecting the location of that paragraph marker will affect the location of the object anchored to it.

Q&A What if I wanted to delete a shape and start over?
With the shape selected, you would press the DELETE key.

Other Ways

1. Choose Insert > Shape in menu bar

To Apply a Shape Style

Word provides a Shape Styles gallery, allowing you to change the appearance of the shape. Because the organization in this project, Heartland Tractor Club, supports many different tractor manufacturers, its letterhead should use a color that is not commonly associated with a particular tractor manufacturer. The next steps apply a shape style that uses a shade of brown.

- With the shape still selected, on the Format tab, under Shape Styles, hover the mouse pointer over the bottom of the Shape Styles gallery to display the expansion arrow, then click the More button in the Shape Styles gallery to expand the gallery (Figure 3–7).

Q&A What if my shape is no longer selected?
Click the shape to select it.

2

- Click the effect in column 5, row 6 in the Shape Styles gallery to apply the selected style to the shape.

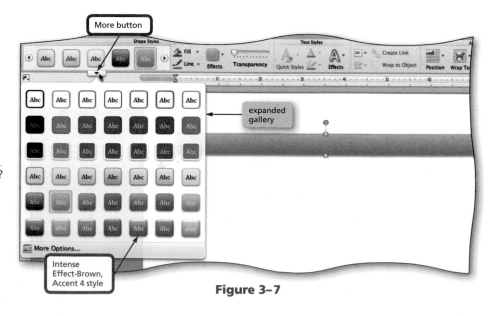

Figure 3–7

To Add Text to a Shape

The next step is to add the organization name to the shape. The following steps add text to a shape.

- CONTROL-click the shape to display a shortcut menu (Figure 3–8).

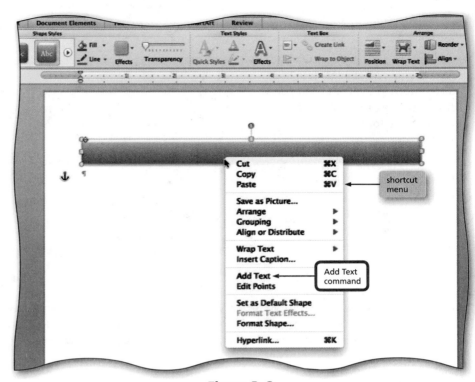

Figure 3–8

- Choose Add Text in the shortcut menu to place an insertion point centered in the shape.

- Type **HEARTLAND TRACTOR CLUB** as the organization name in the shape (Figure 3–9).

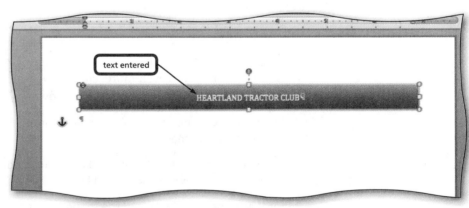

Figure 3–9

To Use the Increase Font Size Button to Increase Font Size

You want the font size of the organization name to be much larger in the shape. In previous chapters, you used the Font Size box arrow on the Home tab, in the Font group to change the font size of text. Word also provides an Increase Font Size button on the Home tab under Font which increases the font size of selected text each time you click the button. The steps on the next page use the Increase Font Size button to increase the font size of the organization name to 22 point.

• Drag through the organization name in the shape to select the text to be formatted.

• Display the Home tab.

• Repeatedly click the Increase Font Size button in the Font group until the Font Size box displays 22 to increase the font size of the selected text (Figure 3–10).

Q&A What if I click the Increase Font Size button too many times, causing the font size to be too big?
Click the Decrease Font Size button until the desired font size is displayed.

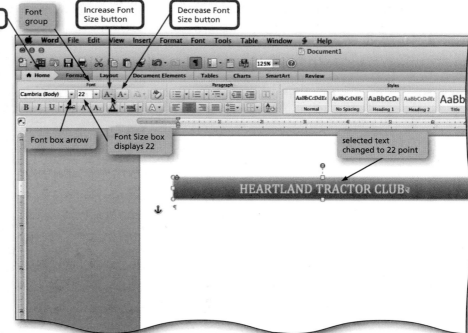

Figure 3–10

Experiment

• Repeatedly click the Increase Font Size and Decrease Font Size buttons on the Home tab under Font and watch the font size of the selected name change in the document window. When you are finished experimenting with these two buttons, set the font size to 22.

Other Ways

1. Press COMMAND-SHIFT->

To Change the Font of Selected Text

The font of the organization name currently is Palatino Linotype. To make the organization name stand out even more, change the font of the name in the letterhead to a font different from the rest of the letter. The following steps change the font of the selected text.

1 With the text selected, on the Home tab, under Font, click the Font box arrow to display the Font pop-up menu.

2 Scroll to and then click Chalkboard in the Font pop-up menu to change the font of the selected text (shown in Figure 3–11).

3 Click anywhere in the text in the shape to remove the selection and place the insertion point in the shape.

Floating versus Inline Objects

When you insert an object, such as a shape, in a document, Word inserts it as either an inline object or a floating object. An **inline object** is an object that is part of a paragraph. With inline objects, you change the location of the object by setting paragraph options, such as centered, right-aligned, and so on. A **floating object** is an object that can be positioned at a specific location in a document or in a layer over or behind text in a document. You have more flexibility with floating objects because you can position a floating object anywhere on the page.

In addition to changing an object from inline to floating and vice versa, Word provides several floating options. All of these options affect how text wraps with the object. Table 3–1 lists the various text wrapping options and explains the function of each one.

Table 3–1 Text Wrapping Options		
Text Wrapping Option	**Object Type**	**How It Works**
In Line with Text	Inline	Object positioned according to paragraph formatting; for example, if paragraph is centered, object will be centered with any text in the paragraph.
Square	Floating	Text wraps around object, with text forming a box around the object.
Tight	Floating	Text wraps around object, with text forming to the shape of the object.
Through	Floating	Object appears at beginning, middle, or end of text. Moving object changes location of text.
Top and Bottom	Floating	Object appears above or below text. Moving object changes location of text.
Behind Text	Floating	Object appears behind text.
In Front of Text	Floating	Object appears in front of text and may cover the text.

Positioning Objects

BTW

If you want to use the Square text wrapping option, you can specify where the object should be positioned on the page. To specify the position, on the Format tab, under Arrange, select the object, click the Position button and then click the desired location in the Position menu.

To Change an Object's Text Wrapping

When you insert a shape in a Word document, the default text wrapping is Through, which means the object appears at the beginning, middle, or end of the text. Because you want the letterhead above the contents of the letter, you change the text wrapping for the shape to Top and Bottom. The following steps change a shape's text wrapping.

1

- If necessary, click the shape to select it.

- Display the Format tab.

- Under Arrange, click the Wrap Text button to display the Wrap Text pop-up menu (Figure 3–11).

- Click Top and Bottom in the Wrap Text pop-up menu so that any text to be entered will be entered below the object.

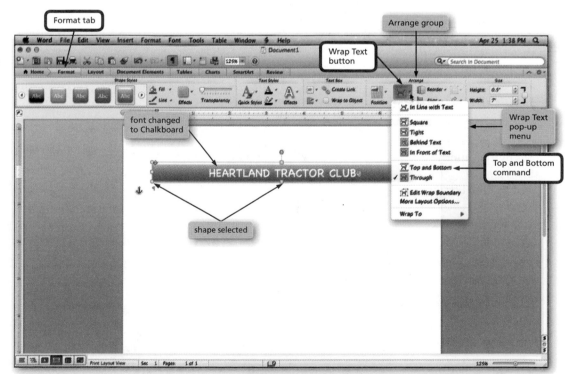

Figure 3–11

Other Ways

1. CONTROL-click object, point to Wrap Text in shortcut menu, click desired wrapping style

2. Choose Format > Shape in menu bar, click Layout, choose desired wrapping style

To Find and Download Clip Art

Files containing graphical images, or graphics, are available from a variety of sources. In the Chapter 1 document, you inserted a digital picture taken with a camera phone. In this project, you insert **clip art**, which is a predefined graphic. In Microsoft Office programs, clip art is located in the **Clip Organizer**, which contains a collection of clip art, photos, animations, sounds, and videos.

The letterhead in this project contains clip art of a tractor (Figure 3–1 on page WD 141). Thus, the next steps find and download a clip art image to be inserted below the shape in the document.

- Click the paragraph mark below the shape to position the insertion point where you want to insert the clip art image.

- Display the Home tab.

- On the Home tab, under Insert, click the Picture button and choose Clip Art Gallery from the menu to display the Clip Gallery.

- In the Search text box, select any text that is displayed, and type **tractor** as the search text, and click the Search button (Figure 3–12).

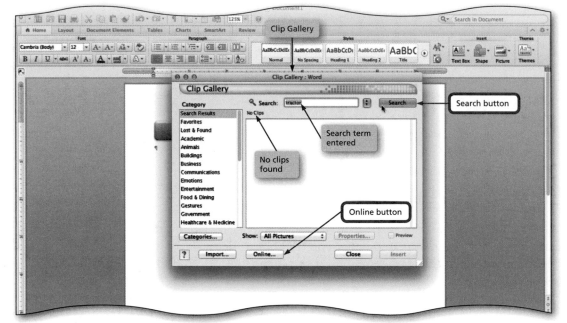

Figure 3–12

- Click the Online button, and then click Yes in the Launch Browser dialog to launch your browser and search for clip art online.

- In the larger Search images and more ... text box, type **tractor** (Figure 3–13) and then click the Search button.

Figure 3–13

3

- Click the Search button to search online for images.

 Q&A Why is my list of clips different from Figure 3–14?
You might have different clip art installed on your hard disk. If you are connected to the Internet, the Clip Gallery displays clips from the Web as well as those installed on your hard disk.

- Click the Next button until you find the page with the tractor image shown in (Figure 3–14) and then click Download to copy the clip art to your Downloads folder.

- Close your browser.

- Close the Clip Gallery.

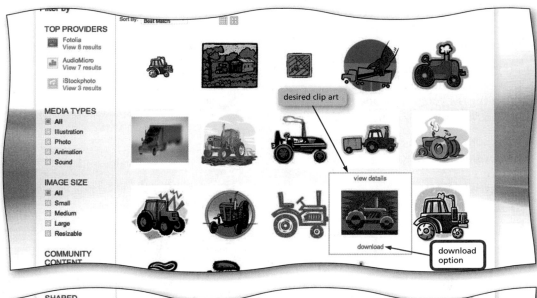

Figure 3–14

To Add Clip Art to the Clip Gallery

You can add downloaded images to the Clip Gallery, to make access to the images easy. The following steps add the image you just downloaded to the Clip Gallery.

1

- If necessary, click the paragraph mark below the shape to position the insertion point where you want to insert the clip art image.

- On the Home tab, under Insert, click Picture, and choose Clip Art Gallery from the menu to display the Clip Gallery dialog (Figure 3–15).

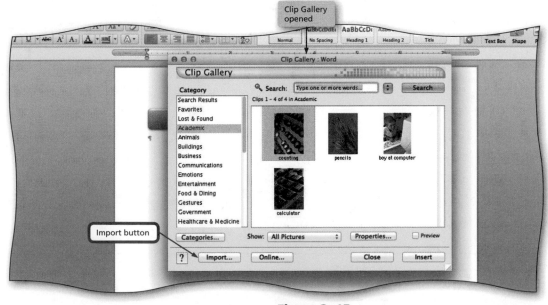

Figure 3–15

- In the Clip Gallery dialog, click the Import button to display the Import dialog.

- Under Favorites, choose the Downloads folder, and then select the file you downloaded, named MC900149887.wmf.

- Make sure the Move into Clip Gallery button is selected (Figure 3–16).

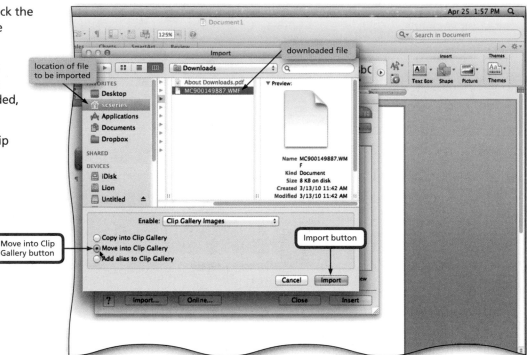

Figure 3–16

- Click the Import button to open the Properties dialog. On the Keywords tab, click New Keyword and enter **tractor** as the keyword text (Figure 3–17) and click OK.

- Click OK to close the Properties dialog and make the Clip Gallery dialog active.

- Click the Close button to close the Clip Gallery dialog.

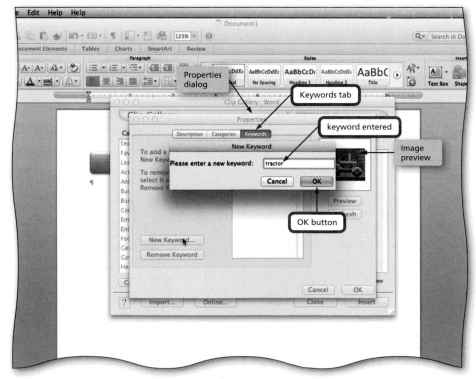

Figure 3–17

To Insert Clip Art

You can insert the downloaded clip art, or any other clip art that is in the Clip Gallery by following these steps.

 1

- On the Home tab, under Insert, choose Picture, and then Clip Art Gallery.

- Enter **tractor** in the Search text box and click the Search button to search for clip art with a keyword of tractor.

- Click the clip art image you wish to insert, in this case the image of the tractor (Figure 3–18).

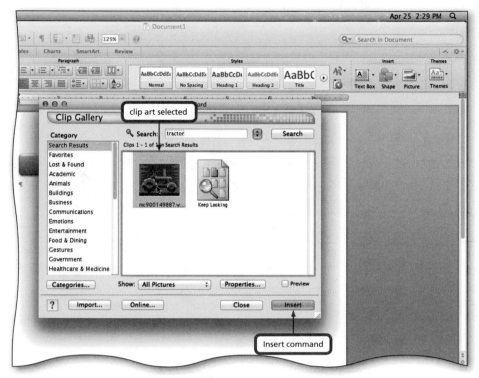

Figure 3–18

 2

- Click the Insert button to insert the clip art in the document at the insertion point (Figure 3–19).

Q&A What else can I do with the Clip Gallery?
With the Clip Gallery you can create, rename, or delete clip art collections; add clips from a camera or a scanner; delete, move, and copy clips; and search for existing clips.

Other Ways

1. Click Media button in Standard toolbar to open Media Browser, click Clip Art, select Category, drag image into document

Figure 3–19

To Resize a Graphic to a Percent of the Original

In this project, the graphic is 35 percent of its original size. Instead of dragging a sizing handle to change the graphic's size, as you learned in Chapter 1, you can set exact size percentages. The following steps resize a graphic to a percent of the original.

- If necessary, click to select the graphic.

- CONTROL-click the graphic, and choose Format Picture from the shortcut menu.

- Click Size, and then under Rotate and scale, set the Height measurement to 35%. The Width measurement should change to 35% automatically (Figure 3–20).

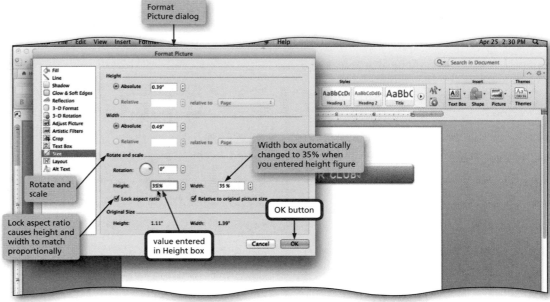

Figure 3–20

Q&A Why did Word automatically fill in the value in the Width box?
When the 'Lock aspect ratio' check box (Format Picture dialog) is selected, Word automatically maintains the size proportions of the graphic.

- Click the OK button to close the dialog and resize the selected graphic (Figure 3–21).

Figure 3–21

Q&A How do I know to use 35 percent for the resized graphic?
The larger graphic consumed too much room on the page. Try various percentages to determine the size that works best in the letterhead design.

Other Ways

1. Click Format Picture tab on ribbon, under Size, enter values, click OK button

2. Choose Format > Picture on menu bar, choose Size, enter values, click OK button

To Change the Color of a Graphic

In Word, you can change the color of a graphic. The clip art currently consists of shades of yellow and brown. Because the clip art in this project will be placed in a rectangle shape, you prefer to use colors that blend better with the current color scheme. The following steps change the color of the graphic to a shade in the current color scheme that matches the color of the shape.

1

- With the graphic still selected (shown in Figure 3–21), on the Format Picture tab, under Adjust, click the Recolor button to display the Recolor gallery (Figure 3–22).

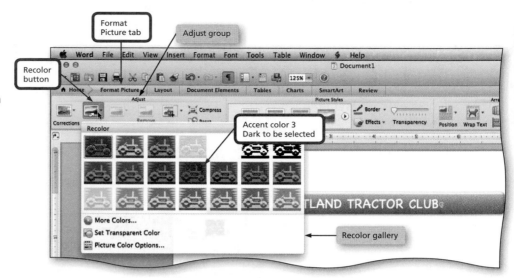

Figure 3–22

2

- Click Accent color 3 Dark in the Recolor gallery (fourth color in second row) to change the color of the selected graphic (Figure 3–23).

Q&A   How would I change a graphic back to its original colors?
With the graphic selected, you would click No Recolor in the Recolor gallery (upper-left color).

Figure 3–23

Other Ways

1. CONTROL-click graphic, click Format Picture on shortcut menu, click Adjust Picture in left pane (Format Picture dialog), select color from Recolor list, click OK button

To Adjust the Brightness and Contrast of a Graphic

In Word, you can adjust the lightness (brightness) of a graphic and also contrast, which is the difference between the lightest and darkest areas of the graphic. The following steps decrease the brightness and contrast of the tractor graphic, each by 20%.

1

- With the graphic still selected (shown in Figure 3–23), on the Format Picture tab, under Adjust, click the Corrections button to display the Corrections gallery (Figure 3–24).

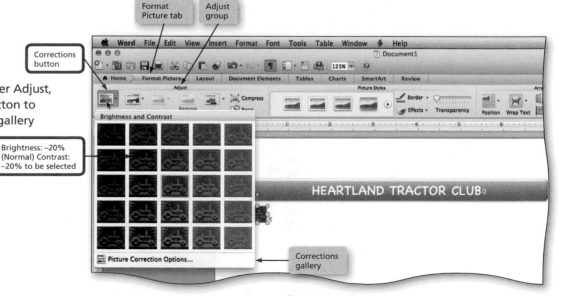

Figure 3–24

- Click Brightness: -20% Contrast: -20% in the Corrections gallery (second image in second row) to change the brightness and contrast of the selected graphic (Figure 3–25).

Q&A Can I remove all formatting applied to a graphic and start over?
Yes. With the graphic selected, you would click the Reset button in the Adjust group on the Format Picture tab.

Other Ways

1. CONTROL-click graphic, click Format Picture in shortcut menu, click Adjust Picture in left pane (Format Picture dialog), adjust settings, click OK button

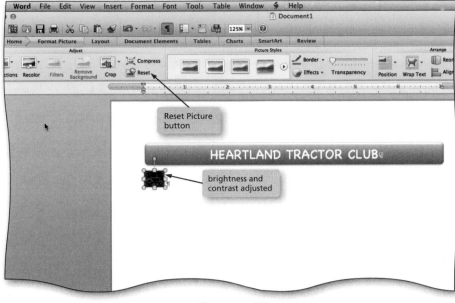

Figure 3–25

To Change the Border Color on a Graphic

The tractor graphic currently has no border (outline). You would like the graphic to have a brown border. The following steps change the border color on a graphic.

- With the graphic still selected, on the Format Picture tab, under Picture Styles, click the Border button arrow to display the Picture Border pop-up menu (Figure 3–26).

2

- Click Accent 4, Darker 50% (row 6, column 8) in the Picture Border pop-up menu to change the picture border color.

Q&A How would I remove a border from a graphic?
With the graphic selected, you would click the No Line in the Picture Border pop-up menu.

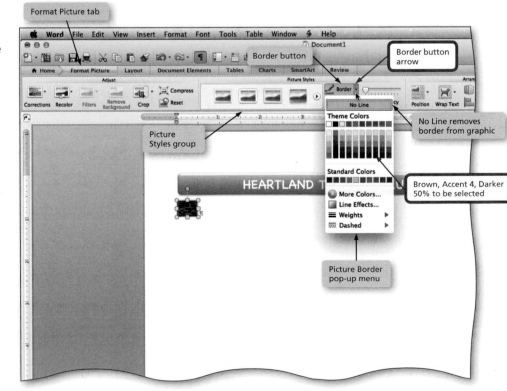

Figure 3–26

To Change an Object's Text Wrapping

The tractor graphic is to be positioned to the left of the organization name in the shape. Clip art, by default, is formatted as an inline graphic, which cannot be moved into a shape. To move the graphic in the shape so that it is not covered by any text, you format it as a floating object with In Front of Text wrapping. The following steps change a graphic's text wrapping.

1 If necessary, click the graphic to select it. If necessary, display the Format Picture tab.

2 Under Arrange, click the Wrap Text button to display the Wrap Text pop-up menu.

Q&A   Do the Format tabs for shapes and text boxes also have a Wrap Text button?
Yes. You can specify how to wrap text with pictures, shapes, and text boxes.

3 Click In Front of Text in the Wrap Text pop-up menu so that you can position the object on top of any item in the document, in this case, on top of the rectangular shape.

Q&A   Why did the graphic jump when I changed the text wrapping?
If the graphic jumps, then Word is set up to align objects with a grid which is by default not visible. The next set of steps will change that setting.

Q&As

For a complete list of the   **BTW**
Q&As found in many of
the step-by-step sequences
in this book, visit the
Office 2011 for Mac Online
Companion Web page at
www.cengagebrain.com,
navigate to the desired
chapter, and click Q&As.

To Move a Graphic

The next step is to move the tractor graphic so that it is positioned to the left of the text on the rectangle shape. In order to have the most control over placement you need to change the grid settings. The following steps change the grid settings and move a graphic.

1

- On the Format Picture tab, under Arrange, click Align and choose Grid Options from the menu.

- In the Grid Options dialog, click to remove check marks from all check boxes under Snap objects (Figure 3–27).

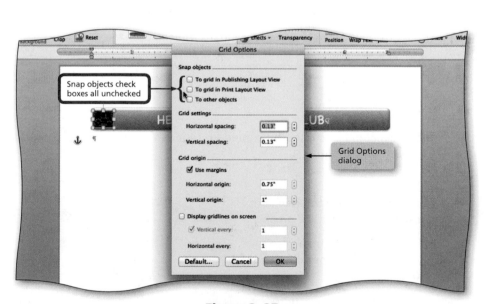

Figure 3–27

2

- Click OK to close the Grid Options dialog.

- Position the mouse pointer in the graphic so that the mouse pointer has a four-headed arrow attached to it (Figure 3–28).

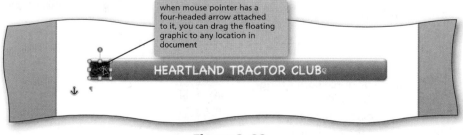

Figure 3–28

• Drag the graphic to the location shown in Figure 3–29. Use the screentip to help locate the graphic. The graphic in Figure 3–29 is located at measurements of .38" and 0.04" for left and top respectively. Your measurements may differ, what is important is relative position.

Q&A What if I moved the graphic to the wrong location?
Repeat these steps. You can drag a floating graphic to any location in a document.

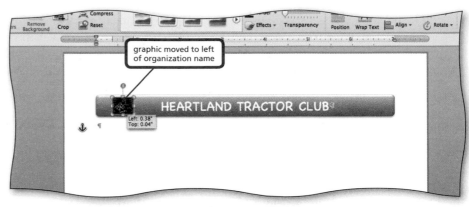

Figure 3–29

To Copy a Graphic

In this project, the same tractor graphic is to be placed to the right of the organization name in the shape. Instead of performing the same steps to insert and format another tractor graphic, you can copy the graphic to the Office Clipboard, paste the graphic from the Office Clipboard, and then move the graphic to the desired location.

You use the same steps to copy a graphic as you used in Chapter 2 to copy text. The following steps copy a graphic.

1 If necessary, click the graphic to select it.

2 In the Standard toolbar, click the Copy button, to copy the selected item to the Clipboard.

To Use Paste Options

The next step is to paste the copied graphic in the document. The following steps paste a graphic using the Paste Options pop-up menu.

• Click the Paste button in the Standard toolbar to paste a copy of the graphic.

• Click the Paste Options button to display the Paste Options pop-up menu (Figure 3–30).

Q&A Why are these paste buttons different from the ones in Chapter 2?
The buttons that appear in the Paste Options menu differ depending on the item you are pasting.

• Click the Keep Source Formatting button in the Paste Options menu to paste the object using the same formatting as the original.

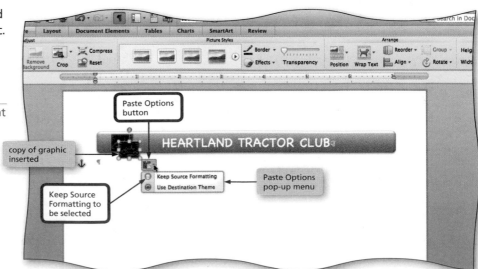

Figure 3–30

To Move a Graphic

The next step is to move the second tractor graphic so that it is positioned to the right of the text in the rectangle shape. The following step moves a graphic.

1 Position the mouse pointer in the graphic so that the mouse pointer has a four-headed arrow attached to it and then drag the graphic to the location shown in Figure 3–31. In Figure 3–31, the graphic is located at left and top measurements of 6.13" and 0.04", respectively.

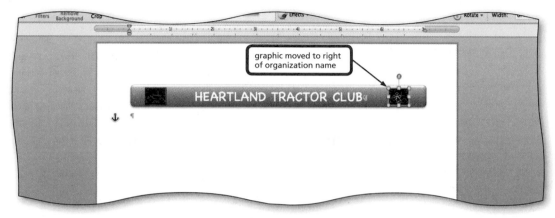

Figure 3–31

To Flip a Graphic

The next step is to flip the clip art image on the right so that the tractor is facing the opposite direction. The following steps flip a graphic horizontally.

1

- If necessary, display the Format Picture tab.
- With the graphic still selected, under Arrange, click the Rotate button to display the Rotate menu (Figure 3–32).

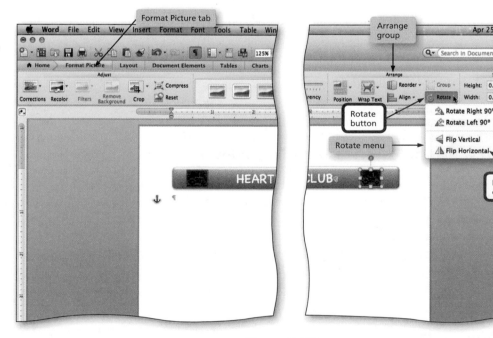

Figure 3–32

2

- Click Flip Horizontal in the Rotate menu, so that Word flips the graphic to display its mirror image (Figure 3–33).

Q&A Can I flip a graphic vertically?
Yes, you would click Flip Vertical in the Rotate menu. You also can rotate a graphic clockwise or counterclockwise by clicking the Rotate Right 90° and Rotate Left 90° commands, respectively, in the Rotate menu.

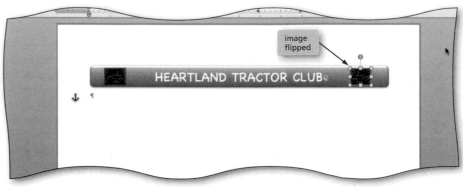

Figure 3–33

To Specify Formatting before Typing and then Enter Text

The contact information for the organization in this project is located on the line below the organization name. The following steps format and then enter the postal address in the letterhead.

1 Position the insertion point on the line below the shape containing the organization name.

2 If necessary, display the Home tab. Under Paragraph, click the Center Text button to center the paragraph.

3 Click the Font Color button arrow to display the Font Color pop-up menu and then click Accent 3, Darker 50% (seventh color in sixth row) in the Font Color menu to change the font color.

4 Click the Font box arrow and select Calibri.

5 If necessary, click the Font Size box arrow and select 11 point.

6 Type `323 Pine Avenue, Graber, OK 74877` and then press the SPACE BAR (shown in Figure 3–34).

To Insert a Symbol from the Symbol Dialog

In the letterhead in this chapter, a small round dot separates the postal address and phone number, and the same type of dot separates the phone number and Web address information. This special symbol (the round dot) is not on the keyboard. Thus, Word provides a method of inserting dots and other symbols, such as letters in the Greek alphabet and mathematical characters.

The following steps insert a dot symbol, called a bullet symbol, between the postal address and phone number in the letterhead.

①

- If necessary, position the insertion point after the space at the end of the address line.

- Click Insert on the menu bar, choose Symbol, and then choose Advanced Symbol to display the Symbol dialog.

②

- If the font in the Font box is not (normal text), click the Font box arrow and then scroll to (normal text) at the top of the list and click it to select this font.

- Click the bullet symbol to select it (Figure 3–34).

- Click the Insert button (Symbol dialog) to place the selected symbol in the document to the left of the insertion point.

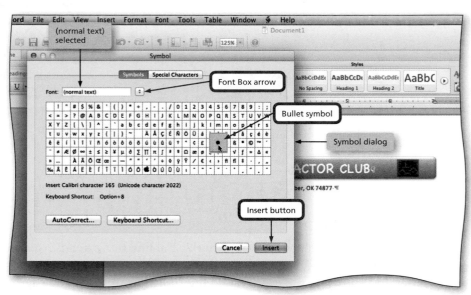

Figure 3–34

Q&A Why is the Symbol dialog still open?
The Symbol dialog remains open, allowing you to insert additional symbols.

③

- Close the Symbol dialog (Figure 3–35).

Figure 3–35

■ Other Ways
1. Click Media Browser button in Standard toolbar, click Symbols icon in Media Browser, select symbol, drag into document

To Add Additional Text

The following steps insert the remainder of text and additional bullets to complete the letterhead header.

① Press the SPACE BAR, type **Phone: (476) 555-9384** and then press the SPACE BAR.

② Click Insert in the menu bar and choose Symbol, then Advanced Symbol to display the Symbol dialog.

③ Insert another bullet symbol at the location of the insertion point, then close the Symbol dialog.

④ Press the SPACE BAR.

⑤ Type **Web address: www.hltclub.com** to finish the text in the letterhead (Figure 3–36 on the next page).

Inserting Special Characters

In addition to symbols, **BTW** you can insert a variety of special characters including dashes, hyphens, spaces, apostrophes, and quotation marks. Click the Special Characters tab in the Symbols dialog box (Figure 3–34), click the desired character in the Character list, click the Insert button, and then click the Close button.

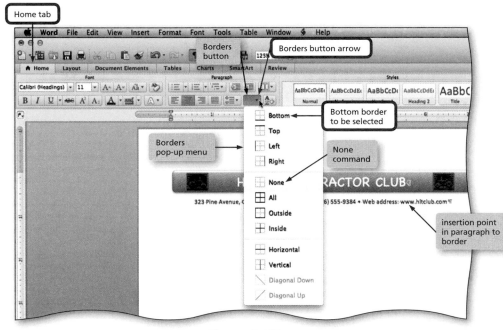

Figure 3–36

To Bottom Border a Paragraph

The letterhead in this project has a horizontal line that extends from the left margin to the right margin immediately below the address, phone, and Web address information, which separates the letterhead from the rest of the letter. In Word, you can draw a solid line, called a border, at any edge of a paragraph. That is, borders may be added above or below a paragraph, to the left or right of a paragraph, or in any combination of these sides. The following steps add a bottom border to the paragraph containing address, phone, and Web information.

- If necessary, display the Home tab.

- With the insertion point in the paragraph to border, on the Home tab, under Paragraph, click the Borders button arrow to display the Borders pop-up menu (Figure 3–37).

- Click Bottom in the Borders pop-up menu to place a border below the paragraph containing the insertion point (Figure 3–38).

Q&A How would I remove an existing border from a paragraph?
If, for some reason, you wanted to remove a border from a paragraph, you would position the insertion point in the paragraph, on the Home tab, under Paragraph, click the Borders button arrow, and then click None in the Borders pop-up menu.

Figure 3–37

Other Ways

1. On Layout tab, under Page Background, click Borders button, click Borders tab (Borders and Shading dialog), select desired border options, click OK button

Figure 3–38

To Clear Formatting

The next step is to position the insertion point below the letterhead, so that you can type the contents of the letter. When you press the RETURN key at the end of a paragraph containing a border, Word moves the border forward to the next paragraph. The paragraph also retains all current settings, such as the center format. Instead, you want the paragraph and characters on the new line to use the Normal style: black font with no border.

In Word, the term, **clear formatting**, refers to returning the formatting to the Normal style. The following steps clear formatting at the location of the insertion point, reset the font to 11 point Calibri, and add space between the border and the next paragraph.

- With the insertion point between the Web address and paragraph mark at the end of the line (as shown in Figure 3–38), press the RETURN key to move the insertion point and paragraph to the next line (Figure 3–39).

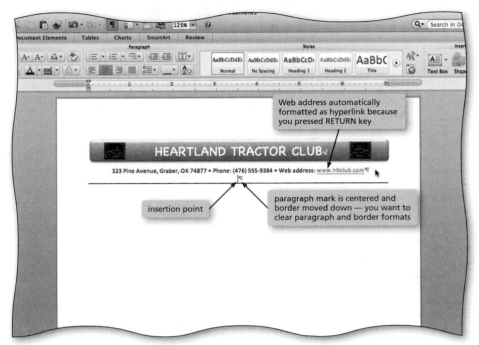

Figure 3–39

- On the Home tab under Font, click the Clear Formatting button to apply the Normal style to the location of the insertion point (Figure 3–40).

- Set the Font to 11 point Calibri.

- Press the RETURN key to insert a blank line after the bordered paragraph.

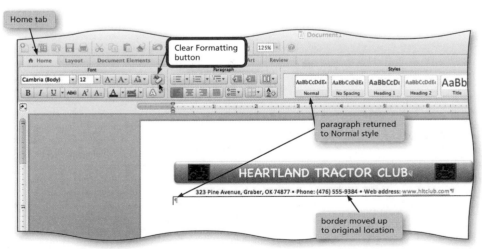

Figure 3–40

Other Ways

1. On Home tab, under Styles, click Normal in Quick Style gallery

AutoFormat as You Type

As you type text in a document, Word automatically formats some of it for you. For example, when you press the RETURN key or SPACE BAR after typing an e-mail address or Web address, Word automatically formats the address as a hyperlink, that is, colored blue and underlined. In Figure 3–39 on the previous page, for example, Word formatted the Web address as a hyperlink because you pressed the RETURN key at the end of the line. Table 3–2 outlines commonly used AutoFormat As You Type options and their results.

Table 3–2 Commonly Used AutoFormat As You Type Options

Typed Text	AutoFormat Feature	Example
Quotation marks or apostrophes	Changes straight quotation marks or apostrophes to curly ones	"the" becomes "the"
Text, a space, one hyphen, one or no spaces, text, space	Changes the hyphen to an en dash	ages 20 - 45 becomes ages 20 – 45
Text, two hyphens, text, space	Changes the two hyphens to an em dash	Two types--yellow and red becomes Two types—yellow and red
Web or e-mail address followed by SPACE BAR or RETURN key	Formats Web or e-mail address as a hyperlink	www.cengage.com becomes www.cengage.com
Three hyphens, underscores, equal signs, asterisks, tildes, or number signs and then RETURN key	Places a border above a paragraph	--- This line becomes _____ This line

Number followed by a period, hyphen, right parenthesis, or greater than sign and then a space or tab followed by text	Creates a numbered list	1. Word
		2. PowerPoint
		
		becomes
		
		  1. Word
		  2. PowerPoint

Asterisk, hyphen, or greater than sign and then a space or tab followed by text	Creates a bulleted list	* Home tab
		* Insert tab
		
		becomes
		
		  • Home tab
		  • Insert tab

Fraction and then a space or hyphen	Condenses the fraction entry so that it consumes one space instead of three	1/2 becomes ½
Ordinal and then a space or hyphen	Makes part of the ordinal a superscript	3rd becomes 3rd

AutoFormat Settings

BTW Before you can use them, AutoFormat options must be enabled. To check if an AutoFormat option is enabled, click Word in the menu bar, choose Preferences, select the AutoFormat as You Type tab, select the appropriate check boxes, and then click the OK button in each open dialog.

To Convert a Hyperlink to Regular Text

The Web address in the letterhead should be formatted as regular text; that is, it should not be blue or underlined. Thus, the following steps remove the hyperlink format from the Web address in the letterhead.

- CONTROL-click the hyperlink (in this case, the Web address) to display a shortcut menu.
- Choose Hyperlink in the shortcut menu (Figure 3–41).

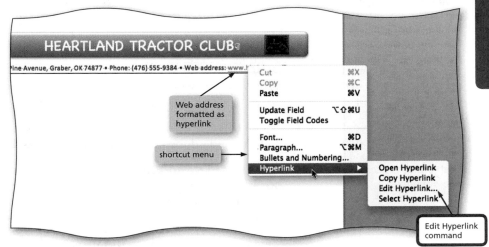

Figure 3–41

- Choose Edit Hyperlink in the submenu to display the Edit Hyperlink dialog (Figure 3–42).
- Click the Remove Link button to remove the hyperlink format from the text.

Q&A   Could I have used the AutoCorrect Options button instead of the Remove Hyperlink command?
Yes. Alternatively, you could have pointed to the small blue box at the beginning of the hyperlink, clicked the AutoCorrect Options button, and then clicked Undo Hyperlink on the AutoCorrect Options menu.

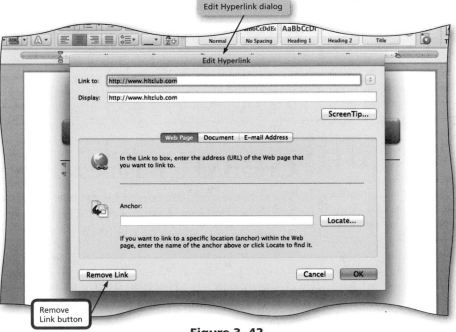

Figure 3–42

- Position the insertion point on the paragraph mark below the border because you are finished with the letterhead (Figure 3–43).

Figure 3–43

To Change Document Properties, then Save and Close a File

The letterhead now is complete. Thus, you should save it in a file. The following steps assume you already have created folders for storing your files, for example, a CIS 101 folder (for your class) that contains a Word folder (for your assignments). Thus, these steps change document properties, save the file in the Word folder in the CIS 101 folder on a USB flash drive using the file name, Heartland Letterhead, and then close the file.

1 Click File in the menu bar and choose Properties to open the Document1 Properties dialog, and then, if necessary, select the Summary tab.

2 Enter your name in the Author property, and enter your course and section in the Subject property. Close the Document1 Properties dialog.

3 With a USB flash drive connected to one of the computer's USB ports, click the Save button on the Standard toolbar to display the Save As dialog.

4 Type `Heartland Letterhead` in the Save As text box to change the file name. Do not press the RETURN key after typing the file name because you do not want to close the dialog at this time.

5 Navigate to the desired save location (in this case, the Word folder in the CIS 101 folder [or your class folder] on the USB flash drive).

6 Click the Save button to save the file in the selected folder on the selected drive with the entered file name.

7 Click File in the menu bar and choose Close to close the document.

Break Point: If you wish to take a break, this is a good place to do so. To resume at a later time, start Word and continue following the steps from this location forward.

Creating a Business Letter

You have created a letterhead for the business letter. The next step is to compose the rest of the content in the business letter. The following pages use Word to create a business letter that contains a table and a bulleted list.

Plan Ahead

Compose an effective business letter.

When composing a business letter, you need to be sure to include all essential elements and to decide which letter style to use.

• **Include all essential letter elements, properly spaced and sized.** All business letters contain the same basic elements, including the date line, inside address, message, and signature block (shown in Figure 3–1 on page WD 141). If a business letter does not use a letterhead, then the top of the letter should include return address information in a heading.

• **Use proper spacing and formats for the contents of the letter below the letterhead.** Use a font that is easy to read, in a size between 8 and 12 point. Add emphasis with bold, italic, and bullets where appropriate, and use tables to present numeric information. Paragraphs should be single-spaced, with double-spacing between paragraphs.

• **Determine which letter style to use.** You can follow many different styles when creating business letters. A letter style specifies guidelines for the alignment and spacing of elements in the business letter.

To Create a New File from an Existing File

The top of the business letter in this chapter contains the letterhead, which you saved in a separate file. You could open the letterhead file and then save it with a new name, so that the letterhead file remains intact for future use. A more efficient technique is to create a new file from the letterhead file. Doing this enables you to save the document the first time using the Save button on the Standard toolbar instead of requiring you to use the Save As command on the File menu. The following steps create a new file from an existing file.

1

- Click File in the menu bar to open the File menu.

- Choose the Open command to display the Open dialog.

2

- If necessary, navigate to the location of the saved Heartland Letterhead file (in this case, the CIS 101 folder on the USB flash drive).

- Click Heartland Letterhead to select the file.

- Click the Open box to display the Open pop-up menu (Figure 3–44).

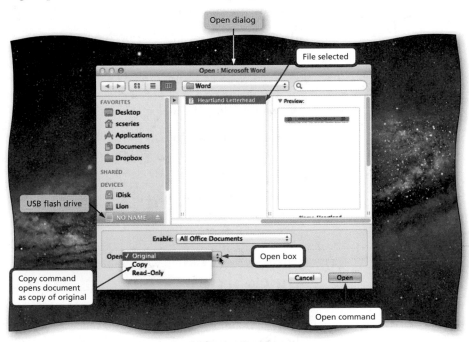

Figure 3–44

3

- Choose Copy from the Open pop-up menu, and then click the Open button to open a new document window that contains a copy of the selected file.

- Click the Print Layout View button to switch to Print Layout view (Figure 3–45).

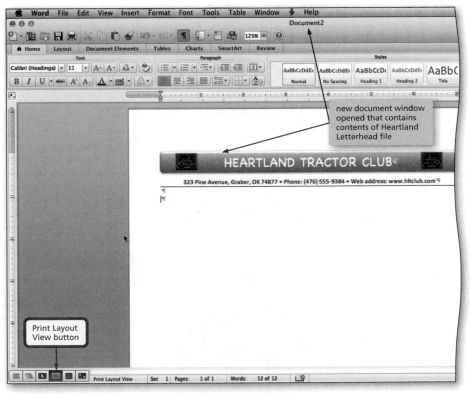

Figure 3–45

New Document Window

BTW If you wanted to open a new blank document window, you could press COMMAND-N or click File > New Blank Document in the menu bar.

To Save a Document

Because you do not want to lose the letterhead at the top of this document, you should save the letter before continuing. The following steps assume you already have created folders for storing your files, for example, a CIS 101 folder (for your class) that contains a Word folder (for your assignments). Thus, these steps save the document in the Word folder in the CIS 101 folder on a USB flash drive using the file name, Heartland Advertisement Letter.

1 With a USB flash drive connected to one of the computer's USB ports, click the Save button on the Standard toolbar to display the Save dialog.

2 Type **Heartland Advertisement Letter** in the File name text box to change the file name. Do not press the RETURN key after typing the file name because you do not want to close the dialog at this time.

3 If necessary, navigate to the desired save location (in this case, the Word folder in the CIS 101 folder [or your class folder] on the USB flash drive).

4 Click the Save button (Save dialog) to save the document in the selected folder on the selected drive with the entered file name.

Quick Styles

Recall that the Normal style in Word places 0 points of blank space after each paragraph and inserts a single line space between each line of text. The business letter should use single spacing for paragraphs and double spacing between paragraphs. Thus, you can use the Normal style for your business letter.

Word has many built-in, or predefined, styles called Quick Styles that you can use to format text (Figure 3–46). The No Spacing style, for example, defines line spacing to single and does not insert any additional blank space between lines when you press the RETURN key.

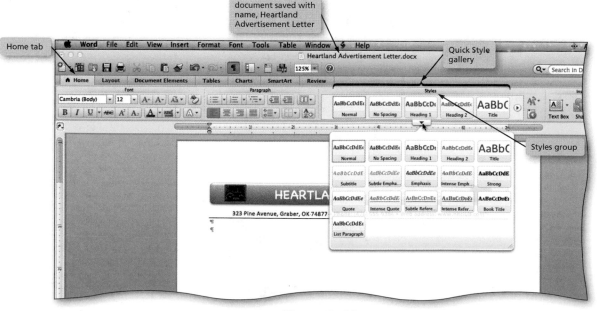

Figure 3–46

To Apply a Quick Style

To apply a Quick Style to a paragraph, first position the insertion point in the paragraph and then apply the style, as the following steps illustrate.

- With the insertion point on the second paragraph mark below the border (shown in Figure 3–43 on page WD 167), on the Home tab, under Styles, click No Spacing in the Quick Style gallery to apply the selected style to the current paragraph.

- Set the Font to 11 point Calibri.

Q&A   Will this style be used in the rest of the document?

Yes. The paragraph formatting, which includes the style, will carry forward to subsequent paragraphs each time you press the RETURN key.

Include all essential letter elements.

Be sure to include all essential business letter elements, properly spaced, in your letter.

- The **date line**, which consists of the month, day, and year, is positioned two to six lines below the letterhead.

- The **inside address**, placed three to eight lines below the date line, usually contains the addressee's courtesy title plus full name, job title, business affiliation, and full geographical address.

- The **salutation**, if present, begins two lines below the last line of the inside address. If you do not know the recipient's name, avoid using the salutation, "To whom it may concern" — it is impersonal. Instead, use the recipient's title in the salutation, e.g., Dear Personnel Director. In a business letter, use a colon (:) at the end of the salutation; in a personal letter, use a comma.

- The body of the letter, the **message**, begins two lines below the salutation. Within the message, paragraphs are single-spaced with one blank line between paragraphs.

- Two lines below the last line of the message, the **complimentary close** is displayed. Capitalize only the first word in a complimentary close.

- Type the **signature block** at least four blank lines below the complimentary close, allowing room for the author to sign his or her name.

Plan Ahead

Determine which letter style to use.

Three common business letter styles are the block, the modified block, and the modified semi-block. Each style specifies different alignments and indentations.

- In the block letter style, all components of the letter begin flush with the left margin.

- In the modified block letter style, the date, complimentary close, and signature block are positioned approximately one-half inch to the right of center or at the right margin. All other components of the letter begin flush with the left margin.

- In the modified semi-block letter style, the date, complimentary close, and signature block are centered, positioned approximately one-half inch to the right of center or at the right margin. The first line of each paragraph in the body of the letter is indented one-half to one inch from the left margin. All other components of the letter begin flush with the left margin.

The business letter in this project follows the modified block style.

Plan Ahead

Using Tab Stops to Align Text

A **tab stop** is a location on the horizontal ruler that tells Word where to position the insertion point when you press the TAB key on the keyboard. Word, by default, places a tab stop at every one-half inch mark on the ruler. These default tab stops are indicated at the bottom of the horizontal ruler by small vertical tick marks (shown in Figure 3–47). You also can set your own custom tab stops. Tab settings are a paragraph format. Thus, each time you press the RETURN key, any custom tab stops are carried forward to the next paragraph.

To move the insertion point from one tab stop to another, press the TAB key on the keyboard. When you press the TAB key, a **tab character** formatting mark appears in the empty space between the tab stops.

When you set a custom tab stop, you specify how the text will align at a tab stop. The tab marker on the ruler reflects the alignment of the characters at the location of the tab stop. Table 3–3 shows types of tab stop alignments in Word and their corresponding tab markers.

Tabs Dialog

BTW You can use the Tabs dialog to set, change the alignment of, and remove custom tab stops, as well as to change the default tab stop distance. To display the Tabs dialog, click Format in the menu bar and choose Tabs. To set a custom tab stop, enter the desired position (Tab dialog) and then click the Set button. To change the alignment of a custom tab stop, click the tab stop position to be changed, click the new alignment, and then click the Set button. To remove an existing custom tab stop, click the tab stop position to be removed and then click the Clear button. To remove all tab stops, click the Clear All button (Tabs dialog).

Table 3–3 Types of Tab Stop Alignments

Tab Stop Alignment	Tab Marker	Result of Pressing Tab Key	Example
Left Tab	[↱▾]	Left-aligns text at the location of the tab stop	toolbar ruler
Center Tab	[↑▾]	Centers text at the location of the tab stop	toolbar ruler
Right Tab	[⬑▾]	Right-aligns text at the location of the tab stop	toolbar ruler
Decimal Tab	[↕•▾]	Aligns text on decimal point at the location of the tab stop	45.72 223.75
Bar Tab	[❘▾]	Aligns text at a bar character at the location of the tab stop	toolbar ruler

To Display the Rulers

One way to set custom tab stops is by using the horizontal ruler. Thus, the following step displays the ruler in the document window.

1 If the rulers are not displayed already, choose Ruler in the View menu.

To Set Custom Tab Stops

The first required element of the business letter is the date line, which in this letter is positioned two lines below the letterhead. The date line contains the month, day, and year, and begins four inches from the left margin, which is approximately one-half inch to the right of center. Thus, you should set a custom tab stop at the 4" mark on the ruler. The following steps set a left-aligned tab stop.

1

- Click the tab selector at the left edge of the horizontal ruler and choose the type of tab you wish to use from the pop-up menu, which is the Left Tab icon in this case.

- Position the mouse pointer on the 4" mark on the ruler, which is the location of the desired custom tab stop (Figure 3–47).

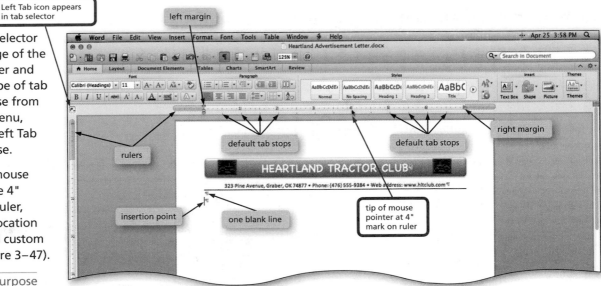

Figure 3–47

Q&A What is the purpose of the tab selector?
Before using the ruler to set a tab stop, ensure the correct tab stop icon appears in the tab selector. Click the tab selector to choose the desired type of tab. The Left Tab icon is the default. For a list of the types of tab stops, see Table 3–3.

2

- Click the 4" mark on the ruler to place a tab marker at that location (Figure 3–48).

Q&A What if I click the wrong location on the ruler?
You can move a custom tab stop by dragging the tab marker to the desired location on the ruler. Or, you can remove an existing custom tab stop by pointing to the tab marker on the ruler and then dragging the tab marker down and out of the ruler.

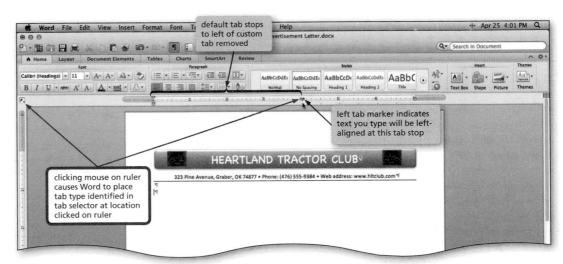

Figure 3–48

Q&A What happened to the default tab stops on the ruler?
When you set a custom tab stop, Word clears all default tab stops to the left of the newly set custom tab stop on the ruler.

■ Other Ways

1. Choose Format > Tabs in menu bar type tab stop position (Tabs dialog), click Set button, click OK button

2. Choose Format > Paragraph, click Line and Page Breaks tab, click Tabs button, type tab stop position, click Set button, click OK button

To Insert the Current Date in a Document

The next step is to enter the current date at the 4" tab stop in the document, as specified in the guidelines for a modified block style letter. In Word, you can insert a computer's system date in a document. The following steps insert the current date in the letter.

- Press the TAB key to position the insertion point at the location of the tab stop in the current paragraph.

- Click Insert in the menu bar, then choose Date and Time to display the Date and Time dialog.

- Select the desired format (Date and Time dialog), in this case 25 April 2013.

- If the Update automatically check box is selected, click the check box to remove the check mark (Figure 3–49).

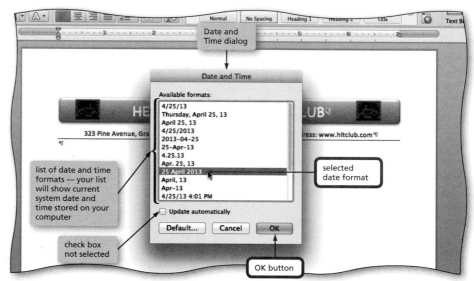

Figure 3–49

Q&A Why should the Update automatically check box not be selected?
In this project, the date at the top of the letter always should show today's date (for example, April 25, 2013). If, however, you wanted the date always to change to reflect the current computer date (for example, showing the date you open or print the letter), then you would place a check mark in this check box.

- Click the OK button to insert the current date at the location of the insertion point (Figure 3–50).

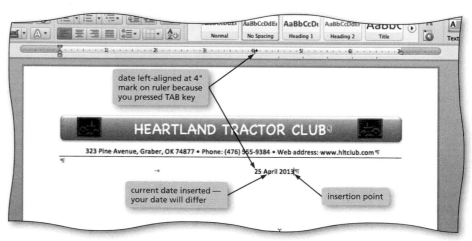

Figure 3–50

To Enter the Inside Address and Salutation

The next step in composing the business letter is to type the inside address and salutation. The following steps enter this text.

1 With the insertion point at the end of the date (shown in Figure 3–50), press the RETURN key three times.

2 Type **Mr. Harvey Wilcox** and then press the RETURN key.

3 Type `Wilcox Tractor Restorations` and then press the RETURN key.

4 Type `3009 North 2850 East Road` and then press the RETURN key.

5 Type `Roundwood, OK 74519` and then press the RETURN key twice.

6 Type `Dear Mr. Wilcox:` to complete the inside address and salutation entries (Figure 3–51).

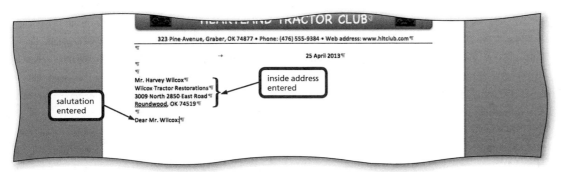

Figure 3–51

To Create an AutoText Entry

If you use the same text or graphic frequently, you can store the text or graphic as an **AutoText entry** and then insert the stored AutoText entry in the open document, as well as in future documents. That is, you can create the entry once as AutoText and then insert the AutoText when you need it. In this way, you avoid entering the text or graphics inconsistently or incorrectly in different locations throughout the same or multiple documents.

The following steps create an AutoText entry for the prospective advertiser's name, Wilcox Tractor Restorations. Later, you will insert the AutoText in the document instead of typing the advertiser's name.

1

• Select the text to be an AutoText entry, in this case Wilcox Tractor Restorations. Do not select the paragraph mark at the end of the text because you do not want the paragraph to be part of the AutoText.

Q&A Why is the paragraph mark not part of the AutoText entry?
Select the paragraph mark only if you want to store paragraph formatting, such as indentation and line spacing, as part of the AutoText.

• In the menu bar, click Tools, then choose AutoCorrect to display the AutoCorrect dialog. Click the AutoText tab.

• Type `wilc` in the Enter AutoText entries here: text box to replace the proposed AutoText entry name (Wilcox Tractor Restorations, in this case) with a shorter AutoText name (Figure 3–52).

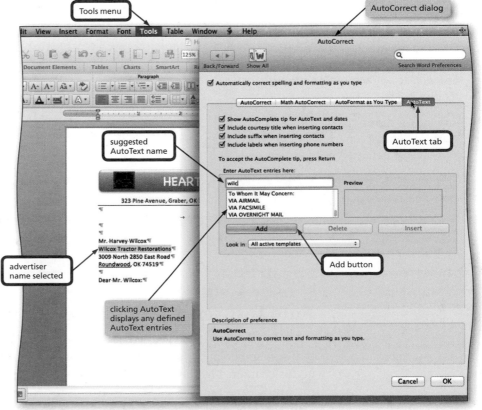

Figure 3–52

• Click the Add button to store the AutoText entry and close the dialog.

To Insert AutoText

In the first sentence in the body of the letter, you want the prospective advertiser name, Wilcox Tractor Restorations, to be displayed. Recall that you stored an AutoText name of wilc for Wilcox Tractor Restorations. Thus, you will type the AutoText name and then instruct Word to replace the name with the stored AutoText entry. The following steps insert AutoText.

• Click to the right of the colon in the salutation and then press the RETURN key twice to position the insertion point one blank line below the salutation.

• Type the beginning of the first sentence as follows, entering the AutoText entry: **We are delighted you are considering advertising your business, wilc** (Figure 3–53).

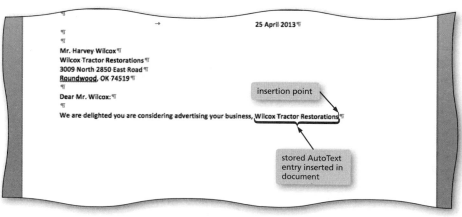

Figure 3–53

• Press the RETURN key to instruct Word to replace the AutoText name (wilc) with the stored AutoText entry (Wilcox Tractor Restorations) (Figure 3–54).

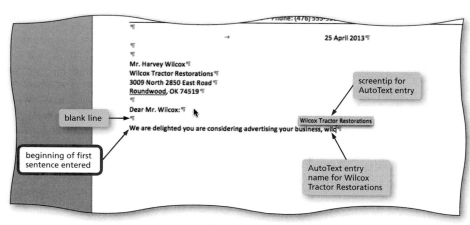

Figure 3–54

AutoText versus AutoCorrect

In Chapter 2, you learned how to use the AutoCorrect feature, which enables you to insert and create AutoCorrect entries, similarly to how you created and inserted AutoText in this chapter. The difference between an AutoCorrect entry and an AutoText entry is that the AutoCorrect feature makes corrections for you automatically as soon as you press the SPACE BAR or type a punctuation mark, whereas you must instruct Word to insert AutoText. That is, you enter the AutoText entry name and then press the RETURN key.

To Insert a Nonbreaking Space

Some compound words, such as proper nouns, dates, units of time and measure, abbreviations, and geographic destinations, should not be divided at the end of a line. These words either should fit as a unit at the end of a line or be wrapped together to the next line.

Word provides two special characters to assist with this task: the nonbreaking space and the nonbreaking hyphen. A **nonbreaking space** is a special space character that prevents two words from splitting if the first word falls at the end of a line. Similarly, a **nonbreaking hyphen** is a special type of hyphen that prevents two words separated by a hyphen from splitting at the end of a line.

The following steps insert a nonbreaking space between the words in the magazine name.

- With the insertion point at the end of the AutoText entry in the document (as shown in Figure 3–54), press the COMMA key and then press the SPACE BAR.

- Type **in** and then press the SPACE BAR. Press COMMAND-I to turn on italics because magazine names should be italicized.

- Type **Heartland** as the first word in the magazine name and then press CONTROL-SHIFT-SPACE BAR to insert a nonbreaking space after the entered word (Figure 3–55).

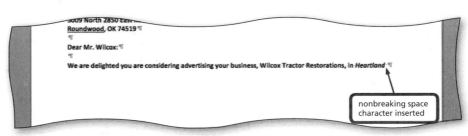

Figure 3–55

- Type **Tractor** and then press CONTROL-SHIFT-SPACE BAR to insert another nonbreaking space after the entered word.

- Type **Magazine** and then press COMMAND-I to turn off italics (Figure 3–56).

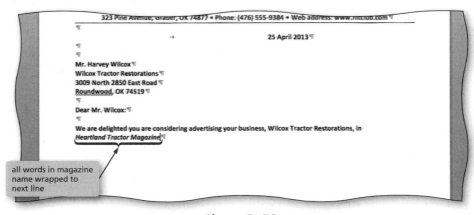

Figure 3–56

Other Ways

1. Choose Insert > Symbol > Advanced Symbol, click Special Characters tab (Symbol dialog), click Nonbreaking Space in Character list, click Insert button, click Close button

To Enter Text

The next step in creating the letter is to enter the rest of the text in the first paragraph. The following steps enter this text.

① Press the COMMA key and then press the SPACE BAR.

② Type this text: **our monthly publication for tractor enthusiasts. The table below outlines advertisement rates per monthly issue:**

Nonbreaking Hyphen

If you wanted to insert a nonbreaking hyphen, you would press COMMAND-SHIFT-HYPHEN.

Press the RETURN key twice to place a blank line between paragraphs (shown in Figure 3–58).

Q&A Why does my document wrap on different words?
Differences in wordwrap may relate to the printer connected to your computer. Thus, it is possible that the same document could wordwrap differently if associated with a different printer.

To Save an Existing Document with the Same File Name

You have made several modifications to the document since you last saved it. Thus, you should save it again. The following step saves the document again.

 Click the Save button on the Standard toolbar to overwrite the previously saved file.

Break Point: If you wish to take a break, this is a good place to do so. You can quit Word now. To resume at a later time, start Word, open the file called Heartland Advertisement Letter, and continue following the steps from this location forward.

Tables

The next step in composing the business letter is to place a table listing the rates for various types of advertisements (shown in Figure 3–1 on page WD 141). A Word **table** is a collection of rows and columns. The intersection of a row and a column is called a **cell**, and cells are filled with data.

The first step in creating a table is to insert an empty table in the document. When inserting a table, you must specify the total number of rows and columns required, which is called the **dimension** of the table. The table in this project has five columns. You often do not know the total number of rows in a table. Thus, many Word users create one row initially and then add more rows as needed. In Word, the first number in a dimension is the number of columns, and the second is the number of rows. For example, in Word, a 5 × 1 (pronounced "five by one") table consists of five columns and one row.

To Insert an Empty Table

The next step is to insert an empty table in the letter. The following steps insert a table with five columns and one row at the location of the insertion point.

- If necessary, scroll the document up so that you will be able to see the table in the document window.

- With the insertion point positioned at the end of the letter, on the Tables tab, under Table Options, click the New button to display the Table pop-up menu.

- Position the mouse pointer on the cell in the first row and fifth column of the grid to preview the desired table dimension (Figure 3–57).

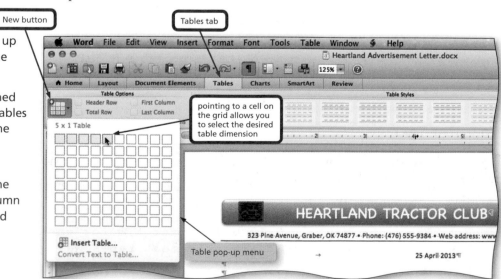

Figure 3–57

2

- Click the cell in the first row and fifth column of the grid to insert an empty table with one row and five columns in the document.

- If necessary, scroll the table up in the document window (Figure 3–58).

Q&A What are the small circles in the table cells?

Each table cell has an **end-of-cell mark,** which is a formatting mark that assists you with selecting and formatting cells. Similarly, each row has an **end-of-row mark,** which you can use to add columns to the right of a table. Recall that formatting marks do not print on a hard copy. The end-of-cell marks currently are left-aligned, that is, positioned at the left edge of each cell.

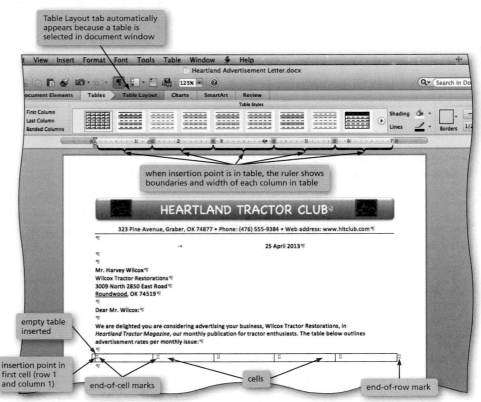

Figure 3–58

To Enter Data in a Table

The next step is to enter data in the cells of the empty table. The data you enter in a cell wordwraps just as text wordwraps between the margins of a document. To place data in a cell, you click the cell and then type.

To advance rightward from one cell to the next, press the TAB key. When you are at the rightmost cell in a row, press the TAB key to move to the first cell in the next row; do not press the RETURN key. The RETURN key is used to begin a new paragraph within a cell. One way to add new rows to a table is to press the TAB key when the insertion point is positioned in the bottom-right corner cell of the table. The following step enters data in the first row of the table and then inserts a blank second row.

1

- With the insertion point in the left cell of the table, type `Type` and then press the TAB key to advance the insertion point to the next cell.

- Type `Dimensions` and then press the TAB key to advance the insertion point to the next cell.

- Type `Word Count` and then press the TAB key to advance the insertion point to the next cell.

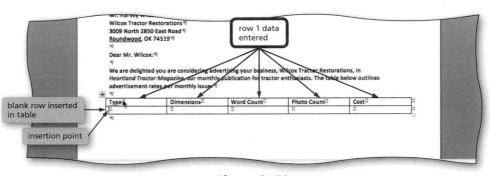

Figure 3–59

- Type `Photo Count` and then press the TAB key to advance the insertion point to the next cell.

- Type `Cost` and then press the TAB key to insert a second row at the end of the table and position the insertion point in the first column of the new row (Figure 3–59).

Q&A How do I edit cell contents if I make a mistake?

Click in the cell and then correct the entry.

Tables

BTW For simple tables, such as the one just created, Word users often drag to select the table dimensions from the Table pop-up menu. For a more complex table, such as one with a varying number of columns per row, Word has a Draw Table feature that allows users to draw a table in the document using a pencil pointer. To use this feature, click the Tables tab on the ribbon and under Draw Borders, click the Draw icon.

To Enter More Data in a Table

The following steps enter the remaining data in the table.

1 Type **Full Page** and then press the TAB key to advance the insertion point to the next cell. Type **9" x 7"** and then press the TAB key to advance the insertion point to the next cell. Type **800** and then press the TAB key to advance the insertion point to the next cell. Type **4** and then press the TAB key to advance the insertion point to the next cell. Type **$650** and then press the TAB key to insert a row at the end of the table and position the insertion point in the first column of the new row.

2 In the third row, type **Half Page** in the first column, **4.5" x 7"** as the dimensions, **400** as the word count, **2** as the photo count, and **$350** as the cost. Press the TAB key to position the insertion point in the first column of a new row.

3 In the fourth row, type **Quarter Page** in the first column, **4.5" x 3.5"** as the dimensions, **200** as the word count, **1** as the photo count, and **$225** as the cost. Press the TAB key.

4 In the fifth row, type **Business Card** in the first column, **2.25" x 3.5"** as the dimensions, **100** as the word count, **0** as the photo count, and **$125** as the cost (Figure 3–60).

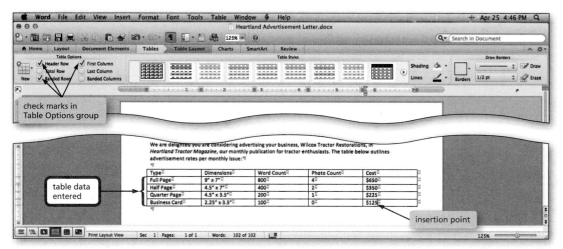

Figure 3–60

To Apply a Table Style

The next step is to apply a table style to the table. Word provides a Table Styles gallery, allowing you to change the basic table format to a more visually appealing style. Word provides a gallery of more than 90 table styles, which include a variety of colors and shading. The following steps apply a table style to the table in the letter.

1
- With the insertion point in the table, be sure the check marks match those in the Table Options group (Tables tab) as shown in Figure 3–60.

Q&A What if the Table tab no longer is the active tab?
Click in the table and then display the Table Layout tab.

Q&A What do the options in the Table Options group mean?
When you apply table styles, if you want the top row of the table (header row), a row containing totals (total row), first column, or last column to be formatted differently, select those check boxes. If you want the rows or columns to alternate with colors, select Banded Rows or Banded Columns, respectively.

- Click the More button in the Table Styles gallery (shown in Figure 3–61) to expand the gallery.
- Scroll down and find Medium Grid 3 - Accent 4 in the Table Styles gallery (Figure 3–61).

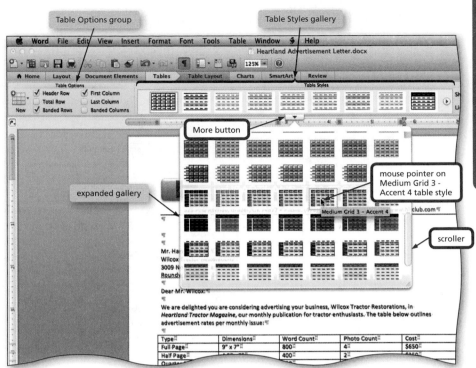

Figure 3–61

- Click Medium Grid 3 - Accent 4 in the Table Styles gallery to apply the selected style to the table (Figure 3–62).

Experiment

- Select and remove check marks from various check boxes in the Table Options group and watch the format of the table change in the document window. When finished experimenting, be sure the check marks match those shown in Figure 3–61.

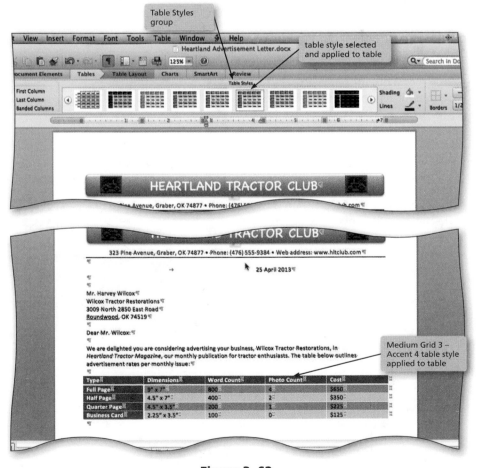

Figure 3–62

To Resize Table Columns to Fit Table Contents

The table in this project currently extends from the left margin to the right margin of the document. You want each column to be only as wide as the longest entry in the table. That is, the first column must be wide enough to accommodate the words, Business Card, and the second column should be only as wide as the title, Dimensions, and so on. The following steps instruct Word to fit the width of the columns to the contents of the table automatically.

- With the insertion point in the table, display the Table Layout tab.

- On the Table Layout tab, under Cell Size, click the AutoFit button to display the AutoFit menu (Figure 3–63).

Q&A What causes the table move handle and table resize handle to appear and disappear from the table?
They appear whenever you position the mouse pointer in the table.

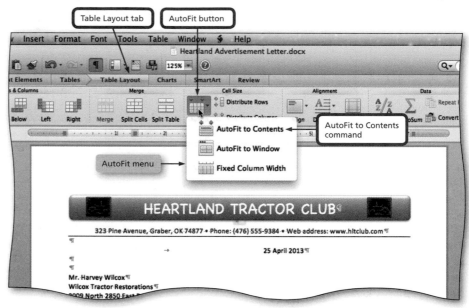

Figure 3–63

- Click AutoFit to Contents in the AutoFit menu, so that Word automatically adjusts the widths of the columns based on the text in the table (Figure 3–64).

Q&A Can I resize columns manually?
Yes, you can drag a **column boundary,** the border to the right of a column, until the column is the desired width. Similarly, you can resize a row by dragging the **row boundary,** the border at the bottom of a row, until the row is the desired height. You also can resize the entire table by dragging the **table resize handle,** which is a small square that appears when you point to the table (shown in Figure 3–65).

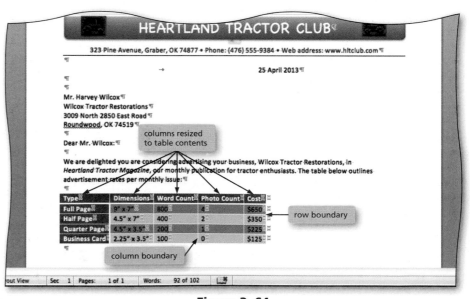

Figure 3–64

Other Ways

1. CONTROL-click table, point to AutoFit on shortcut menu, click AutoFit to Contents
2. Double-click column boundary

Selecting Table Contents

When working with tables, you may need to select the contents of cells, rows, columns, or the entire table. Table 3–4 identifies ways to select various items in a table.

Table 3–4 Selecting Items in a Table	
Item to Select	**Action**
Cell	Point to left edge of cell and click when the mouse pointer changes to a small solid upward-angled pointing arrow.
Column	Point to border at top of column and click when the mouse pointer changes to a small solid downward-pointing arrow.
Row	Point to the left of the row and click when the mouse pointer changes to a right-pointing block arrow.
Multiple cells, rows, or columns adjacent to one another	Drag through cells, rows, or columns.
Multiple cells, rows, or columns not adjacent to one another	Select first cell, row, or column (as described above) and then hold down the **COMMAND** key while selecting next cell, row, or column.
Next cell	Press the **TAB** key.
Previous cell	Press **SHIFT-TAB**.
Table	Point somewhere in the table and then click the table move handle that appears in upper-left corner of the table.

BTW

Resizing Table Columns and Rows

To change the width of a column or the height of a row to an exact measurement, hold down the option key while dragging markers on the ruler.

BTW

Tab Character in Tables

In a table, the TAB key advances the insertion point from one cell to the next. To insert a tab character in a cell, you must press CONTROL-TAB.

To Align Data in Cells

The next step is to change the alignment of the data in cells in the second, third, fourth, and fifth columns of the table. In addition to aligning text horizontally in a cell (left, center, or right), you can align it vertically within a cell (top, center, bottom). When the height of the cell is close to the same height as the text, differences in vertical alignment are not readily apparent, which is the case for this table. The following steps center data in cells.

- Select the cells in the second, third, fourth, and fifth columns by selecting column 2 and then dragging through column 5 (Figure 3–65).

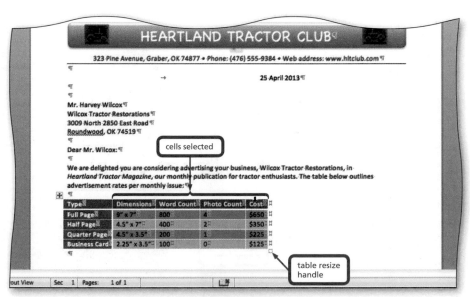

Figure 3–65

- On the Table Layout tab, under Alignment, click the Align button, and then choose Top Center in the menu to center the contents of the selected cells.

- Click in the table to remove the selection (Figure 3–66).

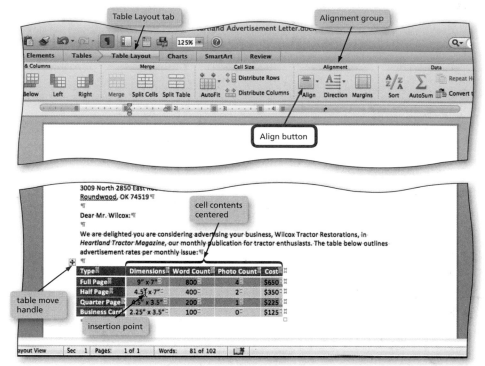

Figure 3–66

To Center a Table

When you first create a table, it is left-aligned, that is, flush with the left margin. In this letter, the table should be centered between the margins. To center a table, you first select the entire table. The following steps select and center a table.

- Position the mouse pointer in the table so that the table move handle appears (shown in Figure 3–66).

- Click the table move handle to select the entire table (Figure 3–67).

Q&A What if the table move handle does not appear?
You also can select a table by placing the insertion point in the table, clicking Table in the menu bar, and then choosing Table.

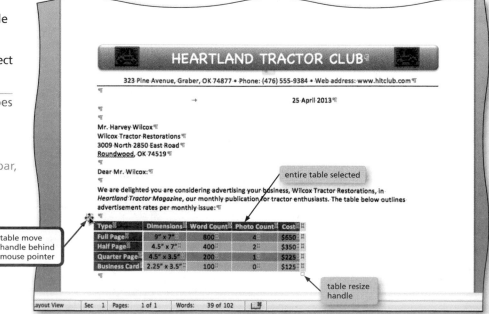

Figure 3–67

2

- On the Home tab, under Paragraph, click the Center button to center the selected table between the left and right margins (Figure 3–68).

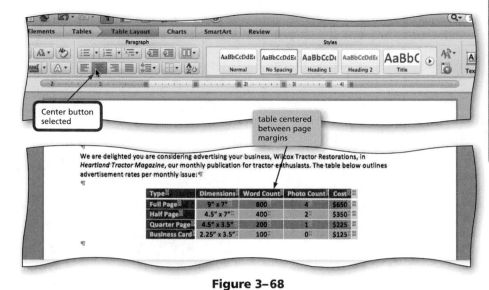

Center button selected

table centered between page margins

Figure 3–68

Other Ways

1. On Table Layout tab under Settings, click Properties button, click Table tab, set alignment, click OK button

To Insert a Row in a Table

The next step is to insert a row at the top of the table because you want to place a title on the table. As discussed earlier, you can insert a row at the end of a table by positioning the insertion point in the bottom-right corner cell and then pressing the TAB key. You cannot use the TAB key to insert a row at the beginning or middle of a table. Instead, you use the Above or Below command. The following steps insert a row in a table.

1

- Position the mouse pointer somewhere in the first row of the table because you want to insert a row above this row (Figure 3–69).

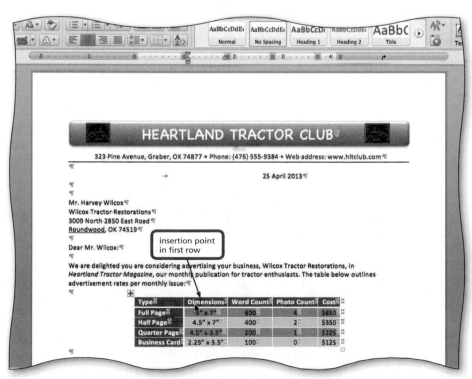

insertion point in first row

Figure 3–69

2

- On the Table Layout tab, under Rows & Columns, click the Above button to insert a row above the row containing the insertion point and then select the newly inserted row (Figure 3–70).

Q&A Do I have to insert rows above the row containing the insertion point?
No. You can insert below the row containing the insertion point by clicking the Below button in the Rows & Columns group on the Table Layout tab.

Q&A Why did the colors in the second row change?
The table style specifies to format the Header row differently, which is the first row.

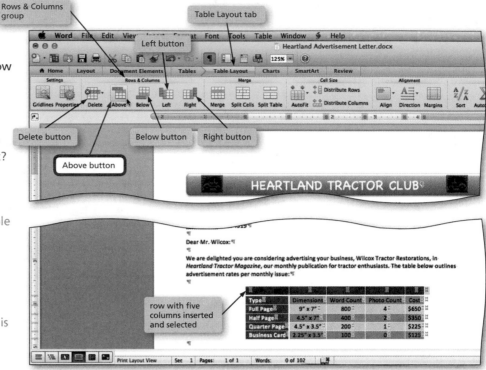

Figure 3–70

TO INSERT A COLUMN IN A TABLE

If, instead of inserting rows, you wanted to insert a column in a table, you would perform the following steps.

1. Position the insertion point in the column to the left or right of where you want to insert the column.

2. On the Table Layout tab, under the Rows & Columns group, click the Left button to insert a column to the left of the current column, or click the Right button to insert a column to the right of the current column. Or you could select the column to the right of where you want the new column, CONTROL-click the selected column, and choose Insert Columns in the shortcut menu.

Moving Tables

BTW If you wanted to move a table to a new location, you would point to the upper-left corner of the table to show the table move handle (four-pointed arrow), then drag the table move handle to the desired new location.

Deleting Table Data

If you want to delete row(s) or delete column(s) from a table, position the insertion point in the row(s) or column(s) to delete, and on the Table Layout tab, under Rows & Columns, click the Delete button, and then click Delete Rows or Delete Columns on the Delete menu. Or, select the row or column to delete, CONTROL-click the selection, and then click Delete Rows or Delete Columns in the shortcut menu.

To delete the contents of a cell, select the cell contents and then press the DELETE key or FUNCTION-DELETE key. You also can drag and drop or cut and paste the contents of cells. To delete an entire table, select the table, and on the Table Layout tab, under Rows & Columns, click the Delete button and then click Delete Table on the Delete menu. To delete the contents of a table and leave an empty table, you would select the table and then press the DELETE key.

To Merge Cells

The top row of the table is to contain the table title, which should be centered above the columns of the table. The row just inserted has one cell for each column, in this case, five cells (shown in Figure 3–70). The title of the table, however, should be in a single cell that spans all rows. Thus, the following steps merge the five cells into a single cell.

- With the cells to merge selected (as shown in Figure 3–70), on the Table Layout tab, under Merge, click the Merge button to merge the five cells into one cell (Figure 3–71).

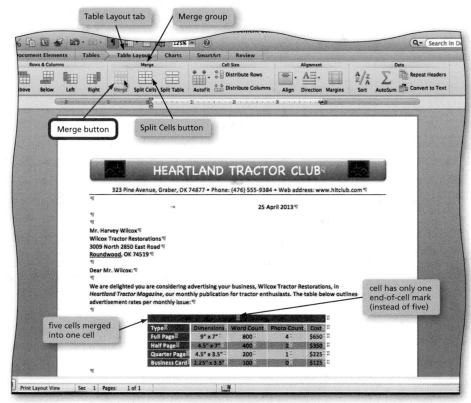

Figure 3–71

- Position the insertion point in the first row and then type `Monthly Issue Advertisement Rates` as the table title (Figure 3–72).

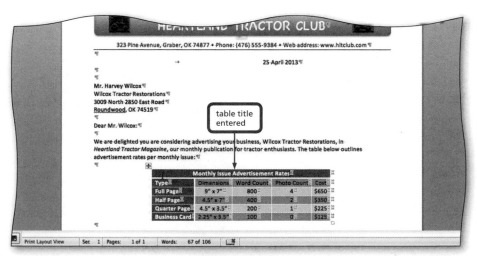

Figure 3–72

Other Ways

1. CONTROL-click selected cells to merge, click Merge Cells in shortcut menu

TO SPLIT TABLE CELLS

Instead of merging multiple cells into a single cell, sometimes you want to split a single cell into multiple cells. If you wanted to split cells, you would perform the following steps.

1. Position the insertion point in the cell to split.
2. On the Table Layout tab, under Merge, click the Split Cells button, or CONTROL-click the cell and then click Split Cells on the shortcut menu, to display the Split Cells dialog.
3. Enter the number of columns and rows into which you want the cell split (Split Cells dialog).
4. Click the OK button.

To Add More Text

The table now is complete. The next step is to enter text below the table. The following steps enter text.

1 Position the insertion point on the paragraph mark below the table and then press the RETURN key.

2 Type `Please note that additional fees will be assessed if the word or photo counts exceed the limits listed above. We offer the following discounts:` and then press the RETURN key (shown in Figure 3–73).

To Bullet a List as You Type

In Chapter 1, you learned how to apply bullets to existing paragraphs. If you know before you type that a list should be bulleted, you can use Word's AutoFormat As You Type feature to bullet the paragraphs as you type them (see Table 3–2 on page WD 164). The following steps add bullets to a list as you type.

- Press the ASTERISK key (*) as the first character on the line (Figure 3–73).

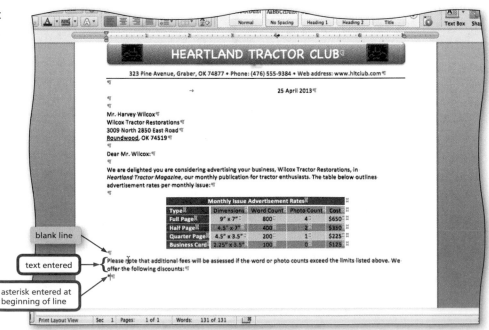

Figure 3–73

2

- Press the SPACE BAR and then type `10 percent discount for any advertisement that runs in three consecutive issues` as the first bulleted item.

- Press the RETURN key to convert the asterisk to a bullet character and to place another bullet character at the beginning of the next line (Figure 3–74).

Q&A   What if I did not want the asterisk converted to a bullet character? You could undo the AutoFormat by clicking the Undo button in the Standard toolbar, pressing COMMAND-Z, clicking the AutoCorrect Options button that appears to the left of the bullet character as soon as you press the RETURN key, and then clicking Undo Automatic Bullets in the AutoCorrect Options menu, or by clicking the Bullets button on the Home tab under Paragraph.

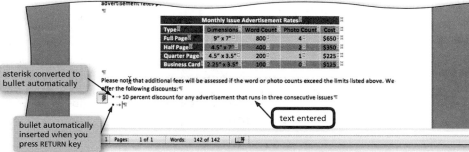

Figure 3–74

3

- Type `5 percent discount for a camera-ready advertisement (prepared using Microsoft Word at the proper size and with all words and photos in final layout form)` and then press the RETURN key.

- Type `3 percent discount if payment in full is submitted with order` and then press the RETURN key.

  Press the RETURN key to turn off automatic bullets as you type (Figure 3–75).

Q&A   Why did automatic bullets stop? When you press RETURN key without entering any text after the automatic bullet character, Word turns off the automatic bullets feature.

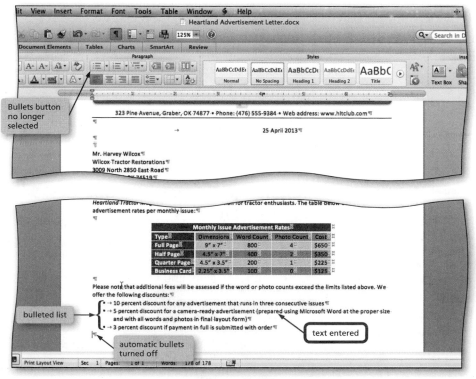

Figure 3–75

Other Ways

1. On Home tab, under Paragraph, click Bullets button

2. CONTROL-click paragraph to be bulleted, point to Bullets and Numbering in shortcut menu, click desired bullet style

To Enter More Text

The following steps enter the remainder of text in the letter.

1 Press RETURN key and then type the paragraph shown in Figure 3–76, making certain you use the AutoText name, wilc, to insert the advertiser name.

2 If necessary, remove the hyperlink from the e-mail address by CONTROL-clicking the e-mail address, choosing Edit Hyperlink from the shortcut menu, and then clicking the Remove Hyperlink button. Press the FUNCTION-RIGHT ARROW keys to position the insertion point at the end of the line.

3 Press RETURN key twice. Press the TAB key to position the insertion point at the 4" mark on the ruler. Type **Sincerely,** and then press RETURN key four times.

4 Press the TAB key to position the insertion point at the 4" mark on the ruler. Type **Frank Urbanczyk** and then press RETURN key.

5 Press the TAB key to position the insertion point at the 4" mark on the ruler. Type **President** as the final text in the business letter (Figure 3–76).

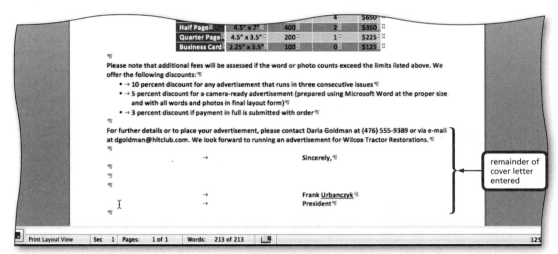

Figure 3–76

To Change Document Properties, Save the Document Again, and Print It

Before saving the letter again, you want to add your name and course and section as document properties if necessary. The following steps change document properties, save the document again, and then print the document.

1 Display the Properties dialog. If necessary, enter your name in the Author property, and enter your course and section in the Subject property. Close the Properties dialog.

2 Click the Save button on the Standard toolbar to overwrite the previously saved file.

3 Click File on the Menu bar and choose Print to display the Print dialog.

4 Verify the printer name that appears in the Printer text box will print a hard copy of the document. If necessary, click the Printer box arrow to display a list of available printer options and then click the desired printer to change the currently selected printer.

5 Click the Print button (Print dialog) to print the letter on the currently selected printer (shown in Figure 3–1 on page WD 141).

Addressing and Printing Envelopes and Mailing Labels

BTWs

For a complete list of the BTWs found in the margins of this book, visit the Office 2011 for Mac Online Companion Web page at www.cengagebrain.com, navigate to the desired chapter, and click BTWs.

With Word, you can print address information on an envelope or on a mailing label. Computer-printed addresses look more professional than handwritten ones.

To Address and Print an Envelope

The following steps address and print an envelope. If you are in a lab environment, check with your instructor before performing these steps.

- Scroll through the letter to display the inside address in the document window.

- Drag through the inside address to select it (Figure 3–77).

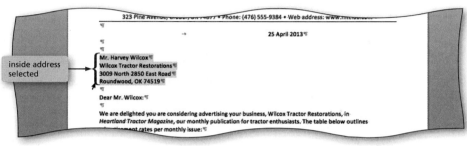

Figure 3–77

- Click Tools in the menu bar, and choose Envelopes to display the Envelope dialog.

- Under Return Address, click to select the Omit option (Figure 3–78).

❸

- Insert an envelope in your printer and click the Print button in the Envelope dialog and then click Print in the Print dialog to print the envelope.

- Click File in the menu bar and choose Close to close the Envelope document that Word created when you printed the document. Click the Don't Save button in the dialog.

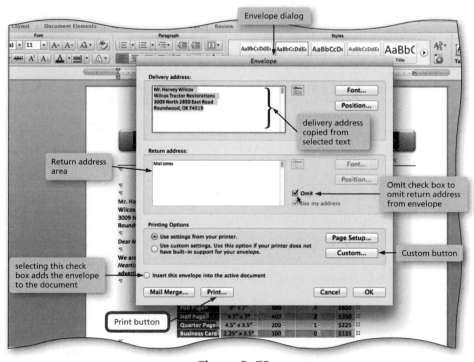

Figure 3–78

Envelopes and Labels

Instead of printing the envelope immediately, you can add it to the document by clicking the 'Insert this envelope into the active document' option (Envelope dialog). To specify a different envelope type (identified by a number on the box of envelopes), click the Custom button under Printing Options (Envelope dialog).

Instead of printing an envelope, you can print a mailing label. To do this, click Tools in the menu bar and then choose Labels to open the Labels dialog. Type the delivery

Quick Reference

BTW For a table that lists how to complete the tasks covered in this book using the mouse, ribbon, shortcut menu, and keyboard, see the Quick Reference Summary at the back of this book, or visit the Office 2011 for Mac Online Companion Web page at www.cengagebrain.com, navigate to the desired application, and click Quick Reference.

address in the Delivery address box. To print the same address on all labels on the page, click 'Full page of the same label' in the Print area. To specify the type of label, click the Options button (Labels dialog). Click the Print button (Labels dialog) to print the label(s).

To Quit Word

This project now is complete. The following steps quit Word.

1 Click Word in the menu bar and then choose Quit Word to close all open documents and quit Word.

2 If a Word dialog appears, click the Save button to save any changes made to the document since the last save.

Chapter Summary

In this chapter, you have learned how to use Word to change margins, insert and format a shape, change text wrapping, download, insert, and format clip art, move and copy graphics, insert symbols, add a border, clear formatting, convert a hyperlink to regular text, create a file from an existing file, set and use tab stops, insert the current date, create and insert AutoText, insert and format tables, and address and print envelopes and mailing labels. The items listed below include all the new Word skills you have learned in this chapter.

1. Change Margin Settings (WD 143)
2. Insert a Shape (WD 144)
3. Apply a Shape Style (WD 146)
4. Add Text to a Shape (WD 147)
5. Use the Increase Font Size Button to Increase Font Size (WD 147)
6. Change an Object's Text Wrapping (WD 149)
7. Find and Download Clip Art (WD 150)
8. Add Clip Art to the Clip Gallery (WD 151)
9. Insert Clip Art (WD 153)
10. Resize a Graphic to a Percent of the Original (WD 154)
11. Change the Color of a Graphic (WD 154)
12. Adjust the Brightness and Contrast of a Graphic (WD 155)
13. Change the Border Color on a Graphic (WD 156)
14. Move a Graphic (WD 157)
15. Use Paste Options (WD 158)
16. Flip a Graphic (WD 159)
17. Insert a Symbol from the Symbol Dialog (WD 160)
18. Bottom Border a Paragraph (WD 162)
19. Clear Formatting (WD 163)
20. Convert a Hyperlink to Regular Text (WD 165)
21. Create a New File from an Existing File (WD 167)
22. Apply a Quick Style (WD 169)
23. Set Custom Tab Stops (WD 170)
24. Insert the Current Date in a Document (WD 172)
25. Create an AutoText Entry (WD 173)
26. Insert AutoText (WD 174)
27. Insert a Nonbreaking Space (WD 175)
28. Insert an Empty Table (WD 176)
29. Enter Data in a Table (WD 177)
30. Apply a Table Style (WD 178)
31. Resize Table Columns to Fit Table Contents (WD 180)
32. Align Data in Cells (WD 181)
33. Center a Table (WD 182)
34. Insert a Row in a Table (WD 183)
35. Insert a Column in a Table (WD 184)
36. Merge Cells (WD 185)
37. Split Table Cells (WD 186)
38. Bullet a List as You Type (WD 186)
39. Address and Print an Envelope (WD 189)

If you have a SAM 2010 user profile, your instructor may have assigned an autogradable version of this assignment. If so, log into the SAM 2010 Web site at www.cengage.com/sam2010 to download the instruction and start files.

Learn It Online

Test your knowledge of chapter content and key terms.

Instructions: To complete the Learn It Online exercises, please visit **www.cengagebrain.com**. At the CengageBrain.com home page, search for *Office 2011 for Mac* using the search box at the top of the page. This will take you to the product page for this book. On the product page, click the Access Now button below the Study Tools heading. On the Book Companion Site Web page, select Word Chapter 3, and then click the link for the desired exercise.

Chapter Reinforcement TF, MC, and SA

A series of true/false, multiple choice, and short answer questions that test your knowledge of the chapter content.

Flash Cards

An interactive learning environment where you identify chapter key terms associated with displayed definitions.

Practice Test

A series of multiple choice questions that test your knowledge of chapter content and key terms.

Who Wants To Be a Computer Genius?

An interactive game that challenges your knowledge of chapter content in the style of a television quiz show.

Wheel of Terms

An interactive game that challenges your knowledge of chapter key terms in the style of the television show *Wheel of Fortune*.

Crossword Puzzle Challenge

A crossword puzzle that challenges your knowledge of key terms presented in the chapter.

Apply Your Knowledge

Reinforce the skills and apply the concepts you learned in this chapter.

Working with Tabs and a Table

Note: To complete this assignment, you will be required to use the Data Files for Students. See the inside back cover of this book for instructions on downloading the Data Files for Students, or contact your instructor for information about accessing the required files.

Instructions: Start Word. Create a new document from the file called Apply 3-1 Projected College Expenses Draft, located on the Data Files for Students. The document is a Word table that you are to edit and format. The revised table is shown in Figure 3–79.

Projected College Expenses

	Freshman	Sophomore	Junior	Senior
Room & Board	3390.00	3627.30	3881.21	4152.90
Tuition & Books	4850.50	5189.50	5552.72	5941.46
Entertainment	635.00	679.45	727.01	777.90
Cell Phone	359.88	365.78	372.81	385.95
Miscellaneous	325.00	347.75	372.09	398.14
Clothing	540.25	577.80	618.29	661.52
Total	$10,100.63	$10,787.58	11,524.13	$12,317.87

Continued >

Figure 3–79

Apply Your Knowledge *continued*

Perform the following tasks:

1. In the line containing the table title, Projected College Expenses, remove the tab stop at the 1" mark on the ruler.

2. Set a centered tab at the 3" mark on the ruler.

3. Bold the characters in the title. Use the Grow Font button to increase their font size to 14. Change their color to Text 2, Darker 25%.

4. In the table, delete the row containing the Food expenses.

5. Insert a new row at the bottom of the table. In the first cell of the new row, enter Total in the cell. Enter these values in the next three cells: Freshman – $10,100.63; Sophomore – $10,787.58; Senior – $12,317.87.

6. Insert a column between the Sophomore and Senior columns. Fill in the column as follows: Column Title – Junior; Room & Board – 3881.21; Tuition & Books – 5552.72; Entertainment – 727.01; Cell Phone – 372.81; Miscellaneous – 372.09; Clothing – 618.29; Total – $11,524.13.

7. In the Table Options group on the Tables tab, these check boxes should have check marks: Header Row, Total Row, Banded Rows, and First Column. The Last Column and Banded Columns check boxes should not be selected.

8. Apply the Medium Grid 3 - Accent 2 style to the table.

9. Make all columns as wide as their contents (AutoFit Contents).

10. Center the cells containing the column headings.

11. Right-align all cells containing numbers in the table.

12. Center the table between the left and right margins of the page.

13. Change the document properties, as specified by your instructor.

14. Save the document using the file name, Apply 3-1 Projected College Expenses Modified and submit it in the format specified by your instructor.

Extend Your Knowledge

Extend the skills you learned in this chapter and experiment with new skills. You may need to use Help to complete the assignment.

Working with Formulas, Clip Art, Sorting, Picture Bullets, Tabs, and Mailing Labels

Note: To complete this assignment, you will be required to use the Data Files for Students. See the inside back cover of this book for instructions on downloading the Data Files for Students, or contact your instructor for information about accessing the required files.

Instructions: Start Word. Create a new document from the file called Extend 3-1 Herbals Letter Draft, located on the Data Files for Students. You will enter formulas in the table, change the clip art to Web clip art, change the table style, sort paragraphs, use picture bullets, move tabs, print mailing labels, and work with the Clip Art Gallery.

Perform the following tasks:

1. Use Help to learn about entering clip art from the Web, sorting, picture bullets, and printing mailing labels.

2. Use Table > Formulas in lthe menu bar to open the Formula dialog (Figure 3–80) to add formulas to the last column in the table so that the total due displays for each item; be sure to enter a number format so that the products are displayed with dollar signs. Then, add formulas to the last row in the

table so that the total quantity and total due are displayed, also with dollar signs. Write down the formulas that Word uses to find the product of values in the rows and to sum the values in a column.

3. Delete the current clip art images in the letterhead. Use the Clip Art Gallery to locate appropriate clip art from the Web, make the clip available offline, and insert an image on each side of the business name in the letterhead.

4. Change the table style. One at a time, select and deselect each check box in the Table Style Options group. Write down the function of each check box: Header Row, Total Row, Banded Rows, First Column, Last Column, and Banded Columns. Select the check boxes you prefer for the table.

5. Sort the paragraphs in the bulleted list. (*Hint:* Use Table > Sort in the menu bar.)

6. Change the bullets in the bulleted list to picture bullets.

7. Move the tab stops in the date line, complimentary close, and signature block from the 3.5" mark to the 4" mark on the ruler.

8. Change the document properties, as specified by your instructor. Save the revised document and then submit it in the format specified by your instructor.

9. Print a single mailing label for the letter.

10. Print a full page of mailing labels, each containing the address shown in Figure 3–80.

11. If your instructor approves, start the Clip Art Gallery. Locate the clip you made available offline in Step 3 and then preview it. What are five of its properties? Add another keyword to the clip. Delete the clip you made available offline.

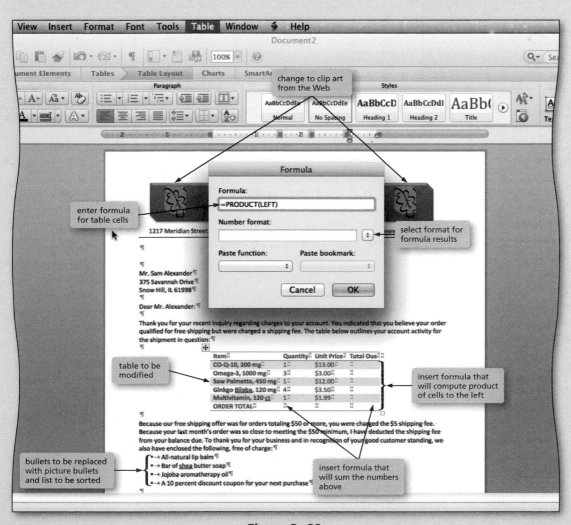

Figure 3–80

Make It Right

Analyze a document and correct all errors and/or improve the design.

Formatting a Business Letter

Note: To complete this assignment, you will be required to use the Data Files for Students. See the inside back cover of this book for instructions on downloading the Data Files for Students, or contact your instructor for information about accessing the required files.

Instructions: Start Word. Create a new document from the file called Make It Right 3-1 Scholarship Letter Draft, located on the Data Files for Students. The document is a business letter that is missing elements and is formatted poorly or incorrectly (Figure 3–81). You are to insert and format clip art in the letterhead, change the color of the text and graphic(s), insert symbols, remove a hyperlink, change the letter style from block to modified block, and format the table.

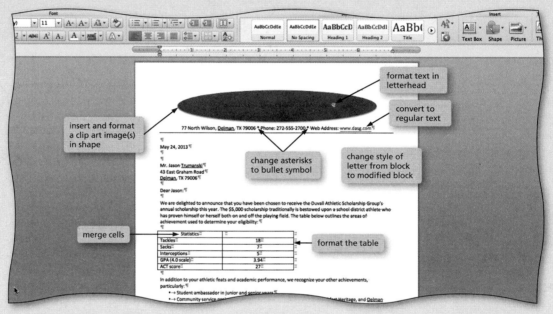

Figure 3–81

Perform the following tasks:

1. Increase the font size of the text in the letterhead. Change the color of the text in the letterhead.

2. Locate and insert at least one appropriate clip art image in the letterhead. If necessary, resize the graphic(s). Move the graphic(s) into the shape.

3. Change the color of the graphic to match the color of the text or shape. Adjust the brightness and contrast of the graphic. Format one color in the graphic as transparent. Change the picture border color.

4. Change the asterisks in the contact information to the dot symbol. Convert the Web address hyperlink to regular text.

5. The letter currently is the block letter style. It should be the modified block letter style. Format the appropriate paragraphs by setting custom tab stops and then positioning those paragraphs at the tab stops. Be sure to position the insertion point in the paragraph before setting the tab stop.

6. Merge the two cells in the first row of the table to one cell and then center the title in the cell. Center the entire table between the page margins. Apply a table style of your choice.

7. Change the document properties, as specified by your instructor. Save the revised document using the file name, Make It Right 3-1 Scholarship Letter Modified, and then submit it in the format specified by your instructor.

In the Lab

Design and/or create a document using the guidelines, concepts, and skills presented in this chapter. Labs are listed in order of increasing difficulty.

Lab 1: Creating a Letter with a Letterhead

Problem: As a consultant for DataLock Storage, you respond to queries from potential customers. One letter you prepare is shown in Figure 3–82.

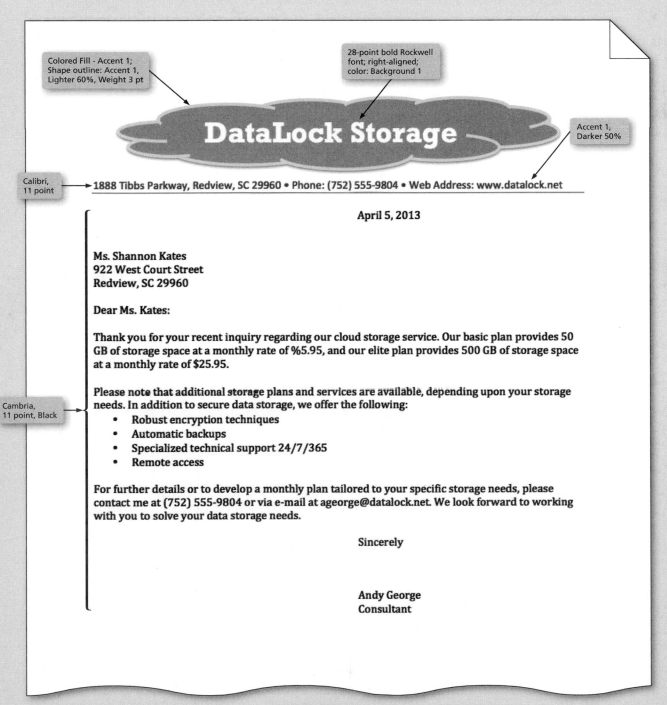

Figure 3–82

Continued >

In the Lab *continued*

Perform the following tasks:

1. Create a new Word document. Change the color scheme to Technic. Set the margins to Normal.

2. Create the letterhead shown at the top of Figure 3–82 on the previous page, following these guidelines:

   a. Insert the cloud shape at an approximate height of 0.95" and width of 5.85". Change text wrapping for the shape to Top and Bottom. Add the company name, DataLock Storage, to the shape. Format the shape and its text as indicated in the figure.

   b. Insert the bullet symbols as shown in the contact information. Remove the hyperlink format from the Web address. If necessary, clear formatting after entering the bottom border.

   c. Save the letterhead with the file name, Lab 3-1 Cloud Storage Letterhead.

3. Create the letter shown in Figure 3–82 using the modified block letter style, following these guidelines:

   a. Apply the No Spacing Quick Style to the document text (below the letterhead).

   b. Set a left-aligned tab stop at the 3.5" mark on the ruler for the date line, complimentary close, and signature block. Insert the current date.

   c. Bullet the list as you type it.

   d. Convert the e-mail address to regular text.

   e. Check the spelling of the letter. Change the document properties, as specified by your instructor. Save the letter with Lab 3-1 Cloud Storage Letter as the file name.

4. If your instructor permits, address and print an envelope or a mailing label for the letter.

In the Lab

Lab 2: Creating a Letter with a Letterhead and Table

Problem: As head librarian at Jonner Public Library, you are responsible for sending confirmation letters for class registrations. You prepare the letter shown in Figure 3–83.

Perform the following tasks:

1. Create a new Word document. Change the color scheme to Pixel. Change the margins to 1" top and bottom and .75" left and right.

2. Create the letterhead shown at the top of Figure 3–83, following these guidelines:

   a. Insert the Curved own Ribbon shape at an approximate height of 1" and width of 7". Change text wrapping for the shape to Top and Bottom. Add the library name to the shape. Format the shape and its text as indicated in the figure.

   b. Insert the clip art image, resize it, change text wrapping to Top and Bottom, move it to the left of the shape, and format it as indicated in the figure. Copy the clip art image and move the copy of the image to the right of the shape, as shown in the figure. Flip the copied image horizontally.

   c. Insert the black small square symbols as shown in the contact information, using the WingDings font. Remove the hyperlink format from the Web address. If necessary, clear formatting after entering the bottom border.

   d. Save the letterhead with the file name, Lab 3-2 Library Letterhead.

3. Create the letter shown in Figure 3–83, following these guidelines:

   a. Apply the No Spacing Quick Style to the document text (below the letterhead).

   b. Set a left-aligned tab stop at the 4" mark on the ruler for the date line, complimentary close, and signature block. Insert the current date.

c. Insert and center the table. Format the table as specified in the figure.

d. Bullet the list as you type it. Convert the e-mail address to regular text.

e. Check the spelling of the letter. Change the document properties, as specified by your instructor. Save the letter with Lab 3-2 Library Letter as the file name.

4. If your instructor permits, address and print an envelope or a mailing label for the letter.

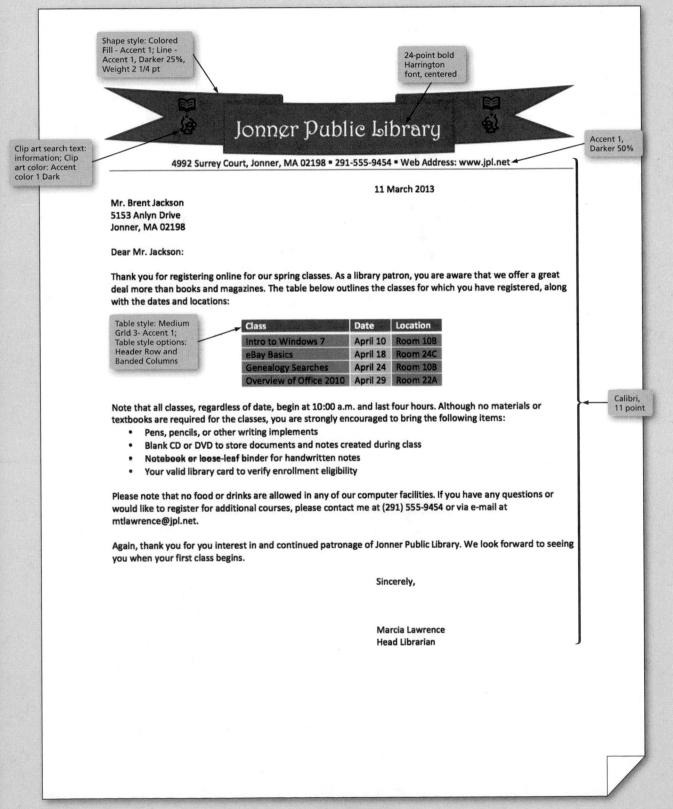

Shape style: Colored Fill - Accent 1; Line - Accent 1, Darker 25%, Weight 2 1/4 pt

24-point bold Harrington font, centered

Clip art search text: information; Clip art color: Accent color 1 Dark

Jonner Public Library

Accent 1, Darker 50%

4992 Surrey Court, Jonner, MA 02198 ▪ 291-555-9454 ▪ Web Address: www.jpl.net

11 March 2013

Mr. Brent Jackson
5153 Anlyn Drive
Jonner, MA 02198

Dear Mr. Jackson:

Thank you for registering online for our spring classes. As a library patron, you are aware that we offer a great deal more than books and magazines. The table below outlines the classes for which you have registered, along with the dates and locations:

Table style: Medium Grid 3- Accent 1; Table style options: Header Row and Banded Columns

Class	Date	Location
Intro to Windows 7	April 10	Room 10B
eBay Basics	April 18	Room 24C
Genealogy Searches	April 24	Room 10B
Overview of Office 2010	April 29	Room 22A

Note that all classes, regardless of date, begin at 10:00 a.m. and last four hours. Although no materials or textbooks are required for the classes, you are strongly encouraged to bring the following items:

Calibri, 11 point

- Pens, pencils, or other writing implements
- Blank CD or DVD to store documents and notes created during class
- Notebook or loose-leaf binder for handwritten notes
- Your valid library card to verify enrollment eligibility

Please note that no food or drinks are allowed in any of our computer facilities. If you have any questions or would like to register for additional courses, please contact me at (291) 555-9454 or via e-mail at mtlawrence@jpl.net.

Again, thank you for you interest in and continued patronage of Jonner Public Library. We look forward to seeing you when your first class begins.

Sincerely,

Marcia Lawrence
Head Librarian

Figure 3–83

In the Lab

Lab 3: Creating a Letter with a Letterhead and Table

Problem: As president of the County Education Board, you communicate with schools in your district. One of the schools has just been awarded a four-star rating.

Instructions: Prepare the letter shown in Figure 3–84. Change the color scheme to Pushpin. Change the margins to 1" top and bottom and .75" left and right. Follow the guidelines in the modified semi-block letter style. Use proper spacing between elements of the letter. After entering the inside address, create an AutoText entry for Fair Grove Elementary School and use the AutoText entry whenever you have to enter the school name. Resize table columns to fit contents. Check the spelling of the letter. Change the document properties, as specified by your instructor. Save the letter with Lab 3-3 Education Board Letter as the file name.

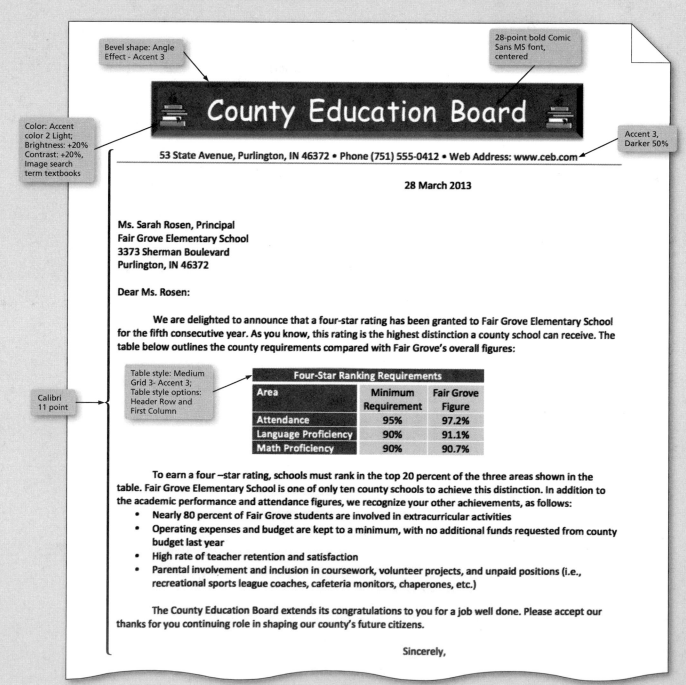

Figure 3–84

Cases and Places

Apply your creative thinking and problem solving skills to design and implement a solution.

Note: To complete these assignments, you may be required to use the Data Files for Students. See the inside back cover of this book for instructions on downloading the Data Files for Students, or contact your instructor for information about accessing the required files.

1: Create a Letter to a Potential Employer

Academic

As a student about to graduate, you are actively seeking employment in your field and have located an advertisement for a job in which you are interested. You decide to write a letter to the potential employer: Ms. Janice Tremont at Home Health Associates, 554 Mountain View Lane, Blue Dust, MO 64319.

The draft wording for the letter is as follows: I am responding to your advertisement for the nursing position in the *Blue Dust Press*. I have tailored my activities and education for a career in geriatric medicine. This month, I will graduate with concentrations in Geriatric Medicine (24 hours), Osteo-pathic Medicine (12 hours), and Holistic Nursing (9 hours). In addition to receiving my bachelor degree in nursing, I have enhanced my education by participating in the following activities: volunteered at Blue Dust's free health care clinic; attended several continuing education and career-specific seminars, including An Aging Populace, Care of the Homebound, and Special Needs of the Elderly; completed one-semester internship at Blue Dust Community Hospital in spring semester of 2012; completed Certified Nursing Assistant (CNA) program at Blue Dust Community College; and worked as nurse's aide for two years during college. I look forward to an interview so that we can discuss the position you offer and my qualifications. With my background and education, I am confident that I will make a positive contribution to Home Health Associates.

The letter should contain a letterhead that uses a shape and clip art, a table (use a table to present the areas of concentration), and a bulleted list (use a bulleted list to present the activities). Insert nonbreaking spaces in the newspaper name. Use the concepts and techniques presented in this chapter to create and format a letter according to the modified block style, creating appropriate paragraph breaks and rewording the draft as necessary. Use your personal information for contact information in the letter. Be sure to check the spelling and grammar of the finished letter. Submit your assignment in the format specified by your instructor.

2: Create a Letter Requesting Donations

Personal

As an alumnus of your historic high school, you are concerned that the building is being considered for demolition. You decide to write a letter to another graduate: Mr. Jim Lemon, 87 Travis Parkway, Vigil, CT 06802.

The draft wording for the letter is as follows: As a member of the class of 1988, you, like many others, probably have many fond memories of our alma mater, Vigil East High School. I recently learned that the building is being considered for demolition because of its age and structural integrity. As a result, I have decided to call upon the many graduating classes of the school to band together and save the historic building from demolition. According to the documents I have reviewed and information from meetings I have attended, a minimum of $214,000 is necessary to save the school and bring it up to code. Once the repairs are made, I plan to start the process of having it declared an historic landmark. You can help by donating your time, skills, or money. We need skilled tradesmen, including carpenters, roofers, plumbers, and electricians, as well as laborers. In addition, we are asking for monetary dona-tions, as follows, although donations in any amount will be accepted gladly: a donation of $100 catego-rizes you as a Save Our School Friend, $250 a Patron, and $500 a Benefactor. Once our monetary goal has been reached, the necessary repairs and replacements will be made as follows: Phase I: roof and exterior, Phase II: electrical and plumbing, and Phase III: interior walls, trim, flooring, and fixtures. I hope you will join our conservation efforts so that Vigil East High School will continue to stand proudly for many more years. If you have questions, please contact me at the phone number or e-mail address above. I hope to hear from you soon.

The letter should contain a letterhead that uses a shape and clip art, a table (use a table to present the Save Our School donor categories), and a bulleted list (use a bulleted list to present the phases). Use the concepts and techniques presented in this chapter to create and format a letter according to the modified block style, creating appropriate paragraph breaks and rewording the draft as necessary. Use your personal information for contact information in the letter and Save Our School as the text in the letterhead. Be sure to check spelling and grammar of the finished letter. Submit your assignment in the format specified by your instructor.

3: Create a Confirmation Letter

Professional

As coordinator for Condor Parks and Recreation, you send letters to confirm registration for activities. You write a confirmation letter to this registrant: Ms. Tracey Li, 52 West 15th Street, Harpville, KY 42194. Condor Parks and Recreation is located at 2245 Community Place, Harpville, KY 42194; phone number is (842) 555-0444; and Web address is www.condorparks.com.

The draft wording for the letter is as follows: Thank you for your interest in our new spring activities recently listed in the *Condor Daily Press*. The courses for which you have enrolled, along with their dates and times are Introductory Golf Clinic on May 5 – 6 from 4:00 – 6:00 p.m. at a cost of $25, Recreational League Volleyball on April 30 – May 28 from 7:30 – 9:00 p.m. at a cost of $130, Pilates on May 30 – June 27 from 8:00 – 9:00 p.m. at a cost of $75, and Intermediate Golf Clinic on June 9 – 10 from 12:00 – 2:00 p.m. at a cost of $30. By paying your annual $25 parks and recreation fee, you also are entitled to the following benefits: free access to racquetball and tennis courts, on a first-come-first-served basis; attendance at any park-sponsored event, including plays, musical performances, and festivals; and free parking at any parks and recreation facility. Please confirm your registration by calling me at [enter your phone number here] or via e-mail at [enter your e-mail address here]. Thank you for your interest in Condor Parks and Recreation offerings. We look forward to seeing you at upcoming events.

The letter should contain a letterhead that uses a shape and clip art, a table (use a table to present the courses enrolled), and a bulleted list (use a bulleted list to present the benefits). Insert nonbreaking spaces in the newspaper name. Use the concepts and techniques presented in this chapter to create and format a letter according to the modified block style, creating appropriate paragraph breaks and rewording the draft as necessary. Be sure to check spelling and grammar of the finished letter. Submit your assignment in the format specified by your instructor.

1 Creating and Editing a Presentation with Clip Art

Objectives

You will have mastered the material in this chapter when you can:

Select a document theme

Create a title slide and a text slide with a multi-level bulleted list

Add new slides and change slide layouts

Insert clips and pictures into a slide with and without a content placeholder

Move and size clip art

Change font size and color

Bold and italicize text

Duplicate a slide

Arrange slides

Select slide transitions

View a presentation in Slide Show view

Print a presentation

1 Creating and Editing a Presentation with Clip Art

Introduction

A PowerPoint **presentation,** also called a **slide show,** can help you deliver a dynamic, professional-looking message to an audience. PowerPoint allows you to produce slides to use in an academic, business, or other environment. One of the more common uses of these slides is to enhance an oral presentation. A speaker may desire to convey information, such as urging students to volunteer at a fund-raising event, explaining changes in employee compensation packages, or describing a new laboratory procedure. The PowerPoint slides should reinforce the speaker's message and help the audience retain the information presented. Custom slides can fit your specific needs and contain diagrams, charts, tables, pictures, shapes, video, sound, and animation effects to make your presentation more effective. An accompanying handout gives audience members reference notes and review material for your presentation.

Project Planning Guidelines

The process of developing a presentation that communicates specific information requires careful analysis and planning. As a starting point, establish why the presentation is needed. Next, analyze the intended audience for the presentation and its unique needs. Then, gather information about the topic and decide what to include in the presentation. Finally, determine the presentation design and style that will be most successful at delivering the message.

Energy-Saving Information

BTW The U.S. Department of Energy's Web site has myriad information available on the topics of energy efficiency and renewable energy. These features can provide news and product research that you can share with audiences with the help of a PowerPoint presentation.

Project — Presentation with Bulleted Lists and Clip Art

In this chapter's project, you will follow proper design guidelines and learn to use PowerPoint to create, save, and print the slides shown in Figures 1–1a through 1–1e. The objective is to produce a presentation, called It Is Easy Being Green, to help consumers understand basic steps they can take to save energy in their homes. This slide show has a variety of clip art and visual elements to add interest and illustrate energy-cutting measures. Some of the text has formatting and color enhancements. Transitions help one slide flow gracefully into the next during a slide show. In addition, you will print a handout of your slides to distribute to audience members.

(a) Slide 1 (Title Slide with Clip Art)

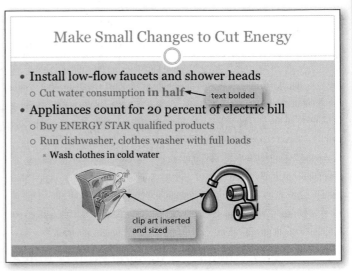

(b) Slide 2 (Multi-Level Bulleted List with Clip Art)

(c) Slide 3 (Title and Picture)

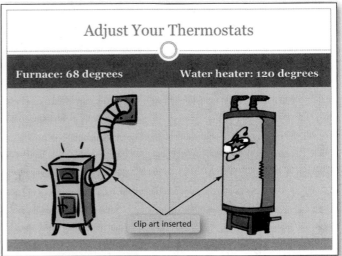

(d) Slide 4 (Comparison Layout and Clip Art)

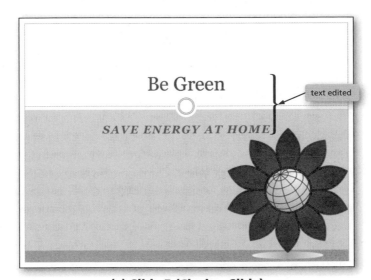

(e) Slide 5 (Closing Slide)

Figure 1–1

BTWs

BTW For a complete list of the BTWs found in the margins of this book, visit the Office 2011 for Mac Online Companion Web page at www.cengagebrain.com, navigate to the desired chapter, and click BTWs.

Overview

As you read this chapter, you will learn how to create the presentation shown in Figure 1–1 on the previous page by performing these general tasks:

- Select an appropriate document theme.
- Enter titles and text on slides.
- Change the size, color, and style of text.
- Insert clips and a photograph.
- Add a transition to each slide.
- View the presentation on your computer.
- Print your slides.

Plan Ahead

General Project Guidelines

When creating a PowerPoint document, the actions you perform and decisions you make will affect the appearance and characteristics of the finished document. As you create a presentation such as the project shown in Figure 1–1, you should follow these general guidelines:

1. **Find the appropriate theme.** The overall appearance of a presentation significantly affects its capability to communicate information clearly. The slides' graphical appearance should support the presentation's overall message. Colors, fonts, and layouts affect how audience members perceive and react to the slide content.

2. **Choose words for each slide.** Use the less is more principle. The less text, the more likely the slides will enhance your speech. Use the fewest words possible to make a point.

3. **Format specific elements of the text.** Examples of how you can modify the appearance, or **format**, of text include changing its shape, size, color, and position on the slide.

4. **Determine where to save the presentation.** You can store a document permanently, or **save** it, on a variety of storage media, including a hard disk, USB flash drive, or CD. You also can indicate a specific location on the storage media for saving the document.

5. **Determine the best method for distributing the presentation.** Presentations can be distributed on paper or electronically. You can print a hard copy of the presentation slides for proofing or reference, or you can distribute an electronic image in various formats.

When necessary, more specific details concerning the above guidelines are presented at appropriate points in the chapter. The chapter also will identify the actions performed and decisions made regarding these guidelines during the creation of the slides shown in Figure 1–1.

For an introduction to Mac OS X and instruction about how to perform basic Mac OS X tasks, read the Office 2011 and Mac OS X chapter at the beginning of this book, where you can learn how to resize windows, change screen resolution, create folders, move and rename files, use Mac OS X Help, and much more.

To Start PowerPoint

If you are using a computer to step through the project in this chapter and you want your screens to match the figures in this book, you should change your screen's resolution to 1280 × 800. For information about how to change a computer's resolution, refer to the Office 2011 and Mac OS X chapter at the beginning of this book.

The following steps, which assume Mac OS X is running, start PowerPoint based on a typical installation. You may need to ask your instructor how to start PowerPoint for your computer. For a detailed example of the procedure summarized below, refer to the Office 2011 and Mac OS X chapter.

1 Click the PowerPoint icon in the Dock to display the PowerPoint Presentation Gallery.

Q&A What is the Welcome to PowerPoint screen I see?
The first time you start PowerPoint, you may see the Welcome to PowerPoint screen. Click Continue to move to the PowerPoint Presentation Gallery.

Q&A   Why do I see a blank PowerPoint presentation rather than the PowerPoint
Presentation Gallery?
The default setting is to show the PowerPoint Presentation Gallery. If you do not
see it, your PowerPoint application has a setting other than the default. You can
skip to step 4.

2   If All is not selected under Themes in the left pane, click to select it.

3   Double-click the White theme in the PowerPoint Presentation Gallery to display a new
blank presentation in the PowerPoint window.

4   If the PowerPoint window is not sized properly, as described in the Office 2011 and Mac
OS X chapter, size the window properly.

5   If the Normal View button in the lower left of the presentation window is not selected,
click it so that your screen is in Normal view.

> For an introduction
> to Office 2011 and
> instruction about how
> to perform basic tasks in
> Office 2011 programs,
> read the Office 2011 and
> Mac OS X chapter at the
> beginning of this book,
> where you can learn how
> to start a program, use the
> ribbon, save a file, open
> a file, quit a program, use
> Help, and much more.

Choosing a Document Theme

You can give a presentation a professional and integrated appearance easily by using
a document theme. A **document theme** provides consistency in design and color
throughout the entire presentation by setting the color scheme, font set, and layout of a
presentation. This collection of formatting choices includes a set of colors (the Theme
Options group, Colors button), a set of heading and content text fonts (the Theme
Options group, Fonts button), and a set of lines and fill effects (the Theme Effects
group). These groups allow you to choose and change the appearance of all the slides
or individual slides in your presentation. The status bar in Figure 1–2 on the next page
shows the current slide number followed by the total number of slides in the document.

Find the appropriate theme.

In the initial steps of this project, you will select a document theme by locating a particular
built-in theme in the Themes group. You could, however, apply a theme at any time while
creating the presentation. Some PowerPoint slide show designers create presentations
using the default Office Theme. This blank design allows them to concentrate on the
words being used to convey the message and does not distract them with colors and
various text attributes. Once the text is entered, the designers then select an appropriate
document theme.

Plan Ahead

To Choose a Document Theme

The document theme identifier shows the theme currently used in the slide show. PowerPoint initially
uses the **Office Theme** until you select a different theme. The steps on the next page change the theme for this
presentation from the Office Theme to the Civic document theme.

1

- Click Themes on the ribbon to display the Themes tab (Figure 1–2).

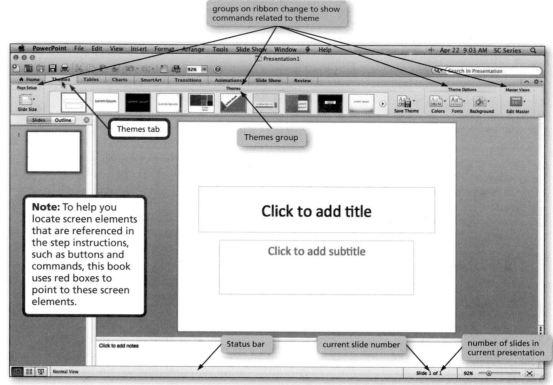

Figure 1–2

2

- Move the mouse into the Themes in-ribbon gallery to make the More button visible.

- Click the More button to expand the gallery, which shows more Built-In theme gallery options (Figure 1–3).

Q&A Are the themes displayed in a specific order?
Yes. They are arranged in alphabetical order running from left to right. If you point to a theme, a ScreenTip with the theme's name appears on the screen.

Q&A What if I change my mind and do not want to select a new theme?
Click anywhere outside the gallery to close the gallery.

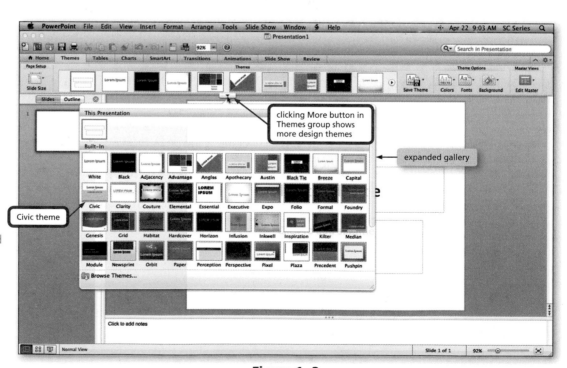

Figure 1–3

- Click the Civic theme to apply this theme to Slide 1 (Figure 1–4).

Q&A If I decide at some future time that this theme does not fit the design of my presentation, can I apply a different theme?

Yes. You can repeat these steps at any time while creating your presentation.

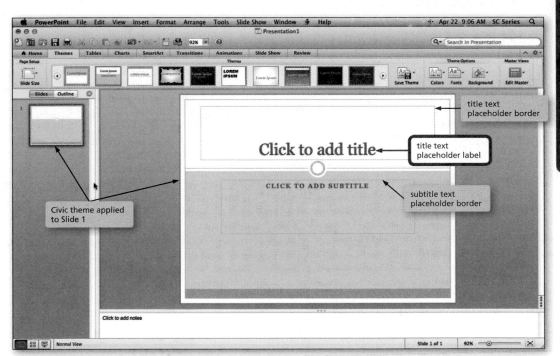

Figure 1–4

Creating a Title Slide

When you open a new presentation, the default **Title Slide** layout appears. The purpose of this layout is to introduce the presentation to the audience. PowerPoint includes eight other built-in standard layouts. The default (preset) slide layouts are set up in **landscape orientation**, where the slide width is greater than its height. In landscape orientation, the slide size is preset to 10 inches wide and 7.5 inches high when printed on a standard sheet of paper measuring 11 inches wide and 8.5 inches high.

Placeholders are boxes with thin borders that are displayed when you create a new slide. Most layouts have both a title text placeholder and at least one content placeholder. Depending on the particular slide layout selected, title and subtitle placeholders are displayed for the slide title and subtitle; a content text placeholder is displayed for text, art, or a table, chart, picture, graphic, or movie. The title slide has two text placeholders where you can type the main heading, or title, of a new slide and the subtitle.

With the exception of a blank slide, PowerPoint assumes every new slide has a title. To make creating a presentation easier, any text you type after a new slide appears becomes title text in the title text placeholder.

The Ribbon and Screen Resolution

PowerPoint may change **BTW** how the groups and buttons within the groups appear on the ribbon, depending on the computer's screen resolution. Thus, your ribbon may look different from the ones in this book if you are using a screen resolution other than 1280 x 800.

Choose the words for the slide.   **Plan Ahead**

No doubt you have heard the phrase, "You get only one chance to make a first impression." The same philosophy holds true for a PowerPoint presentation. The title slide gives your audience an initial sense of what they are about to see and hear. It is, therefore, extremely important to choose the text for this slide carefully. Avoid stating the obvious in the title. Instead, create interest and curiosity using key ideas from the presentation.

Some PowerPoint users create the title slide as their last step in the design process so that it reflects the tone of the presentation. They begin by planning the final slide in the presentation so that they know where and how they want to end the slide show. All the slides in the presentation should work toward meeting this final slide.

To Enter the Presentation Title

The presentation title for this project is It Is Easy Being Green. This title creates interest by introducing the concept of simple energy conservation tasks. The following steps create the slide show's title.

1

• Click the label, Click to add title, located inside the title text placeholder to select the placeholder (Figure 1–5).

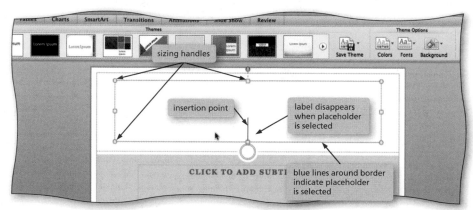

Figure 1–5

2

• Type **It Is Easy Being Green** in the title text placeholder. Do not press the RETURN key (Figure 1–6).

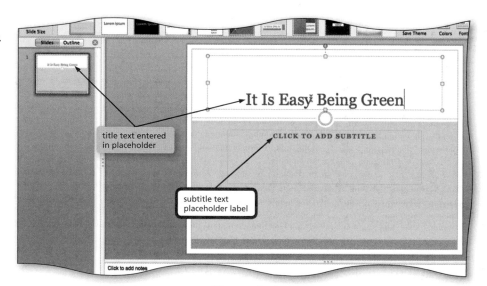

Figure 1–6

Correcting a Mistake When Typing

If you type the wrong letter, press the DELETE key to erase all the characters back to and including the one that is incorrect. If you mistakenly press the RETURN key after typing the title and the insertion point is on the new line, simply press the DELETE key to return the insertion point to the right of the letter n in the word, Green.

When you install PowerPoint, the default setting allows you to reverse up to the last 20 changes by clicking the Undo button on the Standard toolbar. The ScreenTip that appears when you point to the Undo button changes to indicate the type of change just made. For example, if you type text in the title text placeholder and then point to the Undo button, the ScreenTip that appears is Undo Typing. For clarity, when referencing the Undo button in this project, the name displaying in the ScreenTip is referenced. You can reapply a change that you reversed with the Undo button by clicking the Redo button on the Standard toolbar. Clicking the Redo button reverses the last undo action. The ScreenTip name reflects the type of reversal last performed.

Paragraphs

Text in the subtitle text placeholder supports the title text. It can appear on one or more lines in the placeholder. To create more than one subtitle line, you press the RETURN key after typing some words. PowerPoint creates a new line, which is the second paragraph in the placeholder. A **paragraph** is a segment of text with the same format that begins when you press the RETURN key and ends when you press the RETURN key again. This new paragraph is the same level as the previous paragraph. A **level** is a position within a structure, such as an outline, that indicates the magnitude of importance. PowerPoint allows for five paragraph levels.

To Enter the Presentation Subtitle Paragraph

The first subtitle paragraph links to the title by giving further detail that the presentation will focus on energy-saving measures at home. The following steps enter the presentation subtitle.

1

- Click the label, CLICK TO ADD SUBTITLE, located inside the subtitle text placeholder to select the placeholder (Figure 1–7).

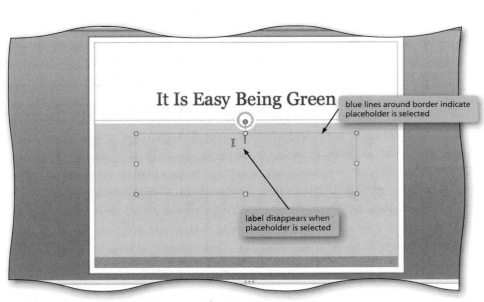

Figure 1–7

2

- Type **Saving Energy at Home** but do not press the RETURN key (Figure 1–8).

Q&A Why did my typing appear in all small capital letters?
The Civic theme automatically converts subtitle text to small caps.

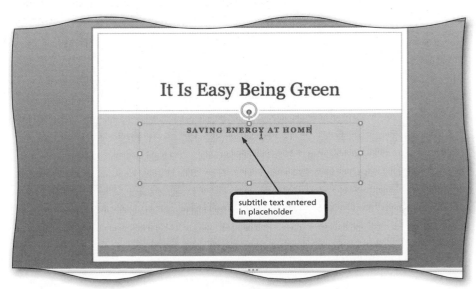

Figure 1–8

Plan Ahead

Identify how to format specific elements of the text.

Most of the time, you use the document theme's text attributes, color scheme, and layout. Occasionally, you may want to change the way a presentation looks, however, and still keep a particular document theme. PowerPoint gives you that flexibility.

Graphic designers use several rules when formatting text.

- Avoid all capital letters, if possible. Audiences have difficulty comprehending sentences typed in all capital letters, especially when the lines exceed seven words. All capital letters leaves no room for emphasis or inflection, so readers get confused about what material deserves particular attention. Some document themes, however, have a default title text style of all capital letters.

- Avoid text with a font size less than 30 point. Audience members generally will sit a maximum of 50 feet from a screen, and at this distance 30-point type is the smallest size text they can read comfortably without straining.

- Make careful color choices. Color evokes emotions, and a careless color choice may elicit the incorrect psychological response. PowerPoint provides a color gallery with hundreds of colors. The built-in document themes use complementary colors that work well together. If you stray from these themes and add your own color choices, without a good reason to make the changes, your presentation is apt to become ineffective.

BTW

Q&As

For a complete list of the Q&As found in many of the step-by-step sequences in this book, visit the Office 2011 for Mac Online Companion Web page at www.cengagebrain.com, navigate to the desired chapter, and click Q&As.

Formatting Characters in a Presentation

Recall that each document theme determines the color scheme, font set, and layout of a presentation. You can use a specific document theme and then change the characters' formats any time before, during, or after you type the text.

Fonts and Font Styles

Characters that appear on the screen are a specific shape and size. Examples of how you can modify the appearance, or **format**, of these typed characters on the screen and in print include changing the font, style, size, and color. The **font**, or typeface, defines the appearance and shape of the letters, numbers, punctuation marks, and symbols. **Style** indicates how the characters are formatted. PowerPoint's text font styles include regular, italic, bold, and bold italic. **Size** specifies the height of the characters and is gauged by a measurement system that uses points. A **point** is 1/72 of an inch in height. Thus, a character with a font size of 36 is 36/72 (or 1/2) of an inch in height. **Color** defines the hue of the characters.

This presentation uses the Civic document theme, which uses particular font styles and font sizes. The Civic document theme default title text font is named Georgia. It has a regular style with no special effects, and its size is 42 point. The Civic document theme default subtitle text font also is Georgia, Bold, small caps, with a font size of 16 point.

To Select a Paragraph

You can use many techniques to format characters. When you want to apply the same formats to multiple words or paragraphs, it is efficient to select the desired text and then make the desired changes to all the characters simultaneously. The first formatting change you will make will apply to the title slide subtitle. The following step selects this paragraph.

• Triple-click the paragraph, SAVING ENERGY AT HOME, in the subtitle text placeholder to select the paragraph (Figure 1–9).

Q&A Can I select the paragraph using a technique other than triple-clicking? Yes. You can move your mouse pointer to the left of the paragraph and then drag to the end of the line.

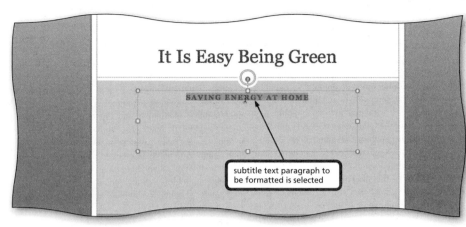

Figure 1–9

To Italicize Text

Different font styles often are used on slides to make them more appealing to the reader and to emphasize particular text. **Italicized** text has a slanted appearance. Used sparingly, it draws the readers' eyes to these characters. The following step adds emphasis to the second line of the subtitle text by changing regular text to italic text.

• With the subtitle text still selected, click the Home tab to make it the active tab, and then click the Italic button in the Font group to italicize that text on the slide (Figure 1–10).

Q&A If I change my mind and decide not to italicize the text, how can I remove this style? Click the Italic button a second time or immediately click the Undo button on the Standard toolbar or press COMMAND-Z.

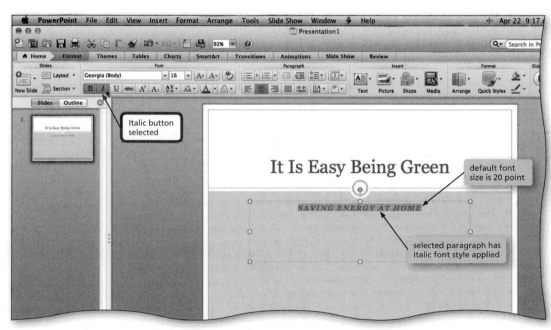

Figure 1–10

Other Ways

1. CONTROL-click selected text, click Format Text in shortcut menu, click Font tab (Format Text dialog), click Italic in Font style list, click OK button

2. Choose Format > Font in menu bar, click Font tab (Format Text dialog), click Italic in Font style list, click OK button

3. Select text, press COMMAND-I

To Increase Font Size

To add emphasis, you increase the font size for the subtitle text. The Increase Font Size button on the Home tab under Font increases the font size in preset increments. The following step uses this button to increase the font size.

- On the Home tab, under Font, click the Increase Font Size button three times to increase the font size of the selected text from 16 to 24 point (Figure 1–11).

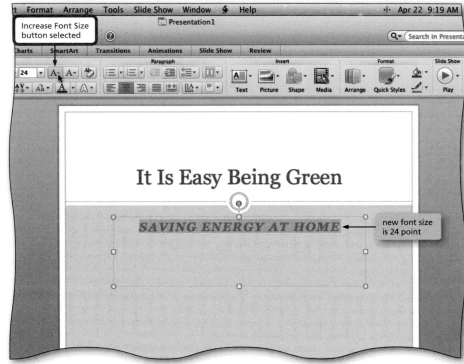

Other Ways

1. On the Home tab, under Font, click Font Size box arrow, click desired font size in Font size list
2. Choose Format > Font in menu bar, click Font tab (Format Text dialog), click 24 in Font size list, click OK button
3. Press COMMAND-SHIFT->

Figure 1–11

To Select a Word

PowerPoint designers use many techniques to emphasize words and characters on a slide. To add emphasis to the energy-saving concept of your slide show, you want to increase the font size and change the font color to bright green for the word, Green, in the title text. You could perform these actions separately, but it is more efficient to select the word and then change the font attributes. The following step selects a word.

- Double-click the word Green to select it (Figure 1–12).

Other Ways

1. Position mouse pointer before first character, press COMMAND-SHIFT-RIGHT ARROW

Figure 1–12

To Change the Text Color

PowerPoint allows you to use one or more text colors in a presentation. To add more emphasis to the word, Green, in the title slide text, and to emphasize the fact that the presentation focuses on green conservation measures, you decide to change the color. The following steps add emphasis to this word by changing the font color from red to bright green.

- With the word, Green, selected, click the Font Color arrow on the Home tab in the Font group to display the Font color gallery (Figure 1–13).

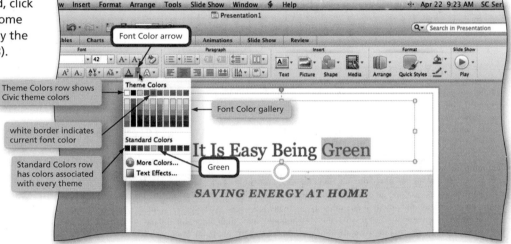

Figure 1–13

- Click the Green color in the Standard Colors row (sixth color) to change the font color to bright green (Figure 1–14).

Q&A What is the difference between the colors shown in the Theme Colors area and the Standard Colors? The 10 colors in the top row of the Theme Colors area are two text, two background, and six accent colors in the Civic theme; the five colors in each column under the top row display different transparencies. The 10 Standard Colors are available in every document theme.

Figure 1–14

- Click outside the selected area to deselect the word.

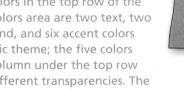

Other Ways

1. CONTROL-click selected text, click Format Text in shortcut menu, click Font Color button, choose Green in Standard Colors row

2. Choose Format > Font in menu bar, click Green under Font Color in Standard Colors row

Organizing Files and Folders

 You should organize and store files in folders so that you easily can find the files later. For example, if you are taking an introductory computer class called CIS 101, a good practice would be to save all PowerPoint files in a PowerPoint folder in a CIS 101 folder. For a discussion of folders and detailed examples of creating folders, refer to the Office for Mac 2011 and Mac OS X chapter at the beginning of this book.

To Save a Presentation

You have performed many tasks while creating this slide and do not want to risk losing work completed thus far. Accordingly, you should save the document.

The following steps assume you already have created folders for storing your files, for example, a CIS 101 folder (for your class) that contains a PowerPoint folder (for your assignments). Thus, these steps save the document in the PowerPoint folder in the CIS 101 folder on a USB flash drive using the file name, Saving Energy. For a detailed example of the procedure summarized below, refer to the Office 2011 and Mac OS X chapter at the beginning of this book.

1 With a USB flash drive connected to one of the computer's USB ports, click the Save button on the Standard toolbar to display the Save As dialog.

2 Type `Saving Energy` in the Save As text box to change the file name. Do not press the RETURN key after typing the file name because you do not want to close the dialog at this time.

3 Navigate to the desired save location (in this case, the PowerPoint folder in the CIS 101 folder [or your class folder] on the USB flash drive).

4 Click the Save button (Save As dialog) to save the document in the selected folder on the selected drive with the entered file name.

Adding a New Slide to a Presentation

With the text for the title slide for the presentation created, the next step is to add the first text slide immediately after the title slide. Usually, when you create a presentation, you add slides with text, clip art, graphics, or charts. Some placeholders allow you to double-click the placeholder and then access other objects, such as media clips, charts, diagrams, and organization charts. You can change the layout for a slide at any time during the creation of a presentation.

To Add a New Text Slide with a Bulleted List

When you add a new slide, PowerPoint uses the Title and Content slide layout. This layout provides a title placeholder and a content area for text, art, charts, and other graphics. A vertical scroll bar appears in the right pane when you add the second slide so that you can move from slide to slide easily. A thumbnail of this slide also appears in the Slides tab. The following step adds a new slide with the Title and Content slide layout.

1

- If necessary, make the Home tab the active tab.

- In the Slides group, click the New Slide button to insert a new slide with the Title and Content layout (Figure 1–15).

Q&A I clicked the New Slide button arrow instead of the New Slide button. What should I do?
Click the Title and Content slide thumbnail in the Layout gallery.

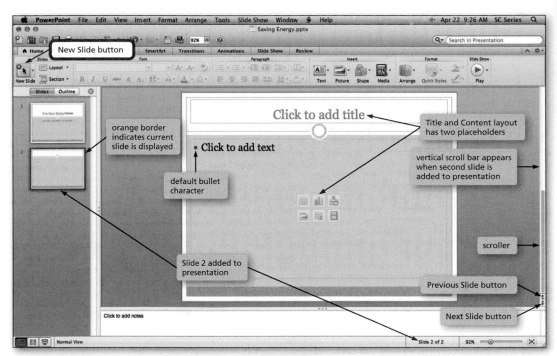

Figure 1–15

● Other Ways

1. Choose Insert > New Slide in menu bar
2. Press COMMAND-SHIFT-N

Choose the words for the slide.   **Plan Ahead**

All presentations should follow the 7 × 7 rule, which states that each slide should have a maximum of seven lines, and each line should have a maximum of seven words. PowerPoint designers must choose their words carefully and, in turn, help viewers read the slides easily.

Avoid line wraps. Your audience's eyes want to stop at the end of a line. Thus, you must plan your words carefully or adjust the font size so that each point displays on only one line.

Creating a Text Slide with a Multi-Level Bulleted List

The information in the Slide 2 text placeholder is presented in a bulleted list with three levels. A **bulleted list** is a list of paragraphs, each of which is preceded by a bullet. A slide that consists of more than one level of bulleted text is called a **multi-level bulleted list slide**. In a multi-level bulleted list, a lower-level paragraph is a subset of a higher-level paragraph. It usually contains information that supports the topic in the paragraph immediately above it.

Two of the Slide 2 bullets appear at the same paragraph level, called the first level: Install low-flow faucets and shower heads, and Appliances count for 20 percent of electric bill. Beginning with the second level, each paragraph indents to the right of the preceding level and is pushed down to a lower level. For example, if you increase the indent of a first-level paragraph, it becomes a second-level paragraph. The second, fourth, and fifth paragraphs on Slide 2 are second-level paragraphs. The last paragraph, Wash clothes in cold water, is a third-level paragraph.

Creating a text slide with a multi-level bulleted list requires several steps. Initially, you enter a slide title in the title text placeholder. Next, you select the content text placeholder. Then, you type the text for the multi-level bulleted list, increasing and decreasing the indents as needed. The next several sections add a slide with a multi-level bulleted list.

To Enter a Slide Title

PowerPoint assumes every new slide has a title. The title for Slide 2 is Make Small Changes to Cut Energy. The following step enters this title.

- Click the label, Click to add title, to select it and then type **Make Small Changes to Cut Energy** in the placeholder. Do not press the RETURN key (Figure 1–16).

Q&A What are those six icons grouped in the middle of the slide?
You can click one of the icons to insert a specific type of content: table, chart, SmartArt graphic, picture, clip art, or media clip.

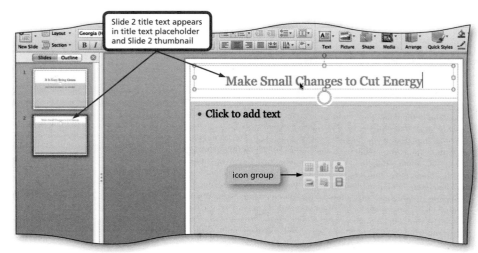

Figure 1–16

To Select a Text Placeholder

Before you can type text into the text placeholder, you first must select it. The following step selects the text placeholder on Slide 2.

- Click the label, Click to add text, to select the text placeholder (Figure 1–17).

Q&A Why does my mouse pointer have a different shape?
If you move the mouse pointer away from the bullet, it will change shape.

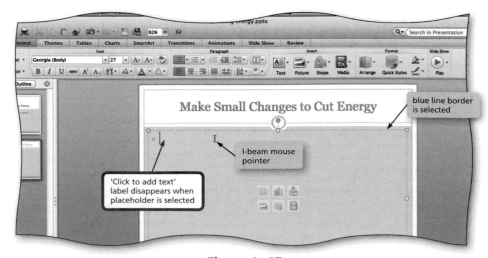

Figure 1–17

To Type a Multi-Level Bulleted List

The content placeholder provides an area for the text characters. When you click inside a placeholder, you then can type or paste text. As discussed previously, a bulleted list is a list of paragraphs, each of which is preceded by a bullet. A paragraph is a segment of text ended by pressing the RETURN key.

The content text placeholder is selected, so the next step is to type the multi-level bulleted list that consists of six paragraphs, as shown in Figure 1–1b on page PPT 3. Creating a lower-level paragraph is called **demoting** text; creating a higher-level paragraph is called **promoting** text. The following steps create a multi-level bulleted list consisting of three levels.

- Type `Install low-flow faucets and shower heads` and then press the RETURN key (Figure 1–18).

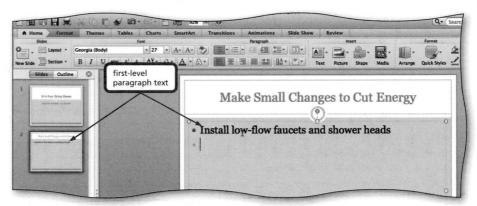

Figure 1–18

- On the Home tab under Paragraph, click the Increase Indent button to indent the second paragraph below the first and create a second-level paragraph (Figure 1–19).

Q&A   Why does the bullet for this paragraph have a different size and color?
A different bullet is assigned to each paragraph level.

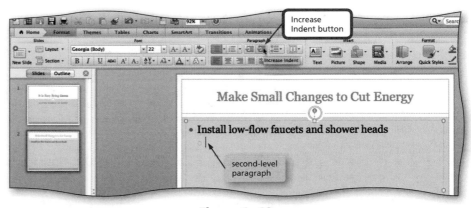

Figure 1–19

- Type `Cut water consumption in half` and then press the RETURN key (Figure 1–20).

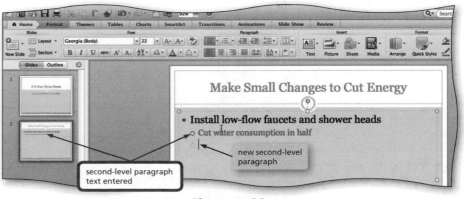

Figure 1–20

4

- On the Home tab under Paragraph, click the Decrease Indent button so that the second-level paragraph becomes a first-level paragraph (Figure 1–21).

Q&A Can I delete bullets on a slide?
Yes. If you do not want bullets to display in a particular paragraph, click the Bullets button on the Home tab under Paragraph or CONTROL-click the paragraph and then click the Bullets and Numbering command from the shortcut menu.

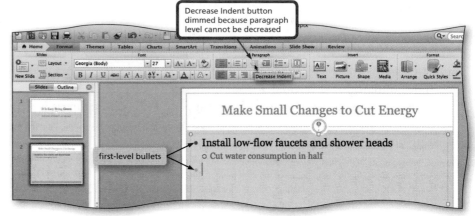

Figure 1–21

Other Ways

1. Press TAB to demote paragraph; press SHIFT-TAB to promote paragraph

To Type the Remaining Text for Slide 2

The following steps complete the text for Slide 2.

1 Type `Appliances count for 20 percent of electric bill` and then press the RETURN key.

2 Click the Increase Indent button in the Paragraph group to demote the paragraph to the second level.

3 Type `Buy ENERGY STAR qualified products` and then press the RETURN key to add a new paragraph at the same level as the previous paragraph.

4 Type `Run dishwasher, clothes washer with full loads` and then press the RETURN key.

5 Click the Increase Indent button in the Paragraph group to demote the paragraph to the third level.

6 Type `Wash clothes in cold water` but do not press the RETURN key (Figure 1–22).

Q&A I pressed the RETURN key in error, and now a new bullet appears after the last entry on this slide. How can I remove this extra bullet?
Press the DELETE key twice.

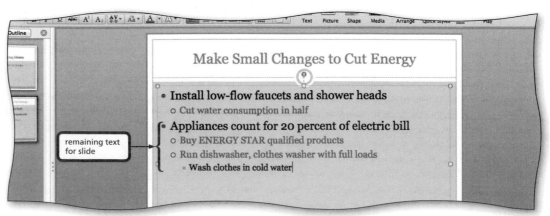

Figure 1–22

To Select a Group of Words

PowerPoint designers use many techniques to emphasize words and characters on a slide. To add emphasis to your slide show's concept of saving natural resources, you want to bold and increase the font size of the words, in half, in the body text. You could perform these actions separately, but it is more efficient to select the words and then change the font attributes. The following steps select two words.

- Position the mouse pointer immediately to the left of the first character of the text to be selected (in this case, the i in the word, in) (Figure 1–23).

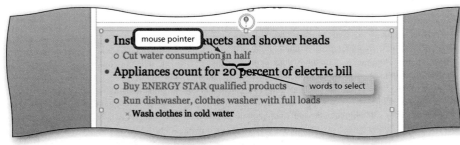

Figure 1–23

- Drag the mouse pointer through the last character of the text to be selected (in this case, the f in half) (Figure 1–24).

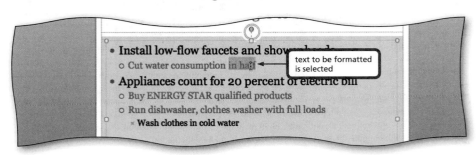

Figure 1–24

Other Ways

1. Click before first word, press COMMAND-SHIFT-RIGHT ARROW

To Bold Text

Bold characters display somewhat thicker and darker than those that display in a regular font style. Clicking the Bold button on the Home tab under Font is an efficient method of bolding text. To add more emphasis to the amount of water savings that can occur by installing low-flow faucets and shower heads, you want to bold the words, in half. The following step bolds this text.

- With the words, in half, selected, click the Bold button on the Home tab under Font to bold the two words (Figure 1–25).

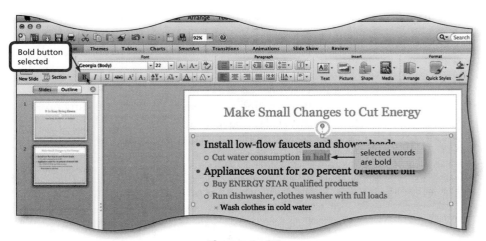

Figure 1–25

Other Ways

1. Choose Format > Font in menu bar, click Font Style box arrow, choose Bold, click OK button

2. Press COMMAND-B

Formatting Words

BTW To format one word, position the insertion point anywhere in the word. Then make the formatting changes you desire. The entire word does not need to be selected for the change to occur.

To Increase Font Size

To add emphasis, you increase the font size for the words, in half. The following step increases the font size from 22 to 24 point.

1 With the words, in half, still selected, click the Increase Font Size button on the Home tab under Font once (Figure 1–26).

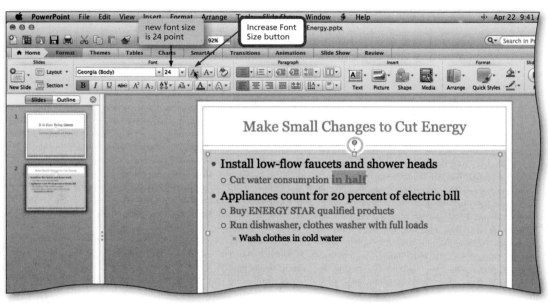

Figure 1–26

Experimenting with Normal View

BTW As you learn to use PowerPoint's features, experiment with using the Outline tab and with closing the Tabs pane to maximize the slide area. To close the Tabs pane, click the x to the right of the Outline tab. To redisplay the Tabs pane, click View in the menu bar and then choose Normal in the View menu.

Adding New Slides and Changing the Slide Layouts

Slide 3 in Figure 1–1c on page PPT 3 contains a photograph and does not contain a bulleted list. When you add a new slide, PowerPoint applies the Title and Content layout. This layout, along with the Title Slide layout for Slide 1, are the default styles. A **layout** specifies the arrangement of placeholders on a slide. These placeholders are arranged in various configurations and can contain text, such as the slide title or a bulleted list, or they can contain content, such as SmartArt graphics, pictures, charts, tables, shapes, and clip art. The placement of the text, in relationship to content, depends on the slide layout. You can specify a particular slide layout when you add a new slide to a presentation or after you have created the slide.

Using the **Layout gallery**, you can choose a slide layout. The 15 layouts in this gallery have a variety of placeholders to define text and content positioning and formatting. Some layouts are for text only (Title Slide, Section Header, and Title Only); some are for text and content (such as Title and Content, Two Content, Comparison, and Content with Caption, and Picture with Caption). The Blank layout has no placeholders. If none of these standard layouts meets your design needs, you can create a **custom layout**. A custom layout specifies the number, size, and location of placeholders, background content, and optional slide and placeholder-level properties.

When you change the layout of a slide, PowerPoint retains the text and objects and repositions them into the appropriate placeholders. Using slide layouts eliminates the need to resize objects and the font size because PowerPoint automatically sizes the objects and text to fit the placeholders.

To Add a Slide with the Title Only Layout

The following steps add Slide 3 to the presentation with the Title Only slide layout style.

1

- On the Home tab, under Slides, click the New Slide button arrow to display the Layout gallery (Figure 1–27).

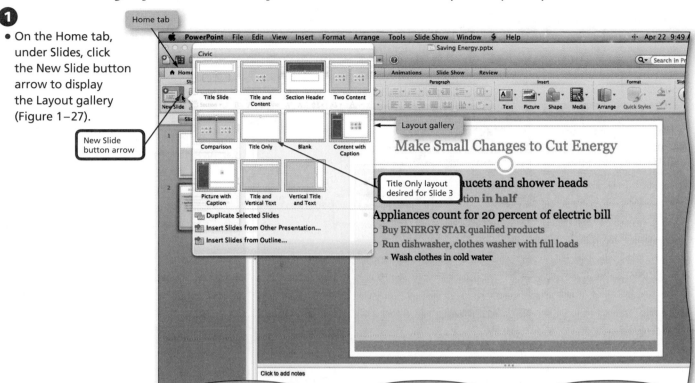

Figure 1–27

2

- Click Title Only to add a new slide and apply that layout to Slide 3 (Figure 1–28).

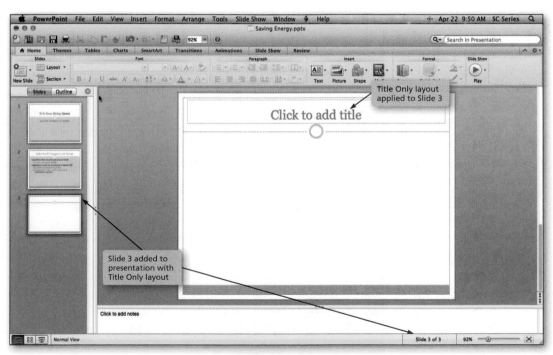

Figure 1–28

Portrait Page Orientation

 BTW If your slide content is dominantly vertical, such as a skyscraper or a person, consider changing the slide layout to a portrait page orientation. To change the orientation, click the Slide Size button on the Themes tab under Page Setup group, choose Page Setup from the pop-up menu, and choose the portrait orientation for slides.

To Enter a Slide Title

The only text on Slide 3 is the title. The following step enters the title text for this slide.

1 Click the label, Click to add title, and then type `Use Energy Efficient Lighting` as the title text but do not press the RETURN key (Figure 1–29).

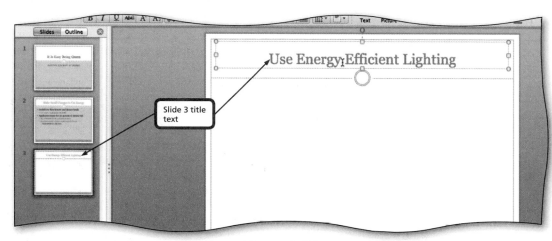

Figure 1–29

To Add a New Slide and Enter a Slide Title and Headings

The text on Slide 4 in Figure 1–1d on page PPT 3 consists of a title and two headings. The appropriate layout for this slide is named Comparison. The following steps add Slide 4 to the presentation with the Comparison layout and then enter the title and heading text for this slide.

1

• Click the New Slide button arrow in the Slides group to display the Layout gallery for the Civic theme (Figure 1–30).

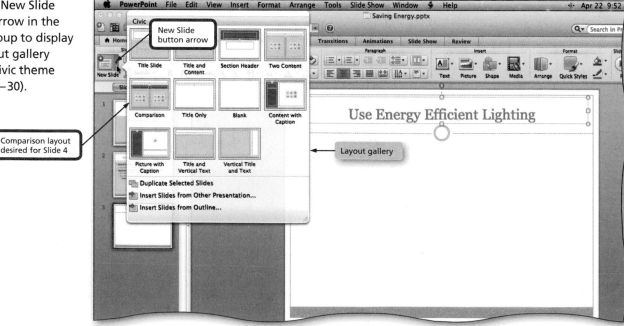

Figure 1–30

2

- Click Comparison to add Slide 4 and apply that layout.

- Click the Click to add title placeholder text.

- Type **Adjust Your Thermostats** in the title text placeholder but do not press the RETURN key.

- Click the left heading placeholder with the label, Click to add text, to select this placeholder (Figure 1–31).

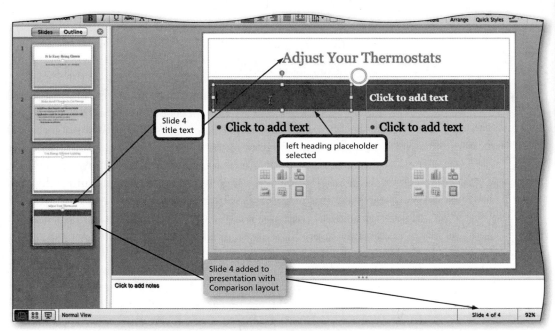

Figure 1–31

3

- Type **Furnace: 68 degrees** but do not press the RETURN key.

- Click the right heading placeholder and then type **Water heater: 120 degrees** but do not press the RETURN key.

- If necessary, triple-click the left heading and click the Decrease Font Size button in the Font group to reduce the font size to 2 to match the right heading (Figure 1–32).

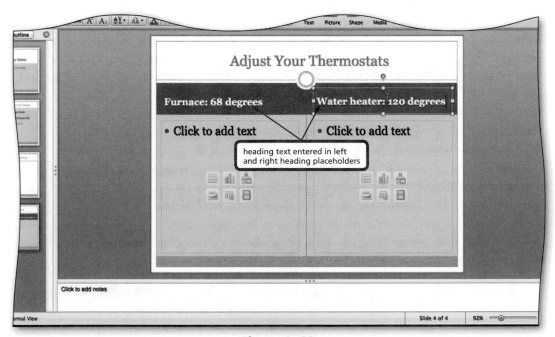

Figure 1–32

Break Point: If you wish to take a break, this is a good place to do so. You can quit PowerPoint now (refer to page PPT 51 for instructions). To resume at a later time, start PowerPoint (refer to pages PPT 4 and PPT 5) for instructions, open the file called Saving Energy (refer to page PPT 52 for instructions), and continue following the steps from this location forward.

PowerPoint Views

The PowerPoint window display varies depending on the view. A **view** is the mode in which the presentation appears on the screen. PowerPoint has four main views: Normal, Slide Sorter, Presenter, and Slide Show. It also has another view, called Notes Page view, used for entering information about a slide.

The default view is **Normal view**, which is composed of three working areas that allow you to work on various aspects of a presentation simultaneously. The left side of the screen has a Tabs pane that consists of a **Slides tab** and an **Outline tab**. These tabs alternate between views of the presentation in a thumbnail, or miniature, view of the slides and an outline of the slide text. You can type the text of the presentation on the Outline tab and easily rearrange bulleted lists, paragraphs, and individual slides. As you type, you can view this text in the **Slide pane**, which shows a large view of the current slide on the right side of the window. You also can enter text, graphics, animations, and hyperlinks directly in the Slide pane. The **Notes pane** at the bottom of the window is an area where you can type notes and additional information. This text can consist of notes to yourself or remarks to share with your audience. If you want to work with your notes in full page format, you can display them in **Notes Page view**.

In Normal view, you can adjust the width of the Slide pane by dragging the **splitter bar** and the height of the Notes pane by dragging the pane borders. After you have created at least two slides, a scroll bar containing **Next Slide** and **Previous Slide** buttons and a **scroller** box will appear on the right edge of the window.

To Move to Another Slide in Normal View

When creating or editing a presentation in Normal view (the view you are currently using), you often want to display a slide other than the current one. Before continuing with developing this project, you want to display the title slide by dragging the scroller on the vertical scroll bar. When you drag the scroller, the **slide indicator** shows the number and title of the slide you are about to display. Releasing the mouse button shows the slide. The following steps move from Slide 4 to Slide 1 using the scroller on the Slide pane.

1

- Position the mouse pointer on the scroller.

- Press and hold down the mouse button so that Slide 4: Adjust Your Thermostats appears in the slide indicator (Figure 1–33).

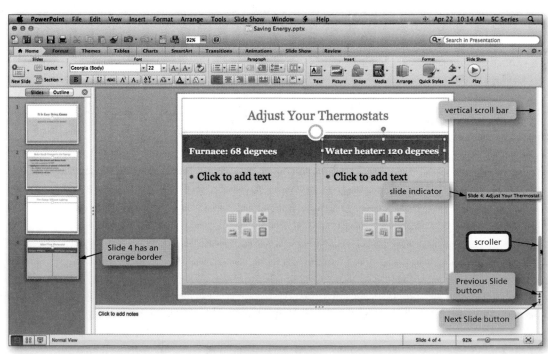

Figure 1–33

• Drag the scroller up
the vertical scroll bar
until Slide 1: It Is Easy
Being Green appears
in the slide indicator
(Figure 1–34).

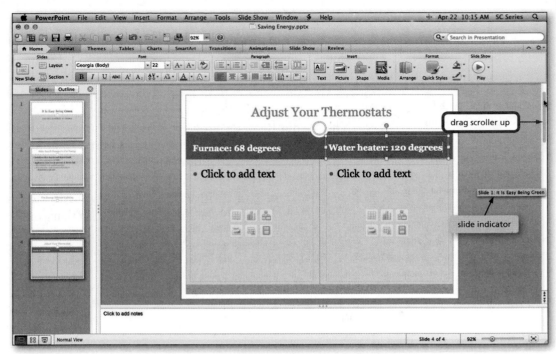

Figure 1–34

• Release the mouse
button so that Slide 1
appears in the Slide
pane and the Slide 1
thumbnail has an
orange border
in the Slides tab
(Figure 1–35).

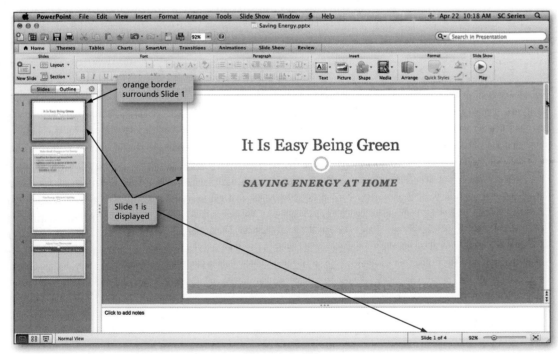

Figure 1–35

Other Ways

1. Click Next Slide button or
   Previous Slide button to
   move forward or back
   one slide

2. Click slide thumbnail on
   Slides tab

3. Press DOWN ARROW or
   UP ARROW

Inserting Clip Art and Photographs into Slides

A **clip** is a single media file that can include art, sound, animation, or movies. Adding a clip can help increase the visual appeal of many slides and can offer a quick way to add professional-looking graphic images and sounds to a presentation without creating these files yourself. Access to media content is available via the Clip Gallery and the Media Browser. You can access clips in PowerPoint using either the Media Organizer or the Clip Gallery.

The **Media Browser** provides a group of various media clips, pictures, audio files, movile files, shape files, and clip art. You can insert a clip into a presentation using the Media Browser. You also can insert clips into a presentation using the **Clip Gallery**. The Clip Gallery also provides access to a group of slides in a document. It also allows you to edit the information stored with a slide (name, keywords, etc.) and search for and import clips from sources online. If you cannot find the clip that you need, you can search for a suitable clip online. You also can add your own clips to slides. You can insert these files directly from a storage medium, such as a USB flash drive, or you can add them to the other files in the Clip Gallery so that you can search for and reuse these images, sounds, animations, and movies. When you create these media files, they are stored on your hard disk in **Favorites**. The Clip Gallery will find these files and create a new collection with these files.

The Media Browser

You can add clips to your presentation in three ways. One way is by selecting one of the slide layouts that includes a content placeholder with a Clip Art Browser button. A second method is by clicking the Picture button in the Insert group on the Home tab. Clicking the Picture button displays a menu from which you can access the Media Browser. The Media Browser allows you to scroll through clips by group, and by media type: photos, audio, movies, clip art, symbols, and shapes. A third way is by opening the Clip Gallery and searching by keyword for the clip you need. Clips have one or more keywords associated with various entities, activities, labels, and emotions. In most instances, the keywords give the name of the clip and related categories. For example, an image of a cow in the Animals category has the keywords animals, cattle, cows, dairies, farms, and Holsteins. You can enter these keywords in the Search for text box to find clips when you know one of the words associated with the image. Otherwise, you might find it necessary to scroll through several categories to find an appropriate clip.

For this presentation, you have been provided with a list of clips that you need to find online and download. The list of clips, and their associated properties, is listed in Table 1–1.

Table 1–1 Clip Art Needed for Presentation

Thumbnail	Identifier	Name/Keyword
	MC900440103.png	green globe
	MC900215338.wmf	faucet
	MC900215847.wmf	dishwasher
	MC900352394.wmf	furnace
	MC900018346.wmf	water heater
	MP900437304.jpg	CFL

Plan Ahead **Adhere to copyright regulations.**

You have permission to use the clips from the Microsoft Clip Gallery and Media Browser. If you want to use a clip from another source, be certain you have the legal right to insert this file in your presentation. Read the copyright notices that may accompany the clip and may be posted on the Web site where you obtained the clip. The owners of these images and files often ask you to give them credit for using their work, which may be satisfied by stating where you obtained the images.

To Find Clips Online Using the Clip Gallery

You have a list of clips that you need for your presentation in Table 1–1 on the previous page. The following steps find clips online and download them to your Downloads folder.

1
- Verify that the Home tab is displayed.
- Click the Picture button on the Home tab under Insert to display the Picture menu (Figure 1–36).

Figure 1–36

2
- Choose Clip Art Gallery to open the Clip Gallery.
- Click in the Search text box, enter the term **green globe** and press RETURN to see the search results (Figure 1–37).

Q&A Why do my search results look different? Clips can be added to the Clip Gallery. Your clip gallery may have additional images added to it.

Figure 1–37

3

- Click the Online button.

- If necessary, click Yes in the Launch Browser dialog to open your default Internet browser.

- Click in the Search text box, then type `green globe` in the Search text box (Figure 1–38).

Figure 1–38

4

- Click the Search button to search for clips with the keywords green globe.

- Point to the desired clip in the Search results (Figure 1–39).

Figure 1–39

5

- Click download to download the clip to your computer. If a window opens with the clip in it, click Preview in the menu bar and then choose Quit Preview to return to your browser.

6

- Select the existing text in the search text box, and replace it with the search text, `faucet`.

- Press the RETURN key to search for clips with the keywords, faucet.

- Point to the desired faucet image and click download to download the clip to your computer (Figure 1–40).

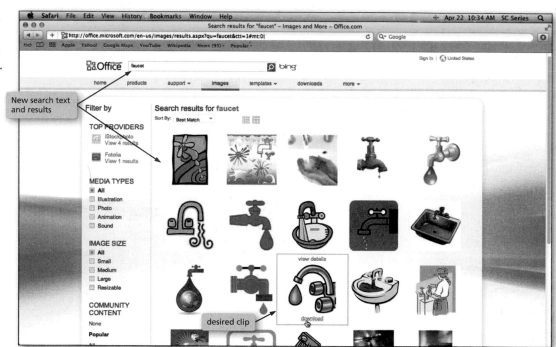

Figure 1–40

7

- Repeat step 6 for the remaining clips, replacing the contents of the Search text box with the search text in the Name/Keyword column in Table 1–1 on page PPT 27.

- After all the clips have been downloaded, click Downloads in the Dock to view the downloaded files (Figure 1–41).

Q&A I don't have a Downloads icon in the Dock. What should I do?
You can use the downloads button in the browser to view a list of downloaded files. Click once to view, and again to close.

8

- If necessary, close the Downloads folder.

- Close the browser and return to the Clip Gallery.

Figure 1–41

To Update the Clip Properties and Import the Clips to the Clip Gallery

With the clips downloaded to the Downloads folder, you now need to import them into the Clip Gallery and Media Browser. Prior to importing, you will update certain properties of the clips to make it easier for you to use them in the Clip Gallery. The following steps update the clip properties and import the clips to the Clip Gallery and Media Browser.

- In the Clip Gallery, if necessary, click on the Favorites Category to make it active.

- Click Import to open the Import dialog. If necessary, navigate to the Downloads folder.

- Select the green globe clip.

- Click Move Into Clip Gallery (Figure 1–42).

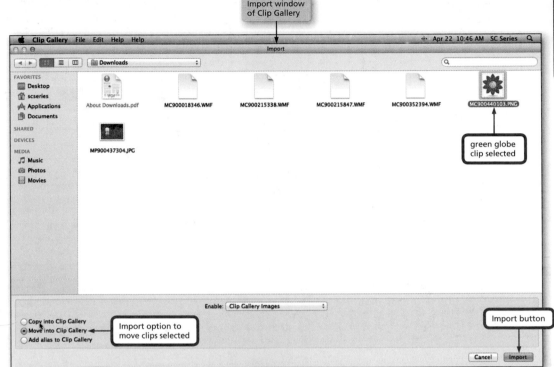

Figure 1–42

- Click the Import button to open the Properties dialog.

- If necessary, click the Description tab, select the contents of the text box, and then enter `green globe` as the description of the clip (Figure 1–43).

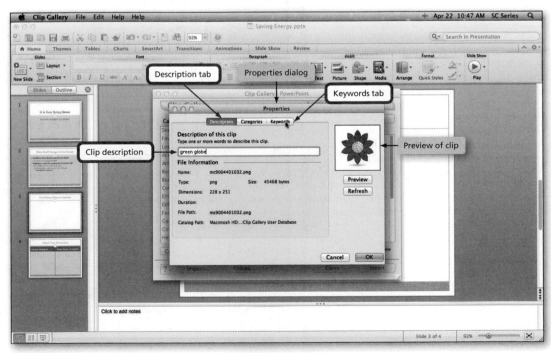

Figure 1–43

3

- Click the Keywords tab, and then click New Keyword to open the New Keyword dialog.

- Enter **green globe** as the new keyword (Figure 1–44).

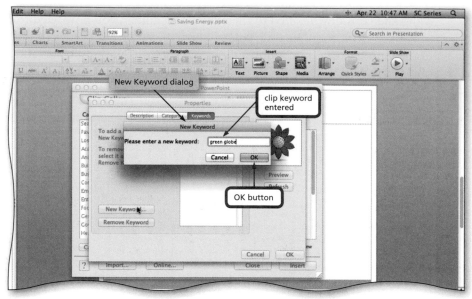

Figure 1–44

4

- Click the OK button to close the New Keyword dialog and return to the Properties dialog (Figure 1–45).

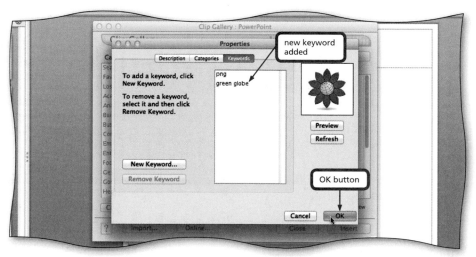

Figure 1–45

5

- Click the OK button to return to the Clip Gallery. You may have to scroll to view the green globe clip (Figure 1–46).

Figure 1–46

6

- Repeat steps 1–3 for each of the remaining clips in Table 1–1 on page PPT 27 (Figure 1–47).

- Click the Close button in the title bar to close the Clip Gallery.

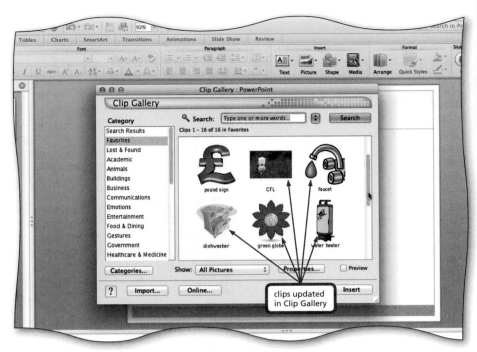

Figure 1–47

Insert a Clip from the Clip Gallery into the Title Slide

Slide 1 uses the Title Slide layout, which has two placeholders for text but none for graphical content. You will add the green globe clip you downloaded earlier to this slide. Later in this chapter, you will size and position it in an appropriate location. The following steps add a clip to Slide 1.

1

- Click Slide 1 in the Slides tab to make it the active slide.

- Click the Picture button on the Home tab under Insert, and choose Clip Art Gallery to open the Clip Gallery.

- If necessary, click the Favorites category.

- Click the green globe clip to select it (Figure 1–48).

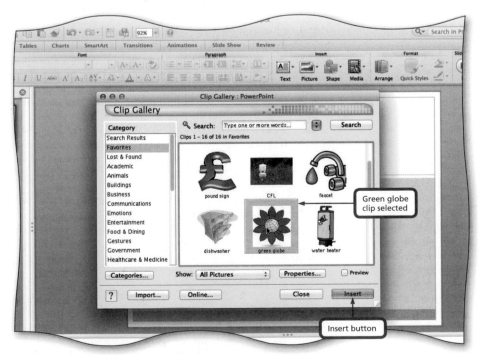

Figure 1–48

● Click the Insert button to insert the clip into the slide (Figure 1–49).

Q&A Why is the green globe clip displayed in this location on the slide?

The slide layout does not have a content placeholder, so PowerPoint inserts the clip in the center of the slide.

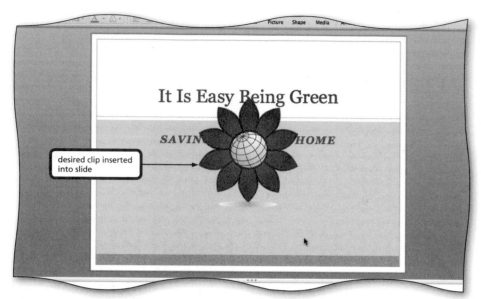

Figure 1–49

To Insert Two Clips from the Clip Gallery into a Slide without a Content Placeholder

The next step is to add two clips to Slide 2. Slide 2 has a bulleted list in the text placeholder, so the icon group does not display in the center of the placeholder. Later in this chapter, you will resize the inserted clips. The Clip Gallery is displayed and will remain open until you close it. The following steps add two clips to Slide 2.

1 Click the Next Slide button to display Slide 2.

2 Click the Picture button on the Home tab under Insert, then click Clip Art Gallery to open the Clip Gallery.

3 Click the Favorites category, then the faucet clip in the Clip Gallery.

4 Double-click the clip to insert it into the slide and keep the Clip Gallery open.

5 Select the dishwasher clip and click Insert to insert it into Slide 2 and close the Clip Gallery (Figure 50).

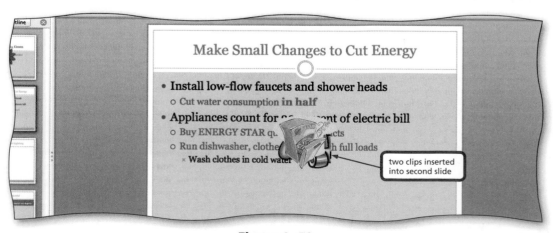

Figure 1–50

To Insert a Clip from the Clip Art Browser into a Content Placeholder

Slide 4 uses the Comparison layout, which has a content placeholder below each of the two headings. You desire to insert clip art into both content placeholders to reinforce the concept that consumers should adjust the heating temperatures of their furnace and water heater. The following steps insert clip art of a furnace into the left content placeholder and a water heater into the right content placeholder on Slide 4.

- Click the Next Slide button twice to display Slide 4.

- Click the Clip Art Browser icon in the left content placeholder to select that placeholder and to open the Media Browser with the Clip Art tab displayed (Figure 1–51).

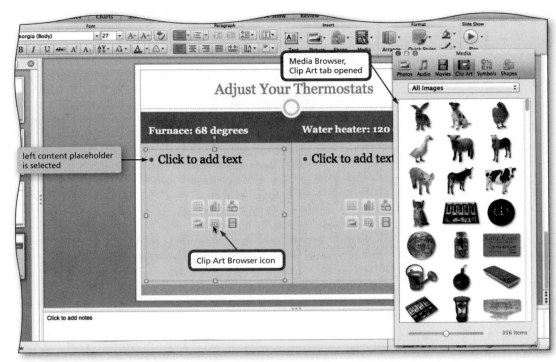

Figure 1–51

2

- Scroll through the list of clips to display the furnace clip shown in Figure 1–52.

- Drag the clip to the slide to insert it into the left content placeholder (Figure 1–52).

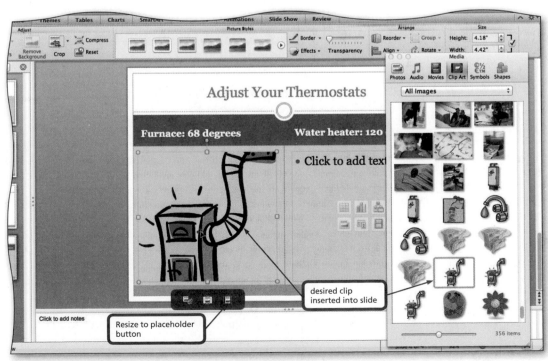

Figure 1–52

3

- Click the Resize to Placeholder button below the clip to resize it to fit the placeholder.

- Click a blank area in the right placeholder to select the placeholder.

- If necessary, scroll through the list of clips to display the water heater clip shown in Figure 1–53 and then drag the clip to the slide to insert it into the right content placeholder.

- Use the Resize to Placeholder button to resize the clip (Figure 1–53).

Figure 1–53

Compressing File Size

When you add a picture to a presentation, PowerPoint automatically compresses this image. Even with this compression applied, a presentation that contains pictures usually has a large file size. To reduce this size, you can compress a picture further without affecting the quality of how it displays on the slide. To compress a picture, select the picture and then click the Compress button in the Adjust group on the Format Picture tab. You can restore the picture's original settings by clicking the Reset Picture button in the Adjust group on the Format Picture tab.

Photographs and the Media Browser

In addition to clip art, you can insert pictures into a presentation. These may include scanned photographs, line art, and artwork from storage media, such as USB flash drives, hard disks, optical discs, and memory cards. To insert a picture into a presentation, the picture must be saved in a format that PowerPoint can recognize. Table 1–2 identifies some of the formats PowerPoint recognizes.

Table 1–2 Primary File Formats PowerPoint Recognizes	
Format	**File Extension**
Windows Bitmap	BMP
Windows Enhanced Metafile	EMF
Compressed Windows Enhanced Metafile	EMZ
Encapsulated Postscript	EPS
FlashPix	FPix,.FPX
Graphics Interchange Format	GIF
Joint Photographic Experts Group (JPEG)	JPEG, JFIF, JPG
Portable Document Format	PDF
Macintosh Picture	PICT, PCT
Portable Network Graphics	PNG
Macintosh Paint	PNTG
Photoshop Document	PSD
QuickTime Image Format	QTIF
Silicon Graphics Incorporated	SGF
Targa	TGA, TPIC
Tagged Image Format	TIFF, TIF
Windows Metafile	WMF
Compressed Windows Metafile	WMZ

To Insert a Photograph from the Clip Art Browser
into a Slide without a Content Placeholder

Next, you will add a photograph to Slide 3. You will not insert this picture into a content placeholder, so it will display in the center of the slide. Later in this chapter, you will resize this picture. To start the process of locating this photograph, you do not need to click the Clip Art Browser icon in the content placeholder because the Clip Art Browser already is displayed. The following steps add a photograph to Slide 3.

1 Click the Previous Slide button to display Slide 3.

2 Scroll through the list of clips until you locate a picture of a light bulb shown in Figure 1–54.

3 Drag the photograph to the slide to insert it into Slide 2 (Figure 1–54).

Q&A Why is my photograph a different size from the one shown in Figure 1–1c on page PPT 3?
The photograph was inserted into the slide and not into a content placeholder. You will resize the picture later in this chapter.

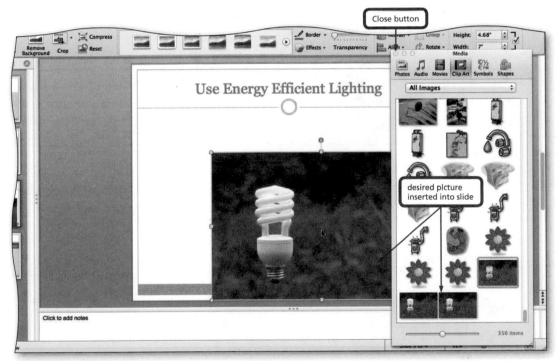

Wrapping Text around a Picture

PowerPoint 2011 does not allow you to wrap text around a picture or other graphics, such as tables, shapes, charts, or graphics. This feature, however, is available in Word 2011.

BTW

Figure 1–54

Break Point: If you wish to take a break, this is a good place to do so. You can quit PowerPoint now (refer to page PPT 51 for instructions). To resume at a later time, start PowerPoint (refer to pages PPT 4 and PPT 5) for instructions, open the file called Saving Energy (refer to page PPT 52 for instructions), and continue following the steps from this location forward.

Resizing Clip Art and Photographs

Sometimes it is necessary to change the size of clip art. **Resizing** includes enlarging or reducing the size of a clip art graphic. You can resize clip art using a variety of techniques. One method involves changing the size of a clip by specifying exact dimensions in a dialog. Another method involves dragging one of the graphic's sizing handles to the desired location. A selected graphic appears surrounded by a **selection rectangle**, which has small squares and circles, called **sizing handles** or move handles, at each corner and middle location.

To Resize Clip Art

On Slides 1 and 2, much space appears around the clips, so you can increase their sizes. Likewise, the photograph on Slide 3 can be enlarged to fill more of the space below the slide title. To change the size, drag the corner sizing handles to view how the clip will look on the slide. Using these corner handles maintains the graphic's original proportions. Dragging the square sizing handles alters the proportions so that the graphic's height and width become larger or smaller. The following steps increase the size of the Slide 1 clip using a corner sizing handle.

- Click the Close button in the Clip Art Browser so that it no longer is displayed.

- Click the Previous Slide button two times to display Slide 1.

- Click the green globe clip to select it and display the selection rectangle.

- Point to the lower-left corner sizing handle on the clip so that the mouse pointer changes to a two-headed arrow (Figure 1–55).

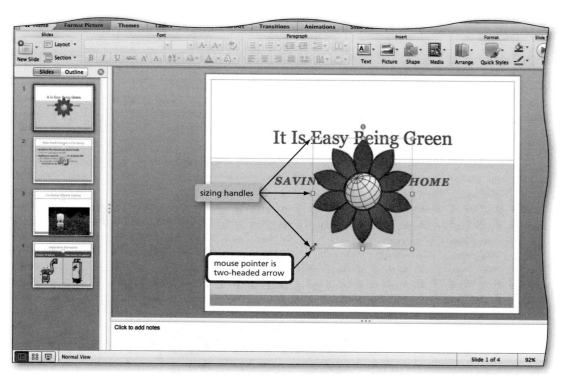

Figure 1–55

- Drag the sizing handle diagonally toward the lower-left corner of the slide until the mouse pointer is positioned approximately as shown in Figure 1–56.

Q&A What if the clip is not the same size as the one shown in Figure 1–47 on page PPT 33?
Repeat Steps 1 and 2.

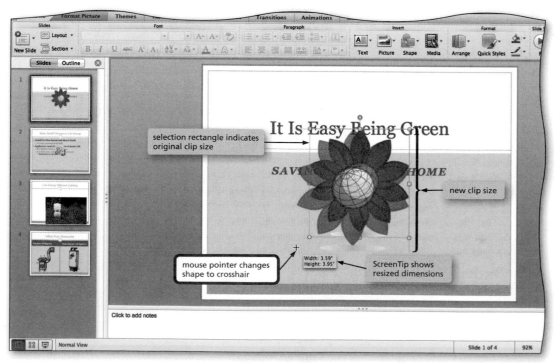

Figure 1–56

3

- Release the mouse button to resize the clip.

- Click outside the clip to deselect it (Figure 1–57).

Q&A   What happened to the Format Picture tab?
When you click outside the clip, PowerPoint deselects the clip and removes the Format Picture tab from the ribbon.

Q&A   What if I want to return the clip to its original size and start again?
With the graphic selected, click the Reset button in the Adjust group on the Format Picture Tab.

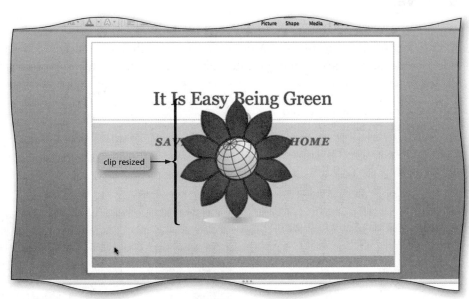

Figure 1–57

To Resize a Photograph

The light bulb picture in Slide 3 can be enlarged slightly to fill much of the space below the slide title. You resize a photograph in the same manner that you resize clip art. The following steps resize this photograph using a sizing handle.

1 Click the Next Slide button twice to display Slide 3.

2 Click the light bulb photograph to select it.

3 Drag the upper-left corner sizing handle on the photograph diagonally outward until the photograph is resized approximately as shown in Figure 1–58, without releasing the mouse button (Figure 1–58).

Minimalist Design

Resist the urge to fill your slides with clip art. Minimalist style reduces clutter and allows the slide content to display prominently. This simple, yet effective design helps audience members with short attention spans to focus on the message. **BTW**

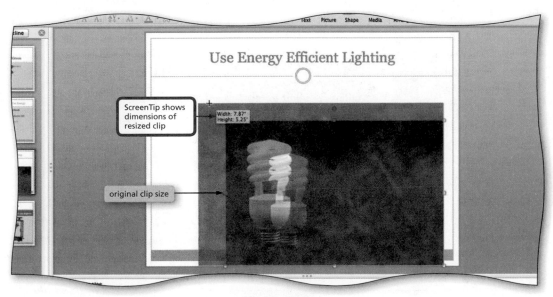

Figure 1–58

4 Release the mouse button to complete the resize task.

To Move Clips

After you insert clip art or a photograph on a slide, you might want to reposition it. The light bulb photograph on Slide 3 could be centered in the space between the slide title and the left and right edges of the slide. The clip on Slide 1 could be positioned in the lower-right corner of the slide. The following steps move these graphics.

- If necessary, click the light bulb photograph on Slide 3 to select it.

- Press and hold down the mouse button and then drag the photograph diagonally downward below the title text (Figure 1–59).

- If necessary, select the photograph and then use the ARROW keys to position it precisely as shown in Figure 1–59.

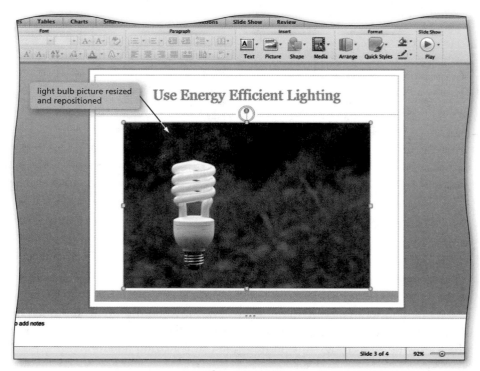

Figure 1–59

- Click the Previous Slide button to display Slide 2.

- Click the dishwasher clip, which is on top of the faucet clip, and then drag the clip to center it under the last bulleted paragraph, Wash clothes in cold water.

- Click the faucet clip and then drag the clip so that the faucet handle is centered under the words, full loads.

- Drag a corner sizing handle on the faucet clip diagonally outward until the clip is resized approximately as shown in Figure 1–60. You may need to drag the clip to position it in the desired location.

- Select the dishwasher clip and then resize and move it so that the clip displays approximately as shown in Figure 1–60.

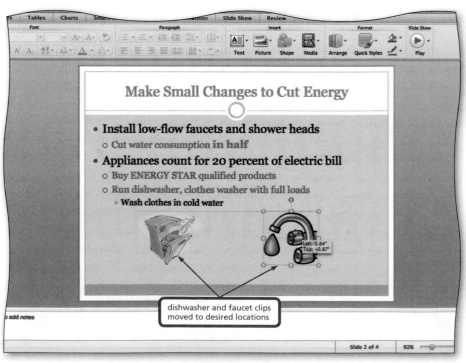

Figure 1–60

- Click the Previous Slide button to display Slide 1.

- Click the globe clip and then drag it to the lower-right corner of the slide. You may want to adjust its size by selecting it and then dragging the corner sizing handles.

- Click outside the clip to deselect it (Figure 1–61).

Figure 1–61

Plan Ahead

Choose a closing slide.

After the last slide appears during a slide show, the default PowerPoint setting is to end the presentation by returning to the PowerPoint window. You can select to have PowerPoint end by displaying a **black slide** after the last slide In your presentation. This black slide appears only when the slide show is running and concludes the slide show, so your audience never sees the PowerPoint window. It is a good idea, however, to end the presentation with a final closing slide to display at the end of the presentation. This slide ends the presentation gracefully and should be an exact copy, or a very similar copy, of your title slide. The audience will recognize that the presentation is drawing to a close when this slide appears. It can remain on the screen when the audience asks questions, approaches the speaker for further information, or exits the room.

Ending a Slide Show with a Closing Slide

All the text for the slides in the Saving Energy slide show has been entered. This presentation thus far consists of a title slide, one text slide with a multi-level bulleted list, a third slide for a photograph, and a fourth slide with a Comparison layout. A closing slide that resembles the title slide is the final slide to create.

To Duplicate a Slide

When two slides contain similar information and have the same format, duplicating one slide and then making minor modifications to the new slide saves time and increases consistency.

Slide 5 will have the same layout and design as Slide 1. The most expedient method of creating this slide is to copy Slide 1 and then make minor modifications to the new slide. The steps on the next page duplicate the title slide.

1

- With Slide 1 selected, on the Home tab under Slides, click the New Slide button arrow to display the Layout gallery (Figure 1–62).

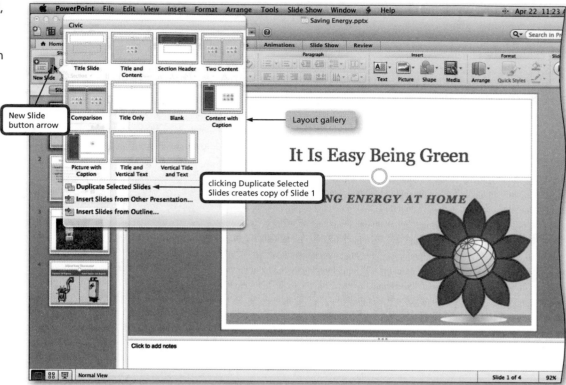

Figure 1–62

2

- Click Duplicate Selected Slides in the Layout gallery to create a new Slide 2, which is a duplicate of Slide 1 (Figure 1–63).

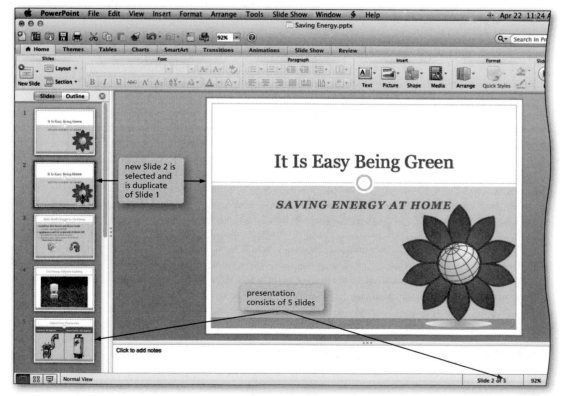

Figure 1–63

Break Point: If you wish to take a break, this is a good place to do so. You can quit PowerPoint now (refer to page PPT 51 for instructions). To resume at a later time, start PowerPoint (refer to pages PPT 4 and PPT 5) for instructions, open the file called Saving Energy (refer to page PPT 52 for instructions), and continue following the steps from this location forward.

To Arrange a Slide

The new Slide 2 was inserted directly below Slide 1 because Slide 1 was the selected slide. This duplicate slide needs to display at the end of the presentation directly after the final title and content slide.

Changing slide order is an easy process and is best performed in the Slides pane. When you click the slide thumbnail and begin to drag it to a new location, a line indicates the new location of the selected slide. When you release the mouse button, the slide drops into the desired location. Hence, this process of dragging and then dropping the thumbnail in a new location is called **drag and drop**. You can use the drag-and-drop method to move any selected item, including text and graphics. The following step moves the new Slide 2 to the end of the presentation so that it becomes a closing slide.

- With Slide 2 selected, drag the Slide 2 slide thumbnail in the Slides pane below the last slide thumbnail but do not release the mouse button (Figure 1–64).

- Release the mouse button to position the slide in its new location.

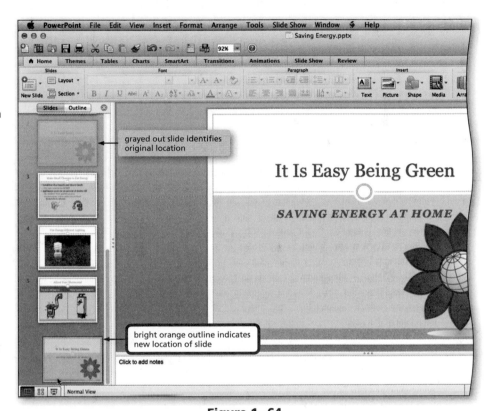

Figure 1–64

Making Changes to Slide Text Content

After creating slides in a presentation, you may find that you want to make changes to the text. Changes may be required because a slide contains an error, the scope of the presentation shifts, or the style is inconsistent. This section explains the types of changes that commonly occur when creating a presentation.

You generally make three types of changes to text in a presentation: additions, replacements, and deletions.

- Additions are necessary when you omit text from a slide and need to add it later. You may need to insert text in the form of a sentence, word, or single character. For example, you may want to add the presenter's middle name on the title slide.

- Replacements are needed when you want to revise the text in a presentation. For example, you may want to substitute the word *their* for the word *there*.

Checking Spelling

 As you review your slides, you should examine the text for spelling errors. In PowerPoint Chapter 3, you will learn to use PowerPoint's built-in spelling checker to help you perform this task.

- Deletions are required when text on a slide is incorrect or no longer is relevant to the presentation. For example, a slide may look cluttered. Therefore, you may want to remove one of the bulleted paragraphs to add more space.

Editing text in PowerPoint basically is the same as editing text in a word processing program. The following sections illustrate the most common changes made to text in a presentation.

Replacing Text in an Existing Slide

When you need to correct a word or phrase, you can replace the text by selecting the text to be replaced and then typing the new text. As soon as you press any key on the keyboard, the selected text is deleted and the new text is displayed.

PowerPoint inserts text to the left of the insertion point. The text to the right of the insertion point moves to the right (and shifts downward if necessary) to accommodate the added text.

Deleting Text

You can delete text using one of three methods. One is to use the DELETE key to remove text just typed. The second is to position the insertion point to the left of the text you want to delete and then hold down the FN key and press the DELETE key. The third method is to drag through the text you want to delete and then press the DELETE key. Use the third method when deleting large sections of text.

To Delete Text in a Placeholder

To keep the ending slide clean and simple, you want to delete a few words in the slide show title and subtitle text. The following steps change It Is Easy Being Green to Be Green and then change Saving Energy at Home to Save Energy.

1

- With Slide 5 selected, position the mouse pointer immediately to the left of the first character of the text to be selected (in this case, the I in the word, It).

- Drag the mouse pointer through the last character of the text to be selected (in this case, the space after the y in Easy) (Figure 1–65).

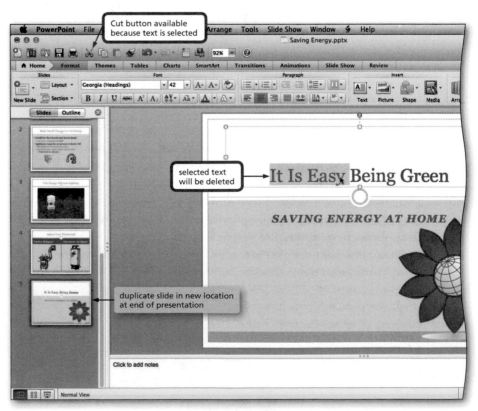

Figure 1–65

- Click the Cut button in the Standard toolbar to delete all the selected text (Figure 1–66).

Figure 1–66

- Select the letters, ing, in the word, Being.

- Click the Cut button (Figure 1–67).

Figure 1–67

4

- Select the letters, ing, in the word, Saving, and then type e to change the word to Save (Figure 1–68).

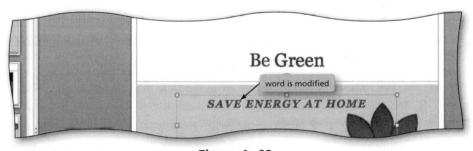

Figure 1–68

Other Ways

1. CONTROL-click selected text, click Cut in shortcut menu

2. Select text, press DELETE or BACKSPACE key

3. Select text, press COMMAND-X

Adding a Transition

PowerPoint provides many animation effects to add interest and make a slide show presentation look professional. **Animation** includes special visual and sound effects applied to text or content. A **slide transition** is a special animation effect used to progress from one slide to the next in a slide show. You can control the speed of the transition effect and add a sound.

PowerPoint provides a variety of transitions arranged into three categories that describe the types of effects: Subtle, Exciting, and Dynamic Content.

To Add a Transition between Slides

In this presentation, you apply the Doors transition in the Exciting category to all slides and change the transition speed from 1.40 seconds to 2 seconds. The following steps apply this transition to the presentation.

1

- Click the Transitions tab on the ribbon and move the mouse into the Transition To This Slide group to make the More button appear (Figure 1–69).

Q&A Is a transition applied now?

No. The first icon in the Transitions group has an orange border, which indicates no transition has been applied.

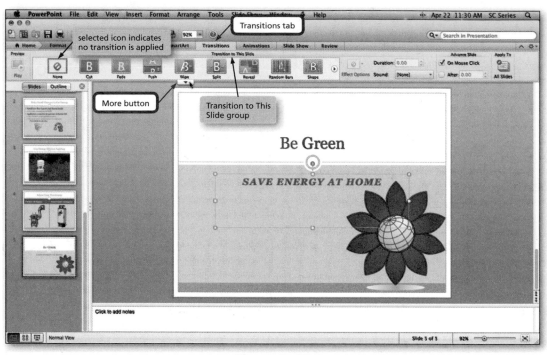

Figure 1–69

2

- Click the More button to expand the Transitions gallery.

- Point to the Doors transition in the Exciting category in the Transitions gallery (Figure 1–70).

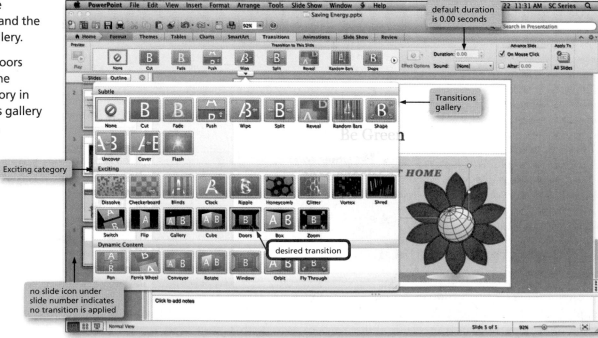

Figure 1–70

3

- Click Doors in the Exciting category in the Transitions gallery to apply this transition to the closing slide.

Q&A Why does a slide icon with an arrow appear next to Slide 5 in the Slides tab?
The icon indicates that a transition animation effect is applied to that slide.

Q&A Why did the time change?
Each transition has a default duration time. The Doors transition time is 1:40 seconds.

- On the Transitions tab, in the Transition to This Slide group, click the Duration up arrow six times to change the transition speed from 01.40 seconds to 02.00 seconds (Figure 1–71).

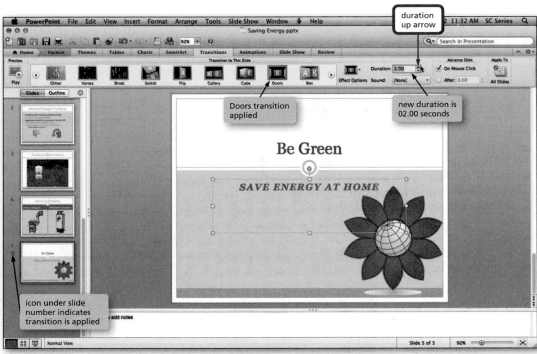

Figure 1–71

4

- In the Preview group, click the Play button to view the transition and the new transition time.

Q&A Can I adjust the duration time I just set?
Yes. Click the Duration up or down arrows or type a speed in the Duration text box and preview the transition until you find the time that best fits your presentation.

5

- Click the All Slides button in the Apply To group to apply the Doors transition and the increased transition time to Slides 1 through 4 in the presentation (Figure 1–72).

Q&A What if I want to apply a different transition and duration to each slide in the presentation?
Repeat Steps 2 and 3 for each slide individually.

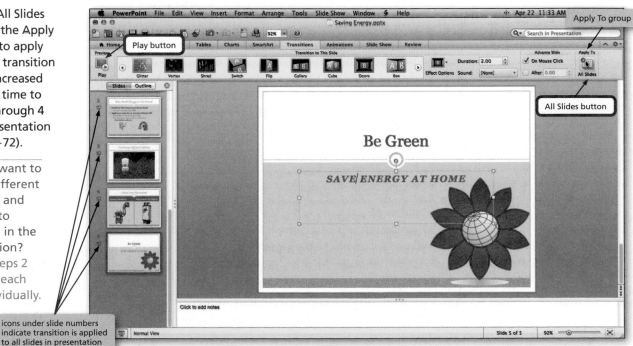

Figure 1–72

To Add an End of Show Slide

The default in PowerPoint is to return you to the application at the end of the slide show. You will add an End of Show slide which will end the show with a black slide, and an instruction to click to exit the show and return to PowerPoint.

- Click PowerPoint in the menu bar and then choose Preferences in the PowerPoint menu to open the PowerPoint Preferences dialog.

- Click the View button at the top of the dialog.

- Under Slide show, click to check End with black slide (Figure 1–73).

- Click the OK button to close the dialog.

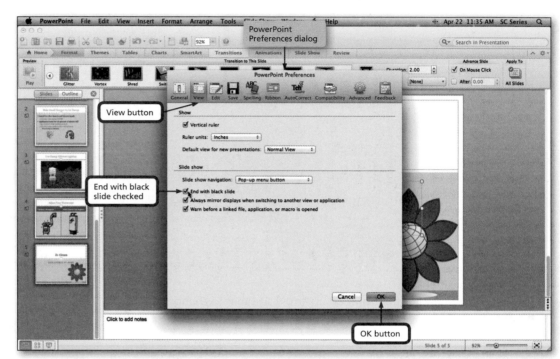

Figure 1–73

Changing Document Properties

PowerPoint helps you organize and identify your files by using **document properties**, which are the details about a file. Document properties, also known as **metadata**, can include information such as the project author, title, subject, and keywords. A **keyword** is a word or phrase that further describes the document. For example, a class name or document topic can describe the file's purpose or content.

Document properties are valuable for a variety of reasons:

- Users can save time locating a particular file because they can view a document's properties without opening the document.

- By creating consistent properties for files having similar content, users can better organize their documents.

- Some organizations require PowerPoint users to add document properties so that other employees can view details about these files.

Five different types of document properties exist, but the more common ones used in this book are standard and automatically updated properties. **Standard properties** are associated with all Microsoft Office documents and include author, title, and subject. **Automatically updated properties** include file system properties, such as the date you create or change a file, and statistics, such as the file size.

To Change Document Properties

The **Document Information Panel** contains areas where you can view and enter document properties. You can view and change information in this panel at any time while you are creating a document. Before saving the presentation again, you want to add your name and course information as document properties. The following steps use the Document Information Panel to change document properties.

- Click File in the menu bar to display the File menu.

- Choose Properties to open the Properties dialog.

- Click the Author text box, if necessary, and then type your name as the Author property. If a name already is displayed in the Author text box, delete it before typing your name.

- Click the Subject text box, if necessary delete any existing text, and then type your course and section as the Subject property.

- If an AutoComplete dialog appears, click its Yes button.

- Click the Keywords text box, if necessary delete any existing text, and then type **energy savings** as the Keywords property (Figure 1–74).

Q&A What types of document properties does PowerPoint collect automatically?
PowerPoint records details such as time spent editing a document, the number of times a document has been revised, and the fonts and themes used in a document.

- Click the OK button to close the Properties dialog.

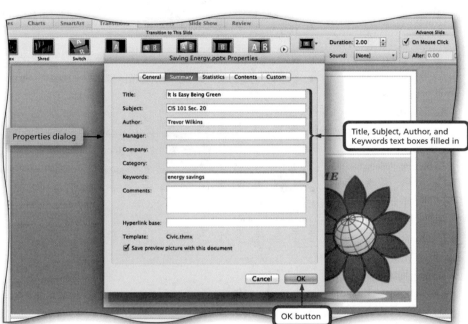

Figure 1–74

To Save an Existing Presentation with the Same File Name

You have made several modifications to the presentation since you last saved it. Thus, you should save it again. The following step saves the document again. For an example of the step listed below, refer to the Office 2011 and Mac OS chapter at the beginning of this book.

 Click the Save button in the Standard toolbar to overwrite the previously saved file.

Saving in a Previous PowerPoint Format

To ensure that your **BTW** presentation will open in PowerPoint 2004 or older versions of this software, you must save your file in PowerPoint 97-2004 format. These files will have the .ppt extension.

Viewing the Presentation in Slide Show View

The Slide Show button, located in the lower-right corner of the PowerPoint window above the status bar, allows you to show a presentation using a computer. The computer acts like a slide projector, displaying each slide on a full screen. The full-screen slide hides the toolbars, menus, and other PowerPoint window elements.

To Start Slide Show View

When making a presentation, you use **Slide Show view**. You can start Slide Show view from Normal view or Slide Sorter view. Slide Show view begins when you click the Slide Show button in the lower-left corner of the PowerPoint window. PowerPoint then shows the current slide on the full screen without any of the PowerPoint window objects, such as the menu bar or toolbars. The following steps start Slide Show view.

- Click the Slide 1 thumbnail in the Slides pane to select and display Slide 1.

- Point to the Slide Show button in the lower-left corner of the PowerPoint window (Figure 1–75).

Q&A Why did I need to select Slide 1?
When you run a slide show, PowerPoint begins the show with the currently displayed slide. If you had not selected Slide 1, then only Slide 5 would have displayed in the slide show.

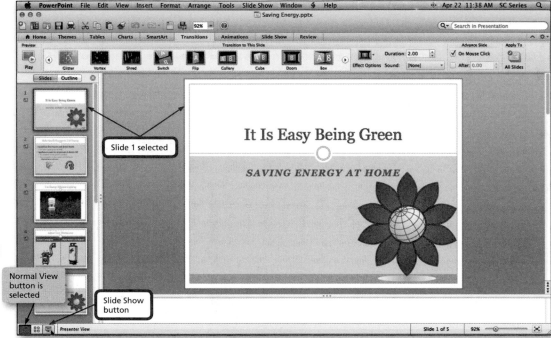

Figure 1–75

- Click the Slide Show button to display the title slide (Figure 1–76).

Q&A Where is the PowerPoint window?
When you run a slide show, the PowerPoint window is hidden. It will reappear once you end your slide show.

Other Ways

1. Click From Start button on the Slide Show tab in the Play Slide Show group

Figure 1–76

To Move Manually through Slides in a Slide Show

After you begin Slide Show view, you can move forward or backward through the slides. PowerPoint allows you to advance through the slides manually or automatically. During a slide show, each slide in the presentation shows on the screen, one slide at a time. Each time you click the mouse button, the next slide appears. The following steps move manually through the slides.

1

• Click each slide until the end of show slide is displayed (Figure 1–77).

2

• Click to exit the slide show and return to Normal view in the PowerPoint window.

Q&A How can I end the presentation at any point?
Press the ESC key at any point to exit a slide show.

Figure 1–77

Other Ways

1. Press RIGHT ARROW, SPACE BAR or DOWN ARROW to advance one slide at a time, or press LEFT ARROW or UP ARROW to go back one slide at a time

To Quit PowerPoint

This project now is complete. The following steps quit PowerPoint. For a detailed example of the procedure summarized below, refer to the Office 2011 and Mac OS chapter at the beginning of this book.

1 Click File in the menu bar and choose Close to close the presentation.

2 If a dialog appears, click the Save button to save any changes made to the document since the last save.

3 Click PowerPoint in the menu bar to display the PowerPoint menu.

4 Choose Quit PowerPoint from the PowerPoint menu to quit PowerPoint.

To Start PowerPoint

Once you have created and saved a document, you may need to retrieve it from your storage medium. For example, you might want to revise the presentation or print it. The steps on the next page start PowerPoint so that you can open and modify the presentation. You may need to ask your instructor how to start PowerPoint for your computer. For a detailed example of the procedure summarized below, refer to the Office 2011 and Mac OS chapter at the beginning of this book.

1 Click the PowerPoint icon in the Dock to start the PowerPoint application and open the PowerPoint Presentation Gallery.

2 Double-click the White Theme to close the gallery and display a blank presentation in the PowerPoint window.

3 If the presentation window is not maximized, click the Maximize button on its title bar to maximize the window.

To Open a Document from PowerPoint

Earlier in this chapter you saved your project on a USB flash drive using the file name, Saving Energy. The following steps open the Saving Energy file from the PowerPoint folder in the CIS 101 folder on the USB flash drive. For a detailed example of the procedure summarized below, refer to the Office 2011 and Mac OS X chapter at the beginning of this book.

1 With your USB flash drive connected to one of the computer's USB ports, click File in the menu bar to display the File menu.

2 Point to Open Recent in the File menu to display the submenu containing a list of recently opened files.

3 Click Saving Energy in the submenu to open the file.

Printing a Presentation

After creating a presentation, you may want to print the slides. Printing a presentation enables you to distribute the document to others in a form that can be read or viewed but typically not edited. It is a good practice to save a presentation before printing it, in the event you experience difficulties printing.

Plan Ahead

Determine the best method for distributing the presentation.

The traditional method of distributing a presentation uses a printer to produce a hard copy. A **hardcopy** or **printout** is information that exists on a physical medium such as paper. For users who can receive fax documents, you can elect to print a hard copy on a remote fax machine. Hard copies can be useful for the following reasons:

- Many people prefer proofreading a hard copy of a document rather than viewing it on the screen to check for errors and readability.

- Hard copies can serve as reference material if your storage medium is lost or becomes corrupted and you need to recreate the document.

Instead of distributing a hard copy of a presentation's slides, users can choose to distribute the presentation as an electronic image that mirrors the original document's appearance. The electronic image of the document can be e-mailed, posted on a Web site, or copied to a portable storage medium such as a USB flash drive. One popular electronic image format, sometimes called fixed format, is PDF by Adobe. In PowerPoint, you can create electronic image files through the Print dialog, accessed from the File menu, and the Save As dialog. Electronic images of documents such as PDF can be useful for the following reasons:

- Users can view electronic images of documents without the software that created the original document (e.g., PowerPoint). Specifically, to view a PDF file, you use a program called Acrobat Reader, which can be downloaded free from Adobe's Web site.

- Sending electronic documents saves paper and printer supplies. Society encourages users to contribute to **green computing,** which involves reducing the environmental waste generated when using a computer.

To Print a Presentation

With the completed presentation saved, you may want to print it. If copies of the presentation are being distributed to audience members, you will print a hard copy of each individual slide on a printer. The following steps print a hard copy of the contents of the saved Saving Energy presentation.

1

- Click File in the menu bar to display the File menu.

- Choose Print in the File menu to open the Print dialog (Figure 1–78).

Q&A How do I preview Slides 2 through 5? Click the Next Slide button in the Print dialog to scroll forward through pages in the document; similarly, click the Previous Slide button to scroll backward through pages.

Q&A How can I print multiple copies of my slides? Increase the number in the Copies box in the Print dialog.

Q&A What if I decide not to print the document at this time? Click Cancel to close the dialog and return to the PowerPoint document window.

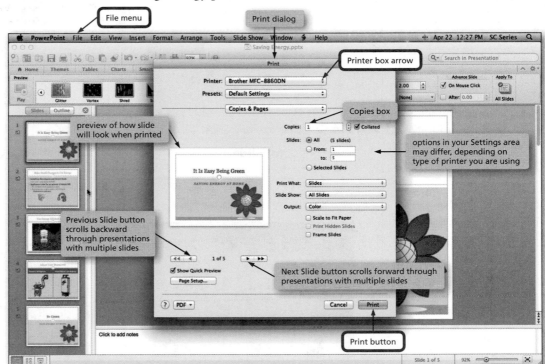

Figure 1–78

2

- Verify the printer name that appears on the Printer button will print a hard copy of the document. If necessary, click the Printer button to display a list of available printer options and then click the desired printer to change the currently selected printer.

3

- Click the Print button in the Print dialog to print the document on the currently selected printer.

- When the printer stops, retrieve the hard copy (Figure 1–79).

Q&A   Do I have to wait until my document is complete to print it?
No, you can follow these steps to print a document at any time while you are creating it.

Q&A   What if I want to print an electronic image of a document Instead of a hard copy?
You would click the PDF button at the bottom of the Print dialog and then select the desired electronic image option such as Save as PDF.

Quick Reference

BTW   For a table that lists how to complete the tasks covered in this book using the mouse, ribbon, shortcut menu, and keyboard, see the Quick Reference Summary at the back of this book, or visit the Office 2011 for Mac Online Companion Web page at www .cengagebrain.com, navigate to the desired application, and click Quick Reference.

Other Ways
1. Press COMMAND-P, press RETURN

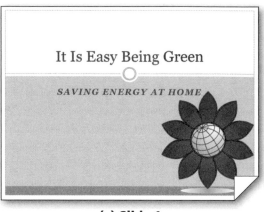

(a) Slide 1

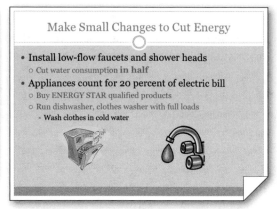

(b) Slide 2

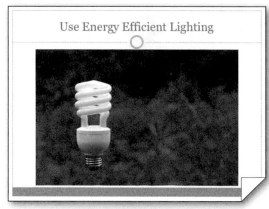

(c) Slide 3

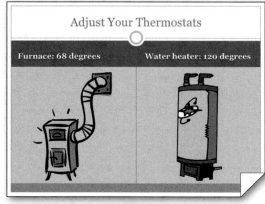

(d) Slide 4

(e) Slide 5

Figure 1–79

To Quit PowerPoint

The project now is complete. The following steps quit PowerPoint. For a detailed example of the procedure summarized below, refer to the Office 2011 and Mac OS chapter at the beginning of this book.

 Click File in the menu bar and choose Close to close the document.

2 If a dialog appears, click the Save button to save any changes made to the document since the last save.

3 Click PowerPoint in the menu bar and choose Quit PowerPoint to quit PowerPoint.

Chapter Summary

In this chapter you have learned how to apply a document theme; create a title slide and text slides with a bulleted list, clip art, and photograph; size and move clip art and a photograph; format and edit text; add a slide transition; view the presentation in Slide Show view; and print slides as handouts. The items listed below include all the new PowerPoint skills you have learned in this chapter.

1. Start PowerPoint (PPT 4)
2. Choose a Document Theme (PPT 5)
3. Enter the Presentation Title (PPT 8)
4. Enter the Presentation Subtitle Paragraph (PPT 9)
5. Select a Paragraph (PPT 10)
6. Italicize Text (PPT 11)
7. Increase Font Size (PPT 12)
8. Select a Word (PPT 12)
9. Change the Text Color (PPT 13)
10. Save a Presentation (PPT 14)
11. Add a New Text Slide with a Bulleted List (PPT 14)
12. Enter a Slide Title (PPT 16)
13. Select a Text Placeholder (PPT 16)
14. Type a Multi-Level Bulleted List (PPT 17)
15. Select a Group of Words (PPT 19)
16. Bold Text (PPT 19)
17. Add a Slide with the Title Only Layout (PPT 21)
18. Add a New Slide and Enter a Slide Title and Headings (PPT 22)
19. Move to Another Slide in Normal View (PPT 24)
20. Find Clips Online Using the Clip Gallery (PPT 28)
21. Update the Clip Properties and Import the Clips to the Clip Gallery (PPT 31)
22. Insert a Clip from the Clip Gallery into the Title Slide (PPT 33)
23. Insert a Clip from the Clip Art Browser into a Content Placeholder (PPT 35)
24. Insert a Photograph from the Clip Art Browser into a Slide without a Content Placeholder (PPT 37)
25. Resize Clip Art (PPT 38)
26. Move Clips (PPT 40)
27. Duplicate a Slide (PPT 41)
28. Arrange a Slide (PPT 43)
29. Delete Text in a Placeholder (PPT 44)
30. Add a Transition between Slides (PPT 46)
31. Add an End of Show Slide (PPT 48)
32. Change Document Properties (PPT 49)
33. Save an Existing Presentation with the Same File Name (PPT 47)
34. Start Slide Show View (PPT 50)
35. Move Manually through Slides in a Slide Show (PPT 51)
36. Quit PowerPoint (PPT 51)
37. Open a Document from PowerPoint (PPT 52)
38. Print a Presentation (PPT 53)

Learn It Online

Test your knowledge of chapter content and key terms.

Instructions: To complete the Learn It Online exercises, please visit **www.cengagebrain.com**. At the CengageBrain.com home page, search for *Office 2011 for Mac* using the search box at the top of the page. This will take you to the product page for this book. On the product page, click the Access Now button below the Study Tools heading. On the Book Companion Site Web page, select PowerPoint Chapter 1, and then click the link for the desired exercise.

Chapter Reinforcement TF, MC, and SA
A series of true/false, multiple choice, and short answer questions that test your knowledge of the chapter content.

Flash Cards
An interactive learning environment where you identify chapter key terms associated with displayed definitions.

Practice Test
A series of multiple choice questions that test your knowledge of chapter content and key terms.

Who Wants To Be a Computer Genius?
An interactive game that challenges your knowledge of chapter content in the style of a television quiz show.

Wheel of Terms
An interactive game that challenges your knowledge of chapter key terms in the style of the television show *Wheel of Fortune*.

Crossword Puzzle Challenge
A crossword puzzle that challenges your knowledge of key terms presented in the chapter.

Apply Your Knowledge

Reinforce the skills and apply the concepts you learned in this chapter.

Modifying Character Formats and Paragraph Levels and Moving a Clip
Note: To complete this assignment, you will be required to use the Data Files for Students. See the inside back cover of this book for instructions on downloading the Data Files for Students, or contact your instructor for information about accessing the required files.

Instructions: Start PowerPoint. Open the presentation, Apply 1-1 Flu Season, from the Data Files for Students.

The two slides in the presentation discuss ways to avoid getting or spreading the flu. The document you open is an unformatted presentation. You are to modify the document theme, indent the paragraphs, resize and move the clip art, and format the text so the slides look like Figure 1–80.

Perform the following tasks:
1. Change the document theme to Perception. On the title slide, use your name in place of Student Name and bold and italicize your name. Increase the title text font size to 60 point. Resize and position the clip as shown in Figure 1–80a.
2. On Slide 2, increase the indent of the second, third, and fifth paragraphs (Cover mouth and nose with a tissue; No tissue? Use your elbow or sleeve; Use soap, warm water for 20 seconds) to second-level paragraphs. Then combine paragraphs six and seven (Drink fluids; Get plenty of rest) to read, Drink fluids and get plenty of rest, as shown in Figure 1–80b.
3. Change the document properties, as specified by your instructor. Save the presentation using the file name, Apply 1-1 Avoid the Flu. Submit the revised document in the format specified by your instructor.

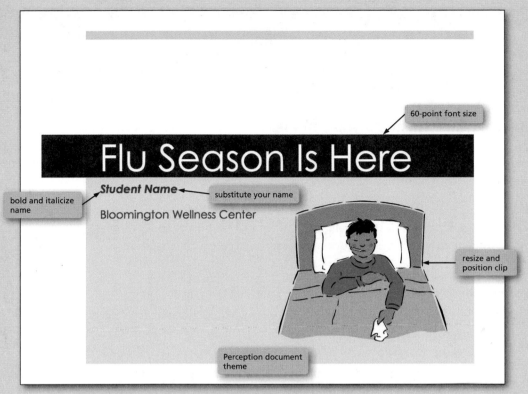

(a) Slide 1 (Title Slide with Clip Art)

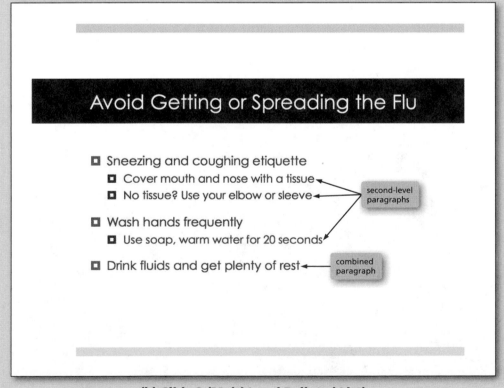

(b) Slide 2 (Multi-Level Bulleted List)

Figure 1–80

Extend Your Knowledge

Extend the skills you learned in this chapter and experiment with new skills. You may need to use Help to complete the assignment.

Changing Slide Theme, Layout, and Text

Note: To complete this assignment, you will be required to use the Data Files for Students. See the inside back cover of this book for instructions on downloading the Data Files for Students, or contact your instructor for information about accessing the required files.

Instructions: Start PowerPoint. Open the presentation that you are going to prepare for your dental hygiene class, Extend 1-1 Winning Smile, from the Data Files for Students.

You will choose a theme, format slides, and create a closing slide.

Perform the following tasks:

1. Apply an appropriate document theme.
2. On Slide 1, use your name in place of Student Name. Format the text on this slide using techniques you learned in this chapter, such as changing the font size and color and also bolding and italicizing words.
3. On Slide 2, change the slide layout and adjust the paragraph levels so that the lines of text are arranged under two headings: Discount Dental and Dental Insurance (Figure 1–81).
4. On Slide 3, create paragraphs and adjust the paragraph levels to create a bulleted list. Edit the text so that the slide meets the 7 × 7 rule, which states that each line should have a maximum of seven words, and each slide should have a maximum of seven lines.
5. Create an appropriate closing slide using the title slide as a guide.
6. The slides contain a variety of clips downloaded via the Online link in the Clip Gallery. Size and move them when necessary.

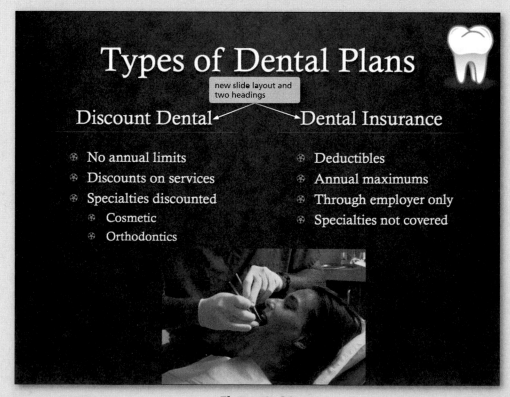

Figure 1–81

7. Apply an appropriate transition to all slides.

8. Change the document properties, as specified by your instructor. Save the presentation using the file name, Extend 1-1 Dental Plans.

9. Submit the revised document in the format specified by your instructor.

Make It Right

Analyze a presentation and correct all errors and/or improve the design.

Correcting Formatting and List Levels

Note: To complete this assignment, you will be required to use the Data Files for Students. See the inside back cover of this book for instructions on downloading the Data Files for Students, or contact your instructor for information about accessing the required files.

Instructions: Start PowerPoint. Open the presentation, Make It Right 1-1 Air Ducts, from the Data Files for Students.

Members of your homeowners' association are having their semiannual meeting, and each member of the board is required to give a short presentation on the subject of energy savings. You have decided to discuss the energy-saving benefits of maintaining the air ducts in your home. Correct the formatting problems and errors in the presentation while keeping in mind the guidelines presented in this chapter.

Perform the following tasks:

1. Change the document theme from Origin, shown in Figure 1–82, to Module.

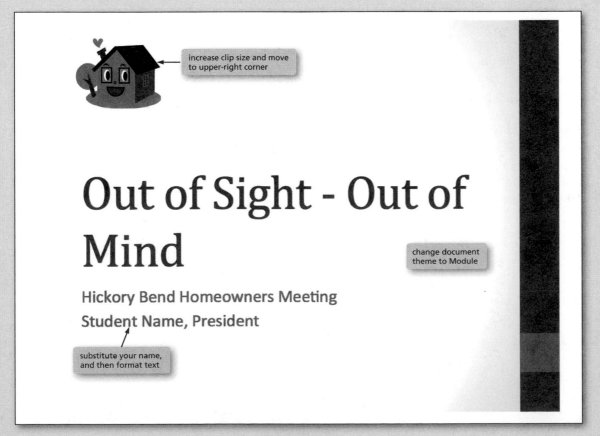

Figure 1–82

Continued >

Make It Right *continued*

2. On Slide 1, replace the words, Shelly Cashman, with your name. Format your name so that it displays prominently on the slide.

3. Increase the size of the clip on Slide 1 and move it to the upper-right corner.

4. Move Slide 2 to the end of the presentation so that it becomes the new Slide 3.

5. On Slide 2, correct the spelling errors and then increase the font size of the Slide 2 title text, Check Hidden Air Ducts, to 54 point. Increase the size of the clip and move it up to fill the white space on the right of the bulleted list.

6. On Slide 3, correct the spelling errors and then change the font size of the title text, Energy Savings, to 54 point. Increase the indent levels for paragraphs 2 and 4. Increase the size of the clips. Center the furnace clip at the bottom of the slide.

7. Change the document properties, as specified by your instructor. Save the presentation using the file name, Make It Right 1-1 Ducts Presentation.

8. Apply the same transition and duration to all slides.

9. Submit the revised document in the format specified by your instructor.

In the Lab

Design and/or create a presentation using the guidelines, concepts, and skills presented in this chapter. Labs 1, 2, and 3 are listed in order of increasing difficulty.

Lab1: Creating a Presentation with Bulleted Lists, a Closing Slide, and Clips

Problem: You are working with upper-level students to host a freshmen orientation seminar. When you attended this seminar, you received some helpful tips on studying for exams. Your contribution to this year's seminar is to prepare a short presentation on study skills. You develop the outline shown in Figure 1–83 and then prepare the PowerPoint presentation shown in Figures 1–84a through 1–84d.

Hit the Books
Studying for an Exam
Sarah Jones

Prepare in Advance
    Location
        Quiet, well-lit
    Timing
        15-minute breaks every hour
    Material
        Quiz yourself

Exam time
    Day of Exam
        Rest properly
        Eat a good meal
        Wear comfy clothes
        Be early
        Be confident

Figure 1–83

Perform the following tasks:

1. Create a new presentation using the Essential document theme.

2. Using the typed notes illustrated in Figure 1–83, create the title slide shown in Figure 1–84a, using your name in place of Sarah Jones. Italicize your name and decrease the font size to 24 point. Reduce the font size of the title text paragraph, Hit the Books, to 66 point. Insert the image on Slide 1 using the Online button in the Clip Gallery.

3. Using the typed notes in Figure 1–83, create the two text slides with bulleted lists and find and insert clips from the Clip Gallery, as shown in Figures 1–84b and 1–84c. Use the Two Content layout for Slide 2, and the Content with Caption layout for Slide 3.

4. Create a closing slide by duplicating Slide 1, deleting your name, replacing the photograph with the photograph shown in Figure 1–84d, and moving the slide to the end of the presentation.

5. On Slide 3, change the font color of the words, Be confident, to Red (second color in the Standard Colors row).

6. Apply the Uncover transition in the Subtle category to all slides. Change the duration to 1.25 seconds.

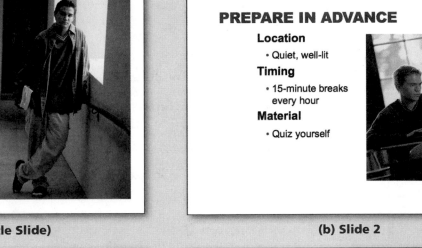

(a) Slide 1 (Title Slide)

(b) Slide 2

(c) Slide 3

(d) Slide 4 (Closing Slide)

Figure 1–84

Continued >

In the Lab *continued*

7. Drag the scroller to display Slide 1. Click the Slide Show button to start Slide Show view. Then click to display each slide.

8. Change the document properties, as specified by your instructor. Save the presentation using the file name, Lab 1-1 Study Skills.

9. Submit the document in the format specified by your instructor.

In the Lab

Lab 2: Creating a Presentation with Bulleted Lists and Clips

Problem: Your health class instructor has assigned every student a different vitamin to research. She hands you the outline shown in Figure 1–85 and asks you to create the presentation about Vitamin D shown in Figures 1–86a through 1–86d on page PPT 63.

Vitamin D

The Sunshine Vitamin
Are You D-ficient?
Presented by Jim Warner

Why is Vitamin D Important?
    We Need Vitamin D
        Vital to our bodies
            Promotes absorption of calcium and magnesium
                For healthy teeth and bones
            Maintains calcium and phosphorus in blood

    Daily Requirements
        How much do we need?
            Child: 5 mcg (200 IU)
            Adult 10-20 mcg (400-600 IU)

Vitamin D Sources
    Sunshine
        Is our primary source
            Vitamin manufactured by our body after exposure
                Three times a week
                For 10-15 minutes

    Foods and Supplements
        Contained in few foods
            Some fish liver oils
            Flesh of fatty fish
        Fortified products
            Milk and cereal
        Available as supplement

Vitamin D History
    Research began in 1924
        Found to prevent rickets
    United States and Canada
        Instituted policy of fortifying foods with Vitamin D
            Milk – food of choice
    Other Countries
        Fortified cereal, bread, margarine

Figure 1–85

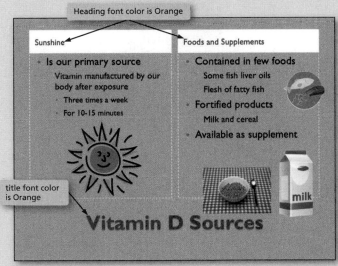

(a) Slide 1 (Title Slide)

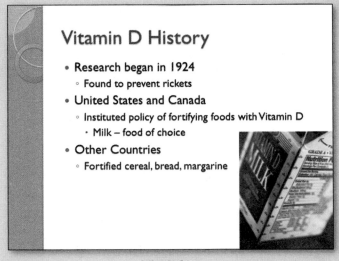

(b) Slide 2

(c) Slide 3

(d) Slide 4

Figure 1–86

Perform the following tasks:

1. Create a new presentation using the Solstice document theme.

2. Using the typed notes illustrated in Figure 1–85, create the title slide shown in Figure 1–86a, using your name in place of Jim Warner. Italicize the title, The Sunshine Vitamin, and increase the font size to 48 point. Change the font size of the first line of the subtitle text, Are You D-ficient?, to 36 point. Change the font color of the title text to Orange (third color in the Standard Colors row) and both lines of the subtitle text to Light Blue (seventh color in the Standard Colors row).

3. Using the typed notes in Figure 1–85, create the three text slides with bulleted lists shown in Figures 1–86b through 1–86d. Change the color of the title text on all slides and the text above the bulleted lists on Slides 2 and 3 to Orange.

4. Add the photographs and clip art shown in Figures 1–86a through 1–86d from the Microsoft Clip Organizer. Adjust the clip sizes when necessary.

5. Apply the Ripple transition in the Exciting category to all slides. Change the duration to 2.00 seconds.

Continued >

In the Lab *continued*

6. Drag the scroll box to display Slide 1. Click the Slide Show button to start Slide Show view. Then click to display each slide.

7. Change the document properties, as specified by your instructor. Save the presentation using the file name, Lab 1-2 Vitamin D.

8. Submit the revised document in the format specified by your instructor.

In the Lab

Lab 3: Creating and Updating Presentations with Clip Art

Problem: You are employed part time at your health club, and the Child Care Center director has asked you to put together a presentation for her to use at the next open house. The club has a large playroom that is perfect for children's parties.

Instructions Part 1: Using the outline in Figure 1–87, create the presentation shown in Figure 1–88. Use the White document theme. On the title slide shown in Figure 1–88a, increase the font size of the title paragraph, Make It a Party!, to 48, change the font color to Red, and change the text font style to italic. Decrease the font size of the entire subtitle paragraph to 28, and change the font color to Blue.

Make It a Party!
　　Host Your Child's
　　Next Birthday Party
　　At The Oaks Health Club

We Do the Work
You Enjoy the Moment
　　Two-hour party
　　Two chaperones
　　Lunch & cake provided
　　Game or craft activity available
　　Decorations

Two Party Packages
　　Package No. 1 - $8/child
　　　　Lunch
　　　　　　Hot Dogs
　　　　　　Pizza
　　Package No. 2 - $12/child
　　　　Lunch including beverage
　　　　　　Hot Dogs
　　　　　　Pizza
　　　　Game
　　　　Craft (age appropriate)

Reserve Your Party Date
　　Reserve 2 weeks in advance
　　Deposit required
　　Party room can hold 20 children
　　Sign up in the Child Care Center

Figure 1–87

Create the three text slides with multi-level bulleted lists, photographs, and clip art shown in Figures 1–88b through 1-88d. Adjust the clip sizes when necessary. Apply the Vortex transition in the Exciting category to all slides and decrease the duration to 3.00 seconds. Change the document properties, as specified by your instructor. Save the presentation using the file name, Lab 1-3 Part One Child Party.

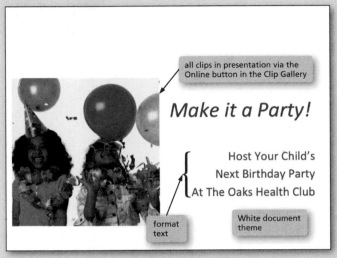

all clips in presentation via the Online button in the Clip Gallery

Make it a Party!

Host Your Child's
Next Birthday Party
At The Oaks Health Club

format text

White document theme

(a) Slide 1 (Title Slide)

We Do the Work
You Enjoy the Moment

- Two-hour party
- Two chaperones
- Lunch & cake provided
- Game or craft activity available
- Decorations

(b) Slide 2

Two Party Packages

Package No. 1 - $8/child
- Lunch
  – Hot Dogs
  – Pizza

Package No. 2 - $12/child
- Lunch including beverage
  – Hot Dogs
  – Pizza
- Game
- Craft (age appropriate)

(c) Slide 3

Reserve Your Party Date

- Reserve 2 weeks in advance
- Deposit required
- Party room can hold 20 children
- Sign up in the Child Care Center

(d) Slide 4

Figure 1–88

Instructions Part 2: The children's parties have proved to be a great perk for members of the health club. A large group of older adults work out at the club and also meet socially once a month. These members have asked about renting the playroom to hold a retirement party for some of their friends. You decide to modify the children's party presentation to promote retirement parties. Use the outline in Figure 1–89 on the next page to modify the presentation created in Part 1 to create the presentation shown in Figure 1–90 on the next page. Required changes are indicated by a yellow highlight.

To begin, save the current presentation with the new file name, Lab 1-3 Part Two Retirement Party. Change the document theme to Waveform. On Slide 3, change the pianist's name from Mr. Winn to your name. Apply the Fade transition in the Subtle category to all slides and change the duration speed to 2.25 seconds. View the slide show. Change the document properties, as specified by your instructor. Submit both Part One and Part Two documents in the format specified by your instructor.

Continued >

In the Lab *continued*

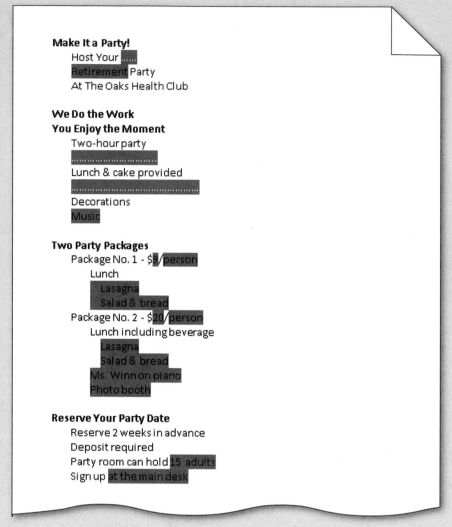

Figure 1–89

(a) Slide 1 (Title Slide)

(b) Slide 2

Figure 1–90 *(continues)*

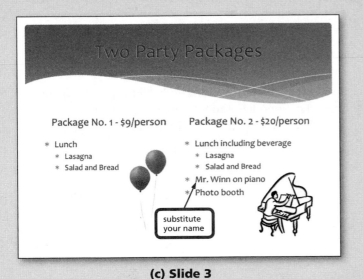

(c) Slide 3

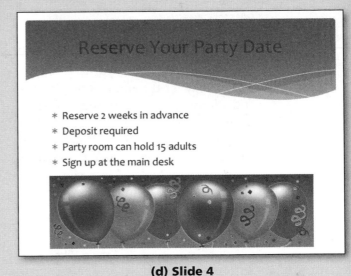

(d) Slide 4

Figure 1–90

Cases and Places

Apply your creative thinking and problem-solving skills to design and implement a solution.

Note: To complete these assignments, you may be required to use the Data Files for Students. See the inside back cover of this book for instructions on downloading the Data Files for Students, or contact your instructor for information about accessing the required files.

As you design the presentations, remember to use the 7×7 rule: a maximum of seven words on a line and a maximum of seven lines on one slide.

1: Design and Create a Presentation about Galileo

Academic

Italian-born Galileo is said to be the father of modern science. After the invention of the telescope by a Dutch eyeglass maker named Hans Lippershey, Galileo made his own telescope and made many discoveries. You decide to prepare a PowerPoint presentation to accompany a speech that is required in your Astronomy class. You create the outline shown in Figure 1–91 about Galileo. Use this outline, along with the concepts and techniques presented in this chapter, to develop and format a slide show with a title slide and three text slides with bulleted lists. Add photographs and clip art from the Clip Gallery (Online button) and apply a transition. Submit your assignment in the format specified by your instructor.

Galileo Galilei
    Father of Modern Science
    Astronomy 201
    Sandy Wendt

Major Role in Scientific Revolution
February 15, 1564 – January 8, 1642
    Physicist
    Mathematician
    Astronomer
    Philosopher

Galileo's Research Years
    1581 – Studied medicine
    1589-1592 - Studied math and physics
    1592-1607 – Padua University
        Developed Law of Inertia
    1609 – Built telescope
        Earth's moon
        Jupiter's moons

Galileo's Later Years
    Dialogue – Two Chief world Systems
        Controversy develops
    1633 – Rome
        Heresy trial
        Imprisoned
    1642 - Dies

Figure 1–91

Continued >

Cases and Places *continued*

2: Design and Create a Presentation Promoting Hiking for Family Fitness

Personal

A great way for the entire family to get exercise is by participating in a hiking adventure. Employees at the local forest preserve district near your home have remodeled the nature center, and you have volunteered to give a presentation at the open house to help families plan their hikes. Use the outline shown in Figure 1–92 and then create an accompanying PowerPoint presentation. Use the concepts and techniques presented in this chapter to develop and format this slide show with a title slide, three text slides with bulleted lists, and clip art. Add photographs and clip art from the Clip Gallery (Online button) and apply a transition. Submit your assignment in the format specified by your instructor.

Take a Hike
 An Adventure with Kids
 Presented by Joshua Lind
 Pines Nature Center

Planning the Adventure
 Trail length – varies by child's age
  Ages 2 to 4: 1 to 2 miles
  Ages 5 to 7: 3 to 4 miles
  Ages 8 to 12: 5 to 7 miles
 Backpack – limit to 20 percent of child's weight

Packing Supplies
 Snacks and Drinks
  Child's favorite healthy foods
   Fruits and nuts
  Water
 Miscellaneous
  Sunscreen
  Insect repellent
  First-aid kit

Wearing the Right Clothes
 Dress in layers
  Children get cold quicker than adults
 Wear long pants and long sleeved shirt
  Protect against insects and cuts
 Wear a hat and comfortable shoes
  Keep body warm

Figure 1–92

3: Design and Create a Landscaping Service Presentation

Professional

The home and garden center where you work is hosting weekend clinics for customers. The owner asks you to give a presentation about the center's new landscaping division and hands you the outline shown in Figure 1–93. Use the concepts and techniques presented in this chapter to develop and format a PowerPoint presentation with a title slide, three text slides with bulleted lists, and clip art. Add photographs and clip art from the Clip Gallery (Online button) and apply a transition. Submit your assignment in the format specified by your instructor.

Barry's Landscaping Service
Bensenville, Indiana

Full-Service Landscaping
    Initial design
    Installation
    Maintenance

Scope of Services
    Landscape design
    Irrigation
    Lighting
    Lawn-care programs
    Tree/shrub maintenance
    Masonry, carpentry
    Water features

Our Promise to You
    Deliver on-time service
    Provide highest level of workmanship
    Give maximum value for your dollar
    Install high quality plants and materials
    Respond quickly to your needs

Figure 1–93

2 Enhancing a Presentation with Pictures, Shapes, and WordArt

Objectives

You will have mastered the material in this chapter when you can:

Change theme colors

Insert a picture to create a background

Format slide backgrounds

Insert and size a shape

Add text to a shape

Apply effects to a shape

Change the font and add a shadow

Format pictures

Apply a WordArt style

Format WordArt

Format text using the Format Painter

2 Enhancing a Presentation with Pictures, Shapes, and WordArt

Introduction

In our visually oriented culture, audience members enjoy viewing effective graphics. Whether reading a document or viewing a PowerPoint presentation, people increasingly want to see photographs, artwork, graphics, and a variety of typefaces. Researchers have known for decades that documents with visual elements are more effective than those that consist of only text because the illustrations motivate audiences to study the material. People remember at least one-third more information when the document they are seeing or reading contains visual elements. These graphics help clarify and emphasize details, so they appeal to audience members with differing backgrounds, reading levels, attention spans, and motivations.

Yoga's Origins

BTW The term, yoga, is derived from the Sanskrit word yuj, meaning to join or unite. Yogis have been practicing this system of exercises and philosophy of mental control for more than 26,000 years.

Project — Presentation with Pictures, Shapes, and WordArt

The project in this chapter follows graphical guidelines and uses PowerPoint to create the presentation shown in Figure 2–1. This slide show, which discusses yoga and meditation, has a variety of illustrations and visual elements. For example, pictures have particular shapes and effects. The enhanced type has a style that blends well with the background and illustrations. Pictures and type are formatted using Quick Styles and WordArt, which give your presentation a professional look.

Overview

As you read through this chapter, you will learn how to create the presentation shown in Figure 2–1 by performing these general tasks:

- Format slide backgrounds.
- Insert and format pictures by applying styles and effects.
- Insert and format shapes.
- Format text using WordArt.
- Print a handout of your slides.

(a) Slide 1 (Title Slide with Picture Background)

(b) Slide 2 (Formatted Picture)

(c) Slide 3 (Formatted Picture)

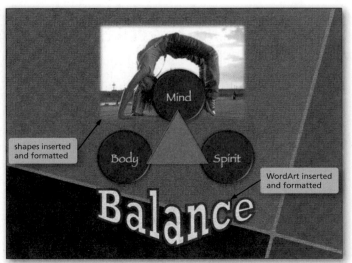

(d) Slide 4 (Inserted and Formatted Shapes)

Figure 2–1

Plan Ahead

General Project Guidelines

When creating a PowerPoint presentation, the actions you perform and decisions you make will affect the appearance and characteristics of the finished document. As you create a presentation with illustrations, such as the project shown in Figure 2–1 on the previous page, you should follow these general guidelines:

1. **Focus on slide text content.** Give some careful thought to the words you choose. Some graphic designers advise starting with a blank screen so that the document theme does not distract from or influence the words.

2. **Apply style guidelines.** Many organizations and publishers establish guidelines for writing styles. These rules apply to capitalization, punctuation, word usage, and document formats. Ask your instructor or manager for a copy of these guidelines or use popular writing guides, such as the *The Chicago Manual of Style, The Associated Press Stylebook*, and *The Elements of Style*.

3. **Use color effectively.** Your audience's eyes are drawn to color on a slide. Used appropriately, color can create interest by emphasizing material and promoting understanding. Be aware of symbolic meanings attached to colors, such as red generally representing danger, electricity, and heat.

4. **Adhere to copyright regulations.** Copyright laws apply to printed and electronic materials. You can copy an existing photograph or artwork if it is in the public domain, if your company owns the graphic, or if you have obtained permission to use it. Be certain you have the legal right to use a desired graphic in your presentation.

5. **Consider graphics for multicultural audiences.** In today's intercultural society, your presentation might be viewed by people whose first language is different from yours. Some graphics have meanings specific to a culture, so be certain to learn about your intended audience and their views.

6. **Use WordArt in moderation.** Used correctly, the graphical nature of WordArt can add interest and set a tone. Format text with a WordArt style only when needed for special emphasis.

When necessary, more specific details concerning the above guidelines are presented at appropriate points in the chapter. The chapter also will identify the actions you perform and decisions made regarding these guidelines during the creation of the presentation shown in Figure 2–1.

Starting PowerPoint

For an introduction to Mac OS X and instruction about how to perform basic Mac OS X tasks, read the Office 2011 and Mac OS X chapter at the beginning of this book, where you can learn how to resize windows, change screen resolution, create folders, move and rename files, use Mac OS X Help, and much more.

Chapter 1 introduced you to starting PowerPoint, selecting a document theme, creating slides with clip art and a bulleted list, and printing a presentation. If you are using a computer to step through the project in this chapter and you want your screens to match the figures in this book, you should change your screen's resolution to 1280 × 800. For information about how to change a computer's resolution, refer to the Office 2011 and Mac OS X chapter at the beginning of this book.

The following steps, which assume Mac OS X is running, start PowerPoint based on a typical installation. You may need to ask your instructor how to start PowerPoint for your computer. For a detailed example of the procedure summarized below, refer to the Office 2011 and Mac OS X chapter.

To Start PowerPoint and Apply a Document Theme

1 Click the PowerPoint icon in the Dock to display the PowerPoint Presentation Gallery.

2 If All is not selected under Themes in the left pane, click to select it.

3 Double-click the Kilter theme in the PowerPoint Presentation Gallery to display a new presentation with the Kilter theme in the PowerPoint window.

4 If the PowerPoint window is not sized properly, as described in the Office 2011 and Mac OS X chapter, size the window properly.

5 If the Normal View button in the lower left of the presentation window is not selected, click it so that your screen is in Normal view.

Focus on slide text content.   **Plan Ahead**

Once you have researched your presentation topic, many methods exist to begin developing slide content.

- Select a document theme and then enter text, illustration, and tables.
- Open an existing presentation and modify the slides and theme.
- Import an outline created in Microsoft Word.
- Start with a blank presentation that uses the default Office Theme. Consider this practice similar to an artist who begins creating a painting with a blank, white canvas.

Experiment using different methods of developing the initial content for slides. Experienced PowerPoint users sometimes find one technique works better than another to stimulate creativity or help them organize their ideas in a particular circumstance.

For an introduction to Office 2011 and instruction about how to perform basic tasks in Office 2011 programs, read the Office 2011 and Mac OS X chapter at the beginning of this book, where you can learn how to start a program, use the ribbon, save a file, open a file, quit a program, use Help, and much more.

Creating Slides and Changing Font Colors and Background Style

In Chapter 1, you selected a document theme and then typed the content for the title and text slides. In this chapter, you will type the slide content for the title and text slides, select a background, insert and format pictures and shapes, and then insert and format WordArt. To begin creating the four slides in this presentation, you will enter text in four different layouts, change the theme colors, and then change the background style.

Apply style guidelines.   **Plan Ahead**

A good stylebook is useful to decide when to use numerals or words to represent numbers, as in the sentence, More than 25 students are waiting for the bus to arrive. Stylebooks also offer rules on forming possessives, capitalizing titles, and using commas. Once you decide on a style to use in your presentation, apply it consistently throughout your presentation.

To Create a Title Slide

Recall from Chapter 1 that the title slide introduces the presentation to the audience. In addition to introducing the presentation, this project uses the title slide to capture the audience's attention by using title text and a background picture. The following steps create the slide show's title slide.

1 Type **Yoga and Meditation** in the title text placeholder.

2 Type **Unify Your Mind,** in the subtitle text placeholder.

3 Press the RETURN key and then type `Body,` as the second line in the subtitle text placeholder.

4 Press the RETURN key and then type `and Spirit` as the third line in the subtitle text placeholder. Change the capital letter 'A' in the word, And, at the beginning of this line to a lowercase 'a' (Figure 2–2).

Q&A   Some stylebooks recommend using lowercase letters when using coordinating conjunctions (for, and, nor, but, or, yet, so) and also when using articles (a, an, the). Why is the case of the word, and, changed in the subtitle text?
By default, PowerPoint capitalizes the first word of each paragraph. For consistency, you can decide to lowercase this word to apply a particular style rule so that the word, and, is lowercase in both the title and subtitle text.

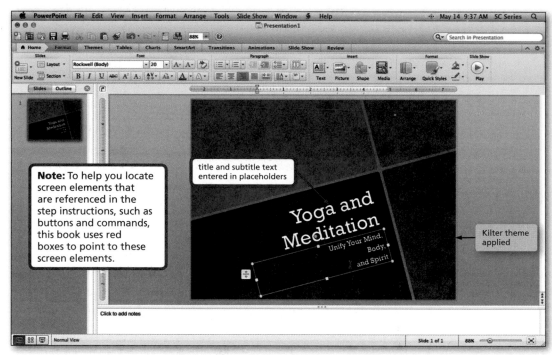

Figure 2–2

Q&As

BTW For a complete list of the Q&As found in many of the step-by-step sequences in this book, visit the Office 2011 for Mac Online Companion Web page at www.cengagebrain.com, navigate to the desired chapter, and click Q&As.

To Create the First Text Slide

The first text slide you create in Chapter 2 emphasizes the relaxation and restoration benefits derived from practicing yoga and meditation. The following steps add a new slide (Slide 2) and then create a text slide using the Picture with Caption layout.

1 On the Home tab, click the New Slide button arrow, and then click Picture with Caption in the Layout gallery to add a new slide with this layout.

2 Type `Relax and Restore` in the title text placeholder.

3 Click the caption placeholder and then type `Calm the mind and boost oxygen levels in the brain` in this placeholder (Figure 2–3).

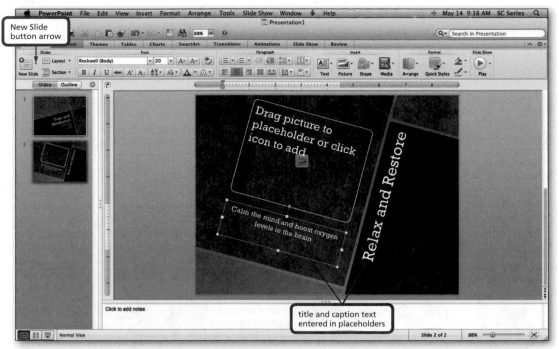

Figure 2–3

To Create the Second Text Slide

The second text slide you create stresses the fact that yoga and meditation strengthen the body in multiple ways. The following steps add a new text slide (Slide 3) that uses the Content with Caption layout.

1 Click the New Slide button arrow and then click Content with Caption in the Layout gallery to add a new slide with this layout.

2 Type `Strengthen Body` in the title text placeholder.

3 Type `Increase flexibility and tone muscles.` in the caption place-holder (Figure 2–4).

BTWs

For a complete list of the BTWs found in the margins of this book, visit the Office 2011 for Mac Online Companion Web page at www.cengagebrain.com, navigate to the desired chapter, and click BTWs.

BTW

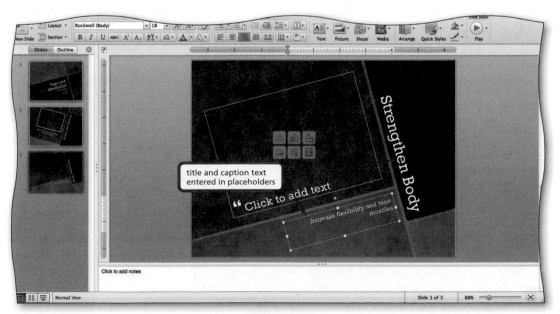

Figure 2–4

To Create the Third Text Slide

Yoga and meditation help create balance in an individual's life. The last slide you create uses graphics to depict the connection among the mind, body, and spirit. You will insert symbols later in this project to create this visual element. For now, you want to create the basic slide. The following step adds a new text slide (Slide 4) that uses the Blank layout.

1 Click the New Slide button arrow and then click Blank in the Layout gallery (Figure 2–5).

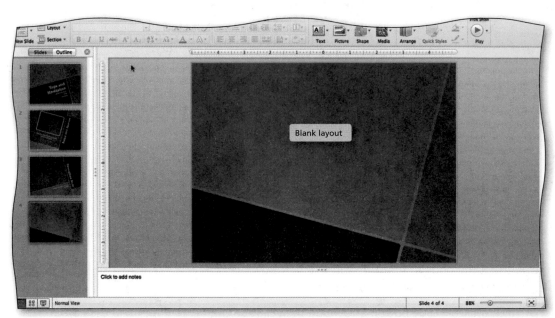

Figure 2–5

Presentation Template Color Scheme

Each presentation template has 12 complementary colors, which collectively are called the **color scheme**. You can apply these colors to all slides, an individual slide, notes pages, or audience handouts. A color scheme consists of four colors for a background and text, six accent colors, and two hyperlink colors. You can customize the theme colors to create your own set and give them a unique name. Table 2–1 explains the components of a color scheme.

Table 2–1 Color Scheme Components	
Component	**Description**
Background color	The background color is the fundamental color of a PowerPoint slide. For example, if the background color is black, you can place any other color on top of it, but the fundamental color remains black. The black background shows everywhere you do not add color or other objects.
Text color	The text color contrasts with the background color of the slide. As a default, the text border color is the same as the text color. Together with the background color, the text and border colors set the tone for a presentation. For example, a gray background with black text and border sets a dramatic tone. In contrast, a red background with yellow text and border sets a vibrant tone.
Accent colors	Accent colors are designed as colors for secondary features on a slide. They often are used as fill colors on graphs and as shadows.
Hyperlink colors	The default hyperlink color is set when you type the text. When you click the hyperlink text during a presentation, the color changes to the Followed Hyperlink color.

To Change the Presentation Theme Colors

The first modification to make is to change the color scheme throughout the presentation. The following steps change the color scheme for the template from an aqua title slide background with white text and blue and orange accents to a dark blue background with white and blue accents.

- Click Themes on the ribbon and then click the Colors button under Theme Options to display the Theme Colors gallery.

- Scroll down to the bottom of the gallery to see the Waveform theme colors (Figure 2–6).

Q&A Why does an orange box surround the Kilter color scheme in the Colors gallery? It shows the Kilter document theme is applied, and those eight colors are associated with that theme.

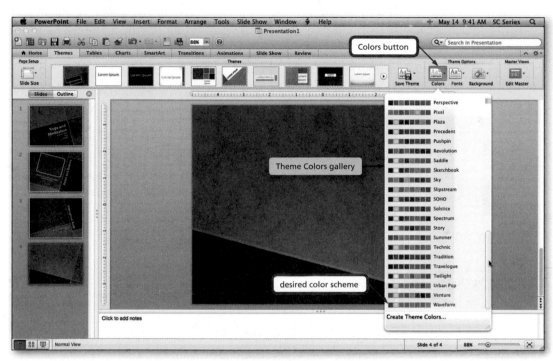

Figure 2–6

- Click Waveform in the Theme Colors gallery to change the presentation theme colors to Waveform (Figure 2–7).

Q&A What if I want to return to the original theme colors? You would click the Theme Colors button and then click Kilter in the Theme Colors gallery.

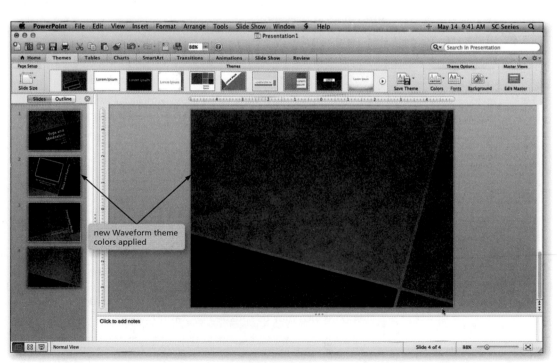

Figure 2–7

To Save a Presentation

You have performed many tasks while creating this slide and do not want to risk losing work completed thus far. Accordingly, you should save the document.

The following steps assume you already have created folders for storing your files, for example, a CIS 101 folder (for your class) that contains a PowerPoint folder (for your assignments). Thus, these steps save the document in the PowerPoint folder in the CIS 101 folder on a USB flash drive using the file name, Yoga. For a detailed example of the procedure summarized below, refer to the Office 2011 and Mac OS X chapter at the beginning of this book.

1 With a USB flash drive connected to one of the computer's USB ports, click the Save button on the Standard toolbar to display the Save As dialog.

2 Type **Yoga** in the File name text box to change the file name. Do not press the RETURN key after typing the file name because you do not want to close the dialog at this time.

3 Navigate to the desired save location (in this case, the PowerPoint folder in the CIS 101 folder [or your class folder] on the USB flash drive).

4 Click the Save button (Save As dialog) to save the document in the selected folder on the selected drive with the entered file name.

Inserting and Formatting Pictures in a Presentation

With the text entered and background formatted in the presentation, the next step is to insert digital pictures into the placeholders on Slides 2 and 3 and then format the pictures. These graphical images draw the viewers' eyes to the slides and help them retain the information presented.

In the following pages, you will perform these tasks:

1. Insert the first digital picture into Slide 3.
2. Insert the second digital picture into Slide 2.
3. Change the look of the first picture.
4. Change the look of the second picture.
5. Resize the second picture.
6. Insert a digital picture into the Slide 1 background.
7. Format slide backgrounds.

Plan Ahead

Adhere to copyright regulations.

You have permission to use the clips from the Microsoft Clip Art Browser. If you want to use a clip from another source, be certain you have the legal right to insert this file in your presentation. Read the copyright notices that accompany the clip and are posted on the Web site. The owners of these images and files often ask you to give them credit for using their work, which may be satisfied by stating where you obtained the images.

To Insert a Picture

The next step in creating the presentation is to insert one of the digital yoga pictures in the picture placeholder in Slide 3. The picture is available on the Data Files for Students. See the inside back cover of this book for instructions on downloading the Data Files for Students, or contact your instructor for information about accessing the required files.

The following steps insert a picture, which, in this example, is located in the PowerPoint Chapter 02 folder on the same USB flash drive that contains the saved presentation, into Slide 3.

- With your USB flash drive connected to one of the computer's USB ports, click the Previous Slide button to display Slide 3.

- Click the Insert Picture from File icon in the content placeholder to display the Choose a Picture dialog.

- Double-click your USB flash drive in the list of available storage devices to display a list of files and folders on the selected USB flash drive. Double-click the Data Files for Students folder, double-click the PowerPoint folder, and then double-click the Chapter 02 folder to display a list of files in that folder.

- Scroll down and then click Hands Yoga to select the file name (Figure 2–8).

Q&A What if the picture is not on a USB flash drive?
Use the same process, but select the drive containing the picture.

Figure 2–8

- Click the Insert button (Choose a Picture dialog) to insert the picture into the content placeholder in Slide 3 (Figure 2–9).

Q&A What are the symbols around the picture?
A selected graphic appears surrounded by a **selection rectangle**, which has small squares and circles, called **sizing handles**, at each corner and middle location.

Q&A What is the gray bar with icons below the picture?
This is the **picture sizing toolbar**, which contains icons for resizing and cropping figures once they have been inserted into the presentation.

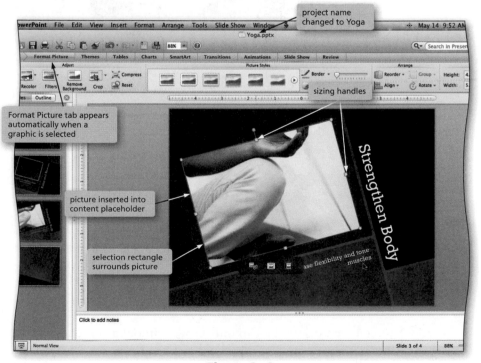

Figure 2–9

To Insert Another Picture into a Content Placeholder

The next step is to insert another digital yoga picture into the Slide 2 content placeholder. This second picture also is available on the Data Files for Students. See the inside back cover of this book for instructions on downloading the Data Files for Students, or contact your instructor for information about accessing the required files.

The following steps insert a picture into Slide 2.

1 Click the Previous Slide button to display Slide 2.

2 With your USB flash drive connected to one of the computer's USB ports, click the Insert Picture from File icon in the content placeholder to display the Choose a Picture dialog.

3 If the list of files and folders on the selected USB flash drive are not displayed in the Insert Picture dialog, double-click your USB flash drive to display them and then navigate to the PowerPoint Chapter 02 folder.

4 Scroll down and then click Green Tank Meditation to select the file name.

5 Click the Insert button (Choose a Picture dialog) to insert the picture into the Slide 2 content placeholder (Figure 2–10).

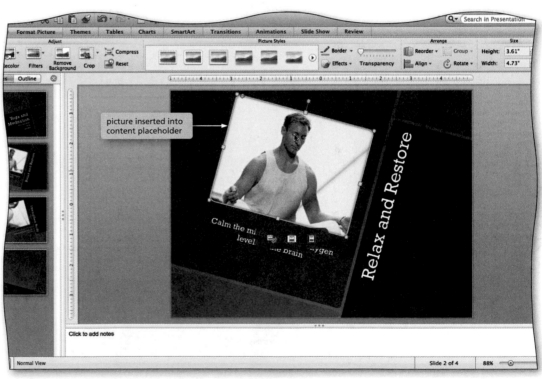

Figure 2–10

To Insert a Picture into a Slide without a Content Placeholder

In Chapter 1, you inserted a clip into a slide without a content placeholder. You also can insert a picture into a slide that does not have a content placeholder. The picture for Slide 4 is available on the Data Files for Students. See the inside back cover of this book for instructions on downloading the Data Files for Students, or contact your instructor for information about accessing the required files. The following steps insert a picture into Slide 4.

• Click the Next Slide button two times to display Slide 4.

• With your USB flash drive connected to one of the computer's USB ports, on the Home tab, under Insert, click the Picture button to display the Picture menu (Figure 2–11).

Figure 2–11

• Choose Picture from File to display the Choose a Picture dialog. If the list of files and folders on the selected USB flash drive are not displayed in the Insert Picture dialog, double-click your USB flash drive to display them and then navigate to the PowerPoint Chapter 02 folder.

• Click Arch Yoga to select the file name (Figure 2–12).

Figure 2–12

❸

• Click the Insert button (Choose a Picture dialog) to insert the picture into Slide 4.

• Move the picture so that it displays approximately as shown in Figure 2–13.

Q&A What is the green circle attached to the selected graphic?
The green circle is a rotate handle. When you drag a graphic's rotate handle, the graphic moves in either a clockwise or counterclockwise direction.

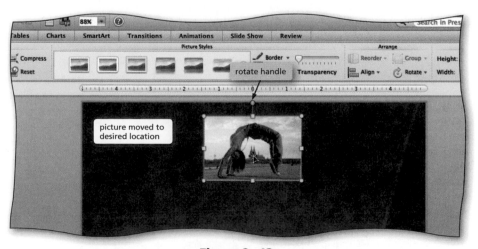

Figure 2–13

To Correct a Picture

A photograph's color intensity can be modified by changing the brightness and contrast. **Brightness** determines the overall lightness or darkness of the entire image, whereas **contrast** is the difference between the darkest and lightest areas of the image. The brightness and contrast are changed in predefined percentage increments. The following step increases the brightness and decreases the contrast to intensify the picture colors.

1

- With the Arch Yoga picture on Slide 4 still selected, click the Corrections button on the Format Picture tab under Adjust to display the Corrections gallery (Figure 2–14).

Q&A Why is a yellow border surrounding the picture in the center of the gallery?
The image on Slide 4 currently has normal brightness and contrast (0%), which is represented by this center image in the gallery.

- Click Brightness: +20% Contrast: −40% (fourth picture in first row of Brightness and Contrast area) to apply this correction to the yoga picture.

Q&A How can I remove all effects from the picture?
Click the Reset button on the Format Picture tab in the Adjust group.

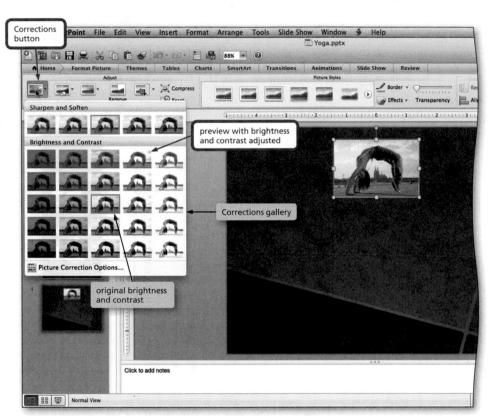

Figure 2–14

Other Ways

1. On Home tab under Adjust, click Corrections button, choose Picture Correction Options, move Brightness or Contrast sliders or enter number in box next to slider (Format Picture dialog)

2. CONTROL-click picture, choose Format Picture in shortcut menu, click Adjust Picture in left pane, move Brightness or Contrast sliders or enter number in box next to slider (Format Picture dialog)

3. Choose Format > Picture in menu bar, click Adjust Picture in left pane, move Brightness or Contrast sliders or enter number in box next to slider (Format Picture dialog)

To Apply a Picture Style

The pictures on Slides 2, 3, and 4 grasp the audience's attention, but you can increase their visual appeal by applying a style. A **style** is a named group of formatting characteristics. PowerPoint provides more than 25 picture styles that enable you easily to change a picture's look to a more visually appealing style, including a variety of shapes, angles, borders, and reflections. The photos in Slides 2, 3, and 4 in this chapter use styles that apply soft edges, reflections, or angled perspectives to the pictures. The following steps apply a picture style to the Slide 4 picture.

- With the Slide 4 picture selected, on the Format Picture tab under Picture styles, click the More button in the Picture Styles gallery to expand the gallery (Figure 2–15).

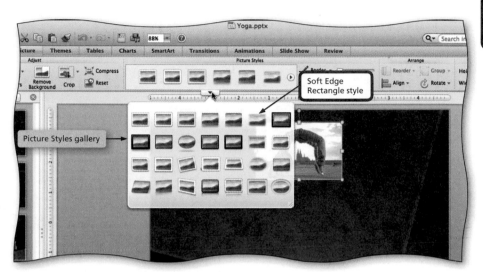

Figure 2–15

- Click Soft Edge Rectangle in the Picture Styles gallery (column 6, row 1) to apply the style to the selected picture (Figure 2–16).

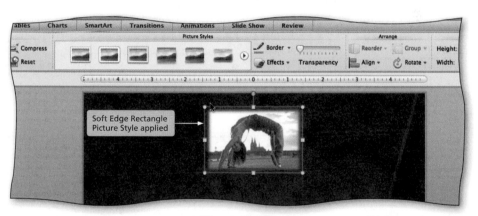

Figure 2–16

To Apply Other Picture Styles

The next step is to apply picture styles to the yoga pictures in Slides 3 and 2. To provide continuity, both of these styles will have a reflection. The following steps apply other picture styles to the Slide 3 and Slide 2 pictures.

1. Click the Previous Slide button to display Slide 3.

2. Click the Slide 3 picture to select it. On the Format Picture tab under Picture Styles, click the More button in the Picture Styles gallery to expand the gallery.

3. Click Reflected Perspective Right (column 2, row 4) in the Picture Styles gallery to apply this style to the picture in Slide 3.

4 Click the Previous Slide button to display Slide 2.

5 Click the Slide 2 picture to select it. On the Format Picture tab, click the More button in the Picture Styles gallery to expand the gallery.

6 Click Reflected Rounded Rectangle (column 5, row 1) in the Picture Styles gallery to apply this style to the picture in Slide 2 (Figure 2–17).

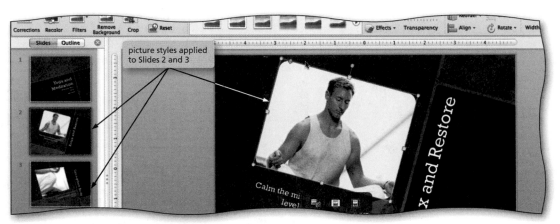

Figure 2–17

To Apply Picture Effects

PowerPoint provides a variety of picture effects so that you can further customize a picture. Effects include shadows, reflections, glow, soft edges, bevel, and 3-D rotation. The difference between the effects and the styles is that each effect has several options, providing you with more control over the exact look of the image.

In this presentation, the photos on Slides 2 and 3 have a green glow effect and have a bevel applied to their edges. The following steps apply picture effects to the selected picture.

1

- With the Slide 2 picture selected, click the Effects button in the Picture Styles group on the Format Picture tab to display the Effects menu.

Q&A What if the Format Picture tab no longer is displayed on my ribbon?
Click the picture to display the Format Picture tab.

- Point to Glow on the Effects menu to display the Glow gallery (Figure 2–18).

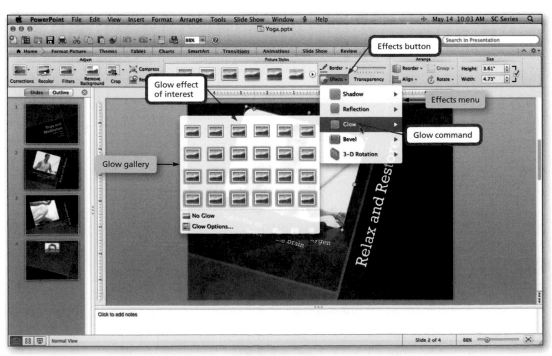

Figure 2–18

2

- Click Accent 1, 11 pt glow (third glow in first row) in the Glow gallery to apply the selected picture effect.

3

- Click the Effects button in the Picture Styles group on the Format Picture tab to display the Effects menu again.

- Point to Bevel on the Effects menu to display the Bevel gallery (Figure 2–19).

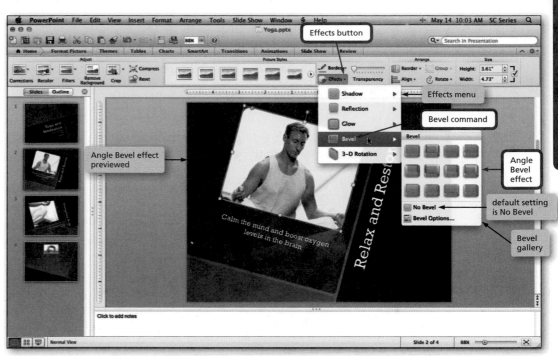

Figure 2–19

4

- Click Angle (leftmost bevel in second row) in the Bevel gallery to apply the selected picture effect (Figure 2–20).

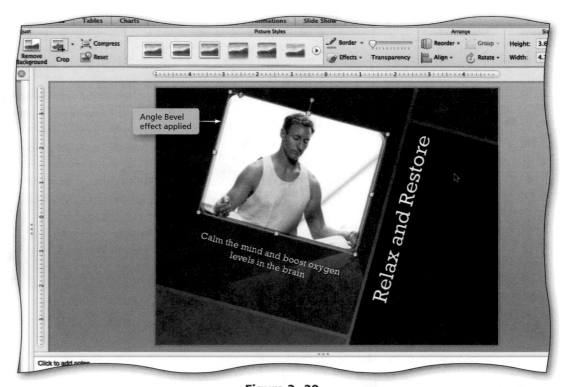

Figure 2–20

■ Other Ways

1. CONTROL-click picture, choose Format Picture in shortcut menu, select desired options (Format Picture dialog), click OK button

2. Choose Format > Picture in menu bar, select desired options (Format Picture dialog), click OK button

To Apply a Picture Style and Effect to Another Picture

In this presentation, the Slide 3 picture also has green glow and bevel effects. The following steps apply the picture style and picture effects to the picture.

1 Click the Next Slide button to display Slide 3 and then click the picture to select it.

2 Click the Effects button on the Format Picture tab under Picture Styles to display the Effects menu and then point to Glow on the Effects menu to display the Glow gallery.

3 Choose Accent 1, 11 pt glow (third glow in first row) in the Glow gallery to apply the picture effect to the picture.

4 Click the Effects button to display the Effects menu again and then point to Bevel on the Effects menu to display the Bevel gallery.

5 Click Convex (third bevel in second row) in the Bevel area to apply the picture effect to the selected picture (Figure 2–21).

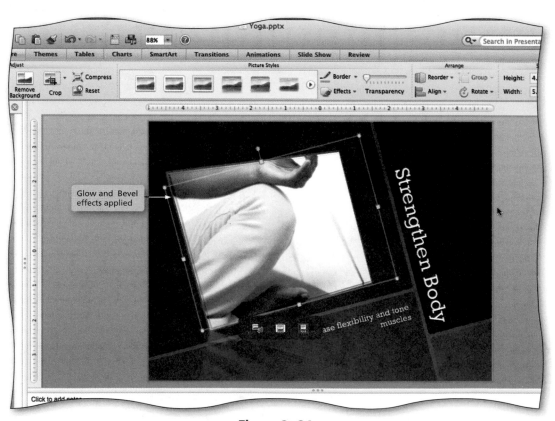

Figure 2–21

To Add a Picture Border

The next step is to add a small border to the Slide 3 picture. Some picture styles provide a border, but the Reflected Rounded Rectangle style you applied to this picture does not. The following steps add a border to the Slide 3 picture.

- With the Slide 3 picture still selected, click the Border button arrow in the Picture Styles group on the Format Picture tab to display the Border pop-up menu.

Q&A What if the Format Picture tab no longer is displayed on my ribbon?
Double-click the picture to display the Format Picture tab.

2

- Point to Weights on the Border pop-up menu to display the Weight list (Figure 2–22).

Q&A Can I make the line width more than 6 pt?
Yes. Click More Lines and then increase the amount in the Width box.

3

- Click 1½ pt to add this line weight to the picture.

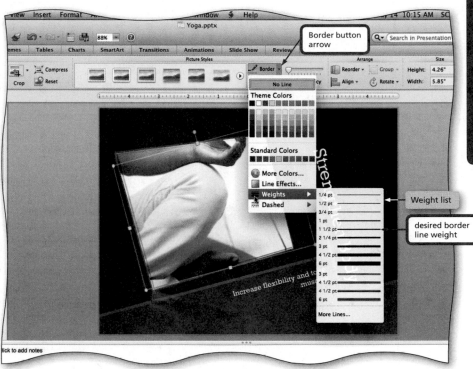

Figure 2–22

To Change a Picture Border Color

The default color for the border you added to the Slide 3 picture is White. Earlier in this chapter, you changed the color scheme to Waveform. To coordinate the border color with the title text color and other elements of this theme, you will use a shade of green in the Waveform color scheme. Any color galleries you display show colors defined in this current color scheme. The following steps change the Slide 3 picture border color.

1

- With the Slide 3 photo still selected, click the Border button arrow again to display the Border pop-up menu (Figure 2–23).

Q&A Why does the Border button change color after I choose a colored border?
Like the Font Color button, the Border button remembers the last color and weight applied and will apply that color and weight to other pictures when the Border button is clicked.

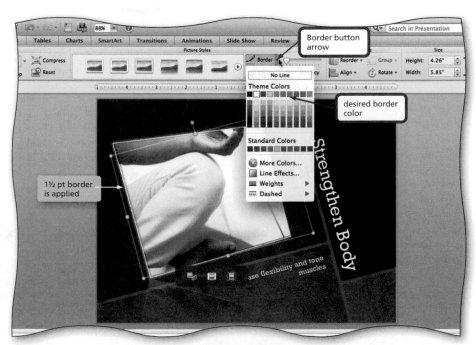

Figure 2–23

• Click Accent 3 (column 7, row 1) in the Border pop-up menu to change the border color (Figure 2–24).

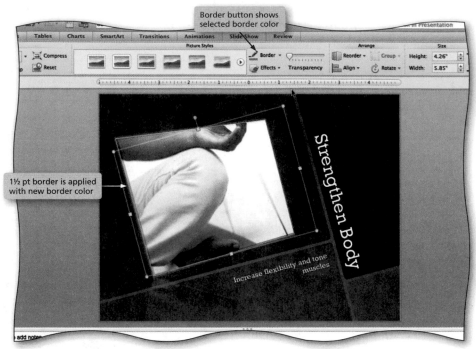

Figure 2–24

To Add a Picture Border and Color to Another Picture

In this presentation, the Slide 2 picture does not have a border as part of the Reflected Perspective Right picture style. The following steps add a border to Slide 2 and change the color.

1 Click the Previous Slide button to display Slide 2 and then click the picture to select it.

2 Click the Border button in the Picture Styles group on the Format Picture tab to change the picture border color and line weight to the last color and line weight selected, in this case the Accent 3 color and 1.5 point line weight (Figure 2–25).

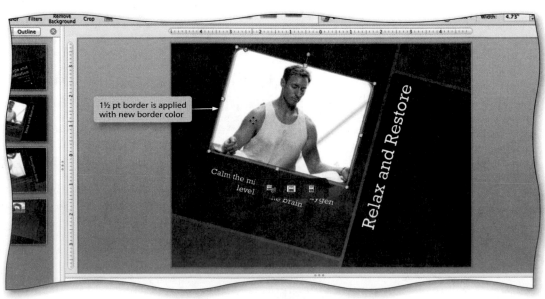

Figure 2–25

To Resize a Graphic by Entering Exact Measurements

The next step is to resize the Slide 3 picture so that it fills much of the empty space in the slide. In Chapter 1, you resized clips by dragging the sizing handles. This technique also applies to changing the size of photos. You also can resize graphics by specifying exact height and width measurements. The yoga picture can be enlarged so that its width measurement is 6.0". When a graphic is selected, its height and width measurements show in the Size group of the Picture Tools Format tab. The following steps resize the Slide 3 picture by entering its desired exact measurements.

- Click the Next Slide button to display Slide 3 and then select the picture. Double-click the measurement in the Width text box on the Format Picture tab in the Size group to select the contents in the text box and then type   6   as the width (Figure 2–26).

Q&A   What if the contents of the Width text box are not selected?
Double-click the left side of the Width text box to select its content.

Figure 2–26

- Press RETURN to resize the picture.

- If necessary, move the photo to the location shown in Figure 2–27.

Q&A   Why did the height size also change?
PowerPoint kept the photo in proportion so that the height changed the same amount as the width changed.

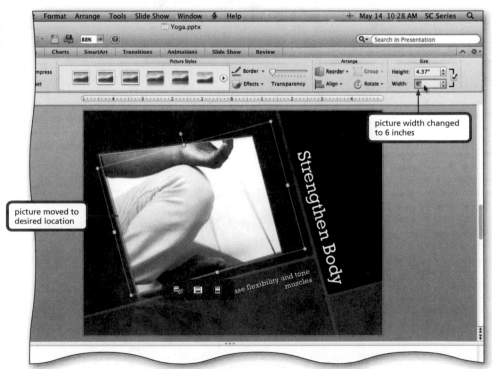

Figure 2–27

To Resize Another Graphic Using Exact Measurements

The Arch Yoga picture on Slide 4 also can be enlarged to fill space at the top of the slide. The yoga picture can be enlarged so that its height and width measurements are 3" and 4.49", respectively. The following steps resize the Slide 4 picture.

1 Click the Next Slide button to display Slide 4 and then select the picture. Double-click the left side of the Height text box on the Format Picture tab in the Size group to select the contents in the text box, type   3   as the height and press RETURN.

2 If necessary, move the photo to the location shown in Figure 2–28.

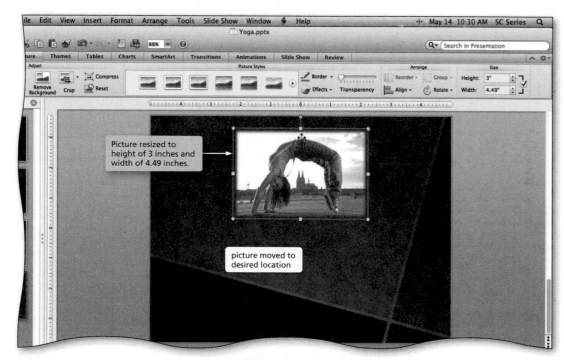

Figure 2–28

To Save an Existing Document with the Same File Name

You have made several modifications to the presentation since you last saved it. Thus, you should save it again. The following step saves the document again. For an example of the step listed below, refer to the Office 2011 and Mac OS chapter at the beginning of this book.

1 Click the Save button in the Standard toolbar to overwrite the previously saved file.

Break Point: If you wish to take a break, this is a good place to do so. You can quit PowerPoint now. To resume at a later time, start PowerPoint, open the file called Yoga, and continue following the steps from this location forward.

Formatting Slide Backgrounds

A slide's background is an integral part of a presentation because it can generate audience interest. Every slide can have the same background, or different backgrounds can be used in a presentation. This background is considered **fill**, which is the content that makes up the interior of a shape, line, or character. Three fills are available: solid, gradient, and picture or texture. **Solid fill** is one color used throughout the entire slide. **Gradient fill** is one color shade gradually progressing to another shade of the same color or one color progressing to another color. **Picture or texture fill** uses a specific file or an image that simulates a material, such as cork, granite, marble, or canvas.

Once you add a fill, you can adjust its appearance. For example, you can adjust its **transparency**, which allows you to see through the background, so that any text on the slide is visible. You also can select a color that is part of the theme or a custom color. You can use **offsets**, another background feature, to move the background from the slide borders in varying distances by percentage. **Tiling options** repeat the background image many times vertically and horizontally on the slide; the smaller the tiling percentage, the greater the number of times the image is repeated.

A background style is a preset combination of fill characteristics that are applied to an entire presentation. You can assign a background style to a presentation, and then customize certain background components for individual slides.

To Choose a Background Style

For each theme, PowerPoint provides 12 **background styles** with designs that may include color, shading, patterns, and textures. **Fill effects** add pattern and texture to a background, which add depth to a slide. The following steps add a background style to the presentation.

- On the Themes tab under Theme Options, click the Background button to display the Background Styles gallery (Figure 2–29).

Q&A Are the backgrounds displayed in a specific order?

Yes. They are arranged in order from light to dark running from left to right. The first row has solid backgrounds; the middle row has darker fills at the top and bottom; the bottom row has fill patterns. If you point to a background, a ScreenTip with the background's name appears on the screen.

- Click Style 7 (third style in second row) to apply the background style to the presentation.

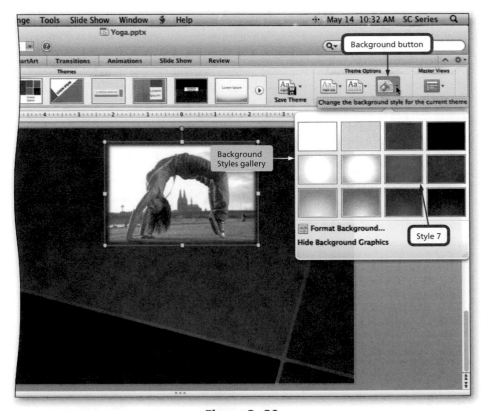

Figure 2–29

To Insert a Texture Fill

A wide variety of texture fills are available to give your presentation a unique look. The 24 pictures in the Textures gallery give the appearance of a physical object, such as water drops, sand, tissue paper, and a paper bag. You also can use your own texture pictures for custom backgrounds. When you insert a fill, PowerPoint assumes you want this custom background on only the current slide displayed. To make this background appear on all slides in the presentation, click the Apply to All button in the Format Background dialog. The steps on the next page insert the Denim fill on Slide 4 in the presentation.

- CONTROL-click anywhere on the Slide 4 blue background to display the shortcut menu (Figure 2–30).

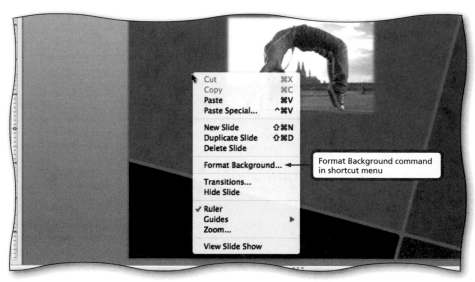

Figure 2–30

- Click Format Background in the shortcut menu to display the Format Background dialog.

- With the Fill pane displaying, click the Picture or Texture tab to show the Picture or Texture pane.

- Click the Choose Texture button in the From texture area to display the Texture gallery (Figure 2–31).

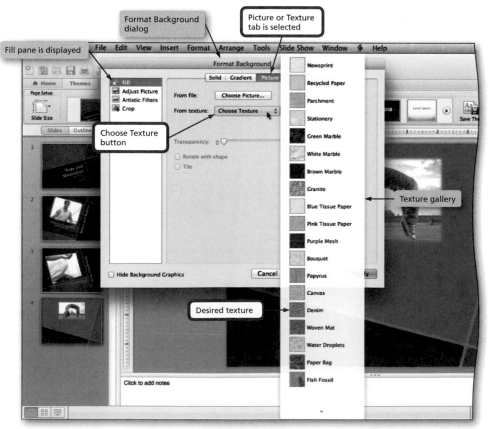

Figure 2–31

3

- Click the Denim background to select it (Figure 2–32).

- Click the Apply button (Format Background dialog) to insert this background on Slide 4.

Q&A The Format Background dialog is covering part of the slide. Can I move this box?
Yes. Click the dialog title and drag it to a different location so that you can view the slide.

Q&A Could I insert this background on all four slides simultaneously?
Yes. You would click the Apply to All button to insert the Denim background on all slides.

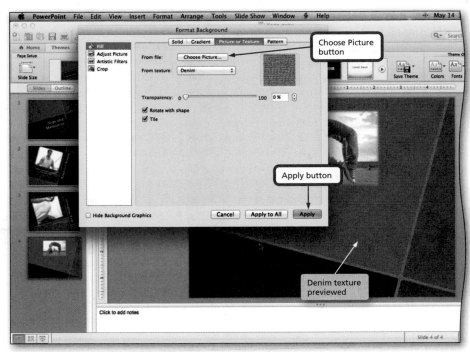

Figure 2–32

> **Other Ways**
> 1. On Themes tab under Theme Options, click Background button, choose Format Background, click Picture or Texture tab (Format Background dialog), select desired background, click Apply button
> 2. Choose Format > Slide Background in menu bar, click Picture or Texture tab (Format Background dialog), select desired background, click Apply button

To Insert a Picture to Create a Background

For variety and interest, you want to use another yoga picture as the Slide 1 background. This picture is stored on the Data Files for Students. PowerPoint will stretch the height and width of this picture to fill the slide area. The following steps insert the picture, Sunrise Yoga, on only Slide 1.

1

- Click the Previous Slide button three times to display Slide 1.

- CONTROL-click the slide and choose Format Background from the shortcut menu.

- With the Fill pane displaying (Format Background dialog), click the Picture or Texture tab.

- Click the Choose Picture button in the From file area (shown in Figure 2–32) to display the Choose a Picture dialog.

- If necessary, double-click your USB flash drive in the list of available storage devices to display a list of files and folders on the selected USB flash drive and then navigate to the PowerPoint Chapter 02 folder.

- Scroll down and then click Sunrise Yoga to select the file name (Figure 2–33).

Q&A What if the picture is not on a USB flash drive?
Use the same process, but select the drive containing the picture.

Figure 2–33

2

- Click the Insert button (Choose a Picture dialog) to insert the Sunrise Yoga picture as the Slide 1 background and keep the Format Background dialog open (Figure 2–34).

Q&A What if I do not want to use this picture?
Click the Undo button in the Standard toolbar.

Q&A Can I move the Format Background dialog to the left so that I can see more of the subtitle text?
Yes. Click the dialog title and then drag the box to the desired location on the slide.

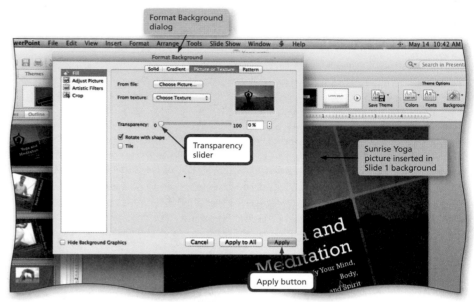

Figure 2–34

To Format the Background Picture Fill Transparency

The Sunrise Yoga picture on Slide 1 is a rich color and conflicts with the title and subtitle text. One method of reducing this richness is to change the transparency. The **Transparency slider** indicates the amount of opaqueness. The default setting is 0, which is fully opaque. The opposite extreme is 100%, which is fully transparent. To change the transparency, you can move the Transparency slider or enter a number in the text box next to the slider. The following step adjusts the transparency to 10%.

1

- On the Picture or Texture tab of the Format Background dialog, click the Transparency slider and drag it to the right until 10% is displayed in the Transparency text box (Figure 2–35).

2

- Click the Apply button (Format Background dialog) to apply the transparency setting and close the dialog.

Q&A Can I move the slider in small increments so that I can get a precise percentage easily?
Yes. Press the INCREMENT ARROWS beside the slider in the dialog to move the slider in one-percent increments.

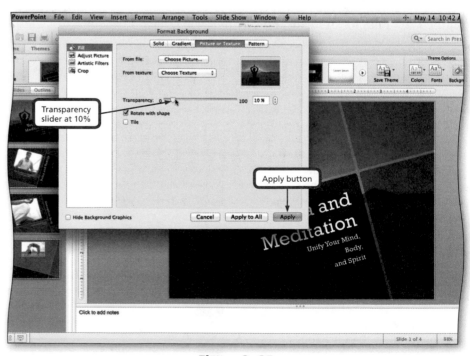

Figure 2–35

To Format the Background Texture Fill Transparency

The Denim texture on Slide 4 is dark and may not offer sufficient contrast with the symbols and text you are going to insert on this slide. You can adjust the transparency of slide texture in the same manner that you change a picture transparency. The following steps adjust the texture transparency to 50%.

- Click the Next Slide button three times to display Slide 4.

- Open the Format Background dialog, click the Picture or Texture tab, click the Transparency slider and drag it to the right until 35% is displayed in the Transparency text box (Figure 2–36).

- Click the Apply button (Format Background dialog).

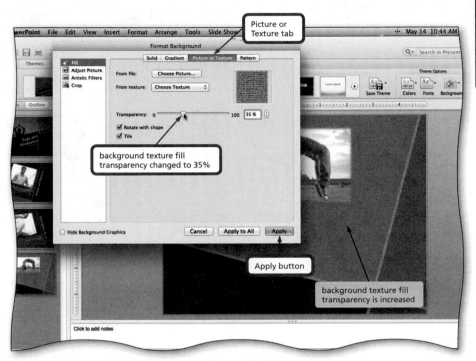

Figure 2–36

Formatting Title and Content Text

Choosing well-coordinated colors and styles for text and objects in a presentation is possible. Once you select a particular Quick Style and make any other font changes, you then can copy these changes to other text using the **Format Painter**. The Format Painter allows you to copy all formatting changes from one object to another.

Introducing the Presentation

Before your audience enters the room, start the presentation and then display Slide 1. This slide should be visually appealing and provide general interest in the presentation. An effective title slide gives a good first impression.

To Change the Subtitle and Caption Font

The default Kilter theme heading, subtitle, and caption text font is Rockwell. To draw more attention to subtitle and caption text and to help differentiate these slide elements from the title text, you want to change the font from Rockwell to Papyrus. To change the font, you must select the letters you want to format. In Chapter 1, you selected a paragraph and then formatted the characters. To format the text in multiple paragraphs quickly and simultaneously, you can select all the paragraphs to be formatted and then apply formatting changes. The steps on the next page change the subtitle and caption font.

• Click the Previous Slide button three times to display Slide 1. Move the mouse pointer to the left of the first subtitle paragraph, Unify Your Mind, until the mouse pointer changes to an I-beam (Figure 2–37).

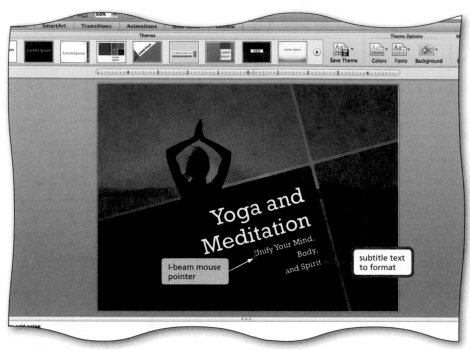

Figure 2–37

• Drag downward to select all three subtitle lines that will be formatted (Figure 2–38).

Figure 2–38

3

- With the text selected, if necessary click the Home tab on the ribbon and then click the Font box arrow in the Font group to display the Font pop-up menu.

- Scroll through the Font pop-up menu and then point to Papyrus (or a similar font) (Figure 2–39).

Q&A Will the fonts in my Font pop-up menu be the same as those shown in Figure 2–39?
Your list of available fonts may differ, depending on what fonts you have installed and the type of printer you are using.

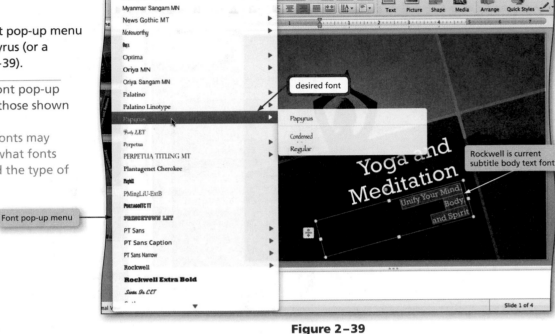

Figure 2–39

4

- Click Papyrus (or a similar font) to change the font of the selected text to Papyrus (Figure 2–40).

Figure 2–40

Other Ways

1. CONTROL-click selected text, click Font in shortcut menu, click Font tab (Format Text dialog), select desired font in Font list, click OK button

2. Choose Format > Font in menu bar, click Font tab (Format Text dialog), select desired font in Font list, click OK button

3. Press COMMAND-T, click Font tab (Format Text dialog), select desired font in the Font list, click OK button

To Shadow Text

A **shadow** helps letters display prominently by adding a shadow behind the text. The following step adds a shadow to the selected subtitle text, Unify Your Mind, Body, and Spirit.

- With the subtitle text still selected, click the Text Effects button on the Home tab under Font to display the Text Effects gallery.

- Point to Shadow to display the Shadow menu (Figure 2–41).

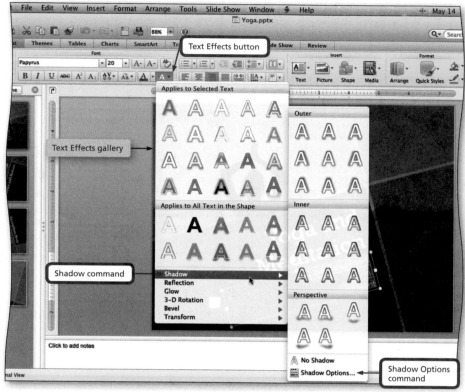

Figure 2–41

- Choose Shadow Options to open the Format Text dialog with Text Shadow selected in the left pane.

- Set Style to Outer, and Angle to 0 degrees.

- Click the Color button to display the Color pop-up menu (Figure 2–42).

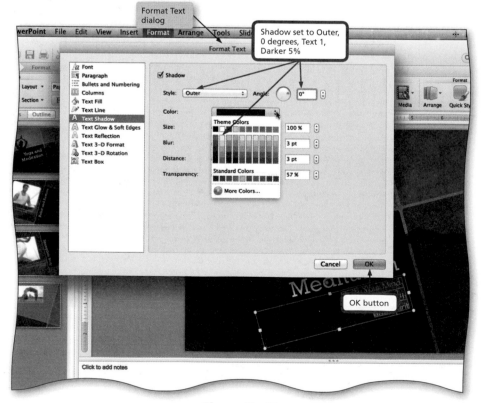

Figure 2–42

3

- Choose Text 1, Darker 5% from the Color pop-up menu.

- Click OK to apply the shadow format to the selected text (Figure 2–43).

Q&A How would I remove a shadow? With the shadowed text selected, you would click the Text Effects button, point to Shadow, and choose No Shadow from the Shadow gallery; or you immediately could click the Undo button in the Standard toolbar.

Figure 2–43

Other Ways

1. CONTROL-click selected text, click Font in shortcut menu, click Text Shadow in left pane (Format Text dialog), select desired shadow settings, click OK button

2. Choose Format > Font, click Font tab (Format Text dialog), click Text Shadow in left pane, select desired shadow settings, click OK button

3. Press COMMAND-T, click Font tab (Format Text dialog), click Text Shadow in left pane, select desired shadow settings, click OK button

---

To Format the Subtitle Text

To increase readability, you can format the Slide 1 subtitle text by bolding the characters and changing the font color to yellow. The following steps format the Slide 1 subtitle text.

1 With the subtitle text selected, click the Bold button on the Home tab under Font to bold the text.

2 Click the Font Color arrow and change the color to Accent 5, Lighter 40% (ninth color in fourth row) (Figure 2–44).

3 Click to deselect the text.

Figure 2–44

To Format the Slide 2 Caption

The caption on a slide should be large enough for audience members to read easily and should coordinate with the font styles in other parts of the presentation. The caption on Slide 2 can be enhanced by changing the font, the font color, and the font size. The following steps format the Slide 2 caption text.

1 Click the Next Slide button to display Slide 2. Triple-click the caption text to select all the characters, click the Font box arrow on the Home tab under Font, and then scroll down and click Papyrus.

2 On the Home tab, under Font, click the Increase Font Size button once to increase the font size to 24 point.

3 Click the Bold button on the Home tab under Font to bold the text (Figure 2–45).

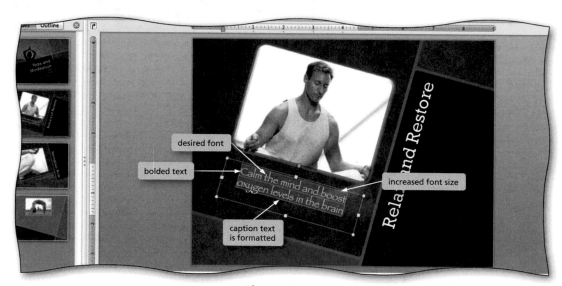

Figure 2–45

Format Painter

To save time and avoid formatting errors, you can use the Format Painter to apply custom formatting to other places in your presentation quickly and easily. You can use this feature in three ways:

- To copy only character attributes, such as font and font effects, select text that has these qualities.
- To copy both paragraph attributes, such as alignment and indentation and character attributes, select the entire paragraph.
- To apply the same formatting to multiple words, phrases, or paragraphs, double-click the Format Painter button and then select each item you want to format. You then can press the ESC key or click the Format Painter button to turn off this feature.

To Format Text Using the Format Painter

To save time and duplicated effort, you quickly can use the Format Painter to copy formatting attributes from the Slide 2 caption text and apply them to Slide 3. The following steps use the Format Painter to copy formatting features.

1

- With the Slide 2 caption text still selected, double-click the Format Painter button in the Standard toolbar.

- Move the mouse pointer into the document area (Figure 2–46).

Q&A Why did my mouse pointer change shape?

The mouse pointer changed shape by adding a paintbrush to indicate that the Format Painter function is active.

Figure 2–46

2

- Click the Next Slide button to display Slide 3. Triple-click the caption placeholder to apply the format to all the caption text, and then click between the words, and, and tone, and press RETURN to move the word, tone, to the second line of the caption (Figure 2–47).

- Press the ESC key to turn off the Format Painter feature.

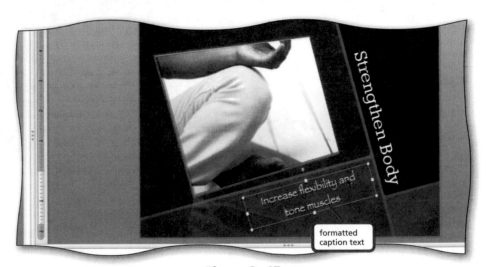

Figure 2–47

Break Point: If you wish to take a break, this is a good place to do so. Be sure to save the Yoga file again and then you can quit PowerPoint. To resume at a later time, start PowerPoint, open the file called Yoga, and continue following the steps from this location forward.

Adding and Formatting a Shape

One method of getting the audience's attention and reinforcing the major concepts being presented is to have graphical elements on the title slide. PowerPoint provides a wide variety of predefined shapes that can add visual interest to a slide. Shape elements include lines, basic geometrical shapes, arrows, equation shapes, flowchart symbols, stars, banners, and callouts. After adding a shape to a slide, you can change its default characteristics by adding text, bullets, numbers, and styles. You also can combine multiple shapes to create a more complex graphic.

Slides 1 and 4 in this presentation are enhanced in a variety of ways. First, a sun shape is added to the Slide 1 title text in place of the letter o. Then a circle shape is inserted on Slide 4 and copied twice, and text is added to each circle and then formatted. Finally, a triangle is inserted on top of the three circle shapes on Slide 4.

Sizing Shapes

PowerPoint's Shapes gallery provides a wide variety of symbols that can help emphasize your major points on each slide. As you select the shapes and then size them, keep in mind that your audience will focus on the largest shapes first. The most important information, therefore, should be placed in or near the shapes with the most visual size.

To Add a Shape

Many of the shapes included in the Shapes gallery can direct the viewer to important aspects of the presentation. For example, the sun shape helps emphasize the presentation's theme of practicing yoga and meditation, and it complements the Sunrise Yoga background picture. The following steps add the Sun shape to Slide 1.

• Click the Previous Slide button two times to display Slide 1. Click the Shape button on the Home tab under Insert to display the Shape pop-up menu. Point to Basic Shapes to display the Basic Shapes gallery (Figure 2–48).

Figure 2–48

• Click the Sun shape in the Basic Shapes area of the Shapes gallery.

Q&A Why did my pointer change shape?
The pointer changed to a plus shape to indicate the Sun shape has been added to the clipboard.

• Position the mouse pointer (a plus shape) above the person's hands in the picture, as shown in Figure 2–49.

Figure 2–49

- Click Slide 1 to insert the Sun shape (Figure 2–50).

Figure 2–50

To Resize a Shape

The next step is to resize the Sun shape. The shape should be reduced so that it is approximately the same size as the letter o in the words Yoga and Meditation. The following steps resize the selected Sun shape.

- With the mouse pointer appearing as a two-headed arrow, drag a corner sizing handle on the Sun shape diagonally inward until the Sun shape is resized approximately as shown in Figure 2–51.

Q&A What if my shape is not selected?
To select a shape, click it.

Q&A What if the shape is the wrong size?
Repeat Step 1.

Figure 2–51

- Release the mouse button to resize the shape.

- Drag the Sun shape on top of the letter o in the word, Yoga (Figure 2–52).

Q&A What if I want to move the shape to a precise location on the slide?
With the shape selected, press the ARROW keys or the COMMAND-ARROW keys to move the shape to the desired location.

Figure 2–52

Other Ways

1. Enter shape height and width in Height and Width text boxes on the Format tab under Size

2. CONTROL-click shape, choose Format Shape in shortcut menu, click Size in left pane, enter shape height and width in Height and Width text boxes (Format Shape dialog), click OK button

3. Choose Format > Shape in menu bar, click Size in left pane, enter shape height and width in Height and Width text boxes (Format Shape dialog), click OK button

To Format a Shape

The next step is to change the color of the Sun shape to orange. The following steps change the color of the Sun shape.

- With the Sun shape still selected, CONTROL-click to display a shortcut menu. Choose Format Shape from the shortcut menu to display the Format Shape dialog.

- Click Fill in the left pane, then click the Color button (Format Shape dialog) (Figure 2–53).

- Choose Orange from the Standard colors in the Color pop-up menu.

- Click OK to close the dialog and change the color of the Sun shape.

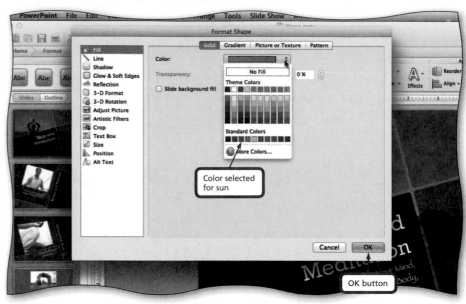

Figure 2–53

To Copy and Paste a Shape

The next step is to copy the Sun shape. The duplicate shape will be placed over the letter o in the word, Meditation. The following steps copy and move the identical second Sun shape.

- With the Sun shape still selected, click the Copy button in the Standard toolbar (Figure 2–54).

Q&A What if my shape is not selected?
To select a shape, click it.

Figure 2–54

2

- Click the Paste button in the Standard toolbar to insert a duplicate Sun shape on Slide 1.

- Drag the second Sun shape on top of the letter o in the word, Meditation, and release the mouse button. If necessary, use the arrow keys to adjust the final placement of the sun so that the letter o is completely covered by the shape (Figure 2–55).

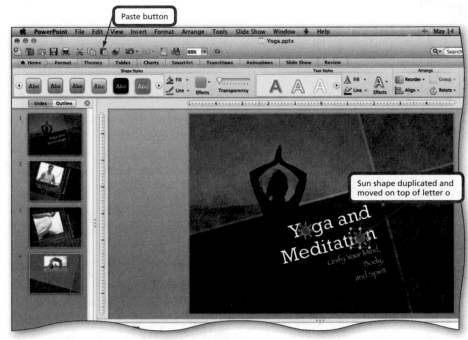

Figure 2–55

Other Ways

1. CONTROL-click selected shape, click Copy in shortcut menu, CONTROL-click, click Paste in shortcut menu

2. Select shape, press COMMAND-C, press COMMAND-V

To Add Other Shapes

Circles, squares, and triangles are among the geometric shapes included in the Shapes gallery. These shapes can be combined to show relationships among the elements, and they can help illustrate the basic concepts presented in your slide show. The following steps add the Oval and Isosceles Triangle shapes to Slide 4.

- Click the Next Slide button three times to display Slide 4 and then click the Shape button on the Home tab in the Insert group to display the Shape menu. Point to Basic Shapes to display a Basic Shapes gallery (Figure 2–56).

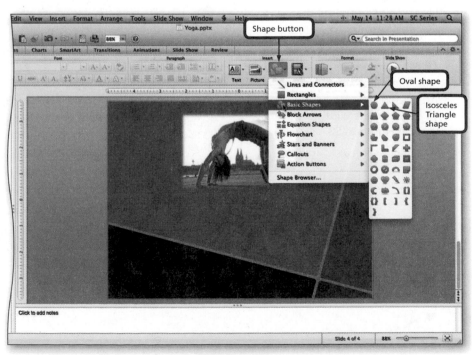

Figure 2–56

- Click the Oval shape in the Basic Shapes area of the Shapes gallery.

- Position the mouse pointer in the center of Slide 4 and then click to insert the Oval shape.

- Press and hold down the SHIFT key and then drag a corner sizing handle until the Oval shape forms a circle and is approximately 1.65" in diameter.

Q&A   Why did I need to press the SHIFT key while enlarging the shape?
Holding down the SHIFT key while dragging draws a perfect circle.

- Move the shape so it is positioned approximately as shown in Figure 2–57.

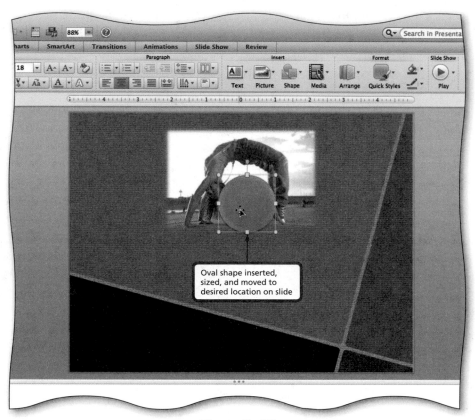

Figure 2–57

- Click the Shape button on the Home tab in the Insert group and then click the Isosceles Triangle shape in the Basic Shapes gallery.

- Position the mouse pointer in the right side of Slide 4 and then click to insert the Isosceles Triangle shape.

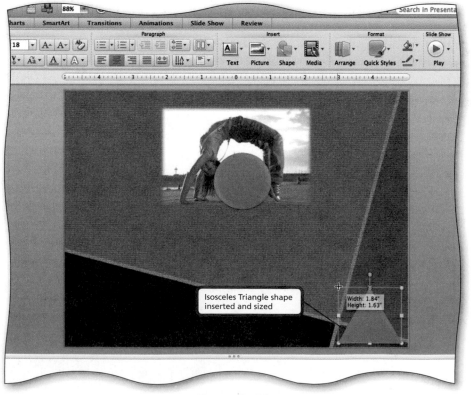

- Resize the shape so that it displays with an approximate height of 1.63" and approximate width of 1.84", as shown in Figure 2–58.

Figure 2–58

To Apply a Shape Style

Formatting text in a shape follows the same techniques as formatting text in a placeholder. You can change font, font color and size, and alignment. The next step is to apply a shape style to the oval so that it appears to have depth. The Shape Styles gallery has a variety of styles that change depending upon the theme applied to the presentation. The following steps apply a style to the Oval shape.

- Click the Oval shape to select it, then display the Format tab (Figure 2–59).

Figure 2–59

2

- Click the More button in the Shape Styles gallery (Format tab under Shape Styles) to expand the Shape Styles gallery (Figure 2–60).

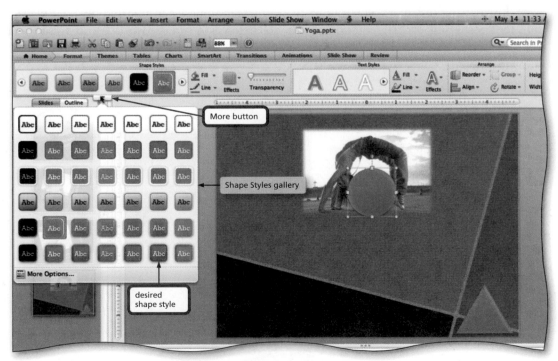

Figure 2–60

- Click the shape style in the sixth row, sixth column to apply the selected style to the Oval shape.

- Click the Fill button arrow on the Format tab under Shape Styles, and select Background 2, Darker 25% (column 3, row 5) from the Theme Colors to change the fill color of the shape (Figure 2–61).

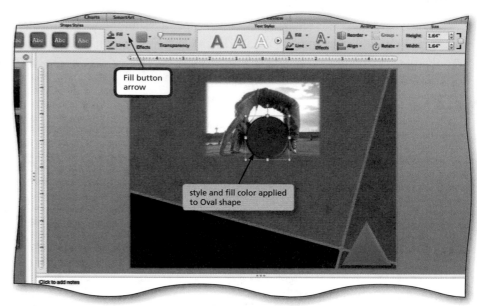

Figure 2–61

Other Ways

1. CONTROL-click shape, click Format Shape in shortcut menu, select Fill in left pane (Format Shape dialog), click Color button, select desired colors, click OK button

2. Choose Format > Shape in menu bar, select Fill in left pane (Format Shape dialog), click Color button, select desired colors, click OK button

To Add Formatted Text to a Shape

Formatting text in a shape follows the same techniques as formatting text in a placeholder. You can change font, font color and size, and alignment. The next step is to add the word, Mind, to the shape, change the font to Papyrus and the font color to Blue-Gray, center and bold the text, and increase the font size to 24 point. The following step adds text to the Oval shape.

- With the Oval shape selected, type **Mind** in the shape.

- Change the font to Papyrus.

- Change the font color to Text 2 (fourth color in first Theme Colors row).

- Change the font size to 24 point and bold the text (Figure 2–62).

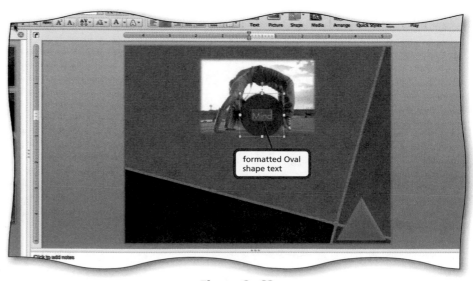

Figure 2–62

To Copy a Shape

Your presentation emphasizes that mind, body, and spirit are equal components in finding balance in life. Each of these elements can be represented by an oval. The following steps copy the Oval shape.

1 Click the edge of the Oval shape so that it is a solid line.

2 Click the Copy button in the Standard toolbar.

3 Click the Paste button in the Standard toolbar two times to insert two duplicate Oval shapes on Slide 4.

4 Move the Oval shapes so they appear approximately as shown in Figure 2–63.

5 In the left oval, select the word, Mind, and then type the word, `Body`, in the oval.

6 In the right oval, select the word, Mind, and then type the word, `Spirit`, in the oval (Figure 2–63). You may need to enlarge the size of the oval shapes slightly so that each word is displayed on one line.

Drawing a Square

Holding down the SHIFT [BTW] key while dragging a Rectangle shape draws a square.

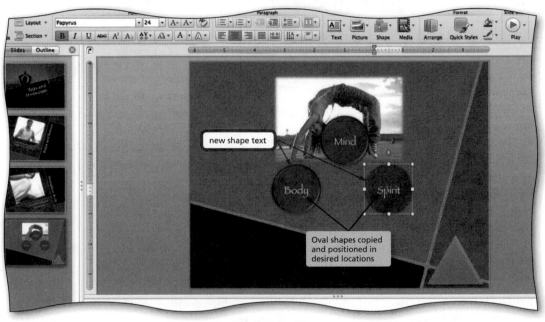

Figure 2–63

To Apply Another Style

The triangle shape helps show the unity among body, mind, and spirit. You can apply a coordinating shape style to the isosceles triangle and then place it on top of the three ovals. The following steps apply a style to the Isosceles Triangle shape.

1 Click the Isosceles Triangle shape on Slide 4 to select it. Display the Format tab.

2 Click the More button in the Shape Styles gallery (on the Format tab under Shape Styles) to expand the Shape Styles gallery and then click the third style in last row to apply that style to the triangle.

3 Use the Fill Color button arrow to change the color of the triangle to Accent 6, Darker 25% from the Theme Colors in the Fill menu.

4 Move the triangle shape to the center of the Ovals.

5 Click the Reorder button on the Format tab in the Arrange group to display the Reorder pop-up menu.

6 Click Bring to Front to display the triangle on top of the ovals. Resize the triangle and adjust positions of the triangle and ovals if necessary so that the shapes display as shown in Figure 2–64.

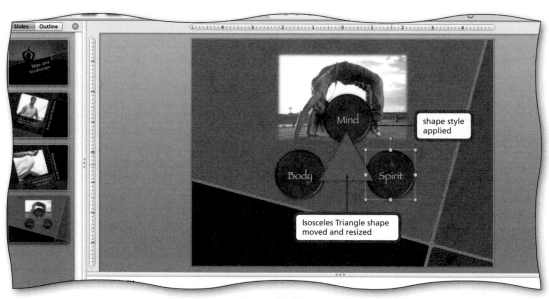

Figure 2–64

Break Point: If you wish to take a break, this is a good place to do so. Be sure to save the Yoga file again and then you can quit PowerPoint. To resume at a later time, start PowerPoint, open the file called Yoga, and continue following the steps from this location forward.

Creating Logos

BTW Many companies without graphic arts departments create their logos using WordArt. The bevels, glows, and shadows allow corporate designers to develop unique images with 3-D effects that give depth to their companies' emblems.

Using WordArt

One method of adding appealing visual elements to a presentation is by using **WordArt** styles. This feature is found in other Microsoft Office applications, including Word and Excel. This gallery of decorative effects allows you to type new text or convert existing text to WordArt. You then can add elements such as fills, outlines, and effects.

As with slide backgrounds, WordArt fill in the interior of a letter can consist of a solid color, texture, picture, or gradient. The WordArt **outline** is the exterior border surrounding each letter or symbol. PowerPoint allows you to change the outline color, weight, and style. You also can add an **effect**, which helps add emphasis or depth to the characters. Some effects are shadows, reflections, glows, bevels, and 3-D rotations.

Plan Ahead

Use WordArt in moderation.

Some WordArt styles are bold and detailed, and they can detract from the message you are trying to present if not used carefully. Select a WordArt style when needed for special emphasis, such as a title slide that audience members will see when they enter the room. WordArt can have a powerful effect, so do not overuse it.

To Insert WordArt

Yoga and meditation can help individuals find balance among the mind, body, and spirit. The symbols on Slide 4 emphasize this relationship, and you want to call attention to the concept. You quickly can add a visual element to the slide by selecting a Text style from the Text Styles gallery and then applying it to a word. The following steps insert WordArt.

 1

- With Slide 4 displaying, click Insert in the menu bar.

- Choose WordArt from the menu to insert the WordArt text box on the slide and display the Format tab for WordArt (Figure 2–65).

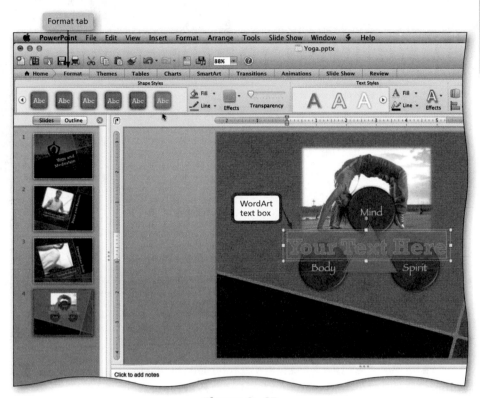

Figure 2–65

2

- Click the More button in the Text Styles gallery to expand the Text Styles gallery (Figure 2–66).

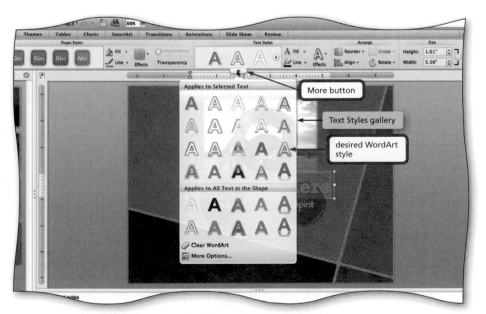

Figure 2–66

- Click the style on the third row, fifth column to apply the style to the text box.

- Type **Balance** in the text box, as the WordArt text (Figure 2–67).

Q&A Why did the Format tab appear automatically in the ribbon?
It appears when you select text to which you could add a WordArt style or other effect.

Figure 2–67

To Change the WordArt Shape

The WordArt text is useful to emphasize the harmony among the mind, body, and spirit. You can further emphasize this word by changing its shape. PowerPoint provides a variety of graphical shapes that add interest to text. The following steps change the WordArt to Triangle Down shape.

- With the Slide 4 WordArt text still selected, click the Effects button on the Format tab in the Text Styles group to display the Effects menu (Figure 2–68).

Figure 2–68

2

• Point to Transform in the Effects menu to display the Transform gallery (Figure 2–69).

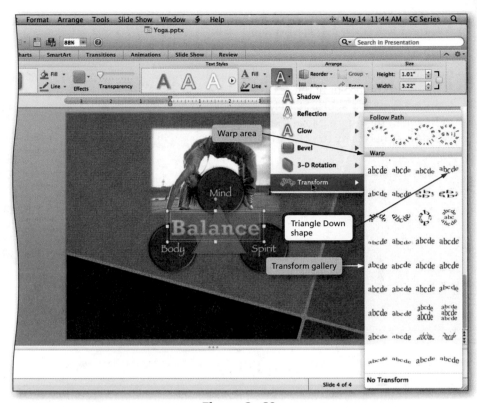

Figure 2–69

3

• Click the Triangle Down shape in the Warp area to apply the Triangle Down shape to the WordArt text (Figure 2–70).

Q&A Can I change the shape I applied to the WordArt?

Yes. Position the insertion point in the text box and then repeat Steps 1 and 2.

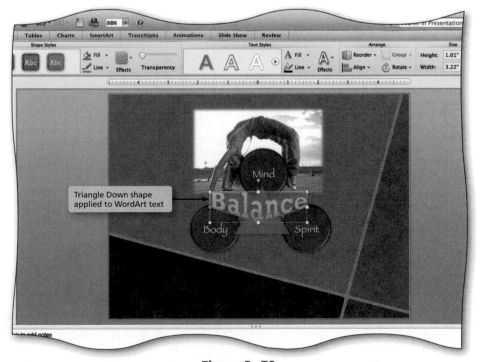

Figure 2–70

4

- Drag the WordArt downward until it is positioned approximately as shown in Figure 2–71.

- Drag a corner sizing handle diagonally outward until the WordArt is resized approximately as shown in the figure. Move the WordArt as necessary to position it as in Figure 2–71.

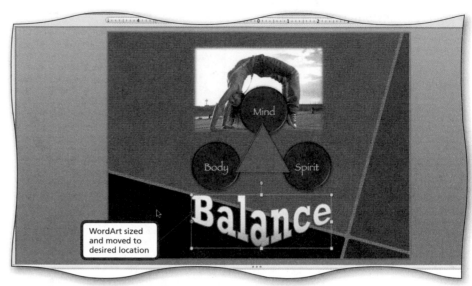

Figure 2–71

To Apply a WordArt Text Fill

The Slide 4 background has a Denim texture for the background, and you want to coordinate the WordArt fill with a similar texture. The following steps add the Blue Tissue Paper texture as a fill for the WordArt characters.

1

- With the WordArt text selected, click the Fill button arrow in the Text Styles group on the Format tab to display the Fill menu.

- From the Fill menu, choose Text Effects to display the Format Text dialog.

- Click Text Fill in the left pane, click the Picture or Texture tab, and then click Choose Texture to display the Texture gallery (Figure 2–72).

2

- Click the Blue Tissue Paper texture to apply this texture as the fill for the WordArt.

- Click the OK button (Format Text dialog) to apply the texture fill to the WordArt.

Q&A Can I apply this texture simultaneously to text that appears in more than one place on my slide? Yes. Select one area of text, press and then hold the COMMAND key while you select the other text, and then apply the texture.

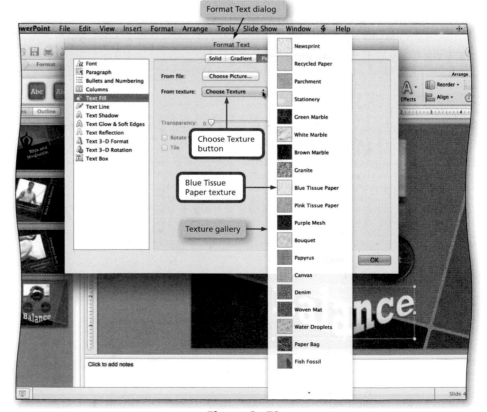

Figure 2–72

To Change the Weight of the WordArt Outline

The letters in the WordArt style applied have a double outline around the edges. To emphasize this characteristic, you can increase the width of the lines. As with font size, lines also are measured in point size, and PowerPoint gives you the option to change the line **weight**, or thickness, starting with ¼ point (pt) and increasing in one-fourth-point increments. Other outline options include modifying the color and the line style, such as changing to dots or dashes or a combination of dots and dashes. The following steps change the WordArt outline weight to 6 pt.

- With the WordArt still selected, click the Line button arrow on the Format tab under Text Styles to display the Line menu.
- Point to Weights in the menu to display the Weights list (Figure 2–73).

Q&A Can I make the line width more than 6 pt?
Yes. Click More Lines and increase the amount in the Width box.

- Click 4 1/2 pt to apply this line weight to the title text outline.

Q&A Must my text have an outline?
No. To delete the outline, click No Outline in the Text Outline gallery.

Figure 2–73

To Change the Color of the WordArt Outline

To add variety, you can change the outline color. The following step changes the WordArt outline color.

- With the WordArt still selected, click the Line button arrow under Text Styles again to display the Line menu.
- Click Background 2 to apply this color to the WordArt outline (Figure 2–74).

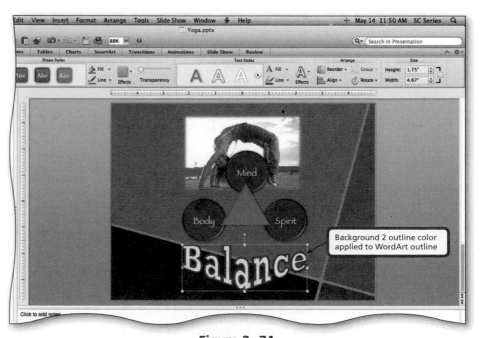

Figure 2–74

To Add a Transition between Slides

A final enhancement you will make in this presentation is to apply the Rotate transition in the Dynamic Content category to all slides and change the transition speed to Slow. The following steps apply this transition to the presentation.

1 Click Transitions on the ribbon. Click the More button in the Transitions to This Slide group to expand the Transitions gallery.

2 Click the Rotate transition in the Dynamic Content category to apply this transition to Slide 4.

3 Click the Duration up arrow in the Timing group 10 times to change the transition speed from 02.00 to 03.00.

4 Click the Play button in the Preview group on the Transitions tab to view the new transition time.

5 Click the All Slides button in the Apply To group to apply this transition and speed to all four slides in the presentation (Figure 2–75).

Figure 2–75

To Change Document Properties

Before saving the presentation again, you want to add your name, class name, and some keywords as document properties. The following steps use the Properties dialog to change document properties.

1 Click File in the menu bar to display the File menu.

2 Choose Properties to open the Properties dialog.

3 Update the contents of the Author and Subject text boxes with your name, course and section.

4 Enter `yoga, meditation` in the Keywords text box.

5 Click OK to close the Properties dialog.

To Print a Presentation

With the completed presentation saved, you may want to print it. If copies of the presentation are being distributed to audience members, you will print a hard copy of each individual slide on a printer. The following steps print a hard copy of the contents of the saved Yoga presentation.

1 Click File in the menu bar to display the File menu.

2 Choose Print in the File menu to open the Print dialog.

3 Verify the printer name that appears in the Printer text box will print a hard copy of the document. If necessary, click the Printer box to display a list of available printer options and then click the desired printer to change the currently selected printer.

4 Click the Print button (Print dialog) to print the document on the currently selected printer. When the printer stops, retrieve the hard copy (Figure 2–76).

(a) Slide 1

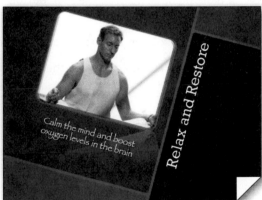

(b) Slide 2

(c) Slide 3

(d) Slide 4

Figure 2–76

To Save an Existing Presentation with the Same File Name

You have made several changes to the presentation since you last saved it. Thus, you should save it again. The following step saves the document again.

1 Click the Save button in the Standard toolbar to overwrite the previously saved file.

To Run an Animated Slide Show

All changes are complete, and the presentation is saved. You now can view the Yoga presentation. The following steps start Slide Show view.

1 Click the Slide 1 thumbnail in the Slides tab to select and display Slide 1.

2 Click the Slide Show button to display the title slide and then click each slide to view the transition effect and slides.

Quick Reference

BTW For a table that lists how to complete the tasks covered in this book using the mouse, ribbon, shortcut menu, and keyboard, see the Quick Reference Summary at the back of this book, or visit the Office 2011 for Mac Online Companion Web page at www. cengagebrain.com, navigate to the desired application, and click Quick Reference.

To Quit PowerPoint

The project now is complete. The following steps quit PowerPoint. For a detailed example of the procedure summarized below, refer to the Office 2011 and Mac OS X chapter at the beginning of this book.

1 Click File in the menu bar and choose Close to close the presentation.

2 If a dialog appears, click the Save button to save any changes made to the document since the last save.

3 Click PowerPoint in the menu bar to display the PowerPoint menu.

4 Choose Quit PowerPoint from the PowerPoint menu to quit PowerPoint.

Chapter Summary

In this chapter you have learned how to add a background style, insert and format pictures, add shapes, size graphic elements, apply styles, and insert WordArt. The items listed below include all the new PowerPoint skills you have learned in this chapter.

1. Change the Presentation Theme Colors (PPT 79)
2. Insert a Picture (PPT 80)
3. Insert a Picture into a Slide without a Content Placeholder (PPT 82)
4. Correct a Picture (PPT 84)
5. Apply a Picture Style (PPT 85)
6. Apply Picture Effects (PPT 86)
7. Add a Picture Border (PPT 88)
8. Change a Picture Border Color (PPT 89)
9. Resize a Graphic by Entering Exact Measurements (PPT 91)
10. Choose a Background Style (PPT 93)
11. Insert a Texture Fill (PPT 94)
12. Insert a Picture to Create a Background (PPT 95)
13. Format the Background Picture Fill Transparency (PPT 96)
14. Format the Background Texture Fill Transparency (PPT 97)
15. Change the Subtitle and Caption Font (PPT 97)
16. Shadow Text (PPT 100)
17. Format Text Using the Format Painter (PPT 102)
18. Add a Shape (PPT 104)
19. Resize a Shape (PPT 105)
20. Format a Shape (PPT 106)
21. Copy and Paste a Shape (PPT 106)
22. Add Other Shapes (PPT 107)
23. Apply a Shape Style (PPT 109)
24. Add Formatted Text to a Shape (PPT 110)
25. Insert WordArt (PPT 113)
26. Change the WordArt Shape (PPT 114)
27. Apply a WordArt Text Fill (PPT 116)
28. Change the Weight of the WordArt Outline (PPT 117)
29. Change the Color of the WordArt Outline (PPT 117)

Learn It Online

Test your knowledge of chapter content and key terms.

Instructions: To complete the Learn It Online exercises, please visit **www.cengagebrain.com.** At the CengageBrain.com home page, search for *Office 2011 for Mac* using the search box at the top of the page. This will take you to the product page for this book. On the product page, click the Access Now button below the Study Tools heading. On the Book Companion Site Web page, select Power-Point Chapter 2, and then click the link for the desired exercise.

Chapter Reinforcement TF, MC, and SA

A series of true/false, multiple choice, and short answer questions that test your knowledge of the chapter content.

Flash Cards

An interactive learning environment where you identify chapter key terms associated with displayed definitions.

Practice Test

A series of multiple choice questions that test your knowledge of chapter content and key terms.

Who Wants To Be a Computer Genius?

An interactive game that challenges your knowledge of chapter content in the style of a television quiz show.

Wheel of Terms

An interactive game that challenges your knowledge of chapter key terms in the style of the television show *Wheel of Fortune*.

Crossword Puzzle Challenge

A crossword puzzle that challenges your knowledge of key terms presented in the chapter.

Apply Your Knowledge

Reinforce the skills and apply the concepts you learned in this chapter.

Changing the Background and Adding Photographs, WordArt, and a Shape Quick Style

Note: To complete this assignment, you will be required to use the Data Files for Students. See the inside back cover of this book for instructions on downloading the Data Files for Students, or contact your instructor for information about accessing the required files.

Instructions: Start PowerPoint. Open the presentation, Apply 2-1 Lab Procedures, from the Data Files for Students.

The four slides in the presentation present laboratory safety procedures for your chemistry class. The document you open is an unformatted presentation. You are to add pictures, which are available on the Data Files for Students. You also will change the background style, change slide layouts, apply a transition, and use the Format Painter so the slides look like Figure 2–77 on the next page.

Perform the following tasks:

1. Change the background style to Style 5 (row 2, column 1).

2. On the title slide (Figure 2–77a), create a background by inserting the picture called Lab Assistant. Change the transparency to 30%.

3. Apply the WordArt style in row 6, column 3 to the title text and increase the font size to 54 point. Also, apply the WordArt Transform text effect, Chevron Up (row 2, column 1 in the Warp area) to this text.

Continued >

Apply Your Knowledge *continued*

4. In the Slide 1 subtitle area, replace the words, Student Name, with your name. Bold and italicize your name and the words, Presented by, and then apply the WordArt style, Fill – Red, Accent 2, Warm Matte Bevel (row 5, column 3). Position this subtitle text and the title text as shown in Figure 2–77a.

5. On Slide 2, change the layout to Two Content and insert the pictures shown in Figure 2–77b called Female in Lab Coat and Female with Goggles. Resize the picture on the left to a height of 4.25". Resize the picture on the right to a height of 3.5". In the left placeholder, apply the Rotated, White picture style to the inserted picture. In the right placeholder, apply the Reflected Bevel, Black picture style to the inserted picture and then change the picture border color to Purple.

6. On Slide 3, change the layout to Two Content and insert the Fire Extinguisher picture shown in Figure 2–77c. Apply the Soft Edge Oval picture style and change the picture brightness to 120% (row 3, column 4 in the Brightness and Contrast area).

7. On Slide 4, change the layout to Picture with Caption and then insert the picture, Hand Washing shown in Figure 2–77d. Increase the subtitle text font size to 18 point. Change the title text font size to 28 point, add a shadow, change font to Engravers MT, and change the font color to Purple.

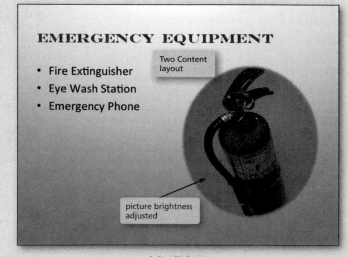

(a) Slide 1

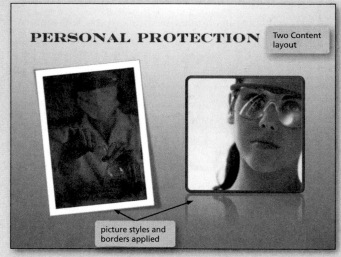

(b) Slide 2

(c) Slide 3

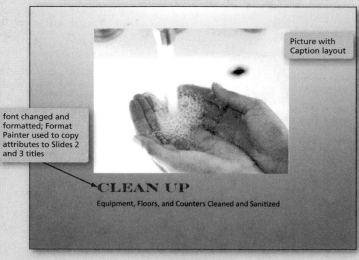

(d) Slide 4

Figure 2–77

8. Use the Format Painter to format the title text on Slides 2 and 3 with the same features as the title text on Slide 4.

9. Apply the Wipe transition in the Subtle category to all slides. Change the duration to 2.00 seconds.

10. Change the document properties, as specified by your instructor. Save the presentation using the file name, Apply 2-1 Chemistry Lab Safety. Submit the revised document in the format specified by your instructor.

Extend Your Knowledge

Extend the skills you learned in this chapter and experiment with new skills. You may need to use Help to complete the assignment.

Changing Slide Backgrounds and Picture Contrast, and Inserting Shapes and WordArt

Note: To complete this assignment, you will be required to use the Data Files for Students. See the inside back cover of this book for instructions on downloading the Data Files for Students, or contact your instructor for information about accessing the required files.

Instructions: Start PowerPoint. Open the presentation, Extend 2-1 Smith Family Reunion, from the Data Files for Students.

You will create backgrounds including inserting a picture to create a background, apply a WordArt Style and Effect, and add shapes to create the presentation shown in Figure 2–78 on page PPT 125.

Perform the following tasks:

1. Change the background style to Denim (row 1, column 3) and change the transparency to 48%. On Slides 2 through 5, change the title text to bold.

2. On the title slide (Figure 2–78a), create a background by inserting the picture called Tree, which is available on the Data Files for Students. If necessary, when formatting the background, turn off the Tile option. Change the transparency to 40%.

3. Apply the WordArt style in Row 3, Column 4, to the title text and increase the font size to 66 point. Also, apply the WordArt Transform text effect, Arch Up (row 1, column 1 in the Follow Path area), to this text.

4. In the Slide 1 subtitle area, insert the Wave shape in the Stars and Banners area. Also, apply the Shape Style in Row 4, Column 7, to the Wave shape. Type **Highlights From Our Last Reunion** and increase the font size to 40 point, change the text to bold italic and change the color to Green. Apply an Inside Right Shadow text style to the Subtitle. Resize and position the shape as shown in Figure 2–78a.

5. On Slide 2, change the layout to Two Content and insert the pictures shown in Figure 2–78b. The pictures to be inserted are called Bocce Ball and Frisbee Catcher and are available on the Data Files for Students. In the left placeholder, resize the photo to a width of 3.59", apply the Rotated White picture style to the inserted picture and change the picture border to Light Green. In the right placeholder, resize the picture to a width of 3.78", and apply the Beveled Oval Black picture style to the inserted picture.

Continued >

Extend Your Knowledge *continued*

6. Insert the Plaque shape in the Basic Shapes area. Also, apply the Shape Style in row 4, column 4 of the Shape Style menu, and apply the Shape Effect, 3-D Rotation, Parallel, Off Axis 1 Right. Type `Cousin Tom & His Frisbee Moves,` increase the font size to 28 point, and bold the text. Resize the shape to a height of 1.25" and a width of 3.78", and move the shape as shown in Figure 2–78b.

7. On Slide 3, change the layout to Picture with Caption and insert the picture shown in Figure 2–78c. The picture to be inserted is called BBQ Grill. Increase the title font size to 44 point. Also, increase the subtitle font size to 32 point, and then bold and italicize this text.

8. On Slide 4, change the layout to Two Content. Resize the two content placeholders to heights of 3.04" each. Do not change the width measurements. Insert the pictures shown in Figure 2–78d. The pictures to be inserted are called Reunion Boys and Reunion Toddler. In the left placeholder, apply the Rotated, White picture effect to the picture. In the right placeholder, apply the Bevel Perspective picture effect. Move the pictures as shown in Figure 2–78d. Bold the slide title.

9. On Slide 5, change the layout to Title and Content and insert the picture shown in Figure 2–78e. The picture to be inserted is called Reunion. Click the Resize button to resize the picture to the placeholder. Enlarge the picture as shown.

10. Insert the Oval Callout and Cloud Callout shapes in the Callouts area. In the Oval Callout shape, type `I hope Grandma makes cookies!` and change the font size to 24 point bold italic. Using a corner resize handle, resize the callout to a width of 3.5" Also add the Shape Style in row 5, column 4 of the shape style menu to this shape. In the Cloud Callout shape, type `I'm looking forward to our next reunion!` and change the font size to 24 point and the style to bold italic. Use a corner resize handle to resize to a height of 3". Move the shapes as shown in Figure 2–78e. Use the adjustment handles (the yellow diamond below each shape) to move the callout arrows as shown in Figure 2–78e. You may need to use Help to learn how to move these arrows.

11. On Slide 6, change the layout to Picture with Caption and insert the picture shown in Figure 2–78f and change the picture correction to Brightness 0% (Normal) Contrast: +20%. The picture to be inserted is called Reunion Tree.

12. Insert the Up Ribbon shape in the Stars and Banners area and type the words `Announcing Our Next Reunion`. Change the font color to Green, the font size to 32 point, and the style to bold italic. Also, apply the Shape Style in column 7, row 4 of the Shape Styles pop-up menu. In the title placeholder, type `Save the date — June 20, 2012` and change the font size to 28 point. Bold this text. Resize the shape to a width of 7.25" and a Height of 1.34".

13. Add the Orbit transition under the Dynamic Content section to Slide 6 only. You may need to use Help to learn how to apply the transition to only one slide. Change the duration to 2.00 seconds.

14. Change the document properties, as specified by your instructor. Save the presentation using the file name, Extend 2-1 Smith Reunion.

15. Submit the revised document in the format specified by your instructor.

(a) Slide 1

(b) Slide 2

(c) Slide 3

(d) Slide 4

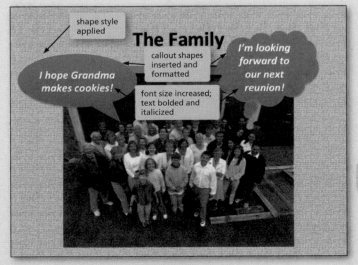

(e) Slide 5

(f) Slide 6

Figure 2–78

Make It Right

Analyze a presentation and correct all errors and/or improve the design.

Changing a Theme and Background Style

Note: To complete this assignment, you will be required to use the Data Files for Students. See the inside back cover of this book for instructions on downloading the Data Files for Students, or contact your instructor for information about accessing the required files.

Instructions: Start PowerPoint. Open the presentation, Make It Right 2-1 New Aerobics Classes, from the Data Files for Students.

Correct the formatting problems and errors in the presentation while keeping in mind the guidelines presented in this chapter.

Perform the following tasks:

1. Change the document theme to Waveform. Apply the Background Style 10 (row 3, column 2) to the presentation.

2. On the title slide, change the title from New Aerobics Classes to New Pool Programs. Type your name in place of Northlake Fitness Center and change the font to bold italic.

3. Move Slide 2 to the end of the presentation so that it becomes the new Slide 5.

4. Adjust the picture sizes, font sizes, and shapes so they do not overlap text and are the appropriate dimensions for the slide content.

5. Apply the Ripple transition to all slides. Change the duration to 02.00.

6. Change the document properties, as specified by your instructor. Save the presentation using the file name, Make It Right 2-1 New Pool Programs.

7. Submit the revised document in the format specified by your instructor.

Figure 2–79

In the Lab

Design and/or create a presentation using the guidelines, concepts, and skills presented in this chapter. Labs 1, 2, and 3 are listed in order of increasing difficulty.

Lab 1: Creating a Presentation Inserting Pictures and Applying Picture Styles

Problem: You are studying German operas in your Music Appreciation class. Wilhelm Richard Wagner (pronounced 'va:gner') lived from 1813 to 1883 and was a composer, conductor, theatre director, and essayist known for his operas. Wagner wrote and composed many operas, and King Ludwig II of Bavaria was one of his biggest supporters. Because you recently visited southern Germany and toured King Ludwig's castles, you decide to create a PowerPoint presentation with some of your photos to accompany your class presentation. These pictures are available on the Data Files for Students. Create the slides shown in Figure 2–80 on the next page from a blank presentation using the White document theme.

Note: To complete this assignment, you will be required to use the Data Files for Students. See the inside back cover of this book for instructions on downloading the Data Files for Students, or contact your instructor for information about accessing the required files.

Instructions: Perform the following tasks:

1. On Slide 1, create a background by inserting the picture called Castle 1, which is available on the Data Files for Students.

2. Type **Fairy Tale Trip to Germany** as the Slide 1 title text. Apply the WordArt style in Row 1, Column 1 of the pop-up menu, and increase the font size to 60 point. Change the text fill to the Papyrus texture, and then change the text line weight to 1½ pt. Also, apply the Transform text effect, Arch Up (in the Follow Path area), to this text. Position this WordArt as shown in Figure 2–80a.

3. Type the title and content for the four text slides shown in Figure 2–80. Apply the Two Content layout to Slides 2 and 3 and the Picture with Caption layout to Slides 4 and 5.

4. On Slide 2, insert the picture called Castle 2 from the Data Files for Students in the right placeholder. Apply the Bevel Perspective picture style. Resize the picture so that it is approximately 4.5" × 6", change the border color to Purple, change the border weight to 6 pt, and then move the picture, as shown in Figure 2–80b.

5. On Slide 3, insert the picture called Castle 3 from the Data Files for Students. Apply the Reflected Bevel, Black picture style and then change the border color to Green. Crop the picture to fill the placeholder. Do not change the border weight.

6. On Slide 4, insert the picture called Castle 4 from the Data Files for Students. Apply the Beveled Oval, Black picture style, change the border color to Blue, and then change the border weight to 6 pt.

7. On Slide 5, insert the picture called Castle 5 from the Data Files for Students. Apply the Moderate Frame, Black picture style, change the border color to Purple, and then change the border weight to 6 pt.

8. For both Slides 4 and 5, increase the title text size to 28 point and the caption text size to 24 point.

9. On Slide 2, change the title text font to Blackmoor LET, change the color to purple, and bold this text. Use the Format Painter to apply these formatting changes to the Slide 3 title text. In Slide 3, insert the Vertical Scroll shape located in the Stars and Banners area, apply the shape style found in column 4, row 3 of the shape style pop-up menu, and change the shape outline weight to 3 pt. Type the text, **Inspiration for Disney's Sleeping Beauty Castle**, and then change the font to Curlz MT, or a similar font. Bold this text, change the color to Dark Blue, and then change the size to 28 point. Increase the scroll shape size, as shown in Figure 2–80c.

Continued >

In the Lab *continued*

picture inserted as background

WordArt style, texture fill, and effect applied

(a) Slide 1

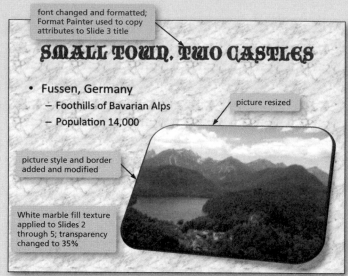

font changed and formatted; Format Painter used to copy attributes to Slide 3 title

picture resized

picture style and border added and modified

White marble fill texture applied to Slides 2 through 5; transparency changed to 35%

(b) Slide 2

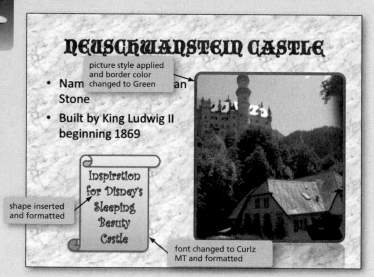

picture style applied and border color changed to Green

shape inserted and formatted

font changed to Curlz MT and formatted

(c) Slide 3

picture style applied and border color and weight changed

font size increased

(d) Slide 4

picture style applied and border color and weight changed

font size increased

(e) Slide 5

Figure 2–80

10. On Slides 2, 3, 4, and 5, change the background style to the White marble fill texture (row 2, column 5) and change the transparency to 35%. Apply the Glitter transition to all slides. Change the duration to 04.50.

11. Change the document properties, as specified by your instructor. Save the presentation using the file name, Lab 2-1 Trip to Germany.

12. Submit the revised document in the format specified by your instructor.

In the Lab

Lab 2: Creating a Presentation with a Shape and with WordArt

Problem: With the economy showing some improvement, many small businesses are approaching lending institutions for loans to expand their businesses. You work part-time for Loans Are Us, and your manager asked you to prepare a PowerPoint presentation for the upcoming Small Business Fair in your community. The pictures for this presentation are available on the Data Files for Students.

Note: To complete this assignment, you will be required to use the Data Files for Students. See the inside back cover of this book for instructions on downloading the Data Files for Students, or contact your instructor for information about accessing the required files.

Instructions: Perform the following tasks:

1. Create a new presentation using the Austin document theme.

2. Type the title and content for the title slide and the three text slides shown in Figure 2–81a–d on the next page. Apply the Title Only layout to Slide 2, the Two Content layout to Slide 3, and the Picture with Caption layout to Slide 4.

3. On both Slides 2 and 4, create a background by inserting the picture called Money. Change the transparency to 35%.

4. On Slide 1, insert the picture called Meeting. Apply the Reflected Bevel, White picture style. Resize the picture so that it is approximately 3.79" × 4.7", change the border color to Dark Blue, change the border weight to 3 pt, and then move the picture, as shown in Figure 2–81a. Increase the title text font size to 60 point, and then apply the WordArt style in Row 6, Column 2, of the WordArt pop-up menu.

5. Increase the subtitle text, Loans Are Us, font size to 28 point and then bold and italicize this text. Apply the WordArt style in Row 6, column 5 of the WordArt pop-up menu.

6. On Slide 2, bold the title text. Insert the pictures called Doc1, Doc2, and Doc3. Resize these pictures so they are approximately 3" × 2.7" and then move them to the locations shown in Figure 2–81b. Insert the Flowchart: Decision shape located in the Flowchart area, apply the Shape style in row 4, column 7 of the Shape Styles pop-up menu, and then resize the shape so that it is approximately 1.5" × 5.83". Change the shape outline weight to 6 pt. Type **Assets, Liabilities & Sales Reports** as the shape text, change the font to Franklin Gothic Medium, or a similar font, change the color to Dark Blue, and then change the size to 24 point.

7. On Slide 3, bold the title text. Insert the picture called Presentation into the right placeholder, apply the Beveled Oval, Black shape picture style, resize the picture so that it is approximately 3.5" × 5.25", crop the picture to fit the placeholder, and then sharpen the picture 50%.

8. On Slide 4, insert the picture called Cash and Credit Card. Change the title text font size to 36 point and bold this text. Break the text as shown in Figure 2–81d. Change the subtitle text font size to 24 point and then bold and italicize these words.

9. Apply the Shape transition to all slides. Change the duration to 01.25.

Continued >

In the Lab continued

(a) Slide 1

(b) Slide 2

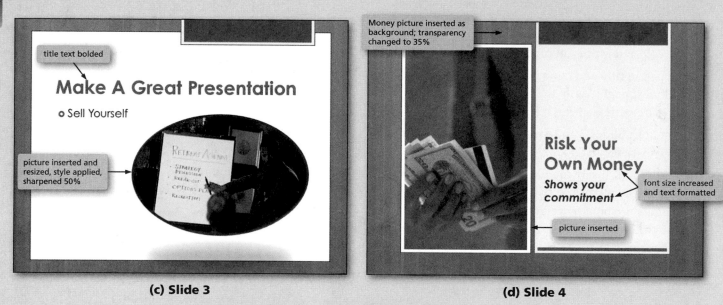

(c) Slide 3

(d) Slide 4

Figure 2–81

10. Change the document properties, as specified by your instructor. Save the presentation using the file name, Lab 2-2 Small Business Loans.

11. Submit the document in the format specified by your instructor.

In the Lab

Lab 3: Creating a Presentation with Pictures and Shapes

Problem: One of your assignments in your child development class is to give a speech about teaching children the value of money, so you decide to create a PowerPoint presentation to add a little interest to your speech. Prepare the slides shown in Figures 2–82a through 2–82e on page PPT 132. The pictures for this presentation are available on the Data Files for Students.

Note: To complete this assignment, you will be required to use the Data Files for Students. See the inside back cover of this book for instructions on downloading the Data Files for Students, or contact your instructor for information about accessing the required files.

Instructions: Perform the following tasks:

1. Create a new presentation using the Median document theme, and then change the presentation theme colors to Flow. This presentation should have five slides; apply the Title Slide layout to Slide 1, the Picture with Caption layout to Slides 2 and 5, the Comparison layout to Slide 3, and the Blank layout to Slide 4.

2. Type the title and content text for the title slide and the four text slides shown in Figure 2–82a–d on the next page.

3. On Slide 1, change the title text font size to 54 point. To make the letter 's' appear smaller than the other letters in the first word of the title slide title text placeholder, change the font size of this letter to 44 point. Insert the Oval shape, resize it so that it is approximately 0.5" × 0.5", and change the shape fill to white, which is the second color in the first row of the Theme Colors in the Fill pop-up menu. Type $, increase the font size to 32 point, change the color to green, and bold this dollar sign. Cover the letter 'o' in the word, Do, with this shape.

4. Insert the picture called Piggy Bank. Apply the Rounded Diagonal Corner, White picture style. Resize the picture so that it is approximately 4.4" × 5.03", change the border color to Light Blue, change the border weight to 3 pt, and then move the picture, as shown in Figure 2–82a. Change the subtitle font size to 32 point and then bold this text.

5. On Slide 2, insert the picture called Child Doing Dishes and then decrease the picture's contrast to –20%. Change the title text size to 36 point and bold this text. Change the caption text size to 32 point.

6. On Slide 3, format the slide background to have the Light horizontal pattern (Hint: you have to click the patterns on the Pattern tab of the Format Background dialog to see their names), with a foreground color of Background 2 and a Background color of Background 2, Darker 10%. Bold the title text. Change the heading title text size in both placeholders to 32 point. In the right placeholder, insert the picture called Father and Daughter and then apply the Reflected Bevel, White picture style. Resize the picture so that it is approximately 3" × 4", crop the picture to fill the placeholder, change the border color to Light Blue, and then change the border weight to 3 pt. Move the picture to the location as shown in Figure 2–82c.

7. On Slide 4, create a background by inserting the picture called Piggy Bank and Coins. Insert the Cloud shape located in the Basic Shapes area and then increase the cloud shape size so that it is approximately 3" × 5.6". Change the shape outline color to Yellow and then change the shape outline weight to 3 pt. Type **Teach your children to save for a big purchase.** as the shape text, and then change the font to Comic Sans MS. Bold and italicize this text and then change the font size to 32 point.

8. On Slide 5, create a background by inserting the picture called Coins. Insert the picture called Father and Child Shopping and then decrease the picture's brightness to –20%. Change the title text font size to 36 point and bold this text.

9. Apply the Box transition to all slides. Change the duration to 02.00. Check the spelling and correct any errors.

10. Change the document properties, as specified by your instructor. Save the presentation using the file name, Lab 2-3 ABCs of Money.

11. Submit the revised document in the format specified by your instructor.

Continued >

In the Lab *continued*

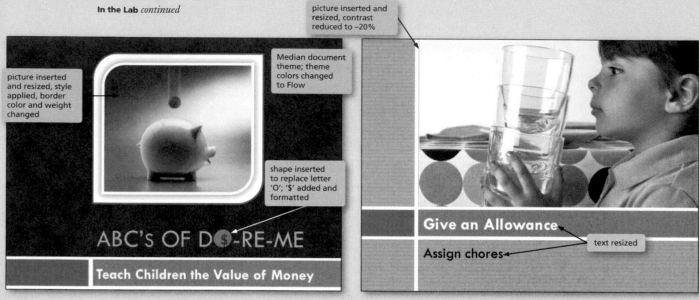

picture inserted and resized, contrast reduced to −20%

picture inserted and resized, style applied, border color and weight changed

Median document theme; theme colors changed to Flow

shape inserted to replace letter 'O'; '$' added and formatted

ABC's OF D$-RE-ME

Teach Children the Value of Money

Give an Allowance

Assign chores

text resized

(a) Slide 1

(b) Slide 2

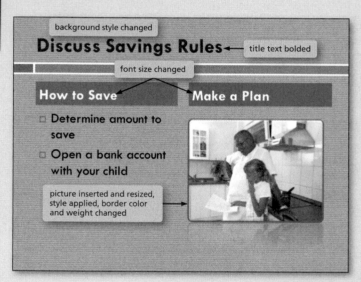

background style changed

Discuss Savings Rules

title text bolded

font size changed

How to Save   Make a Plan

□ Determine amount to save

□ Open a bank account with your child

picture inserted and resized, style applied, border color and weight changed

picture inserted as background

text added and formatted

Teach your children to save for a big purchase

shape inserted and formatted

(c) Slide 3

(d) Slide 4

Coins picture inserted as background

picture inserted and brightness changed to −20%

Take Your Child Shopping

title text font size increased and bolded

(e) Slide 5

Figure 2–82

Cases and Places

Apply your creative thinking and problem-solving skills to design and implement a solution.

Note: To complete these assignments, you may be required to use the Data Files for Students. See the inside back cover of this book for instructions on downloading the Data Files for Students, or contact your instructor for information about accessing the required files.

As you design the presentations, remember to use the 7 × 7 rule: a maximum of seven words on a line and a maximum of seven lines on one slide.

1: Design and Create a Presentation about Acid Rain

Academic

Nature depends on the correct pH balance. Although some rain is naturally acidic with a pH level of around 5.0, human activities have increased the amount of acid in this water. Burning fossil fuels, including coal, oil, and natural gas, produces sulfur dioxide. Exhaust from vehicles releases nitrogen oxides. Both of these gases, when released into the atmosphere, mix with water droplets, forming acid rain. In your science class, you are studying about the causes and effects of acid rain. Create a presentation to show what causes acid rain and what effects it can have on humans, animals, plant life, lakes, and rivers. The presentation should contain at least three pictures appropriately resized. The Data Files for Students contains five pictures called Factory, Rain, Soil, Tree and Clouds, and Vehicles; you can use your own digital pictures or pictures from Office.com if they are appropriate for this topic. These pictures also should have appropriate styles and border colors. Use shapes such as arrows to show what gases are released into the atmosphere. Apply at least three objectives found at the beginning of this chapter to develop the presentation. Add a title slide with a shape and a closing slide. Be sure to check spelling.

2: Design and Create a Presentation about Tutoring

Personal

You have been helping some of your classmates with their schoolwork, and you have decided that you should start a small tutoring business. In the student center, there is a kiosk where students can find out about programs and activities on campus. The student center manager gave you permission to submit a short PowerPoint presentation promoting your tutoring business; this presentation will be added to the kiosk. The presentation should contain pictures appropriately resized. The Data Files for Students contains four pictures called Tutoring 1, Tutoring 2, Tutoring 3, and Tutoring 4, or you can use your own digital pictures or pictures from Office.com if they are appropriate for this topic. Change the contrast and brightness for at least one picture. Insert shapes and WordArt to enhance your presentation. Apply a transition in the Subtle area to all slides and increase the duration. Be sure to check spelling.

3: Design and Create a Presentation on Setting Up Children's Fish Tanks

Professional

Fish make great pets for young children, but there is a lot to learn before they can set up a fish tank properly. The owner of the pet store where you work has asked you to create a presentation for the store to give parents an idea of what they need to purchase and consider when setting up a fish tank. He would like you to cover the main points such as the appropriate size bowl or tank, setup procedures, filtration, water quality, types of fish, care, and feeding. The presentation should contain pictures appropriately resized. The Data Files for Students contains five pictures called Fish 1, Fish 2, Fish 3, Fish 4, and Fish 5, or you can use your own digital pictures or pictures from Office.com if they are appropriate for this topic. Add a title slide and closing slide to complete your presentation. Format the title slide with a shape and change the theme color scheme. Change the title text font on the title slide. Format the background with at least one picture and apply a background texture to at least one slide. This presentation is geared to parents of young children, so keep it colorful, simple, and fun.

3 Reusing a Presentation and Adding Media

Objectives

You will have mastered the material in this chapter when you can:

- Color a picture
- Add an artistic effect to a picture
- Delete and move placeholders
- Align paragraph text
- Copy a slide element from one slide to another
- Change the color of a clip

- Insert and edit a video clip
- Insert audio
- Control audio and video clips
- Check for spelling errors
- Print a presentation as a handout

3 Reusing a Presentation and Adding Media

Introduction

At times, you will need to revise a PowerPoint presentation. Changes may include inserting and adding effects to pictures, altering the colors of clips and pictures, and updating visual elements displayed on a slide. Applying a different theme, changing fonts, and substituting graphical elements can give a slide show an entirely new look. Adding media, including sounds, video, and music, can enhance a presentation and help audience members retain the information being presented.

Project — Presentation with Video, Audio, and Pictures with Effects

The project in this chapter follows graphical guidelines and uses PowerPoint to create the presentation shown in Figure 3–1. The slides in this revised presentation, which discusses Bird Migration, have a variety of audio and visual elements. For example, the pictures have artistic effects applied that soften the pictures and help the audience focus on other elements on the slides. The bird clip has colors that blend well with the background. A short video has been added and has effects to add audience interest. Bird calls integrate with the visual elements. Overall, the slides have myriad media elements and effects that are exciting for your audience to watch and hear.

Overview

As you read through this chapter, you will learn how to create the presentation shown in Figure 3–1 by performing these general tasks:

- Format pictures by recoloring and adding artistic effects.
- Insert and format video and audio clips.
- Modify clip art.
- Vary paragraph alignment.
- Check a presentation for spelling errors.
- Print a handout of your slides.

(a) Slide 1 (Title Slide with Picture Background, Modified Clip, and Animated Clip)

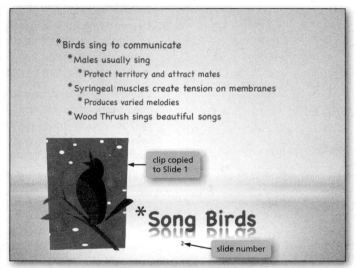

(b) Slide 2 (Bulleted List)

(c) Slide 3 (Picture Background and Video Clip)

(d) Slide 4 (Video Playing Full Screen)

Figure 3–1

Plan Ahead

General Project Guidelines

When creating a PowerPoint presentation, the actions you perform and the decisions you make will affect the appearance and characteristics of the finished document. As you create a presentation with illustrations, such as the project shown in Figure 3–1 on the previous page, you should follow these general guidelines:

1. **Use the color wheel to determine color choices.** Warm colors and cool colors evoke opposite effects on audience members. As you make decisions to color pictures, consider the emotions you want to generate and choose colors that match these sentiments.

2. **Vary paragraph alignment.** Different effects are achieved when text alignment shifts in a presentation. Themes dictate whether paragraph text is aligned left, center, or right in a placeholder, but you can modify these design decisions when necessary.

3. **Use multimedia selectively.** Video, music, and sound files can add interest to your presentation. Use these files only when necessary, however, because they draw the audience's attention away from the presenter and toward the slides. Using too many multimedia files can be overwhelming.

4. **Use handouts to organize your speech.** Effective speakers take much time to prepare their verbal message that will accompany each slide. They practice their speeches and decide how to integrate the material displayed. Viewing the thumbnails, or miniature versions of the slides, will help you associate the slide image with the script. These thumbnails also can be cut out and arranged when organizing the presentation.

5. **Evaluate your presentation.** As soon as you finish your presentation, critique your performance. You will improve your communication skills by eliminating the flaws and accentuating the positives.

When necessary, more specific details concerning the above guidelines are presented at appropriate points in the chapter. The chapter also will identify the actions performed and decisions made regarding these guidelines during the creation of the presentation shown in Figure 3–1.

Starting PowerPoint

For an introduction to Mac OS X and instruction about how to perform basic Mac OS X tasks, read the Office 2011 and Mac OS X chapter at the beginning of this book, where you can learn how to resize windows, change screen resolution, create folders, move and rename files, use Mac OS X Help, and much more.

Chapter 1 introduced you to starting PowerPoint, selecting a document theme, creating slides with clip art and a bulleted list, and printing a presentation. Chapter 2 enhanced slides by adding pictures, shapes, and WordArt. The following steps, which assume Mac OS X is running, start PowerPoint and open the Birds presentation. You may need to ask your instructor how to start PowerPoint for your computer. For a detailed example of the procedure summarized below, refer to the Office 2011 and Mac OS X chapter.

To Start PowerPoint and Open and Save a Presentation

1 Click the PowerPoint icon in the Dock to display the PowerPoint Presentation Gallery. If necessary, click Cancel to close the Presentation Gallery and open a blank document.

2 Close the blank document.

3 Open the presentation, Birds, from the Data Files for Students. See the inside back cover of this book for instructions on downloading the Data Files for Students, or contact your instructor for more information on accessing the required files.

4 Save the presentation using the file name, Bird Migration.

Inserting Pictures and Adding Effects

The Bird Migration presentation consists of four slides that have some text, a clip art image, a formatted background, and a transition applied to all slides. You will insert pictures into two slides and then modify them by adding artistic effects and recoloring. You also will copy the clip art from Slide 2 to Slide 1 and modify the objects in this clip. In Chapter 2, you inserted pictures, made corrections, and added styles and effects; the new effects you apply in this chapter will add to your repertoire of picture enhancements that increase interest in your presentation.

In the following pages, you will perform these tasks:

1. Insert the first digital picture into Slide 1.
2. Insert the second digital picture into Slide 3.
3. Recolor the Slide 3 picture.
4. Recolor and add an artistic effect to the Slide 1 picture.
5. Add a filter to the Slide 3 picture.
6. Send the Slide 3 picture back behind all other slide objects.
7. Send the Slide 1 picture back behind all other slide objects.

> For an introduction to Office 2011 and instruction about how to perform basic tasks in Office 2011 programs, read the Office 2011 and Mac OS X chapter at the beginning of this book, where you can learn how to start a program, use the ribbon, save a file, open a file, quit a program, use Help, and much more.

To Insert and Resize Pictures into Slides without Content Placeholders

The next step is to insert digital pictures into Slides 1 and 3. These pictures are available on the Data Files for Students. See the inside back cover of this book for instructions on downloading the Data Files for Students, or contact your instructor for information about accessing the required files.

The following steps insert pictures into Slides 1 and 3.

1 With Slide 1 displaying and your USB flash drive connected to one of the computer's USB ports, on the Home tab, under Insert, click the Picture button to display the Picture menu, and then choose Picture from File to open the Choose a Picture dialog.

2 Navigate to the picture location (in this case, the PowerPoint folder in the CIS 101 folder [or your class folder] on the USB flash drive).

3 Click Birds in Sky to select the file.

4 Click the Insert button (Choose a Picture dialog) to insert the picture into Slide 1.

5 Resize the picture so that it covers the entire slide (approximately 7.5" × 10").

6 Display Slide 3, click the Picture button to display the Picture menu, choose Picture from File to open the Choose a Picture dialog, and then insert the Bird Reflect picture into Slide 3.

7 Resize the picture so that it covers the entire slide (approximately 7.5" × 10") (Figure 3–2 on the next page).

Inserting Text Boxes

If you want to add text **BTW** in an area of the slide where a content placeholder is not located, you can insert a text box. This object allows you to emphasize or set off text that you consider important for your audience to read. To create a text box, click the Text button in the Insert Group on the Home tab, and choose Text Box from the menu. Click and drag on the slide to create the text box, and then drag this object to the desired location on the slide. Click inside the text box to add or paste text. You also can change the look and style of the text box characters by using formatting features in the Font group on the Home tab.

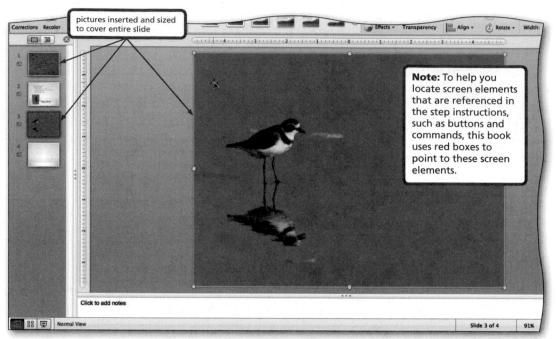

Figure 3–2

Use the color wheel to determine color choices.

The color wheel is one of designers' basic tools. Twelve colors on the wheel are arranged in a specific order, with the three primary colors — red, yellow, and blue — forming a triangle. Between the primary colors are the secondary colors that are formed when the primary colors are mixed. For example, red and yellow mixed together form orange; red and blue form purple; and yellow and blue form green. The six other colors on the wheel are formed when the primary colors are mixed with the secondary colors.

Red, orange, and yellow are considered warm colors, and they display adjacent to each other on one side of the wheel. They are bold and lively, so you should use them when your message is intended to invigorate an audience and create a pleasing effect. Opposite the warm colors are the cool colors: green, blue, and purple. They generate a relaxing, calming atmosphere.

If you put a primary and secondary color together, such as red and purple, your slide will make a very bold and vivid statement. Be certain that effect is one you intend when planning your message.

Q&As

BTW For a complete list of the Q&As found in many of the step-by-step sequences in this book, visit the Office 2011 for Mac Online Companion Web page at www.cengagebrain.com, navigate to the desired chapter, and click Q&As.

Adjusting Picture Colors

PowerPoint allows you to adjust colors to match or add contrast to slide elements by coloring pictures. The Recolor pop-up menu has a wide variety of preset formatting combinations. The thumbnails in the menu display the more common color saturation, color tone, and recolor adjustments. **Color saturation** changes the intensity of colors. High saturation produces vivid colors; low saturation produces gray tones. **Color tone** affects the coolness, called blue, or the warmness, called orange, of pictures. When a digital camera does not measure the tone correctly, a **color cast** occurs, and, as a result, one color dominates the picture. **Recolor** effects convert the picture into a wide variety of hues. The more common are **grayscale**, which changes the color picture into black, white, and shades of gray, and **sepia**, which changes the picture colors into brown, gold, and yellow, reminiscent of a faded photo. You also can fine-tune the color adjustments by clicking Picture Color Options and More Colors commands in the Recolor pop-up menu.

To Color a Picture

The Slipstream theme and text on Slides 1 and 3 have many shades of blue. The inserted pictures, in addition, have blue backgrounds. The following steps recolor the Slide 3 picture to coordinate with the blue colors on the slide.

 1

- With Slide 3 displaying and the Bird Reflect picture selected, click the Recolor button on the Format Picture tab under Adjust, to display the Recolor menu (Figure 3–3).

Q&A Why does the Adjust group look different on my screen?
Your monitor is set to a different resolution. See Chapter 1 for an explanation of screen resolution and the appearance of the ribbon.

Q&A Why are orange borders surrounding the thumbnails in the Color Saturation and Color Tone areas in the pop-up menu?
The image on Slide 3 currently has normal color saturation and a normal color tone.

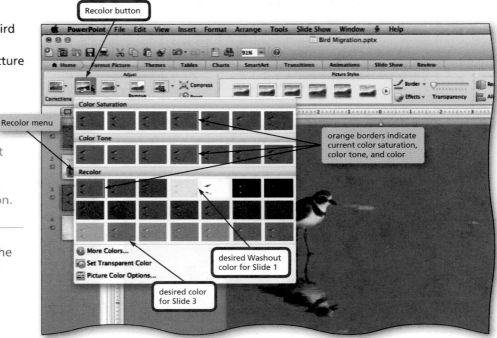

Figure 3–3

2

- Click Accent color 1 Light (second picture in last row of Recolor area) to apply this correction to the Bird Reflect picture (Figure 3–4).

Q&A Could I have applied this correction to the picture if it had been a background instead of a file inserted into the slide?
No. Artistic effects cannot be applied to backgrounds.

Figure 3–4

To Color a Second Picture

The Slide 1 picture has rich hues and is very prominent on the slide. To soften its appearance and to provide continuity with the Slide 3 picture, you can color this picture. The following steps color the picture on the title slide.

1 Display Slide 1 and then click the picture to select it. Click the Recolor button in the Adjust group on the Format Picture tab to display the Recolor pop-up menu.

2 Click Washout (fourth picture in first row of Recolor area) to apply this correction to the Bird Reflect picture (Figure 3–5).

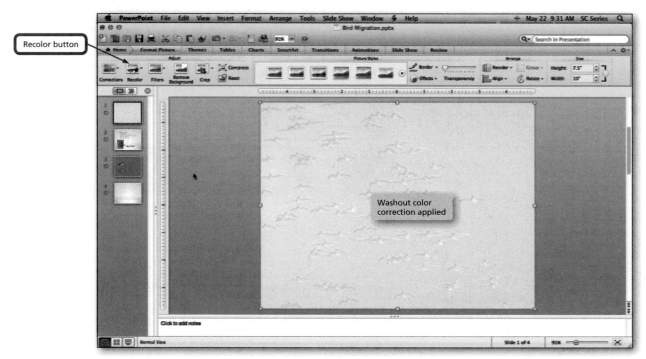

Figure 3–5

To Add an Artistic Effect to a Picture

Artists use a variety of techniques to create effects in their paintings. For example, they can vary the amount of paint on their brushstroke, use fine bristles to add details, mix colors to increase or decrease intensity, and smooth their paints together to blend the colors. You, likewise, can add similar effects to your pictures using PowerPoint's built-in artistic effects. The following steps add an artistic effect to the Slide 1 picture.

1

- With the Birds in Sky picture selected in Slide 1, click the Filters button in the Adjust group on the Format Picture tab to display the Filters pop-up menu (Figure 3–6).

Q&A Why is an orange border surrounding the first thumbnail in the gallery?
The first thumbnail shows a preview of the image on Slide 1 with no artistic effect applied.

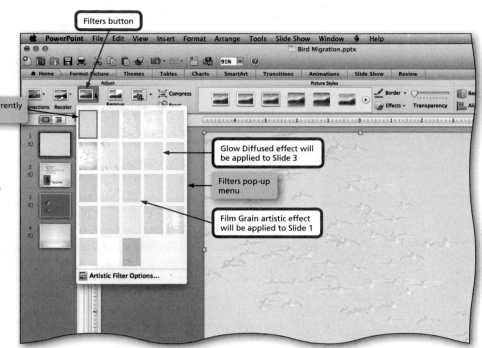

Figure 3–6

2

- Click Film Grain (third picture in third row) to apply this correction to the Birds in Sky picture (Figure 3–7).

Q&A Must I adjust a picture by recoloring and applying an artistic effect?
No. You can apply either a color or an effect. You may prefer at times to mix these adjustments to create a unique image.

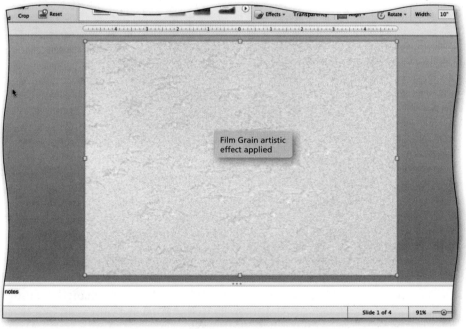

Figure 3–7

To Add an Artistic Effect to a Second Picture

The Slide 3 picture was softened when you applied a blue accent color. You can further change the images and provide continuity with the Slide 1 picture by applying an artistic effect. The following steps add an artistic effect to the Slide 3 picture.

1 Display Slide 3 and then click the picture to select it. If necessary, click the Format Picture tab to display it, and then click the Filters button in the Adjust group to display the Filters pop-up menu.

2 Click Glow Diffused (fourth picture in second row) to apply this effect to the Bird Reflect picture (Figure 3–8).

Figure 3–8

To Change the Stacking Order

The objects on a slide stack on top of each other, much like individual cards in a deck. On Slides 1 and 3, the pictures you inserted are on top of text placeholders. To change the order of these objects, you use the Bring Forward and Send Backward commands. **Bring Forward** moves an object toward the top of the stack, and **Send Backward** moves an object underneath another object. Other commands in the Reorder pop-up menu include **Bring to Front**, which moves a selected object to the top of the stack, and **Send to Back**, which moves the selected object underneath all objects on the slide. The following steps arrange the Slide 3 and Slide 1 pictures by sending them to the bottom of the stack on each slide.

- With the Bird Reflect picture selected in Slide 3, click the Reorder button in the Arrange group to display the Reorder pop-up menu (Figure 3–9).

Q&A How can I see objects that are not on the top of the stack?
Press TAB or SHIFT-TAB to display each slide object.

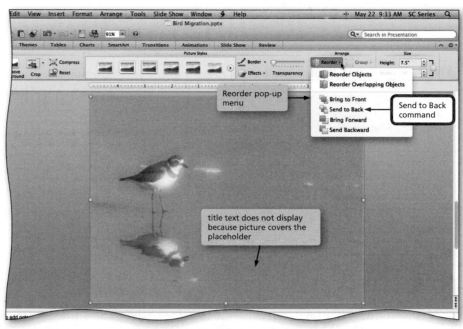

Figure 3–9

❷
- Click Send to Back to move the picture underneath all slide objects (Figure 3–10).

Figure 3–10

- Display Slide 1, select the Birds in Sky picture, and then click the Reorder button in the Arrange group.
- Click Send to Back to move the picture underneath all slide objects (Figure 3–11).

Figure 3–11

Other Ways

1. On Home tab, under Format, click Arrange button, click Send to Back
2. CONTROL-click object, choose Arrange in shortcut menu, click Send to Back
3. Choose Arrange > Send to Back in menu bar

Modifying Placeholders and Deleting a Slide

You have become familiar with inserting text and graphical content in the three types of placeholders: title, subtitle, and content. These placeholders can be moved, resized, and deleted to meet desired design requirements. In addition, placeholders can be added to a slide when needed. After you have modified the placeholder locations, you can view thumbnails of all your slides simultaneously by changing views.

In the following pages, you will perform these tasks:

1. Resize and move the Slide 1 title text placeholder.
2. Delete the Slide 1 subtitle text placeholder.
3. Align the Slide 1 and Slide 3 paragraph text.
4. Delete Slide 4.
5. Change views.

To Resize a Placeholder

The AutoFit button displays on the left side of the Slide 1 title text placeholder because the two lines of text exceed the placeholder's borders. PowerPoint attempts to reduce the font size when the text does not fit, and you can click this button to resize the existing text in the placeholder so the spillover text will fit within the borders. You also can resize the placeholder so that the letters fit within the rectangle. The following step increases the Slide 1 title text placeholder.

1

- With Slide 1 displaying, click somewhere in the title text paragraph to position the insertion point in the paragraph. Click the border of the title text placeholder to select it. Point to the bottom-middle sizing handle so that the mouse pointer changes to a two-headed arrow.

- Drag the bottom border downward to enlarge the text placeholder (Figure 3–12).

Q&A   Can I drag other sizing handles to enlarge or shrink the placeholder?
Yes, you also can drag the left, right, top, and corner sizing handles to resize a placeholder.

Q&A   How do the square sizing handles differ from circle sizing handles?
Dragging a square handle alters the shape of the text box so that it is wider or taller. Dragging a circle handle keeps the box in the same proportion and simply enlarges the overall shape.

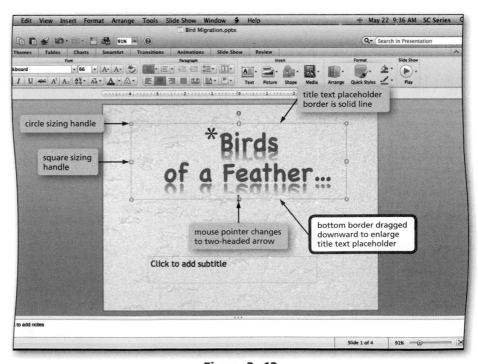

Figure 3–12

To Move a Placeholder

The theme layouts determine where the text and content placeholders display on the slide. If you desire to have a placeholder appear in a different area of the slide, you can move it to a new location. The Slide 1 title text placeholder currently displays in the upper third of the slide, but the text in this placeholder would be more aesthetically pleasing if it were moved toward the center of the slide. The following step moves the Slide 1 title text placeholder.

- With the Slide 1 title text placeholder border displaying as a solid line, point to an area of the bottom border between two sizing handles so that the mouse pointer changes to a four-headed arrow.

Figure 3–13

Q&A What if the placeholder border displays as a dotted line?
Click the border to change the line from dotted to solid.

Q&A Can I click any part of the border, or do I need to click the bottom edge?
You can click any of the four border lines.

- Drag the placeholder downward so that it overlaps part of the subtitle text placeholder (Figure 3–13).

- Release the mouse to set the placeholder in its new location.

To Delete a Placeholder

When you run a slide show, empty placeholders do not display. You may desire to delete unused placeholders from a slide so that they are not a distraction when you are designing slide content. The subtitle text placeholder on Slide 1 is not required for this presentation, so you can remove it. The following steps remove the Slide 1 subtitle text placeholder.

1 Click a border of the subtitle text placeholder so that it displays as a heavier solid blue line (Figure 3–14).

Q&A What if the placeholder border is displaying as a dotted line?
Click the border to change the line from dotted to solid or fine dots.

Figure 3–14

2 Press the DELETE key to remove the placeholder.

Q&A Can I click the Cut button in the Standard toolbar to delete the placeholder?
Yes. Clicking the Cut button deletes the placeholder if it does not contain any text.

Reusing Placeholders

BTW If you need to show the same formatted placeholder on multiple slides, you may want to customize a slide master and insert a placeholder into a slide layout. Using a slide master saves you time because you do not need to type the same information in more than one slide. The slide master is useful when you have extremely long presentations. Every document theme has several slide masters that indicate the size and position of text and object placeholders. Any change you make to a slide master results in changing that component in every slide of the presentation.

Plan Ahead **Vary paragraph alignment.**

Designers use alignment within paragraphs to aid readability and to indicate relationships among slide elements. English language readers are accustomed to seeing paragraphs that are aligned left. When paragraphs are aligned right, the viewer's eyes are drawn to this unexpected text design. If your paragraph is short, consider centering or right-aligning the text for emphasis.

To Align Paragraph Text

The presentation theme determines the formatting characteristics of fonts and colors. It also establishes paragraph formatting, including the alignment of text. Some themes center the text paragraphs between the left and right placeholder borders, while others **left-align** the paragraph so that the first character of a text line is near the left border or **right-align** the paragraph so that the last character of a text line is near the right border. The paragraph also can be **justified** so that the text is aligned to both the left and right borders. When PowerPoint justifies text, it adds extra spaces between the words to fill the entire line.

The words, Birds of a Feather, are centered in the Slide 1 title text placeholder. Later, you will add clip art above the word, Feather, so you desire to left-align the paragraph to make room for this art. In addition, the words in the Slide 3 title text placeholder, Bird Migration, are covering the bird in the picture. You can right-align these words to uncover the bird in the lower-left corner. The following steps change the alignment of the Slide 1 and Slide 3 title placeholders.

- With the Home tab displayed, click somewhere in the title text paragraph of Slide 1 to position the insertion point in the placeholder containing the text to be formatted (Figure 3–15).

Q&A Does it matter where in the placeholder I position the insertion point?
No. When changing the alignment of text in a placeholder, all text in the placeholder containing the insertion point will be formatted.

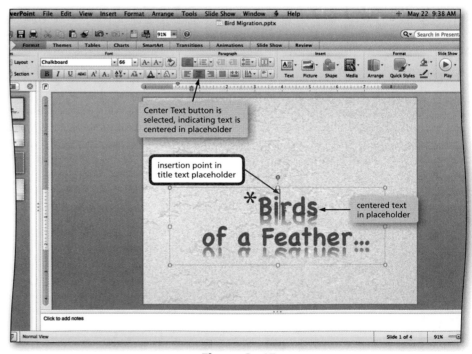

Figure 3–15

2

- Click the Align Text Left button in the Paragraph group to left-align the paragraph (Figure 3–16).

Q&A What if I want to return the paragraph to center alignment?
Click the Center Text button in the Paragraph group on the Home tab.

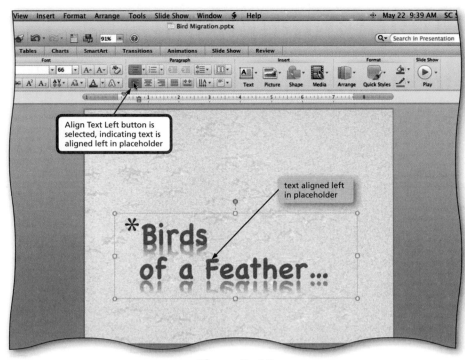

Figure 3–16

3

- Display Slide 3. Click somewhere in the title text paragraph to position the insertion point in the paragraph to be formatted.

4

- Click the Align Text Right button in the Paragraph group to right-align the paragraph.

5

- Move the Slide 3 title text placeholder downward so that it displays approximately as shown in Figure 3–17.

Figure 3–17

Other Ways

1. CONTROL-click paragraph, choose Paragraph in shortcut menu, click

   Alignment box arrow, click Right, click OK button

2. Choose Format > Paragraph in menu bar,

   click Alignment box arrow, click Right, click OK button

3. Press COMMAND-R

To Delete a Slide

The Bird Migration presentation has a blank slide at the end. You decide that you will not use this slide, so you need to remove it from the file. The following steps delete Slide 4 from the presentation.

- CONTROL-click the Slide 4 thumbnail in the Slides tab to display the shortcut menu (Figure 3–18).

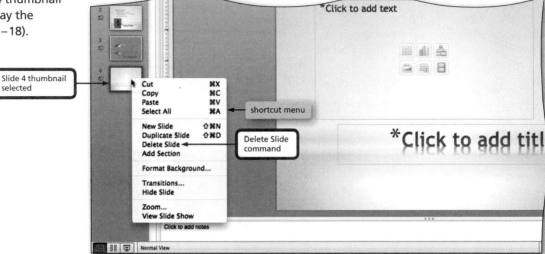

Figure 3–18

- Click Delete Slide to delete Slide 4 from the presentation (Figure 3–19).

Q&A Can I delete multiple slides simultaneously?

Yes. If the slides are sequential, click the first slide you want to delete, press and hold the SHIFT key, click the last slide that you want to delete, CONTROL-click any selected slide, and then click Delete Slide in the shortcut menu. If the slides are not sequential, press and hold the COMMAND key while you click each slide that you want to delete, CONTROL-click any selected slide, and then click Delete Slide in the shortcut menu.

Figure 3–19

Changing Views

You have been using Normal view to create and edit your slides. Once you completed your slides, you reviewed the final products by displaying each slide in Slide Show view, which occupies the full computer screen. You were able to view how the transitions, graphics, and effects will display in an actual presentation before an audience.

PowerPoint has another view to help review a presentation for content, organization, and overall appearance. Slide Sorter view allows you to look at several slides at one time. Switching between Slide Sorter view and Normal view helps you review your presentation, assess whether the slides have an attractive design and adequate content, and make sure they are organized for the most impact. After reviewing the slides, you can change the view to Normal so that you may continue working on the presentation.

To Change Views

You have made several modifications to the slides, so you should check for balance and consistency. The following steps change the view from Normal view to Slide Sorter view, then back to Normal view.

1

- Click the Slide Sorter view button in the lower left of the PowerPoint window to display the presentation in Slide Sorter view (Figure 3–20).

Q&A Why is Slide 3 selected?
It is the current slide in the Slide pane.

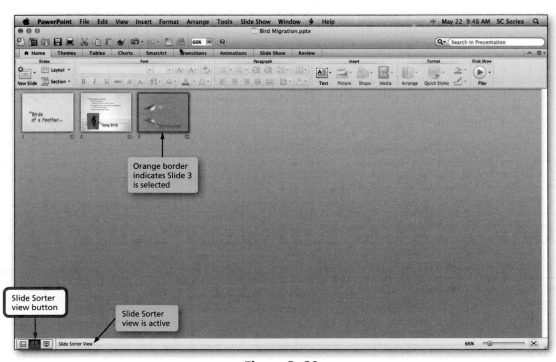

Figure 3–20

2

- Change the zoom to 150% to make the slide content more legible (Figure 3–21).

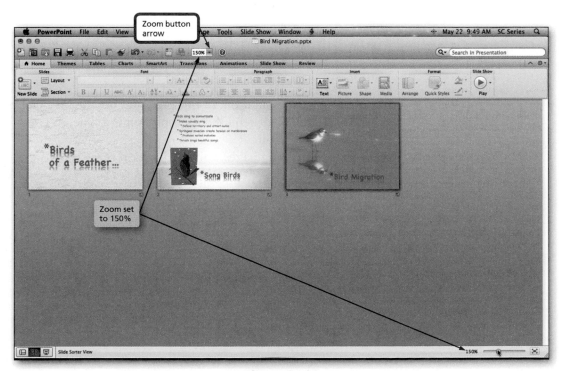

Figure 3–21

3

- Click Slide 1 to make it the active slide (Figure 3–22).

- Click the Normal view button to display the presentation in Normal view.

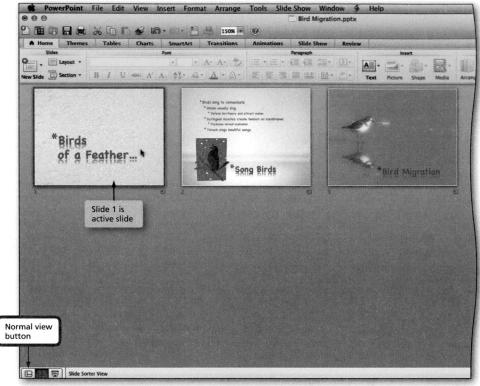

Figure 3–22

Copying and Modifying a Clip

Slide 1 (shown in Figure 3–1a on PPT 137) contains a modified version of a songbird. Occasionally, you may want to remove a picture background and use the foreground content in your presentation. In this presentation, the bird picture has a yellow background that is not required to display on the slide, so you will remove the background from the clip art picture.

In the following pages, you will perform these tasks:

1. Copy the clip from Slide 2 to Slide 1.
2. Remove the background color from the clip.

To Copy a Clip from One Slide to Another

The bird clip on Slide 2 also can display in a modified form on the title slide. The following steps copy this slide element from Slide 2 to Slide 1.

❶

● Display Slide 2. With the Home tab displayed, click the bird clip to select it and then click the Copy button in the Standard toolbar (Figure 3–23).

Q&A Why are some words on Slide 2 underlined with red wavy lines? Those words are not in PowerPoint's main or custom dictionaries, so PowerPoint indicates that they may be misspelled. For example, the word, Syringeal, is spelled correctly, but is not in PowerPoint's dictionaries.

❷

● Display Slide 1 and then click the Paste button in the Standard toolbar to insert the bird clip into the title slide.

Q&A Is the clip deleted from the Office Clipboard when I paste it into the slide?
No.

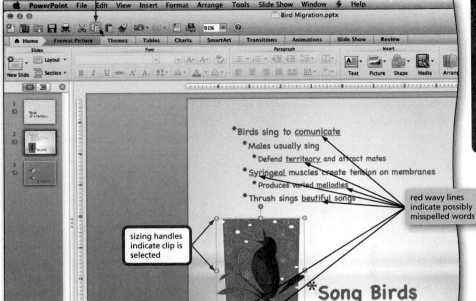

Figure 3–23

❸

● Drag the clip to the location shown in Figure 3–24. Decrease the clip size by dragging one of the corner sizing handles inward until the clip is the size shown in Figure 3–24.

Figure 3–24

Other Ways

1. Edit > Copy (source object), then Edit > Paste (at destination)

2. Press COMMAND-C (source object), then COMMAND-P (at destination)

To Zoom a Slide

You will be modifying small areas of the clip, so it will help you select the relevant pieces if the graphic is enlarged. The following step changes the zoom to 200 percent.

 1

- Click the Zoom button arrow and choose 200% from the pop-up menu to increase the zoom to 200% (Figure 3–25).

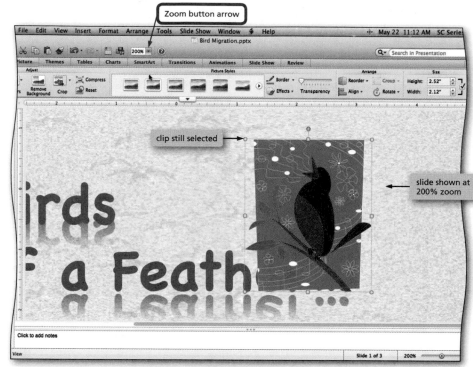

Figure 3–25

Other Ways

1. Choose View > Zoom > Zoom, choose desired zoom (Zoom dialog), click OK button

2. Drag Zoom slider to desired zoom level

To Remove the Clip Background

You want to remove the gold background from the bird picture. The following steps remove the background from the image.

 1

- Click the clip to select it.

- On the Format Picture tab, under Adjust, click the Remove Background button to add background removal lines to the figure.

- Use the sizing handles to drag the lines so that they contain all the content you want to keep.

- Move the mouse onto the picture, so the pointer changes to an arrow with a green circle containing a plus sign (Figure 3–26).

Q&A Why are parts of the picture colored in fuschia?
PowerPoint makes a first estimate at what part of the picture is background, and colors it fuschia. You will be able to fine-tune the selection.

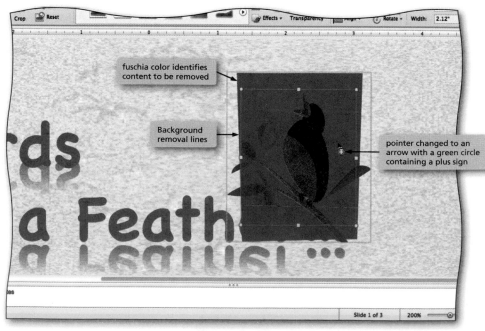

Figure 3–26

2

- Click the tail of the bird to remove the fuschia color from it. (Figure 3–27).

Figure 3–27

3

- Click the remaining components of the picture until you have deselected all the leaves, and stem, as shown in Figure 3–28.

Figure 3–28

4

- Click outside the picture to remove the background.

- Choose Fit from the Zoom pop-up menu (Figure 3–29).

Figure 3–29

Plan Ahead

Use multimedia selectively.

PowerPoint makes it easy to insert multimedia into a presentation. Well-produced video clips add value when they help explain a procedure or show movement that cannot be captured in a photograph. Music can help calm or energize an audience, when appropriate. A sound, such as applause when a correct answer is given, can emphasize an action. Before you insert these files on a slide, however, consider whether they really add any value to your overall slide show. If you are inserting them just because you can, you might want to reconsider your decision. Audiences quickly tire of extraneous sounds and movement on slides, and they will find these media clips annoying. Keep in mind that the audience's attention should focus primarily on the presenter; extraneous or inappropriate media files may divert their attention and, in turn, decrease the quality of the presentation.

Break Point: If you wish to take a break, this is a good place to do so. Be sure to save the Bird Migration file again and then you can quit PowerPoint. To resume at a later time, start PowerPoint, open the file called Bird Migration, and continue following the steps from this location forward.

Adding Media to Slides

Media files can enrich a presentation if they are used correctly. Movies files can have two formats: digital video produced with a camera and editing software or animated GIF (Graphics Interchange Format) files composed of multiple images combined into a single file. Sound files can be from the Media Browser, files stored on your computer, or an audio track on a CD. To hear the sounds, you need a sound card and speakers on your system.

In the following pages, you will perform these tasks:

1. Insert a video file into Slide 3.
2. Add video options that determine the clip's appearance and playback.
3. Insert audio files.
4. Add audio options that determine the clips' appearance and playback.
5. Add a video style to the Slide 3 clip.
6. Resize the video.
7. Insert a movie clip into Slide 1.

To Insert a Video File

Slide 3 has the title, Bird Migration, and you have a short video clip that shows a flock of birds on a beach, and you want to use this clip in your presentation. PowerPoint allows you to insert this clip into your slide so that it will play when you preview the clip or run the slide show. This clip is available on the Data Files for Students. See the inside back cover of this book for instructions on downloading the Data Files for Students, or contact your instructor for more information about accessing the required file. The following steps insert this video clip into Slide 3.

1

- Display Slide 3 and display the Home tab. With your USB flash drive connected to one of the computer's USB ports, click the Media button under Insert to display the Media pop-up menu.

- Choose Movie from File to open the Choose a Movie dialog.

- Navigate to the location of the Data Files for Students.

- Click Wildlife.mov to select the file (Figure 3–30).

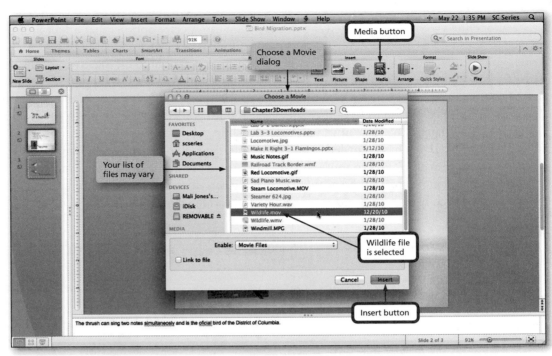

Figure 3–30

2

- Click the Insert button (Choose a Movie dialog) to insert the movie clip into Slide 3 (Figure 3–31).

Q&A Can I adjust the color of a video clip?
Yes. You correct the brightness and contrast, and you also recolor a video clip using the same methods you learned in this chapter to recolor a picture.

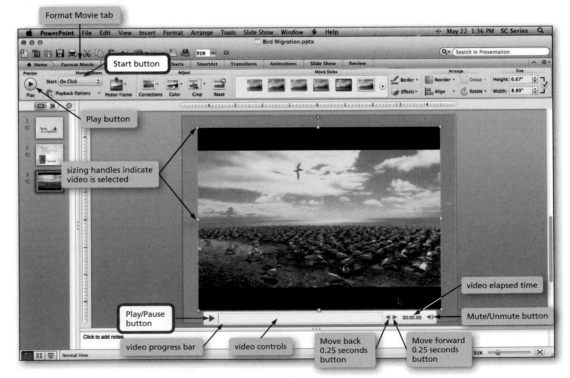

Figure 3–31

To Add Video Options

Once the video clip is inserted into Slide 3, you can specify options that affect how the file is displayed and played. For example, you can have the video play automatically when the slide is displayed, or you can click the slide when you are ready to start the playback. You also can have the video fill the entire slide, which is referred to as **full screen**. If you decide to play the slide show automatically and have it display full screen, you can drag the video frame to the gray area off the slide so that it does not display briefly before going to full screen. You can select the Loop until Stopped option to have the video repeat until you click the next slide, or you can choose to not have the video frame display on the slide until you click the slide.

If your video clip has recorded sounds, the volume controls give you the option to set how loudly this audio will play. They also allow you to mute the sound so that your audience will hear no background noise or music.

The following steps add the options of playing the video full screen automatically when Slide 3 is displayed and also mutes the background music recorded on the video clip.

- If necessary, click Format Movie on the ribbon to display the Format Movie tab. Click the Start button in the Movie Options group to view the Start menu (Figure 3–32).

Q&A   What does the On Click option do?
The video clip would begin playing when a presenter clicks the slide during the slide show.

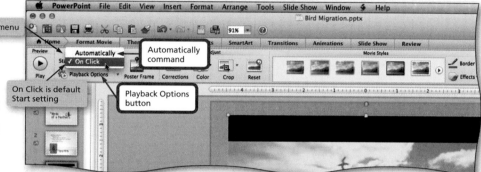

Figure 3–32

- Click Automatically in the Start menu.

- Click the Playback Options button to display the Playback Options pop-up menu (Figure 3–33).

Figure 3–33

3

- Click Play Full Screen to select that option.

- Click the Mute/Unmute button on the control bar of the movie clip to mute the volume of the clip (Figure 3–34).

Figure 3–34

To Insert an Audio File

Avid bird watchers listen to the songs and calls birds make to each other. The Media Browser and Office.com have several of these sounds in audio files that you can download and insert into your presentation. You can also insert an audio clip that you have on a storage device. Once these audio files are inserted into a slide, you can add options that specify how long and how loudly the clip will play; these options are similar to the video options you just selected for the Wildlife video clip. The following steps insert an audio clip from the Data Files for Students into Slide 3.

1

- With your USB flash drive connected to one of the computer's USB ports, click the Media button in the Insert group on the Home tab to display the media pop-up menu.

- Choose Audio from File to open the Choose Audio dialog.

- Navigate to the location of the Data Files for Students.

- Click Glade Birds.wav to select the file (Figure 3–35).

Figure 3–35

2

- Click the Insert button (Choose Audio dialog) to insert the audio clip into Slide 3 (Figure 3–36).

Q&A Why does a sound icon display in the video?
The icon indicates an audio file is inserted.

Q&A Do the Audio Controls buttons have the same functions as the Video Controls buttons that displayed when I inserted the Wildlife clip?
Yes. The controls include playing and pausing the sound, moving back or forward 0.25 seconds, audio progress, elapsed time, and muting or unmuting the sound.

Figure 3–36

● Drag the sound icon to the upper-left corner of the slide (Figure 3–37).

Q&A Must I move the icon on the slide? No. Although your audience will not see the icon when you run the slide show, it is easier for you to see the media elements when they are separated on the slide rather than stacked on top of each other.

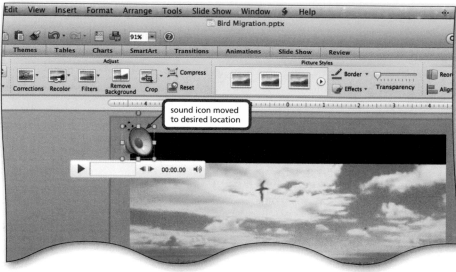

Figure 3–37

Other Ways

1. Choose Insert > Audio in menu bar

To Add Audio Options

Once an audio clip is inserted into a slide, you can specify options that control playback and appearance. As with the video options you applied to the Wildlife clip, the audio clip can play either automatically or when clicked, it can repeat the clip while a particular slide is displayed, and you can drag the sound icon off the slide and set the volume.

The following steps add the options of starting automatically and playing until the slide no longer is displayed, hiding the sound icon on the slide, and increasing the volume.

1

● If necessary, make Format Audio the active tab.

● Click the Start button in the Audio Options group to display the Start menu (Figure 3–38).

2

● Click Automatically in the Start menu.

Q&A Does the On Click option function the same way for an audio clip as On Click does for a video clip? Yes. If you were to select On Click, the sound would begin playing only after the presenter clicks Slide 1 during a presentation.

Figure 3–38

- Click the Playback Options button to display the Playback options menu.

Q&A What is the difference between the Loop Until Stopped option and the Play Across Slides option?

If Loop Until Stopped is chosen, the audio clip repeats for as long as one slide is displayed. In contrast, the Play Across Slides option clip would play only once, but it would continue to play while other slides in the presentation are displayed. Once the end of the clip is reached, the sound would end and not repeat.

- Choose Loop Until Stopped from the menu.

- Click the Playback Options button to display the Playback options menu again (Figure 3–39).

Figure 3–39

- Choose Hide Icon During Show from the menu.

Q&A Why would I want the icon to display during the show?
If you had selected the On Click start option, you would need to find this icon on the slide and click it to start playing the clip.

To Insert an Additional Audio File and Set Options

Having an audio clip play when Slide 1 is displayed would add interest and help set the tone of the presentation. Only one bird appears on that slide, and it appears to be singing heartily. A single bird singing would coordinate nicely with this clip art image. The following steps insert a songbird audio clip into Slide 1 and set playback options.

1 Display Slide 1 and click the Home tab. With your USB flash drive connected to one of the computer's USB ports, click the Media button in the Insert group to display the media pop-up menu.

2 Choose Audio from File to open the Choose Audio dialog, and navigate to the location of the Data Files for Students.

3 Click Birds at dawn.wav, and then click the Insert button (Choose Audio dialog) to insert the audio clip into Slide 1. Move the clip to the bottom-right corner of the slide.

4 On the Format Audio tab, under Audio Options, click the Start button and choose Automatically from the pop-up menu.

5 Click Playback Options and choose Hide Icon During Show.

6 Click Playback Options and choose Loop Until Stopped.

7 Point to the Mute/Unmute button to display the Volume control, then move the Volume slider to the midpoint (Figure 3–40 on the next page).

Playing Audio Continuously

You can play one audio **BTW** file throughout an entire presentation instead of only when one individual slide is displayed. When you select the 'Play across slides' option from the Start button menu in the Audio Options group on the Format Audio tab, the audio clip will play continuously as you advance through the slides in your presentation. If you select this option, be certain the length of the clip exceeds the total time you will display all slides in your slide show.

Figure 3–40

To Add a Video Style

The Wildlife video clip on Slide 3 displays full screen when it is playing, but you can increase the visual appeal of the clip when it is not playing by applying a video style. The video styles are similar to the picture styles you applied in Chapter 2 and include various shapes, angles, borders, and reflections. The following steps apply a video style to the Wildlife clip on Slide 3.

- Display Slide 3 and select the video. Click Format Movie in the ribbon to display the Format Movie tab (Figure 3–41).

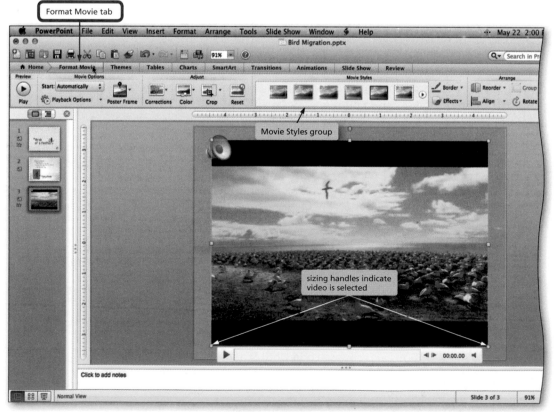

Figure 3–41

2

- With the video selected, click the More button in the Movie Styles group to show the Movie Styles gallery (Figure 3–42).

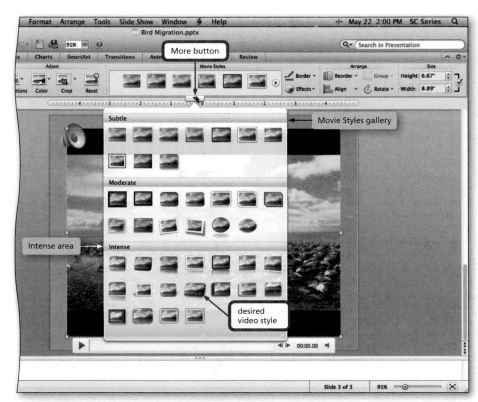

Figure 3–42

3

- Click Bevel Perspective in the Movie Styles gallery (fourth item in second row under Intense) to apply the style to the selected video (Figure 3–43).

Q&A Can I preview the movie clip?
Yes. Point to the clip and then click the Play/Pause button on the Video Controls below the video.

Q&A Can I add a border to a video style?
Yes. You add a border using the same method you learned in Chapter 2 to add a border to a picture. Click the Border button arrow in the Movie Styles group and then select a border line weight and color.

Figure 3–43

To Resize a Video

The Wildlife video size can be decreased to fill the space on the right side of the slide. You resize a video clip in the same manner that you resize clip art and pictures. The following steps resize this video using a sizing handle.

- With the video clip selected, drag the lower-left corner sizing handle on the photograph diagonally inward until the photograph is resized to approximately 5.02" × 6.7".

- Drag the clip to the location shown in Figure 3–44.

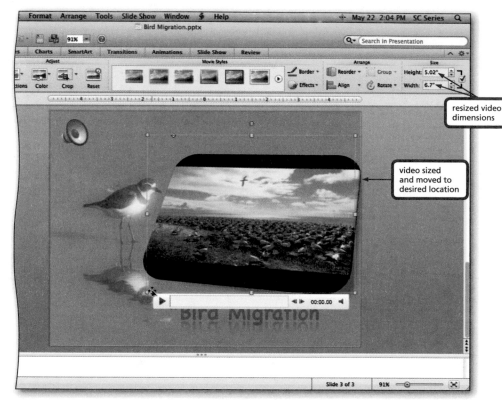

Figure 3–44

To Customize Animation on a Slide

You want the sound and the movie clips on Slide 3 to play simultaneously and automatically. PowerPoint by default will play one (in this case, the audio clip) automatically and wait for user input to start the second. In order to have both the movie and audio clips start automatically, you need to customize the animation on that slide. The following steps customize the animation.

- If necessary, display Slide 3, and then display the Animations tab (Figure 3–45).

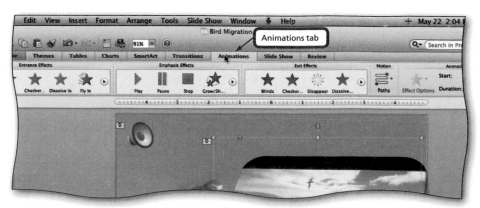

Figure 3–45

- Click the Reorder button in the Animation Options group to open the Custom Animation window.

- Under Animation Order, click Wildlife. mov to select it.

- Click the Timing disclosure triangle to expand the window (Figure 3–46).

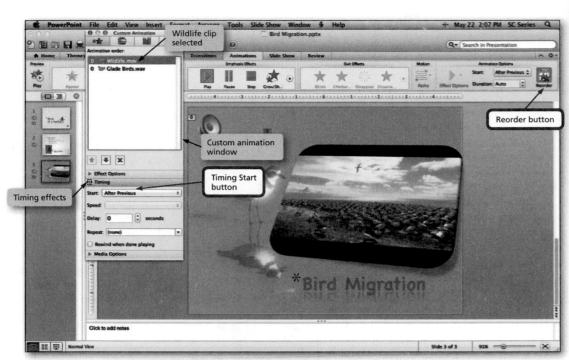

Figure 3–46

- Under Timing, click the Start button to see the pop-up menu (Figure 3–47).

- Choose With Previous to have PowerPoint start both clips when the slide becomes active.

- Click the Close button on the Custom Animation window title bar to close the Custom Animation window.

Figure 3–47

To Insert a Movie Clip

PowerPoint classifies animated GIF files as a type of video or movie because the clips have movement or action. These files are commonplace on Web sites. They also are found in PowerPoint presentations when you want to call attention to material on a particular slide. You can insert them into a PowerPoint presentation in the same manner that you insert video and audio files. They play automatically when the slide is displayed. The following steps insert a music notes video clip into Slide 1.

- Display Slide 1 and then display the Home tab.

- Click the Picture button in the Insert group to display the Picture pop-up menu, and choose Picture from File to open the Choose a Picture dialog.

- If necessary, navigate to the Chapter 3 files on your USB drive.

- Click Music Notes.gif to select the file (Figure 3–48).

Q&A Why does my list of files look different?
The list of picture files can vary depending upon the contents of your USB drive and the organization of those files into folders for each chapter.

Figure 3–48

- Click the Insert button (Choose a Picture dialog) to insert the Music Notes animated GIF clip into Slide 1.

- Resize the clip so that it is approximately 1.03" × 1.51".

- Drag the clip to the location shown in Figure 3–49.

Q&A Why is the animation not showing?
Animated GIF files move only in Slide Show view and Reading view.

Other Ways
1. Insert > Movie in menu bar

Figure 3–49

Break Point: If you wish to take a break, this is a good place to do so. Be sure to save the Bird Migration file again and then you can quit PowerPoint. To resume at a later time, start PowerPoint, open the file called Bird Migration, and continue following the steps from this location forward.

Reviewing and Revising Individual Slides

The text and graphics for all slides in the Bird Migration presentation have been entered. Once you complete a slide show, you might decide to change elements. PowerPoint provides several tools to assist you with making changes. They include finding and replacing text, inserting a synonym, and checking spelling. The following pages discuss these tools.

Replace Dialog

At times, you might want to change all occurrences of a word or phrase to another word or phrase. For example, an instructor may have one slide show to accompany a lecture for several introductory classes, and he wants to update slides with the particular class name and section that appear on several slides. He manually could change the characters, but PowerPoint includes an efficient method of replacing one word with another. The Find and Replace feature automatically locates specific text and then replaces it with desired text.

In some cases, you may want to replace only certain occurrences of a word or phrase, not all of them. To instruct PowerPoint to confirm each change, click the Find Next button in the Replace dialog instead of the Replace All button. When PowerPoint locates an occurrence of the text, it pauses and waits for you to click either the Replace button or the Find Next button. Clicking the Replace button changes the text; clicking the Find Next button instructs PowerPoint to disregard that particular instance and look for the next occurrence of the Find what text.

To Find and Replace Text

While reviewing your slides, you realize that you could give more specific information regarding the type of thrush discussed in Slide 2. The Wood Thrush's songs especially are melodic and beautiful, so you decide to add the word, Wood, to the bird's name. In addition, you want to capitalize the word, Thrush, because it is a specific type of thrush. To perform this action, you can use PowerPoint's Find and Replace feature, which automatically locates each occurrence of a word or phrase and then replaces it with specified text. The word, thrush, displays twice on Slide 2. The following steps use Find and Replace to replace all occurrences of the word, thrush, with the words, Wood Thrush.

- Make Slide 2 the active slide.
- Click Edit in the menu bar to display the Edit menu.
- Point to Find, and then choose Replace to display the Replace dialog.
- Type **thrush** in the Find what text box (Replace dialog).
- Press the TAB key. Type **Wood Thrush** in the Replace with text box (Figure 3–50).

Q&A Do I need to display the slide that contains the words for which I want to search?
No. But to allow you to see the results of this search and replace action, you can display the slide where the changes will occur.

Revising Your Text

Generating ideas, revising slides, editing graphics and text, and then proofreading all slide text are required as part of the development process. A good PowerPoint developer has the ability to write and then revise slide content. Multiple drafts generally are needed to complete a successful presentation. PowerPoint's Find and Replace feature is useful if you need to change all instances of a word throughout a large presentation when you are revising slides.

BTW

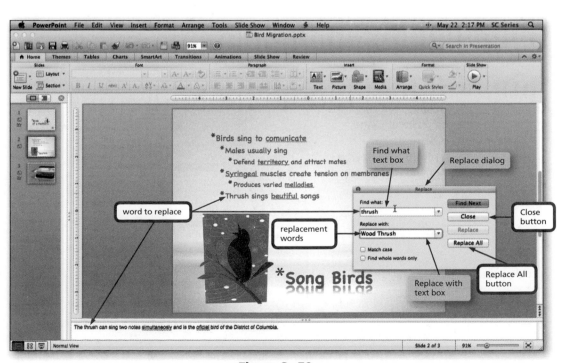

Figure 3–50

2

- Click the Replace All button (Replace dialog) to instruct PowerPoint to replace all occurrences of the Find what word, thrush, with the Replace with words, Wood Thrush (Figure 3–51).

Q&A If I accidentally replaced the wrong text, can I undo this replacement? Yes. Click the Undo button in the Standard toolbar to undo all replacements. If you had clicked the Replace button instead of the Replace All button, PowerPoint would undo only the most recent replacement.

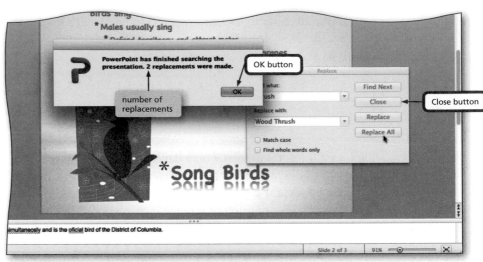

Figure 3–51

3

- Click the OK button in the dialog, and then click the Close button in the Replace dialog to close the Replace dialog.

Other Ways

1. Press SHIFT-COMMAND-H

To Find and Insert a Synonym

When reviewing your slide show, you may decide that a particular word does not express the exact usage you intended or that you used the same word on multiple slides. In these cases, you could find a **synonym**, or word similar in meaning, to replace the inappropriate or duplicate word. PowerPoint provides a **thesaurus**, which is a list of synonyms and antonyms, to help you find a replacement word.

In this project, you want to find a synonym to replace the word, Defend, on Slide 2. The following steps locate an appropriate synonym and replace the word.

1

- With Slide 2 displaying, place the insertion point in the word, Defend, and then CONTROL-click to display a shortcut menu.

- Point to Look Up, and then click Thesaurus on the shortcut menu to open the Toolbox with the Reference Tools window displaying with a list of synonyms for this word (Figure 3–52).

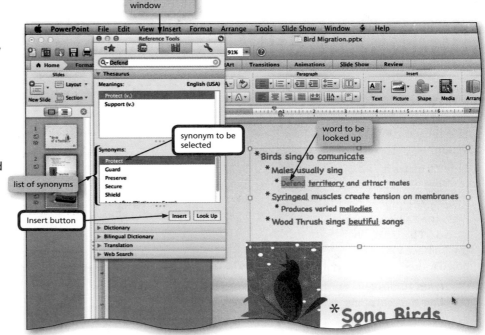

Figure 3–52

- Click the synonym you want (Protect) under Synonyms and then click the Insert button to replace the word, Defend, in the presentation with the word, Protect (Figure 3–53).

- Click the Close button on the Reference Tools title bar to close the Reference Tools window.

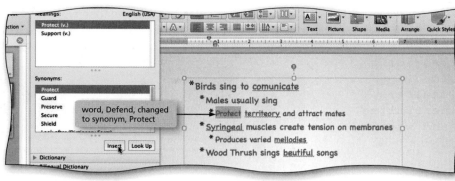

Figure 3–53

Q&A What if I want to find a word with the opposite meaning?
At the bottom of the Synonyms list under Thesaurus in the Reference Tools window you may find one or more antonyms, or words with the opposite meaning.

Other Ways
1. Click Toolbox in Standard toolbar, choose Reference Tools tab
2. Choose Tools > Thesaurus
3. Choose View > Reference Tools
4. Press CONTROL-OPTION-COMMAND-R

To Add Notes

As you create slides, you may find material you want to state verbally and do not want to include on the slide. You can type and format notes in the **Notes pane** as you work in Normal view and then print this information as **notes pages**. After adding comments, you can print a set of speaker notes. These notes will print below a small image of the slide. Charts, tables, and pictures added to the Notes pane also print on these pages. In this project, comments were included on Slide 2 when you opened that file. The following steps add text to the Notes pane on Slides 1 and 3.

1

- Display Slide 1, click Click to add notes in the Notes pane, and then type `More than 10,000 species of birds exist in the world. The largest bird is the ostrich, and the smallest is the hummingbird. They generally live in small groups, but some form huge flocks with thousands of members and a variety of species. Flocks help keep the birds safe while they search for food.` (Figure 3–54).

Q&A What if I cannot see all the lines I typed?
If you have lots of note text, the Notes pane will display the lines you are typing, but earlier lines may scroll up and a scroller will appear in the Notes pane. You can drag the splitter bar up to enlarge the Notes pane, or you can use the scroller to scroll through the notes text.

Figure 3–54

2
- Display Slide 3, click Click to add notes in the Notes pane, and then type `Birds migrate to benefit from warm weather. Some can fly more than 6,000 miles without stopping. We can help bird migration by providing food, shelters, nest sites, and water.` (Figure 3–55).

Slide 3 notes

Birds migrate to benefit from warm weather. Some can fly more than 6,000 miles without stopping. We can help bird migration by providing food, shelters, nest sites, and water.

Figure 3–55

Checking Spelling

After you create a presentation, you should check it visually for spelling errors and style consistency. In addition, you use PowerPoint's Spelling tool to identify possible misspellings on the slides and in the notes. Do not rely on the spelling checker to catch all your mistakes. Although PowerPoint's spelling checker is a valuable tool, it is not infallible. You should proofread your presentation carefully by pointing to each word and saying it aloud as you point to it. Be mindful of commonly misused words such as its and it's, through and though, and to and too.

PowerPoint checks the entire presentation for spelling mistakes using a standard dictionary contained in the Microsoft Office group. This dictionary is shared with the other Microsoft Office applications such as Word and Excel. A custom dictionary is available if you want to add special words such as proper names, cities, and acronyms. When checking a presentation for spelling errors, PowerPoint opens the standard dictionary and the custom dictionary file, if one exists. When a word appears in the Spelling dialog, you can perform one of several actions, as described in Table 3–1.

Table 3–1 Spelling Dialog Buttons and Actions		
Button Name	**When To Use**	**Action**
Ignore	Word is spelled correctly but not found in dictionaries	PowerPoint continues checking the rest of the presentation but will flag that word again if it appears later in document.
Ignore All	Word is spelled correctly but not found in dictionaries	PowerPoint ignores all occurrences of the word and continues checking the rest of the presentation.
Change	Word is misspelled	Click proper spelling of the word in Suggestions list. PowerPoint corrects word, continues checking the rest of the presentation, but will flag that word again if it appears later in document.
Change All	Word is misspelled	Click proper spelling of word in Suggestions list. PowerPoint changes all occurrences of misspelled word and continues checking the rest of the presentation.
Add	Add word to custom dictionary	PowerPoint opens custom dictionary, adds word, and continues checking the rest of the presentation.
Suggest	Correct spelling is uncertain	Lists alternative spellings. Click the correct word from the Suggestions box or type the proper spelling. Corrects the word and continues checking the rest of the presentation.
AutoCorrect	Add spelling error to AutoCorrect list	PowerPoint adds spelling error and its correction to AutoCorrect list. Any future misspelling of word is corrected automatically as you type.
Close	Stop spelling checker	PowerPoint closes spelling checker and returns to PowerPoint window.

The standard dictionary contains commonly used English words. It does not, however, contain many proper names, abbreviations, technical terms, poetic contractions, or antiquated terms. PowerPoint treats words not found in the dictionaries as misspellings.

To Check Spelling

The following steps check the spelling on all slides in the Bird Migration presentation.

1

- Choose Tools > Spelling in the menu bar to open the Spelling dialog (Figure 3–56).

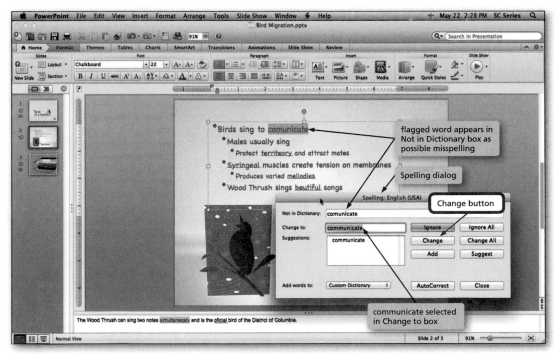

Figure 3–56

2

- With the word, communicate, selected in the Change to box, click the Change button (Spelling dialog) to replace the misspelled flagged word, comunicate, with the selected correctly spelled word, communicate, and then continue the spelling check (Figure 3–57).

Q&A Could I have clicked the Change All button instead of the Change button?

Yes. When you click the Change All button, you change the current and future occurrences of the misspelled word. The misspelled word, comunicate, appears only once in the presentation, so clicking the Change or the Change All button in this instance produces identical results.

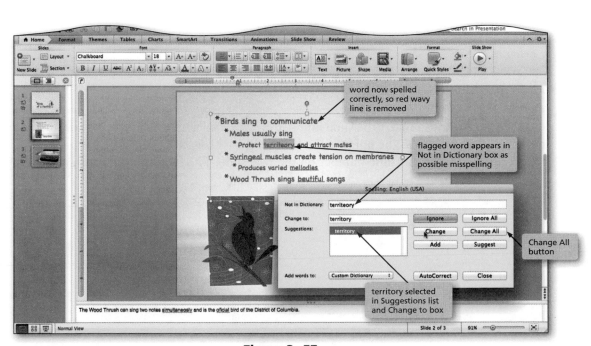

Figure 3–57

- Replace the misspelled word, territeory, with the word, territory that is highlighted in the Suggestions area (Figure 3–58).

- When the word, Syringeal, is flagged, click the Ignore button (Spelling dialog) to skip the correctly spelled word, Syringeal, and then continue the spelling check.

Q&A Syringeal is flagged as a possible misspelled word. Why?
Your custom dictionary does not contain the word, so it is recognized as spelled incorrectly. You can add this word to a custom dictionary to prevent the spelling checker from flagging it as a mistake.

Q&A Could I have clicked the Ignore All button instead of the Ignore button?
Yes. When you click the Ignore All button, you ignore the current and future occurrences of the word.

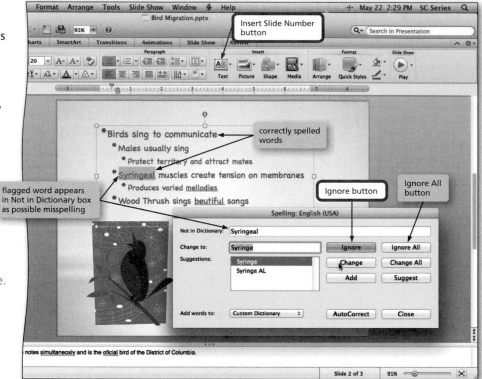

Figure 3–58

- Continue checking all flagged words in the presentation. When a dialog appears notifying you that the spelling check is complete, click the OK button to return to the current slide, Slide 2, or to the slide where a possible misspelled word appeared.

To Insert a Slide Number

PowerPoint can insert the slide number on your slides automatically to indicate where the slide is positioned within the presentation. The number location on the slide is determined by the presentation theme. You have the option to not display this slide number on the title slide. The following steps insert the slide number on all slides except the title slide.

1

- Click Slide 2 in the Slide pane. Display the Home tab and then click the Text button under Insert to display the pop-up menu.

- Choose Slide Number from the menu to display the Header and Footer dialog (Figure 3–59).

Q&A Why did I need to click the Slide pane?
The page number would have been inserted in the Notes pane instead of on the slide.

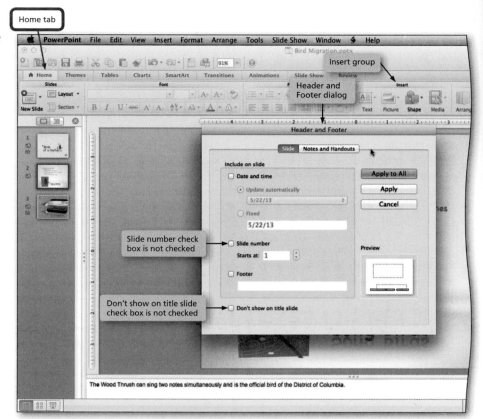

Figure 3–59

2

- Click the Slide number check box (Header and Footer dialog) to place a check mark in it.

- Click the 'Don't show on title slide' check box (Header and Footer dialog) to place a check mark in it (Figure 3–60).

Q&A Where does the slide number display on the slide?
Each theme determines where the slide number is displayed in the footer. In the Slipstream theme, the slide number location is the center of the footer, as indicated by the black box at the bottom of the Preview area.

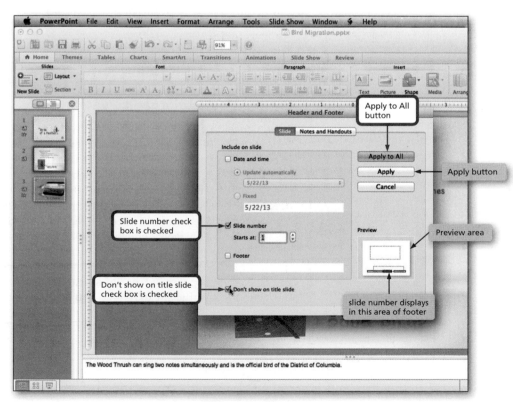

Figure 3–60

3

- Click the Apply to All button (Header and Footer dialog) to close the dialog box and insert the slide number on all slides except Slide 1 (Figure 3–61).

Q&A How does clicking the Apply to All button differ from clicking the Apply button?
The Apply button inserts the slide number only on the currently displayed slide whereas the Apply to All button inserts the slide number on every slide.

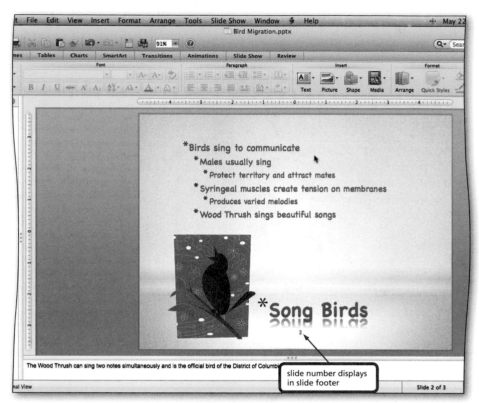

Figure 3–61

Other Ways

1. Click Text button in Home tab, click Header and Footer under Insert

2. Choose Insert > Slide Number in menu bar

3. Choose Insert > Header and Footer in menu bar

Plan Ahead

Use handouts to organize your speech.

As you develop a lengthy presentation with many visuals, handouts may help you organize your material. Print handouts with the maximum number of slides per page. Use scissors to cut each thumbnail and then place these miniature slide images adjacent to each other on a flat surface. Any type on the thumbnails will be too small to read, so the images will need to work with only the support of the verbal message you provide. You can rearrange these thumbnails as you organize your speech. When you return to your computer, you can rearrange the slides on your screen to match the order of your thumbnail printouts. Begin speaking the actual words you want to incorporate in the body of the talk. This process of glancing at the thumbnails and hearing yourself say the key ideas of the speech is one of the best methods of organizing and preparing for the actual presentation. Ultimately, when you deliver your speech in front of an audience, the images on the slides or on your note cards should be sufficient to remind you of the accompanying verbal message.

To Preview and Print a Handout

Printing handouts is useful for reviewing a presentation because you can analyze several slides displayed simultaneously on one page. Additionally, many businesses distribute handouts of the slide show before or after a presentation so attendees can refer to a copy. Each page of the handout can contain reduced images of one, two, three, four, six, or nine slides. The three-slides-per-page handout includes lines beside each slide so that your audience can write notes conveniently. The following steps preview and print a presentation handout.

1

- Click File in the menu bar and choose Print to open the Print dialog.

- Click the Print What button to display the pop-up menu (Figure 3–62).

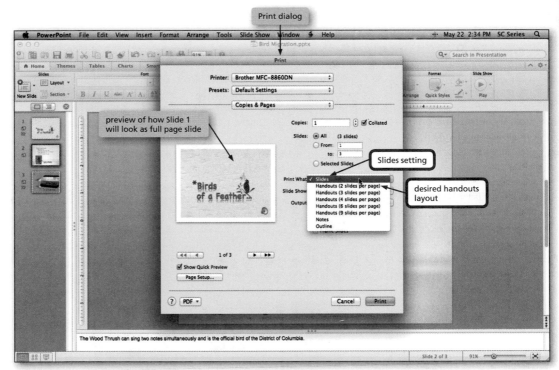

Figure 3–62

2

- Click Handouts (2 slides per page) to select this option and display a preview of the handout (Figure 3–63).

Q&A The current date displays in the upper-right corner of the handout, and the page number displays in the lower-right corner of the footer. Can I change their location or add other information to the header and footer? Yes. Click the Page Setup button near the bottom of the Print dialog, click the Header/Footer button, click the Notes and Handouts tab (Header and Footer dialog), and then decide what header and footer content to include on the handout page.

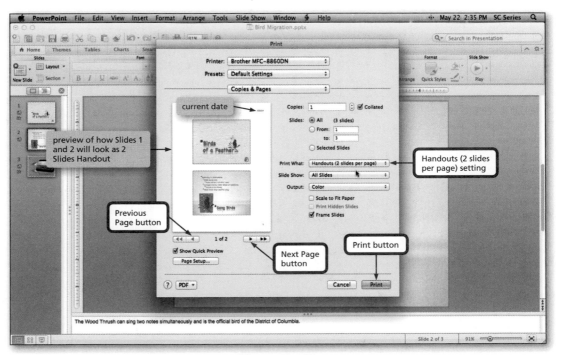

Figure 3–63

3

- Click the Next Page and Previous Page buttons to display previews of the two pages in the presentation.

- Click the Print button (Print dialog) to print the handout.

- When the printer stops, retrieve the printed handout (Figure 3–64).

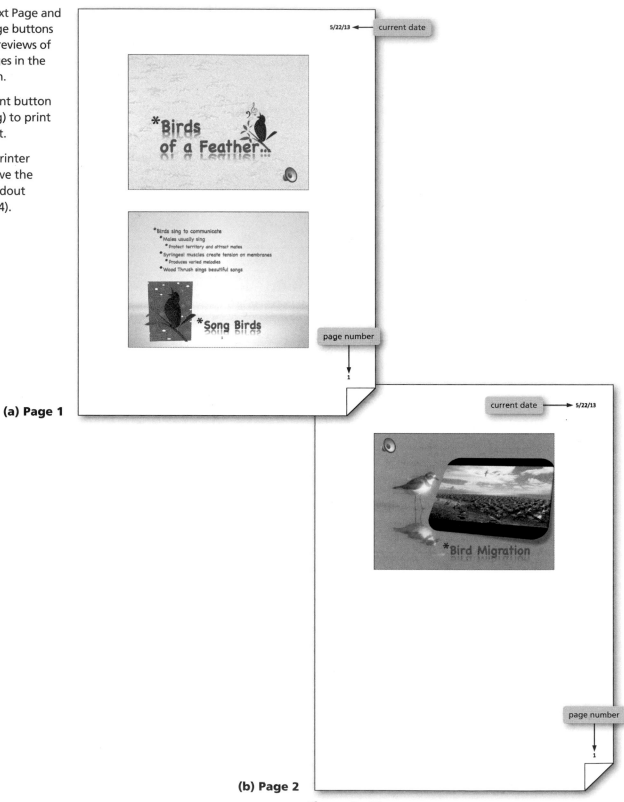

(a) Page 1

(b) Page 2

Figure 3–64

To Print Speaker Notes

Comments added to slides in the Notes pane give the speaker information that supplements the text on the slide. They will print with a small image at the top and the comments below the slide. The following steps print the speaker notes.

- Click File in the menu bar and choose Print to open the Print dialog again, and then click Handouts (2 Slides per page) in the Print What area to display the pop-up menu (Figure 3–65).

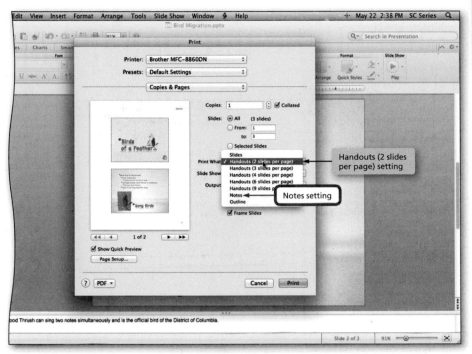

Figure 3–65

- Click Notes in the menu to select this option and display a preview of the current page (Figure 3–66).

- Click the Previous Page and Next Page buttons to display previews of other pages and notes in the presentation.

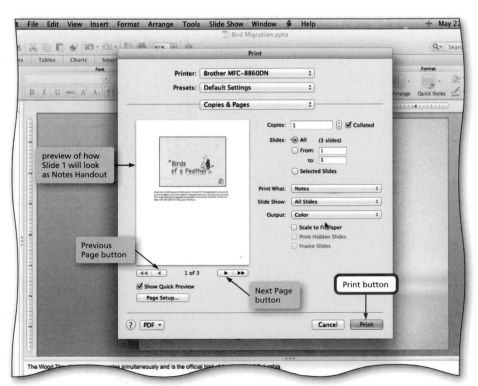

Figure 3–66

3
- Click the Print button in the Print dialog to print the notes.
- When the printer stops, retrieve the printed pages (Figure 3–67).

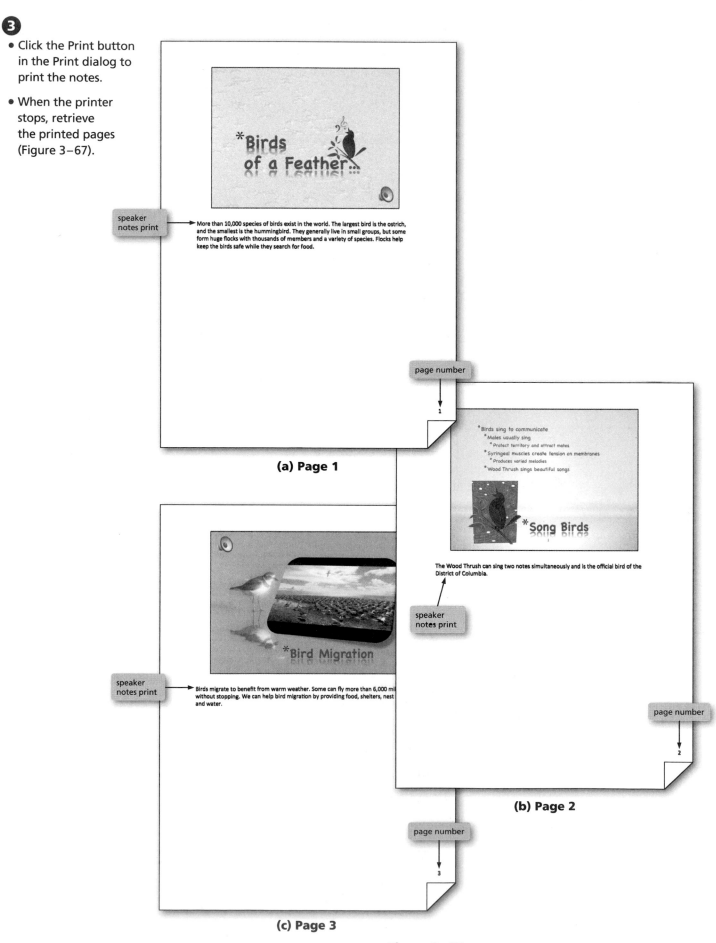

Figure 3–67

Plan Ahead

Evaluate your presentation.

One of the best methods of iarrowmproving your communication skills is to focus on what you learned from the experience. Respond to these questions:

- How successfully do you feel you fulfilled your assignment?
- What strategies did you use to develop your slides and the accompanying oral presentation?
- What revisions did you make?
- If you could go back to the speaking engagement and change one thing, what would it be?
- What feedback did you receive from your instructor or audience?

To Change Document Properties

Before saving the presentation again, you want to add your name, class name, and some keywords as document properties. The following steps use the Properties dialog to change document properties.

1 Click File in the menu bar to display the File menu.

2 Choose Properties to open the Properties dialog.

3 Update the contents of the Author and Subject text boxes with your name, course, and section.

4 Enter `bird, migration, singing` in the Keywords text box.

5 Click the OK button to close the Properties dialog.

To Run a Slide Show with Media

All changes are complete, and the presentation is saved. You now can view the Bird Migration presentation. The following steps start Slide Show view.

1 Click the Slide 1 thumbnail in the Slide pane to select and display Slide 1.

2 On the Home tab under Slide Show, click the Play button to display the title slide, watch the animations, and listen to the bird calls. Allow the audio clip to repeat several times.

3 Press the SPACE BAR to display Slide 2.

4 Press the SPACE BAR to display Slide 3. Listen to the audio clip, watch the video clip, and then allow the audio clip to repeat several times.

5 Press the SPACE BAR to end the slide show and click to exit the slide show.

Quick Reference

For a table that lists how to complete the tasks covered in this book using the mouse, ribbon, shortcut menu, and keyboard, see the Quick Reference Summary at the back of this book, or visit the Office 2011 for Mac Online Companion Web page at www.cengagebrain.com, navigate to the desired application, and click Quick Reference.

To Quit PowerPoint

This project is complete. The following steps quit PowerPoint.

1 Click File in the menu bar and choose Close to close the presentation.

2 If a dialog appears, click the Save button to save any changes made to the presentation since the last save.

3 Choose Quit PowerPoint from the PowerPoint menu to quit PowerPoint.

Chapter Summary

In this chapter you have learned how to enhance an existing presentation by adding video, audio, and pictures with effects. You also learned to modify placeholders, align text, and review a presentation by checking spelling and creating handouts. The items listed below include all the new PowerPoint skills you have learned in this chapter.

1. Color a Picture (PPT 141)
2. Add an Artistic Effect to a Picture (PPT 142)
3. Change the Stacking Order (PPT 144)
4. Resize a Placeholder (PPT 146)
5. Move a Placeholder (PPT 147)
6. Align Paragraph Text (PPT 148)
7. Delete a Slide (PPT 150)
8. Change Views (PPT 151)
9. Copy a Clip from One Slide to Another (PPT 152)
10. Zoom a Slide (PPT 154)
11. Remove the Clip Background (PPT 154)
12. Insert a Video File (PPT 156)
13. Add Video Options (PPT 158)
14. Insert an Audio File (PPT 159)
15. Add Audio Options (PPT 160)
16. Add a Video Style (PPT 162)
17. Resize a Video (PPT 164)
18. Customize Animation on a Slide (PPT 164)
19. Insert a Movie Clip (PPT 166)
20. Find and Replace Text (PPT 167)
21. Find and Insert a Synonym (PPT 168)
22. Add Notes (PPT 169)
23. Check Spelling (PPT 171)
24. Insert a Slide Number (PPT 172)
25. Preview and Print a Handout (PPT 174)
26. Print Speaker Notes (PPT 177)

Learn It Online

Test your knowledge of chapter content and key terms.

Instructions: To complete the Learn It Online exercises, please visit **www.cengagebrain.com.** At the CengageBrain.com home page, search for *Office 2011 for Mac* using the search box at the top of the page. This will take you to the product page for this book. On the product page, click the Access Now button below the Study Tools heading. On the Book Companion Site Web page, select PowerPoint Chapter 3, and then click the link for the desired exercise.

Chapter Reinforcement TF, MC, and SA
A series of true/false, multiple choice, and short answer questions that test your knowledge of the chapter content.

Flash Cards
An interactive learning environment where you identify chapter key terms associated with displayed definitions.

Practice Test
A series of multiple choice questions that test your knowledge of chapter content and key terms.

Who Wants To Be a Computer Genius?
An interactive game that challenges your knowledge of chapter content in the style of a television quiz show.

Wheel of Terms
An interactive game that challenges your knowledge of chapter key terms in the style of the television show *Wheel of Fortune*.

Crossword Puzzle Challenge
A crossword puzzle that challenges your knowledge of key terms presented in the chapter.

Apply Your Knowledge

Reinforce the skills and apply the concepts you learned in this chapter.

Adding Artistic Effects to Pictures, Moving a Placeholder, and Inserting and Controlling Audio Clips
Note: To complete this assignment, you will be required to use the Data Files for Students. See the inside back cover of this book for instructions on downloading the Data Files for Students, or contact your instructor for information about accessing the required files.

Instructions: Start PowerPoint. Open the presentation, Apply 3-1 SAD, from the Data Files for Students.

The five slides in the presentation, shown in Figure 3–68 on the next page, present information about Seasonal Affective Disorder, also known as SAD, which is a mood disorder that occurs generally during the winter months. The document you open is composed of slides containing pictures and clip art, and you will apply filters or modify some of these graphic elements. You also will insert audio clips from the Data Files for Students into the presentation. In addition, you will move the placeholder on the final slide.

Perform the following tasks:

1. Insert the audio clip, Sad piano music, into Slide 1 (Figure 3–68a). Change the volume to the midpoint on the slider, start the clip automatically, and hide the sound icon during the slide show. Then copy this audio clip to Slides 2, 3, and 4 with the same options. Insert the audio clip, Variety hour, into Slide 5, change the volume to the midpoint on the slider, start the clip automatically, and hide the sound icon during the slide show.

Continued >

Apply Your Knowledge *continued*

2. On Slide 2, color the picture by selecting Accent color 2 Dark from the Recolor area, as shown in Figure 3–68b.

3. On Slide 3, apply the Watercolor Sponge filter to the picture, as shown in Figure 3–68c.

4. On Slide 4, increase the contrast to +40%, as shown in Figure 3–68d.

5. On Slide 5, move the WordArt placeholder above the bird in the picture, as shown in Figure 3–68e.

6. On Slide 1, type `Up to 9 percent of U.S. adults may suffer from SAD.` in the Notes pane.

7. Check the slides for spelling errors and then run the revised presentation.

8. Change the document properties, as specified by your instructor. Save the presentation using the file name, Apply 3-1 Seasonal Affective Disorder.

9. Submit the revised document in the format specified by your instructor.

(a) Slide 1

(b) Slide 2

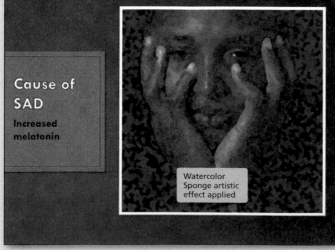

(c) Slide 3

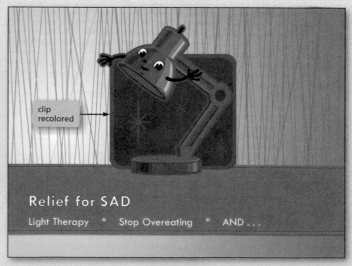

(d) Slide 4

Figure 3–68

(e) Slide 5

Figure 3–68 *(continued)*

Extend Your Knowledge

Extend the skills you learned in this chapter and experiment with new skills. You may need to use Help to complete the assignment.

Formatting a Video Border, Deleting Audio, Adding a Font Effect, and Pausing and Resuming Video Playback

Note: To complete this assignment, you will be required to use the Data Files for Students. See the inside back cover of this book for instructions on downloading the Data Files for Students, or contact your instructor for information about accessing the required files.

Instructions: Start PowerPoint. Open the presentation, Extend 3-1 Nature, from the Data Files for Students.

You will add the Small Caps font effect to the title text on the title slide, delete an audio clip, and format a video border, as shown in Figure 3–69a on the next page. While the slide show is running, you will adjust the video playback to pause and then resume playing the clip.

Perform the following tasks:

1. On Slide 1, move the title text placeholder up so that it is positioned in the upper-right corner of the slide, as shown in Figure 3–69a. Right-align the title text and then add the Small Caps font effect to these letters. *Hint:* Font effects are located in the Format Text dialog.

2. On the title slide, delete the audio clip positioned in the upper-left corner of the slide. The three audio clips on the right side of the slide will remain.

3. Change the video style from Soft Edge Oval to Beveled Oval, Black (in the Moderate area). Then change the video border color to Accent 2 and change the border weight to 10 pt. *Hint:* Click More Lines in the Video Border Weight gallery and then change the Border Style Width.

4. On Slide 2, add a border to each of the six pictures that surround the center deer video frame, and then change the border colors and the border weights. Use Figure 3–69b as a guide. Add the Compound Frame, Black video style (in the Moderate area) to the bird feeder clip.

5. Change the document properties, as specified by your instructor. Save the presentation using the file name, Extend 3-1 Observing Nature.

Continued >

Extend Your Knowledge *continued*

(a) Slide 1   **(b) Slide 2**

Figure 3–69

6. Start the slide show. When a few seconds of the video have elapsed, pause the video and then move your mouse pointer to an area other than the video and listen to the bird audio clips. Then move the mouse pointer over the video clip to display the Video Controls. Resume the video playback.

7. Submit the revised document in the format specified by your instructor.

Make It Right

Analyze a presentation and correct all errors and/or improve the design.

Editing Clips, Finding and Replacing Text, and Correcting Spelling

Note: To complete this assignment, you will be required to use the Data Files for Students. See the inside back cover of this book for instructions on downloading the Data Files for Students, or contact your instructor for information about accessing the required files.

Instructions: Start PowerPoint. Open the presentation, Make It Right 3-1 Flamingos, from the Data Files for Students.

Correct the formatting problems and errors in the presentation while keeping in mind the guidelines presented in this chapter.

Perform the following tasks:

1. On Slide 1 (Figure 3–70), change the audio clip volume to the highest setting and hide the sound icon during the show. Loop this clip for the duration of the slide show.

2. On Slide 2, add the Reflection video effect located in the Reflection Variations area, Medium Reflection 4 pt offset (second reflection in second row) to the video.

3. Copy the flamingo clip from Slide 4 to Slide 3 and then delete Slide 4. Place this clip on the left side of the picture frame and then adjust the picture frame size so it is the appropriate dimension for the slide content.

Figure 3–70

4. Find the word, Antarctica, in the Slide 1 Notes pane, and then replace it with the words, South America. Then find the number, 14, and replace it with the number, 4.

5. Check the slides for spelling errors and then run the revised presentation.

6. Change the document properties, as specified by your instructor. Save the presentation using the file name, Make It Right 3-1 Chilean Flamingos.

7. Submit the revised document in the format specified by your instructor.

In the Lab

Design and/or create a presentation using the guidelines, concepts, and skills presented in this chapter. Labs 1, 2, and 3 are listed in order of increasing difficulty.

Lab 1: Inserting Audio Clips, Coloring a Picture, and Applying Artistic Effects to Pictures

Note: To complete this assignment, you will be required to use the Data Files for Students. See the inside back cover of this book for instructions on downloading the Data Files for Students, or contact your instructor for information about accessing the required files.

Problem: Start PowerPoint. Open the presentation, Lab 3-1 Cooking, from the Data Files for Students. Your college has an outstanding culinary program, and you are preparing a PowerPoint presentation to promote an upcoming seafood cooking class. The slides will feature audio clips and graphics with applied effects. Create the slides shown in Figure 3–71 on the next page.

Continued >

In the Lab *continued*

Instructions: Perform the following tasks.

1. On Slide 1, insert the Mr. Light music audio clip from the data files for students. Change the volume to the lowest setting, play across slides, and hide the sound icon during the show. Move the subtitle text placeholder downward to the location shown in Figure 3–71a and center both paragraphs.

2. On Slide 2, insert the picture called Blackboard and Chef, which is available on the Data Files for Students. Change the color of the picture to Accent Color 3 Dark (Recolor area). Add a border to this picture using Accent 5, and then change the border weight to 6 pt, as shown in Figure 3–71b.

3. On Slide 3, right-align all the text. Insert the Chef video clip from the data files for students and resize this clip so that it is approximately 4.08" × 3.99", as shown in Figure 3–71c. Insert the Pepper Grinder video clip and move it to the location shown in Figure 3–71c. Insert the audio clips, Pepper Grinder and Cartoon Crash, from the data files for students. Start these clips automatically, hide the sound icons during the show, and loop until stopped.

4. On Slide 4, apply the Watercolor Sponge filter to the lobster picture in the left content placeholder and the Plastic Wrap filter to the paella picture in the right content placeholder, as shown in Figure 3–71d.

5. On Slide 5, insert the Bottle Open audio clip from the data files for students. Move the sound icon to the lower-right corner of the slide. Start this clip on click. Center the text in the caption placeholder and then move this placeholder downward to the location shown in Figure 3–71e.

6. Review the slides in Slide Sorter view to check for consistency, and then change the view to Normal.

7. Drag the scroller to display Slide 1. Start Slide Show view and display each slide.

8. Change the document properties, as specified by your instructor. Save the presentation using the file name, Lab 3-1 Cooking Class.

9. Submit the revised document in the format specified by your instructor.

(a) Slide 1

(b) Slide 2

Figure 3–71

(c) Slide 3

(d) Slide 4

(e) Slide 5

Figure 3–71 (continued)

In the Lab

Lab 2: Adding Slide Numbers, Applying Artistic Effects to Pictures, and Recoloring a Video

Note: To complete this assignment, you will be required to use the Data Files for Students. See the inside back cover of this book for instructions on downloading the Data Files for Students, or contact your instructor for information about accessing the required files.

Problem: The Dutch tradition is continuing with Klompen dancers, who take their name from their traditional wooden clog shoes. You attended an annual festival this past spring and captured some video clips of teenagers dancing a traditional dance. In addition, you have some video of a hand-built windmill. In your speech class, you desire to inform your classmates of a few aspects of Dutch life, so you prepare the presentation shown in Figure 3–72 on the next page.

Instructions: Perform the following tasks.

1. Start PowerPoint. Open the presentation, Lab 3-2 Dancers, from the Data Files for Students. On Slide 1, apply the Mosaic Bubbles filter to the tulips picture, as shown in Figure 3–72a. Insert the

Continued >

In the Lab *continued*

audio clip, Spring Music, from the data files for students. Start this clip automatically, hide the sound icon during the show, and change the volume to the midpoint on the slider.

2. On Slide 2, apply the Marker filter to the wooden shoe picture, as shown in Figure 3–72b. Change the Start option for the video clip from On Click to Automatically. Apply the Rotated, Gradient video style (Moderate area) to the video clip, change the video border color to Accent 6, and then change the border width to 18 pt.

3. On Slide 2, type `Many dancers wear traditional, hand-sewn Dutch costumes. Dancers wear thick socks to make the wooden shoes comfortable during this annual event.` in the Notes pane.

4. On Slide 3, insert the video clip called Windmill from the Data Files for Students. Apply the Reflected Bevel, White video style (Intense area). Change the color of the video to Accent color 3 Dark (Recolor area). Start this clip automatically and loop until stopped. Center the text in the title placeholder, as shown in Figure 3–72c.

(a) Slide 1

(b) Slide 2

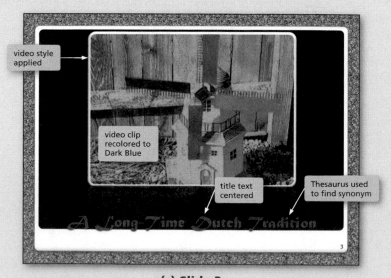

(c) Slide 3

Figure 3–72

5. Use the thesaurus to change the word, Custom, to Tradition. Check the slides for spelling errors.

6. Add the slide number to all slides except the title slide.

7. Review the slides in Slide Sorter view to check for consistency. Then click View > Presenter View in the menu bar to display the current slide and click the Next and Previous buttons to display each slide. Change the view to Normal.

8. Change the document properties, as specified by your instructor. Save the presentation using the file name, Lab 3-2 Klompen Dancers.

9. Submit the revised document in the format specified by your instructor.

In the Lab

Lab 3: Applying Artistic Effects to and Recoloring Pictures, and Inserting Audio

Note: To complete this assignment, you will be required to use the Data Files for Students. See the inside back cover of this book for instructions on downloading the Data Files for Students, or contact your instructor for information about accessing the required files.

Problem: Your Uncle Barney is an avid railroad buff, and he especially is interested in viewing steam locomotives. He has a collection of video clips and photographs of historic steam engines, and he asks you to create a presentation for the next Hessville Train Club meeting he is planning to attend. Start PowerPoint and then open the presentation, Lab 3-3 Locomotives, from the Data Files for Students. Prepare the slides shown in Figures 3–73a through 3–73c on the next page.

Instructions: Perform the following tasks.

1. Delete the subtitle text placeholder on Slide 1. Then insert the picture, Steamer 624, from the Data Files for Students and apply the Glow Diffused filter. Position the picture as shown in Figure 3–73a. Center the title text. Insert the audio clip, Train Whistle By, from the Data Files for Students. Start this clip automatically, hide the sound icon during the show, and loop until stopped.

2. On Slide 2, insert the picture, Locomotive, from the Data Files for Students and resize it so that it fills the entire slide height and width (approximately 7.5" × 10"). Recolor the picture to Accent Color 1 Light as shown in Figure 3–73b.

3. Insert the video clip, Steam Locomotive, from the Data Files for Students. Resize this clip to approximately 4.54" × 8.08" and move the clip to the location shown in Figure 3–73b. Apply the Metal Rounded Rectangle video style (Intense area). Change the color of the border to Accent 2. Start this clip automatically and loop until stopped.

4. On Slide 3, insert the picture, Railroad Track Border, and the video clip, Red Locomotive, from the Data Files for Students. Resize the Red Locomotive clip to approximately 1.5" × 2.89" and move it to the location shown in Figure 3–73c. Also, insert the audio clip, Steam Train Pass, from the Data Files for Students, and move this sound icon to the lower-left corner of the slide. Copy the audio clip, Train Whistle By, from Slide 1 and then move the sound icon to the upper-right corner of the slide. Start both audio clips automatically, hide the sound icons during the show, and loop until stopped.

5. Review the slides in Slide Sorter view. Then click View > Presenter View in the menu bar to display the current slide and click the Next and Previous buttons to display each slide. Change the view to Normal.

6. Change the document properties, as specified by your instructor. Save the presentation using the file name, Lab 3-3 Steam Locomotives.

7. Submit the revised document in the format specified by your instructor.

Continued >

In the Lab *continued*

(a) Slide 1

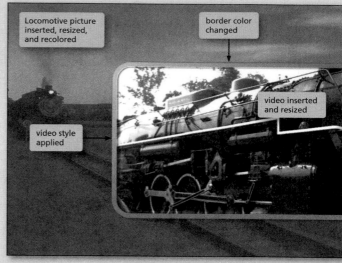

(b) Slide 2

(c) Slide 3

Figure 3–73

Cases and Places

Apply your creative thinking and problem-solving skills to design and implement a solution.

Note: To complete these assignments, you will be required to use the Data Files for Students. See the inside back cover of this book for instructions on downloading the Data Files for Students, or contact your instructor for information about accessing the required files.

As you design the presentations, remember to use the 7 × 7 rule: a maximum of seven words on a line and a maximum of seven lines on one slide.

1: Design and Create a Presentation about Kilauea Volcano

Academic

Most of the volcanic eruptions in Hawaii have occurred within Hawaii Volcanoes National Park. One of these volcanoes, Kilauea, has been erupting since 1983, and visitors to the National Park can drive on two roads to see lava tubes, steam vents, and plants returning to the barren landscape. Rainwater drains through cracks in the ground, is heated, and then is released through fissures and condenses in the cool air. Lava flows in underground tubes, and vents release volcanic gases that consist mainly of carbon dioxide, steam, and sulfur dioxide. During your recent trip to Hawaii Volcanoes National Park, you drove on these roads and captured these geological wonders with your video and digital cameras. You want to share your experience with your Geology 101 classmates. Create a presentation to show the pictures and video clips, which are located in the Data Files for Students and begin with the file name, Case 1. You also can use pictures from Office.com if they are appropriate for this topic. Apply appropriate styles and effects, and use at least three objectives found at the beginning of this chapter to develop the presentation. Be sure to check spelling.

2: Design and Create a Presentation about Surfing

Personal

During your summer vacation, you took surfing lessons and enjoyed the experience immensely. You now want to share your adventure with friends, so you decide to create a short PowerPoint presentation with video clips of the surf and of your paddling on your surfboard to the instruction area in the ocean. You also have pictures of your introductory lesson on shore and of your first successful run catching a wave. The Data Files for Students contains these media files that begin with the file name, Case 2. You also can use your own digital pictures or pictures from Office.com if they are appropriate for this topic. Use the clip, Case 2 - Yellow and Green Surfboard, on one slide. Use at least three objectives found at the beginning of this chapter to develop the presentation. Be sure to check spelling.

3: Design and Create a Presentation to Promote Your Snow Removal Business

Professional

Record snowfalls have wreaked havoc in your neighborhood, so you have decided to earn tuition money by starting a snow removal business. You are willing to clear sidewalks and driveways when snowfall exceeds three inches. To promote your business, you desire to create a PowerPoint presentation to run behind the counter at the local hardware store. The Data Files for Students contains pictures and a video clip that begin with the file name, Case 3. You also can use your own digital pictures or pictures from Office.com if they are appropriate for this topic. Use the clip, Case 3 – Man Shoveling, on one slide. Recolor at least one picture and apply a filter. Be sure to check spelling.

1 Creating a Worksheet and an Embedded Chart

Objectives

You will have mastered the material in this chapter when you can:

- Describe the Excel worksheet
- Enter text and numbers
- Use the Sum button to sum a range of cells
- Copy the contents of a cell to a range of cells using the fill handle
- Apply cell styles
- Format cells in a worksheet

- Create a Clustered Cylinder chart
- Change a worksheet name and worksheet tab color
- Change document properties
- Preview and print a worksheet
- Use the AutoCalculate area to display statistics
- Correct errors on a worksheet

1 Creating a Worksheet and an Embedded Chart

Introduction

Almost any organization collects vast amounts of data. Often, data is consolidated into a summary so that people in the organization better understand the meaning of the data. An Excel worksheet allows data easily to be summarized and charted. A chart conveys a visual representation of data. In this chapter, you will create a worksheet that includes a chart. The data in the worksheet and chart includes data for donations made to a not-for-profit organization that operates in several cities.

Project Planning Guidelines

The process of developing a worksheet that communicates specific information requires careful analysis and planning. As a starting point, establish why the worksheet is needed. Once the purpose is determined, analyze the intended users of the worksheet and their unique needs. Then, gather information about the topic and decide what to include in the worksheet. Finally, determine the worksheet design and style that will be most successful at delivering the message. Details of these guidelines are provided in Appendix A. In addition, each project developed in this book provides practical applications of these planning considerations.

Project — Worksheet with an Embedded Chart

The project in this chapter follows proper design guidelines and uses Excel to create the worksheet shown in Figure 1–1. The worksheet contains fundraising data for the Save Sable River Foundation. The Save Sable River Foundation raises funds to care for the environment and preserve the usability of a river that flows through six cities. The foundation raises funds by using five different fundraising activities. Through a concentrated marketing campaign and providing visible results to the communities, the Save Sable River Foundation quickly became a popular local institution. After several years of successful fundraising, senior management requested an easy-to-read worksheet that shows lifetime fundraising amounts for each fundraising technique by city. In addition, they asked for a chart showing lifetime fundraising amounts because the president of the foundation likes to have a graphical representation that allows him quickly to identify stronger and weaker fundraising activities by city.

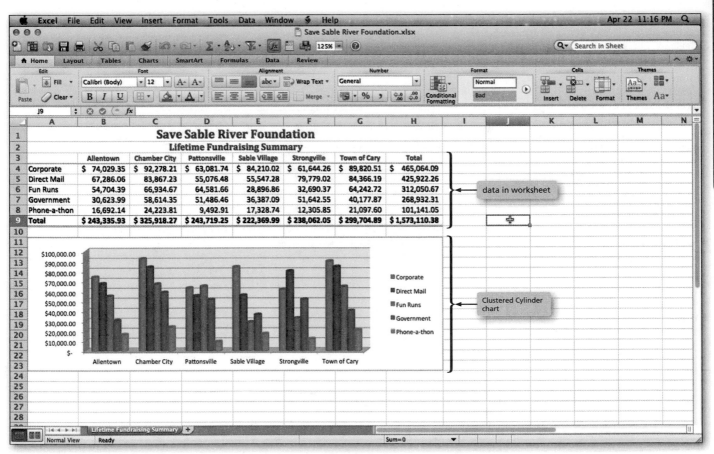

Figure 1–1

The first step in creating an effective worksheet is to make sure you understand what is required. The person or persons requesting the worksheet should supply their requirements in a requirements document. A **requirements document** includes a needs statement, a source of data, a summary of calculations, and any other special requirements for the worksheet, such as charting and Web support. Figure 1–2 on the next page shows the requirements document for the new workbook to be created in this chapter.

Excel 2011 Features

With its what-if analysis tools, research capabilities, collaboration tools, streamlined user interface, smart tags, charting features, Web capabilities, hundreds of functions, and enhanced formatting capabilities, Excel 2011 is one of the easier and more powerful spreadsheet programs available. Its dynamic analytical features make it possible to answer complicated what-if questions and its Web capabilities allow you to create, publish, view, share, and analyze data on an intranet or the World Wide Web.

Worksheet Development Cycle

BTW Spreadsheet specialists do not sit down and start entering text, formulas, and data into a blank Excel worksheet as soon as they have a spreadsheet assignment. Instead, they follow an organized plan, or methodology, that breaks the development cycle into a series of tasks. The recommended methodology for creating worksheets includes: (1) analyze requirements (supplied in a requirements document); (2) design solution; (3) validate design; (4) implement design; (5) test solution; and (6) document solution.

REQUEST FOR NEW WORKBOOK

Date Submitted:	March 22, 2013
Submitted By:	Kevin Li
Worksheet Title:	Save Sable River Foundation Lifetime Fundraising Summary
Needs:	An easy-to-read worksheet that shows a summary of the Save Sable River Foundation's lifetime fundraising efforts for each city in which we operate (Allentown, Chamber City, Pattonsville, Sable Village, Strongville, and the Town of Cary). The worksheet also should include total funds raised for each city, total funds raised for each fundraising activity, and total lifetime funds raised.
Source of Data:	The data for the worksheet is available from the chief financial officer (CFO) of the Save Sable River Foundation.
Calculations:	The following calculations must be made for the worksheet: (a) total lifetime funds raised for each of the six cities; (b) total lifetime funds raised for each of the five fundraising activities; and (c) total lifetime funds raised for the organization.
Chart Requirements:	Below the data in the worksheet, construct a Clustered Cylinder chart that compares the total funds raised for each city within each type of fundraising activity.

Approvals

Approval Status:	X	Approved
		Rejected
Approved By:	Marsha Davis	
Date:	March 29, 2013	
Assigned To:	J. Quasney, Spreadsheet Specialist	

requirements document

Figure 1–2

Overview

BTWs

BTW For a complete list of the BTWs found in the margins of this book, visit the Office 2011 for Mac Online Companion Web page at www.cengagebrain.com, navigate to the desired chapter, and click BTWs.

As you read this chapter, you will learn how to create the worksheet shown in Figure 1–1 on the previous page by performing these general tasks:

- Enter text in the worksheet
- Total data in the worksheet
- Format the text in the worksheet
- Insert a chart into the worksheet
- Identify the worksheet with a worksheet name
- Preview and print the worksheet

General Project Guidelines

Plan Ahead

While creating an Excel worksheet, you need to make several decisions that will determine the appearance and characteristics of the finished worksheet. As you create the worksheet shown in Figure 1–1 on page EX 3, you should follow these general guidelines:

1. **Select titles and subtitles for the worksheet.** Follow the *less is more* guideline. The less text in the titles and subtitles, the more impact the titles and subtitles will have. Use the fewest words possible to specify the information presented in the worksheet to the intended audience.

2. **Determine the contents for rows and columns.** Rows typically contain information that is analogous to items in a list, such as the fundraising techniques used by an organization. Columns typically contain descriptive information about items in rows or contain information that helps to group the data in the worksheet, such as the locations in which the organization operates. Row headings and column headings are usually placed in alphabetical sequence, unless an alternative order is recommended in the requirements document.

3. **Determine the calculations that are needed.** You can decide to total data in a variety of ways, such as across rows or in columns. You also can include a grand total.

4. **Determine where to save the workbook.** You can store a workbook permanently, or **save** it, on a variety of storage media including a hard disk, USB flash drive, CD, or DVD. You also can indicate a specific location on the storage media for saving the workbook.

5. **Identify how to format various elements of the worksheet.** The overall appearance of a worksheet significantly affects its ability to communicate clearly. Examples of how you can modify the appearance, or format, of text include changing its shape, size, color, and position on the worksheet.

6. **Decide on the type of chart needed.** Excel can create many different types of charts, such as cylinder charts and pie charts. Each type of chart relays a different message about the data in the worksheet. Choose a type of chart that relays the message that you want to convey.

7. **Establish where to position and how to format the chart.** The position and format of the chart should command the attention of the intended audience. If possible, position the chart so that it prints with the worksheet data on a single page.

8. **Choose a name for the worksheet.** Each worksheet in a workbook should be named to clarify its purpose. A good worksheet name is succinct, unique to the workbook, and meaningful to any user of the workbook.

9. **Determine the best method for distributing the workbook.** Workbooks and worksheets can be distributed on paper or electronically. The decision regarding how to distribute workbooks and worksheets greatly depends on your intended audience. For example, a worksheet may be printed for inclusion in a report, or a workbook may be distributed using e-mail if the recipient intends to update the workbook.

When necessary, more specific details concerning the above guidelines are presented at appropriate points in the chapter. The chapter also will identify the actions performed and decisions made regarding these guidelines during the creation of the worksheet shown in Figure 1–1.

Worksheet Development

The key to developing a **BTW** useful worksheet is careful planning. Careful planning can reduce your effort significantly and result in a worksheet that is accurate, easy to read, flexible, and useful. When analyzing a problem and designing a worksheet solution, you should follow these steps: (1) define the problem, including need, source of data, calculations, charting, and Web or special requirements; (2) design the worksheet; (3) enter the data and formulas; and (4) test the worksheet.

After carefully reviewing the requirements document (Figure 1–2) and making the necessary decisions, the next step is to design a solution or draw a sketch of the worksheet based on the requirements, including titles, column and row headings, the location of data values, and the Clustered Cylinder chart, as shown in Figure 1–3 on the next page. The dollar signs, 9s, and commas that you see in the sketch of the worksheet indicate formatted numeric values.

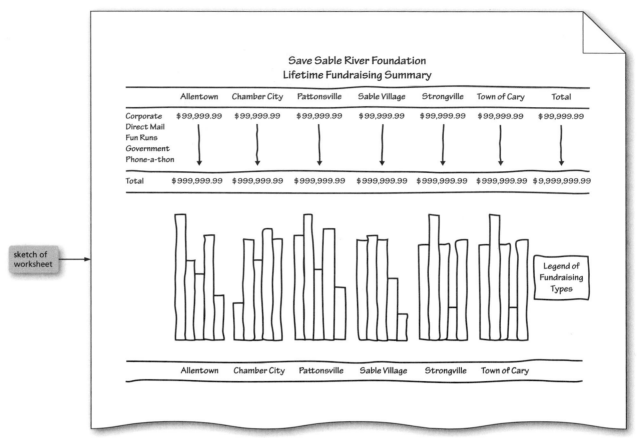

Figure 1–3

With a good understanding of the requirements document, an understanding of the necessary decisions, and a sketch of the worksheet, the next step is to use Excel to create the worksheet and chart.

To Start Excel

If you are using a computer to step through the project in this chapter and you want your screens to match the figures in this book, you should change your screen's resolution to 1280 × 800. For information about how to change a computer's resolution, refer to the Office 2011 and Mac OS X chapter at the beginning of this book.

The following steps, which assume Mac OS X is running, start Excel based on a typical installation. You may need to ask your instructor how to start Excel for your computer. For a detailed example of the procedure summarized below, refer to the Office 2011 and Mac OS X chapter.

1 Click the Excel icon in the Dock to display the Excel Workbook Gallery.

Q&A What is the Welcome to Excel screen I see?
The first time you start Excel, you may see the Welcome to Excel screen. Click Continue to move to the Excel Workbook Gallery.

For an introduction to Mac OS X and instruction about how to perform basic Mac OS X tasks, read the Office 2011 and Mac OS X chapter at the beginning of this book, where you can learn how to resize windows, change screen resolution, create folders, move and rename files, use Mac OS X Help, and much more.

Q&A   Why do I see a blank Excel Workbook rather than the Excel Workbook Gallery?

The default setting is to show the Excel Workbook Gallery. If you do not see it, your Excel application has a setting other than the default. You can skip to step 4.

2 If All is not selected in the Templates pane on the left, click to select it.

3 Double-click the Excel Workbook icon in the Excel Workbook Gallery to display a new blank workbook in the Excel window.

4 If the Excel window is not sized properly, as described in the Office 2011 and Mac OS X chapter, size the window properly.

5 If the Normal View button in the lower left of the workbook window is not selected (shown in Figure 1–4 on the next page), click it so that your screen is in Normal view.

Selecting a Cell

To enter data into a cell, you first must select it. The easiest way **to select a cell** (make it active) is to use the mouse to move the block plus sign mouse pointer to the cell and then click.

An alternative method is to use the arrow keys that are located in the bottom right of most Mac keyboards. An arrow key selects the cell adjacent to the active cell in the direction of the arrow on the key.

You know a cell is selected, or active, when a heavy border surrounds the cell and the active cell reference appears in the Name box on the left side of the formula bar. Excel also changes the active cell's column heading and row heading to a gray color with white labels.

Selecting a Cell

You can select any cell by **BTW** entering its cell reference, such as B4, in the Name box on the left side of the formula bar.

Entering Text

In Excel, any set of characters containing a letter, hyphen (as in a telephone number), or space is considered text. **Text** is used to place titles, such as worksheet titles, column titles, and row titles, on the worksheet.

Select titles and subtitles for the worksheet.   **Plan Ahead**

Worksheet titles and subtitles should be as brief and meaningful as possible. A worksheet title could include the name of the organization, department, or a description of the content of the worksheet. A worksheet subtitle, if included, could include a more detailed description of the content of the worksheet. Examples of worksheet titles are December 2012 Payroll and Year 2013 Projected Budget, and examples of subtitles are Marketing Department and Rent and Utilities, respectively.

Determine the contents of rows and columns.   **Plan Ahead**

As shown in Figure 1–4, data in a worksheet often is identified by row and column titles so that the user of a worksheet easily can identify the meaning of the data. Rows typically contain information that is similar to items in a list. Columns typically contain descriptive information about items in rows or contain information that helps to group the data in the worksheet. Examples of row titles are Product and Total, and examples of column titles are Name and Address.

The Ribbon and Screen Resolution

BTW Excel may change how the groups and buttons within the groups appear on the ribbon, depending on the computer's screen resolution. Thus, your ribbon may look different from the ones in this book if you are using a screen resolution other than 1280 × 800.

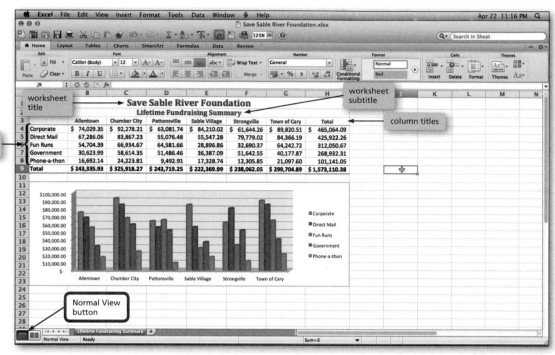

Figure 1–4

To Enter the Worksheet Titles

As shown in Figure 1–4, the worksheet title, Save Sable River Foundation, identifies the organization for which the worksheet is being created in Chapter 1. The worksheet subtitle, Lifetime Fundraising Summary, identifies the type of report.

The following steps enter the worksheet titles in cells A1 and A2. Later in this chapter, the worksheet titles will be formatted so they appear as shown in Figure 1–4.

1

• In the Standard toolbar, click the Zoom button arrow to display the pop-up menu (Figure 1–5).

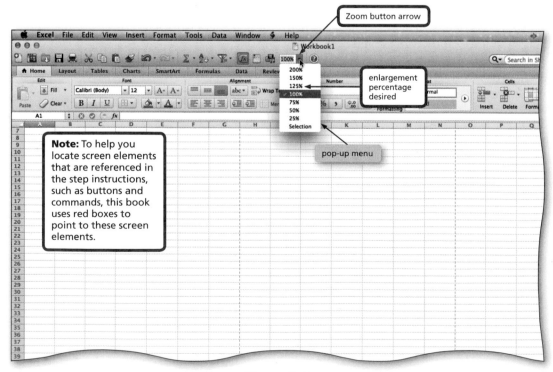

Figure 1–5

2

- Choose 125% from the pop-up menu to enlarge the display of the workbook.

- If necessary, click cell A1 to make cell A1 the active cell (Figure 1–6).

Q&A What if I make a mistake while typing?
If you type the wrong letter and notice the error before clicking the Enter button or pressing the RETURN key, use the DELETE key to delete all the characters back to and including the incorrect letter. To cancel the entire entry before entering it into the cell, click the Cancel button in the formula bar or press the ESC key. If you see an error in a cell after entering the text, select the cell and retype the entry.

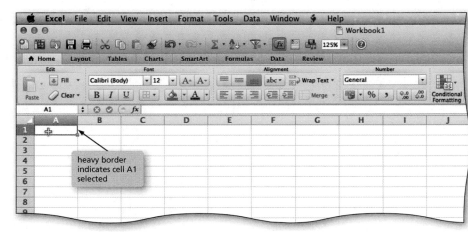

Figure 1–6

3

- Type **Save Sable River Foundation** in cell A1 and then point to the Enter button in the formula bar to prepare to enter text in the active cell (Figure 1–7).

Q&A Why did the appearance of the formula bar change?
Excel displays the title in the formula bar and in cell A1. When you begin typing a cell entry, two buttons in the formula bar turn from gray to colored: the Cancel button and the Enter button. Clicking the **Enter button** completes an entry. Clicking the **Cancel button** cancels an entry.

Q&A What is the vertical line in cell A1?
The text in cell A1 is followed by the insertion point. The **insertion point** is a blinking vertical line that indicates where the next typed character will appear.

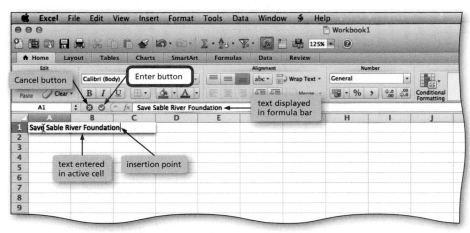

Figure 1–7

4

- Click the Enter button in the formula bar to complete the entry and enter a worksheet title (Figure 1–8).

Q&A Why does the entered text appear in three cells?
When the text is longer than the width of a column, Excel displays the overflow characters in adjacent cells to the right as long as those adjacent cells contain no data. If the adjacent cells contain data, Excel would hide the overflow characters. Excel displays the overflow characters in the formula bar whenever that cell is the active cell.

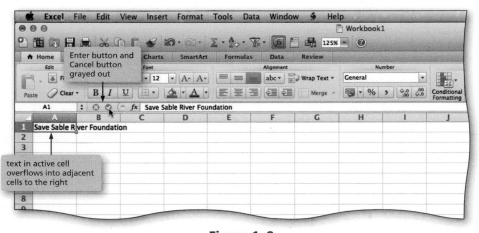

Figure 1–8

- Click cell A2 to select it.

- Type **Lifetime Fundraising Summary** as the cell entry.

- Click the Enter button to complete the entry and enter a worksheet subtitle (Figure 1–9).

Q&A   What happens when I click the Enter button?

When you complete an entry by clicking the Enter button, the insertion point disappears and the cell in which the text is entered remains the active cell.

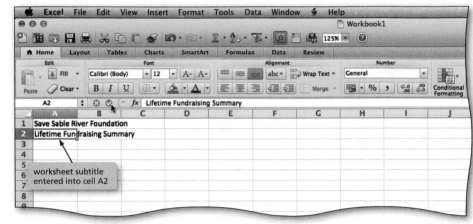

Figure 1–9

Other Ways

1. To complete entry, click any cell other than active cell

2. To complete entry, press RETURN

3. To complete entry, press UP ARROW, DOWN ARROW, LEFT ARROW, or RIGHT ARROW.

4. To complete entry, press HOME, PAGE UP, PAGE DOWN, or END (extended keyboards)

AutoCorrect

Q&As

BTW   For a complete list of the Q&As found in many of the step-by-step sequences in this book, visit the Office 2011 for Mac Online Companion Web page at www.cengagebrain.com, navigate to the desired chapter, and click Q&As.

The **AutoCorrect feature** of Excel works behind the scenes, correcting common mistakes when you complete a text entry in a cell. AutoCorrect makes three types of corrections for you:

1. Corrects two initial capital letters by changing the second letter to lowercase.

2. Capitalizes the first letter in the names of days.

3. Replaces commonly misspelled words with their correct spelling. For example, it will change the misspelled word *recieve* to *receive* when you complete the entry. AutoCorrect will correct the spelling of hundreds of commonly misspelled words automatically.

To Enter Column Titles

The column titles in row 3 (Allentown, Chamber City, Pattonsville, Sable Village, Strongville, Town of Cary, and Total) identify the numbers in each column. In the case of the Save the Sable River Foundation data, the cities identify the funds raised using each fundraising type. The cities, therefore, are placed in columns. To enter the column titles in row 3, select the appropriate cell and then enter the text. The following steps enter the column titles in row 3.

- Click cell B3 to make it the active cell.

- Type **Allentown** to begin entry of a column title in the active cell (Figure 1–10).

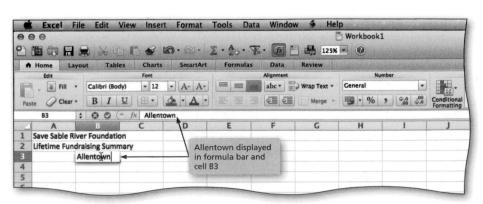

Figure 1–10

2

• Press the RIGHT ARROW key to enter the column title and make the cell to the right the active cell (Figure 1–11).

Q&A Why is the RIGHT ARROW key used to complete the entry in the cell?
If the next entry you want to enter is in an adjacent cell, use the arrow keys to complete the entry in a cell. When you press an arrow key to complete an entry, the adjacent cell in the direction of the arrow (up, down, left, or right) becomes the active cell. If the next entry is in a nonadjacent cell, complete the current entry by clicking the next cell in which you plan to enter data. You also can click the Enter button or press the RETURN key and then click the appropriate cell for the next entry.

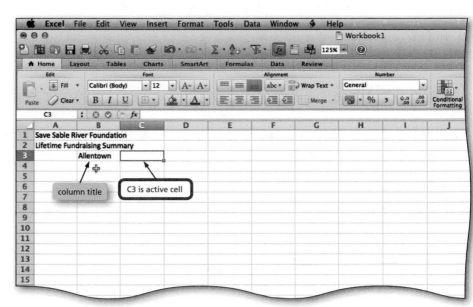

Figure 1–11

3

• Repeat Steps 1 and 2 to enter the remaining column titles; that is, enter **Chamber City** in cell C3, **Pattonsville** in cell D3, **Sable Village** in cell E3, **Strongville** in cell F3, **Town of Cary** in cell G3, and **Total** in cell H3 (complete the last entry in cell H3 by clicking the Enter button in the formula bar) (Figure 1–12).

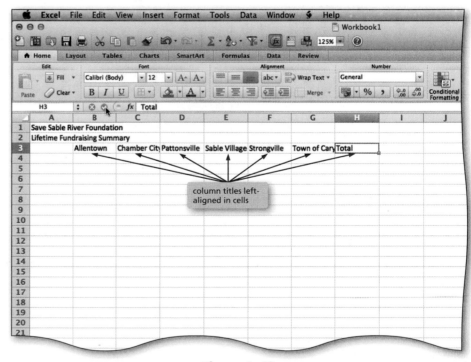

Figure 1–12

To Enter Row Titles

The next step in developing the worksheet for this project is to enter the row titles in column A. For the Save Sable River Foundation data, the list of fundraising activities meets the criterion that information that identifies columns be in a list. It is more likely that in the future, the organization will add more fundraising activities as opposed to more cities. Each fundraising activity, therefore, should be placed in its own row. The row titles in column A (Corporate, Direct Mail, Fun Runs, Government, Phone-a-thon, and Total) identify the numbers in each row.

This process for entering row titles is similar to the process for entering column titles. The following steps enter the row titles in the worksheet.

- Click cell A4 to select it.

- Type **Corporate** and then press the DOWN ARROW key to enter a row title and to make the cell below the current cell the active cell (Figure 1–13).

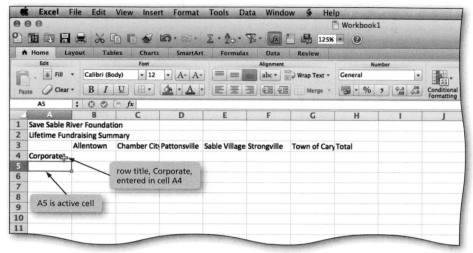

Figure 1–13

- Enter the remaining row titles in column A; **Direct Mail** in cell A5, **Fun Runs** in cell A6, **Government** in cell A7, **Phone-a-thon** in cell A8, **Total** in cell A9, and press the RETURN key (Figure 1–14).

Q&A Why is the text left-aligned in the cells?

When you enter text, Excel automatically left-aligns the text in the cell. Excel treats any combination of numbers, spaces, and nonnumeric characters as text. For example, Excel recognizes the following entries as text:

401AX21, 921–231, 619 321, 883XTY

You can change the text alignment in a cell by realigning it. Other alignment techniques are discussed later in this chapter.

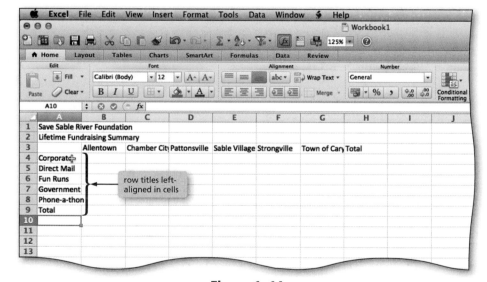

Figure 1–14

Numeric Limitations

BTW In Excel, a number can be between approximately -1×10^{308} and 1×10^{308}. This means it can be between a negative 1 followed by 308 zeros and a positive 1 followed by 308 zeros. To enter a number such as 6,000,000,000,000,000, you can type 6,000,000,000,000,000, or you can type 6E15, which translates to 6×10^{15}.

Entering Numbers

In Excel, you can enter numbers into cells to represent amounts. A **number** can contain only the following characters:

0 1 2 3 4 5 6 7 8 9 + - ( ) , / . $ % E e

If a cell entry contains any other keyboard character (including spaces), Excel interprets the entry as text and treats it accordingly. The use of the special characters is explained when they are used in this book.

To Enter Numbers

The Save Sable River Foundation Lifetime Fundraising Summary numbers used in this chapter are summarized in Table 1–1. These numbers, which represent lifetime fundraising amounts for each of the fundraising activities and cities, must be entered in rows 4, 5, 6, 7, and 8.

Table 1–1 Save Sable River Foundation Lifetime Fundraising Summary						
	Allentown	Chamber City	Pattonsville	Sable Village	Strongville	Town of Cary
Corporate	74029.35	92278.21	63081.74	84210.02	61644.26	89820.51
Direct Mail	67286.06	83867.23	55076.48	55547.28	79779.02	84366.19
Fun Runs	54704.39	66934.67	64581.66	28896.86	32690.37	64242.72
Government	30623.99	58614.35	51486.46	36387.09	51642.55	40177.87
Phone-a-thon	16692.14	24223.81	9492.91	17328.74	12305.85	21097.60

The following steps enter the numbers in Table 1–1 one row at a time.

- Click cell B4 to select it.

- Type `74029.35` and then press the RIGHT ARROW key to enter the data in the selected cell and make the cell to the right the active cell (Figure 1–15).

Q&A Do I need to enter dollar signs, commas, or trailing zeros for the fundraising summary amounts? You are not required to type dollar signs, commas, or trailing zeros. When you enter a dollar value that has cents, however, you must add the decimal point and the numbers representing the cents. Later in this chapter, the numbers will be formatted to use dollar signs, commas, and trailing zeros to improve the appearance and readability of the numbers.

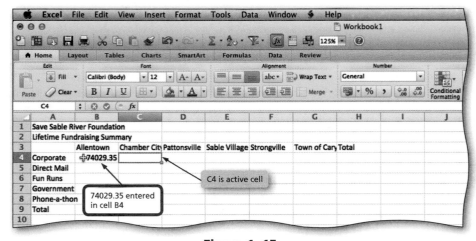

Figure 1–15

- Enter `92278.21` in cell C4, `63081.74` in cell D4, `84210.02` in cell E4, `61644.26` in cell F4, and `89820.51` in cell G4 to complete the first row of numbers in the worksheet (Figure 1–16).

Q&A Why are the numbers right-aligned? When you enter numeric data in a cell, Excel recognizes the values as numbers and right-aligns the values in order to properly vertically align decimal and integer values. For example, values entered below those entered in this step automatically will be right-aligned as well so that the decimals of the values properly align.

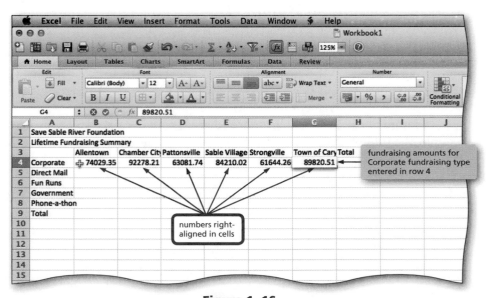

Figure 1–16

3

- Click cell B5 to select it and complete the entry in the previously selected cell.

- Enter the remaining lifetime fundraising summary numbers provided in Table 1–1 on the previous page for each of the four remaining fundraising activities in rows 5, 6, 7, and 8 to finish entering numbers in the worksheet (Figure 1–17).

Q&A   Why did clicking cell B5 complete the entry in cell G4?
Selecting another cell completes the entry in the previously selected cell in the same way as pressing the RETURN key, pressing an arrow key, or clicking the Enter button in the formula bar. In the next set of steps, the entry of the number in cell G4 will be completed by selecting another cell.

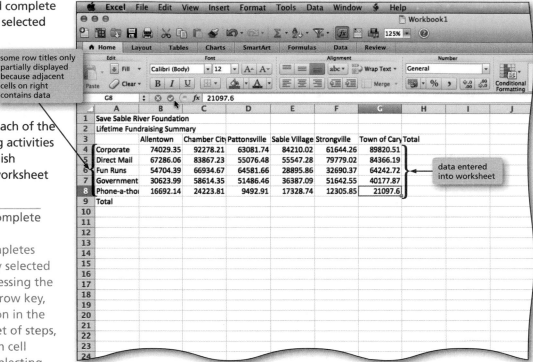

Figure 1–17

Calculating Sums

BTW Excel calculates sums for a variety of data types. For example, Boolean values, such as TRUE and FALSE, can be summed. Excel treats the value of TRUE as 1 and the value of FALSE as 0. Times also can be summed. For example, Excel treats the sum of 1:15 and 2:45 as 4:00.

Calculating a Sum

The next step in creating the worksheet is to perform any necessary calculations, such as calculating the column and row totals.

To Sum a Column of Numbers

As stated in the requirements document in Figure 1–2 on page EX 4, totals are required for each city, each fundraising activity, and the organization. The first calculation is to determine the fundraising total for the fundraising activities in the city of Allentown in column B. To calculate this value in cell B9, Excel must add, or sum, the numbers in cells B4, B5, B6, B7, and B8. Excel's **SUM function** which adds all of the numbers in a range of cells, provides a convenient means to accomplish this task.

A **range** is a series of two or more adjacent cells in a column or row or a rectangular group of cells. For example, the group of adjacent cells B4, B5, B6, B7, and B8 is called a range. Many Excel operations, such as summing numbers, take place on a range of cells.

After the total lifetime fundraising amount for the fundraising activities in the city of Allentown in column B is determined, the totals for the remaining cities and totals for each fundraising activity will be determined. The following steps sum the numbers in column B.

1

- Click cell B9 to make it the active cell and complete the entry in the previously selected cell.

- Click the AutoSum button in the Standard toolbar to display a formula in the formula bar and in the active cell (Figure 1–18).

Q&A How does Excel know which cells to sum?

When you enter the SUM function using the AutoSum button, Excel automatically selects what it considers to be your choice of the range to sum. When proposing the range to sum, Excel first looks for a range of cells with numbers above the active cell and then to the left. If Excel proposes the wrong range, you can correct it by dragging through the correct range before pressing the RETURN key. You also can enter the correct range by typing the beginning cell reference, a colon (:), and the ending cell reference.

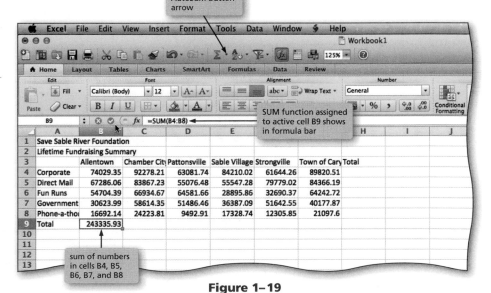

Figure 1–18

2

- Click the Enter button in the formula bar to enter a sum in the active cell (Figure 1–19).

Q&A What is the purpose of the AutoSum button arrow?

If you click the arrow on the right side of the AutoSum button in the Standard toolbar (Figure 1–19), Excel displays a list of often-used functions from which you can choose. The list includes functions that allow you to determine the average, the number of items in the selected range, the maximum value, or the minimum value of a range of numbers.

Figure 1–19

Other Ways

1. Type = S in cell, select SUM from list, select range

Using the Fill Handle to Copy a Cell to Adjacent Cells

Excel also must calculate the totals for Chamber City in cell C9, Pattonsville in cell D9, Sable Village in cell E9, Strongville in cell F9, and the Town of Cary in cell G9. Table 1–2 on the next page illustrates the similarities between the entry in cell B9 and the entries required to sum the totals in cells C9, D9, E9, F9 and G9.

Entering Numbers as Text

 BTW Sometimes, you will want Excel to treat numbers, such as postal codes and telephone numbers, as text. To enter a number as text, start the entry with an apostrophe (').

Table 1–2 Sum Function Entries in Row 9		
Cell	**Sum Function Entries**	**Remark**
B9	=SUM(B4:B8)	Sums cells B4, B5, B6, B7, and B8
C9	=SUM(C4:C8)	Sums cells C4, C5, C6, C7, and C8
D9	=SUM(D4:D8)	Sums cells D4, D5, D6, D7, and D8
E9	=SUM(E4:E8)	Sums cells E4, E5, E6, E7, and E8
F9	=SUM(F4:F8)	Sums cells F4, F5, F6, F7, and F8
G9	=SUM(G4:G8)	Sums cells G4, G5, G6, G7, and G8

To place the SUM functions in cells C9, D9, E9, F9, and G9, you could follow the same steps shown on the previous page in Figures 1–18 and 1–19. A second, more efficient method, however, is to copy the SUM function from cell B9 to the range C9:G9. The cell being copied is called the **source area** or **copy area**. The range of cells receiving the copy is called the **destination area** or **paste area**.

Although the SUM function entries in Table 1–2 are similar, they are not exact copies. The range in each SUM function entry uses cell references that are one column to the right of the previous column. When you copy formulas that include cell references, Excel automatically adjusts them for each new position, resulting in the SUM function entries illustrated in Table 1–2. Each adjusted cell reference is called a **relative reference**.

To Copy a Cell to Adjacent Cells in a Row

The easiest way to copy the SUM formula from cell B9 to cells C9, D9, E9, F9, and G9 is to use the fill handle. The **fill handle** is the small blue square located in the lower-right corner of the heavy border around the active cell. The following steps use the fill handle to copy cell B9 to the adjacent cells C9:G9.

1

- With cell B9 active, point to the fill handle to activate it (Figure 1–20).

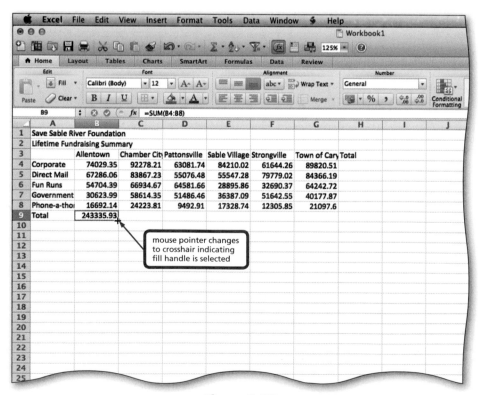

Figure 1–20

2

- Drag the fill handle to select the destination area, range C9:G9, to display a shaded border around the source area and the destination area (Figure 1–21). Do not release the mouse button.

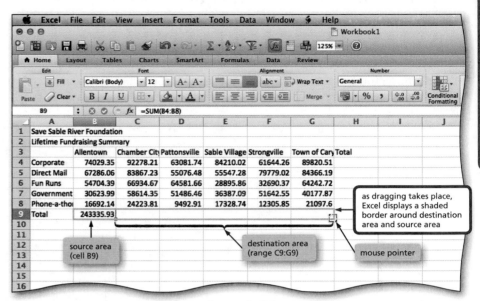

Figure 1–21

3

- Release the mouse button to copy the SUM function from the active cell to the destination area and calculate the sums (Figure 1–22).

Q&A What is the purpose of the AutoFill Options button?

When you copy one range to another, Excel displays an AutoFill Options button (Figure 1–22). The AutoFill Options button allows you to choose whether you want to copy the values from the source area to the destination area with formatting, do so without formatting, or copy only the format. To view the available fill options, click the AutoFill Options button. The AutoFill Options button disappears when you begin another activity in Excel, such as typing data in another cell or applying formatting to a cell or range of cells.

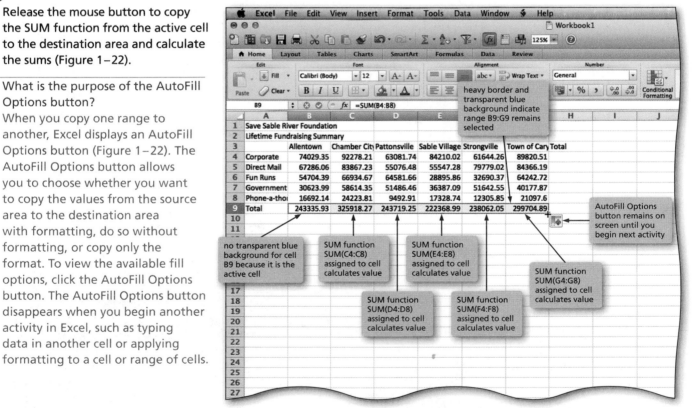

Figure 1–22

Other Ways

1. Select source area, click Copy button in Standard toolbar, select destination area, click Paste button in Standard toolbar

2. CONTROL-click source area, choose Copy in shortcut menu, CONTROL-click destination area, choose Paste in shortcut menu

To Determine Multiple Totals at the Same Time

The next step in building the worksheet is to determine the lifetime fundraising totals for each fundraising activity and total lifetime fundraising for the organization in column H. To calculate these totals, you can use the SUM function much as it was used to total the lifetime fundraising amounts by city in row 9. In this example, however, Excel will determine totals for all of the rows at the same time. The following steps sum multiple totals at once.

- Click cell H4 to make it the active cell (Figure 1–23).

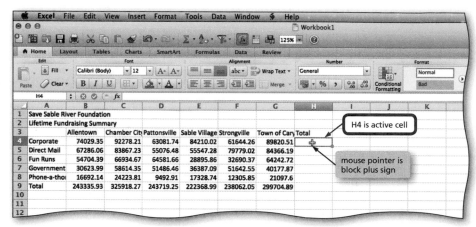

Figure 1–23

- With the mouse pointer in cell H4 and in the shape of a block plus sign, drag the mouse pointer down to cell H9 to highlight the range with a transparent view (Figure 1–24).

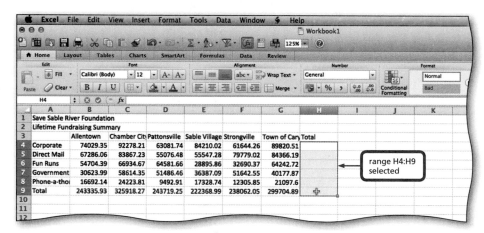

Figure 1–24

- Click the AutoSum button in the Standard toolbar to calculate and display the sums of the corresponding rows (Figure 1–25).

- Select cell A10 to deselect the selected range.

Q&A   How does Excel create unique totals for each row?

If each cell in a selected range is next to a row of numbers, Excel assigns the SUM function to each cell when you click the AutoSum button.

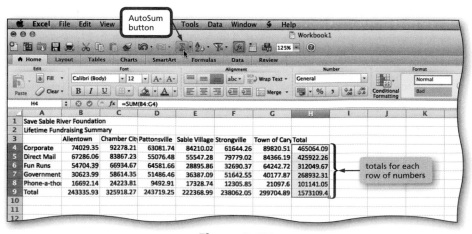

Figure 1–25

To Save a Workbook

You have performed many tasks while creating this workbook and do not want to risk losing work completed thus far. Accordingly, you should save the workbook.

The following steps assume you already have created folders for storing your files, for example, a CIS 101 folder (for your class) that contains an Excel folder (for your assignments). Thus, these steps save the workbook in the Excel folder in the CIS 101 folder on a USB flash drive using the file name, Save Sable River Foundation. For a detailed example of the procedure summarized below, refer to the Office 2011 and Mac OS X chapter at the beginning of this book.

1 With a USB flash drive connected to one of the computer's USB ports, click the Save button in the Standard toolbar to display a dialog.

2 Type **Save Sable River Foundation** in the Save As text box to change the file name. Do not press the RETURN key after typing the file name because you do not want to close the dialog at this time.

3 Use the disclosure button to the right of the Save As text box to navigate to the desired save location (in this case, the Excel folder in the CIS 101 folder [or your class folder] on the USB flash drive).

4 Click the Save button in the dialog to save the document in the selected folder on the selected drive with the entered file name.

Organizing Files and Folders

BTW

You should organize and store files in folders so that you easily can find the files later. For example, if you are taking an introductory computer class called CIS 101, a good practice would be to save all Excel files in an Excel folder in a CIS 101 folder. For a discussion of folders and detailed examples of creating folders, refer to the Office 2011 and Mac OS X chapter at the beginning of this book.

Break Point: If you wish to take a break, this is a good place to do so. You can quit Excel. To resume at a later time, start Excel, open the file called Save Sable River Foundation, and continue following the steps from this location forward.

Formatting the Worksheet

The text, numeric entries, and functions for the worksheet now are complete. The next step is to format the worksheet. You **format** a worksheet to emphasize certain entries and make the worksheet easier to read and understand.

Figure 1–26a shows the worksheet before formatting. Figure 1–26b on the next page shows the worksheet after formatting. As you can see from the two figures, a worksheet that is formatted not only is easier to read but also looks more professional.

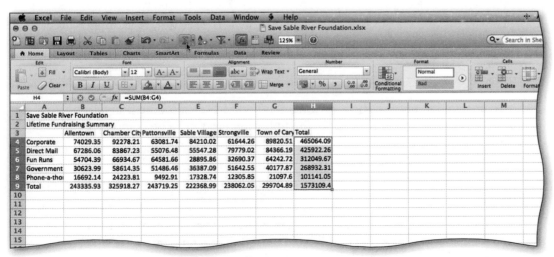

(a) Before Formatting

Figure 1–26

Continued >

(b) After Formatting

Figure 1–26

Plan Ahead

Identify how to format various elements of the worksheet.

By formatting the contents of the worksheet, you can improve its overall appearance. When formatting a worksheet, consider the following formatting suggestions:

- **Increase the font size of cells.** An increased font size gives more impact to the text in a cell. In order to indicate their relative importance, worksheet titles should have the largest font size, followed by worksheet subtitles, and then column and row headings.

- **Change the font color of cells.** Different cell colors help the reader of a worksheet quickly differentiate between the sections of a worksheet. Worksheet titles and subtitles easily should be identifiable from column and row headings. The overuse of too many colors, however, may be distracting to the reader of a worksheet.

- **Center the worksheet titles, subtitles, and column headings.** Centering text in worksheet titles and subtitles over the portion of the worksheet that they represent helps the reader of a worksheet quickly to identify the information that is of interest to them.

- **Modify column widths to best fit text in cells.** Make certain that text in a cell does not overflow into another cell. A column's width should be adjusted to accommodate the largest amount of text used in a cell in the column. Columns that contain data that is similar in nature to other columns should share the same column width.

- **Change the font style of cells.** Use a bold font style to make worksheet titles, worksheet subtitles, column headings, row heading, and totals stand out. Use italics and underline font styles judiciously, as specific rules of grammar apply to their use.

Fonts and Themes

BTW Excel uses default recommended fonts based on the workbook's theme. A theme is a collection of fonts and color schemes. The default theme is named Office, and the two default fonts for the Office theme are Cambria and Calibri. Excel, however, allows you to apply any font to a cell or range as long as the font is installed on your computer.

To change the unformatted worksheet in Figure 1–26a on the previous page to the formatted worksheet in Figure 1–26b, the following tasks must be completed:

1. Change the font, change the font style to bold, increase the font size, and change the font color of the worksheet titles in cells A1 and A2.

2. Center the worksheet titles in cells A1 and A2 across columns A through H.

3. Format the body of the worksheet. The body of the worksheet, range A3:H9, includes the column titles, row titles, and numbers. Formatting the body of the worksheet changes the numbers to use a dollars-and-cents format, with dollar signs in the first row (row 4) and the total row (row 9); adds underlining that emphasizes portions of the worksheet; and modifies the column widths to fit the text in the columns and make the text and numbers readable.

The remainder of this section explains the process required to format the worksheet. Although the formatting procedures are explained in the order described above, you should be aware that you could make these format changes in any order. Modifying the column widths, however, usually is done last because other formatting changes may affect the size of data in the cells in the column.

Font, Style, Size, and Color

The characters that Excel displays on the screen are a specific font, style, size, and color. The **font**, or font face, defines the appearance and shape of the letters, numbers, and special characters. Examples of fonts include Calibri, Cambria, Times New Roman, Arial, and Courier. **Font style** indicates how the characters are emphasized. Common font styles include regular, bold, underline, and italic. The **font size** specifies the size of the characters on the screen. Font size is gauged by a measurement system called points. A single point is about 1/72 of one inch in height. Thus, a character with a **point size** of 10 is about 10/72 of one inch in height. The **font color** defines the color of the characters. Excel can display characters in a wide variety of colors, including black, red, orange, and blue.

When Excel begins, the preset font for the entire workbook is Calibri, with a font size, font style, and font color of 12-point regular black. Excel allows you to change the font characteristics in a single cell, a range of cells, the entire worksheet, or the entire workbook.

Fonts

In general, use no more **BTW** than two font types in a worksheet because the use of more fonts can make a worksheet difficult to read.

To Change a Cell Style

Excel includes the capability of changing several characteristics of a cell, such the font, font size, and font color, all at once by assigning a predefined cell style to a cell. Using the predefined styles that Excel includes provides a consistent appearance to common portions of your worksheets, such as worksheet titles, worksheet subtitles, column headings, and total rows. The following steps assign the Title cell style to the worksheet title in cell A1.

1
- Click cell A1 to make cell A1 the active cell.

- On the Home tab, under Format, point to Normal to display the More button, then click the More button to display the Cell Styles gallery (Figure 1–27).

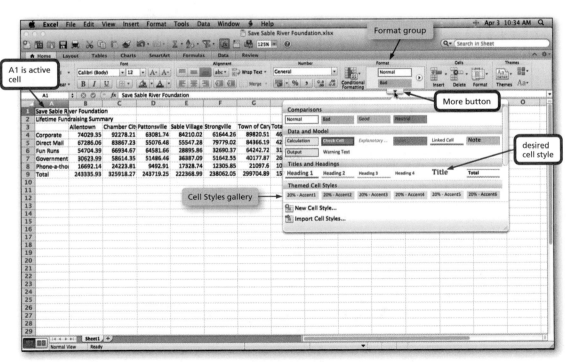

Figure 1–27

2

- Click the Title cell style to apply the cell style to the active cell (Figure 1–28).

Q&A Why do several items in the Font group on the ribbon change?

The changes to the Font box, Bold button, and Font Size box indicate the font changes applied to the active cell, cell A1, as a result of applying the Title cell style.

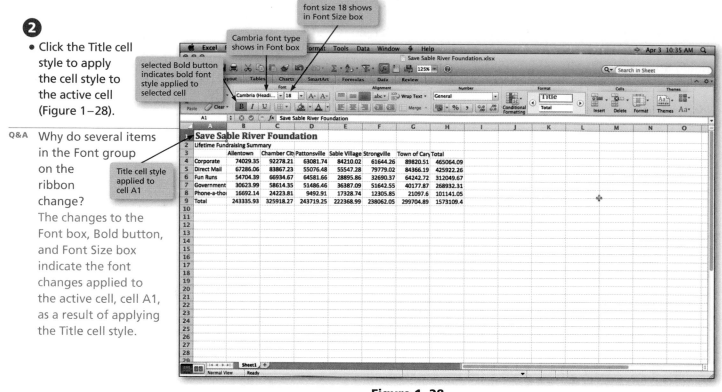

Figure 1–28

To Change the Font

Different fonts often are used in a worksheet to make it more appealing to the reader and to relate or distinguish data in the worksheet. The following steps change the worksheet subtitle's fonts from Calibri to Cambria.

1

- Click cell A2 to make it the active cell.

- On the Home tab, under Font, click the Font button arrow to display the Font gallery (Figure 1–29).

Q&A Which fonts are displayed in the Font gallery?

Because many programs supply additional fonts beyond what comes with the Mac OS X operating system, the number of fonts available on your computer will depend on the programs installed. This book uses only fonts that come with the Mac OS X Lion operating system and Microsoft Office 2011 for Mac.

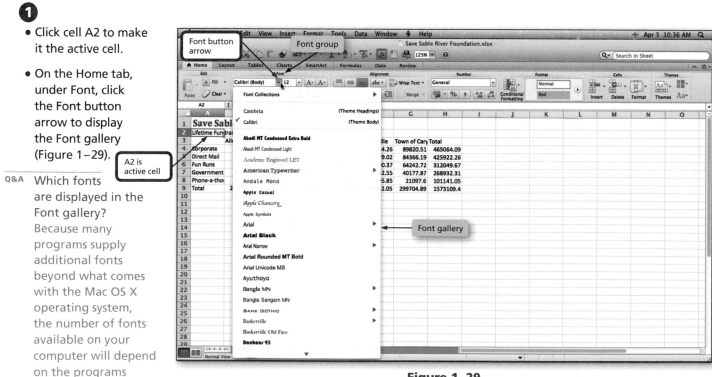

Figure 1–29

2

- Click Cambria to change the font of the worksheet subtitle to Cambria (Figure 1–30).

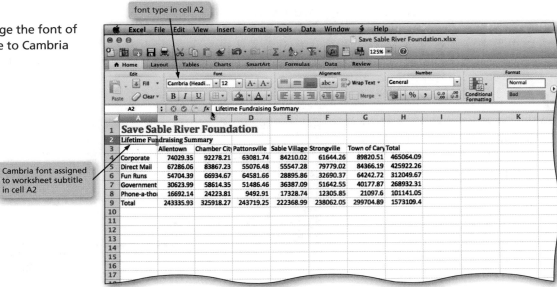

font type in cell A2

Cambria font assigned to worksheet subtitle in cell A2

Figure 1–30

Other Ways

1. CONTROL-click cell, choose Format Cells in shortcut menu, click Font tab (Format Cells dialog), click desired font, click OK button

2. Choose Format > Cells in menu bar, click Font tab (Format Cells dialog), select desired font in Font list, click OK button

To Bold a Cell

You **bold** an entry in a cell to emphasize it or make it stand out from the rest of the worksheet. The following step bolds the worksheet subtitle in cell A2.

1

- With cell A2 active, on the Home tab, under Font, click the Bold button to change the font style of the active cell to bold (Figure 1–31).

Q&A What if a cell already includes a bold style?
If the active cell is already bold, then Excel displays the Bold button with a darker gray background.

Q&A How do I remove the bold style from a cell?
Clicking the Bold button a second time removes the bold font style.

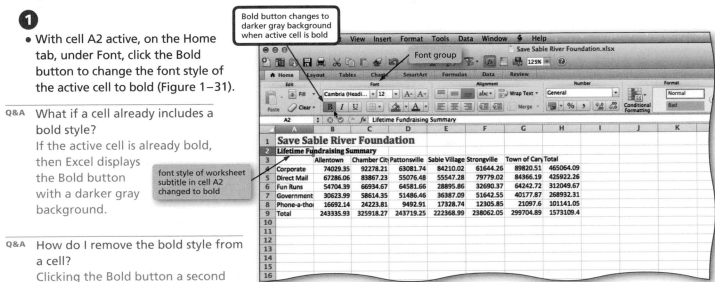

Bold button changes to darker gray background when active cell is bold

Font group

font style of worksheet subtitle in cell A2 changed to bold

Figure 1–31

Other Ways

1. CONTROL-click cell, choose Format Cells in shortcut menu, click Font tab (Format Cells dialog), click Bold, click OK button

2. Press COMMAND-B

To Increase the Font Size of a Cell Entry

Increasing the font size is the next step in formatting the worksheet subtitle. You increase the font size of a cell so that the entry stands out and is easier to read. The following steps increase the font size of the worksheet subtitle in cell A2.

- With cell A2 selected, on the Home tab, under Font, click the Font Size button arrow to display the Font Size list (Figure 1–32).

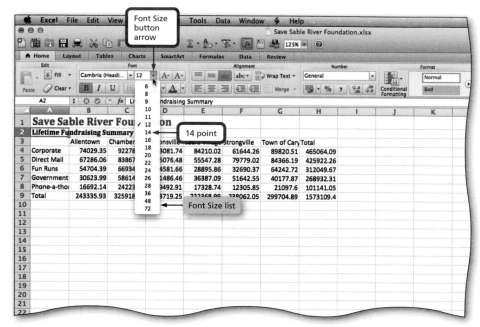

Figure 1–32

- Click 14 in the Font Size list to change the font size in the active cell (Figure 1–33).

Q&A   Can I assign a font size that is not in the Font Size list?
Yes. An alternative to clicking a font size in the Font Size list is to select the value in the Font Size box, type the desired font size, and then press the RETURN key. This procedure allows you to assign a font size not available in the Font Size list to a selected cell entry.

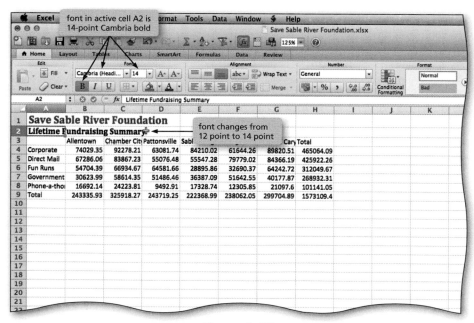

Figure 1–33

Other Ways

1. On Home tab, under Font, click Increase Font Size button or Decrease Font Size button

2. CONTROL-click cell, choose Format Cells on shortcut menu, click Font tab (Format Cells dialog), select font size in Size box, click OK button

To Change the Font Color of a Cell Entry

The next step is to change the color of the font in cell A2 from black to dark blue. The following steps change the font color of a cell entry.

- With cell A2 selected, on the Home tab, under Font, click the Font Color button arrow to display the Font Color pop-up menu (Figure 1–34).

Q&A Which colors does Excel make available on the Font Color pop-up menu?

You can choose from more than 60 different font colors on the Font Color gallery (Figure 1–34). Your Font Color pop-up menu may have more or fewer colors, depending on color settings of your operating system.

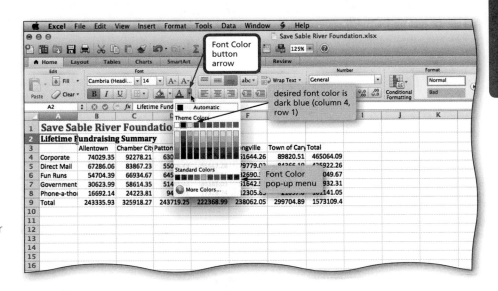

Figure 1–34

- Click Text 2 (column 4, row 1) in the Font Color menu to change the font of the worksheet subtitle in the active cell (Figure 1–35).

Q&A Why does the Font Color button change after I select the new font color?

When you choose a color in the Font Color pop-up menu, Excel changes the Font Color button (on the Home tab under Font) to the chosen color. Thus, to change the font color of the cell entry in another cell to the same color, you need only to select the cell and then click the Font Color button.

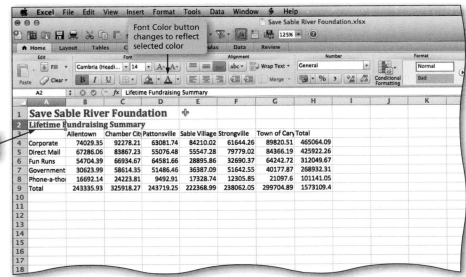

Figure 1–35

Other Ways

1. CONTROL-click cell, choose Format Cells in shortcut menu, click Font tab (Format Cells dialog), select color in Color pop-up, click OK button

To Center Cell Entries Across Columns by Merging Cells

The final step in formatting the worksheet title and subtitle is to center them across columns A through H. Centering a title across the columns used in the body of the worksheet improves the worksheet's appearance. To do this, the eight cells in the range A1:H1 are combined, or merged, into a single cell that is the width of the columns in the body of the worksheet. The eight cells in the range A2:H2 are merged in a similar manner. **Merging cells** involves creating a single cell by combining two or more selected cells. The following steps center the worksheet title and subtitle across columns by merging cells.

- Select cell A1 and then drag to cell H1 to highlight the range to be merged and centered (Figure 1–36).

Q&A What if a cell in the range B1:H1 contains data?
For the Merge button (in the Alignment group on the Home tab) to work properly, all the cells except the leftmost cell in the selected range must be empty.

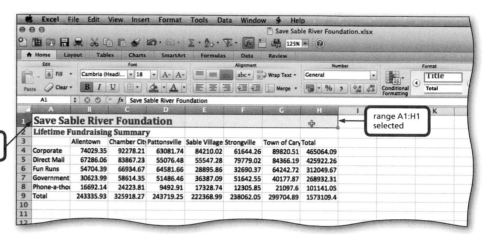

Figure 1–36

- On the Home tab, under Alignment, click the Merge button arrow to display the Merge menu (Figure 1–37).

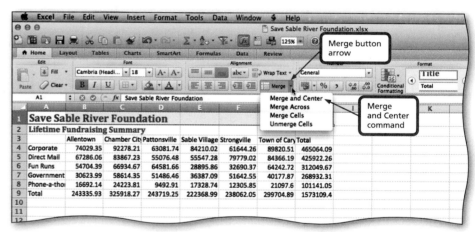

Figure 1–37

- Click Merge and Center to merge cells A1 through H1 and center the contents of the leftmost cell across the selected columns (Figure 1–38).

Q&A What happened to cells B1 through H1?
After the merge, cells B1 through H1 no longer exist. The new cell A1 now extends across columns A through H.

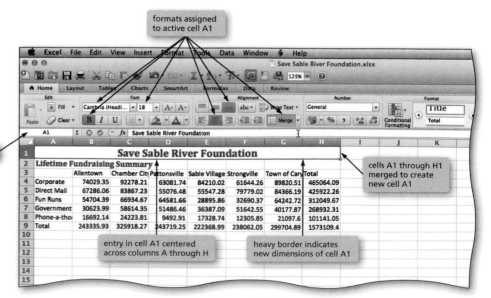

Figure 1–38

4

- Repeat Steps 1 through 3 to merge and center the worksheet subtitle across cells A2 through H2 (Figure 1–39).

Q&A Are cells B1 through H1 and B2 through H2 lost forever?

No. The opposite of merging cells is **splitting a merged cell**. After you have merged multiple cells to create one merged cell, you can unmerge, or split, the merged cell to display the original cells on the worksheet. You split a merged cell by selecting it, clicking the Merge button arrow, and clicking Unmerge Cells. For example, if you click the Merge button arrow a second time in Step 2 and then choose Unmerge Cells, that will split the merged cell A1 into cells A1, B1, C1, D1, E1, F1, G1, and H1. You can also simply click the Merge button to split the merged cells. This is the default action of the button after cells are merged.

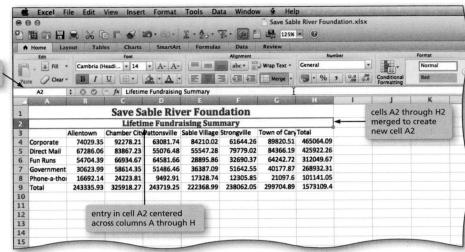

Figure 1–39

To Format Column Titles and the Total Row

The next step to format the worksheet is to format the column titles in row 3 and the total values in row 9. Column titles and the total row should be formatted so anyone who views the worksheet quickly can distinguish the column titles and total row from the data in the body of the worksheet. The following steps format the column titles and total row using cell styles in the default worksheet theme.

1

- Click cell A3 and then drag the mouse pointer to cell H3 to select the range (Figure 1–40).

Q&A Why is cell A3 selected in the range for the column headings?

The style to be applied to the column headings includes an underline that will help to distinguish the column headings from the rest of the worksheet. Including cell A3 in the range ensures that the cell will include the underline, which is visually appealing and further helps to separate the data in the worksheet.

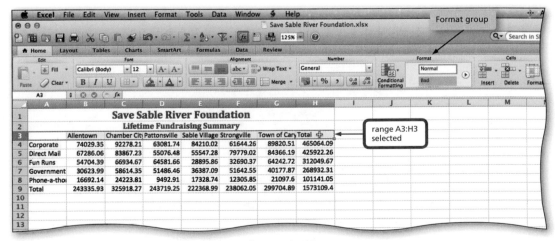

Figure 1–40

- On the Home tab, under Format, click the More button to display the Cell Styles gallery (Figure 1–41).

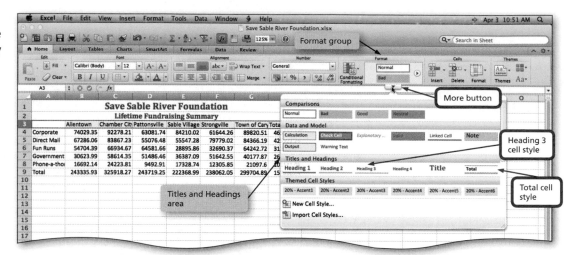

Figure 1–41

- Click the Heading 3 cell style to apply the cell style to the selected range.

- On the Home tab, under Alignment, click the Center Text button to center the column headings in the selected range.

- Click cell A9 and then drag the mouse pointer to cell H9 to select the range (Figure 1–42).

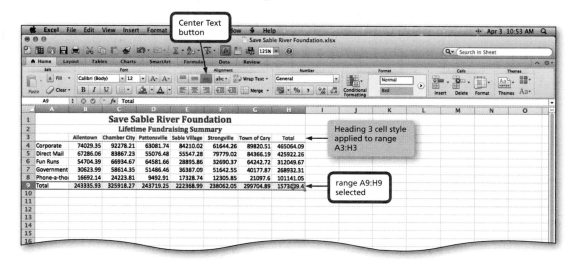

Figure 1–42

Q&A Why should I choose Heading 3 instead of another heading cell style?

Excel includes many types of headings, such as Heading 1 and Heading 2, because worksheets often include many levels of headings above columns. In the case of the worksheet created for this project, the Heading 3 title includes formatting that makes the column titles' font size smaller than the title and subtitle and makes the column titles stand out from the data in the body of the worksheet.

4

- Click the More button to display the Cell Styles gallery and then click the Total cell style in the Titles and Headings area to apply the selected cell style to the cells in the selected range.

- Click cell A11 to select it (Figure 1–43).

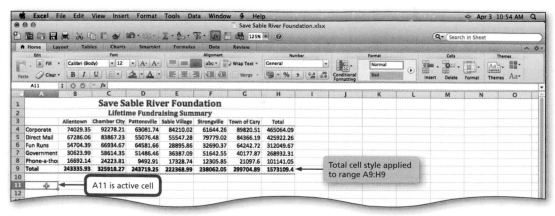

Figure 1–43

To Format Numbers in the Worksheet

As previously noted, the numbers in the worksheet should be formatted to use a dollar-and-cents format, with dollar signs in the first row (row 4) and the total row (row 9). Excel allows you to format numbers in a variety of ways, and these methods are discussed in other chapters in this book. The following steps use buttons on the ribbon to format the numbers in the worksheet.

- Select cell B4 and drag the mouse pointer to cell H4 to select the range (Figure 1–44).

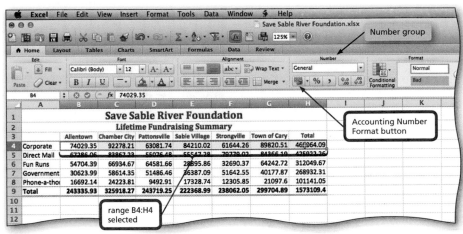

Figure 1–44

- On the Home tab, under Number, click the Accounting Number Format button to apply the Accounting number format to the cells in the selected range.

- Select the range B5:H8 (Figure 1–45).

Q&A What effect does the Accounting number format have on the selected cells?
The Accounting number format causes the cells to be displayed with two decimal places so that decimal places in cells below the selected cells align vertically. Cell widths are adjusted automatically to accommodate the new formatting.

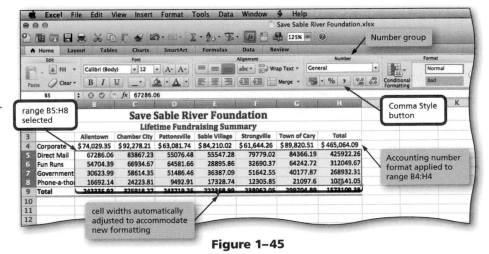

Figure 1–45

- On the Home tab, under Number, click the Comma Style button to apply the Comma Style format to the selected range.

- Select the range B9:H9 to make it the active range (Figure 1–46).

Q&A What effect does the Comma Style format have on the selected cells?
The Comma Style format causes the cells to be displayed with two decimal places and commas as thousands separators.

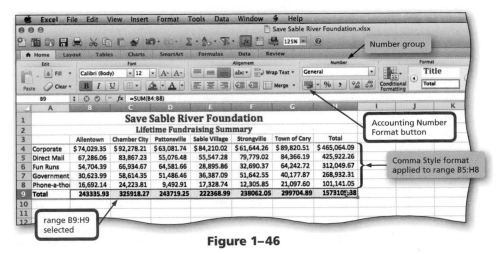

Figure 1–46

4

- On the Home tab, under Number, click the Accounting Number Format button to apply the Accounting number format to the cells in the selected range.

- Select cell A11 (Figure 1–47).

Q&A Why did the column widths automatically adjust again? Because the total row contains larger numbers, the Accounting number format again causes the cell widths automatically to adjust to accommodate the new formatting just as occurred in Step 2.

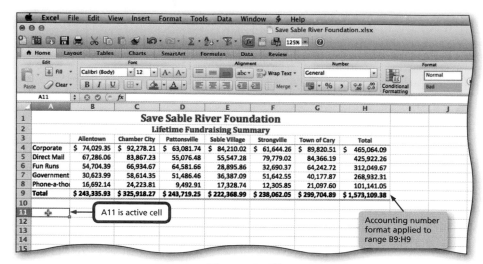

Figure 1–47

Other Ways

1. CONTROL-click selection, choose Format Cells in shortcut menu, click Number tab (Format Cells dialog), choose Accounting in Category list or choose Number and click Use 1000 Separator, click OK button

2. Choose Format > Cells in menu bar, click Number tab (Format Cells dialog), choose Accounting in Category list or choose Number and click Use 1000 Separator, click OK button

---

To Adjust the Column Width

The last step in formatting the worksheet is to adjust the width of column A so that the word Phone-a-thon in cell A8 is shown in its entirety in the cell. Excel includes several methods for adjusting cell widths and row heights, and these methods are discussed later in this book. The following steps adjust the width of column A so that the contents of cell A8 are displayed in the cell.

1

- Point to the boundary on the right side of the column A heading above row 1 to change the mouse pointer to a split double arrow (Figure 1–48).

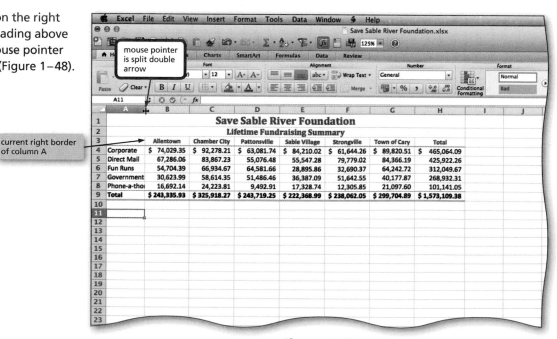

Figure 1–48

2

- Double-click on the boundary to adjust the width of the column to the width of the largest item in the column (Figure 1–49).

Q&A What if none of the items in column A extends through the entire width of the column?
If all of the items in column A were shorter in length than the width of the column when you double-click the right side of the column A heading, then Excel still would adjust the column width to the largest item in the column. That is, Excel would reduce the width of the column to the largest item.

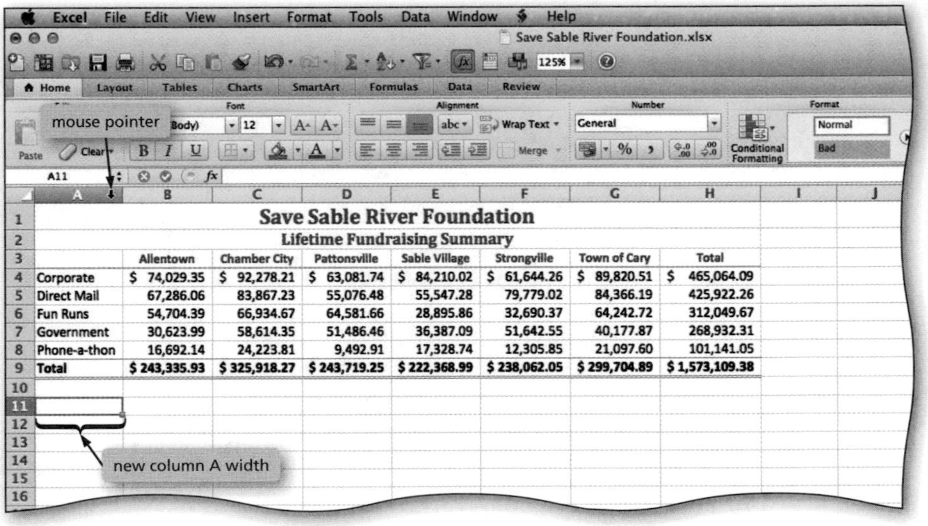

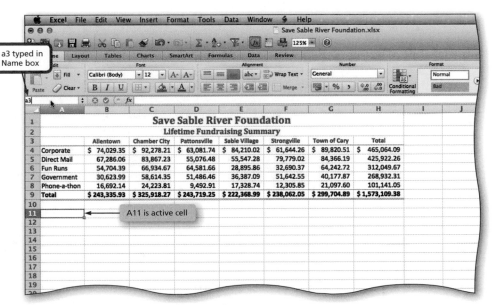

Figure 1–49

Using the Name Box to Select a Cell

The next step is to chart the lifetime fundraising amounts for the five fundraising activities used by the organization. To create the chart, you first must select the cell in the upper-left corner of the range to chart (cell A3). Rather than clicking cell A3 to select it, the next section describes how to use the Name box to select the cell.

To Use the Name Box to Select a Cell

The Name box is located on the left side of the formula bar. To select any cell, click the Name box and enter the cell reference of the cell you want to select. The following steps select cell A3 using the Name box.

1

- Click the Name box in the formula bar and then type **a3** as the cell you wish to select (Figure 1–50).

Q&A Why is cell A11 still selected?
Even though cell A11 is the active cell, Excel displays the typed cell reference a3 in the Name box until you press the RETURN key.

Figure 1–50

● Press the RETURN key to change the active cell in the Name box (Figure 1–51).

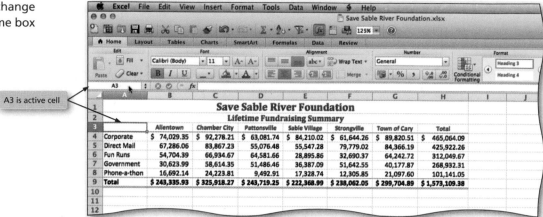

Figure 1–51

Other Ways to Select Cells

As you will see in later chapters, in addition to using the Name box to select any cell in a worksheet, you also can use it to assign names to a cell or range of cells. Excel supports several additional ways to select a cell, as summarized in Table 1–3.

Table 1–3 Selecting Cells in Excel	
Key, Box, or Command	**Function**
ALT-FN-DOWN ARROW	Selects the cell one worksheet window to the right and moves the worksheet window accordingly.
ALT-FN-UP ARROW	Selects the cell one worksheet window to the left and moves the worksheet window accordingly.
ARROW	Selects the adjacent cell in the direction of the arrow on the key.
COMMAND-ARROW	Selects the border cell of the worksheet in combination with the arrow keys and moves the worksheet window accordingly. For example, to select the rightmost cell in the row that contains the active cell, press COMMAND-RIGHT ARROW. On extended keyboards, you also can press the END key, release it, and then press the appropriate arrow key to accomplish the same task.
COMMAND-FN-LEFT ARROW	Selects cell A1 or the cell one column and one row below and to the right of frozen titles and moves the worksheet window accordingly.
Edit > Find command in menu bar	Finds and selects a cell that contains specific contents that you enter in the Find dialog. If necessary, Excel moves the worksheet window to display the cell. You also can press COMMAND-F to display the Find dialog.
Edit > Go To command in menu bar	Selects the cell that corresponds to the cell reference you enter in the Go To dialog and moves the worksheet window accordingly. You also can press CONTROL-G to display the Go To dialog.
COMMAND-LEFT ARROW	Selects the cell at the beginning of the row that contains the active cell and moves the worksheet window accordingly.
Name Box	Selects the cell in the workbook that corresponds to the cell reference you enter in the Name box.
FN-DOWN ARROW	Selects the cell down one worksheet window from the active cell and moves the worksheet window accordingly.
FN-UP ARROW	Selects the cell up one worksheet window from the active cell and moves the worksheet window accordingly.

Break Point: If you wish to take a break, this is a good place to do so. Be sure to save the Save Sable River Foundation file again and then you can quit Excel. To resume at a later time, start Excel, open the file called Save Sable River Foundation, and continue following the steps from this location forward.

Adding a Clustered Cylinder Chart to the Worksheet

As outlined in the requirements document in Figure 1–2 on page EX 4, the worksheet should include a Clustered Cylinder chart to graphically represent the lifetime fundraising for each fundraising activity in which the organization engages. The Clustered Cylinder chart shown in Figure 1–52 on the next page is called an **embedded chart** because it is drawn on the same worksheet as the data.

Plan Ahead

Decide on the type of chart needed.

Excel includes 11 chart types from which you can choose, including column, line, pie, bar, area, X Y (scatter), stock, surface, doughnut, bubble, and radar. The type of chart you choose depends on the type of data that you have, how much data you have, and the message you want to convey.

A line chart often is used to illustrate changes in data over time. Pie charts show the contribution of each piece of data to the whole, or total, of the data. Area charts, like line charts, illustrate changes over time, but often are used to compare more than one set of data and the area under the lines is filled in with a different color for each set of data. An X Y (scatter) chart is used much like a line chart, but each piece of data is represented by a dot and is not connected with a line. A stock chart provides a number of methods commonly used in the financial industry to show stock market data. A surface chart compares data from three columns and/or rows in a three-dimensional manner. A doughnut chart is much like a pie chart, but a doughnut chart allows for comparing more than one set of data, resulting in a chart that looks like a doughnut, with each subsequent set of data surrounding the previous set. A bubble chart is much like an X Y (scatter) chart, but a third set of data results indicates how large each individual dot, or bubble, is on the chart. A radar chart can compare several sets of data in a manner that resembles a radar screen, with each set of data represented by a different color. A column or cylinder chart is a good way to compare values side by side. A Clustered Cylinder chart can go even further in comparing values across categories.

Establish where to position and how to format the chart.

- When possible, try to position charts so that both the data and chart appear on the screen on the worksheet together and so that the data and chart can be printed in the most readable manner possible.

- When choosing/selecting colors for a chart, consider the color scheme of the rest of the worksheet. The chart should not present colors that are in stark contrast to the rest of the worksheet. If the chart will be printed in color, minimize the amount of dark colors on the chart so that the chart both prints quickly and conserves ink.

Cell Values and Charting

When you change a cell **BTW** value on which a chart is dependent, Excel redraws the chart instantaneously, unless automatic recalculation is disabled. To enable or disable automatic recalculation, on the Formulas tab under Calculation, click the Settings button.

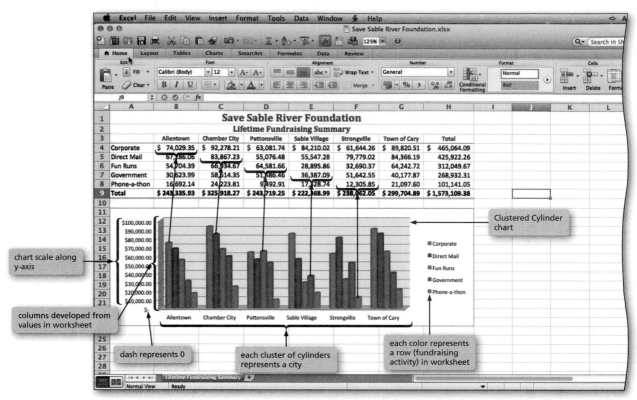

Figure 1–52

In the case of the Save Sable River Foundation Lifetime Fundraising Summary, comparisons of fundraising activities within each city can be made side by side with a Clustered Cylinder chart. The chart uses differently colored cylinders to represent amounts raised for different fundraising activities. Each city uses the same color scheme for identifying fundraising activities, which allows for easy identification and comparison.

- For the city of Allentown, for example, the dark blue cylinder representing Corporate donations shows lifetime donations of $74,029.35.

- For Chamber City, the maroon cylinder representing Direct Mail donations shows lifetime donations of $83,867.23.

- For the city of Pattonsville, the lime green cylinder representing donations for Fun Runs shows lifetime donations of $64,581.66.

- For Sable Village, the purple cylinder representing Government donations shows lifetime donations of $36,387.09.

- For the city of Strongville, the light blue cylinder representing Phone-a-thon donations shows lifetime donations of $12,305.85.

Because the same color scheme is used in each city to represent the five fundraising activities, you easily can compare funds raised by each fundraising activity among the cities. The totals from the worksheet are not represented, because the totals are not in the range specified for charting.

Excel derives the chart scale based on the values in the worksheet and then displays the scale along the vertical axis (also called the **y-axis** or **value axis**) of the chart. For example, no value in the range B4:G8 is less than 0 or greater than $100,000.00, so the scale ranges from 0 to $100,000.00. Excel also determines the $10,000.00 increments of the scale automatically. For the numbers along the y-axis, Excel uses a format that includes representing the 0 value with a dash (Figure 1–52).

To Add a Clustered Cylinder Chart to the Worksheet

The area on the worksheet where the chart appears is called the chart location. As shown in Figure 1–52, the chart location in this worksheet is the range A11:H25; this range is immediately below the worksheet data. Placing the chart below the data on the Save Sable River Foundation Lifetime Fundraising Summary worksheet makes it easier to read the chart along with the data, and the chart and data easily can be printed on one sheet of paper.

The following steps draw a Clustered Cylinder chart that compares the funds raised by fundraising activity for the six cities.

1
- Click cell A3 and then drag the mouse pointer to cell G8 to select the range to be charted (Figure 1–53).

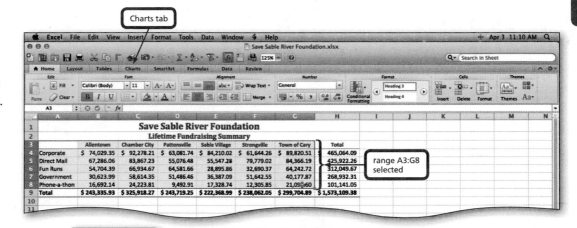

Figure 1–53

2
- Click Charts on the ribbon to display the Charts tab (Figure 1–54).

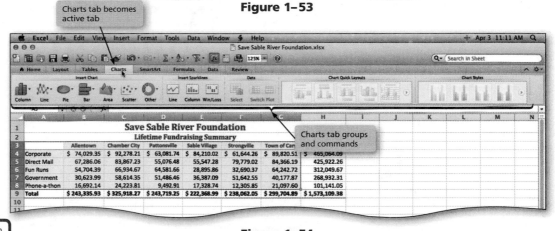

Figure 1–54

3
- On the Charts tab, under Insert Chart, click the Column button to display the Column gallery (Figure 1–55).

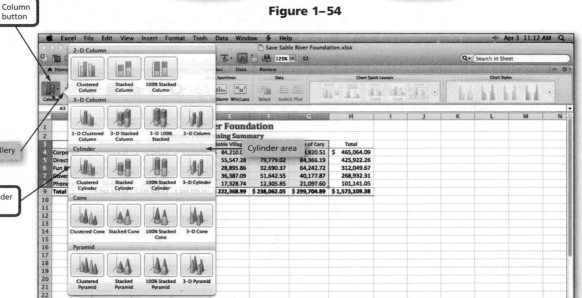

Figure 1–55

4

- Click the Clustered Cylinder chart type in the Cylinder area of the Column gallery to add the selected chart type to the middle of the worksheet in a selection rectangle.

- Press and hold down the mouse button while pointing to the upper-right edge of the selection rectangle to change the mouse pointer to a four-headed arrow (Figure 1–56).

Q&A Why are two new tabs displayed on the ribbon?

When you select objects such as shapes or charts, Excel displays contextual tabs that include special commands that are used to work with the type of object selected. Because a chart is selected, Excel displays the Chart Layout and Format contextual tabs, which include commands to work with charts.

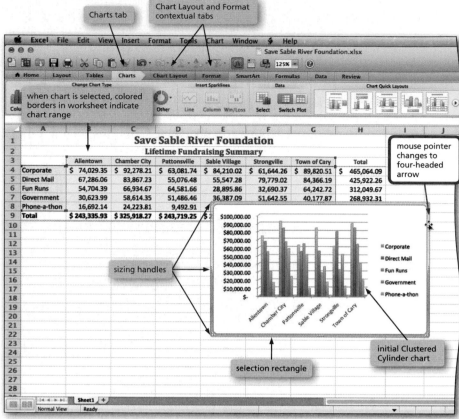

Figure 1–56

5

- Drag the chart to the left to position the upper-left corner of the gray line rectangle over the upper-left corner of cell A11.

- Press and hold down the mouse button while pointing to the middle sizing handle on the right edge of the chart (Figure 1–57).

Q&A How does Excel know which data to use to create the chart?

Excel automatically selects the entries in the topmost row of the chart range (row 3) as the titles for the horizontal axis (also called the **x-axis** or **category axis**) and draws a column for each of the 30 cells in the range containing numbers.

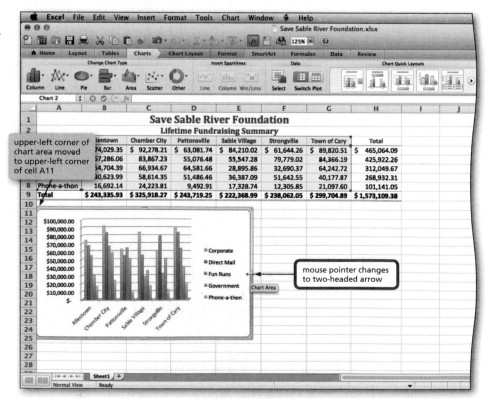

Figure 1–57

6

- While continuing to hold down the mouse button, press the COMMAND key and drag the right edge of the chart to the right edge of column H and then release the mouse button to resize the chart.

- Press and hold down the mouse button while pointing to the middle sizing handle on the bottom edge of the selection rectangle and do not release the mouse button (Figure 1–58).

Q&A Why should I hold the COMMAND key down while I resize a chart?
Holding down the COMMAND key while you drag a chart **snaps** (aligns) the edge of the chart area to the worksheet gridlines. If you do not hold down the COMMAND key, then you can place an edge of a chart in the middle of a column or row.

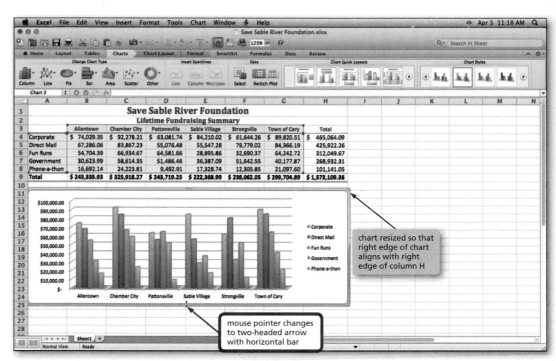

Figure 1–58

7

- While continuing to hold down the mouse button, press the COMMAND key and drag the bottom edge of the chart up to the bottom edge of row 23 and then release the mouse button to resize the chart.

- If necessary, scroll the worksheet so that row 1 displays at the top of the worksheet.

- On the Charts tab, under Chart Styles, click the More button to display the Chart Styles gallery (Figure 1–59).

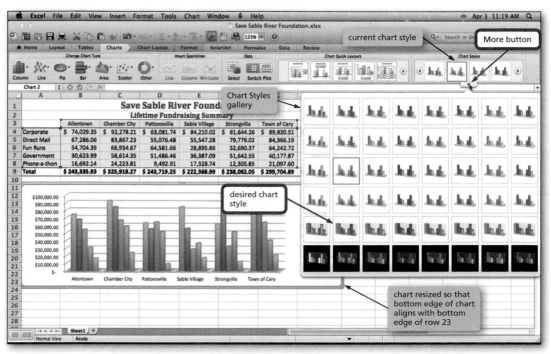

Figure 1–59

8

- In the Chart Styles gallery, click the chart style in column 2, row 5, to apply the chart style to the chart.

- Click cell J9 to deselect the chart and complete the worksheet (Figure 1–60).

Q&A What is the purpose of the items on the right side of the chart? The items to the right of the column chart in Figure 1–60 are the **legend**, which identifies the colors assigned to each bar in the chart. Excel automatically selects the entries in the leftmost column of the chart range (column A) as titles within the legend.

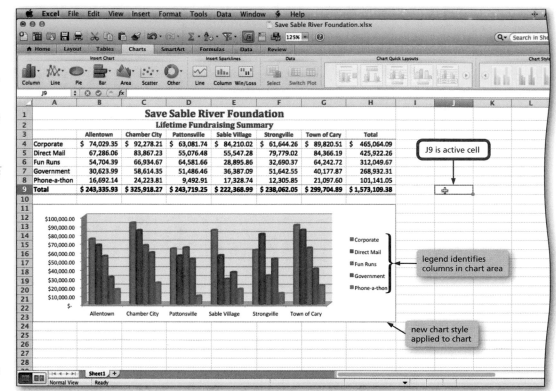

Figure 1–60

Changing the Worksheet Names

The sheet tabs at the bottom of the window allow you to view any worksheet in the workbook. You click the sheet tab of the worksheet you want to view in the Excel window. By default, Excel presets the names of the worksheets to Sheet1, Sheet2, and so on. When Excel is started, the default is for one sheet to show, Sheet1, along with a tab labeled + which creates a new sheet when clicked. The first new sheet will be named Sheet2, the second Sheet3, and so on. The worksheet names become increasingly important as you move toward more sophisticated workbooks, especially workbooks in which you reference cells between worksheets.

Plan Ahead

> **Choose a name for the worksheet.**
>
> Use simple, meaningful names for each worksheet. Worksheet names often match the worksheet title. If a worksheet includes multiple titles in multiple sections of the worksheet, use a name that encompasses the meaning of all of the sections.

To Change the Worksheet Name and Sheet Tab Color

Lifetime Fundraising Summary is a meaningful name for the Save Sable River Foundation Lifetime Fundraising Summary worksheet. The following steps rename worksheet by double-clicking the sheet tab and then change the color of the sheet tab to make it stand out.

- Double-click the sheet tab labeled Sheet1 in the lower-left corner of the window.

- Type **Lifetime Fundraising Summary** as the worksheet name and then press the RETURN key to display the new worksheet name on the sheet tab (Figure 1–61).

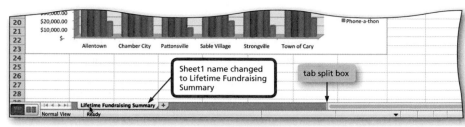

Figure 1–61

Q&A What is the maximum length for a worksheet tab name?

Worksheet names can be up to 31 characters (including spaces) in length. Longer worksheet names, however, mean that fewer sheet tabs will show. To view more sheet tabs, you can drag the tab split box (Figure 1–61) to the right. This will reduce the size of the scroll bar at the bottom of the screen. Double-click the tab split box to reset it to its normal position.

2

- CONTROL-click the sheet tab labeled Lifetime Fundraising Summary in the lower-left corner of the window to display a shortcut menu (Figure 1–62).

- Choose Tab Color in the shortcut menu to display the Tab Color window (Figure 1–63).

Q&A How can I quickly move between worksheet tabs?

You can use the tab scrolling buttons to the left of the sheet tabs (Figure 1–63) to move between worksheets. The leftmost and rightmost scroll buttons move to the first or last worksheet in the workbook. The two middle scroll buttons move one worksheet to the left or right.

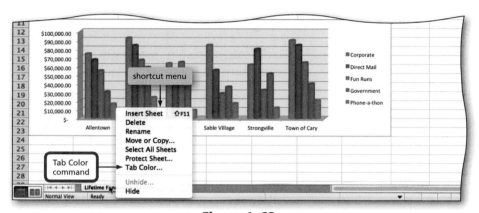

Figure 1–62

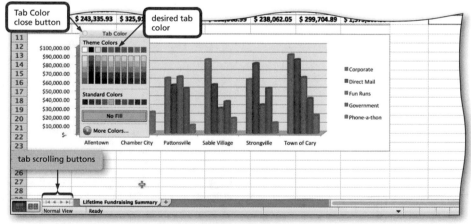

Figure 1–63

3

- Click Accent 2 (column 6, row 1) in the Theme Colors area to change the color of the tab.

- Click the close button on the Tab Color window to close the window (Figure 1–64).

- Click Home on the ribbon to display the Home tab.

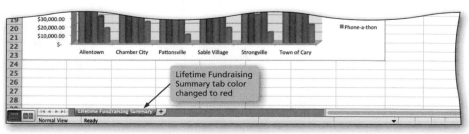

Figure 1–64

Changing Document Properties

Excel helps you organize and identify your files by using **document properties**, which are the details about a file. Document properties, also known as **metadata**, can include information such as the project author, title, subject, and keywords. A **keyword** is a word or phrase that further describes the document. For example, a class name or document topic can describe the file's purpose or content.

Document properties are valuable for a variety of reasons:

- Users can save time locating a particular file because they can view a document's properties without opening the document.

- By creating consistent properties for files having similar content, users can better organize their documents.

- Some organizations require Excel users to add document properties so that other employees can view details about these files.

Five different types of document properties exist, but the more common ones used in this book are standard and automatically updated properties. **Standard properties** are associated with all Microsoft Office documents and include author, title, and subject. **Automatically updated properties** include file system properties, such as the date you create or change a file, and statistics, such as the file size.

To Change Document Properties

The **Document Properties dialog** contains areas where you can view and enter document properties. You can view and change information in this dialog at any time while you are creating a workbook. Before saving the workbook again, you want to add your name and course information as document properties. The following steps use the Document Properties dialog to change document properties.

- Click File in the menu bar to display the File menu.

- Choose Properties to open the Save Sable River Foundation.xlsx Properties dialog (Figure 1–65).

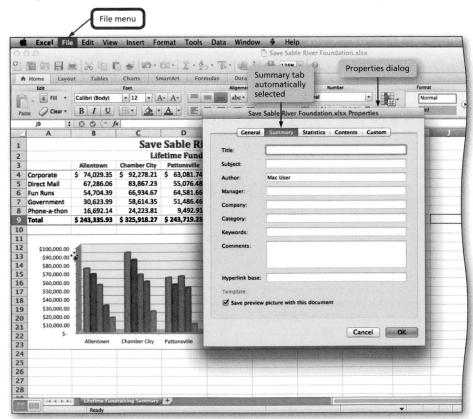

Figure 1–65

- Click the Author text box. If necessary, type your name as the Author property. If another name already is displayed in the Author text box, delete it before typing your name.

- Click the Subject text box, if necessary delete any existing text, and then type your course and section as the Subject property.

- Click the Keywords text box, if necessary delete any existing text, and then type **Lifetime Fundraising Summary** as the Keywords property (Figure 1–66).

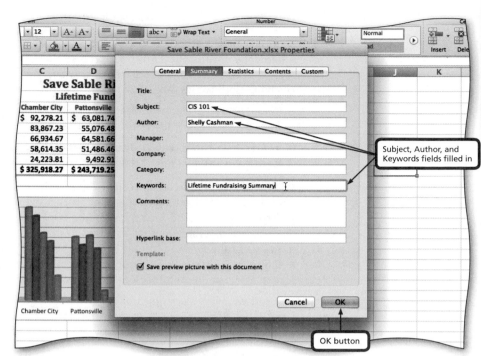

Figure 1–66

Q&A Why are some of the document properties in my Document Properties dialog already filled in?
The person who installed Microsoft Office for Mac 2011 on your computer or network may have set or customized the properties.

Q&A What types of document properties does Excel collect automatically?
Excel records details such as time spent editing a document, the number of times a document has been revised, and the fonts and themes used In a document.

- Click the OK button to close the Document Properties dialog.

To Save an Existing Workbook with the Same File Name

You have made several modifications to the workbook since you last saved it. Thus, you should save it again. The following step saves the workbook again. For an example of the step listed below, refer to the Introduction to Office 2011 and Mac OS X chapter at the beginning of this book.

 Click the Save button in the Standard toolbar to overwrite the previously saved file.

Previewing and Printing a Worksheet

After creating a worksheet, you may want to print it. Printing a worksheet enables you to distribute the worksheet to others in a form that can be read or viewed but typically not edited. It is a good practice to save a workbook before printing a worksheet, in the event you experience difficulties printing.

Conserving Ink and Toner

If you want to conserve ink or toner, you can instruct Excel to print draft quality documents by choosing File > Page Setup in the menu bar, choosing 300 dpi from the Print quality pop-up menu, clicking OK, and then choosing File > Print in the menu bar, and clicking the Print button to print the document.

BTW

Plan Ahead	**Determine the best method for distributing the worksheet.**
	The traditional method of distributing a worksheet uses a printer to produce a hard copy. A **hardcopy or printout** is information that exists on a physical medium such as paper. For users that can receive fax documents, you can elect to print a hard copy on a remote fax machine. Hard copies can be useful for the following reasons:

- Many people prefer proofreading a hard copy of a worksheet rather than viewing it on the screen to check for errors and readability.

- Hard copies can serve as reference material if your storage medium is lost or becomes corrupted and you need to re-create the worksheet.

Instead of distributing a hard copy of a worksheet, users can choose to distribute the worksheet as an electronic image that mirrors the original worksheet's appearance. The electronic image of the worksheet can be e-mailed, posted on a Web site, or copied to a portable storage medium such as a USB flash drive. A popular electronic image format, sometimes called a fixed format, is PDF by Adobe Systems. In Excel for Mac, you can create PDF files through the Print dialog and the Save As dialog. Electronic images of worksheets such as PDF can be useful for the following reasons:

- Users can view electronic images of worksheets without the software that created the original worksheet (e.g., Excel). Specifically, to view a PDF file, you use a program called Acrobat Reader, which can be downloaded free from Adobe's Web site.

- Sending electronic documents saves paper and printer supplies. Society encourages users to contribute to **green computing**, which involves reducing the environmental waste generated when using a computer.

To Preview and Print a Worksheet in Landscape Orientation

With the completed workbook saved, you may want to print it. Because the worksheet is included in a report, you will print a hard copy on a printer. The following steps print a hard copy of the contents of the Save Sable River Foundation Lifetime Fundraising Summary worksheet.

- Click File in the menu bar to display the File menu.

- Choose Print to display the Print dialog.

Q&A   How can I print multiple copies of my document?
Increase the number in the Copies box.

Q&A   What if I decide not to print the document at this time?
Click the Cancel button.

- Verify the printer name that appears in the Printer box will print a hard copy of the document. If necessary, click the Printer box to display a list of available printer options and then choose the desired printer to change the currently selected printer.

- If necessary, click the Show Quick Preview check box to select this option (Figure 1–67).

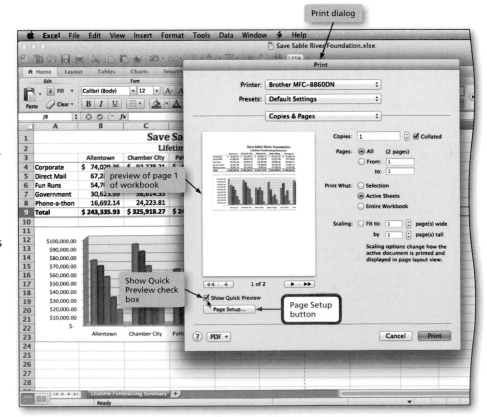

Figure 1–67

2

- Click the Page Setup button in the Print dialog to open the Page Setup dialog.

- On the Page tab, under Orientation, select Landscape (Figure 1–68).

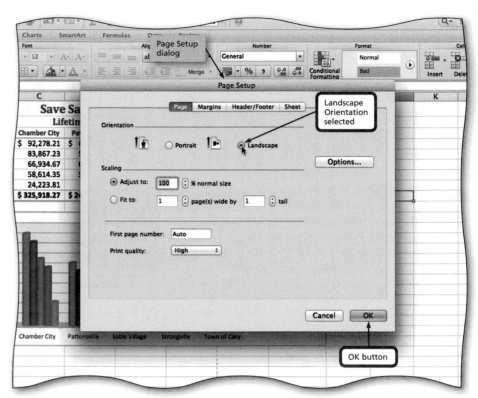

Figure 1–68

3

- Click OK to close the Page Setup dialog (Figure 1–69).

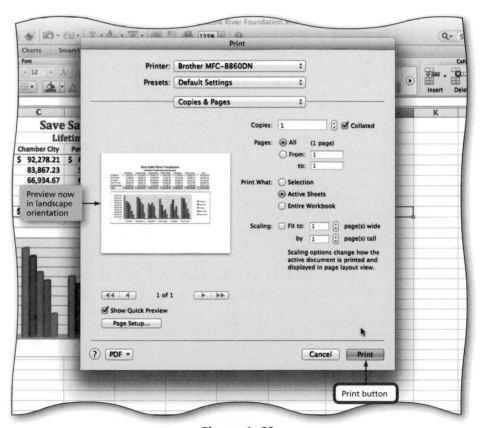

Figure 1–69

4

• Click the Print button in the Print dialog to print the document on the currently selected printer.

• When the printer stops, retrieve the hard copy (Figure 1–70).

Q&A Do I have to wait until my document is complete to print it? No, you can follow these steps to print a document at any time while you are creating it.

Q&A What if I want to print an electronic image of a worksheet instead of a hard copy? You would click the PDF button at the bottom of the Print dialog, choose Save as PDF, specify the filename and location, and click the Save button (Save dialog).

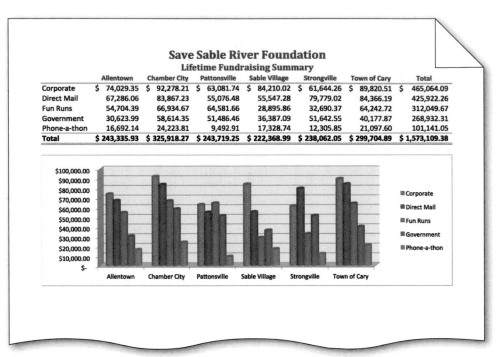

Figure 1–70

Other Ways

1. Click Print button in Standard toolbar

2. Press COMMAND-P, press RETURN

To Quit Excel

The Save Sable River Foundation workbook now is complete. The following steps quit Excel if only one workbook is open. For a detailed example of the procedure summarized below, refer to the Office for Mac 2011 and Mac OS X chapter at the beginning of this book.

1 Click Excel in the menu bar and then choose Quit Excel to close all open workbooks and quit Excel.

2 If an Excel dialog appears, click the Save button to save any changes made to the workbook since the last save.

Starting Excel and Opening a Workbook

Once you have created and saved a workbook, you may need to retrieve it from your storage medium. For example, you might want to revise a worksheet or reprint it. Opening a workbook requires that Excel is running on your computer.

To Start Excel

1 Click the Excel icon in the Dock.

2 Double-click the Excel Workbook icon in the Excel Workbook Gallery to display a new blank document in the Excel window.

The workbook I was working on opened when I started Excel. Why?

Unless you shut down your computer, when Excel is started it will open the most recent workbook you saved.

❸ If the Excel window is not sized properly, as described in the Office 2011 and Mac OS X chapter, size the window properly.

To Open a Workbook from Excel

Earlier in this chapter, you saved your project on a USB flash drive using the file name, Save Sable River Foundation.

The following steps open the Save Sable River Foundation file from the Excel folder in the CIS 101 folder on the USB flash drive. You will only need to follow these steps if your project file does not open when you start Excel. For a detailed example of the procedure summarized below, refer to the Office 2011 and Mac OS X chapter at the beginning of this book.

❶ With your USB flash drive connected to one of the computer's USB ports, click File in the menu bar to display the File menu.

❷ Choose Open to display the Open dialog.

❸ Navigate to the location of the file to be opened (in this case, the Excel folder in the CIS 101 folder [or your class folder] on the USB flash drive). For a detailed example of this procedure, refer to Steps 3a – 3c in the To Save a File in a Folder section in the Office 2011 and Mac OS X chapter at the beginning of this book.

❹ Click Save Sable River Foundation.xlsx to select the file to be opened.

❺ Click the Open button (Open dialog) to open the selected file and display the opened workbook in the Excel window.

Q&A Could I have used the Open Recent command in the File menu to open the file?

Yes. Because the file was recently closed, it should appear in the Open Recent list.

AutoCalculate

You easily can obtain a total, an average, or other information about the numbers in a range by using the **AutoCalculate area** in the lower right of the document window. First, select the range of cells containing the numbers you want to check. Next, click the AutoCalculate area to display the AutoCalculate shortcut menu (Figure 1–71 on the next page). The check mark to the left of the active function (Sum) indicates that the sum of the selected range is displayed in the AutoCalculate area in the status bar. The functions of the AutoCalculate commands in the shortcut menu are described in Table 1–4.

AutoCalculate | BTW

Use the AutoCalculate area in the status bar to check your work as you enter data in a worksheet. If you enter large amounts of data, you can select a range of data and then check the AutoCalculate area to provide insight into statistics about the data you entered. Often, you will have an intuitive feel for whether the numbers are accurate or if you may have made a mistake while entering the data.

Table 1–4 AutoCalculate Shortcut Menu Commands	
Command	Function
Average	AutoCalculate area displays the average of the numbers in the selected range
Count	AutoCalculate area displays the number of nonblank cells in the selected range
Count Nums	AutoCalculate area displays the number of cells containing numbers in the selected range
Max	AutoCalculate area displays the highest value in the selected range
Min	AutoCalculate area displays the lowest value in the selected range
Sum	AutoCalculate area displays the sum of the numbers in the selected range

To Use the AutoCalculate Area to Determine a Maximum

The following steps display the largest amounts of funds raised for any city for the Fun Runs fundraising activity.

- Select the range B6:G6 and then click the AutoCalculate area in the status bar to display the shortcut menu (Figure 1–71).

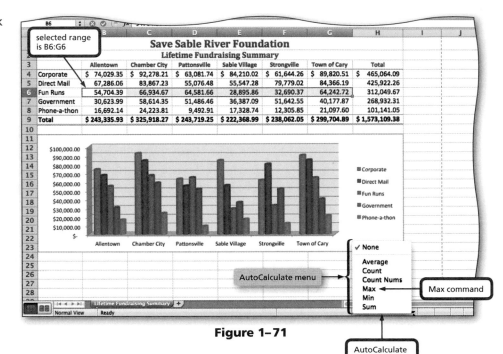

Figure 1–71

- Choose Max in the shortcut menu to display the maximum value in the range B6:G6 in the AutoCalculate area (Figure 1–72).

- Click the AutoCalculate area and then choose None in the shortcut menu to cause the maximum value to no longer appear in the AutoCalculate area. The area appears blank.

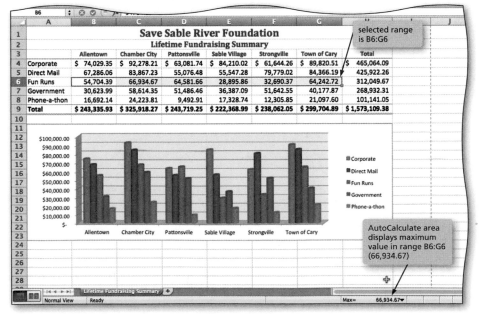

Figure 1–72

Correcting Errors

You can correct errors on a worksheet using one of several methods. The method you choose will depend on the extent of the error and whether you notice it while typing the data or after you have entered the incorrect data into the cell.

Correcting Errors While You Are Typing Data into a Cell

If you notice an error while you are typing data into a cell, press the DELETE key to erase the incorrect characters and then type the correct characters. If the error is a major one, click the Cancel button in the formula bar or press the ESC key to erase the entire entry and then reenter the data from the beginning.

Correcting Errors After Entering Data into a Cell

If you find an error in the worksheet after entering the data, you can correct the error in one of two ways:

1. If the entry is short, select the cell, retype the entry correctly, and then click the Enter button or press the RETURN key. The new entry will replace the old entry.

2. If the entry in the cell is long and the errors are minor, using Edit mode may be a better choice than retyping the cell entry. Use the Edit mode as described below.

   a. Double-click the cell containing the error to switch Excel to Edit mode. In **Edit mode**, Excel displays the active cell entry in the formula bar and a flashing insertion point in the active cell (Figure 1–73). With Excel in Edit mode, you can edit the contents directly in the cell — a procedure called **in-cell editing**.

   b. Make changes using in-cell editing, in the following ways:

      (1) To insert new characters between two characters, place the insertion point between the two characters and begin typing. Excel inserts the new characters at the location of the insertion point.

      (2) To delete a character in the cell, move the insertion point to the right of the character you want to delete and then press the DELETE key or place the insertion point to the left of the character you want to delete and then press FN-DELETE. You also can use the mouse to drag through the character or adjacent characters you want to delete and then press the DELETE key or click the Cut button in the Standard toolbar.

      (3) When you are finished editing an entry, click the Enter button or press the RETURN key.

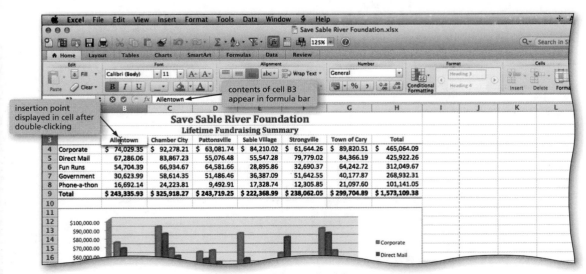

Figure 1–73

In-Cell Editing

BTW An alternative to double-clicking the cell to edit it is to select the cell and then press FN-F2.

While in Edit mode, you may have reason to move the insertion point to various points in the cell, select portions of the data in the cell, or switch from inserting characters to overtyping characters. Table 1–5 summarizes the more common tasks performed during in-cell editing.

	Task	Mouse	Keyboard
	Table 1–5 Summary of In-Cell Editing Tasks		
1	Move the insertion point to the beginning of data in a cell.	Point to the left of the first character and click.	Press FN-LEFT ARROW
2	Move the insertion point to the end of data in a cell.	Point to the right of the last character and click.	Press FN-RIGHT ARROW
3	Move the insertion point anywhere in a cell.	Point to the appropriate position and click the character.	Press RIGHT ARROW or LEFT ARROW
4	Highlight one or more adjacent characters.	Drag the mouse pointer through adjacent characters.	Press SHIFT-RIGHT ARROW or SHIFT-LEFT ARROW
5	Select all data in a cell.	Double-click the cell with the insertion point in the cell if there are no spaces in the data in the cell.	
6	Delete selected characters.	Click the Cut button in the Standard toolbar.	Press DELETE
7	Delete characters to the left of the insertion point.		Press DELETE
8	Delete characters to the right of the insertion point.		Press FN-DELETE

Editing the Contents of a Cell

BTW Rather than using in-cell editing, you can select the cell and then click the formula bar to edit the contents.

Undoing the Last Cell Entry

Excel provides the Undo command in the Standard toolbar (Figure 1–74), which allows you to erase recent cell entries. Thus, if you enter incorrect data in a cell and notice it immediately, click the Undo button and Excel changes the cell entry to what it was prior to the incorrect data entry.

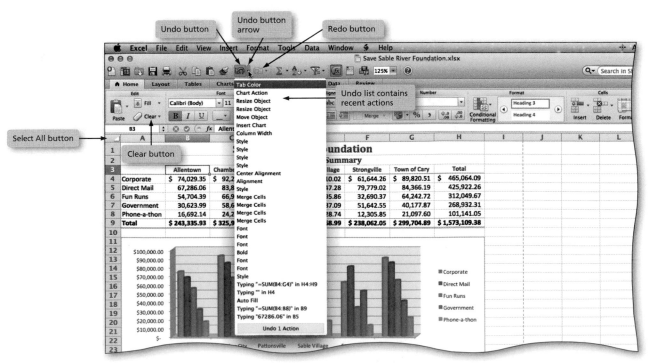

Figure 1–74

Excel remembers the last 100 actions you have completed. Thus, you can undo up to 100 previous actions by clicking the Undo button arrow to display the Undo list and then clicking the action to be undone (Figure 1–74). You can drag through several actions in the Undo list to undo all of them at once. If no actions are available for Excel to undo, then the Undo button is dimmed and inoperative.

The Redo button, next to the Undo button in the Standard toolbar, allows you to repeat previous actions.

Clearing a Cell or Range of Cells

If you enter data into the wrong cell or range of cells, you can erase, or clear, the data using one of the first four methods listed below. The fifth method clears the formatting from the selected cells.

To Clear Cell Entries Using the Fill Handle

1. Select the cell or range of cells and then point to the fill handle so the mouse pointer changes to a crosshair.
2. Drag the fill handle back into the selected cell or range until a shadow covers the cell or cells you want to erase. Release the mouse button.

To Clear Cell Entries Using the Shortcut Menu

1. Select the cell or range of cells to be cleared.
2. CONTROL-click the selection.
3. Choose Clear Contents in the shortcut menu.

To Clear Cell Entries Using the Delete Key

1. Select the cell or range of cells to be cleared.
2. Press the DELETE key.

To Clear Cell Entries and Formatting Using the Clear Button

1. Select the cell or range of cells to be cleared.
2. On the Home tab, under Edit, click the Clear button (Figure 1–74).
3. Choose Contents in the menu.

To Clear Formatting Using the Cell Styles Button

1. Select the cell or range of cells from which you want to remove the formatting.
2. On the Home tab, under Format, click the Styles button and select Normal in the Cell Styles gallery.

The Clear button on the Home tab in the Edit group is the only command that clears both the cell entry and the cell formatting. As you are clearing cell entries, always remember that you should *never press the* SPACE BAR *to clear a cell*. Pressing the SPACE BAR enters a blank character. A blank character is text and is different from an empty cell, even though the cell may appear empty.

Getting Back to Normal

If you accidentally assign BTW unwanted formats to a range of cells, you can use the Normal cell style selection in the Cell Styles gallery. On the Home tab under Format, click Normal in the Cell Styles gallery. Doing so changes the format to Normal style. To view the characteristics of the Normal style, CONTROL-click the style in the Cell Styles gallery and then click Modify.

Excel Help

At any time while using BTW Excel, you can find answers to questions and display information about various topics through Excel Help. Used properly, this form of assistance can increase your productivity and reduce your frustrations by minimizing the time you spend learning how to use Excel. For instruction about Excel Help and exercises that will help you gain confidence in using it, read the Office 2011 and Mac OS X chapter at the beginning of this book.

Clearing the Entire Worksheet

If the required worksheet edits are extremely extensive, you may want to clear the entire worksheet and start over. To clear the worksheet or delete an embedded chart, you would use the following steps.

To Clear the Entire Worksheet

1. Click the Select All button on the worksheet (Figure 1–74 on page EX 48).
2. On the Home tab, under Edit, click the Clear button and then choose All on the Clear menu to delete both the entries and formats.

The Select All button selects the entire worksheet. Instead of clicking the Select All button, you can press COMMAND-A. To clear an unsaved workbook, click the workbook's close button. Click the No button if the Excel dialog asks if you want to save changes. To start a new, blank workbook, choose New on the File menu.

To delete an embedded chart, you would complete the following steps.

To Delete an Embedded Chart

1. Click the chart to select it.
2. Press the DELETE key.

To Quit Excel

The project now is complete. The following steps quit Excel. For a detailed example of the procedure summarized below, refer to the Office for Mac 2011 and Mac OS X chapter at the beginning of this book.

1 Click Excel in the menu bar and then choose Quit Excel to close all open workbooks and quit Excel.

2 If an Excel dialog appears, click the Save button to save any changes made to the workbook since the last save.

Quitting Excel

BTW Do not forget to remove your USB flash drive from the USB port after quitting Excel, especially if you are working in a laboratory environment. Nothing can be more frustrating than leaving all of your hard work behind on a USB flash drive for the next user.

Quick Reference

BTW For a table that lists how to complete the tasks covered in this book using the mouse, ribbon, menu bar, shortcut menu, and keyboard, see the Quick Reference Summary at the back of this book, or visit the Office 2011 for Mac Online Companion Web page at www.cengagebrain. com, navigate to the desired application, and click Quick Reference.

Chapter Summary

In this chapter you have learned how to enter text and numbers to create a worksheet, how to select a range, how to use the Sum button, format cells, insert a chart, preview and print a worksheet, and correct errors on a worksheet. The items listed below include all the new Excel skills you have learned in this chapter.

1. To Start Excel (EX 6)
2. Enter the Worksheet Titles (EX 8)
3. Enter Column Titles (EX 10)
4. Enter Row Titles (EX 11)
5. Enter Numbers (EX 12)
6. Sum a Column of Numbers (EX 14)
7. Copy a Cell to Adjacent Cells in a Row (EX 16)
8. Determine Multiple Totals at the Same Time (EX 18)
9. Save a Workbook (EX 19)
10. Change a Cell Style (EX 21)
11. Change the Font (EX 22)
12. Bold a Cell (EX 23)
13. Increase the Font Size of a Cell Entry (EX 24)
14. Change the Font Color of a Cell Entry (EX 25)
15. Center Cell Entries Across Columns by Merging Cells (EX 25)
16. Format Column Titles and the Total Row (EX 27)
17. Format Numbers in the Worksheet (EX 29)
18. Adjust the Column Width (EX 30)
19. Use the Name Box to Select a Cell (EX 31)
20. Add a Clustered Cylinder Chart to the Worksheet (EX 35)
21. Change the Worksheet Name and Sheet Tab Color (EX 38)
22. Change Document Properties (EX 40)
23. Save an Existing Workbook with the Same File Name (EX 41)
24. Preview and Print a Worksheet in Landscape Orientation (EX 42)
25. Quit Excel (EX 44, 50)
26. Start Excel (EX 44)
27. Open a Workbook from Excel (EX 45)
28. Use the AutoCalculate Area to Determine a Maximum (EX 46)
29. Clear Cell Entries Using the Fill Handle (EX 49)
30. Clear Cell Entries Using the Shortcut Menu (EX 49)
31. Clear Cell Entries Using the Delete Key (EX 49)
32. Clear Cell Entries and Formatting Using the Clear Button (EX 49)
33. Clear Formatting Using the Cell Styles Button (EX 49)
34. Clear the Entire Worksheet (EX 50)
35. Delete an Embedded Chart (EX 50)

If you have a SAM 2010 user profile, your instructor may have assigned an autogradable version of this assignment. If so, log into the SAM 2010 Web site at www.cengage.com/sam2010 to download the instruction and start files.

Learn It Online

Test your knowledge of chapter content and key terms.

Instructions: To complete the Learn It Online exercises, please visit **www.cengagebrain.com**. At the CengageBrain.com home page, search for *Office 2011 for Mac* using the search box at the top of the page. This will take you to the product page for this book. On the product page, click the Access Now button below the Study Tools heading. On the Book Companion Site Web page, select Excel Chapter 1, and then click the link for the desired exercise.

Chapter Reinforcement TF, MC, and SA

A series of true/false, multiple choice, and short answer questions that test your knowledge of the chapter content.

Flash Cards

An interactive learning environment where you identify chapter key terms associated with displayed definitions.

Practice Test

A series of multiple choice questions that test your knowledge of chapter content and key terms.

Who Wants To Be a Computer Genius?

An interactive game that challenges your knowledge of chapter content in the style of a television quiz show.

Wheel of Terms

An interactive game that challenges your knowledge of chapter key terms in the style of the television show *Wheel of Fortune*.

Crossword Puzzle Challenge

A crossword puzzle that challenges your knowledge of key terms presented in the chapter.

Apply Your Knowledge

Reinforce the skills and apply the concepts you learned in this chapter.

Changing the Values in a Worksheet

Instructions: Start Excel. Open the workbook Apply 1–1 Clothes Campus Third Quarter Expenses (Figure 1–75a). See the inside back cover of this book for instructions for downloading the Data Files for Students, or see your instructor for information on accessing the files required in this book.

1. Set the zoom to 125%. Make the changes to the worksheet described in Table 1–6 so that the worksheet appears as shown in Figure 1–75b. As you edit the values in the cells containing numeric data, watch the totals in row 7, the totals in column F, and the chart change.

2. Change the worksheet title in cell A1 to the Title cell style and then merge and center it across columns A through F. Use the commands on the Home tab under Font on the ribbon to change the worksheet subtitle in cell A2 to 16-point Cambria red, bold font and then center it across columns A through F. Use the Accent 2 theme color (column 6, row 1 in the Font Color gallery) for the red font color. Center the column titles in B3:F3.

3. Apply the worksheet name, Third Quarter Expenses, to the sheet tab and apply the Accent 2 theme color to the sheet tab.

4. Change the document properties as specified by your instructor. Save the workbook using the file name, Apply 1–1 Clothed for Campus Third Quarter Expenses. Close the workbook and exit Excel. Submit the revised workbook as specified by your instructor.

Table 1–6 New Worksheet Data	
Cell	**Change Cell Contents To**
A1	Clothed for Campus
B4	7829.50
C4	19057.83
D5	24217.92
E5	25859.62
E6	35140.84

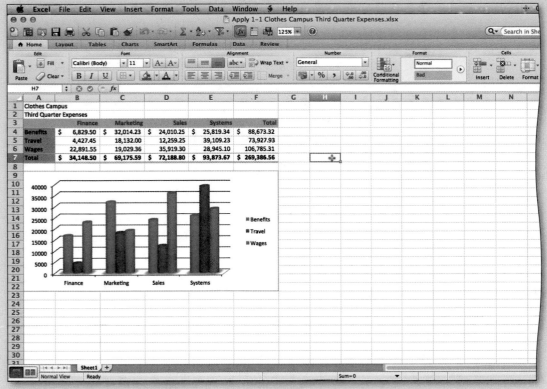

(a) Before

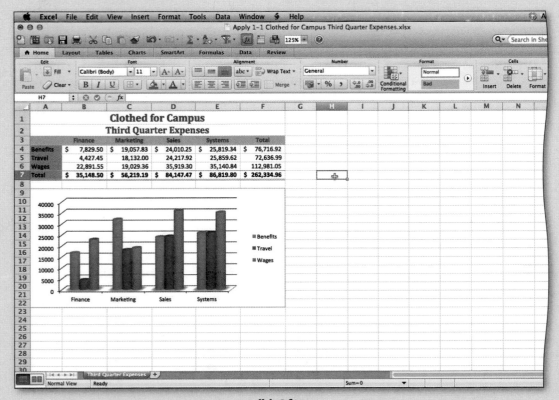

(b) After

Figure 1–75

Extend Your Knowledge

Extend the skills you learned in this chapter and experiment with new skills. You may need to use Help to complete the assignment.

Formatting a Worksheet and Adding Additional Charts

Instructions: Start Excel. Open the workbook Extend 1–1 Pack Right Moving Supplies. See the inside back cover of this book for instructions for downloading the Data Files for Students, or see your instructor for information on accessing the files required in this book. Perform the following tasks to format cells in the worksheet and to add two charts to the worksheet.

1. Set the zoom to 125%. Use the commands in the Font group on the Home tab on the ribbon to change the font of the title in cell A1 to 22-point Arial Black, Accent 3, bold, and the subtitle of the worksheet to 14-point Arial, Accent 2, bold.

2. Select the range A3:G8, click the Charts tab on the ribbon, and then click the Area button under Insert Chart on the ribbon to view the Area chart options (Figure 1–76).

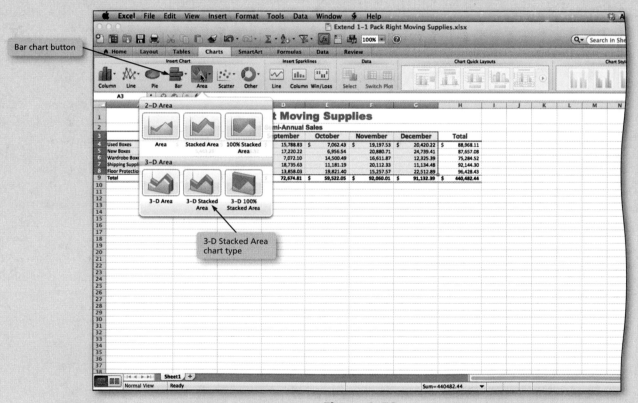

Figure 1–76

3. Insert a 3-D Stacked Area chart by clicking the 3-D Stacked Area chart type in the gallery. Move the chart either below or to the right of the data in the worksheet. Apply a chart style of your choice to the chart.

4. Deselect the chart and reselect the range A3:G8, and then follow Step 3 above to insert a Clustered Cone chart from the Bar gallery in the worksheet. Move the chart either below or to the right of the data so that the chart does not overlap the Stacked Area in 3-D chart. Make sure to make the values on the horizontal axis readable by expanding the size of the chart. Choose a different chart style for this chart than the one you selected for the Stacked Area in 3-D chart.

5. Resize each chart so that it snaps to the worksheet gridlines. You may need to scroll the worksheet to resize and view the charts. Preview the worksheet.

6. Apply a worksheet name to the sheet tab and apply a color of your choice to the sheet tab.

7. Change the document properties as specified by your instructor. Save the workbook using the file name, Extend 1–1 Pack Right Moving Supplies Charts. Close the workbook and exit Excel. Submit the revised workbook as specified by your instructor.

Make It Right

Analyze a workbook and correct all errors and/or improve the design.

Fixing Formatting Problems and Data Errors in a Worksheet

Instructions: Start Excel. Open the workbook Make It Right 1–1 Pets. See the inside back cover of this book for instructions for downloading the Data Files for Students, or see your instructor for information on accessing the files required for this book. Correct the following formatting problems and data errors (Figure 1–77) in the worksheet, while keeping in mind the guidelines presented in this chapter.

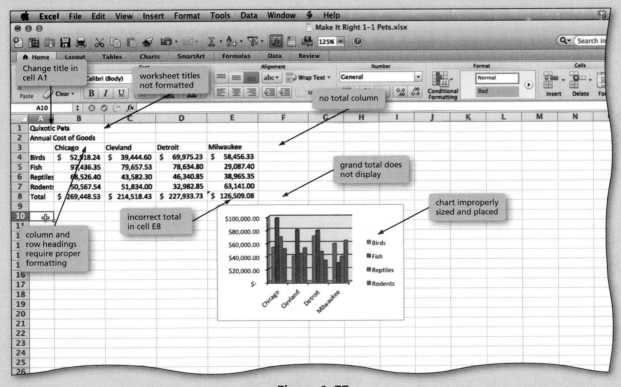

Figure 1–77

1. Set the zoom to 125%

2. Merge and center the worksheet title and subtitle appropriately.

3. Format the worksheet title with a cell style appropriate for a worksheet title.

4. Format the subtitle using commands on the Home tab under the Font group and apply the Accent 2 color to the subtitle.

5. Correct the typographical error in cell A1 by changing Quixotic to Exotic. Correct the spelling mistake in cell C3 by changing Clevland to Cleveland.

Continued >

6. Add a column header for totals in column F and create the necessary totals in column F.

7. Apply proper formatting to the column headers and total row, including centering the column headers.

8. Adjust the column sizes so that all data in each column is visible.

9. Create the grand total for the annual cost of goods.

10. The SUM function in cell E8 does not sum all of the numbers in the column. Correct this error by editing the range for the SUM function in the cell.

11. Resize and move the chart so that it is below the worksheet data and does not extend past the right edge of the worksheet data. Be certain to snap the chart to the worksheet gridlines by holding down the COMMAND key as you resize the chart to the right edge of column F and the bottom of row 22.

12. Apply a worksheet name to the sheet tab and apply the Accent 5 color to the sheet tab.

13. Change the document properties as specified by your instructor. Save the workbook using the file name, Make It Right 1–1 Exotic Pets Annual Cost of Goods. Close the workbook and exit Excel. Submit the revised workbook as specified by your instructor.

In the Lab

Design and/or create a workbook using the guidelines, concepts, and skills presented in this chapter. Labs 1, 2, and 3 are listed in order of increasing difficulty.

Lab 1: Annual Revenue Analysis Worksheet

Problem: You work as a spreadsheet specialist for A Healthy Body Shop, a high-end total fitness center franchise. Your manager has asked you to develop an annual revenue analysis worksheet similar to the one shown in Figure 1–78.

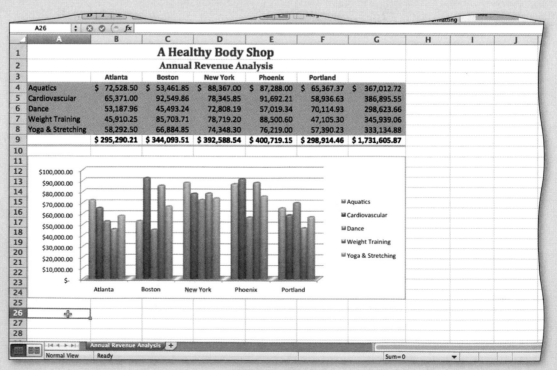

Figure 1–78

Instructions: Perform the following tasks.

1. Start Excel and open a new blank workbook. Set the zoom to 125%. Enter the worksheet title, A Healthy Body Shop, in cell A1 and the worksheet subtitle, Annual Revenue Analysis, in cell A2. Beginning in row 3, enter the franchise locations, fitness activities, and annual revenues shown in Table 1–7.

Table 1–7 A Healthy Body Shop Annual Revenues

	Atlanta	Boston	New York	Phoenix	Portland
Aquatics	72528.50	53461.85	88367.00	87288.00	65367.37
Cardiovascular	65371.00	92549.86	78345.85	91692.21	58936.63
Dance	53187.96	45493.24	72808.19	57019.34	70114.93
Weight Training	45910.25	85703.71	78719.20	88500.60	47105.30
Yoga & Stretching	58292.50	66884.85	74348.30	76219.00	57390.23

2. Create totals for each franchise location, fitness activity, and company grand total.

3. Format the worksheet title with the Title cell style. Center the title across columns A through G.

4. Format the worksheet subtitle to 14-point Constantia, Text 2 font color, bold font, and center it across columns A through G.

5. Use Cell Styles to format the range A3:G3 with the Heading 3 cell style, the range A4:G8 with the 40% - Accent 6 cell style (you may have to scroll down to find this), and the range A9:G9 with the Total cell style. Center the column headers in row 3. Apply the Accounting Number format to the range B4:G4 and the range B9:G9. Apply the Comma Style to the range B5:G8. Adjust any column widths to the widest text entry in each column.

6. Select the range A3:F8 and then insert a Clustered Cylinder Column chart. Apply the style in row 4, column 2 of the Chart Styles gallery to the chart. Move and resize the chart so that it appears in the range A11:G24.

7. Apply the worksheet name, Annual Revenue Analysis, to the sheet tab and apply the Accent 6, Darker 25% color to the sheet tab. Change the document properties, as specified by your instructor.

8. Save the workbook using the file name Lab 1-1 A Healthy Body Shop Annual Revenue Analysis.

9. Preview and print the worksheet in landscape orientation.

10. Make the following two corrections to the sales amounts: 62,675.45 for New York Weight Training (cell D7), 67,238.56 for Portland Cardiovascular (cell F5). After you enter the corrections, the company totals in cell G8 should equal $1,723,864.05.

11. Preview and print the revised worksheet in landscape orientation. Close the workbook without saving the changes and exit Excel.

12. Submit the assignment as specified by your instructor.

In the Lab

Lab 2: Semiannual Sales Analysis Worksheet

Problem: As the chief accountant for Play 'em Again, a reseller of cell phones, DVDs, electronic games, MP3 players, and accessories, you have been asked by the vice president to create a worksheet to analyze the semiannual sales for the company by products across sales channels (Figure 1–79 on the following page). The sales channels and corresponding revenue by product for the year are shown in Table 1–8 on the next page.

Continued >

In the Lab *continued*

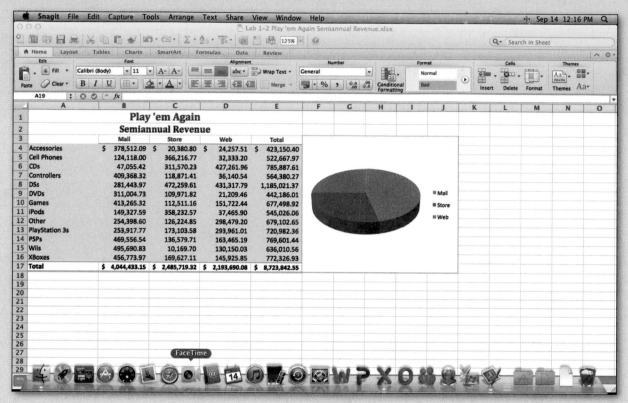

Figure 1–79

Instructions: Perform the following tasks.

1. Open a new Excel file and create the worksheet shown in Figure 1–79 using the data in Table 1–8.

2. Use the SUM function to determine total revenue for the three sales channels, the totals for each product, and the company total. Add column and row headings for the total row and total column, as appropriate.

Table 1–8 Play 'em Again Semiannual Revenue

	Mail	Store	Web
Accessories	378512.09	20380.80	24257.51
Cell Phones	124118.00	366216.77	32333.20
CDs	47055.42	311570.23	427261.96
Controllers	409368.32	118871.41	36140.54
DSs	281443.97	472259.61	431317.79
DVDs	311004.73	109971.82	21209.46
Games	413265.32	112511.16	151722.44
iPods	149327.59	358232.57	37465.90
Other	254398.60	126224.85	298479.20
PlayStation 3s	253917.77	173103.58	293961.01
PSPs	469556.54	136579.71	163465.19
Wiis	495690.83	10169.70	130150.03
XBoxes	456773.97	169627.11	145925.85

3. Format the worksheet title with the Title cell style and center it across columns A through E. Use the Font group on the ribbon to format the worksheet subtitle to 16-point Cambria red, bold font. Center the subtitle across columns A through E.

4. Format the range B3:E3 with the Heading 3 cell style and center the text in the cells. Format the range A4:E16 with the 20% - Accent4 cell style, and the range B17:E17 with the Total cell style. Format cells B4:E4 and B17:E17 with the Accounting Number Format and cells B5:E16 with the Comma Style numeric format. Adjust the column widths of columns A through E to accommodate the largest entry in each.

5. Create a pie chart that shows the revenue contributions of each sales channel. Chart the sales channel names (B3:D3) and corresponding totals (B17:D17). That is, select the range B3:D3, and then while holding down the COMMAND key, select the range B17:D17. Insert the 3-D Pie chart, as shown in Figure 1–79, by using the Pie button in the Chart Type group on the Charts tab. Use the chart location F3: J17.

6. Apply the worksheet name, Semiannual Revenue, to the sheet tab and apply the Accent 4, Lighter 80% color to the sheet tab. Change the document properties, as specified by your instructor.

7. Save the workbook using the file name, Lab 1-2 Play 'em Again Semiannual Revenue. Print the worksheet in landscape orientation.

8. Two corrections to the figures were sent in from the accounting department. The correct revenue is $118,124.45 for Cell Phones sold through the mail (cell B5) and $43,573.67 for iPods sold over the Web (cell D11). After you enter the two corrections, the company total in cell E17 should equal $8,725,956.77. Print the revised worksheet in landscape orientation.

9. Use the Undo button twice to change the worksheet back to the original numbers in Table 1–8. Use the Redo button twice to change the worksheet back to the revised state.

10. Close Excel without saving the latest changes. Start Excel and open the workbook saved in Step 7. Double-click cell C14 and use in-cell editing to change the PSPs Store revenue (cell C14) to $128,857.32. Write the company total in cell E17 at the top of the first printout. Click the Undo button.

11. Click cell A1 and then click the Merge button on the Home tab under Alignment on the ribbon to split cell A1 into cells A1, B1, C1, D1, and E1. Use the Merge button to merge the cell range A1:E1 into one again.

12. Close the workbook without saving the changes. Submit the assignment as specified by your instructor.

In the Lab

Lab 3: Projected College Cash Flow Analysis Worksheet

Problem: Attending college is an expensive proposition and your resources are limited. To plan for your four-year college career, you have decided to organize your anticipated resources and expenses in a worksheet. The data required to prepare your worksheet is shown in Table 1–9.

Table 1–9 College Cost and Resources				
Resources	Freshman	Sophomore	Junior	Senior
529 Plans	2700.00	2889.00	3091.23	3307.62
Financial Aid	5250.00	5617.50	6010.73	6431.48
Job	3100.00	3317.00	3549.19	3797.63
Parents	3700.00	3959.00	4236.13	4532.66
Savings	4250.00	4547.50	4865.83	5206.43
Other	1100.00	1177.00	1259.39	1347.55

Continued >

In the Lab *continued*

Table 1–9 College Cost and Resources *(continued)*				
Expenses	**Freshman**	**Sophomore**	**Junior**	**Senior**
Activities Fee	500.00	535.00	572.45	612.52
Books	650.00	695.50	744.19	796.28
Clothes	750.00	802.50	858.68	918.78
Entertainment	1650.00	1765.50	1889.09	2021.32
Room & Board	7200.00	7704.00	8243.28	8820.31
Tuition	8250.00	8827.50	9445.43	10106.60
Miscellaneous	1100.00	1177.00	1259.39	1347.55

Instructions Part 1:   Using the numbers in Table 1–9, create the worksheet shown in columns A through F in Figure 1–80. Set the zoom to 125%. Format the worksheet title as Calibri 24-point bold purple. Merge and center the worksheet title in cell A1 across columns A through F. Format the worksheet subtitles in cells A2 and A11 as Calibri 16-point bold red. Format the ranges A3:F3 and A12:F12 with the Heading 2 cell style and center the text in the cells. Format the ranges A4:F9 and A13:F19 with the 20% - Accent 2 cell style, and the ranges A10:F10 and A20:F20 with the Total cell style.

Change the name of the sheet tab and apply the Dark Purple color from the Standard Colors area to the sheet tab. Update the document properties, including the addition of at least one keyword to the properties, and save the workbook using the file name, Lab 1-3 Part 1 College Resources and Expenses. Print the worksheet. Submit the assignment as specified by your instructor.

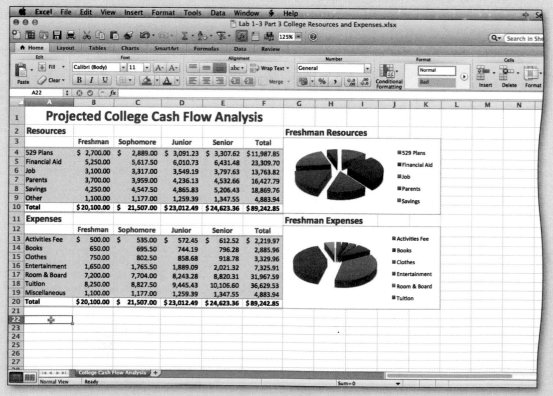

Figure 1–80

After reviewing the numbers, you realize you need to increase manually each of the Sophomore-year expenses in column C by $400, except for the Activities Fee. Change the Sophomore-year expenses to reflect this change. Manually change the Parents resources for the Sophomore year by the amount required to cover the increase in costs. The totals in cells F10 and F20 should equal $91,642.87. Print the worksheet. Close the workbook without saving changes.

Instructions Part 2: Open the workbook Lab 1–3 Part 1 College Resources and Expenses and then save the workbook using the file name, Lab 1-3 Part 2 College Resources and Expenses. Set the zoom to 125%. Insert a 3-D Exploded Pie chart in the range G3:K10 to show the contribution of each category of resources for the Freshman year. Chart the range A4:B9 and apply the chart style in column 2, row 4 of the Chart Styles gallery to the chart. Add the Pie chart title as shown in cell G2 in Figure 1–80. Insert a 3-D Exploded Pie chart in the range G12:K20 to show the contribution of each category of expenses for the Freshman year. Chart the range A13:B19 and apply the same chart style to the chart. Add the Pie chart title shown in cell G11 in Figure 1–80. Save the workbook. In the Print dialog, click the Scaling: check box to shrink the sheet to a single page, and then print the worksheet in landscape orientation. Submit the assignment as specified by your instructor.

Instructions Part 3: Open the workbook Lab 1-3 Part 2 College Resources and Expenses and then save the workbook using the file name, Lab 1-3 Part 3 College Resources and Expenses. A close inspection of Table 1–9 shows that both cost and financial support figures increase 7% each year. Use Excel Help to learn how to enter the data for the last three years using a formula and the Copy and Paste buttons in the Standard toolbar. For example, the formula to enter in cell C4 is =B4*1.07. Enter formulas to replace all the numbers in the range C4:E9 and C13:E19. If necessary, reformat the tables, as described in Part 1. The worksheet should appear as shown in Figure 1–80, except that some of the totals will be off by approximately 0.01 due to rounding errors. Save the workbook. Submit the assignment as specified by your instructor. Close the workbook without saving changes.

Cases and Places

Apply your creative thinking and problem solving skills to design and implement a solution.

1: Analyzing Quarterly Expenses

Academic

To estimate the funds needed by your school's Travel Club to make it through the upcoming quarter, you decide to create a report for the club itemizing the expected quarterly expenses. The anticipated expenses are listed in Table 1–10. Use the concepts and techniques presented in this chapter to create the worksheet and an embedded Clustered Cylinder chart. Be sure to use an appropriate chart style that compares the quarterly cost of each expense. Total each expense item and each quarter. Include a grand total for all of the expenses. Use the AutoCalculate area to determine the average amount spent per quarter on each expense. Manually insert the averages with appropriate titles in an appropriate area on the worksheet.

Table 1–10 Travel Club Quarterly Expenses				
	1st Quarter	**2nd Quarter**	**3rd Quarter**	**4th Quarter**
Copies and Supplies	75	50	80	150
Meeting Room Rent	400	425	400	425
Miscellaneous	150	100	175	70
Refreshments	130	155	150	225
Speaker Fees	200	200	400	500
Travel	450	375	500	375

Continued >

Cases and Places *continued*

2: Create a 3-D Exploded Pie Chart to Summarize Property Values

Personal

Your wealthy Aunt Nicole owns several properties of varying value. She would like to see the values of the properties in a worksheet and chart that helps her to better understand her investments. She has asked you to develop a worksheet totaling the values of the properties and also to include other relevant statistics. The property values are: Property 1, $56,671.99; Property 2, $82,276.58; Property 3, $60,135.45; Property 4, $107,373.39; and Property 5, $87,512.82. Create a 3-D Exploded pie chart to illustrate the relative property values. Use the AutoCalculate area to find the average, maximum, and minimum property values and manually enter them and their corresponding identifiers in an appropriate area of the worksheet. Use the AutoSum button to total the property values.

3: Analyzing Historical Yearly Sales

Business

You are working part-time for Noble's Mobile Services. Your manager has asked you to prepare a worksheet to help her analyze historical yearly sales by type of product (Table 1–11). Use the concepts and techniques presented in this chapter to create the worksheet and an embedded 3-D Clustered Column chart that includes proper numerical formatting, totaling, and formatting of the worksheet.

Table 1-11 Noble's Mobile Services Historical Yearly Sales				
	2008	**2009**	**2010**	**2011**
Camera Phones	92598	10487	136791	176785
Headsets	9035	8909	4886	6512
Music Phones	57942	44923	54590	67696
Other Accessories	27604	38793	24483	33095
Satellite Radios	17161	19293	30763	44367
Standard Mobile Phones	8549	9264	7600	6048
Wireless PDAs	57963	68059	103025	87367

2 Formulas, Functions, and Formatting

Objectives

You will have mastered the material in this chapter when you can:

- Enter formulas using the keyboard
- Enter formulas using Point mode
- Apply the AVERAGE, MAX, and MIN functions
- Verify a formula using Range Finder
- Apply a theme to a workbook
- Apply a date format to a cell or range

- Add conditional formatting to cells
- Change column width and row height
- Check the spelling in a worksheet
- Set margins, headers, and footers in Page Layout view
- Preview and print versions of a worksheet

2 Formulas, Functions, and Formatting

Introduction

In Chapter 1, you learned how to enter data, sum values, format a worksheet to make it easier to read, and draw a chart. This chapter continues to highlight these topics and presents some new ones.

The new topics covered in this chapter include using formulas and functions to create a worksheet. A **function** is a prewritten formula that is built into Excel. Other new topics include option buttons, verifying formulas, applying a theme to a worksheet, adding borders, formatting numbers and text, using conditional formatting, changing the widths of columns and heights of rows, spell checking, using alternative types of worksheet displays and printouts, and adding page headers and footers to a worksheet. One alternative worksheet display and printout shows the formulas in the worksheet instead of the values. When you display the formulas in the worksheet, you see exactly what text, data, formulas, and functions you have entered into it.

Project — Worksheet with Formulas and Functions

The project in this chapter follows proper design guidelines and uses Excel to create the worksheet shown in Figure 2–1. The Mobile Masses Store opened its doors when consumer demand for mobile devices, such as mobile phones and PDAs, had just begun. The store's owners pay each employee on a biweekly basis. Before the owners pay the employees, they summarize the hours worked, pay rate, and tax information for each employee to ensure that the business properly compensates its employees. This summary includes information such as the employee names, hire dates, number of dependents, hours worked, hourly pay rate, net pay, and tax information. As the complexity of the task of creating the summary increases, the owners want to use Excel to create a biweekly payroll report.

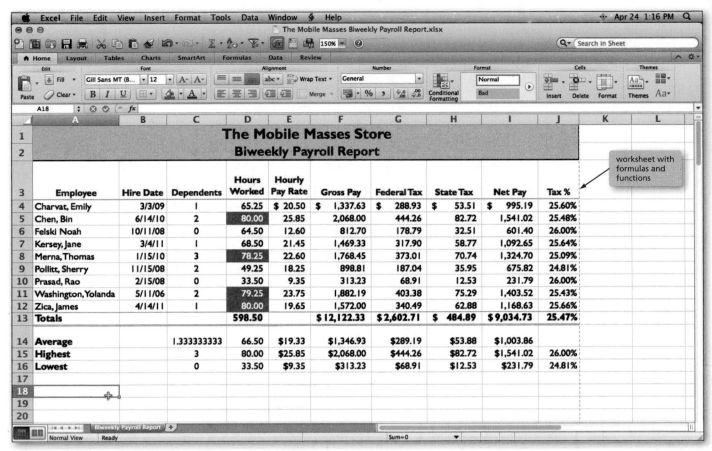

Figure 2–1 Worksheet

Recall that the first step in creating an effective worksheet is to make sure you understand what is required. The people who will use the worksheet usually provide the requirements. The requirements document for The Mobile Masses Store Biweekly Payroll Report worksheet includes the following needs: source of data, summary of calculations, and other facts about its development (Figure 2–2 on the following page).

REQUEST FOR NEW WORKSHEET

Date Submitted:	April 16, 2013
Submitted By:	Samuel Snyder
Worksheet Title:	The Mobile Masses Store Biweekly Payroll Report
Needs:	An easy-to-read worksheet that summarizes the company's biweekly payroll (Figure 2-3 on page EX 68). For each employee, the worksheet is to include the employee's name, hire date, dependents, hours worked, hourly pay rate, gross pay, federal tax, state tax, net pay, and total tax percent. The worksheet also should include totals and the average, highest value, and lowest value for column of numbers specified below.
Source of Data:	The data supplied by Samuel includes the employee names, hire dates, hours worked, and hourly pay rates. This data is shown in Table 2-1 on page EX 71.
Calculations:	The following calculations must be made for each of the employees: 1. Gross Pay = Hours Worked × Hourly Pay Rate 2. Federal Tax = 0.22 × (Gross Pay − Dependents * 24.32) 3. State Tax = 0.04 × Gross Pay 4. Net Pay = Gross Pay − (Federal Tax + State Tax) 5. Tax % = (Federal Tax + State Tax) / Gross Pay 6. Compute the totals for hours worked, gross pay, federal tax, state tax, and net pay. 7. Compute the total tax percent. 8. Use the AVERAGE function to determine the average for dependents, hours worked, hourly pay rate, gross pay, federal tax, state tax, and net pay. 9. Use the MAX and MIN functions to determine the highest and lowest values for dependents, hours worked, hourly pay rate, gross pay, federal tax, state tax, net pay and total tax percent.

Approvals

Approval Status:	X	Approved
		Rejected
Approved By:	Julie Adams	
Date:	April 23, 2013	
Assigned To:	J. Quasney, Spreadsheet Specialist	

Figure 2–2

Overview

As you read this chapter, you will learn how to create the worksheet shown in Figure 2–1 on the previous page by performing these general tasks:

- Enter formulas and apply functions in the worksheet
- Add conditional formatting to the worksheet
- Apply a theme to the worksheet
- Set margins, and add headers and footers to a worksheet
- Work with the worksheet in Page Layout view
- Change margins on the worksheet
- Print a section of the worksheet

General Project Decisions

☐ **Plan Ahead**

While creating an Excel worksheet, you need to make several decisions that will determine the appearance and characteristics of the finished worksheet. As you create the worksheet necessary to meet the requirements shown in Figure 2–2, you should follow these general guidelines:

1. **Plan the layout of the worksheet.** Rows typically contain items analogous to items in a list. A name could serve as an item in a list, and, therefore, each name could be placed in a row. As a list grows, such as a list of employees, the number of rows in the worksheet will increase. Information about each item in the list and associated calculations should appear in columns.

2. **Determine the necessary formulas and functions needed.** Calculations result from known values. Formulas for such calculations should be known in advance of creating a worksheet. Values such as the average, highest, and lowest values can be calculated using Excel functions as opposed to relying on complex formulas.

3. **Identify how to format various elements of the worksheet.** The appearance of the worksheet affects its ability to express information clearly. Numeric data should be formatted in generally accepted formats, such as using commas as thousands separators and parentheses for negative values.

4. **Establish rules for conditional formatting.** Conditional formatting allows you to format a cell based on the contents of the cell. Decide under which circumstances you would like a cell to stand out from related cells and determine in what way the cell will stand out.

5. **Specify how the hard copy of a worksheet should appear.** When it is possible that a person will want to create a hard copy of a worksheet, care should be taken in the development of the worksheet to ensure that the contents can be presented in a readable manner. Excel prints worksheets in landscape or portrait orientation, and margins can be adjusted to fit more or less data on each page. Headers and footers add an additional level of customization to the printed page.

When necessary, more specific details concerning the above guidelines are presented at appropriate points in the chapter. The chapter also will identify the actions performed and decisions made regarding these guidelines during the creation of the worksheet shown in Figure 2–1 on page EX 65.

In addition, using a sketch of the worksheet can help you visualize its design. The sketch for The Mobile Masses Store Biweekly Payroll Report worksheet includes a title, a subtitle, column and row headings, and the location of data values (Figure 2–3 on the following page). It also uses specific characters to define the desired formatting for the worksheet, as follows:

1. The row of Xs below the leftmost column defines the cell entries as text, such as employee names.

2. The rows of Zs and 9s with slashes, dollar signs, decimal points, commas, and percent signs in the remaining columns define the cell entries as numbers. The Zs indicate that the selected format should instruct Excel to suppress leading 0s. The 9s indicate that the selected format should instruct Excel to display any digits, including 0s.

3. The decimal point means that a decimal point should appear in the cell entry and indicates the number of decimal places to use.

4. The slashes in the second column identify the cell entry as a date.

Aesthetics versus Function

The function, or purpose, **BTW** of a worksheet is to provide a user with direct ways to accomplish tasks. In designing a worksheet, functional considerations should come before visual aesthetics. Avoid the temptation to use flashy or confusing visual elements within the worksheet. One exception to this guideline occurs when you may need to draw the user's attention to an area of a worksheet that will help the user more easily complete a task.

5. The dollar signs that are not adjacent to the Zs in the first row below the column headings and in the total row signify a fixed dollar sign. The dollar signs that are adjacent to the Zs below the total row signify a floating dollar sign, or one that appears next to the first significant digit.

6. The commas indicate that the selected format should instruct Excel to display a comma separator only if the number has enough digits to the left of the decimal point.

7. The percent sign (%) in the far-right column indicates a percent sign should appear after the number.

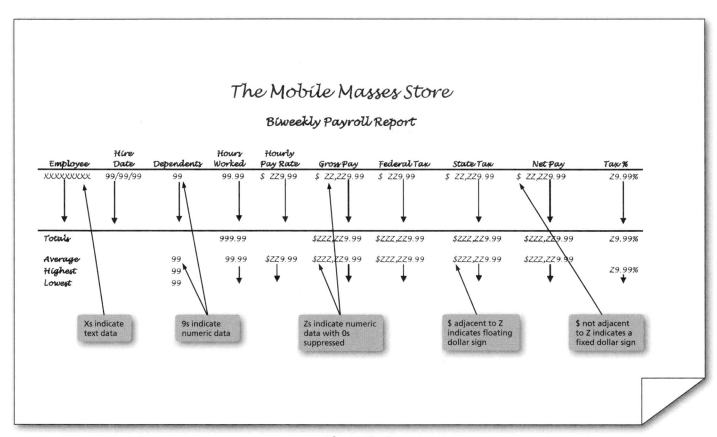

Figure 2–3

With a good comprehension of the requirements document, an understanding of the necessary decisions, and a sketch of the worksheet, the next step is to use Excel to create the worksheet.

To Start Excel

If you are using a computer to step through the project in this chapter and you want your screens to match the figures in this book, you should change your screen's resolution to 1280 × 800. For information about how to change a computer's resolution, refer to the Office 2011 and Mac OS X chapter at the beginning of this book.

The following steps, which assume Mac OS X is running, start Excel based on a typical installation. You may need to ask your instructor how to start Excel for your computer. For a detailed example of the procedure summarized below, refer to the Office 2011 and Mac OS X chapter.

1 Click the Excel icon in the Dock to display the Excel Workbook Gallery.

2 If All is not selected in the Templates pane on the left, click to select it.

3 Double-click the Excel Workbook icon in the Excel Workbook Gallery to display a new blank workbook in the Excel window.

4 If the Excel window is not sized properly, as described in the Office 2011 and Mac OS X chapter at the beginning of this book, size the window properly.

5 If the Normal View button in the lower left of the workbook window is not selected, click it so that your screen is in Normal view.

Entering the Titles and Numbers into the Worksheet

The first step in creating the worksheet is to enter the titles and numbers into the worksheet. The following sets of steps enter the worksheet title and subtitle and then the biweekly payroll report data shown in Table 2–1 on page EX 71.

> For an introduction to Office 2011 and instruction about how to perform basic tasks in Office 2011 programs, read the Office 2011 and Mac OS X chapter at the beginning of this book, where you can learn how to start a program, use the ribbon, save a file, open a file, quit a program, use Help, and much more.

To Enter the Worksheet Title and Subtitle

The following steps enter the worksheet title and subtitle into cells A1 and A2.

1 Set the zoom to 150%.

Q&A Why change the zoom to 150%?
Change the zoom when you cannot see clearly the content you are working on. Setting the zoom to a larger number makes rows and columns of numbers easier to read and edit. A smaller number for the zoom can be useful when evaluating the layout of components such as data and supporting charts, on the worksheet. Keep in mind that the zoom affects how the spreadsheet displays on the screen, not how it prints out on paper. Adjust the zoom to the level that best suits your working needs.

2 If necessary, select cell A1. Type **The Mobile Masses Store** in the selected cell and then press the DOWN ARROW key to enter the worksheet title.

3 Type **Biweekly Payroll Report** in cell A2 and then press the DOWN ARROW key to enter the worksheet subtitle (Figure 2–4 on page EX 71).

The employee names and the row titles Totals, Average, Highest, and Lowest in the leftmost column begin in cell A4 and continue down to cell A16. The employee data is entered into rows 4 through 12 of the worksheet. The remainder of this section explains the steps required to enter the column titles, payroll data, and row titles, as shown in Figure 2–4, and then save the workbook.

To Enter the Column Titles

The column titles in row 3 begin in cell A3 and extend through cell J3. Some of the column titles in Figure 2–3 on the next page include multiple lines of text, such as Hours Worked in cell D3. To start a new line in a cell, press CONTROL-OPTION-RETURN after each line, except for the last line, which is completed by clicking the Enter button, pressing the RETURN key, or pressing one of the arrow keys. When you see CONTROL-OPTION-RETURN in a step, press the RETURN key while holding down both the CONTROL and OPTION keys and then release all three keys. The steps on the next page enter the column titles.

The Ribbon and Screen Resolution

BTW Excel may change how the groups and buttons within the groups appear on the ribbon, depending on the computer's screen resolution. Thus, your ribbon may look different from the ones in this book if you are using a screen resolution other than 1280 × 800.

1 With cell A3 selected, type **Employee** and then press the RIGHT ARROW key to enter the column heading.

2 Type **Hire Date** in cell B3 and then press the RIGHT ARROW key to enter the column heading.

3 Type **Dependents** and then press the RIGHT ARROW key to enter the column heading.

4 In cell D3, type **Hours** and then press CONTROL-OPTION-RETURN to enter the first line of the column heading. Type **Worked** and then press the RIGHT ARROW key to enter the column heading.

5 Type **Hourly** in cell E3 and then press CONTROL-OPTION-RETURN to begin a new line in the cell. Type **Pay Rate** and then press the RIGHT ARROW key to enter the column heading.

6 Type **Gross Pay** in cell F3 and then press the RIGHT ARROW key to enter the column heading.

7 Type **Federal Tax** in cell G3 and then press the RIGHT ARROW key to enter the column heading.

8 Type **State Tax** in cell H3 and then press the RIGHT ARROW key to enter the column heading.

9 Type **Net Pay** in cell I3 and then press the RIGHT ARROW key to enter the column heading.

10 Type **Tax %** in cell J3 to enter the column heading.

BTWs

BTW For a complete list of the BTWs found in the margins of this book, visit the Office 2011 for Mac Online Companion Web page at www.cengagebrain.com, navigate to the desired chapter, and click BTWs.

Four-Digit Years

BTW By default, Excel for Mac uses a two-digit year value. Use four-digit years, if necessary, to ensure that Excel interprets year values the way you intend.

To Enter the Biweekly Payroll Data

The biweekly payroll data in Table 2–1 includes a hire date for each employee. Excel considers a date to be a number and, therefore, it displays the date right-aligned in the cell. The following steps enter the data for each employee: name, hire date, dependents, hours worked, and hourly pay rate.

1 Select cell A4, type **Charvat, Emily,** and then press the RIGHT ARROW key to enter the employee name.

2 Type **3/3/09** in cell B4 and then press the RIGHT ARROW key to enter a date in the selected cell.

3 Type **1** in cell C4 and then press the RIGHT ARROW key to enter a number in the selected cell.

4 Type **65.25** in cell D4 and then press the RIGHT ARROW key to enter a number in the selected cell.

5 Type **20.50** in cell E4 and then click cell A5 to enter a number in the selected cell.

6 Enter the payroll data in Table 2–1 for the eight remaining employees in rows 5 through 12 (Figure 2–4).

Q&As

BTW For a complete list of the Q&As found in many of the step-by-step sequences in this book, visit the Office 2011 for Mac Online Companion Web page at www.cengagebrain.com, navigate to the desired chapter, and click Q&As.

Q&A In step 5, why did the data that was entered as 20.50 display as 20.5?
The Excel default for number formatting is the General formatting. General formatting deletes trailing zeros by default. You will change the formatting in a later step.

Table 2–1 The Mobile Masses Store Biweekly Payroll Report Data

Employee	Hire Date	Dependents	Hours Worked	Hourly Pay Rate
Charvat, Emily	3/3/09	1	65.25	20.50
Chen, Bin	6/14/10	2	80.00	25.85
Felski, Noah	10/11/08	0	64.50	12.60
Kersey, Jane	3/4/11	1	68.50	21.45
Merna, Thomas	1/15/10	3	78.25	22.60
Pollitt, Sherry	11/15/08	2	49.25	18.25
Prasad, Rao	2/15/08	0	33.50	9.35
Washington, Yolanda	5/11/06	2	79.25	23.75
Zica, James	4/14/11	1	80.00	19.65

Formatting Worksheets **BTW**

With early worksheet programs, users often skipped rows to improve the appearance of the worksheet. With Excel it is not necessary to skip rows because you can increase row heights to add white space between rows.

To Enter the Row Titles

The following steps add row titles for the rows that will contain the totals, average, highest, and lowest amounts.

1 Select cell A13. Type **Totals** and then press the DOWN ARROW key to enter a row header.

2 Type **Average** in cell A14 and then press the DOWN ARROW key to enter a row header.

3 Type **Highest** in cell A15 and then press the DOWN ARROW key to enter a row header.

4 Type **Lowest** in cell A16 and then press the RETURN key to enter a row header. Select cell F4 to prepare to enter a formula in the cell (Figure 2–4).

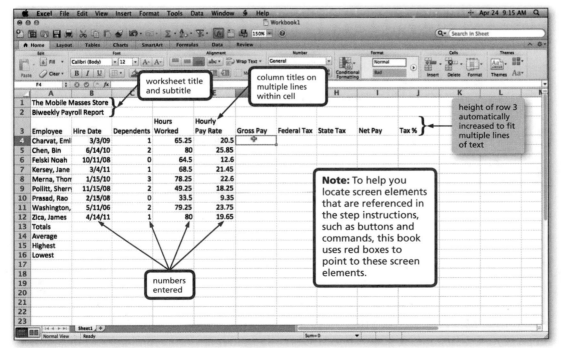

Figure 2–4

Wrapping Text **BTW**

If you have a long text entry, such as a paragraph, you can instruct Excel to wrap the text in a cell. This method is easier than pressing COMMAND-OPTION-RETURN to end each line of text within the paragraph. To wrap text, select the cell, click the Wrap Text button on the Home tab under Alignment and choose Wrap Text from the menu. If you want to control where each line ends in the cell, rather than letting Excel wrap the text based on the cell width, you must end each line with COMMAND-OPTION-RETURN.

To Change Document Properties

As discussed in Chapter 1, the first time you save a workbook, you should change the document properties. The following steps change the document properties.

1 Click File in the menu bar to display the File menu.

2 Choose Properties to open the Workbook1 Properties dialog.

3 Click the Author text box. If necessary, type your name as the Author property. If another name already is displayed in the Author text box, delete it before typing your name.

4 Click the Subject text box, if necessary delete any existing text, and then type your course and section as the Subject property.

5 Click the Keywords text box, if necessary delete any existing text, and then type **Biweekly Payroll Report** as the Keywords property.

6 Click the OK button to close the Document Properties dialog.

Entering Numbers in a Range

BTW An efficient way to enter data into a range of cells is to select a range and then enter the first number in the upper-left cell of the range. Excel responds by accepting the value and moving the active cell selection down one cell. When you enter the last value in the first column, Excel moves the active cell selection to the top of the next column.

To Change the Sheet Name and Save the Workbook

The following steps change the sheet name to Biweekly Payroll Report, change the sheet tab color, and save the workbook on a USB flash drive in the Excel folder (for your assignments) using the file name, The Mobile Masses Biweekly Payroll Report.

1 Double-click the Sheet1 tab and then enter **Biweekly Payroll Report** as the sheet name and then press the RETURN key.

2 CONTROL-click the tab to display the shortcut menu and then choose Tab Color in the shortcut menu to display the Tab Color window. Click Accent 1, Darker 25% (column 5, row 5) in the Theme Colors area to apply a new color to the sheet tab.

3 Click the close button in the Tab Color window title bar to close the window.

4 With a USB flash drive connected to one of the computer's USB ports, click the Save button in the Standard toolbar to display the Save As dialog.

5 Type **The Mobile Masses Biweekly Payroll Report** in the File name text box to change the file name. Do not press the RETURN key after typing the file name because you do not want to close the dialog at this time.

6 Navigate to the desired save location (in this case, the Excel folder in the CIS 101 folder [or your class folder] on the USB flash drive).

7 Click the Save button (Save As dialog) to save the document in the selected folder on the selected drive with the entered file name.

Entering Formulas

One of the reasons Excel is such a valuable tool is that you can assign a **formula** to a cell, and Excel will calculate the result. Consider, for example, what would happen if you had to multiply 65.25 by 20.5 and then manually enter the product for Gross Pay, 1,337.625, in cell F4. Every time the values in cells D4 or E4 changed, you would have to recalculate the product and enter the new value in cell F4. By contrast, if you enter a formula in cell F4 to multiply the values in cells D4 and E4, Excel recalculates the product whenever new values are entered into those cells and displays the result in cell F4.

Determine the formulas and functions needed.

As you have learned, formulas and functions simplify the creation and maintenance of worksheets because Excel performs calculations for you. When formulas and functions are used together properly, the amount of data that a user manually must enter in a worksheet greatly can be diminished:

- **Utilize proper algebraic notation.** Most Excel formulas are the result of algebraic calculations. A solid understanding of algebraic operators and the order of operations is important to writing sound formulas.

- **Utilize the fill handle and copy and paste operations to copy formulas.** The fill handle and the Excel copy and paste functionality help to minimize errors caused by retyping formulas. When possible, if a similar formula will be used repeatedly in a worksheet, avoid retyping the formula and instead use the fill handle.

- **Be careful about using invalid and circular cell references.** An invalid reference occurs when Excel does not understand a cell reference used in a formula, resulting in Excel displaying a #REF! error message in the cell.

A formula in a cell that contains a reference back to itself is called a **circular reference**. Excel often warns you when you create a circular reference. In almost all cases, circular references are the result of an incorrect formula. A circular reference can be direct or indirect. For example, placing the formula =A1 in cell A1 results in a direct circular reference. An indirect circular reference occurs when a formula in a cell refers to another cell or cells that include a formula that refers back to the original cell.

- **Employ the Excel built-in functions whenever possible.** Excel includes prewritten formulas called **functions** to help you compute a range of values and statistics. A function takes a value or values, performs an operation, and returns a result to the cell. The values that you use with a function are called **arguments**. All functions begin with an equal sign and include the arguments in parentheses after the function name. For example, in the function =AVERAGE(C4:C12), the function name is AVERAGE, and the argument is the range C4:C12. Become familiar with the extensive number of built-in functions. When you have the choice, always use built-in functions instead of writing and typing a formula version of your mathematical expression. Such a practice reduces the possibility of errors and simplifies the formula used in a cell, resulting in improved readability.

Automatic Recalculation

Every time you enter **BTW** a value into a cell in the worksheet, Excel automatically recalculates all formulas. You can change to manual recalculation by clicking the Settings button on the Formulas tab under Calculation, and then clicking Calculate Manually. In manual calculation mode, pressing COMMAND-= (the COMMAND key plus the EQUAL key) instructs Excel to recalculate all formulas.

To Enter a Formula Using the Keyboard

The formulas needed in the worksheet are noted in the requirements document as follows:

1. Gross Pay (column F) = Hours Worked × Hourly Pay Rate
2. Federal Tax (column G) = 0.22 × (Gross Pay – Dependents × 24.32)
3. State Tax (column H) = 0.04 × Gross Pay
4. Net Pay (column I) = Gross Pay – (Federal Tax + State Tax)
5. Tax % (column J) = (Federal Tax + State Tax) / Gross Pay

The gross pay for each employee, which appears in column F, is equal to hours worked in column D times hourly pay rate in column E. Thus, the gross pay for Emily Charvat in cell F4 is obtained by multiplying 65.25 (cell D4) by 20.50 (cell E4) or =D4*E4. The steps on the next page enter the initial gross pay formula in cell F4 using the keyboard.

1

• With cell F4 selected, type `=d4*e4` in the cell to display the formula in the formula bar and in the current cell and to display colored borders around the cells referenced in the formula (Figure 2–5).

Q&A What occurs on the worksheet as I enter the formula?

The **equal sign** (=) preceding d4*e4 alerts Excel that you are entering a formula or function and not text. Because the most common error when entering a formula is to reference the wrong cell in a formula mistakenly, Excel colors the borders of the cells referenced in the formula. The coloring helps in the reviewing process to ensure the cell references are correct. The **asterisk** (*) following d4 is the arithmetic operator that directs Excel to perform the multiplication operation.

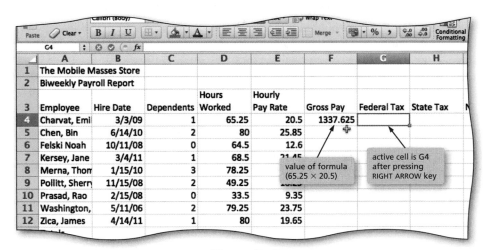

Figure 2–5

2

• Press the RIGHT ARROW key to complete the arithmetic operation indicated by the formula, to display the result in the worksheet, and to select the cell to the right (Figure 2–6). The number of decimal places shown in cell F4 may be different, but these values will be adjusted later in this chapter.

Figure 2–6

Arithmetic Operations

Table 2–2 describes multiplication and other valid Excel arithmetic operators.

Arithmetic Operator	Meaning	Example of Usage	Meaning
–	Negation	–78	Negative 78
%	Percentage	=23%	Multiplies 23 by 0.01
^	Exponentiation	=3 ^ 4	Raises 3 to the fourth power
*	Multiplication	=61.5 * C5	Multiplies the contents of cell C5 by 61.5
/	Division	=H3 / H11	Divides the contents of cell H3 by the contents of cell H11
+	Addition	=11 + 9	Adds 11 and 9
–	Subtraction	=22 – F15	Subtracts the contents of cell F15 from 22

Table 2–2 Summary of Arithmetic Operators

Order of Operations

When more than one arithmetic operator is involved in a formula, Excel follows the same basic order of operations that you use in algebra. Moving from left to right in a formula, the **order of operations** is as follows: first negation (–), then all percentages (%), then all exponentiations (^), then all multiplications (*) and divisions (/), and finally, all additions (+) and subtractions (–).

As in algebra, you can use parentheses to override the order of operations. For example, if Excel follows the order of operations, 8 * 3 + 2 equals 26. If you use parentheses, however, to change the formula to 8 * (3 + 2), the result is 40, because the parentheses instruct Excel to add 3 and 2 before multiplying by 8. Table 2–3 illustrates several examples of valid Excel formulas and explains the order of operations.

Troubling Formulas

If Excel does not accept a formula, remove the equal sign from the left side and complete the entry as text. Later, after you have entered additional data in the cells reliant on the formula or determined the error, reinsert the equal sign to change the text back to a formula and edit the formula as needed.

Table 2–3 Examples of Excel Formulas

Formula	Meaning
=G15	Assigns the value in cell G15 to the active cell.
=2^4 + 7	Assigns the sum of 16 + 7 (or 23) to the active cell.
=100 + D2 or =D2 +100 or =(100 + D2)	Assigns 100 plus the contents of cell D2 to the active cell.
=25% * 40	Assigns the product of 0.25 times 40 (or 10) to the active cell.
– (K15 * X45)	Assigns the negative value of the product of the values contained in cells K15 and X45 to the active cell. You do not need to type an equal sign before an expression that begins with minus signs, which indicates a negation.
=(U8 – B8) * 6	Assigns the product of the difference between the values contained in cells U8 and B8 times 6 to the active cell.
=J7 / A5 + G9 * M6 – Z2 ^ L7	Completes the following operations, from left to right: exponentiation (Z2 ^ L7), then division (J7 / A5), then multiplication (G9 * M6), then addition (J7 / A5) + (G9 * M6), and finally subtraction (J7 / A5 + G9 * M6) – (Z2 ^ L7). If cells A5 = 6, G9 = 2, J7 = 6, L7 = 4, M6 = 5, and Z2 = 2, then Excel assigns the active cell the value –5; that is, 6 / 6 + 2 * 5 – 2 ^ 4 = –5.

To Enter Formulas Using Point Mode

The sketch of the worksheet in Figure 2–3 on page EX 68 calls for the federal tax, state tax, net pay, and tax % for each employee to appear in columns G, H, I, and J, respectively. All four of these values are calculated using formulas in row 4:

Federal Tax (cell G4) = 0.22 × (Gross Pay – Dependents × 24.32) or =0.22*(F4–C4*24.32)

State Tax (cell H4) = 0.04 × Gross Pay or = 0.04* F4

Net Pay (cell I4) = Gross Pay – (Federal Tax + State Tax) or =F4-(G4+H4)

Tax % (cell J4) = (Federal Tax + State Tax) / Gross Pay or =(G4+H4)/F4

An alternative to entering the formulas in cells G4, H4, I4, and J4 using the keyboard is to enter the formulas using the mouse and Point mode. **Point mode** allows you to select cells for use in a formula by using the mouse. The steps on the following pages enter formulas using Point mode.

- With cell G4 selected type
  `=0.22*(` to begin the formula
  and then click cell F4 to add a
  cell reference in the formula
  (Figure 2–7).

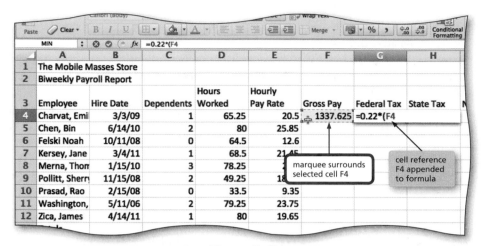

Figure 2–7

2

- Type `–` (minus sign) and then click
  cell C4 to add a subtraction operator
  and a reference to another cell to
  the formula.

- Type `*24.32)` to complete the
  formula (Figure 2–8).

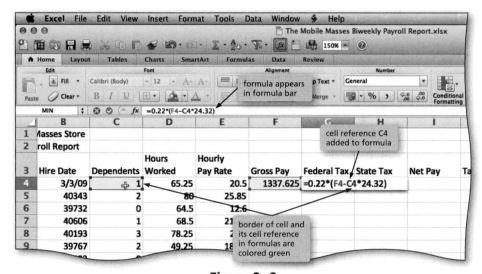

Figure 2–8

- Click the Enter button in the formula
  bar and then select cell H4 to prepare
  to enter the next formula.

- Type `=0.04*` and then click
  cell F4 to add a cell reference to
  the formula (Figure 2–9).

Q&A Why should I use Point mode to
enter formulas?

Using Point mode to enter formulas
often is faster and more accurate
than using the keyboard to type
the entire formula when the cell
you want to select does not require
you to scroll. In many instances, as
in these steps, you may want to use
both the keyboard and mouse when
entering a formula in a cell. You can
use the keyboard to begin the formula, for example,
and then use the mouse to select a range of cells.

Figure 2–9

4

- Click the Enter button in the formula bar and then select cell I4 to prepare to enter the next formula.

- Type = (equal sign) and then click cell F4 to begin the formula and add a cell reference to the formula.

- Type – ((minus sign followed by an open parenthesis) and then click cell G4 to add a cell reference to the formula.

- Type + (plus sign) and then click cell H4 to add an addition operator and cell reference to the formula.

- Type) (close parenthesis) to complete the formula (Figure 2–10).

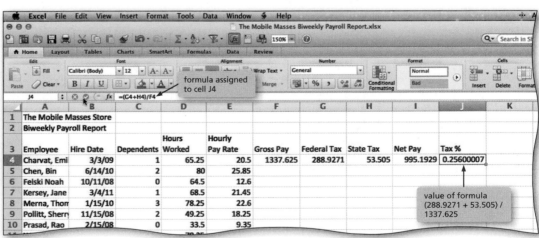

Figure 2–10

5

- Click the Enter button in the formula bar to enter the formula in cell I4.

- Select cell J4. Type = ((equal sign followed by an open parenthesis) and then click cell G4 to add a reference to the formula.

- Type + (plus sign) and then click cell H4 to add an addition operator and cell reference to the formula.

- Type) / (close parenthesis followed by a forward slash), and then click cell F4 to add a division operator and cell reference to the formula.

- Click the Enter button in the formula bar to enter the formula in cell J4 (Figure 2–11).

Figure 2–11

Q&A Why do eight decimal places show in cell J4?

The actual value assigned by Excel to cell J4 from the division operation in step 5 is 0.256000075, with nine decimal places. While not all the decimal places appear in Figure 2–11, Excel maintains all of them for computational purposes. Thus, if referencing cell J4 in a formula, the value used for computational purposes is 0.256000075, not 0.25600007. The General cell format is set to display up to 11 digits, depending on the width of the column. If you change the width of column J, more significant digits of the value will be displayed.

To Copy Formulas Using the Fill Handle

The five formulas for Emily Charvat in cells F4, G4, H4, I4, and J4 now are complete. You could enter the same five formulas one at a time for the eight remaining employees. A much easier method of entering the formulas, however, is to select the formulas in row 4 and then use the fill handle to copy them through row 12. When performing copying operations in Excel, the source area is the cell, or range, from which data or formulas are being copied. When a range is used as a source, sometimes it is called the source range. The destination area is the cell, or range, to which data or formulas are being copied. When a range is used as a destination, sometimes it is called the destination range. Recall from Chapter 1 that the fill handle is a small rectangle in the lower-right corner of the active cell or active range. The following steps copy the formulas using the fill handle.

- Select the source range, F4:J4 in this case, and then point to the fill handle.

- Drag the fill handle down through cell J12 and continue to hold the mouse button to select the destination range (Figure 2–12).

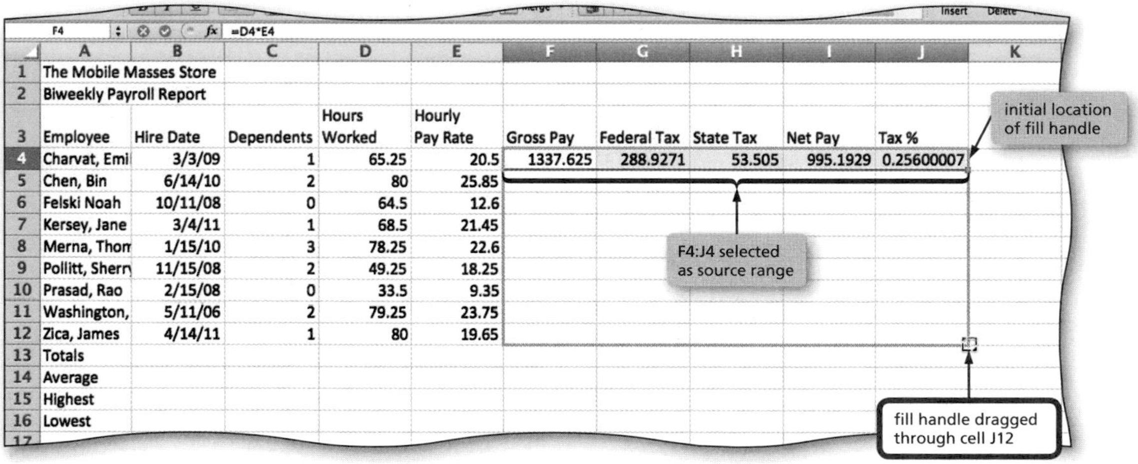

Figure 2–12

❷

- Release the mouse button to copy the formulas to the destination range (Figure 2–13).

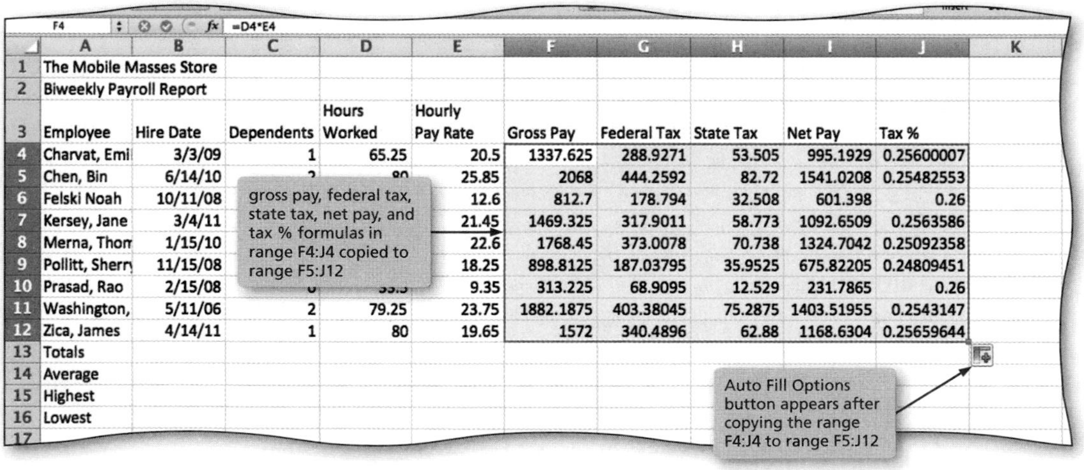

Q&A How does Excel adjust the cell references in the formulas in the destination area? Recall that when you copy a formula, Excel adjusts the cell references so that the new formulas contain references corresponding to the new location and perform calculations using the appropriate values. Thus, if you copy downward, Excel adjusts the row portion of cell references. If you copy across, then Excel adjusts the column portion of cell references. These cell references are called **relative cell references**.

Figure 2–13

Other Ways

1. CONTROL-click source area, choose Copy in shortcut menu, CONTROL-click destination area, choose Paste in shortcut menu

2. Select source area, click Copy button in Standard toolbar, select destination area, click Paste button in Standard toolbar

Option Buttons

Excel displays option buttons in a workbook while you are working on it to indicate that you can complete an operation using automatic features such as AutoCorrect, Auto Fill, error checking, and others. For example, the Auto Fill Options button shown in Figure 2–13 appears after a fill operation, such as dragging the fill handle. When an error occurs in a formula in a cell, Excel displays the Trace Error button next to the cell and identifies the cell with the error by placing a green triangle in the upper left of the cell.

Table 2–4 summarizes the option buttons available in Excel. When one of these buttons appears on your worksheet, click the button arrow to produce the list of options for modifying the operation or to obtain additional information.

Table 2–4 Options Buttons in Excel		
Button	**Name**	**Menu Function**
	Auto Fill Options	Gives options for how to fill cells following a fill operation, such as dragging the fill handle.
	Insert Options	Lists formatting options following an insertion of cells, rows, or columns.
	Paste Options	Specifies how moved or pasted items should appear (for example, with original formatting, without formatting, or with different formatting).
	Trace Error	Lists error-checking options following the assignment of an invalid formula to a cell.

The Paste Options Button

The Paste Options button BTW provides powerful functionality. When performing copy and paste operations, the button allows you great freedom in specifying what it is you want to paste. For example, you could choose to paste an exact copy of what you copied, including the cell contents and formatting. You also could copy just formulas, just formatting, just the cell values, a combination of these options, or a picture of what you copied.

To Determine Totals Using the AutoSum Button

The next step is to determine the totals in row 13 for the hours worked in column D, gross pay in column F, federal tax in column G, state tax in column H, and net pay in column I. To determine the total hours worked in column D, the values in the range D4 through D12 must be summed. To do so you can either enter the function =sum(d4:d12) in cell D13 or select cell D13 and use the AutoSum button in the Standard toolbar to perform the calculation. Recall that a function is a prewritten formula that is built into Excel. Similar SUM functions can be used in cells F13, G13, H13, and I13 to total gross pay, federal tax, state tax, and net pay, respectively. The following steps determine totals in cell D13 and the range F13:I13.

1 Select the cell to contain the sum, cell D13 in this case. Click the AutoSum button in the Standard toolbar to sum the contents of the range D4:D12 in cell D13 and then click the Enter button to display a total in the selected cell.

2 Select the range to contain the sums, range F13:I13 in this case. Click the AutoSum button to display totals in the selected range (Figure 2–14 on the next page).

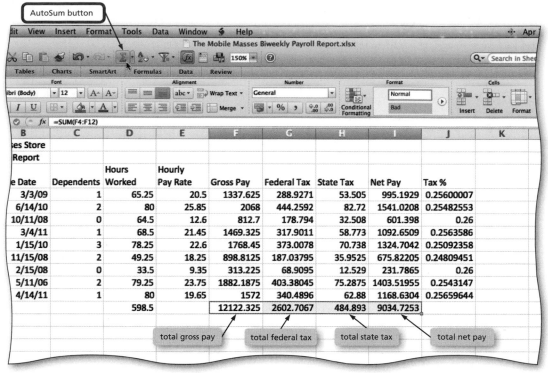

Figure 2–14

To Determine the Total Tax %

With the totals in row 13 determined, the next step is to copy the Tax % formula in cell J12 to cell J13 as performed in the following steps.

1 Select the cell to be copied, J12 in this case, and then point to the fill handle.

2 Drag the fill handle down through cell J13 to copy the formula (Figure 2–15).

Q&A Why was the formula I13/F13 not copied to cell J13 earlier?

The formula, I13/F13, was not copied to cell J13 when cell J4 was copied to the range J5:J12 because both cells involved in the computation (I13 and F13) were blank, or zero, at the time. A **blank cell** in Excel has a numerical value of zero, which would have resulted in an error message in cell J13. Once the totals were determined, both cells I13 and F13 (especially F13, because it is the divisor) had nonzero numerical values.

	A	B	C	D	E	F	G	H	I	J	K
1	The Mobile Masses Store										
2	Biweekly Payroll Report										
3	Employee	Hire Date	Dependents	Hours Worked	Hourly Pay Rate	Gross Pay	Federal Tax	State Tax	Net Pay	Tax %	
4	Charvat, Emi	3/3/09	1	65.25	20.5	1337.625	288.9271	53.505	995.1929	0.25600007	
5	Chen, Bin	6/14/10	2	80	25.85	2068	444.2592	82.72	1541.0208	0.25482553	
6	Felski Noah	10/11/08	0	64.5	12.6	812.7	178.794	32.508	601.398	0.26	
7	Kersey, Jane	3/4/11	1	68.5	21.45	1469.325	317.9011	58.773	1092.6509	0.2563586	
8	Merna, Thon	1/15/10	3	78.25	22.6	1768.45	373.0078	70.738	1324.7042	0.25092358	
9	Pollitt, Sherry	11/15/08	2	49.25	18.25	898.8125	187.03795	35.9525	675.82205	0.24809451	
10	Prasad, Rao	2/15/08	0	33.5	9.35	313.225	68.9095		7865	0.26	
11	Washington,	5/11/06	2	79.25	23.75	1882.1875	403.38045		1955	0.2543147	
12	Zica, James	4/14/11	1	80	19.65	1572	340.4896	62.88	1168.6304	0.25659644	
13	Totals			598.5		12122.325	2602.7067	484.893	9034.7253	0.25470359	
14	Average										
15	Highest										
16	Lowest										
17											
18											

formula is =(G12+H12)/F12

formula is =(G13+H13)/F13

Auto Fill Options button appears after copying cell J12 to cell J13

Figure 2–15

Using the AVERAGE, MAX, and MIN Functions

The next step in creating The Mobile Masses Biweekly Payroll Report worksheet is to compute the average, highest value, and lowest value for the number of dependents listed in the range C4:C12 using the AVERAGE, MAX, and MIN functions in the range C14:C16. Once the values are determined for column C, the entries can be copied across to the other columns.

With Excel, you can enter functions using one of six methods: (1) the keyboard or mouse, (2) the Formula Builder button in the formula bar, (3) the AutoSum button arrow, (4) the Insert button in the Function group on the Formulas tab, (5) the Function command on the Insert menu, and (6) the Name box area in the formula bar (Figure 2–16). The method you choose will depend on your typing skills and whether you can recall the function name and required arguments.

In the following pages, each of the first three methods will be used. The keyboard and mouse method will be used to determine the average number of dependents (cell C14). The Formula Builder button in the formula bar method will be used to determine the highest number of dependents (cell C15). The AutoSum button arrow method will be used to determine the lowest number of dependents (cell C16).

Statistical Functions BTW

Excel usually considers a blank cell to be equal to 0. The statistical functions, however, ignore blank cells. Excel thus calculates the average of three cells with values of 10, blank, and 8 to be 9 [(10 + 8) / 2] and not 6 [(10 + 0 + 8) / 3].

To Determine the Average of a Range of Numbers Using the Keyboard and Mouse

The **AVERAGE function** sums the numbers in the specified range and then divides the sum by the number of cells with numeric values in the range. The following steps use the AVERAGE function to determine the average of the numbers in the range C4:C12.

1

- Select the cell to contain the average, cell C14 in this case.

- Type **=av** in the cell to display the Formula AutoComplete list. Press the DOWN ARROW key to highlight the required function (Figure 2–16).

Q&A What is happening as I type?

As you type the equal sign followed by the characters in the name of a function, Excel displays the Formula AutoComplete list. This list contains those functions that alphabetically match the letters you have typed. Because you typed =av, Excel displays all the functions that begin with the letters av.

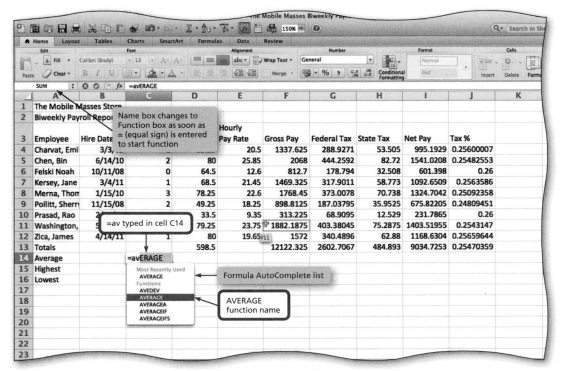

Figure 2–16

● Click AVERAGE in the Formula
AutoComplete list to select the
function.

● Select the range to be averaged,
C4:C12 in this case, to insert the
range as the argument to the
function (Figure 2–17).

Q&A As I drag, why does the function
in cell C14 change?

When you click cell C4, Excel
appends cell C4 to the left
parenthesis in the formula bar and
surrounds cell C4 with a marquee.
When you begin dragging, Excel
appends to the argument a colon
(:) and the cell reference of the cell
where the mouse pointer is located.

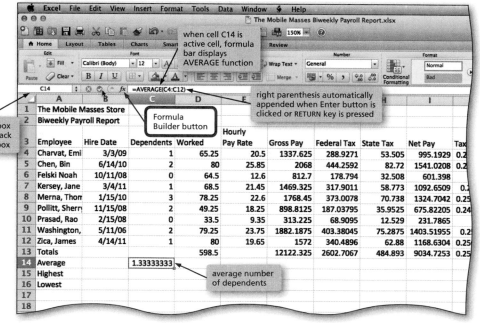

Figure 2–17

● Click the Enter button to compute
the average of the numbers in the
selected range and display the result
in the selected cell (Figure 2–18).

Q&A Can I use the arrow keys to
complete the entry instead?

No. When you use Point
mode you cannot use the
arrow keys to complete the
entry. While in Point mode,
the arrow keys change the selected
cell reference in the range you are
selecting.

Q&A What is the purpose of the
parentheses in the function?

The AVERAGE function requires
that the argument (in this case, the
range C4:C12) be included within
parentheses following the function
name. Excel automatically appends
the right parenthesis to complete the AVERAGE function
when you click the Enter button or press the RETURN key.

Figure 2–18

● **Other Ways**

1. On Formulas tab, under
   Function, click AutoSum
   button arrow, choose
   Average

2. Click Formula Builder
   button in formula bar,
   click AVERAGE

3. Click AutoSum button
   arrow in Standard toolbar,
   click Average

To Determine the Highest Number in a Range of Numbers Using the Formula Builder

The next step is to select cell C15 and determine the highest (maximum) number in the range C4:C12. Excel includes a function called the **MAX function** that displays the highest value in a range. Although you could enter the MAX function using the keyboard and Point mode as described in the previous steps, an alternative method to entering the function is to use the Formula Builder in the formula bar. The following steps use the Formula Builder in the formula bar to enter the MAX function.

- Select the cell to contain the maximum number, cell C15 in this case.

- Click the Formula Builder button in the formula bar to display the Formula Builder window.

- Double-click MAX in the function list in the Formula Builder to select it (Figure 2–19). If the MAX function is not displayed in the function list, scroll the list until the function is displayed.

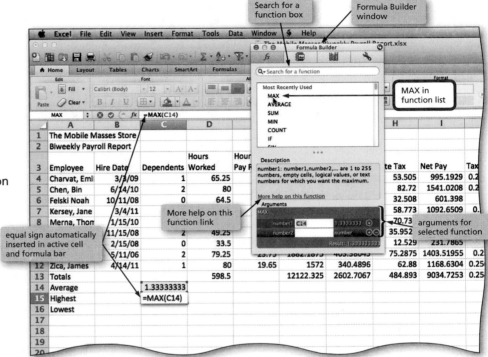

Figure 2–19

- Type **c4:c12** in the number1 box (Formula Builder) to enter the first argument of the function (Figure 2–20).

Q&A Why did numbers appear in the Formula Builder?
As shown in Figure 2–20, Excel displays the value the MAX function will return to cell C15 in the Formula Builder. It also lists the first few numbers in the selected range, next to the number1 box.

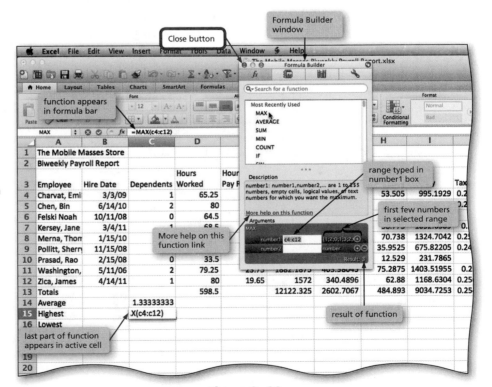

Figure 2–20

3

- Click the Close button in the Formula Builder window to display the highest value in the chosen range in the selected cell and in the formula bar (Figure 2–21).

Q&A Why should I not just enter the highest value that I see in the range C4:C12 in cell C15?
In this example, rather than entering the MAX function, you visually could scan the range C4:C12, determine that the highest number of dependents is 3, and manually enter the number 3 as a constant in cell C15. Excel would display the number the same as in Figure 2–21. Because it contains a constant, however, Excel will continue to display 3 in cell C15, even if the values in the range C4:C12

change. If you use the MAX function, Excel will recalculate the highest value in the range C4:C12 each time a new value is entered into the worksheet.

MAX function determines highest value in range C4:C12

	A	B	C	D	E	F	G	H
1	The Mobile Masses Store							
2	Biweekly Payroll Report							
3	Employee	Hire Date	Dependents	Hours Worked	Hourly Pay Rate	Gross Pay	Federal Tax	State Tax
4	Charvat, Emi	3/3/09	1	65.25	20.5	1337.625	288.9271	53.505
5	Chen, Bin	6/14/10	2	80	25.85	2068	444.2592	82.72
6	Felski Noah	10/11/08	0	64.5	12.6	812.7	178.794	32.508
7	Kersey, Jane	3/4/11	1	68.5	21.45	1469.325	317.9011	58.773
8	Merna, Thom	1/15/10	3	78.25	22.6	1768.45	373.0078	70.738
9	Pollitt, Sherr	11/15/08	2	49.25	18.25	898.8125	187.03795	35.9525
10	Prasad, Rao	2/15/08	0	33.5	9.35	313.225	68.9095	12.529
11	Washington,	5/11/06	2	79.25	23.75	1882.1875	403.38045	75.2875
12	Zica, James	4/14/11	1	80	19.65	1572	340.4896	62.88
13	Totals			598.5		12122.325	2602.7067	484.893
14	Average		1.33333333					
15	Highest		3					
16	Lowest							
17								

C15 =MAX(C4:C12)

highest value in range C4:C12

Figure 2–21

Other Ways

1. On Formulas tab, under Function, click AutoSum button arrow, choose Max
2. Click AutoSum button arrow in Standard toolbar, click Max
3. Type **=MAX** in cell

To Determine the Lowest Number in a Range of Numbers Using the AutoSum Menu

The next step is to enter the **MIN function** in cell C16 to determine the lowest (minimum) number in the range C4:C12. Although you can enter the MIN function using either of the methods used to enter the AVERAGE and MAX functions, the following steps perform an alternative using the AutoSum button in the Standard toolbar.

1

- Select cell C16 to prepare to enter the next function.

- In the Standard toolbar, click the AutoSum button arrow to display the AutoSum pop-up menu (Figure 2–22).

Q&A Why should I use the AutoSum pop-up menu?
Using the AutoSum pop-up menu allows you to enter one of five often-used functions easily into a cell, without having to memorize its name or the required arguments.

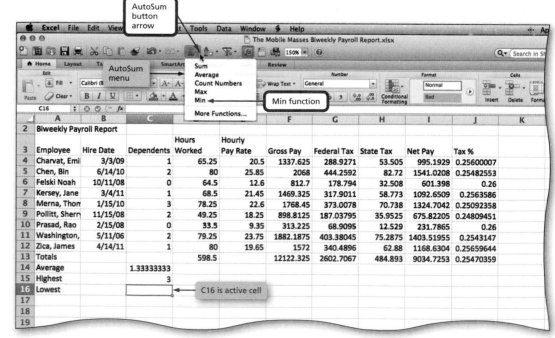

Figure 2–22

2

- Click Min to display the MIN function in the formula bar and in the active cell (Figure 2–23).

Q&A Why does Excel select the range C14:C15?

The range C14:C15 automatically selected by Excel is not correct. Excel attempts to guess which cells you want to include in the function by looking for ranges that are adjacent to the selected cell and that contain numeric data.

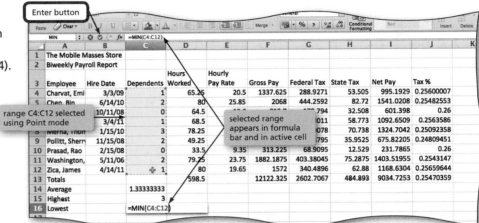

Figure 2–23

3

- Click cell C4 and then drag through cell C12 to display the function with the new range in the formula bar and in the selected cell (Figure 2–24).

Figure 2–24

4

- Click the Enter button to determine the lowest value in the range C4:C12 and display the result in the formula bar and in the selected cell (Figure 2–25).

Q&A How can I learn about other functions?

Excel has more than 400 additional functions that perform just about every type of calculation you can imagine. These functions are categorized in the Formula Builder shown in Figure 2–19 on page EX 83. To view the categories, scroll through the function list: the functions are grouped by category. To obtain a description of a selected function, select its name in the Formula Builder. Excel displays the description of the function in the Description area of the Formula Builder.

Figure 2–25

 Other Ways

1. On Formulas tab, under Function, click AutoSum button arrow, choose Min

2. Click Formula Builder button in formula bar (if necessary, select Statistical category), choose MIN

3. Choose View > Formula Builder in menu bar, choose MIN (Formula Builder)

4. Type `=MIN` in cell

To Copy a Range of Cells Across Columns to an Adjacent Range Using the Fill Handle

The next step is to copy the AVERAGE, MAX, and MIN functions in the range C14:C16 to the adjacent range D14:J16. The following steps use the fill handle to copy the functions.

- Select the source range from which to copy the functions, in this case C14:C16.

- Drag the fill handle in the lower-right corner of the selected range through cell J16 and continue to hold down the mouse button to begin a fill operation (Figure 2–26).

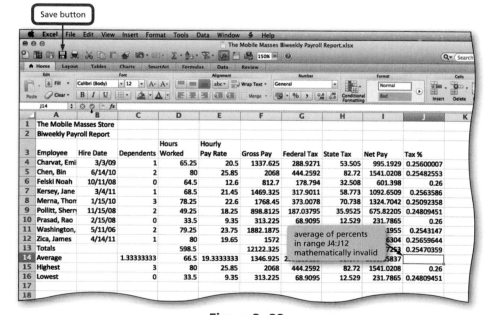

Figure 2–26

- Release the mouse button to copy the three functions to the selected range (Figure 2–27).

Q&A How can I be sure that the function arguments are proper for the cells in range D14:J16?
Remember that Excel adjusts the cell references in the copied functions so that each function refers to the range of numbers above it in the same column. Review the numbers in rows 14 through 16 in Figure 2–27. You should see that the functions in each column return the appropriate values, based on the numbers in rows 4 through 12 of that column.

Figure 2–27

- Select cell J14, press the DELETE key and then click the Enter button to delete the average of the Tax % (Figure 2–28).

Q&A Why is the formula in cell J14 deleted?
The average of the Tax % in cell J14 is deleted because an average of percentages of this type is mathematically invalid.

Figure 2–28

Other Ways

1. CONTROL-click source area, choose Copy in shortcut menu, CONTROL-click destination area, choose Paste in shortcut menu

2. Select source area, click Copy button in Standard toolbar, select destination area, click Paste button in Standard toolbar

3. Select source area, choose Edit > Copy in menu bar, select destination area, choose Edit > Paste in menu bar

4. Select source area, press COMMAND-C, select destination area, press COMMAND-V

To Save a Workbook Using the Same File Name

Earlier in this project, an intermediate version of the workbook was saved using the file name, The Mobile Masses Biweekly Payroll Report. The following step saves the workbook a second time, using the same file name.

1 Click the Save button in the Standard toolbar to overwrite the previously saved file.

Break Point: If you wish to take a break, this is a good place to do so. You can quit Excel now. To resume at a later time, start Excel, open the file called Mobile Masses Biweekly Payroll Report, and continue following the steps from this location forward.

Verifying Formulas Using Range Finder

One of the more common mistakes made with Excel is to include a wrong cell reference in a formula. An easy way to verify that a formula references the cells you want it to reference is to use the Excel Range Finder. Use **Range Finder** to check which cells are referenced in the formula assigned to the active cell. Range Finder allows you to make immediate changes to the cells referenced in a formula.

To use Range Finder to verify that a formula contains the intended cell references, double-click the cell with the formula you want to check. Excel responds by highlighting the cells referenced in the formula so that you can check that the cell references are correct.

Entering Functions
You can drag the Formula **BTW** Builder (Figure 2–20 on page EX 83) out of the way in order to select a range. You also can click the green Maximize button on the Formula Builder title bar to collapse the Formula Builder. After selecting the range, click the green Maximize button again to expand the Formula Builder.

To Verify a Formula Using Range Finder

The following steps use Range Finder to check the formula in cell J4.

1

- Double-click cell J4 to activate Range Finder (Figure 2–29).

2

- Press the ESC key to quit Range Finder and then click anywhere in the worksheet, such as cell A18, to deselect the current cell.

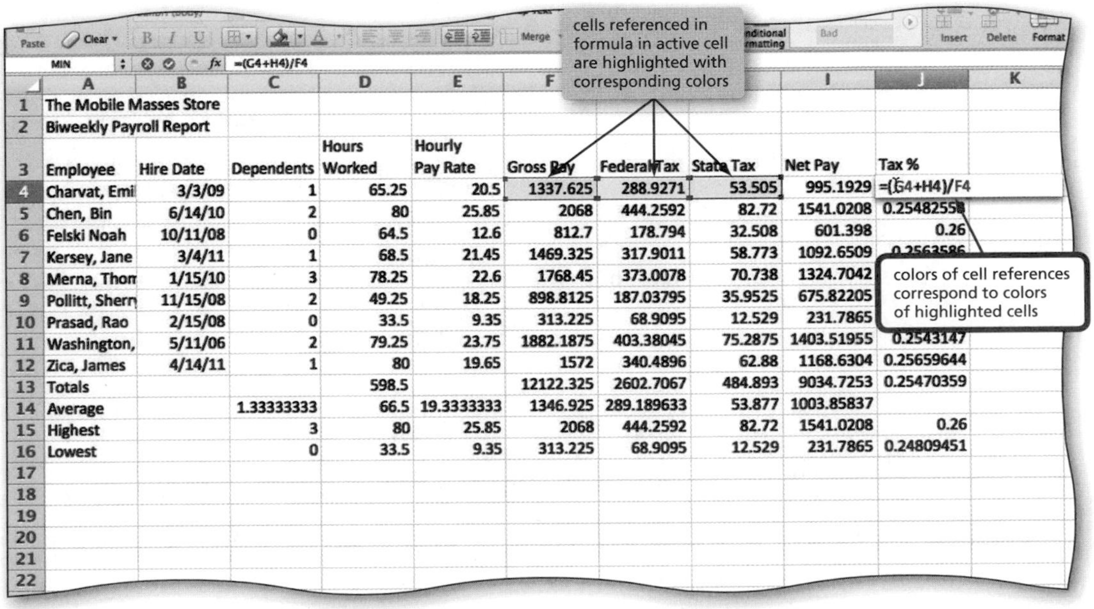

Figure 2–29

Formatting the Worksheet

Although the worksheet contains the appropriate data, formulas, and functions, the text and numbers need to be formatted to improve their appearance and readability.

In Chapter 1, cell styles were used to format much of the worksheet. This section describes how to change the unformatted worksheet in Figure 2–30a to the formatted worksheet in Figure 2–30b using a theme and other commands on the ribbon. The colors and fonts that are used in the worksheet shown in Figure 2–30b are those that are associated with the Solstice theme.

(a) Unformatted Worksheet

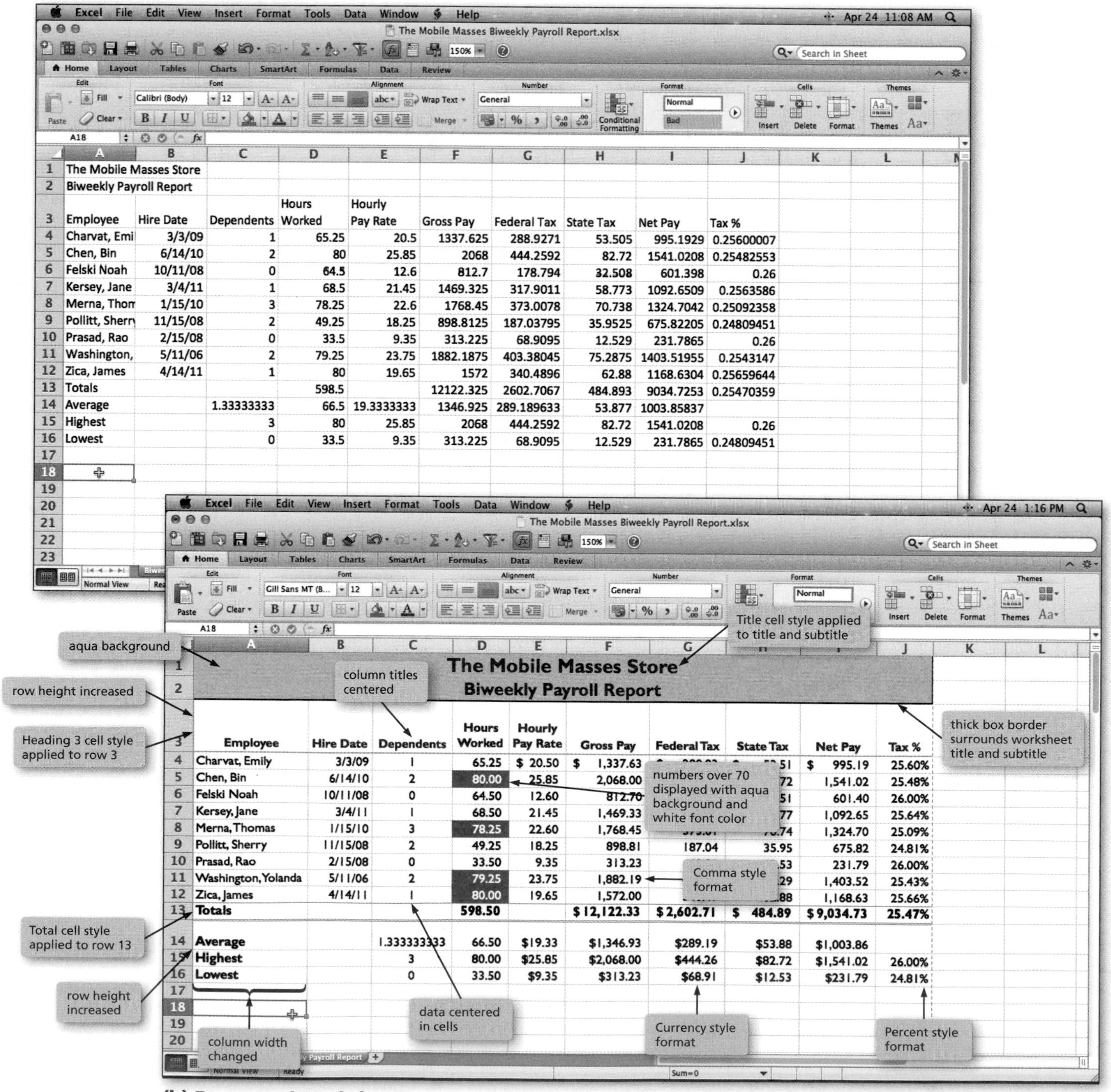

(b) Formatted Worksheet

Figure 2–30

☐ **Plan Ahead**

Identify how to format various elements of the worksheet.

As you have learned, applying proper formatting to a worksheet improves its appeal and readability. The following list includes additional worksheet formatting considerations.

- **Consider using cell borders and fill colors for various portions of the worksheet.** Cell borders, or box borders, draw a border around a cell or range of cells to set the cell or range off from other portions of the worksheet. For example, worksheet titles often include cell borders. Similarly, the use of a fill color in a cell or range of cells sets off the cell or range from other portions of the worksheet and provides visual impact to draw the user's eye toward the cell or range.

- **Use good judgment when centering values in columns.** If a cell entry is short, such as the dependents in column C, centering the entries within their respective columns improves the appearance of the worksheet.

- **Consider the use of a different theme.** A **theme** is a predefined set of colors, fonts, chart styles, cell styles, and fill effects that can be applied to an entire workbook. Every new workbook that you create is assigned a default theme named Office. Excel, however, includes a variety of other themes that provide a range of visual effects for your workbooks.

- **Apply proper formatting for cells that include dates.** Excel provides a number of date formats so that date values can be formatted to meet your needs. How you decide to format a date depends on a number of factors. For example, dates that include years both before and after the year 2000 should be formatted with a four-digit year. Your organization or department may insist on the use of certain standard date formats. Industry standards also may indicate how you should format date values.

The following outlines the formatting suggested in the sketch of the worksheet in Figure 2–3 on page EX 68.

1. Workbook theme — Solstice
2. Worksheet title and subtitle
   a. Alignment — center across columns A through J
   b. Cell style — Title
   c. Font size — title 18; subtitle 16
   d. Background color (range A1:J2) — Accent 1, Lighter 60%
   e. Border — thick box border around range A1:J2
3. Column titles
   a. Cell style — Heading 3
   b. Alignment — center
4. Data
   a. Dates in column B — mm/dd/yy format
   b. Alignment — center data in range C4:C12
   c. Numbers in column D — Comma style and two decimal places; if a cell in range D4:D12 is greater than 70, then cell appears with background color of aqua and a font color of white
   d. Numbers in top row (range E4:I4) — Accounting number format
   e. Numbers below top row (range E5:I12) — Comma style and decimal places
5. Total line
   a. Cell style — Total
   b. Numbers — Accounting number format

6. Average, highest, and lowest rows

    a. Font style of row titles in range A14:A16 — bold

    b. Numbers — Currency style with floating dollar sign in the range E14:I16

7. Percentages in column J

    a. Numbers — Percentage style with two decimal places

8. Column widths

    a. Columns A, B, and C — best fit

    b. Column H — 10.22 characters

    c. Column D, E, and J — 7.56 characters

9. Row heights

    a. Row 3 — 48.00 points

    b. Row 14 — 27.00 points

    c. Remaining rows — default

To Change the Workbook Theme

The Solstice theme includes fonts and colors that provide the worksheet a professional and subtly colored appearance. The following steps change the workbook theme to the Solstice theme.

1

• On the Home tab, under Themes, click the Themes button to display the Themes pop-up menu.

• Scroll to the bottom of the Built-in themes area (Figure 2–31).

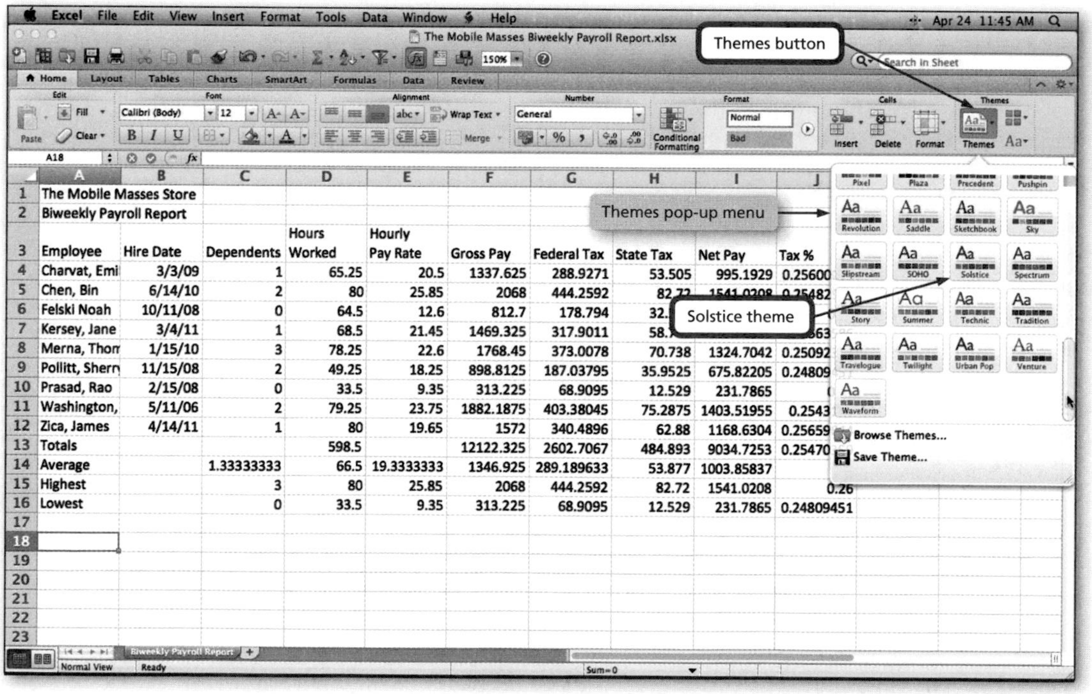

Q&A Why should I change the theme of a workbook? A company or department may standardize on a specific theme so that all of their documents have a similar appearance. Similarly, an individual may want to have a theme that sets his or her work apart from the work of others. Other Office programs, such as Word and PowerPoint, include the same themes included with Excel, meaning that all of your Microsoft Office documents can share a common theme.

Figure 2–31

2

- Click Solstice in the Themes menu to change the workbook theme (Figure 2–32).

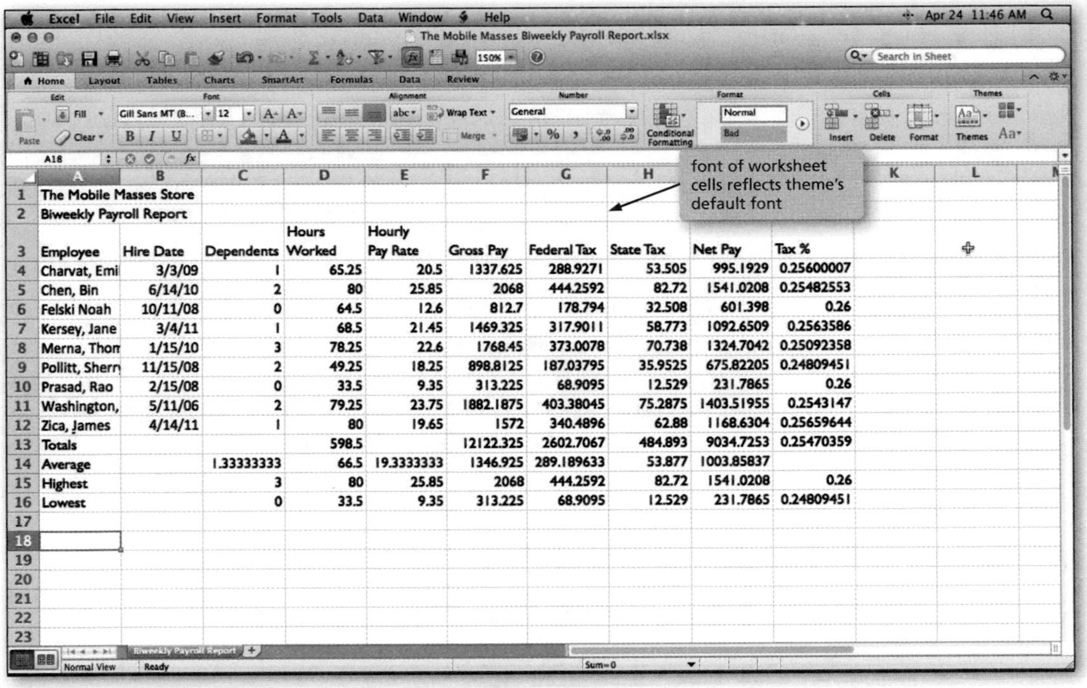

Q&A Why did the cells in the worksheet change?

The cells in the worksheet originally were formatted with the default font for the default Office theme. The default font for the Solstice theme is different from the default font for the Office theme and, therefore, changed on the worksheet when you changed the theme. If you had modified the font for any of the cells, those cells would not receive the default font for the Solstice theme.

Figure 2–32

To Format the Worksheet Titles

The following steps merge and center the worksheet titles, apply the Title cells style to the worksheet titles, and decrease the font size of the worksheet subtitle.

1 Select the range to be merged, A1:J1 in this case, and then, on the Home tab under Alignment, click the Merge button to merge and center the text in the selected range.

2 Select the range A2:J2 and then click the Merge button to merge and center the text in the selected range.

3 Select the range to contain the Title cell style, in this case A1:A2. On the Home tab, under Format, point to Normal to display the downward pointing More button, click the More button to display the Cell Styles gallery, and click the Title cell style to apply the cell style to the selected range.

4 Select cell A2 and then, on the Home tab under Font, click the Decrease Font Size button to decrease the font size of the selected cell to the next lowest font size (Figure 2–33 on the following page).

Q&A What is the effect of clicking the Decrease Font Size button?

When you click the Decrease Font Size button, Excel assigns the next lowest font size in the Font Size gallery to the selected range. The Increase Font Size button works in a similar manner but causes Excel to assign the next highest font size in the Font Size gallery to the selected range.

Color Selection

Knowing how people perceive colors helps you emphasize parts of your worksheet. Warmer colors (red and orange) tend to reach toward the reader. Cooler colors (blue, green, and violet) tend to pull away from the reader. Bright colors jump out of a dark background and are easiest to see. White or yellow text on a dark blue, green, purple, or black background is ideal.

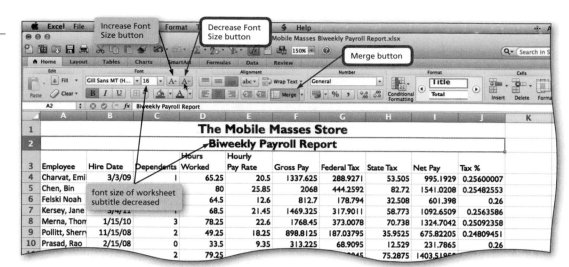

Figure 2–33

To Change the Background Color and Apply a Box Border to the Worksheet Title and Subtitle

The final formats assigned to the worksheet title and subtitle are the aqua background color and thick box border (Figure 2–30b on page EX 88). The following steps complete the formatting of the worksheet titles.

1
- Select the range A1:A2 and then on the Home tab, under Font, click the Fill Color button arrow to display the Fill Color pop-up menu (Figure 2–34).

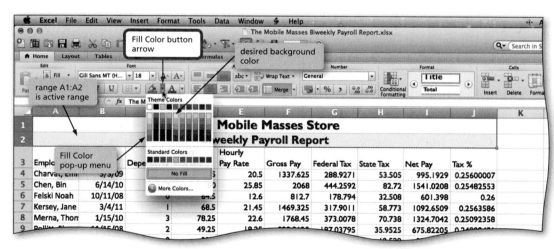

Figure 2–34

2
- Click Accent 1, Lighter 60% (column 5, row 3) in the Fill Color pop-up menu to change the background color of the range of cells (Figure 2–35).

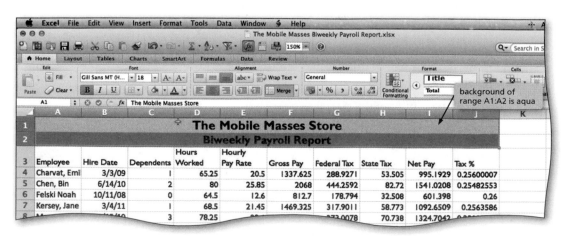

Figure 2–35

❸
- On the Home tab, under Font, click the Borders button arrow to display the Borders pop-up menu (Figure 2–36).

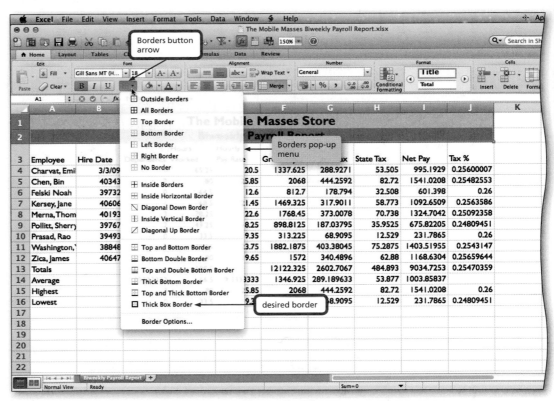

Figure 2–36

❹
- Click Thick Box Border in the Borders pop-up menu to display a thick box border around the selected range.

- Click anywhere in the worksheet, such as cell A18, to deselect the current range (Figure 2–37).

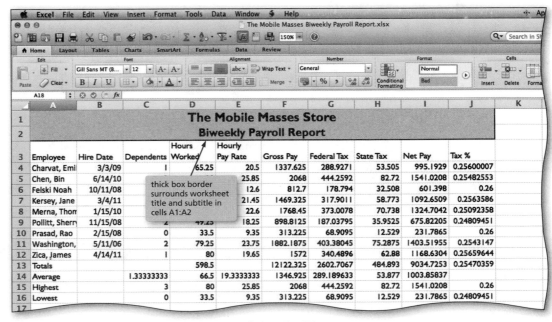

Figure 2–37

Other Ways

1. CONTROL-click range, click Format Cells in shortcut menu, click appropriate tab (Format Cells dialog), click desired format, click OK button

2. Choose Format > Cells in menu bar, click appropriate tab (Format Cells dialog), click desired format, click OK button

3. Press COMMAND-1, click appropriate tab (Format Cells dialog), click desired format, click OK button

Background Colors

BTW The most popular background color is blue. Research shows that the color blue is used most often because this color connotes serenity, reflection, and proficiency.

To Apply a Cell Style to the Column Headings and Format the Total Rows

As shown in Figure 2–30b on page EX 88, the column titles (row 3) should have the Heading 3 cell style and the totals row (row 13) should have the Total cell style. The summary information headings in the range A14:A16 should be bold. The following steps assign these styles and formats to row 3 and row 13 and the range A14:A16.

1 Select the range to be formatted, cells A3:J3 in this case.

2 Apply the Heading 3 cell style to the range A3:J3.

3 On the Home tab, under Alignment, click the Center Text button to center the column headings.

4 Apply the Total cell style to the range A13:J13.

5 Bold the range A14:A16 (Figure 2–38).

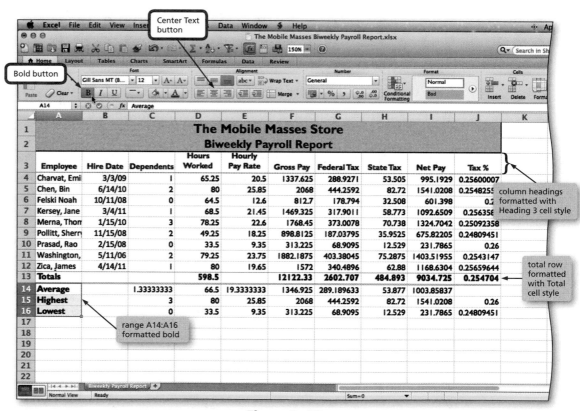

Figure 2–38

To Center Data in Cells

With the column titles and total rows formatted, the next step is to center the Dependents numbers in column C. The following step centers the data in the range C4:C16.

1

- Select the range C4:C16 and then on the Home tab under Alignment, click the Center Text button to center the data in the selected range.

- Select cell E4 to deselect the selected range (Figure 2–39).

Q&A Can I format an entire column at once?
Yes. Rather than selecting the range C4:C16 in Step 1, you could have clicked the column C heading immediately above cell C1, and then, on the Home tab under Alignment, clicked the Center Text button. In this case, all cells in column C down to the last cell in the worksheet would have been formatted to use center alignment. This same procedure could have been used to format the dates in column B.

	The Mobile Masses Store								
	Biweekly Payroll Report								
Employee	**Hire Date**	**Dependents**	**Hours Worked**	**Hourly Pay Rate**	**Gross Pay**	**Federal Tax**	**State Tax**	**Net Pay**	**Tax %**
Charvat, Emi	3/3/09	1	65.25	20.5	1337.625	288.9271	53.505	995.1929	0.25600007
Chen, Bin	6/14/10	2	80	25.85	2068	444.2592	82.72	1541.0208	0.25482553
Felski Noah	10/11/08	0	64.5	12.6	812.7	178.794	32.508	601.398	0.26
Kersey, Jane	3/4/11	1	68.5	21.45	1469.325	317.9011	58.773	1092.6509	0.2563586
Merna, Thor	1/15/10	3	78.25	22.6	1768.45	373.0078	70.738	1324.7042	0.25092358
Pollitt, Sherri	11/15/08	2			898.8125	187.03795	35.9525	675.82205	0.24809451
Prasad, Rao	2/15/08	0			313.225	68.9095	12.529	231.7865	0.26
Washington,	5/11/06	2	7		1882.1875	403.38045	75.2875	1403.51955	0.2543147
Zica, James	4/14/11	1	80	19.65	1572	340.4896	62.88	1168.6304	0.25659644
Totals			598.5		12122.33	2602.707	484.893	9034.725	0.254704
Average		1.33333333	66.5	19.3333333	1346.925	289.189633	53.877	1003.85837	
Highest		3	80	25.85	2068	444.2592	82.72	1541.0208	0.26
Lowest		0	33.5	9.35	313.225	68.9095	12.529	231.7865	0.24809451

range C4:C16 centered

Figure 2–39

Other Ways

1. CONTROL-click range, choose Format Cells in shortcut menu, click appropriate tab (Format Cells dialog), click desired format, click OK button

2. Press CONTROL-1, click appropriate tab (Format Cells dialog), click desired format, click OK button

TO FORMAT DATES AND CENTER DATA IN CELLS

The default date format in Excel 2011 is the format this worksheet will use. There will be occasions when you will need to change the format of dates. The following steps will format dates.

1. Select the range to contain the new date format, cells B4:B12 in this case.

2. Click Format in the menu bar and then choose Cells from the menu to display the Format Cells dialog.

3. If necessary, click the Number tab (Format Cells dialog), click Date in the Category list, and then choose the desired format for the selected date entries.

4. Click the OK button (Format Cells dialog) to format the dates in the current column using the selected date format style.

Figure 2–40 on the next page shows the Format Cells dialog with the Date Category on the Number tab selected.

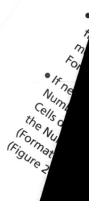

3

- Select the range to contain the Comma style format, cells D4:D16 in this case.

- Click the Comma Style button to assign the Comma style format to the selected range (Figure 2–43).

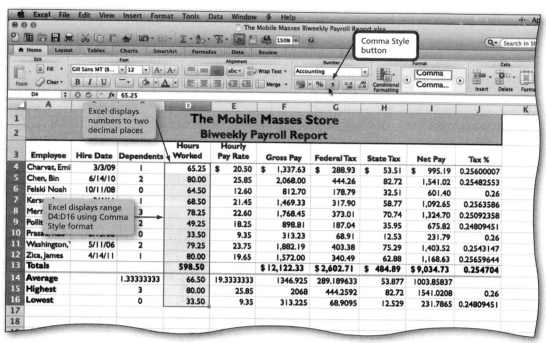

Figure 2–43

To Apply a Currency Style Format with a Floating Dollar Sign Using the Format Cells Dialog

The following steps use the Format Cells dialog to apply the Currency style format with a floating dollar sign to the numbers in the range E14:I16.

1

- Select the range E14:I16 and then CONTROL-click the selected cells to display a shortcut menu.

- Choose Format Cells from the shortcut menu to display the Format Cells dialog.

- If necessary, click the Number tab (Format Cells dialog) to display the Number pane (Format Cells dialog) (Figure 2–44).

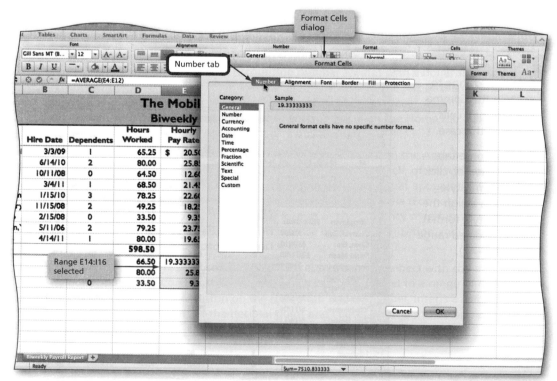

Figure 2–44

2

- Click Currency in the Category list to select the necessary number format category, and then click the third style ($1,234.10) in the Negative numbers list (Format Cells dialog) to select the desired currency format for negative numbers (Figure 2–45).

Q&A How do I select the proper format?
You can choose from 12 categories of formats. Once you select a category, you can select the number of decimal places, whether or not a dollar sign should be displayed, and how negative numbers should appear. Selecting the appropriate negative numbers format is important, because doing so adds a space to the right of the number in order to align the numbers in the worksheet on the decimal points. Some of the available negative number formats do not align the numbers in the worksheet on the decimal points.

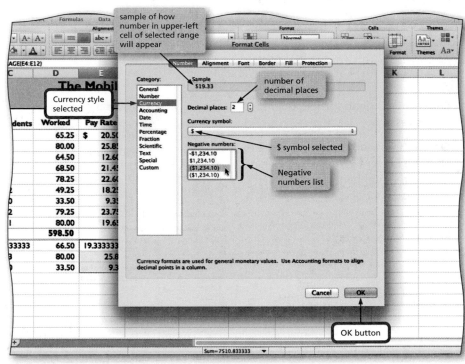

Figure 2–45

3

- Click the OK button (Format Cells dialog) to assign the Currency style format with a floating dollar sign to the selected range (Figure 2–46).

Q&A What is the difference between using the Accounting number style and Currency style?
When using the Accounting Number Style button, a fixed dollar sign always appears on the left side of the cell. The Currency style assigned using the Format Cells dialog uses a floating dollar sign that appears immediately to the left of the first digit. Cell E4, for example, has a fixed dollar sign, while cell E14 has a floating dollar sign.

ire Date	Dependents	Hours Worked	Hourly Pay Rate	Gross Pay	Federal Tax	State Tax	Net Pay	Tax %
3/3/09	1	65.25	$ 20.50	$ 1,337.63	$ 288.93	$ 53.51	$ 995.19	0.25600007
6/14/10	2	80.00	25.85	2,068.00	444.26	82.72	1,541.02	0.25482553
10/11/08	0	64.50	12.60	812.70	178.79	32.51	601.40	0.26
3/4/11	1	68.50	21.45	1,469.33	317.90	58.77	1,092.65	0.2563586
1/15/10	3	78.25	22.60	1,768.45	373.01	70.74	1,324.70	0.25092358
11/15/08	2	49.25	18.25	898.81	187.04	35.95	675.82	0.24809451
2/15/08	0	33.50	9.35	313.23	68.91	12.53	231.79	0.26
5/11/06	2	79.25	23.75	1,882.19	403.38	75.29	1,403.52	0.2543147
4/14/11	1	80.00	19.65	1,572.00	340.49	62.88	1,168.63	0.25659644
		598.50		$12,122.33	$2,602.71	$ 484.89	$9,034.73	0.254704
		66.50	$19.33	$1,346.93	$289.19	$53.88	$1,003.86	
		80.00	$25.85	$2,068.00	$444.26	$82.72	$1,541.02	0.26
		33.50	$9.35	$313.23	$68.91	$12.53	$231.79	0.24809451

Excel displays range E14:116 using Currency style format with floating dollar signs

weekly Payroll Report

Ready   Sum=$7,510.83

Figure 2–46

Other Ways

1. Choose Format > Cells in menu bar, click Number tab (Format Cells dialog), click Currency in Category list, select format, click OK button

2. Press CONTROL-1, click Number tab (Format Cells dialog), click Currency in Category list, select format, click OK button

3. Press CONTROL-SHIFT-DOLLAR SIGN ($)

To Apply a Percent Style Format and Use the Increase Decimal Button

The next step is to format the Tax % in column J. Currently, Excel displays the numbers in column J as a decimal fraction (for example, 0.25600007 in cell J4). The following steps format the range J4:J16 to the Percent style format with two decimal places.

- Select the range to format, cell J4:J16 in this case.

- On the Home tab under Number, click the Percent Style button to display the numbers in the selected range as a rounded whole percent.

Q&A What is the result of clicking the Percent Style button?

The Percent Style button instructs Excel to display a value as a percentage, determined by multiplying the cell entry by 100, rounding the result to the nearest percent, and adding a percent sign. For example, when cell J4 is formatted using the Percent Style buttons, Excel displays the actual value 0.256000075 as 26%.

e Date	Dependents	Hours Worked	Hourly Pay Rate	Gross Pay	Federal Tax	State Tax	Net Pay	Tax %
3/3/09	I	65.25	$ 20.50	$ 1,337.63	$ 288.93	$ 53.51	$ 995.19	25.60%
6/14/10	2	80.00	25.85	2,068.00	444.26	82.72	1,541.02	25.48%
0/11/08	0	64.50	12.60	812.70	178.79	32.51	601.40	26.00%
3/4/11	I	68.50	21.45	1,469.33	317.90	58.77	1,092.65	25.64%
V15/10	3	78.25	22.60	1,768.45	373.01	70.74	1,324.70	25.09%
15/08	2	49.25	18.25	898.81	187.04	35.95	675.82	24.81%
15/08	0	33.50	9.35	313.23	68.91	12.53	231.79	26.00%
11/06	2	79.25	23.75	1,882.19	403.38	75.29	1,403.52	25.43%
14/11	I	80.00	19.65	1,572.00	340.49	62.88	1,168.63	25.66%
		598.50		$12,122.33	$2,602.71	$ 484.89	$9,034.73	25.47%
	1.33333333	66.50	$19.33	$1,346.93	$289.19	$53.88	$1,003.86	
	3	80.00	$25.85	$2,068.00	$444.26	$82.72	$1,541.02	26.00%
	0	33.50	$9.35	$313.23	$68.91	$12.53	$231.79	24.81%

Percent Style button
Increase Decimal button
Decrease Decimal button
Percent
Excel displays range J4:J16 using Percent style format with two decimal places

Figure 2–47

- Under Number, click the Increase Decimal button two times to display the numbers in the selected range with two decimal places (Figure 2–47).

Other Ways

1. CONTROL-click range, click Format Cells in shortcut menu, click Number tab (Format Cells dialog), click Percentage in Category list, select format, click OK button

2. Choose Format > Cells in menu bar, click Number tab (Format Cells dialog), click Percentage in Category list, select format, click OK button

3. Press CONTROL-1, click Number tab (Format Cells dialog), click Percentage in Category list, select format, click OK button

4. Press CONTROL-SHIFT-PERCENT SIGN (%)

Conditional Formatting

The next step is to emphasize the values greater than 70 in column D by formatting them to appear with an aqua background and white font color.

Plan Ahead

Establish rules for conditional formatting.

Excel lets you apply formatting that appears only when the value in a cell meets conditions that you specify. This type of formatting is called **conditional formatting**. You can apply conditional formatting to a cell, a range of cells, the entire worksheet, or the entire workbook. Usually, you apply conditional formatting to a range of cells that contains values you want to highlight, if conditions warrant.

- A **condition**, which is made up of two values and a relational operator, is true or false for each cell in the range. If the condition is true, then Excel applies the formatting. If the condition is false, then Excel suppresses the formatting. What makes conditional formatting so powerful is that the cell's appearance can change as you enter new values in the worksheet.

- As with worksheet formatting, follow the less-is-more rule when considering conditional formatting. Use conditional formatting to make cells and ranges stand out and raise attention. Too much conditional formatting can result in confusion for the reader of the worksheet.

Conditional Formatting

BTW You can assign any format to a cell, a range of cells, a worksheet, or an entire workbook conditionally. If the value of the cell changes and no longer meets the specified condition, Excel suppresses the conditional formatting.

To Apply Conditional Formatting

The following steps assign conditional formatting to the range D4:D12, so that any cell value greater than 70 will cause Excel to display the number in the cell with an aqua background and a white font color.

- Select the range D4:D12.

- On the Home tab under Format, click the Conditional Formatting button to display the Conditional Formatting pop-up menu (Figure 2–48).

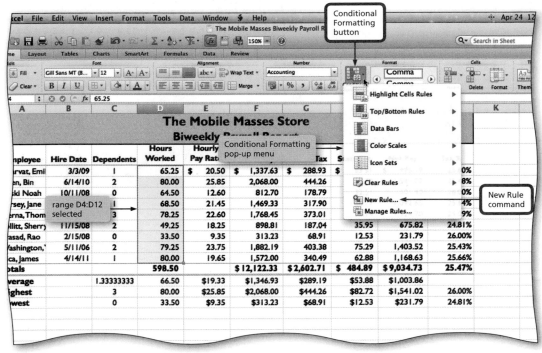

Figure 2–48

2

- Choose New Rule in the Conditional Formatting menu to display the New Formatting Rule dialog.

- Choose Classic in the Style box.

- Set the rule conditions to Format only cells that contain, Cell value, greater than, 70 to set a conditional format for cells in the selected range that contain values greater than 70 (Figure 2–49).

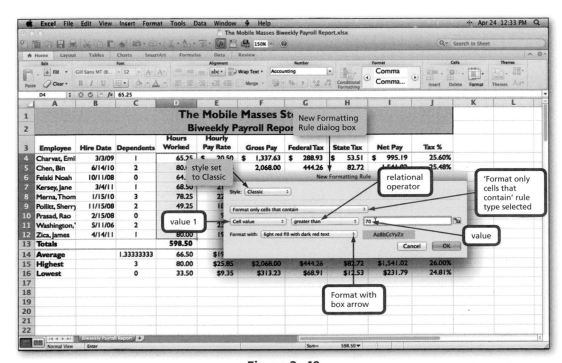

Figure 2–49

- In the 'Format with' area, click the box arrow and choose custom format to open the Format Cells dialog.

- If necessary, click the Font tab. Click the Color box arrow (Format Cells dialog) to display the Color pop-up menu and then click Background 1 (column 1, row 1) in the Color pop-up menu to select the white font color.

- Click the Fill tab (Format Cells dialog) to display the Fill pane, click the Color box arrow in the Background area, and then click Accent 1, Darker 25% (column 5, row 5) to select the background color (Figure 2–50).

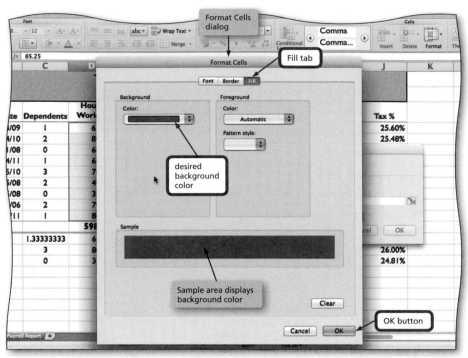

Figure 2–50

- Click the OK button (Format Cells dialog) to close the Format Cells dialog and display the New Formatting Rule dialog with the desired font and background colors displayed in the Preview box (Figure 2–51).

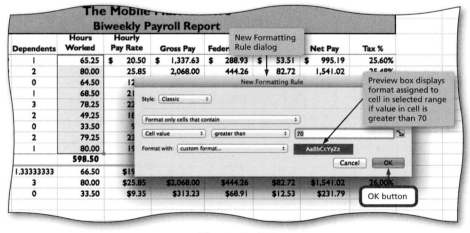

Figure 2–51

⑤

- Click the OK button to assign the conditional format to the selected range.

- Click anywhere in the worksheet, such as cell A18, to deselect the current range (Figure 2–52).

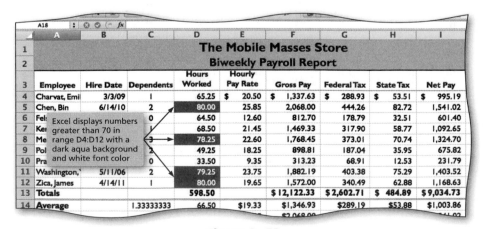

Figure 2–52

Conditional Formatting Operators

As shown in Figure 2–49 on page EX 101, the second text box in the New Formatting Rule dialog allows you to select a relational operator, such as less than, to use in the condition. The eight different relational operators from which you can choose for conditional formatting in the New Formatting Rule dialog are summarized in Table 2–5.

Table 2–5 Summary of Conditional Formatting Relational Operators	
Relational Operator	**Description**
between	Cell value is between two numbers.
not between	Cell value is not between two numbers.
equal to	Cell value is equal to a number.
not equal to	Cell value is not equal to a number.
greater than	Cell value is greater than a number.
less than	Cell value is less than a number.
greater than or equal to	Cell value is greater than or equal to a number.
less than or equal to	Cell value is less than or equal to a number.

Changing the Widths of Columns and Heights of Rows

When Excel starts and displays a blank worksheet on the screen, all of the columns have a default width of 10 characters, or 0.90 inches. A character is defined as a letter, number, symbol, or punctuation mark in 12-point Calibri font, the default font used by Excel. An average of 10 characters in 12-point Calibri font will fit in a cell.

Another measure of the height and width of cells is pixels, which is short for picture element. A **pixel** is a dot on the screen that contains a color. The size of the dot is based on your screen's resolution. At the resolution of 1280 × 800 used in this book, 1280 pixels appear across the screen and 800 pixels appear down the screen for a total of 1,024,000 pixels. It is these 1,024,000 pixels that form the font and other items you see on the screen.

Rows in Excel are measured in points or inches. The default row height in a blank worksheet is 15 points or 0.21 inches. You can change the width of the columns or height of the rows at any time to make the worksheet easier to read or to ensure that Excel displays an entry properly in a cell.

Hidden Rows and Columns

For some people, trying **BTW** to unhide a range of columns or rows using the mouse can be frustrating. An alternative is to use the menu bar: select the columns or rows on either side of the hidden columns or rows (and including the hidden columns or rows), then choose Format > Column (or Format > Row) and choose Unhide.

To Change the Widths of Columns

When changing the column width, you can set the width manually or you can instruct Excel to size the column to best fit. **Best fit** means that the width of the column will be increased or decreased so that the widest entry will fit in the column. Sometimes, you may prefer more or less white space in a column than best fit provides. To change the white space, Excel allows you to change column widths manually.

When the format you assign to a cell causes the entry to exceed the width of a column, Excel automatically changes the column width to best fit. If you do not assign a format to a cell or cells in a column, the column width will remain 10 characters. To set a column width to best fit, double-click the right boundary of the column heading above row 1.

The steps on the following pages change the column widths: column A, B, and C to best fit; column H to 10.22 characters; and columns D, E, and J to 7.56 characters.

- Drag through column headings A, B, and C above row 1 to select the columns.

- Point to the boundary on the right side of column heading C to cause the mouse pointer to become a split double arrow (Figure 2–53).

Q&A What if I want to make a large change to the column width? If you want to increase or decrease column width significantly, you can CONTROL-click a column letter and then use the Column Width command in the shortcut menu to change the column's width. To use this command, however, you must select one or more entire columns.

columns A, B, and C selected

mouse pointer pointing to right boundary of column C

Figure 2–53

Employee	Hire Date	Dependents	Hours Worked	Hourly Pay Rate	Gross Pay	Federal Tax	State Tax	Net Pay	Tax %
					The Mobile Masses Store				
					Biweekly Payroll Report				
Charvat, Emi	3/3/09	1	65.25	$ 20.50	$ 1,337.63	$ 288.93	$ 53.51	$ 995.19	25.60%
Chen, Bin	6/14/10	2	80.00	25.85	2,068.00	444.26	82.72	1,541.02	25.48%
Felski Noah	10/11/08	0	64.50	12.60	812.70	178.79	32.51	601.40	26.00%
Kersey, Jane	3/4/11	1	68.50	21.45	1,469.33	317.90	58.77	1,092.65	25.64%
Merna, Thom	1/15/10	3	78.25	22.60	1,768.45	373.01	70.74	1,324.70	25.09%
Pollitt, Sherry	11/15/08	2	49.25	18.25	898.81	187.04	35.95	675.82	24.81%
Prasad, Rao	2/15/08	0	33.50	9.35	313.23	68.91	12.53	231.79	26.00%
Washington,`	5/11/06	2	79.25	23.75	1,882.19	403.38	75.29	1,403.52	25.43%
Zica, James	4/14/11	1	80.00	19.65	1,572.00	340.49	62.88	1,168.63	25.66%
Totals			598.50		$12,122.33	$2,602.71	$ 484.89	$9,034.73	25.47%
Average		1.33333333	66.50	$19.33	$1,346.93	$289.19	$53.88	$1,003.86	
Highest		3	80.00	$25.85	$2,068.00	$444.26	$82.72	$1,541.02	26.00%
Lowest		0	33.50	$9.35	$313.23	$68.91	$12.53	$231.79	24.81%

- Double-click the right boundary of column heading C to change the width of the selected columns to best fit.

- Point to the boundary on the right side of the column H heading above row 1.

- When the mouse pointer changes to a split double arrow, drag until the ScreenTip indicates Width: 10.50 (0.94 inches). Do not release the mouse button (Figure 2–54).

mouse pointer pointing to right boundary of column H

ScreenTip shows proposed column width

Width: 10.50 (0.94 inches)

column widths A, B, and C set to best fit

dotted line shows proposed right border of column H

Employee	Hire Date	Dependents	Hours Worked	Hourly Pay Rate	Gross Pay	Federal Tax	State Tax	Net Pay	Tax %
					The Mobile Masses Store				
					Biweekly Payroll Report				
Charvat, Emily	3/3/09	1	65.25	$ 20.50	$ 1,337.63	$ 288.93	$ 53.51	$ 995.19	25.60%
Chen, Bin		2	80.00	25.85	2,068.00	444.26	82.72	1,541.02	25.48%
Felski No		0	64.50	12.60	812.70	178.79	32.51	601.40	26.00%
Kersey, Ja		1	68.50	21.45	1,469.33	317.90	58.77	1,092.65	25.64%
Merna, Thomas	1/15/10	3	78.25	22.60	1,768.45	373.01	70.74	1,324.70	25.09%
Pollitt, Sherry	11/15/08	2	49.25	18.25	898.81	187.04	35.95	675.82	24.81%
Prasad, Rao	2/15/08	0	33.50	9.35	313.23	68.91	12.53	231.79	26.00%
Washington, Yolanda	5/11/06	2	79.25	23.75	1,882.19	403.38	75.29	1,403.52	25.43%
Zica, James	4/14/11	1	80.00	19.65	1,572.00		62.88	1,168.63	25.66%
Totals			598.50		$12,1…		484.89	$9,034.73	25.47%
Average		1.333333333	66.50	$19.33	$1,3…		$53.88	$1,003.86	
Highest		3	80.00	$25.85	$2,068.00	$444.26	$82.72	$1,541.02	26.00%
Lowest		0	33.50	$9.35	$313.23	$68.91	$12.53	$231.79	24.81%

Figure 2–54

Q&A What happens if I change the column width to zero (0)?
If you decrease the column width to 0, the column is hidden. **Hiding cells** is a technique you can use to hide data that might not be relevant to a particular report or sensitive data that you do not want others to see. To instruct Excel to display a hidden column, position the mouse pointer to the right of the column heading boundary where the hidden column is located and then drag to the right.

3

- Release the mouse button to change the column width.

- Click the column D heading above row 1 to select the column.

- While holding down the COMMAND key, click the column E heading and then the column J heading above row 1 so that nonadjacent columns are selected (Figure 2–55).

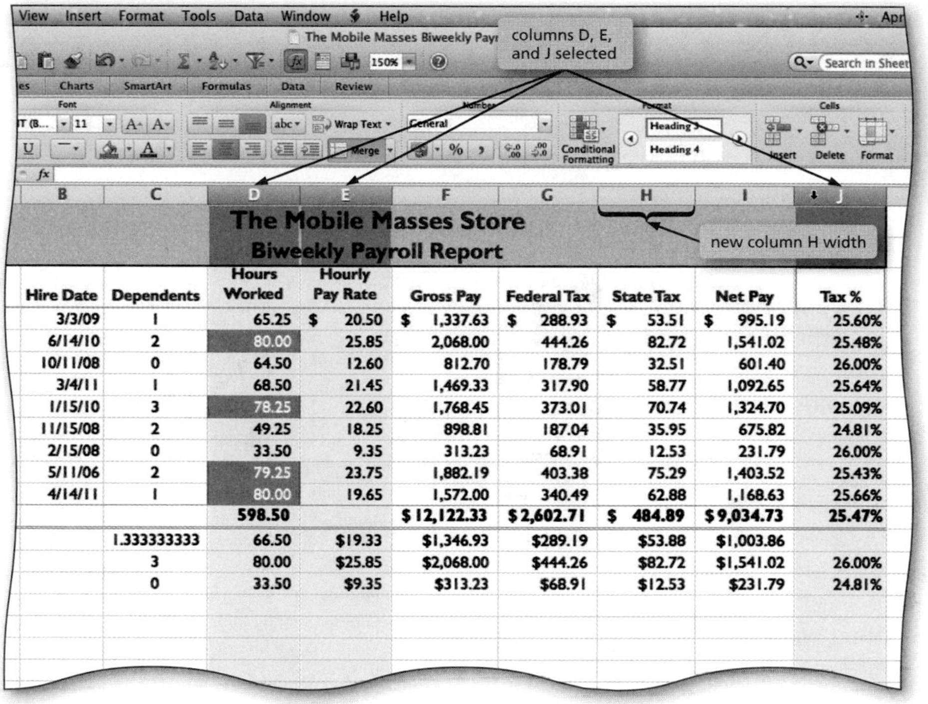

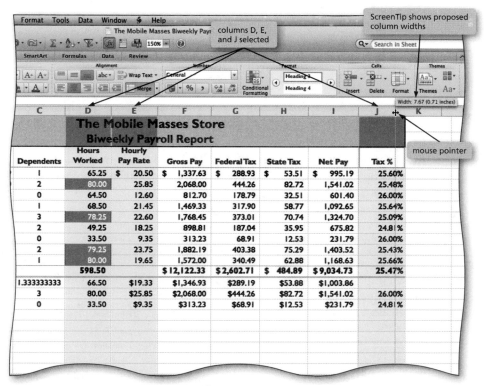

Figure 2–55

4

- If necessary, scroll the worksheet to the right so that the right border of column J is visible. Point to the boundary on the right side of the column J heading above row 1.

- Drag until the ScreenTip indicates Width: 7.67 (0.71 inches). Do not release the mouse button (Figure 2–56).

Figure 2–56

- Release the mouse button to change the column widths of columns D, E, and J.

- If necessary, scroll the worksheet to the left so that the left border of column A is visible.

- Click anywhere in the worksheet, such as cell A18, to deselect the columns (Figure 2–57).

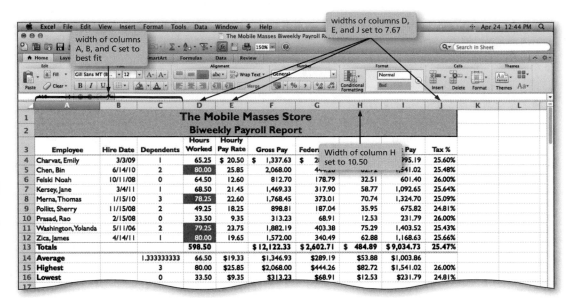

Figure 2–57

Other Ways

1. CONTROL-click column heading or drag through multiple column headings and CONTROL-click, choose Column Width in shortcut menu, enter desired column width, click OK button

2. Choose Format > Column > Width in menu bar, enter desired column width, click OK button

To Change the Heights of Rows

When you increase the font size of a cell entry, such as the title in cell A1, Excel automatically increases the row height to best fit so that it can display the characters properly. Recall that Excel did this earlier when multiple lines were entered in a cell in row 3, and when the cell style of the worksheet title and subtitle was changed.

You also can increase or decrease the height of a row manually to improve the appearance of the worksheet. The following steps improve the appearance of the worksheet by increasing the height of row 3 to 48.00 points and increasing the height of row 14 to 27.00 points.

- Point to the boundary below row heading 3.

- Drag down until the ScreenTip indicates Height: 48.00 (0.67 inches). Do not release the mouse button (Figure 2–58).

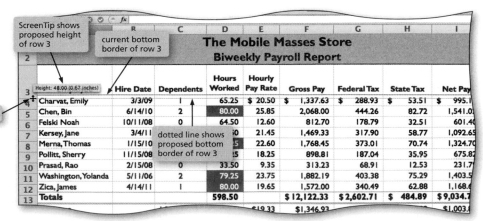

Figure 2–58

2

- Release the mouse button to change the row height.

- Point to the boundary below row heading 14.

- Drag down until the ScreenTip indicates Height: 27.00 (0.37 inches). Do not release the mouse button (Figure 2–59).

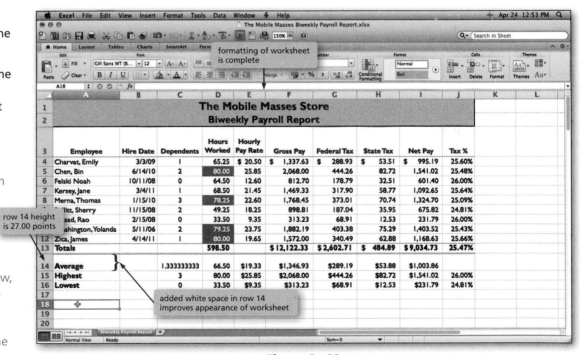

Figure 2–59

3

- Release the mouse button to change the row height.

- Click anywhere in the worksheet, such as cell A18, to deselect the current cell (Figure 2–60).

Q&A Can I hide a row? Yes. As with column widths, when you decrease the row height to 0, the row is hidden. To instruct Excel to display a hidden row, position the mouse pointer just below the row heading boundary where the row is hidden and then drag down. To set a row height to best fit, double-click the bottom boundary of the row heading.

Figure 2–60

● Other Ways

1. On Home tab under Cells, click Format button, choose Row Height, enter desired row height, click OK button

2. CONTROL-click row heading or drag through multiple row headings and CONTROL-click, choose Row Height in shortcut menu, enter desired row height, click OK button

3. Choose Format > Row > Height in menu bar, enter desired row height, click OK button

Break Point: If you wish to take a break, this is a good place to do so. Be sure to save the The Mobile Masses Biweekly Payroll Report file again and then you can quit Excel. To resume at a later time, start Excel, open the file called The Mobile Masses Biweekly Payroll Report and continue following the steps from this location forward.

Spell Checking

BTW While Excel's spell checker is a valuable tool, it is not infallible. You should proofread your workbook carefully by pointing to each word and saying it aloud as you point to it. Be mindful of misused words such as its and it's, through and though, and to and too. Nothing undermines a good impression more than a professional looking report with misspelled words.

Checking Spelling

Excel includes a **spell checker** you can use to check a worksheet for spelling errors. The spell checker looks for spelling errors by comparing words on the worksheet against words contained in its standard dictionary. If you often use specialized terms that are not in the standard dictionary, you may want to add them to a custom dictionary using the Spelling dialog.

When the spell checker finds a word that is not in either dictionary, it displays the word in the Spelling dialog. You then can correct it if it is misspelled.

To Check Spelling on the Worksheet

To illustrate how Excel responds to a misspelled word, the following steps misspell purposely the word, Employee, in cell A3 as the word, Empolyee, as shown in Figure 2–61.

1

• Click cell A3 and then type **Empolyee** to misspell the word Employee.

• Select cell A1 so that the spell checker will begin checking at the selected cell.

• Click Review on the ribbon to display the Review tab.

• In the Proofing group, click the Spelling button to run the spell checker and display the misspelled word in the Spelling dialog (Figure 2–61).

Q&A What happens when the spell checker finds a misspelled word?

When the spell checker identifies that a cell contains a word not in its standard or custom dictionary, it selects that cell as the active cell and displays the Spelling dialog. The Spelling dialog lists the word not found in the dictionary and a list of suggested corrections (Figure 2–61).

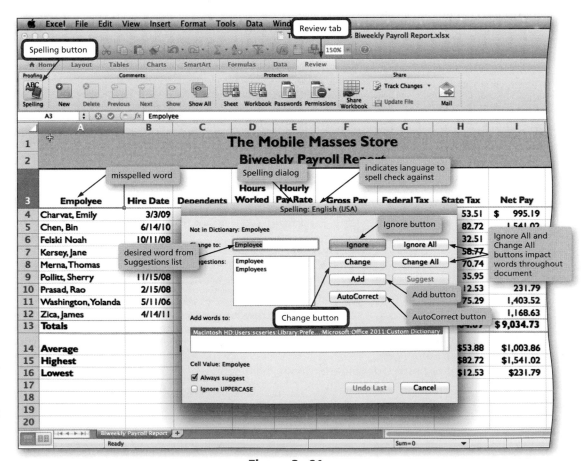

Figure 2–61

2

- Click the Change button (Spelling dialog) to change the misspelled word to the correct word (Figure 2–62).

- Click the Close button (Spelling dialog) to close the Spelling dialog.

- If the Microsoft Excel dialog is displayed, click the OK button.

3

- Click anywhere in the worksheet, such as cell A18, to deselect the current cell.

- Display the Home tab.

- Click the Save button in the Standard toolbar to save the workbook.

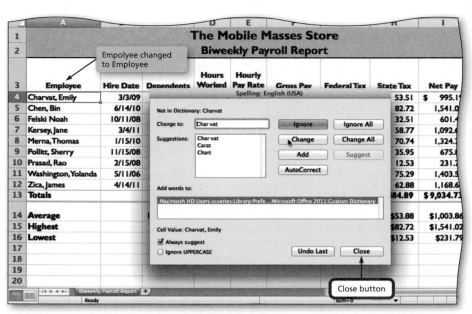

Figure 2–62

Q&A **What other actions can I take in the Spelling dialog?**
If one of the words in the Suggestions list is correct, click it and then click the Change button. If none of the suggestions is correct, type the correct word in the Change to box and then click the Change button. To change the word throughout the worksheet, click the Change All button instead of the Change button. To skip correcting the word, click the Ignore button. To have Excel ignore the word for the remainder of the worksheet, click the Ignore All button.

Other Ways

1. Choose Tools > Spelling in menu bar, select correct spelling, click OK button

Additional Spell Checker Considerations

Consider these additional guidelines when using the spell checker:

- To check the spelling of the text in a single cell, double-click the cell to make the formula bar active and then click the Spelling button in the Proofing group on the Review tab.

- If you select a single cell so that the formula bar is not active and then start the spell checker, Excel checks the remainder of the worksheet, including notes and embedded charts.

- If you select a cell other than cell A1 before you start the spell checker, Excel will display a dialog when the spell checker reaches the end of the worksheet, asking if you want to continue checking at the beginning.

- If you select a range of cells before starting the spell checker, Excel checks the spelling of the words only in the selected range.

- To check the spelling of all the sheets in a workbook, CONTROL-click any sheet tab, choose Select All Sheets in the shortcut menu, and then start the spell checker.

- To add words to the dictionary such as your last name, click the Add button in the Spelling dialog (Figure 2–61) when Excel identifies the word as not in the dictionary.

- Click the AutoCorrect button (Spelling dialog) to add the misspelled word and the correct version of the word to the AutoCorrect list. For example, suppose that you misspell the word, do, as the word, dox. When the spell checker displays the Spelling dialog with the correct word, do, in the Change to box, click the AutoCorrect button. Then, anytime in the future that you type the word dox, Excel automatically will change it to the word, do.

Error Checking

Always take the time **BTW** to check the formulas of a worksheet before submitting it to your supervisor. You can check formulas by clicking the Check for Errors on the Formulas tab under Audit Formulas. You also should test the formulas by employing data that tests the limits of formulas. Experienced spreadsheet specialists spend as much time testing a workbook as they do creating it, and they do so before placing the workbook into production.

Preparing to Print the Worksheet

Excel allows for a great deal of customization in how a worksheet appears when printed. For example, the margins on the page can be adjusted. A header or footer can be added to each printed page as well. Excel also has the capability to work on the worksheet in Page Layout view. **Page Layout view** allows you to create or modify a worksheet while viewing how it will look in printed format. The default view that you have worked in up until this point in the book is called **Normal view**.

Plan Ahead

Specify how the printed worksheet should appear.

Before printing a worksheet, you should consider how the worksheet will appear when printed. In order to fit as much information on the printed page as possible, the margins of the worksheet should be set to a reasonably small width and height. While the current version of a worksheet may print on one page, you may add more data in the future that causes the worksheet to extend to multiple pages. It is, therefore, a good idea to add a page header to the worksheet that prints in the top margin of each page. A **header** is common content that prints on every page of a worksheet. Landscape orientation is a good choice for large worksheets because the printed worksheet's width is greater than its length.

To Change the Worksheet's Margins, Header, and Orientation in Page Layout View

The following steps change to Page Layout view, narrow the margins of the worksheet, change the header of the worksheet, and set the orientation of the worksheet to landscape. Often, you may want to reduce margins so that the printed worksheet better fits the page. **Margins** are those portions of a printed page outside the main body of the printed document and always are blank when printed. Recall that in Chapter 1, the worksheet was printed in landscape orientation. The current worksheet also is too wide for a single page and requires landscape orientation to fit on one page in a readable manner.

- Click the Page Layout View button in the lower left of the document window to view the worksheet in Page Layout view (Figure 2–63).

Q&A What are some key features of Page Layout view?
Page Layout view shows the worksheet divided into pages. A gray background separates each page. The white areas surrounding each page indicate the print margins. The top of each page includes a Header area, and the bottom of each page includes a Footer area. Page Layout view also includes a ruler at the top and side of the page that assist you in placing objects on the page, such as charts and pictures.

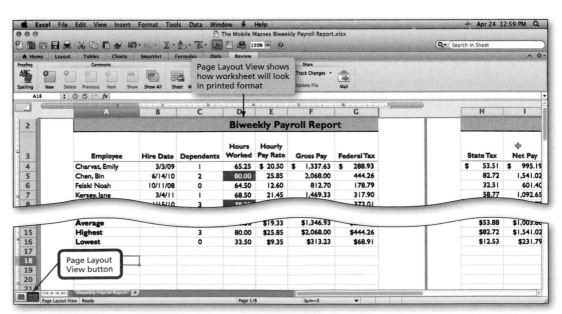

Figure 2–63

2

- Display the Layout tab.

- In the Page Setup group, click the Margins button to display the Margins pop-up menu (Figure 2–64).

Q&A Could I also have used the Layout tab to change to Page Layout view?
Yes. Under View on the Layout tab, you can click the Page Layout button to change to Page Layout view, or the Normal button to change back to Normal view.

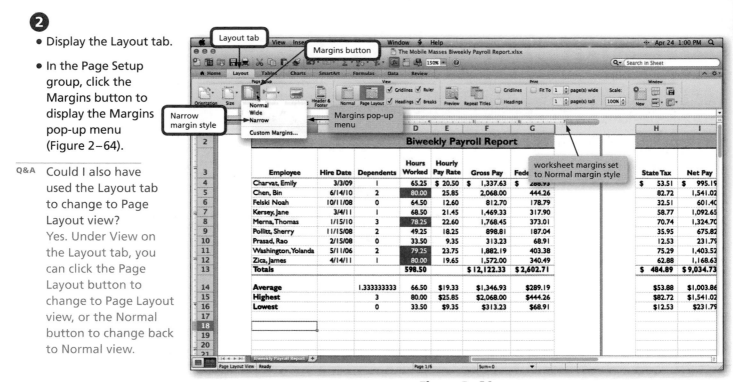

Figure 2–64

3

- Choose Narrow on the Margins pop-up menu to change the worksheet margins to the Narrow margin style.

- If necessary, drag the scroller on the right side of the worksheet to the top so that row 1 of the worksheet is displayed.

- Double-click above the worksheet title in cell A1 in the center of the Header area to make the header active and display the Header toolbar.

Q&A My header toolbar is sitting on top of the header. What should I do?
Using your mouse, point to the background of the toolbar, and then drag the header toolbar to a different location in your window.

- Type **Samuel Snyder** and then press the RETURN key. Type **Chief Financial Officer** to complete the worksheet header (Figure 2–65).

Q&A What else can I place in a header?
You can add text, page number information, date and time information, the file path of the workbook, the file name of the workbook, the sheet name of the workbook, and pictures to a header.

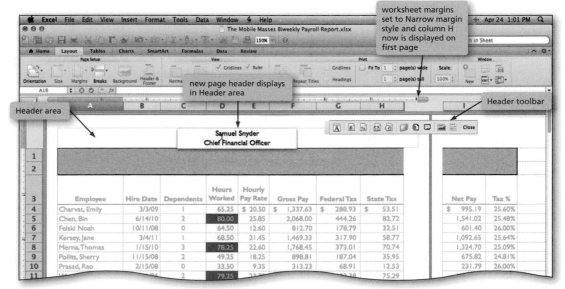

Figure 2–65

- Click Close on the Header toolbar to deselect the header. On the Layout tab, under Page Setup, click the Orientation button to display the Orientation pop-up menu (Figure 2–66).

Q&A Why do I need to deselect the header? Excel disables almost all of the buttons on the ribbon as you edit a header or footer. In addition to the commands on the Layout tab (Figure 2–65 on the previous page), only a few commands remain available on the Home tab on the ribbon. To continue working in Excel, therefore, you should select a cell in the worksheet so that all of the commands on the ribbon are available for your use.

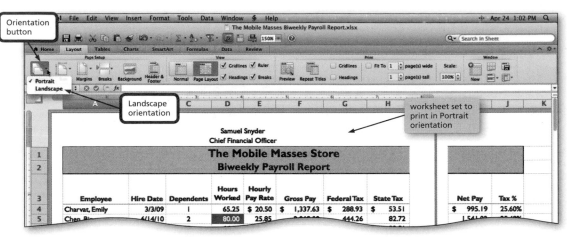

Figure 2–66

- Choose Landscape on the Orientation pop-up menu to change the worksheet's orientation to landscape (Figure 2–67).

Q&A Do I need to change the orientation every time I want to print the worksheet? No. Once you change the orientation and save the workbook, Excel will save the orientation setting for that workbook until you change it. When you open a new workbook, Excel sets the orientation to portrait.

Figure 2–67

Other Ways

1. Choose File > Page Setup, click Page tab (Page Setup dialog), choose Portrait or Landscape, click OK button

Printing the Worksheet

Excel provides other options for printing a worksheet. The following sections print the worksheet and print a section of the worksheet.

To Center the Worksheet Contents on the Page

The header content is centered on the page, while the worksheet content is not. Centering the worksheet content will better line up the header content and the title of the worksheet. The following steps center the worksheet content on the page.

- On the Layout tab, under Page Setup, click the Margins button and select Custom Margins to display the Page Setup dialog with the Margins tab active.

- Click to check the Horizontally check box under Center on page (Page Setup dialog; Figure 2–68).

- Click the OK button to close the dialog and center the worksheet contents on the page (see Figure 2–69 on the next page).

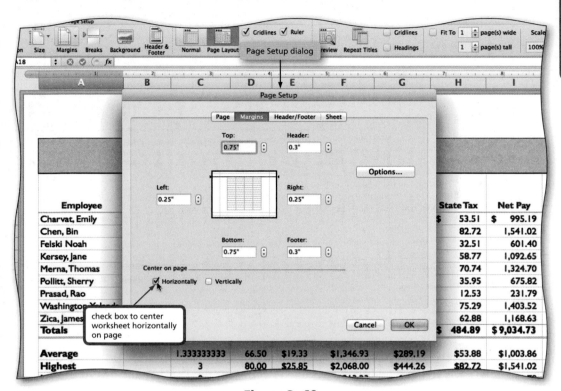

Figure 2–68

Other Ways

1. Choose File > Print in menu bar, click Page Setup button (Print dialog), click Margins tab (Page Setup dialog), click Horizontally under Center on Page, click OK button

To Print a Worksheet

The following steps print the worksheet.

1. Click File in the menu bar to display the File menu.

2. Choose Print to display the Print dialog.

3. Verify the printer name that appears in the Printer box will print a hard copy of the document. If necessary, click the Printer disclosure button to display a list of available printer options and then choose the desired printer to change the currently selected printer.

4. Click the Print button in the Print dialog to print the document on the currently selected printer.

5. When the printer stops, retrieve the hard copy (Figure 2–69 on the next page).

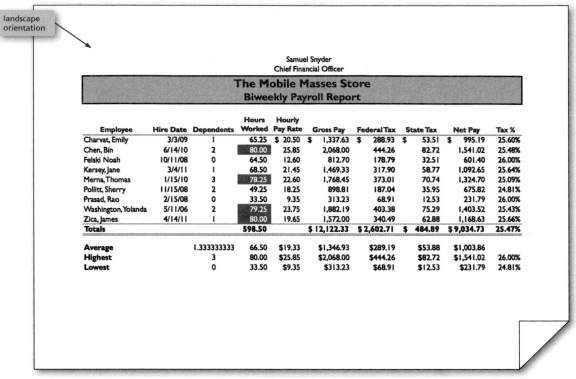

Figure 2–69

To Print a Section of the Worksheet

You might not always want to print the entire worksheet. You can print portions of the worksheet by selecting the range of cells to print and then clicking Selection in the Print What area in the Print dialog. The following steps print the range A3:F16.

- Select the range to print, cells A3:F16 in this case.

- Click File in the menu bar and choose Print to display the Print dialog.

- Click Selection in the Print What: area to instruct Excel to print only the selected range (Figure 2–70).

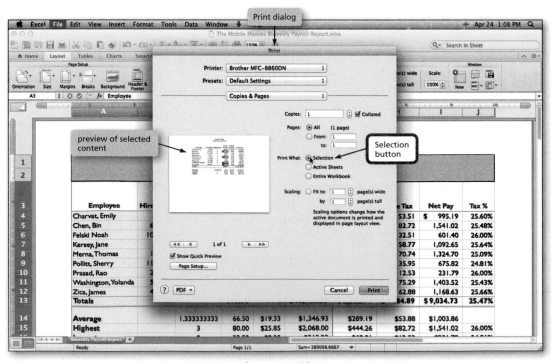

Figure 2–70

2

- Click the Print button (Print dialog) to print the selected range of the worksheet on the currently selected printer (Figure 2–71).
- Click the Normal View button in the lower-left document window to return to Normal view.
- Click cell A18 to deselect the range A3:F16.

Q&A What are my options for telling Excel what to print?
Excel includes three options to allow you to determine what should be printed (Figure 2–70). As shown in the previous steps, the Selection button instructs Excel to print the selected range. The Active Sheets button instructs Excel to print the active worksheet (the worksheet currently on the screen) or the selected worksheets. Finally, the Entire Workbook button instructs Excel to print all of the worksheets in the workbook.

Samuel Snyder
Chief Financial Officer

header prints

Employee	Hire Date	Dependents	Hours Worked	Hourly Pay Rate	Gross Pay
Charvat, Emily	3/3/09	1	65.25	$ 20.50	$ 1,337.63
Chen, Bin	6/14/10	2	80.00	25.85	2,068.00
Felski, Noah	10/11/00	0	64.50	12.60	812.70
Kersey, Jane	3/4/11	1	68.50	21.45	1,469.33
Merna, Thomas	1/15/10	3	78.25	22.60	1,768.45
Pollitt, Sherry	11/15/08	2	49.25	18.25	898.81
Prasad, Rao	2/15/08	0	33.50	9.35	313.23
Washington, Yolanda	5/11/06	2	79.25	23.75	1,882.19
Zica, James	4/14/11	1	80.00	19.65	1,572.00
Totals			**598.50**		**$ 12,122.33**
Average		1.333333333	66.50	$19.33	$1,346.93
Highest		3	80.00	$25.85	$2,068.00
Lowest		0	33.50	$9.35	$313.23

selected range prints

Figure 2–71

Other Ways

1. Select range, choose File > Print Area in menu bar, click Set Print Area, set range to print, click Print button

Displaying and Printing the Formulas Version of the Worksheet

Thus far, you have been working with the **values version** of the worksheet, which shows the results of the formulas you have entered, rather than the actual formulas. Excel also can display and print the **formulas version** of the worksheet, which shows the actual formulas you have entered, rather than the resulting values.

The formulas version is useful for debugging a worksheet. **Debugging** is the process of finding and correcting errors in the worksheet. Viewing and printing the formulas version instead of the values version makes it easier to see any mistakes in the formulas.

When you change from the values version to the formulas version, Excel increases the width of the columns so that the formulas and text do not overflow into adjacent cells on the right. The formulas version of the worksheet, thus, usually is significantly wider than the values version. To fit the wide printout on one page, you can use landscape orientation, which has already been selected for the workbook, and the Fit to option in the Page sheet in the Page Setup dialog.

Values versus Formulas **BTW**

When completing class assignments, do not enter numbers in cells that require formulas. Most instructors will check both the values version and formulas version of your worksheets. The formulas version verifies that you entered formulas, rather than numbers, in formula-based cells.

To Display the Formulas in the Worksheet and Fit the Printout on One Page

The following steps change the view of the worksheet from the values version to the formulas version of the worksheet and then print the formulas version on one page.

- Press CONTROL-ACCENT MARK (`) to display the worksheet with formulas.
- Scroll to the right until column J appears.
- Click File in the menu bar, and then choose Print to display the Print dialog (Figure 2–72).

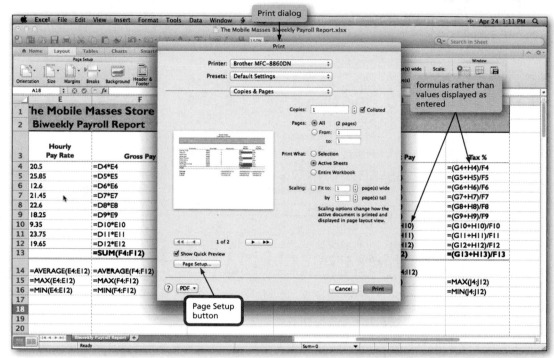

Figure 2–72

- Click the Page Setup button to display the Page Setup dialog.
- Click the Page tab to make it active.
- If necessary, click Landscape in the Orientation area to select it.
- If necessary, click Fit to in the Scaling area to select it (Figure 2–73).

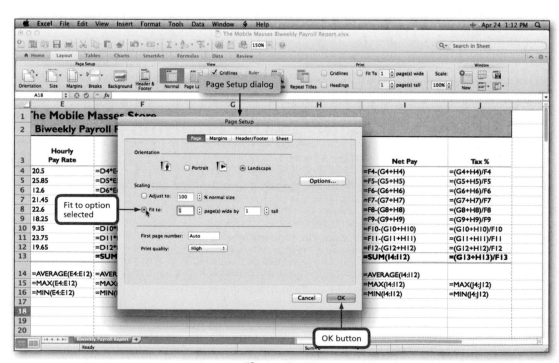

Figure 2–73

❸

- Click the OK button to close the Page Setup dialog.

- If necessary, in the Print dialog, select the Active Sheets option in the Print What area of the dialog. Click the Print button (Print dialog) to print the formulas in the worksheet on one page in landscape orientation (Figure 2–74).

❹

- After viewing and printing the formulas version, press CONTROL-ACCENT MARK (`) to instruct Excel to display the values version.

- Scroll to the left until column A appears.

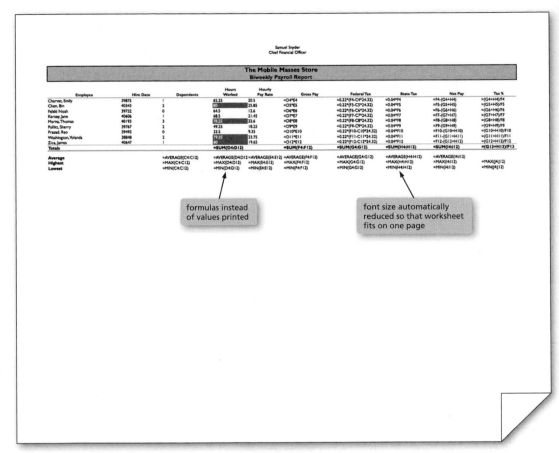

Figure 2–74

To Change the Print Scaling Option Back to 100%

Depending on your printer, you may have to change the Print Scaling option back to 100% after using the Fit to option. Doing so will cause the worksheet to print at the default print scaling of 100%. The following steps reset the Print Scaling option so that future worksheets print at 100%, instead of being resized to print on one page.

❶ Click File in the menu bar, and then choose Page Setup to display the Page Setup dialog.

❷ Click Adjust to in the Scaling area to select the Adjust to setting.

❸ If necessary, type 100 in the Adjust to box to adjust the print scaling to a new percentage.

❹ Click the OK button (Page Setup dialog) to set the print scaling to normal.

❺ Display the Home tab.

Q&A What is the purpose of the Adjust to box in the Page Setup dialog?
The Adjust to box allows you to specify the percentage of reduction or enlargement in the printout of a worksheet. The default percentage is 100%. When you click the Fit to option, this percentage automatically changes to the percentage required to fit the printout on one page.

Quick Reference

BTW For a table that lists how to complete the tasks covered in this book using the mouse, ribbon, shortcut menu, menu bar, and keyboard, see the Quick Reference Summary at the back of this book, or visit the Office 2011 for Mac Online Companion Web page at www.cengagebrain. com, navigate to the desired application, and click Quick Reference.

To Save the Workbook and Quit Excel

With the workbook complete, the following steps save the workbook and quit Excel.

1 Click the Save button in the Standard toolbar.

2 Click Excel in the menu bar and then choose Quit Excel to close all open workbooks and quit Excel.

3 If an Excel dialog appears, click the Save button to save any changes made to the workbook since the last save.

Chapter Summary

In this chapter you have learned how to enter formulas, calculate an average, find the highest and lowest numbers in a range, verify formulas using Range Finder, added borders, align text, format numbers, change column widths and row heights, and add conditional formatting to a range of numbers. In addition, you learned to spell check a worksheet, print a section of a worksheet, and display and print the formulas version of the worksheet using the Fit to option. The items listed below include all the new Excel skills you have learned in this chapter.

1. Enter a Formula Using the Keyboard (EX 73)
2. Enter Formulas Using Point Mode (EX 75)
3. Copy Formulas Using the Fill Handle (EX 78)
4. Determine the Average of a Range of Numbers Using the Keyboard and Mouse (EX 81)
5. Determine the Highest Number in a Range of Numbers Using the Formula Builder (EX 83)
6. Determine the Lowest Number in a Range of Numbers Using the AutoSum Menu (EX 84)
7. Copy a Range of Cells Across Columns to an Adjacent Range Using the Fill Handle (EX 86)
8. Verify a Formula Using Range Finder (EX 87)
9. Change the Workbook Theme (EX 90)
10. Change the Background Color and Apply a Box Border to the Worksheet Title and Subtitle (EX 92)
11. Center Data in Cells (EX 94)
12. Apply an Accounting Number Format and Comma Style Format Using the Ribbon (EX 97)
13. Apply a Currency Style Format with a Floating Dollar Sign Using the Format Cells Dialog (EX 98)
14. Apply a Percent Style Format and Use the Increase Decimal Button (EX 100)
15. Apply Conditional Formatting (EX 101)
16. Change the Widths of Columns (EX 103)
17. Change the Heights of Rows (EX 106)
18. Check Spelling on the Worksheet (EX 108)
19. Change the Worksheet's Margins, Header, and Orientation in Page Layout View (EX 110)
20. Center the Worksheet Contents on the Page (EX 113)
21. Print a Section of the Worksheet (EX 114)
22. Display the Formulas in the Worksheet and Fit the Printout on One Page (EX 116)

 If you have a SAM 2010 user profile, your instructor may have assigned an autogradable version of this assignment. If so, log into the SAM 2010 Web site at www.cengage.com/sam2010 to download the instruction and start files.

Learn It Online

Test your knowledge of chapter content and key terms.

Instructions: To complete the Learn It Online exercises, please visit **www.cengagebrain.com**. At the CengageBrain.com home page, search for *Office 2011 for Mac* using the search box at the top of the page. This will take you to the product page for this book. On the product page, click the Access Now button below the Study Tools heading. On the Book Companion Site Web page, select Excel Chapter 2, and then click the link for the desired exercise.

Chapter Reinforcement TF, MC, and SA

A series of true/false, multiple choice, and short answer questions that test your knowledge of the chapter content.

Flash Cards

An interactive learning environment where you identify chapter key terms associated with displayed definitions.

Practice Test

A series of multiple choice questions that test your knowledge of chapter content and key terms.

Who Wants To Be a Computer Genius?

An interactive game that challenges your knowledge of chapter content in the style of a television quiz show.

Wheel of Terms

An interactive game that challenges your knowledge of chapter key terms in the style of the television show *Wheel of Fortune.*

Crossword Puzzle Challenge

A crossword puzzle that challenges your knowledge of key terms presented in the chapter.

Apply Your Knowledge

Reinforce the skills and apply the concepts you learned in this chapter.

Profit Analysis Worksheet

Instructions: The purpose of this exercise is to open a partially completed workbook, enter formulas and functions, copy the formulas and functions, and then format the worksheet titles and numbers. As shown in Figure 2–75, the completed worksheet analyzes the costs associated with a police department's fleet of vehicles.

	A	B	C	D	E	F	G
1			**Village of Scott Police Department**				
2			**Monthly Vehicle Cost-per-Mile Summary**				
3	Vehicle ID	Miles Driven	Cost per Mile	Maintenance Cost	Mileage Cost	Total Cost	Total Cost per Mile
4	670543	2,007	$ 0.49	$ 242.80	$ 983.43	$ 1,226.23	$ 0.61
5	979253	3,192	0.48	446.37	1,532.16	1,978.53	0.62
6	948173	3,802	0.65	472.47	2,471.30	2,943.77	0.77
7	837625	2,080	0.62	432.25	1,289.60	1,721.85	0.83
8	824664	2,475	0.56	369.88	1,386.00	1,755.88	0.71
9	655385	3,294	0.50	352.05	1,647.00	1,999.05	0.61
10	836417	3,640	0.70	417.80	2,548.00	2,965.80	0.81
11	993617	3,395	0.70	390.39	2,376.50	2,766.89	0.81
12	779468	4,075	0.55	442.17	2,241.25	2,683.42	0.66
13	**Totals**	27,960		$ 3,566.18	$16,475.24	$20,041.42	$ 0.72
14	Highest	4,075	$0.70	$472.47	$2,548.00	$2,965.80	$0.83
15	Lowest	2,007	$0.48	$242.80	$983.43	$1,226.23	$0.61
16	Average	3,107	$0.58	$396.24	$1,830.58	$2,226.82	$0.72

Figure 2–75

Continued >

Apply Your Knowledge *continued*

1. Start Excel. Open the workbook Apply 2-1 Village of Scott Police Department. See the inside back cover of this book for instructions for downloading the Data Files for Students or see your instructor for information on accessing the files required in this book.

2. Use the following formulas in cells E4, F4, and G4:

   Mileage Cost (cell E4) = Miles Driven * Cost per Mile or = B4 * C4

   Total Cost (cell F4) = Maintenance Cost + Mileage Cost or = D4 + E4

   Total Cost per Mile (cell G4) = Total Cost / Miles Driven or = F4 / B4

   Use the fill handle to copy the three formulas in the range E4:G4 to the range E5:G12.

3. Determine totals for the miles driven, maintenance cost, mileage cost, and total cost in row 13. Copy the formula in cell G12 to G13 to assign the formula in cell G12 to G13 in the total line. If necessary, reapply the Total cell style to cell G13.

4. In the range B14:B16, determine the highest value, lowest value, and average value, respectively, for the values in the range B4:B12. Use the fill handle to copy the three functions to the range C14:G16.

5. Format the worksheet as follows:

   a. change the workbook theme to Foundry by using the Themes button

   b. cell A1 — change to Title cell style

   c. cell A2 — change to a font size of 16

   d. cells A1:A2 — Accent 6 background color and a thick box border

   e. cells C4:G4 and D13:G13 — Accounting number format with two decimal places and fixed dollar signs by using the Accounting Number Format button on the Home tab under Number

   f. cells C5:G12 — Comma style format with two decimal places by using the Comma Style button on the Home tab under Number

   g. cells B4:B16 — Comma style format with no decimal places

   h. cells C14:G16 — Currency style format with floating dollar signs by using Format > Cells in the menu bar

   i. cells G4:G12 — apply conditional formatting so that cells with a value greater than 0.80 appear with a rose background color (Accent 6) and black text

6. Switch to Page Layout View and delete any current text in the Header area. Enter your name, course, laboratory assignment number, and any other information, as specified by your instructor, in the Header area. Center the worksheet on the page horizontally, using the Page Setup dialog, accessed on the Print dialog, and then print the worksheet in landscape orientation. Change the document properties, as specified by your instructor. Save the workbook using the file name, Apply 2-1 Village of Scott Police Department Complete.

7. Use Range Finder to verify the formula in cell G13.

8. Print the range A3:D16. Press CONTROL+ACCENT MARK (`) to change the display from the values version of the worksheet to the formulas version. Print the formulas version in landscape orientation on one page (Figure 2–76) by using the Fit to option in the Page sheet in the Page Setup dialog box. Press CONTROL+ACCENT MARK (`) to change the display of the worksheet back to the values version. Close the workbook without saving it.

9. Submit the workbook and results as specified by your instructor.

Mali Jones
Apply 2-1 Village of Scott Police Department Complete

Village of Scott Police Department
Monthly Vehicle Cost-per-Mile Summary

Vehicle ID	Miles Driven	Cost per Mile	Maintenance Cost	Mileage Cost	Total Cost	Total Cost per Mile
670543	2007	0.49	242.8	=B4*C4	=D4+E4	=F4/B4
979253	3192	0.48	446.37	=B5*C5	=D5+E5	=F5/B5
948173	3802	0.65	472.47	=B6*C6	=D6+E6	=F6/B6
837625	2080	0.62	432.25	=B7*C7	=D7+E7	=F7/B7
824664	2475	0.56	369.88	=B8*C8	=D8+E8	=F8/B8
655385	3294	0.5	352.05	=B9*C9	=D9+E9	=F9/B9
836417	3640	0.7	417.8	=B10*C10	=D10+E10	=F10/B10
993617	3395	0.7	390.39	=B11*C11	=D11+E11	=F11/B11
779468	4075	0.55	442.17	=B12*C12	=D12+E12	=F12/B12
Totals	=SUM(B4:B12)		=SUM(D4:D12)	=SUM(E4:E12)	=SUM(F4:F12)	=F13/B13
Highest	=MAX(B4:B12)	=MAX(C4:C12)	=MAX(D4:D12)	=MAX(E4:E12)	=MAX(F4:F12)	=MAX(G4:G12)
Lowest	=MIN(B4:B12)	=MIN(C4:C12)	=MIN(D4:D12)	=MIN(E4:E12)	=MIN(F4:F12)	=MIN(G4:G12)
Average	=AVERAGE(B4:B12)	=AVERAGE(C4:C12)	=AVERAGE(D4:D12)	=AVERAGE(E4:E12)	=AVERAGE(F4:F12)	=AVERAGE(G4:G12)

Figure 2-76

Extend Your Knowledge

Extend the skills you learned in this chapter and experiment with new skills. You may need to use Help to complete the assignment.

Applying Conditional Formatting to Cells

Instructions: Start Excel. Open the workbook Extend 2-1 State Wildlife Department Employee Ratings. See the inside back cover of this book for instructions for downloading the Data Files for Students, or see your instructor for information on accessing the files required in this book. Perform the following tasks to apply three types of conditional formatting to cells in a worksheet:

1. Select the range C4:C18. Click the Conditional Formatting button on the Home tab in the Format group and then click New Rule in the Conditional Formatting list. Select 'Classic' in the Style area, and 'Format only top or bottom ranked values' (New Formatting Rule dialog), as shown in Figure 2-77 on the next page. Enter any value between 10 and 25 in the text box , and click the Percent check box to select it. From the 'Format with' list, choose custom format to open the Format Cells dialog, then select a blue background color. Click the Font tab (Format Cells dialog) and choose the Automatic font color for this conditional format. Click the OK button and view the worksheet.

2. With range C4:C18 selected, apply a conditional format to the range that uses a green background color with Automatic font color to highlight cells with scores that are below average.

Continued >

Extend Your Knowledge *continued*

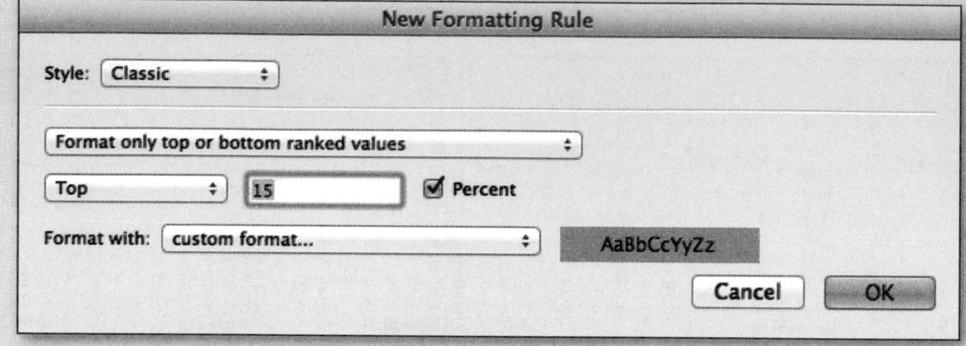

Figure 2–77

3. With range D4:D18 selected, apply conditional formats to the range that use an orange background color with Automatic font color to highlight cells that contain Exemplary or Exceeds Requirements.

4. With range B4:B18 selected, apply a conditional format to the range that uses a red background color with Automatic font color to highlight cells with duplicate student names.

5. Change the document properties as specified by your instructor. Save the workbook using the file name, Extend 2-1 State Wildlife Department Employee Ratings Complete. Submit the revised workbook as specified by your instructor.

Make It Right

Analyze a workbook and correct all errors and/or improve the design.

Correcting Formatting, Functions, and Formulas in a Worksheet

Instructions: Start Excel. Open the workbook Make It Right 2-1 Dion Designwear Profit Analysis. See the inside back cover of this book for instructions for downloading the Data Files for Students, or see your instructor for information on accessing the files required for this book.

In this exercise you will learn how to correct formatting, functions, and formula problems in a worksheet (Figure 2–78).

Perform the following tasks:

1. Add a thick box border around the title and subtitle so that they appear more separated from the rest of the worksheet.

2. Adjust the width of column D to 8.00 (0.84 inches) so that the word in the column header does not wrap.

3. Spell check the worksheet and correct any spelling mistakes that are found, but ignore any spelling mistakes found with the worksheet title and the product descriptions.

4. Center the values in the Product column.

5. The averages in several columns do not include the product in row 4. Adjust the functions in these cells so that all products are included in the calculation.

6. The total sales calculations should be:

Total Sales = Units Sold * (Cost + Profit)

Adjust the formulas in the range F4:F13 so that the correct formula is used.

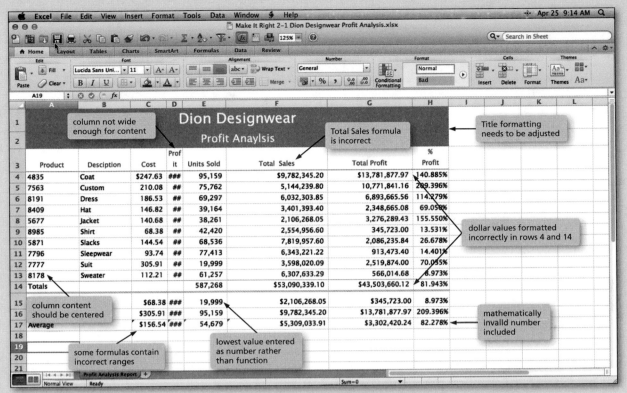

Figure 2–78

7. The value for the lowest value in column E was entered as a number rather than as a function. Replace the value with the appropriate function.

8. The currency values in rows 4 and 14 are currently formatted with the Currency format (floating dollar sign). They should be formatted with the Accounting Number Format button (Home tab under Number). The Accounting number format displays a fixed dollar sign. After making the currency changes, adjust columns F and G to best fit.

9. Delete the function in the cell containing the average of % Profit because it is mathematically invalid.

10. Change the document properties as specified by your instructor. Save the workbook using the file name, Make It Right 2–1 Dion Designwear Profit Analysis Corrected. Submit the revised workbook as specified by your instructor.

In the Lab

Design and/or create a workbook using the guidelines, concepts, and skills presented in this chapter. Labs 1, 2, and 3 are listed in order of increasing difficulty.

Lab 1: Accounts Receivable Balance Worksheet

Problem: You are a part-time assistant in the accounting department at Aficionado Guitar Parts, a Chicago-based supplier of custom guitar parts. You have been asked to use Excel to generate a report that summarizes the monthly accounts receivable balance (Figure 2–79 on the next page). A chart of the balances also is desired. The customer data in Table 2–6 on the next page is available for test purposes.

Continued >

In the Lab *continued*

Customer	Beginning Balance	Credits	Payments	Purchases
Cervantes, Katriel	803.01	56.92	277.02	207.94
Cummings, Trenton	285.05	87.41	182.11	218.22
Danielsson, Oliver	411.45	79.33	180.09	364.02
Kalinowski, Jadwiga	438.37	60.90	331.10	190.39
Lanctot, Royce	378.81	48.55	126.15	211.38
Raglow, Dora	710.99	55.62	231.37	274.71
Tuan, Lin	318.86	85.01	129.67	332.89

Table 2–6 Aficionado Guitar Parts Accounts Receivable Data

Instructions Part 1: Create a worksheet similar to the one shown in Figure 2–79. Include the five columns of customer data in Table 2–6 in the report, plus two additional columns to compute a service charge and a new balance for each customer. Assume no negative unpaid monthly balances.

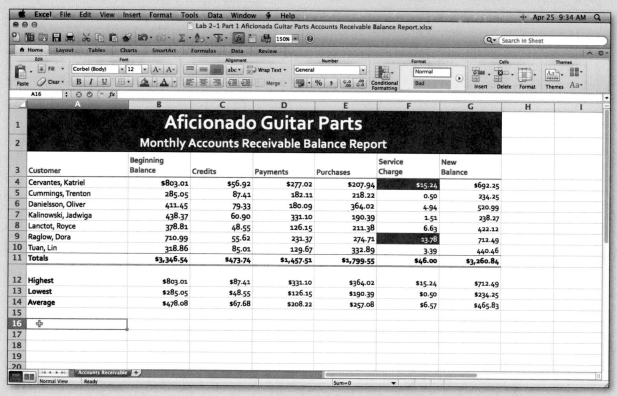

Figure 2–79

Perform the following tasks:

1. Enter and format the worksheet title **Aficionado Guitar Parts** and worksheet subtitle **Monthly Accounts Receivable Balance Report** in cells A1 and A2. Change the theme of the worksheet to the Module theme. Apply the Title cell style to cells A1 and A2. Change the font size in cell A1 to 28 points. Merge and center the worksheet title and subtitle across columns A through G. Change the background color of cells A1 and A2 to the Red standard color. Change the font color of cells A1 and A2 to the White theme color. Draw a thick box border around the range A1:A2.

2. Change the width of column A to 20.00 characters. Change the widths of columns B through G to 12.00 characters. Change the heights of row 3 to 36.00 points and row 12 to 30.00 points.

3. Enter the column titles in row 3 and row titles in the range A11:A14, as shown in Figure 2–79. Center the column titles in the range A3:G3. Apply the Heading 3 cell style to the range A3:G3. Apply the Total cell style to the range A11:G11. Bold the titles in the range A12:A14. Change the font size in the range A3:G14 to 12 points.

4. Enter the data in Table 2–6 in the range A4:E10.

5. Use the following formulas to determine the service charge in column F and the new balance in column G for the first customer. Copy the two formulas down through the remaining customers.

   a. Service Charge (cell F4) = 3.25% * (Beginning Balance – Payments – Credits)

   b. New Balance (G4) = Beginning Balance + Purchases – Credits – Payments + Service Charge

6. Determine the totals in row 11.

7. Determine the maximum, minimum, and average values in cells B12:B14 for the range B4:B10, and then copy the range B12:B14 to C12:G14.

8. Format the numbers as follows: (a) assign the Currency style with a floating dollar sign to the cells containing numeric data in the ranges B4:G4 and B11:G14, and (b) assign a number style with two decimal places and a thousand's separator (currency with no dollar sign) to the range B5:G10.

9. Use conditional formatting to change the formatting to white font on a red background in any cell in the range F4:F10 that contains a value greater than 10.

10. Change the worksheet name from Sheet1 to Accounts Receivable and the sheet tab color to the Red standard color. Change the document properties, as specified by your instructor. Change the worksheet header with your name, course number, and other information as specified by your instructor.

11. Spell check the worksheet. Preview and then print the worksheet in landscape orientation. Save the workbook using the file name, Lab 2-1 Part 1 Aficionado Guitar Parts Accounts Receivable Balance Report.

12. Print the range A3:D14. Print the formulas version on another page. Close the workbook without saving the changes. Submit the assignment as specified by your instructor.

Instructions Part 2: In this part of the exercise, you will create a 3-D Bar chart on a new worksheet in the workbook (Figure 2–80). If necessary, use Excel Help to obtain information on inserting a chart on a separate sheet in the workbook.

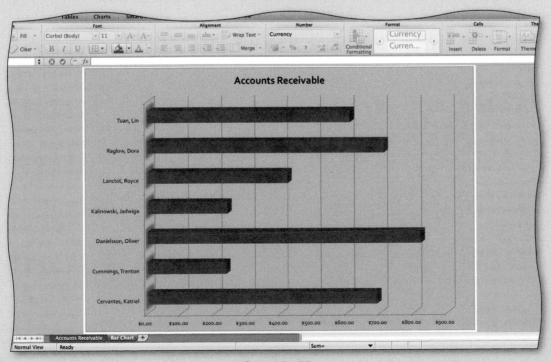

Figure 2–80

Continued >

In the Lab continued

1. Open the workbook Lab 2-1 Part 1 Aficionado Guitar Parts Accounts Receivable Balance Report workbook created in Part 1. Save the workbook using the file name, Lab 2-1 Part 2 Aficionado Guitar Parts Accounts Receivable Balance Report.

2. Use the COMMAND key and mouse to select the nonadjacent chart ranges A4:A10 and G4:G10. That is, select the range A4:A10 and while holding down the COMMAND key, select the range G4:G10.

3. On the Charts tab, under Insert Chart, click the Bar button and then select 3-D Clustered Bar in the 3-D Bar area. When the chart is displayed on the worksheet, choose Move Chart from the Chart menu. When the Move Chart dialog appears, click New sheet and then type Bar Chart for the sheet name. Click the OK button (Move Chart dialog). Change the sheet tab color to the Green standard color.

4. When the chart is displayed on the new worksheet, click the Series 1 series label and then press the DELETE key to delete it. Click the Chart Area, which is a blank area near the edge of the chart, click the Fill button on the Format tab under Chart Element Styles, and then select Accent 5, Lighter 60% in the gallery (column 9, row 3). Click one of the bars in the chart. On the Format tab, under Chart Element Styles, click the Fill button and then select the Green standard color. Click the Chart Title button on the Chart Layout tab under Labels, and then select Title Above Chart in the pop-up menu. If necessary, use the scroll bar on the right side of the worksheet to scroll to the top of the chart. Click the edge of the chart title to select it and then type **Accounts Receivable** as the chart title.

5. Drag the Accounts Receivable tab at the bottom of the worksheet to the left of the Bar Chart tab to reorder the sheets in the workbook. Preview and print the chart.

6. Click the Accounts Receivable sheet tab. Change the following beginning balances: customer Oliver Danielsson to $702.13 and customer Lin Tuan to $482.74. The company also decided to change the service charge from 3.25% to 2.75% for all customers. After copying the adjusted formula in cell F4 to the range F5:F10, click the Auto Fill Options button and then click Fill without Formatting to maintain the original formatting in the range F5:F10. The total new balance in cell G11 should equal $3,720.82.

7. Select both sheets by holding down the SHIFT key and then clicking the Bar Chart tab. Preview and print the selected sheets. Save the workbook. Submit the assignment as specified by your instructor.

Lab 2: Sales Summary Worksheet

Problem: You have been asked to build a worksheet for a start-up company, Electry Auto, that analyzes the financing needs for the company's first six months in business. The company plans to begin operations in January with an initial investment of $500,000.00. The expected revenue and costs for the company's first six months are shown in Table 2–7. The desired worksheet is shown in Figure 2–81. The initial investment is shown at the starting balance for January (cell B4). The amount of financing required by the company is shown as the lowest ending balance (cell F12).

Table 2–7 Electry Auto Start-Up Financing Needs Data		
Month	**Revenue**	**Costs**
January	105000	220000
February	82000	260000
March	200000	255000
April	250000	320000
May	325000	420000
June	510000	540000

Instructions Part 1: Perform the following tasks to build the worksheet shown in Figure 2–81.

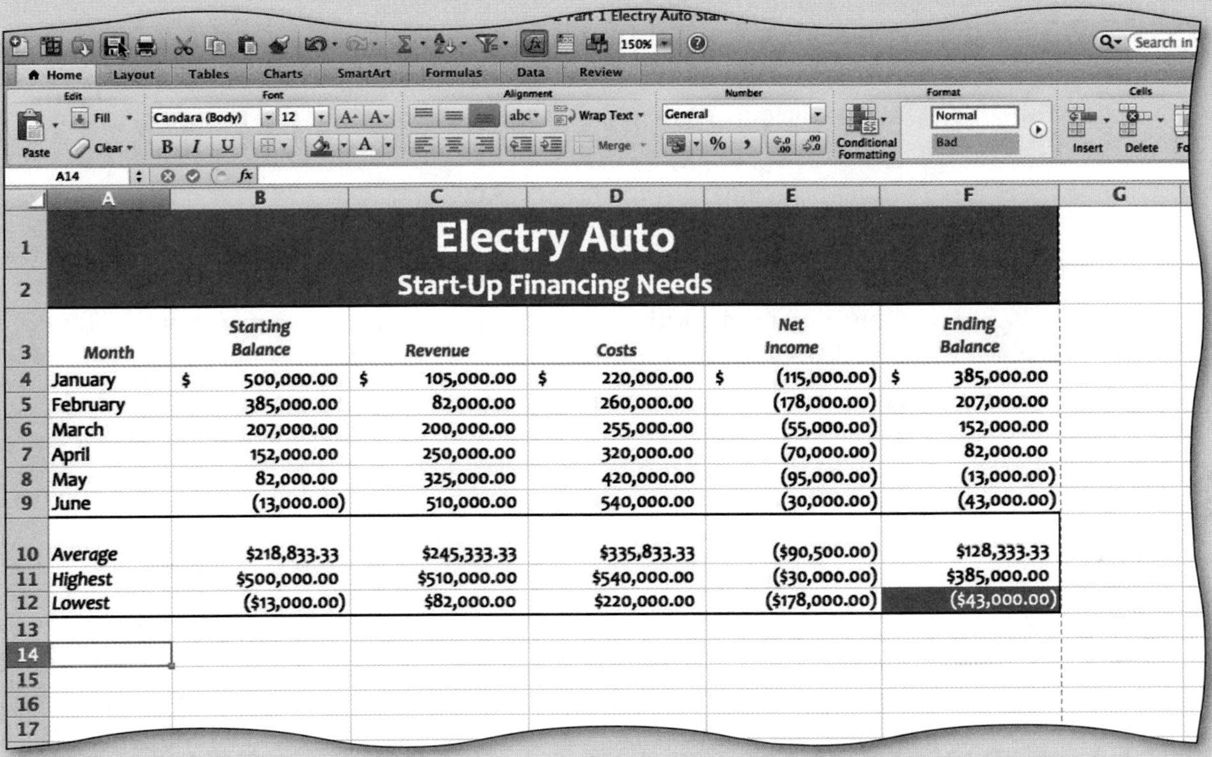

	Electry Auto				
	Start-Up Financing Needs				
Month	**Starting Balance**	**Revenue**	**Costs**	**Net Income**	**Ending Balance**
January	$ 500,000.00	$ 105,000.00	$ 220,000.00	$ (115,000.00)	$ 385,000.00
February	385,000.00	82,000.00	260,000.00	(178,000.00)	207,000.00
March	207,000.00	200,000.00	255,000.00	(55,000.00)	152,000.00
April	152,000.00	250,000.00	320,000.00	(70,000.00)	82,000.00
May	82,000.00	325,000.00	420,000.00	(95,000.00)	(13,000.00)
June	(13,000.00)	510,000.00	540,000.00	(30,000.00)	(43,000.00)
Average	$218,833.33	$245,333.33	$335,833.33	($90,500.00)	$128,333.33
Highest	$500,000.00	$510,000.00	$540,000.00	($30,000.00)	$385,000.00
Lowest	($13,000.00)	$82,000.00	$220,000.00	($178,000.00)	($43,000.00)

Figure 2–81

1. Start Excel. Apply the Waveform theme to a new workbook.
2. Increase the width of columns B through F to 14.00.
3. Enter the worksheet title `Electry Auto` in cell A1 and the worksheet subtitle `Start-Up Financing Needs` in cell A2. Enter the column titles in row 3, as shown in Figure 2–81. In row 3, use CONTROL-OPTION-RETURN to start a new line in a cell.
4. Enter the start-up financing needs data described in Table 2–7 in columns A, C, and D in rows 4 through 9. Enter the initial starting balance (cell B4) of 500000.00. Enter the row titles in the range A10:A12, as shown in Figure 2–81.
5. For the months of February through March, the starting balance is equal to the previous month's ending balance. Obtain the starting balance for February by setting the starting balance of February to the ending balance of January. Use a cell reference rather than typing in the data. Copy the formula for February to the remaining months.
6. Obtain the net income amounts in column E by subtracting the costs in column D from the revenues in column C. Enter the formula in cell E4 and copy it to the range E5:E9. Obtain the ending balance amounts in column F by adding the starting balance in column B to the net income in column E. Enter the formula in cell F4 and copy it to the range F5:F9.
7. In the range B10:B12, use the AVERAGE, MAX, and MIN functions to determine the average value, highest value, and lowest value in the range B4:B9. Copy the range B10:B12 to the range C10:F12.
8. One at a time, merge and center the worksheet title and subtitle across columns A through F. Select cells A1 and A2 and change the background color to light blue (column 7 in the Standard Colors area in the Fill Color pop-up menu). Apply the Title cell style to cells A1 and A2. Change the worksheet title in cell A1 to 28-point white (column 1, row 1 on the Font Color pop-up menu). Change the worksheet subtitle to the same color. Assign a thick box border to the range A1:A2.

Continued >

In the Lab *continued*

9. Center the titles in row 3, columns A through F. Apply the Heading 3 cell style to the range A3:F3. Use the Italic button to italicize the column titles in row 3 and the row titles in the range A10:A12.

10. Assign a thick box border to the range A10:F12. Change the background and font color for cell F12 to the same colors applied to the worksheet title in Step 8.

11. Change the column width of columns B through F to 15.00 characters.

12. Change the row heights of row 3 to 36.00 points and row 10 to 30.00 points.

13. Assign the Accounting number format to the range B4:F4. Assign the Comma style format to the range B5:F9. Assign a Currency format with a floating dollar sign and a negative numbers format that matches the format in B5:F9 to the range B10:F12.

14. Rename the sheet tab as Start-Up Financing Needs. Apply the Light Blue color to the sheet tab. Change the document properties, as specified by your instructor. Change the worksheet header with your name, course number, and other information as specified by your instructor. Center the worksheet on the page horizontally, using the Page Setup dialog. Save the workbook using the file name Lab 2-2 Part 1 Electry Auto Start-Up Financing Needs. Print the entire worksheet in landscape orientation. Next, print only the range A3:B9.

15. Display the formulas version by pressing CONTROL+ACCENT MARK (`). Print the formulas version using the Fit to option in the Scaling area on the Page tab in the Page Setup dialog. After printing the worksheet, reset the Scaling option by selecting the Adjust to button on the Page tab in the Page Setup dialog box and changing the percent value to 100%. Change the display from the formulas version to the values version by pressing CONTROL+ACCENT MARK (`). Do not save the workbook.

16. Submit the revised workbook as requested by your instructor.

Instructions Part 2: In this part of the exercise, you will change the revenue amounts until the lowest ending balance is greater than zero, indicating that the company does not require financing in its first six months of operation. Open the workbook created in Part 1 and save the workbook as Lab 2-2 Part 2 Electry Auto Start-Up Financing Needs. Manually increment each of the six values in the revenue column by $1,000.00 until the lowest ending balance in cell F12 is greater than zero. The value of cell F12 should equal $5,000.00. All six values in column C must be incremented the same number of times. Update the worksheet header and save the workbook. Print the worksheet. Submit the assignment as specified by your instructor.

Instructions Part 3: In this part of the exercise, you will change the monthly costs until the lowest ending balance is greater than zero, indicating that the company does not require financing in its first six months of operation. Open the workbook created in Part 1 and then save the workbook as Lab 2-1 Part 3 Electry Auto Start-Up Financing Needs. Manually decrement each of the six values in the costs column by $1,000.00 until the lowest ending balance in cell F12 is greater than zero. Decrement all six values in column C the same number of times. Your worksheet is correct when the lowest ending balance in cell F12 is $5,000.00. Update the worksheet header and save the workbook. Print the worksheet. Submit the assignment as specified by your instructor.

Lab 3: Stock Club Investment Analysis

Problem: Several years ago, you and a large group of friends started a stock club. Each year every member invests more money per month. You have decided to create a portfolio worksheet (Figure 2–82) that summarizes the club's current stock holdings so that you can share the information with your group of friends. The club's portfolio is summarized in Table 2–8. Table 2–8 also shows the general layout of the worksheet to be created.

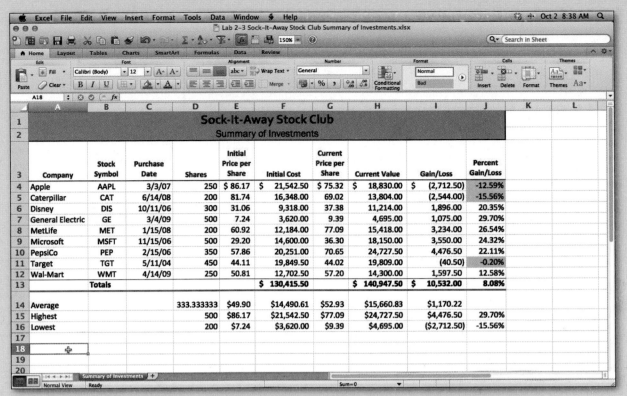

Figure 2–82

Table 2–8 Sock-It-Away Stock Club

Company	Stock Symbol	Purchase Date	Shares	Initial Price per Share	Initial Cost	Current Price per Share	Current Value	Gain/ Loss	Percent Gain/ Loss
Apple	AAPL	3/3/2007	250	86.17	Formula A	75.32	Formula B	Formula C	Formula D
Caterpillar	CAT	6/14/2008	200	81.74		69.02			
Disney	DIS	10/11/2006	300	31.06		37.38			
General Electric	GE	3/4/2009	500	7.24		9.39			
MetLife	MET	1/15/2008	200	60.92		77.09			
Microsoft	MSFT	11/15/2006	500	29.20		36.30			
PepsiCo	PEP	2/15/2006	350	57.86		70.65			
Target	TGT	5/11/2004	450	44.11		44.02			
Wal-Mart	WMT	4/14/2009	250	50.81		57.20			
Totals			Formula E						
Average			Formula F						
Highest			Formula G						
Lowest			Formula H						

Instructions: *Perform the following tasks:*

1. Start Excel. Enter the worksheet titles Sock-It-Away Stock Club in cell A1 and Summary of Investments in cell A2.

2. Enter the column titles and data in Table 2–8 beginning in row 3.

3. Change the column widths and row heights as follows: column A — 13; column B — 8.17; columns E and G — 7.50; columns F, H, and I — 13.00; column J — 8.33; row 3 — 56.00 points; row 14 — 27.00 points.

Continued >

4. Enter the following formulas in row 4 and then copy them down through row 12:

   a. Enter Formula A in cell F4: Initial Cost = Shares × Initial Price per Share

   b. Enter Formula B in cell H4: Current Value = Shares × Current Price Per Share

   c. Enter Formula C in cell I4: Gain/Loss = Current Value − Initial Cost

   d. Enter Formula D in cell J4: Percent Gain/Loss = Gain/Loss / Initial Cost

5. Compute the totals (Formula E) for initial cost, current value, gain/loss, and percent gain loss. For the percent gain/loss in cell J13, copy cell J12 to J13 using the fill handle.

6. In cells D14, D15, and D16, enter Formulas F, G, and H using the AVERAGE, MAX, and MIN functions. Copy the three functions across through the range J14: J16. Delete the invalid formula in cell J14.

7. Format the worksheet as follows:

   a. Apply the Spectrum theme to the worksheet.

   b. Format the worksheet title with Title cell style. Merge and center across columns A through J.

   c. Format the worksheet subtitle with Franklin Gothic Book font, 14 point font size, Text 1 theme font color. Merge and center across columns A through J.

   d. Format the worksheet title and subtitle background with Accent 2, Lighter 60% theme color and a thick box border.

   e. Format row 3 with the Heading 3 cell style and row 13 with the Total cell style. Center the entries in row 3.

   f. Format the data in rows 4 through 12: center data in column B; range E4:I4 — Accounting number format style with fixed dollar sign; range E5:I12 — Comma style; range J4:J13 — Percentage style with two decimal places; cells F13, H13, and I13 — Accounting Number format with fixed dollar sign.

   g. Format E14:I16 — Currency format with floating decimal places, negative values in parentheses with black font color; J15:J16 — Percentage style with two decimal places.

   h. Format J4:J12 — apply conditional formatting so that if a cell in range is less than 0, then cell appears with a pink background color.

8. Spell check the worksheet. Change the name of the sheet tab to Summary of Investments and apply the Accent 2, Darker 25% theme color to the sheet tab. Update the document properties, and save the workbook using the file name, Lab 2-3 Sock-It-Away Stock Club Summary of Investments. Print the worksheet in landscape orientation. Print the formulas version on one page. Close the workbook without saving changes. Submit the assignment as specified by your instructor.

Cases and Places

Apply your creative thinking and problem-solving skills to design and implement a solution.

1: Analyzing Emergency Student Loans

Academic

The Student Assistance office at your school provides emergency loans at simple interest. The data obtained from six types of loans and the desired report format are shown in Table 2–9. The required formulas are shown in Table 2–10. Use the concepts and techniques presented in this chapter to create and format the worksheet. Include total, average, maximum, and minimum values for Principal, Interest, and Amount Due.

Table 2–9 Emergency Student Loan Data and Worksheet Layout

Loan Type	Principal	Rate	Time in Years
Academic Supplies	$40,000	7.5%	.4
Medical Emergency	$25,500	12%	.33
Personal Emergency	$12,750	8.25%	.5
Room and Board	$27,000	6.5%	1
Travel Expenses	$4,550	12%	.5
Tuition Reimbursement	$107,000	6%	1

Table 2–10 Emergency Student Loan Formulas

Interest = Principal × Rate × Time

Amount Due = Principal + Interest

Average = AVERAGE function

Minimum = MIN function

Maximum = MAX function

2: Analyzing Energy Consumption

Personal

Your parents believe that your late night studying sessions and household appliance usage contribute to excessive electricity bills. You have decided to try to prove them wrong by analyzing your daily and monthly electricity consumption. You research the energy consumption of your personal items and appliance usage to obtain consumption costs per hour for each item. Table 2–11 contains the data and format for the report you want to create.

Use the concepts and techniques presented in this project to create and format the worksheet. Include an embedded 3-D Pie chart that shows the cost per month. Use Microsoft Excel Help to create a professional looking 3-D Pie chart with title and data labels.

Table 2–11 Appliance Electricity Usage Costs

Appliance	Cost per Hour	Hours Used Daily	Total Cost Per Day	Total Cost per Month (30 Days)
Clothes dryer	$0.325	1		
Computer	$0.02	6		
DVD player	$0.035	1		
Light bulbs	$0.043	8		
Refrigerator	$0.035	24		
Stereo	$0.02	5		
Television	$0.04	4		
Washing machine	$0.03	2		

3: Analyzing Profit Potential

Professional

You work for HumiCorp, an online retailer of home humidifiers. Your manager wants to know the profit potential of their inventory based on the items in inventory listed in Table 2–12 on the next page. Table 2–12 contains the format of the desired report. The required formulas are shown in Table 2–13 on the next page. Use the concepts and techniques developed in this chapter to create and format the worksheet. The company just received 67 additional desk-sized humidifiers and shipped out 48 room-sized humidifiers. Update the appropriate cells to reflect the change in inventory.

Cases and Places *continued*

Table 2–12 HumiCorp Inventory Profit Potential Data and Worksheet Layout

Item	Units on Hand	Unit Cost	Total Cost	Unit Price	Total Value	Potential Profit
Desk	187	27.58	Formula A	Formula B	Formula C	Formula D
Filtered home-sized	42	324.14				
Filtered room-sized	118	86.55				
Home-sized	103	253.91				
Room-sized	97	53.69				
Total	—	—	—	—	—	—
Average	Formula E					
Lowest	Formula F					
Highest	Formula G					

Table 2–13 HumiCorp Inventory Profit Potential Formulas

Formula A = Units on Hand × Unit Cost
Formula B = Unit Cost × (1 / (1 − .66))
Formula C = Units on Hand × Unit Price
Formula D = Total Value − Total Cost
Formula E = AVERAGE function
Formula F = MIN function
Formula G = MAX function

3 What-If Analysis, Charting, and Working with Large Worksheets

Objectives

You will have mastered the material in this chapter when you can:

Rotate text in a cell

Create a series of month names

Copy, paste, insert, and delete cells

Format numbers using format symbols

Freeze and unfreeze rows and columns

Show and format the system date

Use absolute and mixed cell references in a formula

Use the IF function to perform a logical test

Create Sparkline charts

Use the Format Painter button to format cells

Create a 3-D Pie chart on a separate chart sheet

Rearrange worksheet tabs

Change the worksheet view

Answer what-if questions

Goal seek to answer what-if questions

3 What-If Analysis, Charting, and Working with Large Worksheets

Introduction

Worksheets normally are much larger than those created in the previous chapters, often extending beyond the size of the Excel window. Because you cannot see the entire worksheet on the screen at one time, working with a large worksheet sometimes can be frustrating. This chapter introduces several Excel commands that allow you to control what is displayed on the screen so that you can view critical parts of a large worksheet at one time. One command allows you to freeze rows and columns so that Excel always displays them on the screen. Another command splits the worksheet into separate windowpanes so that you can view different parts of a worksheet on the screen at one time.

When you set up a worksheet, you should use cell references in formulas whenever possible, rather than constant values. The use of a cell reference allows you to change a value in multiple formulas by changing the value in a single cell. The cell references in a formula are called assumptions. Assumptions are values in cells that you can change to determine new values for formulas. This chapter emphasizes the use of assumptions and shows how to use Excel to answer what-if questions, such as what happens to the six-month operating income if you decrease the marketing expenses assumption by 3 percent? Being able to analyze quickly the effect of changing values in a worksheet is an important skill in making business decisions.

This chapter also introduces you to techniques that will enhance your ability to create worksheets and draw charts. From your work in Chapter 1, you are aware of how easily you can create charts. This chapter covers additional charting techniques that allow you to convey a message in a dramatic pictorial fashion, such as Sparkline charts and an exploded 3-D pie chart. This chapter also covers other methods for entering values in cells, such as allowing Excel to enter values for you based on a pattern of values that you create, and formatting these values. In addition, you will learn how to use absolute cell references and how to use the IF function to assign a value to a cell based on a logical test.

Project — Financial Projection Worksheet with What-If Analysis and Chart

The project in the chapter follows proper design guidelines and uses Excel to create the worksheet and pie chart shown in Figures 3–1a and 3–1b. Modern Music Shops operates several stores that sell and service musical instruments. Each June and December, the director of finance and accounting submits a plan to the management team to show projected monthly sales revenues, costs of goods sold, gross margin, expenses, and operating income for the next six months. The director requires an easy-to-read worksheet that shows financial projections for the next six months. The worksheet should allow for quick analysis if projections for certain numbers change, such as the percentage of expenses allocated to marketing. In addition, a 3-D pie chart is required that shows the projected operating income contribution for each of the six months.

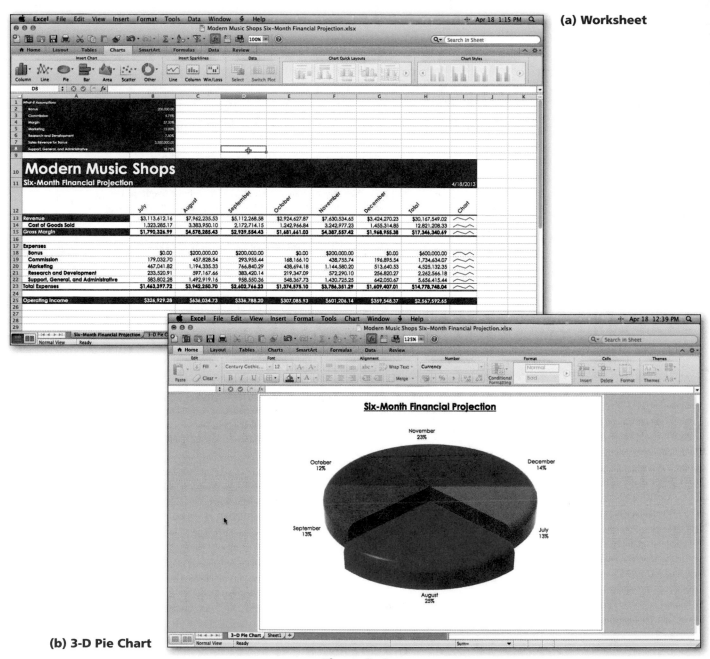

(a) Worksheet

(b) 3-D Pie Chart

Figure 3–1

The requirements document for the Modern Music Shops Six-Month Financial Projection worksheet is shown in Figure 3–2 on the next page. It includes the needs, source of data, summary of calculations, chart requirements, and other facts about its development.

REQUEST FOR NEW WORKBOOK

Date Submitted:	April 9, 2013
Submitted By:	Marcus Olek
Worksheet Title:	Modern Music Shops' Six-Month Financial Projection
Needs:	The needs are: (1) a worksheet (Figure 3-3a on page EX 138) that shows Modern Music Shops' projected monthly sales, cost of goods sold, gross margin, expenses, and operating income for a six-month period; and (2) a 3-D Pie chart (Figure 3-3b on page EX 138) that shows the projected contribution of each month's operating income to the six-month period operating income.
Source of Data:	The data supplied by the Finance department includes projections of the monthly sales and expenses (Table 3-1 on page EX 139) that are based on prior years. All the remaining numbers in the worksheet are determined from these 13 numbers using formulas.
Calculations:	The following calculations must be made for each month: 1. Cost of Goods Sold = Revenue − Revenue × Margin 2. Gross Margin = Revenue − Cost of Goods Sold 3. Bonus Expense = $200,000.00 if the Revenue exceeds the Revenue for Bonus; otherwise Bonus Expense = 0 4. Commission Expense = Commission Assumption × Revenue 5. Marketing Expense = Marketing Assumption × Revenue 6. Research and Development = Research and Development Assumption × Revenue 7. Support, General, and Administrative Expense = Support, General, and Administrative Assumption × Revenue 8. Total Expenses = Sum of Expenses 9. Operating Income = Gross Margin − Total Expenses
Chart Requirements:	Show Sparkline charts for Revenue and each of the items noted in the calculations area above. A 3-D Pie chart is required on a separate sheet (Figure 3-3b) to show the contribution of each month's operating income to the six-month period operating income. The chart should also emphasize the month with the greatest operating income.

Approvals

Approval Status:	X	Approved
		Rejected
Approved By:		Farah Qadir, CFO
Date:		April 16, 2013
Assigned To:		J. Quasney, Spreadsheet Specialist

Figure 3–2

Overview

As you read this chapter, you will learn how to create the worksheet shown in Figure 3–1 on the previous page by performing these general tasks:

- Create a series of month names
- Use absolute cell references in a formula
- Use the IF function to perform a logical test
- Create Sparkline charts in a range of cells
- Use the Format Painter button to format cells
- Create a 3-D pie chart on a separate chart sheet
- Answer what-if questions
- Manipulate large worksheets

General Project Decisions

Plan Ahead

While creating an Excel worksheet, you need to make several decisions that will determine the appearance and characteristics of the finished worksheet. As you create the worksheet required to meet the requirements shown in Figure 3–2, you should follow these general guidelines:

1. **Plan the layout of the worksheet.** Worksheets that include financial data associated with time frames typically include dates, such as months, quarters, or years, as column headers. What-if assumptions should not clutter the worksheet, but placing them in an easily located portion of the worksheet allows for quicker creation of new projections.

2. **Determine the necessary formulas and functions needed.** Often, financial calculations rely on strict definitions and commonly accepted formulas for performing the calculations. Look for such situations and always use the accepted formulas. When using a what-if section on a worksheet, make certain to create formulas that use the what-if criteria. When a requirement necessitates a calculation only under a certain condition, a function can check for the condition and make the calculation when necessary.

3. **Specify how to best utilize Sparkline charts.** Sparkline charts allow worksheet users quickly to visualize information in a small chart within a cell. The use of multiple Sparkline charts in the worksheet will provide the user with a visual comparison of the various data items for each month. The user, therefore, can see trends for each line item over time and also compare relationships among various line items.

4. **Identify how to format various elements of the worksheet.** Format separate parts of a worksheet, such as what-if assumptions, in a manner that indicates that they are separate from the main area of the worksheet. Other financial items, such as sales revenue and expenses, are distinct categories of financial data and should be separated visually. Totals and subtotals should stand out to draw the reader's attention.

5. **Specify how charts should convey necessary information.** As you have learned, different chart types convey different messages and are appropriate in different situations. For example, a 3-D pie chart is a good way to compare visually a small set of numbers. Often one or two slices of a pie chart displays as exploded, meaning that the slice appears pulled away from the cart, in order to emphasize the slice to the user. Format chart data points so that the worksheet user's eye is drawn to important information.

6. **Perform what-if analysis and goal seeking using the best techniques.** What-if analysis allows you quickly to answer questions regarding various predictions. A what-if area of a worksheet allows users of the worksheet efficiently to ask questions. Goal seeking allows you automatically to modify values in a what-if area of a worksheet based on a goal that you have for another cell in the worksheet.

When necessary, more specific details concerning the above guidelines are presented at appropriate points in the chapter. The chapter also will identify the actions you perform and decisions made regarding these guidelines during the creation of the worksheet shown in Figure 3–1 on page EX 135.

Using a sketch of the worksheet can help you visualize its design. The sketch of the worksheet consists of titles, column and row headings, location of data values, calculations, and a rough idea of the desired formatting (Figure 3–3a on the next page). The sketch of the 3-D pie chart shows the expected contribution of each month's operating income to the six-month operating income (Figure 3–3b on the next page). The assumptions will be entered at the top of the worksheet (Figure 3–3a). The projected monthly sales revenue will be entered in row 13 of the worksheet. The projected monthly sales revenue and the assumptions shown in Table 3–1 on page EX 139 will be used to calculate the remaining numbers in the worksheet.

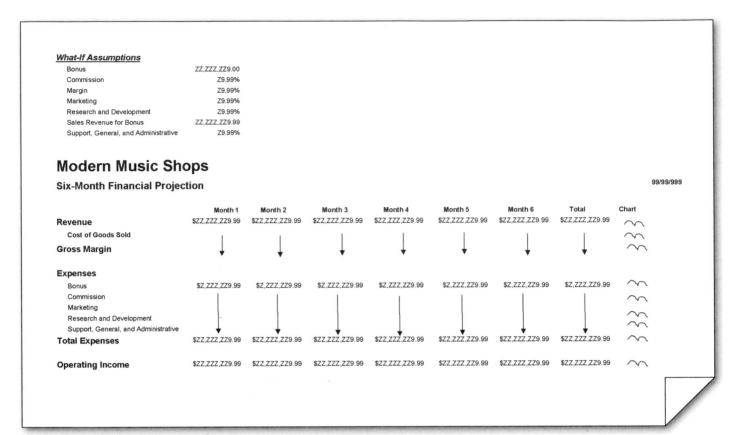

**What-If Assumptions**

Bonus	ZZ,ZZZ,ZZ9.00
Commission	Z9.99%
Margin	Z9.99%
Marketing	Z9.99%
Research and Development	Z9.99%
Sales Revenue for Bonus	ZZ,ZZZ,ZZ9.99
Support, General, and Administrative	Z9.99%

Modern Music Shops

Six-Month Financial Projection   99/99/999

	Month 1	Month 2	Month 3	Month 4	Month 5	Month 6	Total	Chart
Revenue	$ZZ,ZZZ,ZZ9.99	$ZZ,ZZZ,ZZ9.99	$ZZ,ZZZ,ZZ9.99	$ZZ,ZZZ,ZZ9.99	$ZZ,ZZZ,ZZ9.99	$ZZ,ZZZ,ZZ9.99	$ZZ,ZZZ,ZZ9.99	
Cost of Goods Sold								
Gross Margin								
Expenses								
Bonus	$Z,ZZZ,ZZ9.99	$Z,ZZZ,ZZ9.99	$Z,ZZZ,ZZ9.99	$Z,ZZZ,ZZ9.99	$Z,ZZZ,ZZ9.99	$Z,ZZZ,ZZ9.99	$Z,ZZZ,ZZ9.99	
Commission								
Marketing								
Research and Development								
Support, General, and Administrative								
Total Expenses	$ZZ,ZZZ,ZZ9.99	$ZZ,ZZZ,ZZ9.99	$ZZ,ZZZ,ZZ9.99	$ZZ,ZZZ,ZZ9.99	$ZZ,ZZZ,ZZ9.99	$ZZ,ZZZ,ZZ9.99	$ZZ,ZZZ,ZZ9.99	
Operating Income	$ZZ,ZZZ,ZZ9.99	$ZZ,ZZZ,ZZ9.99	$ZZ,ZZZ,ZZ9.99	$ZZ,ZZZ,ZZ9.99	$ZZ,ZZZ,ZZ9.99	$ZZ,ZZZ,ZZ9.99	$ZZ,ZZZ,ZZ9.99	

Figure 3–3 (a) Worksheet Sketch

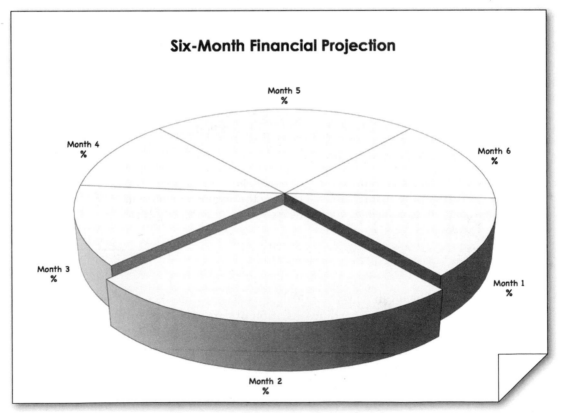

Six-Month Financial Projection

Month 5 %

Month 4 %

Month 6 %

Month 3 %

Month 1 %

Month 2 %

Figure 3–3 (b) 3-D Pie Chart Sketch

With a solid understanding of the requirements document, an understanding of the necessary decisions, and a sketch of the worksheet, the next step is to use Excel to create the worksheet.

Table 3–1 Modern Music Shops Six-Month Financial Projections Data and What-If Assumptions	
Projected Monthly Total Sales Revenues	
July	$3,113,612.16
August	7,962,235.53
September	5,112,268.58
October	2,924,627.87
November	7,630,534.65
December	3,424,270.23
What-If Assumptions	
Bonus	$200,000.00
Commission	5.75%
Margin	57.50%
Marketing	15.00%
Research and Development	7.50%
Sales Revenue for Bonus	$3,500,000.00
Support, General, and Administrative	18.75%

To Start Excel

If you are using a computer to step through the project in this chapter and you want your screens to match the figures in this book, you should change your screen's resolution to 1280 × 800. For information about how to change a computer's resolution, refer to the Office 2011 and Mac OS X chapter at the beginning of this book.

The following steps, which assume Mac OS X is running, start Excel based on a typical installation. You may need to ask your instructor how to start Excel for your computer. For a detailed example of the procedure summarized below, refer to the Office 2011 and Mac OS X chapter.

1 Click the Excel icon in the Dock to display the Excel Workbook Gallery.

2 If All is not selected in the Templates pane on the left, click to select it.

3 Double-click the Excel Workbook icon in the Excel Workbook Gallery to display a new blank workbook in the Excel window.

Q&A What if Excel automatically opens a workbook when I start Excel?
If you had a workbook open when you last quit Excel, Excel will, by default, open that workbook when started. You can choose Close in the File menu to close that workbook, and then choose New in the File menu to open a new workbook.

4 If the Excel window is not sized properly, as described in the Office 2011 and Mac OS X chapter, size the window properly.

5 If the Normal View button in the lower left of the workbook window is not selected, click it so that your screen is in Normal view.

For an introduction to Mac OS X and instruction about how to perform basic Mac OS X tasks, read the Office 2011 and Mac OS X chapter at the beginning of this book, where you can learn how to resize windows, change screen resolution, create folders, move and rename files, use Windows Help, and much more.

For an introduction to Office 2011 and instruction about how to perform basic tasks in Office 2011 programs, read the Office 2011 and Mac OS X chapter at the beginning of this book, where you can learn how to start a program, use the ribbon, save a file, open a file, quit a program, use Help, and much more.

The Ribbon and Screen Resolution

BTW | Excel may change how the groups and buttons within the groups appear on the ribbon, depending on the computer's screen resolution. Thus, your ribbon may look different from the ones in this book if you are using a screen resolution other than 1280 × 800.

BTWs

BTW | For a complete list of the BTWs found in the margins of this book, visit the Excel 2011 BTW Web page (scsite.com/ex2011/btw).

Rotating Text in a Cell

BTW | In Excel, you use the Alignment pane of the Format Cells dialog as shown in Figure 3–5 on page EX 141, to position data in a cell by centering, left-aligning, or right-aligning; indenting; aligning at the top, bottom, or center; and rotating. If you enter 90 in the Degrees box in the Orientation area, the text will appear vertically and read from bottom to top in the cell.

To Enter the Worksheet Titles, Change Document Properties, Apply a Theme, and Save the Workbook

The worksheet contains two titles, initially in cells A8 and A9. In the previous chapters, titles were centered across the worksheet. With large worksheets that extend beyond the size of a window, it is best to enter titles left-aligned as shown in the sketch of the worksheet in Figure 3–3a on page EX 138 so the user can more easily find the worksheet title. The following steps enter the worksheet titles, change document properties, change the workbook theme to Plaza, and then save the workbook.

1 Set the zoom to 125%.

2 Select cell A8 and then type `Modern Music Shops` as the worksheet title.

3 Select cell A9 and then type `Six-Month Financial Projection` as the worksheet subtitle and then press the RETURN key to enter the worksheet subtitle.

4 Change the document properties as specified by your instructor.

5 Apply the Plaza theme to the workbook.

6 With a USB flash drive connected to one of the computer's USB ports, click the Save button in the Standard toolbar to display the Save As dialog.

7 Type `Modern Music Shops Six-Month Financial Projection` in the File name text box to change the file name. Do not press the RETURN key after typing the file name because you do not want to close the dialog at this time.

8 Navigate to the desired save location (in this case, the Excel folder in the CIS 101 folder [or your class folder] on the USB flash drive).

9 Click the Save button (Save As dialog) to save the document in the selected folder on the selected drive with the entered file name.

Rotating Text and Using the Fill Handle to Create a Series

The data on the worksheet, including month names and the What-If Assumptions section, now can be added to the worksheet.

Plan Ahead

Plan the layout of the worksheet.

Excel allows you to rotate text in a cell. Rotated text often provides a strong visual appeal. Rotated text also allows you to fit more text into a smaller column width. Chapters 1 and 2 used the fill handle to copy a cell or a range of cells to adjacent cells. The fill handle also allows creation of a series of numbers, dates, or month names automatically. Using the fill handle in this way eliminates the need to type in such data, saving time and eliminating typographical errors.

To Rotate Text and Use the Fill Handle to Create a Series of Month Names

The design of the worksheet calls specifically for only six months of data. Because there always will be only six months of data in the worksheet, the months should be placed across the top of the worksheet as column headings rather than as row headings. The data for the worksheet includes more data items regarding each month than there are months, and, possibly, more expense categories could be added in the future. A proper layout, therefore, includes placing months as column headings.

When you first enter text, its angle is zero degrees (0°), and it reads from left to right in a cell. Excel allows you to rotate text in a cell counterclockwise by entering a number between 1° and 90°.

The following steps enter the month name, July, in cell B10; format cell B10 (including rotating the text); and then use the fill handle to enter the remaining month names in the range C10:G10.

1

- If necessary, select the Home tab and then click cell B10 because this cell will include the first month name in the series of month names.

- Type **July** as the cell entry and then click the Enter button in the formula bar.

- CONTROL-click cell B10 to display a shortcut menu (Figure 3–4).

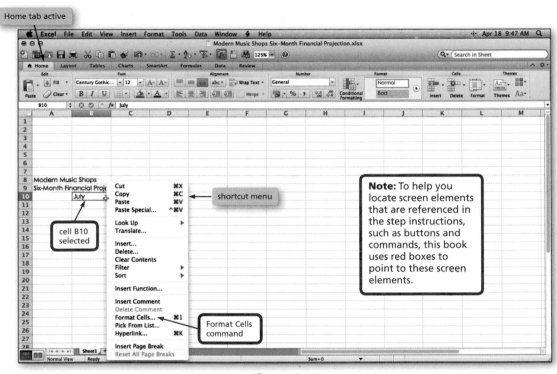

Figure 3–4

2

- Choose Format Cells from the shortcut menu to display the Format Cells dialog.

- Click the Alignment tab to display the Alignment pane. Click the 45° point in the Orientation area (Format Cells dialog) to move the Text hand in the Orientation area to the 45° point and to display a new orientation in the Degrees box (Figure 3–5).

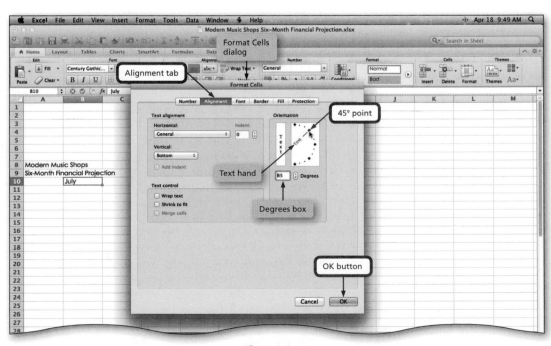

Figure 3–5

• Click the OK button (Format Cells dialog) to rotate the text in the active cell and automatically increase the height of the current row to best fit the rotated text.

• Point to the fill handle on the lower-right corner of cell B10 to display the crosshair mouse pointer in preparation of filling the month series (Figure 3–6).

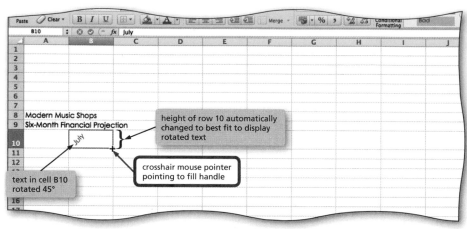

Figure 3–6

4

• Drag the fill handle to the right to select the range to fill, C10:G10 in this case. Do not release the mouse button (Figure 3–7).

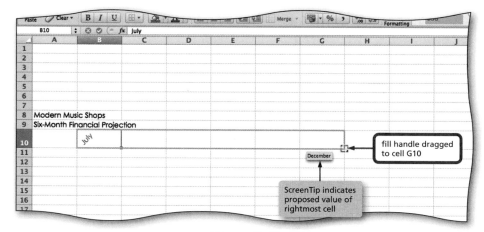

Figure 3–7

• Release the mouse button to create a month name series in the selected range and copy the format of the selected cell to the selected range.

• Click the Auto Fill Options button below the lower-right corner of the fill area to display the Auto Fill Options menu (Figure 3–8).

Q&A What if I do not want to copy the format of cell B10 during the auto fill operation?

In addition to creating a series of values, dragging the fill handle instructs Excel to copy the format of cell B10 to the range C10:G10. With some fill operations, you may not want to copy the formats of the source cell or range to the destination cell or range. If this is the case, click the Auto Fill Options button after the range fills and then select the option you desire in the Auto Fill Options menu (Figure 3–8).

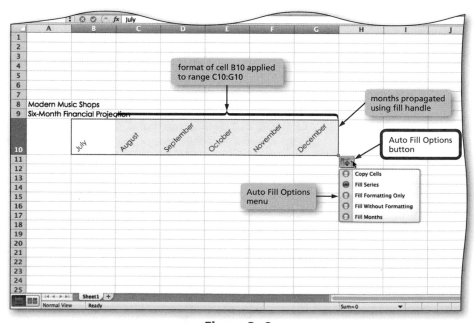

Figure 3–8

6

- Click the Auto Fill Options button to hide the Auto Fill Options menu.

- Select cell H10, type **Total**, and then press the RIGHT ARROW key to enter a column heading.

- Type **Chart** in cell I10 and then press the RIGHT ARROW key to enter a column heading.

Q&A Why is the word Total automatically formatted with a 45° rotation?
Excel tries to save you time by automatically recognizing the adjacent cell format in cell G10 and applying it to cell H10. Such behavior also occurs when typing the column heading in cell I10.

Other Ways
1. Enter start month in cell, apply formatting, CONTROL-drag fill handle in direction to fill, click Fill Months in shortcut menu

Using the Auto Fill Options Menu

As shown in Figure 3–8, Fill Series is the default option that Excel uses to fill an area, which means it fills the destination area with a series, using the same formatting as the source area. If you choose another option in the Auto Fill Options menu, then Excel immediately changes the contents of the destination range. Following the use of the fill handle, the Auto Fill Options button remains active until you begin the next Excel operation. Table 3–2 summarizes the options in the Auto Fill Options menu.

The Mighty Fill Handle
If you drag the fill handle BTW to the left or up, Excel will decrement the series rather than increment the series. If you drag the fill handle back into the middle of a cell, Excel erases the contents of the cell.

Table 3–2 Options Available in the Auto Fill Options Menu	
Auto Fill Option	**Description**
Copy Cells	Fill destination area with contents using format of source area. Do not create a series.
Fill Series	Fill destination area with series using format of source area. This option is the default.
Fill Formatting Only	Fill destination area using format of source area. No content is copied unless fill is series.
Fill Without Formatting	Fill destination area with contents, without the formatting of source area.
Fill Months	Fill destination area with series of months using format of source area. Same as Fill Series and shows as an option only if source area contains a month.

You can create several different types of series using the fill handle. Table 3–3 illustrates several examples. Notice in examples 4 through 7, 9, and 11 that, if you use the fill handle to create a series of numbers or nonsequential months, you must enter the first item in the series in one cell and the second item in the series in an adjacent cell. Excel still creates the series, however, if the first two items are in a range and the cells between the items are empty. Next, select both cells and drag the fill handle through the destination area.

Custom Fill Sequences
You can create your BTW own custom lists for use with the fill handle. For example, if you often type in the same list of products or names into Excel, you can create a custom fill sequence. You then can type the first product or name and then use the fill handle automatically to fill in the remaining products or names. To create a custom fill sequence, click Excel in the menu bar and choose Preferences. Click Custom Lists in the Formulas and Lists area (Excel Preferences dialog) to open the Custom Lists dialog.

Table 3–3 Examples of Series Using the Fill Handle		
Example	**Contents of Cell(s) Copied Using the Fill Handle**	**Next Three Values of Extended Series**
1	4:00	5:00, 6:00, 7:00
2	Qtr2	Qtr3, Qtr4, Qtr1
3	Quarter 1	Quarter 2, Quarter 3, Quarter 4
4	22-Jul, 22-Sep	22-Nov, 22-Jan, 22-Mar
5	2012, 2013	2014, 2015, 2016
6	1, 2	3, 4, 5
7	625, 600	575, 550, 525
8	Mon	Tue, Wed, Thu
9	Sunday, Tuesday	Thursday, Saturday, Monday
10	4th Section	5th Section, 6th Section, 7th Section
11	−205, −208	−211, −214, −217

To Increase Column Widths

In Chapter 2, you increased column widths after the values were entered into the worksheet. Sometimes, you may want to increase the column widths before you enter the values and, if necessary, adjust them later. The following steps increase the column widths.

- Move the mouse pointer to the boundary between column heading A and column heading B so that the mouse pointer changes to a split double arrow in preparation of adjusting the column widths.

- Drag the mouse pointer to the right until the ScreenTip displays the desired column width, Width: 36.00 (3.57 inches) in this case. Do not release the mouse button (Figure 3–9).

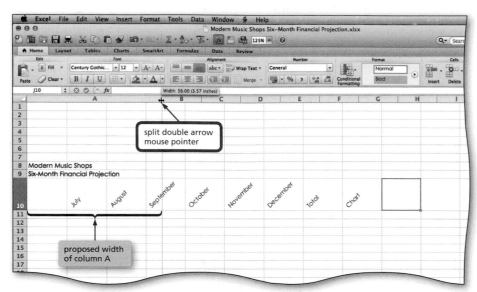

Figure 3–9

- Release the mouse button to change the width of the column.

- Click column heading B to select the column and then drag through column heading G to select the range in which to change the widths.

- Release the mouse button, then move the mouse pointer to the boundary between column headings B and C in preparation of resizing column B, and then drag the mouse to the right until the ScreenTip displays the desired width, Width: 14.86 (1.51 inches) in this case. Do not release the mouse button (Figure 3–10).

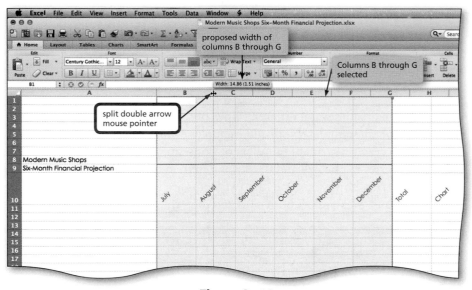

Figure 3–10

- Release the mouse button to change the width of the selected columns.

- If necessary, scroll the worksheet so that column H is visible and then use the technique described in Step 1 to increase the width of column H to 16.00 (1.62 inches).

To Enter and Indent Row Titles

Excel allows you to indent text in cells. Often, indentation sets off titles, such as row titles, from other titles to create a hierarchy, such as you may find in a table of contents in a book. The following steps enter the row titles in column A and indent several of the row titles.

- If necessary, scroll the worksheet so that column A and row 23 are visible and then enter the row titles in the range A11:A23 but without the indents.

- Select cell A12 and then, on the Home tab under Alignment, click the Increase Indent button to increase the indentation of the text in the selected cell.

- Select the range A16:A20 and then click the Increase Indent button to increase the indentation of the text in the selected range (Figure 3–11).

- Select cell A1 to deselect the current cells.

Q&A What happens when I click the Increase Indent button?
The Increase Indent button on the Home tab under Alignment indents the contents of a cell to the right by three spaces each time you click it. The Decrease Indent button decreases the indent by three spaces each time you click it.

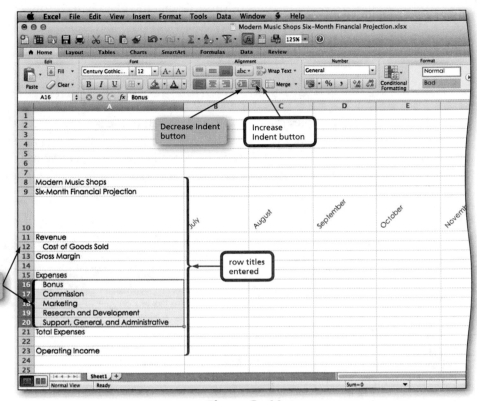

Figure 3–11

Other Ways

1. To indent, CONTROL-click range, choose Format Cells in shortcut menu, click Alignment tab (Format Cells dialog), click Left (Indent) in Horizontal list, type number of spaces to indent in Indent text box, click OK button (Format Cells dialog)

2. Choose Format > Cells in menu bar, click Alignment tab (Format Cells dialog), click Left (Indent) in Horizontal list, type number of spaces to indent in Indent text box, click OK button (Format Cells dialog)

Copying a Range of Cells to a Nonadjacent Destination Area

The What-If Assumptions section should be placed in an area of the worksheet that is accessible easily yet does not impair the view of the main section of the worksheet. As shown in Figure 3–3a on page EX 138, the What-If Assumptions should be placed above the calculations in the worksheet. Additionally, the row titles in the Expenses area are the same as the row titles in the What-If Assumptions table, with the exception of the two additional entries in cells A4 (Margin) and A7 (Sales Revenue for Bonus). Hence, the

Fitting Entries in a Cell

BTW

An alternative to increasing column widths or row heights is to shrink the characters in a cell to fit the current width of the column. To shrink to fit, choose Format > Cells in the menu bar, click the Alignment tab, then click Shrink to fit in the Text control area. After shrinking entries to fit in cells, consider using the Zoom box in the Standard toolbar to make the entries more readable.

What-If Assumptions table row titles can be created by copying the range A16:A20 to the range A2:A6 and then inserting two rows for the additional entries in cells A4 and A7. The source area (range A16:A20) is not adjacent to the destination area (range A2:A6). The first two chapters used the fill handle to copy a source area to an adjacent destination area. To copy a source area to a nonadjacent destination area, however, you cannot use the fill handle.

A more versatile method of copying a source area is to use the Copy button and Paste button in the Standard toolbar. You can use these two buttons to copy a source area to an adjacent or nonadjacent destination area.

To Copy a Range of Cells to a Nonadjacent Destination Area

The Copy button copies the contents and format of the source area to the **clipboard**, a reserved place in the computer's memory that allows you to collect text and graphics from an Office document and then paste them into almost any other type of document. The Paste button copies the item from the clipboard to the destination area.

The following steps enter the what-if area row heading and use the Copy and Paste buttons to copy the range A16:A20 to the nonadjacent range A2:A6.

- With cell A1 selected, type **What-If Assumptions** as the new row title.

- Select the range A16:A20 and then click the Copy button in the Standard toolbar to copy the values and formats of the selected range, A16:A20 in this case, to the clipboard.

- Select cell A2, the top cell in the destination area (Figure 3–12).

Q&A Why do I not need to select the entire destination area?
You are not required to select the entire destination area (range A2:A6) before clicking the Paste button in the Standard toolbar. Excel needs to know only the upper-left cell of the destination area. In the case of a single column range, such as A2:A6, the top cell of the destination area (cell A2) also is the upper-left cell of the destination area.

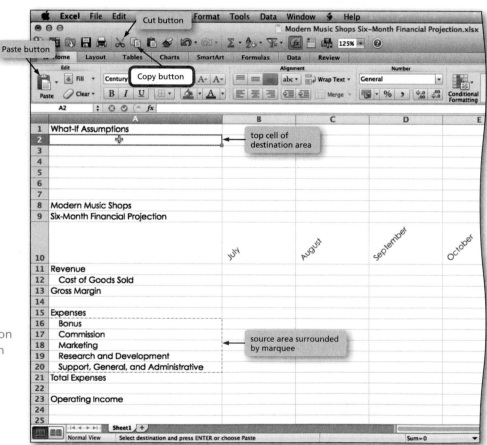

Figure 3–12

2

- Click the Paste button in the Standard toolbar to copy the values and formats of the last item placed on the clipboard, range A16:A20 in this case, to the destination area, A2:A6 in this case (Figure 3–13).

Q&A   What if data already existed in the destination area?

When you complete a copy, the values and formats in the destination area are replaced with the values and formats of the source area. Any data contained in the destination area prior to the copy and paste is lost. If you accidentally delete valuable data, immediately click the Undo button in the Standard toolbar.

3

- Press the ESC key to remove the marquee from the source.

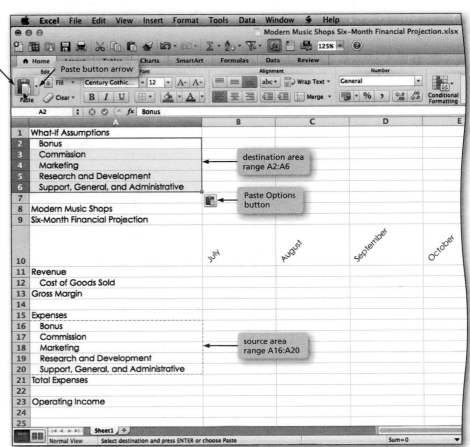

Figure 3–13

Other Ways

1. CONTROL-click source area, choose Copy in shortcut menu, CONTROL-click destination area, choose Paste in shortcut menu

2. Choose Edit > Copy in menu bar, select destination area, choose Edit > Paste in menu bar

3. Select source area, press COMMAND-C, select destination area, press COMMAND-V

Using the Paste Menu and the Paste Options Menu

After you click the Paste button, Excel immediately displays the Paste Options button, as shown in Figure 3–13. If you click the Paste Options button and select an option in the Paste Options menu (shown in Figure 3–14a on the next page), Excel modifies the most recent paste operation based on your selection. Table 3–4 on page EX 149 summarizes the options available in the Paste Options menu. You can use combinations of the options in the Paste Options menu to customize your paste operation. That is, after clicking one of the options in the Paste Options menu, you can open the menu again to further adjust your paste operation.

Q&As

For a complete list of the Q&As found in many of the step-by-step sequences in this book, visit the Excel 2011 Q&A Web page (scsite.com/ex2011/qa).

BTW

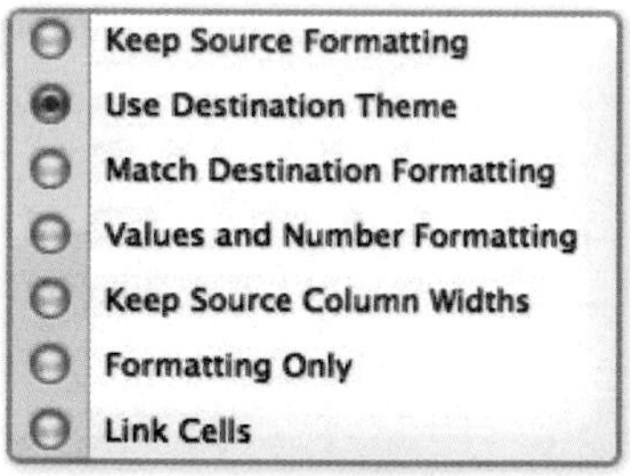

(a)

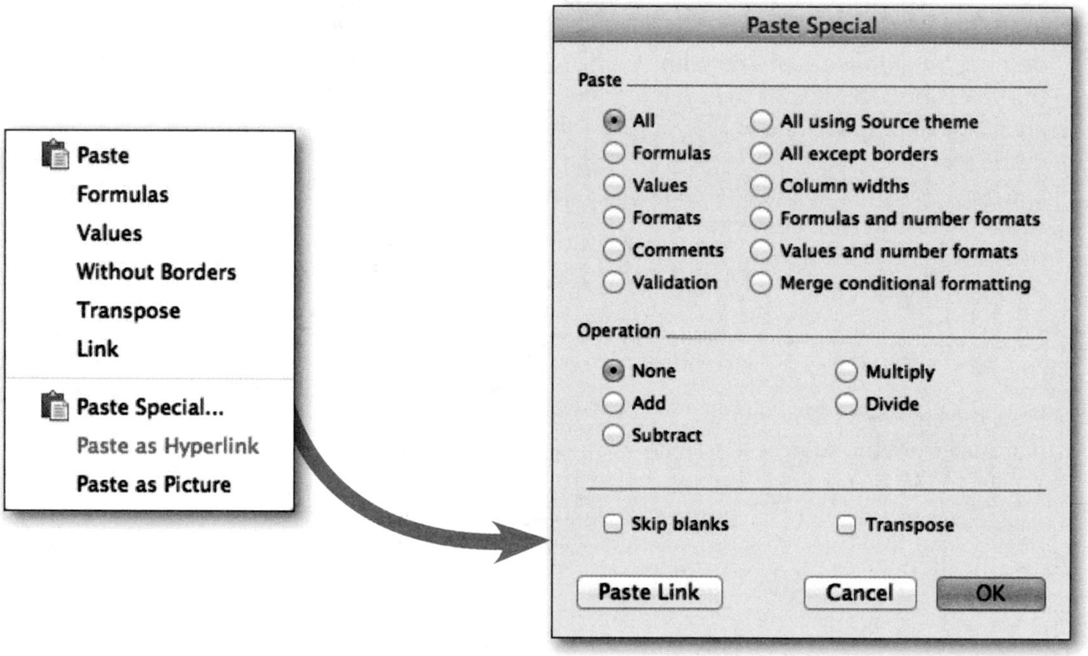

(b)

Figure 3–14

Copying and Pasting from Other Programs

BTW If you have data you need in Excel, but the data is stored in another program, copying and pasting likely will help you. You might need to experiment before you are successful because Excel might attempt to copy formatting or other information that you did not intend to paste from the other program. Using the various Paste buttons likely will solve most of such problems.

Move It or Copy It

BTW Contrary to popular belief, move and copy operations are not the same. When you move a cell, the data in the original location is cleared and the format of the cell is reset to the default. When you copy a cell, the data and format of the copy area remains intact. In short, you should copy cells to duplicate entries and move cells to rearrange entries.

In addition to the Paste Options menu, the Paste button arrow on the Home tab under Edit includes an arrow that, when clicked, displays additional Paste options such as Paste Special and Paste as Picture. These options are shown in Figure 3–14b and summarized in Table 3–4.

Table 3–4 Paste Options Available

Location	Paste Option	Description
Paste Options pop-up menu	Keep Source Formatting	Pastes contents, format, and styles of source area.
	Use Destination Theme	Pastes contents of source area using the theme applied to destination area.
	Match Destination Formatting	Pastes contents of source area using all formatting applied to destination area.
	Values & Number Formatting	Pastes contents and format of source area for numbers or formulas, but use format of destination area for text.
	Keep Source Column Widths	Pastes contents and format of source area. Change destination column widths to source column widths.
	Formatting Only	Pastes format of source area, but not the contents.
	Link Cells	Pastes an absolute reference to the location of the source cells, rather than the contents of the source cells. When the source cells are updated, the destination cells will be updated.
Paste menu	Paste	Copy contents and format of source area. This option is the default.
	Formulas	Copy formulas from the source area, but not the contents and format.
	Values	Copy contents of source area, but not the formatting for formulas.
	Without Borders	Copy contents and format of source area, but not any borders.
	Transpose	Copy the contents and format of the source area, but transpose, or swap, the rows and columns.
	Link	Pastes an absolute reference to the location of the source cells, rather than the contents of the source cells. When the source cells are updated, the destination cells will be updated.
	Paste as Hyperlink	Pastes a link to a specific place in another Office document.
	Paste as Picture	Pastes a bitmap image of the contents of the source cells.
Paste Special (Paste)	All	Paste all contents, including formatting and linked data.
	Formulas	Paste formulas only.
	Values	Paste only the values displayed in the cell(s).
	Formats	Paste only the cell formatting.
	Comments	Paste only comments attached to the cell.
	Validation	Paste only the data validation rules from the copied cells to the paste area.
	All using Source theme	Paste all contents using the theme applied to source data.
	All except borders	Pastes all contents except for applied cell borders.
	Column widths	Pastes the width of a column or range of columns to the destination column or range of columns.
	Formulas and number formats	Pastes the formulas and applied number formats to the destination cell(s).
	Values and number formats	Pastes the values and applied number formats to the destination cell(s).
	Merge Conditional formatting	Combines conditional formatting from the copied cells with any conditional formatting present in the destination cells.
Paste Special (Operation)	None	Pastes without applying any mathematical operation.
	Add	Adds the values in source area to values in destination cells.
	Subtract	Subtracts the values in the source cells from the values in the destination cells.
	Multiply	Multiplies the values in the source cells by the values in the destination cells.
	Divide	Divides the values in the destination cells by the values in the source cells.
Paste Special (Additional Options)	Skip blanks	Does not replace values In destination cells with blanks In source cells.
	Transpose	Changes columns of source cells to rows, or rows of source cells to columns.
	Paste Link	Pastes an absolute reference to the location of the source cells, rather than the contents of the source cells. When the source cells are updated, the destination cells will be updated.

Using Drag and Drop to Move or Copy Cells

You also can use the mouse to move or copy cells. First, you select the source area and point to the border of the cell or range. You know you are pointing to the border of the cell or range when the mouse pointer changes to a hand. To move the selected cell or cells, drag the selection to the destination area. To copy a selection, hold down the OPTION key while dragging the selection to the destination area. You know Excel is in copy mode when a small plus sign appears next to the hand mouse pointer. Be sure to release the mouse button before you release the OPTION key. Using the mouse to move or copy cells is called **drag and drop**.

Using Cut and Paste to Move Cells

Another way to move cells is to select them, click the Cut button in the Standard toolbar (Figure 3–12 on page EX 146) to remove them from the worksheet and copy them to the Office Clipboard, select the destination area, and then click the Paste button in the Standard toolbar. You also can use the Cut command in the shortcut menu, instead of the Cut button.

Inserting and Deleting Cells in a Worksheet

At any time while the worksheet is on the screen, you can insert cells to enter new data or delete cells to remove unwanted data. You can insert or delete individual cells; a range of cells, rows, and columns; or entire worksheets.

To Insert a Row

According to the sketch of the worksheet in Figure 3–3a on page EX 138, two rows must be inserted in the What-If Assumptions table, one between Commission and Marketing for the Margin assumption and another between Research and Development and Support, General, and Administrative for the Sales Revenue for Bonus assumption. The following steps insert the new rows into the worksheet.

1

- CONTROL-click row heading 4, the row below where you want to insert a row, to display the shortcut menu (Figure 3–15).

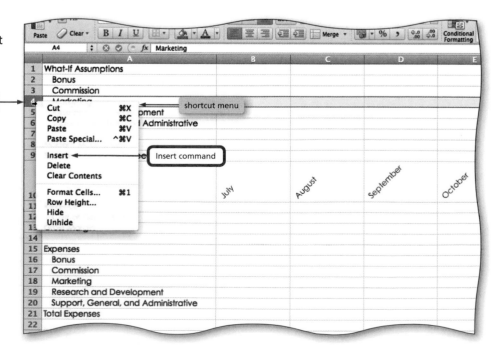

Figure 3–15

2

- Click Insert in the shortcut menu to insert a new row in the worksheet by shifting the selected row and all rows below it down one row.

- Select cell A4 in the new row and then enter **Margin** to enter a new row title (Figure 3–16).

Q&A What is the resulting format of the new row?

The cells in the new row inherit the formats of the cells in the row above them. You can change this behavior by clicking the Insert Options button that appears immediately below the blank inserted row. Following the insertion of a row, the Insert Options button allows you to select from the following options: (1) Format Same As Above; (2) Format Same As Below; and (3) Clear Formatting. The Format Same as Above option is the default. The Insert Options button remains active until you begin the next Excel operation. Excel does not display the Insert Options button if the initial row does not contain any formatted data.

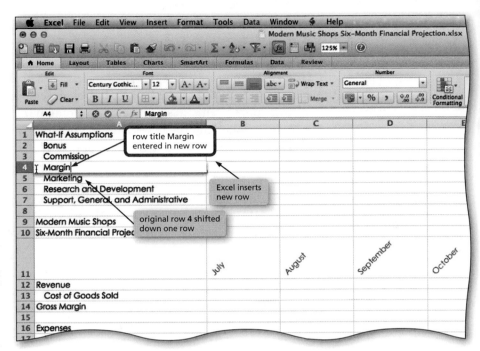

Figure 3–16

3

- CONTROL-click row heading 7 to display a shortcut menu and then click Insert in the shortcut menu to insert a new row in the worksheet.

- Select cell A7 in the new row and then enter **Sales Revenue for Bonus** to enter a new row title (Figure 3–17).

Q&A What would happen if cells in the shifted rows were included in formulas?

If the rows that shift down include cell references in formulas located in the worksheet, Excel automatically would adjust the cell references in the formulas to their new locations. Thus, in Step 2, if a formula in the worksheet references a cell in row 7 before the insert, then Excel adjusts the cell reference in the formula to row 8 after the insert.

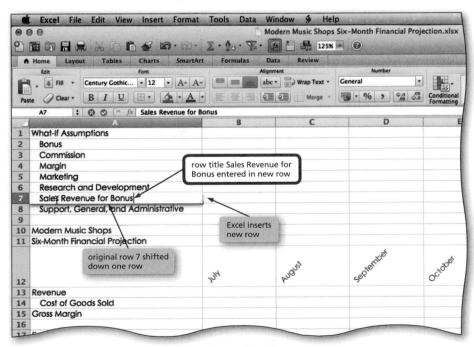

Figure 3–17

Inserting Multiple Rows

BTW If you want to insert multiple rows, you have two choices. You can repeatedly insert single rows by using the Insert command in the shortcut menu or Insert > Row in the menu bar. Alternatively, you can select any number of existing rows to choose the number of rows that you want to insert. For instance, if you want to insert five rows, select five existing rows in the worksheet, CONTROL-click the rows, and then click Insert in the shortcut menu.

Ranges and Undo

BTW The incorrect use of copying, deleting, inserting, and moving ranges of cells have the potential to render a worksheet useless. Carefully review the results of these actions before continuing on to the next task. If you are not sure the result of the action is correct, click the Undo button in the Standard toolbar.

Inserting Columns

You insert columns into a worksheet in the same way you insert rows. To insert columns, select one or more columns immediately to the right of where you want Excel to insert the new column or columns. Next, click the INSERT BUTTON arrow under Cells on the Home tab, and then click Insert Columns in the Insert list or CONTROL-click the selected column(s), then click Insert in the shortcut menu. The Insert command in the shortcut menu requires that you select an entire column (or columns) to insert a column (or columns). Following the insertion of a column, Excel displays the Insert Options button, which allows you to modify the insertion in a fashion similar to that discussed earlier when inserting rows.

Inserting Single Cells or a Range of Cells

The INSERT COMMAND in the shortcut menu, the INSERT BUTTON arrow on the Home tab under Cells, or the Insert > Cells command in the menu bar allows you to insert a single cell or a range of cells. You should be aware that if you shift a single cell or a range of cells, however, it no longer lines up with its associated cells. To ensure that the values in the worksheet do not get out of order, spreadsheet experts recommend that you insert only entire rows or entire columns.

Deleting Cells, Columns, and Rows

The DELETE button on the Home tab under Cells deletes the selected cells, but does not shift any other cells to compensate. The DELETE command removes the cells from the worksheet and shifts the remaining rows up (when you delete rows) or shifts the remaining columns to the left (when you delete columns). If formulas located in other cells reference cells in the deleted row or column, Excel does not adjust these cell references. Clicking the DELETE button arrow on the Home tab under Cells brings up the Delete dialog, which does give you the option of shifting cells right, down, or deleting entire rows or columns. The DELETE COMMAND in the shortcut menu also displays the Delete dialog. Deleting removes cells (including the data and format) from the worksheet. Deleting cells is not the same as clearing cells. The Clear command, described in Chapter 1 on page EX 49, clears the data from the cells, but the cells remain in the worksheet. Excel displays the error message #REF! in those cells to indicate a cell reference error. For example, if cell A7 contains the formula =A4+A5 and you delete row 5, Excel assigns the formula =A4+#REF! to cell A6 (originally cell A7) and displays the error message #REF! in cell A6. Excel also displays an Error Options button when you select the cell containing the error message #REF!, which allows you to select options to determine the nature of the problem.

To Enter Numbers with Format Symbols

The next step in creating the Six-Month Financial Projection worksheet is to enter the what-if assumptions values in the range B2:B8. The numbers in the table can be entered and then formatted as in Chapters 1 and 2, or each one can be entered with format symbols. When a number is entered with a **format symbol**, Excel immediately displays it with the assigned format. Valid format symbols include the dollar sign ($), comma (,), and percent sign (%).

If you enter a whole number, it appears without any decimal places. If you enter a number with one or more decimal places and a format symbol, Excel displays the number with two decimal places. Table 3–5 illustrates several examples of numbers entered with format symbols. The number in parentheses in column 4 indicates the number of decimal places.

Table 3–5 Numbers Entered with Format Symbols

Format Symbol	Typed in Formula Bar	Displays in Cell	Comparable Format
'	374,149	374,149	Comma(0)
	5,833.6	5,833.60	Comma(2)
$	$58917	$58,917	Currency(0)
	$842.51	$842.51	Currency(2)
	$63,574.9	$63,574.90	Currency(2)
%	85%	85%	Percent(0)
	12.80%	12.80%	Percent(2)
	68.4222%	68.42%	Percent(2)

The following step enters the numbers in the What-If Assumptions table with format symbols.

1

- Enter 200,000.00 in cell B2, 5.75% in cell B3, 57.50% in cell B4, 15.00% in cell B5, 7.50% in cell B6, 3,500,000.00 in cell B7, and 18.75% in cell B8 to display the entries using formats based on the format symbols entered with the numbers (Figure 3–18).

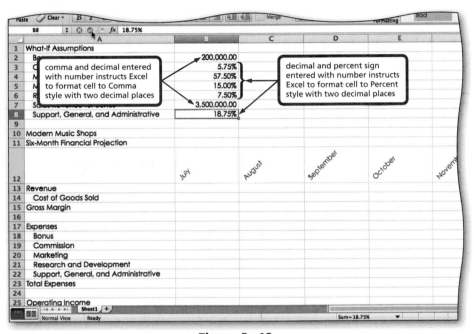

Figure 3–18

Other Ways

1. CONTROL-click range, choose Format Cells in shortcut menu, click Number tab (Format Cells dialog), click category in Category list, select desired format, click OK button (Format Cells dialog)

2. Press COMMAND-1, click Number tab (Format Cells dialog), click category in Category list, select desired format, click OK button (Format Cells dialog)

To Freeze Column and Row Titles

Freezing worksheet titles is a useful technique for viewing large worksheets that extend beyond the window. Normally, when you scroll down or to the right, the column titles in row 12 and the row titles in column A that define the numbers no longer appear on the screen. This makes it difficult to remember what the numbers in these rows and columns represent. To alleviate this problem, Excel allows you to **freeze the titles**, so that Excel displays the titles on the screen, no matter how far down or to the right you scroll.

The steps on the following page use the Freeze Panes button on the Layout tab under Window to freeze the worksheet title and column titles in rows 10, 11, and 12, and the row titles in column A.

1

- Scroll the worksheet to ensure that Excel displays row 10 as the first row and column A on the screen.

- Select cell B13 to select the cell on which to freeze panes.

- Display the Layout tab and then click the Freeze Panes button to display the Freeze Panes pop-up menu (Figure 3–19).

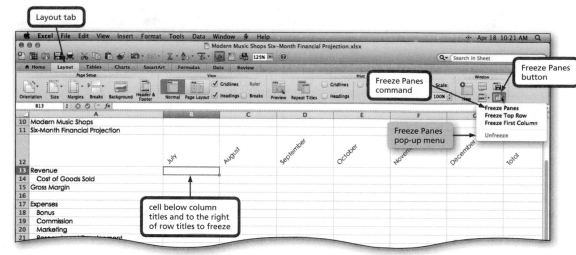

Figure 3–19

Q&A Why should I ensure that row 10 is the first row displayed?

Before freezing the titles, it is important that Excel display the first row that you want frozen as the first row displayed. For example, if cell B13 was selected while displaying row 1, then Excel would freeze the what-if assumptions and only show a few rows of data in the Six-Month Financial Project area of the worksheet. To ensure that you can view as much data as possible, always scroll to a row that maximizes the view of your important data before freezing panes.

2

- Click Freeze Panes in the Freeze Panes pop-up menu to freeze rows and columns to the left and above the selected cell, column A and rows 10 through 12 in this case (Figure 3–20).

Q&A What happens after I click the Freeze Panes command?

Excel displays a thin black line on the right side of column A, indicating the split between the frozen row titles in column A and the rest of the worksheet. It also displays a thin black line below row 12, indicating the split between the frozen column titles in rows 10 through 12 and the rest of the worksheet (Figure 3–20).

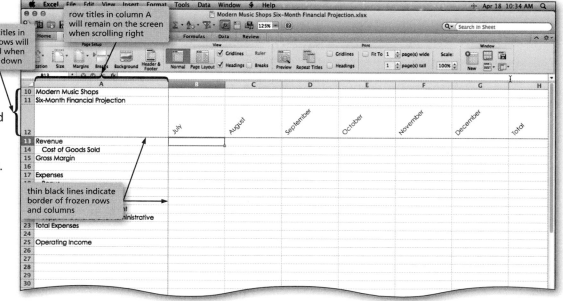

Figure 3–20

Other Ways

1. Choose Window > Freeze Panes in menu bar

To Enter the Projected Monthly Sales

The following steps enter the projected revenue, listed earlier in Table 3–1 on page EX 139, in row 13.

1 Display the Home tab.

2 Enter `3113612.16` in cell B13, `7962235.53` in cell C13, `5112268.58` in cell D13, `2924627.87` in cell E13, `7630534.65` in cell F13, and `3424270.23` in cell G13 (Figure 3–21).

3 Make H13 the active cell.

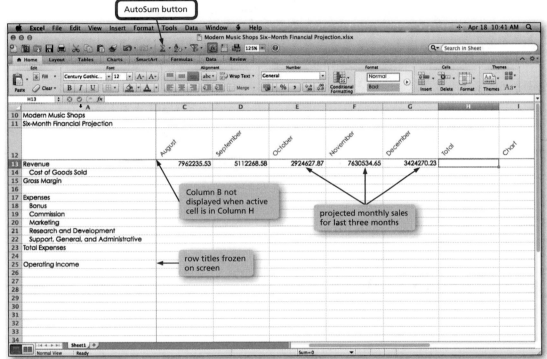

Figure 3–21

To Enter and Format the System Date

The sketch of the worksheet in Figure 3–3a on page EX 138 includes a date stamp on the right side of the heading section. A **date stamp** shows the date a workbook, report, or other document was created or the period it represents. In business, a report often is meaningless without a date stamp. For example, if a printout of the worksheet in this chapter were distributed to the company's analysts, the date stamp would show when the six-month projections were made, as well as what period the report represents.

A simple way to create a date stamp is to use the NOW function to enter the system date tracked by your computer in a cell in the worksheet. The **NOW function** is one of 22 date and time functions available in Excel. When assigned to a cell, the NOW function returns a number that corresponds to the system date and time beginning with December 31, 1899. For example, January 1, 1900 equals 1, January 2, 1900 equals 2, and so on. Noon equals .5. Thus, noon on January 1, 1900 equals 1.5 and 6 P.M. on January 1, 1900 equals 1.75. If the computer's system date is set to the current date, which normally it is, then the date stamp is equivalent to the current date.

The following steps enter the NOW function and then change the format from mm/dd/yy hh:mm to mm/dd/yyyy.

- Scroll to make column I completely visible.

- Select cell I11 and then click the Formula Builder button in the formula bar to display the Formula Builder window.

- Scroll down in the list of available functions to find NOW in the list of functions.

- Double-click the NOW function to insert the function into the worksheet (Figure 3–22).

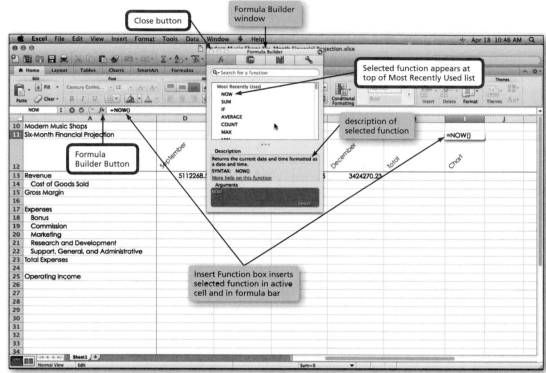

Figure 3–22

- Click the Close button on the Formula Builder window to close the Formula Builder window and to display the system date and time in the selected cell, using the default date and time format mm/dd/yy hh:mm.

- CONTROL-click cell I11 to display a shortcut menu (Figure 3–23).

Q&A Why does the date appear with the mm/dd/yy hh:mm format?
Excel automatically formats the result of the NOW function as a date, using the date and time format, mm/dd/yy hh:mm, where the first mm is the month, dd is the day of the month, yy is the year, hh is the hour of the day, and mm is the minutes past the hour.

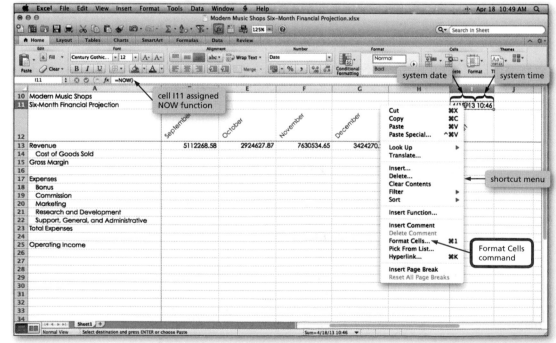

Figure 3–23

3

- Click Format Cells in the shortcut menu to display the Format Cells dialog.

- If necessary, click the Number tab (Format Cells dialog) to display the Number pane.

- Click Date in the Category list (Format Cells dialog) to display the types of date formats in the Type list. Scroll down in the Type list and then click 3/14/2001 to display the selected format in the Sample area of the dialog (Figure 3–24).

Q&A Why do the dates in the Type box show March 14, 2001 instead of the current date?
The date March 14, 2001 is used as a sample date in the Format Cells dialog.

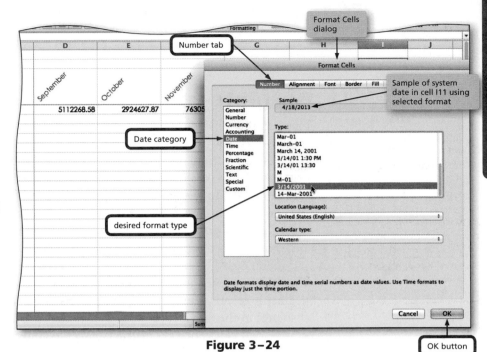

Figure 3–24

4

- Click the OK button (Format Cells dialog) to display the system date in the format mm/dd/yyyy.

- Double-click the border between columns I and J to change the width of the column to best fit (Figure 3–25).

Q&A How does Excel format a date?
In Figure 3–25, the date is displayed

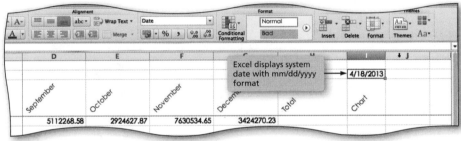

Figure 3–25

right-aligned in the cell because Excel treats a date as a number formatted to display as a date. If you assign the General format (Excel's default format for numbers) to a date in a cell, the date is displayed as a number with two decimal places. For example, if the system time and date is 9:00 AM on November 13, 2013 and the cell containing the NOW function is assigned the General format, then Excel displays the following number in the cell:

41591.375

Number of days since December 31, 1899

Time of day is 9:00 AM (Portion of day complete)

The whole number portion of the number (41591) represents the number of days since December 31, 1899. The decimal portion of the number (.375) represents 9:00 AM as the time of day, at which point 37.5% of the day is complete. To assign the General format to a cell, click General in the Category list in the Format Cells dialog (Figure 3–24).

5

- Click the Save button to save the worksheet.

Other Ways

1. CONTROL-click cell, choose Format Cells in shortcut menu, click Number tab (Format Cells dialog), click Date in Category list, select desired format, click OK button (Format Cells dialog)

2. Press COMMAND-1, click Number tab (Format Cells dialog), click Date Category list, select desired format, click OK button (Format Cells dialog)

3. Press CONTROL-SHIFT-# to format date to dd-mon-yy (6-Apr-13, for example)

Break Point: If you wish to stop working through the chapter at this point, you can quit Excel now and then resume the project at a later point in time by starting Excel, opening the file called Modern Music Shops Six-Month Financial Projection, and continuing to follow the steps from this location forward.

Absolute versus Relative Addressing

The next sections describe the formulas and functions needed to complete the calculations in the worksheet.

As you learned in Chapters 1 and 2, Excel modifies cell references when copying formulas. While copying formulas, however, sometimes you do not want Excel to change cell references. To keep a cell reference constant when copying a formula or function, Excel uses a technique called absolute cell referencing. To specify an absolute cell reference in a formula, enter a dollar sign ($) before any column letters or row numbers you want to keep constant in formulas you plan to copy. For example, $B$4 is an absolute cell reference, whereas B4 is a relative cell reference. Both reference the same cell. The difference becomes apparent when they are copied to a destination area. A formula using the **absolute cell reference** $B$4 instructs Excel to keep the cell reference B4 constant (absolute) in the formula as it copies it to the destination area. A formula using the **relative cell reference** B4 instructs Excel to adjust the cell reference as it copies it to the destination area. A cell reference with only one dollar sign before either the column or the row is called a **mixed cell reference**. When planning formulas, be aware of when you need to use absolute, relative, and mixed cell references. Table 3–6 gives some additional examples of each of these types of cell references.

Table 3–6 Examples of Absolute, Relative, and Mixed Cell References		
Cell Reference	**Type of Reference**	**Meaning**
$B$4	Absolute cell reference	Both column and row references remain the same when you copy this cell, because the cell references are absolute.
B$4	Mixed reference	This cell reference is mixed. The column reference changes when you copy this cell to another column because it is relative. The row reference does not change because it is absolute.
$B4	Mixed reference	This cell reference is mixed. The column reference does not change because it is absolute. The row reference changes when you copy this cell reference to another row because it is relative.
B4	Relative cell reference	Both column and row references are relative. When copied to another cell, both the column and row in the cell reference are adjusted to reflect the new location.

The next step is to enter the formulas that calculate the following values for July: cost of goods sold (cell B14), gross margin (cell B15), expenses (range B18:B22), total expenses (cell B23), and the operating income (cell B25). The formulas are based on the projected monthly revenue in cell B13 and the assumptions in the range B2:B8.

To Enter a Formula Containing Absolute Cell References

The formulas for each column (month) are the same, except for the reference to the projected monthly revenue in row 13, which varies according to the month (B13 for July, C13 for August, and so on). Thus, the formulas for July can be entered in column B and then copied to columns C through G. Table 3–7 shows the formulas for determining the July cost of goods sold, gross margin, expenses, total expenses, and operating income in column B.

Table 3–7 Formulas for Determining Cost of Goods Sold, Margin, Expenses, Total Expenses, and Operating Income for July

Cell	Row Title	Formula	Comment
B14	Cost of Goods Sold	=B13 * (1 − B4)	Revenue times (1 minus Margin %)
B15	Gross Margin	= B13 − B14	Revenue minus Cost of Goods Sold
B18	Bonus	=IF(B13 >= B7, B2, 0)	Bonus equals value in B2 or 0
B19	Commission	=B13 * B3	Revenue times Commission %
B20	Marketing	=B13 * B5	Revenue times Marketing %
B21	Research and Development	=B13 * B6	Revenue times Research and Development %
B22	Support, General, and Administrative	=B13 * B8	Revenue times Support, General, and Administrative %
B23	Total Expenses	=SUM(B18:B22)	Sum of July Expenses
B25	Operating Income	=B15 − B23	Gross Margin minus Total Expenses

As the formulas are entered as shown in Table 3–7 in column B for July and then copied to columns C through G (August through December) in the worksheet, Excel will adjust the cell references for each column automatically. Thus, after the copy, the August Commission expense in cell C19 would be =C13 * C3. While the cell reference C13 (February Revenue) is correct, the cell reference C3 references an empty cell. The formula for cell C7 should read =C13 * B3, rather than =C13 * C3, because B3 references the Commission % value in the What-If Assumptions table. In this instance, a way is needed to keep a cell reference in a formula the same, or constant, when it is copied.

The following steps enter the cost of goods formula = B13*(1 − $B$4) in cell B14 using Point mode. To enter an absolute cell reference, you can type the dollar sign ($) as part of the cell reference or enter it by pressing COMMAND-T with the insertion point in or to the right of the cell reference to change it to absolute.

- Click CONTROL-FN-LEFT ARROW to select cell B13, then click cell B14 to select the cell in which to enter the first formula.

Q&A Why does pressing CONTROL-FN-LEFT ARROW select cell B13?
When the titles are frozen and you press CONTROL-FN-LEFT ARROW, Excel selects the upper-left cell of the unfrozen section of the worksheet. For example, in Step 1 of the previous steps, Excel selected cell B13. When the titles are unfrozen, pressing CONTROL-FN-LEFT ARROW selects cell A1.

- Type = (equal sign), select cell B13, type *(1−b4 to continue entering the formula, and then press COMMAND-T to change the most recently typed cell reference, in this case cell b4, from a relative cell reference to an absolute cell reference. Type) to complete the formula (Figure 3–26).

Q&A Is an absolute reference required in this formula?
No, because a mixed cell reference could have been used. The formula in cell B14 will be copied across columns, rather than down rows. So, the formula entered in cell B14 in Step 1 could have been entered as =B13*(1−$B4), rather than =B13*(1−$B$4). To change the absolute cell reference to a mixed cell reference, continue to press COMMAND-T until you achieve the desired cell reference.

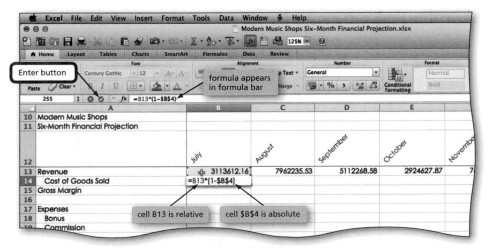

Figure 3–26

2

- Click the Enter button in the formula bar to display the result, 1323285.168, instead of the formula in B14 (Figure 3–27).

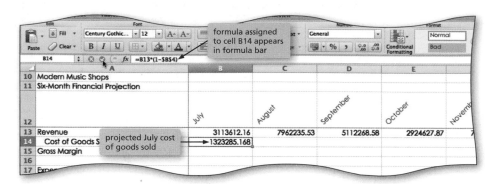

Figure 3–27

3

- Click cell B15 to select the cell in which to enter the next formula, type = (equal sign), click cell B13, type – (minus sign), and then click cell B14 to add a reference to the cell to the formula.

- Click the Enter button in the formula bar to display the result in the selected cell, in this case gross margin for July, 1790326.992, in cell B15 (Figure 3–28).

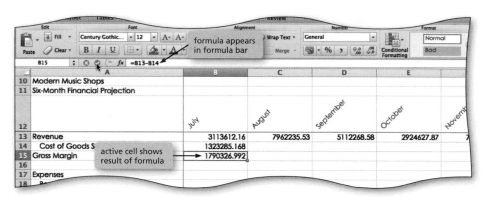

Figure 3–28

Logical Operators in IF Functions

 IF functions can use logical operators, such as AND, OR, and NOT. For example, the three IF functions =IF(AND(A1>C1, B1<C2), "OK", "Not OK") and =IF(OR(K5>J5, C3<K6), "OK", "Not OK") and =IF(NOT(B10<C10), "OK", "Not OK") use logical operators. In the first example, both logical tests must be true for the value_if_true OK to be assigned to the cell. In the second example, one or the other logical tests must be true for the value_if_true OK to be assigned to the cell. In the third example, the logical test B10<C10 must be false for the value_if_true OK to be assigned to the cell.

Making Decisions — The IF Function

According to the Request for New Workbook in Figure 3–2 on page EX 136, if the projected July revenue in cell B13 is greater than or equal to the sales revenue for bonus in cell B7 (3,500,000.00), then the July bonus value in cell B18 is equal to the bonus value in cell B2 (200,000.00); otherwise, cell B18 is equal to 0. One way to assign the July bonus value in cell B18 is to check to see if the revenue in cell B13 equals or exceeds the sales revenue for the bonus amount in cell B7 and, if so, then to enter 200,000.00 in cell B18. You can use this manual process for all six months by checking the values for the corresponding months.

Because the data in the worksheet changes each time a report is prepared or the figures are adjusted, however, it is preferable to have Excel assign the monthly bonus to the entries in the appropriate cells automatically. To do so, cell B18 must include a formula or function that displays 200,000.00 or 0.00 (zero), depending on whether the projected July revenue in cell B13 is greater than, equal to, or less than the sales revenue for bonus value in cell B7.

The **IF function** is useful when you want to assign a value to a cell based on a logical test. For example, using the IF function, cell B18 can be assigned the following IF function:

$$=IF(B13>=\$B\$7, \$B\$2, 0)$$

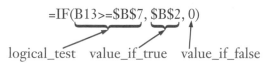

logical_test   value_if_true   value_if_false

The IF function instructs Excel that, if the projected July revenue in cell B13 is greater than or equal to the sales revenue for bonus value in cell B7, then Excel should display the value 200000 in cell B2, in cell B18. If the projected July revenue in cell B13 is less than the sales revenue for bonus value in cell B7, then Excel displays a 0 (zero) in cell B18.

The general form of the IF function is:

=IF(logical_test, value_if_true, value_if_false)

The argument, logical_test, is made up of two expressions and a comparison operator. Each expression can be a cell reference, a number, text, a function, or a formula. Valid comparison operators, their meaning, and examples of their use in IF functions are shown in Table 3–8. The argument, value_if_true, is the value you want Excel to display in the cell when the logical test is true. The argument, value_if_false, is the value you want Excel to display in the cell when the logical test is false.

Table 3–8 Comparison Operators		
Comparison Operator	Meaning	Example
=	Equal to	=IF(B12 = 200, F3 * H4, E10 + F3)
<	Less than	=IF(G56 * Q56 < D12, $M$10, B9 ^ 5)
>	Greater than	=IF(MIN(A12:A52) > 75, 0, 1)
>=	Greater than or equal to	=IF($T$9 >= B7, P3 - H12, 1000)
<=	Less than or equal to	=IF(C9 * G2 <= 99, $T35, 350 * C9)
<>	Not equal to	=IF(G15 <> 1, "No","Yes")

To Enter an IF Function

The following steps assign the IF function =IF(B13>=$B$7,$B$2,0) to cell B18. This IF function determines whether or not the worksheet assigns a bonus for July.

1

- Click cell B18 to select the cell for the next formula.

- Click the Formula Builder button in the formula bar to display the Formula Builder window.

- Scroll to the Logical section of the function list, and then click IF in the list to select the required function (Figure 3–29).

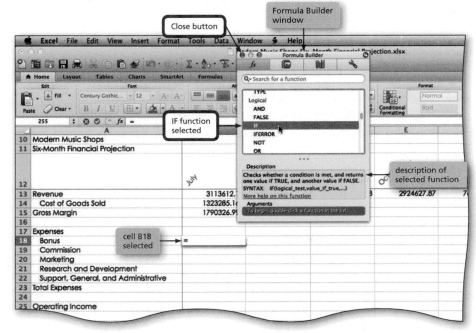

Figure 3–29

2

- Double-click the IF function to expand the Arguments section of the Formula Builder window.

- Type b13>=b7 in the value1 test box to enter a logical test for the IF function.

- Type b2 in the then box to enter the result of the IF function if the logical test is true.

- Type 0 in the else box to enter the result of the IF function if the logical test is false (Figure 3–30).

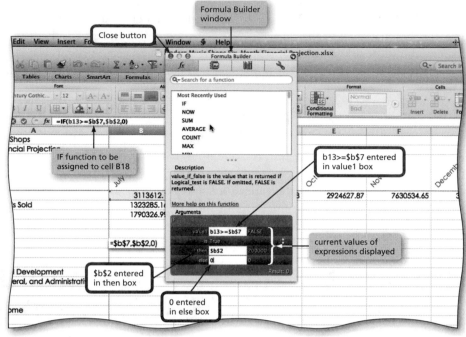

Figure 3–30

3

- Click the Close button on the Formula Builder window to insert the IF function in the selected cell (Figure 3–31).

Q&A Why is the value 0 displayed in cell B18?

The value that Excel displays in cell B18 depends on the values assigned to cells B13, B2, and B7. For example, if the value for July revenue in cell B13 is increased above 3,500,000.00, then the IF function in cell B18 will cause Excel to display 200,000.00. If you change the sales revenue for bonus in cell B7 from 3,500,000.00 to another number and the value in cell B13 is greater than or equal to the value in cell B7, it will change the results in cell B18 as well.

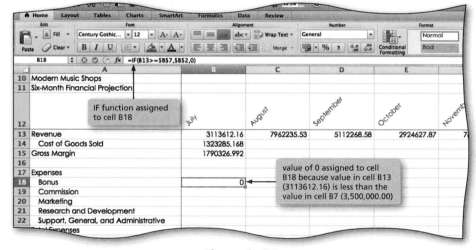

Figure 3–31

To Enter the Remaining July Formulas

The July commission expense in cell B19 is equal to the revenue in cell B13 times the commission assumption in cell B3 (5.75%). The July marketing expense in cell B20 is equal to the projected July revenue in cell B13 times the marketing assumption in cell B5 (15.00%). Similar formulas determine the remaining July expenses in cells B21 and B22.

The total expenses value in cell B23 is equal to the sum of the expenses in the range B18:B22. The operating income in cell B25 is equal to the gross margin in cell B15 minus the total expenses in cell B23. The formulas are short, and therefore, they are typed in the following steps, rather than entered using Point mode.

1 Select cell B19. Type `=b13*$b$3` and then press the DOWN ARROW key to enter the formula in the selected cell. Type `=b13*$b$5` and then press the DOWN ARROW key to enter the formula in the selected cell. Type `=b13*$b$6` and then press the DOWN ARROW key to enter the formula in the selected cell. Type `=b13*$b$8` and then press the DOWN ARROW key to enter the formula in the selected cell.

2 With cell B23 selected, click the AutoSum button in the Standard toolbar twice to insert a SUM function in the selected cell. Select cell B25 to prepare to enter the next formula. Type `=b15-b23` and then press the RETURN key to enter the formula in the selected cell.

3 Press CONTROL-ACCENT MARK (`) to display the formulas version of the worksheet (Figure 3–32).

4 When you are finished viewing the formulas version, press CONTROL-ACCENT MARK (`) to display the values version of the worksheet.

Q&A   Why should I view the formulas version of the worksheet?
Viewing the formulas version (Figure 3–32) of the worksheet allows you to check the formulas assigned to the range B14:B25. Recall that formulas were entered in lowercase. You can see that Excel converts all the formulas from lowercase to uppercase.

Error Messages

When Excel cannot calculate a formula, it displays an error message in a cell. These error messages always begin with a number sign (#). The more commonly occurring error messages are as follows: #DIV/0! (tries to divide by zero); #NAME? (uses a name Excel does not recognize); #N/A (refers to a value not available); #NULL! (specifies an invalid intersection of two areas); #NUM! (uses a number incorrectly); #REF (refers to a cell that is not valid); #VALUE! (uses an incorrect argument or operand); and ##### (refers to cells not wide enough to display entire entry).

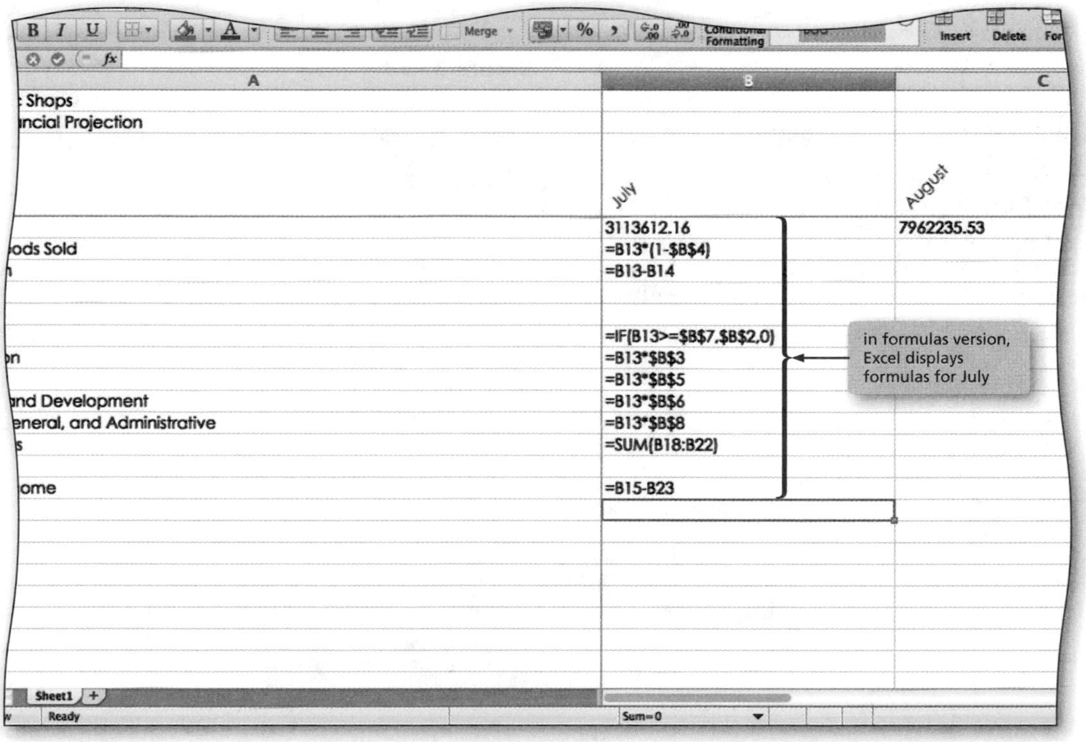

BTW

Figure 3–32

To Copy Formulas with Absolute Cell References Using the Fill Handle

The steps on the next page use the fill handle to copy the July formulas in column B to the other five months in columns C through G.

● Select the range B14:B25 and then point to the fill handle in the lower-right corner of the selected cell, B25 in this case, to display the crosshair mouse pointer (Figure 3–33).

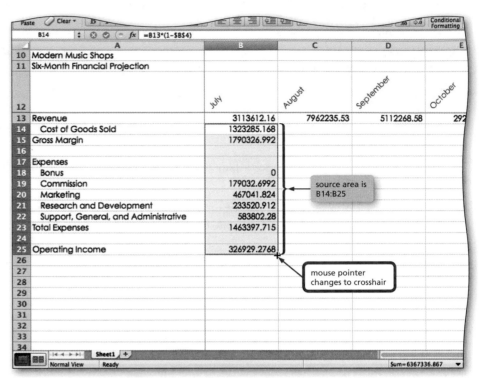

Figure 3–33

● Drag the fill handle to the right to copy the formulas from the source area, B14:B25 in this case, to the destination area, C14:G25 in this case, and display the calculated amounts and Auto Fill Options button (Figure 3–34).

Q&A What happens to the formulas after performing the copy operation? Because the formulas in the range B14:B25 use absolute cell references, the formulas still refer to the current values in the Assumptions table when the formulas are copied to the range C14:G25.

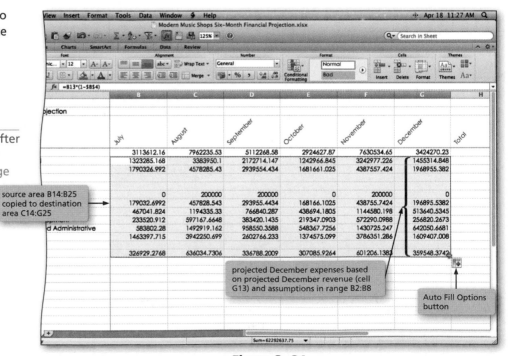

Figure 3–34

To Determine Row Totals in Nonadjacent Cells

The following steps determine the row totals in column H. To determine the row totals using the AutoSum button, select only the cells in column H containing numbers in adjacent cells to the left. If, for example, you select the range H14:H25, Excel will display 0s as the sum of empty rows in cells H16, H17, and H24.

1 Scroll the window to the right to view the full width of column H.

2 Select the range H13:H15. While holding down the COMMAND key, select the range H18:H23 and cell H25, as shown in Figure 3–35.

3 Click the AutoSum button in the Standard toolbar to display the row totals in the selected ranges (Figure 3–35).

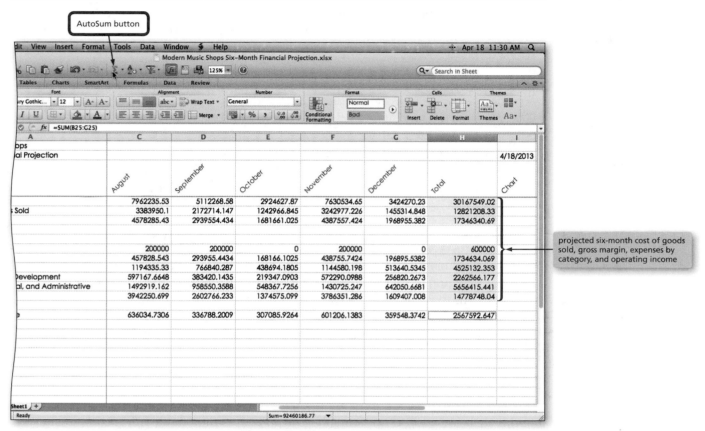

Figure 3–35

To Unfreeze the Worksheet Titles and Save the Workbook

All the text, data, and formulas have been entered into the worksheet. The following steps unfreeze the titles to allow you to work with the worksheet without frozen rows and columns, and save the workbook using its current file name, Modern Music Shops Six-Month Financial Projection.

1 Press CONTROL-FN-LEFT ARROW to select cell B13 and view the upper-left corner of the screen.

2 On the Layout tab under Window, click the Freeze Panes button to display the pop-up menu.

3 Choose Unfreeze in the pop-up menu to unfreeze the frozen columns and rows.

4 Display the Home tab and then click the Save button in the Standard toolbar to save the workbook.

Nested Forms of the IF Function

A **nested IF function** is one in which the action to be taken for the true or false case includes yet another IF function. The second IF function is considered to be nested, or layered, within the first. Study the nested IF function below, which determines the eligibility of a student to go on a field trip. The school permits the student to attend the field trip if the student's age is at least 14 and the student has provided a signed permission form. Assume the following in this example: (1) the nested IF function is assigned to cell L9, which instructs Excel to display one of three messages in the cell; (2) cell L7 contains a student's age; and (3) cell L8 contains a Y or N, based on whether the person provided a signed permission form.

=IF(L7>=14, IF(L8="Y","Allowed","Can Travel, but No Permission"),"Too Young to Travel")

The nested IF function instructs Excel to display one, and only one, of the following three messages in cell L9: (1) Allowed; or (2) Can Travel, but No Permission; or (3) Too Young to Travel.

You can nest IF functions as deep as you want, but after you get beyond a nest of three IF functions, the logic becomes difficult to follow and alternative solutions, such as the use of multiple cells and simple IF functions, should be considered.

Adding and Formatting Sparkline Charts

Sometimes you may want to condense a range of data into a small chart in order to show a trend or variation in the range. Excel's standard charts may be too large or extensive for your needs. An Excel **Sparkline chart** provides a simple way to show trends and variations in a range of data within a single cell. Excel includes three types of Sparkline charts: Line, Column, and Win/Loss. Because they exist in only one cell, you should use Sparkline charts to convey succinct, eye-catching summaries of the data they represent.

To Add a Sparkline Chart to the Worksheet

Each of the rows of monthly data, including those containing formulas, provides useful information easily summarized by a Line Sparkline chart. A Line Sparkline chart is a good choice because it shows trends over the six-month period for each row of data.

The following steps add a Line Sparkline chart to cell I13 and then use the fill handle to create Line Sparkline charts in the range I14:I25 that represent the monthly data in rows 13 through 25.

1

- Scroll the worksheet so that both columns B and I are displayed on the screen.

- Select cell I13 to prepare to insert a Sparkline chart in the cell.

- On the Charts tab, under Insert Sparklines, click Line to display the Insert Sparklines dialog (Figure 3–36).

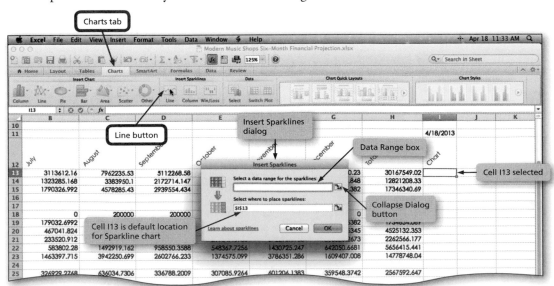

Figure 3–36

2

- Drag through the range B13:G13 to select the range. Do not release the mouse (Figure 3–37).

Q&A What happened to the Create Sparklines dialog?
When a dialog includes a Collapse Dialog button (Figure 3–36), selecting cells or a range collapses the dialog so that only the current text box is displayed. Once the selection is made, the dialog expands back to its original size. You also can click the Collapse Dialog button to make your selection and then click the Expand Dialog button (Figure 3–37) to expand the dialog.

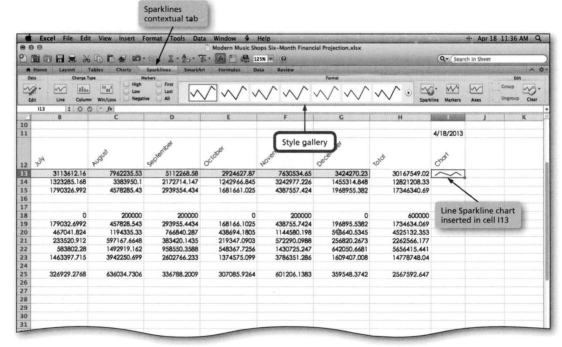

Figure 3–37

3

- Release the mouse button to insert the selected range, B13:G13 in this case, in the Data Range text box.

- Click the OK button (Create Sparklines dialog) to insert a Line Sparkline chart in the selected cell and display the Sparklines contextual tab (Figure 3–38).

Figure 3–38

To Format and Copy a Sparkline Chart

Just as with standard charts, Excel provides formatting options for Sparkline charts. Sparkline chart formatting is restricted greatly as compared to standard charts. As shown in Figure 3–38, the Format group on the Sparklines tab allows you to specify the style and color for the parts of a Sparkline chart as well as to highlight various points in the chart. Markers provide a point on the chart for each cell represented in the chart.

The steps on the next page format the Sparkline chart in cell I13 using the Accent 1, (no dark or light) Sparkline chart style.

- On the Sparklines tab, under Format, point to the Style gallery to display the More button. Click the More button to display the Sparkline Style gallery (Figure 3–39).

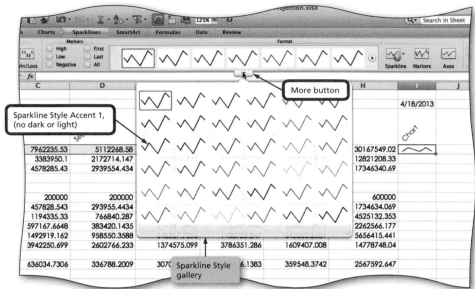

Figure 3–39

- Click Sparkline Style Accent 1, (no dark or light) in the Sparkline Style gallery to apply the style to the Sparkline chart in the selected cell, I13 in this case.

- Point to the fill handle in cell I13 and then drag through cell I25 to copy the Line Sparkline chart.

- Select cell I27 (Figure 3–40).

Q&A Why do Sparkline charts not appear in cells I16, I17, and I24?
Excel does not draw Sparkline charts if the range for the Sparkline chart contains no data. In this case the ranges B16:G16, B17:G17, and B24:G24 do not contain data, so Excel draws no Sparkline chart. If you add data to cells in those ranges, then Excel automatically would draw Line Sparkline charts for the rows to which you added data because the Sparkline charts were defined for cells I16, I17, and I24 by the drag operation.

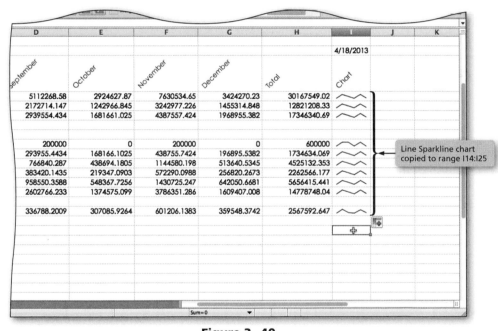

Figure 3–40

Formatting the Worksheet

The worksheet created thus far shows the financial projections for the six-month period, from July to December. Its appearance is uninteresting, however, even though some minimal formatting (formatting assumptions numbers, changing the column widths, formatting the date, and formatting the Sparkline chart) was performed earlier. This section will complete the formatting of the worksheet to make the numbers easier to read and to emphasize the titles, assumptions, categories, and totals as shown in Figure 3–41.

Identify how to format various elements of the worksheet.   **Plan Ahead**

A worksheet, such as the one presented in this chapter, should be formatted in the following manner: (1) format the numbers; (2) format the worksheet title, column titles, row titles, and total rows; and (3) format the assumptions table. Numbers in heading rows and total rows should be formatted as Currency style with a floating dollar sign. Other dollar amounts should be formatted with a Comma style. An assumptions table should be diminished in its formatting so that it does not distract from the main calculations and data in the worksheet. Assigning the data in an assumptions table a smaller font size would set it apart from other data formatted with a larger font size.

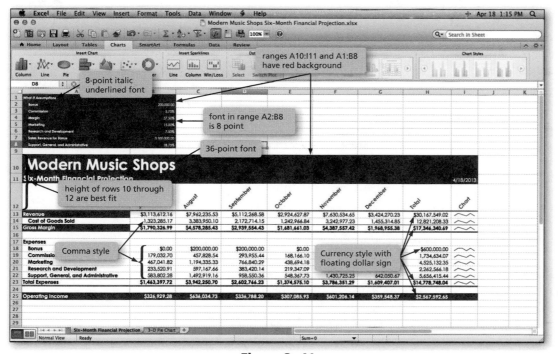

Figure 3–41

To Assign Formats to Nonadjacent Ranges

The numbers in the range B13:H25 are to be formatted as follows:

- Assign the Currency style with a floating dollar sign to rows 13, 15, 18, 23, and 25.
- Assign a Comma style to rows 14 and 19 through 22.

The following steps assign formats to the numbers in rows 13 through 25.

- Select the range B13:H13 as the first range to format.

- While holding down the COMMAND key, select the nonadjacent ranges B15:H15, B18:H18, B23:H23, and B25:H25, and then release the COMMAND key.

- Click Format in the menu bar to display the Format menu.

- Choose Cells to display the Format Cells dialog.

- Click Currency in the Category list (Format Cells dialog), if necessary select 2 in the Decimal places box, if necessary click $ in the Currency symbol list to ensure a dollar sign shows in the cells to be formatted, and click the black font color ($1,234.10) in the Negative numbers list to prepare the desired Currency style for the selected ranges (Figure 3–42).

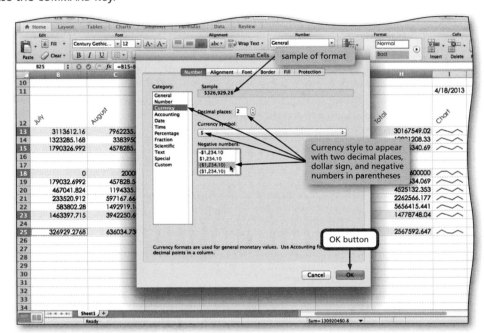

Figure 3–42

Q&A   Why was the particular style chosen for the negative numbers?
In accounting, negative numbers often are shown with parentheses surrounding the value rather than with a negative sign preceding the value. Thus, the format (1,234.10) in the Negative numbers list was clicked. The data being used in this chapter contains no negative numbers. You must select a format for negative numbers, however, and you must be consistent if you are choosing different formats in a column; otherwise, the decimal points may not line up.

Q&A   Why is the Format Cells dialog used to create the format for the ranges in this step?
The requirements for this worksheet call for a floating dollar sign. To assign a Currency style with a floating dollar sign, use the Format Cells dialog rather than the Accounting Style button in the Number group on the Home tab, which assigns a fixed dollar sign.

2

- Click the OK button (Format Cells dialog) to close the Format Cells dialog and apply the desired format to the selected ranges.

- Select the range B14:H14 as the next range to format.

- While holding down the COMMAND key, select the range B19:H22, and then release the COMMAND key to select nonadjacent ranges.

- Click Format in the menu bar and then choose Cells to display the Format Cells dialog.

- Click Currency in the Category list (Format Cells dialog), if necessary select 2 in the Decimal places box, click None in the Currency symbol list so a dollar sign does not show in the cells to be formatted, and click the black font color (1,234.10) in the Negative numbers list (Figure 3–43).

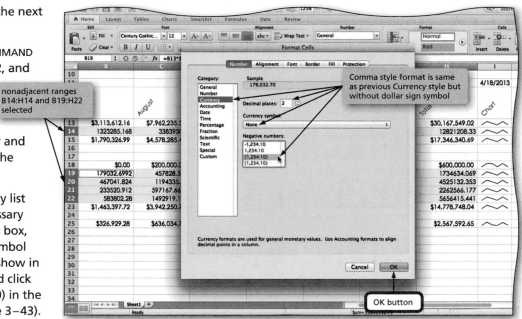

Figure 3–43

3

- Click the OK button (Format Cells dialog) to close the Format Cells dialog and apply the desired format to the selected ranges.

- Select cell B27 to select an empty cell and display the formatted numbers as shown in Figure 3–44.

Q&A Why is the Format Cells dialog used to create the style for the ranges in Steps 2 and 3? The Format Cells dialog is used to assign the Comma style, because the Comma Style button in the Number Group on the Home tab assigns a format that displays a dash (–) when a cell has a value of 0. The specifications for this worksheet call for displaying a value of 0 as 0.00 (see cell B18 in Figure 3–41) rather than as a dash. To create a Comma style using the Format Cells dialog, you can assign a Currency style with no dollar sign.

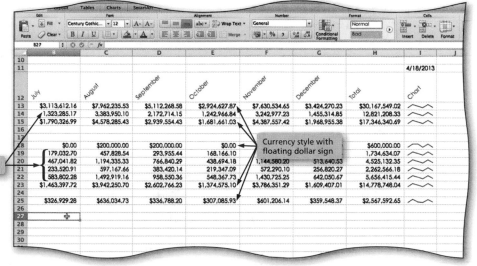

Figure 3–44

Other Ways

1. CONTROL-click range, choose Format Cells in shortcut menu, click Number tab (Format Cells dialog), click category in Category list, select format, click OK button (Format Cells dialog)

2. Press COMMAND-1, click Number tab (Format Cells dialog), click category in Category list, select format, click OK button (Format Cells dialog)

To Format the Worksheet Titles

The following steps emphasize the worksheet titles in cells A10 and A11 by changing the font, size, and color. The steps also format all of the row headers in column A with a bold font style.

- Press CONTROL-FN-LEFT ARROW to select cell A1 and then click the column A heading to select the column.

- On the Home tab, under Font, click the Bold button to bold all of the data in the selected column.

- Select cell A10, and on the Home tab under Font, click the Font Size box arrow, and then click 36 in the Font Size list to increase the font size of the selected cell.

- Select cell A11, and increase the font size of the selected cell to 18 (Figure 3–45).

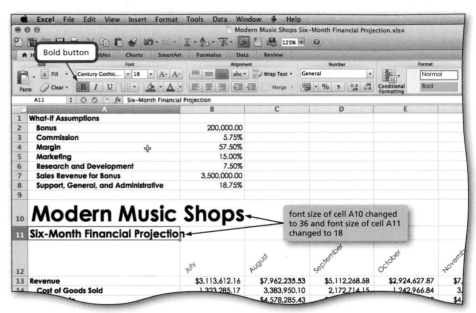

Figure 3–45

- Select the range A10:I11 and then on the Home tab, under Font, click the Fill Color button arrow to display the Fill Color pop-up menu.

- Click Accent 2, Lighter 25% (column 6, row 5) in the Fill Color pop-up menu to add a background color to the selected range.

- On the Home tab, under font, click the Font Color button arrow and then select Background 1 (column 1, row 1) in the Font Color pop-up menu to change the font color of the selected range (Figure 3–46).

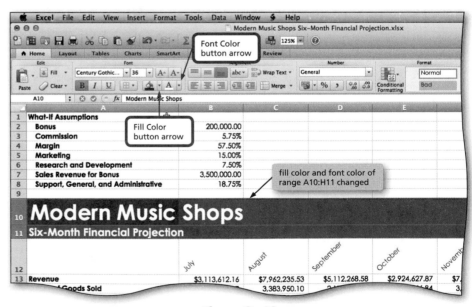

Figure 3–46

Other Ways

1. CONTROL-click range, choose Format Cells in shortcut menu, click Fill tab (Format Cells dialog) to color background (or click Font tab to color font), click OK button

2. Press COMMAND - 1, click Fill tab (Format Cells dialog) to color background (or click Font tab to color font), click OK button

To Assign Cell Styles to Nonadjacent Rows and Colors to a Cell

The next step to improving the appearance of the worksheet is to format the heading in row 12 and the totals in rows 15, 23, and 25. The following steps format the heading in row 13 with the Heading 3 cell style and the totals in rows 15, 23, and 25 with the Total cell style. Cell A13 also is formatted with a background color and font color.

1 Select the range A12:I12 and apply the Heading 2 cell style.

2 Select the range A15:I15 and while holding down the COMMAND key, select the ranges A23:I23 and A25:I25.

3 Apply the Total cell style to the selected nonadjacent ranges.

4 Select cell A13, click the Fill Color button arrow and then click the Accent 2, Lighter 25% color (column 6, row 5) in the Fill Color pop-up menu.

5 Click the Font Color button arrow and then click the Background 1 color (column 1, row 1) in the Font Color pop-up menu (Figure 3–47).

Work Days

Assume that you have **BTW** two dates, one in cell A1 and the other in cell A2. Assume further that the date in cell A1 is your starting date and the date in cell A2 is the ending date. To calculate the work days between the two dates (excluding weekends), use the following formula: =NETWORKDAYS(A1, A2).

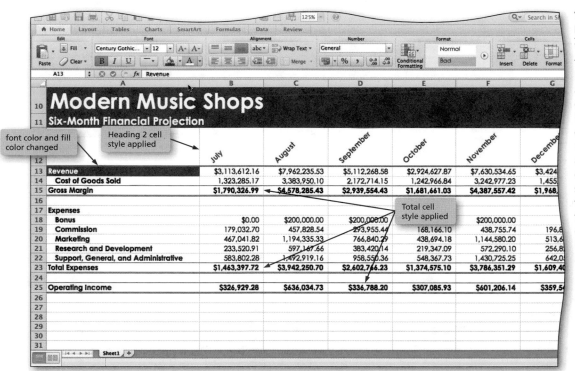

Figure 3–47

The Fill and Font Color Buttons

You may have noticed **BTW** that the color bar at the bottom of the Fill Color and Font Color buttons on the Home tab in the Font group (Figure 3–46) changes to the most recently selected color. To apply this same color to a cell background or text, select a cell and then click the Fill Color button to use the color as a background or click the Font Color button to use the color as a font color.

To Copy a Cell's Format Using the Format Painter

Using the Format Painter, you can format a cell quickly by copying a cell's format to another cell or a range of cells. The steps on the next page format cells A15 and the range A25:I25 using the Format Painter.

1

- If necessary, click cell A13 to select a source cell for the format to paint.

- Double-click the Format Painter button in the Standard toolbar and then move the mouse pointer onto the worksheet to cause the mouse pointer to change to a block plus sign with a paintbrush (Figure 3–48).

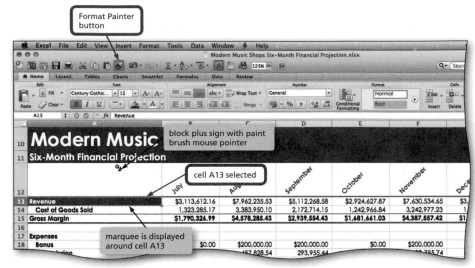

Figure 3–48

2

- Click cell A15 to assign the format of the source cell, A13 in this case, to the destination cell, A15 in this case (Figure 3–49).

Figure 3–49

3

- With the mouse pointer still a block plus sign with a paintbrush, drag through the range A25:I25 to assign the format of the source cell, A13 in this case, to the destination range, A25:I25 in this case.

- Press the ESC key to stop the Format Painter.

- Apply the Currency style to the range B25:H25 to cause the cells in the range to appear with a floating dollar sign, two decimal places, and negative numbers with black font in parentheses, and then, if necessary, scroll the worksheet so that column A is displayed (Figure 3–50).

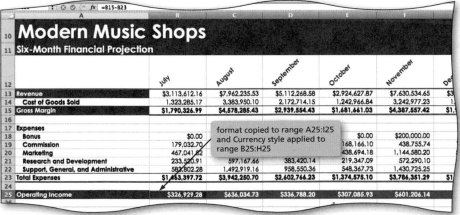

Q&A Why does the Currency style need to be reapplied to the range B25:H25? Sometimes, the use of the Format Painter results in unintended outcomes. In this case, the changing of the background fill color and font color for the range B25:H25 resulted in the loss of the Currency style because the format being copied did not include the Currency style. Reapplying the Currency style to the range results in the proper number style, fill color, and font color.

Figure 3–50

Other Ways

1. Select source cell, click Copy button in Standard toolbar, select destination cell, click Paste button arrow in the Edit group on the Home tab, choose Paste Special in Paste pop-up menu, click Formats (Paste Special dialog), click OK button

2. CONTROL-click source cell, choose Copy in shortcut menu, CONTROL-click destination cell, choose Paste Special, click Formats (Paste Special idalog), click OK button

To Format the What-If Assumptions Table and Save the Workbook

The last step to improving the appearance of the worksheet is to format the What-If Assumptions table in the range A1:B8. The specifications in Figure 3–41 on page EX 169 require an 8-point italic underlined font for the title in cell A1 and 8-point font in the range A2:B8. The following steps format the What-If Assumptions table.

① Press CONTROL-FN-LEFT ARROW to select cell A1.

② On the Home tab, under Font, click the Font Size button arrow and then click 8 in the Font Size list to decrease the font size of the selected cell.

③ On the Home tab, under Font, click the Italic button and then click the Underline button to italicize and underline the text in the selected cell.

④ Select the range A2:B8, click the Font Size button arrow in the Font group on the Home tab, and then click 8 in the Font Size list to apply a smaller font size to the selected range.

⑤ Select the range A1:B8 and then click the Fill Color button on the Home tab under Font to apply the most recently used background color to the selected range.

⑥ Click the Font Color button on the Home tab under Font to apply the most recently used font color to the selected range.

⑦ Click cell D8 to deselect the range A2:B8 and display the What-If Assumptions table, as shown in Figure 3–51.

⑧ Save the workbook.

Q&A What happens when I click the Italic and Underline buttons?
Recall that when you assign the italic font style to a cell, Excel slants the characters slightly to the right, as shown in cell A1 in Figure 3–51. The **underline** format underlines only the characters in the cell, rather than the entire cell, as is the case when you assign a cell a bottom border.

Painting a Format to Nonadjacent Ranges

BTW

Double-click the Format Painter button in the Standard toolbar and then drag through the nonadjacent ranges to paint the formats to the ranges. Click the Format Painter button again to deactivate it.

Selecting Nonadjacent Ranges

BTW

One of the more difficult tasks to learn is selecting nonadjacent ranges. To complete this task, do not hold down the COMMAND key when you select the first range because Excel will consider the current active cell to be the first selection, and you may not want the current active cell in the selection. Once the first range is selected, hold down the COMMAND key and drag through the nonadjacent ranges. If a desired range is not visible in the window, use the scroll arrows to view the range. You need not hold down the COMMAND key while you scroll.

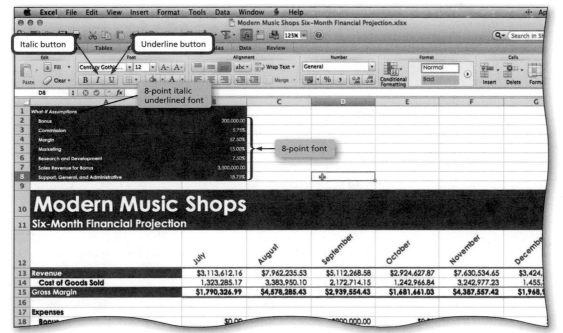

Figure 3–51

Break Point: If you wish to stop working through the chapter at this point, you can quit Excel now and then resume the project at a later point in time by starting Excel, opening the file called Modern Music Shops Six-Month Financial Projection, and continuing to follow the steps from this location forward.

Charts

BTW When you change a value on which a chart is dependent, Excel immediately redraws the chart based on the new value. With bar charts, you can drag the bar in the chart in one direction or another to change the corresponding value in the worksheet.

Adding a 3-D Pie Chart to the Workbook

The next step in the chapter is to draw the 3-D Pie chart on a separate sheet in the workbook, as shown in Figure 3–52. Use a **pie chart** to show the relationship or proportion of parts to a whole. Each slice (or wedge) of the pie shows what percent that slice contributes to the total (100%).

The 3-D Pie chart in Figure 3–52 shows the contribution of each month's projected operating income to the six-month projected operating income. The 3-D Pie chart makes it easy to evaluate the contribution of one month in comparison to the other months.

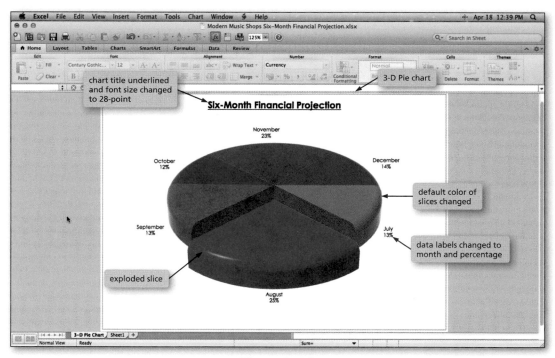

Figure 3–52

Chart Items

BTW When you rest the mouse pointer over a chart item, such as a legend, bar, or axis, Excel displays a chart tip containing the name of the item.

Unlike the 3-D Column chart created in Chapter 1, the 3-D Pie chart shown in Figure 3–52 is not embedded in the worksheet. Instead, the Pie chart resides on a separate sheet, called a **chart sheet**, which contains only the chart.

In this worksheet, the ranges to chart are the nonadjacent ranges B12:G12 (month names) and B25:G25 (monthly operating incomes). The month names in the range B12:G12 will identify the slices of the Pie chart; these entries are called **category names**. The range B25:G25 contains the data that determines the size of the slices in the pie; these entries are called the **data series**. Because six months are being charted, the 3-D Pie chart contains six slices.

The sketch of the 3-D Pie chart in Figure 3–3b on page EX 138 also calls for emphasizing the month of August by offsetting its slice from the main portion. A Pie chart with one or more slices offset is called an **exploded Pie chart**.

As shown in Figure 3–52, the default 3-D Pie chart also has been enhanced by rotating it, changing the colors of the slices, adding a bevel, and modifying the chart title and labels that identify the slices.

To Draw a 3-D Pie Chart on a Separate Chart Sheet

The following steps draw the 3-D Pie chart on a separate chart sheet.

 1

- Select the range B12:G12 to identify the range of the category name of the 3-D Pie Chart.

- If necessary, scroll the worksheet so that row 25 is displayed, and while holding down the COMMAND key, select the range B25:G25.

- Display the Charts tab.

- Click the Pie button under Insert Chart to display the Pie pop-up menu (Figure 3–53).

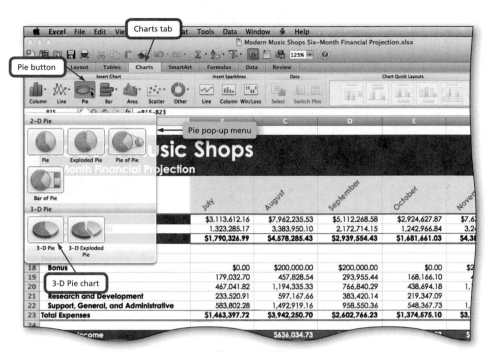

Figure 3–53

2

- Choose 3-D Pie in the Pie pop-up menu to select the desired chart type.

- When Excel draws the chart, CONTROL-click the chart border to display a shortcut menu.

- Choose Move Chart from the shortcut menu to display the Move Chart dialog (Figure 3–54).

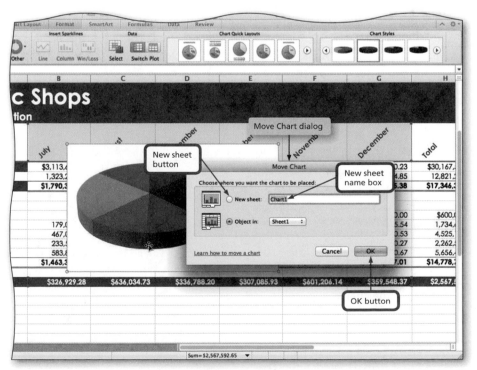

Figure 3–54

- Click the New sheet button (Move Chart dialog) and then type `3-D Pie Chart` in the New sheet text box to enter a sheet tab name for the chart sheet.
- Click the OK button (Move Chart dialog) to move the chart to a new chart sheet with a new sheet name, 3-D Pie Chart in this case (Figure 3–55).

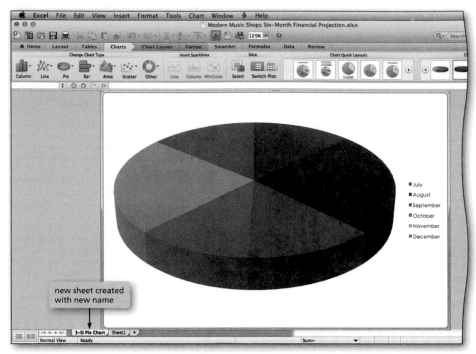

Figure 3–55

To Insert a Chart Title and Data Labels

The next step is to insert a chart title and labels that identify the slices. Before you can format a chart item, such as the chart title or data labels, it must be selected. The following steps insert a chart title, remove the legend, and add data labels.

- If the chart is not already selected, click anywhere in the chart area outside the chart to select the chart.
- Display the Chart Layout tab and then click the Chart Title button in the Labels group to display the Chart Title pop-up menu.
- Click the Overlap Title at Top command in the Chart Title pop-up menu to add a chart title centered at the top of the chart.
- If necessary, select the text in the chart title and then type `Six-Month Financial Projection` to add a new chart title (Figure 3–56).

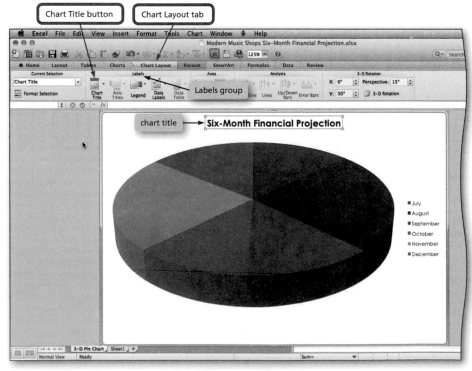

Figure 3–56

2

- Select the text in the new title and then display the Home tab.

- Under the Font group, click the Underline button to assign an underline font style to the chart title (Figure 3–57).

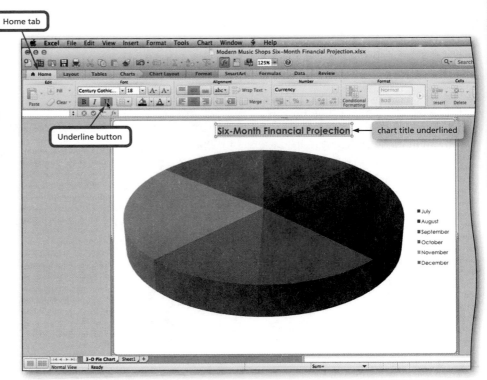

Figure 3–57

3

- Display the Chart Layout tab and, in the Labels group, click the Legend button to display the Legend pop-up menu (Figure 3–58).

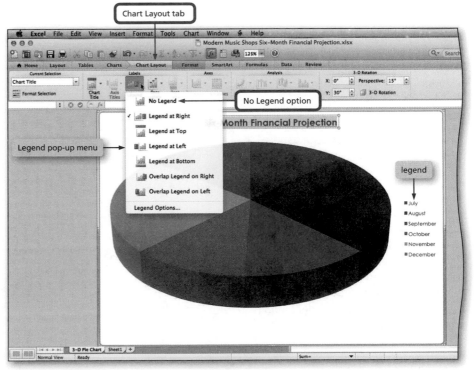

Figure 3–58

- Choose the No Legend option in the Legend pop-up menu to turn off the legend on the chart.

- On the Chart Layout tab, under Labels, click the Data Labels button and then choose Outside End in the pop-up menu to display data labels outside the chart at the end of each slice (Figure 3–59).

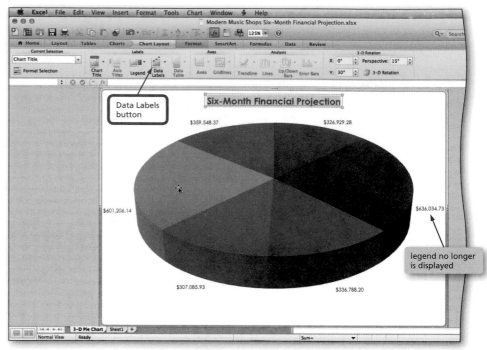

Figure 3–59

- If necessary, CONTROL-click any data label to select all of the data labels on the chart and to display a shortcut menu.

- Choose the Format Data Labels command in the shortcut menu to display the Format Data Labels dialog.

- If necessary, click the Series Name, Value, and Show Leader Lines check boxes to deselect them (Format Data Labels dialog) and then click the Category Name and Percentage check boxes to cause the data labels to be displayed with category names and percentage values, rather than currency values. Under Label options, ensure that check boxes are deselected (Figure 3–60).

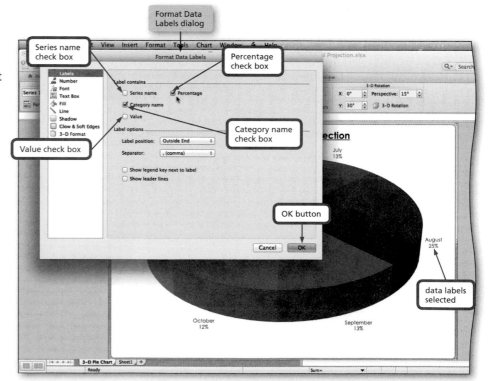

Figure 3–60

- Click the OK button to close the Format Data Labels dialog and to display the chart (Figure 3–61).

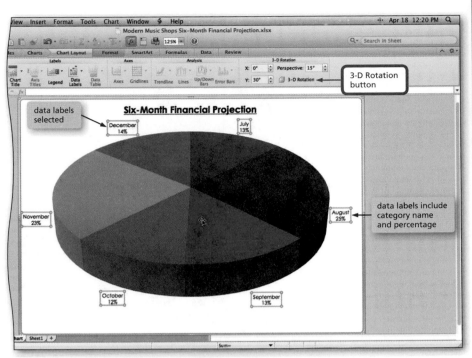

Figure 3–61

To Rotate a 3-D Pie Chart

With a three-dimensional chart, you can change the view to better show the section of the chart you are trying to emphasize. Excel allows you to control the rotation angle, elevation, perspective, height, and angle of the axes.

When Excel initially draws a Pie chart, it always positions the chart so that one of the dividing lines between two slices is a straight line pointing to 12 o'clock (or 0°). As shown in Figure 3–61, the line that divides the December and July slices currently is set to 0°. This line defines the rotation angle of the 3-D Pie chart.

To obtain a better view of the offset August slice, the largest slice, the 3-D Pie chart can be rotated 90° to the left. The following steps rotate the 3-D Pie chart.

- On the Chart Layout tab, under 3-D Rotation, click the 3-D Rotation button to display the Format Chart Area dialog.

- Click and hold the Increase X Rotation button in the Rotation area of the Format Chart Area dialog until the X rotation is at 90° to rotate the chart (Figure 3–62).

Q&A What happens as I click the Increase X Rotation button?
Excel rotates the chart 1° in a clockwise direction each time you click the Increase X Rotation button. The Y box in the Rotation area allows you to control the tilt, or elevation, of the chart. You can tilt the chart towards or away from your view in order to enhance the view of the chart.

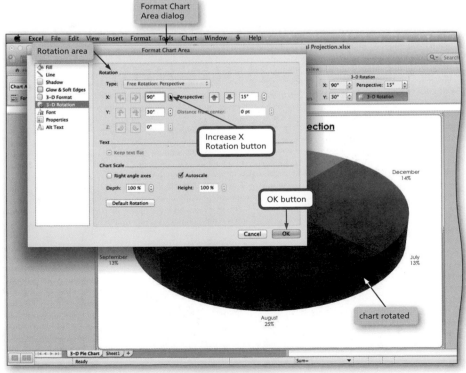

Figure 3–62

2

- Click the OK button to close the dialog and display the rotated chart (Figure 3–63).

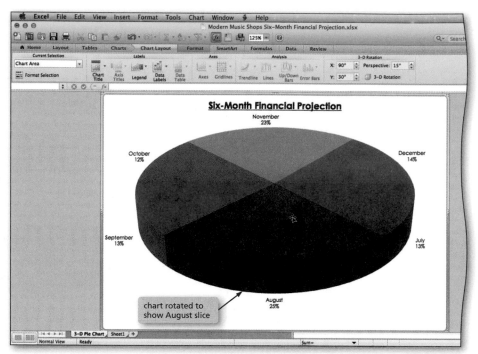

Figure 3–63

To Apply a 3-D Format to a Pie Chart

Excel allows you to apply dramatic 3-D visual effects to charts. The chart shown in Figure 3–63 could be enhanced with a bevel along the top edge. A bevel is a curve that is applied to soften the appearance of a straight edge. Excel also allows you to change the appearance of the material from which the surface of the chart appears to be constructed. The following steps apply a bevel to the chart and change the surface of the chart to a softer-looking material.

1

- CONTROL-click the chart to display a shortcut menu (Figure 3–64).

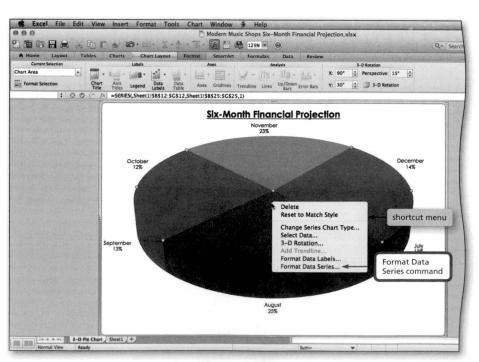

Figure 3–64

2

- Choose the Format Data Series command in the shortcut menu to display the Format Data Series dialog and then click the 3-D Format category (Format Data Series dialog) on the left side of the dialog to display the 3-D Format pane.

- Click the Top button (Format Data Series dialog) in the Bevel area to display the Top Bevel pop-up menu (Figure 3–65).

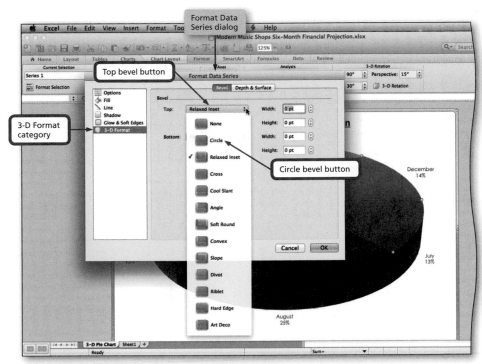

Figure 3–65

3

- Click the Circle bevel button (Format Data Series dialog) to add a top bevel to the chart.

- Type 50 pt in the uppermost Width box in the Bevel area (Format Data Series dialog) and then type 50 pt in the uppermost Height box in the Bevel area of the dialog to increase the width and height of the bevel on the chart (Figure 3–66).

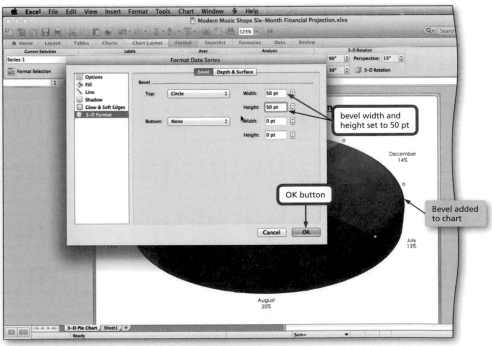

Figure 3–66

- Click the Depth and Surface tab (Format Data Series dialog) to display the Depth and Surface pane.

- Click the Material button in the Surface area (Format Data Series dialog) to display the Material pop-up menu (Figure 3–67).

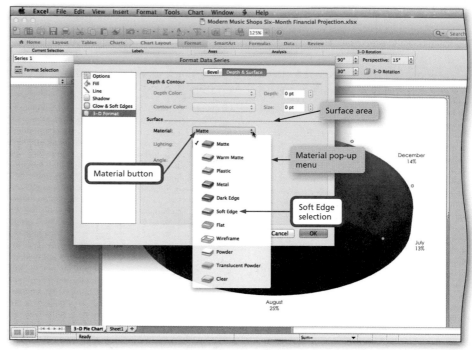

Figure 3–67

- Click the Soft Edge button in the Material pop-up menu and then click the OK button (Format Data Series dialog) to apply the desired material and close the Format Data Series dialog (Figure 3–68).

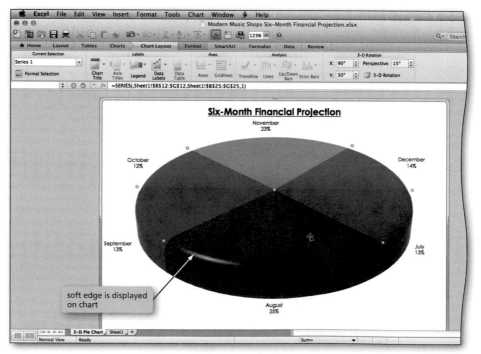

Figure 3–68

To Explode a 3-D Pie Chart and Change the Color of a Slice

The next step is to emphasize the slice representing August by **offsetting**, or exploding, it from the rest of the slices so that it stands out. The following steps explode the largest slice of the 3-D Pie chart and then change its color.

1

- Click the slice labeled August twice (do not double-click) to select only one slice of the 3-D Pie chart, the August slice in this case.

- CONTROL-click the slice labeled August to display a shortcut menu (Figure 3–69).

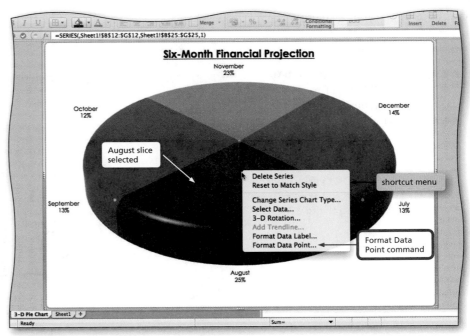

Figure 3–69

2

- Choose Format Data Point in the shortcut menu to display the Format Data Point dialog.

- Click the Options category on the left side to display the Options pane.

- Click the Increase Point Explosion button until the Point explosion box reads 28% to set how far the slice in the 3-D Pie chart should be offset from the rest of the chart (Figure 3–70).

Q&A Should I offset more slices?
You can offset as many slices as you want, but remember that the reason for offsetting a slice is to emphasize it. Offsetting multiple slices tends to reduce the impact on the reader and reduces the overall size of the Pie chart.

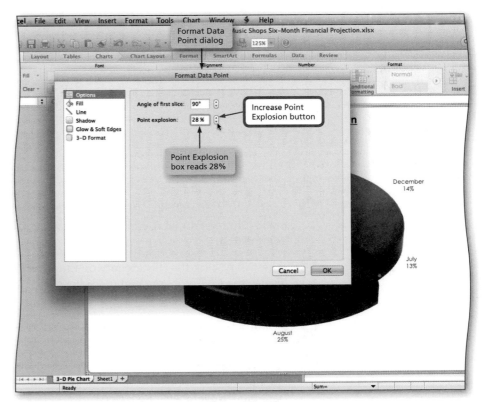

Figure 3–70

3

- Click the Fill category (Format Data Point dialog) on the left side of the dialog to display the Fill pane.

- If necessary, click the Solid tab to display the Fill Color area and then click the Color button to display the Color pop-up menu.

- Click the Blue color in the Standard Colors area and then click the OK button (Format Data Point dialog) to change the color of the selected slice and close the dialog (Figure 3–71).

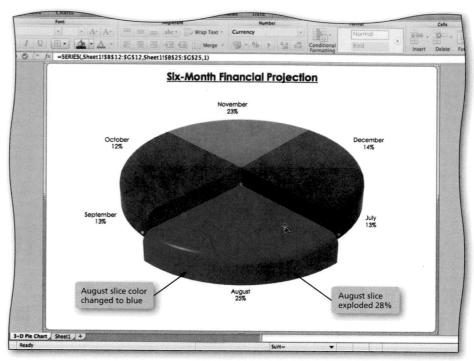

Figure 3–71

Other Ways

1. CONTROL-click slice, choose Format Data Point from shortcut menu
2. Select slice, choose Format > Data Point from menu bar
3. Select slice, press COMMAND-1

Exploding a 3-D Pie Chart

If you click a 3-D Pie chart so that all of the slices are selected, you can drag one of the slices to explode all of the slices.

To Change the Colors of the Remaining Slices

The colors of the remaining slices also can be changed to enhance the appeal of the chart. The following steps change the color of the remaining five chart slices.

1 CONTROL-click the slice labeled July to select only the July slice, and display a shortcut menu. Choose Format Data Point from the shortcut menu to display the Format Data Point dialog.

2 If necessary, click the Fill category on the left side of the dialog, click the Solid tab to display the Fill Color area and then click the Color button to display the Color pop-up menu.

3 Click the Yellow color in the Standard Colors area in the Color pop-up menu to change the color of the slice.

4 Repeat Steps 1 through 3 for the remaining four slices. Assign the following colors in the Standard Colors area in the color gallery to each slice: September – Green; October – Dark Blue; November – Red; December – Dark Purple.

5 Click anywhere outside the Chart Area to deselect the December slice and deselect the chart (Figure 3–72). The completed chart appears as shown in Figure 3–72.

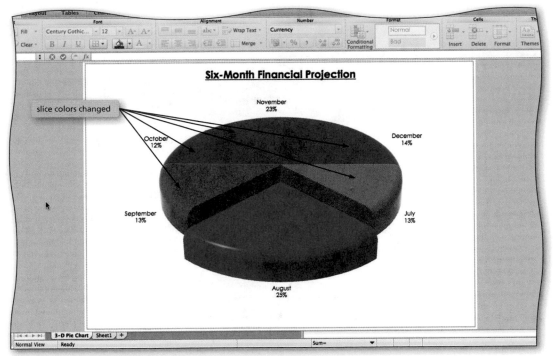

Figure 3–72

Renaming and Reordering the Sheets and Coloring Their Tabs

The final step in creating the workbook is to reorder the sheets and modify the tabs at the bottom of the screen.

To Rename the Sheets and Color Their Tabs

The following steps rename the sheets and color the sheet tabs.

1 Change the sheet tab color of the 3-D Pie Chart sheet to Accent 3, Lighter 60%, (column 7, row 3) and then close the Tab Color window.

2 Double-click the tab labeled Sheet1 at the bottom of the screen.

3 Type `Six-Month Financial Projection` as the new sheet name and then press the RETURN KEY.

4 Change the sheet tab color of the Six-Month Financial Projection sheet to Accent 2, Lighter 75% (column 6, row 3), close the Tab Color window and then select cell D8 (Figure 3–73).

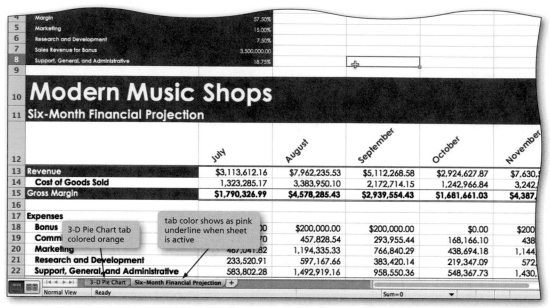

Figure 3–73

To Reorder Sheet Tabs

Change the order of sheets in a workbook so that they appear with the most important worksheets first. The following steps reorder the sheets so that the worksheet precedes the chart sheet in the workbook.

- Drag the Six-Month Financial Projection tab to the left in front of the 3-D Pie Chart tab to rearrange the sequence of the sheets (Figure 3–74).

	Modern Music Shops					
	Six-Month Financial Projection					
		July	August	September	October	November
13	Revenue	$3,113,612.16	$7,962,235.53	$5,112,268.58	$2,924,627.87	$7,630,5
14	Cost of Goods Sold	1,323,285.17	3,383,950.10	2,172,714.15	1,242,966.84	3,242,9
15	Gross Margin	$1,790,326.99	$4,578,285.43	$2,939,554.43	$1,681,661.03	$4,387,5
16						
17	Expenses					
18	Bonus	$0.00	$200,000.00	$200,000.00	$0.00	$200
19	Commission	179,032.70	457,828.54	293,955.44	168,166.10	438
20	Marketing	467,041.82	1,194,335.33	766,840.29	438,694.18	1,144
21	Research and Development	233,520.91	597,167.66	383,420.14	219,347.09	572
22	Support, General, and Administrative	583,802.28	1,492,919.16	958,550.36	548,367.73	1,430

Six-Month Financial Projection tab moved to left of 3-D Pie Chart tab

Figure 3–74

Other Ways

1. To move sheet, CONTROL-click sheet tab, click Move or Copy in shortcut menu

To Check Spelling in Multiple Sheets

By default, the spell checker checks the spelling only in the selected sheets. It will check all the cells in the selected sheets, unless you select a range of two or more cells. Before checking the spelling, the following steps select both sheets in the workbook so that both worksheets in the workbook are checked for spelling errors.

1 With the Six-Month Financial Projection sheet active, press CONTROL-FN-LEFT ARROW to select cell A1. Hold down the COMMAND key and then click the 3-D Pie Chart tab to select multiple sheets.

2 Display the Review tab, and under Proofing, click the Spelling button to check spelling in the selected sheets.

3 Correct any errors and then click the OK button (Spelling dialog or "The spell check is complete" dialog) when the spell check is complete.

4 Save the workbook.

To Preview and Print the Workbook

After checking the spelling, the next step is to preview and print the sheets. As with spelling, Excel previews and prints only the selected sheets. In addition, because the worksheet is too wide to print in portrait orientation, the orientation must be changed to landscape. The following steps adjust the orientation and scale, preview the workbook, and then print the workbook.

1 Ready the printer. If both sheets are not selected, hold down the COMMAND key and then click the tab of the inactive sheet.

2 Click File in the menu bar and choose Print to open the Print dialog.

3 Click the Page Setup button to open the Page Setup dialog.

4 If necessary, click the Page button to display the Page pane. Choose Landscape under Orientation.

5 Under Scaling, select 'Fit to' and set to 1 page wide by 1 page tall to cause the sheets to print on one page each.

6 Click the Margins tab (Page Setup dialog) to display the Margins pane, and select Horizontally under Center on page. Click the OK button to close the Page Setup dialog and return to the Print dialog.

7 If necessary, click the Printer button to display a list of available Printer options and then click the desired printer to change the currently selected printer.

8 Click the Print button (Print dialog) to print the worksheet and chart in landscape orientation on the currently selected printer.

9 When the printer stops, retrieve the printed worksheet and chart (Figure 3–75a and Figure 3–75b on the following page).

10 CONTROL-click the Six-Month Financial Projection tab. Click Ungroup Sheets in the shortcut menu to deselect the 3-D Pie Chart tab.

11 Save the workbook.

Checking Spelling

Unless you first select a BTW range of cells or an object before starting the spell checker, Excel checks the entire selected worksheet, including all cell values, cell comments, embedded charts, text boxes, buttons, and headers and footers.

Conserving Ink and Toner

If you want to conserve BTW ink or toner, you can instruct Excel to print draft quality documents by choosing File > Print in the menu bar to open the Print dialog, clicking the Copies & Pages button, and selecting Print Settings from the pop-up menu. Under Basic Print Settings, place a check mark in the Toner Save Modecheck box, and then click the Print button.

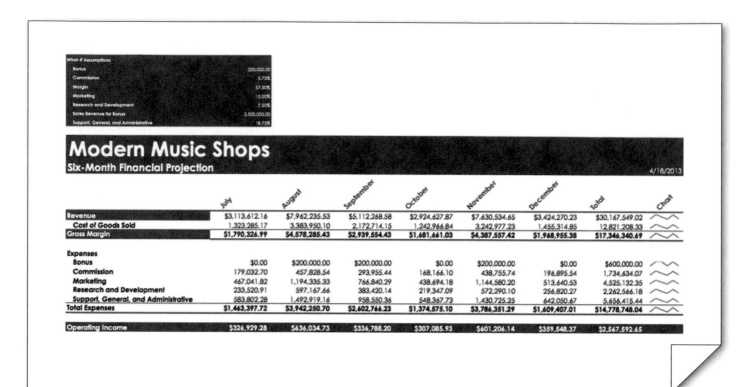

What-If Assumptions
Bonus	200,000.00
Commission	5.75%
Margin	57.50%
Marketing	15.00%
Research and Development	7.50%
Sales Revenue for Bonus	3,500,000.00
Support, General, and Administrative	18.75%

Modern Music Shops
Six-Month Financial Projection
4/18/2013

	July	August	September	October	November	December	Total	Chart
Revenue	$3,113,612.16	$7,962,235.53	$5,112,268.58	$2,924,627.87	$7,630,534.65	$3,424,270.23	$30,167,549.02	
Cost of Goods Sold	1,323,285.17	3,383,950.10	2,172,714.15	1,242,966.84	3,242,977.23	1,455,314.85	12,821,208.33	
Gross Margin	$1,790,326.99	$4,578,285.43	$2,939,554.43	$1,681,661.03	$4,387,557.42	$1,968,955.38	$17,346,340.69	
Expenses								
Bonus	$0.00	$200,000.00	$200,000.00	$0.00	$200,000.00	$0.00	$600,000.00	
Commission	179,032.70	457,828.54	293,955.44	168,166.10	438,755.74	196,895.54	1,734,634.07	
Marketing	467,041.82	1,194,335.33	766,840.29	438,694.18	1,144,580.20	513,640.53	4,525,132.35	
Research and Development	233,520.91	597,167.66	383,420.14	219,347.09	572,290.10	256,820.27	2,262,566.18	
Support, General, and Administrative	583,802.28	1,492,919.16	958,550.36	548,367.73	1,430,725.25	642,050.67	5,656,415.44	
Total Expenses	$1,463,397.72	$3,942,250.70	$2,602,766.23	$1,374,575.10	$3,786,351.29	$1,609,407.01	$14,778,748.04	
Operating Income	$326,929.28	$636,034.73	$336,788.20	$307,085.93	$601,206.14	$359,548.37	$2,567,592.65	

(a) Worksheet

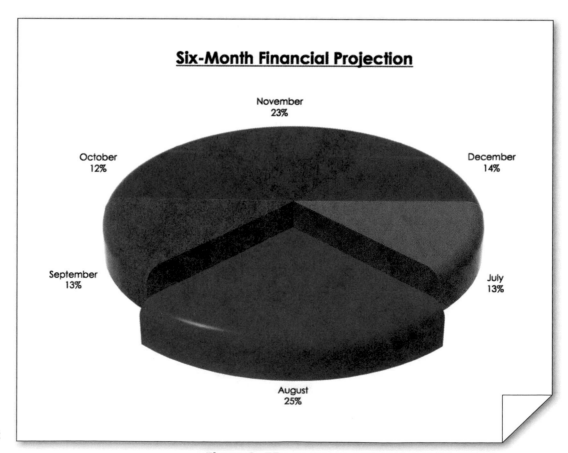

Six-Month Financial Projection

November 23%
October 12%
December 14%
September 13%
July 13%
August 25%

(b) 3-D Pie Chart

Figure 3–75

Changing the View of the Worksheet

With Excel, you easily can change the view of the worksheet. For example, you can magnify or shrink the worksheet on the screen. You also can view different parts of the worksheet through windowpanes.

To Shrink and Magnify the View of a Worksheet or Chart

You can magnify (zoom in) or shrink (zoom out) the appearance of a worksheet or chart by using the Zoom button on the View tab in the Zoom group. When you magnify a worksheet, Excel enlarges the view of the characters on the screen, but displays fewer columns and rows. Alternatively, when you shrink a worksheet, Excel is able to display more columns and rows. Magnifying or shrinking a worksheet affects only the view; it does not change the window size or printout of the worksheet or chart. The following steps shrink and magnify the view of the worksheet.

1

- If cell A1 is not active, press CONTROL-FN-LEFT ARROW.

- In the Standard toolbar, click the Zoom button arrow to display a list of magnifications in the Zoom pop-up menu (Figure 3–76).

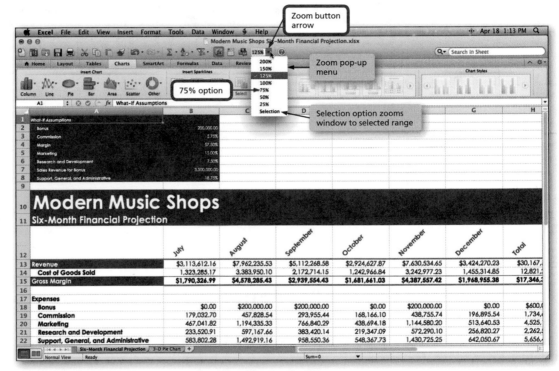

Figure 3–76

2

- Choose 75% from the pop-up menu to shrink the display of the worksheet (Figure 3–77).

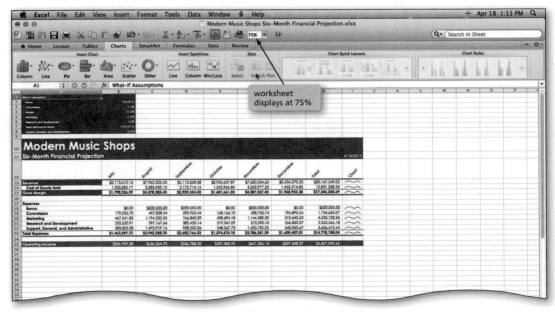

Figure 3–77

3

- Choose 100% in the pop-up menu to display the worksheet at 100% (Figure 3–78).

- Choose 125% in the pop-up menu to display the worksheet at 125%.

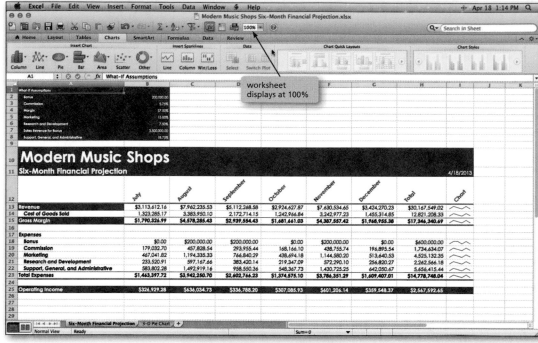

Figure 3–78

To Split a Window into Panes

When working with a large worksheet, you can split the window into two or four panes to view different parts of the worksheet at the same time. Splitting the Excel window into four panes at cell D13 allows you to view all four corners of the worksheet easily. The following steps split the Excel window into four panes.

1

- Select cell D13, the intersection of the four proposed panes, to select the cell at which to split the window.

- Display the Layout tab (Figure 3–79).

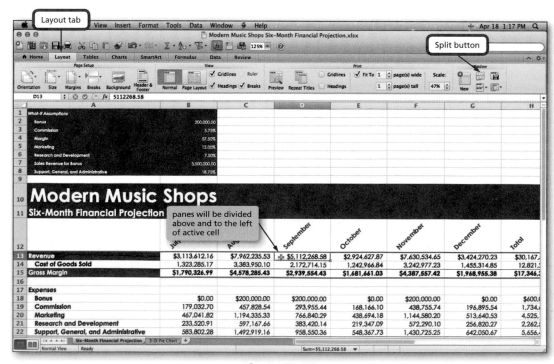

Figure 3–79

2

- On the Layout tab, under Window, click the Split button to divide the window into four panes.

- Use the horizontal and vertical scrollers to show the four corners of the worksheet at the same time (Figure 3–80).

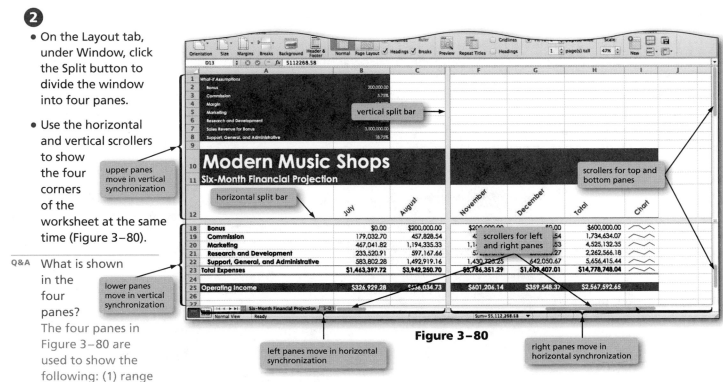

Figure 3–80

Q&A What is shown in the four panes?

The four panes in Figure 3–80 are used to show the following: (1) range A1:C12 in the upper-left pane; (2) range F1:J12 in the upper-right pane; (3) range A18:C27 in the lower-left pane; and (4) range F18:J27 in the lower-right pane. The vertical split bar is the vertical bar going up and down the middle of the window. The horizontal split bar is the horizontal bar going across the middle of the window. If you use the scrollers below the window and to the right of the window to scroll the window, you will see that the panes split by the horizontal split bar scroll together vertically. The panes split by the vertical split bar scroll together horizontally. To resize the panes, drag either split bar to the desired location in the window.

> **Other Ways**
> 1. Drag horizontal split box and vertical split box to desired locations

To Remove the Panes from the Window

The following step removes the panes from the workbook window.

1 Position the mouse pointer at the intersection of the horizontal and vertical split bars.

2 When the mouse pointer changes to a four-headed arrow, double-click to remove the four panes from the window.

What-If Analysis

The automatic recalculation feature of Excel is a powerful tool that can be used to analyze worksheet data. Using Excel to scrutinize the impact of changing values in cells that are referenced by a formula in another cell is called **what-if analysis** or **sensitivity analysis**. When new data is entered, Excel not only recalculates all formulas in a worksheet but also redraws any associated charts.

In the workbook created in this chapter, many of the formulas are dependent on the assumptions in the range B2:B8. Thus, if you change any of the assumption values, Excel immediately recalculates all formulas. Excel redraws the 3-D Pie chart as well, because it is based on these numbers.

Zooming

BTW

You can use the Zoom box in the Standard toolbar or View > Zoom in the menu bar to zoom from 25% to 200% to reduce or enlarge the display of a worksheet.

To Analyze Data in a Worksheet by Changing Values

A what-if question for the worksheet in Chapter 3 might be *what* would happen to the six-month operating income in cell H25 *if* the Bonus, Commission, Support, General, and Administrative assumptions in the What-If Assumptions table were changed as follows: Bonus $200,000.00 to $150,000.00; Commission 5.75% to 4.00%; Support, General, and Administrative 18.75% to 15.75%? To answer a question like this, you need to change only the first, second, and seventh values in the What-If Assumptions table, as shown in the following steps. The steps also divide the window into two vertical panes. Excel instantaneously recalculates the formulas in the worksheet and redraws the 3-D Pie chart to answer the question.

- Press CONTROL-FN-LEFT ARROW to select cell A1.

- Drag the vertical split box from the lower-right corner of the screen to the left so that the vertical split bar is positioned at the right edge of column C to split the screen vertically as shown in Figure 3–81.

- Drag the horizontal split box from the upper-right corner of the screen down so that the horizontal split bar is positioned under row 11 as shown in Figure 3–81 to split the screen horizontally.

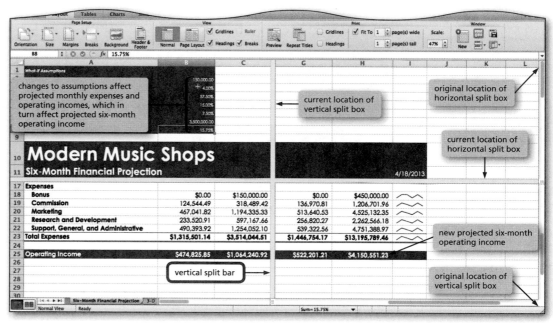

Figure 3–81

- Use the horizontal and vertical scrollers in the lower-right pane to view the total operating income in cell H25 in the lower-right pane.

- Enter **150000** in cell B2, **4%** in cell B3, and **15.75%** in cell B8 (Figure 3–81), which causes the six-month operating income in cell H25 to increase from $2,567,592.65 to $4,150,551.23.

To Goal Seek

If you know the result you want a formula to produce, you can use **goal seeking** to determine the value of a cell on which the formula depends. The following steps close and reopen the Modern Music Shops Six-Month Financial Projection workbook. They then use the Goal Seek command to determine the Support, General, and Administrative percentage in cell B8 that will yield a six-month operating income of $3,000,000.00 in cell H25, rather than the original $2,567,592.65.

1

- Close the workbook without saving the changes and then reopen it.

- Drag the vertical split box from the lower-right corner of the screen to the left so that the vertical split bar is positioned as shown in Figure 3–82 to split the screen vertically.

- Drag the horizontal split box from the upper-right corner of the screen down so that the horizontal split bar is positioned as shown in Figure 3–82 to split the screen horizontally.

- Use the scrollers in the lower-right pane to view the total operating income in column H in the lower-right pane.

- Select cell H25, the cell that contains the six-month operating income. Display the Data tab and then click the What-If button under Analysis to display the What-If menu (Figure 3–82).

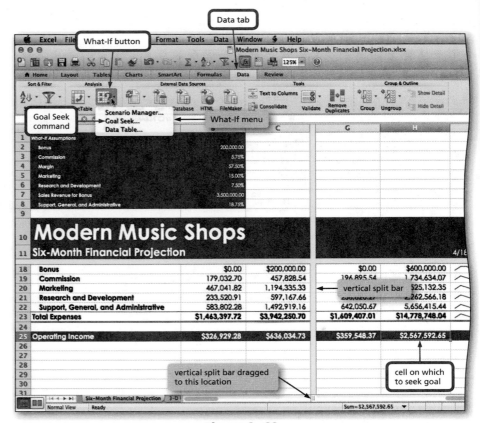

Figure 3–82

2

- Click Goal Seek to display the Goal Seek dialog with the Set cell box set to the selected cell, H25 in this case.

- In the Goal Seek dialog, click the To value text box, type 3,000,000 and then click the 'By changing cell' box to select the box.

- Click cell B8 on the worksheet to assign the current cell, $B$8 in this case, to the 'By changing cell' box (Figure 3–83).

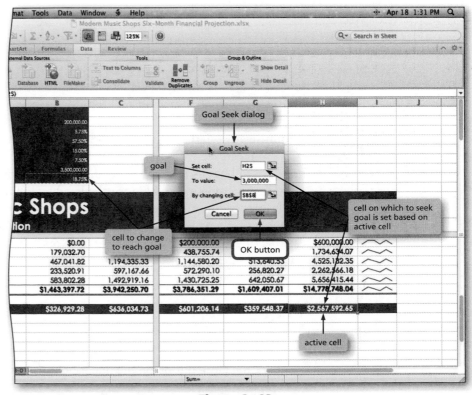

Figure 3–83

3

- Click the OK button (Goal Seek dialog) to goal seek for the sought-after value in the 'To value' box, $3,000,000.00 in cell H25 in this case (Figure 3–84).

Q&A What happens when I click the OK button? Excel immediately changes cell H25 from $2,567,592.65 to the desired value of $3,000,000.00. More importantly, Excel changes the Support, General, and Administrative assumption in cell B8 from 18.75% to 17.32% (Figure 3–84). Excel also displays the Goal Seek Status dialog. If you click the OK button, Excel keeps the new values in the worksheet. If you click the Cancel button, Excel redisplays the original values.

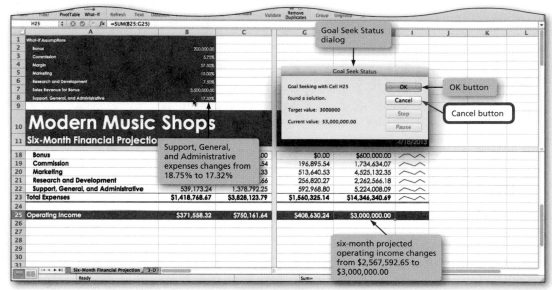

Figure 3–84

4

- Click the Cancel button in the Goal Seek Status dialog to redisplay the original values in the worksheet.

Goal Seeking

Goal seeking assumes you can change the value of only one cell referenced directly or indirectly to reach a specific goal for a value in another cell. In this example, to change the six-month operating income in cell H25 to $3,000,000.00, the Support, General, and Administrative percentage in cell B8 must decrease by 1.43% from 18.75% to 17.32%.

You can see from this goal seeking example that the cell to change (cell B8) does not have to be referenced directly in the formula or function. For example, the six-month operating income in cell H25 is calculated by the function =SUM(B25:G25). Cell B8 is not referenced in this function. Instead, cell B8 is referenced in the formulas in rows 18 through 22, on which the monthly operating incomes in row 25 are based. Excel thus is capable of goal seeking on the six-month operating income by varying the value for the Support, General, and Administrative assumption.

To Quit Excel

With the workbook complete, the following steps quit Excel.

1 Click the Close button on the upper-right corner of the title bar.

2 If the Microsoft Excel dialog is displayed, click the Don't Save button.

Chapter Summary

In this chapter you learned how to work with large worksheets that extend beyond the document window, how to use the fill handle to create a series, about new formatting techniques, about the difference between absolute cell references and relative cell references, how to use the IF function, and how to rotate text in a cell, freeze titles, add Sparkline charts, change the magnification of the worksheet, show different parts of the worksheet at the same time through multiple panes, create a 3-D Pie chart, and improve the appearance of a 3-D Pie chart. This chapter also introduced you to using Excel to do what-if analysis by changing values in cells and goal seeking. The items listed below include all the new Excel skills you have learned in this chapter.

1. Rotate Text and Use the Fill Handle to Create a Series of Month Names (EX 141)
2. Increase Column Widths (EX 144)
3. Enter and Indent Row Titles (EX 145)
4. Copy a Range of Cells to a Nonadjacent Destination Area (EX 146)
5. Insert a Row (EX 150)
6. Enter Numbers with Format Symbols (EX 152)
7. Freeze Column and Row Titles (EX 153)
8. Enter and Format the System Date (EX 155)
9. Enter a Formula Containing Absolute Cell References (EX 158)
10. Enter an IF Function (EX 161)
11. Copy Formulas with Absolute Cell References Using the Fill Handle (EX 163)
12. Unfreeze the Worksheet Titles and Save the Workbook (EX 165)
13. Add a Sparkline Chart to the Worksheet (EX 166)
14. Format and Copy a Sparkline Chart (EX 167)
15. Assign Formats to Nonadjacent Ranges (EX 170)
16. Format the Worksheet Titles (EX 172)
17. Copy a Cell's Format Using the Format Painter (EX 173)
18. Draw a 3-D Pie Chart on a Separate Chart Sheet (EX 177)
19. Insert a Chart Title and Data Labels (EX 178)
20. Rotate a 3-D Pie Chart (EX 181)
21. Apply a 3-D Format to a Pie Chart (EX 182)
22. Explode a 3-D Pie Chart and Change the Color of a Slice (EX 184)
23. Reorder Sheet Tabs (EX 188)
24. Check Spelling in Multiple Sheets (EX 188)
25. Shrink and Magnify the View of a Worksheet or Chart (EX 191)
26. Split a Window into Panes (EX 192)
27. Analyze Data in a Worksheet by Changing Values (EX 194)
28. Goal Seek (EX 194)

 If you have a SAM 2010 user profile, your instructor may have assigned an autogradable version of this assignment. If so, log into the SAM 2010 Web site at www.cengage.com/sam2010 to download the instruction and start files.

Learn It Online

Test your knowledge of chapter content and key terms.

Instructions: To complete the Learn It Online exercises, please visit **www.cengagebrain.com**. At the CengageBrain.com home page, search for *Office 2011 for Mac* using the search box at the top of the page. This will take you to the product page for this book. On the product page, click the Access Now button below the Study Tools heading. On the Book Companion Site Web page, select Excel Chapter 3, and then click the link for the desired exercise.

Chapter Reinforcement TF, MC, and SA
A series of true/false, multiple choice, and short answer questions that test your knowledge of the chapter content.

Flash Cards
An interactive learning environment where you identify chapter key terms associated with displayed definitions.

Practice Test
A series of multiple choice questions that test your knowledge of chapter content and key terms.

Who Wants To Be a Computer Genius?
An interactive game that challenges your knowledge of chapter content in the style of a television quiz show.

Wheel of Terms
An interactive game that challenges your knowledge of chapter key terms in the style of the television show *Wheel of Fortune*.

Crossword Puzzle Challenge
A crossword puzzle that challenges your knowledge of key terms presented in the chapter.

Apply Your Knowledge

Reinforce the skills and apply the concepts you learned in this chapter.

Understanding Logical Tests and Absolute Cell Referencing
Instructions Part 1: Determine the truth value (true or false) of the following logical tests, given the following cell values: B4 = 30; W3 = 100; H5 = 32; L2 = 25; and M8 = 15. Enter true or false.

a. M8 > B4   Truth value: _____

b. W3 = L2   Truth value: _____

c. L2 + 15 * B4 / 10 <> W3   Truth value: _____

d. H5 – L2 < B4 / M8   Truth value: _____

e. (M8 + B4) * 2 <> W3 – (M8 / 3) * 2   Truth value: _____

f. M8 + 300 > B4 * H5 + 10   Truth value: _____

g. H5 * L2 >= 2 * (W3 + 25)   Truth value: _____

h. B4 = 10 * (M8 / 5)   Truth value: _____

Instructions Part 2: Write cell J49 as a relative reference, absolute reference, mixed reference with the column varying, and mixed reference with the row varying.

_____ _____ _____ _____

Instructions Part 3: Start Excel. Open the workbook Apply 3-1 Absolute Cell References. See the inside back cover of this book for instructions for downloading the Data Files for Students, or see your instructor for information on accessing the files required in this book. You will re-create the numerical grid pictured in Figure 3–85.

Perform the following tasks:

1. Enter a formula in cell C7 that multiplies the sum of cells C3 through C6 times cell C2. Write the formula so that when you copy it to cells D7 and E7, Excel adjusts all the cell references according to the destination cells. Verify your formula by checking it with the values found in cells C7, D7, and E7 in Figure 3–85.

2. Enter a formula in cell F3 that multiplies cell B3 times the sum of cells C3 through E3. Write the formula so that when you copy the formula to cells F4, F5, and F6, Excel adjusts all the cell references according to the destination cells. Verify your formula by checking it with the values found in cells F3, F4, F5, and F6 in Figure 3–85.

3. Enter a formula in cell C8 that multiplies the sum of cells C3 through C6 times cell C2. Write the formula so that when you copy the formula to cells D8 and E8, cell C2 remains absolute. Verify your formula by checking it with the values found in cells C8, D8, and E8 in Figure 3–85.

4. Enter a formula in cell G3 that multiplies the sum of cells C3, D3, and E3 times cell B3. Write the formula so that when you copy the formula to cells G4, G5, and G6, cell B3 remains absolute. Verify your formula by checking it with the values found in cells G3, G4, G5, and G6 in Figure 3–85.

5. Apply the worksheet name, Cell References, to the sheet tab and apply the Accent 2 theme color to the sheet tab.

6. Change the document properties, as specified by your instructor. Change the worksheet header with your name, course number, and other information as specified by your instructor. Save the workbook using the file name, Apply 3-1 Absolute Cell References Complete, and submit the workbook as requested by your instructor.

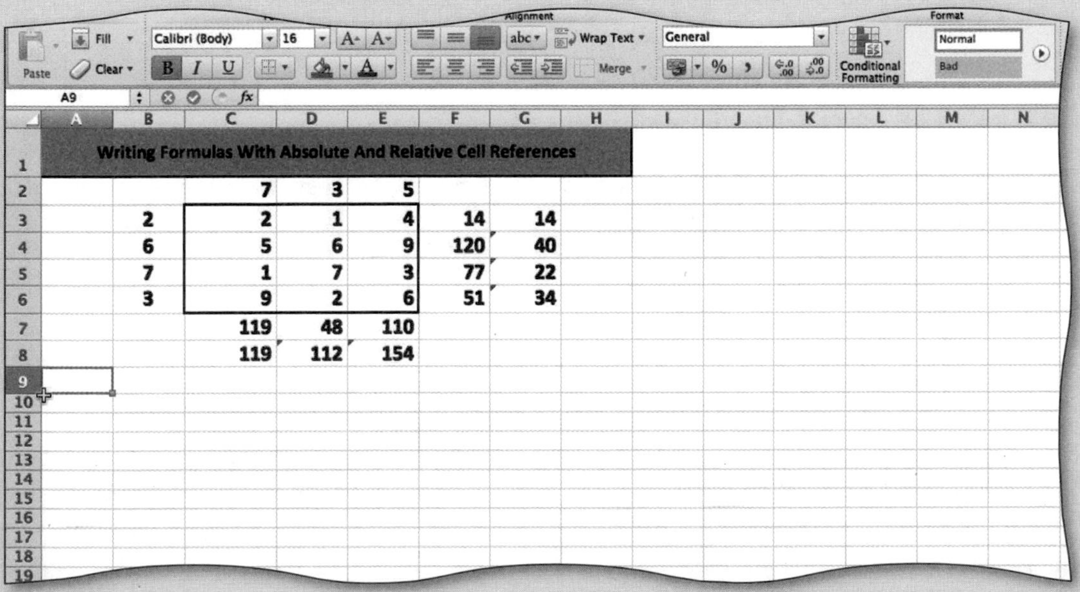

Figure 3–85

Extend Your Knowledge

Extend the skills you learned in this chapter and experiment with new skills. You may need to use Help to complete the assignment.

Nested IF Functions and More About the Fill Handle

Instructions Part 1:   Start Excel and create a new Excel workbook. You will use nested IF functions to determine values for sets of data.

1. Using the Formula Builder, enter the following IF function in cell B1:

    IF(A1="TX", "Central", "Time Zone Error")

    Close the Formula Builder window.

2. Select cell B1, select the text "Time Zone Error" in the formula bar, click the INSERT BUTTON in the Function group on the Formulas tab, choose Logical, then click IF, and enter the following IF function:

    IF(A1="OR", "Pacific", "Time Zone Error")

3. Select cell B1, select "Time Zone Error" in the formula bar, click the INSERT BUTTON in the Function group on the Formulas tab, choose Logical, then click IF, and enter the following IF function:

    IF(A1="VA", "Eastern", "Time Zone Error")

4. Verify that the formula in cell B1 appears as follows:

    =IF(A1="TX","Central", IF(A1="OR","Pacific", IF(A1="VA","Eastern","Time Zone Error")))

5. Use the fill handle to copy the nested IF function down through cell B6. Enter the following data in the cells in the range A1:A6 and then write down the results that display in cells B1 through B6 for each set. Set 1: A1 = TX; A2 = NY; A3 = OR; A4 = MI; A5 = TX; A6 = VA. Set 2: A1= WI; A2 = OR; A3 = IL; A4 = VA; A5 = NJ; A6 = TX.

    Set 1 Results: _____

    Set 2 Results: _____

6. Save the workbook using the file name, Extend 3-1 Create Series Complete Part 1, and submit the workbook as specified by your instructor.

Instructions Part 2:   Start Excel. Open the workbook Extend 3-1 Create Series. See the inside back cover of this book for instructions for downloading the Data Files for Students, or see your instructor for information on accessing the files required in this book.

Perform the following tasks:

1. Use the fill handle on one column at a time to propagate the twelve series through row 14, as shown in Figure 3–86. For example, in column A, select cell A2 and drag the fill handle down to cell A14. In column C, hold down the OPTION key to repeat Saturday through cell C14. In column D, select the range D2:D3 and drag the fill handle down to cell D14. Likewise, in columns G through L, select the two adjacent cells in rows 2 and 3 before dragging the fill handle down to the corresponding cell in row 14.

2. Select cell D19. While holding down the OPTION key, one at a time drag the fill handle three cells to the right, to the left, up, and down to generate four series of numbers beginning with zero and incremented by one.

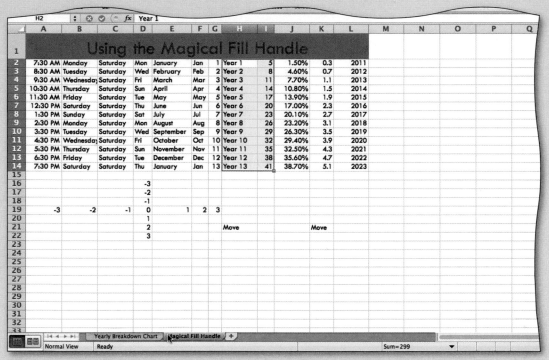

Figure 3–86

3. Select cell H19. Point to the cell border so that the mouse pointer changes to a hand icon with a plus sign. Drag the mouse pointer down to cell H21 to move the contents of cell H19 to cell H21.

4. Select cell H21. Point to the cell border so that the mouse pointer changes to a hand icon with a plus sign. While holding down the OPTION key, drag the mouse pointer to cell K21 to copy the contents of cell H21 to cell K21.

5. Select cell K19. Drag the fill handle in to the center of cell K19 so that the cell is shaded and the cell contents are deleted.

6. Apply a worksheet name to the sheet tab and apply a color of your choice to the sheet tab.

7. Select cell range H2:I14, click the Pie button in the Insert Chart group on the Charts tab to display the Pie pop-up menu, click 3-D Pie in the Pie pop-up menu.

8. CONTROL-click the border of the chart and choose Move Chart in the shortcut menu to open the Move Chart dialog, click the New sheet OPTION button (Move Chart dialog), and then click the OK button (Move Chart dialog) to move the 3-D Pie chart to a new worksheet.

9. Click the Chart Title button in the Labels group on the Chart Layout tab, click Title Above Chart in the Chart Title pop-up menu, select the title, and change the chart title to "Yearly Breakdown".

10. Click the Data Labels button in the Labels group on the Chart Layout tab, click Outside End in the Data Labels pop-up menu to add data points to the chart.

11. Apply a chart sheet name to the sheet tab and apply a color of your choice to the tab.

12. Change the document properties, as specified by your instructor. Change the worksheet header with your name, course number, and other information as specified by your instructor. Save the workbook using the file name, Extend 3-1 Create Series Complete Part 2, and submit the workbook as specified by your instructor.

Make It Right

Analyze a workbook and correct all errors and/or improve the design.

Inserting Rows, Moving a Range, and Correcting Formulas in a Worksheet

Instructions: Start Excel. Open the workbook Make It Right 3-1 SpeedyOfficeSupply.com Annual Projected Net Income. See Sthe inside back cover of this book for instructions for downloading the Data Files for Students, or see your instructor for information on accessing the files required for this book. Correct the following design and formula problems (Figure 3–87a) in the worksheet.

1. The Shipping Cost in cell C8 is computed using the formula =B2*B8 (Shipping % × Sales). Similar formulas are used in cells C9, C10, and C11. The formula in cell C8 was entered and copied to cells C9, C10, and C11. Although the result in cell C8 is correct, the results in cells C9, C10, and C11 are incorrect. Edit the formula in cell C8 by changing cell B2 to an absolute cell reference. Copy the corrected formula in cell C8 to cells C9, C10, and C11. After completing the copy, click the Auto Fill Options button arrow that is displayed below and to the right of cell C11 and choose Fill Without Formatting.

2. The Discount amounts in cells D8, D9, D10, and D11 are computed using the IF function. The Discount amount should equal the amount in cell B3*B8 (Discount % × Sales) if the corresponding Sales in column B is greater than or equal to $2,500,000. If the corresponding Sales in column B is less than $2,500,000, then the Discount amount is 5%*B8 (5% × Sales). The IF function in cell D8 was entered and copied to cells D9, D10, and D11. The current IF functions in cells D8, D9, D10, and D11 are incorrect. Edit and correct the IF function in cell D8. Copy the corrected formula in cell D8 to cells D9, D10, and D11. After completing the copy, click the Auto Fill Options button arrow that is displayed below and to the right of cell D11 and choose Fill Without Formatting.

3. The Processing Costs in cell E8 is computed using the formula =B4*B8 (Proc. Costs % × Sales). The formula in cell E8 was entered and copied to cells E9, E10, and E11. Although the result in cell E8 is correct, the results in cells E9, E10, and E11 are incorrect. Edit and correct the formula in cell E8 by changing cell B4 to an absolute cell reference. Copy the corrected formula in cell E8 to cells E9, E10, and E11. After completing the copy, click the Auto Fill Options button arrow that displays below and to the right of cell E11 and choose Fill Without Formatting. Ensure that the range B9:E11 is formatted with the Accounting Number format.

4. Change the design of the worksheet by moving the Assumptions table in the range A1:B4 to the range A14:B17, as shown in Figure 3–87b. To complete the move, drag the Assumptions table to the range A14:B17. Use Figure 3–87b to verify that Excel automatically adjusted the cell references based on the move. Use the Undo button and Redo button in the Standard toolbar to move the Assumptions table back and forth while the results of the formulas remain the same.

5. Apply a worksheet name to the sheet tab and apply the orange, Accent 3 color to the sheet tab.

6. Change the document properties, as specified by your instructor. Change the worksheet header with your name, course number, and other information as specified by your instructor. Save the workbook using the file name, Make It Right 3-1 SpeedyOfficeSupply.com Annual Projected Net Income Complete, and submit the revised workbook as specified by your instructor.

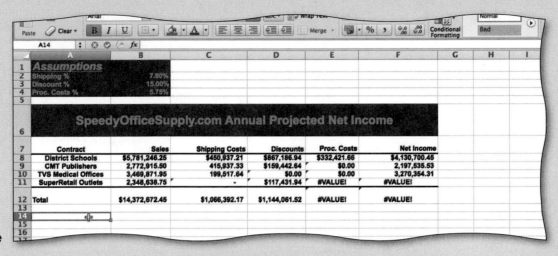

(a) Before

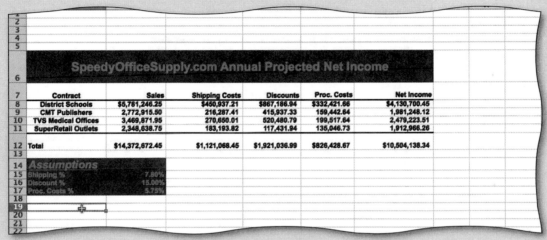

(b) After

Figure 3–87

In the Lab

Create a workbook using the guidelines, concepts, and skills presented in this chapter. Labs are listed in order of increasing difficulty.

Lab 1: Six-Year Financial Projection

Problem: Your supervisor in the Finance department at Med Supply Online Warehouse has asked you to create a worksheet that will project the annual gross margin, expenses, total expenses, operating income, income taxes, and net income for the next six years based on the assumptions in Table 3–9. The desired worksheet is shown in Figure 3–88 on the following page. In Part 1 you will create the worksheet. In Part 2 you will create a chart to present the data, shown in Figure 3–89 on page EX 206. In Part 3 you will use Goal Seek to analyze three different sales scenarios.

Table 3–9 Med Supply Online Warehouse Financial Projection Assumptions	
Units Sold in Prior Year	1,589,712
Unit Cost	$59.50
Annual Sales Growth	4.50%
Annual Price Decrease	3.80%
Margin	38.80%

Continued >

In the Lab *continued*

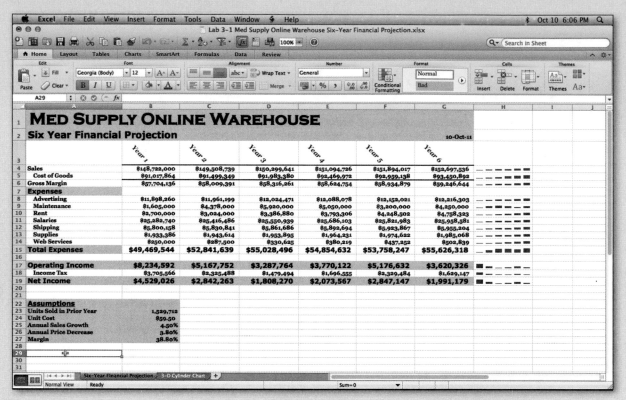

Figure 3–88

Instructions Part 1:

1. Start Excel. Apply the Civic theme to the worksheet by using the Themes button in the Themes group on the Home tab. Bold the entire worksheet by selecting the entire worksheet and using the Bold button in the Font group on the Home tab.

2. Enter the worksheet title Med Supply Online Warehouse in cell A1 and the subtitle Six-Year Financial Projection in cell A2. Format the worksheet title in cell A1 to 36-point Copperplate Gothic Bold (or a similar font). Format the worksheet subtitle in cell A2 to 20-point Verdana (or a similar font). Enter the system date in cell G2 using the NOW function. Format the date to the 14-Mar-01 style.

3. Change the following column widths: A = 25.00 characters; B through H = 15.00 characters. Change the heights of rows 7, 15, 17, 19, and 22 to 18.00 points.

4. Enter the six column titles Year 1 through Year 6 in the range B3:G3 by entering Year 1 in cell B3 and then dragging cell B3's fill handle through the range C3:G3. Format cell B3 as follows: (a) increase the font size to 14; (b) center and italicize it; and (c) angle its contents clockwise. Use the Format Painter button in the Standard toolbar to copy the format assigned to cell B3 to the range C3:G3.

5. Enter the row titles in the range A4:A19. Change the font in cells A7, A15, A17, and A19 to 14-point Verdana (or a similar font). Add thick bottom borders to the ranges B3:G3 and B5:G5. Use the Increase Indent button on the Home tab in the Alignment group to increase the indent of the row titles in cell A5, the range A8:A14, and cell A18.

6. Enter the table title Assumptions in cell A22. Enter the assumptions in Table 3–9 on the previous page in the range A23:B27. Use format symbols when entering the numbers. Change the font size of the table title in cell A22 to 14-point Verdana and underline it.

7. Select the range B4:G19, CONTROL-click the selected cells and choose Format Cells from the shortcut menu to display the Format Cells dialog. Use the Number category (Format Cells dialog) to assign the Comma style with no decimal places and negative numbers enclosed in parentheses to the range B4:G19.

8. Complete the following entries:

a. Year 1 Sales (cell B4) = Units Sold in Prior Year * (Unit Cost / (1 – Margin)) or = B23*(B24/(1–B27))

b. Year 2 Sales (cell C4) = Year 1 Sales * (1 + Annual Sales Growth) * (1 – Annual Price Decrease) or =B4*(1+$B$25)*(1–$B$26)

c. Copy cell C4 to the range D4:G4.

d. Year 1 Cost of Goods (cell B5) = Year 1 Sales * (1 – Margin) or =B4 * (1 – $B$27)

e. Copy cell B5 to the range C5:G5.

f. Gross Margin (cell B6) = Year 1 Sales – Year 1 Cost of Goods or =B4 – B5

g. Copy cell B6 to the range C6:G6.

h. Year 1 Advertising (cell B8) = 500 + 8% * Year 1 Sales or =500+8%*B4

i. Copy cell B8 to the range C8:G8.

j. Maintenance (row 9): Year 1 = 1,605,000; Year 2 = 4,378,000; Year 3 = 5,920,000; Year 4 = 5,050,000; Year 5 = 3,200,000; Year 6 = 4,250,000

k. Year 1 Rent (cell B10) = 2,700,000

l. Year 2 Rent (cell C10) = Year 1 Rent + (12% * Year 1 Rent) or =B10+(12%*B10)

m. Copy cell C10 to the range D10:G10.

n. Year 1 Salaries (cell B11) = 17% * Year 1 Sales or =17%*B4

o. Copy cell B11 to the range C11:G11.

p. Year 1 Shipping (cell B12) = 3.9% * Year 1 Sales or =3.9%*B4

q. Copy cell B12 to the range C12:G12.

r. Year 1 Supplies (cell B13) = 1.3% * Year 1 Sales or =1.3%*B4

s. Copy cell B13 to the range C13:G13.

t. Year 1 Web Services (cell B14) = 250,000

u. Year 2 Web Services (cell C14) = Year 1 Web Services + (15% * Year 1 Web Services) or =B14+(15%*B4)

v. Copy cell C14 to the range D14:G14.

w. Year 1 Total Expenses (cell B15) = SUM(B8:B14)

x. Copy cell B15 to the range C15:G15.

y. Year 1 Operating Income (cell B17) = Year 1 Gross Margin – Year 1 Total Expenses or =B6–B15

z. Copy cell B17 to the range C17:G17.

aa. Year 1 Income Taxes (cell B18): If Year 1 Operating Income is less than 0, then Year 1 Income Taxes equal 0; otherwise Year 1 Income Taxes equal 45% * Year 1 Operating Income or =IF(B17 < 0, 0, 45%*B17)

bb. Copy cell B18 to the range C18:G18.

cc. Year 1 Net Income (cell B19) = Year 1 Operating Income – Year 1 Income Taxes or = B17–B18

dd. Copy cell B19 to the range C19:G19.

Continued >

In the Lab *continued*

   ee. In cell H4, insert a Sparkline Column chart using the Column button in the Insert Sparklines group on the Charts tab for cell range B4:G4.

   ff. Repeat step ee for the ranges H5:H6, H8:H15, and H17:H19.

9. Change the background colors as shown in Figure 3–88 on page EX 204. Use Accent 3, Lighter 40% for the background colors.

10. Zoom to: (a) 200%; (b) 75%; (c) 25%; and (d) 100%.

11. Change the document properties, as specified by your instructor. Change the worksheet header with your name, course number, and other information as specified by your instructor. Save the workbook using the file name, Lab 3-1 Med Supply Online Warehouse Six-Year Financial Projection.

12. Preview the worksheet. Use the Orientation button on the Layout tab in the Page Setup group to fit the printout on one page in landscape orientation. Preview the formulas version (CONTROL + `) of the worksheet in landscape orientation using the Fit to option. Press CONTROL + ` to instruct Excel to display the values version of the worksheet. Save the workbook again and close the workbook.

13. Submit the workbook as specified by your instructor.

Instructions Part 2:

1. Start Excel. Open the workbook Lab 3-1 Med Supply Online Warehouse Six-Year Financial Projection.

2. Use the nonadjacent ranges B3:G3 and B19:G19 to create a 3-D Cylinder chart. Click the Column button on the Charts tab in the Insert Chart Type group, and choose Clustered Cylinder (row 3, column 1) from the pop-up menu. When the chart is displayed, CONTROL-click the chart border, choose Move Chart from the shortcut menu to open the Move Chart dialog. Click the New Sheet button and click OK to move the chart to a new sheet.

3. Select the legend on the right side of the chart and delete it. Add the chart title by clicking the Chart Title button in the Labels group on the Chart Format tab. Click Line Above Chart in the Chart Title pop-up menu. Format the chart title as shown in Figure 3–89.

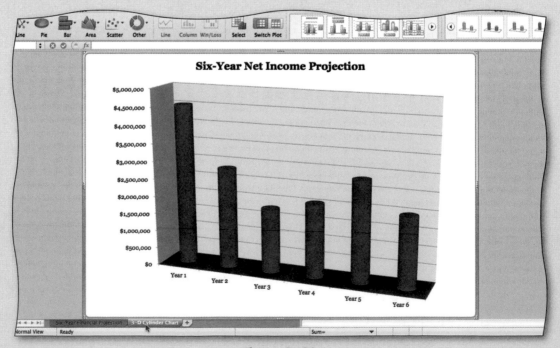

Figure 3–89

4. To change the color of the cylinders, click one of the cylinders and use the Fill button in the Chart Element Styles group on the Format tab to change the fill color to Accent 1, Darker 25%. To change the color of the wall, click the wall behind the cylinders and use the Fill button to change the chart wall color to Background 1, Darker 15%. Use the same procedure to change the color of the base of the wall to Background 2, Darker 90%.

5. Rename the sheet tabs Six-Year Financial Projection and 3-D Cylinder Chart. Rearrange the sheets so that the worksheet is leftmost and color their tabs as shown in Figure 3–89.

6. Click the Six-Year Financial Projection tab to display the worksheet. Save the workbook using the same file name (Lab 3-1 Med Supply Online Warehouse Six -Year Financial Projection) as defined in Part 1. Submit the workbook as requested by your instructor.

Instructions Part 3:

1. Start Excel. Open the workbook Lab 3-1 Med Supply Online Warehouse Six-Year Financial Projection. Do not save the workbook in this part of the In the Lab exercise. Divide the window into two panes by dragging the horizontal split box between rows 6 and 7. Use the scroll bars to show both the top and bottom of the worksheet. Using the numbers in columns 2 and 3 of Table 3–10, analyze the effect of changing the annual sales growth (cell B25) and annual price decrease (cell B26) on the net incomes in row 19. The resulting answers are in column 4 of Table 3–10. Submit the workbook or results of the what-if analysis for each case as requested by your instructor.

Table 3–10 Med Supply Online Warehouse Data to Analyze and Results			
Case	Annual Sales Growth	Annual Price Decrease	Year 6 Resulting Net Income in Cell G19
1	8.45%	5.75%	2,617,163
2	14.75%	23.00%	(2,623,699)
3	25.50%	2.65%	14,917,086

2. Close the workbook without saving it, and then reopen it. Use the What-If button in the Analysis group on the Data tab to goal seek. Determine a margin (cell B27) that would result in a Year 6 net income of $4,000,000 (cell G19). You should end up with a margin of 40.83% in cell B27. Submit the workbook with the new values or the results of the goal seek as requested by your instructor. Do not save the workbook with the latest changes.

In the Lab

Lab 2: Analysis of Indirect Expense Allocations

Problem: Your classmate works part time as an advisor for the ReachOut Neighbors not-for-profit group. She has asked you to assist her in creating an indirect expense allocation worksheet (Figure 3–90 on the next page) that will help the not-for-profit administration better evaluate the branch offices described in Table 3–11.

Table 3–11 ReachOut Neighbor Worksheet Data							
	Chicago Branch Office	Dallas Branch Office	Houston Branch Office	Jacksonville Branch Office	Los Angeles Branch Office	New York Branch Office	Reno Branch Office
Total Donations	735356	98190	178435	212300	175350	752900	1845230
Distributed Goods and Services	529750	60891	135589	150895	96050	589590	1629350
Direct Expenses	57550	22530	14750	25300	42670	58600	65000
Square Footage	15500	775	7550	8250	950	6275	8600

Continued >

In the Lab *continued*

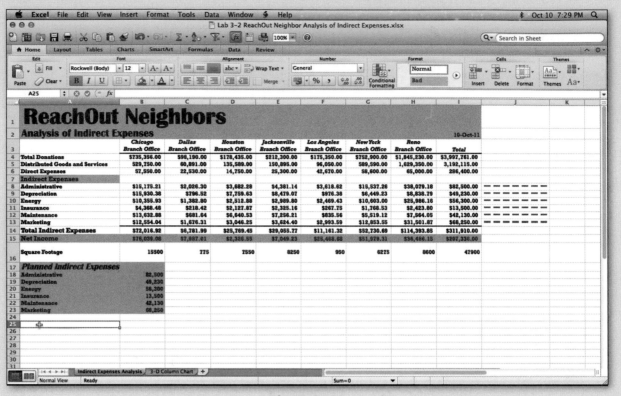

Figure 3–90

Instructions Part 1:   Do the following to create the worksheet shown in Figure 3–90.

1. Apply the Foundry theme to the worksheet. Bold the entire worksheet by selecting the entire worksheet and using the Bold button on the Home tab in the Font group.

2. Change the following column widths: A = 30.00; B through I = 13.00; J = 20.00.

3. Enter the worksheet titles in cells A1 and A2 and the system date in cell I2. Format the date to the 14-Mar-01 style.

4. Enter the column titles, row titles, and the first three rows of numbers in Table 3–11 on the previous page in rows 3 through 6. Add the column heading Total to cell I3. Center and italicize the column headings in the range B3:I3. Add a thick bottom border to the range B3:I3. Sum the individual rows 4, 5, and 6 in the range I4:I6.

5. Enter the Square Footage row as shown in Table 3–11 with the comma format symbol in row 16. Sum row 16 in cell I16. Use the Format Painter button in the Standard toolbar to format cell I16. Change the height of row 16 to 42.00. Vertically center the range A16:I16 through the use of the Format Cells dialog.

6. Enter the remaining row titles in the range A7:A17 as shown in Figure 3–90. Increase the font size in cells A7, A14, and A15 to 14 point.

7. Copy the row titles in range A8:A13 to the range A18:A23. Enter the numbers shown in the range B18:B23 of Figure 3–90 with format symbols.

8. The planned indirect expenses in the range B18:B23 are to be prorated across the branch office as follows: Administrative (row 8), Energy (row 10), and Marketing (row 13) on the basis of Total Donations (row 4); Depreciation (row 9), Insurance (row 11), and Maintenance (row 12) on the basis of Square Footage (row 16). Use the following formulas to accomplish the prorating:

   a. Chicago Branch Office Administrative (cell B8) = Administrative Expenses * Chicago Branch Office Total Donations / ReachOut Neighbors Total Donations or =$B$18*B4/$I$4

b. Chicago Branch Office Depreciation (cell B9) = Depreciation Expenses * Chicago Branch Office Square Footage / Total Square Footage or =$B$19*B16/$I$16

c. Chicago Branch Office Energy (cell B10) = Energy Expenses * Chicago Branch Office Total Donations / ReachOut Neighbor Total Donations or =$B$20*B4/$I$4

d. Chicago Branch Office Insurance (cell B11) = Insurance Expenses * Chicago Branch Office Square Footage / Total Square Footage or =$B$21*B16 /$I$16

e. Chicago Branch Office Maintenance (cell B12) = Maintenance Expenses * Chicago Branch Office Square Footage / Total Square Footage or =$B$22*B16/$I$16

f. Chicago Branch Office Marketing (cell B13) = Marketing Expenses * Chicago Branch Office Total Donations / ReachOut Neighbor Total Donations or =$B$23*B4/$I$4

g. Chicago Branch Office Total Indirect Expenses (cell B14) = SUM(B8:B13)

h. Chicago Branch Office Net Income (cell B15) = Total Donations – (Distributed Goods and Services + Direct Expenses + Total Indirect Expenses) or =B4-(B5+B6+B14)

i. Copy the range B8:B15 to the range C8:H15.

j. Sum the individual rows 8 through 15 in the range I8:I15.

9. Add a thick bottom border to the range B13:I13. Assign the Currency style with two decimal places and show negative numbers in parentheses to the following ranges: B4:I4; B8:I8; and B14:I15. Assign the Comma style with two decimal places and show negative numbers in parentheses to the following ranges: B5:I6 and B9:I13.

10. Change the font in cell A1 to 48-point Britannic Bold (or a similar font). Change the font in cell A2 to 22-point Britannic Bold (or a similar font). Change the font in cell A17 to 18-point italic Britannic Bold.

11. Use the background color Accent 1, Lighter 40% and the font color Background 2, Darker 75% for cell A7 and the ranges A1:I2; A15:I15; and A17:B23 as shown in Figure 3–90.

12. Insert a Sparkline Win/Loss chart for the range B8:H8 in cell J8. Copy the cell J8 to the cell range J9:J13.

13. Rename the Sheet1 sheet as Indirect Expenses Analysis and color its tab Accent 1.

14. Update the document properties with your name, course number, and name for the workbook. Change the worksheet header with your name, course number, and other information as specified by your instructor. Save the workbook using the file name, Lab 3-2 ReachOut Neighbor Analysis of Indirect Expenses.

15. Preview the worksheet. Use the Orientation button in the Page Setup group on the Layout tab to fit the printout on one page in landscape orientation using the Fit to option. Preview the formulas version (CONTROL + `) of the worksheet in landscape orientation using the Fit to option. Press CONTROL + ` to instruct Excel to display the values version of the worksheet. Save the workbook again and close the workbook.

16. Divide the window into four panes and show the four corners of the worksheet. Remove the four panes. Close the workbook but do not save the workbook.

Instructions Part 2:   Start Excel. Open Lab 3-2 ReachOut Neighbor Analysis of Indirect Expenses. Draw a 3-D Column Chart (Figure 3–91 on the next page) on a separate sheet that shows the contribution of each category of indirect expense to the total indirect expenses. That is, chart the nonadjacent ranges A8:A13 (category names) and I8:I13 (data series). Show labels that include value of the column. Do not show the legend. Format the 3-D Column Chart as shown in Figure 3–91. You will need to open the Format Chart Area dialog by clicking the 3-D Rotation button on the chart Layout tab, and the select Right Angle Axes and deselect Autoscale in the Chart Scale area to square the chart on the sheet. Rename the chart sheet 3-D Column Chart and set the sheet tab color to Accent 6, Darker 10%. Move the chart tab to the right of the worksheet tab. Save the workbook using the file name, Lab 3-2 ReachOut Neighbor Analysis of Indirect Expenses. Submit the workbook as specified by your instructor.

Continued >

In the Lab *continued*

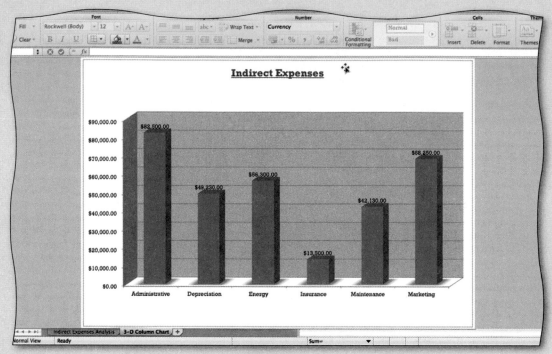

Figure 3–91

Instructions Part 3: Start Excel. Open Lab 3-2 ReachOut Neighbor Analysis of Indirect Expenses.

1. Using the numbers in Table 3–12, analyze the effect of changing the planned indirect expenses in the range B18:B23 on the net incomes for each branch office. You should end with the following totals in cell I15: Case 1 = $5,846.00 and Case 2 = $124,346.00. Submit the workbook or results for each case as requested by your instructor.

2. Use the What-If button on the Data tab in the Analysis group to goal seek. Determine a planned indirect Marketing expense (cell B23) that would result in a total net income of $50,000 (cell I15). You should end up with a planned indirect Marketing expense of $225,586 in cell B23. Submit the workbook with the new values or the results of the goal seek as specified by your instructor.

Table 3–12 ReachOut Neighbor Indirect Expense Allocations What-If Data		
	Case 1	Case 2
Administrative	124000	66500
Depreciation	156575	75000
Energy	72525	56000
Insurance	46300	67000
Maintenance	75000	48000
Marketing	39000	82400

In the Lab

Lab 3: Modifying a Weekly Inventory Worksheet

Problem: As a summer intern at Dinah's Candle Depot, you have been asked to modify the weekly inventory report shown in Figure 3–92a. The workbook, Lab 3-3 Dinah's Weekly Inventory Report, is included with the Data Files for Students. See the inside back cover of this book for instructions for downloading the Data Files for Students, or see your instructor for information on accessing the files required for this book.

The major modifications to the payroll report to be made in this exercise include: (1) reformatting the worksheet; (2) adding computations of quantity to order based on reorder level and weeks to arrive; (3) adding calculations to suggest changes in ordering; (4) adding current and last month sales for inventory items; (5) adding and deleting inventory items; and (6) changing inventory item information. The final inventory report is shown in Figure 3–92b.

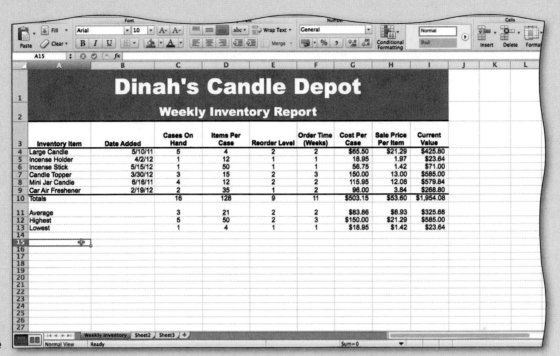

(a) Before

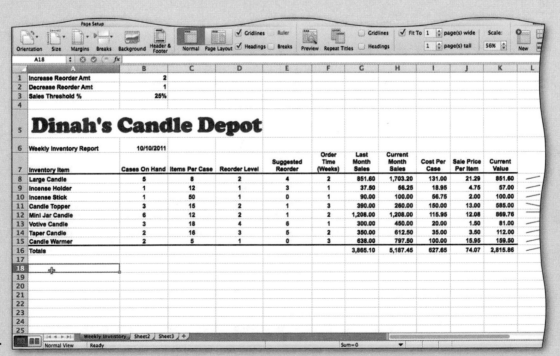

(b) After

Figure 3–92

Continued >

In the Lab *continued*

Instructions Part 1:

1. Start Excel. Open the workbook, Lab 3-3 Dinah's Weekly Inventory Report and then save the workbook using the file name Lab 3-3 Dinah's Weekly Inventory Report Complete.

2. Select the worksheet by clicking the Select All button. Click the Clear button on the Home tab in the Edit group and then click Formats in the Clear menu to clear the formatting. Bold the entire worksheet.

3. Delete rows 11 through 13 to remove the statistics below the Totals row. Change all the row heights back to the default height (15.00).

4. Insert four rows above row 1 by selecting rows 1 through 4, CONTROL-clicking the selection, and clicking Insert in the shortcut menu.

5. Change the row heights as follows: row 5 = 48.00; row 6 = 26.00; and 7 = 38.00. For the range B7:I7, change the format so that the text wraps. Center the range B7:I7.

6. Delete column B by CONTROL-clicking the column heading and clicking DELETE in the shortcut menu.

7. Insert a new column between columns D and E. Change the column widths as follows: A = 25.00; E = 13.00; and F through I = 8.67. Enter the new column E title Suggested Reorder in cell E7.

8. Insert two new columns between columns F and G. Enter the new column G title Last Month Sales in cell G7. Enter the new column H title Current Month Sales in cell H7.

9. Enhance the worksheet title in cell A5 by using a 36-point purple Cooper Black (or a similar font) font style as shown in Figure 3–92b on the previous page.

10. Assign the NOW function to cell B6 and format it to the 3/14/2001 style.

11. Delete item Car Air Freshener (row 13). Change Mini Jar Candle's (row 12) cases on hand to 6. Change Large Candle's (row 8) items per case to 8 and cost per case to $131.00. Change Incense Stick's (row 10) sale price per item to $2.00 and Incense Holder's (row 9) sale price per item to $4.75.

12. Freeze column A and rows 1 through 7 by selecting cell B8, clicking the Freeze Panes button in the Window group on the Layout tab and then clicking Freeze Panes in the Freeze Panes pop-up menu.

13. In columns G and H, enter the current month and last month sales values listed in Table 3–13.

14. Insert three new rows immediately above the Totals row. Add the new items data as listed in Table 3–14.

Table 3–13 Dinah's Candle Depot Monthly Sales Values		
Inventory Item	**Last Month Sales**	**Current Month Sales**
Large Candle	851.6	1703.2
Incense Holder	37.5	56.25
Incense Stick	90	100
Candle Topper	390	260
Mini Jar Candle	1208	1208

Table 3–14 Dinah's Candle Depot New Items

Inventory Item	Cases On Hand	Items Per Case	Reorder Level	Order Time (Weeks)	Last Month Sales	Current Month Sales	Cost Per Case	Sale Price Per Item
Votive Candle	3	18	4	1	300	450	20	1.5
Taper Candle	2	16	3	2	350	612.5	35	3.5
Candle Warmer	2	5	1	3	638	797.5	100	15.95

15. Center the range B8:F15. Use the Currency category in the Format Cells dialog to assign a Comma style (no dollar signs) with two decimal places and negative numbers within parentheses to the range G8:K16. Draw a thick bottom border in the ranges A7:K7 and A15:K15.

16. As shown in Figure 3–92b on page EX 211, enter and format the Increase Reorder Amt (2), the Decrease Reorder Amt (1), and the Sales Threshold % (25%) information in the range A1:B3. Use format symbols where applicable.

17. Remove any Totals in the range B16:F16. Update and add totals as necessary so that totals appear in the range G16:K16.

18. In cell E8, enter an IF function that applies the following logic and then copy it to the range E9:E15. If (Current Month Sales – Last Month Sales) / Current Month Sales >= Sales Threshold %, then Reorder Level + Increase Reorder Amt, otherwise Reorder Level – Decrease Reorder Amt or =IF((H8-G8)/H8 >= $B$3, D8+$B$1,D8-$B$2).

19. In cell L8, insert a Sparkline Line chart for range G8:H8. Copy cell L8 to the range L9:L16.

20. Unfreeze the worksheet by clicking the Freeze Panes button on the Layout tab in the Window group and then clicking Unfreeze Panes in the Freeze Panes pop-up menu.

21. Preview the worksheet. Use the Orientation button on the Layout tab in the Page Setup group to fit the printout on one page in landscape orientation.

22. Change the document properties, as specified by your instructor. Change the worksheet header, adding your name, course number, and other information as specified by your instructor. Save the workbook.

23. Use the Zoom button in the Standard toolbar to change the view of the worksheet. One by one, select all the percents in the Zoom pop-up menu. When you are done, return the worksheet to 100% magnification.

24. Preview the formulas version (CONTROL + `) in landscape orientation. Close the worksheet without saving the latest changes.

25. Submit the workbook as specified by your instructor.

Instructions Part 2: Start Excel. Open Lab 3-3 Dinah's Weekly Inventory Report Complete. Do not save the workbook in this part. Using the numbers in Table 3–15, analyze the effect of changing the Sales Threshold in cell B3. The first case should result in a Suggested Reorder in cell E15 of 0. The second case should result in a Suggested Reorder in cell E15 of 3. Close the workbook without saving changes. Submit the results of the what-if analysis as specified by your instructor.

Table 3–15 The Dinah's Candle Depot's Sales Threshold Cases	
Case	Sales Threshold
1	30%
2	15%

Continued >

In the Lab *continued*

Instructions Part 3:   Submit results for this part as requested by your instructor.

1. Start Excel. Open Lab 3-3 Dinah's Weekly Inventory Report Complete. Select cell E8. Write down the formula that Excel displays in the formula bar. Select the range D8:D15. Point to the border surrounding the range and drag the selection to the range E17:E24. Click cell E8, and write down the formula that Excel displays in the formula bar below the one you wrote down earlier. Compare the two formulas. What can you conclude about how Excel responds when you move cells involved in a formula? Click the Undo button on the Quick Access Toolbar.

2. CONTROL-click the range D8:D15 and then click Delete in the shortcut menu. When Excel displays the Delete dialog, click Shift cells left and then click the OK button. What does Excel display in cell D8? Click cell D8 and then point to the Trace Error button that is displayed to the left of the cell. Write down the ScreenTip that is displayed. Click the Undo button on the Quick Access Toolbar.

3. CONTROL-click the range D8:D15 and then click Insert in the shortcut menu. When Excel displays the Insert dialog, click 'Shift cells right' and then click the OK button. What does Excel display in the formula bar when you click cell F8? What can you conclude about how Excel responds when you insert cells next to cells involved in a formula? Close the workbook without saving the changes.

Cases and Places

Apply your creative thinking and problem solving skills to design and implement a solution.

1: Bachelor Degree Expense and Resource Projection

Academic

Attending college with limited resources can be a trying experience. One way to alleviate some of the financial stress is to plan ahead. Develop a worksheet following the general layout in Table 3–16 that shows the projected expenses and resources for four years of college. Use the formulas listed in Table 3–17 and the concepts and techniques presented in this chapter to create the worksheet.

Table 3–16 Bachelor Degree Expense and Resource Projection					
Expenses	**Freshman**	**Sophomore**	**Junior**	**Senior**	**Total**
Room & Board	$12,550.00	Formula A			—
Tuition & Books	16,450.00	Formula A			—
Clothes	785.00	Formula A			—
Entertainment	1,520.00	Formula A			—
Miscellaneous	936.00	Formula A			—
Total Expenses	—	—	—	—	—
Resources	**Freshman**	**Sophomore**	**Junior**	**Senior**	**Total**
Savings	Formula B				
Parents	Formula B				—
Job	Formula B				—
Loans	Formula B				—
Scholarships	Formula B				—
Total Resources	—	—	—	—	—

Table 3–16 Bachelor Degree Expense and Resource Projection (continued)

Assumptions

Savings	10.00%
Parents	12.00%
Job	11.00%
Loans	35.00%
Scholarships	32.00%
Annual Rate Increase	8.25%

Table 3–17 Bachelor Degree Expense and Resource Projection Formulas

Formula A = Prior Year's Expense * (1 + Annual Rate Increase)

Formula B = Total Expenses for Year * Corresponding Assumption

After creating the worksheet: (a) perform what-if analysis by changing the percents of the resource assumptions; (b) perform a what-if analysis to determine the effect on the resources by increasing the Annual Rate Increase to 9.95% (answer = $149,520.41); and (c) with the original assumptions, goal seek to determine what the Annual Rate Increase would be for the total expenses to be $175,000 (answer = 20.77%). Submit the workbook and results of the what-if analysis as specified by your instructor.

2: Fuel Cost Analysis

Personal

You are thinking about buying a new vehicle, and you want to make sure that you get the most fuel savings you can find. You know that there are hybrid vehicles available and so you decide to research them as well as gas-only cars. Your friends also are interested in the results. Together, you decide to research the fuel costs associated with various types of vehicles. Research the gas mileage for six vehicles: three should run only on gas, and the others should be hybrid vehicles, combining gas and battery power. After you find the gas mileage for each vehicle, you will use formulas to calculate the fuel cost for 1 month, 1 year, and three years. Assume that in a typical month, you will drive 400 miles and that the average price of gas is $2.69 per gallon. Develop a worksheet following the general layout in Table 3–18 that shows the fuel cost analysis. Use the formulas listed in Table 3–19 on the next page and the concepts and techniques presented in this chapter to create the worksheet. Add a 3-D line chart showing the cost comparisons as an embedded chart.

Table 3–18 Fuel Cost Analysis

Vehicle	Miles Per Gallon	1 Month	1 Year	3 Year
Ford Expedition	17	Formula A	Formula B	Formula C
Dodge RAM 1500	20	—	—	—
Honda Civic	31	—	—	—
Chevy Silverado Hybrid	21	—	—	—
Ford Fusion Hybrid	41	—	—	—
Honda Civic Hybrid	45	—	—	—
Assumptions				
Distance per Month	400			
Price of Gas	$2.69			

Continued >

Cases and Places *continued*

Table 3–19 Fuel Cost Analysis Formulas
Formula A = (Distance per Month / Miles per Gallon)*Price of Gas
Formula B = ((Distance per Month / Miles per Gallon)*Price of Gas)*12
Formula C = ((Distance Per Month / Miles per Gallon)*Price of Gas)*36

3: Quarterly Income Projections

Professional

Notable Web Site Design is one of the largest Web site design and Web site hosting companies in the Midwest. The company generates revenue from Web site design and selling Web site hosting space on their Web servers. A fixed percentage of the total net revenue is spent on administrative, equipment, marketing, payroll, and production expenses. A bonus is expensed if the total net revenue for the quarter exceeds $14,000,000. The company's projected receipts and expenditures for the next four quarters are shown in Table 3–20.

With this data, you have been asked to prepare a worksheet similar to Figure 3–88 on page EX 204 for the next management team meeting. The worksheet should show total net revenues, total expenditures, and operating income for each quarterly period. Include a 3-D Pie chart on a separate sheet that shows the quarterly income contributions to the annual operating income. Use the concepts and techniques presented in this chapter to create and format the worksheet and chart.

During the meeting, one manager lobbied to reduce marketing expenditures by 1.25% and payroll costs by 2.75%. Perform a what-if analysis reflecting the proposed changes in expenditures. The changes should result in an operating income of $22,425,581 for the year. Using the original assumptions shown in Table 3–20, another manager asked to what extent marketing would have to be reduced to generate an annual operating income of $21,000,000. Marketing would have to be reduced by 1.92% from 13.50% to 11.58%.

Submit the workbook and results of the what-if analysis as specified by your instructor.

Table 3–20 Notable Website Design Operating Income Projection by Quarter				
Revenues	**Quarter 1**	**Quarter 2**	**Quarter 3**	**Quarter 4**
Site Design	12,247,999	15,234,813	16,567,102	10,619,201
Web Hosting	1,678,153	5,901,988	4,718,231	1,569,378
Expenditures				
Administrative	10.50%			
Bonus	250,000.00			
Equipment	17.75%			
Marketing	13.50%			
Payroll	22.50%			
Production	6.30%			
Revenue for Bonus	14,000,000.00			

1 Managing E-Mail Messages with Outlook

Objectives

You will have mastered the material in this chapter when you can:

Start and quit Outlook

Compose, address, and send an e-mail message

Open, read, print, and close an e-mail message

Reply to an e-mail message

Forward an e-mail message

Delete an e-mail message

Check spelling as you type an e-mail message

Save an e-mail message in the Drafts folder

Retrieve a saved e-mail message

Attach a file to an outgoing e-mail message

Copy another person when sending an e-mail message

Preview and save a file attachment

Create an e-mail folder

Move and copy received e-mail messages to a folder

1 Managing E-Mail Messages with Outlook

Introduction

E-mail (short for **electronic mail**) is the transmission of messages and files over a computer network. Today, e-mail is a communication method for both personal and business use. An **e-mail program**, such as Microsoft Outlook for Mac 2011, is software in the user's computer that can access the mail servers in a local or remote network. Outlook is used to compose, send, receive, store, print, and delete e-mail messages. Finally, you can organize messages so that you easily can find and respond to them later.

To use Outlook, you must have an e-mail account. An **e-mail account** is an account used to connect to an e-mail service via an Internet service provider. An **Internet service provider (ISP)** delivers Internet access to a geographic location, either regionally or nationally. An e-mail account could be set up by your employer or school, or through a Web application such as Google's Gmail, Yahoo! Mail, or Windows Live Hotmail. Outlook does not create or issue e-mail accounts; it merely provides you with access to them. You may be able to establish e-mail service through your cable or telephone company.

In Outlook, an e-mail account is contained in an e-mail profile. An **e-mail profile** includes the e-mail account(s), data files, and settings that contain information about where a user's e-mail is stored. A **personal folders file (.pst or .olm file)** is a data file that stores a user's Outlook items, including e-mail messages, on your computer. A data file is created automatically when you set up an e-mail profile in Outlook, called an Outlook profile. If you are using Outlook on a home computer and starting it for the first time, the Welcome to Outlook:mac 2011 screen opens. From this screen you can add an e-mail account or import an existing account. Outlook can automatically configure most account settings for the e-mail account you want to use. (The process is discussed later in this chapter.) If you are using Outlook on a classroom computer, your instructor will provide the necessary information on how to begin using Outlook.

> ### Project Planning Guidelines
>
> The process of composing an e-mail message that communicates specific information requires some analysis and planning. As a starting point, establish why the e-mail message is needed. Once the purpose is determined, analyze the intended readers of the e-mail message and their unique needs. Then, gather information about the topic and decide what to include in the e-mail message. Details of these guidelines are provided in Appendix A. In addition, each project in this book provides practical applications of these planning considerations.

Project — Composing and Sending E-Mail Messages

The project in this chapter follows the general guidelines for using Outlook to compose, open, and reply to e-mail messages, as shown in Figure 1–1. To communicate with individuals and groups, you typically send or receive some kind of message. Phone calls, faxes, letters, e-mail, and text messages are examples of ways to communicate a message. E-mail is a convenient way to send information to multiple people simultaneously, instantly, and inexpensively.

As a student assistant to the director of the Business and Computer Division at Condor Harbor Community College (CHCC), you use Outlook to communicate with faculty, staff, and fellow classmates. This chapter uses the communications features of Microsoft Outlook for Mac 2011 to compose, send, read, reply to, and forward e-mail messages regarding an upcoming New Student Orientation program. Your responsibilities include collecting information from instructors who are participating in the orientation program, coordinating the resources needed, and scheduling student volunteers to work at the orientation program. Using Outlook, you open e-mail messages from instructors and students regarding these activities. You reply to e-mail messages and include a document containing the schedule that the recipient, or receiver of the e-mail message, can open. To organize messages, you create folders in which to store them.

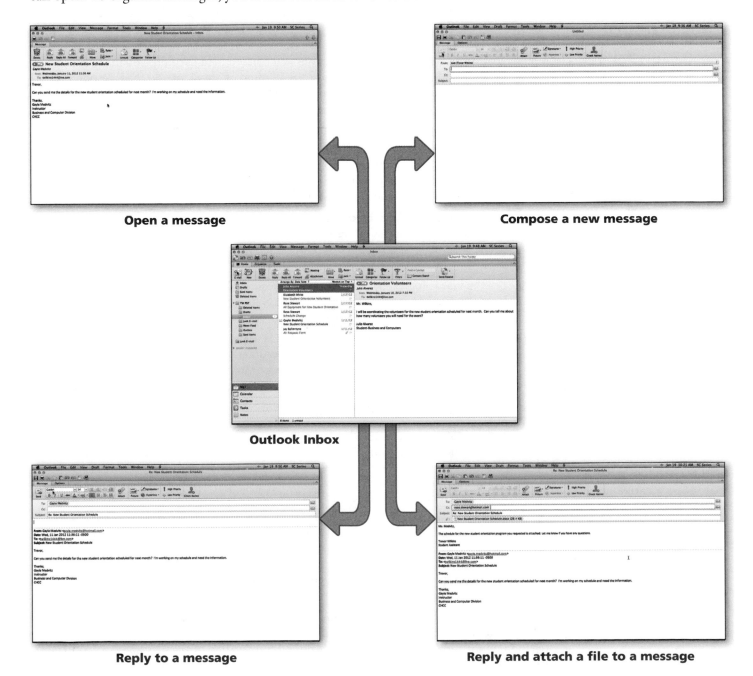

Open a message

Compose a new message

Outlook Inbox

Reply to a message

Reply and attach a file to a message

Figure 1–1

Overview

As you read this chapter, you will learn how to communicate using e-mail by performing these general tasks:

- Compose and send an e-mail message.
- Open, read, and print an e-mail message.
- Reply to an e-mail message.
- Forward an e-mail message.
- Save an e-mail message.
- Attach a file to an e-mail message.
- Send an e-mail message to multiple recipients.
- Organize e-mail messages in folders.

Plan Ahead

General Project Guidelines

When creating an e-mail message, the actions you perform and decisions you make will affect the appearance and characteristics of the finished message. As you read, respond to, and create e-mail messages, such as those shown in Figure 1–1 on the previous page, you should follow these general guidelines:

1. **Determine the best method for reading e-mail messages you receive.** Although e-mail messages are sent electronically, you can read them on the computer in several ways or print them if you need a paper copy.

2. **Organize the e-mail message.** An e-mail message typically is organized into two areas: the message header and the message area.

3. **Choose the words for the subject line.** The subject line should indicate the main purpose or topic of the e-mail message. Use as few words as possible and never leave the subject line blank because it provides important information for the person receiving the e-mail message.

4. **Choose the words for the message text.** The message text should be clear and concise. Use as few words as possible to make a point. Brief or short message text is more likely to be read than lengthy text.

5. **Ensure that the content of the e-mail message is appropriate for the recipient.** An e-mail message sent to a close friend may be considerably different from one sent to an instructor, coworker, or client. Shortening words or using abbreviations (such as u for you, r for are, and 2 for to) may be appropriate for personal e-mail messages, but should be avoided when sending work-related e-mail messages. These types of abbreviations are too informal for the workplace and often are viewed as unprofessional.

6. **Alert the recipient(s) when sending large file attachments.** An **attachment** is a file, such as a document or picture, which is sent along with an e-mail message. Recipients can open attachments only if they have the appropriate software installed on their computer. Be aware when sending large file attachments that some e-mail services only allow file attachments up to a certain size.

7. **Be aware of computer viruses and how they spread.** A **virus** is a malicious computer program that can damage files and the operating system. One way that viruses spread is through virus-infected e-mail attachments. You only should open attachments when the e-mail message is from someone you know or when you are expecting the attachment. If you receive an e-mail attachment, you should use an **antivirus program**, which is a program that checks files for viruses, to verify that the attachment is virus free.

When necessary, more specific details concerning the above guidelines are presented at appropriate points in the chapter. The chapter also will identify the actions performed and decisions made regarding these guidelines during the creation of the messages shown in Figure 1–1.

Outlook Account Settings

The first time you start Outlook on a home computer, the opening screen gives you the choice to add or import an account, or to view What's New in Outlook for Mac. If you choose to add a new e-mail account, you will be prompted to provide the e-mail address for that account. An **e-mail address** identifies a user so that he or she can receive Internet e-mail. Just as you address a letter when using the postal system, you address an e-mail message with the e-mail address of the person receiving the message, or the **recipient**. Likewise, when someone sends you a message, he or she must have your e-mail address.

An e-mail address is divided into two parts. The first part contains a **user name**, which is a unique combination of characters, such as letters of the alphabet and numbers, which identifies a specific user. The last part is a **domain name**, which is the unique name associated with a specific Internet address and is provided by your ISP or school. In an Internet e-mail address, an @ (pronounced *at*) symbol separates the user name from the domain name. A possible e-mail address for someone named Kiley Barnhill, for example, would be kbarnhill@scsite.com, which would be read as k barnhill at s c site dot com. Figure 1–2 shows the parts of an e-mail address.

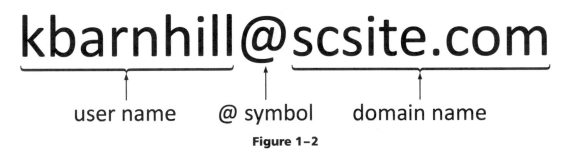

Figure 1–2

After entering an e-mail address, you enter a password for the account. A **password** is a combination of letters, numbers, and symbols that verifies your identity. Typically, the ISP provides a password when you set up your e-mail service. Most people change the password so that they can remember it easily. After you enter the password, the Accounts dialog displays with some information already filled in.

Figure 1–3 on the next page shows the initial screen when you first start Outlook, and then shows typical entries in the Accounts dialog, which is part of the initial account setup. You also can display this dialog by clicking Tools in the menu bar and choosing Accounts. Notice in Figure 1–3 that the entered password is displayed as asterisks or bullets, which keeps your password private, preventing anyone from learning your password as you type it.

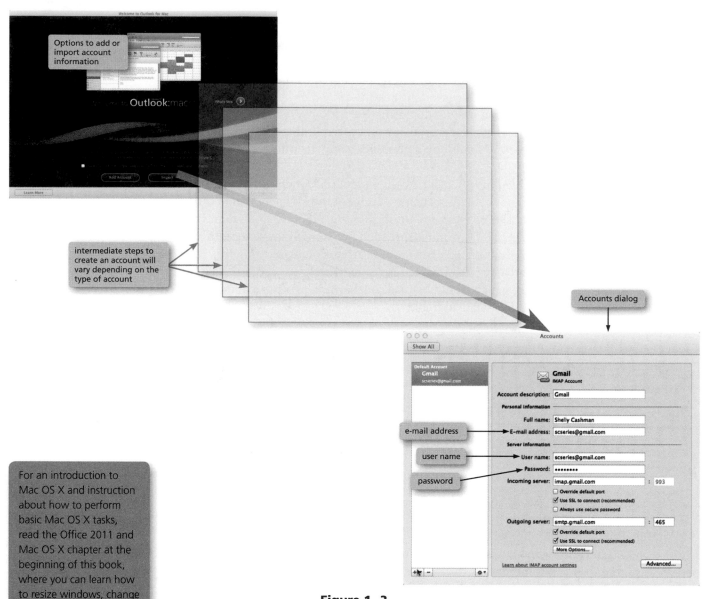

Figure 1–3

For an introduction to Mac OS X and instruction about how to perform basic Mac OS X tasks, read the Office 2011 and Mac OS X chapter at the beginning of this book, where you can learn how to resize windows, change screen resolution, create folders, move and rename files, use Mac OS X Help, and much more.

For an introduction to Office 2011 and instruction about how to perform basic tasks in Office 2011 programs, read the Office 2011 and Mac OS X chapter at the beginning of this book, where you can learn how to start a program, use the ribbon, save a file, open a file, quit a program, use Help, and much more.

To Start Outlook

If you are using a computer to step through the project in this chapter and you want your screens to match the figures in this book, you should change your screen's resolution to 1280 × 800. For information about how to change a computer's resolution, refer to the Office 2011 and Mac OS X chapter at the beginning of this book.

The following steps, which assume that Mac OS X is running and you have an e-mail profile set up in Outlook, start Outlook based on a typical installation. You may need to ask your instructor how to start Outlook for your computer. For a detailed example of the procedure summarized below, refer to the Office 2011 and Mac OS X chapter.

1 Click the Outlook icon in the Dock to open Outlook.

2 If the Outlook window is not maximized, click the green Zoom button next to the Minimize button on its title bar to maximize the window.

3 If the Inbox window is not displayed, click the Mail button in the Navigation Pane to display your Inbox.

Note: If you are stepping through this project on a computer and you want your screens to appear the same as in the figures, then you should ask your instructor for assistance with opening or importing the TW.pst mailbox from the Data Files for Students. See the inside back cover of this book for instructions for downloading the Data Files for Students or see your instructor for information about accessing files for this book.

To Open an Outlook Data File

The e-mail messages you work with in this chapter are stored in a personal folders (.pst) file named TW.pst, which is an Outlook mailbox available on the Data Files for Students. See the inside back cover of this book for instructions on downloading the Data Files for Students, or contact your instructor for information about accessing the required files. The following steps show how to open this personal folders file in Outlook, display the Inbox for the TW file, and then make your TW mailbox match the figures in this chapter. In this example, the TW mailbox is located in the Chapter1 folder in the Outlook folder in the Data Files for Students folder on a USB flash drive.

1
- With your USB flash drive connected to one of the computer's USB ports, click File in the menu bar to display the File menu.

- Choose Import to display the Begin Import screen of the Import dialog, and click Outlook Data File (.pst or .olm) (Figure 1–4).

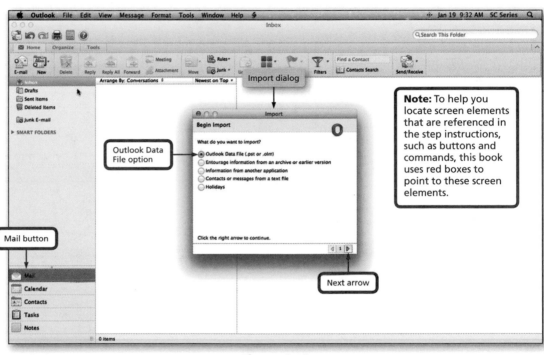

Figure 1–4

2
- Click the Next arrow at the lower right of the screen to move to the Choose a File Type screen and select Outlook for Windows Data File (.pst) (Figure 1–5).

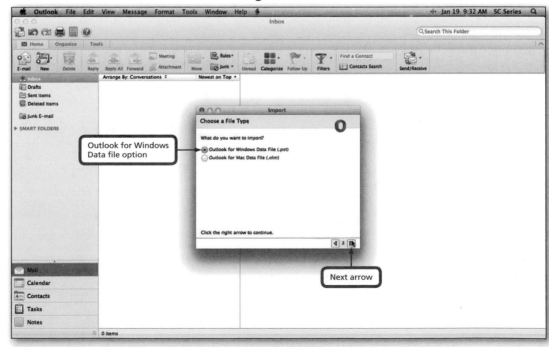

Figure 1–5

• Click the Next arrow to open the 'Choose the Outlook for Windows Data File (.pst) to import' screen of the Import dialog.

• Navigate to the mailbox location (in this case, the Chapter 1 folder in the Outlook folder in the Data Files for Students folder on a USB flash drive). For a detailed example of this procedure, refer to Steps 3a–3c in the To Save a File in a Folder section in the Office 2011 and Mac OS X chapter on pages OFF 31–32 at the beginning of this book.

• Select the TW.pst file (Figure 1–6).

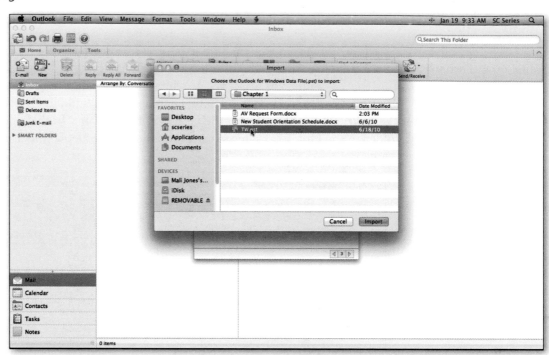

Figure 1–6

• Click the Import button (Import dialog) to import the data file (Figure 1–7).

• When the Import Complete screen appears, click the Done button.

• Click the disclosure triangle beside the TW PST folder to view the contained folders.

• Click Inbox below the TW PST heading in the Navigation Pane to view the TW PST Inbox.

Q&A What is the Navigation Pane?
The **Navigation Pane** is a pane along the left side of the Outlook window that contains shortcuts to your Outlook folders and gives you quick access to them. You use the Navigation Pane to browse all your Outlook folders using one of its views: Mail, Calendar, Contacts, Tasks, or Notes. The contents of the Navigation Pane change depending on the folder you are using.

Q&A What is the Inbox?
The **Inbox** is the Outlook folder that contains incoming e-mail messages.

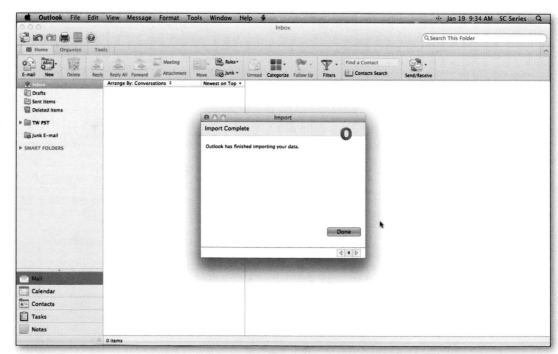

Figure 1–7

5

- Click the Arrange By: bar at the top of the message list in the Inbox to display the pop-up menu.

- If Date Sent is not selected with a check mark, click Date Sent to select it.

- If Show in Groups is selected with a check mark, click Show in Groups to remove the check mark and deselect this command. (Figure 1–8).

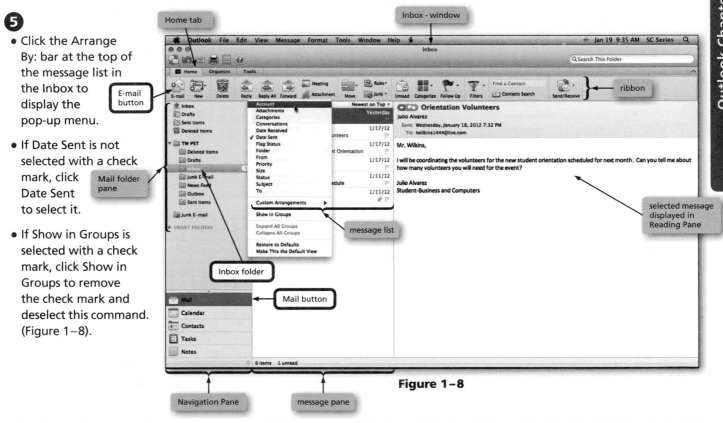

Figure 1–8

Composing and Sending E-Mail Messages

Composing an e-mail message consists of four basic steps — open a new message window, enter message header information, enter the message text, and add a signature.

Organize the e-mail message.

An e-mail message typically is organized into two areas: the message header and the message area.

- The information in the **message header** routes the message to its recipients and identifies the purpose or contents of the message. The message header contains the e-mail address of the recipient(s), the primary person or persons to whom you are sending the message; it also may contain a courtesy copy or carbon copy (cc), which includes one or more additional recipients; and the **subject line**, which states the reason for the message.

- The **message area**, where you type an e-mail message, consists of a greeting line or salutation, the message text, an optional closing, and a signature line(s).

- A **greeting line** or salutation sets the tone of the message and can be formal or informal, depending on the nature of the message. You can use a comma (,) or a colon (:) at the end of the greeting line.

- The **message text** informs the recipient or summarizes or requests information.

- A **closing** signals an end to the message using courtesy words such as or. Because the closing is most appropriate for formal e-mail messages, it is optional.

- A **signature line(s)** identifies the sender and may contain additional information, such as a job title and phone number(s). In a signature, the name usually is provided on one line followed by other information listed on separate lines.

Plan Ahead

The Outlook Window

The chapters in this book **BTW** begin with the Outlook window appearing as it did at the initial installation of the software. Your Outlook window may look different depending on your screen resolution and other Outlook settings.

To Compose an E-Mail Message

The first step in this project is to send an e-mail message to Rose Stewart, a faculty member at the college, asking her to send you the morning agenda for the new student orientation program. The following steps compose a new e-mail message to Rose Stewart.

1

- Click the E-mail button on the Home tab to open the Untitled window (Figure 1–9).

Q&A I got a message about not having set up an e-mail account. What should I do?

You need to set up an e-mail profile with an active e-mail account before you can compose and send e-mail messages.

See your instructor if you do not yet have an account set up, or click Tools in the menu bar, choose Accounts, and fill in the required information to set up an account.

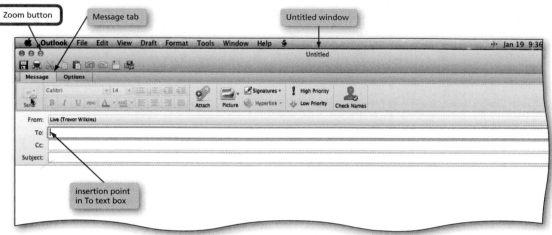

Figure 1–9

2

- If necessary, click the Zoom button in the Untitled window to maximize the window.

- With the insertion point in the To text box, type `rose.stewart@hotmail.com` (with no spaces), to enter the e-mail address of the recipient.

Q&A Why does Rose Stewart's complete e-mail address appear when I start typing the address?

As you type in the To: text box, Outlook uses a feature called **AutoComplete**, which begins to suggest possible matches based on names you have typed before and names in sent and received mail. AutoComplete suggests the complete address before you finish typing. You can press the RETURN key to add the suggested e-mail address to the To: text box.

- Click the Subject text box to position the insertion point in the Subject text box.

- Type **Draft Agenda** as the subject.

- Press the TAB key to move the insertion point into the message area (Figure 1–10).

Q&A Why does the message title change to Draft Agenda?

The message title corresponds to the Subject text. When you enter subject text, the message title is updated.

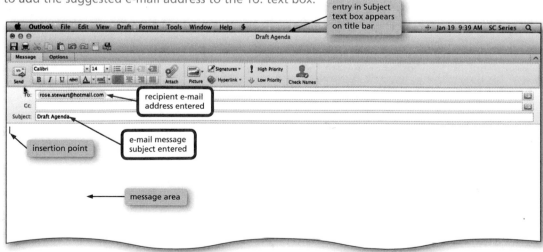

Figure 1–10

Q&A What if I make an error while typing an e-mail message?

Press the DELETE key until you have deleted the error and then retype the text correctly. You also can click the Undo button in the Standard toolbar to undo your most recent action.

- Type **Ms. Stewart,** as the greeting line.

- Press the RETURN key to move the insertion point to the beginning of the next line.

- Press the RETURN key again to insert a blank line between the greeting line and the message text (Figure 1–11).

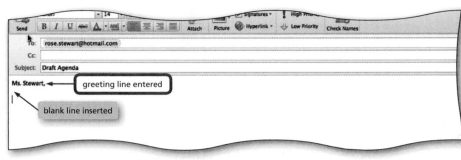

Figure 1–11

Q&A   Why did a blank space appear between the greeting line and the insertion point?

Each time you press the RETURN key, Outlook creates a new paragraph. When you press the RETURN key on a line with no text, Outlook inserts blank space between the two paragraphs.

- Type **Could you please send me the proposed agenda for the new student orientation program scheduled for next month?** to enter the message text.

- Press the RETURN key two times to insert a blank line below the message text.

- Type **Thanks,** as the closing and then press the RETURN key to move the insertion point to the next line.

- Type **Trevor Wilkins** as signature line 1.

- Press the RETURN key to move the insertion point to the next line and then type **Student Assistant** as signature line 2 (Figure 1–12).

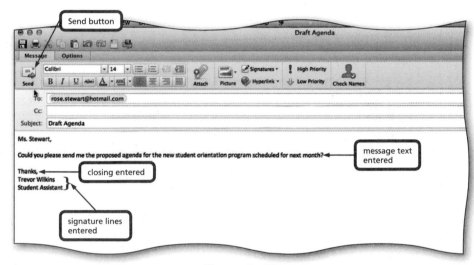

Figure 1–12

Q&A   Do I always need to type my last name in the signature of an e-mail message?

No. If you and your recipient know each other, you can type only your first name as the signature.

Other Ways

1. Click New button on Home tab, choose E-mail Message
2. Choose File > New > E-mail Message in menu bar
3. Press COMMAND-N

To Send an E-Mail Message

The message to Rose Stewart is created and ready to be sent. The following step sends the completed e-mail message to Rose Stewart.

- Click the Send button on the Message tab to send the e-mail message and close the message window.

Q&A   What happened to the e-mail message?

E-mail messages are sent automatically when you click Send in a new message window.

Other Ways

1. Press COMMAND-RETURN

How E-Mail Messages Travel from Sender to Receiver

Q&As

BTW For a complete list of the Q&As found in many of the step-by-step sequences in this book, visit the Office 2011 for Mac Online Companion Web page at www.cengagebrain.com, navigate to the desired chapter, and click Q&As.

When you send someone an e-mail message, it travels across the Internet to the computer at your ISP that handles outgoing e-mail messages. This computer, called the **outgoing e-mail server,** examines the e-mail address on your message, selects the best route for sending the message across the Internet, and then sends the e-mail message. Many outgoing e-mail servers use **SMTP (Simple Mail Transfer Protocol)**, which is a communications protocol, or set of rules for communicating with other computers. An e-mail program such as Outlook contacts the outgoing e-mail server and then transfers the e-mail message(s) in its Outbox to that server. If the e-mail program cannot contact the outgoing e-mail server, the e-mail message(s) remains in the Outbox until the program can connect to the server.

As an e-mail message travels across the Internet, routers direct the e-mail message to a computer at your recipient's ISP that handles incoming e-mail messages. (A **router** is a device that forwards data on a network.) The computer handling incoming e-mail messages, called the **incoming e-mail server,** stores the e-mail message(s) until your recipient uses an e-mail program such as Outlook to retrieve the e-mail message(s). Some e-mail servers use **POP3**, the latest version of **Post Office Protocol (POP)**, a communications protocol for incoming e-mail. Figure 1–13 shows how an e-mail message may travel from a sender to a receiver.

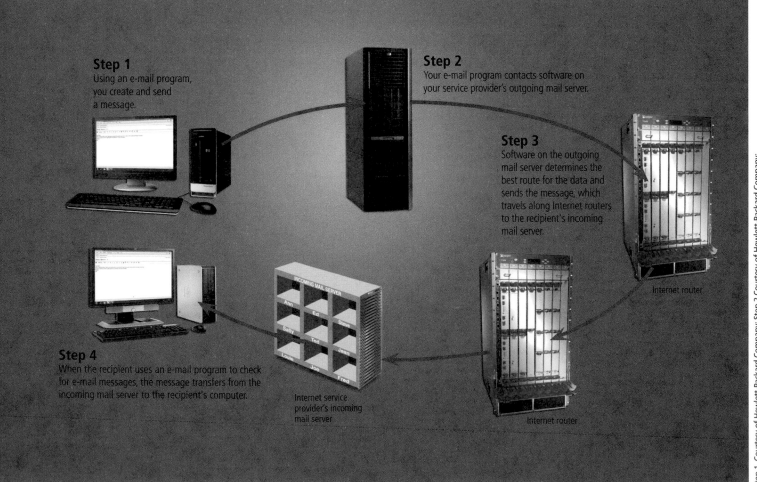

Step 1
Using an e-mail program, you create and send a message.

Step 2
Your e-mail program contacts software on your service provider's outgoing mail server.

Step 3
Software on the outgoing mail server determines the best route for the data and sends the message, which travels along Internet routers to the recipient's incoming mail server.

Internet router

Step 4
When the recipient uses an e-mail program to check for e-mail messages, the message transfers from the incoming mail server to the recipient's computer.

Internet service provider's incoming mail server

Internet router

Figure 1–13

In some cases, the user provides Outlook information about the outgoing and incoming e-mail servers when setting up an e-mail account; you also can ask Outlook to try to configure these settings automatically. You can verify these Internet e-mail settings in the Accounts dialog, which is displayed by choosing Accounts from the Tools menu in the menu bar. Figure 1–14 shows the Accounts dialog for Kiley Barnhill. Notice that this account uses a POP3 incoming mail server and an SMTP outgoing mail server with the same domain name as in the e-mail address.

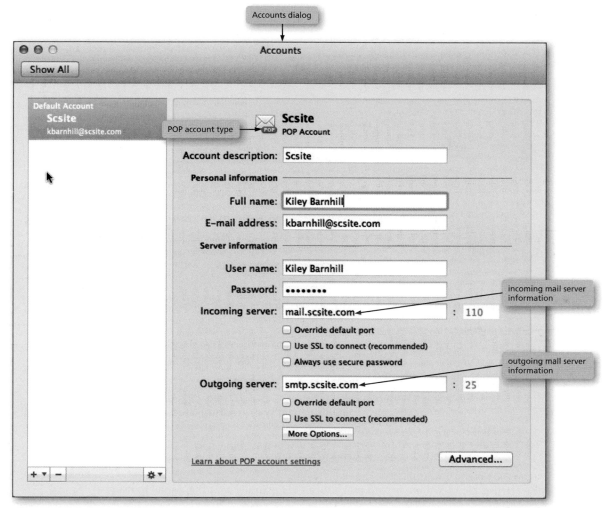

Figure 1–14

Working with Incoming Messages

When you receive e-mail messages, Outlook directs them to the Inbox and displays them in the **message pane,** which lists the contents of the selected folder, in this case the Inbox (Figure 1–15 on the next page). The list of messages displayed in the message pane is called the **message list**. A highlighted e-mail message in the message list displays the selected message header, which appears in bold with a **closed envelope icon** to the left of the e-mail message if the e-mail message is unread (unopened). An **open envelope icon** indicates a previously read (opened) message. The circled number next to the Inbox folder shows how many unread messages are stored in the Inbox. The e-mail messages on your computer may be different.

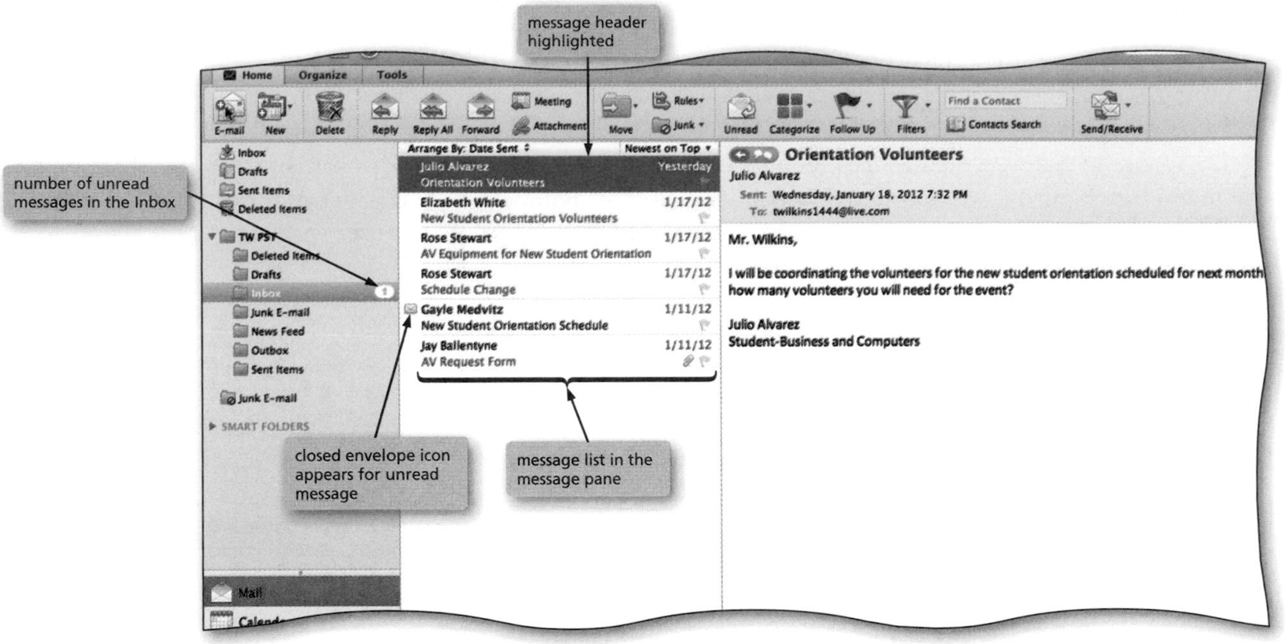

Figure 1–15

You can read incoming messages in three ways: in an open window, in the Reading Pane, or as a hard copy. A **hard copy** (**printout**) is information presented on a physical medium such as paper.

Junk E-Mail Filters

BTW The Outlook Junk E-mail Filter is turned on by default and evaluates whether an incoming message should be sent to the Junk E-mail folder. By scanning message information such as the content, time the message was sent, and who sent the message, this feature determines whether a message might be spam and diverts it to the Junk E-mail folder. To change junk e-mail settings, click the Junk button on the Home tab, and then click Junk E-mail Protection to display the Junk E-mail Protection dialog. Choose the level of protection you want and click the OK button.

Plan Ahead

Determine the best method for reading e-mail messages you receive.

Popular methods for reading an e-mail message are to either display it in the Reading Pane or to open it in its own message window. These methods are easy and quick. Reading electronic documents also saves paper and printer supplies. You should be aware of problems, however, that can be caused by reading e-mail messages.

- **Know the sender.** If you receive an e-mail message from someone you do not know, you should not open it because it might trigger a virus. Unsolicited e-mail messages, known as **spam** or **junk e-mail**, are e-mail messages sent from an unknown sender to many e-mail accounts, usually advertising a product or service such as low-cost medication, low-interest loans, or free credit reports. Spam quickly can fill an Inbox with unwanted messages. If a suspicious e-mail message appears to come from someone you know and trust, contact them first to make sure they actually sent the e-mail message.

- **Do not click a hyperlink in an e-mail message from an unknown sender.** A **hyperlink** is a word, phrase, symbol, or picture in an e-mail message or on a Web page that, when clicked, directs you to another document or Web site. One way spammers (senders of spam) verify your e-mail address is by sending messages that request you to click a hyperlink to direct you to a Web site. After spammers know that your e-mail address is valid, they are likely to send you many more e-mail messages.

The next several pages in this chapter read and reply to an e-mail message. The following pages follow these general tasks:

1. Read an e-mail message in the Reading Pane.

2. Open, print, and close an e-mail message.

3. Reply to and forward an e-mail message.

4. Delete an e-mail message.

5. Check the spelling of an e-mail message.

6. Save an e-mail message.

7. Attach a file to an outgoing e-mail message.

To Read an E-Mail Message in the Reading Pane

You can read an e-mail message without opening it by displaying its contents in the Reading Pane. The **Reading Pane** appears on the right side of the Outlook window by default and displays the contents of a message without opening the message. The following step displays an e-mail message from Gayle Medvitz in the Reading Pane.

- If necessary, click the message header from Gayle Medvitz in the Inbox message list to select the e-mail message and display its contents in the Reading Pane (Figure 1–16).

Q&A What happens to the message icon when I select another message?
Outlook automatically marks messages as read after you preview the message in the Reading Pane and select another message to view. A read message is displayed in the message list with an open envelope and is not bold. An unread message is displayed with a closed envelope icon and appears in bold in the message list.

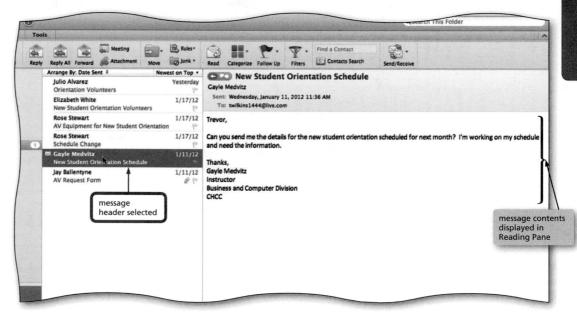

Figure 1–16

To Open an E-Mail Message in a Window

The next step is to open the message in its own window for further evaluation. The following step opens the message from Gayle Medvitz.

- Double-click the Gayle Medvitz message in the message list to display the selected e-mail message in its own window (Figure 1–17).

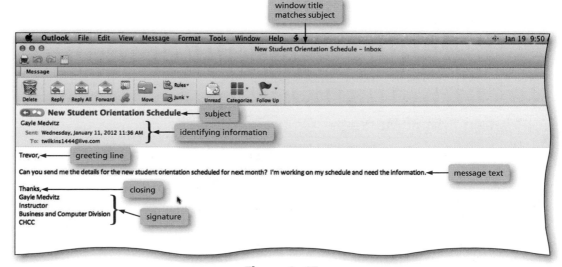

Figure 1–17

Other Ways

1. CONTROL-click message header, choose Open Message in shortcut menu

2. Select message header, press COMMAND-O

To Close an E-Mail Message

You are finished with the e-mail message from Gayle Medvitz, so you can close it. The following steps close the New Student Orientation Schedule – Inbox window.

- Click the Close button on the title bar of the message window to close the window (Figure 1–18).

Q&A What happened to the icon beside the message from Gayle Medvitz?
After viewing a message in its own window, the icon indicating the message is unread is removed by Outlook.

Q&A Can I change the message status from unread to read or from read to unread?
Yes, CONTROL-click the message you want to change and select the Mark as Read or Mark as Unread command in the shortcut menu.

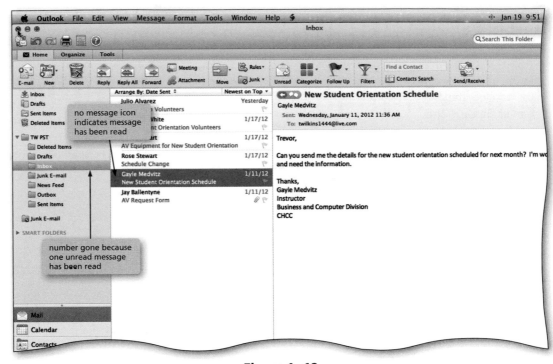

Figure 1–18

Q&A Why did the number next to the Inbox folder change?
When you close a message window, the message header (Gayle Medvitz, in this case) in the message pane no longer appears in bold, the closed envelope icon is deleted to indicate the message has been opened, and the number next to the Inbox folder changes to reflect the number of unread messages.

Other Ways

1. Choose File > Close in menu bar
2. Press COMMAND-W

To Print an E-Mail Message

Occasionally, you may want to print the contents of an e-mail message. A hard copy of an e-mail message can serve as reference material if your storage medium becomes corrupted and you need to re-create the message or refer to the message when your computer is not readily available. A printed copy of an e-mail message also serves as a **backup**, which is an additional copy of a file or message that you store for safekeeping. You can print the contents of an e-mail message from an open message window or directly from the Inbox window.

You would like to have a hard copy of the message from Gayle Medvitz so that you can keep it with other documents relating to the orientation topic. The following steps print the e-mail message from Gayle Medvitz.

1

• In the message list, CONTROL-click the e-mail message from Gayle Medvitz to display a shortcut menu that presents a list of possible actions (Figure 1–19).

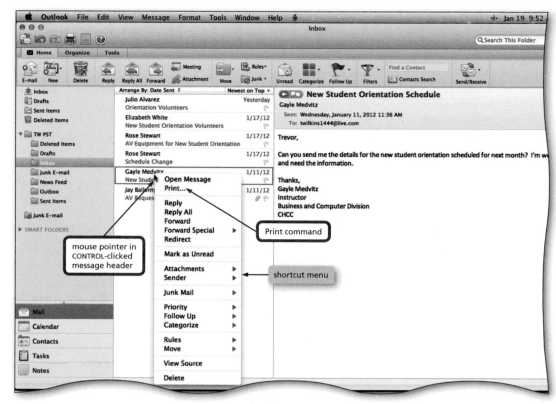

Figure 1–19

2

• Click Print in the shortcut menu to display the Print dialog (Figure 1–20).

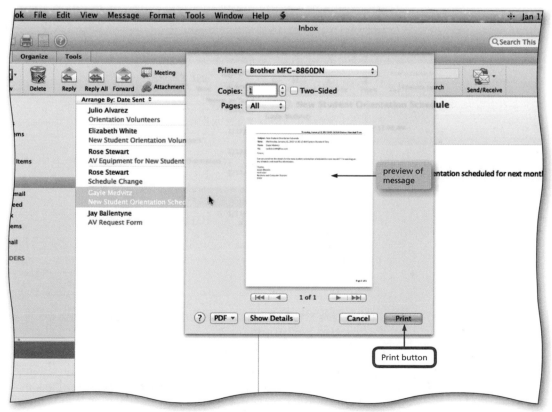

Figure 1–20

• Click the Print button to send the e-mail message to the currently selected printer.

• When the printer stops, retrieve the hard copy (Figure 1–21).

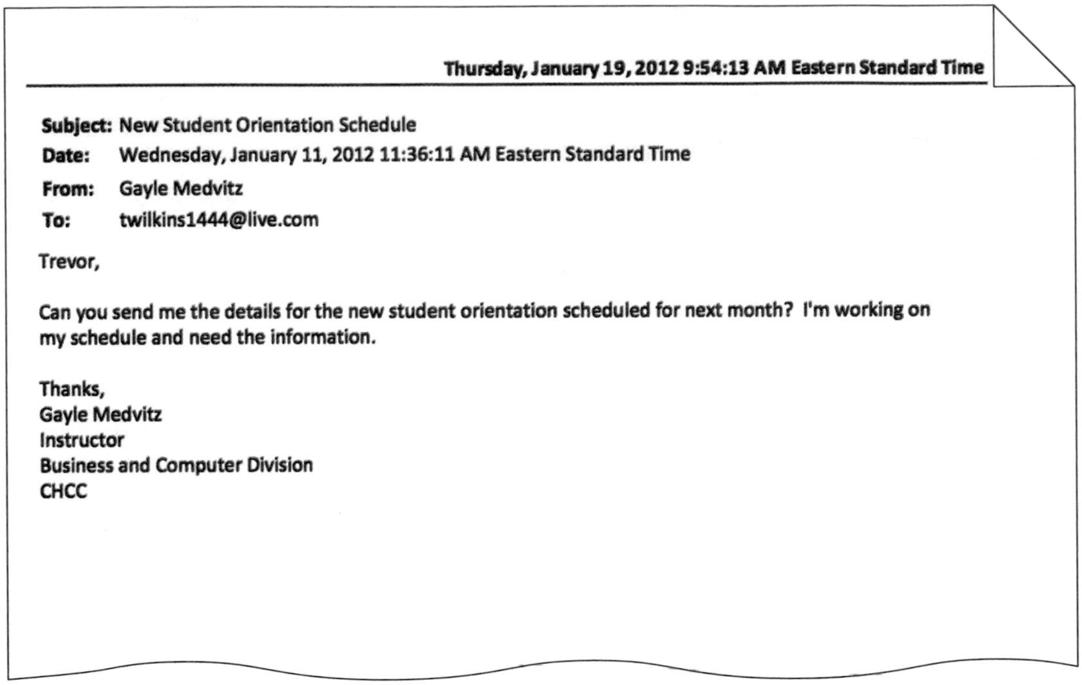

Thursday, January 19, 2012 9:54:13 AM Eastern Standard Time

Subject: New Student Orientation Schedule
Date: Wednesday, January 11, 2012 11:36:11 AM Eastern Standard Time
From: Gayle Medvitz
To: twilkins1444@live.com

Trevor,

Can you send me the details for the new student orientation scheduled for next month? I'm working on my schedule and need the information.

Thanks,
Gayle Medvitz
Instructor
Business and Computer Division
CHCC

Other Ways
1. Click Print button in Standard toolbar
2. Choose File > Print in menu bar
3. Press COMMAND-P

Figure 1–21

To Print Multiple Copies of an E-Mail Message

You may need to print multiple copies of an e-mail message if you want to distribute the message to more than one person, or if you want to file one copy for later use and keep a second copy as a backup. If you wanted to print multiple copies of an e-mail message, you would follow these steps.

1. CONTROL-CLICK the message you want to print and then click Print in the shortcut menu.
2. Change the number in the Copies box in the Open dialog to the number of desired copies, such as a 2 for 2 copies.
3. Click the Print button to print the message and close the dialog.

Responding to E-Mail Messages

In this chapter, you respond to e-mail messages by replying to and forwarding them. Thus, the next step is to respond to an e-mail message that has already been received.

Plan Ahead

Ensure that the content of the e-mail message is appropriate for the recipient.

An e-mail message you send to a close friend may be much less formal than one you send to an instructor, coworker, or client. For example, conversational language to a friend, such as "Can't wait to see you!" is not appropriate in professional e-mail messages. All standard grammar rules apply, however, such as punctuation, capitalization, and spelling, no matter the audience.

When responding to e-mail messages, you have three options in Outlook: Reply, Reply All, or Forward. Table 1–1 lists the response options and their actions.

Table 1–1 Outlook Response Options	
Response Option	**Action**
Reply	Opens the RE: reply window and sends a reply to the person who sent the message.
Reply All	Opens the RE: reply window and sends a reply to everyone listed in the message header.
Forward	Opens the FW: message window and sends a copy of the selected message to additional people, if you want to share information with others. The original message text is included in the message window.

You reply to messages you already have received. You can forward an e-mail message to additional recipients to share information with others. You should receive permission from the sender before forwarding a message, in case the sender intended the original message to remain private. A message that you forward is similar to a new message in that you send the message to someone other than the original sender of the message. A reply sends the message to the person who sent the message.

To Reply to an E-Mail Message

The message from Gayle Medvitz is asking for information and requires a reply. The following steps reply to the e-mail message from Gayle Medvitz.

1

- If necessary, click the Gayle Medvitz message header in the message list to select it and display its contents in the Reading Pane (Figure 1–22).

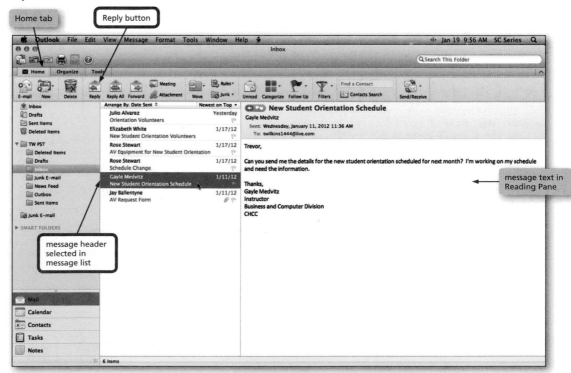

Figure 1–22

2

- Click the Reply button on the Home tab to open the RE: New Student Orientation Schedule window.

- If the message window is not maximized, click the green Zoom button next to the Minimize button on its title bar to maximize the window (Figure 1–23).

Q&A Why does Re: appear at the beginning of the subject line and in the title bar?
The Re: indicates this message is a reply to another message. The subject of the original message appears after the Re.

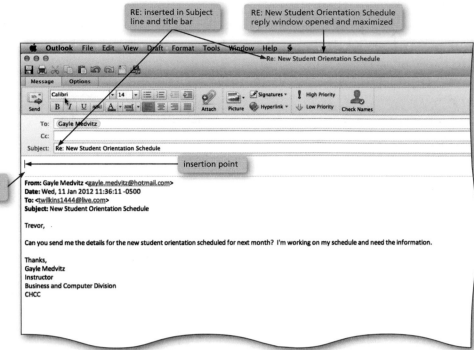

Figure 1–23

3

- If necessary, click the message area below the message header to position the insertion point at the top of the message area.

- Type `Good morning,` as the greeting line.

- Press the RETURN key two times to place a blank line between the greeting line and the message text.

- Type `We are finalizing the schedule today. I will send it to you as soon as we are finished.` to enter the message text.

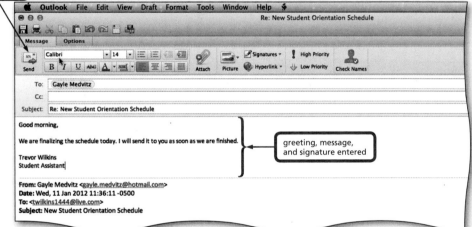

Figure 1–24

- Press the RETURN key two times to place a blank line between the message text and the signature lines.

- Type `Trevor Wilkins` as signature line 1 and then press the RETURN key to move the insertion point to the next line.

- Type `Student Assistant` as signature line 2 (Figure 1–24).

4

- Click the Send button on the Message tab to send the e-mail message and display the Inbox window.

Q&A Why did a left-pointing purple arrow appear beside the message in the Inbox?
The left-pointing purple arrow indicates you replied to the message.

Other Ways

1. CONTROL-click message header, click Reply

2. Choose Message > Reply from menu bar

3. Click message header, press COMMAND-R

To Forward an E-Mail Message

Elizabeth White has sent you an e-mail message offering to volunteer for the New Student Orientation program. Because she is not sure you can authorize her volunteer service, she mentions that you can forward her message to the appropriate person. In fact, Julio Alvarez is the person handling the volunteers for the program. The following steps forward Elizabeth White's message to Julio Alvarez.

1

- In the Inbox window, click the Elizabeth White message header in the message list to select the e-mail message (Figure 1–25).

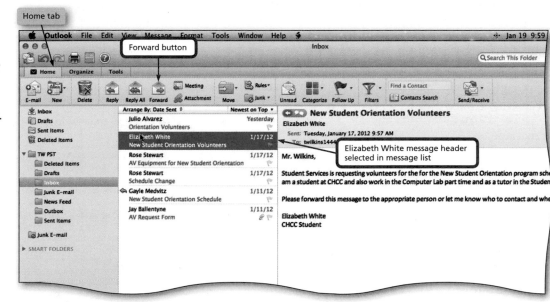

Figure 1–25

2

- Click the Forward button on the Home tab to display the FW: New Student Orientation Volunteers window.

- Type **julioa1776@ hotmail.com** (with no spaces) in the To text box as the recipient's e-mail address (unless you are stepping through this task — in that case, enter an actual e-mail address) (Figure 1–26).

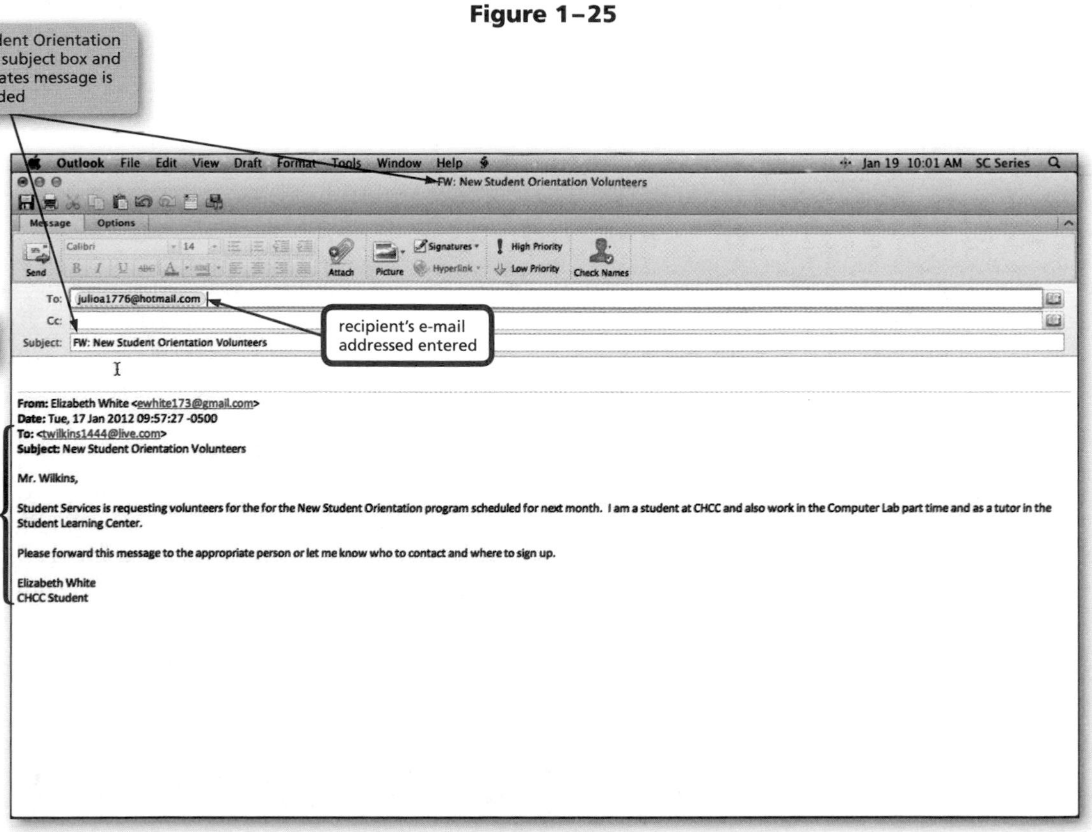

Q&A Why does the original message appear in the message area of the window?

By default, Outlook is configured to automatically display the original message below the new message area for all message replies and forwards.

Figure 1–26

• Click the message area above the original message text and then type `Julio,` as the greeting line.

• Press the RETURN key two times to enter a blank line before the message text.

• Type `I received the message below from Elizabeth White, a new student at CHCC. Because you have been working on the orientation program, could you please handle this request?` to enter the message text.

• Press the RETURN key two times to place a blank line between the message text and the signature lines.

• Type `Trevor Wilkins` as signature line 1 and then press the ENTER key to move the insertion point to the next line.

• Type `Student Assistant` as signature line 2 (Figure 1–27).

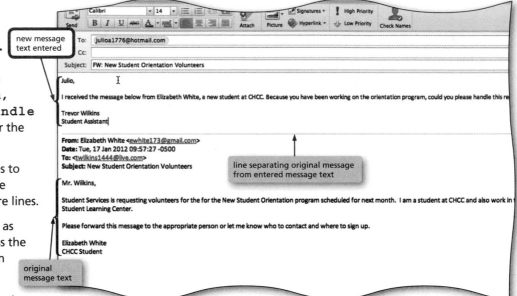

Figure 1–27

Other Ways

1. CONTROL-click message header, choose Forward in shortcut menu

2. Choose Message > Forward in menu bar

3. Click message header, press COMMAND-F

Message Formats

As shown in Figure 1–27, Outlook's default (preset) message format is HTML (Hypertext Markup Language), which is a format that allows you to view pictures and text formatted with color and various fonts and font sizes. **Formatting** refers to changing the appearance of text in a document such as the font (typeface), font size, color, and alignment of the text in a document.

Before you send an original e-mail message, reply to an e-mail message, or forward an e-mail message, consider which message format you want to use. A **message format** determines whether an e-mail message can include pictures or formatted text, such as bold, italic, and colored fonts. Select a message format that is appropriate for your message and your recipient. Outlook offers two message formats: HTML and Plain Text, summarized in Table 1–2. If you select the HTML format, for example, the e-mail program your recipient uses must be able to display formatted messages or pictures.

Table 1–2 Message Formats	
Message Format	**Description**
HTML	HTML format is the default format for new messages in Outlook. HTML lets you include pictures and basic formatting, such as text formatting, numbering, bullets, and alignment. HTML is the recommended format for Internet mail because the more popular e-mail programs use it.
Plain Text	Plain Text format is recognized by all e-mail programs and is the most likely format to be allowed through a company's virus-filtering program. Plain Text does not support basic formatting, such as bold, italic, colored fonts, or other text formatting. It also does not support pictures displayed directly in the message.

Be aware of computer viruses and how they are spread.

Your message may be blocked by the recipient's e-mail server. Some e-mail servers are set up to automatically block messages in the HTML format using antivirus software. If you have concerns about whether the recipient's server is set up to block messages formatted as HTML, use Plain Text as the message format.

Plan Ahead

To Change the Message Format and Send the Message

The next step in this project is to change the message format of the e-mail message before forwarding it to Julio Alvarez. You want to make sure that your reply is not blocked by an antivirus program, so you will change the message format to Plain Text. The following steps change the message format to Plain Text and then send the message.

- In the message window, click the Options tab.

- Click the Format button to display a dialog that asks if you are sure you want to turn off HTML formatting (Figure 1–28).

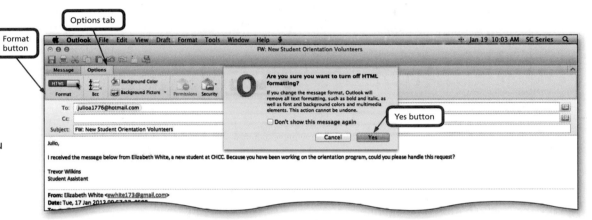

Figure 1–28

- Click the Yes button in the dialog to confirm turning off HTML formatting and to select the Plain Text message format (Figure 1–29).

Q&A What happened to the line separating the existing message and the new message?
When Plain Text is selected as the message format, all formatting such as text color, font type, and size is removed.

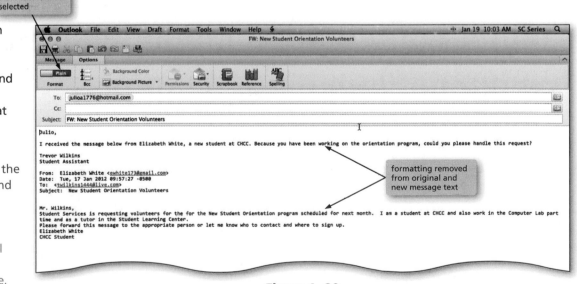

Figure 1–29

- Click the Message tab, and then click the Send button to send the e-mail message and display the Inbox window.

Q&A Why did a forward-pointing blue arrow appear beside the message in the Inbox?
The forward-pointing blue arrow indicates you forwarded the message.

To Delete an E-Mail Message

Now that you have forwarded Elizabeth White's message, you no longer need to keep it in your Inbox and you decide to delete it. When you delete a message from a folder, Outlook removes the message from the folder and moves it to the Deleted Items folder. The following steps delete the e-mail message from Elizabeth White.

1
- If necessary, click the Elizabeth White message header in the message list to select the e-mail message (Figure 1–30).

Q&A Why does the Navigation Pane contain two Deleted Items folders?
The imported .pst file contains a Deleted Items folder. The other deleted Items folder is the default Deleted Items folder, where all deleted items are placed.

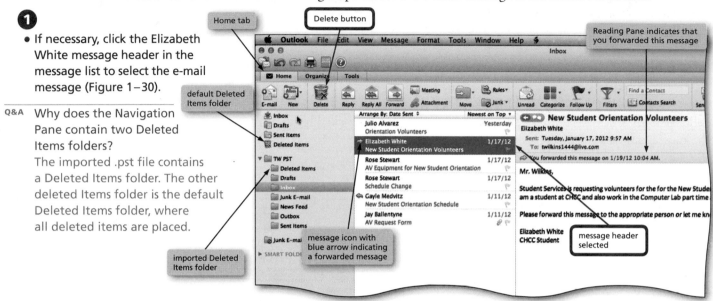

Figure 1–30

2
- Click the Delete button on the Home tab to move the e-mail message from the current folder (Inbox, in this case) to the default Deleted Items folder.

- If you want to verify the location of the deleted file, click the default Deleted Items folder in the Navigation Pane to display the Deleted Items message list in the message pane, which shows all deleted e-mail messages (Figure 1–31).

Q&A Is the e-mail message permanently deleted when I click the Delete button?

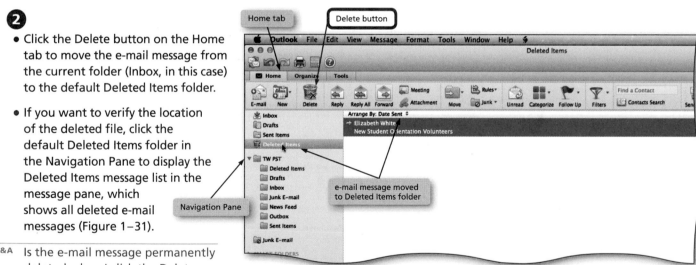

Figure 1–31

No, after Outlook moves the e-mail message to the Deleted Items folder, it stores the deleted e-mail message in that folder until you permanently delete the message. One way to permanently delete a message is to select the Deleted Items folder to view its contents in the message pane and then select the item to be deleted. Click the Delete button on the Home tab, and then click the Yes button in the Microsoft Office Outlook dialog to permanently delete the selected item from Outlook.

Other Ways
1. Drag selected e-mail message to Deleted Items folder
2. Click e-mail message, press DELETE
3. Click e-mail message, press COMMAND-DELETE

Break Point: If you wish to take a break, this is a good place to do so. You can quit Outlook now (refer to page OUT 37 for instructions). To resume at a later time, start Outlook (refer to page OUT 6 for instructions), and then continue to follow the steps from this location forward.

Spelling and Grammar Check

As you type text in an e-mail message, Outlook checks your typing for possible spelling and grammar errors and flags any potential errors in the message text with a red, green, or purple dotted underlines. A red dotted underline means the flagged text is not in Outlook's main dictionary (because it is a proper name or misspelled). A green dotted underline indicates the text may be incorrect grammatically. A purple dotted underline indicates the text may contain a contextual spelling error such as the misuse of homophones (words that are pronounced the same but have different spellings or meanings, such as one and won). Although you can check the entire message for spelling and grammar errors at once, you also can check these flagged errors as they appear on the screen.

A flagged word is not necessarily misspelled. For example, many names, abbreviations, and specialized terms are not in Outlook's main dictionary. In these cases, you instruct Outlook to ignore the flagged word. As you type, Outlook also detects duplicate words while checking for spelling errors. For example, if your e-mail message contains the phrase, to the store, Outlook places a green dotted underline below the second occurrence of the word, the.

The following pages illustrate how to ignore a correctly typed word and correct an incorrectly typed word in a reply to an e-mail message.

To Reply to an E-Mail Message

You are ready to reply to Gayle Medvitz's e-mail message and send her a copy of the orientation schedule, which now is complete. The following steps begin the reply to the e-mail message.

1 If necessary, click the Inbox folder under TW PST to display its contents in the message list.

2 Click the Gayle Medvitz message header to select the e-mail message.

3 Click the Reply button on the Home tab to send a second reply to Gayle Medvitz.

4 If necessary, maximize the message window to provide more room to work.

To Check the Spelling of a Correctly Typed Word

As you start typing the e-mail message, you will notice that Gayle Medvitz's last name has a red dotted line below it even though it is spelled correctly, indicating the word is not in Outlook's main dictionary. The steps on the next page ignore the error and remove the red dotted line.

- Type **Ms. Medvitz,** as the greeting line and then press the RETURN key, which causes Outlook to place a red dotted line below the proper name (in this case, Medvitz) (Figure 1–32).

Q&A Why does a red dotted line appear below Medvitz even though it is spelled correctly?
Outlook places a red dotted line below any word that is not in the main dictionary when Outlook checks for spelling errors.

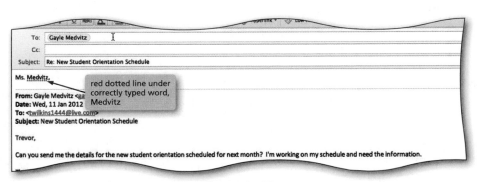

Figure 1–32

- CONTROL-click the proper name, Medvitz, to display a shortcut menu that presents a list of suggested spelling corrections for the flagged word, and then point to the Ignore Spelling command to prepare for selecting it (Figure 1–33).

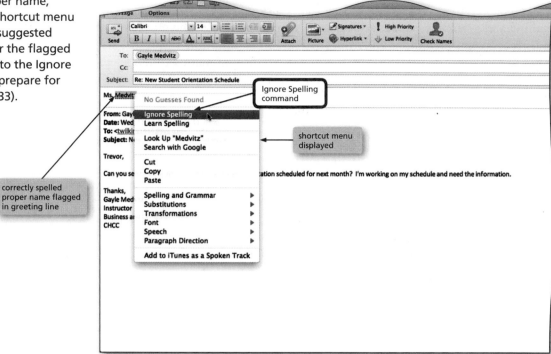

Figure 1–33

- Click Ignore Spelling in the shortcut menu to ignore this flagged error, close the shortcut menu, and remove the red dotted line beneath the name (in this case, Medvitz) (Figure 1–34).

Q&A What if Outlook does not flag my spelling and grammar errors with dotted underlines?

To verify that the check spelling and grammar as you type features are enabled, click Edit in the menu bar and choose Spelling and Grammar. Make sure that Check Spelling While Typing and Check Grammar With Spelling are both checked. If you want Outlook to automatically try to correct spelling errors, check the Correct Spelling Automatically command.

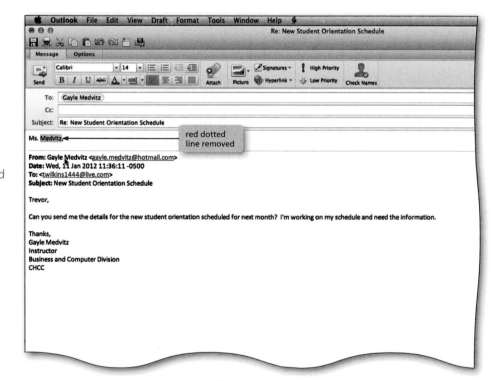

Figure 1–34

To Check the Spelling of Misspelled Text

In the following steps, the word, program, has been misspelled intentionally as profram to illustrate Outlook's check spelling as you type feature. If you are performing the steps in this project, your e-mail message may contain different misspelled words, depending on the accuracy of your typing. The following steps check the spelling of a misspelled word.

● Click Edit in the menu bar and choose Spelling and Grammar to show the Spelling and Grammar submenu.

● If necessary, click to remove the check mark beside Correct Spelling Automatically.

● Press the DOWN ARROW key to move the insertion point to the blank paragraph below the greeting line.

● Press the RETURN key, type `The schedule for the new student orientation profram` to begin entering the message text, and then press the SPACEBAR so that a red dotted line appears below the misspelled word.

● CONTROL-click the flagged word (profram, in this case) to display a shortcut menu that presents a list of suggested spelling corrections for the flagged word, and then point to program to prepare for selecting it (Figure 1–35).

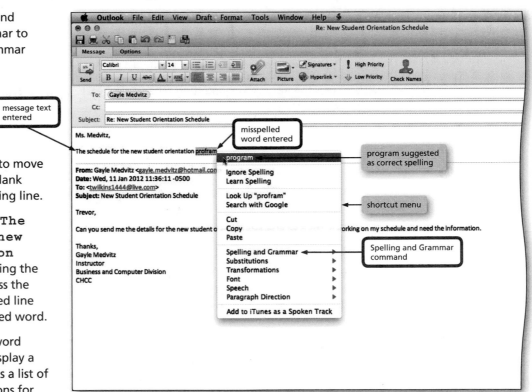

Figure 1–35

Q&A What should I do if the correction I want to use is not in the list on the shortcut menu?
You can click outside the shortcut menu to close the shortcut menu and then retype the correct word, or you can click Spelling and Grammar on the shortcut menu and choose Check Document Now to display the Spelling dialog.

● Click program on the shortcut menu to replace the misspelled word in the e-mail message with a correctly spelled word (Figure 1–36).

● Press the RIGHT ARROW key to deselect the replaced word and move the insertion point.

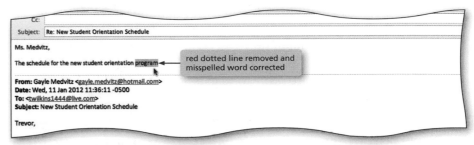

Figure 1–36

Other Ways

1. Choose Edit > Spelling and Grammar > Check Spelling Now

To Enter More Text

In the e-mail message, the text yet to be entered includes the remainder of the message text and the signature lines. The following steps enter the remainder of the message text and signature lines.

1 Press SPACE BAR, then type `you requested is attached. Let me know if you have any questions.` to continue entering the message text.

2 Press the RETURN key two times to move the insertion point one blank line below the message text.

3 Type `Trevor Wilkins` as signature line 1.

4 Press the RETURN key and then type `Student Assistant` as signature line 2 (Figure 1–37).

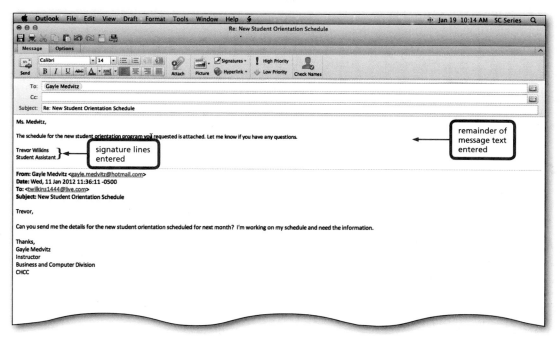

Figure 1–37

Saving and Closing an E-Mail Message

Occasionally, you begin composing a message but cannot complete the process. You may be waiting for information from someone else to include in the message, or you might prefer to complete the message later after you have time to evaluate its content. One option is to save the message, which stores the message in the Drafts folder until you are ready to send it. The Drafts folder is the default location for all saved messages.

To Save and Close an E-Mail Message without Sending It

The orientation schedule that Gayle Medvitz requested still is being drafted, so you are not ready to send the e-mail message to her. The following steps save the RE: New Student Orientation Schedule message in the Drafts folder for completion at a later time.

1

- Click the Save button in the Standard toolbar to save the message in the default Drafts folder.

Q&A   How does Outlook know where to store the saved message?
The default Drafts folder is the folder where Outlook automatically stores all saved messages.

2

- Click the Close button on the title bar to close the RE: New Student Orientation Schedule window (Figure 1–38).

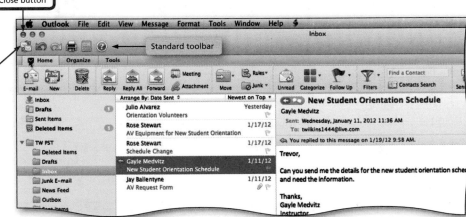

Figure 1–38

Q&A   What happens if I click the Close button without saving the message?
If you create a message and then click the Close button, Outlook displays a dialog asking you if you want to save the changes. If you click Save as Draft, Outlook saves the file to the Drafts folder and closes the message window. If you click Continue Writing, Outlook returns you to the message for additional editing. If you click Discard Changes, Outlook discards the e-mail message and closes the message window.

3

- If you want to view the saved message, click the Drafts folder to view any saved messages (Figure 1–39).

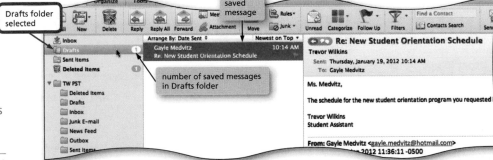

Figure 1–39

Q&A   Do I need to view the messages in the Drafts folder?
No, they are stored in the Drafts folder until you need them.

Q&A   Why is this draft not saved in the TW PST draft folder?
The Draft folder in the TW PST folder contains any items that were in the TW PST draft folder at the time the .pst file was created. The contents of the TW PST folder and its subfolders are not actively associated with the e-mail account you are using with Outlook, but rather are available to review and respond to using the e-mail account you set up in Outlook.

Opening and Modifying a Saved E-Mail Message

The Word document containing the New Orientation Schedule that Gayle Medvitz requested has been completed. The next step is to modify the saved message to Gayle Medvitz by attaching the Word file. You also want to include Rose Stewart as a courtesy copy recipient. By including her e-mail address as a courtesy copy in the message header, Rose Stewart receives a copy of the message but is not the primary recipient. As such, she neither is required to reply nor is a reply expected from her.

To Open a Saved E-Mail Message

To complete the message to Gayle Medvitz, you first must open it. The following steps open the previously saved New Student Orientation Schedule message, located in the Drafts folder.

- If necessary, click the default Drafts folder in the Mail folder list to display the message header for the Gayle Medvitz e-mail message in the message list (Figure 1–40).

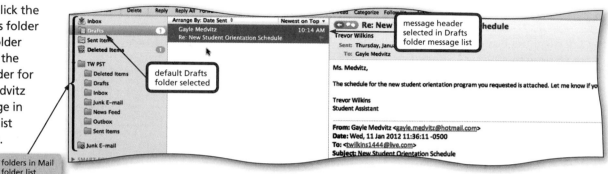

Figure 1–40

- Double-click the Gayle Medvitz message header in the Drafts folder to open the e-mail message (Figure 1–41).

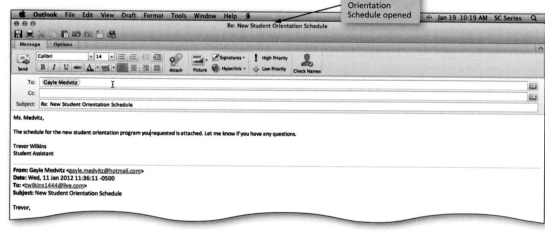

Figure 1–41

Other Ways

1. CONTROL-click message, click Open Message
2. With message selected, press COMMAND-O

To Include a Courtesy Copy Recipient in an E-Mail Message

The following step includes Rose Stewart as a courtesy copy recipient of the message to Gayle Medvitz.

- Click the Cc text box to select it and then begin typing `rose.stewart@ hotmail.com` (with no spaces), and then select the address from the Contacts and Recent Addresses box to include a courtesy copy e-mail address in the message header (Figure 1–42).

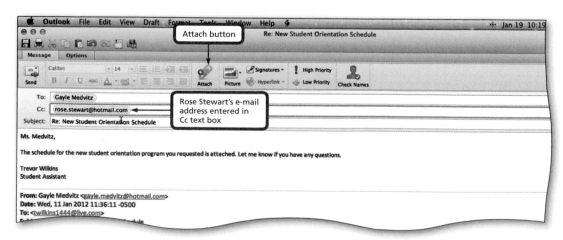

Figure 1–42

To Attach a File to an E-Mail Message

Many of the messages you receive and respond to are likely to contain an attachment, that is, a file such as a document or picture sent along with a message. You typically attach a file to an e-mail message to provide additional information to a recipient.

Before you send the e-mail message, you need to attach a file to the message to Gayle Medvitz to include the schedule she requested. The following steps attach a file to an e-mail message.

- Click the Attach button on the Message tab to display a dialog.

- If Devices is not displayed in the Navigation Pane, drag the Navigation Pane scroller in the dialog until Devices appears.

- If necessary, scroll through the dialog until your USB flash drive appears in the list of available storage devices, and then click the USB flash drive to select it.

- If necessary, navigate to the folder containing the data files for this chapter, and then double-click that folder to open it and display the data files for this chapter.

- Click New Student Orientation Schedule.docx to select the file to attach (Figure 1–43).

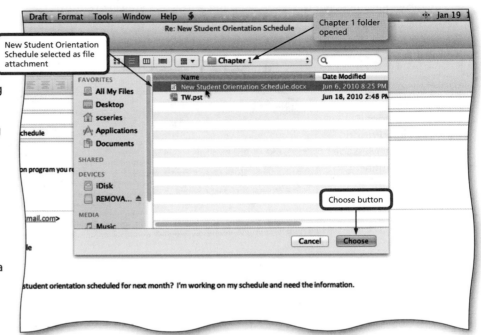

Figure 1–43

- Click the Choose button to attach the selected file to the e-mail message and close the dialog (Figure 1–44).

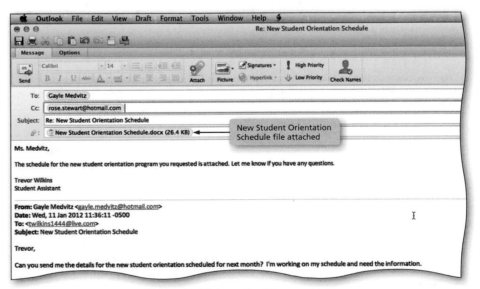

Figure 1–44

Other Ways

1. Choose Draft > Attachments > Add from menu bar

2. Press COMMAND-E

To Set Message Importance for a Single E-Mail Message and Send the Message

Outlook provides the option to assign an **importance level** to a message, which indicates to the recipient the priority level of an e-mail message. The default importance level for all new messages is normal importance, but you can change the importance level to high or low, depending on the priority level of the e-mail message. A message sent with **high importance** displays a red exclamation point in the message header and indicates to the recipient that the message requires a higher priority than other messages he or she might have received. The **low importance** option displays with a blue arrow and indicates to the recipient a low priority for the message.

Your e-mail message to Gayle Medvitz and Rose Stewart requires their immediate attention so you decide to send the message with high importance. The following steps set the high importance option for a single e-mail message and then send the message.

1

- With the message to Gayle Medvitz and Rose Stewart open, click the High Priority button on the Message tab to add a high importance level to the e-mail message (Figure 1–45).

Q&A How would I set a low importance to an e-mail message? Click the Low Priority button on the Message tab.

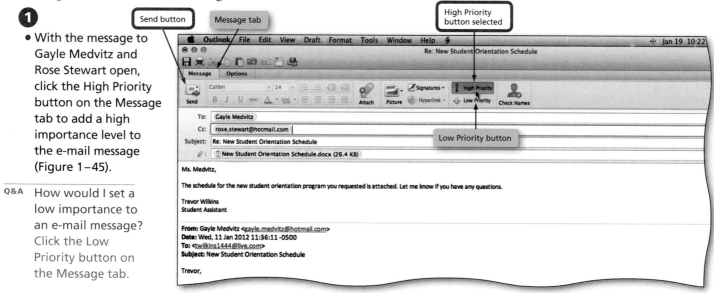

Figure 1–45

2

- Click the Send button on the Message tab to send the e-mail message.

Q&A What happens to the e-mail message I just sent?
After Outlook closes the message window, it stores the e-mail message reply in the Outbox folder while it sends the message to the two recipients. You might not see the message in the Outbox because Outlook usually stores it there only briefly. Next, Outlook moves the message to the Sent Items folder. The original message in the message list now shows an open envelope icon with a purple arrow to indicate a reply was sent.

Outlook Help

BTW At any time while using Outlook, you can find answers to questions and display information about various topics through Outlook Help. Used properly, this form of assistance can increase your productivity and reduce your frustrations by minimizing the time you spend learning how to use Outlook. For instruction about Outlook Help and exercises that will help you gain confidence in using it, read the Office 2011 and Mac OS X chapter at the beginning of this book.

File Attachments

Users typically attach a file to an e-mail message to provide additional information to the recipient. The **Attachment Preview** feature in Outlook allows you to preview an attachment you receive in an e-mail message from either the Reading Pane in an unopened message or the message area of an opened message.

Outlook has built-in previewers for several file types, such as other Office programs, pictures, text, and Web pages. Outlook includes attachment previewers that work with other Microsoft Office programs so that users can preview an attachment without opening it. These attachment previewers are turned on by default. To preview an attached file created in an Office 2011 application, you must have that Office application installed on your computer. For example, to preview an Excel attachment in Outlook, you must have Excel installed. Third-party software vendors may provide previewers that support additional attachment file types.

The previewers in Microsoft Office for Mac 2011 are designed to provide additional security against potentially harmful code, allowing you to preview attachments more safely. Turning off the attachment previewers removes that layer of protection. Using Attachment Preview, you quickly can see the contents of the attachment without opening it, thus eliminating the need to save the attachment. If you do not have the program that was used to create the attached file, you cannot open an attachment.

If Outlook does not have a built-in previewer for an attachment's file type, Outlook displays a message explaining why it cannot preview the attachment. It also asks if you want to save the file and open it with the program in which it was created.

To Preview and Save an Attachment

When you receive a message with an attachment, you can preview an attached file without opening it to see its contents. After Trevor Wilkins receives the e-mail message and attachment from Jay Ballentyne, he previews the contents of the attached file and then saves the attachment in a folder on his computer. The following steps preview and store the attachment from Jay Ballentyne.

- If necessary, click Inbox to display the TW Inbox.

- In the message list, click the message header from Jay Ballentyne with the AV Request Form subject line to select the e-mail message and display its contents in the Reading Pane (Figure 1–46).

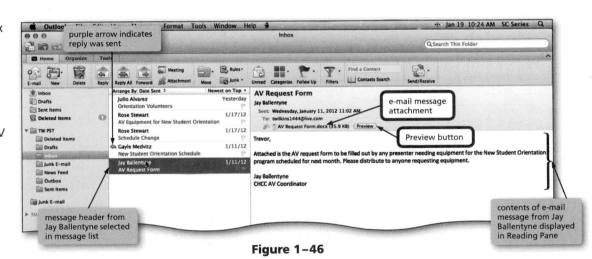

Figure 1–46

2

- In the Reading Pane, click the Preview button to preview the document in a new window (Figure 1–47).

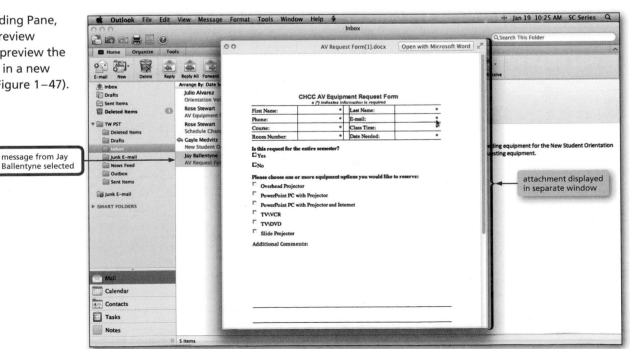

Figure 1–47

- Click the Close button to close the window containing the attachment preview.

- CONTROL-click the attachment and choose Save As from the shortcut menu to display a dialog.

- Navigate to the location to which you wish to save the file, in this case the Chapter 1 folder in the Outlook folder on the USB flash drive (Figure 1–48).

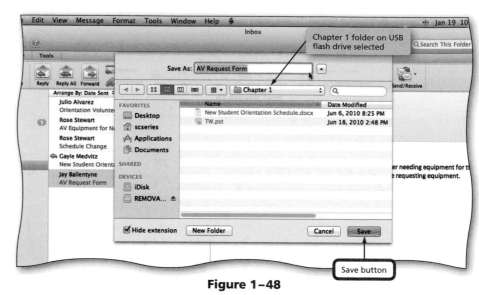

4

- Click the Save button in the dialog to save the attached file and close the dialog.

Figure 1–48

Q&A After I save the attachment, is there a way to keep the e-mail message but not the attachment?

Yes. CONTROL-click the attachment in the Reading Pane and then click Remove in the shortcut menu to remove the attachment from the e-mail message.

Other Ways

1. Choose Message > Attachments >Save

Using Outlook Folders to Organize the Inbox

Keeping track of incoming messages and other Outlook items can be a challenge, especially if you receive many e-mail messages. Outlook provides a basic set of **folders**, which are containers that store Outlook items of a specific type, such as messages, appointments, or contacts. For example, the Inbox is a mail folder created to store e-mail messages. One way to organize your Outlook items is to create folders.

To Create a New Folder in the Inbox Folder

You anticipate receiving several messages throughout the semester from faculty and classmates and want to create a folder in the Inbox folder, known as a subfolder, to store these e-mail messages. The following steps create a subfolder called Volunteers in Trevor Wilkins' Inbox folder.

1

- If it is not already selected, click the Inbox folder under TW PST to select it.

- Click the New button on the Home tab to display the New pop-up menu (Figure 1–49).

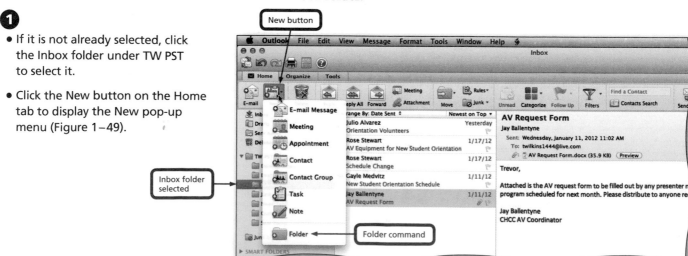

Figure 1–49

● Click Folder in the menu to
create a new folder in the Inbox
(Figure 1–50).

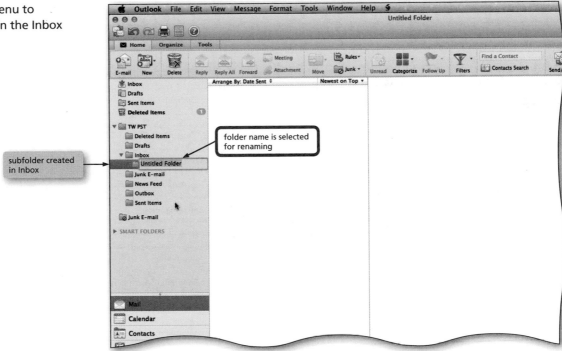

Figure 1–50

● Type **Volunteers** as the
subfolder name, and press RETURN
(Figure 1–51).

Q&A Why is the Volunteers folder
indented below the Inbox folder?
A folder within a folder is called
a subfolder. When you create a
subfolder, Outlook indents the
folder in the list to indicate that
it is a subfolder of a main folder.

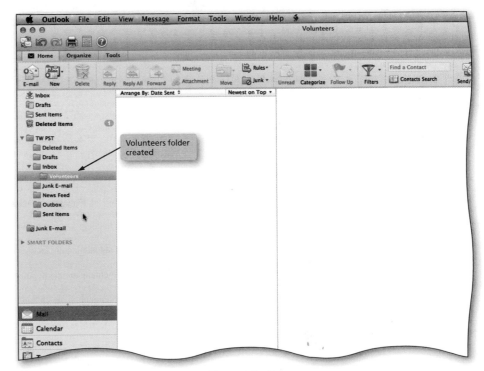

Figure 1–51

🔖 **Other Ways**

1. CONTROL-click Inbox,
   choose New Folder

2. Select Inbox, choose File >
   New > Folder

3. Press SHIFT-COMMAND-N

To Move an E-Mail Message to a Folder

With the folder for e-mail messages regarding volunteers created, the next step is to move messages about volunteers to that folder. Specifically, you will move the message from Julio Alvarez from the Inbox folder to the Volunteers folder. In this case, the Inbox folder is called the source folder, and the Volunteers folder is called the destination folder. A **source folder** is the location of the document or message to be moved or copied. A **destination folder** is the location where you want to move or copy the file or message. The steps on the next page move the message from Julio Alvarez to the Volunteers folder.

- In the Inbox folder (source folder), click the message header from Julio Alvarez in the Inbox message list to select the e-mail message.

- Click the Move button in the Home tab to display the Move menu (Figure 1–52).

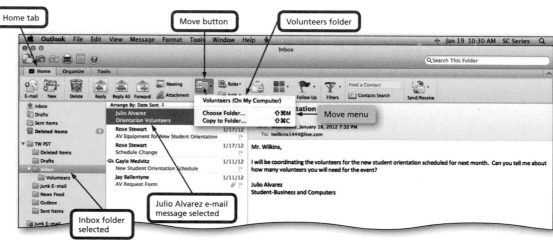

Figure 1–52

- Click Volunteers on the Move menu to move the selected message from the source folder (Inbox folder, in this case) to the destination folder (Volunteers folder, in this case).

- In the Navigation Pane, click the Volunteers folder to display its contents (Figure 1–53).

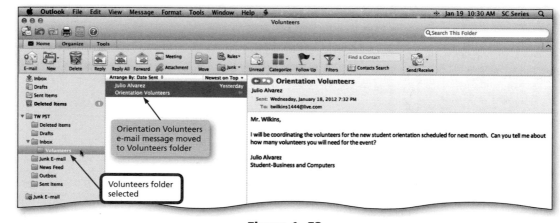

Figure 1–53

Q&A Can I move more than one message at a time?
Yes. Click the first message to select it. While holding the COMMAND key, click additional messages to select them. Click the Move button on the Home tab and then click the destination folder to select it.

Q&A Can I copy the e-mail messages instead of moving them?
Yes. Select the message(s) to copy and click the Move button on the Home tab. Click Copy to Folder on the menu to display the Copy Items dialog. Select the destination folder (the folder you want to copy the e-mail message to) and then click the OK button to copy the selected message to the destination folder.

Other Ways

1 CONTROL-click selected message, choose Move in shortcut menu, choose folder

2 Press SHIFT-COMMAND-M, type name of destination folder in Search box, click Move button

Outlook Chapter 1

To Quit Outlook

This project now is complete. The following step quits Outlook. For a detailed example of the procedure summarized below, refer to the Office 2011 and Mac OS X chapter at the beginning of this book.

1 If you have an e-mail message open, click the Close button on the left side of the title bar to close the message window.

2 Click Outlook in the menu bar and choose Quit Outlook.

Other Ways

1. Press COMMAND-Q

Quick Reference

For a table that lists how **BTW** to complete the tasks covered in this book using the mouse, ribbon, shortcut menu, menu bar, and keyboard, see the Quick Reference Summary at the back of this book, or visit the Office 2011 for Mac Online Companion Web page at www.cengagebrain .com, navigate to the desired application, and click Quick Reference.

Chapter Summary

In this chapter, you learned how to use Outlook to read, open, print, reply to, forward, format, delete, save, and send e-mail messages. You also learned to check spelling in an e-mail. You viewed and saved file attachments as well as attached a file to an e-mail message. You learned how to add a courtesy copy to an e-mail message and set the importance of e-mail messages. Finally, you created a folder in the Inbox and moved an e-mail message to the new folder. The items listed below include all the new Outlook skills you have learned in this chapter.

1. Start Outlook (OUT 6)
2. Open an Outlook Data File (OUT 7)
3. Compose an E-Mail Message (OUT 10)
4. Send an E-Mail Message (OUT 11)
5. Read an E-Mail Message in the Reading Pane (OUT 15)
6. Open an E-Mail Message in a Window (OUT 15)
7. Close an E-Mail Message (OUT 16)
8. Print an E-Mail Message (OUT 16)
9. Print Multiple Copies of an E-Mail Message (OUT 18)
10. Reply to an E-Mail Message (OUT 19)
11. Forward an E-Mail Message (OUT 21)
12. Change the Message Format and Send the Message (OUT 23)
13. Delete an E-Mail Message (OUT 24)
14. Check the Spelling of a Correctly Typed Word (OUT 25)
15. Check the Spelling of Misspelled Text (OUT 27)
16. Save and Close an E-Mail Message without Sending It (OUT 28)
17. Open a Saved E-Mail Message (OUT 30)
18. Include a Courtesy Copy Recipient in an E-Mail Message (OUT 30)
19. Attach a File to an E-Mail Message (OUT 31)
20. Set Message Importance for a Single E-Mail Message and Send the Message (OUT 32)
21. Preview and Save an Attachment (OUT 33)
22. Create a New Folder in the Inbox Folder (OUT 34)
23. Move an E-Mail Message to a Folder (OUT 36)
24. Quit Outlook (OUT 37)

 If you have a SAM 2010 user profile, your instructor may have assigned an autogradable version of this assignment. If so, log into the SAM 2010 Web site at www.cengage.com/sam2010 to download the instruction and start files.

Learn It Online

Test your knowledge of chapter content and key terms.

Instructions: To complete the Learn It Online exercises, start your browser, click the Address bar, and then enter the Web address `scsite.com/out2011/learn`. When the Outlook 2011 Learn It Online page is displayed, click the link for the exercise you want to complete and then read the instructions.

Chapter Reinforcement TF, MC, and SA
A series of true/false, multiple choice, and short answer questions that test your knowledge of the chapter content.

Flash Cards
An interactive learning environment where you identify chapter key terms associated with displayed definitions.

Practice Test
A series of multiple choice questions that test your knowledge of chapter content and key terms.

Who Wants To Be a Computer Genius?
An interactive game that challenges your knowledge of chapter content in the style of a television quiz show.

Wheel of Terms
An interactive game that challenges your knowledge of chapter key terms in the style of the television show *Wheel of Fortune*.

Crossword Puzzle Challenge
A crossword puzzle that challenges your knowledge of key terms presented in the chapter.

Apply Your Knowledge

Reinforce the skills and apply the concepts you learned in this chapter.

Creating an E-Mail Message with an Attachment
Note: To complete this assignment, you will be required to use the Data Files for Students. See the inside back cover of this book for instructions on downloading the Data Files for Students, or contact your instructor for information about accessing the required files.

Instructions: Start Outlook. You are to send an e-mail addressed to selected customers of Hickory Ridge Day Care for Pets who might be interested in boarding their pets. You also attach a file named Day Care for Pets Flyer from the Data Files for Students.

Perform the following tasks:
1. Create a new e-mail message addressed to your instructor and enter `Hickory Ridge Day Care for Pets Bulletin` as the subject.
2. Enter `Greetings,` as the greeting line, checking spelling as you type.
3. Insert a blank line, and then enter `Hickory Ridge Day Care for Pets would like to acquaint you with our newly upgraded facility. We have expanded our facilities to include a climate controlled playroom and a security system to monitor our facility 24/7. Please stop by with your pet any time between 7 am and 5 pm for a visit. We would love to see you and your pet.` as the message text, checking spelling as you type.
4. Enter your name as the signature.
5. Attach the Day Care for Pets Flyer file to the e-mail message.
6. Save the e-mail message on a USB flash drive using the file name, Day Care for Pets Bulletin. Submit the e-mail message, shown in Figure 1–54, in the format specified by your instructor.

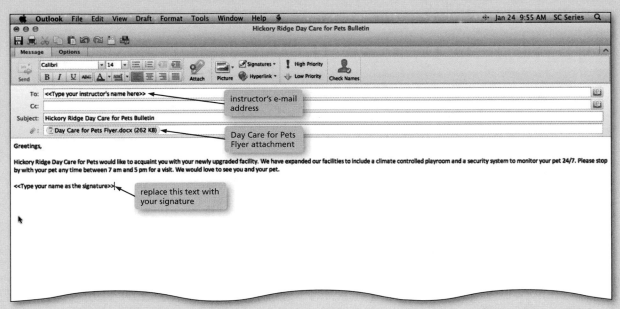

Figure 1–54

Extend Your Knowledge

Extend the skills you learned in this chapter and experiment with new skills. You may need to use Help to complete the assignment.

Managing E-Mail Messages

Note: To complete this assignment, you will be required to use the Data Files for Students. See the inside back cover of this book for instructions on downloading the Data Files for Students, or contact your instructor for information about accessing the required files.

Instructions: Start Outlook. Open the Extend 1-1.pst mailbox file from the Data Files for Students. You will create three folders, rename the folders, and then move messages into the appropriate folders. You also will apply a follow-up flag for the messages in one of the folders. Use Outlook Help to learn about how to add a flag to a message for follow-up and how to create an Outlook Data File for Mac (.olm).

Perform the following tasks:

1. Create three new subfolders in the Inbox folder. Name one folder New folder 1, another folder New folder 2, and the third folder New folder 3. Make sure that only mail items are contained in the new folders.

2. In the Navigation Pane, rename the newly created folders. Rename New folder 1 to USB Problems. Rename New folder 2 to Monitor Problems. Rename New folder 3 to Printer Problems. (*Hint:* To rename the folders, right-click the folder you want to rename in the Navigation Pane to open a shortcut menu. Select Rename Folder on the shortcut menu. Type the new name of the folder, and then press the RETURN key.)

3. Based on the message headers and content of the e-mail messages in the Extend 1-1 mailbox, move each message to one of the folders you created. Mark all the messages as unread. Figure 1–55 on the next page shows the mailbox with the messages moved to the new folders.

4. In the Monitor Problems folder, assign a flag for follow-up for next week to all messages.

5. Export the Inbox mailbox to an Outlook data file (.olm) on a USB flash drive using the file name, Extend 1-1.olm, and then submit it in the format specified by your instructor.

Continued >

Extend Your Knowledge *continued*

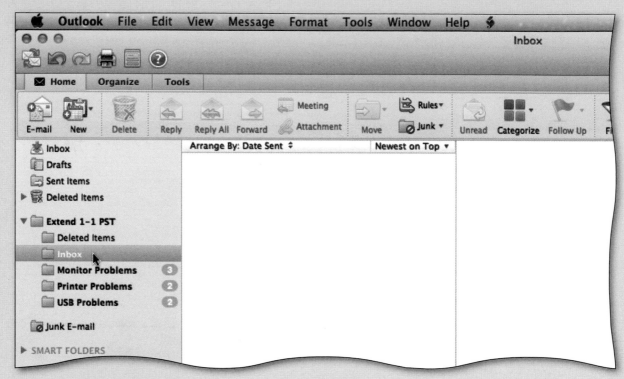

Figure 1–55

Make It Right

Analyze a document and correct all errors and/or improve the design.

Correcting Errors and Changing the Format of an E-Mail Message

Note: To complete this assignment, you will be required to use the Data Files for Students. See the inside back cover of this book for instructions on downloading the Data Files for Students, or contact your instructor for information about accessing the required files.

Instructions: In Outlook, open the Outlook data file, Make It Right 1-1.pst, from the Data Files for Students. The Dietary Needs for the Upcoming Conference message contains spelling errors. To see the red dotted line under the misspelled words, click at the end of the message and press the SPACE BAR. The e-mail message was sent using the HTML message format, as shown in Figure 1–56.

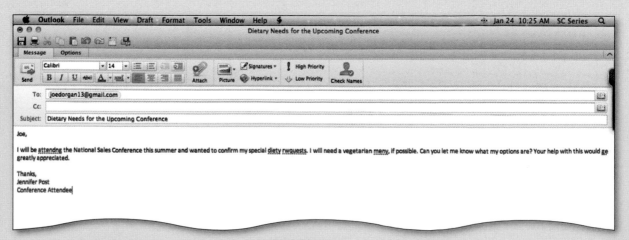

Figure 1–56

Copy the body of the message by selecting the body of the message and then clicking the Copy button in the Standard toolbar. Create a new e-mail message and then paste the copied text into the body of the new message. Address the e-mail to yourself. Check for the spelling and grammar errors and correct each spelling error (red dotted underline) and grammar error (green or blue dotted underlines). In most cases, you can make the correction by CONTROL-clicking the flagged text and then clicking the appropriate correction in the shortcut menu. In some cases, however, you may need to make the correction by hand.

Change the format of the e-mail message to Plain Text, and then send the message to yourself. Save the message on a USB flash drive as Make It Right 1-1.eml by dragging the message from the Sent items folder in Outlook to the USB flash drive in a Finder window, and then submit it in the format specified by your instructor.

In the Lab

Design and/or create an e-mail message using the guidelines, concepts, and skills presented in this chapter. Labs are listed in order of increasing difficulty.

Lab 1: Composing and Saving an E-Mail Message with High Importance

Problem: After returning from an illness that required you to miss a class at school, you need to contact your instructor. Create an e-mail message to your instructor requesting information about missed class assignments and change the message format to Plain Text. Because you need this information immediately, send the e-mail message with high importance. Also, send a Cc (courtesy copy) to yourself. Figure 1–57 shows the completed e-mail message.

Instructions: Perform the following tasks:

1. Open the Untitled window to create a new e-mail message.

2. Address the e-mail message to your instructor and send a Cc (courtesy copy) to yourself.

3. Type **Missed Class Assignments** as the subject.

4. Change the format of the message to Plain Text.

5. Type the message text as shown in Figure 1–57, inserting blank lines where they appear in the figure. Use your name as the signature. If Outlook flags any misspelled words as you type, check their spelling and correct them.

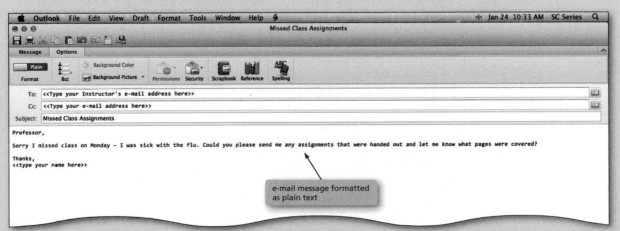

Figure 1–57

Continued >

In the Lab *continued*

6. Apply High Importance to this message and send the message.

7. Save the message in the Drafts folder.

8. Save the message on a USB flash drive as Missed Class Assignments.eml by dragging the message from the Sent items folder in Outlook to the USB flash drive in a Finder window, and then submit it in the format specified by your instructor.

In the Lab

Lab 2: Composing, Sending, and Replying to an E-Mail Message

Problem: As a part-time employee in the Computer Help Center for your school, you have been asked to compile a list of keyboard shortcuts for Outlook 2011. First, you compose the e-mail message shown in Figure 1–58, and then you attach a file. The document to be attached is named Outlook 2011 Keyboard Shortcuts.

Note: To complete this assignment, you may be required to use the Data Files for Students. See the inside back cover of this book for instructions on downloading the Data Files for Students, or contact your instructor for information about accessing the required files.

Instructions: Perform the following tasks:

1. Create a new e-mail message. Address the message to yourself with a courtesy copy to your instructor.

2. Enter the subject, message text, and signature shown in Figure 1–58a. Insert blank lines where they are shown in the figure. If Outlook flags any misspelled words as you type, check their spelling and correct them.

3. Attach the Outlook 2011 Keyboard Shortcuts file to the e-mail message.

4. Send the e-mail message with high importance and use the HTML format for the message.

5. When you receive the Keyboard Shortcuts for Outlook 2011 e-mail message, move it to a new folder in your Inbox named Shortcuts.

6. Open the message in the Shortcuts folder, and then compose the reply. Figure 1–58b shows a reply from a student named Dana Cooper to a student named Heather Moore. Copy the text of the e-mail message shown in Figure 1–58b, but replace Heather's e-mail address with your own. Be sure to remove your instructor's e-mail address from the Cc text box, if necessary. If Outlook flags any misspelled words as you type, check their spelling and correct them.

7. If necessary, change the format of the e-mail message to Plain Text, and then send the message to yourself.

8. When you receive the RE: Keyboard Shortcuts for Outlook 2011 message, move it to the Shortcuts folder in your Inbox folder.

9. Save the e-mail message on a USB flash drive using your last name plus *Lab 2* as the file name. For example, if your last name is Smith, the file name would be Smith Lab 2.eml. Submit the file in the format specified by your instructor.

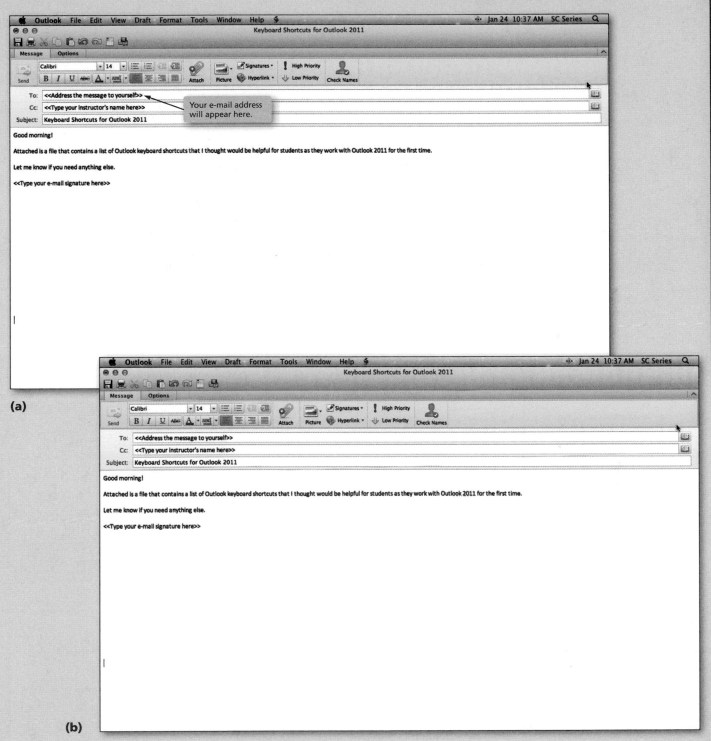

(a)

(b)

Figure 1–58

In the Lab

Lab 3: Creating and Sending an E-Mail Message to Several People

Problem: Your boss at Maple Valley Bakery has asked you to send e-mail messages to a few new customers inviting them to a pastry and coffee event the bakery is hosting. For one e-mail message, you need to attach a document named Maple Valley Bakery Flyer. You prepare the e-mail messages shown in Figure 1–59.

Note: To complete this assignment, you may be required to use the Data Files for Students. See the inside back cover of this book for instructions on downloading the Data Files for Students, or contact your instructor for information about accessing the required files.

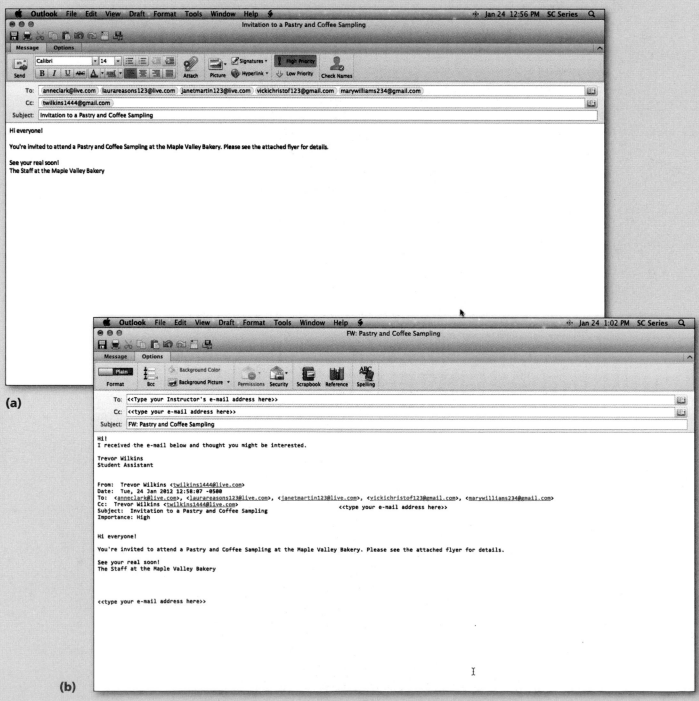

(a)

(b)

Figure 1–59

Instructions: Perform the following tasks:

1. Create a new e-mail message. Address the message to the following recipients:

   anneclark@live.com

   laurareasons123@live.com

   janetmartin123@live.com

   vickichristof123@gmail.com

   marywilliams234@gmail.com

2. Enter your e-mail address so that you send a courtesy copy to yourself.

3. Enter the subject, message text, and signature shown in Figure 1–59a. Insert blank lines where they are shown in the figure. If Outlook flags any misspelled words as you type, check their spelling and correct them.

4. Attach the Maple Valley Bakery Flyer document to the e-mail message.

5. Save the e-mail message in the Drafts folder.

6. Send the e-mail message with high importance and use the HTML format for the message.

7. When you receive the Invitation to a Pastry and Coffee Sampling e-mail message, move it to a new folder in your Inbox named Events.

8. Select the message in the Events folder, and then forward to your instructor the message shown in Figure 1–59b. If Outlook flags any misspelled words as you type, check their spelling and correct them.

9. If necessary, change the format of the e-mail message to Plain Text, and then send yourself a courtesy copy.

10. Save the response e-mail message on a USB flash drive using your last name plus *Lab 3* as the file name. For example, if your last name is Smith, the file name would be Smith Lab 3 .eml. Submit the file in the format specified by your instructor.

Cases and Places

Apply your creative thinking and problem solving skills to design and implement a solution.

Note: To complete these assignments, you may be required to use the Data Files for Students. See the inside back cover of this book for instructions on downloading the Data Files for Students, or contact your instructor for information about accessing the required files.

1: Compose, Print, and Send a Message for a Campus Event

Academic

As an employee of the student union, you are responsible for creating and sending e-mail messages informing student leaders about upcoming lectures and presentations at the union. This month, the union has two lectures and one presentation scheduled. The presentation is about travel in Washington, DC. The e-mail message should include an attachment of a digital photo. The Data Files for Students contain a photo named DC.jpg or you can use your own digital photo if it is appropriate for the topic of the e-mail message. The e-mail message should be addressed to yourself and your instructor. The subject should contain the text, Spring Lectures at the Union. The message text consists of the following, in any order: The student union is sponsoring three events in its lecture series on our nation's capital this month. Enjoy a panoramic presentation about tourism in Washington, DC. Experience the varieties of culinary offerings. Learn about the upcoming festivals and cultural events

Continued >

Cases and Places *continued*

throughout the Washington, DC, metropolitan area. Use the concepts and techniques presented in this chapter to create this e-mail message. Be sure to check spelling and grammar before you send the message. Submit your assignment in the format specified by your instructor.

2: Compose an E-Mail Message to a Relative or Friend and Attach a File

Personal

Being involved with your studies, extracurricular activities, and college life in general can limit the time you have to communicate with family and friends. Compose and send an e-mail message to a close relative or friend. The e-mail message should contain information about your class schedule, activities, and new friends that you have made. Attach a picture of the school to the message. You can use the file College.jpg or you can use your own digital photo of your school. Compose the message in HTML format. The subject should be Campus Life or you can use your own subject. The message text consists of at least the following information: This semester I am taking 15 credits, so my schedule is very full. I also am involved in the Student Government Association. I met a student who went to high school in a neighboring town, and we found we have many mutual friends. Attached is a picture of one of our buildings so you can get a sense of how beautiful the campus is. Add a greeting line, closing, and other appropriate text. Use the concepts and techniques presented in this chapter to create this e-mail message. Be sure to check spelling and grammar before you send the message. Submit your assignment in the format specified by your instructor.

3: Forward an E-Mail Message to Multiple Recipients Informing Them about an Event

Professional

As an IT recruiter for local executive search firm, you receive many e-mail messages regarding job and career fairs throughout your community. You recently received an e-mail message, IT Recruitment Fair.msg, inviting you to attend an employment fair sponsored by the Chamber of Commerce and held at a local high school. The Career Fair also provides job seekers with a free résumé review service and access to a job search database. More than 100 employers representing various industries will be represented and attending would be a wonderful networking opportunity. Your schedule is full and you cannot attend. The e-mail message asks that you forward the invitation to anyone you think might be interested in attending. In a folder window, open the message file IT Recruitment Fair.msg from the Data Files for Students in the Cases and Places folder. Replace nikitanner123@gmail.com in the To box with your own e-mail address and send the e-mail message to yourself. Now you can forward the e-mail message to your coworkers.

Forward the e-mail message to three coworkers who you think might benefit from attending, telling them about the benefits of such an event. Their e-mail addresses are as follows:

davidclark@live.com

angelareasons123@live.com

marcimartin123@live.com

Send a courtesy copy to your boss, in case she might want to send additional people to the event or perhaps attend the event herself. Her e-mail address is susanwilliams234@gmail.com. Print the forwarded message and submit it in the format specified by your instructor.

2 Managing Calendars

Objectives

You will have mastered the material in this chapter when you can:

Open the Calendar folder

Describe the components of the Outlook Calendar

Navigate the Calendar using the mini calendar

View specific dates on the mini calendar

Create a personal calendar

Enter, save, move, edit, and delete appointments

Set the status of and a reminder for an appointment

Create and edit events

Move and delete events

Create and edit meetings and respond to meeting requests

Display the calendar in Day, Work, Week, and Month views

Print the calendar in Grid and List views

2 Managing Calendars

Introduction

Whether you are a student at a local college, an activity coordinator in your community, or a business professional, you can take advantage of the Outlook Calendar to schedule and manage appointments, events, and meetings. In particular, you can use Calendar to keep track of your class schedule and appointments, and to schedule meetings. If you are traveling and do not have electronic access to your calendar, you can print a copy to keep with you. You can use Outlook to view or print a daily, weekly, or monthly calendar.

In addition to using Calendar in your academic or professional life, you will find it helpful for scheduling personal time. Most people have multiple appointments to keep each day, week, or month. Calendar can organize activity-related information in a structured, readable manner.

Project — Appointments, Events, and Meetings in Calendar

Time management is a part of everyday life. Many people constantly are rearranging appointments, work schedules, and vacations in an attempt to use their time efficiently. Managing your schedule using a calendar can increase productivity, while maximizing free time. Outlook is the perfect tool to maintain both a professional and a personal schedule. The **Calendar** is the Outlook folder that contains your personal schedule of appointments, events, and meetings. In this project, you use the basic features of Calendar to create a calendar for appointments, classes, work schedules, and extracurricular activities for Trevor Wilkins (Figure 2–1). In addition to creating a calendar for Trevor, you will learn how to print a daily, weekly, or monthly calendar.

Overview

As you read through this chapter, you will learn how to create the calendar shown in Figure 2–1 by performing these general tasks:

- Enter appointments on specific dates.
- Create one-time and recurring appointments.
- Move appointments to new dates.
- Create one-time and recurring events.
- Schedule a meeting with others.
- Respond to a meeting request.
- View and print the calendar.

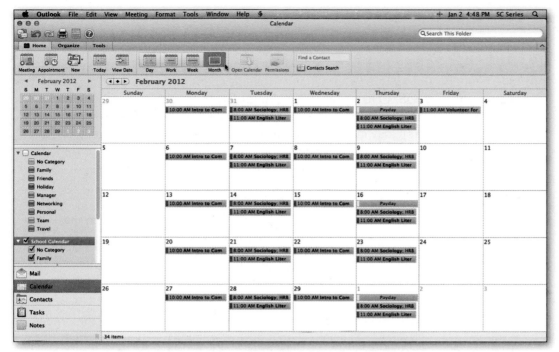

Figure 2–1

General Project Guidelines

When creating a calendar, the actions you perform and decisions you make will affect the appearance and characteristics of the finished calendar. As you create an appointment, event, or meeting to develop a schedule, you should follow these general guidelines:

1. **Determine what you need to schedule.** People use a calendar to keep track of their schedule and to organize and manage their time. For students, a class list with room numbers and class times would be a good start toward managing their school schedule. For business professionals, the calendar is a dynamic tool that requires frequent updating to keep track of appointments and meetings. You also may want to keep track of personal items, such as birthdays and family gatherings.

2. **Determine where to store your calendar items.** Any information you add to the Outlook Calendar is called a calendar item, or item for short. Outlook stores items in a folder named Calendar by default. If you are creating personal, academic, or business items, you may want to create separate calendars for each group.

3. **Determine if an activity is recurring.** A recurring activity is one that happens on a regular basis. Classes most likely recur throughout the semester. Work schedules can change week-by-week or month-by-month. Family events, such as birthdays and anniversaries, also can be recurring events on the calendar.

4. **Create an agenda before scheduling a meeting.** An agenda is a list of items to be discussed in a meeting. A poorly organized meeting may be the least productive tool in the business world, while a carefully planned meeting with a defined agenda can be a productive use of time, helping meeting participants stay focused and on schedule.

5. **Set calendar item options.** When creating items on a calendar, determine how to display the time of an appointment or event, such as busy or out of the office, so that the calendar is an accurate indication of your time. Also, decide whether to set a reminder for the item and how often it recurs, if at all.

6. **Determine the best method for distributing a calendar.** Consider whether you need to share a calendar with others. If you do, you can share calendars electronically in Outlook or print a calendar and distribute printed copies.

When necessary, more specific details concerning the above guidelines are presented at appropriate points in the chapter. The chapter also will identify the actions performed and decisions made regarding these guidelines during the creation of the calendar shown in Figure 2–1.

For an introduction to Mac OS X and instruction about how to perform basic Mac OS X tasks, read the Office 2011 and Mac OS X chapter at the beginning of this book, where you can learn how to resize windows, change screen resolution, create folders, move and rename files, use Mac OS X Help, and much more.

To Start Outlook

If you are using a computer to step through the project in this chapter and you want your screens to match the figures in this book, you should change your screen's resolution to 1280 × 800. For information about how to change a computer's resolution, refer to the Office 2011 and Mac OS X chapter at the beginning of this book.

The following steps, which assume Mac OS X is running, start Outlook based on a typical installation. You may need to ask your instructor how to start Outlook for your computer. For a detailed example of the procedure summarized below, refer to the Office 2011 and Mac OS X chapter at the beginning of this book.

1 Click the Outlook icon in the Dock to open Outlook.

2 If the Outlook window is not maximized, click the green Zoom button next to the Minimize button on its title bar to maximize the window.

3 Click the Calendar button in the Navigation Pane to display the Calendar window in Day view. If the calendar is not in Day view, click the Day button on the Home tab of the ribbon.

4 If the mini calendar is not displayed at the top of the Navigation Pane, click the divider at the top of the Navigation Pane and drag it downward until the mini calendar is displayed (Figure 2–2).

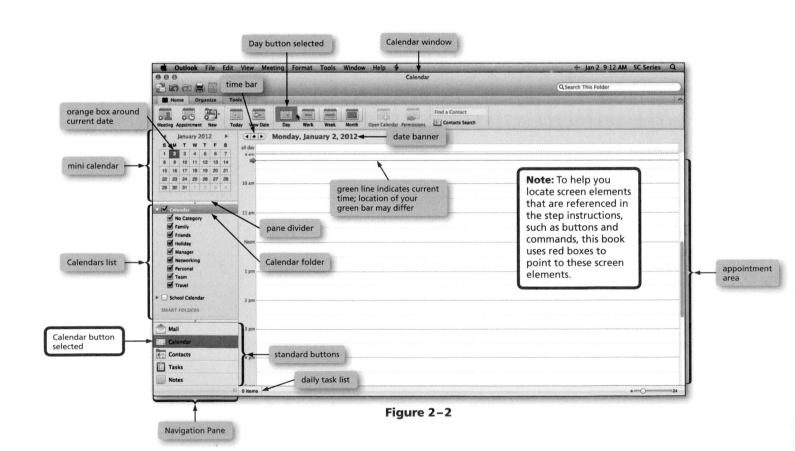

Figure 2–2

Calendar Window

The Calendar window shown in Figure 2–2 includes a variety of features to help you work efficiently. It contains many elements similar to the windows in other Office programs, as well as some that are unique to Outlook. The main elements of the Calendar window are the Navigation Pane, the appointment area, and the daily task list.

The Navigation Pane includes buttons for Mail, Calendar, Contacts, Tasks, and Notes, and two other panes: the mini calendar and the Calendars list. The **mini calendar** shows a calendar for the current month with an orange box around the current date, scroll arrows to advance from one month to another, and any date on which an item is scheduled in bold. The **Calendars list** shows available calendars and the various categories available for each calendar. The appointment area contains a date banner, a day heading, and a time bar. The appointment area displays 30-minute time slots by default when viewing Calendar in Day, Work, or Week view, and is not available in Month view. The time bar has Previous and Next buttons that allow you to move back or forward one unit (day, work week, or week), and the diamond Today button in the center allows you to view the range that includes today's date. The task list displays a list of current tasks, appears below the appointment area, and is only visible in Day, Work, and Week views.

Calendar Items

An **item** is any element in Outlook that contains information. Examples of calendar items include appointments, events, and meetings. All calendar items start as an appointment. Outlook defines an **appointment**, such as a doctor's appointment, as an activity that does not involve other people or resources, such as conference rooms. Outlook defines an **event**, such as a seminar or vacation, as an activity that occurs at least once and lasts 24 hours or longer. An appointment becomes an event when you schedule it for the entire day. An annual event, such as a birthday, anniversary, or holiday, occurs yearly on a specific date. Events do not occupy time slots in the appointment area and, instead, are displayed in a banner below the day heading when viewing the calendar in Day, Work, or Week view. An appointment becomes a **meeting** when people and other resources, such as meeting rooms, are involved.

Items are organized into Calendar folders. Calendar folder contents are displayed on the calendar. Display contents of a folder by clicking on the box beside the calendar folder name. Make a calendar folder the active calendar by clicking on the calendar folder name itself. Items will be displayed, or not displayed, and greyed out, or not, depending on how the calendar folders are selected. Figure 2–3 on the next page shows how different selection options change what is displayed on the calendar.

For an introduction to Office 2011 and instruction about how to perform basic tasks in Office 2011 programs, read the Office 2011 and Mac OS X chapter at the beginning of this book, where you can learn how to start a program, use the ribbon, save a file, open a file, quit a program, use Help, and much more.

Using Calendars

For those with Microsoft BTW Exchange accounts, other users can give you access to their calendars. This allows you to make appointments, check free times, schedule meetings, and refer to contact information. This is especially useful when you are scheduling meetings or events that depend on other people's schedules.

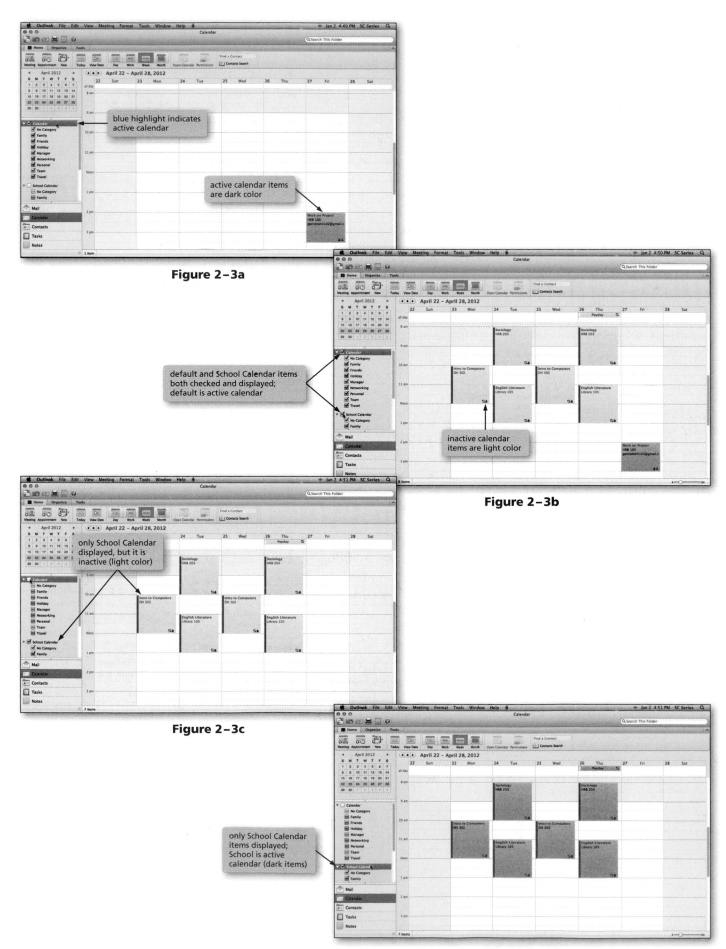

Figure 2–3a

Figure 2–3b

Figure 2–3c

Figure 2–3d

When you create items on your calendar, it is helpful to show your time using the appointment status information. You can set the appointment status for a calendar item using the Status button on the Appointment tab on the ribbon, which provides four options for showing your time on the calendar: Free, Tentative, Busy, and Out of Office. For example, if you are studying or working on a project, you might show your time as busy because you are unable to perform other tasks at the same time. On the other hand, a dental appointment or a class would show your time as Out of Office because you need to leave your home or office to attend. Table 2–1 describes the items you can schedule on your calendar and the appointment status option associated with each item. Each calendar item also can be one-time or recurring.

Table 2–1 Calendar Items		
Calendar Item	**Description**	**Show As Default**
One-time appointment	Default calendar item, involves only your schedule and does not invite other attendees or require resources such as a conference room	Busy
Recurring appointment	Occurs at regular intervals, such as weekly, biweekly, monthly, or bimonthly	Busy
One-time event	Occurs at least once and lasts 24 hours or longer, such as a vacation or conference	Free
Recurring event	Occurs at regular intervals, such as weekly, biweekly, monthly, or bimonthly, such as holidays	Free
One-time meeting	Includes people and other resources, such as meeting rooms	Busy
Recurring meeting	Occurs at regular intervals, such as weekly, biweekly, monthly, or bimonthly, such as staff meetings or department meetings	Busy

The Ribbon and Screen Resolution

Outlook may change **BTW** how the groups and buttons within the groups appear on the ribbon, depending on the computer's screen resolution. Thus, your ribbon may look different from the ones in this book if you are using a screen resolution other than 1280 × 800.

Determine where to store your calendar items.

When you schedule an appointment, Outlook adds the appointment to the Calendar folder by default. If you are creating personal, academic, and business items, you may want to create a separate calendar for each group. Users often create multiple calendars to keep personal items separate from academic or business items.

Plan Ahead

To Create a Personal Folder

As in other Outlook folders, such as the Inbox, you can create multiple folders within the Calendar folder. In certain situations, you may need to keep more than one calendar, such as one for business items and another for personal items.

The following steps create a folder to store your class and school-related information, separate from your default folder, Calendar.

1

- With the Calendar window open, click Organize on the ribbon to display the Organize tab (Figure 2–4).

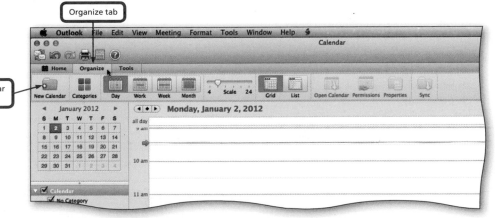

Figure 2–4

• Click the New Calendar button to create a new Untitled Folder in the Navigation Pane.

• Type **School Calendar** and press RETURN to enter a name for the new folder. Click the disclosure arrow beside Calendar to collapse the Calendar folder (Figure 2–5).

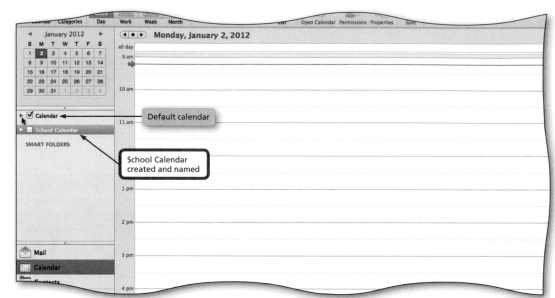

Figure 2–5

To Display a Personal Calendar

Now that the School Calendar folder has been created, the next step is to make sure that any entries in the School Calendar appear in the appointment area. The following step displays entries from both the Calendar and the School Calendar folders in the appointment area.

• In the Calendars pane, click the check box beside School Calendar to place a check mark in the check box, and make sure that the default Calendar folder also has a check mark so that both the Calendar and the School Calendar folders are selected in the calendar list and displayed in the appointment area (Figure 2–6).

Figure 2–6

To Remove the Default Calendar from the Appointment Area

While working with the School Calendar, you may want to display only that calendar in the Outlook window to see only school-related calendar items. The following step removes the default Calendar from the appointment area.

- Click Calendar in the Calendars list to remove the check mark from the Calendar check box, so that the default calendar no longer is displayed in the appointment area (Figure 2–7).

Q&A   Why does my view look different from what is shown?
Figure 2–6 shows Day view. If this is not the current view, click the Day button on the Home tab.

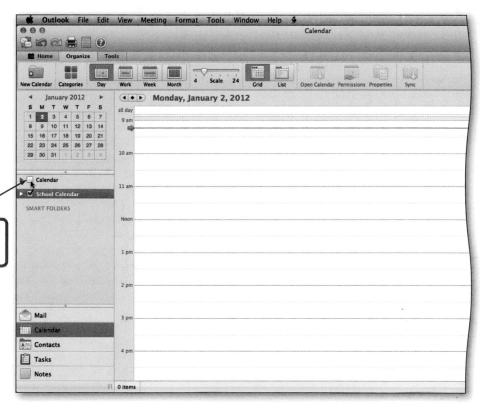

check mark removed so default calendar contents no longer displayed

Figure 2–7

Viewing the Calendar

Each Microsoft Outlook 2011 folder displays the items it contains in a layout called a view. You can change the arrangement and format of the folder contents by changing the view. Recall that the default view of the Calendar folder is Week view. Some people may prefer a different view of their calendar, such as daily or monthly. For instance, you might want to view all the items for a given month at one time, in which case Month view would work best.

In this section, you will navigate to a specific date and then examine the different ways to view a calendar. Although the Outlook window looks different in each view, you can accomplish the same tasks in each view: you can add, edit, or delete appointments, events, and meetings.

Q&As

For a complete list of the Q&As found in many of the step-by-step sequences in this book, visit the Office 2011 for Mac Online Companion Web page at www.cengagebrain.com, navigate to the desired chapter, and click Q&As.

BTW

To Go to a Specific Date

The next step in this project is to display a date that is not visible in the current view so that you can view that date in the appointment area. One option is to use the View Date button, which allows you to navigate to a specific date and display that date in the appointment area. The following steps display a specific date, in this case January 15, 2012, in the appointment area in a calendar.

- Display the Home tab, and then click the View Date button to display a pop-up calendar (Figure 2–8).

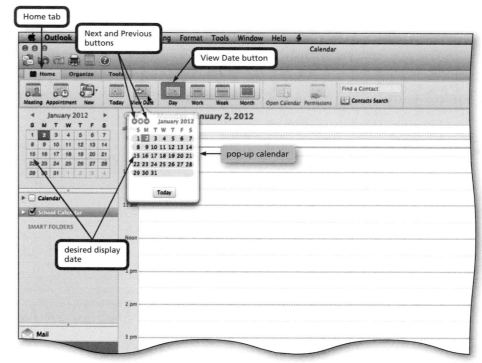

Figure 2–8

- If necessary, use the Next or Previous buttons on the time bar in the pop-up menu to display January 2012.

- Click the date of interest, in this case January 15, 2012 in the pop-up calendar to display the date in the current calendar (Figure 2–9).

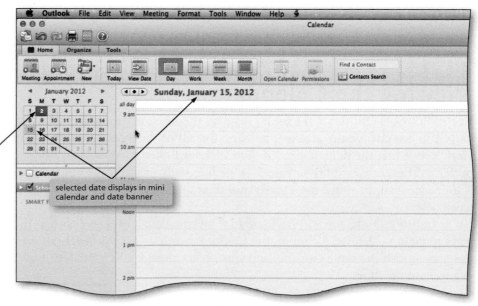

Figure 2–9

Other Ways

1. Click Next or Previous buttons in mini calendar to display the desired month, then click the desired date

To Display the Calendar in Work View

In Outlook, you can display several calendar days at once so that you can see multiple appointments at the same time. **Work view** shows five workdays (Monday through Friday) in a columnar style. Hours that are not part of the default workday (9:00 AM – 5:00 PM) appear shaded when viewing the calendar in Day, Work, and Week view. The following step displays the calendar in Work view.

1

- Click the Work button on the Home tab to display the work week in the appointment area for the selected date (Figure 2–10).

Q&A Why is Monday, January 16, through Friday, January 20, highlighted on the mini calendar?
The calendar days displayed in the appointment area are highlighted on the mini calendar.

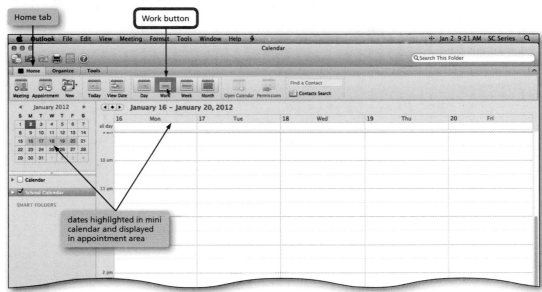

Figure 2–10

Other Ways
1. Choose View > Work Week   2. Press CONTROL-COMMAND-2

To Display the Calendar in Week View

The advantage of displaying a calendar in **Week view** is to see how many appointments are scheduled for any given week, including weekends. In Week view, the seven days of the selected week appear in the appointment area. The following step displays the calendar in Week view.

1

- Click the Week button on the Home tab to display the full week, including weekends, in the appointment area (Figure 2–11).

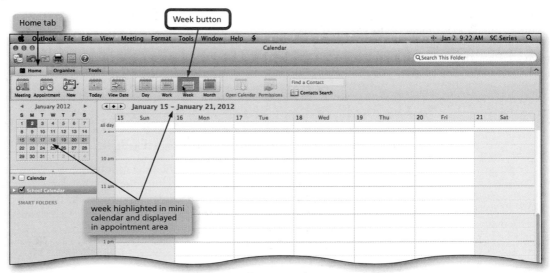

Figure 2–11

Other Ways
1. Choose View > Week   2. Press CONTROL-COMMAND-3

To Display the Calendar in Month View

Month view resembles a standard monthly calendar page and displays a schedule for an entire month. Appointments are listed in each date in the calendar. The following step displays the calendar in Month view.

1
- Click the Month button on the Home tab to display one full month in the appointment area (Figure 2–12).

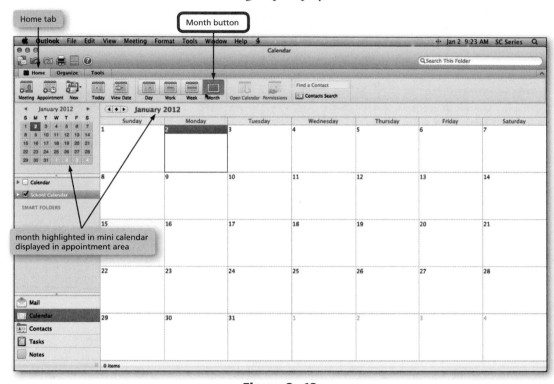

Figure 2–12

BTWs

 BTW For a complete list of the BTWs found in the margins of this book, visit the Office 2011 for Mac Online Companion Web page at www.cengagebrain.com, navigate to the desired chapter, and click BTWs.

Creating and Editing Appointments

Recall that every item you schedule in Outlook Calendar begins as an appointment. In Outlook, you easily can change an appointment to an event or a meeting. This section describes how to navigate to a specific date, schedule a dental visit as a one-time appointment, and enter classes in a class schedule as recurring appointments, starting with January 1, 2012.

Plan Ahead **Determine what you need to schedule.**

As mentioned previously, you can schedule appointments, events, and meetings using Outlook Calendar. You can create appointments either directly in the appointment area or use the New Appointment button. One method may be more efficient than the other, depending on the item you are scheduling and how much detail you need to enter for the calendar item you are creating.

Creating Appointments in the Appointment Window

A **one-time appointment**, such as a lunch date, doctor's appointment, or conference call, is an appointment that occurs only once on a calendar. A **recurring appointment**, such as a class in a class schedule, repeats on the calendar at regular intervals. You can create an appointment by double-clicking a time slot in the appointment area to open the Appointment window. You also can click the Appointment button on the Home tab to open the Appointment window. From the Appointment window, you can enter specific details about the appointment, such as location and recurrence pattern. The **recurrence pattern** schedules the Outlook appointment on the calendar at regular intervals for a designated period of time.

Outlook also allows you to configure a **reminder**, similar to an alarm clock reminder, which is an alert window that briefly appears on your screen as a reminder of an upcoming appointment. Depending on how Outlook Calendar is configured, you may hear a chime or other sound as part of the reminder.

Another option when creating an appointment is to set the **appointment status**, which is how the time for a calendar item is marked on your calendar. The default appointment status setting is Busy, as indicated in the previous steps, but you can change the status to more accurately reflect your time.

Keeping Appointments Private

Besides setting the status of an appointment, you can designate an appointment as private so that other users cannot view or access the appointment. Use the Private button on the Appointment tab to mark an appointment as private.

BTW

To Create a One-Time Appointment Using the Appointment Window

When you click a day on the mini calendar in the Navigation Pane, Outlook displays the calendar for the date selected in Day view in the appointment area. Day view shows a daily view of a specific date in half-hour increments. The following steps create a one-time conference call appointment on the default calendar on January 16 using the appointment area to open the Appointment window.

- Click the Day button on the Home tab to display the daily view of the calendar in the appointment area.

- Click 16 in the January mini calendar to display the selected date in the appointment area (Figure 2–13).

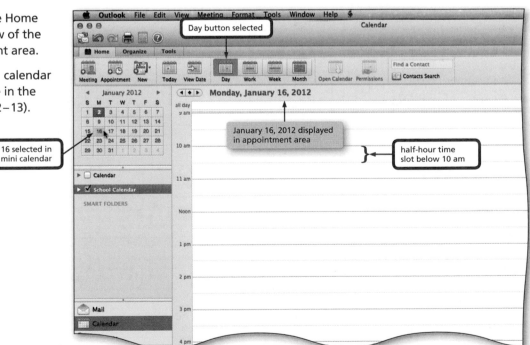

Figure 2–13

2

- Double-click in the half-hour slot under 10:00 am to open the Appointment window (Figure 2–14).

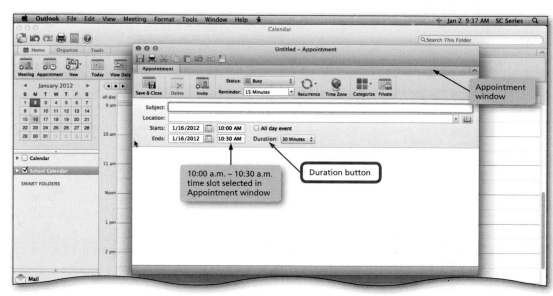

Figure 2–14

3

- Type **Conference Call** as the appointment subject.

- Click the Duration button to display the duration pop-up menu (Figure 2–15).

Q&A Why did the title of the window change from Untitled – Appointment to Conference Call – Appointment?
The title bar displays the name of the appointment. Because the name of the appointment changed, the name on the title bar also changed.

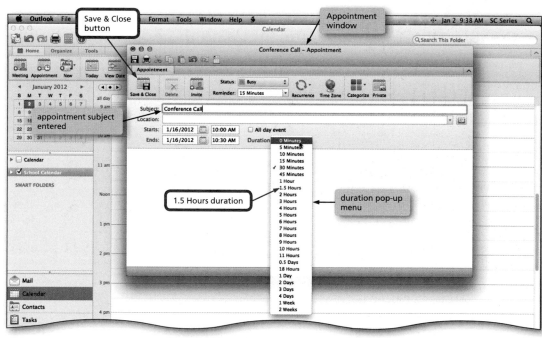

Figure 2–15

4

- Choose 1.5 Hours from the pop-up menu, and then click the Save & Close button to close the Appointment window and enter the conference call appointment in the appointment area (Figure 2–16).

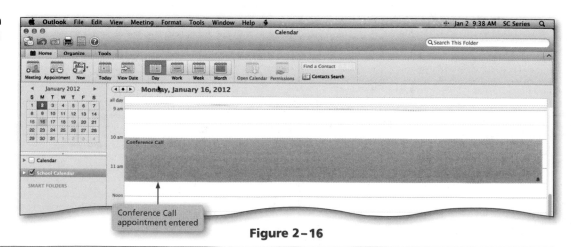

Figure 2–16

To Create Another One-Time Appointment Using the Appointment Window

You volunteered to work at the annual blood drive from 11:00 AM until 4:00 PM on Tuesday, January 17. The following steps enter the blood drive appointment using the Appointment button on the Home tab to open the Appointment window.

1 Click the Appointment button on the Home tab to open the Untitled – Appointment window.

2 Type `Volunteer for Blood Drive` in the Subject text box as the appointment subject, and press the TAB key to move the insertion point to the Location text box.

3 Type `Student Activities Center` in the Location text box as the location of the event.

4 Click the Starts calendar button to display a calendar for the current month, and click 17 to select the start date.

Q&A Why did the end date in the Ends date text box change to the same date as the Starts date text box?

Outlook automatically sets appointments to occur during a single day, with a default duration of 30 minutes.

5 Click 8 in the Starts time text box and type `11` to set the start time to 11:00 a.m.

6 Change the duration to 5 Hours (Figure 2–17).

Q&A Why did I not have to specify an End date for the appointment?

When you specify a Start date, Outlook uses the same date for the End date by default.

Q&A Why did I not have to specify an End time for the appointment?

When you specify a Start time and duration, Outlook calculates the appropriate End time automatically.

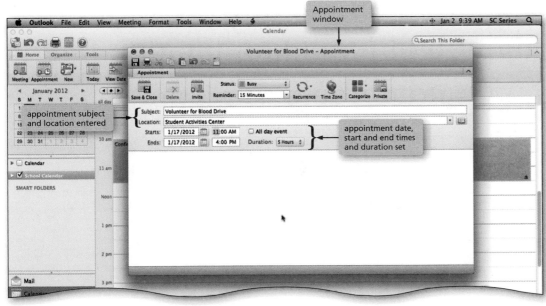

Figure 2–17

Other Ways

1. Choose File > New > Appointment in menu bar

2. Click in appointment area, press COMMAND-N

Plan Ahead

Set Calendar item options.

When creating items on your calendar, you can set a number of options that determine how the Calendar is displayed and how it handles an appointment. Table 2–2 lists the options available when creating an item on your calendar. Consider setting one or all of the options shown in Table 2–2.

Setting Appointment Options

Searching for Calendar Items

BTW To find a calendar item, click the Search This Folder text box in the upper-right corner of the calendar. Type a word or phrase contained in the calendar item you are seeking. Items that contain the text you typed are listed with the search text highlighted. When you are finished, click the Close button on the Search tab.

The Appointment window provides the ability to set options for an appointment. Table 2–2 lists the main settings available in the Appointment window, and Table 2–3 lists the options for indicating your availability on the Calendar.

Table 2–2 Main Elements of the Appointment Window	
Option	**Description**
Status	Indicates your availability on a specific date and time; if you want to show others your availability when they schedule a meeting with you during a specific time, this must be set accurately. The ability to show others your availability is applicable if you are working with a Microsoft Exchange Account, which allows others to view your calendar.
Reminder	Alerts you at a specific time prior to the item's occurrence
Recurrence	If an item on your calendar repeats at regularly scheduled intervals, set the Recurrence options so that you only have to enter the item once on your calendar
Time Zone	Use the time zone option to specify the time zone for the meeting time, if you have participants in more than one time zone.
Invite	Clicking Invite changes the appointment to a meeting, and allows you to send invitations for the meeting to other people by specifying an e-mail address
Categorize	Use categories to organize Outlook items
Private	Applicable if you are working with a Microsoft Exchange Account, which allows others to view your calendar; this option keeps everything but the date and time of an item visible to the owner only

Table 2–3 Calendar Item Status Options	
Calendar Item Status Options	**Description**
Free	Shows time in white in Day, Week, Work, or Month view
Tentative	Shows time with a slashed bar to the left in Day, Week, Work, or Month view
Busy	Shows time block in blue/gray in Day, Week, Work, or Month view
Out of Office	Shows time with a purple bar to the left in Day, Week, Work, or Month view

The following pages illustrate how to set these various appointment options.

To Change the Status of an Appointment

To make sure your time is displayed accurately on the calendar, you change the appointment status from the default of Busy to Out of Office, meaning you are not in the office for the time of the blood drive appointment. The following steps change the status of an appointment.

1

• Click the Status button in the Volunteer for Blood Drive – Appointment window to display the list of appointment status options (Figure 2–18).

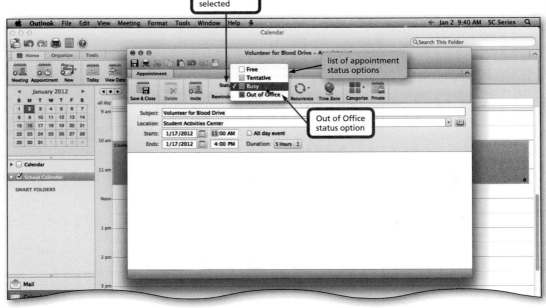

Figure 2–18

2

• Click Out of Office to change the appointment status from Busy to Out of Office (Figure 2–19).

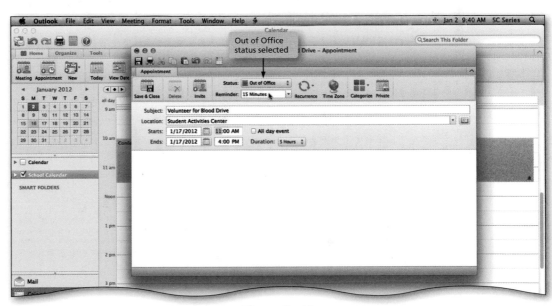

Figure 2–19

Other Ways

1. Click appointment, click Status button on Appointment tab, set status

2. Double-click appointment, click Status button (Appointment window), change status

3. CONTROL-click appointment, choose Show As in shortcut menu

4. Press COMMAND-O, change status

To Set a Reminder for an Appointment

With the start and end date and time for the blood drive appointment set and the appointment status selected, you want to schedule a reminder so that you do not forget the appointment. Recall that a reminder works similar to an alarm clock with options such as Snooze and Dismiss. When the reminder is displayed, you also can open the item for further review. The following steps set a 30-minute reminder for the blood drive appointment.

- Click the Reminder box arrow to display a list of available reminder intervals (Figure 2–20).

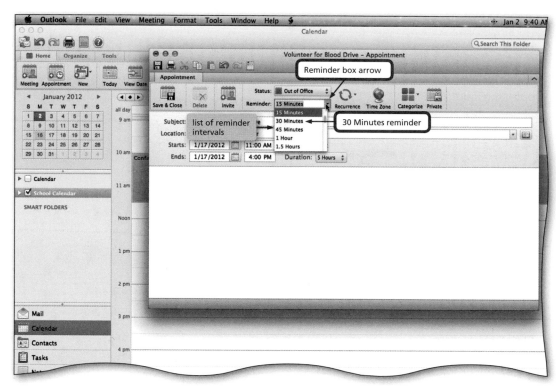

Figure 2–20

- Click 30 Minutes to set a reminder for 30 minutes prior to the start time of the appointment (Figure 2–21).

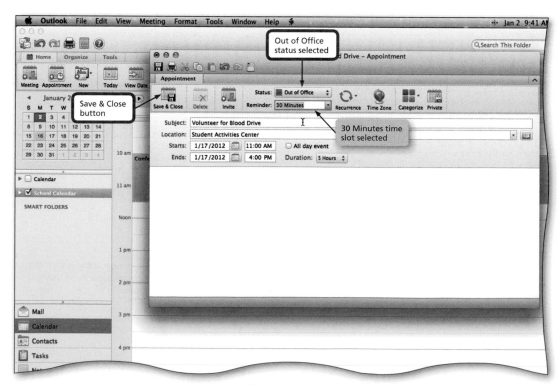

Figure 2–21

3

- Click the Save & Close button to save and close the Volunteer for Blood Drive – Appointment window and place the appointment on the calendar.

- Click 17 on the mini calendar to display January 17, 2012 in the appointment area (Figure 2–22).

Q&A Do I have to click the date in the appointment area when I save an appointment?
It is not necessary to click the date in the appointment area, but it is good practice to verify your appointments to ensure the details are accurate.

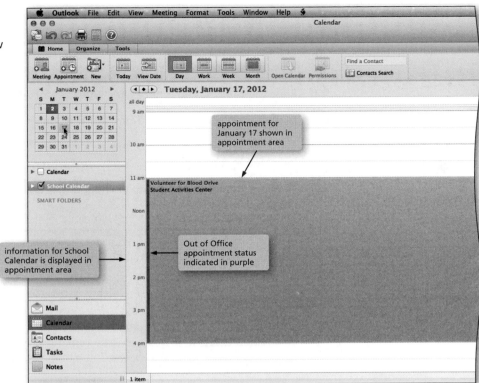

Figure 2–22

To Create the Remaining One-Time Appointments and View the Calendar

With the Volunteer for Blood Drive appointment created, the next step is to add the other appointments listed in Table 2–4, which shows appointments for various student activities on campus. The following steps create the remaining one-time appointments in the Appointment window using the data in Table 2–4.

Table 2–4 Additional One-Time Appointments

Subject	Location	Start & End Date	Start Time	End Time	Status	Reminder
Interview for student activity position	Activity Center	1/18/2012	9:00 AM	10:30 AM	Out of Office	10 minutes
International Student Fundraiser	RFB 400	1/19/2012	11:00 AM	12:00 PM	Tentative	30 minutes
Internship Opportunities	DH 100	1/20/2012	9:30 AM	11:00 AM	Tentative	5 minutes

1 Click the Appointment button on the Home tab to open the Untitled – Appointment window.

2 Enter the subject for the first appointment in Table 2–4 in the Subject text box and then press the TAB key to move the insertion point to the Location text box.

3 Enter the location for the first appointment as indicated.

4 Press the TAB key and use the Calendar button to enter the date of the appointment.

5 Select the hour of the start time, and enter the hour of the start time from the table.

6 Press the TAB key and, if necessary, enter the minutes of the start time from the table.

7 Press the TAB key, and if necessary, type **a** for AM or **p** for PM.

8 Move to and update the end time for the appointment.

9 Click Status button to change the appointment status for the first appointment as indicated in the table.

10 Click the Reminder box arrow to change the reminder for the first appointment as indicated in the table.

11 Click the Save & Close button to save the appointment.

12 Repeat Steps 1 through 11 for the two remaining one-time appointments in the table.

13 Click the Week button on the Home tab to view the completed calendar (Figure 2–23).

Q&A   What is the bell icon I see in the lower-right corner of appointments?
The bell indicates that a reminder is set. When the reminder is due, an alert is displayed on screen and a sound plays. To set a reminder to display on screen without sound, choose Outlook > Preferences, and uncheck the Reminder box under Sounds.

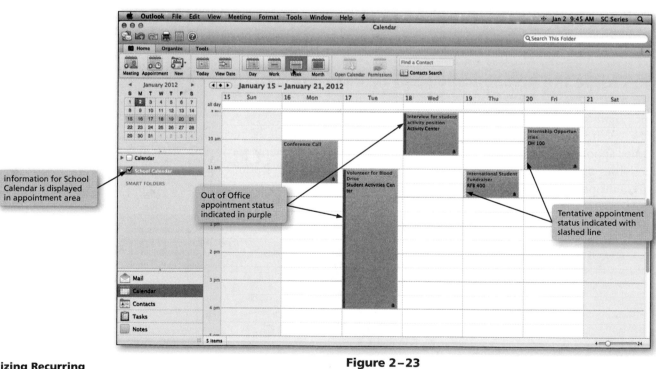

Figure 2–23

Recognizing Recurring Appointments

BTW The Recurrence symbol appears on recurring appointments and events. You can double-click an item with a Recurrence symbol to edit one or more occurrences of the appointment or event.

Creating Recurring Appointments

Many appointments are **recurring appointments**, meaning they happen at regular intervals for a designated period of time. For example, a class held every Monday and Wednesday from 9:00 AM to 11:00 AM is a recurring appointment. Your college classes occur two times per week, at regular weekly intervals during the semester, and entering these recurring appointments for each occurrence during the semester would be time-consuming. You want to add the classes to the calendar as recurring appointments so that you can keep track of time throughout the entire semester. Adding these classes as recurring appointments enables you to enter the appointment information one time, with it automatically recurring at a set interval for a specified period of time. You will create the appointment only once and configure the recurrence pattern to designate the rate of recurrence, in this case weekly, and on what day(s) of the week the class occurs.

To Create Another Appointment Using the Appointment Window

The following steps create an appointment for the Introduction to Computers class.

1 Click the Appointment button on the Home tab to open the Untitled – Appointment window.

2 Type **Intro to Computers** in the Subject text box and then press the TAB key to move the insertion point to the Location text box.

3 Type **DH 302** in the Location text box as the location for the class.

4 Click the Starts Calendar button to display a pop-up calendar of available dates, and then click 23 to select Mon 1/23/2012 as the day the first class meets.

5 Change the start time for the class to 10:00.

6 Change the end time for the class to 12:00 PM.

To Set Recurrence Options for an Appointment

Now that the appointment for the first class is created, you will establish a recurring pattern so that you do not have to enter the class schedule every week. The following steps configure a recurring pattern for the Introduction to Computers class, which meets every Monday and Wednesday until the end of the semester.

1

- Click the Recurrence button to display the Recurrence pop-up menu (Figure 2–24).

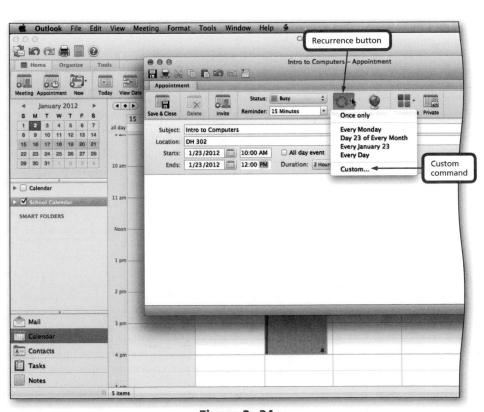

Figure 2–24

2

- Choose Custom from the pop-up menu to display a dialog.

- If necessary, click the Repeats button, then choose Weekly to set the recurrence pattern.

- In the Every text box , type 1 if it does not already appear in the text box to schedule the frequency of the recurrence pattern.

- In the On area, click W to schedule the class two times per week (Mondays and Wednesdays) (Figure 2–25).

Q&A   Why is the Monday check box already selected in the Recurrence pattern area?
Monday is already selected because that was the date you entered for the day the class starts. If the class started on Tuesday, then the Tuesday check box would be selected when you set the recurrence pattern.

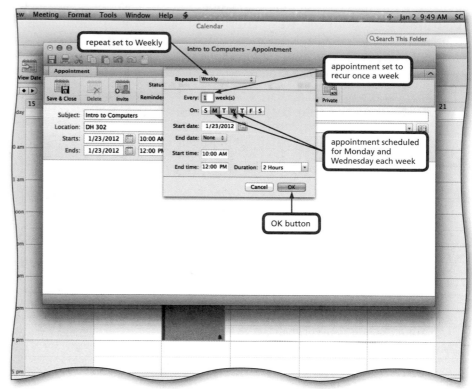

Figure 2–25

Q&A   Why does the Start date text box contain a date?
When you display the Appointment Recurrence dialog, Outlook automatically sets the range of recurrence with the date the appointment starts.

3

- Click the End Date calendar button, then click By from the pop-up menu.

- Click the End date calendar button and use the Previous and Next buttons on the pop-up calendar to navigate to May (Figure 2–26).

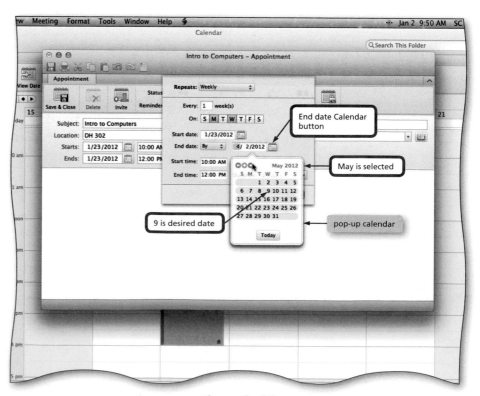

Figure 2–26

- Click 9 to replace the displayed end date with a new date (Figure 2–27).

Q&A What if I do not know the end date, but I know how many times the class meets?
You can click the End after option button and then type the number of times the class meets in the End after text box.

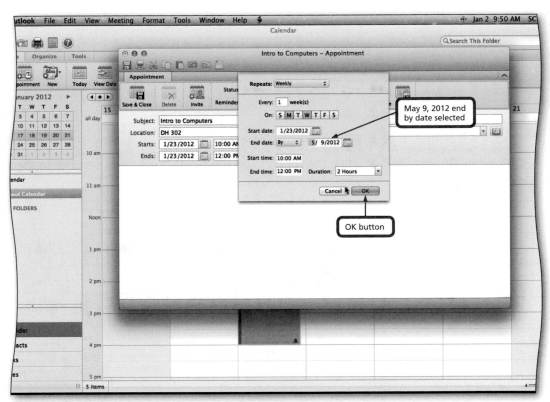

Figure 2–27

⑤

- Click the OK button to close the dialog and set the recurrence pattern (Figure 2–28).

Q&A Why is the value in the Reminder box set for 15 minutes?
The default reminder time for all calendar items is 15 minutes.

Q&A Why did the appointment title bar change to Intro to Computers Appointment Series?
When you set a recurring pattern, the title bar changes to reflect a series.

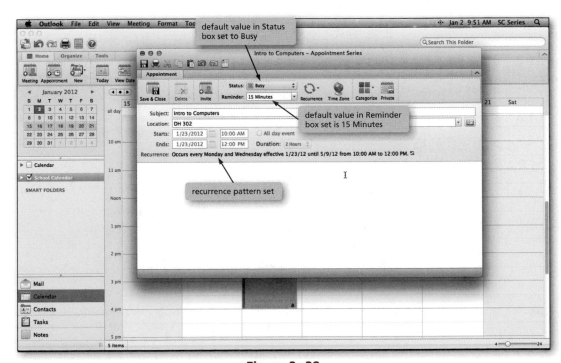

Figure 2–28

Moving a Recurring Appointment

BTW If you move a recurring appointment, you move only the selected instance of the appointment. To move all instances of a recurring appointment, open the appointment, click the Edit Series button (Appointment tab | Options group), click the Recurrence button, and then change the recurrence pattern.

To Set Status Options and a Reminder for an Appointment

Next, you will set a reminder 30 minutes prior to the class and mark your time as Out of Office because you will be in class during this time. The following steps set the Status and Reminder options.

1 Click the Status button to display the list of appointment status options.

2 Click Out of Office to change the appointment status from Busy to Out of Office.

3 Click the Reminder box arrow to display a list of available reminder intervals.

4 Click 30 Minutes to set a reminder for 30 minutes prior to the start time of the appointment (Figure 2–29).

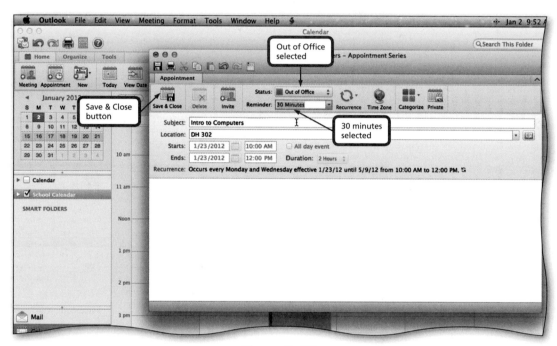

Figure 2–29

To Save the Appointment

With all the information about the Introduction to Computers class entered, you must save the appointment. The following steps save the Intro to Computers – Appointment Series and close the window.

1 Click the Save & Close button to save the recurring appointment on the calendar and close the window.

2 Click 23 on the mini calendar to display the January 23, 2012 recurring appointment in the appointment area in Week view (Figure 2–30).

Q&A Do I need to display the appointment after I save it?
No, this step was included to view the appointment on the calendar.

Q&A What is the new icon I see beside the reminder icon?
This icon indicates that this is a recurring appointment.

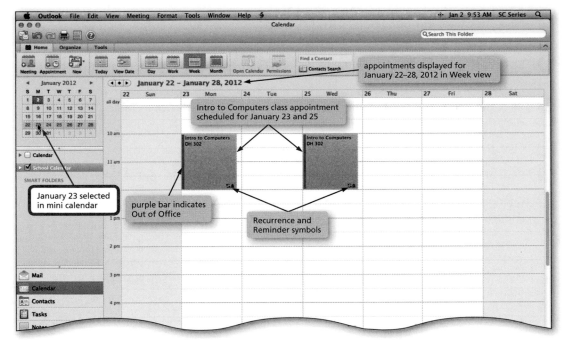

Figure 2–30

To Create More Recurring Appointments

With the Intro to Computers class appointment series created, the next step is to create recurring class appointments for the remainder of your class schedule using the appointment information in Table 2–5. The following steps create the remaining class schedule.

Table 2–5 Recurring Appointments								
Appointment (Class)	Location	Start Date	End Date	Start Time	End Time	Show As	Reminder	Recurrence
Sociology	HRB 203	1/24/2012	Set in Recurrence	8:00 AM	10:00 AM	Out of Office	30 minutes	Weekly, every Tuesday and Thursday; end by Thursday, 5/3/2012
English Literature	Library 105	1/24/2012	Set in Recurrence	11:00 AM	1:00 PM	Out of Office	15 minutes	Weekly, every Tuesday and Thursday; end by Thursday, 5/3/2012

1 Click the Day button on the ribbon to display the daily view of the calendar in the appointment area.

2 Click 24 in the mini calendar to select January 24 and to display the selected date in the appointment area.

3 Click the Appointment button on the Home tab to open the Untitled – Appointment window.

4 Type `Sociology` as the appointment subject and then press the TAB key to move to the Location field.

5 Enter the location shown in Table 2–5.

6 Change the start and end times to match the start and end times for the class shown in Table 2–5.

7 Click the Status button to display the list of appointment status options and then click the option shown Table 2–5 on the previous page.

8 Select the Reminder box arrow to display the list of time slots and then click the option shown in Table 2–5.

9 Click the Recurrence button and set the recurrence pattern shown in Table 2–5, and then click the OK button to close the Recurrence dialog.

10 Click the Save & Close button to close the Appointment window.

11 Repeat Steps 3 through 10 to add the information in the second row of Table 2–5.

12 Change to Week view, and scroll up if necessary to see both appointments in the calendar (Figure 2–31).

Q&A   What if I have appointments that recur other than weekly?
You can set daily, weekly, monthly, or yearly recurrence patterns in the Recurrence dialog. A recurring appointment can be set to have no end date, to end after certain number of occurrences, or to end by a certain date.

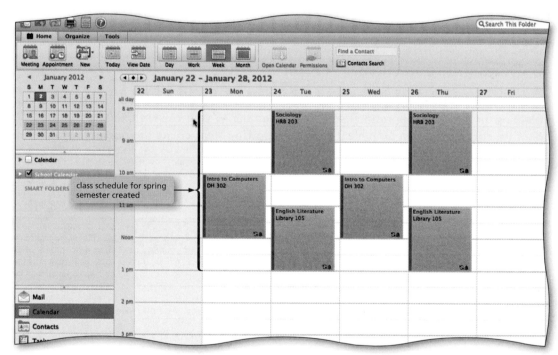

Figure 2–31

To Create Another One-Time Appointment Using the Appointment Window

You signed up for a college trip to New York on January 14th, and need to enter the trip information on your calendar. Buses leave from the front parking lot at 7:00 AM and will return by 11:00 PM the same day. The following steps create an appointment for the date and time of the New York trip.

1 Open the Appointment window.

2 Enter `New York Trip` in the Subject text box.

3 Enter `Bus pickup in front parking lot` in the Location text box

4 Set the start date to January 14, 2012.

5 Set the start time to 7:00 a.m. and the end time to 11:00 p.m.

6 Save the appointment and close the Appointment window. Scroll to January 14 in Day view to confirm the appointment information (Figure 2–32).

Q&A Why is it important to verify the appointment?

It is important to verify that you did not make inadvertent mistakes while adding the appointment to your calendar. Errors might cause you to miss an important appointment.

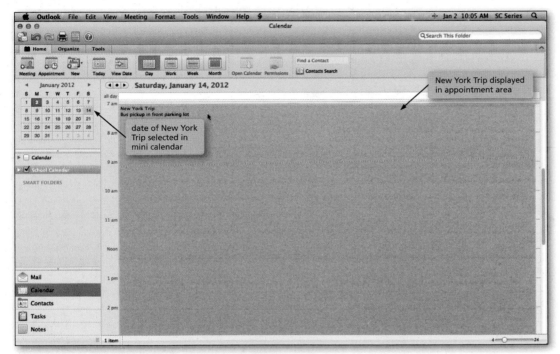

Figure 2–32

Editing Appointments

Schedules often need to be rearranged, and Outlook provides several ways to edit appointments. You can change the subject and location by clicking the appointment and editing the information directly in the appointment area, or by double-clicking the appointment and making corrections using the Appointment window. You can specify whether all occurrences in a series of recurring appointments need to be changed, or a single occurrence should be altered.

To Move an Appointment to a Different Time on the Same Day

Outlook provides several ways to move appointments. Suppose, for instance, that you cannot attend the conference call appointment at 10:00 AM on Monday, January 16, 2012. The appointment needs to be rescheduled to 1:00 PM for the same amount of time (two hours, in this case). Instead of deleting and then retyping the appointment, you can drag it to a new time slot. The following step moves the conference call appointment to a new time slot.

- Click 16 in the January 2012 mini calendar in the Navigation Pane to display the selected date in the appointment area.

- Position the mouse pointer on the conference call appointment to prepare to move the appointment.

- Drag the conference call appointment to the 1:00 PM time slot on the same day to reschedule the appointment (Figure 2–33).

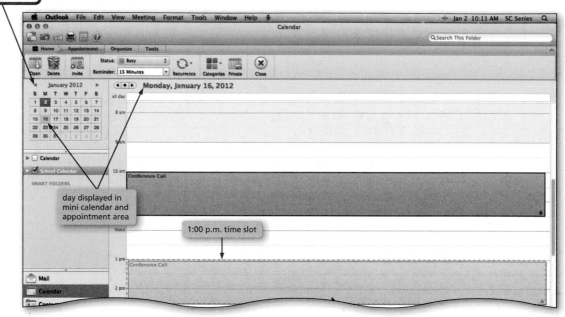

Figure 2–33

Other Ways

1. Double-click appointment, change time in Appointment window, click Save & Close

2. CONTROL-click appointment, choose Open, change time in Appointment window, click Save & Close

3. Press COMMAND-O, change time in Appointment window, click Save & Close

To Move an Appointment to a Different Date

If you are moving an appointment to a new date but remaining in the same time slot, you can drag the appointment to the new date in appointment area. The following step moves an appointment to a new date in the same time slot.

- Click the Month button on Home tab of the ribbon to change to Month view.

- In the appointment area, drag the selected appointment on January 16, 2012 to the 25 in the January 2012 calendar (Figure 2–34).

- Release the mouse button to move the appointment to the new date.

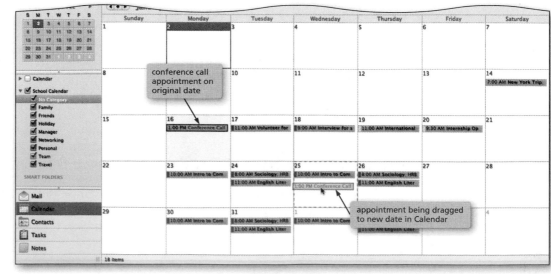

Figure 2–34

To Move an Appointment to a Different Month

The blood drive, originally scheduled for January 17, 2012, has been rescheduled to February 3, 2012. To move an appointment to another month, you must open the Appointment window. The following steps open the Volunteer for Blood Drive appointment and move it to February 3, 2012.

- Click 17 in the January 2012 mini calendar in Navigation Pane to display the selected date in Day view in the appointment area (Figure 2–35).

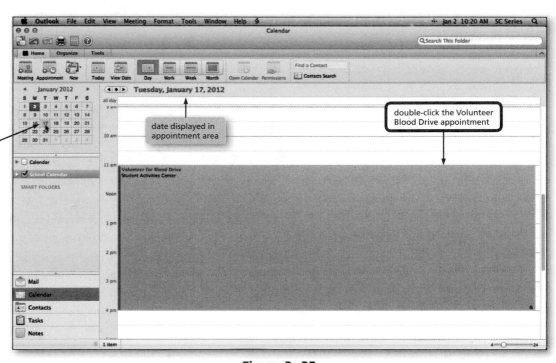

Figure 2–35

- Double-click the Volunteer for Blood Drive appointment in the appointment area to open the Appointment window.

- Click the Starts calendar button to display the calendar for selecting a start date.

- Click the Next button to display the calendar for February 2012 (Figure 2–36).

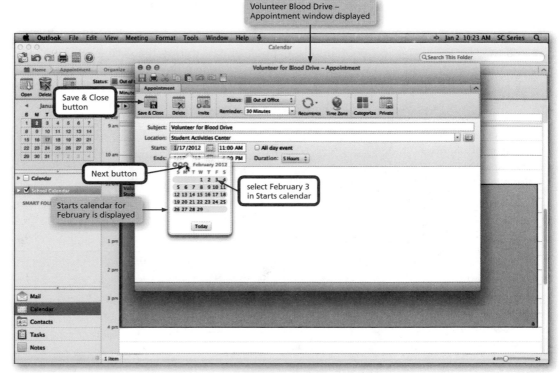

Figure 2–36

- Click 3 in the Starts calendar for February to display the selected date in both the Starts and Ends boxes.

- Click the Save & Close button to save the change to the appointment and close the window.

- Scroll to February in the mini calendar and click 3 to verify the appointment change (Figure 2–37).

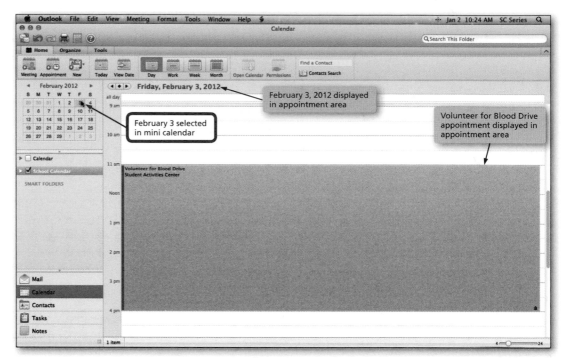

Figure 2–37

To Delete a Single Occurrence of a Recurring Appointment

Appointments sometimes are canceled and must be deleted from the schedule. For example, the schedule created thus far in this project contains class appointments during the spring semester. The college is closed for Spring Break from April 9 – 13, 2012 and no classes will meet during that time. The classes scheduled during Spring Break need to be deleted. The following steps delete only the classes scheduled during Spring Break.

- Click the Next button on the mini calendar until April 2012 is displayed.

- Click 9 on the mini calendar to display April 9, 2012 in the appointment area.

- Click the Intro to Computers appointment in the appointment area to display the Appointment Series tab (Figure 2–38).

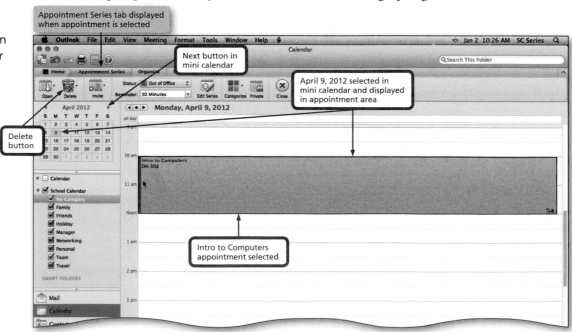

Figure 2–38

- Click the Delete button on the Appointment Series tab to display the Delete menu (Figure 2–39).

- Click Occurrence on the Delete menu and then click Delete in the dialog that displays to delete only the selected occurrence from the calendar.

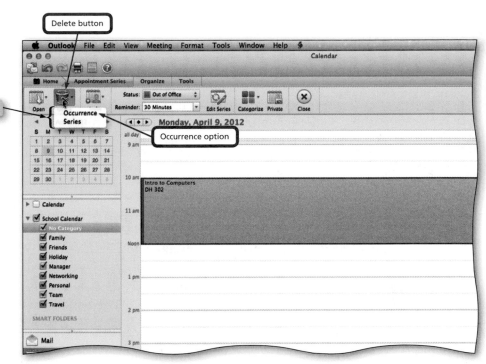

Figure 2–39

❹

- Click the Week button on the ribbon to display appointments for the week of April 8 – April 14, 2012.

- Repeat Steps 2 through 3 to delete the remaining classes from the week of April 8, 2012 (Figure 2–40).

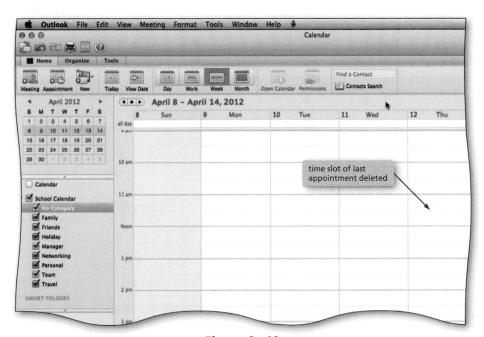

Figure 2–40

Other Ways

1. Click appointment, press DELETE, click Delete button in dialog

2. CONTROL–click appointment, click Delete in shortcut menu, choose Delete Occurrence, click Delete button in dialog

Break Point: If you wish to take a break, this is a good place to do so. To resume at a later time, start Outlook and continue following the steps from this location forward.

Creating and Editing Events

Outlook's Calendar folder allows you to keep track of important events. Recall that events are activities that last 24 hours or longer. Examples of events include conferences, vacations, and holidays. Events can be one-time or recurring. In Outlook, events differ from appointments in one primary way — they do not appear in individual time slots in the appointment area. Instead, when you schedule an event, its description appears in a small banner below the day heading. Similar to an appointment, the event status can be indicated as time that is free, busy, tentative, or out of the office during the event. See Table 2–3 on page OUT 63 for a complete description of these options.

To Create a One-Time Event in the Appointment Window

A Computer Expo is being held at the Convention Center from May 9, 2012 through May 11, 2012 that you want to attend. Because the conference will last for several days, Outlook will schedule the conference as an event. You begin to schedule an event by creating an appointment. Because you are not certain you can attend the event, you decide to show your time as Tentative. The following steps create an event for the convention on the calendar.

1

- Click the Appointment button on the Home tab to open the Untitled – Appointment window.

- Type **Computer Expo** in the Subject text box, and then press the TAB key to move the insertion point to the Location text box.

- Type **Convention Center** as the location of the event (Figure 2–41).

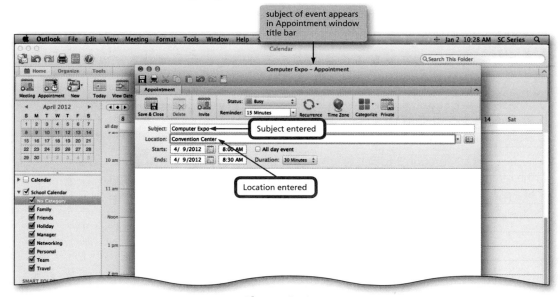

Figure 2–41

2

- Click the Starts Calendar button to display the Starts calendar.

- Click the Next button until the May 2012 calendar is displayed.

- Click 9 in the May calendar to display Wed 5/9/2012 as the day the Computer Expo starts.

- Click 'All day event' to place a check mark in the 'All day event' check box and change the appointment to an event (Figure 2–42).

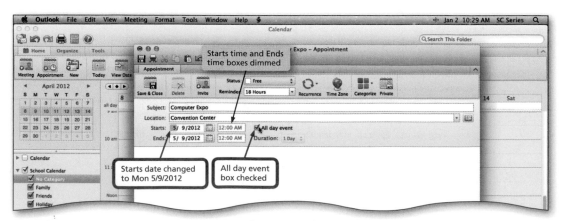

Figure 2–42

3

- Click the Ends Calendar button to display the Ends calendar.

- Click 11 in the May calendar as the end date to set the end date (Figure 2–43).

Q&A Why does the Status box display the time as Free?

The default appointment status for events is Free because events do not occupy blocks of time during the day on the calendar.

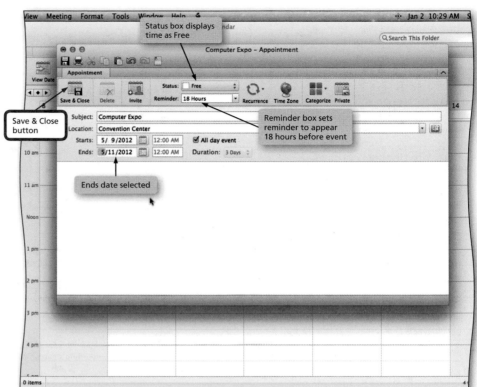

Figure 2–43

4

- Click the Status button to display a list of appointment status options.

- Click Tentative to set the appointment status.

- Click the Reminder box arrow to display the list of reminder durations.

- Scroll to and click None to set no reminder (Figure 2–44).

Q&A Why is the event reminder set for 18 hours?

The default reminder for events is 18 hours.

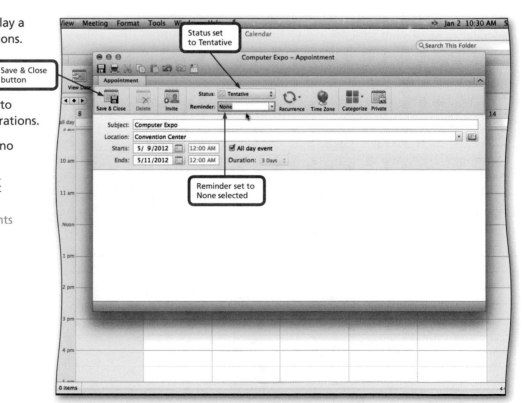

Figure 2–44

5

- Click the Save & Close button to save the event and close the Appointment window.

- If necessary, click the Next button on the mini calendar to scroll to May 2012.

- Click 9 to display May 9, 2012 in the appointment area and to view the Computer Expo event banner (Figure 2–45).

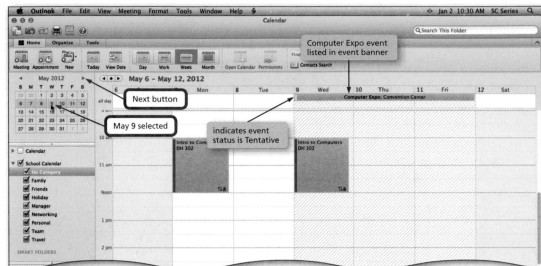

Figure 2–45

Q&A   Why is the Computer Expo event displayed at the top of the calendar?

Events do not occupy time slots on the calendar, so they appearas banners at the top of the calendar on the day they occur.

Q&A   Why does the appointment area display diagonal lines in some time slots?

When you show the time for an event as Tentative, the appointment displays light diagonal lines to indicate the tentative status of the time on your calendar.

To Move a One-Time Event to a New Date and Change the Event Status

The Computer Expo, originally scheduled for May 9, has been postponed to a later date. You need to move the Computer Expo event to a new date. Because you will be off campus for the Computer Expo, you also want the calendar to show your time for the Computer Expo as Out of Office. The following steps move the one-time event to a new date and change the status to Out of Office.

1

- Double-click the Computer Expo event in the event banner to open the window for the selected event.

2

- Click the Starts calendar button to display the Starts pop-up calendar.

- Click 11 under May 2012 to change the Computer Expo start time.

- Click the Status button to display the list of appointment status options and then click Out of Office to change the event status from Tentative to Out of Office (Figure 2–46).

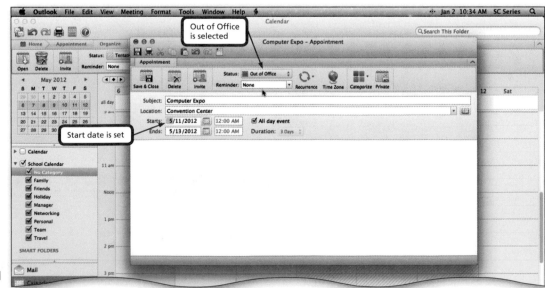

Q&A   Why did the end date change when I changed the start date?

Outlook automatically calculates the new end date when you change the start date.

Figure 2–46

3

- Click the Save & Close button to save the changes to the selected event and close the window.

- If necessary, click 11 on the mini calendar to display May 11, 2012 in the appointment area and view the Computer Expo event banner Figure 2–47).

Q&A Why did the reminder not change when I changed the appointment status? When the appointment status changes after you create the appointment, the reminder does not automatically change as it does when you create the appointment for the first time.

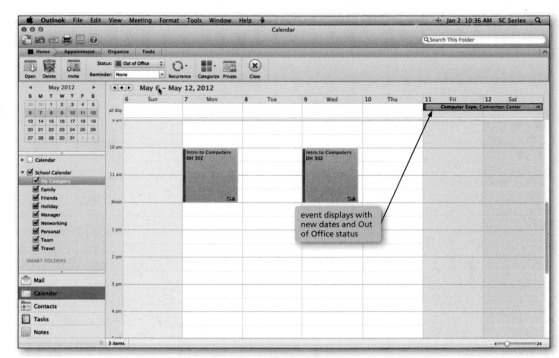

Figure 2–47

To Delete a One-Time Event

Because your schedule has changed, you no longer can attend the Computer Expo event. You need to delete the Computer Expo event from your calendar. The following step deletes the Computer Expo event from your calendar.

- If necessary, click the Computer Expo event banner in the appointment area of the calendar to select it and display the Appointment tab on the ribbon.

- Click the Delete button on the Appointment tab and then the Delete button in the dialog that appears to delete the Computer Expo event from the calendar (Figure 2–48).

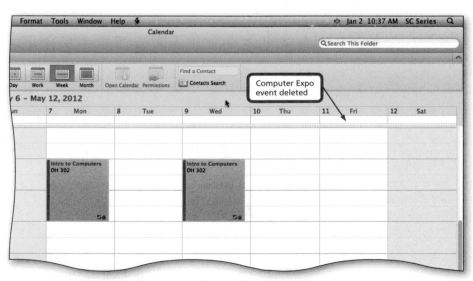

Figure 2–48

To Create a Recurring Event Using the Appointment Window

A recurring event is similar to a recurring appointment in that it occurs at regular intervals on your calendar. However, editing a recurring event is slightly different from editing one-time events. You can specify whether all occurrences in a series of recurring events need to be changed or if a single occurrence should be altered.

You want to add your pay schedule to the calendar to keep track of when you receive a paycheck. The following steps create a recurring event for your pay schedule.

- If necessary, click Home on the ribbon to display the Home tab.

- Click the Appointment button to display the Untitled – Appointment window.

- In the Subject text box, type **Payday** as the subject.

- Press the TAB key two times to select the month in the Starts date box (Figure 2–49).

Q&A Do I need to add a location to the Payday event?

No, an event such as a payday, birthday, or anniversary does not have a location.

Q&A Why do the title and tab bars indicate that this is an Appointment window?

The title bar and tab display both events and appointments as Appointments.

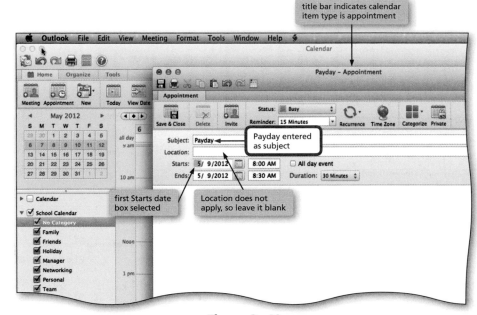

Figure 2–49

- Type **1/6/2012** as the first payday in the Starts date box.

- Click 'All day event' to place a check mark in the 'All day event' check box and to change the appointment to an event (Figure 2–50).

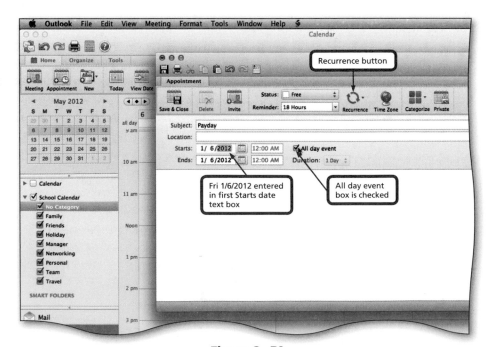

Figure 2–50

3

- Click the Recurrence button to display the Recurrence menu, and choose Custom to display the dialog (Figure 2–51).

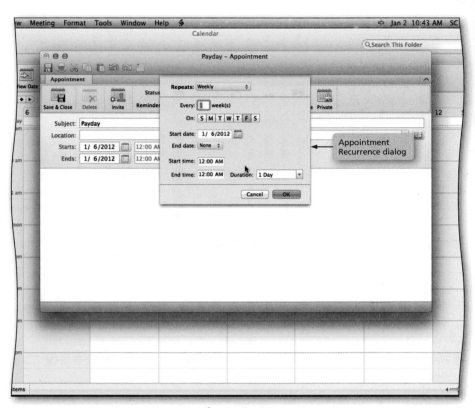

Figure 2–51

4

- If necessary, click the Repeats button, then click Weekly (Appointment Recurrence dialog) to set the Recurrence pattern.

- In the Every text box, type   2   to have the event appear on the calendar every two weeks.

- If necessary, in the On area, click F to schedule the event on Fridays.

- If necessary, make sure that only Friday is selected.

- If necessary, for the End date option, select None so that the event remains on the calendar indefinitely (Figure 2–52).

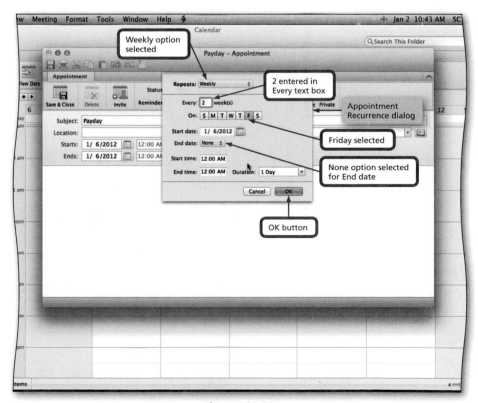

Figure 2–52

- Click the OK button to accept the recurrence settings and close the Appointment Recurrence dialog.

- Click the Reminder box arrow to display a list of reminder time slots.

- Scroll to the top of the list and click None to remove the reminder from the event (Figure 2–53).

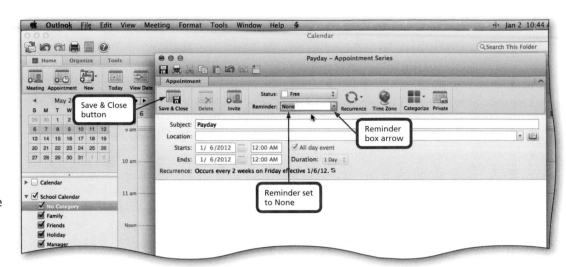

Figure 2–53

Q&A Why was the reminder removed from the event?
The Payday event does not require a reminder.

- Click the Save & Close button to save the event and close the window.

- Click the Next or Previous button as necessary on the mini calendar to navigate to January 2012, then click 2 to display the Payday event banner in the appointment area. (Figure 2–54).

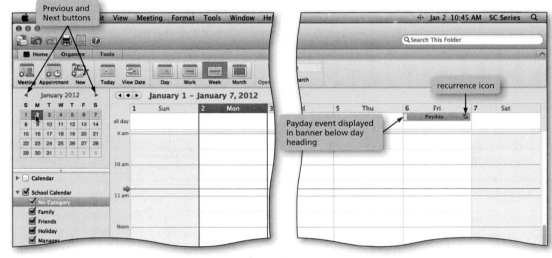

Figure 2–54

To Move a Recurring Event to a Different Day

Your school is changing the day it pays employees from Friday to Thursday. Because this will affect all Payday events in the series, you will change the date in the Payday event series from Friday to Thursday. The following steps change the date for all occurrences in a series.

❶

- Click Day on the Home tab and then click 6 in the mini calendar to display January 6, 2012 and the Payday event banner in the appointment area.

- In the appointment area, click the Payday event banner to display the Appointment Series tab (Figure 2–55).

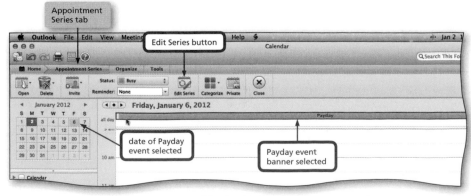

Figure 2–55

2

- Click the Edit Series button to display the Payday - Appointment Series window.

- Click the Recurrence button to display the Appointment Recurrence menu.

- Choose Custom from the menu to display the dialog.

- In the On area, click T to select Thursday.

- Click F to deselect Friday.

- Click the Start date calendar button and click 5 to change the start date to Thu 1/5/2012 (Figure 2–56).

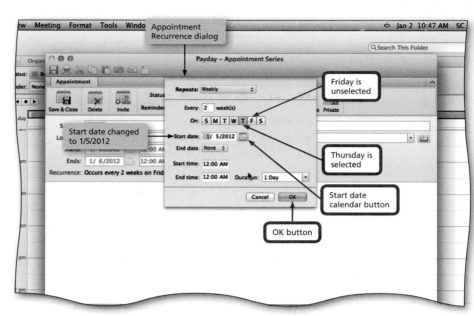

Figure 2–56

3

- Click the OK button to close the dialog and change the event day.

- Click Save & Close to save the changes and close the Appointment window.

- Click 19 in the mini calendar to view the Payday event in the calendar (Figure 2–57).

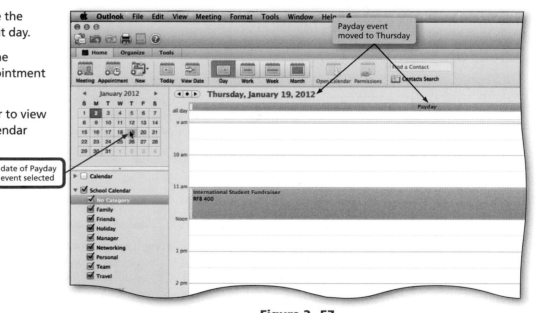

Figure 2–57

Other Ways

1. CONTROL-click event, choose Go to Series, click Recurrence button

TO DELETE A RECURRING EVENT

Deleting a recurring event is similar to deleting a recurring appointment. If you choose to delete a recurring event, you would use the following steps.

1. Scroll to the month of the event in the mini calendar and click the date of the event.

2. Click the event to display the Appointment Series tab.

3. Click the Delete button (Appointment Series tab) to display the Delete menu.

4. Click Series on the Delete menu and then click Delete in the dialog to delete the event from the calendar.

Entering Locations
 As you enter appointments, events, and meetings, you can include location information by entering it in the Location box. After entering one or more locations, you can click the Location box arrow and select a location from the list.

Creating and Editing Meetings

Outlook Calendar includes many items that help you manage your time in a given day, week, or month. In addition to appointments and events, you likely will have to schedule meetings with other people or reply to a meeting invitation you received indicating to the sender whether you can attend. As defined earlier, a meeting is an appointment that includes people to whom you send an invitation. A meeting also can include resources such as conference rooms. The person who creates the meeting and sends the invitations is known as the **meeting organizer**. The meeting organizer schedules a meeting by creating a **meeting request**, which is an e-mail invitation to the meeting and arrives in each attendee's Inbox. Responses to a meeting request arrive in the Inbox of the meeting organizer. The Untitled – Meeting request window is similar to the Untitled – Appointment window with a few exceptions. The meeting request window includes the To text box, where you enter an e-mail address for **attendees**, who are people invited to the meeting, and the Send button, which sends the invitation for the meeting to the attendees. When a meeting request arrives in the attendee's Inbox, it displays an icon different from an e-mail message icon.

Plan Ahead

Create an agenda before scheduling a meeting.

Have a list of topics for discussion prepared and estimate the time for each item and an ending time. When creating the agenda, consider who will attend the meeting and where it will be held.

- **Be sure you include everyone you need to attend the meeting.** Invite only those people whose attendance is absolutely necessary to ensure that all of the agenda items can be addressed at the meeting.

- **Be sure you have a location for the meeting.** Confirm that the location of the meeting is available and that the room is the appropriate size for the number of people invited. Also, make sure the room can accommodate any multimedia equipment that might be needed for the meeting, such as a projector or telephone and video conferencing capabilities.

To View the School Calendar in Overlay Mode

Before you schedule a meeting on your main calendar, you want to make sure no scheduling conflicts exist on the School Calendar. Outlook provides overlay mode, which allows you to view entries from more than one calendar in the appointment area. The following steps display the default Calendar and School Calendar, then make the Calendar folder the active folder.

1
- Click the Calendar check box to display any items in the Calendar folder on the Calendar (Figure 2–58).

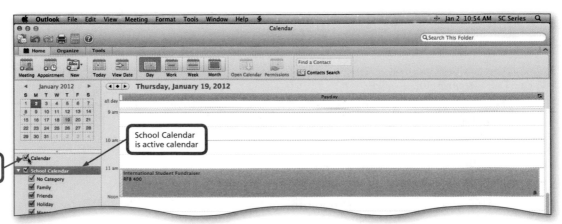

Figure 2–58

2

- Click Calendar in the Navigation Pane to make it the active calendar folder displaying in the calendar pane (Figure 2–59).

Q&A Why do the School Calendar items appear faded when I select Calendar in the Navigation Pane?
Items from the active calendar appear darker, while items from other selected calendars appear lighter.

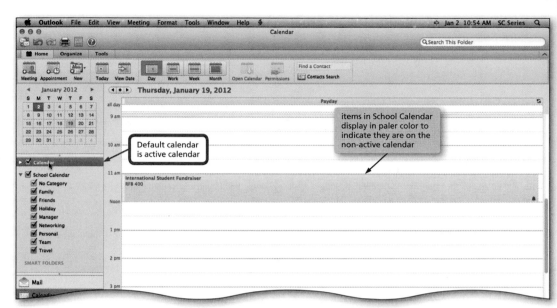

Figure 2–59

To Create and Send a Meeting Request

You want to meet with your advisor, Jay Ballentyne, to discuss your course selection for the next semester. Rather than send an e-mail message requesting the meeting, you decide to use Outlook Calendar to create this meeting. Meetings can be scheduled on your main calendar or supplemental calendars, even though meetings scheduled on your secondary calendars will be not be tallied. In order to complete the next several sets of steps, you will need to have an e-mail account set up in Outlook. The following steps display the main calendar, create a meeting request, and send an invitation to your advisor. You also will use overlay mode to see if any conflicts appear on your schedule. If you are completing this project on a personal computer, use the e-mail address of your instructor instead of Jay Ballentyne's e-mail address.

1

- Click the Meeting button on the Home tab to open the Untitled – Meeting window.

- If necessary, maximize the Untitled – Meeting window to provide as much room as possible to work (Figure 2–60).

Q&A Why does the message header include the text, "This invitation has not been sent"?
When scheduling a meeting with other people, invitations are sent to them. This notice reminds you that you have not yet sent the invitation to the meeting.

Figure 2–60

2

- Click the To text box and then type `jay.ballentyne@hotmail.com` (substitute your instructor's e-mail address for Jay Ballentyne's e-mail address) as the invitee to this meeting.

- Press the TAB key to move the insertion point to the Subject text box.

- Type `Course Selection for Next Semester` as the subject of the meeting.

- Press the TAB key to move the insertion point to the Location text box.

- Type `RCF 200` as the location of the meeting.

- Press the TAB key to select the month in the Starts date text box (Figure 2–61).

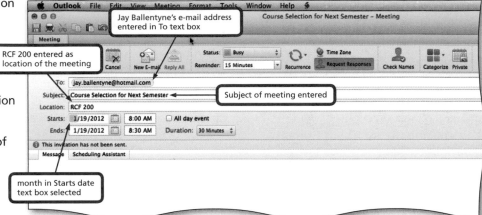

Figure 2–61

3

- Type `4/23/2012` as the start date of the meeting, and then press the TAB key four times to select the time in the Starts time text box.

- Type `12:30 pm` as the start time for the meeting, and then press the TAB key to select the time in the Ends time text box.

- Type `1:30 pm` as the end time for the meeting (Figure 2–62).

Figure 2–62

4

- Click the Send button to send the invitation to Jay Ballentyne (or your instructor) and add the meeting to the calendar.

- If necessary, click the Week button on the Home tab, then click the appropriate scroll arrow on the mini calendar to display the April 2012 calendar.

- Click 23 on the mini calendar to display April 23, 2012 in the meeting area and view the meeting (Figure 2–63).

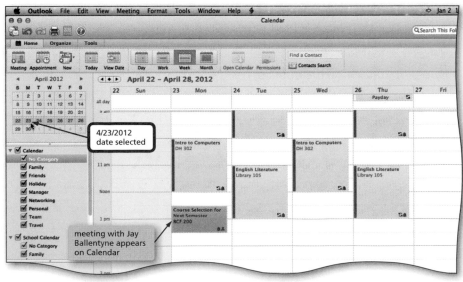

Figure 2–63

Other Ways

1. Choose File > New > Meeting in menu bar

To Change the Time of a Meeting and Send an Update

Your schedule has changed, which means you need to change the time of the meeting with Jay Ballentyne and send an update to inform her of the change. Though the invitee can propose a new time, only the originator can change or delete the meeting. Other reasons to update a meeting request may be that you have added or removed attendees or resources, changed the meeting to a recurring series, or moved the meeting to a different date or time. The following steps change the time of the meeting and send an update to the attendee.

- Double-click the meeting with Jay Ballentyne (or your instructor) to open the Course Selection for Next Semester – Meeting window.

- Click the Starts time text box and type **1:30** as the new start time (Figure 2–64).

Figure 2–64

- Click the Send Update button to send the new information, close the meeting request, and view the updated meeting in the appointment area (Figure 2–65).

Q&A What if I need to cancel the meeting?
Click the meeting in the appointment area to display the Meeting tab on the ribbon, click the Cancel button and then click the Send Cancellation button to send the cancellation notice and remove the meeting from the calendar.

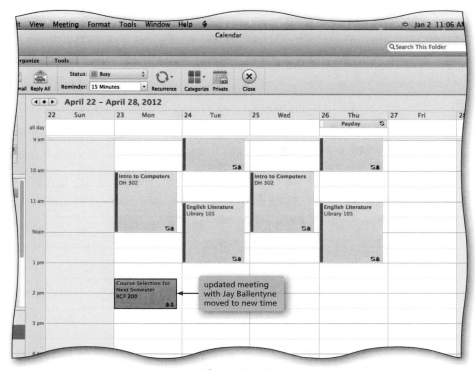

Figure 2–65

Other Ways

1. Drag meeting to new time in appointment area, click Send Update

To Reply to a Meeting Request

You and another student, (in this example, Gillian Winston), are working on a project for your social studies class. Using Outlook Calendar, Gillian has sent you a meeting request to meet and work on the project together. You accept the invitation by replying to the meeting request from Gillian. Outlook allows you to choose from four response options: Accept, Tentative, Decline, or Propose New Time. The following steps accept the meeting request from Gillian Winston. To complete these steps, you and another student must exchange meeting requests, and use the meeting request sent to you in place of the meeting request from Gillian Winston in these steps. If you do not have any meeting requests, read these steps without performing them.

1

- Click the Mail button in the Navigation Pane to display the default Inbox folder.

- Click Inbox to open the Inbox.

- If necessary, click the invitation from Gillian Winston in the message list to select the invitation and display the contents in the reading pane (Figure 2–66).

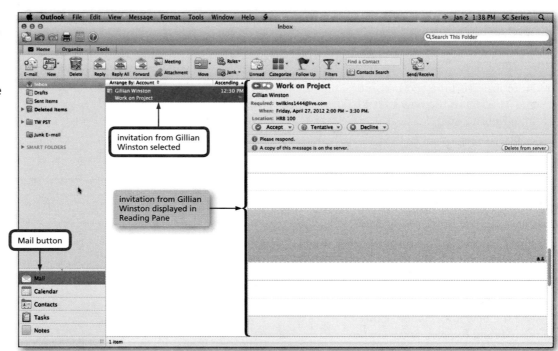

Figure 2–66

2

- Double-click the Gillian Winston message header to open the invitation.

- Click the Accept button on the Meeting tab to display the options for accepting the meeting (Figure 2–67).

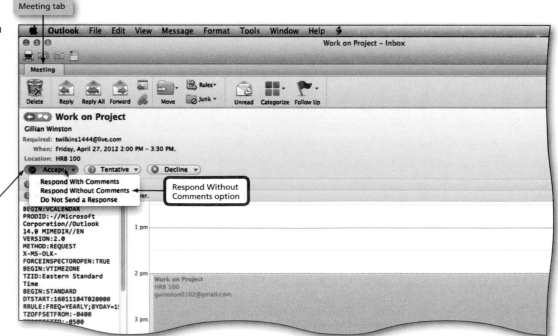

Figure 2–67

3

- Click Respond Without Comments to send the accept response and add the meeting to the calendar.

- Click the Calendar button in the Navigation pane to display the calendar.

- Navigate to April using the mini calendar and click on 27 to display the calendar in Week view with the meeting added to the calendar.

Q&A   What happened to the meeting invitation in the Inbox?
When you accept or tentatively accept a meeting request, the invitation is deleted from the Inbox and the meeting is added to your calendar. The meeting response is in the Sent Items folder.

Q&A   What happens when I decline a meeting request?
When a meeting request is declined, the meeting request is removed from your Inbox and the meeting is not added to your calendar. The reply is placed in the Sent Items folder.

Q&A   What should I do if I have a conflict with the meeting time?
You can choose Respond With Comments on either the Tentative or Decline menus, and propose an alternate time for the meeting to the host.

To Cancel a Meeting

You no longer need to meet with Jay Ballentyne and want to cancel the meeting. The following steps cancel a meeting.

1

- Click the Course Selection for Next Semester meeting on April 23 in the appointment area to select the meeting and then display the Meeting tab on the ribbon (Figure 2–68).

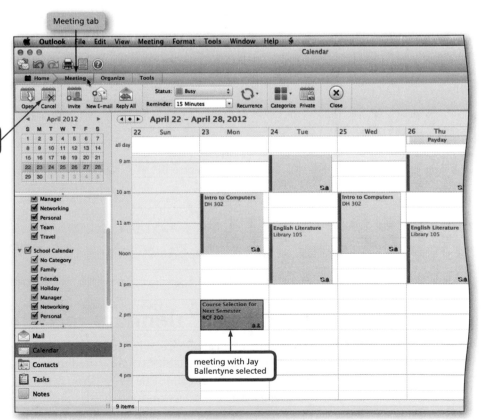

Figure 2–68

● Click the Cancel button on the
  Meeting tab to open the window for
  the selected meeting (Figure 2–69).

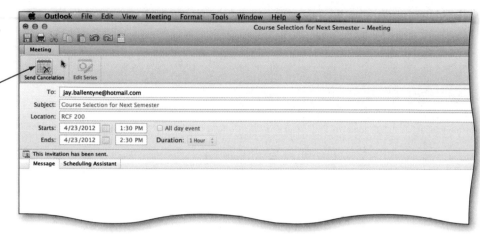

Figure 2–69

● Click the Send Cancellation button
  on the Meeting tab to send the
  cancellation notice and delete
  the meeting from your calendar
  (Figure 2–70).

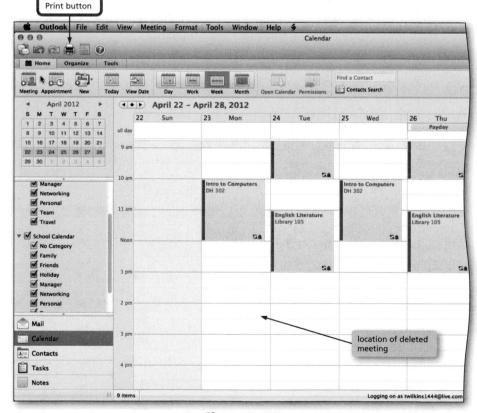

Figure 2–70

Printing Calendars in Different Views

All or part of a calendar can be printed in a number of different views, or **print styles**.
Printing a calendar enables you to distribute the calendar to others in a form that can be
read or viewed, but cannot be edited. You can print a monthly, daily, or weekly view of
your calendar and select options such as the date range and fonts used. You also can view
your calendar in a list by changing the current view from Calendar view to List view. This
section prints your calendar from Calendar view in the Weekly Calendar style, and then
changes the current view to List view and prints the calendar in Table style. Table 2–6
lists the print styles available for printing your calendar from Calendar view.

Table 2-6 Print Styles for Calendar View

Print Style	Description
Day	Prints a daily appointment schedule for a specific date including one day per page, and a two-month calendar
Work Week	Prints a five-day work week calendar with one week per page and an hourly schedule, similar to the Day style
Week	Prints a seven-day weekly calendar with one week per page and an hourly schedule, similar to the Day style
Month	Prints five weeks per page of a particular month or date range

---

Determine the best method for distributing a calendar.　　　**Plan Ahead**

The traditional method of distributing a calendar uses a printer to produce a hard copy. A **hard copy** or **printout** is information that exists on a physical medium such as paper. Hard copies can serve as reference material if your storage medium is lost or becomes corrupted and you need to re-create the calendar.

To Print the Calendar in Weekly Calendar Style

In this exercise, you will be working with the School Calendar, so you need to make that the active calendar and close the default calendar. Also, you want a hard copy of your first week of classes so that you can see all your appointments for the first week of the semester. The following steps display the School Calendar, and then print the calendar for the first week of classes.

- Click the Calendar check box in the Navigation Pane to display only the School calendar.

- Click School Calendar to select it as the active calendar. (Make sure School Calendar remains checked.)

- Click View Date on the Home tab, and navigate to January 2012.

- If necessary, click Week to make Week the active view.

- Click 29 to make 1/29/2012 the active date on the calendar.

- Click the Print button in the Standard toolbar to open the Print dialog. If necessary, click the Show Details button to display the detailed Print dialog.

- Click Week in the Style box to display the Style pop-up menu (Figure 2–71).

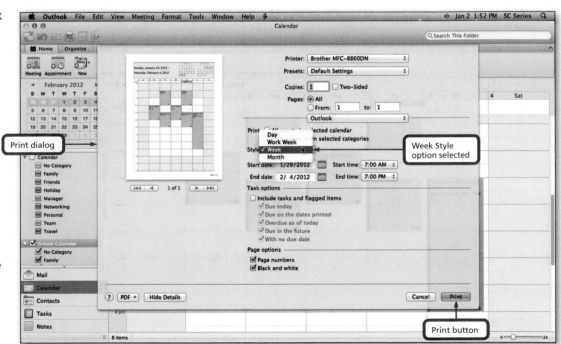

Figure 2–71

2

- Select Week from the Style pop-up menu.

- Verify the printer name that appears on the Printer button will print a hard copy of the calendar. If necessary, click the Printer button to display a list of available printer options and then click the desired printer to change the currently selected printer (Figure 2–72).

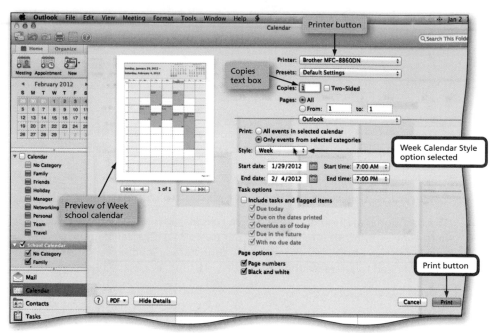

Figure 2–72

3

- Click the Print button in the dialog to print the calendar on the currently selected printer.

- When the printer stops, retrieve the hard copy (Figure 2–73).

Q&A How can I print multiple copies of my calendar?
Increase the number in the Copies text box on the Print dialog, and then click the Print button to send the calendar to the printer and return to the calendar.

Q&A What if I decide not to print the calendar at this time?
Click Cancel in the Print dialog to return to the calendar window.

 Other Ways

1. Choose File > Print in menu bar, set print options, click Print button

2. Press COMMAND-P, set print options, click Print button

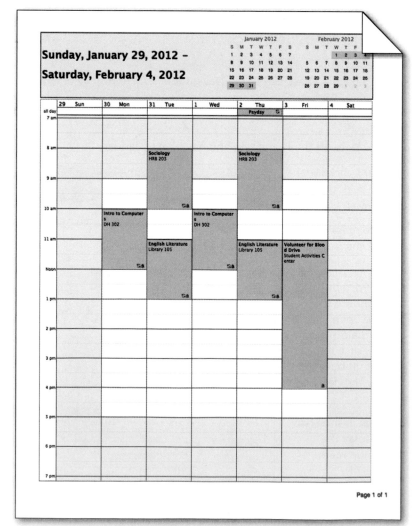

Figure 2–73

To Change the Current View to List View

You can print a list of all your calendar items for a given day, week, work week, or month using List view, which prints your calendar in a memo format. To print a calendar in this view, you must change the current view to List view. The following step changes the view from Calendar view to List view and then print the calendar in the Table style.

- With the School Calendar selected in the Navigation Pane, click Organize on the ribbon to display the Organize tab.

- If necessary, click Week to display a weekly calendar.

- Click the List button to display the calendar entries in list view (Figure 2–74).

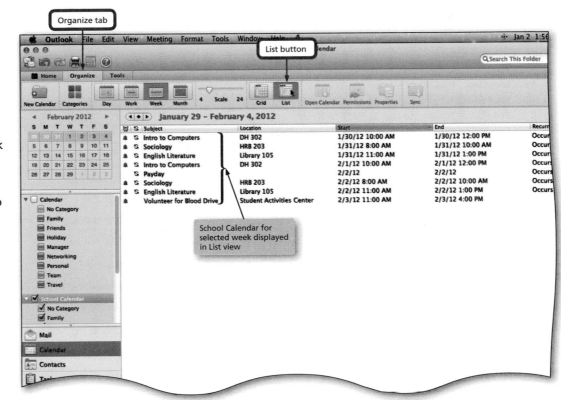

Figure 2–74

To Print the Calendar from List View

Now that the calendar view is displaying all your calendar items in a list, you want to print the calendar in this format. The following steps print the calendar in List view.

1 Click the Print button in the Standard toolbar to open the Print dialog. If necessary, click the Show Details button to display the detailed Print dialog.

2 Select Memo from the Style pop-up menu.

3 Verify the printer name in the Printer box will print a hard copy of the calendar in Memo style. If necessary, click the Printer box to display a list of available printer options and then click the desired printer to change the currently selected printer.

4 Click the Print button to send the list of appointments to the selected printer.

5 When the printer stops, retrieve the hard copy (Figure 2–75 on the next page).

6 Click Grid on the ribbon to return to Calendar view.

Changing Settings before Printing

To change the margins, page orientation, or paper size before printing, choose Page Setup in the File menu to display the Page Setup dialog box. **BTW**

Other Ways

1. Press COMMAND-P, click Print button

Monday, January 2, 2012 2:00:34 PM Eastern Standard Time

Subject: Intro to Computers
Location: DH 302
Start time: Monday, January 30, 2012 10:00 AM
End time: Monday, January 30, 2012 12:00 PM
Recurrence: Occurs every Monday and Wednesday effective 1/23/12 until 5/9/12 from 10:00 AM to 12:00 PM.

Subject: Sociology
Location: HRB 203
Start time: Tuesday, January 31, 2012 8:00 AM
End time: Tuesday, January 31, 2012 10:00 AM
Recurrence: Occurs every Tuesday and Thursday effective 1/24/12 until 5/3/12 from 8:00 AM to 10:00

Subject: English Literature
Location: Library 105
Start time: Tuesday, January 31, 2012 11:00 AM
End time: Tuesday, January 31, 2012 1:00 PM
Recurrence: Occurs every Tuesday and Thursday effective 1/24/12 until 5/3/12 from 11:00 AM to 1:00

Subject: Intro to Computers
Location: DH 302
Start time: Wednesday, February 1, 2012 10:00 AM
End time: Wednesday, February 1, 2012 12:00 PM
Recurrence: Occurs every Monday and Wednesday effective 1/23/12 until 5/9/12 from 10:00 AM to 12:00 PM.

Subject: Payday
Start time: Thursday, February 2, 2012
End time: Thursday, February 2, 2012
Recurrence: Occurs every 2 weeks on Thursday effective 1/5/12.

Subject: Sociology
Location: HRB 203
Start time: Thursday, February 2, 2012 8:00 AM
End time: Thursday, February 2, 2012 10:00 AM
Recurrence: Occurs every Tuesday and Thursday effective 1/24/12 until 5/3/12 from 8:00 AM to 10:00

Subject: English Literature
Location: Library 105
Start time: Thursday, February 2, 2012 11:00 AM
End time: Thursday, February 2, 2012 1:00 PM
Recurrence: Occurs every Tuesday and Thursday effective 1/24/12 until 5/3/12 from 11:00 AM to 1:00

Subject: Volunteer for Blood Drive

1

Monday, January 2, 2012 2:00:34 PM Eastern Standard Time

Location: Student Activities Center
Start time: Friday, February 3, 2012 11:00 AM
End time: Friday, February 3, 2012 4:00 PM

Figure 2–75

Exporting and Importing Folders

The calendar now is ready to be saved on a USB flash drive. Saving your work on an external storage device allows you to take your schedule to another computer where you will import the calendar for use on a secondary computer.

With many programs, a single file, such as a letter or spreadsheet, can be saved directly on an external storage device. With Outlook, each appointment, task, or contact is a separate file. Rather than saving numerous individual files, Outlook uses the **Import and Export Wizard** to guide you through the process of saving an entire folder including any subfolders, which are folders within another folder. Transferring a subfolder to a USB flash drive is called **exporting**. Adding a subfolder to your Outlook mailbox is called **importing**. Subfolders can be imported from a Windows version of Outlook (.pst file) or a Mac version of Outlook (.olm file). Subfolders can be imported and exported from any Outlook item. When you export a folder, Outlook for Mac saves the folder (and its subfolders as specified) to a given location, adding the extension **.olm** to the exported file. An **.olm file** is a data file that stores all Outlook 2011 for Mac items in a specific location.

Shortcut Keys

To print a complete ‎BTW list of shortcut keys in Outlook, click Help in the menu bar, type shortcut keys in the search text box, and press the RETURN key. Click the Outlook keyboard shortcuts link, then click the Show All link in the upper-right corner of the Help window. Click the Action (gear) button and choose Print from the Action menu, and then click the Print button in the dialog.

To Export a Subfolder to a USB Flash Drive

The following steps export a Calendar subfolder to a USB flash drive.

1

- Connect the USB flash drive containing the Data Files for Students to one of the computer's USB ports.

- Click File in the menu bar, and choose Export to display the Export wizard.

- If necessary, choose Outlook for Mac Data File (.olm), 'Items of the following types', and the check boxes as shown in Figure 2–76.

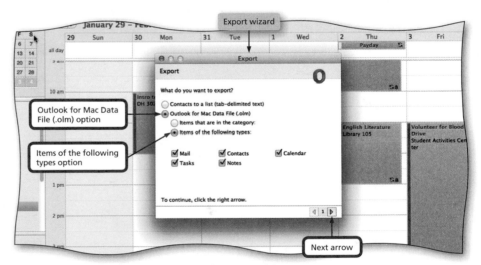

Figure 2–76

2

- Click the Next arrow in the Export wizard and if necessary choose 'No, do not delete items' (Figure 2–77).

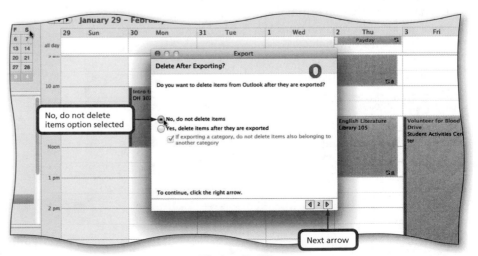

Figure 2–77

- Click the Next arrow in the Export Wizard to display the Save dialog.
- If necessary click the Save As disclosure button to expand the dialog.
- Navigate to the location of your Data Files for Students, in this case, on the USB flash drive in the Chapter 2 folder of the Data Files for Students folder (Figure 2–78).

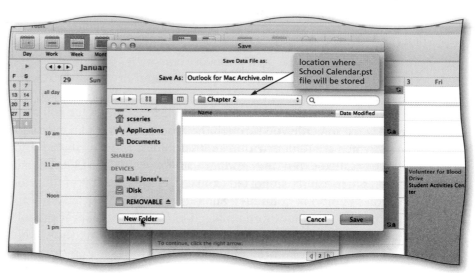

Figure 2–78

- Type `School Calendar.olm` in the Save As text box (Figure 2–79).

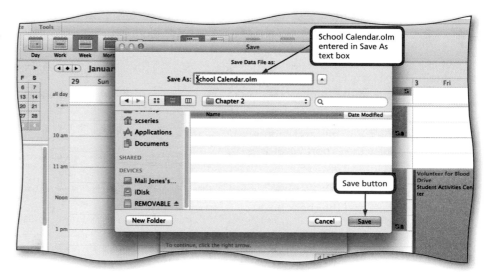

Figure 2–79

- Click the Save button to specify the name and location of the file, close the Save dialog, and return to the Export wizard. When Outlook is done exporting the file, the Done button will be highlighted (Figure 2–80).

- Click the Done button to close the wizard.

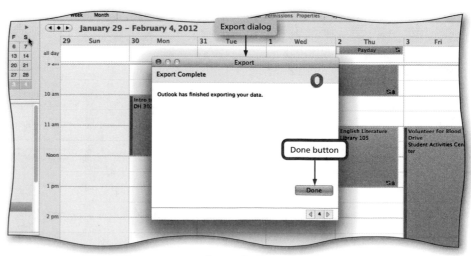

Figure 2–80

To Import a Personal Subfolder

You may want to transfer your school calendar from one computer to another. For example, you may want to have your calendar on a notebook computer and a desktop computer. To do this, you need to export your calendar, as shown earlier, and then import that calendar to another computer. To import a calendar, you would perform the following steps.

1. Select the folder into which you want to import the data file.
2. Click File in the menu bar and choose Import to display the Import dialog.
3. Select the Outlook Data File, and then click the Next arrow.
4. Choose the format of the Data File (.pst or .olm) and then click the Next arrow.
5. Navigate to the location where the data file is stored.
6. Select the file to import and click the Import button.
7. When the file is finished importing, click the Done button to close the dialog.

To Delete a Personal Subfolder

The School Calendar subfolder now has been exported to a USB flash drive. A copy of the School Calendar. olm file still is stored on the hard disk of your computer, and appears in Outlook's Folder List. To delete a subfolder from the computer entirely, use the Delete command. The following steps delete a personal subfolder. If you did not complete the previous set of steps, do not delete the School Calendar subfolder.

- CONTROL-click the School Calendar button in the Navigation Pane to display a shortcut menu.

- Choose Delete from the shortcut menu (Figure 2–81).

- Click the Delete button in the Microsoft Outlook dialog to delete the folder.

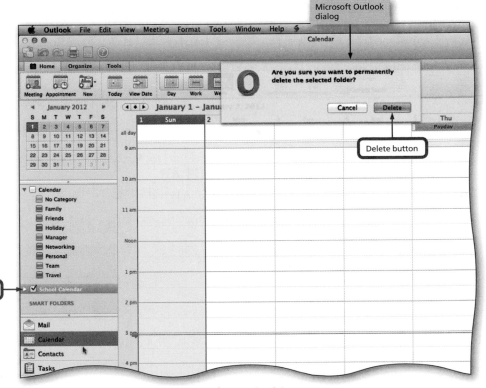

Figure 2–81

Other Ways

1. Select calendar in Navigation Pane, choose Edit > Delete in menu bar, click Delete

2. Select calendar in Navigation Pane, press COMMAND-DELETE

Quick Reference

 For a table that lists how to complete the tasks covered in this book using the mouse, ribbon, shortcut menu, and keyboard, see the Quick Reference Summary at the back of this book, or visit the Office 2011 for Mac Online Companion Web page at www.cengagebrain.com, navigate to the desired application, and click Quick Reference.

To Quit Outlook

With the project complete, the final step is to quit the Outlook program and return to the Mac OS X desktop. The following steps quit Outlook.

1 Click the Close button on the left side of the title bar to close the Calendar.

2 Click Outlook in the menu bar, and choose Quit Outlook.

Chapter Summary

In this chapter, you have learned how to use Outlook to create a personal schedule by entering appointments, creating recurring appointments, moving appointments to new dates, and scheduling events. You also learned how to invite attendees to a meeting, accept a meeting request, and propose and change the time of a meeting. To review your schedule, you learned to view and print your calendar in different views. Finally, you learned how to export your personal folder to an external storage device. The following list includes all the new Outlook skills you have learned in this chapter.

1. Create a Personal Folder (OUT 53)
2. Display a Personal Calendar (OUT 54)
3. Remove the Default Calendar from the Appointment Area (OUT 55)
4. Go to a Specific Date (OUT 56)
5. Display the Calendar in Work View (OUT 57)
6. Display the Calendar in Week View (OUT 57)
7. Display the Calendar in Month View (OUT 58)
8. Create a One-Time Appointment Using the Appointment Window (OUT 59)
9. Change the Status of an Appointment (OUT 63)
10. Set a Reminder for an Appointment (OUT 64)
11. Set Recurrence Options for an Appointment (OUT 67)
12. Move an Appointment to a Different Time on the Same Day (OUT 73)
13. Move an Appointment to a Different Date (OUT 74)
14. Move an Appointment to a Different Month (OUT 75)
15. Delete a Single Occurrence of a Recurring Appointment (OUT 76)
16. Create a One-Time Event in the Appointment Window (OUT 78)
17. Move a One-Time Event to a New Date and Change the Event Status (OUT 80)
18. Delete a One-Time Event (OUT 81)
19. Create a Recurring Event Using the Appointment Window (OUT 82)
20. Move a Recurring Event to a Different Day (OUT 84)
21. Delete a Recurring Event (OUT 85)
22. View the School Calendar in Overlay Mode (OUT 86)
23. Create and Send a Meeting Request (OUT 87)
24. Change the Time of a Meeting and Send an Update (OUT 89)
25. Reply to a Meeting Request (OUT 90)
26. Cancel a Meeting (OUT 91)
27. Print the Calendar in Weekly Calendar Style (OUT 93)
28. Change the Current View to List View (OUT 95)
29. Export a Subfolder to a USB Flash Drive (OUT 97)
30. Import a Personal Subfolder (OUT 99)
31. Delete a Personal Subfolder (OUT 99)

 If you have a SAM 2010 user profile, your instructor may have assigned an autogradable version of this assignment. If so, log into the SAM 2010 Web site at www.cengage.com/sam2010 to download the instruction and start files.

Learn It Online

Test your knowledge of chapter content and key terms.

Instructions: To complete the Learn It Online exercises, start your browser, click the Address bar, and then enter the Web address **scsite.com/out2011/learn.** When the Outlook 2011 Learn It Online page is displayed, click the link for the exercise you want to complete and then read the instructions..

Chapter Reinforcement TF, MC, and SA
A series of true/false, multiple choice, and short answer questions that test your knowledge of the chapter content.

Flash Cards
An interactive learning environment where you identify chapter key terms associated with displayed definitions.

Practice Test
A series of multiple choice questions that test your knowledge of chapter content and key terms.

Who Wants To Be a Computer Genius?
An interactive game that challenges your knowledge of chapter content in the style of a television quiz show.

Wheel of Terms
An interactive game that challenges your knowledge of chapter key terms in the style of the television show *Wheel of Fortune*.

Crossword Puzzle Challenge
A crossword puzzle that challenges your knowledge of key terms presented in the chapter.

Apply Your Knowledge

Reinforce the skills and apply the concepts you learned in this chapter.

Editing a Calendar
Note: To complete this assignment, you will be required to use the Data Files for Students. See the inside back cover of this book for instructions on downloading the Data Files for Students, or contact your instructor for information about accessing the required files.

Instructions: Start Outlook. Edit the calendar provided in the file called Apply Your Knowledge 2-1 Calendar, located on the Data Files for Students. The Apply Your Knowledge 2-1 Calendar is a personal calendar with appointments for personal activities, class schedules, and events in 2012. Many of the scheduled items have changed and you now need to revise these scheduled items.

Perform the following tasks:
1. Create a folder called Apply Your Knowledge and import the Apply Your Knowledge 2-1 Calendar folder into the newly created folder.
2. Display only the Apply Your Knowledge 2-1 Calendar in the Outlook Calendar window. Use Week view to display the calendar.
3. Change Kelly's Birthday Party from February 17 to February 19. The party is at the same time.
4. Reschedule the work on February 9 to February 12. The work starts at 12:00 PM and continues until 4:00 PM.
5. Reschedule the two-hour Chemistry Study Lab on Wednesday evenings from 5:00 PM – 7:00 PM to 6:00 PM – 8:00 PM in CHM 225.
6. Change Intramural Basketball from Mondays and Wednesdays to Tuesdays and Thursdays at the same time.

Continued >

Apply Your Knowledge *continued*

7. Print the final calendar in Month view, shown in Figure 2–82, and then submit the printout to your instructor.

8. Export the Apply Your Knowledge 2–1 Calendar folder to a USB flash drive and then delete the folder from the hard disk.

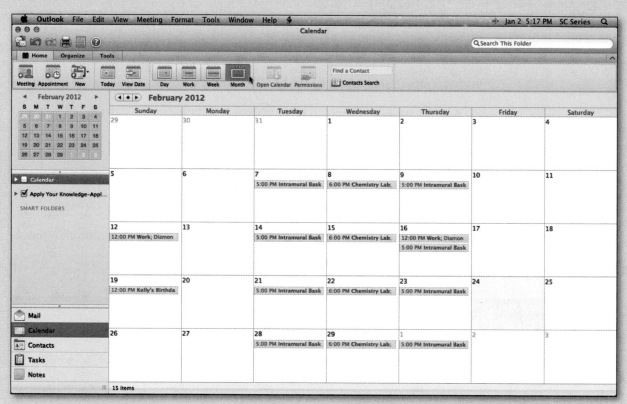

Figure 2–82

Extend Your Knowledge

Extend the skills you learned in this chapter and experiment with new skills. You may need to use Help to complete the assignment.

Sharing and Publishing Calendars

Instructions: Start Outlook. Create a new blank calendar and then add appointments to the new calendar. A sample calendar is shown in Figure 2–83 on the next page.

Perform the following tasks:

1. Start Outlook and create a new blank calendar named Extend Your Knowledge 2-1.

2. Add three appointments to the new calendar. At least one appointment should be a weekly recurring appointment and end after six occurrences.

3. Use Help to learn about assigning and creating new categories

4. Assign the appointments created to three different categories, 2 which exist currently in Outlook, and one which you create yourself.

5. Print four versions of your calendar, one which shows all appointments, and three additional calendars, each showing one appointment or appointment series only.

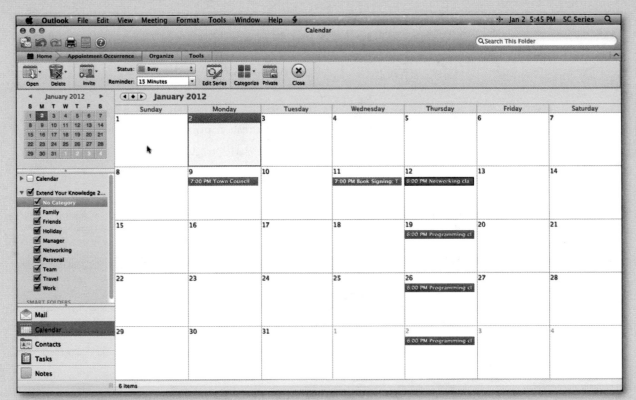

Figure 2–83

6. Remove the three appointments added in Step 2.

7. Submit your answers in the format specified by your instructor.

Make It Right

Analyze a calendar and correct all errors and/or improve the design.

Correcting Appointment Times

Note: To complete this assignment, you may be required to use the Data Files for Students. See the inside back cover of this book for instructions on downloading the Data Files for Students, or contact your instructor for information about accessing the required files.

Instructions: Start Outlook. Import the Make It Right 2-1 Calendar folder in the Data Files for Students folder into Outlook. While reviewing your Outlook calendar, you realize that you created several appointments incorrectly. You will identify and open the incorrect appointments, edit them so that they reflect the correct information, and then save all changes.

Perform the following tasks:

1. Display only the Make It Right 2-1 Calendar in the Outlook Calendar window.

2. While adding a dentist appointment to the Calendar, you inadvertently recorded the appointment time as 2:00 AM instead of 2:00 PM. Edit the appointment on April 2, 2012, and change the Start time to 2:00 PM. The appointment still will last one hour.

3. The Yoga class scheduled for Wednesday, April 25, 2012 is a recurring appointment on your calendar. Change the appointment to reflect the Yoga class meeting every Thursday starting April 19, 2012 through the end of June from 7:00 PM until 9:00 PM.

Continued >

Make It Right *continued*

4. Your monthly homeowner's association board meeting has modified their meeting schedule to meet on the second Tuesday of each month instead of on the thirteenth of each month. Update the calendar to reflect this change.

5. An appointment during the week of April 16, 2012, has been added to your calendar two times with the same start time and end time. Remove one of these appointments from the calendar.

6. Print the calendar using the Monthly style for April 8, 2012 to May 12, 2012 (Figure 2–84).

7. Export the Make It Right 2–1 Calendar folder to a USB flash drive and then delete the folder from the hard disk.

8. Submit the calendar in a format specified by your instructor.

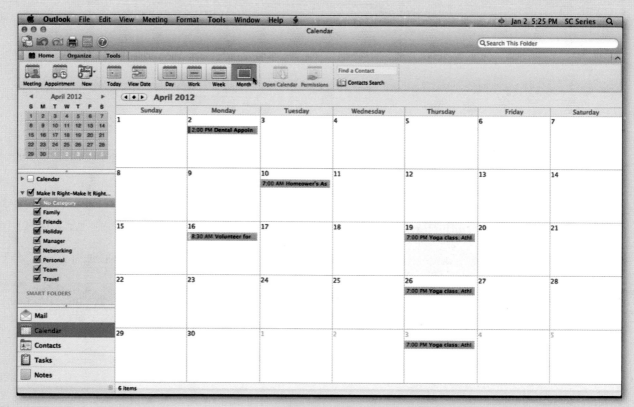

Figure 2–84

In the Lab

Design, create, modify, and/or use a document using the guidelines, concepts, and skills presented in this chapter. Labs are listed in order of increasing difficulty.

Lab 1: Creating Recurring Events

Problem: You are a graduate assistant for the English Department at your college and have been asked to create a list of faculty birthdays. Table 2–7 lists each faculty member's birthday. Enter the birthdays as recurring events (these events should occur one time per year).

Perform the following tasks:

1. Create a personal Calendar subfolder named English Department Birthdays.

2. Create the events in the calendar, using the information listed in Table 2–7.

3. For each event, show the time as Free.

4. For each event, set the reminder to one day.

5. Set each event to recur yearly on the same day.

6. Each event should be an all-day event.

7. Print the English Department Birthdays calendar using the Calendar Details style, and submit it in a format specified by your instructor.

Table 2–7 Employee Birthday Information	
Employee Name	**Birthday**
Shannon Brown	1/6/1952
Brett Lipinski	2/17/1980
Sloan McLoughlin	3/29/1975
Joseph Kelly	5/6/1963
Emma Thompson-Wright	6/5/1979
Madelyn Judowski	8/26/1968

In the Lab

Lab 2: Creating a Calendar

Problem: You are the owner of a small hardware store. Your store has experienced rapid growth during the last several months, and with spring approaching, you need to change to regular from seasonal stock. As the owner, you also have administrative duties to perform, such as staff meetings, payroll, advertising, and sales campaigns. To make your schedule even more hectic, you coach your child's spring soccer team. You need to create a schedule of appointments to help you keep track of your various jobs and responsibilities each day (Figure 2–85).

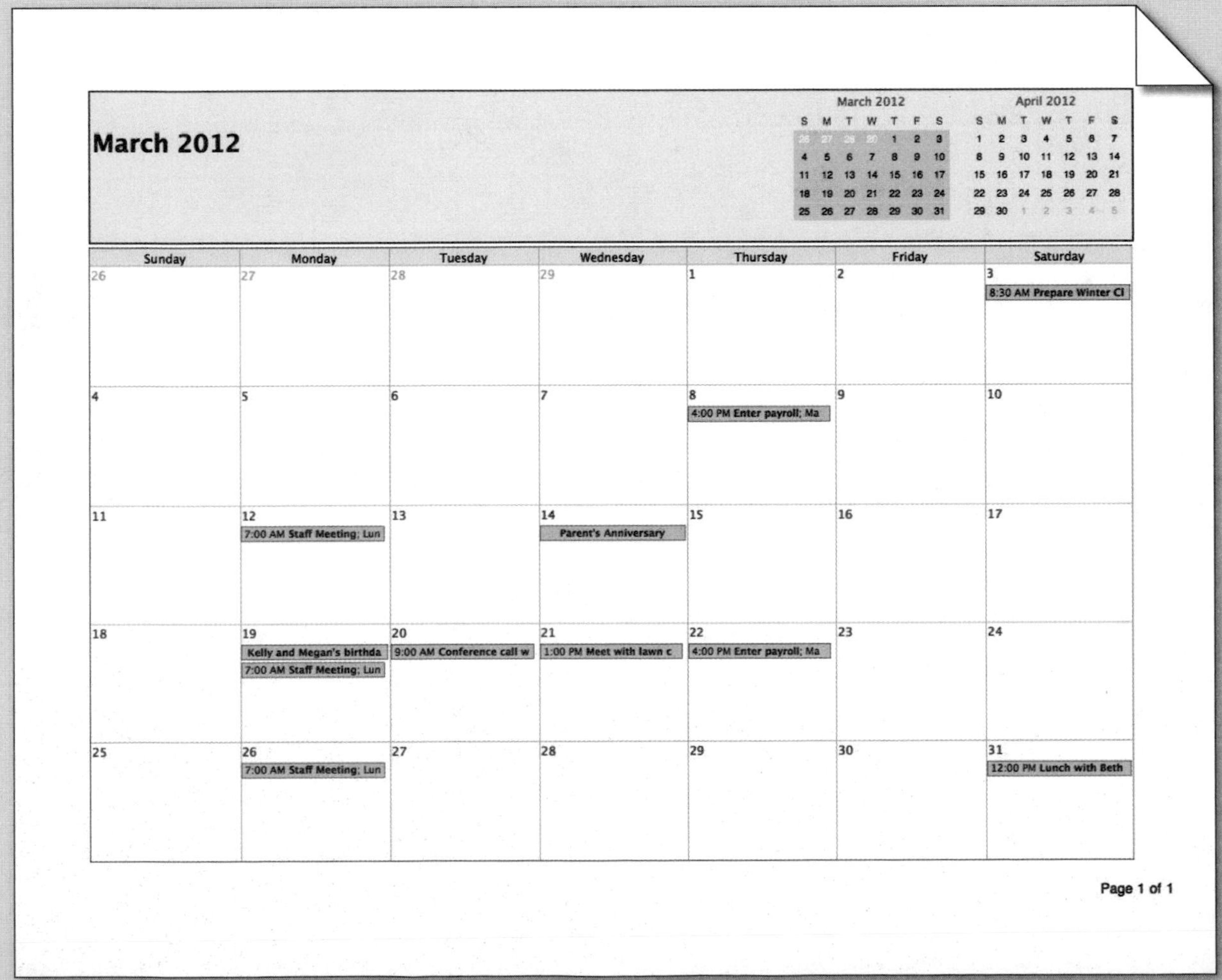

Figure 2–85

Continued >

In the Lab *continued*

Perform the following tasks:

1. Create a personal Calendar subfolder named A-1 Hardware.
2. Enter the calendar items in the calendar, using the information listed in Table 2–8.

Table 2–8 Calendar Appointment Information

Description	Location	Date	Time	Status	Reminder	Recurrence
Staff meeting	Lunchroom	Every Monday from March 12, 2012 – June 12, 2012	7:00 AM – 8:00 AM	Busy	30 minutes	Weekly, end by June 12, 2012
Prepare Winter Closeout Sale	Manager's Office	March 3, 2012	8:30 AM – 10:30 AM	Busy	10 minutes	None
Enter payroll	Manager's Office	Start March 8, 2012, every Thursday	4:00 PM – 5:00 PM	Busy	15 minutes	Every two weeks, no end date
Kelly & Megan's birthday		March 19, 2012	All-day event	Free	None	Yearly
Parents Anniversary		March 14, 2012	All-day event	Free	1 day	Yearly
Conference call with Liz and Greg		March 20, 2012	9:00 AM – 10:00 AM	Tentative	15 minutes	None
Meet with lawn care supplier		March 21, 2012	1:00 PM – 2:00 PM	Out of Office	30 minutes	None
Lunch with Beth		March 31, 2012	12:00 PM – 1:00 PM	Out of Office	15 minutes	None

3. Print the Appointment calendar for the month of March, and then submit the printout in the format specified by your instructor.

In the Lab

Lab 3: Creating a Schedule

Problem: Start Outlook. Create a new Calendar folder using your name as the name of the new folder. You are to create a schedule of classes and other appointments using the information in Table 2–9. This calendar is for the spring semester that begins Monday, January 30, 2012, and ends Friday, May 11, 2012. The calendar you create is shown in Figure 2–86.

Table 2–9 Appointment Information							
Subject	Location	Start Date	Time	Status	Reminder	Recurrence	End After
Doctor Appointment	Drs. office	2/3/2012	2:00 PM – 3:00 PM	Out of Office	30 minutes	None	
Work		1/31/2012	7:00 AM – 3:30 PM	Out of Office	1 hour	Weekly, T, Th, Sa	No end date
Volunteer for New Student Orientation	Student Union	1/21/2012	8:30 AM – 12:00 PM	Out of Office	15 minutes	None	
Chemistry	Science 300	1/30/2012	8:00 AM – 9:30 AM	Busy	15 minutes	Weekly, M, W	30 classes
Technical Report Writing	HRB 201	1/30/2012	11:30 AM – 1:00 PM	Busy	10 minutes	Weekly, M, W	30 classes
Marketing	HRB 300	1/31/2012	7:00 PM – 8:30 PM	Busy	30 minutes	Weekly, T, Th	30 classes

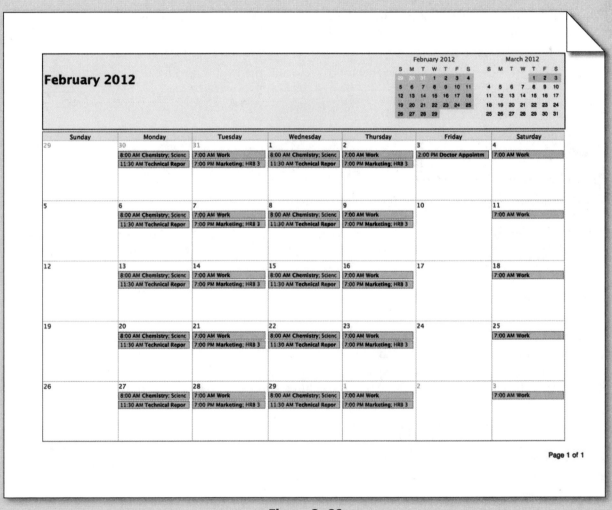

Figure 2–86

Perform the following tasks:

1. Create a one-time appointment for the first item in Table 2–9. Enter the text in the Subject column, Doctor Appointment, as the appointment subject. Enter the location, start date, and time as shown in Table 2–9. Show the time as Out of Office in your calendar and set a 30-minute reminder.

Continued >

In the Lab *continued*

2. Create a recurring appointment for the Work item in Table 2–9 on the previous page. Enter the subject, start date, and time as shown. Show the time as Out of Office in your calendar and set a one-hour reminder. Set the appointment to recur weekly on Tuesdays, Thursdays, and Saturdays with no end date.

3. Create a one-time appointment for the Volunteer for New Student Orientation item in Table 2–9. Enter the subject, start date, and time as shown. Show the time as Out of Office in your calendar and set a 15-minute reminder.

4. Create a recurring appointment for the Chemistry item in Table 2–9. Enter the subject, start date, and time as shown. Show the time as busy and set a 15-minute reminder. Set the appointment to recur weekly on Mondays and Wednesdays for 30 occurrences.

5. Create a recurring appointment for the Technical Report Writing item in Table 2–9. Enter the subject, start date, and time as shown. Show the time as busy and set a 10-minute reminder. Set the appointment to recur weekly on Mondays and Wednesdays for 30 occurrences.

6. Create a recurring appointment for the Marketing item in Table 2–9. Enter the subject, start date, and time as shown. Show the time as busy and set a 30-minute reminder. Set the appointment to recur weekly on Tuesdays and Thursdays for 30 occurrences.

7. Print the February 2012 calendar in Month view, and then submit it in the format specified by your instructor.

Cases and Places

Apply your creative thinking and problem solving skills to design and implement a solution.

Note: To complete these assignments, you may be required to use the Data Files for Students. See the inside back cover of this book for instructions on downloading the Data Files for Students, or contact your instructor for information about accessing the required files.

1: Create a Personal Schedule

Academic

Create a personal schedule for the next month using the information provided in Table 2–10. Include your appointments for work, classes, and study time. You also can include any extracurricular activities in which you participate. Use recurring appointments when possible. Schedule all-day activities as events. Print the calendar in Monthly Style and submit it in the format specified by your instructor.

Table 2–10 Academic Calendar Items

Description	Location	Date	Time	Status	Reminder	Recurrence
Financial Planning Workshop	Columbia Inn	March 11, 2012	1:00 PM – 4:00 PM	Busy	30 minutes	None
Spring Fling	Quad	March 3, 2012	12:00 PM – 2:00 PM	Out of Office	10 minutes	None
Department Meeting		Every Monday	2:00 PM – 3:00 PM	Busy	5 minutes	Weekly, end after 12 occurrences
Petition to Graduate		March 15, 2012	All Day Event	Free	1 day	None
Parents Anniversary		October 20, 2012	All Day Event	Free	1 day	Yearly
NJCAA D3 Women's Lacrosse Nationals		March 6, 2012 – March 8, 2012	All Day Event	Tentative	None	None
SGA Meeting		March 21, 2012	11:30 PM – 12:30 PM	Out of Office	30 minutes	None
Work Schedule		2/28/2012	2:00 PM – 5:30 PM	Out of Office	15 minutes	Tuesdays and Thursdays

2: Create a Work Schedule for Employees

Professional

At work, you are in charge of scheduling snack bar coverage for your local athletic club for the month of May. Create a schedule of work times for four employees. Brett works Mondays, Wednesdays, and Fridays from 9:00 AM to 5:00 PM; Megan works Tuesdays, Thursdays, and Saturdays from 9:00 AM to 5:00 PM; Joe works from 12:00 PM until 9:00 PM on Mondays, Wednesdays, and Fridays. Pat completes the schedule working from 12:00 PM until 9:00 PM on Tuesdays, Thursdays, and Saturdays. Print the calendar in Monthly Style and submit it in the format specified by your instructor.

3: Create Meeting Invitations

Personal

Create a personal calendar to keep track of several items relating to your schedule outside of class or work. Use Table 2–11 to add these items to your personal calendar.

Table 2–11 Personal Calendar Items						
Description	Location	Date	Time	Show As	Reminder	Recurrence
Open House at your child's new school	Jenna's School	April 3, 2012	1:00 PM – 4:00 PM	Out of Office	30 minutes	None
Annual Physical	Medical Plan	April 5, 2012	12:00 PM – 2:00 PM	Out of Office	10 minutes	None
Air Conditioning Yearly Service	Home	April 4, 2012	2:00 PM – 3:00 PM	Busy	5 minutes	Yearly, on the first Wednesday in April
Performance Evaluation	Manager's Office	April 16, 2012	All Day Event	Free	1 day	None
Car Payment Due		April 15, 2012	All Day Event	Free	1 day	Monthly, 15th day of every month

Appendix A

Project Planning Guidelines

Using Project Planning Guidelines

The process of communicating specific information to others is a learned, rational skill. Computers and software, especially Microsoft Office 2011 for Mac, can help you develop ideas and present detailed information to a particular audience.

Using Microsoft Office 2011 for Mac, you can create projects such as Word documents, PowerPoint presentations, and Excel spreadsheets. Productivity software such as Microsoft Office 2011 for Mac minimizes much of the laborious work of drafting and revising projects. Some communicators handwrite ideas in notebooks, others compose directly on the computer, and others have developed unique strategies that work for their own particular thinking and writing styles.

No matter what method you use to plan a project, follow specific guidelines to arrive at a final product that presents information correctly and effectively (Figure A–1). Use some aspects of these guidelines every time you undertake a project, and others as needed in specific instances. For example, in determining content for a project, you may decide that a chart communicates trends more effectively than a paragraph of text. If so, you would create this graphical element and insert it in an Excel spreadsheet, a Word document, or a PowerPoint slide.

Determine the Project's Purpose

Begin by clearly defining why you are undertaking this assignment. For example, you may want to track monetary donations collected for your club's fund-raising drive. Alternatively, you may be urging students to vote for a particular candidate in the next election. Once you clearly understand the purpose of your task, begin to draft ideas of how best to communicate this information.

Analyze Your Audience

Learn about the people who will read, analyze, or view your work. Where are they employed? What are their educational backgrounds? What are their expectations? What questions do they have?

PROJECT PLANNING GUIDELINES

1. DETERMINE THE PROJECT'S PURPOSE
Why are you undertaking the project?

2. ANALYZE YOUR AUDIENCE
Who are the people who will use your work?

3. GATHER POSSIBLE CONTENT
What information exists, and in what forms?

4. DETERMINE WHAT CONTENT TO PRESENT TO YOUR AUDIENCE
What information will best communicate the project's purpose to your audience?

Figure A–1

Design experts suggest drawing a mental picture of these people or finding photos of people who fit this profile so that you can develop a project with the audience in mind.

By knowing your audience members, you can tailor a project to meet their interests and needs. You will not present them with information they already possess, and you will not omit the information they need to know.

Example: Your assignment is to raise the profile of your college's nursing program in the community. How much do they know about your college and the nursing curriculum? What are the admission requirements? How many of the applicants admitted complete the program? What percent pass the state board exams?

Gather Possible Content

Rarely are you in a position to develop all the material for a project. Typically, you would begin by gathering existing information that may reside in spreadsheets or databases. Web sites, pamphlets, magazine and newspaper articles, and books could provide insights of how others have approached your topic. Personal interviews often provide perspectives not available by any other means. Consider video and audio clips as potential sources for material that might complement or support the factual data you uncover.

Determine What Content to Present to Your Audience

Experienced designers recommend writing three or four major ideas you want an audience member to remember after reading or viewing your project. It also is helpful to envision your project's endpoint, the key fact you wish to emphasize. All project elements should lead to this ending point.

As you make content decisions, you also need to think about other factors. Presentation of the project content is an important consideration. For example, will your brochure be printed on thick, colored paper or posted on the Web? Will your PowerPoint presentation be viewed in a classroom with excellent lighting and a bright projector, or will it be viewed on a notebook computer monitor? Determine relevant time factors, such as the length of time to develop the project, how long readers will spend reviewing your project, or the amount of time allocated for your speaking engagement. Your project will need to accommodate all of these constraints.

Decide whether a graph, photo, or artistic element can express or emphasize a particular concept. The right hemisphere of the brain processes images by attaching an emotion to them, so audience members are more apt to recall these graphics long term rather than just reading text.

As you select content, be mindful of the order in which you plan to present information. Readers and audience members generally remember the first and last pieces of information they see and hear, so you should place the most important information at the top or bottom of the page.

Summary

When creating a project, it is beneficial to follow some basic guidelines from the outset. By taking some time at the beginning of the process to determine the project's purpose, analyze the audience, gather possible content, and determine what content to present to the audience, you can produce a project that is informative, relevant, and effective.

Appendix B

Publishing Office 2011 Web Pages Online

With the Office 2011 programs Word 2011 and Excel 2011, you use the Save As Web Page command in the File menu to save a Web page to a Web site, network location, or FTP site. **File Transfer Protocol (FTP)** is an Internet standard that allows computers to exchange files with other computers on the Internet.

You should contact your network system administrator or technical support staff at your Internet access provider to determine if their Web server supports Web folders, FTP, or both, and to obtain necessary permissions to access the Web server.

Using an Office Program to Publish Office 2011 Web Pages

When publishing online, someone first must assign the necessary permissions for you to publish the Web page. If you are granted access to publish online, you must obtain the Web address of the Web server, a user name, and possibly a password that allows you to connect to the Web server. The steps in this appendix assume that you have access to an online location to which you can publish a Web page.

TO CONNECT TO AN ONLINE LOCATION

To publish a Web page online, you first must connect to the online location. To connect to an online location using Mac OS X Lion, you can perform the following steps.

1. In the Finder, click Go on the menu bar to display the Go menu.

2. In the Go menu, choose Connect to Server to open the Connect to Server dialog.

3. Enter the server address in the Server Address text box. The address needs to contain both the protocol and the actual server address. If you were connecting to an ftp server, for example, the entry would be ftp://server.address.com, where ftp:// is the protocol, and server.address.com is the server address or IP address of the server.

4. Click the Connect button to open a dialog which prompts you for your Name and Password.

5. Enter your Username and Password, and click Connect.

6. When successfully connected, a window will open with a title bar containing username@serveraddress. The server will also appear in the navigation bar of Finder windows in the Shared section.

7. When you wish to disconnect, open a Finder window and click the Eject icon in the navigation pane next to the ftp server.

To Save a Web Page to an Online Location

The online location now can be accessed easily from Mac programs, including Microsoft Office programs. After creating a Microsoft Office file you wish to save as a Web page, you must save the file to the online location to which you connected in the previous steps. To save a Microsoft Word document as a Web page, for example, and publish it to the online location, you would perform the following steps.

1. Click File on the ribbon to display the File menu and then choose Save As Web Page to display the Save As Web Page dialog.

2. Type the Web page file name in the Save As text box. Do not press the RETURN key because you do not want to close the dialog at this time.

3. Click the Format box arrow and then click Web Page (.htm) to select the Web Page format.

4. If necessary, scroll to display the name of the online location in the Shared group in the navigation pane.

5. Double-click the online location name in the navigation pane to select that location as the new save location and display its contents in the right pane.

6. If necessary, navigate to the folder on the server to which you wish to save your Web page.

7. Click the Save button (Save As dialog).

The Web page now has been published online. To view the Web page using a Web browser, contact your network or system administrator for the Web address you should use to connect to the Web page.

Appendix C

Saving to the Web Using Windows Live SkyDrive

Introduction

Windows Live SkyDrive, also referred to as **SkyDrive**, is a free service that allows users to save files to the Web, such as documents, presentations, spreadsheets, databases, videos, and photos. Using SkyDrive, you also can save files in folders, providing for greater organization. You then can retrieve those files from any computer connected to the Internet. Some Office 2011 programs including Word, PowerPoint, and Excel can save files directly to an Internet location such as SkyDrive. SkyDrive also facilitates collaboration by allowing users to share files with other SkyDrive users (Figure C–1).

Figure C–1

Note: An Internet connection is required to perform the steps in this appendix.

To Save a File to Windows Live SkyDrive

You can save files directly to SkyDrive from within Word, PowerPoint, and Excel using the File menu. The following steps save an open Word document (Koala Exhibit Flyer, in this case) to SkyDrive. These steps require you to have a Windows Live account. Contact your instructor if you do not have a Windows Live account.

- Start Word and then open a document you want to save to the Web (in this case, the Koala Exhibit Flyer).

- Click File in the menu bar to display the File menu (Figure C–2).

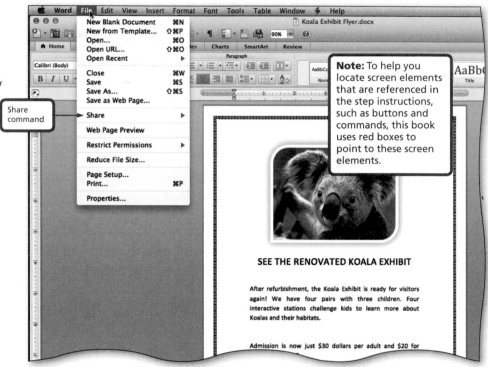

Figure C–2

❷

- Choose Share on the menu to display the Share submenu (Figure C–3).

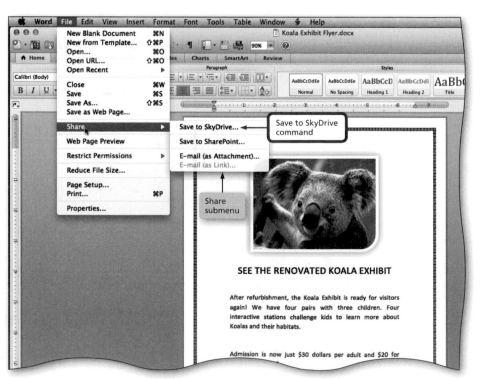

Figure C–3

- Click Save to SkyDrive in the Share submenu to display the Windows Live Sign In dialog (Figure C–4).

Q&A What if the Sign In dialog does not appear?

If you already are signed into Windows Live, the Sign In dialog will not be displayed. Instead, the contents of your Windows Live SkyDrive will be displayed. If you already are signed into Windows Live, proceed to Step 5.

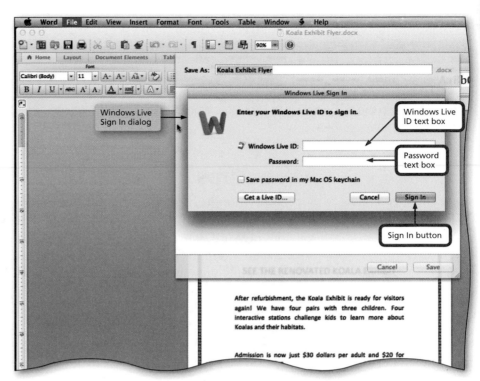

Figure C–4

- Enter your Windows Live ID in the Windows Live ID text box (Windows Live login dialog).

- Enter your Windows Live password in the Password text box.

- Click the Sign In button to sign into Windows Live and display the contents of your Windows Live SkyDrive in the Personal Folders area of the dialog.

- If necessary, click the folder to set the save location for the document, in this case the Documents folder.

- Type **Koala Exhibit Web** in the Save As text box to enter the file name (Figure C–5).

Q&A What if the Documents folder does not exist?

Click another folder to select it as the save location. Record the name of this folder so that you can locate and retrieve the file later in this appendix.

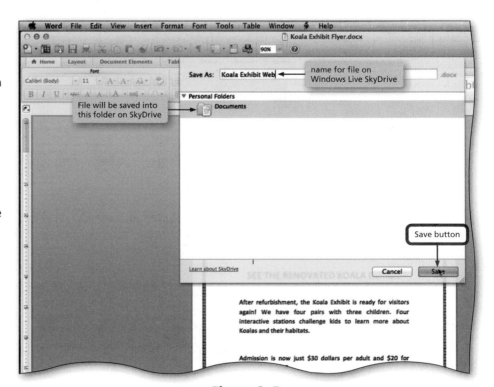

Figure C–5

Q&A My SkyDrive shows personal and shared folders. What is the difference?

Personal folders are private and are not shared with anyone. Shared folders can be viewed by SkyDrive users to whom you have assigned the necessary permissions.

- Click the Save button (Save As dialog) to save the file to Windows Live SkyDrive.

Q&A Is it necessary to rename the file?
It is good practice to rename the file. If you download the file from SkyDrive to your computer, having a different file name will preserve the original file.

- Click Word on the menu bar, then click Quit Word to quit the application.

Web Apps

Microsoft has created a scaled-down, Web-based version of its Microsoft Office suite, called **Microsoft Office Web Apps,** or **Web Apps**. Web Apps contains Web-based versions of Word, PowerPoint, Excel, and OneNote that can be used to view and edit files that are saved to SkyDrive. Web Apps allows users to continue working with their files even while they are not using a computer with Microsoft Office installed. In addition to working with files located on SkyDrive, Web Apps also enables users to create new Word documents, PowerPoint presentations, and Excel spreadsheets. After returning to a computer with the Microsoft Office suite, some users choose to download files from SkyDrive and edit them using the associated Microsoft Office program.

> **Note:** As with all Web applications, SkyDrive and Office Web Apps are subject to change. Consequently, the steps required to perform the actions in this appendix might be different from those shown.

To Download a File from Windows Live SkyDrive

Files saved to SkyDrive can be downloaded from a Web browser using any computer with an Internet connection. The following steps download the Koala Exhibit Web file using a Web browser.

- Click the Safari icon in the Dock to start Safari.

- Replace the content in the Address bar with `skydrive.live.com` and then press the RETURN key to display a SkyDrive Web page requesting you sign in to your Windows Live account (Figure C–6). (If the contents of your SkyDrive are displayed instead, you already are signed in and can proceed to Step 3 on the next page.)

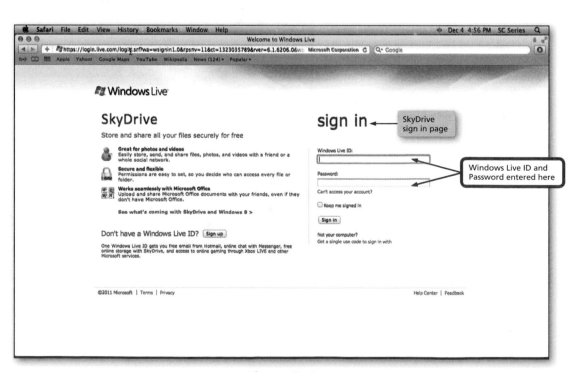

Figure C–6

Q&A Why does the Web address change after I enter it in the Address bar?
The Web address changes because you are being redirected to sign into Windows Live
before you can access SkyDrive.

2

- If necessary, enter
your Windows Live ID
and password in the
appropriate text boxes
and then click the Sign
in button to sign into
Windows Live and
display the contents
of your SkyDrive
(Figure C–7).

Q&A What if my screen
shows the contents
of a particular folder,
instead of all folders?
To display all folders
on your SkyDrive, click
Files under SkyDrive in
the upper left corner
of the window.

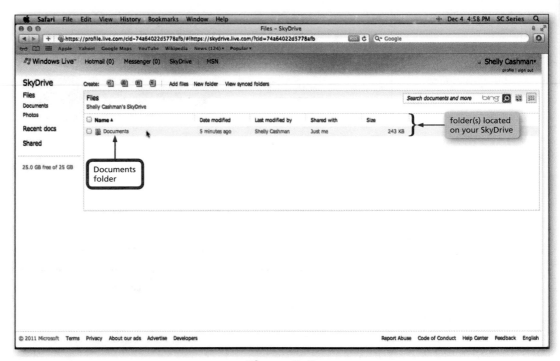

Figure C–7

3

- Click the Documents
folder, or the link
corresponding to the
folder containing
the file you wish to
open, to select the
folder and display its
contents (Figure C–8).

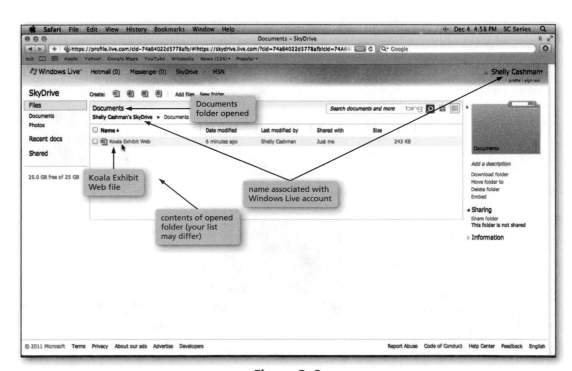

Figure C–8

- Click the check box next to the file to select the file.
- Click Open in Word to display a dialog (Figure C–9).

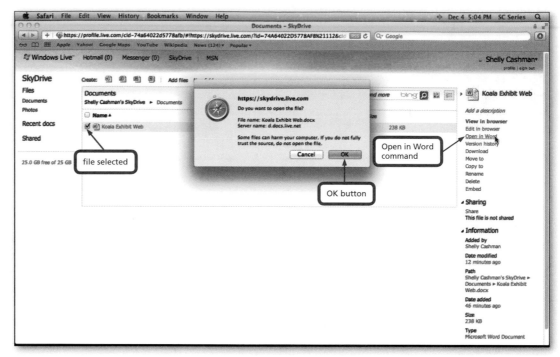

Figure C–9

- Click the OK button to open the Windows Live Sign In dialog.
- Enter your Windows Live ID and password in the appropriate text boxes and then click Sign In to open the file in Microsoft Word on your computer.

Q&A What if I want to save the file on my computer's hard disk? Refer to the Office 2011 and Mac OS X chapter at the beginning of this book.

Q&A What if I click the name of the file rather than the checkbox and the Open in Word link? Clicking the name of the file will open the file in the Word Web App rather than in the Word application on your computer (See Figure C–12).

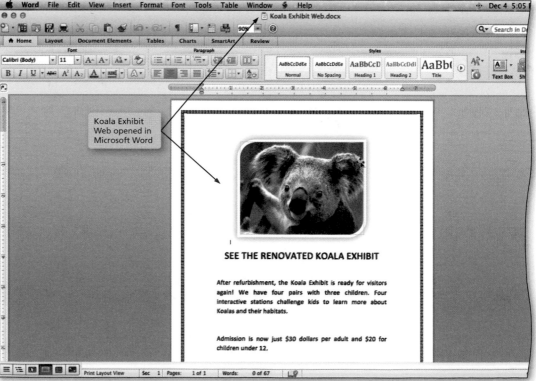

Figure C–10

Collaboration

In today's workplace, it is common to work with others on projects. Collaborating with the members of your team often requires sharing files. It also can involve multiple people editing and working with a certain set of files simultaneously. Placing files on SkyDrive in a public or shared folder enables others to view or modify the files. The members of the team then can view and edit the files simultaneously using Web Apps, enabling the team to work from one set of files (Figure C–11). Collaboration using Web Apps not only enables multiple people to work together, it also can reduce the amount of time required to complete a project.

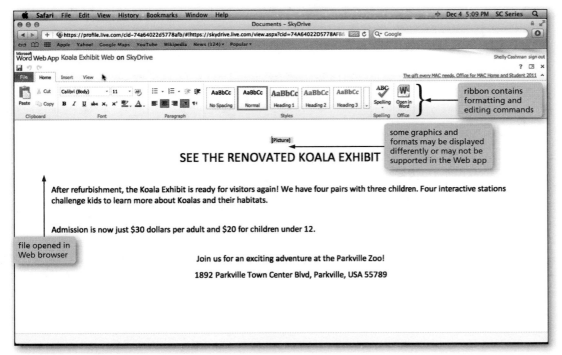

Figure C–11

Capstone Project: Wee Ones Day Care

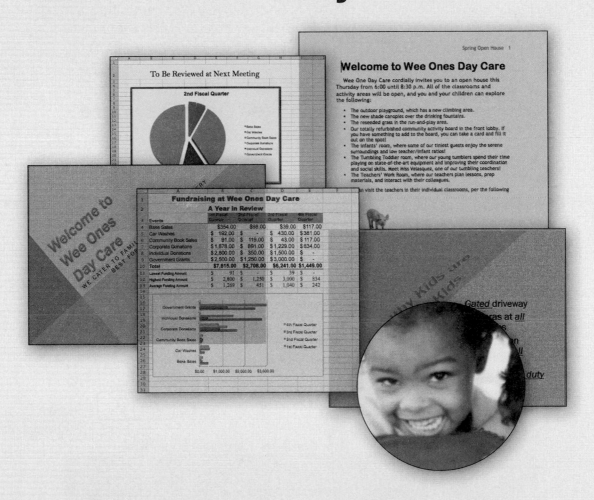

The Capstone Project consists of an integrated, comprehensive set of problems relating to a single scenario. Students apply concepts and skills presented in this book to create solutions to the problems using Word, PowerPoint, and Excel.

Wee Ones Day Care, which is located in downtown Springfield, Rhode Island, provides day care for children ages up to 8 years old. The children's activities include arts and crafts, field trips, and organized outdoor games. As the executive assistant to the owner, Elizabeth Jordan, you provide many office support tasks to keep the day care center running.

Word Capstone Project

Creating a One-Page Flyer with a Picture and a Table

Problem: Wee Ones Day Care hosts an open house for parents four times a year and distributes a flyer to announce each of these open houses. The owner of the day care center has asked you to produce the flyer for the upcoming open house.

Instructions Part 1:   Open a blank document and use Publishing Layout view to change the theme to Slipstream. Enter the text and table of the flyer and modify the text and table as shown in Figure 1–1. Locate the clip art by opening the Clip Art Browser, selecting the Animals category, and then dragging the pig image into the flyer. Change the document properties to reflect your name as author.

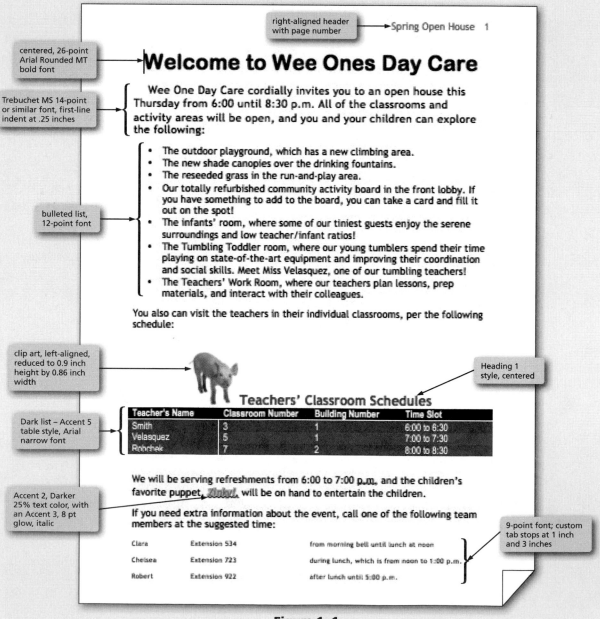

Figure 1–1

Instructions Part 2:   The owner of the day care is pleased with your flyer, but she has some changes for you. Check the spelling of your document, but be sure not to change the spelling of the puppet's name. Adjust the table to Autofit to Contents, change the teachers' names to "R. Smith" and "S. Robchek," respectively, and center the table. Then, bold the teachers' names and italicize their respective time slots in the table. The grass area in the playground is not ready for use; as such, delete the third bullet from the bulleted list and move the first bullet so that it is the second bullet in the list. Position the clip art to the middle right of the page and set it to a Tight text wrap. Delete the tab stop at the 3-inch mark and use a comma between each of the extensions and suggested times. Change the custom tab stops for the last three lines of text so that the text is more evenly aligned across the page. Miss Velasquez will not be attending the event. Search and replace her name with "Chardon," the last name of the other tumbling teacher. Last, find a synonym for the text, tiniest, which is used within the bulleted list, and change the theme to Kilter.

PowerPoint Capstone Project

Creating a Presentation with Images and a Transition

Problem: During each open house at Wee Ones Day Care, you give an orientation presentation to the parents who come to visit. The owner, Elizabeth Jordan, has asked you to ensure that the PowerPoint presentation for the upcoming open house showcases the day care and highlights its offerings.

Instructions Part 1: Use the typed notes shown in Figure 1–2 on page CAP 4 to start the new presentation shown in Figure 1–3 on page CAP 5. Apply the Angles theme, change the theme colors to Inspiration, and use a Title Slide layout for Slide 1, the Two Content layout for Slide 2, and the Content with Caption layout for Slides 3 and 4.

On Slide 1, shown in Figure 1–3 (a), change the font size of the title, Welcome to Wee Ones Day Care, to 48 point, adjusting the text as shown in Figure 1–3 (a). Apply the text effect shown (first row, third column in the Applies to All Text in the Shape section) to the title and then italicize the text. Apply the Newsprint texture fill to the subtitle text. (*Hint:* On the Format tab, click the Fill button arrow in the Shape Styles group, then click Fill Effects. With Fill selected in the left navigation pane of the Format Picture dialog, click the Picture or Texture tab, then select the Newsprint texture.) Center the text and then change the font size to 18-pt. Insert the Explosion 1 shape and apply the shape Quick Style (third row, sixth column) shown in Figure 1–3 (a). Add the text, apply bold, change the font size to 20 point and then position and resize the shape as necessary.

On Slide 2, shown in Figure 1–3 (b), use the Clip Art Gallery to insert the 'smiling' photo in the People category into the right placeholder. Use the Corrections button on the Format Picture tab to soften the picture by 25%, and use the Recolor button to change the color tone to a temperature of 4700K. Then, add a Reflected Bevel, White picture style, an Accent 3, Darker 25% picture border, and a Relaxed Inset bevel effect. Insert the Style 5 theme background to all slides.

On Slide 3, shown in Figure 1–3 (c), adjust the title text to match the figure. Insert a Striped Right Arrow shape and position it to point to the craft tables bullets. Add the text, Look!, and then format the text as 32 point, Accent 6, Darker 25% color. Change the shape style to the Quick Style shown (fourth row, seventh column). Delete the subtitle placeholder.

On Slide 4, shown in Figure 1–3 (d), format the list as bullets, and then underline and italicize the word, Gated. Use the Format Painter button to underline and italicize the indicated words in the subsequent bullets. Delete the subtitle placeholder. Open the Format Background dialog box and apply the Denim texture shown in Figure 1–3 (d). Set the Transparency to 40%.

Instructions Part 2: Elizabeth Jordan reviewed your presentation and has suggested a few changes. On Slide 2, change the border color of the image to Accent 4, Darker 25% as shown in Figure 1–4 (a) on page CAP 6. Then, apply the Push transition to all the slides and increase the duration to 04.00.

On the Safety slide, Slide 4, replace the text, Safety is our concern, with Healthy Kids Are Happy Kids. Apply the text effect that appears in the second row, second column of the Applies to All Text in the Shape section. Change the font size to 40 point. Center the text and then apply the Stop Warp transform text effect. Reposition and resize the title placeholder. Format the text with the Inside Center Shadow text effect.

Continued >

PowerPoint Capstone Project *continued*

To accommodate some last-minute content, duplicate Slide 2, position the new slide as Slide 4, delete the image, locate the photo shown in Figure 1–4 (b) on page CAP 6 using the Clip Art Gallery (*Hint:* search for 'roller coaster'), and insert this image into the placeholder. Change the size of the image to approximately 5.6" × 4.83", and then using a button below the image, resize the picture to fit the placeholder. Apply the Bevel Perspective picture style. Replace the text on the slide with the following content, formatted as bulleted text. (*Hint:* You may need to click the Increase Indent button once.) Be sure to resize the placeholder so that each bulleted item appears on a single line. Submit the assignment as requested by your instructor.

Title: Special Events for Older Children
Field trip to Roger Williams Zoo
Fundraisers for local charities
Carnival Night

Slide #1

Welcome to Wee Ones Day Care

We cater to families who want the very best for their children

Slide #2

Activities for the Little Ones

Outdoors

- Playground
- Tetherball

Indoors

- Computer games
- Story nook

Nap time

- Individual mats
- Blankets and pillows

Slide #3

Adventures for the Older Children

- Supervised Internet exploration
- Writing centers
- Craft tables
  - Paints
  - Beading
  - Pottery tools

Slide #4

Safety is our concern!

- Gated driveway
- Cameras at all entrances
- Identification process for all visitors
- Staff nurse on duty

Figure 1–2

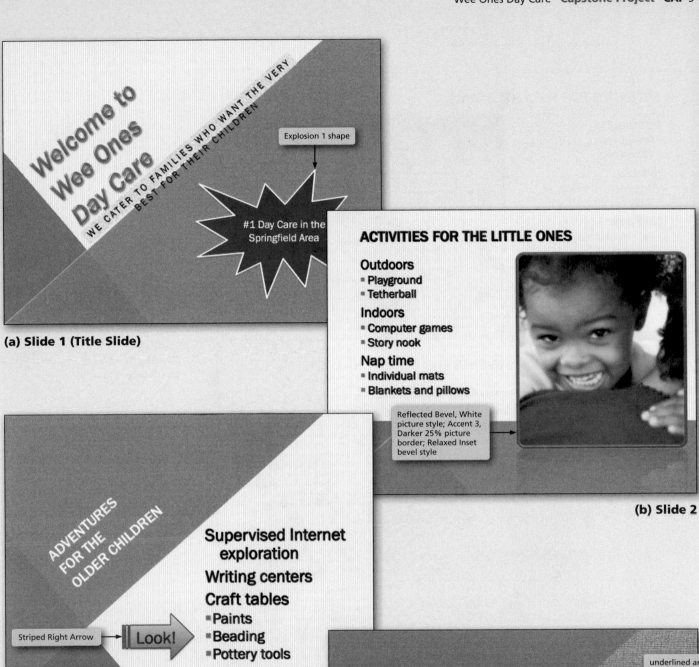

(a) Slide 1 (Title Slide)

(b) Slide 2

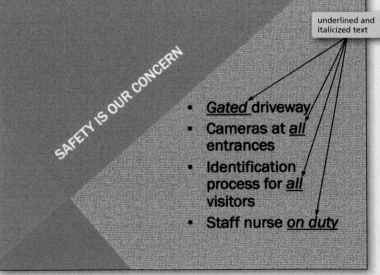

(c) Slide 3

(d) Slide 4

Figure 1–3

Continued >

PowerPoint Capstone Project *continued*

(a) Slide 2 (Modified)

(b) Slide 4 (Duplicated and Modified Slide 2)

(c) Slide 5 (Original Slide 4 Modified)

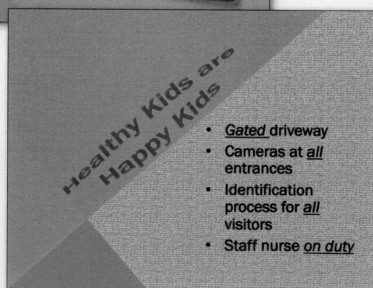

Figure 1–4

Excel Capstone Project

Analyzing and Presenting Fundraising Data

Problem: The teachers at Wee Ones Day Care have been running fundraisers throughout the year so that the day care can fund the many field trips that the children take. Over the last year, money has come in from different events, including bake sales, car washes, community book sales, and similar activities. In addition, cash donations were received from individuals and business groups, and grants were received from several government agencies in the city. The owner of the day care has asked you to organize the information about the money that has flowed from these events and prepare a basic spreadsheet, as shown in Figure 1–5 on the next page, for use by the administration team.

Instructions Part 1:   Start Excel and enter the text from Table 1–1. Place the text, Events, from the top-left of the table in cell A1. Place the remainder of the table in the adjacent rows and columns in the worksheet. Format the range B2:E2 with Currency formatting with floating dollar signs. (*Hint:* choose Cells on the Format menu, click Currency category on Number tab.) Format the range B3:E7 with the Accounting number format. Change the column width of column A to 1.75 inches. Change the width of columns B, C, D, and E to 1 inch.

Double-click the Sheet1 tab, and rename the tab Fundraising Overview. Change the tab color to Red. (*Hint:* Point to Format on the Sheet menu, then click Tab Color.)

Table 1–1 Sources of Money at Wee Ones Day Care				
Events	**1st Quarter**	**2nd Quarter**	**3rd Quarter**	**4th Quarter**
Bake Sales	354	98	39	117
Car Washes	192	0	430	381
Community Book Sales	91	119	43	117
Corporate Donations	1678	891	1229	834
Individual Donations	2800	0	1500	0
Government Grants	2500	1250	3000	0

Insert two new rows above row 1. Enter the text Fundraising at Wee Ones Day Care in cell A1 and the text A Year in Review in cell A2. Merge and center the cell A1 text across columns A through E, and do the same for the cell A2 text. Format cells A1:E2 with the Title style; change the font size of the text in row 2 to 16. Format cells A3:E3 with the Heading 3 style. Apply the Essential theme to the workbook.

To align the column widths to their best fit, double-click the left column border for column B, and for columns C through F.

Instructions Part 2:   In cell A10, enter Total and apply the Total format to the range A10:E10. In cell A11, enter Lowest Funding Amount. In cell A12, enter Highest Funding Amount, and in cell A13, enter Average Funding Amount. Bold the text in cells A11, A12, and A13, and change the font in those cells to Arial Narrow, size 10 font. Increase the width of column A to 2.15 inches. Change cells B4:E10 to font size 14 point.

In cell B10, use the Sum function to sum the values in the range B4:B9. Copy the formula in cell B10 to the range C10:E10 and if necessary, apply the Currency format with fixed dollar signs to the numbers in the range B10:E10.

Continued >

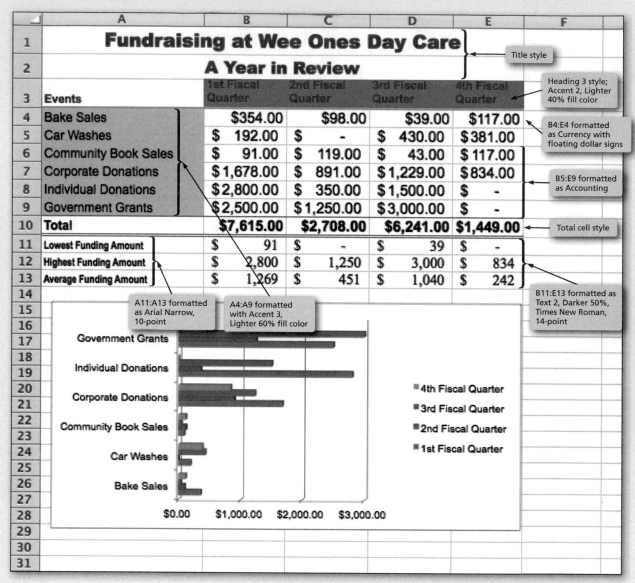

Figure 1–5

In cell B11, use the Insert Function button on the Formulas tab under Function to insert the MIN function (in the Statistical group) for the range B4:B9. Use the fill handle to copy the formula from cell B11 to the range C11:E11.

In cell B12, enter `= (max(B4:B9))`. Copy the formula in cell B12 to the range C12:E12. In cell B13, use the AutoSum button arrow in the Standard toolbar to insert the AVERAGE function for the range B4:B9. Use the fill handle to copy the formula from cell B13 to the range C13:E13.

Select the range B11:E13. Format the range with Accounting formatting. Use the Decrease Decimal button on the Home tab under Number to remove all decimal places from the values in the cells. Change the font color of the text to Text 2, Darker 50%; change the font to Times New Roman; and change the font size to 14 point.

One of the school's instructors reviews the entries in the spreadsheet and asks you to change cell C8 to 350 to reflect updated records and to change the header text in the range B3:E3 to make the header text clearer. Delete the contents of cell C8, and enter 350. Using the Search in Sheet box, find all cells containing the word Quarter, replace all instances with the words Fiscal Quarter, and then use the Wrap Text button on the Home tab under Alignment to wrap the text.

Highlight the range B3:E3, and using the Fill Color arrow on the Home tab under Font, select Accent 2, Lighter 40%. Highlight the range A4:A9 and apply the Accent 3, Lighter 60% fill color.

To create a chart to make your spreadsheet more effective, use the range A3:E9 and the Bar button (on the Charts tab under Insert Chart) to create a 3-D Clustered Bar chart. Style the chart using the style in the second column, first row in the Chart Styles group. Use the Axes button on the Chart Layout tab to open the Format Axis dialog for the horizontal axis by pointing to Horizontal Axis, then clicking Axis Options. If necessary, select Scale in the left navigation, and then change the Major unit to 1000. Select the chart, click the Align button to make sure that the Snap to Grid command is selected on the Format tab under Arrange, and size and position the chart as shown in Figure 1–5.

Before you turn in the spreadsheet and chart for Elizabeth Jordan's first review, spell check your work and change the document properties as specified by your instructor. Save the workbook, and print your work in formula view.

Instructions Part 3:   After considering your work further, you decide to make some changes before you give the spreadsheet file to Elizabeth Jordan for her final approval.

Use the Colors button on the Home tab under Themes to select the Breeze color scheme for the workbook theme. For the range A4:A9, apply the Accent 5, Lighter 40% fill color.

Use the Format Painter button on the Standard toolbar to copy the formatting of cell E3 to F3. Enter the text, Trend, in cell F3. Use the Line button (on the Charts tab under Insert Sparklines) to create a Sparkline chart in F4 for the range B4:E4. Use the fill handle to build the same type of chart in each of the cells in the range F5:F9. Highlight the range F4:F9, and use the Sparkline button (Sparklines tab, Format group) to change the Weight to the fifth option from the top.

To showcase the team's efforts in the second quarter, insert a new sheet, and rename the Sheet1 tab to Second Fiscal Quarter. From the Fundraising Overview tab, use the range A3:A9 and the range C3:C9 to create a Pie chart (Charts tab, Insert Chart group). Use the Move Chart command on a shortcut menu to move the chart to the Second Fiscal Quarter sheet.

On the Second Fiscal Quarter sheet, use the Pie button in the Change Chart Type group to change the chart to a 3-D Pie. Use the Themes button (on the Home tab under Themes) to select the Waveform theme. Select the chart and change the Point explosion to 10%. (*Hint:* Select Series "2nd Fiscal Quarter" and then click the Format Selection button.) With Chart Area as the current selection, apply the chart style in the sixth column, first row in the Chart Element Styles gallery. Change the border line weight to 6 pt and apply the Angle Bevel effect. Use the Align button to make sure that the Snap to Grid command is selected (Format tab under Arrange), and size and position the chart as shown in Figure 1–6 on the next page.

Resize row 2 to 50.00 pixels. In cell A2, enter To Be Reviewed at Next Meeting. Select cells A2:H2, use the Merge button (on the Home tab under Alignment) to merge and center the text, and then change the font of the text to Bell MT, 28 pt.

To prepare a polished spreadsheet for printing, you have some final tasks to complete: Use the Header & Footer button on the Layout tab under Page Setup to insert the current time and current date in the center section of the header. (*Hint:* Use the Customize Header button.) Next, use the Margins button to select Narrow margins and the Orientation button to select Landscape orientation.

You want to make a further good impression on your boss. Before you turn in the spreadsheet and chart for her review, spell check your work. Save the workbook, and print your work in non-formula view and then formula view.

Continued >

Excel Capstone Project *continued*

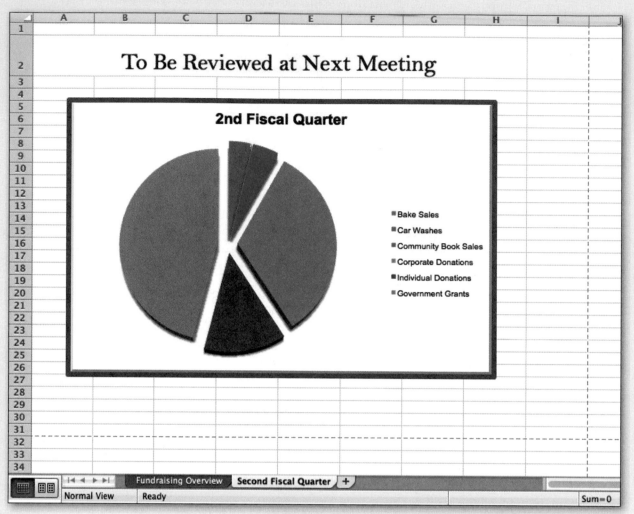

Figure 1–6

Change the document properties as specified by your instructor. Change the worksheet header with your name, course number, and other information as specified by your instructor. Save the workbook using the current file name. Close the workbook. Submit the assignment as requested by your instructor.

Index

Quick Reference Summary

Table 1: Microsoft Word 2011 for Mac Quick Reference Summary

Task	Page Number	Mouse	Ribbon	Shortcut Menu	Menu Bar	Keyboard Shortcut
All Caps	WD 85		Change Case button (Home tab | Font group), UPPERCASE		Format > Change Case > UPPERCASE; Format > Font, Font tab (Font dialog), Effects area, All caps	COMMAND-SHIFT-A; SHIFT-FN-F3
AutoCorrect Entry, Create	WD 22, WD 90				Tools > AutoCorrect; Word > Preferences > AutoCorrect	
AutoCorrect Options Button, Use	WD 89	Point to AutoCorrect Options button in flagged word				
AutoText, Insert	WD 174					type AutoText entry name, press RETURN
AutoText Entry, Create	WD 173				Tools > AutoCorrect, AutoText tab (AutoCorrect dialog)	
Bibliographical List, Create	WD 108		Bibliography button (Document Elements tab | References group)			
Bibliography Style, Change	WD 92		Bibliography Style button arrow (Document Elements tab | References group)			
Bold	WD 33		Bold button (Home tab | Font group)	Font, Font tab (Font dialog), Bold in Font style list	Format > Font, Font tab (Font dialog), Bold in Font style list	COMMAND-B
Border Paragraph	WD 162		Borders button arrow (Home tab | Paragraph group); Borders button (Layout tab | Page Background), Borders tab (Borders and Shading dialog)		Format > Borders and Shading, Borders tab (Borders and Shading dialog)	
Bullets, Apply	WD 27, WD 186		Bulleted List button (Home tab | Paragraph group)	Bullets and Numbering	Format > Bullets and Numbering, Bulleted tab (Bullets and Numbering dialog)	* (asterisk), SPACE BAR

Table 1: Microsoft Word 2011 for Mac Quick Reference Summary *(continued)*

Task	Page Number	Mouse	Ribbon	Shortcut Menu	Menu Bar	Keyboard Shortcut
Center	WD 18		Center Text button (Home tab | Paragraph group)	Paragraph, Indents and Spacing tab (Paragraph dialog), Alignment pop-up menu	Format > Paragraph, Indents and Spacing tab (Paragraph dialog), Alignment pop-up menu	COMMAND-E
Change Case	WD 22		Change Case button (Home tab | Font group)	Font, Font tab, Effects area (Font dialog)	Format > Font, Font tab, Effects area (Font dialog)	SHIFT-F3
Change Spacing before or after Paragraph	WD 46		Spacing Before or Spacing After box arrow (Page Layout tab | Paragraph group)	Paragraph, Indents and Spacing tab (Paragraph dialog), Before and After boxes	Format > Paragraph, Indents and Spacing tab, Before and After boxes	OPTION-COMMAND-M
Citation, Edit	WD 95	Click citation, Citations Options box arrow, Edit This Citation				
Citation, Insert	WD 93	Toolbox button in Standard toolbar, Citations pane	Manage button (Document Elements tab | References group), + button (Citations pane)			
Clear Formatting	WD 163		Clear Formatting button (Home tab | Font group)			COMMAND-SPACE BAR, COMMAND-Q
Click and Type	WD 83	Position mouse pointer at desired location, when I-beam pointer appears, double-click				
Clip Art, Add to Clip Gallery	WD 151		Picture button (Home tab | Insert group), Clip Art Gallery, Import button (Clip Gallery dialog), choose file, click Import (Clip Gallery dialog)			
Clip Art, Find and Download	WD 150		Picture button (Home tab | Insert group), enter search text, click Online button (Clip Gallery dialog)			
Clip Art, Insert	WD 153	Media button in Standard toolbar, Clip Art tab (Media Browser), Category button, drag image into document	Picture button (Home tab | Insert group)			
Color Text	WD 30		Font Color button arrow (Home tab | Font group)	Font, Font tab (Font dialog), Font color	Format > Font, Font tab (Font dialog), Font color	
Copy	WD 114	Copy button in Standard toolbar		Copy	Edit > Copy	COMMAND-C
Count Words	WD 103	Word Count indicator at bottom of document window			Tools > Word Count	

Table 1: Microsoft Word 2011 for Mac Quick Reference Summary *(continued)*

Task	Page Number	Mouse	Ribbon	Shortcut Menu	Menu Bar	Keyboard Shortcut
Custom Dictionary, Set Default, View or Modify Entries	WD 121				Word > Preferences > Spelling and Grammar, Dictionaries button	
Date, Insert Current	WD 172				Insert > Date and Time	
Document Properties, Change	WD 52				File > Properties	
Document Properties, Print	WD 123				File > Print, Copies & Pages button (Print dialog), Print What, Document properties	COMMAND-P
Double-Space	WD 78		Line Spacing button (Home tab | Paragraph group), 2.0	Paragraph, Indents and Spacing tab (Paragraph dialog), Line Spacing	Format > Paragraph, Indents and Spacing tab (Paragraph dialog), Line Spacing	COMMAND-2
Double-Underline	WD 85		Underline button arrow (Home tab | Font group)	Font, Font tab, Underline style (Font dialog)	Format > Font, Underline style (Font dialog)	COMMAND-SHIFT-D
Endnote, Insert	WD 98		Endnote button (Document Elements tab | Citations group)		Insert > Footnote, Endnotes (Footnote and Endnote dialog)	
Envelope, Address and Print	WD 189				Tools > Envelopes	
Field, Convert to Regular Text	WD 110	Click field, click box arrow, Convert Bibliography to Static Text				
Find Text	WD 116	Click Page Number indicator at bottom of document window, Find tab	Find button (Home tab | Editing group)		View > Sidebar > Search Pane; Edit > Find > Find	COMMAND-F
Font, Change	WD 21		Font box arrow (Home tab | Font group)	Font, Font tab (Font dialog)	Font menu; Format > Font, Font tab (Font dialog)	COMMAND-D
Font Size, Change	WD 20		Font Size box arrow (Home tab | Font group)	Font, Font tab, Size box (Font dialog)	Format > Font, Font tab, Size box (Font dialog)	COMMAND-D
Font Size, Decrease	WD 85, WD 147		Decrease Font Size button (Home tab | Font group)			COMMAND-SHIFT-<
Font Size, Decrease 1 point	WD 85					COMMAND-[
Font Size, Increase	WD 85, WD 147		Increase Font Size button (Home tab | Font group)			COMMAND-SHIFT->
Font Size, Increase 1 point	WD 80, WD 85					COMMAND-]

Table 1: Microsoft Word 2011 for Mac Quick Reference Summary *(continued)*

Task	Page Number	Mouse	Ribbon	Shortcut Menu	Menu Bar	Keyboard Shortcut
Footer, Insert	WD 81	Double-click dimmed footer area	Footer button (Document Elements tab | Header and Footer group)		View > Header and Footer	
Footnote, Insert	WD 97		Footnote button (Document Elements tab | Citations group)		Insert > Footnote	COMMAND-OPTION-F
Formatting Marks, Show or Hide	WD 10	'Show all nonprinting characters' (¶) button in Standard toolbar			Word > Preferences, View, Nonprinting characters, All check box	
Go to a Page	WD 118	Select Browse Object button on vertical scroll bar, Go To icon; Click Page Number indicator at bottom of window, click Go To tab			Edit > Find > Go To	COMMAND-OPTION-G
Graphic, Adjust Brightness and Contrast	WD 155		Corrections button (Format Picture tab | Adjust group)	Format Picture, Adjust Picture in left pane (Format Picture dialog)		
Graphic, Change Border Color	WD 156		Border button (Format Picture tab | Picture Styles group)			
Graphic, Change Color	WD 154		Recolor button (Format Picture tab | Adjust group)	Format Picture, Adjust Picture in left pane (Format Picture dialog)		
Graphic, Flip	WD 159		Rotate button (Format Picture tab | Arrange group)			
Graphic, Move	WD 157	Drag graphic				
Graphic, Resize	WD 38, WD 40, WD 154	Drag sizing handle	Height and Width text boxes (Format Picture tab | Size group)	Format Picture, Size	Format > Picture, Size	
Hanging Indent, Create	WD 85, WD 109	Drag Hanging Indent marker on ruler	Line Spacing button (Home tab | Paragraph group), Line Spacing Options, Indentation area, Special button (Paragraph dialog)	Paragraph, Indents and Spacing tab (Paragraph dialog), Special, Hanging	Format > Paragraph, Indents and Spacing tab, Special button	COMMAND-T
Hanging Indent, Remove	WD 85	Drag Hanging Indent marker on ruler	Line Spacing button (Home tab | Paragraph group), Line Spacing Options, Indentation area, Special button (Paragraph dialog)	Paragraph, Indents and Spacing tab (Paragraph dialog) , Special button, Hanging	Format > Paragraph, Indents and Spacing tab, Special, Hanging	COMMAND-SHIFT-T
Header and Footer, Close	WD 82	Close button in header or footer; double-click main body text			View > Header and Footer	

Table 1: Microsoft Word 2011 for Mac Quick Reference Summary (*continued*)

Task	Page Number	Mouse	Ribbon	Shortcut Menu	Menu Bar	Keyboard Shortcut
Header, Switch to	WD 80	Double-click dimmed header area	Header button (Document Elements tab | Header and Footer group)		View > Header and Footer	
Hyperlink, Convert to Regular Text	WD 165	Undo Hyperlink (AutoCorrect Options menu)		Hyperlink, Edit Hyperlink, Remove Link		
Indent, Decrease	WD 85	Drag First Line Indent marker on ruler	Decrease Indent button (Home tab | Paragraph group)	Paragraph, Indents and Spacing tab (Paragraph dialog)		COMMAND-SHIFT-M
Indent, First-Line	WD 86	Drag First Line Indent marker on ruler		Paragraph, Indents and Spacing tab (Paragraph dialog)	Format > Paragraph, Indents and Spacing tab (Paragraph dialog)	TAB at beginning of paragraph
Indent, Increase	WD 85		Increase Indent button (Home tab | Paragraph group)			CONTROL-SHIFT-M; TAB
Insertion Point, Move Down/ Up One Line	WD 15					DOWN ARROW/ UP ARROW
Insertion Point, Move Down/ Up One Paragraph	WD 15					COMMAND-DOWN ARROW/ COMMAND-UP ARROW
Insertion Point, Move Down/ Up One Page	WD 15	Next Page/Previous Page button at bottom of scroll bar; Click anywhere below the scroller on the vertical scroll bar/Click anywhere above the scroller on the vertical scroll bar				FN-UP ARROW / FN-DOWN ARROW or PAGE DOWN/ PAGE UP
Insertion Point, Move Down/ Up One Screen	WD 15	Next Page/Previous Page button at bottom of scroll bar; Click anywhere below the scroller on the vertical scroll bar/Click anywhere above the scroller on the vertical scroll bar				FN-UP ARROW / FN-DOWN ARROW or PAGE DOWN/ PAGE UP
Insertion Point, Move Left/ Right One Character	WD 15					LEFT ARROW/ RIGHT ARROW
Insertion Point, Move Left/ Right One Word	WD 15					OPTION-LEFT ARROW; OPTION-RIGHT ARROW
Insertion Point, Move to Beginning/ End of Document	WD 15					COMMAND-FN-LEFT ARROW or COMMAND-FN-RIGHT ARROW; COMMAND-HOME or COMMAND-END

Table 1: Microsoft Word 2011 for Mac Quick Reference Summary *(continued)*

Task	Page Number	Mouse	Ribbon	Shortcut Menu	Menu Bar	Keyboard Shortcut
Insertion Point, Move to Beginning/ End of Line	WD 15					COMMAND-LEFT ARROW / COMMAND-RIGHT ARROW or HOME/ END
Insertion Point, Move to Bottom/Top of Document Window	WD 15					COMMAND-FN-DOWN ARROW / COMMAND-FN-UP ARROW
Italicize	WD 29		Italic button (Home tab | Font group)	Font, Font tab (Font dialog)	Format > Font, Font tab (Font dialog)	COMMAND-I
Justify Paragraph	WD 85		Justify Text button (Home tab | Paragraph group)	Paragraph, Indents and Spacing tab, Alignment button (Paragraph dialog)	Format > Paragraph, Indents and Spacing tab, Alignment button (Paragraph dialog)	COMMAND-J
Left-Align Paragraph	WD 85		Align Text Left button (Home tab | Paragraph group)	Paragraph, Indents and Spacing tab, Alignment button (Paragraph dialog)	Format > Paragraph, Indents and Spacing tab, Alignment button (Paragraph dialog)	COMMAND-L
Line Spacing, Change	WD 6, WD 78		Line Spacing button (Home tab | Paragraph group)	Paragraph, Indents and Spacing tab, (Paragraph dialog)	Format > Paragraph, Indents and Spacing tab, (Paragraph dialog)	COMMAND-[number of desired line spacing, i.e., 2 for double-spacing], OPTION-COMMAND-M
Mailing Label, Print	WD 189				Tools > Labels	
Margin Settings, Change	WD 7	Drag margin boundary on ruler	Margins button (Layout tab | Margins group)		Format > Document, Margins tab	
Move Text	WD 51	Drag and drop selected text; Cut/Paste buttons in Standard toolbar		Cut, Paste	Edit > Cut, then Edit > Paste	COMMAND-X, COMMAND-V
New File, Create from Existing	WD 167				File > Open, select file, choose Copy (Open box arrow, Open dialog)	
Nonbreaking Hyphen, Insert	WD 175					COMMAND-SHIFT-HYPHEN
Nonbreaking Space, Insert	WD 175				Insert > Symbol > Advanced Symbol, Special Characters tab (Symbol dialog)	CONTROL-SHIFT-SPACE BAR
Normal Style, Apply	WD 5, WD 163		Normal (Home tab | Styles group); Clear Formatting button (Home tab | Font group)			

Table 1: Microsoft Word 2011 for Mac Quick Reference Summary *(continued)*

Task	Page Number	Mouse	Ribbon	Shortcut Menu	Menu Bar	Keyboard Shortcut
Normal Style, Modify	WD 76			CONTROL-click style in Styles gallery, Modify	Format > Style, select style, Modify button (Style dialog)	
Open a Document	WD 49				File > Open or FIle > Open Recent	COMMAND-O
Page Border, Add	WD 45		Borders button (Layout tab | Page Background group)		Format > Document, Layout tab, Borders button, Page Border tab	
Page Break, Insert	WD 107		Break button (Layout tab | Page Setup group), Page Break		Insert > Break > Page Break	COMMAND-SHIFT-RETURN
Page Number, Insert	WD 81		Page # button (Header and Footer tab | Insert group), or Page # button (Document Elements tab, Header and Footer group)		Insert > Page Numbers	
Paste	WD 114	Paste button in Standard toolbar		Paste	Edit > Paste	COMMAND-V
Paste Options, Use	WD 158	After pasting, click Paste Options button near pasted object				
Paste Options Menu, Display	WD 115	Paste Options button by moved/copied text				
Picture, Apply Style	WD 41		More button (Format Picture tab | Picture Styles group)			
Picture Effects, Apply	WD 42		Effects button (Format Picture tab | Picture Styles group)	Format Picture	Format > Picture	
Picture, Insert	WD 36		Picture button (Home tab | Insert group), Picture from File			
Preview a Document	WD 125				File > Print, Show Quick Preview (Print dialog)	COMMAND-P
Print Document	WD 54	Print button in Standard toolbar			File > Print	COMMAND-P
Quick Style, Apply	WD 169		Style name in Quick Styles gallery (Home tab | Styles group)			
Quit Word	WD 48				Word > Quit Word	COMMAND-Q
Readability, Show Statistics	WD 121				Word > Preferences > Spelling and Grammar, Show readability statistics (Spelling and Grammar dialog)	

Table 1: Microsoft Word 2011 for Mac Quick Reference Summary (*continued*)

Task	Page Number	Mouse	Ribbon	Shortcut Menu	Menu Bar	Keyboard Shortcut
Redo	WD 28	Redo button in Standard toolbar				COMMAND-Y
Remove Character Formatting	WD 85					CONTROL-SPACE BAR
Remove Space after Paragraph	WD 78		Line Spacing button (Home tab | Paragraph group)	Paragraph, Indents and Spacing tab (Paragraph dialog)	Format > Paragraph, Indents and Spacing tab (Paragraph dialog)	
Replace Text	WD 117	Click Page number indicator at bottom of document window, click Replace tab			View > Sidebar > Search Pane; Edit > Find > Replace	COMMAND-SHIFT-H
Reference Tools Toolbox, Use to Look Up Information	WD 122	Toolbox button in Standard toolbar, Reference Tools pane		CONTROL-click word, choose Look Up, Definition; CONTROL-click word, Look Up, Web Search		
Right-Align	WD 81		Align Text Right button (Home tab | Paragraph group)	Paragraph, Indents and Spacing tab, (Paragraph dialog), Alignment	Format > Paragraph, Indents and Spacing tab (Paragraph dialog), Alignment	COMMAND-R
Rulers, Display or Hide	WD 86				View > Ruler	
Save	WD 15	Save button in Standard toolbar			File > Save or FIle > Save As	COMMAND-S
Save Document, Same File Name	WD 35	Save button in Standard toolbar			File > Save	COMMAND-S
Scroll, Page by Page	WD 15, WD 113	Previous Page/Next Page button on vertical scroll bar; Click anywhere above the scroller on the vertical scroll bar/ Click anywhere below the scroller on the vertical scroll bar				COMMAND-PAGE UP or COMMAND-PAGE DOWN
Scroll, Up/ Down One Object	WD 15	Select Browse Object button at bottom of vertical scroll bar, select object icon, click scroll Previous/Next buttons				
Scroll, Up/ Down One Screen	WD 15	Click above/below scroll box on vertical scroll bar				
Select Block of Text	WD 35	Click beginning, SHIFT-click end				

Table 1: Microsoft Word 2011 for Mac Quick Reference Summary (continued)

Task	Page Number	Mouse	Ribbon	Shortcut Menu	Menu Bar	Keyboard Shortcut
Select Character(s)	WD 35	Drag through characters				SHIFT-RIGHT ARROW or SHIFT-LEFT ARROW
Select Entire Document	WD 35	In left margin, triple-click				COMMAND-A
Select Graphic	WD 35	Click graphic				
Select Group of Words	WD 31	Drag mouse pointer through words				OPTION-SHIFT-RIGHT ARROW repeatedly
Select Line	WD 35	Click in left margin; drag mouse pointer through line				FN-LEFT ARROW, SHIFT-DOWN ARROW; FN-RIGHT ARROW, SHIFT-COMMAND-LEFT ARROW
Select Multiple Paragraphs	WD 35	Drag mouse pointer in left margin				SHIFT-DOWN ARROW
Select Nonadjacent Items	WD 181	Select first item, hold down COMMAND key while selecting next item(s)				
Select Paragraph	WD 35	Move mouse to left of paragraph until mouse pointer changes to a right-pointing black arrow, triple-click paragraph				COMMAND-SHIFT-DOWN ARROW or COMMAND-SHIFT-UP ARROW
Select Sentence	WD 35	COMMAND-click				
Select Word	WD 35	Double-click word; Drag through word				OPTION-SHIFT-RIGHT ARROW or OPTION-SHIFT-LEFT ARROW
Shade Paragraph	WD 24			Borders and Shading, Shading tab (Borders and Shading dialog)	Format > Borders and Shading, Shading tab (Borders and Shading dialog)	
Shape, Add Text	WD 147			Add Text		
Shape, Apply Style	WD 146		More button in Shape Styles gallery (Format tab | Shape Styles group)			
Shape, Insert	WD 144		Shape button (Home tab | Insert group)		Insert > Shape	
Single-Space Lines	WD 85		Line Spacing button (Home tab | Paragraph group), 1.0	Paragraph, Indents and Spacing tab (Paragraph dialog), Line spacing button	Format > Paragraph, Indents and Spacing tab (Paragraph dialog), Line spacing button	COMMAND-1
Small Caps	WD 85			Font, Font tab, Small caps (Font dialog)	Format > Font, Font tab, Small caps (Font dialog)	COMMAND-SHIFT-K

Table 1: Microsoft Word 2011 for Mac Quick Reference Summary (continued)

Task	Page Number	Mouse	Ribbon	Shortcut Menu	Menu Bar	Keyboard Shortcut
Source, Edit	WD 95, WD 110	Click citation, Citation Options box arrow, Edit this Citation	Manage button (Document Elements tab | References group), Action button (Toolbox), Edit Source			
Source, Enter	WD 100	Toolbox button in Standard toolbar, Citations pane, Action button, Citation Source Manager, New (Source Manager dialog)	Manage Sources button (Document Elements tab | References group), Manage button, Action button (Citations pane, Toolbox), New Button			
Spelling and Grammar, Check at Once	WD 120	Spelling and Grammar check icon at bottom of document window		Spelling	Tools > Spelling and Grammar	OPTION-COMMAND-L
Spelling, Check as You Type	WD 12			CONTROL-click flagged word, choose correction from list		
Style, Modify	WD 76, WD 99			CONTROL-click style in Styles gallery, Modify; CONTROL-click text, Style, Modify button (Style dialog)	Format > Style, select style, Modify button (Style dialog)	
Style, Update to Match Selection	WD 79			CONTROL-click style in Quick Style gallery, Update to Match Selection		
Subscript	WD 85		Subscript button (Home tab | Font group)	Font, Font tab, Subscript (Font dialog)		COMMAND-EQUAL SIGN
Superscript	WD 85		Superscript button (Home tab | Font group)	Font, Font tab, Superscript (Font dialog)		COMMAND-SHIFT-PLUS SIGN
Symbol, Insert	WD 160				Insert > Symbol > Advanced Symbol	
Synonym, Find and Insert	WD 119	Toolbox button in Standard toolbar, Reference Tools icon, enter word, click Thesaurus		Synonyms, click desired word	Tools > Thesaurus	CONTROL-OPTION-COMMAND-R
Tab Stops, Set Custom	WD 170	Click tab selector at left edge of ruler, choose type of tab, click desired tab stop on ruler			Format > Tabs; Format > Paragraph, Tabs button, type tab stop position, Set button	
Table, Align Data in Cells	WD 181		Align button (Table Layout tab | Alignment group)			

Table 1: Microsoft Word 2011 for Mac Quick Reference Summary (continued)

Task	Page Number	Mouse	Ribbon	Shortcut Menu	Menu Bar	Keyboard Shortcut
Table, Apply Style	WD 178		More button in Table Styles gallery (Table Layout tab | Table Styles group)			
Table, Center	WD 182		Select table, Center Paragraph button (Home tab | Paragraph group); Properties button (Table Layout tab | Settings group), Table tab (Table Properties dialog), Center	Table Properties, Table tab (Table Properties dialog), Center	Table > Table Properties, Table tab (Table Properties dialog), Center	
Table, Delete Cell Contents	WD 184	Cut button in Standard toolbar		Cut	Edit > Cut	DELETE; COMMAND-X
Table, Delete Entire	WD 184		Delete button (Table Layout tab | Rows & Columns group), Delete Table			
Table, Delete Row or Column	WD 184		Delete button (Table Layout tab | Rows & Columns group)	Delete Rows or Delete Columns		
Table, Insert	WD 176		New button (Tables tab | Table Options group), choose desired dimensions in grid			
Table, Insert Column	WD 184		Left or Right button (Table Layout tab | Rows & Columns group)	Select column to right of new column, Insert Columns		
Table, Insert Row	WD 183		Above or Below button (Table Layout tab | Rows & Columns group)	Select row below new row, Insert Rows		
Table, Merge Cells	WD 185		Merge button (Table Layout tab | Merge group)	Merge Cells		
Table, Select Cell	WD 181	When mouse pointer changes to a small solid upward angled pointing arrow, click left edge of cell				
Table, Select Column	WD 181	When mouse pointer changes to a small solid downward-pointing arrow, click top border of column				
Table, Select Entire	WD 181	Click table move handle			Table > Select > Table	
Table, Select Multiple Cells, Rows, or Columns, Adjacent	WD 181	Drag through cells, rows, or columns				

Table 1: Microsoft Word 2011 for Mac Quick Reference Summary (*continued*)

Task	Page Number	Mouse	Ribbon	Shortcut Menu	Menu Bar	Keyboard Shortcut
Table, Select Multiple Cells, Rows, or Columns, Nonadjacent	WD 181	Select first cell, row, or column, hold COMMAND key while selecting next cell, row, or column				
Table, Select Next Cell	WD 181					TAB
Table, Select Previous Cell	WD 181					SHIFT-TAB
Table, Select Row	WD 181	When mouse pointer changes to a right-pointing black arrow, click to left of row				
Table, Split Cells	WD 186		Split Cells button (Table Layout tab | Merge group)	Split Cells		
Table Columns, Resize to Fit Table Contents	WD 180	Double-click column boundary	AutoFit button (Table Layout tab | Cell Size group), AutoFit to Contents	AutoFit, AutoFit to Contents		
Text Effect, Apply	WD 23		Text Effects button (Home tab | Font group)	Font, Font tab (Font dialog), Text Effects button	Format > Font, Font tab (Font dialog), Text Effects button	
Text Wrapping, Change	WD 149		Wrap Text button (Format tab | Arrange group)	Wrap Text	Format > Shape, click Layout in left pane (Format Shape dialog)	
Theme Colors, Change	WD 33		In Publishing Layout view, Colors button (Home tab | Themes group)			
Toolbox, Show	WD 75	Toolbox button in Standard toolbar	'Manage the styles that are used in this document' button (Home tab | Styles group)		View > (specific Toolbox)	
Underline	WD 32		Underline button (Home tab | Font group)	Font, Font tab (Font dialog), Underline style	Format > Font (Font dialog), Font tab, Underline style	COMMAND-U
Underline Words, Not Spaces	WD 85			Font, Font tab (Font dialog), Underline style, Words only	Format > Font (Font dialog), Font tab, Underline style, Words only	COMMAND-SHIFT-W
Undo	WD 28	Undo button in Standard toolbar				COMMAND-Z
View One Page	WD 44	Zoom button arrow in Standard toolbar, Whole Page			View > Zoom, Whole page	
Zoom Document	WD 38	Zoom box arrow in Standard toolbar; Zoom slider in lower-right of document window	Zoom button (View tab | Zoom group)		View > Zoom	

Table 2: Microsoft PowerPoint 2011 for Mac Quick Reference Summary

Task	Page Number	Mouse	Ribbon	Shortcut Menu	Menu Bar	Keyboard Shortcut
Audio File, Insert	PPT 159		Media button (Home tab | Insert group)			
Audio Options, Add	PPT 160		Format Audio tab | Audio Options group			
Clip Art, Copy	PPT 152	Copy button in Standard toolbar		Copy	Edit > Copy	COMMAND-C
Clip Art, Find and Download	PPT 28		Picture button (Home tab | Insert group), Clip Art Gallery, Online button, Search text box, enter criteria, Search button, Download			
Clip Art, Insert	PPT 33	Clip Art icon in slide (drag clip art from Media Browser Clip Art pane)	Picture button (Home tab | Insert group), Clip Art Gallery			
Clip Art, Photo, or Shape, Move	PPT 40	Drag				ARROW KEYS move selected image in small increments
Clip Object, Remove Background	PPT 154		Remove Background button (Format Picture tab | Adjust group)			
Copy	PPT 152	Copy button in Standard toolbar		Copy	Edit > Copy	COMMAND-C
Document Properties, Change	PPT 49				File > Properties	
End of Show Slide, Add	PPT 48				PowerPoint > Preferences, View button, End with black slide	
Font, Change	PPT 97		Font box arrow (Home tab | Font group)	Font, Font tab	Format > Font, Font tab	COMMAND-T, Font tab
Font, Change Color	PPT 13		Font Color button or Font Color button arrow (Home tab | Font group)	Format Text, Font Color button	Format > Font, Font Color	
Font Size, Decrease	PPT 102		Decrease Font Size button or Font Size box arrow (Home tab | Font group)			COMMAND-SHIFT-<
Font Size, Increase	PPT 12		Increase Font Size button or Font Size box arrow (Home tab | Font group)	Font, Font tab	Format > Font, Font tab	COMMAND-SHIFT->
Format Painter, Use	PPT 102	Format Painter button in Standard toolbar				
Handout, Print	PPT 174				File > Print, Print What button, Handouts	COMMAND-P, Print What button, Handouts

Table 2: Microsoft PowerPoint 2011 for Mac Quick Reference Summary *(continued)*

Task	Page Number	Mouse	Ribbon	Shortcut Menu	Menu Bar	Keyboard Shortcut
List Level, Decrease	PPT 18		Decrease Indent button (Home tab | Paragraph group)			SHIFT-TAB
List Level, Increase	PPT 17		Increase Indent button (Home tab | Paragraph group)			TAB
Movie Clip (Animated GIF), Insert	PPT 166		Picture button (Home tab | Insert group)		Insert > Photo, Picture from File	
Next Slide	PPT 24	Next Slide button on vertical scroll bar or next slide thumbnail on Slides tab; drag scroller down on vertical scroll bar				DOWN ARROW
Normal View	PPT 151	Normal View button at lower-left PowerPoint window			View > Normal	COMMAND-1
Notes, Add	PPT 169	In Normal view, click Notes pane and type notes				
Notes, Print	PPT 177				File > Print, Print What button, Notes	COMMAND-P, Print What button, Notes
Open Presentation	PPT 52				File > Open or Open Recent	COMMAND-O
Paste	PPT 106, PPT 153	Paste button in Standard toolbar		Paste		COMMAND-V
Photo, Insert	PPT 28, PPT 37	Picture icon on slide (drag photo from Media Browser Photos pane)	Picture button (Home tab | Insert group), Photo Browser			
Picture, Add an Artistic Effect	PPT 142		Filters button (Format Picture tab | Adjust group)	Format Picture, Adjust Picture	Format > Picture, Adjust Picture	
Picture, Add Border	PPT 88		Border button arrow (Format Picture tab | Picture Styles group)	Format Picture, Line	Format > Picture, Line	
Picture Border, Change Color	PPT 89		Border button arrow (Format Picture tab | Picture Styles group)	Format Picture, Line (Format Picture dialog)	Format > Picture, Line (Format Picture dialog)	
Picture, Correct	PPT 84		Corrections button (Format Picture tab | Adjust group)	Format Picture, Adjust Picture	Format > Picture, Adjust Picture	
Picture Effects, Apply	PPT 86		Effects button (Format Picture tab | Picture Styles group)	Format Picture	Format > Picture	
Picture, Insert	PPT 80	Insert Picture from File icon in placeholder	Picture button (Home tab | Insert group), Picture from File		Insert > Photo > Picture from File	

Table 2: Microsoft PowerPoint 2011 for Mac Quick Reference Summary *(continued)*

Task	Page Number	Mouse	Ribbon	Shortcut Menu	Menu Bar	Keyboard Shortcut
Picture, Recolor	PPT 141		Recolor button (Format Picture tab | Adjust group)	Format Picture, Adjust Picture	Format > Picture, Adjust Picture	
Picture Style, Apply	PPT 84		More button (Format Picture tab | Picture Styles group)			
Placeholder, Delete	PPT 147	Select placeholder, Cut button in Standard toolbar		Delete		Select placeholder, DELETE
Placeholder, Move	PPT 147	Drag				
Placeholder, Resize	PPT 146	Drag sizing handles				
Presentation Theme, Change Color	PPT 79		Colors button (Themes tab | Theme Options group)			
Presentation Theme, Choose	PPT 5		More button (Themes tab | Themes group)			
Previous Slide	PPT 25	Previous Slide button on vertical scroll bar; Previous slide thumbnail on Slides tab; drag scroller up on vertical scroll bar				UP ARROW
Print a Presentation	PPT 53	Print button in Standard toolbar			File > Print	COMMAND-P
Quit PowerPoint	PPT 51				PowerPoint > Quit PowerPoint	COMMAND-Q
Resize	PPT 38, PPT 91	Drag sizing handles	Enter height and width values (Format Picture tab | Size)	Format Picture, Size (enter height and width)	Format > Picture, Size (enter height and width)	
Save a Presentation	PPT 14	Save button in Standard toolbar			File > Save; File > Save As	COMMAND-S
Shape, Add	PPT 104	Click Media Browser button in Standard toolbar, Shapes tab (Media Browser), drag shape onto slide	Shape button (Home tab | Insert)		Insert > Shape	
Shape, Apply Style	PPT 109		More button (Format tab | Shape Styles group)	Format Shape	Format > Shape	
Shape, Format	PPT 106			Format Shape	Format > Shape	
Slide Number, Insert	PPT 172		Text button (Home tab | Insert group), Slide Number or Header and Footer		Insert > Slide Number or Insert > Header and Footer	
Slide Show, End	PPT 51	Click black ending slide		End Show		ESC; HYPHEN; RIGHT ARROW; DOWN ARROW

Table 2: Microsoft PowerPoint 2011 for Mac Quick Reference Summary *(continued)*

Task	Page Number	Mouse	Ribbon	Shortcut Menu	Menu Bar	Keyboard Shortcut
Slide Show View	PPT 50	Slide Show button at lower-right PowerPoint window	From Start button or From Current Slide button (Slide Show tab | Play Slide Show group)		Slide Show > Play from Start or Play from Current Slide	SHIFT-COMMAND-RETURN or COMMAND-RETURN
Slide Sorter View	PPT 151	Slide Sorter button at lower-left PowerPoint window	Slide Sorter button (View tab | Presentation Views group)			COMMAND-2
Slide, Add	PPT 14		New Slide button (Home tab | Slides group)		Insert > New Slide	COMMAND-SHIFT-N
Slide, Arrange	PPT 43	Drag slide in Slides tab or Outline tab to new position, or in Slide Sorter view drag to new position				
Slide, Delete	PPT 150			Delete Slide		DELETE
Slide, Duplicate	PPT 41		New Slide button arrow (Home tab | Slides group), Duplicate Selected Slides			
Slide, Format Background	PPT 93		Background button (Themes tab | Theme Options group)	Format Background	Format > Slide Background	
Slide, Insert Picture as Background	PPT 95		Background button (Theme tab | Theme Options group)	Format Background, Fill pane, Picture or Texture tab (Format Background dialog), Choose Picture button	Format > Slide Background, Fill, Picture or Texture tab (Format Background dialog), Choose Picture button	
Slide, Insert Texture Fill	PPT 93		Background button (Themes tab | THeme Options group)	Format Background, Fill, Picture or Texture	Format > Slide Background, Fill, Picture or Texture	
Slide, Select Layout	PPT 21		Layout button or New Slide button arrow (Home tab | Slides group)			
Spelling, Check	PPT 171			Spelling (or click correct word on shortcut menu)	Tools > Spelling	OPTION-COMMAND-L
Stacking Order, Change	PPT 144		Reorder button (Format Picture tab | Arrange group), Bring to Front, Send to Back, Bring Forward or Send Backward	Arrange, Bring to Front, Send to Back, Bring Forward or Send Backward	Arrange > Bring to Front or Send to Back	
Synonym, Find and Insert	PPT 168	Toolbox icon in Standard toolbar, Reference Tools tab		Look Up, or click desired synonym in shortcut menu	Tools > Thesaurus or View > Reference Tools	CONTROL-OPTION-COMMAND-R
Text, Add Shadow	PPT 100		Text Effects button (Home tab | Font group)	Font, Font tab, Text Shadow	Format > Font, Font tab, Text Shadow	COMMAND-T, Font tab, Text Shadow

Table 2: Microsoft PowerPoint 2011 for Mac Quick Reference Summary *(continued)*

Task	Page Number	Mouse	Ribbon	Shortcut Menu	Menu Bar	Keyboard Shortcut
Text, Align Horizontally	PPT 148		Align Text buttons (Home tab | Paragraph group)	Paragraph, Alignment	Format > Paragraph, Alignment	COMMAND-R (right), COMMAND-L (left), COMMAND-E (center)
Text, Bold	PPT 19		Bold button (Home tab | Font group)	Font, Font tab, Font Style box	Format > Font, Font Style box	COMMAND-B
Text, Change Color	PPT 13		Font Color button or Font Color button arrow (Home tab | Font group)	Format Text, Font Color button	Format > Font, Font Color	
Text, Delete	PPT 44	Cut button in Standard toolbar		Cut	Edit > Cut	COMMAND-X; DELETE
Text, Find and Replace	PPT 167				Edit > Find > Replace	SHIFT-COMMAND-H
Text, Italicize	PPT 11		Italic button (Home tab | Font group)	Font, Font tab	Format > Font, Font tab	COMMAND-I
Text, Select Paragraph	PPT 10	Triple-click paragraph; drag mouse pointer over paragraph				
Text, Select Word	PPT 12	Double-click word				COMMAND-SHIFT-RIGHT ARROW
Transition, Add	PPT 46		Transitions tab | Transition to This Slide group			
Transparency, Change	PPT 96		Background button (Themes tab | Theme Options group) Format Background, Adjust Picture (Format Background dialog), Transparency slider	Format Background, Fill or Adjust Picture (Format Background dialog) Transparency slider	Format > Slide Background, Fill or Adjust Picture (Format Background dialog) Transparency slider	
Video File, Insert	PPT 156		Media button (Home tab | Insert group)			
Video Options	PPT 158		Format Movie tab | Movie Options group			
Video Style, Add	PPT 162		More button (Format Movie tab | Movie Styles group)			
WordArt, Add Text Effects	PPT 114		Effects button (Format tab | Text Styles group)	Format Text		
WordArt, Change Outline Weight or Color	PPT 117		Line button arrow (Format tab | Text Styles group)	Format Text		
WordArt, Insert	PPT 113		Text Styles gallery (Format tab | Text Styles group)		Insert > WordArt	
Zoom for Viewing Slides	PPT 154	Drag Zoom slider on status bar; Zoom box in Standard toolbar			View > Zoom	

Table 3: Microsoft Excel 2011 for Mac Quick Reference Summary

Task	Page Number	Mouse	Ribbon	Shortcut Menu	Menu Bar	Keyboard Shortcut
Accounting Number Format, Apply	EX 29		Accounting Number Format button (Home tab | Number group)	Format Cells, Number tab	Format > Cells, Number tab	
All Data in a Cell, Select	EX 48	Double-click if there are no spaces in data				
Auto Fill	EX 16	Drag fill handle, Auto Fill Options button				
AutoCalculate	EX 45	Select range, click AutoCalculate area, click calculation command				
AutoSum	EX 14	AutoSum button in Standard toolbar	AutoSum button (Formulas tab | Function group)			
Average Function	EX 81	AutoSum button arrow in Standard toolbar; Formula builder button in formula bar, AVERAGE	AutoSum button arrow (Formulas tab | Function group)		View > Formula Builder, AVERAGE	Type =av, press DOWN ARROW
Background Color, Change	EX 92		Fill Color button arrow (Home tab | Font group)	Format Cells, Fill tab (Format Cells dialog)	Format > Cells, Fill tab (Format Cells dialog)	COMMAND-1
Best Fit	EX 30	Double-click column boundary		Column Width		
Bold	EX 23		Bold button (Home tab | Font group)	Format Cells, Font tab, Bold font style	Format > Cells, Font tab, Bold font style	COMMAND-B
Cell, Select	EX 7	Click cell; Name box, type cell reference, press RETURN				Use arrow keys
Cell Entries, Clear Selected	EX 48	Drag fill handle to the left or up	Clear button (Home tab | Edit group), Clear Contents	Clear Contents	Edit > Clear	DELETE
Cell Reference, Add	EX 76	Begin typing formula, click cell				
Cell Style, Change	EX 21		Cell Styles gallery (Home tab | Format group)			
Cells, Merge and Center	EX 25		Merge button arrow (Home tab | Alignment group), Merge and Center	Format Cells, Alignment tab, Center Across Selection	Format > Cells, Alignment tab, Center Across Selection	
Characters to Left of Insertion Point, Delete	EX 48					DELETE

Table 3: Microsoft Excel 2011 for Mac Quick Reference Summary *(continued)*

Task	Page Number	Mouse	Ribbon	Shortcut Menu	Menu Bar	Keyboard Shortcut
Characters to Right of Insertion Point, Delete	EX 48					FN-DELETE
Characters, Highlight	EX 48	Drag through adjacent characters				SHIFT-RIGHT ARROW or SHIFT-LEFT ARROW
Chart, Add	EX 35, EX 177		Insert Chart group | Charts tab			
Chart, Delete Selected	EX 50			Delete		DELETE
Chart, Resize	EX 37	Drag edges of chart (hold down COMMAND key to snap to gridlines)				
Chart, Rotate	EX 181		3-D Rotation button (Chart Layout tab | 3-D Rotation)			
Color Text	EX 24		Font Color button arrow (Home tab | Font group)	Format Cells, Font tab, Color box		
Column Width, Adjust	EX 103	Drag column heading boundary; double-click column boundary to adjust to widest item in column				
Column, Delete	EX 152		Delete button arrow (Home tab | Cells group)			
Column, Insert	EX 152		Insert button arrow (Home tab | Cells group),	(CONTROL-click column to right) Insert		
Comma Style Format, Apply	EX 29		Comma Style button (Home tab | Number group)	Format Cells, Number tab, Number category (Format Cells dialog), Use 1000 Separator	Format > Cells, Number tab, Number category (Format Cells dialog), Use 1000 Separator	
Conditional Formatting	EX 101		Conditional Formatting button (Home tab | Format group)			
Copy Range of Cells	EX 17	Select range, drag fill handle or Copy button on Standard toolbar, then Paste button (Standard toolbar)	Copy button (Home tab | Clipboard group) |	Copy, select destination, Paste	Edit > Copy | Edit > Paste	COMMAND-C | COMMAND-V
Currency Style Format, Apply	EX 98			Format Cells, Number tab, Currency	Format > Cells, Number tab, Currency	CTRL-SHIFT-dollar sign ($)
Date, Format	EX 95		Number style box (Home tab | Number group), Date	Format Cells, Number tab, Date	Format > Cells, Number tab, Date	

Table 3: Microsoft Excel 2011 for Mac Quick Reference Summary *(continued)*

Task	Page Number	Mouse	Ribbon	Shortcut Menu	Menu Bar	Keyboard Shortcut
Date, Insert Today's	EX 156	Formula Builder button in formula bar, NOW function			View > Formula Builder, NOW	Type = NOW, press DOWN ARROW
Document Properties, Change	EX 40				File > Properties	
Document Properties, Set or View	EX 40				File > Properties	
Entry, Complete	EX 10	Click Enter button in formula bar; Click any other cell				Press RETURN or any ARROW KEY
Fill Color, Change	EX 172		Fill Color button arrow (Home tab | Font group)	Format Cells, Font tab, Fill tab, Color	Format > Cells, Font tab, Fill tab, Color	COMMAND-1, Fill tab, Color
Fill Series	EX 143	After dragging Fill handle, Auto Fill Options button, Fill Series option				
Font, Change	EX 22		Font box arrow on Home tab	Format Cells, Font tab	Format > Cells, Font tab	
Font Color, Change	EX 25		Font Color button arrow (Home tab | Font group)	Format Cells, Font tab, Color box		
Font Size, Decrease	EX 24		Decrease Font Size button (Home tab | Font group); Font Size box arrow (Home tab | Font group)	Format Cells, Font tab, Size box		
Font Size, Increase	EX 24		Increase Font Size button (Home tab | Font group); Font Size box arrow (Home tab | Font group)	Format Cells, Font tab, Size box		
Format Painter, Use	EX 173	Double-click Format Painter button in Standard toolbar, move mouse pointer to destination cell(s)				
Formulas Version	EX 115					CONTROL-ACCENT MARK (`)
Highlight Cells	EX 27	Drag mouse pointer				
In-Cell Editing	EX 48	Double-click cell				
Insertion Point, Move	EX 48	Click				Use arrow keys
Insertion Point, Move to Beginning of Data in Cell	EX 48	Point to left of first character and click				FN-LEFT ARROW or HOME

Table 3: Microsoft Excel 2011 for Mac Quick Reference Summary (continued)

Task	Page Number	Mouse	Ribbon	Shortcut Menu	Menu Bar	Keyboard Shortcut
Insertion Point, Move to Ending of Data in Cell	EX 48	Point to right of last character and click				FN-RIGHT ARROW or END
Italicize Text	EX 175		Italic button (Home tab | Font group)	Format Cells, Font tab, Font style	Format > Cells, Font tab, Font style	COMMAND-I
Margins, Change	EX 110	Drag margin markers on ruler	Margins button (Layout tab | Page Setup group)		File > Page Setup, Margins tab (Page Setup dialog)	
Max Function	EX 83	AutoSum button arrow in Standard toolbar; Formula builder button in formula bar, MAX	AutoSum button arrow (Formulas tab | Function group)		View > Formula Builder, MAX	Type =MAX, press DOWN ARROW
Min Function	EX 84	AutoSum button arrow in Standard toolbar; Formula builder button in formula bar, MIN	AutoSum button arrow (Formulas tab | Function group)		View > Formula Builder, MIN	Type =MIN, press DOWN ARROW
Multiple Sheets, Select	EX 189	COMMAND-click tab; SHIFT-click tab				
New Line in Cell, Start	EX 69					CONTROL-OPTION-RETURN
Numbers, Format	EX 29		Number format buttons (Home tab | Number group); Number format box (Home tab | Number group)	Format Cells, Number tab	Format > Cells, Number tab	
Open Workbook	EX 45				File > Open; File > Open Recent	COMMAND-O
Page Orientation, Change	EX 110		In Page Layout view, Orientation button (Layout tab | Page Setup group)		File > Page Setup	
Panes, Freeze	EX 153		Freeze Panes button (Layout tab | Window group), Freeze		Window > Freeze Panes	
Panes, Split a Window into	EX 192	Drag horizontal or vertical split box to desired location	Split button (Layout tab | Window group)			
Panes, Unfreeze	EX 165		Freeze Panes button (Layout tab | Window group), Unfreeze		Window > Unfreeze Panes	
Percent Style Format, Apply	EX 100		Percent Style button (Home tab | Number group)	Format Cells, Number tab, Percentage	Format > Cells, Number tab, Percentage	CONTROL-SHIFT-percent sign (%)
Print Scaling Option	EX 116				File > Print, Fit to (Scaling area, Print dialog)	

Table 3: Microsoft Excel 2011 for Mac Quick Reference Summary *(continued)*

Task	Page Number	Mouse	Ribbon	Shortcut Menu	Menu Bar	Keyboard Shortcut
Print Section of Worksheet	EX 114				Select section, File > Print, Selection (Print What area, Print dialog)	
Print Worksheet	EX 42	Print button in Standard toolbar			File > Print	COMMAND-P, RETURN
Quit Excel	EX 44				Excel > Quit Excel	COMMAND-Q
Range Finder	EX 87	Double-click cell				
Range, Deselect	EX 3, EX 18	Click outside range				ESC
Range, Select	EX 18	Drag fill handle through range				
Redo	EX 48	Redo button in Standard toolbar				COMMAND-Y
Row Height, Change	EX 106	Drag row heading boundary	Format button (Home tab | Cells group), Row Height	Row Height	Format > Row > Height	
Row, Delete	EX 152		Delete button arrow (Home tab | Cells group), Rows			
Row, Insert	EX 150		Insert button arrow (Home tab | Cells group), Rows	(CONTROL-click row heading below row to insert), Insert		
Save Workbook	EX 19	Save button in Standard toolbar			File > Save	COMMAND-S
Save Workbook, New Name	EX 19				File > Save As	SHIFT-COMMAND-S
Save Workbook, Same Name	EX 41	Save button in Standard toolbar			File > Save	COMMAND-S
Select Cell	EX 31	Click cell or click Name box, type cell reference, press RETURN			Edit > Go To	Use arrow keys
Select Entire Worksheet	EX 50	Click Select All button				COMMAND-A
Select Nonadjacent Cells or Ranges	EX 97	Select first cell or range, hold down COMMAND key while selecting second cell or range				
Selected Characters, Delete	EX 47	Cut button in Standard toolbar		Delete	Edit > Delete	DELETE
Sheet Name, Change	EX 38	Double-click sheet tab, type name				

Table 3: Microsoft Excel 2011 for Mac Quick Reference Summary *(continued)*

Task	Page Number	Mouse	Ribbon	Shortcut Menu	Menu Bar	Keyboard Shortcut
Sheet Tab, Change Color	EX 38			Tab Color		
Sparkline Chart, Add	EX 166		Line button (Charts tab | Insert Sparklines group)			
Spelling	EX 108		Spelling button (Review tab | Proofing group)		Tools > Spelling	
Sum	EX 14		AutoSum button in Standard toolbar			Type =s, select SUM, select range
Text, Delete after Typing but before Pressing the RETURN Key	EX 9, EX 47	Cancel button in formula bar				ESC
Text, Delete while Typing	EX 9					DELETE
Text, Indent	EX 145		Increase Indent button (Home tab | Alignment group)	Format Cells, Alignment tab, Indent box in Text alignment area (Format Cells dialog)	Format > Cells, Alignment tab, Indent box in Text alignment area (Format Cells dialog)	
Text, Rotate	EX 141			Format Cells, Alignment tab, Orientation area	Format > Cells, Alignment tab, Orientation area	
Underline Text	EX 175		Underline button (Home tab | Font group)	Format Cells, Font tab, Underline	Format > Cells, Underline	COMMAND-U
Undo	EX 48	Undo button in Standard toolbar				CONTROL-Z
Workbook Theme, Change	EX 90		Themes button (Home tab | Themes group)			
Worksheet Name, Change	EX 38	Double-click sheet tab, type name				
Worksheet, Clear	EX 50		Select All button, Clear button (Home tab | Edit group)			COMMAND-A, Clear button (Home tab | Edit group)
Worksheet, Preview	EX 42				File > Print, Show Quick Preview	COMMAND-P, Show Quick Preview
Zoom a Worksheet or Chart	EX 191	Zoom button arrow in Standard toolbar		View > Zoom		

Table 4: Microsoft Outlook 2011 for Mac Quick Reference Summary

Task	Page Number	Mouse	Ribbon	Shortcut Menu	Menu Bar	Keyboard Shortcut
Appointment, Change Date for	OUT 74	Double-click appointment, change date *or* Drag appointment to different date in		Open, change date		COMMAND-O, change date
Appointment, Change Time for	OUT 73	Double-click appointment, change time *or* Drag appointment to different time slot		Open, change time		COMMAND-O, change time
Appointment, Create	OUT 59	Drag to select time slots, type appointment title; Double-click time slot	New button (Home tab), Appointment; Appointment button (Home tab)		File > New > Appointment	COMMAND-N
Appointment, Delete	OUT 76		Delete button (Appointment Series tab)	Delete, Delete button in dialog		DELETE, Delete button in dialog
Appointment, Save	OUT 70		Save & Close button (Appointment tab)			
Appointment, Set Recurrence Options for	OUT 67		Recurrence button (Appointment tab)			
Appointment, Set Reminder for	OUT 64		Reminder box arrow (Appointment tab)			
Appointment, Set Status for	OUT 63		Status button (Appointment tab)	Show As		
Attach File to E-Mail Message	OUT 31		Attach button (Message tab)		Draft > Attachments > Add	COMMAND-E
Attachment, Preview	OUT 33	Preview button in Reading Pane				
Attachment, Save	OUT 33			Save As	Message > Attachments > Save	
Calendar, Display Different Month in	OUT 75	Click Previous or Next button in mini calendar				
Date, Go to	OUT 55	Click date in mini calendar	View Date button (Home tab)			
Day View, Display in Calendar	OUT 59		Day button (Home tab)			
Default Calendar, Remove from Appointment Area	OUT 55	Remove check mark from default Calendar check box in Calendars list				

Table 4: Microsoft Outlook 2011 for Mac Quick Reference Summary (continued)

Task	Page Number	Mouse	Ribbon	Shortcut Menu	Menu Bar	Keyboard Shortcut
Display Calendar in List View	OUT 95		List button (Organize tab)			
E-Mail Message, Compose New	OUT 10		E-mail button (Home tab) or New button (Home tab), E-Mail Message		File > New > E-Mail Message	COMMAND-N
E-Mail Message, Close	OUT 16	Click Close button on message title bar			File > Close	COMMAND-W
E-Mail Message, Delete	OUT 24	Drag e-mail to Deleted Items folder	Delete button (Home tab)			DELETE
E-Mail Message, Forward	OUT 21		Forward button (Home tab)	Forward	Message > Forward	COMMAND-F
E-Mail Message, Move to Folder	OUT 35	Drag message to folder	Move button (Home tab)	Move		SHIFT-COMMAND-M
E-Mail Message, Open	OUT 15	Double-click message in message list		Open Message		COMMAND-O
E-Mail Message, Read in Reading Pane	OUT 15	Message header in message list				
E-Mail Message, Reply	OUT 19		Reply button (Home tab)	Reply	Message > Reply	COMMAND-R
E-Mail Message, Send	OUT 11		Send button (Message tab)			COMMAND-RETURN
Event, Create	OUT 78		Appointment button (Home tab), All day event check box			
Event, Delete	OUT 81		Delete button (Appointment tab)			
Event, Save	OUT 84		Save & Close button (Appointment tab)			
Event, Set Recurrence Options for	OUT 82		Recurrence button (Appointment tab)	Go to Series, Recurrence button		
Export Calendar Subfolder	OUT 97				File > Export	
File, Attach to E-Mail Message	OUT 31		Attach button (Message tab)		Draft > Attachments > Add	COMMAND-E
Folder, Create in Inbox	OUT 34		New button (Home tab), Folder	New Folder	File > New > Folder	SHIFT-COMMAND-N

Table 4: Microsoft Outlook 2011 for Mac Quick Reference Summary *(continued)*

Task	Page Number	Mouse	Ribbon	Shortcut Menu	Menu Bar	Keyboard Shortcut
Importance, Set to High for E-Mail Message	OUT 32		High Priority button (Message tab)			
List View, Display for Calendar	OUT 95		List button (Organize tab)			
Meeting, Cancel	OUT 91		Cancel button (Meeting tab), Send Cancellation button			
Meeting Time, Change and Send an Update	OUT 89	Double-click meeting, change time in Starts and/ or Ends boxes, Send Update button *or* Drag meeting to new time, Send Update button				
Meeting, Create and Send a Request	OUT 87		Meeting button (Home tab)		File > New > Meeting	
Message Format, Change to Plain Text	OUT 23		Format button (Options tab), Yes button (Outlook dialog)			
Month View, Display in Calendar	OUT 58		Month button (Home tab)		View > Month	CONTROL-COMMAND-4
Outlook Data File, Export	OUT 97				File > Export	
Outlook Data File, Import	OUT 7				File > Import, Outlook Data File	
Personal Calendar, Delete	OUT 99		Delete Calendar button (Folder tab | Actions group)	Delete, Delete button (Outlook dialog)	Edit > Delete, Delete button (Outlook dialog)	COMMAND-DELETE, Delete button (Outlook dialog)
Personal Calendar, Display	OUT 54	In Navigation Pane, check box next to calendar				
Personal Calendar, Hide	OUT 55	In Navigation Pane, uncheck box next to calendar				
Personal Folder, Create	OUT 53		New Calendar button (Organize tab)			
Personal Subfolder, Delete	OUT 99			Delete, Delete button (Outlook dialog)	Edit > Delete, Delete button (Outlook dialog)	
Print Calendar in List View	OUT 95	List button (Organize tab), Print button in Standard toolbar			List button (Organize tab), File > Print	List button (Organize tab), COMMAND-P

Table 4: Microsoft Outlook 2011 for Mac Quick Reference Summary *(continued)*

Task	Page Number	Mouse	Ribbon	Shortcut Menu	Menu Bar	Keyboard Shortcut
Print Calendar in Week Style	OUT 93	Week button (Home tab), Print button in Standard toolbar			Week button (Home tab), File > Print	Week button (Home tab), COMMAND-P
Print E-Mail Message	OUT 16	Print button in Standard toolbar		Print		COMMAND-P
Quit Outlook	OUT 37				Outlook > Quit Outlook	COMMAND-Q
Reply to E-Mail Message	OUT 19		Reply button (Home tab)	Reply	Message > Reply	COMMAND-R
Save Appointment	OUT 70		Save & Close button (Appointment tab)			
Save Attachment	OUT 33			Save As	Message > Attachments > Save	
Save E-Mail Message in Drafts Folder	OUT 28	Save button in Standard toolbar; Close button, Yes button (Outlook dialog)			File > Save	
Spelling, Check as You Type	OUT 25, OUT 27			CONTROL-click error, click correct word on shortcut menu	Edit > Spelling and Grammar	
Week View, Display in Calendar	OUT 57		Week button (Home)		View > Week	CONTROL-COMMAND-ALT-3
Work Week View, Display in Calendar	OUT 57		Work button (Home tab)		View > Work Week	CONTROL-COMMAND-2